Economics of Securities Law
Volume II

Economic Approaches to Law

Series Editors: Richard A. Posner

Judge, United States Court of Appeals for the Seventh Circuit and Senior Lecturer, University of Chicago Law School, USA

Francesco Parisi

Oppenheimer Wolff and Donnelly Professor of Law University of Minnesota Law School, USA and Professor of Economics, University of Bologna, Italy

Wherever possible, the articles in these volumes have been reproduced as originally published using facsimile reproduction, inclusive of footnotes and pagination to facilitate ease of reference.

For a list of all Edward Elgar published titles visit our website at www.e-elgar.com

Economics of Securities Law Volume II

Edited by

Geoffrey P. Miller

Stuyvesant Comfort Professor of Law
New York University Law School, USA

ECONOMIC APPROACHES TO LAW

An Elgar Research Collection
Cheltenham, UK • Northampton, MA, USA

Published by
Edward Elgar Publishing Limited
The Lypiatts
15 Lansdown Road
Cheltenham
Glos GL50 2JA
UK

Edward Elgar Publishing, Inc.
William Pratt House
9 Dewey Court
Northampton
Massachusetts 01060
USA

A catalogue record for this book is available from the British Library

Library of Congress Control Number: 2015952677

MIX
Paper from responsible sources
FSC® C013056
FSC www.fsc.org

ISBN 978 1 78347 181 2 (2 volume set)

Printed and bound in Great Britain by TJ International Ltd, Padstow

Contents

Acknowledgements

The editor and publishers wish to thank the authors and the following publishers who have kindly given permission for the use of copyright material.

American Bar Association via the Copyright Clearance Center's RightsLink service for article: Henry T.C. Hu and Bernard Black (2006), 'Empty Voting and Hidden (Morphable) Ownership: Taxonomy, Implications, and Reforms', *Business Lawyer*, **61** (3), May, 1011–70.

American Economic Association for article: Robert J. Shiller (2003), 'From Efficient Markets Theory to Behavioral Finance', *Journal of Economic Perspectives*, **17** (1), Winter, 83–104.

Blackwell Publishing Ltd for articles: David Hirshleifer (2001), 'Investor Psychology and Asset Pricing', *Journal of Finance*, **LVI** (4), August, 1533–97; Rafael La Porta, Florencio Lopez-de-Silanes and Andrei Shleifer (2006), 'What Works in Securities Laws?', *Journal of Finance*, **LXI** (1), February, 1–32.

Columbia Law Review for article: John C. Coffee, Jr. (1991), 'Liquidity versus Control: The Institutional Investor as Corporate Monitor', *Columbia Law Review*, **91** (6), October, 1277–368.

Duke Law Journal for article: James D. Cox (1986), 'Insider Trading and Contracting: A Critical Response to the "Chicago School"', *Duke Law Journal*, **1986** (4), September, 628–59.

Elsevier Ltd for articles: Michael C. Jensen and Richard S. Ruback (1983), 'The Market for Corporate Control: The Scientific Evidence', *Journal of Financial Economics*, **11** (1–4), April, 5–50; Lawrence R. Glosten and Paul R. Milgrom (1985), 'Bid, Ask and Transaction Prices in a Specialist Market with Heterogeneously Informed Traders', *Journal of Financial Economics*, **14** (1), March, 71–100; Malcolm Baker, Jeffrey Wurgler and Yu Yuan (2012), 'Global, Local, and Contagious Investor Sentiment', *Journal of Financial Economics*, **104** (2), May, 272–87.

Harvard Business School Publishing for article: Henry G. Manne (1966), 'In Defense of Insider Trading', *Harvard Business Review*, **44**, November–December, 113–22.

Harvard Law Review Association via the Copyright Clearance Center's Rightslink service for articles: Frank H. Easterbrook and Daniel R. Fischel (1981), 'The Proper Role of a Target's Management in Responding to a Tender Offer', *Harvard Law Review*, **94** (6), April, 1161–204; Lucian A. Bebchuk (1982), 'The Case for Facilitating Competing Tender Offers', *Harvard Law Review*, **95**, 1028–56.

Northwestern University School of Law for article: David D. Haddock and Jonathan R. Macey (1986), 'A Coasian Model of Insider Trading', *Northwestern University Law Review*, **80** (6), 1449–72.

Stanford Law Review via the Copyright Clearance Center's RightsLink service for articles: Dennis W. Carlton and Daniel R. Fischel (1983), 'The Regulation of Insider Trading', *Stanford Law Review*, **35**, May, 857–95; Stephen J. Choi and A.C. Pritchard (2003), 'Behavioral Economics and the SEC', *Stanford Law Review*, **56** (1), October, 1–73.

University of Chicago Press for article: Henry G. Manne (1965), 'Mergers and the Market for Corporate Control', *Journal of Political Economy*, **73** (2), April, 110–20.

University of Illinois Law Review for article: Jennifer H. Arlen and William J. Carney (1992), 'Vicarious Liability for Fraud on Securities Markets: Theory and Evidence', *University of Illinois Law Review*, **1992** (3), 691–740.

Virginia Law Review via the Copyright Clearance Center's RightsLink service for article: Marcel Kahan and Edward Rock (2011), 'The Insignificance of Proxy Access', *Virginia Law Review*, **97**, 1347–434.

Yale Law Journal for article: Roberta Romano (1998), 'Empowering Investors: A Market Approach to Securities Regulation', *Yale Law Journal*, **107**, 2359–430.

Every effort has been made to trace all the copyright holders but if any have been inadvertently overlooked the publishers will be pleased to make the necessary arrangement at the first opportunity.

In addition the publishers wish to thank the Library of Indiana University at Bloomington, USA for its assistance in obtaining these articles.

Part I
Takeovers

[1]

MERGERS AND THE MARKET FOR CORPORATE CONTROL[1]

HENRY G. MANNE
George Washington University Law School

In recent years many of the traditional economic justifications of our antitrust laws have been seriously questioned. A new sophistication has developed, and economic activities frequently held illegal by the courts are now thought by many to be consistent with our antitrust goals. The rules against tie-ins, vertical mergers, predatory competition, among others, have to a greater or lesser degree had their theoretical foundations considerably weakened. Recently even cartels, the most venerable victim of American antitrust laws, have found their near champion.[2]

One practice, however, remains generally condemned in both the economic literature and the most recent Supreme Court rulings. Mergers among competitors would seem to have no important saving grace. The position has gained considerable legal currency that any merger between competing firms is at least suspect and perhaps per se illegal. The latter result seems especially likely when one of the combining firms already occupies a substantial position in the relevant market. Antitrust problems in the merger field seem more and more to be confined to discussions of relevant product and geographic markets and perhaps to the issue of quantitative substantiality.[3]

Presumably there is still a so-called failing-company defense to an illegal merger charge. The announced justification for this doctrine was that, if indeed the merged company was failing, then it was not actually a competitor in the industry.[4] But there are strong suggestions that even that defense may be unavailable when a large corporation is making the acquisition, or when there is any chance of absorption by a non-competing firm, or when the acquired company has not "failed" enough.[5]

[1] Helpful criticisms and suggestions on this article by Professors Armen A. Alchian, Joseph Aschheim, Donald Dewey, and Joseph P. McKenna are gratefully acknowledged.

A companion article to this one by the same author, entitled "Some Theoretical Aspects of Share Voting," appears in *Columbia Law Review*, LXIV (1964), 1427–45. That article analyzes the strategies available to shareholders when different techniques for taking over control of a corporation are used.

[2] Donald Dewey, "The Economic Theory of Anti-Trust: Science or Religion?" *Virginia Law Review*, L (1964), 413–34. This article also contains references to the other iconoclastic literature (pp. 426–27).

[3] Among the recent articles and cases bearing out this conclusion are the following: Donald Dewey, *op. cit.*; Richard E. Day, "Conglomerate Mergers and the 'Curse of Bigness,'" *North Carolina Law Review*, XLII (1964), 511–66; James A. Rahl, "Current Anti-Trust Developments in the Merger Field," *Anti-Trust Bulletin*, VIII (1963), 493–515; United States v. El Paso Natural Gas Company, 376 U.S. 651 (1964); and United States v. First National Bank and Trust Company of Lexington, 376 U.S. 665 (1964).

[4] International Shoe Company v. Federal Trade Commission, 280 U.S. 291, 294 (1929); but see Derek C. Bok, "Section 7 of the Clayton Act and the Merging of Law and Economics," *Harvard Law Review*, LXXIV (1960), 226–355, esp. p. 340, where concern for the interests in the failing company is argued to be the most likely reason for the doctrine.

[5] Derek C. Bok, *op. cit.*, pp. 339–47; and see cases cited in anonymous comment, "An Updating of the 'Failing Company' Doctrine in the Amended Section 7 Setting," *Michigan Law Review*, LXI (1963), 566–83.

There is also a "solely for investment" defense to Clayton Act charges. This appears as an explicit proviso in the third paragraph of Section 7, 15 U.S.C.A. sec. 18 (1962). But the famous du Pont–

There is general agreement among economists that the courts' approach to horizontal mergers is correct.[6] Professor Donald Dewey, who appears slightly regretful about the severe treatment of mergers by our courts and administrative agencies, concedes that no important economies can be attained through a merger which cannot be gained either by internal growth or, at worst, by a cartel, if that were legal. But Dewey is certainly not as severe in his personal indictment of horizontal mergers as most other economists. He has argued that most mergers "have virtually nothing to do with either the creation of market power or the realization of scale economies. They are merely a civilized alternative to bankruptcy or the voluntary liquidation that transfers assets from falling to rising firms."[7]

Consistent with his alternative-to-bankruptcy explanation of mergers, Dewey points out that, "[i]f the capital market were perfect and a merger conferred no monopoly power, a rising firm would be indifferent between the two forms of expansion."[8] Thus a rapidly expanding industry with a relatively short life cycle of its firms would be characterized by substantial external growth of successful firms. Mergers then would "most commonly indicate not the decline of competition but its undoubted vigor."[9]

Dewey's argument is, however, only a partial redemption of mergers, since a great many have occurred in industries in which the life cycle of firms is not as short as in the southern textile industry, which he mentions as his example. Further, Dewey's defense of mergers seems to be limited to those cases in which bankruptcy or liquidation is imminent. But, if a merger can be justified at this stage of the firm's life, presumably it is also desirable before bankruptcy becomes imminent in order to avoid that eventuality. If, as Dewey suggests, mergers actually are superior to bankruptcy as a method of "shifting assets from fall-

G. M. case, United States v. E. I. Du Pont de Nemours and Company, 353 U.S. 586 (1957), seems to have very substantially weakened the force of this proviso. Also see Swift and Co. v. F.T.C., 8 Fed. 2d 595, 599, reversed on other grounds, 272 U.S. 554 (1925), where it is stated: "It would be difficult to conceive of any case where one corporation purchased all the stock of its competitor solely for investment. Such a case would be a rare one."

There was once thought to be an illegal purpose requirement for convictions under the Sherman Act. See Eugene V. Rostow, "Monopoly under the Sherman Act: Power or Purpose?" *Illinois Law Review*, XLIII (1949), 745–92. But recent Supreme Court decisions in the merger field have left little vitality to that notion. Cf. United States v. First National Bank and Trust Company of Lexington, 376 U.S 665, 669 (1964).

[6] See George J. Stigler, "Mergers and Preventive Anti-Trust Policy," *Pennsylvania Law Review*, CIV (1955), 176–84 (Stigler too recognizes the possibility that some mergers may increase competition, but he finds it "most uncommon" [p. 181]); M. A. Adelman, "The Anti-Merger Act, 1950–60," *American Economic Review*, LI (May, 1961), 236–54 ("The horizontal elements of mergers . . . have been treated severely and—if maintaining competition is the object—rationally" [p. 238]).

[7] "Mergers and Cartels: Some Reservations about Policy," *Market Economic Review*, LI (May, 1961), 257. Dewey analyzed four relatively unimportant cases of scale economies that can be realized only through a consolidation, but he concluded, in substantial agreement with Stigler and Adelman, "that the present experiment discouraging growth by mergers should be continued" with a ban in any industry not generally considered a good example of workable competition (p. 261).

Jesse W. Markham has remarked that some mergers are the "means by which some entrepreneurs make their exit from the industry, selling their undepreciated assets to other entrepreneurs. . . . Since 1930 most mergers appear to have been of the ordinary business variety in that they had neither monopoly nor promotional gains as their objective" ("Survey of the Evidence and Findings on Mergers," in *Business Concentration and Price Policy* [New York: National Bureau of Economic Research, 1955], p. 181). He concluded that "while some mergers impair a competitive enterprise system, others may be an integral part of it" (p. 182).

[8] "Mergers and Cartels . . . ," *op. cit.*, p. 257.

[9] *Ibid.*

ing to rising firms," and if mergers were completely legal, we should anticipate relatively few actual bankruptcy proceedings in any industry which was not itself contracting. The function so wastefully performed by bankruptcies and liquidations would be economically performed by mergers at a much earlier stage of the firm's life.

THE CORPORATE-CONTROL MARKET

The conventional approach to a merger problem takes corporations merely as decision-making units or firms within the classical market framework. This approach dictates a ban on many horizontal mergers almost by definition. The basic proposition advanced in this paper is that the control of corporations may constitute a valuable asset; that this asset exists independent of any interest in either economies of scale or monopoly profits; that an active market for corporate control exists; and that a great many mergers are probably the result of the successful workings of this special market.

Basically this paper will constitute an introduction to a study of the market for corporation control. The emphasis will be placed on the antitrust implications of this market, but the analysis to follow has important implications for a variety of economic questions. Perhaps the most important implications are those for the alleged separation of ownership and control in large corporations. So long as we are unable to discern any control relationship between small shareholders and corporate management, the thrust of Berle and Means's famous phrase remains strong. But, as will be explained below, the market for corporate control gives to these shareholders both power and protection commensurate with their interest in corporate affairs.

A fundamental premise underlying the market for corporate control is the existence of a high positive correlation between corporate managerial efficiency and the market price of shares of that company.[10] As an existing company is poorly managed—in the sense of not making as great a return for the shareholders as could be accomplished under other feasible managements—the market price of the shares declines relative to the shares of other companies in the same industry or relative to the market as a whole. This phenomenon has a dual importance for the market for corporate control.

In the first place, a lower share price facilitates any effort to take over high-paying managerial positions. The com-

[10] The claim of a positive correlation between managerial efficiency and the market price of shares would seem at first blush to raise an empirical question. In fact, however, the concept of corporate managerial efficiency, with its overtones of an entrepreneurial function, is one for which there are no objective standards. But there are compelling reasons, apart from empirical data, for believing that this correlation exists. Insiders, those who have the most reliable information about corporate affairs, are strongly motived financially to perform a kind of arbitrage function for their company's stock. That is, given their sense of what constitutes efficient management, they will cause share prices to rise or decline in accordance with that standard.

The contention is often made that stock-market prices are not accurate gauges, since far more trades take place without reliable information than with it. But there is reason to believe that intelligence rather than ignorance ultimately determines the course of individual share prices. Stock-market decisions tend to be of the one-out-of-two-alternatives variety, such as buy or not buy, hold or sell, or put or call. To the extent that decisions on these questions are made by shareholders or potential shareholders operating without reliable information, over a period of time the decisions will tend to be randomly distributed and the effect will therefore be neutral. Decisions made by those with a higher degrees of certainty will to that extent not meet a canceling effect since they will not be made on a random basis. Over some period of time it would seem that the average market price of a company's shares must be the "correct" one.

pensation from these positions may take the usual forms of salary, bonuses, pensions, expense accounts, and stock options. Perhaps more important, it may take the form of information useful in trading in the company's shares; or, if that is illegal, information may be exchanged and the trading done in other companies' shares. But it is extremely doubtful that the full compensation recoverable by executives for managing their corporations explains more than a small fraction of outsider[11] attempts to take over control. Take-overs of corporations are too expensive generally to make the "purchase" of management compensation an attractive proposition.[12]

It is far more likely that a second kind of reward provides the primary motivation for most take-over attempts. The market price of shares does more than measure the price at which the normal compensation of executives can be "sold" to new individuals. Share price, or that part reflecting managerial efficiency, also measures the potential capital gain inherent in the corporate stock. The lower the stock price, relative to what it could be with more efficient management, the more attractive the take-over becomes to those who believe that they can manage the company more efficiently. And the potential return from the successful take-over and revitalization of a poorly run company can be enormous.[13]

Additional leverage in this operation can be obtained by borrowing the funds with which the shares are purchased, although American commercial banks are generally forbidden to lend money for this purpose. A comparable advantage can be had from using other shares rather than cash as the exchange medium. Given the fact of special tax treatment for capital gains, we can see how this mechanism for taking over control of badly run corporations is one of the most important "get-rich-quick" opportunities in our economy today.

But the greatest benefits of the take-over scheme probably inure to those least conscious of it. Apart from the stock market, we have no objective standard of managerial efficiency. Courts, as indicated by the so-called business-judgment rule, are loath to second-guess business decisions or remove directors from office. Only the take-over scheme provides some assurance of competitive efficiency among corporate managers and thereby affords strong protection to the interests of vast numbers of small, non-controlling shareholders. Compared to this mechanism, the efforts of the SEC and the courts to protect shareholders through the development of a fiduciary duty concept and the shareholder's derivative suit seem small indeed. It is true that sales by dissatisfied shareholders are necessary to trigger the mechanism and that these shareholders may suffer considerable losses. On the other hand, even greater capital losses are prevented by the existence of a competitive market for corporate control.[14]

[11] "Outsider" here refers to anyone not presently controlling the affairs of the corporation, even though it may include one or more individuals on the corporation's board of directors.

[12] To the extent that executive compensation increases with higher share prices, the take-over is most attractive at the time when it is also most expensive. Indeed, the danger of a take-over may account for managers' voluntarily decreasing their compensation when the company's share price is down.

[13] The clearest modern illustration is probably furnished by Louis Wolfson's successful venture into Montgomery Ward. For details of this and other large stock price gains associated with corporation "raids" see David Karr, *Fight for Control* (New York: Ballantine Books, 1956).

[14] Unfortunately the suppression of this market would be the consequence of proposals made by sev-

There are several mechanisms for taking over the control of corporations. The three basic techniques are the proxy fight, direct purchase of shares, and the merger. The costs, practical difficulties, and legal consequences of these approaches vary widely. The selection of one or another or some combination of these techniques frequently represents a difficult strategy decision. An attempt will be made in this paper to analyze some of the considerations involved in a selection of one device over another.

PROXY FIGHTS

The most dramatic and publicized of the take-over devices is the proxy fight; it is also the most expensive, the most uncertain, and the least used of the various techniques. Indeed it is somewhat difficult to describe the necessary conditions under which a proxy fight rather than some other take-over form will be indicated. At first blush, the proxy fight appears to be inexpensive since one does not have to own a large number of shares (or for that matter any shares) in order to wage a fight. But this fact is most relevant when the take-over is for the purpose of gaining the incumbents' compensation. If the outsider wants capital gains, he will be interested in owning more, not fewer, shares. This suggests that proxy fights will be relatively more often used when the issue is not one of management policies but of distribution of insiders' compensation.[15]

Even as a device for settling internal power struggles, actual proxy fights constitute only a small percentage of threatened fights.[16] The parties will generally prefer to negotiate a settlement in accordance with their respective strengths than incur the costs of soliciting proxies. The more reliable the information about relative strengths available, the more will settlement be likely to occur. This suggests that proxy fights will be relatively more common when there is widespread distribution of the company's shares than when there are relatively large holdings.

In a number of cases the outsider would probably like to own more shares and take over control without waging or threatening a proxy fight. But if he is unable to accumulate sufficient capital to purchase control directly, he may settle for half a loaf. In effect he indicates his willingness to share the capital-gain potential with all other shareholders in exchange for enough of their votes to put him into control.

When a proxy fight is announced, the shares tend to rise in price, reflecting a rise in both the market value of the vote and the discounted value of potential gain in the underlying share interest if

---

eral writers in the field. For a review and a criticism of this literature see Henry G. Manne, "The 'Higher Criticism' of the Modern Corporation," *Columbia Law Review*, LXII (1962), 399–432. For another defense of this market see Harry G. Johnson, *The Canadian Quandary* (Toronto: McGraw-Hill Book Co., 1963), pp. xvii–xviii.

[15] The courts draw a similar distinction for purposes of determining when contestants in a proxy fight may recover their expenses from the corporate treasury. Generally they may recover if the contest is found to be one of policy rather than a "purely personal power contest" (Rosenfeld v. Fairchild Engine & Airplane Corp., 309 N.Y. 168, 129 N.E. 2d 291 [1955]). It does not seem to be too difficult, however, to establish the existence of a "policy" controversy to the court's satisfaction.

[16] In the SEC's fiscal year 1962 seventeen companies were involved in proxy contests, while a total of 253 persons, both management and non-management, filed statements as participants. The respective figures for 1961 were thirty-two proxy contests and 463 participant filings. Many non-management filings are multiple; that is, several people are involved in the same fight. But no breakdown beyond the total number of participants is available. Therefore, it is impossible to prove the point made in the text from published data. See *27th and 28th Annual Reports* (Washington: Securities and Exchange Commission, 1961 and 1962).

the outsider wins.[17] Other outsiders will find it in their interest to retain their shares or purchase shares, to vote for the outsider seeking control, and to share in the capital appreciation. It may be cheaper to elicit the support of these voters through expenditures on persuasion than through outright purchase of the shares. But to the outsider seeking control, every voter represents another person with whom he must share the potential gain resulting from his more efficient management. These voters are analogous to, or substitutes for, the capital or credit with which the outsider would otherwise purchase control directly.

Proxy-fight expenses have always included direct expenses of mailings, advertising, telephone calls, and visits to large shareholders. But since the Securities Exchange Act of 1934, the cost of waging a proxy fight has probably increased substantially. Prior to the act, the proxy system operated largely through broker intermediaries acting as full agents for the beneficial owners of the shares. To the brokers was delegated not merely the ministerial job of voting but the more important responsibility of deciding how to vote. That practice has been largely replaced because of the SEC philosophy that the proxy system should duplicate actual meetings of shareholders as closely as possible. Thus, today, "giving a proxy" is really tantamount to voting. And, since the shareholder himself is voting, it is also felt that he should be fully and truthfully informed about all aspects of the corporation's affairs. This has tremendously increased the cost of soliciting proxies. But while the incumbents finance the bulk of their proxy solicitation expenses from corporate funds, the outsider will have this advantage only if he wins.[18]

DIRECT PURCHASE OF SHARES

The second mechanism for taking over control of a corporation is the direct purchase of the requisite number of shares of the corporations. There are several techniques that may be used in the direct

[17] See Henry G. Manne, *op. cit.*, pp. 410–13. It is possible, of course, for the vote price to be rising while the market value of the underlying investment interest is declining, though this would seem to be uncommon.

[18] The SEC rules on proxy solicitations have aided the insiders in unexpected and curious ways. Outsiders in a proxy fight are not privy to the particulars of corporate information as are the insiders, so they must frequently "guess" why the company is not doing as well as it should. These "guesses" will take the form of broad accusations and innuendoes directed at the incumbents. Outsiders would like the opportunity to include in their proxy solicitation such general statements as "the incumbents are wasting corporate assets"; "the incumbents are paying themselves fraudulently high salaries"; or "the officers of the company have been negligent in failing to acquire new opportunities for the corporation." The SEC generally refuses to allow such statements to be mailed to shareholders unless the insurgents can prove the truthfulness of the allegations. Frequently there is no way the insurgents can find that proof, short of discovery proceedings in a suit, though they might in all good faith suspect the facts alleged. Therefore, the practice has developed of filing shareholder derivative suits when a proxy fight is decided upon. Then the solicitation materials may legally say, "A shareholder's derivative suit is presently pending in the Federal District Court for the Southern District of New York charging the officers and directors with waste of corporate assets"; or "a suit to force the officers to pay back part of their salaries has been filed by a shareholder in Delaware"; etc.

Not only has the Securities Exchange Act increased the cost of waging a proxy fight because of the additional materials that must be cleared through the SEC, but it has also increased uncertainty because of the panoply of SEC regulations. For instance, the Chicago and North Western Railroad's successful fight against the Union Pacific's first bid for control of the Rock Island Railroad was recently voided on the grounds, among others, that unsolicited advice by a broker to his customer advising acceptance of the C. & N.W.'s offer constituted an illegal solicitation of proxies (Union Pacific Railroad Company v. Chicago and North Western Railway Company, 226 F. Supp. 400 [N.D., Ill., 1964]).

purchase of shares. The most obvious is outright purchase on the open market of the requisite percentage of shares.[19] The outsider might also try to buy the shares from large individual owners, thus preserving secrecy and allowing negotiation on price. Finally, he may make a bid for tenders, that is, a request that shareholders make an offer to sell their shares to him at a certain price, usually above the market. This last form of direct purchase is most apposite when the shares are widely held and there is a chance of a fast increase in market price if the news spreads that there is a heavy buyer in the market for the company's shares. A tender bid is usually stated to be effective only if a minimum percentage of shares is offered at the announced price. Also, the bid will ordinarily be for less than 100 per cent of the shares in order to avoid the problem of many individual shareholders trying to be the sole hold-out. In practice, private negotiation for large blocks of shares may be combined with either open-market purchases or a tender bid.

There are few serious legal problems with any of the direct purchase techniques. In fact, about the only one which has arisen with any regularity in recent years results from Professor Adolf A. Berle's contention that control is a corporate asset.[20] The implication of this notion is that any premium received by an individual for a sale of control belongs in equity to all of the shareholders. As a general proposition, the courts have refused to follow this thesis; and there are numerous judicial statements to the effect that one may claim a premium for control.[21]

A number of legal writers, following Berle, continue to press for a rule of equality in share purchase price when an outsider buys control in a corporation.[22] The economic results of such a rule could be most unfortunate. Many holders of

[19] This percentage may range from less than 51 per cent if the purchaser is only interested in establishing a foundation for a proxy fight; to 51 per cent when only simple control is desired; to $66\frac{2}{3}$ or 75 per cent, when state law requires that percentage for approval of a merger or reorganization; to 80 per cent, the figure required for consolidation of income statements under the Internal Revenue Code as well as for tax-free reorganizations; to 90 per cent, the figure required for simplified mergers of subsidiaries into parent companies in Delaware (95 per cent in New York); or 100 per cent if no minority interests are wanted.

[20] Adolf A. Berle and Gardiner C. Means, *The Modern Corporation and Private Property* (New York: Macmillan Co., 1933), p. 244; Adolf A. Berle, "'Control' in Corporate Law," *Columbia Law Review*, LVIII (1958), 1212–25, esp. 1221.

[21] The difficult cases have been those in which control carried with it peculiar advantages not normally assumed to be part of the standard compensation of corporate managers. The problem is illustrated by the now classic case of Perlman v. Feldmann, 219 F. 2d 172 (2d Cir., 1955), in which only a controlling block of shares was purchased, but at a price reflecting the value of the right to allocate the company's steel production to the purchaser at a time when quasi-official price controls existed. The court found the control seller liable to the other shareholders for a part of the premium received over the normal market price of the shares. The most convincing factor, not emphasized by the court, was that the company had probably been receiving a full free-market price for its steel, with the difference over the controlled price taken in the form of interest-free loans and guaranteed future orders. Indications were that the new controllers would sell to themselves at the "quasi-legal" price and discontinue these other valuable practices. Thus the premium paid for the control block of shares was given partly in exchange for a right more appropriately thought of as belonging equally to each share than to the control group. That is, if a "gray-market" profit was to be made, it should go to all the shareholders. The court was explicit, however, that the seller could retain that part of the premium received for control not covering the power to allocate steel.

[22] Richard W. Jennings, "Trading in Corporate Control," *California Law Review*, XLIV (1956), 1–39; and Noyes Leech, "Transactions in Corporate Control," *University of Pennsylvania Law Review*, CIV (1956), 725–839. For a sharply opposing viewpoint see Wilbur G. Katz, "The Sale of Corporate Control," *Chicago Bar Record*, XXXVIII (1957), 376–80; also Alfred Hill, "The Sale of Controlling Shares," *Harvard Law Review*, LXX (1957), 986–1039.

control blocks of shares would refuse to sell at a share price which did not pay them a premium at least sufficient to compensate them for the loss of net values presently being received from their position in the corporation. If all non-controlling shareholders must accordingly be paid a premium over the market price of their shares, then in a substantial number of cases the purchaser will not conclude the bargain. This further suggests that, if control is securely held in one block, the "market price" of traded shares is the price for an underlying share interest without an aliquot portion of control. That is, if one person owns 51 per cent of the shares of a company, nothing will be paid for the vote attached to the other shares,[23] no matter how actively the shares may be traded on the market. The less securely control is held in one block, the more likely are non-controlling shareholders to participate in the "premium," and the less will an outsider be willing to pay one shareholder for control. Both proxy fights and competitive tender bids are more likely to occur under these conditions, since each of them gives shareholders the power to sell their votes at a premium.

MERGERS

The third major mechanism for taking over control of the corporation is the merger. Here, by definition, the acquiring concern will be a corporation and not an individual, and the medium of exchange used to buy control will typically be shares of the acquiring company rather than cash. Another major difference between the merger and other take-over forms is that, almost without exception, a merger requires the explicit approval of those already in control of the corporation.[24] And most statutes require more than a simple majority vote by shareholders to effectuate a merger. If the merger occurs after an acquisition of shares in a tender bid, then the tender bid and not the merger is the actual mechanism for changing control.

The requirement of management's approval for a merger generates some peculiar results. Generally speaking, managers' incentives and interests coincide with those of their shareholders in every particular except one: they have no incentive, as managers, to buy management services for the company at the lowest possible price.[25] Even if the market for corporate control is working perfectly, so long as the cost to the corporation of the incumbent managers' inefficiency is below the cost to an outsider of taking over control, the insiders will remain secure in the positions with protected high salaries.[26]

In the case of tender bids, as we have seen, a premium for control may be paid; and in the proxy fight situation, in one

[23] This holds true only to the extent that 51 per cent is the relevant majority. If a higher percentage is necessary for some purpose, minority votes will have some value so long as the requisite percentage is not already controlled.

[24] There is a slight possibility that outsiders might be able to force a merger vote by shareholders under the Securities Exchange Act's "Stockholder's Proposal" Rule, although the SEC seems to take the position that such a proposal may only be advisory, not mandatory, on the board, if passed. See Louis Loss, *Securities Regulation* (Boston: Little, Brown & Co., 1961), p. 908.

[25] To the extent that the same individuals are also shareholders, their motivation will reflect a conflict. If their ownership interest is great enough, they may sacrifice the emoluments of management in order to improve their position as shareholders. The decision will simply reflect the greater of the two conflicting interests.

[26] This may furnish some proof for the notion that executive compensation is a function of size. If the cost of taking over control is a function of the number of shareholders, as it certainly is in the case of proxy fights, it is likely that managers may be able to claim larger compensation to the extent of the higher cost to outsiders of buying control.

sense at least, the premium is paid in the form of expenditures necessary to persuade shareholders to vote a certain way. But the merger has considerable cost advantages over the other two forms of take-over, not the least being the ability to use shares rather than cash as the purchasing medium.

The shareholders should ordinarily be willing to accept any offer of a tax-free exchange of new marketable shares worth more than their old shares. But the managers are in a position to claim almost the full market value of control, since they have it in their power to block the merger by voting against it.[27] When we find incumbents recommending a control change, it is generally safe to assume that some side payment is occurring.

Side payments are often not simple transactions at law because of the rule that directors and officers may not sell their positions shorn of the share interest necessary to insure a transfer of control.[28] The most obvious kind of side payment to managers is a position within the new structure either paying a salary or making them privy to valuable market information.[29] This arrangement, easily established with mergers, can look like normal business expediency, since the argument can always be made that the old management provides continuity and a link with the past experience of the corporation.

There is still another very important reason why mergers may be more desirable than proxy fights or take-over bids as a way of operating in the corporate-control market. This is a market in which reliable information about valuable opportunities will be extremely difficult to discover. For reasons already mentioned, the corporate insiders will generally have no incentive to advertise this kind of information. Blatant cases will, of course, be evident from casual observation of industrial affairs and the stock market.[30]

The great problem in the corporate-control market is finding reliable information about new opportunities. There have generally been a few individual operators in this market, and perhaps they have found the more obvious cases of bad management. But to guarantee effective competitition in the market for corporate control, it seems clear that corporations must be allowed to function therein. Managers of a competing firm, unlike free-wheeling individual participants in the market for corporate control, almost automatically know a great deal of the kind of information crucial to a take-over decision. Careful analysis of cost conditions in their own firm and the market price of shares of other corporations in the same industry will provide information that can be relied upon with some degree of confidence.

Since, in a world of uncertainty, profitable transactions will be entered into

[27] The greater the shareholdings of mangement, the more likely they are to approve a merger offer with little or no side payment.

[28] Essex Universal Corp. v. Yates 305 F.2d (2d Cir., 1962).

[29] See, e.g., Smith v. The Good Music Station, 129 A.2d 242 (Del. Ch. 1957), and Borak v. J. I. Case Co., 317 Fed. 2d 838, at 844 (7th Cir., 1963), aff'd 377 U.S. 426 (1964). There are no reported cases of differential numbers of shares being offered controlling and non-controlling shareholders in a merger. Such an arrangement may be illegal under state statutes, and it is not likely to receive the high-majority-share vote required for most mergers.

[30] The most obvious example is that of a corporation whose total assets in liquidation would be worth more than the aggregate market value of all of its shares. This situation can continue to exist only because no individual shareholder believes there is any way of claiming the premium, since the managers will take no step toward liquidation and there is no indication that the corporation will not continue to be badly run. Perhaps the classic case of this sort was the take-over by Louis Wolfson of the Capital Transit Corporation. For this and other examples see Karr, *op. cit.*, p. 150.

more often by those whose information is relatively more reliable,[31] it should not surprise us that mergers within the same industry have been a principal form of changing corporate control. Reliable information is often available to suppliers and customers as well. Thus many vertical mergers may be of the control takeover variety rather than of the "foreclosure of competitors" or scale-economies type. Undoubtedly many more mergers, both horizontal and vertical, would have occurred but for our antitrust laws. The managers of corporations have considerable incentive to exploit such opportunities for their corporation, just as they are motivated to find any good new investment opportunity. And there are both legal and practical barriers to the individuals' utilizing such opportunities for themselves.

CONCLUSIONS

Mergers seem in many instances to be the most efficient of the three devices for corporate take-overs. Consequently, they are of considerable importance for the protection of individual non-controlling shareholders and are desirable from a general welfare-economics point of view. Certainly they are more desirable than the increased number of bankruptcies that would undoubtedly ensue if this avenue of taking over control were totally closed.

This is not to suggest that the antitrust norm of competition in the product market need be entirely sacrificed to the norm of competition in the market for corporate control. Rather it points up some of the serious problems with current antitrust doctrine. The market for corporate control implies a number of important advantages which must be compared to those existing in present antitrust enforcement. Among the advantages of the former, as we have seen, are a lessening of wasteful bankruptcy proceedings, more efficient management of corporations, the protection afforded non-controlling corporate investors, increased mobility of capital, and generally a more efficient allocation of resources.

The greatest difficulty in assessing the proper role for the market for corporate control comes in the area of horizontal mergers, where, as previously indicated, this market may operate most effectively.[32] It may be that, so long as entry into an industry is kept open, there is no reason at all for rules against mergers, at least short of a monopolization charge under Section 2 of the Sherman Act. It is extremely unlikely, however, that Congress or the courts would ever adopt such a rule.

Far more likely is an *ad hoc* recognition of the importance of the market for corporate control in individual cases.[33] Courts or agencies might begin to look at such factors as the average life cycle of firms in the industry, the amount of total new investment in the industry, the condition of the acquired firms in terms of both financial and managerial strength, the number of bankruptcies in the industry, and the amount of proxy-fight and tender-bid activity. These fac-

[31] Cf. H. B. Malmgren, "Information, Expectations, and the Theory of the Firm," *Quarterly Journal of Economics*, LXXIX (1961), 399–421; and George J. Stigler, "The Economics of Information," *Journal of Political Economy*, LXIX (1961), 213–25.

[32] The case for a free market in corporate control as between supplier and customer firms seems quite strong, since the arguments in favor of present anti-merger policy are perhaps weakest there. See Robert Bork, "Vertical Integration and the Sherman Act: The Legal History of an Economic Misconception," *University of Chicago Law Review*, XXII (1954), 157–201.

[33] This might be done either through the resurrection of the "business-purpose" doctrine or, in Clayton Act cases, by beefing up the "solely-for-investment" proviso. See n. 5 above.

tors would then have to be weighed on the scales with the more traditional approach in terms of number of firms in the industry, concentration ratios, size of the acquiring firm, and its acquisitions history. But no longer does the tendency to hold most mergers illegal per se seem justified.

One real problem will be in devising statistical methods for distinguishing mergers motivated by a quest for monopoly profit from those merely trying to establish more efficient management in poorly run companies. But if the theoretical aspects of these transactions are well enough understood, this should not be insuperable. There may be different effects on the prices of shares depending on the motive behind the merger. In the normal merger for acquisition of control, something will be paid by the acquiring company for the control opportunity. Since this factor does not figure largely in the market price of even badly run companies until the possibility of a takeover is known, the exchange ratio in the merger will appear to be too favorable to the acquired company, judged by the relative premerger announcement prices. The price of the shares of the acquiring company in such a merger should then tend to decrease and those of the acquired company to increase upon the announcement of the merger. If, on the other hand, the merger is motivated by a quest for market power, or by economies of scale available to both corporations, then the price of stock of each company should increase on the announcement of the merger terms. The first of these two results conforms to what seems most frequently to occur when mergers are announced, though no data are presently available on this subject.[34] The study of the economics of the market for corporate control is still in its infancy.

[34] A study of the effect of mergers on stock prices has been completed by the staff of the Subcommittee on Anti-Trust and Monopoly of the Senate Judiciary Committee. That study was unavailable at the time of writing this article.

Another possible approach to proof in this area is to determine if actual changes in the management personnel ultimately follow the merger. In mergers for market power, there is little reason to believe that this will occur very quickly; whereas, if the position is in the nature of a side payment, as it would be if the merger was motivated more by the control potential, we might anticipate somewhat earlier efforts to "ease out" the old managers of the acquired company.

[2]

VOLUME 94 APRIL 1981 NUMBER 6

HARVARD LAW REVIEW

THE PROPER ROLE OF A TARGET'S MANAGEMENT IN RESPONDING TO A TENDER OFFER

Frank H. Easterbrook and Daniel R. Fischel***

Under existing federal and state law, a corporation's managers can resist and often defeat a premium tender offer without liability to either the corporation's shareholders or the unsuccessful tender offeror. Professors Easterbrook and Fischel argue that resistance by a corporation's managers to premium tender offers, even if it triggers a bidding contest, ultimately decreases shareholder welfare. Shareholders would be better off, the authors claim, were such resistance all but proscribed. The authors consider, but find wanting, a number of potential criticisms of their analysis; they conclude by proposing a rule of mangerial passivity capable of controlling resistance in actual cases.

A cash tender offer typically presents shareholders of the "target" corporation with the opportunity to sell many if not all of their shares quickly and at a premium over the market price.[1] Notwithstanding the apparent benefit both to shareholders of the target and to the acquirer when such offers succeed, the target's management may oppose the offer, arguing that the premium is insufficient or that the corporation would be harmed by its new owners. To defeat the offer, management may file suits against the offeror, sell new shares to dilute the offeror's holdings, manufacture an antitrust prob-

* Assistant Professor of Law, University of Chicago.

** Assistant Professor of Law, Northwestern University. The Authors thank Walter J. Blum, Michael Bradley, Lea Brilmayer, Dennis W. Carlton, Peter Dodd, Richard A. Epstein, Mayer Freed, Leo Herzel, Gregg A. Jarrell, Edmund W. Kitch, Douglas M. Kraus, John H. Langbein, Douglas Laycock, Bernard D. Meltzer, Daniel Polsby, Richard A. Posner, Stephen Presser, David S. Ruder, Myron Scholes, Kenneth E. Scott, Stephen M. Shapiro, Matthew L. Spitzer, Robert S. Stillman, Harry Watson, and participants at the law and economics workshops of Harvard and the University of Chicago Law Schools for their helpful comments. The Law and Economics Program of the University of Chicago provided support for the writing of this Article; David Glazer furnished assistance in the research.

[1] *See, e.g.*, Panter v. Marshall Field & Co., 486 F. Supp. 1168 (N.D. Ill. 1980), *appeal docketed*, No. 80-1375 (7th Cir. Mar. 21, 1980). *Marshall Field* involved a shareholder's suit against management for defeating a tender offer with a premium exceeding 100% of the price just prior to formulation of offer plans.

lem by acquiring one of the offeror's competitors, or engage in a wide variety of other defensive tactics.[2] Sometimes the resistance leads to the target's being acquired at a price above the initial bid, either by the original bidder or by a "white knight,"[3] and sometimes the resistance defeats the takeover attempt altogether.[4]

The ability of management to engage in defensive tactics in response to a cash tender offer is a relatively recent development in contests for corporate control. Prior to the enactment of the Williams Act[5] in 1968, offerors were free to structure offers in a manner designed to force shareholders to decide quickly whether to sell all or part of their shares at a premium.[6] The target's management consequently had little time to mobilize a defensive strategy to impede the offer. The Williams Act, however, has deprived the offeror of this advantage of speed by regulating the conditions under which the offer can be made.[7] More than half the states have enacted

---

[2] The common defensive stratagems are set out in E. ARANOW, H. EINHORN & G. BERLSTEIN, DEVELOPMENTS IN TENDER OFFERS FOR CORPORATE CONTROL 193–206 (1977); A. FLEISCHER, TENDER OFFERS: DEFENSES, RESPONSES AND PLANNING (1978); M. LIPTON & E. STEINBERGER, TAKEOVERS AND FREEZEOUTS §§ 6.4–6.6.3 (1978 & Supp. 1980); Hochman & Folger, *Deflecting Takeovers: Charter and By-Law Techniques*, 34 BUS. LAW. 537 (1979); Nathan & Sobel, *Corporate Stock Repurchases in the Context of Unsolicited Takeover Bids*, 35 BUS. LAW. 1545 (1980).

[3] The recent battle between J. Ray McDermott, Inc., and Wheelabrator-Frye, Inc., for control of Pullman, Inc., provides a notable illustration of the "white knight" phenomenon. McDermott initiated the bidding at $28 per share in July 1980. Wheelabrator-Frye won the fight several months later with a bid of $52.50 per share, covering more than five times the number of shares McDermott offered to purchase initially. *See* McDermott, Inc. v. Wheelabrator-Frye, Inc., No. 80-2306 (7th Cir. Sept. 25, 1980); Wall St. J., Aug. 22, 1980, at 2, col. 2; *id.*, Sept. 17, 1980, at 4, col. 2; *id.*, Sept. 18, 1980, at 55, col. 1.

[4] *See, e.g.*, Lewis v. McGraw, 619 F.2d 192 (2d Cir.), *cert. denied*, 101 S. Ct. 354 (1980); Panter v. Marshall Field & Co., 486 F. Supp. 1168 (N.D. Ill. 1980), *appeal docketed*, No. 80-1375 (7th Cir. Mar. 21, 1980); Labaton Co. v. Universal Leaf Tobacco Co., [1979 Transfer Binder] FED. SEC. L. REP. (CCH) ¶ 96,943 (S.D.N.Y. 1979); Berman v. Gerber Prods. Co., 454 F. Supp. 1310 (W.D. Mich. 1978); Grossman, Faber & Miller, P.A. v. Cable Funding Corp., [1974–1975 Transfer Binder] FED. SEC. L. REP. (CCH) ¶ 94,913 (D. Del. 1974); Northwest Indus. v. B.F. Goodrich Co., 301 F. Supp. 706 (N.D. Ill. 1969).

[5] 15 U.S.C. §§ 78g, 78l–78n, 78s (1976).

[6] Before 1968 offerors could limit the time an offer would be available, require that tenders be irrevocable, or specify that if the offer should be oversubscribed the first shares to be tendered would be the first to be purchased. Offers with such terms produced considerable pressure for shareholders to tender quickly, lest they lose the opportunity to realize the favorable terms.

[7] *See* 15 U.S.C. § 78n(d)(5) (1976) (indirectly compelling every offer to remain open for at least seven days by allowing shareholders to withdraw any shares they have tendered during that time); 17 C.F.R. 240.14d-7(a)(1) (1980) (rule promulgated by the Securities and Exchange Commission extending the minimum period to 15 business

tender offer statutes that go beyond the Williams Act in placing restrictions on the ability of an offeror to wage a tender offer.[8] The effect of state and federal regulation of tender offers has been to give the target's management the time to undertake a defensive strategy.[9]

The reaction of shareholders to managerial resistance depends on the outcome. Few protest when resistance leads to a takeover at a higher price. When resistance thwarts the takeover attempt altogether, however, litigation usually follows. Although defeat of the takeover attempt may deprive the target's shareholders of a substantial premium, shareholders' suits against management to recover this loss are almost always unsuccessful.[10] Relying on the business judgment rule, courts typically have held that the target's management has the right, and even the duty, to oppose a tender offer it determines to be contrary to the firm's best interests.[11] Commentators generally have applauded the results of these cases.[12]

---

days); 17 C.F.R. 240.14d-7(a)(2) (1980) (SEC rule requiring the offer to remain open for 10 business days after another bidder makes a tender offer for the same class of securities). For a criticism of the Williams Act, see Fischel, *Efficient Capital Market Theory, the Market for Corporate Control, and the Regulation of Cash Tender Offers*, 57 TEX. L. REV. 1 (1978).

[8] To the extent that the state statutes are less hospitable to hostile takeover bids than the Williams Act, they are of doubtful constitutionality. *Compare* Kennecott Corp. v. Smith, 637 F.2d 181 (3d Cir. 1980), *and* MITE Corp. v. Dixon, 633 F.2d 486 (7th Cir. 1980), *appeal docketed sub nom.* Edgar v. MITE Corp., 49 U.S.L.W. 3533 (U.S. Jan. 15, 1981) (No. 80-1188), *and* Great W. United Corp. v. Kidwell, 577 F.2d 1256 (5th Cir. 1978), *rev'd on other grounds sub nom.* Leroy v. Great W. United Corp., 443 U.S. 173 (1979), *and* Dart Indus. v. Conrad, 462 F. Supp. 1 (S.D. Ind. 1978) (unconstitutional), *with* Telvest, Inc. v. Bradshaw, 618 F.2d 1029 (4th Cir. 1980) (probably constitutional), *and* AMCA Int'l Corp. v. Krouse, 482 F. Supp. 929 (S.D. Ohio 1979) (constitutional), *and* Unitrode Corp. v. Dynamics Corp. of Am., 399 N.E.2d 5 (Mass. 1980) (construing state statute to avoid constitutional problems). *See generally* Note, *Securities Law and the Constitution: State Tender Offer Statutes Reconsidered*, 88 YALE L.J. 510 (1979).

[9] This has been recognized in several recent decisions that have held state tender offer statutes to be unconstitutional. *See* Kennecott Corp. v. Smith, 637 F.2d 181 (3d Cir. 1980); MITE Corp. v. Dixon, 633 F.2d 486 (7th Cir. 1980), *appeal docketed sub nom.* Edgar v. MITE Corp., 49 U.S.L.W. 3533 (U.S. Jan. 15, 1981) (No. 80-1188).

[10] *See, e.g.*, Lewis v. McGraw, 619 F.2d 192 (2d Cir.), *cert. denied*, 101 S. Ct. 354 (1980); Panter v. Marshall Field & Co., 486 F. Supp. 1168 (N.D. Ill. 1980), *appeal docketed*, No. 80-1375 (7th Cir. Mar. 21, 1980); Berman v. Gerber Prods. Co., 454 F. Supp. 1310 (W.D. Mich. 1978). *See also* Treadway Cos. v. Care Corp., 638 F.2d 357 (2d Cir. 1980), *rev'g in part* 490 F. Supp. 668 (S.D.N.Y. 1980), *discussed at* note 101 *infra*.

[11] *E.g.*, Panter v. Marshall Field & Co., 486 F. Supp. 1168 (N.D. Ill. 1980), *appeal docketed*, No. 80-1375 (7th Cir. Mar. 21, 1980).

[12] *See, e.g.*, Herzel, Schmidt & Davis, *Why Corporate Directors Have a Right to*

We argue in this Article that current legal rules allowing the target's management to engage in defensive tactics in response to a tender offer decrease shareholders' welfare. The detriment to shareholders is fairly clear where defensive tactics result in a defeat of a takeover, causing shareholders to lose the tender premium. Even where resistance leads to a higher price paid for the firm's shares, however, shareholders as a whole do not necessarily benefit. The value of any stock can be understood as the sum of two components: the price that will prevail in the market if there is no successful offer (multiplied by the likelihood that there will be none) and the price that will be paid in a future tender offer (multiplied by the likelihood that some offer will succeed). A shareholder's welfare is maximized by a legal rule that enables the sum of these two components to reach its highest value. Any approach that looks only at the way in which managers can augment the tender offeror's bid, given that a tender offer has already been made, but disregards the effect of a defensive strategy on the number of offers that will be made in the future and the way in which the number of offers affects the efficiency with which corporations are managed, ignores much that is relevant to shareholders' welfare.

We attempt in Part I to furnish what the existing legal literature and case law lacks: a framework for understanding how defensive tactics affect the number of tender offers, the price if an offer is made, and the price of stock in the event no offer is made. Our investigation leads to the conclusion that shareholders' welfare is maximized by an externally imposed legal rule severely limiting the ability of managers to resist a tender offer even if the purpose of resistance is to trigger a bidding contest. In Part II we consider and reject a number of the arguments which have been raised against our analysis of the proper role of a target's management in response to a tender offer. Finally, in Part III we propose a rule of managerial passivity that could be applied to control resistance to tender offers, and show that such a rule would not be inconsistent with the prevailing principles of fiduciary duty that apply to managers or with the business judgment rule.

Resist Tender Offers, 3 CORP. L. REV. 107 (1980); Lipton, *Takeover Bids in the Target's Boardroom*, 35 BUS. LAW. 101 (1979); Steinbrink, *Management's Response to the Takeover Attempt*, 28 CASE W. L. REV. 882 (1978). *See also* A. FLEISCHER, *supra* note 2; Hochman & Folger, *supra* note 2; M. LIPTON & E. STEINBERGER, *supra* note 2. Other authors, although skeptical about the motivation for resistance, would allow defensive tactics in certain circumstances. *See, e.g.*, Gelfond & Sebastian, *Reevaluating the Duties of Target Management in a Hostile Tender Offer*, 60 B.U.L. REV. 403 (1980); Lynch & Steinberg, *The Legitimacy of Defensive Tactics in Tender Offers*, 64 CORNELL L. REV. 901 (1979).

I. Defensive Tactics and Shareholder Welfare

A cash tender offer at a premium over the market price gives each shareholder the opportunity to obtain, with certainty, a return exceeding the current market value of the target's stock. It would be possible, if overly simple, to stop at this point and conclude that tender offers are beneficial to the target's shareholders. Simple ideas do not always survive scrutiny, and this one has been subject to challenge on the ground that the market price of shares does not reflect their real worth. Instead, it is argued, the price of shares must be too low at the time of the offer, for how else could the prospective acquirer offer to pay a premium? We address these concerns in Section A below. In subsection 1 we examine how the price of shares comes to reflect their value. In subsection 2 we discuss why bidders might offer more than the market price. We then use the principles explained in Section A to show in Section B how shareholders would be best off if managers did not resist tender offers.

A. Tender Offers and the Markets for Stock and Managers

1. Efficient Capital Market Theory and the Price of Tender Offers. — It is very unlikely that price and "value" will diverge in large markets for shares. If there were such divergences, investors could reap substantial gains by identifying and buying underpriced shares and selling overpriced shares.[13] Since there are many sophisticated investors with ample capital, the arbitrage process would proceed quite quickly, and it would become impossible to make systematic gains by finding undervalued shares. As investors bought and sold on the basis of what they knew, their very activity would drive the price toward the correct one. The change in the price would reduce the gains available from identifying mispriced shares. Indeed, once information about a firm reached the market, prices would adjust quickly whether or not anyone traded, because no trader with rational expectations would sell for less than the price he expected the shares to reach once the news became widespread.

The process of estimation and trading leads to prices that embody all of the available information about the value of the shares. Commonly referred to as the "efficient capital market hypothesis," the proposition that it is not possible to make abnormal gains by identifying and trading in mispriced stocks

[13] A share is "underpriced" or "overpriced" in relation to some future price. We do not imply that a share has any intrinsic value.

has been widely accepted.[14] It means that the price of shares reflects the collective wisdom of all traders about the value of the stock, and it also means that there is no reliable way to determine the direction, amount, or even existence of any difference between today's and tomorrow's price. If capital markets are efficient, as the evidence shows them to be,[15] then any statement that a given stock is really worth more than its

[14] *See* note 15 *infra*. The statement that investors do not usually profit by acquiring new information in an efficient capital market raises interesting problems. If the price of shares fully incorporates information about the firm, then no one has an incentive to gather additional information. Yet information-gathering, followed by trading, is the process by which prices come to embody the information. The more closely price follows information, it seems, the less information there will be, and consequently the more profitable it becomes to gather new information and beat the market. The matter is not, however, paradoxical. Market participants will simply secure information to the point where the marginal dollar invested in research equals the gain to be had from making better projections. There will not be an equilibrium with perfect information, but there is an "equilibrium degree of disequilibrium." Grossman & Stiglitz, *On the Impossibility of Informationally Efficient Markets*, 70 AM. ECON. REV. 393 (1980). *See also* Langbein & Posner, *Market Funds and Trust-Investment Law: II*, 1977 AM. B. FOUNDATION RESEARCH J. 1, 7–12. Because information spreads quickly through the market, this equilibrium will be an optimal guess about tomorrow's price of shares. Even though some people can make a living by acquiring and trading on information, it is unlikely that anyone could improve on the informativeness of the share's price as a method of summarizing the available supply of knowledge.

[15] Several kinds of evidence support the proposition that stock markets are efficient: (1) Stock prices cannot be predicted by any mechanical rule, and the trend of past prices provides no guidance about the trend of future prices. This indicates that the current price already embodies any information obtainable from trends. (2) Stock prices adjust rapidly to newly disclosed information, and the price adjustments are unbiased in the sense that they do not systematically overshoot or undershoot the eventual price. In most cases, the price adjustments actually precede the release of new information, and there is thus no change at all when an apparently significant disclosure is made. This indicates that "information leakage," *see* Hirshleifer & Riley, *The Analytics of Uncertainty and Information — An Expository Survey*, 17 J. ECON. LITERATURE 1375, 1403–11 (1979), and the concomitant trading that occurs in anticipation of announcements make the announcements themselves superfluous. In short, stock prices embody all of the "public" information and more. (3) Changes in firms' accounting practices, and hence in their apparent profits, have no effect on price. This indicates that markets discount firms' attempts to manipulate information pertinent to price. Similarly, other changes of form, such as stock splits, also have no effect on price, if adjusted for changes in dividend rate. (4) Market professionals are unable to do better than casual investors in predicting stock movements. Professionally managed mutual funds, for example, do not perform better than portfolios selected at random. (5) The elaborate disclosures required by the SEC do not make investors better off; returns are no higher now than they were in the 1920's. *See generally* J. LORIE & M. HAMILTON, THE STOCK MARKET: THEORIES AND EVIDENCE 70–98 (1973); Fama, *Efficient Capital Markets: A Review of Theory and Empirical Work*, 25 J. FINANCE 383 (1970); Jensen, *Capital Markets: Theory and Evidence*, 3 BELL J. ECON. & MANAGEMENT SCI. 357 (1972); Note, *The Efficient Capital Market Hypothesis, Economic Theory and the Regulation of the Securities Industry*, 29 STAN. L. REV. 1031, 1034–57 (1977).

price is not believable;[16] if a guess better than the market's guess could be devised, the cost of making the improvement (including the payments to researchers and analysts) would exceed the gains from the knowledge.

It may be helpful to think of stock prices as reflecting estimates of the probabilities of future states of the world. To a great extent, price movements depend on the state of the economy, the rate of interest, demand for the firm's product, the skill (or luck) of the firm's managers, and so on. The price of the stock on any given day will be a composite of the prices the stock would assume under different assumptions about the future. Suppose that the fortunes of one firm depend on the success of some innovative process. If the process works, the future earnings of that firm will be worth $100 per share; if it flops, the earnings will be worth only $20. If failure is 3 times as likely as success, then the shares will trade for $40.[17] The price of the shares will rise or fall as new information sheds light on either the probability of success (an increase to 1 chance in 2 will lead to a price of $60) or the profits if the venture succeeds. Changes in the interest rate would affect the way in which these earnings streams are discounted to present value, thus affecting the price of shares. Other influences work in a similar way.

This illustrates why the constant, sometimes violent, movement of share prices is consistent with the proposition that markets are efficient. When price changes, the change does not show that the old price was wrong; it shows only that new information has been incorporated into the price of the stock.

We can conclude from this, with some confidence, that a tender offer at a price higher than the prevailing one also

---

[16] For an argument that a market averages people's weighted beliefs about the future and that the resulting prices are a better estimate of the correct probabilities than any of the participants' estimates, see Verrecchia, *Consensus Beliefs, Information Acquisition, and Market Information Efficiency*, 70 AM. ECON. REV. 874 (1980).

[17] The $40 figure is simply the average of the two outcomes weighted by their relative probabilities of occurrence: $(75\% \times 20) + (25\% \times 100) = 40$. We assume here that investors are risk neutral (indifferent to risk). A person is risk neutral if he would pay the same amount for a ticket that entitled him to $1 as he would for a ticket that entitled him to participate in a coin flip in which he would receive $2 for calling the coin correctly. If he would pay more for the $2 ticket, he is risk preferring; if he would pay less for the $2 ticket, he is risk averse. In the example, the shares will trade for less than $40 if the shareholders are risk averse, more than $40 if they are risk preferring. Whether shareholders act if risk averse depends on the extent to which the risks of a particular stock can be eliminated by diversifying (*i.e.*, owning a basket of many stocks). Both theory and evidence suggest that if the risks are diversifiable, shareholders will be indifferent to them; otherwise they will be risk averse. *See* J. LORIE & M. HAMILTON, *supra* note 15, at 171–259.

exceeds the value of the stock. True, the target's managers may know something about the firm's prospects not yet incorporated into the price of the shares.[18] But the disparity between price and worth could not last long. If a bidder tried to steal the target by capitalizing on its special information, the target's managers could defeat the offer by disclosing the information to the public.[19] The price would adjust to reflect the new information, and the offer would succeed only if it were higher than the new price. Tender offers at a premium thus must benefit the target's shareholders.

2. *Agency Costs and Takeovers.* — Although the efficiency of capital markets implies that shareholders gain from tender offers, it also seems to imply that bidders are irrational. Why can a bidder identify underpriced stocks if market professionals cannot? The bidder's knowledge would be shared by the target's management in most cases, and management could release the information, causing a price adjustment. The simple fact that the bidder has made an offer might cause the information to leak to the market. Unless stock markets are substantially inefficient,[20] the bidder will not be able to acquire a company for less than its value under current conditions.

Commentators have proposed a bewildering number of explanations for mergers and takeovers. They include gains from

---

[18] If there were no prohibitions against insider trading, shares would not sell for less than a price incorporating all information, since insider trades would move prices to reflect even corporate secrets. *See* Fischel, *supra* note 7, at 24.

[19] If the firm needed to act in secret to realize the value of its knowledge, management would be dutybound not to reveal the information. *See, e.g.*, SEC v. Texas Gulf Sulphur Co., 401 F.2d 833, 843–44, 850 n.12 (2d Cir. 1968) (en banc) (secrecy needed to enable acquisition of land under which the corporation had discovered valuable ore of which the landowner was not aware), *cert. denied*, 404 U.S. 1005 (1971). The existence of a duty to maintain secrecy, even in the face of a tender offer for less than the eventual price of the stock, may constitute an exception to our more general conclusion that shareholders' welfare would be maximized by managerial passivity in response to tender offers. It is *not* an exception, however, if there is a competitive market in acquisitions or if shareholders have rational expectations about the prospects of their firms. Competitive bidders would protect the shareholders' interests fully. For the technical argument about rational expectations, see S. Grossman & O. Hart, The Allocational Role of Takeover Bids in Situations of Asymmetric Expectations (U. Pa. Wharton School, White Center for Financial Research, Working Paper No. 6-80, Jan. 1980). For an empirical argument that shareholders do have rational expectations, see Bradley, *Interfirm Tender Offers and the Market for Corporate Control*, 53 J. BUS. 345 (1980).

[20] The qualification is important. Stocks traded over the counter may not always have sufficiently liquid markets (or may not be the subject of sufficiently frequent scrutiny) to ensure that their prices reflect all available information. If markets for particular stocks are not efficient, it is not possible to say that every tender bid at a premium is beneficial to shareholders. Even so, however, all of the arguments about agency costs apply to these firms, and they support a rule of managerial passivity.

increasing the ability of firms to employ information that would leak if conveyed between independent entities, "synergy" gains as the combined firms obtain the value of some savings in joint operations, and tax benefits. None of these explanations is implausible, and none is inconsistent with a belief that tender offers improve shareholders' welfare.[21] But the savings and benefits attributable to each could be achieved by friendly merger as well as by hostile tender offer. Since a tender offer is by far the more costly device,[22] one must consider whether some source of benefit both accounts for large cash premiums and explains why a friendly merger did not occur.

The most probable explanation for unfriendly takeovers emphasizes their role in monitoring the performance of corporate managers. The tender bidding process polices managers whether or not a tender offer occurs, and disciplines or replaces them if they stray too far from the service of the shareholders.[23] We offer the following explanation both to show what we mean by agency costs[24] and to illustrate how the tender bidding process influences these costs.

Corporate managers (which include both officers and members of the board), like all other people, work harder if they

---

[21] The suggestion that offerors are attempting to realize the gains from nonpatentable information appears in Jarrell & Bradley, *The Economic Effects of Federal and State Regulations of Cash Tender Offers*, 23 J.L. & ECON. 371 (1980). They view this as a welfare-increasing process. "Synergy," if it exists, also obviously increases welfare. Tax reasons may seem more problematic. The acquired firm may have a valuable tax loss or cash that can be passed to shareholders at the capital gains rate through an acquisition. Moreover, a tender offer may capitalize the target's earnings stream, distributing it as capital gains. Even tax-motivated takeovers improve efficiency: they free up assets that the target may be holding as cash (or investing suboptimally) to avoid a distribution at high tax rates. The tender offeror receives and can invest these assets without recognizing taxable gain. And, of course, a firm may have acquired a tax loss as a result of suboptimal management. Finally, even though a firm with inferior managers could achieve tax savings through an acquisition, it is the firm with the best combination of tax advantages *and* good management that can make the highest bid for the target. Given competition among acquirers, any tax-motivated takeover is unlikely to reduce the efficiency with which the target's assets are used.

[22] The average cost of a tender offer before 1975 was 13% of the total postoffer market price of the shares. Smiley, *Tender Offers, Transactions Costs and the Theory of the Firm*, 58 REV. ECON. & STATISTICS 22, 30 (1976).

[23] *See* Manne, *Mergers and the Market for Corporate Control*, 73 J. POL. ECON. 110 (1965).

[24] This use of "agency costs" was introduced by Jensen & Meckling, *Theory of the Firm: Managerial Behavior, Agency Costs and Ownership Structure*, 3 J. FINANCIAL ECON. 305 (1976). *See also* Alchian & Demsetz, *Production, Information Costs, and Economic Organization*, 62 AM. ECON. REV. 777 (1972).

can enjoy all of the benefits of their efforts. In a corporation, however, much of the benefit of each manager's performance inures to someone else, whether it be shareholders, bondholders, or other managers. The investors must be given a substantial share of the gains to induce them to put up their money.[25] Because no single manager receives the full benefit of his work, he may find that, at the margin, developing new ventures and supervising old ones takes too much effort to be worthwhile; each manager may reason that someone else is apt to do the work if he does not or to take the rewards even if he does well. No manager will be completely vigilant. So some managers will find it advantageous to shirk responsibilities, consume perquisites, or otherwise take more than the corporation promised to give them. One especially important way in which managers' performance falls short of the ideal is in choosing the firm's other agents. Because no manager can obtain all of the benefits available to the firm from making good decisions, none takes all cost-justified steps to recruit and train those employees best suited for their jobs. As a result, many firms will have some employees less than completely dedicated to their jobs and other employees who, although fully dedicated, ought not to be in the positions they hold. These agency costs of less than optimal management cause the firm's shares to trade for less than the price they would achieve if agency costs were zero.

Shareholders might be able to reap substantial gains from improving the performance of managers as their agents.[26] But this improvement is difficult to achieve, and the difficulty is

[25] Any siphoning of benefits by the managers is an agency cost even if the managers put the existing resources of the firm to their socially optimal use. Unless all of the benefits of new investment are returned to those who supply the firm's capital, there will be too little investment in the future. The reduction in the incentive to invest is a real social cost.

[26] This is not to suggest that there is something undesirable in the fact that many firms are controlled by managers rather than by stockholders. This "separation of ownership and control," criticized so harshly in A. BERLE & G. MEANS, THE MODERN CORPORATION AND PRIVATE PROPERTY (1932), and, less thoughtfully, in R. NADER, M. GREEN & J. SELIGMAN, TAMING THE GIANT CORPORATION (1976), is nothing but another way of describing the division of labor. The separation enables skilled managers to run enterprises even though they lack personal wealth, and it enables those who have wealth to invest even though they lack managerial skills. Moreover, this division of labor also enables investors to diversify their portfolios, in turn lowering risk and making investment more attractive. *See* Langbein & Posner, *Market Funds and Trust-Investment Law*, 1976 AM. B. FOUNDATION RESEARCH J. 1; Posner, *The Rights of Creditors of Affiliated Corporations*, 43 U. CHI. L. REV. 499 (1976).

Corporations are contractual undertakings, and the founders of a corporation can select that set of arrangements which maximizes their welfare. Separation of ownership and control would not emerge or survive if it did not serve important functions. *See* R. WINTER, GOVERNMENT AND THE CORPORATION (1978). If separation were not highly functional, investors would not entrust their money to managers. (Surely the reason why outsiders (tender bidders) play an important role. The agency costs typically will go undetected by individual shareholders. Most shareholders are passive investors seeking liquid holdings. They have little interest in managing the firm and less incentive to learn the details of management. No one shareholder can collect all or even a little of the gains available from monitoring the firm's managers. The benefits would be dispersed among all stockholders according to their investments, not according to their monitoring efforts. Because other shareholders take a free ride on any one shareholder's monitoring, each shareholder finds it in his self-interest to be passive. He simply sells his shares if he is dissatisfied.

The free riding problems that inhibit monitoring by shareholders are aggravated by the difficulty any shareholder would face in doing anything about the firm's managers once he discovered the existence of excessive agency costs. The shareholder who makes the discovery has no authority to compel the firm to change its ways. He must either persuade the managers or induce his fellow shareholders to oust the managers and install new ones. Yet persuasion is lost on misbehaving managers who need not listen. The cry of "turn the rascals out" also is not of much use, because other shareholders still find it in their self-interest to be passive. The shareholder who has made the discovery must persuade his fellow shareholders to invest a significant amount of time in studying the corporation's affairs. These shareholders would be willing to do so only if their attention and study could yield a benefit. But here, too, free riding makes things difficult. Each shareholder will recognize that his votes will not affect the outcome of any dispute unless he has a large bloc of shares. As a result, each shareholder's self-interest leads him to ignore the controversy; it is costly to become informed, and the cost produces little prospect of benefit. If each shareholder reasons in the same way, as he should, the managers of the firm will prevail in any contest about their operation of the company. And that is the pattern in the market. Shareholders routinely vote for managers or pay no attention to elections. Successful campaigns against managers are rare, and they seldom succeed even if one dissident shareholder holds a large bloc of stock that he can vote in his own favor.[27]

---

managers of large corporations have no monopsony power over investment opportunities.) The point we make in the text is consistent with a belief that, if shareholders were required to "control" corporations more tightly than they do now, the price of shares would be still lower.

[27] The proclivity of money managers and trustees to vote for corporate management — much maligned in the legal literature — doubtless accounts for some of management's lopsided success. But, for the reasons we have given in text, share-

Corporate managers recognize that they can improve the performance of the firm by reducing agency costs. Managers monitor each other's performance and reward achievements; bonuses and salary adjustments could be a form of "ex post settling up" that substantially alleviates incentive problems, as Eugene Fama has argued.[28] Gary Becker and George Stigler have supplied a strong argument that if managers enjoy especially favorable salaries or other terms of employment, they may be disciplined by the prospect of being fired.[29] Pensions and retirement bonuses also help to coax good performance from managers.[30]

These devices, although more useful than monitoring by shareholders, still are imperfect. They depend on the ability of the firm to discriminate good performance from inferior performance by each employee. But because managers typically work in teams, it is hard to determine the contribution of each person.[31] The output of one group of managers depends on the quality of information and options supplied by another group, and so on. The attempt to determine the marginal contribution of each manager is bound to be difficult and costly. Worse, the attempt to meter the contributions of each manager, and to dispense rewards accordingly, encounters the free rider problem we have discussed. Because no manager can obtain all of the benefits of monitoring his col-

holders would not be better off under a regime requiring trustees to make a "reasoned judgment" on contested matters or to pass voting rights through to the beneficial owners. If, as we have argued, the shareholders' self-interest has led them to be ignorant and passive, a rule compelling them or their nominees to become informed cannot make them better off. *See* Langbein & Posner, *supra* note 14.

[28] *See* Fama, *Agency Problems and the Theory of the Firm*, 88 J. POL. ECON. 288, 295–306 (1980). Fama neglects, however, the problem of the discount rate. If inferior management is not discovered for some time after the event, it may be impossible to achieve a satisfactory ex post settling up.

[29] *See* Becker & Stigler, *Law Enforcement, Malfeasance, and Compensation of Enforcers*, 3 J. LEGAL STUD. 1, 9–10 (1974).

[30] The incentive provided by such devices obviously increases as the manager nears retirement. So, too, does the need to give the manager an incentive. As a manager becomes older, the effect on his future earnings of today's shirking and malfeasance becomes smaller, and in the period just before retirement the manager's incentive to work hard is smallest of all. *See* Becker & Stigler, *supra* note 29; Klein, Crawford & Alchian, *Vertical Integration, Appropriable Rents, and the Competitive Contracting Process*, 21 J.L. & ECON. 297, 304 & n.17 (1978). Although ERISA bars the forfeiture of pensions for misconduct and shirking, it does not prevent firms from withholding retirement bonuses from its employees. *See* Hepple v. Roberts & Dybdahl, Inc., 622 F.2d 962 (8th Cir. 1980).

[31] This explains why stock options and other profit sharing plans, which attempt to minimize agency costs by making managers "owners," cannot be very effective. In a large corporation, any one manager's efforts are likely to have only a trivial effect on the price of the firm's shares.

leagues, each one will be less than fully dedicated to the task.[32] Even the most dedicated manager will find it difficult to fire or discipline an old friend when the benefits of ruthlessness accrue to distant and unknown shareholders.

The methods of metering and monitoring within a firm are thus unlikely to work well unless the management team as a whole is subject to supervision and, if necessary, discharge. The prospect that the team's work will be judged as a whole gives senior managers a powerful incentive to create and use intra-management control devices. Yet, as we have explained, shareholder monitoring cannot supply the necessary supervision.

Tender offers are a method of monitoring the work of management teams. Prospective bidders monitor the performance of managerial teams by comparing a corporation's potential value with its value (as reflected by share prices) under current management. When the difference between the market price of a firm's shares and the price those shares might have under different circumstances becomes too great, an outsider can profit by buying the firm and improving its management. The outsider reduces the free riding problem because it owns a majority of the shares. The source of the premium is the reduction in agency costs, which makes the firm's assets worth more in the hands of the acquirer than they were worth in the hands of the firm's managers.

All parties benefit in this process. The target's shareholders gain because they receive a premium over the market price.[33]

---

[32] Alchian & Demsetz, *supra* note 24, suggests that there would always be inefficient management unless the ultimate supervisor received all of the firm's profits. As we have explained in the text, in a publicly held corporation the shareholders (who have the residual entitlement to profits) lack the incentive to serve as monitors.

[33] *But see* Grossman & Hart, *Takeover Bids, the Free-Rider Problem, and the Theory of the Corporation*, 11 BELL J. ECON. 42 (1980). While recognizing the power of the tender offer in disciplining management, Grossman and Hart believe that an offeror could not induce the shareholders to part with their shares unless it had some way of appropriating to itself the gains from the acquisition. They observe that, if the offeror plans to profit by improving the firm's management, then it must expect the postacquisition price of shares to be even higher than the offer price. Consequently, they reason, a shareholder will prefer the postoffer price to the tender price, and he will not tender if his holdings are so small that they cannot affect the success of the offer. And, of course, if everyone reasons in the same way, the offer will fail. Grossman and Hart conclude that offerors should be able to "dilute" the price of shares after the acquisition in order to overcome this tendency not to tender. Shareholders, knowing that dilution could follow the acquisition, will tender their shares, and thus the threat of dilution need never be carried out.

This argument is not compelling. The tender offeror has two potent devices that overcome the holdout problem. First, the offeror may specify that the offer is contingent on receipt of a sufficiently large percentage of the shares so that any share-

The bidder obtains the difference between the new value of the firm and the payment to the old shareholders. Nontendering shareholders receive part of the appreciation in the price of the shares.[34]

More significantly for our purposes, shareholders benefit even if their corporation never is the subject of a tender offer. The process of monitoring by outsiders poses a continuous threat of takeover if performance lags. Managers will attempt to reduce agency costs in order to reduce the chance of takeover, and the process of reducing agency costs leads to higher prices for shares.[35] We now explore how different responses to takeover bids influence the size of the benefit derived from monitoring by outsiders in advance of any offer.

B. The Consequences of Management's Defensive Tactics

1. Resistance and Agency Costs. — The argument presented above establishes that takeovers are beneficial to both shareholders and society. It follows that any strategy designed to prevent tender offers reduces welfare. If the company adopts a policy of intransigent resistance and succeeds in maintaining its independence, the shareholders lose whatever pre-

---

holder's decision could affect the success of the offer. Since each shareholder knows that all other shareholders will reason the same way he does, he will tender in order to obtain the premium. Second, the offeror can acquire all of the shares with a freezeout merger after it obtains control. *See* DEL. CODE ANN. tit. 8, § 262(f) (1974); MODEL BUS. CORP. ACT § 81(a)(3) (1978). *But cf.* Singer v. Magnavox Co., 380 A.2d 969 (Del. 1977) (requiring merger price to be fair). *See* Brudney & Chirelstein, *A Restatement of Corporate Freezeouts*, 87 YALE L.J. 1354, 1359–65 (1978) (criticizing restrictions on two-step freezeouts). Once the shareholders understand that holding out will not enable them to obtain more than the tender offer price, they have an incentive to tender their shares to obtain the premium as soon as possible.

The idea of dilution is nonetheless important in establishing rules with respect to management's response to a tender offer. The ability of the offeror to obtain the shares for less than their value in the hands of new management can be thought of as dilution, and the existence of this dilution is essential to the profitability (and hence the existence) of tender offers. *See* p. 1177 *infra*. The available evidence suggests that share prices are "diluted" in this way. *See* Bradley, *supra* note 19.

[34] The price of shares typically increases substantially after a tender offer, *see* note 76 *infra*, and state law often requires the tender offeror to pay at least the tender offer price in order to complete a freezeout merger. *See* Roland Int'l Corp. v. Najjar, 407 A.2d 1032, 1037 (Del. 1979) (requiring "entire fairness" for freezeout merger); Singer v. Magnavox Co., 380 A.2d 969 (Del. 1977) (requiring business purpose); DEL. CODE ANN. tit. 8, § 262 (1974) (establishing appraisal rights). These restrictions on freezeouts give controlling shareholders incentives to pay minority shareholders a proportional interest in the gains produced by the acquisition.

[35] Fischel, *supra* note 7; Manne, *supra* note 23. At least one court has recognized the power of tender offer threats in increasing the price of shares. Dart Indus. v. Conrad, 462 F. Supp. 1, 8–9 (S.D. Ind. 1978).

mium over market value the bidder offered or would have offered but for the resistance or the prospect of resistance. This lost premium reflects a foregone social gain from the superior employment of the firm's assets.

The target's managers, however, have a substantial interest in preserving their company's independence and thus preserving their salaries and status; the less effective they have been as managers, the greater their interest in preventing a takeover. They may disguise a policy of resistance to all offers as a policy of searching for a better offer than any made so far. Extensive manuals describe both the stratagems of resistance and the methods of disguise.[36] There is no signal that separates intransigent resistance from honest efforts to conduct an auction for the shareholders' benefit. The fact that the first tender offer or any subsequent offer is defeated supplies little information, because any auctioneer understands that determined efforts to collect the highest possible price may lead to no sale at all in the short run.[37]

Even resistance that ultimately elicits a higher bid is socially wasteful. Although the target's shareholders may receive a higher price, these gains are exactly offset by the bidder's payment and thus by a loss to the bidder's shareholders. Shareholders as a group gain nothing; the increase in the price is simply a transfer payment from the bidder's shareholders to the target's shareholders. Indeed, because the process of resistance consumes real resources, shareholders as a whole lose by the amount targets spend in resistance plus the amount bidders and any rivals spend in overcoming resistance.[38] These additional costs can be substantial.[39]

---

[36] *See* authorities collected note 2 *supra*. *See also* Lipton, *supra* note 12, at 120–30. New defensive strategies are constantly being invented. The latest is lobbying for legislation to block the acquisition. *See* Wall St. J., Feb. 13, 1981, at 19, col. 4.

[37] Even if the target's management intends to conduct an auction, its noncooperative response to the offer may lead to an inferior disposition of the target's assets. *See* Polinsky, *Controlling Externalities and Protecting Entitlements: Property Right, Liability Rule, and Tax-Subsidy Approaches*, 8 J. LEGAL STUD. 1 (1979) (arguing that noncooperative behavior sometimes frustrates the transfer of resources to the highest valuing users).

[38] As a general matter, expenditures that influence the distribution of trading gains but do not generate better performance are simple waste. Society as a whole would pay to prevent traders from fighting over the gains of trades that are bound to occur anyway. For rigorous demonstrations of this, see Fama & Laffer, *Information and Capital Markets*, 44 J. BUS. 289 (1971); Hirshleifer, *The Private and Social Value of Information and the Reward to Inventive Activity*, 61 AM. ECON. REV. 561 (1971). Tender offers at premiums over the market price fall into the class of trades that are bound to occur eventually.

[39] Defensive acquisitions — ones that create antitrust problems for the bidder, but would not otherwise have been made by the target — can be costly to consummate

This argument may appear to be inconsistent with fiduciary principles. If resistance touches off an auction, it may drive up the price paid for the target's shares.[40] Ordinarily managers are charged with the duty of maximizing the returns to the firm's shareholders without regard to adverse consequences to other firms' shareholders or to society at large. The standard economic assumption since Adam Smith introduced the invisible hand has been that the firm's rational pursuit of its self-interest yields more gains for it than losses for its rivals. The result is efficient because the winners gain more than enough to compensate the losers.

But this is not invariably true, and the recent experience with pollution provides an example. When a firm treats the air as a free good, society as a whole may lose more than the firm gains. As long as the firm is entitled to disregard the effects on third parties of the pollution it emits, it will consume too much clean air in producing its products.

A related "externality" arises when a target's management resists a tender offer. The resulting increase in the prices paid for target firms will generally discourage prospective bidders for other targets; when the price of anything goes up, the

---

and may involve inferior uses of the newly acquired assets. Litigation against the offeror, extensive mailings to and solicitation of shareholders, and other defensive tactics can be quite costly to both the target and the bidder. For example, in the recent contest for control of Pullman, the fees paid to lawyers, investment bankers, and similar participants in the fight were $17 million. When Mead Corporation defeated Occidental Petroleum's bid in 1979, the cost was $15 million. *See* Wall St. J., Dec. 2, 1980, at 1, col. 6; *id.* at 23, col. 2. There is a further cost of resistance if the contest prolongs the period before the acquisition can be completed, for that delays the achievement of the gains the acquisition will produce.

[40] Bidding usually serves the function of allocating goods to their highest valued uses; the best indication of the ability to put something to a valuable use is the willingness to pay for it. In the housing market, for example, sellers regularly hire brokers, who conduct an extended "auction" of the house to solicit the highest bid. In the end the owner receives more money, and the house is sold to the person who values it most highly. But a housing auction and a management-run auction for a corporation differ in a number of important respects. Shareholders wishing to auction off their corporation would not employ the firm's managers as their agents in the auction because the managers' interests potentially conflict with the shareholders' interests. *See* pp. 1198–99 *infra*. In addition, the market for corporate shares is far more efficient than the market for parcels of real estate. The former establishes even without an auction the value of corporations as currently managed. There is thus no need to expend resources to duplicate what the market provides for free — an accurate estimate of current value. Given the existence of a market price for shares, we know that the transfer of the target firm to a higher bidding offeror produces gains for both society and the target's shareholders. Even if the first bidder cannot put the target's assets to the best possible use, those assets could be resold and eventually would end up in possession of the firm that valued them most highly. *See* Coase, *The Problem of Social Cost*, 3 J.L. & ECON. 1 (1960). Indeed, the first bidder's failure in that situation to resell the target's assets to another higher valuing firm would constitute inferior management that would expose the bidder itself to takeover.

quantity demanded falls. Changes in the incentives of bidders affect the utility of monitoring by outsiders, and that affects the size of agency costs and in turn the pre-offer price of potential targets' stock. In order to explore the nature of these effects, it would be useful to ask what rational shareholders would do if, *before* a tender offer was in prospect, they could bind the management to resist or to acquiesce in any offer.

Consider the effects of two polar rules. Under the first rule, management is passive in the face of tender offers. If there are no competing bidders, the first tender offeror will prevail at the lowest premium that will induce the shareholders to surrender their shares. Under the second rule, management uses all available means to resist the offer. This resistance creates an auction, so that no bidder can acquire the target without paying a price almost as high as the shares would be worth under the best practicable management.[41] For example, shares of firm *X* are trading for $40. Outsiders could manage the firm better so that the shares would be valued at $90 each.[42] A bid of $50 would induce a substantial majority of *X*'s shareholders to tender their shares. Under the first paradigm rule — managerial acquiescence — the bid of $50 would ensure success. Under the second paradigm — resistance — a tender offeror could not acquire *X* for much less than $90 per share.

Which of these rules maximizes the welfare of *X*'s shareholders? If the question is asked ex post, after a tender offer has been made, then plainly the shareholders would prefer the second rule and the bidding war. But if the shareholders were asked which strategy the managers should pursue ex ante, prior to the offer, they would have substantial reasons to choose acquiescence. It is easy to see why. If the target's shareholders obtain *all* the gains from the transaction, no one has an incentive to make a tender offer, and thus no one will offer a premium for the shares.[43] The shareholders will be

---

[41] Neither rule accurately describes a real possibility. There would always be some competition among offerors no matter what the target's management does, and this competition would ensure that the bidder pays more than the absolute minimum demanded by shareholders. At the same time, no defensive strategy would enable the target's shareholders to receive the last nickel of gain, both because there is substantial uncertainty about the value of the assets in the new owners' hands and because the bidder who can make the best use of the assets would not have to pay much more than the last offer of the bidder who could put the assets to the second highest use. Nonetheless, the paradigm rules reveal tendencies; if one rule is clearly inferior to the other, it follows that other rules similar to the inferior one should be avoided.

[42] The shares would be valued at more than $90 were there no agency costs.

[43] Indeed, there will be inefficiently little investment in monitoring by prospective offerors whenever the target's existing shareholders can capture *any* of the benefits of

stuck with their \$40 shares. Under the strategy of acquiescence, however, the shareholders obtain \$50 and are better off.[44]

Prospective offerors must do substantial research to identify underpriced corporations and to determine how their management can be improved. They may engage investment banking houses and investigate the affairs of many corporations before finding one whose management could be improved. The position of a tender offeror is particularly precarious because, at the time it makes a bid, its investment in information about the target is sunk. Perhaps the first bidder will invest \$10 per share in finding out about many potential targets and then exploring the prospects of *X* in depth. If it can acquire *X* for \$50 per share, it reaps a profit as high as \$30 per share (\$90 minus \$10 investigation costs, minus \$50 tender price). The bidder's profit falls to nothing when the tender offer price reaches \$80 per share. Once the offeror announces its bid, however, other potential acquirers learn the target's identity. The bid itself, and the accompanying disclosures under federal and state law, may reveal much of what the offeror has learned.[45] If the offeror does not supply other bidders with valuable information, the target's management may do so as part of a strategy to set up an auction. But any other bidder need not bear costs as high as those already incurred by the first bidder. The subsequent bidders take a free ride, making

---

the monitor's endeavors. *Cf.* Grossman & Hart, *supra* note 33, at 54–58 (the optimal "dilution factor" for society in takeovers is infinite, meaning that the offeror should be allowed to confiscate the value of untendered shares in order to ensure that all shares will be tendered).

44 This analysis can be generalized. As we noted at the outset, p. 1164 *supra*, the value of any stock can be understood as the sum of two components: (i) the price that will prevail in the market if there is no successful offer multiplied by the likelihood that there will be none, and (ii) the price that will be paid in a future tender offer multiplied by the likelihood that some offer will succeed. If the shareholders could bind the firm's managers to follow a single rule, they would want them to follow a strategy that maximized ex ante share value, $(p)T + (1 - p)M$, where p is the probability that a tender offer will succeed, T is the tender offer price, and M is the market price of the shares in the event of no takeover. The shareholders would not look solely at T, because any rule increasing the size of T decreases p and M. Using the numerical example from the text, as T rises toward \$90, p falls toward zero, since a prospective offeror would not engage in the costly and risky efforts necessary to investigate prospective targets and make a tender offer if it did not anticipate being able to enjoy a substantial part of the gains.

45 Grossman & Hart, *Disclosure Laws and Takeover Bids*, 35 J. FINANCE 323, 327–33 (1980); Grossman & Hart, *supra* note 33, at 58 & n.25; Jarrell & Bradley, *supra* note 21. Indeed, the existence of an offer by itself tells other prospective bidders where to look, even if it conveys no other information. These other bidders can confine their study to the target firm, although the first offeror undoubtedly incurred costs in examining the records and prospects of many firms.

a profit even if the price rises to $80 per share. As a result, no firm wants to be the first bidder unless it has some advantage, such as speed,[46] over subsequent bidders to compensate for the fact that only it had to incur monitoring costs. And, of course, if there is no first bidder there will be no later bidders and no tender premium.

Perhaps most important of all, requiring bidders to pay a high premium will lead to a decrease in the price of the target's shares. A bidder facing the prospect of paying a high premium is less likely to monitor other firms, and the decrease in searching for targets leads to a decrease in the number of bids.[47] Then the price of *X*'s stock is likely to decrease because, with the reduction in monitoring, agency costs rise.

For instance, assume that a bid of 20% over the market price will attract enough shares under the acquiescence paradigm to achieve success, but under the resistance paradigm the premium must be 50% or more. As before, firm *X*'s shares would trade for $90 under the best practicable management. The shareholder choosing one of the paradigm rules to bind the managers would ask: How effective will outside monitoring be in inducing my managers to come as close to optimality as possible? The governing rule would influence managers' performance; if takeovers are more costly, there will be fewer diligent managers in any given firm. Agency costs will tend to increase to the point where further increases precipitate a takeover.

Under a rule of acquiescence, where a premium of 20% carries the day, excess agency costs cannot for long exceed $15 per share. If the price falls below $75 per share ($90 divided by 1.2), then potential bidders will begin to see the prospect of a profitable takeover. The farther the price falls below $75, the more profitable and hence the more likely a takeover. Things look quite different to the shareholder, though, under the resistance paradigm. Then the price could fall to $60 ($90 divided by 1.5) in the market without attracting any interest from potential bidders. The more effective resistance is in raising the premiums after tender offers are made, the lower

[46] If the making of a bid itself triggers an auction, the initial bidder is at a disadvantage unless the period for tendering is very short. Before the enactment of the Williams Act and state tender offer statutes, offers typically were open for only a few days. *See* pp. 1162–63 *supra*. Speed was the essence of success. The statutes creating delays have made auctions more effective in increasing tender premiums, but in the process they have decreased the number of successful tender offers. Jarrell & Bradley, *supra* note 21, at 398–403; *see* Fischel, *supra* note 7. Managerial tactics that intensify the bidding war simply aggravate the problem a prospective offeror faces in determining whether to invest in monitoring.

[47] The available data show that the number of offers decreases as resistance increases. *See* Jarrell & Bradley, *supra* note 21, at 398–403.

the share price can fall without attracting interest by bidders.[48] The shareholder trying to choose a set of instructions to management consequently would conclude that his welfare is best served by instructions to acquiesce. Such instructions give managers the greatest incentive to perform optimally.[49]

2. *The Acquiescence Paradigm as an Implicit Shareholder Agreement.* — Our argument implies that resistance is costly to shareholders and that logically they should seek to avoid those costs by instructing managers to acquiesce in tender offers. Theoretically, shareholders could assure acquiescence by insisting on appropriate provisions in the articles of incorporation or bylaws. Such provisions would facilitate monitoring of managerial performance, and consequently the price of shares of corporations with antiresistance provisions should rise relative to other firms. Moreover, corporations must compete in the capital markets for funds, and they could obtain these funds at lower cost if their articles constrained the defensive maneuvers of management.

Yet articles of incorporation rarely if ever contain antiresistance provisions. To the contrary, they sometimes contain provisions to make acquisition difficult. Classified boards, cumulative voting, supermajority consent rules, and similar provisions may frustrate the tender offeror's attempts to take control after it has purchased a majority of the common stock.[50] These provisions raise the effective price of an ac-

[48] Of course, the shareholder would not think that resistance versus acquiescence is the sole determinant of agency costs. Many other things, including monitoring within management teams, influence the size of these costs. *See* p. 1172 *supra*. But to the extent that a rule about resistance to tender offers affects these costs, the *direction* of the influence is plain.

[49] We have constructed the analysis in this subsection on the basis of a number of simplifying and highly unrealistic assumptions. We have assumed that managers are not attempting to defeat all offers and in their efforts to conduct an auction never misjudge the price bidders would pay and so never erroneously defeat the offers. We have assumed that managers never attempt to use resistance to appropriate to themselves some portion of the additional premium available in an auction. If these assumptions are relaxed, then the shareholder's choice of which instructions to issue to management becomes even easier. When managers have a right to resist, they can sell nonresistance for soft jobs, comfortable consulting contracts, and substantial severance bonuses. *E.g.*, Singer v. Magnavox Co., 380 A.2d 969 (Del. 1977) (resistance dropped after management obtained employment contracts). It would be very difficult for a court to separate these disguised bribes from the many economically desirable employment and consulting arrangements worked out in mergers. The shareholder could prevent that misappropriation of his gains — and the accompanying transactions costs borne by the target — by issuing binding instructions to acquiesce in tender offers.

[50] M. LIPTON & E. STEINBERGER, *supra* note 2, § 6.2 (1978 & Supp. 1980), provides a catalogue of structural provisions designed to make takeovers difficult and costly. *See also* Hochman & Folger, *supra* note 2.

quisition and increase the offeror's risk. Managers sometimes recommend to shareholders that such provisions be added to the articles of incorporation, and shareholders routinely follow these recommendations.

But these facts hardly suggest that shareholders approve of management resistance. The great majority of public corporations have *not* adopted "porcupine" provisions making acquisitions more difficult, and general principles of fiduciary duty restrict managers' options to do so.[51] More important, shareholders would find it impossible to instruct managers to acquiesce in tender offers because of the very agency and monitoring problems that lead to the offers. Individual shareholders do not have the incentive to attempt to insert antiresistance provisions into the bylaws or articles of incorporation or to oppose management on suggested porcupine provisions, because no shareholder or coalition of shareholders can capture the full value of such an action to the shareholders as a group. If such a provision were inserted, managers could probably delete it again by amendment.[52] Even if one shareholder waged a campaign on behalf of shareholders' interests, few others would pay any attention, because no one shareholder's vote is likely to affect the outcome. Dissatisfied shareholders are more likely to sell their stock than attempt to change the corporation's bylaws or otherwise oppose management.[53]

The situation here is similar to the situation in many other areas of corporate law that recognize shareholders' inability to monitor managers' performance. The Trust Indenture Act,[54] Bankruptcy Code,[55] state corporation codes, and other statutes

---

[51] Numerous courts have recognized that managers' attempts to perpetuate themselves in control breach their fiduciary duty. *See, e.g.*, Lerman v. Diagnostic Data, Inc., 421 A.2d 906 (Del. Ch. 1980) (holding that managers may not change proxy election rules if the change entrenches them in office); Cheff v. Mathes, 41 Del. Ch. 494, 199 A.2d 548 (1964); Auerbach v. Bennett, 47 N.Y.2d 619, 393 N.E.2d 994, 419 N.Y.S.2d 920 (1979). Supporters of defensive action against tender offers repeatedly counsel managers not to be candid about their objectives, lest candor lead to a finding of violation of fiduciary responsibilities. *E.g.*, M. Lipton & E. Steinberger, *supra* note 2, § 6.1.1 (1978 & Supp. 1980) ("Preparation of a 'black book' of procedures to be used in the event of a takeover attempt is not desirable because it may be used to embarrass management in litigation by creating a 'credibility gap' for a management that states it has acted in good faith and carefully considered a raider's offer."); Lipton, *supra* note 12, at 120–30 (elaborate script for camouflaging the target's reasons for resisting an offer).

[52] Grossman & Hart, *supra* note 33, does not take proper account of this problem in arguing that the founders of a corporation will select rules that make takeovers attractive.

[53] *See* pp. 1170–71 *supra*.

[54] 15 U.S.C. §§ 77aaa–77bbbb (1976 & Supp. III 1979).

[55] 11 U.S.C. §§ 101–766, 1101–1146 (Supp. III 1979).

provide standard form "contracts" of the sort shareholders would be likely to choose if they were in a position to do so. With respect to tender offers, as elsewhere, the instructions to managers must be imposed from outside the corporation.[56]

II. The Arguments Supporting the Right of Target Management to Adopt a Defensive Strategy

Our analysis cuts against the grain of many cases and a substantial amount of commentary. The rationales offered to support the right of target management to resist tender offers can be grouped in four categories: (1) tender offers do not increase welfare; (2) the target's shareholders benefit from price increases when tender offers are defeated; (3) the target's management has obligations to noninvestor groups that may be adversely affected by a tender offer; and (4) the target's management is obligated to prevent unlawful conduct. In the sections that follow, we consider and reject each of these rationales as a basis for resistance.[57]

A. The Arguments That Tender Offers Do Not Increase Welfare

Our argument relies on the premise that tender offers increase social welfare by moving productive assets to higher-valued uses and to the hands of better managers. Numerous commentators, however, have reached a contrary conclusion. It has been observed, for instance, that many target companies are "well run," have substantial amounts of cash from successful operations, and that the offeror retains the target's management after acquiring control.[58] These observations are invoked to support an assertion that the acquired firms were not doing poorly; consequently, the argument concludes, tender offers do not move assets to better managers.

This is unpersuasive. It amounts to second-guessing the market. Unless the acquirer is giving away its money, the premium price paid for the shares indicates a real gain in the productivity of the assets. If General Motors is willing to bid $100 for a ton of steel owned by General Electric, and GE

[56] This is not, however, a general argument for governmental control of the provisions of corporate charters. Far from it. Once the market for corporate control and the market for shares are operating efficiently, corporate managers will be led to choose whatever provisions of internal government maximize shareholders' wealth. *See* R. Winter, *supra* note 26.

[57] We do not consider again the argument that defensive tactics are beneficial because they raise the offer price, viewed ex post. *See* pp. 1175–80 & notes 38–49 *supra*.

[58] *See, e.g.*, Lipton, *supra* note 12.

sells, we would count this as a value-increasing transaction despite the fact that GE otherwise would have put the steel to "good use" (perhaps $90 worth). The highly subjective observation that acquired firms are well run does not exclude the possibility that, in new hands, the firms would be better run. Only proof that markets are not efficient in pricing shares could support the argument that tender offers do not improve the use of resources.

That acquired firms often are cash rich, perhaps implying successful past operations, also does not demonstrate that takeovers are undesirable. To the contrary, that a firm holds a substantial cash position indicates agency costs. Cash can be invested. The acquirer usually invests the cash it obtains in the takeover, thus putting idle resources to work. The retention of the target's management after a takeover also is not significant. Although the management may keep their old titles, they often lose effective control to officers of the acquirer. Retention in office may be a form of bribe, paid to secure acquiescence in the takeover, rather than a signal of satisfactory performance.[59]

Martin Lipton has advanced a related argument: Tender offers decrease social welfare because they "adversely affect long-term planning and thereby jeopardize the economy."[60] But he fails to demonstrate how long-term planning is "adversely affected," let alone the economy jeopardized. The threat of takeovers does not prevent managers from engaging

[59] Retention also would be expected under the specific information approach taken by Jarrell & Bradley, *supra* note 21.

[60] Lipton, *supra* note 12, at 105. Lipton states that the issue is "[w]hether the long-term interest of the nation's corporate system and economy should be jeopardized in order to benefit speculators interested not in the vitality and continued existence of the business enterprise in which they have bought shares, but only in a quick profit on the sale of those shares." *Id.* at 104. As discussed in the text, Lipton is simply wrong in concluding that tender offers injure the long-term interests of the corporate system and economy. Moreover, his attack on speculators (arbitrageurs) who are interested "only in a quick profit on the sale of [their] shares," *id.*, is unwarranted. Arbitrageurs perform a constructive role by purchasing and selling shares. They offer shareholders who wish to sell their shares at a profit in advance of a tender offer (and thereby avoid the risk that the offer will be defeated, oversubscribed, or never made) the opportunity to do so. By constantly searching for firms that are likely to be the subject of a tender offer, arbitrageurs also make the market more efficient. Finally, arbitrageurs, by selling their shares to an offeror, contribute to the transfer of assets to those who can manage them more efficiently. That the arbitrageurs are not interested in "the vitality and continued existence of the corporate enterprise in which they have bought shares," *id.*, hardly distinguishes them from the typical shareholder of the large publicly held corporation. Arbitrageurs, like other shareholders, buy and sell shares in order to make a profit. By doing so, they contribute to market efficiency, provide a necessary check on suboptimal management, and facilitate the transfer of control to more capable managers.

in long-range planning. If the market perceives that management has developed a successful long-term strategy, this will be reflected in higher share prices that discourage takeovers. To be sure, the risk of a tender offer ensures that corporate managers will be unable to assume that they can continue in office indefinitely. But this risk of displacement does not reduce welfare. Precisely the opposite is true; some insecurity of tenure is necessary to spur managers to their best performance. Society benefits from an active takeover market, therefore, because it simultaneously provides an incentive to all corporate managers to operate efficiently and a mechanism for displacing inefficient managers.

Harold Williams, former Chairman of the Securities and Exchange Commission, has argued that tender offers decrease welfare because they divert resources that otherwise could be used for capital investments and instead are used only to rearrange the ownership of existing corporate assets.[61] The answer to this argument is that funds used to finance a tender offer are not necessarily diverted from investment to consumption. They are merely shifted from the acquiring corporation to the target's shareholders. The acquiring corporation could equally well have distributed these funds as dividends or put them to other non-investment uses. There is also no reason to assume that the target's shareholders will use these funds for consumption rather than capital investment. The shareholders may reinvest what they receive from the tender offeror. There is, therefore, no reason to conclude a priori that an active takeover market diverts funds from capital investment.[62]

Tender offers have also been characterized as "raids" in which the offeror pays a premium for a working majority of the shares in order to loot the firm to the detriment of the minority shareholders.[63] It is unlikely, however, that any

[61] Speech by Harold Williams Before the Seventh Annual Securities Regulation Institute (Jan. 17, 1980), *reprinted in* [1979–1980 Transfer Binder] FED. SEC. L. REP. (CCH) ¶ 82,445. The Director of Policy Planning of the Federal Trade Commission has made a similar argument. Reich, *Pie-Slicers vs. Pie-Enlargers*, WASH. MONTHLY, Sept. 1980, at 13.

[62] Williams' argument is based on the premise that we should encourage firms with accumulated cash to make new capital outlays in plant and research and development, rather than encouraging these firms to take over other existing firms. This argument, however, would deny shareholders the right to the most profitable rate of return by forcing firms to make new capital outlays when a takeover or merger would be more profitable. Williams' related concern that the tender offer dollars paid to target shareholders may not be invested because of the dearth of new equity issues in recent years would be best answered by tax measures to encourage new equity, such as lowering the 70% maximum individual income tax on dividends.

[63] This argument was raised most frequently during debates on the Williams Act and is still frequently made on behalf of the target's managers. Its classic expression

tender offer for a substantial percentage of a company's shares will be motivated by a desire to loot the acquired corporation. A looter generates no new value, and thus cannot afford to pay a premium price for all shares. Even if a bidder seeks less than all shares, it cannot pay a significant premium for those it obtains. If, for example, the offeror acquires for $15 per share 70% of a firm whose shares had been trading for $10, it cannot hope to make a profit by looting. Also, looting from minority shareholders violates established rules,[64] and a bidder would not be likely to escape detection if it violated these rules.

Another argument against tender offers portrays them as reducing the welfare of the shareholders of the acquirers by more than the premium paid to the target's shareholders. In this view, tender offers represent self-aggrandizing empire building by acquiring managers who err in deciding what firms to acquire or what price to pay.[65] The difficulty with this view is its implicit assumption that product and labor market constraints (and the tender offer process itself) do not discipline managers. A corporation headed by an empire-building management team that did not maximize profits would fare poorly in the product market and would have lower share prices; its managers would fare poorly in the employment market. The corporation itself would become a takeover candidate.

Finally, it has been suggested that takeovers create monopolies.[66] Profit increases that come about because of monop-

is the statement by Senator Harrison Williams in commenting on an earlier version of the Williams Act:

> In recent years we have seen proud old companies reduced to corporate shells after white-collar pirates have seized control with funds from sources which are unknown in many cases, then sold or traded away the best assets, later to split up most of the loot among themselves . . . .
>
> The ultimate responsibility for preventing this kind of industrial sabotage lies with the management and the shareholders of the corporation that is so threatened. But the leniency of our laws places management and shareholders at a distinct disadvantage in coming to grips with the enemy.

111 CONG. REC. 28257–58 (1965).

Looting may be seen as similar to stealing, which redistributes rather than increases welfare. However, if looting were prevalent, a decrease in welfare would actually occur, as the risk of looting perpetrated by managers with no interest in running acquired companies well was factored into the price of shares ex ante. This would lead to a reduction in all share prices.

[64] *See, e.g.*, Gerdes v. Reynolds, 28 N.Y.S.2d 622 (Sup. Ct. 1941).

[65] Marris & Mueller, *The Corporation, Competition, and the Invisible Hand*, 18 J. ECON. LITERATURE 32, 36–37, 42, 46 (1980) (discussing other articles).

[66] *See, e.g.*, 1 *Mergers and Economic Concentration: Hearings on S. 600 Before the Subcommittee on Antitrust, Monopoly and Business Rights of the Senate Judiciary Committee*, 96th Cong., 1st Sess. 61–106 (1979) (testimony of Assistant Attorney General John Shenefield) [hereinafter cited as *Merger Hearings*]. *But see* G. BENSTON, CONGLOMERATE MERGERS 26–31 (1980).

olization produce reductions in social welfare. This view, however, is contradicted by the evidence. Most tender offers raise no antitrust problems, and one careful study has shown that takeovers generally reduce concentration in the acquired firms' markets.[67]

The raider, managerialist, and monopolist models of tender offers are also contradicted by data on stock price movements. Most of the movement in the price of a stock is correlated with movement in the market as a whole and depends on general economic conditions. But the movements in individual stock prices net of movements in the market give a rough picture of the fortunes of the issuing companies, and data about these movements for individual companies — called cumulative average residuals, or CAR's — are powerful indicators of a company's performance.

Each of the views of tender offers, including the welfare-maximizing view that we advance, implies a particular pattern of acquirers' and targets' CAR's. The proposition that tender offers move assets to better uses implies that, because the acquirers are looking for targets with suboptimal performance, the prices of the targets' shares would decline relative to the market for a period prior to the offer. The targets' CAR's would begin to rise again, shortly before the offer was announced, as information leaked to the market. The CAR's of the untendered shares would show significant gains over the preannouncement position. The offeror's CAR's should show little abnormal movement, because offerors should not be able to make more than a competitive return (given the extent of risk) on their investment in the target.

If, on the other hand, tender offers are conducted to raid the assets of the targets, the CAR's of targets would be steady until word of the offer leaked to the market; then they would decrease, as investors feared the worst. The CAR's of the minority, untendered shares would plummet after the acquisitions were completed. The CAR's of offerors should rise, in anticipation of gains from looting, once word reached the market.

If tender offers harm the acquirers because their management acquires the wrong firms or pays prices that are too high, then the acquirers' CAR's should be steady or declining until word leaks, after which they would decrease. The CAR's of the targets would be steady until shortly before the offer, when

[67] Goldberg, *The Effect of Conglomerate Mergers on Competition*, 16 J.L. & ECON. 137 (1973). *See also* R. POSNER & F. EASTERBROOK, ANTITRUST 921–42 (2d ed. 1981).

they would increase. Untendered shares would not appreciate in price.

Finally, if tender offers are an instrument of monopolization, the CAR's of both firms should be steady before word of the acquisition spreads, and then both CAR's should rise in anticipation of monopoly profits.[68]

A great deal of evidence has been accumulated on the movement of CAR's before and after tender offers.[69] The evidence shows that the CAR's of acquired firms decline steadily for approximately forty months before the offer. A month or two before the offer, they begin to rise. After the offer has been completed, the nontendered shares continue to trade at a significant increase over the pre-offer price. The CAR's of the offerors rise when the offer is made. The estimates of gains to targets' shareholders run from 14% to 50%; the estimated gains to offerors' shareholders are 5% to 10%.[70]

---

[68] The CAR's we have described for the various views of tender offers will not necessarily describe the status of every target firm but rather will describe averages. For instance, the raid theory does not require that pre-offer market-line residuals of every target be steady. An occasional pre-offer decreasing or increasing residual is compatible with the raid theory. However, because average residuals are zero (indicating that share prices track market price movements), we would expect on average flat CAR's for targets under the raid theory. This is because the raid theory suggests no reason why acquirers would be looking for firms whose performance is not average.

[69] Bradley, *Interfirm Tender Offers and the Market for Corporate Control*, 53 J. BUS. 345 (1980); Dodd, *Merger Proposals, Management Discretion, and Stockholder Wealth*, 8 J. FINANCIAL ECON. 105 (1980); Dodd & Ruback, *Tender Offers and Shareholder Returns*, 5 J. FINANCIAL ECON. 351 (1977); Ellert, *Mergers, Antitrust Law Enforcement and Stockholder Returns*, 31 J. FINANCE 715 (1976); Jarrell & Bradley, *supra* note 21; Kummer & Hoffmeister, *Valuation Consequences of Cash Tender Offers*, 33 J. FINANCE 505 (1978); Mandelker, *Risk and Return: The Case of Merging Firms*, 1 J. FINANCIAL ECON. 303 (1974). Other studies are summarized in R. POSNER & K. SCOTT, ECONOMICS OF CORPORATION LAW AND SECURITIES REGULATION 228–31 (1980); G. BENSTON, *supra* note 66, at 35–45; 2 *Merger Hearings*, *supra* note 66, at 9–48 (testimony of Richard Posner).

[70] Dodd & Ruback, *supra* note 69, found that targets' shareholders received average premiums of 21% and acquirers' shareholders obtained nominal gains. Bradley, *supra* note 69, at 346, concluded that the targets' shareholders received a premium of 49% (relative to the price two months before the offer), while bidders' shareholders obtained an appreciation of 9% over the same period. Dodd, *supra* note 69, found gains of 33.96% to targets' shareholders relative to the price 10 days before the offer. Mandelker, *supra* note 69, at 314, found gains of 14% for the targets' shares and no abnormal gains for offerors. Jarrell & Bradley, *supra* note 21, at 389–90, found premiums of 30% to 70% for the targets' shareholders.

These results obviously differ on the extent of the gains. But differences such as this should be expected. The studies concentrate on different samples of offers in different years, and they use different periods of reference for computing price changes. It should not be surprising, therefore, that some studies also appear to find that takeovers produce little effect. Firth, *The Profitability of Takeovers and Mergers*, 89 ECON. J. 316, 323 (1979), concluded that in the United Kingdom from 1972 to 1974 offerors suffered losses that almost exactly offset the gains of the targets' shareholders.

In the judgment of the market, then, tender offers increase welfare. They rescue firms with declining CAR's but do not hurt the acquiring firms. Most of the gain goes to shareholders of the target, who benefit whether or not they tender. After the acquisition has been completed, the minority untendered shares of the target continue to trade at prices significantly higher than the pre-offer price.[71] The acquiring firms' prices increase continuously before the acquisition — not the pattern we would expect if bidders were managed by self-aggrandizing men.[72] This pattern of security prices is inconsistent with the raiding, managerialist, and monopolist views of tender offers but is consistent with the value-maximizing approach that we adopt.[73]

B. The Argument That Share Price Increases Justify Resistance from Target's Management

Several commentators have noted that even if a tender bid fails, the share price of the target often rises, sometimes to more than the tender offer price.[74] If shareholders so benefit, the argument goes, then management is justified in resisting tender offers. Although the data marshalled to support this

---

Firth speculated that the market structure of the United Kingdom might be different in some respect from that of the United States but otherwise was at a loss to explain his findings. Other scholars conclude that bidders suffer slight losses. Dodd, *supra* note 69, found that successful bidders appear to sustain losses of 7.22%. Marris & Mueller, *supra* note 65, at 42, 46, summarizes other studies indicating that bidders may be slightly optimistic. But this, too, is consistent with our approach; if an auction occurs, the prize goes to the highest bidder, and the highest bid is the most likely to suffer from unfulfillable expectations.

[71] Although the nontendering shareholders receive substantial gains, Bradley, *supra* note 69, at 346, finds that they do not receive quite as much as the tendering shareholders. This tends to confirm the argument of Grossman & Hart, *supra* note 33, at 46, that corporations will allow acquirers to "dilute" the nontendered shares slightly in order to encourage a majority of shareholders to tender.

[72] Both Mandelker, *supra* note 69, and Ellert, *supra* note 69, found that the CAR's of acquiring firms increased substantially in the four to eight years before the offer. This suggests that offerors are doing relatively well and that the offer serves to bring new assets within the control of the offerors' superior managers.

[73] Most of those who argue that tender offers do not increase welfare neglect the wealth of recent data. For example, Gelfond & Sebastian, *supra* note 12, at 453–58, asserts that tender offers do not move assets to higher valued uses yet cites none of the recent relevant studies of CAR movements. And Lipton, *supra* note 12, at 106–09, ignores not only these studies but the earlier profit studies as well. It was in the beginning of the 1970's that economists developed the procedures necessary to discriminate among the possible explanations for tender offers. Any analysis that overlooks these results is of dubious validity.

[74] Dodd & Ruback, *supra* note 69, at 362–63; Jarrell & Bradley, *supra* note 21, at 397–98; Lipton, *supra* note 12, at 106–09, 132–33.

point varies in quality,[75] the premiums offered in unsuccessful offers appear to be less than the appreciation after the offer is defeated.[76] This fact calls for explanation.

The most plausible reason for a price increase following the tender offer's defeat is that the market sees the defeat as simply one round in an extended auction. The market anticipates that in the future another offeror — one not saddled with the first offeror's higher costs of information — will acquire the target. Many management-induced withdrawals are followed by higher offers,[77] and share prices increase as the eventual acquisition becomes more likely.[78]

Another possible explanation for the price increase following a defeated tender offer is that the offer itself served to rouse the target's management to action. The offer warned management to improve its performance, and either the offer or the accompanying public disclosure may have provided the target's management with the information to do so.[79]

Regardless of the cause of the price increase, shareholders in general have little cause for rejoicing. The price rise comes about because someone is taking a free ride on information generated by the first offeror. Free riding of this sort reduces the incentive to make the first offer, and, for the reasons we have developed earlier, decreases the amount of monitoring,

---

[75] In particular, Lipton's data is unpersuasive. *See* Lipton, *supra* note 12, at 106–09, 132–33. Lipton studied 36 unsolicited tender offers that were defeated between 1973 and 1979. Nineteen of the 36 target firms were trading at a higher price than the rejected offer as of June 1979. But Lipton does not attempt to determine whether the price changes resulted from general market movements or from the defeat of the tender offer. Nor does he consider the possibility that the price of the firm's shares would have been still higher if the tender offer had succeeded. Finally, by focusing on share price after an offer is defeated, Lipton ignores the ex ante interest of shareholders in keeping prices high. *See* pp. 1177–80 & notes 41–49 *supra*.

[76] *See* Bradley, *supra* note 19, at 348, 368–72. Bradley found that unsuccessful offers had a premium of 29%, while the shares appreciated 45% relative to their price two months before the offer. He concluded that this finding demonstrates that shareholders have rational expectations — that is, that they refuse to take an offer if the shares will become more valuable on the defeat of the offer. *Id.* at 375.

[77] *See* Lipton, *supra* note 12, at 106–08.

[78] The data discussed in note 70 *supra* appear to support the explanation. However, to test our hypothesis precisely would require dividing targets into two classes — those in which managers demonstrate a plan to defeat all offers, and those in which managers attempt to elicit a higher offer. We predict that the price of the former will plummet when the tender offer is withdrawn, while the price of the latter will rise relative to the pre-offer price. No such research has been done, perhaps because of the considerable difficulty of separating firms accurately into these two categories.

[79] *See* Dodd & Ruback, *supra* note 69; Grossman & Hart, *Disclosure Laws and Takeover Bids*, *supra* note 45; Jarrell & Bradley, *supra* note 21.

decreases the number of offers, and harms shareholders in the long run.[80]

C. The Argument That Directors Have a Duty to Protect the Interests of Noninvestor Groups

Several commentators have argued that directors of a target company, when confronted with a tender offer, have a duty to consider the interests of various noninvestor groups such as employees, customers, creditors, and the community in general.[81] Even if a tender offer presents shareholders with an opportunity to sell at a profit, these commentators would allow management to resist the tender offer if it believed that the offer would adversely affect these noninvestor groups.

This proposal is deeply flawed. First, its advocates make no attempt to explain why a successful tender offer should be deleterious to the corporation's employees, suppliers, or creditors. Takeovers improve economic efficiency, and that improvement usually enhances the position of those who deal with the firm. The new owners cannot improve the firm's performance by discarding valuable employees or suppliers or by harming the interests of creditors.[82] The new owner would harm itself in the process of harming the firm. Second, even if the new owners have new policies concerning employees, plant location, and so on, how can existing managers know whether these policies are detrimental on balance? Most likely the existing managers have little information about the operational decisions to be made by their successors. And if they had such information, what could they do with it?[83] Which

[80] *See* p. 1175 *supra* (defensive strategies are not beneficial even though they raise the offer price).

[81] Lipton, *supra* note 12; Steinbrink, *supra* note 12; Speech of Harold Williams Before the Seventh Annual Securities Regulation Institute, *supra* note 61.

[82] If maintaining good community relations is in the interest of the firm, then the new owners will maintain the existing policies. And if the target's community relations were not in the firm's interests, then the old management was diverting shareholders' wealth to friends or other favorites. If the existence of such diversion were demonstrable, it would amount to a breach of the managers' fiduciary duty to shareholders whether or not a takeover occurred.

[83] Managers should not be allowed to consider whether creditors, suppliers, or employees will be displaced in deciding whether to oppose a tender offer. The risk of displacement is an inevitable and indispensable characteristic in any free market economy. Any attempt by management to minimize this risk by preventing new owners from having the opportunity to operate more efficiently, with existing or (if necessary) new inputs of production, is anticompetitive. Such behavior is more characteristic of medieval guilds than of free markets.

Moreover, as we have emphasized, outsiders have no incentive to discard existing policies that are in the firm's best interests. *Cf.* McKenzie, *Frustrating Business Mobility*, REG., May/June 1980, at 32 (arguing that proposed laws that attempt to groups are to be considered by management? Should management be obligated to balance losses to existing noninvestor groups against the (presumably greater) gains to other noninvestor groups as a result of the tender offer?[84] Even if these hurdles can be overcome, how should management balance the effect of a tender offer on noninvestor groups with the impact on shareholders?[85]

Finally, the proposed approach amounts to rejection of the idea that agents (managers) are accountable to their principals (shareholders). So long as it continues to be lawful to form corporations for profit, shareholders are entitled to hire managers dedicated to the shareholders' interests alone. The duty of management is to operate efficiently and thus maximize the return to shareholders.[86] Maximization of shareholders' wealth ultimately works to the advantage of workers and suppliers, because shareholders gain only from the firm's mutually beneficial transactions with those persons. If the proposed approach were adopted, however, management would, in certain

minimize employee and community dislocation by preventing businesses from moving to areas where they can operate more efficiently are anticompetitive and hurt the communities and workers they attempt to protect).

[84] The argument has been made that defense is justified because the target firms are run by "locals," with appropriate concern for their home towns, and that the new "outside" owners will disregard these ties. *Cf.* Herald Co. v. Seawell, 472 F.2d 1081 (10th Cir. 1972) (directors of newspaper have obligation to public and employees in addition to stockholders). This argument is overly provincial. Why should the old suppliers or the community in which the firm operates count for more than the new suppliers or new home base chosen by new management?

[85] If a successful tender offer would give shareholders a 20% return on their investment, but might cost certain employees their jobs, should management oppose the tender offer? What if the premium is larger but a longtime creditor might lose a valuable source of business? The number of problems could be multiplied indefinitely. Our point is that although management, at least in nonconflict-of-interest situations, is best situated to determine what actions will maximize the return to shareholders, it is hardly qualified or authorized to balance shareholders' interests against the uncertain effects of an acquisition on various vaguely defined noninvestor groups.

[86] This is unquestionably the prevailing view. *See* Dodge v. Ford Motor Co., 204 Mich. 459, 507, 170 N.W. 668, 684 (1919) ("A business corporation is organized and carried on primarily for the profit of the stockholders. The powers of the directors are to be employed for that end. The discretion of directors is to be exercised in the choice of means to attain that end and does not extend to a change in the end itself . . . ."); *Corporate Director's Guidebook*, 33 BUS. LAW. 1595, 1621 (1978); Hetherington, *Facts and Legal Theory: Shareholders, Managers and Corporate Responsibility*, 21 STAN. L. REV. 248, 279–80 (1969). The most recent cases continue to adhere to this view. One court, for example, held that United States Steel Corporation had no common law or contractual obligation to consider the effects of plant closures on employees or the communities in which the plants were located. Local 1330, United Steel Workers v. United States Steel Corp., 631 F.2d 1264, 1279–82 (6th Cir. 1980). *But cf.* Herald Co. v. Seawell, 472 F.2d 1081 (10th Cir. 1972) (holding that directors of newspapers have obligation to public and employees in addition to stockholders).

cases, sacrifice the interest of the shareholders to the interests of noninvestor groups.[87] Such a result, far more than the separation of ownership and control or any other characteristic of the modern corporation, would greatly prejudice shareholders by decreasing the incentive of management to act in their best interest. A manager responsible to two conflicting interests is in fact answerable to neither. A principle of divided loyalty ultimately would harm everyone by reducing the willingness of people to entrust their money to managers.[88]

D. *The Argument That Directors Have a Duty to Prevent Violations of Law*

A final justification for resistance to tender offers is target management's alleged duty to prevent unlawful conduct.[89] In furtherance of this duty, managers have instituted litigation against offerors to prevent asserted violations by the offerors of the antitrust laws and the Williams Act. In many cases, the expense and delay caused by the litigation are sufficient to defeat the tender offer, even if the underlying claim is frivolous.

But what is the source of management's duty? If managers act on behalf of shareholders, the duty must come from a need to prevent injury to these shareholders. If a given act involves a violation of law, penalties may follow. Managers' duty calls for them to minimize the sum of penalty costs and the cost of compliance with the rule.[90] But the first link in the chain is the possibility of injury. There is no duty to spend the firm's resources to prevent some *other* party from exposing itself to a penalty. Indeed, unless a party is actually injured by a violation, it generally does not have even the right to sue. The question, therefore, is what injury (in penalties or other costs) the target corporation or its shareholders could suffer if the offeror violates the law.

With respect to alleged antitrust violations, it is difficult to see how the shareholders will suffer "loss or damage by a

[87] Jensen & Meckling, *Rights and Production Functions: An Application to Labor-managed Firms and Codetermination*, 52 J. BUS. 469 (1979), makes a convincing argument that programs in which noninvestors have claims to the firm's income will make all claimants (including the nonowners) worse off.

[88] This defect in the proposal for management responsibility to noninvestor groups is shared by similar proposals to place representatives of various constituent groups on the board of directors. Apart from the insoluble practical problems of determining who should be on the board and how votes should be allocated, constituent representation plans inevitably have the effect of decreasing management's accountability to shareholders.

[89] *See, e.g.*, Lipton, *supra* note 12; Steinbrink, *supra* note 12.

[90] *See* Engel, *An Approach to Corporate Social Responsibility*, 32 STAN. L. REV. 1, 37–58 (1979).

violation of the antitrust laws."[91] The acquired company suffers no "loss or damage" because it generally becomes richer rather than poorer.[92] Only the acquirer can violate the Clayton Act;[93] the target's shareholders are not exposed to any risk of penalty.

Shareholders who receive and hold the offeror's stock could conceivably be injured, however, if the new combined firm is assessed treble damages for an antitrust violation. But this possible future injury would not serve as the justification for an antitrust suit brought by the target's management. There is no assurance that such damages will be assessed. The shareholders could avoid any risks by selling in the market. That the bidder's stock is worth more than the target's shares surrendered in the offer suggests strongly that the possible future liability is less than the apparent future gains from the offer. Because the target's management has a duty to the tendering shareholders who risk losing the tender offer premium if the offer is defeated, it cannot logically raise the uncertain prospect of antitrust liability as a reason why shareholders should be compelled to forego a sure gain. Management's proper course if it believes that a successful tender offer would violate the antitrust laws is to refer the matter to the Department of Justice.[94]

Suits to redress alleged violations of section 13(d) of the Williams Act[95] present a more difficult problem. Because Congress has enacted the statute to ensure that shareholders of a target company receive accurate information concerning the offeror and its plans,[96] the offeror's noncompliance may injure the target's shareholders. It is by no means clear, however,

---

[91] To obtain injunctive relief under § 16 of the Clayton Act, 15 U.S.C. § 26 (1976), a party must establish "loss or damage by a violation of the antitrust laws." *See* Brunswick Corp. v. Pueblo Bowl-O-Mat, Inc., 429 U.S. 477 (1977). The Court held there that a plaintiff cannot recover damages unless it can demonstrate antitrust injury; that is, it must prove that its injury resulted from that which made the defendant's conduct unlawful. After *Brunswick* a strong argument can be made that a target company has not suffered any antitrust injury resulting from the tender offer, even if an illegal combination results. *See* Fischel, *supra* note 7, at 38. This same point has been made more recently in 2 P. AREEDA & D. TURNER, ANTITRUST LAW ¶ 346b, at 248–49 (1978), and was apparently adopted in A.D.M. Corp. v. Sigma Instruments, Inc., 628 F.2d 753, 754 (1st Cir. 1980).

[92] *See* Missouri Portland Cement Co. v. Cargill, Inc., 498 F.2d 851, 866–67 (2d Cir.), *cert. denied*, 419 U.S. 883 (1974).

[93] Section 7 applies only to acquiring firms. 15 U.S.C. § 18 (1976).

[94] Management also could inform the shareholders of its belief and let them make their own decision whether to tender.

[95] 15 U.S.C. § 78m(d)(1) (1976).

[96] For critical analyses of this requirement that an offeror disclose its plans, see Fischel, *supra* note 7, at 12–13; Grossman & Hart, *Disclosure Laws and Takeover Bids*, *supra* note 45; Jarrell & Bradley, *supra* note 21.

that management should be allowed to represent shareholders' interests under the Williams Act by bringing suit; the interests of the two groups may conflict in this situation,[97] and there is too great a risk that a management-initiated suit will be a dilatory tactic intended to defeat a tender offer beneficial to shareholders.[98] Here, as with antitrust concerns, management's best course is to refer the matter to the appropriate government agency, in this case the Securities and Exchange Commission.

III. THE BUSINESS JUDGMENT RULE AND MANAGERIAL PASSIVITY

Our thesis that managers of target companies should acquiesce when confronted with a tender offer has not been adopted by courts and state legislatures. As we indicated at the outset, courts have generally gone in the opposite direction, holding that directors have not only the right but also the duty to resist tender offers that they believe to be not in the best interests of their shareholders.[99] Although some decisions find particular defensive tactics to be unlawful,[100] they are exceptions to the general rule permitting or even requiring defensive strategies.

The most significant conceptual impediment to judicial, and perhaps even legislative, adoption of a rule requiring managerial passivity has been the notion that assessing the economic merits of tender offers, like judging the merits of any other prospect facing the corporation, is peculiarly within the ability of management. This sense that decisions regarding the future of the corporation are best made by its managers is embodied in the business judgment rule[101] — a common law

---

[97] For a discussion of the conflict of interest between managers and shareholders when a tender offer has been made, see pp. 1197–98 *infra*.

[98] Another barrier to a suit to enjoin a tender offer for a violation of § 13(d), 15 U.S.C. § 78m(d)(1) (1976), by the offeror is that the Williams Act contains no such express private right of action. *Compare* Dan River, Inc. v. Unitex Ltd., 624 F.2d 1216 (4th Cir. 1980) (holding that a target may sue under § 13(d)), *and* Kirsch Co. v. Bliss Laughlin Indus., [1980 Transfer Binder] FED. SEC. L. REP. (CCH) ¶ 97,580 (W.D. Mich. July 1, 1980) (same), *with* Gateway Indus. v. Agency Rent A Car, Inc., [1980 Binder] FED. SEC. L. REP. (CCH) ¶ 97,540 (N.D. Ill. June 10, 1980) (no private right of action under § 13(d)).

[99] *See* p. 1163 *supra*.

[100] Klaus v. Hi-Shear Corp., 528 F.2d 225 (9th Cir. 1975); Podesta v. Calumet Indus., [1978 Transfer Binder] FED. SEC. L. REP. (CCH) ¶ 96,433–34 (N.D. Ill.); Condec Corp. v. Lunkenheimer Co., 230 A.2d 769 (Del. Ch. 1967).

[101] *See* p. 1163 *supra*. The precise meaning of the rule is in dispute. *Compare* Veasey & Manning, *Codified Standard — Safe Harbor or Uncharted Reef*, 35 BUS.

doctrine that, at least outside the realm of tender offers, has long insulated managerial decisions from judicial scrutiny. Under the business judgment rule, managers enjoy considerable freedom to direct the corporation as they see fit. Without some showing of either bad faith or self-dealing, courts almost uniformly refuse to subject the decisions of managers to review on the merits.

Our purpose in this Part is to harmonize our proposal of managerial passivity with the business judgment rule and demonstrate that the rule should never serve to justify a decision to oppose a tender offer. We also attempt to provide some guidelines for courts to use in determining whether management has engaged in conduct for the purpose of defeating a tender offer.

A. The Rationale and Limits of the Business Judgment Rule

The shareholder-owners (and also bondholders) of a corporation must select agents (managers) to run its affairs. If the corporation is publicly held, the managers are unlikely to own a significant proportion of the firm's securities. As we have repeatedly emphasized, agency costs are an inevitable consequence of this relationship. Yet courts generally do not scrutinize managers' conduct. Quite the contrary, after satisfying themselves that particular business decisions were made in good faith by the managers and were not tainted by self-dealing, courts invoking the business judgment rule typically decline to inquire further. While it may at first appear anom-

LAW. 919 (1980), *with* Arsht & Hinsey, *Codified Standard — Same Harbor But Charted Channel: A Response*, 35 BUS. LAW. ix (July 1980).

The recent case of Treadway Cos. v. Care Corp., 638 F.2d 357 (2d Cir. 1980), *rev'g in part* 490 F. Supp. 668 (S.D.N.Y. 1980), illustrates the strength of the business judgment rule, once it has been invoked. Care acquired 31% of Treadway's stock and indicated an intent to obtain control. Treadway's management responded by "selling" a large block of shares to a third party; the buyer obtained a commitment by Treadway to repurchase the shares. The district court concluded that this deal was inexplicable except as a strategem to frustrate Care and to maintain Treadway's managers in office, and it found that Treadway had made no serious study of the consequences of a takeover by Care. It enjoined Treadway from voting these new shares. The court of appeals reversed, relying on the business judgment rule. It found that the plaintiffs had not carried their initial burden of establishing that the directors had an interest in the transaction or acted in bad faith. *Id.* at 380–88. It therefore was irrelevant that the directors could not establish that they had a proper purpose in issuing the shares.

Treadway is not a tender offer case — it involved an attempted takeover through a proxy contest by a minority shareholder. Such a situation raises some prospect that the new controlling party will not look after the interests of the majority of the shareholders. The case is, therefore, not strictly inconsistent with the analysis of the business judgment rule that we offer below. It is, nonetheless, at odds with the spirit of our proposal.

alous for courts to give managers such broad discretion given the inevitability of agency costs, there is no tension between the rule and shareholders' welfare.

The application of the business judgment rule contributes to the efficient management that shareholders desire. There is no reason to think that courts generally could improve the performance of managers. Courts lack the experience and information necessary to make business decisions. Although sometimes a court might be able to detect inferior decision-making or other agency costs, the burden of inquiry in the run of cases almost certainly would carry costs larger than the gains available in the few cases where courts could improve matters. Even if judges were well suited to the task of reviewing business judgments, the ratio of suits to improvements would be high, because plaintiff-shareholders, just like courts, would lack the information necessary to challenge managerial decisions intelligently.

Moreover, it is doubtful that shareholders would gain from having better decisions made on the basis of additional information developed in litigation. Many business decisions are made on the basis of suggestive but inconclusive information. Rational shareholders would not have it otherwise, however, for their welfare is maximized by decisions that yield the highest profits net of the costs of gathering information and making the decisions. Yet after things go awry, it is easy for a shareholder to contend that managers gathered too little information. If information-gathering and deciding costs are disregarded — as they often are by courts — then a different business decision may be preferred over the one management actually took. But because shareholders would not want managers to disregard information-gathering and deciding costs in search of better decisions, they also would not favor a legal rule that paid too little attention to those costs.

There is no reason to believe that judicial scrutiny is more effective in policing management than various market forces, which provide incentives to management to operate efficiently and keep share prices high. One mechanism creating such an incentive is the market for corporate control, particularly the tender offer market, which we have discussed at length. Indeed, the ability of shareholders freely to trade their shares, and thereby vote on current management, is no doubt the most powerful check on agency costs.[102] Other market incentives exist to ensure that management will generally act in the best interests of shareholders. Competition in the product and

[102] *See* R. WINTER, *supra* note 26.

services market, for example, ensures that a firm that is inefficiently managed will not survive over time. Similarly, the market for managerial services provides managers with considerable incentive to operate efficiently so as to increase the market value of their own services.[103] Finally, various compensation packages, such as stock option plans, by making managers owners, also attempt to provide management with incentives to keep share prices high by linking managerial compensation to the firm's performance.[104] In light of these various incentives to keep share prices high, management's interest in maximizing share price corresponds (if imperfectly) to the shareholders' interest in maximum return on their investment. There is little need to add to these automatic devices a process of judicial review that is costly and unlikely to identify or correct real errors of business judgment.

But market forces are not fully effective in making the interests of managers and shareholders coincide. Some self-dealing transactions pose an especially great risk of malfeasance. The clearest example of this may be emptying the corporate treasury and fleeing to Honduras with the proceeds. At the same time, courts are especially adept at discovering fraud, deceit, or pocket-lining in business transactions. An inquiry into fraud does not require an examination of the wisdom of any business decision.

For these reasons, the rules that govern the managers' duty of *care* have been distinguished from the rules governing the duty of *loyalty*. When managers have acute conflicts of interest, they must bear the burden, unaided by any presumption or deference, of establishing that the transaction was "fair" (beneficial) to the firm.[105] The duty of loyalty and the duty of care thus are treated differently, with the business judgment rule covering only the latter. This limitation on the scope of the business judgment rule, like the basis of the rule itself, rests on principles that maximize the welfare of shareholders.

---

[103] Poor management may lead to reductions in the managers' salaries and bonuses. Other managers may also fire the shirkers. Fama, *supra* note 28; Jensen & Meckling, *supra* note 24. Managers with a history of poor performance will also command lower salaries at other firms.

[104] Stock option plans, however, cannot eliminate the problem of suboptimal management. *See* note 31, *supra*.

[105] *E.g.*, Lewis v. S.L. & E., Inc., 629 F.2d 764 (2d Cir. 1980); Wilderman v. Wilderman, 315 A.2d 610 (Del. Ch. 1978); Ross Transport, Inc. v. Crothers, 185 Md. 573, 45 A.2d 267 (1946). *See also* Maldonado v. Flynn, 413 A.2d 1251 (Del. Ch.) (refusing to apply the business judgment rule to a motion to dismiss a derivative suit), *contingently dismissed on res judicata grounds*, 417 A.2d 378 (Del. Ch. 1980) (in light of Maldonado v. Flynn, 483 F. Supp. 274 (S.D.N.Y. 1980)).

B. Defensive Tactics and the Business Judgment Rule

In view of the recognized limits on the scope of the business judgment rule, it is surprising that courts have invoked the rule so freely as a basis for refusing to review the defensive conduct of managers faced with a hostile tender offer. A frequent consequence of a successful takeover attempt is the replacement of incumbent managers. For acquirers, replacement of target management is typically a significant motive for making the tender offer in the first place; for the target's shareholders, such offers present the most effective means of manifesting disapproval of management. Given the serious and unavoidable conflict of interest that inheres in any decision on one's own ouster, courts ought not to make available to a manager resisting a tender offer — and, in effect, fighting against his own replacement — the same deference accorded to the decisions of a manager in good standing.

Indeed, unlike transactions involving a conflict of managerial interest outside the realm of tender offers, efforts undertaken by target management primarily to resist a takeover bid should not even be susceptible of the justification that they happen to benefit the target. Such efforts to resist should instead be proscribed completely. Conflicts transactions outside the realm of tender offers are not similarly interdicted because they typically involve corporate decisions that shareholders, as a practical matter, simply cannot make.[106] But in deciding whether to accept or reject a tender offer, managers enjoy no particular comparative advantage over shareholders. The decision does not involve management of the corporation's affairs in any meaningful sense and thus can be made by shareholders even though they are not involved in those affairs to any significant degree.

Moreover, the rationales underlying the policy of judicial restraint embodied in the business judgment rule in no way counsel against implementation of a rule of managerial passivity. The deference accorded managerial decisions under the

---

[106] The decision whether to oppose a tender offer is different from other "interested" director transactions such as the setting of salaries or the making of contracts with a related entity. Because of the dangers presented by a conflict of interest in these latter situations, courts are likely to scrutinze these transactions closely to prevent harmful self-dealing. But it could not seriously be argued that the best way to minimize the risks created by a conflict of interest would be for shareholders to establish the salaries of directors or make contracts for the corporation. These types of decisions, regardless of the inevitable conflict of interest, must be made by management as agents for the firm; the shareholders themselves have neither the time, the expertise, nor the interest to become involved with running the corporation's affairs.

business judgment rule reflects, in part, the inability of courts to make better business decisions than managers and, in part, the inefficiency that would result were managers encouraged to disregard the costs of gathering information and making decisions. A rule of managerial passivity does not require courts to make business decisions at all, let alone better decisions than managers. To implement a rule of passivity, all a court need do is determine whether managers were passive.[107] It need not gather costly information nor induce managers to incur inefficiently large costs of decisionmaking to stave off litigation. Under a rule of passivity, managerial decisions would be subject to attack only if designed to defeat takeover bids, and not for being inadequately researched.[108]

C. The Role of Management in Responding to a Tender Offer Compared with the Role of Management in Other Fundamental Corporate Changes

Our proposal that managers should be passive in response to a tender offer might appear to be at odds with the broad

---

[107] See pp. 1201–03 *infra*.

[108] Some commentators have suggested, however, that if the decision to oppose a tender offer is taken pursuant to the recommendations of a truly independent committee of the board of directors, courts should apply the business judgment rule. Gelfond & Sebastian, *supra* note 12; *see* Speech by Harold Williams Before the Seventh Annual Securities Regulation Institute, *supra* note 61. This proposal fails to take account of several considerations. "Independent" directors may not be so independent in passing on such matters, for they effectively serve at the pleasure of the managers whose jobs are at stake in a takeover. These managers provide the information on which the outside directors will act. *See* Galef v. Alexander, 615 F.2d 51 (2d Cir. 1980); Maldonado v. Flynn, 413 A.2d 1251 (Del. Ch.), *contingently dismissed on res judicata grounds*, 417 A.2d 378 (Del. Ch. 1980) (in light of Maldonado v. Flynn, 483 F. Supp. 274 (S.D.N.Y. 1980)). *But cf.* Lewis v. Anderson, 615 F.2d 778 (9th Cir. 1980) (good faith exercise of business judgment by special litigation committee is immune from judicial scrutiny); Auerbach v. Bennett, 47 N.Y.2d 619, 393 N.E.2d 994, 419 N.Y.S.2d 920 (1979) (no judicial inquiry into actions of special litigation committee appointed by board of directors). More important, however, the independent director proposal assumes that directors, even if disinterested, have the right to decide for the shareholders, ex post, whether or not the shareholders may sell their shares. By making this assumption, however, the independent director proposal disregards the need for a binding policy of acquiescence in order to maximize shareholders' welfare ex ante. Any attempt to resist a tender offer will have the effect of increasing the amount of agency costs by raising the offerors' costs and decreasing the number of offers. And the resulting decrease in the effectiveness of monitoring will lead to a fall in the price of shares when the assessment is made ex ante. This decline in share price will occur regardless of whether the managers (or disinterested directors) decide to resist. *See* pp. 1175–80 *supra*. For shareholder wealth to be maximized ex ante, the decision whether or not to sell when a tender offer is made must be made by the shareholders and by shareholders alone.

discretion that management has in negotiating a merger or deciding whether the firm should be sold or liquidated.[109] The difference in treatment is justified, however, by the differences between the role played by the board in tender offers and its role in these other situations.

By statute,[110] the board of directors negotiates a merger as the firm's agent. So long as the board continues to exercise agency authority, there is little reason to second-guess its decision to disapprove a merger. Only at great cost, if at all, could a court determine whether rejection of a proposed merger was a mistake. The performance of the board in its role as agent is policed by market forces. If the board attempts to siphon the benefits of the merger to itself, or obstinately refuses to negotiate based on a policy of being independent, the prospective partner can simply make a tender offer. The tender offer, therefore, is an essential safety valve to ensure that managers evaluate merger proposals in the best interests of the shareholders.[111] A legal rule that allowed the target's management the same discretion in responding to a tender offer as it has in responding to a merger proposal, therefore, would decrease the number of mergers as well as the number of tender offers, because a valuable check on management would be lost.

The analogy to the lack of any obligation on the part of management to make a periodic decision whether to sell or liquidate is similarly irrelevant. A tender offer presents shareholders with a concrete price at a premium over market. The offeror has borne the necessary costs of investigation, and the target's shareholders obtain the benefit. In contrast, the board could not decide whether to sell or liquidate without investing substantial sums in getting an estimate of realizable proceeds. The advice of investment bankers or other experts is inexact and quite expensive. Constant expenditure of funds for this purpose is not likely to be justified.

If it could somehow be determined that the firm is worth more sold or liquidated than as a going concern, then it should

[109] Several commentators have suggested that the rules concerning tender offers be modeled on the role of the board in mergers. *E.g.*, Lipton, *supra* note 12; Herzel, Schmidt & Davis, *supra* note 12. It has also been suggested that since directors have no obligation to make a periodic decision whether to sell or liquidate, they should similarly have no obligation to accept a tender offer. Lipton, *supra* note 12.

[110] State corporation statutes typically provide that a vote of the directors is necessary to submit a merger proposal to the shareholders. *See, e.g.*, DEL. CODE ANN. tit. 8, § 251(b) (1974).

[111] This safety valve aspect of tender offers is implicitly recognized by state corporation statutes, which typically require that directors approve a merger proposal but impose no similar approval requirement in the case of tender offers.

be sold or liquidated. This is a fundamental principle of bankruptcy law.[112] True, management of a solvent firm has no duty to sell or liquidate in this situation. But if it does not, the company will be an attractive tender offer candidate. The offeror then can sell or liquidate and thereby appropriate the resulting gains for itself and for remaining minority shareholders. Again, therefore, the tender offer acts as a safety valve and helps to induce managers to serve the shareholders' interests.

D. The Meaning of Managerial Passivity

Although we have concluded that shareholders would want management to be passive in the face of a tender offer, we have not attempted to define precisely what we mean by passivity. Doubtless, managers must carry out the corporation's ordinary business. Perhaps, too, management should be able to issue a press release urging shareholders to accept or reject the offer.[113] The offeror also will convey its views to the shareholders, who can act on these messages in light of the self-interest of both the management and the offeror.[114] But almost any other defensive actions expend the target's resources and produce no gain to investors. Thus, management should not propose antitakeover charter or bylaw amendments, file suits against the offeror, acquire a competitor of the offeror in order to create an antitrust obstacle to the tender offer, buy or sell shares in order to make the offer more costly, give away to some potential "white knight" valuable corporate information that might call forth a competing bid, or initiate any other defensive tactic to defeat a tender offer.[115]

Our proposal for managerial passivity does not mean, however, that managers must go to sleep when they suspect an

[112] N. Buchanan, The Economics of Corporate Enterprise chs. 14–15 (1940).

[113] SEC Rule 14e-2, 17 C.F.R. 240.14e-2 (1980), requires the target's management to inform the shareholders of its position with respect to a tender offer within 10 days of its announcement. This release of information may lead to a change in share prices, and defeat of the offer, if significant facts previously were unknown to traders. *See* p. 1168 *supra*.

[114] Section 14(e) of the Williams Act prohibits false and deceptive statements by both a target and an offeror. 15 U.S.C. § 78n(e) (1976).

[115] It is irrelevant to our analysis whether the incumbent management has a "policy" dispute with the offeror. We question, therefore, the approach in the line of Delaware cases which hold that directors can lawfully expend resources to defend their positions when corporate policy is at stake. *E.g.*, Cheff v. Mathes, 41 Del. Ch. 494, 199 A.2d 548 (1964); Kois v. Carey, 39 Del. Ch. 47, 158 A.2d 136 (1960); Martin v. American Potash & Chem. Corp., 33 Del. Ch. 232, 92 A.2d 295 (1952); *see* Fischel, *supra* note 7, at 35, 40–42.

imminent tender offer. A requirement of managerial somnolence would deprive the corporation of valuable business opportunities and might give firms a device for hindering their competitors' operations. Yet many legitimate business decisions could have the effect of making the corporation less attractive to the bidder and thus could be called resistance. It is also possible, however, that many business decisions, ostensibly taken for the purpose of seizing valuable business opportunities, are actually undertaken for the purpose of defeating the tender offer. Distinguishing resistance from passivity will be simple in some cases and hard in others.

Management will frequently leave clues, however, that suggest its motive. The recent decision in *Panter v. Marshall Field & Co.*[116] illustrates this process. Marshall Field operates a number of high quality department and specialty stores. Although frequently the subject of overtures to merger, Field has rejected each one.[117] Field also made a number of acquisitions in the past, apparently for the purpose of creating antitrust problems for potential bidders.[118] Field resisted again when Carter Hawley Hale, another retailer, prepared to make a cash tender offer. Field filed suit urging that the acquisition would violate the securities or antitrust laws; it urged its shareholders not to tender, arguing that the price was too low; it made several defensive acquisitions that not only aggravated a potential antitrust problem but also made Field less attractive as Carter's merger partner;[119] Field's board authorized the management to take "such action as they deemed necessary" in order to defeat the offer altogether.[120]

Under our view that managers should be passive in response to a tender offer, *Marshall Field* is an easy case. Management's departure from passivity was unmistakeable and constituted a clear breach of fiduciary duty.[121] But how would the case have proceeded if Field had issued a public statement of neutrality while proceeding with the acquisition? A prophylactic rule that would prevent management from making profitable acquisitions would harm shareholders, yet applica-

[116] 486 F. Supp. 1168 (N.D. Ill. 1980), *appeal docketed*, No. 80-1375 (7th Cir. Mar. 21, 1980).

[117] *Id.*, slip op. at 1177.

[118] *Id.*

[119] *Id.* at 1177–84, 1188–90.

[120] *Id.* at 1180–84.

[121] The district court, however, held that the directors of Marshall Field did not violate any fiduciary duty. *Id.* at 1194–95. This holding was based on the premise, erroneous in our view, that the business judgment rule provides management with the right, and even the duty, to resist a tender offer that it deems to be not in the best interests of the firm or its shareholders.

tion of the usual business judgment rule would give managers free rein to carry out disguised programs of resistance.

The timing of managerial action provides a useful, if imperfect, basis for resolving this dilemma. On the one hand, courts could simply presume, subject to rebuttal by a litigant who established the contrary, that any plans or programs set in motion before target managers had reason to believe that there would be a takeover attempt were not undertaken with a view to resisting the tender offer.[122] Such plans would presumptively comply with the rule of passivity and would thus enjoy the freedom from judicial scrutiny otherwise available under the business judgment rule.[123] On the other hand, if actions that materially hindered either the offer or the acquisition were taken immediately after management first had reason to know of an impending offer, then courts could presume that the actions were undertaken with a view to defeating the offer.[124] The target's managers could be allowed to overcome the presumption, but only by a substantial demonstration that their actions were undertaken for the economic benefit of the target rather than for the purpose of defeating the offer.

---

[122] The business judgment rule should not apply, however, to unambiguous preventive defense tactics such as shark-repellant charter and bylaw amendments. This type of resistance (which, we have emphasized, is a form of suboptimal management) should be prohibited per se.

[123] The principal problem with any such approach is that it creates an incentive for managers to take their defensive steps in advance — to build moats and barricades. They could, for example, insert in the bylaws of the firm provisions that make takeover costly; a bonus of $20 million to be paid to any person involuntarily transferred from one job to another, or a mandatory dividend of $20 per share whenever one person gains more than 25% of the shares would be possible (if farfetched) provisions. These second-best responses could in principle be as effective as existing defensive strategies in preventing takeovers, yet we know (from the fact that they are not now employed) that they are more costly to the target than today's antitakeover devices. Our proposal is hardly desirable if it simply drives managers to construct new methods of resistance or new ways of disguising old methods. We conclude, nonetheless, that problems of second-best solutions are not a sufficient objection to the analysis presented here. Similar objections could be raised to most other legal rules. The rule against price-fixing cartels, for example, might induce firms to substitute territorial or customer allocations that are costly to design, enforce, and disguise. Yet society has sufficient confidence in the benefits of the rule against price fixing that the risk of such undetectable devices seems worth running. The same is true with tender offers.

[124] *See* cases cited note 4 *supra*. In some cases, however, management will resist a tender offer in order to prevent the offer from interfering with plans set in motion before the takeover attempt. *See* Crouse-Hinds Co. v. InterNorth, Inc., 634 F.2d 690 (2d Cir. 1980). Resistance in this situation is inconsistent with our proposal of managerial passivity and should be prohibited.

This allocation of burdens places on the management — which has a clear conflict of interest and superior access to information about the reasons for and consequences of its deeds — the responsibility of justification. It meets two essential criteria: it does not incapacitate management from seizing profitable business opportunities just because another firm is attempting to acquire the target, and it also does not freely allow defensive strategems. We do not doubt that the standard would prove troublesome in some cases, but it would resolve most cases, such as *Marshall Field*, quickly and inexpensively.

[3]

COMMENT

THE CASE FOR FACILITATING COMPETING TENDER OFFERS

*Lucian A. Bebchuk**

Last year in this journal, Professors Easterbrook and Fischel advocated a rule that would require management to be passive in the face of a takeover bid, and argued that even resistance that triggers a bidding contest is undesirable. They reasoned that bidding contests curtail the search for takeover targets and thus are ultimately detrimental to shareholder welfare. In this Comment, Mr. Bebchuk maintains that bidding contests are consistent with a substantial level of search, and argues that facilitating competing bids is desirable for both target shareholders and society. Consequently, he endorses regulations that provide time for competing bids, and supports a rule that would allow management to solicit competing bids as long as it does not obstruct the initial or any subsequent tender offer.

In a recent article,[1] Professors Easterbrook and Fischel argue that the facilitation of competing bids in corporate takeovers is undesirable.[2] Their argument is based on the effect that bidding contests have on the search for takeover targets by prospective acquirers.[3] Increases in the prices that must be paid for targets, they emphasize, reduce the return on search by prospective acquirers and thus discourage an activity that benefits both targets' shareholders and the economy.[4] They contend that bidding contests for targets are therefore contrary to the long-run interests of targets' shareholders and of society. Accordingly, even resistance by a target's management that succeeds in triggering a bidding contest and securing a high premium is counterproductive.[5] Easterbrook and Fischel therefore advocate a rule that would require a target's management to remain passive in the face of a tender offer.[6]

---

* S.J.D. and Ph.D. candidate, Harvard Law School and Harvard University Department of Economics. I am indebted to Professor Victor Brudney for his advice. I also benefited from comments by Professor Robert Clark and Louis Kaplow on a draft of this Comment.

[1] Easterbrook & Fischel, *The Proper Role of a Target's Management in Responding to a Tender Offer*, 94 HARV. L. REV. 1161 (1981).

[2] *Id.* at 1175–80.

[3] *Id.* at 1176–80.

[4] *Id.* at 1173–74, 1176–80.

[5] *Id.* at 1164, 1175–80.

[6] *Id.* at 1164, 1201–04.

Whether or not bidding contests are desirable, there are strong reasons for opposing defensive tactics, such as creation of antitrust obstacles, that obstruct the resisted offer.[7] These tactics can be abused, as Easterbrook and Fischel observe, by a management seeking to perpetuate its control.[8] Obstructing tactics also preclude shareholders from making their own decision whether to accept the offer.[9] These concerns justify the prohibition of such tactics,[10] even if Easterbrook's and Fischel's thesis on bidding contests is rejected.

The Easterbrook and Fischel thesis provides the sole ground, however, for barring management's solicitation of a competing bid from a "white knight."[11] This important and widely used tactic cannot be employed by management to avoid a takeover altogether, and it leaves shareholders free to accept any offer; it can only increase the price they will be offered for their shares. The Easterbrook and Fischel thesis also has implications for the regulation of offerors. Various provisions of the Williams Act[12] and state tender offer statutes regulate tender offers in ways that facilitate competing bids;[13] if bidding contests are counterproductive, it follows that these provisions are undesirable.[14]

This Comment critically examines Easterbrook's and Fis-

---

[7] Obstructing tactics include creation of antitrust or regulatory obstacles, adoption of an antitakeover charter or bylaw amendments, repurchase of stock, issuance of stock to a friendly party, and litigation against the offeror. *See* E. ARANOW & H. EINHORN, TENDER OFFERS FOR CORPORATE CONTROL 234–76 (1973); A. FLEISCHER, TENDER OFFERS: DEFENSES, RESPONSES, AND PLANNING 113–55 (1981); M. LIPTON & E. STEINBERGER, TAKEOVERS & FREEZEOUTS 296–320 (1978). A relatively new obstructing tactic is the granting of "lock-up" options to a "white knight." *See* Mobil Corp. v. Marathon Oil Co., [Current Transfer Binder] FED. SEC. L. REP. (CCH) ¶ 98,399, at 92,385 (6th Cir. Dec. 23, 1981).

[8] Easterbrook & Fischel, *supra* note 1, at 1175; *see* Gelfond & Sebastian, *Reevaluating the Duties of Target Management in a Hostile Tender Offer*, 60 B.U.L. REV. 403 (1980); Gilson, *A Structural Approach to Corporations: The Case Against Defensive Tactics in Tender Offers*, 33 STAN. L. REV. 819 (1981); Lynch & Steinberg, *The Legitimacy of Defensive Tactics in Tender Offers*, 64 CORNELL L. REV. 901 (1979).

[9] *See* Gilson, *supra* note 8, at 845–48, 856–62; Lynch & Steinberg, *supra* note 8, at 933–38.

[10] For a recent, comprehensive argument that these concerns warrant a prohibition of obstructing tactics, see Gilson, *supra* note 8.

[11] *See* Easterbrook & Fischel, *supra* note 1, at 1201.

[12] 15 U.S.C. §§ 78*l*(i), 78m(d)–(e), 78n(d)–(f) (1976).

[13] *See infra* notes 91–92, 95–96. Primarily, the regulations provide time, which is necessary for making competing offers.

[14] The undesirability of regulations that facilitate competing bids is implied by Easterbrook & Fischel, *supra* note 1, at 1179 n.46. A similar view is expressed by Jarrel & Bradley, *The Economic Effects of Federal and State Regulations of Cash Tender Offers*, 23 J.L. & ECON. 371 (1980).

chel's stimulating analysis and their intriguing thesis.[15] It argues that facilitating competing tender offers is desirable both to targets' shareholders and to society. Time is essential for competing offers, and such offers will be further facilitated if potential buyers can receive information from the target's management.[16] This Comment therefore supports a rule of auctioneering that: (1) provides, by regulating offerors, time for making competing bids; and (2) allows incumbent management to solicit such bids by providing information about the target to potential buyers.

Part I discusses the various motives for takeovers, explaining that the motive on which Easterbrook and Fischel concentrate is not the only and probably not even the dominant one. Part II examines a rule of auctioneering from the perspective of targets' shareholders. The analysis shows that the rule does not deny searchers significant rewards relative to search costs and that it thus is consistent with a substantial level of search. Part II then demonstrates that the rule greatly increases premiums in unsolicited takeovers, as well as in negotiated acquisitions. The rule is particularly crucial because, faced with only one potential buyer, a target's dispersed shareholders may be subject to a bargaining disadvantage.

Part III considers a rule of auctioneering from the perspective of social welfare. The rule has several socially beneficial effects, such as the allocation of targets' assets to their most valuable use. Moreover, abandoning the rule in order to enhance rewards for searchers may lead to socially excessive investment in search. On the basis of this analysis, Part IV concludes that competing bids should be facilitated, and outlines the implications of that conclusion for the regulation of offerors and the role of incumbent management.

I. Motives for Takeovers

Offerors initiating takeover bids may have one or more of the following motives. First, the motive on which Easterbrook and Fischel focus is the prospect of increasing the target's profits by replacing its management.[17] The new management

---

[15] The recent article by Gilson, *supra* note 8, at 870–75, also criticizes the Easterbrook and Fischel view that facilitating competing bids is undesirable. This Comment was written prior to the appearance of Professor Gilson's impressive article. The footnotes to this Comment indicate where the analyses overlap.

[16] *See infra* pp. 1052, 1054–55.

[17] *See* Easterbrook & Fischel, *supra* note 1, at 1169–73. This explanation of takeovers was first suggested by Manne, *Mergers and the Market for Corporate Control*, 73 J. POL. ECON. 110, 113 (1965).

may be more dedicated to profit-maximization and less inclined to pursue its own interests, and may thus reduce the level of agency costs.[18] Alternatively, the new management may be more able and imaginative than the incumbents.[19] This "managerial gains" explanation is consistent with the evidence that successful tender offers are accompanied by an increase in the combined stock market value of the acquirer and the target.[20] That evidence, however, does not single out managerial gains as the cause of increased valuation. Although the expectation of managerial gains may explain some or even many takeovers, there is no basis for denying the significance of other motives.

A second and frequent motive for takeovers is the prospect of "synergistic gains." Synergistic gains encompass all increases in the combined future profits of the acquirer and the target that a takeover produces through means other than an improvement in management. The takeover may create economies of scale in production, in marketing, or in control, or it may produce such financial advantages as a reduced cost of capital.[21] The acquirer may possess some skills or nonpatentable information that are useful to the target.[22] Finally, the takeover may yield tax savings[23] or an increase in combined

---

[18] Agency costs refer to the decrease in a company's value caused by the managers' divergence from profit-maximization due to their concern for their own perquisites, leisure, and so forth. Agency costs exist because shareholders are unable to monitor perfectly their agents, the managers. *See* Jensen & Meckling, *Theory of the Firm: Managerial Behavior, Agency Costs and Ownership Structure*, 3 J. FIN. ECON. 305 (1976).

[19] The distinction between gains resulting from a reduction in agency costs and those resulting from superior talent of the new management is important for the following reason. Because agency costs are the result of a deliberate choice by the management to pursue its own interests, the mere threat of a takeover can induce incumbents to be more dedicated to the goal of profit-maximization. Thus, the takeover mechanism reduces agency costs indirectly as well, even in companies that are not subject to a takeover. In contrast, gains from superior talent of the acquirer's management (as well as "synergistic gains") cannot be realized unless the target is actually acquired; no threat can induce the incumbents to perform better than they are able to.

[20] *See, e.g.*, Bradley, *Interfirm Tender Offers and the Market for Corporate Control*, 53 J. BUS. 345 (1980); Dodd & Ruback, *Tender Offers and Stockholder Returns*, 5 J. FIN. ECON. 351 (1977); Kummer & Hoffmeister, *Valuation Consequences of Cash Tender Offers*, 33 J. FIN. 505 (1978); *see also* Easterbrook & Fischel, *supra* note 1, at 1186–88 (discussing this evidence).

[21] *See* P. STEINER, MERGERS: MOTIVES, EFFECTS, POLICIES 58–69 (1975); Lintner, *Expectations, Mergers and Equilibrium in Purely Competitive Securities Markets*, 61 AM. ECON. REV. 101 (1971) (separate May issue).

[22] *See* Jarrel & Bradley, *supra* note 14, at 382–84.

[23] *See* P. STEINER, *supra* note 21, at 75–95. The most important sources of tax savings are unused tax-loss carryovers, investment credits, and depreciation allowances that either the acquirer or the target may have and that can be used to reduce

market power,[24] in which case the synergistic gains — and the resulting increase in the firms' stock market value — do not reflect any social gains.

Synergistic gains have been recognized by many commentators as an important and pervasive motive for takeovers.[25] While acknowledging the possibility of synergistic gains, Easterbrook and Fischel suggest that they are an improbable explanation of hostile takeovers because they are likely to be realized through a friendly merger.[26] But any motive for a negotiated merger might also lead a prospective acquirer to make a hostile tender offer. Incumbent management may refuse to participate in merger negotiations or may insist on terms that the prospective acquirer is not willing to accept.

Third, a firm may attempt an acquisition because it has information suggesting that the target's stock is currently undervalued.[27] The recent wave of bids for oil companies, for example, may well have occurred because the prices of the companies' shares did not fully reflect the value of their oil reserves.[28] To the extent that the takeover process leads the market to revise its valuation of the target, the process will be accompanied by an increase in the combined stock market value of the target and the acquirer.[29] It must be emphasized,

---

the tax liability of the other company. For a recent example of acquisitions motivated by tax savings, see Friedman, *The Truck-Leasing Triangle*, N.Y. Times, Jan. 7, 1982, at D1, col. 3 (tax savings resulting from combinations of insurance brokers and truck lessors).

[24] Because most takeovers are of the conglomerate type, increased market power is presumably not a dominant source of synergistic gains. Still, there are some horizontal and vertical acquisitions, and even conglomerate mergers may have some anticompetitive effects. *See* P. STEINER, *supra* note 21, at 69–74, 218–87 (problems of reciprocity and reduction in potential competition created by conglomerate mergers).

[25] *See, e.g.*, P. STEINER, *supra* note 21, at 47–95; Bradley, *supra* note 20; Gilson, *supra* note 8, at 873–74; Jarrel & Bradley, *supra* note 14, at 382–84; Lintner, *supra* note 21; Shay, *Setting the 'Right' Premium In an Efficient Market*, MERGERS & ACQUISITIONS, Spring 1981, at 23.

[26] *See* Easterbrook & Fischel, *supra* note 1, at 1169.

[27] *See id.* at 1160; Grossman & Hart, *The Allocational Role of Takeover Bids in Situations of Asymmetric Information*, 36 J. FIN. 253 (1981).

[28] *See, e.g.*, *The New Urge to Merge*, NEWSWEEK, July 27, 1981, at 50, 50, 54. In a recent ruling against Mobil's bid for Marathon Oil, the Sixth Circuit reasoned:

> Mobil Corporation did not convince the District Court that the merger would benefit the economy, increase operating efficiency, bring advantages of scale, or substitute better management. *Mobil's reasons for the acquisition*, according to the testimony of its President, Mr. Tavoulareas, and others, *seem to be that Marathon stock was underpriced in the market* and that Marathon's valuable Yates Field in Texas would provide Mobil with additional needed domestic crude oil reserves.

Marathan Oil Co. v. Mobil Corp., 5 TRADE REG. REP. (CCH) (Trade Cas.) ¶ 64,420, at 75,070 (6th Cir. Dec. 23, 1981) (emphasis added).

[29] *See* Grossman & Hart, *supra* note 27. A speculative motive is thus consistent

however, that the takeover does not increase the target's true value; it only makes the market aware of an already existing value. The takeover merely accelerates an adjustment in the market price that would ultimately occur anyway. A "speculative" acquisition may produce a social benefit — it does "correct" the market price — but the benefit is smaller than the stock gains accompanying the acquisition.

Finally, the managers of the offeror may be motivated in part by the prospect of expanding the size of the enterprise under their control.[30] It is widely accepted that managers prefer to increase the size of their firm because their income, perquisites, and prestige ususally increase with firm size.[31] Although the expansion motive may not dominate in many or even any takeovers, it may often exist alongside other motives. Easterbrook and Fischel deny the existence of this motive and argue that the acquirer itself will be subject to a takeover if its management is not profit maximizing.[32] But although the takeover threat reduces managements' divergence from profit-maximization, there is no doubt that some divergence may exist in every firm.[33] The expansion motive is consistent with both the economic theory of the firm and the existing empirical evidence.[34]

The remainder of this Comment assumes that the dominant motives for tender offers are gains from synergy and from improved management, and that takeovers, by and large, increase social welfare. It should be kept in mind, however, that many offerors are at least partially motivated by tax savings, speculative profit, and preference for expansion —

---

with the evidence, *see* sources cited *supra* note 20, that takeovers are accompanied by an increase in the combined stock market value of the target and the acquirer.

30 *See, e.g.*, R. MARRIS, THE ECONOMIC THEORY OF 'MANAGERIAL' CAPITALISM 122–24 (1964); Marris & Mueller, *The Corporation, Competition, and the Invisible Hand*, 18 J. ECON. LITERATURE 32, 41–45 (1980).

31 *See, e.g.*, W. BAUMOL, BUSINESS BEHAVIOR, VALUE AND GROWTH 45–52 (rev. ed. 1967); R. MARRIS, *supra* note 30, at 46–109; Baumol, *On the Theory of Expansion of the Firm*, 52 AM. ECON. REV. 1078 (1962); Marris & Mueller, *supra* note 30, at 40–45.

32 *See* Easterbrook & Fischel, *supra* note 1, at 1173.

33 *See, e.g.*, Jensen & Meckling, *supra* note 18, at 312–13 (some agency costs exist whenever management and ownership do not overlap). Because the tender offer process is frictional, it cannot perfectly police incumbent managements. *See also infra* note 81 (discussing implications of friction in the tender offer process).

34 Several empirical studies find that, on average, acquirers make little or no gain, or that they even lose. *See, e.g.*, Dodd & Ruback, *supra* note 20. At any rate, even if the evidence were conclusive that acquirers, *on average*, earned profits from takeovers, it would not rule out the possibility, well grounded in the economic theory of the firm, that a significant number of acquirers' managements are *in part* motivated by the prospect of expanding their firm.

private benefits that do not entirely represent social gains. It also should be emphasized that takeover gains may depend substantially on the acquirer's identity. The magnitude of synergistic gains clearly depends on the "fit" between the acquirer and the target, and acquirers may well differ in their ability to improve the management of the target.

II. The Perspective of Targets' Shareholders

The optimal legal rule for shareholders of potential targets is one that maximizes the value of their shares. The value of a firm's stock depends on: (1) the firm's performance under its present management; and (2) the probability that a merger or a takeover will occur multiplied by the premium expected from such an event.[35] This Part examines the effects of a rule of auctioneering on the factors that determine the shareholders' wealth.

A. The Effect on Search by Potential Offerors

An increase in the likelihood of a takeover benefits the shareholders of potential targets in two ways.[36] First, it increases the probability that they will receive a premium. Second, strengthening the takeover threat may induce present managements to be more profit maximizing. The more that prospective offerors search, the greater is the likelihood that a potential takeover target will be identified. The amount of search that will be conducted depends on its costs and benefits.

Easterbrook and Fischel object to a rule of auctioneering because they are concerned that it will severely curtail the search for potential targets and consequently the number of offers.[37] The first bidder incurs search costs to identify the target. Subsequent bidders, alerted to the target's existence by the first bidder's offer, will not bear these costs. Easterbrook and Fischel suggest that a bidding contest all but denies the first bidder any return on its search. Therefore, under a rule of auctioneering, firms have hardly any incentive to be the

---

35 *See* Easterbrook & Fischel, *supra* note 1, at 1164. Their criterion is similar, except that it does not incorporate the probability of a merger and the premium expected in a merger.

36 *Id.* at 1173–74.

37 *Id.* at 1177–78. Indeed the model they present suggests that a rule of auctioneering will eliminate search by offerors altogether. They note that their model does not accurately describe reality, but they claim that it "reveal[s] tendencies." *Id.* at 1173 n.41.

first bidder; search for targets and takeovers will be severely diminished.

Undoubtedly, bidding contests have some adverse effect on the amount of search done by prospective offerors. The following analysis suggests, however, that a rule of auctioneering is consistent with a substantial amount of search.

The prevailing rule of auctioneering does not eliminate significant returns to the search for targets. First, searchers are rewarded by the opportunity to invest profitably in the stock of targets they discover.[38] A searcher that has identified a target may, and often does, start purchasing the target's shares in the market prior to making a tender offer.[39] The searcher may purchase five percent of the target's stock without being required by the Williams Act to disclose the purchases.[40] Whether the searcher wins or loses a subsequent bidding contest over the target, it will earn a gain on its pre-offer purchases of the target's stock.[41] The gain is likely to be substantial and may approach two to three percent of the target's value.[42]

---

[38] *See* Gilson, *supra* note 8, at 871.

[39] For a recent example, see Cole, *IC Offers $451 Million for Sunbeam*, N.Y. Times, Sept. 22, 1981, at D1, col. 3 (before making an unsolicited offer for the Sunbeam Corporation, IC Industries purchased 4.5% of Sunbeam's stock).

[40] As amended, § 13(d)(1) of the Williams Act requires any person who obtains more than five percent beneficial interest in a company to file with the SEC. 15 U.S.C. § 78n(d)(1) (1976).

[41] If the searcher holds X shares of the target and the target is acquired through a tender offer for all shares at a premium of $\$Y$ per share, the searcher will gain $\$XY$ on its pre-offer purchase, regardless of the acquirer's identity. If the acquirer is a competing bidder, the searcher will earn $\$XY$ by tendering the stock it holds to the winner. If the searcher itself acquires the target, it will have to pay $\$XY$ less than it would have paid if it were a second bidder and had not made a pre-offer purchase of the target's stock.

Even if no tender offer is successful and the target remains independent, the postoffer price of its shares is likely to exceed the pre-offer price that the searcher paid for its holdings. *See* Dodd & Ruback, *supra* note 20, at 362–63; Jarrel & Bradley, *supra* note 14, at 397–98.

[42] Jarrel & Bradley, *supra* note 14, at 373, 389–90, finds that the average takeover premium between 1968 (when the Williams Act was enacted) and 1977 was 52.8% in takeovers not subject to state tender offer statutes, and 73.1% in takeovers subject to such statutes. Several other empirical studies examine the gains that targets' shareholders realize on their stock as a result of takeovers. These studies, however, use samples that include pre-1968 takeovers, and thus presumably underrepresent the gains to targets' shareholders in the post-1968 period, when the Williams Act facilitated competing bids. Nonetheless, even the findings of these studies suggest that the searcher can profit substantially from pre-offer purchases of the target's stock. *See* Bradley, *supra* note 20, at 345–46 (an average premium of 49% and average gain on nontendered shares of 36% between 1962 and 1977); Dodd & Ruback, *supra* note 20, at 356–67 (an average gain of 20.6% on target's stock in successful tender offers

Second, a searcher may discover a target whose acquisition will bring greater synergistic or managerial gains to the searcher than to any other potential acquirers. If a searcher discovers a target with assets it values more highly than do other potential buyers, it will win any bidding contest even if the searcher has no advantage as first bidder. This contest will leave the searcher with a surplus, for it will have to pay only slightly more for the target than other bidders would be willing to pay; it need not pay as much as its own valuation of the target.[43] Because acquirers may vary significantly in their valuation of a target, that surplus may be substantial.

Third, although a rule of auctioneering goes far toward placing competing potential acquirers on equal footing, it unfortunately cannot always ensure that the first bidder will have no systematic advantage. Because the period for making competing bids is necessarily limited, the first bidder will have much more time to study the target than will other potential buyers. The first bidder may thus have an informational advantage, at least over those other potential buyers to which management does not provide information about the target.[44] Additionally, the initial offeror may have a strategic advantage by virtue of being the first to commit itself to a possible contest.[45]

Not only does the prevailing rule of auctioneering maintain substantial rewards for search, but also the search costs that first bidders incur do not seem to be at all large.[46] The search

between 1958 and 1976); Kummer & Hoffmeister, *supra* note 20, at 511 (an average gain of 18.6% to targets' shareholders between 1958 and 1974).

[43] The possibility of such a gain is noted by Easterbrook & Fischel, *supra* note 1, at 1177 n.41.

[44] While the prevailing rule of auctioneering allows management to provide information to potential competing offerors, unfortunately management may elect not to do so or to provide information to a particular "white knight" but not to other potential buyers. *See infra* p. 1055.

[45] *See generally* T. SCHELLING, THE STRATEGY OF CONFLICT 21–52 (1960) (discussing irreversible steps that produce strategic advantages). For example, consider a case in which both *A*, the first bidder, and *B*, another potential offeror, value the target by $X per share, and *B* is aware of *A*'s valuation of the target. *A* has already incurred the transaction costs involved in making a tender offer, and now *B* is considering whether to make these expenditures and advance a rival bid. Because the transaction costs involved in *A*'s bid are sunk, *A* will be prepared to raise its bid for the target to anything less than $X per share. Thus, to win a contest over the target, *B* will have to bid $X per share in addition to spending the transaction costs involved in making a bid. Consequently, *B*'s rational decision will be not to enter into a contest with *A*, even though *B*'s valuation of the target is the same as *A*'s. Admittedly, the strategic advantage a first bidder may have is small, but it should be considered in light of the small size of the search costs that first bidders incur.

[46] *See* Gilson, *supra* note 8, at 870. Easterbrook and Fischel fear that first bidders incur substantial search costs. *See* Easterbrook & Fischel, *supra* note 1, at 1178–79.

for targets involves analysis of data about different companies, most of which is publicly available. Because prospective acquirers often lack appropriate in-house resources, the search is frequently done for them by investment bankers.[47] When investment bankers conduct the search in addition to processing the offer, the search costs are a fraction of their total fees. Investment bankers' fees, in turn, are often less than one percent of the target's value.[48] Moreover, these fees are usually contingent upon the success of the acquisition attempt; if the first bidder does not gain control over the target, it usually will have to pay the investment banker only a very small, often negligible, amount.[49]

The conclusion that searchers receive significant rewards relative to search costs is supported by the evidence. A large number of acquisitions do occur under the prevailing rule of auctioneering,[50] a fact that reflects a substantial underlying

[47] *See, e.g.*, Feinberg, *Poaching is the new name of the game*, INST'L INVESTOR, Nov. 1980, at 37, 41. An investment banker's search is often undertaken at the invitation of a prospective acquirer interested in buying a company with certain characteristics. The investment banker will then study and screen companies that may fit the client's plans. Alternatively, an investment banker may, on its own initiative, identify and study a company whose acquisition may be profitable, and then look for an appropriate buyer and approach it with the acquisition idea. Easterbrook and Fischel recognize that search for targets may actually be done by investment bankers. *See* Easterbrook & Fischel, *supra* note 1, at 1178.

Some search may also be conducted for prospective acquirers by other outside professionals, such as management consulting firms. Merger brokers, who are very active in purchases of small, privately held companies, are less involved in the search for potential takeover targets (that is, publicly traded companies with clear separation between management and ownership).

[48] *See* Carrington, *Merger Advisers Say the Big Fees They're Charging Are Warranted*, Wall St. J., July 17, 1981, at 29; *Deals of the Year*, FORTUNE, Jan. 25, 1982, at 36. Investment bankers provide several important services to a prospective acquirer throughout the tender offer process. Thus, when an investment banker's total fee includes a search component, it constitutes only a limited, and possibly minor, fraction of the total fee.

[49] *See* Carrington, *supra* note 48; *Deals of the Year*, *supra* note 48, at 36.

[50] In 1981, there were 166 acquisitions of publicly traded companies, of which 60 were by takeover. Letter from Tomislava Simic, Director of Research, W.T. Grimm Co., to Lucian Bebchuk (Jan. 25, 1982) (on file in Harvard Law School Library) (data collected by firm specializing in mergers). In addition, there were 646 acquisitions of parts — divisions, subsidiaries, or product lines — of publicly traded companies (divestitures). *Id.* The search by prospective acquirers is reflected not only in takeovers but in acquisitions of all kinds. A prospective acquirer that has identified a company as a candidate for beneficial acquisition may well approach the company's management and negotiate acquisition of the company or of the part of the company that is particularly valuable to the prospective acquirer. *See infra* p. 1042. It should be noted, however, that not all acquisitions are the result of prior search by the buyer. The seller initiates a significant share of acquisitions (probably even the majority of divestitures), and these acquisitions thus reflect prior search by the seller's management for an appropriate buyer. *See infra* p. 1046.

level of search.[51] Undoubtedly, any enhancement of the rewards to searchers will raise the investment in search: publicly available data about companies will be examined even more intensely than at present, and perhaps some new and costly methods of search will be adopted. The number of unidentified acquisition opportunities that incremental search will discover, however, presumably declines as the level of search rises. Therefore, because current search activity is substantial, it is far from clear that a given increase in the incentives for search will substantially increase the number of identified targets.

Finally, it should be emphasized that, if an increase in existing rewards for search is desirable, some enhancement may be accomplished without abandoning the rule of auctioneering. This can be done by raising the percentage of the target's stock that may be purchased without disclosure. Although the increase must be limited in order not to frustrate competing bids,[52] it will still substantially raise the profits that searchers can earn on pre-offer purchases of the target's stock. From the perspective of targets' shareholders, abandonment of the rule of auctioneering to enhance further rewards for search is justified only if the resulting increase in offer frequency can be expected to be so large that it will outweigh the loss of the rule's significant positive effect on premiums.

B. The Effect on Premiums in Unsolicited Takeovers

Because Easterbrook and Fischel believe that a rule of auctioneering will severely curtail search for targets and thus unsolicited takeovers, they pay little attention to the effect of the rule on premiums in the takeovers that do occur.[53] As the

---

[51] The number of acquisitions reflects only a fraction of the potential targets that prospective offerors identify. A company will be acquired only if: (1) it is identified as one whose acquisition will produce a gain; and (2) this gain exceeds the transaction costs that will be incurred in an acquisition. Thus, when the gain that can be produced by an acquisition is below the threshold level of transaction costs, there will be no offer and no acquisition. This will occur regardless whether a rule of auctioneering is maintained or abandoned; the existence of competition is immaterial simply because no net gain can be made from an acquisition.

At present, an important source of transaction costs is management's ability to employ obstructing tactics. Thus, a prohibition of such tactics, which this Comment supports without regard to its effect on offer frequency, can be expected to increase the number of offers. The increase in offer frequency will result not from an increase in search, but rather from an expansion of the set of companies that can be profitably acquired.

[52] *See infra* p. 1054.

[53] *See* Easterbrook & Fischel, *supra* note 1, at 1178–80.

preceding Section demonstrated, however, the rule is entirely consistent with a substantial amount of search; it is therefore necessary to consider carefully the rule's effect on premiums.

Competition among potential buyers generally raises the price a seller will receive. Such competition is especially important for the sellers in a corporate takeover, however, because targets' ownership is usually dispersed. Dispersed target shareholders who face only one potential buyer, the initial offeror, are subject to a particular disadvantage that a sole owner would not suffer. If the target had a sole owner, the owner could bargain with the buyer over division of the gains from the acquisition. But the dispersed shareholders are presumably unable to organize and threaten to block the takeover, insisting on receiving some specific share of the gains.[54]

When each small shareholder decides whether to tender or to hold out, he will ignore the effect of his decision on the success of the tender offer in attracting the number of shares necessary for control. The shareholder will consider whether, assuming the offer is successful, he will be better off tendering his shares or holding out. Takeovers are frequently the first stage of a two-step merger and are followed by a freezeout, in which nontendering shareholders receive cash or securities for their shares.[55] Given the current legal rules governing corporate freezeouts, the value of the consideration paid to nontendering shareholders, while presumably higher than the shares' pre-offer price, is unlikely to exceed, and may be lower than, the value of the tender offer.[56] Indeed, some recent tender

---

[54] It is assumed here that, as this Comment recommends, management is barred from blocking tender offers. If management could block a takeover, it could, of course, threaten to do so unless shareholders receive some specific premium. Giving *management* bargaining power by allowing it to block a takeover is not, however, an acceptable solution to the problem of shareholders' inability to organize and bargain with the offeror as a sole owner would. Management may well use its power not to bargain for a higher premium, but rather either to avoid a takeover altogether or to extract personal benefits from the offeror in return for abstaining from blocking.

[55] *See, e.g.*, Dodd & Ruback, *supra* note 20, at 352.

[56] In a freezeout, the acquirer is constrained by the appraisal rights of the nontendering shareholders. Appraisal statutes, however, generally exclude from the required compensation any element of value arising from the expectation or accomplishment of a merger. *See, e.g.*, DEL. CODE ANN. tit. 8, § 262(f) (Supp. 1980); N.Y. BUS. CORP. LAW § 623(h)(4) (McKinney 1963). The appraisal process may thus ensure that nontendering shareholders receive the value of their shares in the independent target, but it is not designed to give them any share of the gains from the target's acquisition. *See* Brudney & Chirelstein, *Fair Shares in Corporate Mergers and Takeovers*, 88 HARV. L. REV. 297, 304–06, 336–37 (1974).

Professors Brudney and Chirelstein propose the imposition of a fairness requirement that the acquirer pay the same price per share on freezeout as it offered on tender. *Id.* at 337–40. This requirement would significantly reduce the pressure on offers have been accompanied by the offeror's announcement that it contemplated a freezeout in which nontendering shareholders would receive securities with a significantly lower value than that of the initial offer.[57] The threat of a subsequent freezeout may thus pressure shareholders to tender their shares for the premium offered,[58] even if the premium is one they would likely reject were they able to organize.[59]

The existence of large shareholders, who take into account the effect of their decisions on the success of the tender offer, may strengthen the bargaining position of the target's shareholders. But as long as the majority of the target's stock is owned by small shareholders with insignificant holdings, a potential buyer that does not face competition may well acquire the target for a low premium constituting only a small fraction of the takeover's gains. Only a competing offer, or the threat of such an offer, will enable the dispersed target's shareholders to get a substantial share of those gains.[60]

---

the target's shareholders to tender. But it has not been adopted by the courts. *See, e.g.*, Tanzer v. International Gen. Indus., 402 A.2d 382, 393–95 (Del. Ch. 1979). At any rate, even if the rule were adopted, the pressure to tender, albeit much weaker, would still exist. If the tender offer is successful and a freezeout follows, holding out will result in receiving the tender price, but at a later point in time.

[57] For example, in the recent takeover of Marathon Oil by U.S. Steel, U.S. Steel offered $125 in cash for tendered shares and announced that it was contemplating a subsequent freezeout in which nontendered shares would be converted into the right to receive $100 of U.S. Steel notes. *See* N.Y. Times, Dec. 2, 1981, at D4, cols. 1–3 (notice of supplement of U.S. Steel's offer). The premium in that takeover was sizable, nonetheless, because Mobil had also made a bid and additional potential buyers were waiting in the wings.

[58] Pressure to tender is likely to exist even if the offeror is not expected to arrange a freezeout following the offer's execution. Although nontendering stockholders will be able to retain their shares in such a case, the value of those shares after the offer's execution is likely to be lower than the value of the tender offer. This will certainly be true of the shares' value in the acquirer's eyes, if the acquirer will not arrange a freezeout. The reason why an acquirer may value nontendered shares at less than the price it will have to pay for them in a freezeout is presumably that control over the target enables the acquirer to siphon directly to itself part of the takeover's gains.

[59] Gilson, *supra* note 8, at 859–62, examines the pressure on shareholders to tender and suggests that it is unlikely to result in acceptance of offers that will make the shareholders worse off than they were before the offer. I agree with Professor Gilson. The freezeout threat is unlikely to lead shareholders to accept such offers because the price in a freezeout presumably will be at least as high as the shares' pre-offer price. The argument made here, however, is that shareholders might be pressured into accepting offers that, though making them better off, provide them with only a small fraction of the takeover's gains.

[60] It is possible to argue that the existence of some pressure on shareholders to tender is essential for the takeover process to function. As explained above, each small shareholder, when making his tender decision, compares (1) the expected price of nontendered shares immediately following the offer's execution (assuming the offer will be successful), with (2) the offer's value. If (1) is lower than (2), shareholders will

Even if the target's shareholders did not have the bargaining disadvantage of dispersed ownership — if they were in the position of a sole owner — a rule of auctioneering would still increase premiums substantially. First, in the absence of any buyers other than the initial offeror, the distribution of any part of the takeover's gains is subject to bargaining between the offeror and the seller. A rule of auctioneering will compel the initial offeror to pay at least the premium that other potential buyers are willing to pay. Moreover, the initial offeror may not be the firm that attaches the highest value to the target's assets. In that case a rule of auctioneering will lead to a takeover by a firm that values the target more highly and can thus pay a higher premium.

It should be pointed out that the beneficial impact of a rule of auctionering on premiums is not limited to those instances in which competing bids are actually made. Under the prevailing rule of auctioneering, many unsolicited offers are not challenged by competing bids.[61] The premiums in such cases are still affected by the rule, however, because they are augmented by the first bidders to eliminate or reduce the threat of competing offers. If that threat did not exist, the bidders would offer much smaller premiums. Thus, a rule of auctioneering significantly raises the premiums in all unsolicited takeovers.

C. *The Effect on Negotiated Acquisitions*

Not all acquisitions are the result of unsolicited tender offers. An acquisition may also be the product of negotiations

---

be pressured to tender, even if that is not in their collective self-interest. On the other hand, if (1) exceeds (2), shareholders will be induced to hold out, even if acceptance of the offer is in their collective self-interest. (And if (1) and (2) are equal, many shareholders who ignore the effect of their decision on the offer's success will still not bother to tender). Thus, the argument goes, takeovers of companies with dispersed ownership will not be possible, no matter how generous the offers are, unless offerors can treat nontendering shareholders less favorably than tendering ones. *Cf.* Grossman & Hart, *Takeover bids, the free-rider problem, and the theory of the corporation*, 11 BELL J. ECON. 42 (1980) (dilution of the rights of nontendering shareholders is essential for the takeover process to function).

This Comment does not address the question whether pressure on shareholders to tender is essential for takeovers. The analysis merely demonstrates the existence of pressure to tender under the current state of the law and consequently concludes that, at present, competition among acquirers is crucial if a target's shareholders are to receive a significant share of the takeover's gains. If such pressure is indeed essential for takeovers, the above conclusion will simply become one of greater generality.

[61] *See, e.g.*, Austin, *Tender Offer Update: 1978-1979*, MERGERS & ACQUISITIONS, Summer 1980, at 13, 17; Bradley, *supra* note 20; Dodd & Ruback, *supra* note 20; Kummer & Hoffmeister, *supra* note 20.

between the target's management and the acquirer. After identifying a target, a prospective acquirer may well approach its management with an offer of acquisition.[62] The initiative for acquisition negotiations may also come from the target's management. Once the management and the prospective acquirer agree on terms, a negotiated acquisition will be consummated by a merger[63] or a friendly takeover.[64]

At present, most acquisitions are negotiated and not the result of unfriendly takeovers.[65] To determine whether a rule governing takeovers is desirable from the perspective of tar-

---

[62] A negotiated acquisition may have some advantages over an unfriendly takeover, even if the target's management cannot obstruct the latter. First, in the acquisition negotiations the prospective acquirer is likely to receive from the management some nonpublic information about the target. This information would reduce the prospective acquirer's uncertainty about the gains the considered acquisition may produce, and thus would enable it better to judge whether the acquisition is profitable. *See* J. FREUND, ANATOMY OF A MERGER: 230–41, 248–80 (1975); Gilson, *supra* note 8, at 850–51. Second, because a negotiated acquisition may be consummated not only through a friendly takeover but also through a statutory merger, a consolidation, or a sale of the target's assets, it may be better designed to maximize tax savings. *See generally* B. BITTKER & J. EUSTICE, FEDERAL INCOME TAXATION OF CORPORATIONS AND SHAREHOLDERS ¶¶ 14.01 to .57 (4th ed. 1979) (discussing tax-exempt corporate reorganizations).

Management's present ability to employ obstructing tactics provides another reason why a prospective acquirer may try to negotiate with the management rather than initiate an unfriendly tender offer. The prospective acquirer may fear that management will obstruct an unsolicited takeover bid, and may therefore seek management's approval of its acquisition. Indeed, the prospective acquirer may also try to ensure, by promising some personal benefits to the management, that the management will obstruct any tender offer initiated by other potential buyers. Thus, adopting the recommended prohibition of obstructing tactics will reduce the proportion of negotiated acquisitions, although it will not eliminate them.

[63] Merger refers here to all forms of acquisition, including consolidation and sale of substantially all assets, that require board and shareholder approval.

[64] Because the consummation of a friendly takeover requires much less time than does a merger, the former method of acquisition is usually adopted when the parties are interested in a speedy consummation. There may be a legitimate business reason for a quick resolution. But the motive behind the choice of a speedy technique may also be an improper one. *See infra* notes 70–71.

[65] *See* Freund & Greene, *Substance over Form S-14: A Proposal to Reform SEC Regulation of Negotiated Acquisitions*, 36 BUS. LAW. 1483, 1485–86 (1981). A substantial share of acquisitions are through mergers. *See supra* note 50. And even among takeovers a significant fraction is not hostile. *See* Bradley, *supra* note 20, at 347; Kummer & Hoffmeister, *supra* note 20, at 505.

As explained above, *see supra* note 62, adopting a prohibition against obstructing tactics will increase the proportion of unfriendly takeovers over negotiated acquisitions. However, this Section studies negotiated acquisitions in order to establish that the rule of auctioneering increases premiums in all acquisitions. This point will not be undermined, of course, if negotiated acquisitions are replaced by unfriendly takeovers; the preceding Section has already demonstrated that the rule significantly increases premiums in such takeovers.

gets' shareholders, it is therefore essential to take into account the rule's effect on negotiated acquisitions. The following analysis demonstrates that the prevailing rule of auctioneering increases the premiums not only in unsolicited takeovers, but in *all* acquisitions as well.

It should be noted first that, if the rule of auctioneering is abandoned, many negotiated acquisitions, especially those initiated by the buyer, will be replaced by unsolicited takeovers; more importantly, these will be low-premium takeovers. A prospective acquirer that has identified a target will be induced to make a low-premium tender offer immediately.[66] If the offeror approaches the management, management may start negotiating with other potential buyers. An immediate bid, however, will free the offeror from the threat of competing offers. In the absence of competition, the offeror will be able to acquire the target for a small premium.[67]

The premiums in negotiated acquisitions that will occur even if the rule of auctioneering is abandoned will be substantially lower than they would have been under the rule. The premiums in negotiated acquisitions are affected by the rule of auctioneering because they are determined against the background of a possible unfriendly tender offer by the acquirer or by a competing potential buyer. The rule's effect on the premium in a negotiated acquisition depends on the extent to which management abuses its role as a bargaining agent for the shareholders. To examine the rule's effect, therefore, this Section considers two polar cases. In one, management is concerned solely with maximizing the benefits the acquisition will confer on the shareholders. In the other, management is not at all concerned with the shareholders' premium and pursues only its own, different interests. Management may be at least partly concerned with the shareholders' premium because it may have incentives to increase the firm's value;[68] although

---

[66] *See* Gilson, *supra* note 8, at 875.

[67] If the rule of auctioneering is abandoned, low-premium unfriendly takeovers will be more likely to occur even when the target's management initiates acquisition negotiations. A prospective acquirer that has been approached by management and recognizes the potential for beneficial acquisition will be induced to launch an unfriendly bid immediately. To be sure, management may have simultaneously approached other potential buyers. But if the prospective acquirer acts quickly and if sufficient time for making competing bids is not provided, the prospective acquirer may be relatively free from the threat of competition.

[68] Managers may receive part of their compensation in the firm's securities and may have thus accumulated a significant amount of such securities. Additionally, the managers' performance may affect their future job prospects. *See* Easterbrook & Fischel, *supra* note 1, at 1172; Fama, *Agency Problems and the Theory of the Firm*, 88 J. POL. ECON. 288 (1980).

such an increase is rarely management's sole objective, it may well be one objective.

Consider first the case in which management is fully dedicated to the shareholders' interests. A rule of auctioneering enhances the ability of the management to advance these interests in the acquisition negotiations. The premium in a negotiated acquisition is the result of bargaining between the target's management and the acquirer, and thus depends on the parties' bargaining positions. If competing bids are impeded, the acquirer's bargaining postion will be significantly strengthened relative to that of the management. The acquirer will never be willing to pay more than it would have to spend to gain control of the target in an unfriendly takeover in which management actively seeks competing bids, and a rule of auctioneering substantially raises this ceiling.

A rule of auctioneering also increases the premium in the case in which management completely disregards the shareholders' interests. In this case management will not bargain with the acquirer for a higher premium. Instead, it will extract personal benefits in return for approving a premium smaller than other potential buyers would be willing to pay. The shareholders may be quite vulnerable to such abuse.[69] It is very difficult to prove that management's judgment has been skewed by self-interest, and the need for shareholder ratification may be an inadequate protection against a tainted merger agreement. The tainted acquisition, however, is subject to the threat that another potential buyer will initiate a tender offer before the acquisition is consummated.

A rule of auctioneering, coupled with a prohibition of obstructing tactics, would enhance this threat and enable it to serve as an important check on the self-serving management and its partner. The prohibition will prevent disloyal management from obstructing tender offers that other potential buyers may initiate. The rule of auctioneering, in turn, ensures that the tainted acquisition cannot be consummated before other potential buyers have had time to initiate tender offers. Even if potential competing buyers face no obstructions, they do need time to study the target's acquisition, especially because they will receive no information from the target's management. Because consummation of a merger usually requires at least two months,[70] disloyal management and

[69] *See, e.g.*, Brudney & Chirelstein, *supra* note 56, at 340–44 (discussing acquisitions tainted by side payments to management, and shareholders' vulnerability to such abuse).

[70] *See* Freund & Greene, *supra* note 65, at 1499–500. The consummation of a merger requires substantial time because shareholders' approval is needed. It is

its partner may choose the route of a friendly takeover in order to speed consummation of the acquisition.[71] The rule of auctioneering ensures that, even in this scenario, time will be available for tender offers by other potential buyers. The smallest premium that shareholders might receive, in the presence of totally disloyal management, is the minimum premium necessary to gain control over the target in a friendly takeover; the rule of auctioneering and the prohibition of obstructing tactics substantially raise this floor.

In sum, a rule of auctioneering increases premiums in all acquisitions, unfriendly or negotiated, through merger or takeover, whether management is loyal or self-serving. By ensuring that no acquisition can occur before potential competing buyers have time to advance rival tender offers, the rule increases premiums in all acquisitions. By allowing management to solicit competing offers, the rule further raises premiums in some, although not all, acquisitions. Premiums are raised in unfriendly takeovers in which management actually seeks competing offers, and in negotiated acquisitions in which management uses the threat of soliciting bids, at least in part, to bargain for increased premiums. Management's power to solicit competing bids does not, of course, raise premiums in those negotiated acquisitions in which management refrains from solicitation solely in return for personal benefits from the acquirer. In no case, however, can the existence of this power reduce the shareholders' premium. The concluding Part of this Comment verifies this proposition.

Finally, it is important to point out that, while the positive effect of a rule of auctioneering on premiums reduces the

---

necessary to prepare bulky proxy statements, to file them with the SEC, to wait for and respond to the comments of the SEC's staff, and then to solicit the shareholders' votes. In most cases, materials cannot be mailed to stockholders until one month after filing with the SEC, and another month is usually required for the solicitation of votes.

Until shareholders' approval of the merger is obtained, competing potential acquirers can enter the picture. The press release concerning the merger agreement will alert competitors, which will start studying the target. If the management receives a merger offer with a higher premium, existence of the offer must be highlighted in the merger proxy statement; the chances of gaining shareholders' ratification will therefore decline. Moreover, the competing potential buyer may well initiate a tender offer and succeed in purchasing, before the shareholders' vote, enough shares to gain control over the target or at least to defeat the merger proposal.

[71] *See* Freund & Easton, *The Three-Piece Suitor: An Alternative Approach to Negotiated Corporate Acquisitions*, 34 BUS. LAW. 1679 (1979); Freund & Greene, *supra* note 65. These authors explain that the technique of friendly takeover is adopted in negotiated acquisitions mainly as a means of reducing the threat of potential competing buyers.

incentives for search by prospective acquirers, it encourages search by targets' management. If acquisition of a company can produce gains, management may look for an appropriate acquirer. One reason why management may do so is that it has incentives to increase the firm's value. As a result of these incentives, an acquisition with a substantial premium may be in management's interest.[72] Because a rule of auctioneering raises the premiums expected in an acquisition of the target, it increases the incentive for management to look for such an opportunity.

III. The Perspective of Social Welfare

Part II emphasized that a rule of auctioneering benefits targets' shareholders by increasing premiums. As Easterbrook and Fischel note, however, an increase in the premiums paid to targets' shareholders produces no net social gain; the increase is exactly offset by a loss to the acquirers' shareholders.[73] This Part therefore inquires whether a rule of auctioneering can be opposed from the perspective of social welfare. From that point of view, the desirable legal rule is one that maximizes aggregate social welfare, regardless where the gains and losses fall.[74]

A. The Effect on Search by Potential Offerors

Again, the only possible objection to a rule of auctioneering is that it reduces the number of acquisitions by decreasing incentives for search. The previous Part already questioned the magnitude of that reduction in the number of acquisitions.

---

[72] Target management's search for an appropriate acquirer may also be motivated by the expectation of receiving from the acquirer some personal benefits for management's cooperation. Thus, the recommended prohibition of obstructing tactics, which will eliminate management's ability to extract personal benefits from the acquirer in return for refraining from obstructing, will reduce management's incentive to search. Nonetheless, because obstructing tactics may be very harmful to the shareholders, the prohibition is on the whole clearly desirable. The encouragement of search by targets' managements — or by prospective acquirers — should not be pursued by all possible means. The attractiveness of a rule of auctioneering from the perspective of targets' shareholders is that it encourages search by targets' management *in addition to* substantially increasing premiums.

[73] *See* Easterbrook & Fischel, *supra* note 1, at 1175.

[74] The welfare criterion used here is the Kaldor-Hicks (Potential Pareto-Superiority) criterion, according to which a change from rule *B* to rule *A* is desirable if the individuals who benefit from the change could hypothetically compensate the losers out of their gains. *See generally Symposium on Efficiency as a Legal Concern*, 8 Hofstra L. Rev. 485 (1980) (articles on the application of the Kaldor-Hicks criterion to legal rules).

It assumed, however, that any increase in search is desirable from the perspective of targets' shareholders, even if the resulting increase in offer-frequency is quite limited. But that is not necessarily the case from society's point of view.

The search for targets has the direct social benefit of yielding acquisitions that produce social gains. It also benefits society indirectly by inducing incumbent managements to be more profit maximizing. Therefore, there is no doubt that some amount of search is socially desirable. It is also clear, however, that search should not increase without limit. Search is costly, and its marginal benefit presumably declines as its level increases. Increments in search are socially desirable only up to the point at which the marginal social cost and benefit of extra search are equal. To induce the socially optimal level of search, the private incentives for searchers must equal, *at the margin*, the social benefits from their activity.

Consider the incentives for search in a situation in which premiums are negligible, so that all the stock market gains produced by a takeover are realized by the searcher-acquirer. On the one hand, the private rewards for extra search exceed its *direct* social benefit. First, the stock market gains produced by takeovers do not entirely represent social gains created by these takeovers. A takeover may be motivated by a prior undervaluation of the target, in which case the increase in stock value simply reflects a revision in the market's estimate of the target's true value.[75] The increase in stock value may also result from tax savings or from enhanced market power,[76] and thus come at the expense of tax revenues or consumers. Second, acquirers' managers may be induced to search by their preference for expansion, in addition to being motivated by the prospect of gains for their firms.[77] On the other hand, searchers do not capture the *indirect* social benefit from a marginal dollar spent on search — that is, the extent to which this extra search, by strengthening the takeover threat, will increase incumbents' devotion to shareholders' interests. In sum, the marginal private rewards for search may, or may not, exceed the marginal social benefit from it.

Hence, if competing bids are impeded, with the low premiums that result, it is possible that there will be socially excessive investment in search. To determine the desirable level of incentives for search, it is necessary to have more information than is presently available about its marginal so-

---

[75] *See supra* pp. 1032–33.
[76] *See supra* notes 23–24.
[77] *See supra* p. 1033.

cial benefits and private rewards. Until such understanding is acquired, it should not be presumed that an abandonment of the rule of auctioneering will move society closer to the optimal level of search, or even that there is underinvestment in search at present.

B. Other Welfare Effects

Even if the reduction in search caused by a rule of auctioneering is undesirable, the case for the rule remains strong. While the rule's upward effect on premiums is socially neutral, the rule does have substantial socially beneficial effects.

First, acquirers may vary substantially in the amount of synergistic or managerial gains they can produce, and a rule of auctioneering increases the likelihood that the target will be acquired by the firm to which its assets are most valuable.[78] When the initial offeror cannot put the target's assets to the best possible use, the rule facilitates an acquisition by a firm that values the target more highly. Additionally, the rule increases the likelihood that the initial offeror will be the most efficient user of the target's assets.[79]

Although Easterbrook and Fischel note that bidding contests allocate targets' assets to their most valuable uses, they attach no weight to this consideration. They suggest that, if the acquirer cannot put the target's assets to the best possible use, the assets can be resold and will eventually end up in the possession of the firm that values them most highly.[80] Easterbrook and Fischel, however, ignore the fact that transfer of the assets from the acquirer to that firm may involve substantial delay, incur significant transaction costs, or even never occur.[81] The transfer of corporate assets is an imperfect and

---

[78] *See* Gilson, *supra* note 8, at 872–74.

[79] An investment banker may identify and study a target on its own initiative in order to approach a potential buyer later with the acquisition idea. A rule of auctioneering reduces the likelihood that any potential buyer other than the one that values the target most highly will be able to acquire the target. Therefore, because investment bankers usually receive a fee contingent on the success of the acquisition attempt, the rule greatly increases the investment banker's incentive to look for the potential buyer to which the target's assets are most valuable.

Alternatively, the target may be identified by a potential buyer (or an investment banker searching on its behalf). The finder will first purchase in the market some amount of the target's stock, which is bound to appreciate if the target will be subject to a premium takeover. Then, if the finder is clearly not the potential buyer that values the target most highly, the rule of auctioneering may induce it not to make an acquisition attempt that is likely to fail, but instead to pass the information about the target to other potential acquirers.

[80] *See* Easterbrook & Fischel, *supra* note 1, at 1176 n.40.

[81] The managers of the acquirer, *A*, may prefer to retain the target's assets and

frictional process; indeed, the imperfection and friction, and the desire to reduce them, are a main concern of both Easterbrook's and Fischel's article and this Comment.

Second, a rule of auctioneering encourages socially desirable investment in potential targets. Easterbrook and Fischel urge us to adopt an ex ante perspective and realize that the gains from takeovers are a consequence of prior search for targets and that incentives for search are thus desirable.[82] Take the ex ante perspective one step back and one finds that the potential gains from a target's acquisition would not exist, waiting to be discovered by prospective acquirers, if not for individuals' prior decisions to establish and invest in the target. Therefore, the gains from the acquisition can also be attributed to these investment decisions, and not only to the search for targets. The same logic suggests that to induce an optimal level of investment in potential targets requires that targets' shareholders receive the social gains resulting from their investment. By providing targets' shareholders with a larger share of the gains produced when their companies are acquired, a rule of auctioneering moves society closer to the desirable level of investment in potential targets.[83]

Third, a rule of auctioneering encourages managements of potential targets to look for an appropriate acquirer.[84] Because search by managements of potential targets is presumably not motivated by speculation regarding the target's value or by preference for expansion, an increase in such search is likely to be socially desirable.

Finally, a rule of auctioneering improves the information

not sell them to firm *B*, which places the greatest value on those assets, to avoid reducing the size of the enterprise under their control. *See* sources cited *supra* note 31. Easterbrook and Fischel argue that, if *A* will not sell the target's assets to *B*, *A* itself will be subject to a takeover by *B*. *See* Easterbrook & Fischel, *supra* note 1, at 1176 n.40. But because takeovers are costly, not every company holding some assets that are valued more highly by another firm will be taken over. Note that to acquire only the target's assets through a takeover, *B* (which may be smaller than *A*) will have to acquire *A* in its entirety (an acquisition that may create antitrust problems), and then divest itself of the "original" *A*. At any rate, a series of takeovers is a very inefficient substitute for a bidding contest that will enable *B*, the firm to which the target's assets are most valuable, to acquire those assets in a relatively prompt and inexpensive way.

[82] *See* Easterbrook & Fischel, *supra* note 1, at 1177–78.

[83] To the extent that an acquirer is "unique" in that it can produce greater synergistic or managerial gains than others, the acquirer's shareholders should be rewarded with the social gains resulting from the acquirer's existence. A bidding contest is compatible with that goal. The contest does not require the acquirer to pay as much as its own valuation of the target, but rather only slightly more than the target's value to other potential acquirers. Thus, the acquirer captures the gains from the acquisition that other potential buyers cannot produce.

[84] *See supra* pp. 1045–46 & note 72.

that constitutes the basis for acquisition decisions, and thus reduces the likelihood of an acquisition that produces no gain, or even a loss. Under a rule of auctioneering, a prospective acquirer may well approach a company's management, initiate acquisition negotiations, and request specific information about the company. When management cooperates, a socially useful transfer of information follows. The prospective acquirer is likely to receive nonpublic information that it could not otherwise obtain and that will make it better able to judge whether an acquisition will be beneficial.[85] If the rule of auctioneering is abandoned, however, a prospective acquirer that has identified what seems to be a promising target will be induced to launch an immediate unsolicited bid.[86] An attempt to verify through target management that potential gains exist will create the danger, which an immediate bid will eliminate, that the management will start looking for other potential buyers.

IV. Conclusion and Implications

Although Easterbrook's and Fischel's article contributes to the analysis of the rules governing takeovers,[87] their thesis that it is undesirable to facilitate competing bids is unpersuasive. This Comment demonstrates that a rule of auctioneering has significant benefits. The rule benefits targets' shareholders by substantially raising the premium they can expect if their company is acquired, whether through a merger or through a takeover. The rule increases social welfare by enhancing in a number of ways the efficiency with which society's resources are used.

This Comment also addresses the concern that the rule has a grave impact on the search for targets. Under the prevailing rule of auctioneering, significant incentives for search are maintained, and consequently a substantial amount of search is conducted. Even if it is desirable to enhance the incentives for search, some enhancement can be accomplished without abandoning the rule. Although abandonment of the rule of auctioneering would further encourage search, the increase in search may be socially undesirable. And in any event, it is

---

85 *See* J. Freund, *supra* note 62, at 230–41, 248–80; Gilson, *supra* note 8, at 850–51.

86 *See supra* p. 1043.

87 In particular, Easterbrook and Fischel demonstrate that the rationale behind the business judgment rule is inapplicable to management's resistance to takeovers, and refute arguments that may be made for allowing management to employ obstructing tactics. *See* Easterbrook & Fischel, *supra* note 1, at 1182–99.

far from clear that the resulting increase in the number of acquisitions will be substantial.

Admittedly, no conclusive proof can be offered that the positive effects of a rule of auctioneering outweigh its possibly adverse effect on the search for targets. But the analysis does suggest that the rule is desirable from the perspectives of both targets' shareholders and social welfare. The legal system should therefore continue to facilitate competing tender offers.

Before examining the implications of this conclusion, a qualification should be emphasized. Although the facilitation of competing bids significantly serves the interests of society and targets' shareholders, it is not sufficient to protect those interests fully. The concerns created by the dispersed ownership of targets are only mitigated and not eliminated by the existence of competition among acquirers.

One source of concern is that shareholders may lack adequate information to evaluate tender offers. Incapable of concerted action, shareholders are unable to demand from an offeror information that a sole owner would insist on.[88] Another source of concern is that shareholders' tender decisions may deviate from what is in their collective self-interest. To be sure, a rule of auctioneering does improve the terms of the tender offers that targets' shareholders face. Nonetheless, while a rational sole owner may at times choose not to accept, at least temporarily, the offers made to him, this course of action might be much more difficult for a target's dispersed shareholders.[89] Examination of these problems and whatever legal intervention they require, however, is beyond the scope of this Comment.

A. The Regulation of Offerors

The regulation of offerors should be designed to facilitate competing tender offers, and present regulation generally goes in the right direction.[90] Primarily, the regulation of offerors

---

[88] This problem may be addressed by regulation requiring an offeror to provide target shareholders with the information that a sole owner would be likely to demand. It is not possible to examine here whether current disclosure requirements are appropriate in light of this criterion. *See* 17 C.F.R. § 240.14d-6 (1981) (disclosure requirements prescribed by the SEC).

[89] Allowing incumbent management to block tender offers is clearly not the way to address this problem. *See supra* note 54.

[90] Tender offers are at present regulated by both the Williams Act, 15 U.S.C. §§ 78*l*(i), 78m(d)–(e), 78n(d)–(f) (1976), and state tender offer statutes. This Comment does not address questions of the state statutes' constitutionality and the desirability of two sets of regulations. *See State Takeover Statutes and the Williams Act*, 32 BUS. LAW. 187 (1976); Note, *Securities Law and the Constitution: State Tender Offer*

should provide the time necessary for realizing the potential benefits from competition among acquirers. Even when management provides potential buyers with information about the target, potential buyers need time to verify and assess that information and to decide if they should make a competing offer. They need even more time if they do not receive management's cooperation, which may possibly be denied because the initial offeror promised management some personal benefits. And if alternative offers are made, shareholders need time to evaluate them.

Given that time is essential, it is still necessary to explain why it has to be provided by regulatory intervention. One could argue that the offeror and the target's shareholders should be free to consummate a transaction as quickly as they wish. If the acquirer asks for an acceptance within a very short period and the shareholders believe a better offer may be forthcoming, so the argument goes, they may simply hold out.

As explained, however, the dispersed shareholders of a target might find it difficult to refuse an offer even if refusal is in their collective self-interest. If the shareholders could cooperate, they presumably would often agree among themselves to wait for some limited period and explore the possibility of a better offer. Because transaction costs make such an agreement impossible, delay should be secured by regulation preventing shareholders from committing themselves to an acquirer during a cooling-off period. This period can be provided by allowing shareholders to withdraw tendered shares for some specified time after an offer is made.[91] It is also possible to extend the period by requiring that an offer be published some prescribed time before its effective date.[92]

Statutes Reconsidered, 88 YALE L.J. 510 (1979). The concern here is with the desirable substantive content of the regulation of offerors.

[91] *See* 15 U.S.C. § 78n(d)(5) (1976) (tendered shares can be withdrawn within seven days after an offer is made); 17 C.F.R. § 240.14d-7(a)(1) (1981) (SEC rule extending the withdrawal period to 15 business days). A number of state tender offer statutes prescribe longer withdrawal periods. *See* E. ARANOW, H. EINHORN & G. BERLSTEIN, DEVELOPMENTS IN TENDER OFFERS FOR CORPORATE CONTROL 240–42 (1977).

[92] The proposed Federal Securities Code drafted by the American Law Institute requires offerors to publish a "definitive notice" of the tender offer at least 10 days before the tender offer is made. FED. SEC. CODE § 606 (d)(2) (Proposed Official Draft 1978). Almost all state tender offer statutes require that the offeror file information concerning the offer with the state securities commissioner, or at least furnish it to the target company, some given time (usually varying between 10 and 30 days) before making the offer. *See* E. ARANOW, H. EINHORN & G. BERLSTEIN, *supra* note 91, at 212. The problem with the waiting periods produced by the state filing and

How long a delay should regulations prescribe? The danger from mandating too short a period is clear. In many cases, time pressure would impede competing offers, and an additional delay would therefore secure a higher price for shareholders and possibly a more valuable use of the target's assets. On the other hand, lengthening the delay period imposes costs. A quick resolution of the target's fate will enable all parties involved to know where they stand, and to plan their future actions, at an earlier time. The acquirer, for one, will be able to implement promptly its plans for the use of the target's assets. In addition, offerors that keep their offers open bear the costs of the uncertainty of changing circumstances.

Adoption of the recommended ban on obstructing tactics will provide a basis for lengthening the delay period. First, the ban will alleviate the concern that a longer delay will give management more time to construct obstructions. Second, the ban will prevent dedicated management from gaining an extension in order to secure a competing offer, which in turn will make a longer regulatory delay desirable. The appropriateness of the current delay period should be reconsidered in light of all the considerations discussed above. While this Comment does not recommend a specific figure, the fifteen-business-day period prescribed by the present federal regulation[93] does seem more likely to be insufficient than excessive.[94]

In addition to the standard delay period prescribed for all offers, an effort should be made to identify particular circumstances in which an extension is warranted. One such case arises when a competing bid is made very close to the end of the standard delay period. Because shareholders will need time to compare the alternative offers, it is desirable to mandate a short additional delay.[95]

---

notification requirements is that the disclosure of the offer is not made to the *public*. Thus, trading in the target's stock may continue with little or no information being supplied to the market. *See* Freund & Greene, *supra* note 65, at 1497–98; *State Takeover Statutes and the Williams Act*, *supra* note 90, at 196–97. Moreover, the facilitation of competing bids will be served by a public disclosure, so that all potential competing buyers will be alerted even if the target's management does not contact them.

[93] *See supra* note 91.

[94] The proposed Federal Securities Code extends the present delay period. It prescribes a 10-day advance publication of the offer. FED. SEC. CODE § 606(d)(2) (Proposed Official Draft 1978). Additionally, it requires offers to be open for at least 20 days, *id.* § 606(e), and allows shareholders to withdraw tendered shares at any time until two days before expiration of the offer, *id.* § 606(h).

[95] *See* 17 C.F.R. § 240.14d-7(a)(2) (1981) (SEC rule allowing withdrawal of tendered shares within 10 business days after another bidder makes a tender offer for the same class of securities).

Finally, to facilitate competition among acquirers, it is necessary to limit the amount of the target's stock that a prospective acquirer may purchase secretly.[96] As explained above, allowing prospective offerors to make an undisclosed purchase of *some* amount of stock is instrumental in inducing search for targets. That amount of stock must be quite limited, however, lest the searcher lock up the target for itself or at least erect significant obstacles against competitors. A prospective acquirer that has purchased the specified amount of the target's stock should disclose its acquisition intentions and thus enable other potential buyers to make their own offers to the shareholders within the prescribed delay period.

B. The Role of Incumbent Management

Although the possibility that resistance by management will facilitate competing bids is not a ground for concern — quite the contrary — there is a strong basis for opposition to obstructing tactics. Management cannot be trusted to use these tactics primarily to gain a limited delay that will facilitate a bidding contest. First, it may employ these tactics to avoid a takeover altogether and perpetuate its control. Alternatively, it may use them to distort an existing contest among prospective acquirers: it may obstruct other contenders in order to favor one that offers a better deal for management but worse terms for the shareholders. Therefore, time for making competing bids should be provided solely by regulatory mandate, and incumbent management should be barred from actions that obstruct any tender offer.

While management should not obstruct existing offers, this Comment recommends that it be assigned the auctioneering role of expanding the set of offers shareholders face. Management should be allowed to look, on its own or through investment bankers, for other potential buyers and to provide them with information about the target that will facilitate their decisions to make competing bids. Indeed, management should be required, as part of its fiduciary duty, diligently to seek a higher offer if achieving such an offer appears feasible.

Once a regulatory delay is prescribed, why is management's auctioneering ever necessary? Potential acquirers may have difficulties in gathering, within the limited delay period, all

---

[96] *See* 15 U.S.C. § 78n(d)(1) (1976) (requiring disclosure of an acquisition of more than 5% of a company's stock). The original disclosure threshold was 10% ownership, *see* Williams Act, Pub. L. No. 90-439, § 2, 82 Stat. 454, 455–56 (1968); the 5% threshold was established in 1970, *see* Act of Dec. 22, 1970, Pub. L. No. 91-567, § 3, 84 Stat. 1497, 1497.

the information necessary for deciding whether to make a competing bid, and management can provide them with that information. The extent to which management's solicitation is essential depends in each case on the amount of information about the target that offerors need and on the extent to which they can obtain this information promptly without management's cooperation. Although competing bidders may often be able to come forward on their own, in many cases management's solicitation is likely to be helpful or even crucial for the facilitation of competing bids.

Thus, management often can make a desirable use of the power to auctioneer, either by actually facilitating competing bids or by employing the threat of auctioneering to bargain for a higher premium in a negotiated acquisition. That management can use a specific power in a desirable way, however, does not necessarily mean that it will elect to do so. Therefore, it is necessary to examine whether the possibility of managerial abuse may provide a reason for denying management the power to auctioneer.

Management's self-interest may affect its use of the auctioneering power in two ways. First, management may solicit a bid from a particular "white knight" not out of concern for the takeover's premium, but out of self-interest. The "white knight" may have promised to retain the management (either in return for the management's cooperation or for genuine business reasons) or to present it with some other personal benefits. But regardless of the management's motives, it performs a desirable role whenever it solicits a competing bid. As long as management cannot obstruct other contenders, the "white knight" will win the contest only if it is willing to pay the largest premium. Thus, the possibility that management's auctioneering will be motivated by self-serving preference among potential acquirers is not a ground for concern.

The second way in which management's self-interest may affect its use of the power to auctioneer is more troubling. Management that is negotiating with a prospective acquirer may agree to abstain from soliciting competing bids solely in return for the promise of personal benefits. In this case management's power to auctioneer does not, of course, serve any useful purpose. It should be emphasized, however, that the self-serving management can do nothing more than be passive; this cannot, in comparison with a situation in which management is *required* to be passive, reduce the premium shareholders will receive or lead to a less efficient allocation of the target's assets.

Clearly, the power to auctioneer would not serve its intended purpose if managements used it solely to extract personal benefits in return for abstaining from auctioneering. This Comment recommends that management be allowed to auctioneer, however, because there are reasons to expect management in a significant number of cases to use its power, at least partially, in a desirable way. In the face of an unsolicited tender offer, management may well elect to solicit a competing bid, either because of the incentives it has to increase the firm's value or because an acquisition by a particular "white knight" serves its self-interest better than one by the initial offeror. And in a negotiated acquisition, management may, because of the incentives to increase the firm's value, use the threat of auctioneering at least in part to bargain for an increased premium. Finally, although a duty to look for better offers in the face of a takeover bid would be difficult to enforce, imposing such a duty may further increase the frequency with which managements make a desirable use of the power to auctioneer.

[4]

Journal of Financial Economics 11 (1983) 5–50. North-Holland Publishing Company

THE MARKET FOR CORPORATE CONTROL

The Scientific Evidence*

Michael C. JENSEN

University of Rochester, Rochester, NY 14627, USA

Richard S. RUBACK

Massachusetts Institute of Technology, Cambridge, MA 02139, USA

Received March 1983, final version received April 1983

This paper reviews much of the scientific literature on the market for corporate control. The evidence indicates that corporate takeovers generate positive gains, that target firm shareholders benefit, and that bidding firm shareholders do not lose. The gains created by corporate takeovers do not appear to come from the creation of market power. With the exception of actions that exclude potential bidders, it is difficult to find managerial actions related to corporate control that harm shareholders. Finally, we argue the market for corporate control is best viewed as an arena in which managerial teams compete for the rights to manage corporate resources.

1. The analytical perspective

1.1. Definition

Corporate control is frequently used to describe many phenomena ranging from the general forces that influence the use of corporate resources (such as legal and regulatory systems and competition in product and input markets) to the control of a majority of seats on a corporation's board of directors. We define corporate control as the rights to determine the management of corporate resources — that is, the rights to hire, fire and set the compensation of top-level managers [Fama and Jensen (1983a, b)]. When a

*The authors are, respectively, Professor and Director, Managerial Economics Research Center, Graduate School of Management, University of Rochester, and Assistant Professor, Sloan School of Management, Massachusetts Institute of Technology. We have benefited from the comments of Paul Asquith, Fischer Black, Michelle Bonnice, Michael Bradley, Andrew Christie, Frank Easterbrook, Richard Leftwich, Paul Malatesta, Terry Marsh, Robert Merton, Wayne Mikkelson, Walter Oi, Charles Plosser, Katherine Schipper, G. William Schwert, Clifford Smith, René Stulz, Jerold Warner, Martin Zimmerman, and especially Harry DeAngelo, Linda DeAngelo and John Long. This research is sponsored by the Managerial Economics Research Center of the University of Rochester, Graduate School of Management.

0304–405x/83/$03.00 © Elsvier Science Publishers

bidding firm acquires a target firm, the control rights to the target firm are transferred to the board of directors of the acquiring firm. While corporate boards always retain the top-level control rights, they normally delegate the rights to manage corporate resources to internal managers. In this way the top management of the acquiring firm acquires the rights to manage the resources of the target firm.

1.2. Managerial competition

We view the market for corporate control, often referred to as the takeover market, as a market in which alternative managerial teams compete for the rights to manage corporate resources. Hence, the takeover market is an important component of the managerial labor market; it complements the internal and external managerial labor markets discussed by Fama (1980). Viewing the market for corporate control as the arena in which management teams compete is a subtle but substantial shift from the traditional view, in which financiers and activist stockholders are the parties who (alone or in coalition with others) buy control of a company and hire and fire management to achieve better resource utilization. The managerial competition model instead views competing management teams as the primary activist entities, with stockholders (including institutions) playing a relatively passive, but fundamentally important, judicial role. Arbitrageurs and takeover specialists facilitate these transactions by acting as intermediaries to value offers by competing management teams, including incumbent managers. Therefore, stockholders in this system have relatively little use for detailed knowledge about the firm or the plans of competing management teams beyond that normally used for the market's price setting function. Stockholders have no loyalty to incumbent managers; they simply choose the highest dollar value offer from those presented to them in a well-functioning market for corporate control, including sale at the market price to anonymous arbitrageurs and takeover specialists. In this perspective, competition among managerial teams for the rights to manage resources limits divergence from shareholder wealth maximization by managers and provides the mechanism through which economies of scale or other synergies available from combining or reorganizing control and management of corporate resources are realized.

Takeovers can occur through merger, tender offer, or proxy contest, and sometimes elements of all three are involved. In mergers or tender offers the bidding firm offers to buy the common stock of the target at a price in excess of the target's previous market value. Mergers are negotiated directly with target manager's and approved by the target's board of directors before going to a vote of target shareholders for approval. Tender offers are offers to buy shares made directly to target shareholders who decide individually whether to tender their shares for sale to the bidding firm. Proxy contests occur when an insurgent group, often led by a dissatisfied former manager or large stockholder, attempts to gain controlling seats on the board of directors.

1.3. Overview of the issues and evidence

Manne's (1965) seminal article initiated an interest in how the market for control influences large corporations, and knowledge about many facets of the market for corporate control has recently increased considerably. This body of scientific knowledge about the corporate takeover market provides answers to the following questions:

1. How large are the gains to shareholders of bidding and target firms?
2. Does opposition to takeover bids by the managers of target firms reduce shareholder wealth?
3. Do takeovers create market power in product markets?
4. Does antitrust opposition to takeovers impose costs on merging firms?
5. Is shareholder wealth affected by proxy contests?
6. Are corporate voting rights valuable?

A brief overview of the evidence provides a useful guide to the more detailed discussion that follows. Numerous studies estimate the effects of mergers and tender offers on the stock prices of the participating firms. Tables 1 and 2 present a summary of stock price changes (measured net of marketwide price movements) for successful and unsuccessful takeovers in these studies. The returns in the tables represent our synthesis of the evidence. Discussion of the details of the studies and the issues that lie behind the estimates in the tables is contained in section 2, 'The Wealth Effects of Takeover Activities'.

Table 1

Abnormal percentage stock price changes associated with successful corporate takeovers.[a]

Takeover technique	Target (%)	Bidders (%)
Tender offers	30	4
Mergers	20	0
Proxy contests	8	n.a.[b]

[a]Abnormal price changes are price changes adjusted to eliminate the effects of marketwide price changes.
[b]Not applicable.

Table 2

Abnormal percentage stock price changes associated with unsuccessful corporate takeover bids.[a]

Takeover technique	Targets (%)	Bidders (%)
Tender offers	−3	−1
Mergers	−3	−5
Proxy contests	8	n.a.[b]

[a]Abnormal price changes are price changes adjusted to eliminate the effects of marketwide price changes.
[b]Not applicable.

Table 1 shows that target firms in successful takeovers experience statistically significant abnormal stock price changes of 20% in mergers and 30% in tender offers. Bidding firms realize statistically significant abnormal gains of 4% in tender offers and zero in mergers. Table 2 shows that both bidders and targets suffer small negative abnormal stock price changes in unsuccessful merger and tender offer takeovers, although only the −5% return for unsuccessful bidders in mergers is significantly different from zero. Stockholders in companies that experience proxy contests earn statistically significant average abnormal returns of about 8%. Somewhat surprisingly, these returns are not substantially lower when the insurgent group loses the contest.

The contrast between the large stock price increases for successful target firms and the insignificant stock price changes for unsuccessful targets indicates that the benefits of mergers and tender offers are realized only when control of the target firm's assets is transferred to a bidding firm. This suggests that stockholders of potential target firms are harmed when target managers oppose takeover bids or take other actions that reduce the probability of a successful acquisition. Moreover, since target managers replaced after takeovers lose power, prestige and the value of organization-specific human capital, they have incentives to oppose a takeover bid even though shareholders might benefit substantially from acquisition. However, management opposition to a takeover bid will benefit stockholders if it leads to a higher takeover price or otherwise increased stock prices. Thus, the effect of management opposition on shareholder wealth is an empirical matter.

The evidence indicates that the effect of unsuccessful takeover attempts varies across takeover techniques, and the reasons for these differences are not currently known. In unsuccessful mergers the target's stock price falls to about its pre-offer level. In unsuccessful tender offers the target's stock price remains substantially above its pre-offer level, unless a subsequent bid does not occur in the two years following the initial offer. If such a subsequent bid does not occur, the target's stock price reverts to its pre-offer level. Finally, in proxy contests the 8% increase in equity values does not depend on the outcome of the contest.

The abnormal stock price changes summarized in tables 1 and 2 indicate that transfer of the target-firm control rights produces gains. The evidence reviewed in section 3, 'Antitrust and the Source of Merger Gains', indicates that the merger gains do not come from the creation of product market power. This is an important finding since the evidence also indicates antitrust opposition to takeovers imposes costs on merging firms by restricting transfers of corporate control. The takeover gains apparently come from the realization of increased efficiencies or synergies, but the evidence is not sufficient to identify their exact sources.

Section 4 contains a discussion of conflicts of interest between management and stockholders as well as estimates of the effects on stock prices of various managerial actions and proxy contests, and estimates of the value of corporate voting rights. Evidence presented in section 4 indicates that some actions that reduce the probability of takeovers, such as corporate charter changes, do not reduce shareholder wealth. In contrast, managerial actions that eliminate potential bidders, such as targeted large-block repurchases or standstill agreements, apparently are costly to shareholders. Section 5 discusses unsettled issues and suggests directions for future research.

2. The wealth effects of takeover activities

Numerous studies estimate the effects of takeovers on stock prices of bidder and target firms around the time of announcement of takeover attempts. Such 'event studies' use estimates of the abnormal stock price changes around the offer announcement date as a measure of the economic effects of the takeover. Abnormal returns are measured by the difference between actual and expected stock returns. The expected stock return is measured conditional on the realized return on a market index to take account of the influence of marketwide events on the returns of individual securities.[1]

Early event studies of takeovers, including Mandelker (1974), Ellert (1976), and Langetieg (1978), use the effective date of merger (the date of final

[1]Fama, Fisher, Jensen and Roll (1969) first used this methodology in their study of the price effects of stock splits. Brown and Warner (1980, 1983) provide a detailed discussion of the techniques and various methodological issues regarding their use and interpretation. For simplicity we avoid discussing the details of the abnormal return estimation technique used in each of the studies summarized here. The techniques used in the papers to calculate the abnormal returns are generally similar and, more importantly, the results appear robust with respect to the various estimation techniques used although Malatesta (1983) raises some interesting questions regarding the effects of the use of constrained estimation techniques. The methodologically oriented reader is referred to the original studies for details on these matters.

approval by target shareholders) as the event date. The expected price effects will occur on or before the first public announcement of a takeover. Therefore, because the announcement date occurs at random times prior to the effective date, using the latter as the event date makes it difficult to identify changes in security prices that are due to the takeover event itself. [See Dodd and Ruback (1977).] Because of this difficulty, we focus on studies that, following Dodd and Ruback, analyze abnormal returns around the time of the first public announcement of a takeover.

Table 3 summarizes the estimated abnormal returns for successful and unsuccessful bidding and target firms around announcements of tender offers and mergers. Panel A of table 3 reports the results of the tender offer studies. The results of the merger studies are contained in panels B.1 through B.3 of table 3, which provide measures of abnormal price changes for different time periods around the merger offer announcement. The table identifies the author(s) and year of publication of each study, the time period of the sample, the timing of the event period over which the abnormal returns are estimated, the sample size and *t*-statistic. In some cases the abnormal returns are obtained from studies whose primary purpose is to examine other issues,[2] for example, the antitrust implications of mergers. In some of these cases the numbers of interest for table 3 are not directly presented and we have calculated the relevant abnormal returns and *t*-statistics from data in the articles. In several cases authors have provided estimates not published in the study. Italicized *t*-values are calculated by us using the methods described in footnote a to table 3. Unavailable data are denoted by 'n.a.'.

2.1 Target-firm stockholder returns

Successful target returns. The thirteen studies summarized in table 3 indicate that targets of successful takeover attempts realize substantial and statistically significant increases in their stock prices. The estimates of positive abnormal returns to targets of *successful tender offers*[3] in the month or two surrounding the offer shown in table 3, panel A, are uniformly positive ranging from 16.9% to 34.1%, and the weighted average abnormal return across the seven studies is 29.1%.[4]

For targets of *successful mergers*, the estimated abnormal returns immediately around the merger announcement in panel B.1 of table 3 range

[2]Eckbo (1983), Malatesta (1983), Wier (1983), Ruback (1983a), Bradley (1980), Bradley, Desai and Kim (1982, 1983), and Jarrell and Bradley (1980).

[3]Various definitions of a successful offer are used by the authors. Generally an offer is considered successful if the bidder acquires a substantial fraction of the number of shares initially sought.

[4]The weighted average abnormal return uses sample sizes as weights and ignores the issues associated with overlapping samples. Available data do not allow the calculation of *t*-values for any of the weighted averages.

Table 3
Abnormal returns associated with mergers and tender offers; sample size and *t*-statistic[a] are given in parentheses.

Study	Sample period	Event period	Bidding firms: Successful (%)	Bidding firms: Unsuccessful (%)	Target firms: Successful (%)	Target firms: Unsuccessful (%)
Panel A. Tender offers: Announcement effects						
Dodd and Ruback (1977)	1958–1978	Offer announcement month	+2.83 (124, 2.16)	+0.58 (48, 1.19)	+20.58 (133, 25.81)	+18.96 (36, 12.41)
		The month of and month following offer announcement	+3.12 (124, *2.24*)	−1.71 (48, −*0.76*)	+21.15 (133, *15.75*)	+16.31 (36, *6.32*)
Kummer and Hoffmeister (1978)	1956–1974	Offer announcement month	+5.20 (17, *1.96*)	n.a.	+16.85 (50, *10.88*)	+21.09 (38, *11.87*)
Bradley[b] (1980)	1962–1977	Twenty days before through twenty days after the offer announcement	+4.36 (88, *2.67*)	−2.96 (46, −*1.31*)	+32.18 (161, *26.68*)	+47.26 (97, *30.42*)
Jarrell and Bradley (1980)	1962–1977	Forty days before through twenty days after the offer announcement	+6.66 (88, *3.35*)	n.a.	+34.06[c] (147, *25.48*)	n.a.
Bradley, Desai and Kim (1983)	1963–1980	Ten days before through ten days after the offer announcement	n.a.	−0.27 (94, 0.24)	n.a.	+35.55[d] (112, 36.61)
Bradley, Desai and Kim (1982)	1962–1980	Ten days before through ten days after the offer announcement	+2.35 (161, 3.02)	n.a.	+31.80 (162, 36.52)	n.a.
Ruback (1983a)	1962–1981	Five days before through the offer announcement	n.a.	−0.38 (48, −0.63)	n.a.	n.a.
Weighted average abnormal return[e, h]			+3.81 (478, n.a.)	−1.11 (236, n.a.)	+29.09 (653, n.a.)	+35.17 (283, n.a.)

(*continued overleaf*)

Table 3 (continued)

Study	Sample period	Event period	Bidding firms: Successful (%)	Bidding firms: Unsuccessful (%)	Target firms: Successful (%)	Target firms: Unsuccessful (%)
Panel B.1.	*Mergers: Two-day announcement effects*					
Dodd (1980)	1970–1977	The day before and day of the offer announcement	−1.09 (60, −2.98)	−1.24 (66, −2.63)	+13.41 (71, 23.80)	+12.73 (80, 19.08)
Asquith (1983)	1962–1976	The day before and day of the offer announcement	+0.20 (196, 0.78)	+0.50 (89, 1.92)	+6.20 (211, 23.07)	+7.00 (91, 12.83)
Eckbo (1983)	1963–1978	The day before through the day after the offer announcement	+0.07[f] (102, −0.12)	+1.20[g] (57, 2.98)	+6.24[f] (57, 9.97)	+10.20[g] (29, 15.22)
Weighted average abnormal return[h]			−0.05 (358, n.a.)	+0.15 (212, n.a.)	+7.72 (339, n.a.)	+9.76 (200, n.a.)
Panel B.2.	*Mergers: One-month announcement effects*					
Dodd (1980)	1970–1977	Twenty days before through the first public announcement	+0.80 (60, 0.67)	+3.13 (66, 2.05)	+21.78 (71, 11.93)	+22.45 (80, 10.38)
Asquith (1983)	1962–1976	Nineteen days before through the first public announcement day	+0.20 (196, 0.25)	+1.20 (87, 1.49)	+13.30 (211, 15.65)	+11.70 (91, 6.71)
Eckbo (1983)	1963–1978	Twenty days before through ten days after the public announcement	+1.58[f] (102, 1.48)	+4.85[g] (57, 3.43)	+14.08[f] (57, 6.97)	+25.03[g] (29, 12.61)
Asquith,[i] Bruner and Mullins (1983)	1963–1979	Twenty days before the announcement day through the announcement day	+3.48 (170, 5.30)	+0.70 (41, 0.41)	+20.5 (35, 9.54)	+10.0 (19, 3.45)
Malatesta (1983)	1969–1974	Public announcement month	+0.90 (256, 1.53)	n.a.	+16.8 (83, 17.57)	n.a.
Weighted average abnormal return[h]			+1.37 (784, n.a.)	+2.45 (251, n.a.)	+15.90 (457, n.a.)	+17.24 (219, n.a.)

Panel B.3. Mergers: Total abnormal returns from offer announcement through outcome

Dodd (1980)	1970–1977	Ten days before offer announcement through ten days after outcome date	−7.22 (60, *−2.50*)	−5.50 (66, *−2.05*)	+33.96 (71, *7.66*)	+3.68 (80, *0.96*)
Asquith (1983)	1962–1976	The day before offer announcement through outcome date	−0.10 (196, *−0.05*)	−5.90 (89, *−3.15*)	+15.50 (211, *6.01*)	−7.50 (91, *−1.54*)
Wier[j] (1983)	1962–1979	Ten days before offer announcement through ten days after cancellation date	n.a.	+3.99 (16, *0.89*)	n.a.	−9.02 (17, *−1.82*)
Weighted average abnormal return[h]			−1.77 (256, n.a.)	−4.82 (171, n.a.)	+20.15 (282, n.a.)	−2.88 (188, n.a.)

[a]Not available = n.a.

The non-italicized t-statistics were obtained directly from the cited study or calculated using standard errors reported in the study. In the absence of this information, we have approximated the t-statistics. The italicized t-statistics in panel A are calculated as: $t=\bar{X}\sqrt{N}/S\sqrt{T}$, where $\bar{X}$ is the reported abnormal return, N is the number of observations in the sample, T is the number of days over which the abnormal returns are cumulated, and S is the per day per observation standard deviation. $S=2.39\%$ and is calculated as the average of the implied per day observation standard deviation in all of the studies. The italicized t-statistics in panel **B**.w were calculated as: $t=\bar{X}\sqrt{N}/S\sqrt{\bar{T}}$, where $\bar{T}$ is the average number of days in the average cumulative return, and the standard deviation is from the original study.

[b]These data are plotted in Bradley (1980). Bradley provided the numerical values in private correspondence.

[c]The abnormal return for successful targets is measured over the period forty days before through five days after the offer announcement.

[d]The abnormal return for unsuccessful targets in the announcement month.

[e]The weighted average excludes the announcement month results of Dodd and Ruback (1977) and includes their results for the month of and month following the announcement.

[f]Includes mergers which were not challenged by antitrust authorities.

[g]Sample consists of mergers that were challenged by antitrust authorities. Eckbo (1983) reports that most of these acquisitions were not completed.

[h]The abnormal returns are weighted by samples in calculating the weighted average. Overlapping sample problems are ignored.

[i]Asquith, Bruner and Mullins (1983) provided the data for successful and unsuccessful target firms in private correspondence.

[j]Sample includes only mergers that are cancelled after antitrust complaints under Section 7 of the Clayton Act.

from 6.2% to 13.4%, and the weighted average abnormal return is 7.7%[5] Abnormal returns measured over holding periods of approximately one month surrounding the merger announcement are presented in panel B.2. The weighted average one-month return is 15.9% which is about twice the magnitude of the two-day abnormal returns. This comparison suggests that almost half of the abnormal returns associated with the merger announcements occur prior to their public announcement.[6]

Panel B.3 presents abnormal returns from the first public announcement through the outcome day that incorporate all effects of changing information regarding the offer that occur after the initial announcement. These returns are the most complete measures of the profitability of the mergers to target shareholders in table 3,[7] but they underestimate the gains to target shareholders because they do not include the premium on shares purchased by the bidder prior to the completion of the merger.[8] Dodd (1980) and Asquith (1983) report these total abnormal returns for successful targets as 34% and 15.5% respectively, and the weighted average of the two estimates is 20.2%.

Unsuccessful target returns. The weighted average abnormal returns to stockholders of target firms involved in *unsuccessful tender offers* shown in table 3, panel A, is 35.2%. The comparable one-month abnormal return for targets of *unsuccessful mergers* in panel B.2 is 17.2%. As panels A, B.1 reveal, these weighted average abnormal returns for targets of unsuccessful takeover attempts are approximately equal to those for targets of successful takeovers. Hence, on average the market appears to reflect approximately equal expected gains for both successful and unsuccessful takeovers at the time of the first public announcement. However, one-month announcement abnormal returns are an insufficient measure of stock price changes associated with unsuccessful takeover attempts because they do not include

[5]The *Wall Street Journal* publication date is conventionally used as the announcement date even though the actual announcement of the offers often occurs on the day prior to the publication day.

[6]Keown and Pinkerton (1981) also find that roughly half of the price adjustment occurs prior to the public announcement date. They incorrectly conclude that 'impending merger announcements are poorly held secrets' and that the pre-announcement price adjustments reflect insider trading and the leakage of inside information. They provide no tests of the plausible alternative hypothesis that the price adjustments prior to the 'announcement day' are unbiased responses to public information that increases the probability of a takeover. For many purposes the relatively crude characterization of an event as the *Wall Street Journal* announcement date or the company's formal announcement date is satisfactory. However, for many events there is literally no single 'event day', only a series of occurrences that increase or decrease the probability of an outcome such as a takeover. Inferences about insider trading or leakage require careful consideration of these issues.

[7]Interestingly the target stock price changes appear to capture all of the target value changes associated with the merger. See Kim and McConnell (1977) and Asquith and Kim (1982) who find no merger announcement effects on publicly-traded bond prices.

[8]See Ruback (1982) for calculation of gains to target shareholders that appropriately includes the proceeds to the tendering shareholders on repurchased shares.

the stock price response to the information that the offer failed. The correct measure of the wealth effects, therefore, is the cumulative return from the offer through the termination announcement. The weighted average return to *unsuccessful merger* targets from the initial announcement through the outcome date presented in panel B.3 is -2.9%. Thus, all of the announcement gains are lost over the time that the merger failure becomes known.

In contrast to the behavior of stock prices of targets of unsuccessful mergers, stock prices of targets of *unsuccessful tender offers* remain substantially above their pre-offer level even after the failure of the offer. Unfortunately, the tender offer studies do not present data on the cumulative abnormal return for unsuccessful tender offers from the initial announcement through the outcome date. Nevertheless, some information can be extracted from the abnormal returns following the initial announcement. Dodd and Ruback (1977) find an abnormal return of -2.65% for targets of unsuccessful tender offers in the month following the initial announcement, but the cumulative abnormal return over the entire year following the announcement is only -3.25% ($t=0.90$).

Bradley, Desai and Kim (1983) analyze the post-failure price behavior of a sample of 112 targets of *unsuccessful tender offers* that they segment into two categories: 86 targets that received subsequent takeover offers and 26 targets that did not receive such offers.[9] Returns in the announcement month for the two subsamples are 29.1% and 23.9% respectively, and both are statistically significant. From the announcement month of the initial unsuccessful offer through the following two years, the average abnormal return for the targets that *received* subsequent offers is 57.19% ($t=10.39$). In contrast, the average abnormal return over the same two-year period for targets that *did not receive* subsequent offers is an insignificant -3.53% ($t=-0.36$), and recall this return includes the announcement effects. Thus, the positive abnormal returns associated with unsuccessful tender offers appear to be due to the anticipation of subsequent offers; target shareholders realize additional positive abnormal returns when a subsequent offer is made, but lose the initial announcement gains if no subsequent offer occurs.[10]

Summary: The returns to targets. In summary, the evidence indicates that targets of *successful tender offers* and *mergers* earn significantly positive abnormal returns on announcement of the offers and through completion of the offers. Targets of *unsuccessful tender offers* earn significantly positive

[9]These data seem to indicate that the probability of becoming a takeover target rises substantially after an initial unsuccessful offer occurs.

[10]This evidence casts doubt on the earlier conjectures by Dodd and Ruback (1977) that unsuccessful tender offers lead to target shareholder gains through the disciplining of existing inefficient managers. It is also inconsistent with the argument made by DeAngelo, DeAngelo and Rice (1982) that part of the target price change in takeover offers represents the value of implicit information about target profitability that is revealed by the offer announcement.

abnormal returns on the offer announcement and through the realization of failure. However, those targets of unsuccessful tender offers that do not receive additional offers in the next two years lose all previous announcement gains, and those targets that do receive new offers earn even higher returns. Finally, targets of *unsuccessful mergers* appear to lose all positive returns earned in the offer announcement period by the time failure of the offer becomes known.

2.2 Bidding-firm stockholder returns

Successful bidders. The abnormal returns for bidders in *successful tender offers* summarized in panel A of table 3 are all significantly positive and range from 2.4% to 6.7%, with a weighted average return of 3.8%. Thus, bidders in successful tender offers realize significant percentage increases in equity value, although this increase is substantially lower than the 29.1% return to targets of successful tender offers.

The evidence on bidder returns in *mergers* is mixed and therefore more difficult to interpret than that for bidders in tender offers. On the whole it suggests that returns to bidders in mergers are approximately zero. The two-day abnormal returns associated with the announcement of a merger proposal summarized in panel B.1 of table 3 differ considerably across studies. Dodd (1980) finds a significant abnormal return of −1.09% for 60 successful bidders on the day before and the day of the first public announcement of the merger — indicating that merger bids are, on average, negative net present value investments for bidders. However, over the same two-day period, Asquith (1983) and Eckbo (1983) report slightly positive, but statistically insignificant, abnormal returns — suggesting that merger bids are zero net present value investments. In contrast to the mixed findings for the immediate announcement effects, all five estimates of the one-month announcement effects in panel B.2 of table 3 are positive, but only the estimate of 3.48% by Asquith, Bruner and Mullins (1983) is significantly different from zero. The weighted averages are 1.37% for the one-month announcement effects and −0.05% for the two-day announcement effects.

Panel B.3 of table 3 contains the results of two studies that report the total abnormal return for successful bidding firms from the initial announcement day through the outcome announcement day. If the initial announcement is unanticipated, and there are no other information effects, this cumulative abnormal return includes the effects of all revisions in expectations and offer prices and therefore is a complete measure of the equity value changes for successful bidders. The weighted average of the two estimates is −1.77%, and the individual estimates are −7.22% for 60 successful bidders and −0.1% for 196 successful bidders.

The estimated abnormal returns to successful bidding firms in all six studies summarized in panels B.1 through B.3 of table 3 suggest that mergers are zero net present value investments for bidders[11] — except for the Dodd (1980) estimates in panels B.1 and B.3. It is difficult to understand the reason for the substantial difference between Dodd's estimates and the others. His sample period and methodology are similar to those of the other studies, although his sample is restricted to acquisition proposals for NYSE firms that 'are initially announced in the form of a merger' and is therefore somewhat more restrictive than others. His sample 'does not include merger proposals that were preceded by a tender offer and does not include "defensive mergers" where a target firm finds a merger partner in response to a tender offer by a third firm' [Dodd (1980, p. 107)]. Lacking obvious clues to explain the difference in Dodd's estimates, we're left with the conjecture that his results are sample specific even though there is no apparent reason why this should be induced by his sample selection criteria.[12]

Malatesta (1983) provides estimates of total abnormal *dollar* returns to the equity holders of successful bidding firms in the period 1969–1974 that are consistent with Dodd's results. He reports an average loss of about $28 million ($t = -1.85$) in the period four months before through the month of announcement of the merger outcome (indicated by announcement of board/management approval) of the merger.

Unsuccessful bidders. Inferences about the profitability of takeover bids can also be made from the behavior of bidding-firm stock prices around the time of termination announcements for unsuccessful acquisition attempts. Positive abnormal returns to a bidding firm in response to the announcement that a takeover attempt is unsuccessful (for reasons other than bidder cancellation) are inconsistent with the hypothesis that takeovers are positive net present value investments. Dodd reports insignificant average abnormal returns of 0.9% for 19 bidders on the day before and day of announcement of merger termination initiated by targets. If mergers are positive return projects, these target-termination announcement returns should be negative. Dodd also reports positive termination announcement returns of 1.38% for 47 bidders in his bidder-termination subsample. These positive returns are consistent with the hypothesis that bidders maximize shareholder wealth and cancel mergers after finding out they overvalued the target on the initial offer.

Ruback (1983a) uses data on unsuccessful bidders to test directly for value-maximizing behavior of bidders. He argues that wealth-maximizing bidders

[11]There are, however, classic examples which seem to contradict the conclusion that merger bids are zero net present value investments. For example, see the detailed examination of the 1981 DuPont–Conoco merger by Ruback (1982) in which DuPont paid $7.54 billion, the largest takeover in U.S. corporate history. The value of DuPont fell by $789 million (−9.9%) over the takeover period, and $641 million of the decline occurred on the day of the announcement of DuPont's first offer.

[12]After discussing the issues with us, Dodd was kind enough to recheck and replicate his results — no data or computer programming errors were found.

will abandon takeover attempts when increments in the offer price would make the takeover a negative net present value investment. For 48 bidders in competitive tender offers (defined by the presence of multiple bidders), he finds the average potential gain to the unsuccessful bidder from matching the successful offer price is −$91 million ($t = -4.34$). The potential gain is calculated as the abnormal bidder equity value change associated with the original announcement of the unsuccessful bid minus the additional cost if the higher successful bid were matched. Furthermore, 41 bidders did not match higher offer prices that would have resulted in a negative net present value acquisition.[13] These results are consistent with value-maximizing behavior by bidding firms.

Problems in measuring bidder returns. There is reason to believe the estimation of returns is more difficult for bidders than for targets. Since stock price changes reflect changes in expectations, a merger announcement will have no effect if its terms are fully anticipated in the market. Furthermore, targets are acquired once at most, whereas bidders can engage in prolonged acquisition programs. Malatesta (1981, 1983) and Schipper and Thompson (1983a) point out that the present value of the expected benefits of a bidder's acquisition program is incorporated into the share price when the acquisition program is announced or becomes apparent to the market. Thus, the gain to bidding firms is correctly measured by the value change associated with the initial information about the acquisition program and the incremental effect of each acquisition. The abnormal returns to bidding firms associated with mergers reported in table 3 measure only the incremental value change of each acquisition and are therefore potentially incomplete measures of merger value to successful bidders.

Bidding firms do not typically announce acquisition programs explicitly; this information is generally revealed as the bidders pursue takeover targets. However, Schipper and Thompson (1983a) find that for some firms the start of a takeover program can be approximately determined. They examine the stock price behavior of 30 firms that announced acquisition programs during the period 1953 through 1968. The information that these firms intended to pursue an acquisition program was revealed either in annual reports or specific announcements to the financial press, or in association with other corporate policy changes. For 13 firms in their sample, Schipper and Thompson are unable to identify a specific month in which the acquisition program was adopted. For these firms, December of the program-adoption year is used as the announcement month. Four of the remaining 17 firms

[13]In the remaining 7 observations, the unsuccessful bidders did not match the successful offer price even though the data suggest that the matching would have been a positive net present value investment. The average potential gain for these 7 observations is $23 million ($t = 0.64$). The low t-value suggests that these 'mistakes' are not statistically significant. However, as noted in Ruback (1983a), the measured potential gains are likely to underestimate the actual potential gains when the probability of success is less than one.

had multiple announcements of their programs and the date of the last announcement is used for these firms.

The difficulties in identifying the exact announcement date imply that the capitalized values of the acquisition program are impounded into stock prices prior to the Schipper and Thompson 'announcement month'. Consistent with the hypothesis that mergers are positive net present value investments for bidding firms, they find abnormal returns of 13.5% ($t=2.26$) for their sample of 30 firms in the 12 months prior to and including the 'event month'. However, the imprecise announcement month, the resultant necessity for measuring abnormal returns over a 12-month interval, and contemporaneous changes in corporate policy make it difficult to determine with confidence the association between positive abnormal returns and initiation of the acquisition program. For example, suppose 'good luck' provided bidder management with additional resources to try new projects such as mergers. As Schipper and Thompson discuss, in this case stock prices would show the pattern evidenced in their study even if the mergers have zero net present value.[14]

Asquith, Bruner and Mullins (1983) also examine the profitability of merger programs. They focus on the abnormal returns associated with the first four bids after the initiation of a merger program, arguing that the earlier bids in a merger program should contain more information about the profitability of the program than later bids. This suggests that the price response associated with the first few bids should be greater than the price response associated with later bids. They analyze the abnormal returns for successive merger bids (up to four) of 156 firms that initiated merger programs in the period 1963–1979 after eight years without a bid. Their results indicate that merger bids (both successful and unsuccessful) are positive net present value investments, as evidenced by significant average bidder gains of 2.8% ($t=5.20$) in the 20 days prior to and including the first public announcement. However, there is little evidence that the major gain to the acquisition program is capitalized into the bidder's stock price on announcement of the early mergers. The returns, sample size and t-statistics by merger sequence number are:

	Merger sequence number			
	1	2	3	4
Abnormal return (N, t-statistic)	2.4% (70, 2.21)	3.7% (59, 3.13)	2.4% (47, 1.37)	2.8% (38, 2.38)

[14]Schipper and Thompson conclude that negative abnormal stock price changes for their acquiring firms around times of restrictive regulatory changes help resolve this ambiguity and

In addition to the problems caused by prior capitalization of the gains from takeover bids, measuring the gains to bidding firms is also difficult because bidders are generally much larger than target firms. Thus, even when the dollar gains from the takeover are split evenly between bidder and target firms, the dollar gains to the bidders translate into smaller percentage gains. Asquith, Bruner and Mullins (1983) report that the abnormal returns of bidding firms depend on the relative size of the target. For 99 mergers in which the target's equity value is 10% or more of the bidder's equity value, the average abnormal return for *bidders* is 4.1% ($t=4.42$) over the period 20 days before through the day of announcement. For the 115 remaining mergers in which the target's equity value is less than 10% of the bidder's equity value, the average abnormal return for bidders is 1.7% ($t=2.00$). Furthermore, the precision of the estimated gains is lower for bidders than for targets because the normal variation in equity value for the (larger) bidder is greater, relative to a given dollar gain, than it is for the target. Thus, even if the gains are split equally, the relative sizes of bidding and target firms imply that both the average abnormal return and its t-statistic will be smaller for bidding firms.

Returns to bidders also show evidence of other measurement problems. Several studies show indications of systematic reductions in the stock prices of bidding firms in the year following the event. These post-outcome negative abnormal returns are unsettling because they are inconsistent with market efficiency and suggest that changes in stock price during takeovers overestimate the future efficiency gains from mergers. Table 4 presents the cumulative abnormal returns in the year following takeovers in six different studies. One of the post-announcement abnormal returns in the two tender offer studies in panel A of table 4 is not significantly different from zero. In addition, the post-outcome abnormal returns for the merger studies reported in panel B of table 4 provide evidence of systematic reductions in stock price. Langetieg (1978) and Asquith (1983) report significant negative abnormal returns in the year following the outcome announcement. Malatesta (1983) finds insignificant negative abnormal returns in the year following the merger announcement for his entire sample, although he finds significant negative abnormal returns for bidders in mergers occurring after 1970 and for bidders with smaller equity value.

There are several potential explanations for the negative post-outcome abnormal returns. One hypothesis is that the studies impose ex post selection bias by using information that is not available at the announcement date to

make the evidence that the programs were positive net present value projects for acquirers 'more compelling'. However, this conclusion cannot be drawn. Negative returns on the imposition of regulatory changes that impose higher future costs on bidders would also be observed if the original acquisition programs were negative net present value projects as long as the regulatory changes do not cause the bidders to abandon their acquisition programs.

Table 4

Summary of post-outcome abnormal returns for tender offers and mergers; sample size and t-statistic[a] are given in parentheses.

			Bidding firms		Target firms	
Study	Sample period	Event period	Successful (%)	Unsuccessful (%)	Successful (%)	Unsuccessful (%)
Panel A. Tender offers						
Dodd and Ruback (1977)	1958–1978	Month after through 12 months after the offer announcement	−1.32 (124, −0.41)	−1.60 (48, −0.52)	+7.95 (133, 0.85)	−3.25 (36, 0.90)
Bradley, Desai and Kim (1983)	1962–1980	Month after through 12 months after the offer announcement	n.a.	−7.85[b] (94, −2.34)	n.a.	+3.04 (112, 0.90)
Panel B. Mergers						
Mandelker (1974)	1941–1962	Month after through 12 months after the effective date	+0.60 (241, 0.31)	n.a.	n.a.	n.a.
Langetieg (1978)	1929–1969	Month after through 12 months after the effective date	−6.59 (149, −2.96)	n.a.	n.a.	n.a.
Asquith (1983)	1962–1976	Day after through 240 days after the outcome announcement	−7.20 (196, −4.10)	−9.60 (89, −5.41)	n.a.	−8.7 (91, −2.11)
Malatesta (1983)	1969–1974	Month after through 12 months after approval for entire sample	−2.90 (121, −1.05)	n.a.	n.a.	n.a.
		Month after through 12 months after approval for mergers occurring after 1970	−13.7 (75, −2.88)	n.a.	n.a.	n.a.
		Month after through 12 months after approval for firms with equity value under $300 million	−7.70 (59, −1.51)	n.a.	n.a.	n.a.

[a]Not available = n.a.

The t-statistics either come directly from the cited study or were calculated from implied standard deviations available in the cited study, or come from an earlier draft of the study.

[b]This abnormal return covers the period from the day after through 180 days after the offer.

select samples. Alternatively, the negative drift could be caused by non-stationary parameters or other forms of model misspecification, but Langetieg (1978) finds these factors do not explain the negative post-outcome returns in his sample. Schipper and Thompson (1983a) argue that regulatory changes that reduced the profitability of mergers could explain the negative abnormal returns, but Malatesta (1983) finds significant negative abnormal post-outcome returns of −13.7% ($t = 2.88$) for mergers occurring after the regulatory changes. Explanation of these post-event negative abnormal returns is currently an unsettled issue.

Summary: The returns to bidders. The reported positive returns to *successful bidders* in *tender offers* and the generally negative returns to *unsuccessful bidders* in both *mergers* and *tender offers* are consistent with the hypothesis that mergers are positive net present value projects. The measurement of returns to bidders in mergers is difficult, and perhaps because of this the results are mixed. The evidence suggests, however, that returns to *successful bidding* firms in *mergers* are zero. Additional work on this problem is clearly warranted.

2.3. The total gains from takeovers

The evidence indicates that shareholders of target firms realize large positive abnormal returns in completed takeovers. The evidence on the rewards to bidding firms is mixed, but the weight of the evidence suggests zero returns are earned by successful bidding firms in mergers and that statistically significant but small positive abnormal returns are realized by bidders in successful tender offers. Since targets gain and bidders do not appear to lose, the evidence suggests that takeovers create value. However, because bidding firms tend to be larger than target firms, the sum of the returns to bidding and target returns do not measure the gains to the merging firms. The dollar value of small percentage losses for bidders could exceed the dollar value of large percentage gains to targets.

Malatesta (1983) and Bradley, Desai and Kim (1982) measure the changes in total dollar value associated with completed takeovers. Malatesta examines a matched sample of targets and their bidders in 30 successful mergers and finds a significant average increase of $32.4 million ($t = 2.07$) in their combined equity value in the month before and month of outcome announcement. The acquired firms earned $18.6 million ($t = 5.41$) of the combined increase in equity value, and acquiring firms earned $13.8 million ($t = 0.91$). Bradley, Desai and Kim (1982) report positive but statistically insignificant total dollar gains to bidders and targets in 162 tender offers of $17.2 million ($t = 1.26$). However, the average percentage change in total value of the combined target and bidder firms is a significant 10.5% ($t = 6.58$). This evidence indicates that changes in corporate control increase the combined market value of assets of the bidding and target firms.

3. Antitrust and the source of merger gains

The evidence indicates that, on average, takeovers result in an upward revaluation of the target's equity, and that shareholders of target firms realize a substantial increase in wealth as a result of completed takeovers. Understanding the source of the gains to merging firms is important since acquisition attempts often meet strong opposition, sometimes from target management, sometimes from antitrust authorities. Target managers, for example, often argue that target shareholders are harmed by takeovers; indeed, the common use of the emotion-laden term 'raider' to label the bidding firm suggests that the bidder's gains are coming at the expense of the target firm's shareholders. The evidence summarized above indicates that this argument is false; the bidder's gains (if any) do not appear to be simple wealth transfers from target shareholders.[15] Acquisition attempts are also opposed by target firms, competitors, and antitrust authorities, among others, who argue that mergers are undesirable because they reduce competition and create monopoly power.[16] Such opposition has delayed merger completion, caused merger cancellations, and resulted in court-ordered divestiture of previously completed acquisitions.[17] In addition, the evidence indicating positive net benefits to merging firms, together with the zero or positive abnormal returns to bidding firms, is inconsistent with the hypothesis that takeovers are motivated by non-value-maximizing behavior by the managers of bidding firms.

3.1. The source of takeover gains

Various sources of gains to takeovers have been advanced. Potential reductions in production or distribution costs, often called synergies, could occur through realization of economies of scale, vertical integration, adoption of more efficient production or organizational technology,[18] increased utilization of the bidder's management team, and reduction of agency costs by bringing organization-specific assets under common ownership.[19]

[15]See Bradley (1980) for an extended discussion of these issues in the context of tender offers.

[16]Arguments by target management that a takeover should be prohibited on antitrust grounds seems particularly self-interested and inconsistent with maximization of shareholder wealth.

[17]For example, the Justice Department's request for additional information from Mobil during the Conoco takeover prohibited Mobil from buying Conoco common stock and prevented Mobil from actively competing with DuPont and Seagram for control of Conoco, even though Mobil's offer was approximately one billion dollars higher. Ruback (1982) analyzes this takeover in detail.

[18]See Chandler (1962, 1977) and Williamson (1975, 1981) for discussion of advantages of the multidivisional form of organization which seems common to merged firms. Bradley, Desai and Kim (1982) investigate the role of specialized resources in merger gains.

[19]See Klein, Crawford and Alchian (1978) for discussion of the agency costs of outside ownership of organization-specific assets.

Financial motivations for acquisitions include the use of underutilized tax shields, avoidance of bankruptcy costs, increased leverage, and other types of tax advantages.[20] Takeovers could increase market power in product markets. Finally, takeovers could eliminate inefficient target management. Each of these hypotheses predicts that the combined firm generates cash flows with a present value in excess of the sum of the market values of the bidding and target firms. But the abnormal returns do not identify which components of the present value of net cash flows have changed. Studies of the abnormal returns to takeover participants cannot, therefore, distinguish between these alternative sources of gains.

Two important exceptions are the studies by Stillman (1983) and Eckbo (1983), which use the equity price changes of firms that *compete* in product markets with the merged target to reject the hypothesis that takeovers create market power. The market power hypothesis implies that mergers increase product prices thereby benefiting the merging firms and other competing firms in the industry. Higher prices allow competing firms to increase their own product prices and/or output, and therefore the equity values of competing firms should also rise on the offer announcement.

Stillman (1983) examines the abnormal returns for rival firms in 11 horizontal mergers. The small sample size arises from his sample selection criteria. Of all mergers challenged under Section 7 of the Clayton Act, these 11 are the merger complaints in unregulated industries whose rivals were identified in the proceedings and for which constraints on data availability were met. While this screening process creates a small sample, it reduces ambiguity about the applicability of the test and the identity of rivals. He finds no statistically significant abnormal returns for rival firms in nine of the mergers examined. Of the remaining two mergers, one exhibits ambiguous results and the other is consistent with positive abnormal returns for rivals. Stillman's evidence, therefore, is inconsistent with the hypothesis that the gains from mergers are due to the acquisition of market power.

Eckbo (1983) uses the stock price reaction of rivals at the announcement of the antitrust challenge as well as at the announcement of the merger to test the market power hypothesis. Eckbo's final sample consists of 126 challenged horizontal mergers and, using product line classifications rather than records of court and agency proceedings, he identifies an average of 15 rivals for each merger. He also identifies rivals for 65 unchallenged horizontal mergers and 58 vertical mergers.

Eckbo's results indicate that rival firms have positive abnormal returns around the time of the first public announcement of the *merger*. Rivals of unchallenged mergers realized abnormal returns of 1.1% ($t=1.20$) and rivals of challenged mergers realized abnormal returns of 2.45% ($t=3.02$) in the

[20]See Benston (1980, p. 21).

period 20 days prior to and 10 days following the first public announcement. These results are consistent with the market power hypothesis.

Eckbo uses the stock price reactions of *rivals* at announcement of the *antitrust challenge* to reject the market power hypothesis. The market power hypothesis predicts negative abnormal returns for rival firms at the time the complaint is filed because the complaint reduces the probability of completion of the merger (which, it is assumed, would have generated market power), and the concomitant increase in output prices is then less probable. In the period 20 days before through 10 days after the antitrust challenge, the rivals to 55 challenged mergers realize statistically insignificant average abnormal returns of 1.78% ($t = 1.29$). This finding is inconsistent with the market power hypothesis, which implies the returns of rivals should be significantly negative at the complaint announcement. Furthermore, Eckbo reports that rivals with a positive market reaction to the initial merger announcement do not tend to have negative abnormal returns at the time of complaint. Thus, Eckbo's evidence is inconsistent with the market power hypothesis.

Although the evidence in Eckbo (1983) and Stillman (1983) is inconsistent with the market power hypothesis, identification of the actual source of the gains in takeovers has not yet occurred. There is evidence in Asquith (1980, 1983), Malatesta (1983), Langetieg (1978), Ellert (1976), and Mandelker (1974) that target firms experience negative abnormal returns in the period prior to approximately six months before the acquisition.[21] This below normal performance is consistent with the hypothesis that inefficient target management caused target firms to perform badly, but there is currently no evidence that directly links these negative pre-merger returns to inefficiency. Eckbo's results, moreover, are inconsistent with the target inefficiency hypothesis. His evidence indicates that the gains are more general, extending to rivals in the industry as well as to the specific target firm, and removal of inefficient target management is unlikely to be an industry-wide phenomenon.

It would be surprising to find that all the gains reflected in table 3 are due to a single phenomenon such as elimination of inefficient target management. Some of the gains are also likely to result from other synergies in combining two or more independent organizations, and discovery of the precise nature of these synergies is a complicated task. Ruback (1982), for example, examines the DuPont–Conoco merger to determine the source of the revaluation that occurred; the stockholders of the target, Conoco, realized gains of about $3.2 billion whereas stockholders of the bidder, DuPont, incurred losses of almost $800 million. The DuPont–Conoco merger, therefore, 'created' about $2.4 billion of additional market value. Ruback

[21]The declines reported by Asquith (1983), Malatesta (1983), Langetieg (1978) and Ellert (1976) are statistically significant.

explores a variety of different explanations for the revaluations, including synergy, the release of new information, undervalued oil reserves, replacement of inefficient target management, and departures from stockholder wealth maximization by the management of DuPont. None of these hypotheses provide an adequate explanation for the revaluation, although it is impossible to reject the hypothesis that DuPont had some special new information about Conoco's assets. These results suggest it is difficult to identify the source of the gains from takeovers — even in the context of a single takeover.

Information effects of various kinds might also play a role in explaining the behavior of stock prices at times of takeovers. For example, DeAngelo, DeAngelo and Rice (1982) conjecture that information effects associated with bidder management's possession of inside information about its own value might help explain the difference in bidder returns in tender offers and merger proposals. The evidence indicates that bidders in successful tender offers earn small positive returns and that successful merger bidders earn approximately zero returns. Tender offers are frequently cash offers,[22] and mergers are usually stock and other security exchange offers. When bidder management's inside information (unrelated to the acquisition) indicates its stock is undervalued it will prefer a cash offer and vice versa for a stock offer.[23] Therefore, astute market participants will interpret a cash offer as good news and a stock offer as bad news about the bidder's value and incorporate this information into bidder stock prices along with the estimated value of the acquisition. This argument implies that returns to bidders in cash tender offers will be higher than in mergers, if other aspects of the deals are approximately equivalent.

The inside information argument is as yet untested. However, it implies that stock prices fall when new shares are sold and rise when shares are repurchased, and this implication is consistent with the price effects associated with intrafirm capital structure changes found by a growing number of authors. For example, prices generally fall on the exchange of common and preferred stock for bonds [Masulis (1980a)], on the call and conversion of convertible bonds to stock [Mikkelson (1981, 1983)], on the issuance of convertible debt [Dann and Mikkelson (1982)], on the issuance of stock through rights offerings [Smith (1977)], and on the sale of common stock in secondary offering [Scholes (1972)], while prices generally rise on repurchases of common stock [Dann (1981), Vermaelen (1981), Masulis (1980b) and Rosenfeld (1982)]. The only inconsistent evidence is the

[22]Bradley (1980), Jarrell and Bradley (1980) and Bradley, Desai and Kim (1983) sample only cash offers; Dodd and Ruback (1977) and Ruback (1983a) sample both cash and security exchange tender offers.

[23]See Myers and Majluf (1981) who argue that sale of shares by a target through merger can reveal negative information about the target's value.

significant negative returns associated with targeted buybacks of large blocks of stock documented by DeAngelo and Rice (1983) and Bradley and Wakeman (1983). However, the targeted buyback evidence seems well explained by other factors, as discussed in section 4.5 below.

3.2. The costs of antitrust actions

The evidence indicates that merger gains do not come from the acquisition of market power, but rather from some source of efficiencies that also appears to be available to rival firms in the industry. Given this evidence it is of interest to examine the effects of antitrust actions on merging firms.

In their studies of antitrust merger actions, Ellert (1976), Wier (1983) and Eckbo (1983) demonstrate that antitrust opposition to takeovers imposes substantial costs on target firm shareholders. Wier examines the abnormal returns for firms involved in mergers which were opposed by antitrust authorities under Section 7 of the Clayton Act. Her sample contains mergers involving 16 bidding firms and 17 target firms that were cancelled after antitrust complaints. The cumulative abnormal return from 30 days before through the proposal announcement is 9.25%. During the period *following* the proposal announcement through the complaint period and the cancellation day, all the previous target firm announcement gains are eliminated; the cumulative abnormal return is −12.43%. Bidding firms in her sample appear to show no abnormal returns at the time of proposal announcement or cancellation.

Wier (1983) also examines the abnormal returns associated with the announcement of antitrust complaints for 111 completed mergers, and her data reveal significant abnormal returns of −2.58% for the day before through the day after the complaint announcement. Ellert (1976) reports an abnormal return of −1.83% ($t=-3.24$) in the complaint month for 205 defendants in antitrust merger cases over the period 1950–1972. Similarly, Eckbo (1983) reports an average abnormal return of −9.27% ($t=-7.61$) for 17 target firms on the day before through the day after the announcement of an antitrust complaint. In addition, Wier finds that the abnormal return for 32 firms that completed their mergers and were later convicted of antitrust violations is −2.27% ($t=-4.11$) from the day before through the day after the conviction announcement. However, she finds no significant abnormal returns on announcement of the outcome for 30 firms whose antitrust suits were dismissed and for 66 firms that settled their antitrust suits. Dismissal or settlement of a suit, unless fully expected, would generally represent good news. As Wier points out, the absence of significant abnormal returns at these announcements is puzzling.

There is also evidence consistent with the hypothesis that Federal Trade Commission antitrust actions benefit rivals of merging firms by restricting competition. Eckbo (1983) finds that rivals of mergers challenged by the Federal Trade Commission earn essentially zero abnormal returns on the day of the merger announcement and significantly positive abnormal returns on the day of the complaint announcement. In contrast, rivals of mergers challenged by the Justice Department earn significantly positive abnormal returns on the merger announcement and essentially zero abnormal returns on the complaint announcement. Eckbo (1983) concludes: 'This evidence strongly contradicts the [market power] hypothesis and gives some support to a "rival producer protection" rationale for the behavior of the FTC towards these mergers.'

In sum, the negative abnormal returns associated with antitrust complaints, Section 7 convictions, and cancellations of mergers induced by antitrust actions indicate that antitrust opposition to takeovers imposes substantial costs on the stockholders of merging firms. This finding is particularly interesting given that the evidence indicates merger gains do not arise from the creation of market power but rather from the acquisition of some form of efficiencies.

3.3. The effects of takeover regulation

In addition to antitrust regulation, the imposition of security regulations governing takeovers appears to have reduced the profitability of takeovers. The effect of changes in tender offer regulations (such as the Williams Amendment and state tender offer laws) on the abnormal returns to bidding and target firms, is examined in Smiley (1975) and Jarrell and Bradley (1980). Smiley finds that the Williams Amendment increased the abnormal returns to target firms by 13%. Jarrell and Bradley find that the target's average abnormal return increased after the Williams Amendment and the bidder's average abnormal return decreased. They find that average abnormal returns for 47 target firms prior to the Williams Amendment were 22% ($t=12.9$) in the period 40 days before through five days after the first public announcement of the takeover. In comparison, the average abnormal return for 90 targets subject to regulation under the Williams Amendment is 40% ($t=19.2$) and the returns to 20 targets subject to both the Williams Amendment and state tender offer laws is 35% ($t=5.1$). For bidders, the average abnormal return in the period 40 days before through 20 days after the first public announcement is 9% ($t=3.5$) for 28 unregulated offers, 6% ($t=2.1$) for 51 offers regulated by the Williams Amendment, and 4% ($t=0.7$) for 9 offers regulated by the Williams Amendment and state tender offer laws. Asquith, Bruner and Mullins (1983) provide similar evidence. For mergers prior to October 1, 1969, they report average abnormal returns to bidders of 4.40% over the period 20 days before through the first public announcement and average abnormal returns of 1.7% to bidders in mergers after October 1, 1969.

The evidence seems to indicate that the regulations increased the returns to the target's shareholders at the expense of the shareholders of bidding firms, but the tests are not sufficient to draw this conclusion from the data. Suppose the regulations have no effect whatsoever except to eliminate the low-value offers. By raising transactions costs and imposing restrictions on takeovers, the regulations could simply truncate the distribution of takeovers that would actually occur. This truncation of less profitable takeovers would reduce the returns to shareholders of firms that do not become targets and have no effect on the returns to those that do become targets, but it would increase the *measured* average abnormal returns for targets of completed takeovers. The effect of such truncation on the abnormal returns to bidding firms is less clear since no well-developed theory exists that determines the division of the net benefits between target and bidding firms.

Schipper and Thompson (1983a) examine the effect of four regulatory changes that occurred in 1968–1970: Accounting Principle Board Opinions 16 and 17, the 1969 Tax Reform Act, the 1968 Williams Amendment, and its 1970 extension. Each of these regulatory changes restricts bidders and thereby reduces the profitability of bidding firms. The abnormal return for bidders engaged in merger programs at the time of four regulatory changes is interesting because, in an efficient market, the effect of the regulatory changes is impounded in the bidder's stock price on announcement of the changes. They find an average abnormal return of -1.3% ($t=4.5$) during the 15 months in which events related to regulatory change occurred between January 1967 and December 1970. Schipper and Thompson (1983b) use an alternative technique to estimate the effects of the regulatory changes. They report that the Williams Amendment reduced the equity values of acquiring firms by about 6%. The Schipper and Thompson event-type tests are more precise than the comparison of abnormal returns to bidders before and after regulation, and they indicate that the regulatory changes impose costs on bidding firms. Their approach cannot be used to assess the effect of the regulations on target firms because it is difficult, if not impossible, for the market to identify future target firms.[24] If market participants cannot identify targets prior to the bids, appreciable changes in stock price will not be observed for targets of future takeovers at times of regulatory changes.

4. Manager–stockholder conflicts of interest

4.1. Corporate control: The issues

Takeovers serve as an external control mechanism that limits major

[24]Palepue (1983) uses a binary logit model to identify determinants of the probability of acquisition. While he finds several variables that are statistically significant, the overall explanatory power of the model is negligible.

managerial departures from maximization of stockholder wealth.[25] It is unlikely, however, that the threat of takeover ensures complete coherence of managerial actions and maximization of stockholder wealth. Because of the existence of other control mechanisms, the inability of the takeover market to eliminate all departures from maximization of stockholder wealth does not imply that these departures are prevalent in modern corporations.[26] The limitations of the takeover market also do not imply that the departures, when they occur, are costly to shareholders; some of the costs are borne by managers themselves through reductions in their salaries.[27]

Measurement of the costs of manager–stockholder conflict by direct examination of managerial decisions is difficult for reasons that include the difficulty in identifying the benefits to managers that emanate from particular decisions, the difficulty in determining the information base for the decision, errors in the stock market assessment of value, and the difficulty in ex post auditing of decisions. For example, suppose the announcement of a capital investment is associated with a decline in the firm's stock price, suggesting that the investment reduces shareholder wealth. There is no particular reason in this case to suspect that the decision benefits managers.[28] Furthermore, the price decline could be an error due to the market's lack of inside information possessed by managers. Alternatively, even if the investment is value-maximizing, the decline in price could result from an exogenous reduction in profitability that the investment reveals to the market. Finally, even when the investment proves to be a negative net present value

[25]The average abnormal returns to target shareholders in tables 1 and 3 are not measures of the extent of managerial departures from stockholder wealth maximization. For example, in addition to the gains from eliminating inefficient managers, they include the gains from efficiency innovations and synergies available to the combined firm.

[26]See Fama and Jensen (1983a, b, c) and Jensen (1983) for discussions of agency costs, control and survival in a theory of organizations that views conflicts of interests in a general fashion.

[27]See Jensen and Meckling (1976, p. 328) and Fama (1980). However, unless the cost of perfectly enforcing managerial contracts is zero, the agency costs of managerial discretion will not be zero. Zero costs of managerial discretion imply zero costs of constructing a managerial performance measurement, evaluation and compensation system that perfectly reflects in the manager's salary all deviations from shareholder wealth maximization. Contrary to Fama's (1980) argument, this implication holds even for the monitoring performed by the managerial labor market. Consider, for example, a case in which the value of a manager's human capital that is specific to his current organization is large relative to the value of his general human capital. (The value of general human capital means the value of human capital in its highest-value use outside the manager's current organization.) In this case, fluctuations in the value of his general human capital, even if they perfectly reflect the manager's deviations from maximization of shareholder wealth, will have no direct effect on his welfare. Therefore, the managerial labor market will not eliminate the agency costs between managers and stockholders in such situations.

[28]For example, the evidence presented by Mikkelson (1981, 1983) and Masulis (1980a) indicates that call and conversion of convertible bonds to common stock and exchange of common and preferred stock for bonds is associated with statistically significant stock price declines. Except for cases in which managerial compensation depends on earnings per share, it is difficult to see how managers benefit from such capital structure changes.

investment, it is difficult, given uncertainty, to distinguish between managerial incompetence, managerial opportunism or mere bad luck.

Some evidence on the costs of managerial departures from maximization of stockholder wealth can be obtained by focusing on changes in the rules that govern manager–stockholder interactions. Corporate charter changes that affect the probability of a future outside takeover are good examples. The evidence summarized in section 2 indicates that shareholders in successful takeover targets realize substantial wealth increases. Managers of potential targets, however, can suffer welfare losses in takeovers — for example, through their displacement as managers and the resulting loss of organization-specific human capital. In such situations, managers have incentives to take actions that reduce the probability of an outside takeover and thereby benefit themselves at the expense of shareholders.

However, the conflict between shareholder interests managerial opposition to takeovers is not clear cut. Corporate charter changes that increase the ability of target managers to control the outcome of a takeover bid can enable managers to extract a higher offer price from the bidder or to solicit higher offers from other bidders. Jarrell and Bradley (1980) and DeAngelo and Rice (1983) argue that uncoordinated wealth-maximizing decisions by individual shareholders can result in takeovers that grant a larger share of the takeover gains to the shareholders in the bidding firm.

Suppose a firm has 100 shares of common stock with a market price of \$9.50 per share and a total market value of \$950. Economies with total value of \$50 can be realized only if the firm is merged with firm A. Firm A makes a two-part takeover bid, offering \$12 per share for up to 51 shares and \$7 per share for the remaining 49 shares.[29] Note that if the offer is successful, the bidder obtains the target firm for \$955 — an amount only \$5 over its market value. Shareholders of firm A therefore receive \$45 of the \$50 total takeover gain. As table 5 illustrates, each shareholder faces the classic 'prisoner's dilemma' problem. Acting independently, each shareholder maximizes his wealth by tendering, although all target shareholders are better off if nobody tenders until they receive a larger fraction of the takeover gains.[30] This problem is reduced by requiring bidders to get

[29]Such two-part offers were used in the Conoco, Marathon and Brunswick takeover attempts, perhaps to reduce minority shareholder blocking power. Dodd and Ruback (1977) present evidence that non-selling target shareholders receive positive abnormal returns of 17.4% ($t=6.68$) in subsequent 'cleanup' offers of outside minority interests. DeAngelo, DeAngelo and Rice (1982) find abnormal returns of 30.4% to minority shareholders and indications of minority blocking power in going private transactions. (See section 4.7 below.) Others have argued [see Grossman and Hart (1980)] that shareholders face free-rider problems when there is a holdout premium available. They argue that if holdout premiums exist, free-rider problems prevent takeovers from succeeding even when they are profitable for all parties. In such a situation shareholders as a group would be better off if two-part offers are made by potential bidders.

[30]If less than 51% of the shares are tendered and the offer is therefore unsuccessful, the tendering shareholder receives \$12 per share as compared to the \$9.50 market value if he does not tender. This assumes, for simplicity, that the bidder does not abandon the takeover effort. If

Table 5
Per share dollar payoff to individual shareholder who either tenders his shares or keeps his shares.

	Offer outcome	
Individual action	Unsuccessful ($)	Successful ($)
Tender	12.00	9.55
Don't tender	9.50	7.00

simultaneous approval of more target shareholders, and enabling management to act as agent for target shareholders can help accomplish this. If antitakeover amendments increase the bargaining power of target managers to elicit a higher offer price they could benefit target shareholders.[31]

It is worth noting that firm A in the example cannot take advantage of the target shareholder's prisoner's dilemma problems to acquire the target at less than its market value of $950 (perhaps by offering $12 for 51 shares and $5 for the rest for a total of $857). If firm A attempts this action, competition from other firms will drive the total offer to the target's current market value of $950 if there are no gains from merger. Thus as Bradley (1980) argues, competition prevents corporate raiding or corporate piracy.[32]

The remainder of this section discusses several studies that estimate the effects on stock price of managerial actions that can affect the probability that a firm will be a takeover target — including changes in the state of incorporation, adoption of antitakeover charter amendments, managerial opposition to takeovers, going private transactions, standstill agreements, and targeted large block repurchases. The results of the studies are mixed. On the one hand, there is little or no evidence of a decline in stock price that is associated with either changes in the state of incorporation, or adoption of antitakeover charter amendments, and outside selling shareholders gain substantially in going private transactions. On the other hand, there is

abandonment occurs the target firm could then become the bidder and use the same strategy to take over firm A. If the offer is successful and 100% of the shares are tendered, the shareholder expects to receive a minimum of $9.55 per share ($12 per share on 51% of his shares and $7 per share on 49% of his shares if he tenders immediately). If he does not tender immediately he will receive only $7 per share. Since, independent of the outcome, immediate tendering has higher value, the optimal non-collusive decision is to tender.

[31]For simplicity we have assumed the $50 gain is independent of the takeover bargaining procedures. Easterbrook and Fischel (1982a) examine the implications of various gain-sharing rules for the creation of gains.

[32]The timing of the offer expiration is obviously important to the bidding process because it could limit competition and is worthy of additional analysis.

evidence that shareholders are harmed by targeted large block repurchases and standstill agreements. Overall, the evidence indicates that negative returns are associated with managerial actions regarding takeovers (1) if the action eliminates a takeover bid or causes a takeover failure, or (2) if the action does not require formal stockholder approval either through voting or tendering decisions.

4.2. Changes in state of incorporation

Corporate charters specify the governance rules for corporations, including rules that establish conditions for mergers (such as the percentage of stockholders that must approve a takeover). Individual states specify constraints on charter rules that differ from state to state. This variation in state law means that changing the state of incorporation affects the contractual arrangement among shareholders effected through the corporate charter, and these changes can affect the probability that a firm will become a takeover target.

Dodd and Leftwich (1980) investigate changes in stockholder returns associated with changes in the state of incorporation for 140 firms during the period 1927–1977. Of these firms, 126 reincorporated in Delaware, a state that provides few constraints on charter rules and therefore provides greater contractual freedom for shareholders and managers. Delaware also provides a set of well-defined legal precedents that facilitate contracting and resolution of disputes. Only six firms left Delaware, and there were only eight changes in states of incorporation that did not involve Delaware.

One explanation for reincorporation in Delaware is that managers use Delaware's minimal restrictions on charter rules to exploit shareholders. An alternative explanation is that the more lenient Delaware code enables managers to take actions to increase shareholder wealth that are not possible (or are more costly) under the more restrictive charters in other states. For example, for a portion of the sample period Delaware required only simple majority stockholder approval for mergers, while many other states required greater than majority approval. Under these conditions, reincorporation in Delaware reduces the costs of merger approval and thereby raises the probability of becoming a bidder or a target in a takeover.

Dodd and Leftwich attempt to isolate the first public announcement of a change in the state of incorporation, but in many instances it is likely that the announcement date they identify is not the first public announcement of the reincorporation. Therefore, the market reaction to the change is likely to be incorporated in stock prices prior to the 'event day' and this prior response reduces the power of their tests. They find abnormal returns to shareholders of firms that changed their state of incorporation of about 30% ($t = 7.90$) over the period 24 months prior to and including the announcement month — abnormal returns that seem too large to be caused solely by changes in the state of incorporation. Dodd and Leftwich use a variety of tests to determine the source of these gains, including examination of 50 firms for which precise *Wall Street Journal* announcement dates are obtainable, analysis of changes in systematic risk, and elimination of the largest positive abnormal return for each firm over the 25-month interval. These additional tests suggest that firms changed their state of incorporation after a period of superior performance and that the change itself is associated with small positive abnormal returns. Importantly, they find no evidence of a decline in stockholder wealth at times when the state of incorporation is changed — an observation inconsistent with the hypothesis that the changes are motivated by managerial exploitation of shareholders.

4.3. Antitakeover amendments

Firms can amend their charters to make the conditions for shareholder approval of mergers more stringent. These antitakeover amendments include super-majority provisions and provisions for the staggered election of board members. By increasing the stringency of takeover conditions, such amendments can reduce the probability of being a takeover target and therefore reduce shareholder wealth. However, as explained above, by increasing the plurality required for takeover approval, the amendments could benefit shareholders by enabling target management to better represent their common interests in the merger negotiations.

DeAngelo and Rice (1983) and Linn and McConnell (1983) examine the effect of the adoption of antitakeover amendments on stock prices of the adopting firms. DeAngelo and Rice examine 100 firms that adopted super-majority, staggered board, fair price, and lock-up provisions over the period 1974–1978. Shareholders of these firms realized statistically insignificant abnormal returns of -0.16% ($t=-0.41$) on the day of and the day after the mailing date of the proxy containing the proposals. Over the period 10 days before through 11 days after the proxy mailing date the cumulative abnormal returns are an insignificant -0.90% ($t=-0.70$). These results suggest the adoption of antitakeover provisions does not reduce stockholder wealth, although DeAngelo and Rice point out that the results might be positively biased if the proposal of the amendment communicates to target shareholders an increased probability of a takeover attempt and its associated gains.

Linn and McConnell (1983) find no significant abnormal returns on the proxy mailing date for a sample of 388 firms that adopted antitakeover amendments ove the period 1960–1980. They argue, however, that it is difficult to identify the precise date on which information about the antitakeover provisions is released. The information could be released on the date the board approves the amendments (which occurs prior to the proxy mailing date) or on the date of stockholder approval (which follows the proxy mailing date). Hence, they examine the abnormal stock returns throughout the amendment process. For 170 firms in which the day of board approval is available, the cumulative abnormal returns from the day of board approval through the day before the proxy mailing date is an insignificant 0.71% ($t=1.20$). For 307 firms they find significant average abnormal returns of 1.43% ($t=3.41$) over the period from the proxy mailing date through the day before the stockholders meeting. In the 90-day period beginning with the stockholders meeting, the cumulative abnormal returns are an insignificant 0.86% ($t=1.65$). These results provide weak evidence in favor of the hypothesis that antitakeover amendments increase stockholder wealth. The results also suggest that the proxy mailing date is not the date when the information is incorporated in stock prices, a finding that is inconsistent with market efficiency.

Linn and McConnell also examine the abnormal returns to 49 firms that removed previously enacted antitakeover amendments. Over the period between board approval and proxy mailing, these firms experienced a statistically significant average abnormal return of −3.63% ($t=-2.33$). This result implies shareholders benefit from the presence of antitakeover amendments, but leaves a puzzle in understanding why they were removed in these 49 cases. In a related test, Linn and McConnell examine the abnormal stock returns of 120 firms incorporated in Delaware when the fraction of shareholders required to approve a merger was reduced by Delaware from two-thirds to a simple majority. The average abnormal return in the month of the change in the Delaware law is −1.66% ($t=-2.15$), and each of these 120 firms subsequently adopted antitakeover amendments. However, these 120 firms were selected because they adopted antitakeover amendments. This selection bias means that these returns are also consistent with the hypothesis that changes in the Delaware law on average had no effect on stockholder wealth.

Consistent with the DeAngelo and Rice results, the Linn and McConnell results imply that on average antitakeover amendments do not decrease stockholder wealth. In addition, the Linn and McConnell evidence is weakly supportive of the hypothesis that on the average such amendments increase shareholder wealth.[33]

4.4. *Managerial opposition to takeovers*

Target firm managers can make outside takeovers more difficult in ways

[33]H. DeAngelo and E. Rice have suggested to us that when a super-majority provision grants acquisition blocking power to a manager or other stockholder (for example a manager holding 21% of the stock when an 80% super-majority provision is implemented) the stock price effects will be more pronounced. This hypothesis has not as yet been studied.

other than through adoption of antitakeover corporate charter amendments. Since target shareholders benefit from takeovers, explicit managerial actions to prevent a takeover *independent of the price offered* appear to be an instance of managerial pursuit of self-interest at the expense of shareholders. Managerial opposition to a takeover in order to elicit a larger premium can increase the benefits of the takeover for shareholders. Such opposition can take the form of press releases and mailings that present the manager's position, the initiation of certain court actions, and the encouragement of competing bids.[34] However, it is difficult to argue that actions which *eliminate* a potential bidder are in the stockholder's best interests. Actions that can eliminate a takeover bid include cancellation of a merger proposal by target management without referral to shareholders, initiation of antitrust complaints, standstill agreements, or premium repurchases of the target's stock held by the bidder.

Kummer and Hoffmeister (1978) examine the abnormal returns associated with tender offers that are opposed and unopposed by target management. The average abnormal return of target shareholders in the announcement month is 16.45% ($t=15.16$) for the 44 successful targets in which managers did not oppose the offer, versus 19.80% ($t=13.62$) for 21 targets in which managers opposed the offer. Thus, managerial resistance is associated with higher premiums for offers that proved successful. However, fifteen of the 21 targets in which managers opposed the offer were not acquired within ten months, and the shareholders of these firms incurred abnormal losses of 11.7% in the ten months following the initial offer. This pattern of abnormal returns is consistent with our earlier interpretation of the stock price behavior of unsuccessful targets and with the results of Bradley, Desai and Kim (1983): Stock prices rise at the announcement of the initial bid and then decline if future takeover bids do not materialize. The Kummer and Hoffmeister results are consistent with the hypothesis that, on average, management opposition benefits target shareholders. The question remains, however, whether the shareholders of the targets of unsuccessful takeover bids could be made better off by less intensive managerial opposition — opposition that would allow their mergers to succeed without reducing the higher premiums in the otherwise successful offers. There appears to be an interesting free-rider problem here; although it might pay targets in general to establish a credible opposition threat, the costs to a particular target's

[34]See Easterbrook and Fischel (1981a, b, 1982a, b), Gilson (1981, 1982a, b), Bebchuk (1982a, b) and the references therein for discussion of various antitakeover tactics of target management and arguments regarding whether target management should remain passive in the presence of tender offers or whether they should take actions to help run an auction for the firm by encouraging competing bids. The effects of target management actions on the rewards to investment in takeover activities and therefore on the overall frequency of bids is an important aspect of this issue.

shareholders imply they would not want a manager to let an above market offer fail.

The higher average return to targets with managerial opposition to takeovers is also consistent with the hypothesis that such opposition harms stockholders of target firms by reducing the frequency of takeover offers. For example, the higher returns could arise because only the more highly profitable takeovers are pursued when bidders believe managerial opposition will lower the probability of success and raise the expected costs.[35] If managerial opposition simply raises costs, bids will be lower than they would be otherwise and low profit takeovers would not occur. As explained earlier, this truncation of the distribution of takeovers would raise the measured average profitability of manager-opposed takeovers. Since the target's board and management must approve a merger offer before it can go to a shareholder vote, hostile takeovers must be accomplished by gaining control of the board either through tender offers or other accumulation of shares or proxies. The evidence in tables 1 and 3 indicates that premiums to targets in tender offers are greater than premiums to targets in mergers. This could be due to the truncation phenomenon. Moreover the truncation hypothesis is consistent with the evidence that the gains to *bidders* are also larger in tender offers.

Dodd's (1980) evidence indicates that managerial opposition harms stockholders. He partitions his sample into 26 mergers that appear to be terminated by targets and 54 mergers that are terminated by either bidders or an unidentified party. In the target-terminated subsample, the cumulative abnormal returns from ten days prior to the first public announcement of the offer through ten days after termination is about +11% for the target firms. In contrast, the abnormal return over the same period for the 'bidder-terminated' subsample is an insignificant 0.2%. The average abnormal target return on the day before and day of termination announcement is a significant −5.57% for the cancellations by the target and a significant −9.75% for the cancellations by the bidder. If targets cancel mergers in anticipation of more profitable future takeover bids that will benefit stockholders, the abnormal returns to targets on announcement of cancellation would be positive rather than negative. The negative returns are consistent with the hypothesis that target managers who cancel such mergers are not acting in the stockholder's interest. In addition, the complete loss of gains to targets where bidders cancel indicates that when bidders back out (perhaps because they find they overestimated the value of the target), the target price returns to its pre-offer level.

[35]The costs associated with making an unsuccessful takeover bid sometimes go far beyond the search costs and the administrative, legal and other out of pocket expenses. See Ruback (1983b) for a discussion of the losses incurred by Gulf when they withdrew their bid for Cities Service.

4.5. Targeted large block stock repurchases

Currently available evidence suggests that managerial opposition to a takeover does not reduce shareholder wealth unless the resistance eliminates potential takeover bids. Two papers, Dann and DeAngelo (1983) and Bradley and Wakeman (1983), examine the effect on stockholder returns of privately negotiated or targeted stock repurchases. In a privately negotiated or targeted repurchase, a firm repurchases a block of its common stock from an individual holder, generally at a premium. These premiums can be interpreted as payments to potential bidders to cease takeover activity. The evidence indicates that such repurchases are associated with significantly negative abnormal stock returns for the shareholders of the repurchasing firm, and significantly positive abnormal returns for the sellers. Dann and DeAngelo report an average premium over the market price of 16.4% on 41 negotiated repurchases involving a premium, and for these 41 repurchases they report an average abnormal return on the repurchasing firm's stock of -1.76% ($t=-3.59$) on the day before and day of announcement. For 17 instances of non-premium targeted large block repurchases in which the price was equal to or below the market price, Dann and DeAngelo report insignificant average abnormal returns of -0.34% ($t=-0.33$) on the day before and day of announcement. Bradley and Wakeman report abnormal returns of -2.85% ($t=-5.82$) for 61 firms that repurchased a single block of common stock and abnormal returns of 1.40% ($t=2.24$) for 28 selling firms. They also present regression estimates indicating the total value of non-participating shareholders' stock declines dollar for dollar with increases in the premium paid to the seller, and that selling firm shareholders gain commensurately. The combined evidence presented by Dann and DeAngelo, and Bradley and Wakeman indicates that premium targeted large block repurchases reduce the wealth of non-participating stockholders.

The reductions in shareholder wealth associated with targeted repurchases suggest that explicit managerial actions to eliminate takeover bidders are costly to non-participating stockholders. Bradley and Wakeman reinforce this interpretation by examining 21 firms whose targeted repurchases were associated with a takeover cancellation. For these firms the average abnormal return the day prior to through the day after announcement of the repurchase is -5.50% ($t=-7.14$). Over the same event period, 40 firms that made targeted repurchases unaccompanied by merger cancellations experienced average abnormal returns of -1.39% ($t=-1.97$). Thus, targeted repurchases are more costly to non-participating stockholders when they are used to thwart takeover attempts.

The evidence on the negative effect of targeted repurchases on shareholder wealth is especially interesting when contrasted with the large positive abnormal returns ranging from 12.4% to 18.9% from the day before to 30 days after the announcement of non-targeted repurchase tender offers documented by Masulis (1980), Dann (1981), Vermaelen (1981) and Rosenfeld (1982).[36] Moreover, Dann and Vermaelen document positive abnormal returns of 4.1% and 3.4% for 121 and 243 open-market repurchases over the same event interval. Bradley and Wakeman report abnormal returns of 1.9% for repurchases from insiders, 1.6% for repurchases of small shareholdings, and 0.6% for 40 targeted repurchases where no merger bid is involved (all over the same 32-day event period). All these estimates of repurchase effects are positive and are in striking contrast to the average abnormal returns of −12.5% over the same 32-day event interval for two targeted share repurchases which involve a merger bid. The evidence provides fairly strong indications that targeted large block repurchases at premiums over market price reduce the wealth of non-participating shareholders.

4.6. Standstill agreements

Dann and DeAngelo (1983) examine the effects of standstill agreements on stock prices. Standstill agreements are voluntary contracts in which a firm agrees to limit its holdings of another firm, and, therefore, not to mount a takeover attempt. The 30 firms in their sample that obtained standstill agreements earned average abnormal returns of −4.52% ($t=-5.72$) on the day before and day of announcement of the agreement. In addition, the 19 firms entering standstill agreements that were unaccompanied by repurchases earned average abnormal returns of −4.04% ($t=-4.49$) in the same event period. Bradley and Wakeman (1983) present regression evidence suggesting that the 'news of the merger termination and the announcement of a standstill agreement have the same informational content'. This evidence also supports the hypothesis that managerial opposition that thwarts takeover bids reduces the wealth of non-participating stockholders.

4.7. Going private transactions

DeAngelo, DeAngelo and Rice (1982) examine the returns to stockholders in 72 'going private' proposals for firms listed on the New York or American Stock Exchanges in the period 1973–1980. In pure going private proposals the public stock ownership is replaced by full equity ownership by an incumbent management group and the stock is delisted. In leveraged buyouts (also included in their sample) management shares the equity with private outside investors. They find abnormal returns for the public stockholders of 30.4% ($t=12.4$) in the period 40 days before through the announcement of the going private proposal — gains that are virtually identical to the 29.1% weighted average returns in interfirm tender offers shown in table 3, panel A.

[36]Sample sizes range from 119 to 199.

They argue that the gains from going private are due to 'savings of registration and other public ownership expenses, and improved incentives for corporate decision makers under private ownership'. There is no evidence that outside stockholders are harmed in these transactions, which are commonly labeled 'minority freezeouts'. Moreover, the fact that stockholder litigation occurred in over 80% of the going private proposals that did not involve third parties provides a hint that these premiums are due to the blocking power typically accorded minority stockholders in going private transactions.

4.8. Direct evidence on stockholder control

The evidence on takeovers and actions that affect the probability of takeovers suggests that takeovers serve to limit managerial departures from maximization of stockholder wealth. Conflicts of interest between owners and managers can, however, be limited in the absence of takeovers through mergers or tender offers. Stockholders elect the board of directors and the board of directors directly monitors managers. Stockholders can change managers by electing a different board of directors, and voting rights and proxy contests are therefore important aspects of the general control process.

In this section we first examine the empirical evidence on internal transfers of control provided in the study by Dodd and Warner (1983) of the abnormal equity returns around the time of 96 proxy fights over the period 1962–1978. We then discuss the Lease, McConnell and Mikkelson (1983) study of the value of voting rights.

Proxy contests. In a proxy fight, dissident shareholders solicit votes to elect directors who differ from management's proposed slate. If the proxy fight results in dissidents obtaining a majority of seats on the board of directors, some change in corporate control occurs. Since both takeovers and proxy fights transfer control over assets, it is likely that the announcement of a proxy fight will be associated with an increase in equity value if the assets are to be put to superior uses. However, in a takeover the bidder offers a premium to target shareholders so that the stock price of the target can rise even if no higher value uses for the target's assets exists — the premium representing in this case a wealth transfer from bidding firm shareholders to target firm shareholders. Thus, examination of changes in equity value associated with proxy fights provides direct evidence on the gains resulting from changes in management and presumably, therefore, from changes in managerial decisions on resource utilization.

Dodd and Warner (1983) study a sample of 96 proxy contests in the period 1962–1978. They report that stockholders of firms realize a significant positive average abnormal return of 1.2% ($t=2.52$) on the day before and day of the first *Wall Street Journal* announcement of a control contest.

Furthermore, Dodd and Warner argue that information about the forthcoming proxy contest is available prior to the initial *Wall Street Journal* announcement, and that 1.2% is therefore a downward-biased estimate of the abnormal stock price increase due to the contest. Over the period 59 days before through the initial announcement of the contest the abnormal return is 11.9% ($t=5.09$). The significant positive abnormal return on the announcement day and the period prior to it suggests that proxy contests increase equity values and redirect the assets of the firm to more profitable uses. This implication is strengthened by the positive abnormal returns of 8.2% ($t=2.78$) over the period 59 days prior to contest announcement through the day of the election outcome announcement in the *Wall Street Journal*.

If the gains to stockholders associated with a proxy fight are due solely to potential changes in management, equity prices should decline when dissidents do not obtain board representation. The results in Dodd and Warner indicate that the acquisition of even partial dissident representation on the board is associated with positive abnormal returns, and complete failure to obtain representation results in negative abnormal returns. In 56 contests in which dissidents obtained seats on the board of directors, the abnormal return on the day before and day of the outcome announcement is 1.1% ($t=2.38$). Alternatively, in the 40 contests in which the dissidents failed to obtain seats, stock prices fell by 1.4% ($t=-1.67$) on the day before and day of the outcome announcement. However, the holding-period returns throughout the entire control contest indicate that the positive average effect of the contest is realized regardless of the outcome. Over the period sixty days prior to the initial announcement through the outcome announcement, the average abnormal return for contests in which dissidents win seats is virtually identical to that for contests in which dissidents win no seats. (These contest period estimates, of course, have much higher standard errors than the outcome announcement effects.)

Thus, while the relation between the revision in stock prices and announcement of the election outcome supports the importance of board representation, the magnitude of the revision is small relative to the total gains. The combined implication of the Dodd and Warner results is that, independent of the outcome, control contests increase equity values and the increase is larger when the dissidents win seats.

The value of control. We define corporate control as the rights to determine the management of corporate resources, and these rights are vested in the corporation's board of directors. Lease, McConnell and Mikkelson (1983) examine an important aspect of control, the value of rights to vote in elections to select the board of directors and to vote on other matters that require stockholder approval. They identify 30 firms that have two classes of common stock that differ only in their voting rights. Both classes have identical claims to dividends and are treated equally on liquidation. They calculate the ratio of month end prices for the two classes of stock over the time in which the two classes traded in the period 1940–1978. For 18 firms with voting and non-voting common stock and without voting preferred stock, the average premium for the voting stock is 3.79%. Of the 360 month end price ratios in their sample, 336 indicate that the voting stock traded at a premium. For the 9 firms without voting preferred stock that have two classes of voting common stock which differ only in voting rights, the common stock with superior voting rights traded at an average premium of 6.95% and 393 of the 468 month end price ratios indicate a premium for the stock with superior voting rights. Finally, for four firms with voting preferred, the class of common stock with superior voting rights traded at an average discount of 1.17%.

While the discount for stock with superior voting rights in firms that have voting preferred remains an unexplained puzzle, the weight of the Lease, McConnell and Mikkelson evidence indicates that voting rights are valuable. In addition, Dodd and Warner (1983) present evidence that voting rights are valuable. For 42 proxy contests with record dates that follow the initial announcement of the proxy contest, they report that stock prices fall on average by 1.4% ($t = -3.02$) on the day after the record date (the day the stock goes ex-vote).

5. Unsettled issues and directions for future research

Careful examination of the reaction of stock prices to various control-related events has greatly increased our understanding of the market for corporate control. Nevertheless, much remains to be learned, and the measurement of effects on stock prices will continue to play an important role in this research effort. We are, however, reaching the point of rapidly diminishing returns from efforts that focus *solely* on stock price effects. Further progress toward understanding the market for corporate control will be substantially aided by efforts that examine other organizational, technological and legal aspects of the environment in addition to the effects of takeovers on stock prices. Of course, the relationship between these other factors and stock price effects will be of continuing importance to future research. This section is devoted to discussion of a number of unsettled issues and suggests some directions for future research.

5.1. Competition among management teams

In our view the takeover market is an arena in which alternative management teams compete for the rights to manage corporate resources.[37]

[37]This phenomenon is made particularly evident by the simultaneous mutual tender offers that have become common recently, the so-called 'Pac Man' defense. See Herzel and Schmidt (1983) for a penetrating discussion of these offers.

In small takeovers management teams can consist of a single proprietor (with staff) or a partnership of managers. Competing management teams are also commonly organized in the corporate form, especially in large takeovers. In these cases the managerial team consists of the top-level internal managers and a board of directors. The board acts as the top-level control device and is the repository of the control rights acquired by the team. The competition among management teams is complex, and it is not yet fully described by theory or evidence. The following discussion, however, suggests an analytical approach and directions for future research.

The contractual setting. Analysis of the competition among management teams in the market for corporate control must begin with a specification of the analytically important aspects of the institutional and contractual environment.[38] In particular, the nature of the rights of each of the parties in the set of contracts that define the open corporation are important to the functioning of the market for corporate control. The corporation is a legal entity that serves as the nexus for a set of contracts among independent agents. One implication of this view is that the corporation has no owners. Instead, stockholders are agents in the nexus of contracts who specialize in riskbearing. Indeed, unrestricted common stock residual claims are the unique contractual aspect of the open corporate form that distinguishes it from all other forms of organization. Its residual claims are unrestricted in the sense that they are freely alienable and do not require the claimant to have any other role in the organization — in contrast, for example, to the residual claims of closed corporations that are generally restricted to agents with other roles in the organization. This unrestricted alienability enables separation of the riskbearing and management functions and therefore facilitates the realization of the benefits of specialization of these two functions. In this view, control of the agency problems of separation of residual riskbearing from management functions requires separation of the management function (initiation and implementation) from the control function (ratification and monitoring). Observation indicates this always occurs and that boards of directors or trustees are the common institutional device for accomplishing this separation.

The board of directors in the open corporation is elected by vote of the residual claimants who, while retaining the rights to ratify certain major decisions by shareholder vote, delegate most management and control rights to the board. The board in turn delegates most of its management and control rights to the internal managers while retaining the rights to ratify certain major decisions. Most importantly, the board of directors always retains the top-level control rights, that is, the rights to hire, fire and set the compensation of the top-level managers. Board membership consists of

[38]This discussion draws on the analysis in Jensen and Meckling (1976, 1979), Fama (1980), and especially Fama and Jensen (1983a, b).

internal managers and external agents with expertise of value to the organization. Moreover, the complex contractual arrangements that define the open corporation are embedded in a legal system that further defines the contracts and rights of the parties. For example, the legal system imposes fiduciary responsibility on board members and managers and delineates the legal rights and remedies available to shareholders who challenge the actions of board members and managers.

The unrestricted alienability of the common stock residual claims of the open corporation is essential to the existence of the market for control. Unrestricted alienability allows the existence of a stock market that facilitates transfer and valuation of the claims at low cost. Low cost transferability makes it possible for competing outside managers to bypass the current management and board of directors to acquire the rights to manage the corporation's resources. These control rights can be acquired by direct solicitation of stockholders, either through tender offers or proxy solicitation. Outside management teams can also acquire the management rights by merger negotiations with the target's management and board subject to ratification by vote of the stockholders.

The internal control system has its foundation in the corporate charter and is strengthened or weakened by day to day operating practices and procedures and by the quality of the individuals who hold board seats and positions in top management. Competition from alternative management teams in the market for corporate control serves as a source of external control on the internal control system of the corporation. Alternative institutional forms such as professional partnerships, non-profit organizations and mutuals do not receive the benefits of competition from alternative management teams in an external control market.[39] Of course, internal competition in each of these organizations and the external regulatory environment (such as in banking) contributes to the control function. But the corporation alone receives the benefits of the private external control market in addition to the internal control mechanisms.

When a breakdown of the internal control system imposes large costs on shareholders from incompetent, lazy or dishonest managers, takeover bids in the market for corporate control provide a vehicle for replacing the entire internal control system. Competing managers who perceive the opportunity to eliminate the inefficiencies can offer target shareholders a higher-valued alternative than current management while benefiting their own shareholders and themselves. Similar incentives come into play when the acquisition of substantial synergy gains requires displacement of an efficient current management team.

[39]Fama and Jensen (1983a, b, c) provide detailed analyses of these alternative organizational forms and their survival properties. Mayers and Smith (1981, 1982) and Smith (1982) provide a discussion of conflict resolution, contracting practices and the differences between mutual and corporate organizational forms in the insurance and banking industries.

Management teams receive the assistance of legal and financial institutions with expertise in both offensive and defensive takeover strategies. Sometimes this assistance is acquired under direct contract (for example, legal services) and on other occasions the assistance is provided by independent agents acting in their own interest. Takeover specialists, sometimes referred to as 'raiders' — who acquire specialized expertise in takeover strategy and in ferreting out and amassing a controlling block of shares — perform an important function in facilitating transfers of control. Such agents may or may not take control of a firm. They can succeed solely by developing expertise in discovering companies where potential takeover gains exist and in amassing blocks of shares sufficient to enable other management teams to acquire the control rights. The takeover specialists' gains come from transferring their shares to these other acquirers at the takeover price. Arbitrageurs perform an important role by specializing in valuing the competing offers and providing a market that allows investors to delegate both the valuation and riskbearing function during the takeover period.

5.2. Directions for future research

Many interesting and important research issues are suggested by the managerial competition view of the market for corporate control. It also suggests new perspectives on a number of unresolved issues that promise significant advances in the development of a theory of organizations.[40]

Examination of the costs and benefits to competing management teams of success or failure in the takeover market will aid in understanding the forces that determine when and why takeovers are initiated, and why target managers oppose or acquiesce to such proposals. Factual knowledge about the career paths and compensation experience of bidder and target management personnel will be valuable in such efforts. For example: How does management turnover frequency in takeover situations compare with that in non-takeover conditions? Do target managers lose their jobs more frequently in unfriendly takeovers than in friendly or 'white knight' acquisitions? What happens to the managers of targets who successfully avoid takeover? When target managers remain with the merged firm, how do they fare in compensation, rank and rapidity of promotion in the merged firm? How do target managers who leave the merged entity fare in the external labor market? What happens to managers of successful and unsuccessful bidding firms, and how does their experience (compensation, promotion, etc.) relate to the stock price effects of the outcomes? What is the relative frequency with which takeovers are motivated by inefficient target management versus the acquisition of other economies or synergies? What

[40]See Jensen (1983) for a discussion and overall perspective on organisation theory and methodology and the emerging revolution in the science of organizations.

are the synergies that contribute to takeover gains? How are takeover frequency and terms affected by (1) antitakeover amendments, (2) golden parachutes (that is, contractual employment guarantees and compensation in the event of control changes), and (3) various other managerial actions to oppose takeovers?

The definition of the market for corporate control as the arena in which managers compete for resources to manage raises a variety of questions regarding the form of the competition. Takeover strategies, both offensive and defensive, have received relatively little attention in the academic literature. The managerial competition model provides an interesting framework for the evaluation of alternative strategies. For example, bidders in hostile takeovers typically try to reduce the time that the offer is outstanding by keeping it secret prior to its announcement and by structuring offers (e.g., two-part offers) so that early tendering is beneficial to shareholders. Incumbent managers attempt to lengthen the time that an offer is outstanding. These opposing strategies are consistent with managerial competition; the bidder tries to reduce the incumbent management team's ability to compete, and targets want more time to respond to the bid or to seek out other bidders that offer better opportunities for themselves and their shareholders. This is consistent with the observation that potential targets prepare takeover defenses prior to the occurrence of a hostile bid.

The managerial competition perspective also helps explain the types of defensive strategies used by target firms. For example, suppose the incumbent management team has reliable information that its equity is underpriced. If this information cannot be made public, the managerial competition model predicts that incumbent managers will attempt to find a white knight. The information could be released to the white knight, perhaps through a confidential information center, and both the incumbent management team and the shareholders of the target would benefit. While this analysis is preliminary and speculative, the interactions between the incentives of competing management teams and the strategies they adopt is an interesting area for future research. Knowledge resulting from such research will allow us to understand better the determinants of the offer, such as structure (single or two part, cash or exchange of securities), timing, type of offer (tender, merger, or proxy contest), and tax effects. Understanding takeover strategy also requires more detailed knowledge of the effects of voting rules [see Easterbrook and Fischel (1983)], the determinants of effective control, the effects of institutional ownership, and the effects of specialized takeover agents and arbitrageurs [see Wyser-Pratte (1982)].

Detailed knowledge of the control market should also provide insights regarding the reasons for spinoffs and divestitures, and why joint ventures, which can be thought of as partial mergers, are used in some cases and not in others. Why, for example, are joint ventures often used for new ventures and not for ongoing operations, for example, by divestiture of a corporate division into a joint venture with outside partners? A thorough understanding of spinoffs, divestitures, takeovers and joint ventures should also help us understand the discounts and premiums on closed-end funds and, in particular, why closed-end funds selling at substantial discounts are not either liquidated or turned into open-end funds [see Thompson (1978)].

Finally, a number of more familiar issues require substantial additional research to complete our knowledge. No one as yet has studied the prices paid by white knights in mergers; folklore holds that embattled target managers search out such friendly merger partners to rescue them from an unfriendly takeover. But if the takeover premiums paid by white knights are generally no lower than other offers, shareholders are not harmed. In addition, precise measurement of the returns to bidders in takeovers is still an unsettled issue. Finally, knowledge of the sources of takeover gains still eludes us.

5.3. Conclusions

Many controversial issues regarding the market for corporate control have yet to be settled and many new issues have yet to be studied. It is clear, however, that much is now known about this market. Indeed, it is unlikely that any set of transactions has been studied in such detail. In brief, the evidence seems to indicate that corporate takeovers generate positive gains, that target firm shareholders benefit, and that bidding firm shareholders do not lose. Moreover, the gains created by corporate takeovers do not appear to come from the creation of market power. Finally, it is difficult to find managerial actions related to corporate control that harm stockholders; the exceptions are those actions that eliminate an actual or potential bidder, for example, through the use of targeted large block repurchases or standstill agreements.

While research on the market for corporate control has mushroomed, it is, in our opinion, a growth industry. Much exciting and valuable knowledge remains to be discovered, and there are valuable prospects for beneficial interdisciplinary exchange among lawyers, economists, accountants, and organization theorists. An important result of this research will be a greatly expanded set of knowledge about the functioning of this enormously productive social invention: the corporation.[41]

[41]See also Meckling and Jensen (1982).

References

Asquith, Paul, 1980, A two-event study of merger bids, market uncertainty, and stockholder returns, Ph.D. dissertation (University of Chicago, Chicago, IL).

Asquith, Paul, 1983, Merger bids, uncertainty, and stockholder returns, Journal of Financial Economics 11, this issue.
Asquith, Paul, Robert F. Bruner and David W. Mullins, Jr., 1983, The gains to bidding firms from merger, Journal of Financial Economics 11, this issue.
Asquith, Paul and E. Han Kim, 1982, The impact of merger bids on the participating firms' security holders, Journal of Finance 37, 1209–1228.
Bebchuk, Lucian, 1982a, The case for facilitating competing tender offers: A reply and extension, Stanford Law Review 35, 23ff.
Bebchuk, Lucian, 1982b, The case for facilitating competing tender offers, Harvard Law Review 95, 1028ff.
Benston, George J., 1980, Conglomerate mergers: Causes, consequences, and remedies (American Enterprise Institute for Public Policy Research, Washington, DC).
Bradley, Michael, 1980, Interfirm tender offers and the market for corporate control, Journal of Business 53, 345–376.
Bradley, Michael, Anand Desai and E. Han Kim, 1982, Specialized resources and competition in the market for corporate control, Working paper (University of Michigan, Ann Arbor, MI).
Bradley, Michael, Anand Desai and E. Han Kim, 1983, The rationale behind interfirm tender offers: Information or synergy?, Journal of Financial Economics 11, this issue.
Bradley, Michael and L. MacDonald Wakeman, 1983, The wealth effects of targeted share repurchases, Journal of Financial Economics 11, this issue.
Brown, Stephen J. and Jerold B. Warner, 1980, Measuring security price performance, Journal of Financial Economics 8, 205–258.
Brown, Stephen J. and Jerold B. Warner, 1983, Using daily stock returns in event studies, Unpublished manuscript (University of Rochester, Rochester, NY).
Chandler, Alfred D., Jr., 1962, Strategy and structure (MIT Press, Cambridge, MA).
Chandler, Alfred D., Jr., 1977, The visible hand: The managerial revolution (Belknapp Press, Cambridge, MA).
Dann, Larry Y., 1981, Common stock repurchases: An analysis of returns to bondholders and stockholders, Journal of Financial Economics 9, 113–138.
Dann, Larry Y. and Harry DeAngelo, 1983, Standstill agreements, privately negotiated stock repurchases, and the market for corporate control, Journal of Financial Economics 11, this issue.
Dann, Larry Y. and Wayne H. Mikkelson, 1982, Convertible debt issuance, capital structure change and leverage-related information: Some new evidence, Unpublished manuscript (Amos Tuck School of Business, Hanover, NH).
DeAngelo, Harry, Linda DeAngelo and Edward M. Rice, 1982, Going private: Minority freezeouts and stockholder wealth, Managerial Economics Research Center working paper no. MERC 82-18 (Graduate School of Management, University of Rochester, Rochester, NY).
DeAngelo, Harry and Edward M. Rice, 1983, Antitakeover charter amendments and stockholder wealth, Journal of Financial Economics 11, this issue.
Dodd, Peter, 1980, Merger proposals, management discretion and stockholder wealth, Journal of Financial Economics 8, 105–138.
Dodd, Peter and Richard Leftwich, 1980, The market for corporate charters: 'Unhealthy competition' versus federal regulation, Journal of Business 53, 259–283.
Dodd, Peter and Richard Ruback, 1977, Tender offers and stockholder returns: An empirical analysis, Journal of Financial Economics 5, 351–374.
Dodd, Peter and Jerold B. Warner, 1983, On corporate governance: A study of proxy contests, Journal of Financial Economics 11, this issue.
Easterbrook, Frank H. and Daniel R. Fischel, 1981a, The proper role of a target's management in responding to a tender offer, Harvard Law Review 94, 1161–1203.
Easterbrook, Frank H. and Daniel R. Fischel, 1981b, Takeover bids, defensive tactics, and shareholders' welfare, The Business Lawyer 36, 1733–1750.
Easterbrook, Frank H. and Daniel R. Fischel, 1982a, Corporate control transactions, Yale Law Journal 91, 698–737.
Easterbrook, Frank H. and Daniel R. Fischel, 1982b, Auctions and sunk costs in tender offers, Stanford Law Review 35, 1–21.
Easterbrook, Frank H. and Daniel R. Fischel, 1983, Voting in corporate law, Journal of Law and Economics 26, June, forthcoming.

Eckbo, B. Espen, 1983, Horizontal mergers, collusion, and stockholder wealth, Journal of Financial Economics 11, this issue.
Ellert, J.C., 1975, Antitrust enforcement and the behavior of stock prices, Unpublished dissertation (University of Chicago, Chicago, IL).
Ellert, J.C., 1976, Mergers, antitrust law enforcement and stockholder returns, Journal of Finance 31, 715–732.
Fama, Eugene F., 1980, Agency problems and the theory of the firm, Journal of Political Economy 88, 288–307.
Fama, Eugene F., Larry Fisher, Michael C. Jensen and Richard Roll, 1969, The adjustment of stock prices to new information, International Economic Review 10, 1–21.
Fama, Eugene F. and Michael C. Jensen, 1983a, Separation of ownership and control, Journal of Law and Economics 26, June, forthcoming.
Fama, Eugene F. and Michael C. Jensen, 1983b, Agency problems and residual claims, Journal of Law and Economics 26, June, forthcoming.
Fama, Eugene F. and Michael C. Jensen, 1983c, Organizational forms and investment decisions, Managerial Economics Research Center working paper no. MERC 83-03, April (Graduate School of Management, University of Rochester, Rochester, NY).
Gilson, Ronald J., 1981, A structural approach to corporations: The case against defensive tactics in tender offers, Stanford Law Review 33, 819–891.
Gilson, Ronald J., 1982a, The case against shark repellent amendments: Structural limitations on the enabling concept, Stanford Law Review 34, 775–836.
Gilson, Ronald J., 1982b, Seeking competitive bids versus pure passivity in tender offer defense, Stanford Law Review 35, 51–67.
Grossman, S. and O. Hart, 1980, Takeover bids, the free-rider problem, and the theory of the corporation, Bell Journal of Economics, Spring, 42–64.
Herzel, Leo and John R. Schmidt, 1983, Simultaneous mutual tender offers, Unpublished manuscript, March (Mayer, Brown and Platt, Chicago, IL).
Jarrell, Gregg and Michael Bradley, 1980, The economic effects of federal and state regulations of cash tender offers, Journal of Law and Economics 23, 371–407.
Jensen, Michael C., 1983, Organization theory and methodology, Accounting Review 58, 319–339.
Jensen, Michael C. and William H. Meckling, 1976, Theory of the firm: Managerial behavior, agency costs and ownership structure, Journal of Financial Economics 3, 305–360.
Jensen, Michael C. and William H. Meckling, 1979, Rights and production functions: An application to labor-managed firms and codetermination, Journal of Business 52, 469–506.
Keown, Arthur J. and John M. Pinkerton, 1981, Merger announcements and insider trading activity: An empirical investigation, Journal of Finance 36, 855–869.
Kim, H. and J. McConnell, 1977, Corporate mergers and co-insurance of corporate debt, Journal of Finance 32, 349–363.
Klein, Benjamin, Robert Crawford and Armen A. Alchian, 1978, Vertical integration, appropriable rents, and the competitive contracting process, Journal of Law and Economics 21, 297–326.
Kummer, D. and R. Hoffmeister, 1978, Valuation consequences of cash tender offers, Journal of Finance 33, 505–516.
Langetieg, T., 1978, An application of a three-factor performance index to measure stockholders gains from merger, Journal of Financial Economics 6, 365–384.
Lease, Ronald C., John J. McConnell and Wayne H. Mikkelson, 1983, The market value of control in publicly-traded corporations, Journal of Financial Economics 11, this issue.
Linn, Scott C. and John J. McConnell, 1983, An empirical investigation of the impact of 'antitakeover' amendments on common stock prices, Journal of Financial Economics 11, this issue.
Malatesta, Paul H., 1981, Corporate mergers, Unpublished Ph.D. dissertation (University of Rochester, Rochester, NY).
Malatesta, Paul H., 1983, The wealth effect of merger activity and the objective functions of merging firms, Journal of Financial Economics 11, this issue.
Mandelker, Gershon, 1974, Risk and return: The case of merging firms, Journal of Financial Economics 1, 303–335.

Manne, Henry G., 1965, Mergers and the market for corporate control, Journal of Political Economy 73, 110–120.
Masulis, Ronald W., 1980a, The effects of capital structure change on security prices: A study of exchange offers, Journal of Financial Economics 8, 139–178.
Masulis, Ronald W., 1980b, Stock repurchase by tender offer: An analysis of the causes of common stock price changes, Journal of Finance 35, 305–319.
Mayers, David and Clifford W. Smith, Jr., 1981, Contractual provisions, organizational structure, and conflict control in insurance markets, Journal of Business 54, 407–434.
Mayers, David and Clifford W. Smith, Jr., 1982, Toward a positive theory of insurance, Monograph 1982-1 (Salomon Brothers Center for the Study of Financial Institutions, New York University, New York, NY).
Meckling, William H. and Michael C. Jensen, 1982, Reflections on the corporation as a social invention, in: Controlling the giant corporation: A symposium (Center for Research in Government Policy and Business, Graduate School of Management, University of Rochester, Rochester, NY).
Mikkelson, Wayne H., 1981, Convertible calls and security returns, Journal of Financial Economics 9, 237–264.
Mikkelson, Wayne H., 1983, Capital structure change and decreases in stockholders' wealth, Proceedings of Conference on Corporate Capital Structures in the United States (National Bureau of Economic Research, Cambridge, MA) forthcoming.
Myers, Stewart C. and Nicholas J. Majluf, 1981, Stock issues and investment policy when firms have information that investors do not have, Working paper no. 1258-81 (Massachusetts Institute of Technology, Cambridge, MA).
Palepue, Krishna, 1983, The determinants of acquisition likelihood, Unpublished manuscript (Harvard University, Boston, MA).
Rosenfeld, Ahron, 1982, Repurchase offers: Information adjusted premiums and shareholders' response, Working paper (Krannert Graduate School of Management, Purdue University, West Lafayette, IN).
Ruback, Richard S., 1982, The Conoco takeover and stockholder returns, Sloan Management Review 23, 13–33.
Ruback, Richard S., 1983a, Assessing competition in the market for corporate acquisitions, Journal of Financial Economics 11, this issue.
Ruback, Richard S., 1983b, The Cities Service takeover: A case study, Journal of Finance, May, forthcoming.
Schipper, Katherine and Rex Thompson, 1983a, Evidence on the capitalized value of merger activity for acquiring firms, Journal of Financial Economics 11, this issue.
Schipper, Katherine and Rex Thompson, 1983b, The impact of merger-related regulations on the shareholders of acquiring firms, Journal of Accounting Research 21, forthcoming.
Scholes, Myron, 1972, Market for securities: Substitution versus price pressure and the effects of information on share prices, Journal of Business 45, 179–211.
Smiley, Robert, 1975, The effect of the Williams amendment and other factors on transactions costs in tender offers, Industrial Organization Review 3, 138–145.
Smith, Clifford W., Jr., 1977, Alternative methods for raising capital: Rights versus underwritten offerings, Journal of Financial Economics 5, 273–307.
Smith, Clifford W., Jr., 1982, Pricing mortgage originations, Areuea Journal 10, 313–330.
Stillman, Robert, 1983, Examining antitrust policy toward horizontal mergers, Journal of Financial Economics 11, this issue.
Thompson, Rex, 1978, Closed-end investment companies: The implications of discounts and premiums for efficiency in the capital markets and the market for corporate control, Ph.D. dissertation (University of Rochester, Rochester, NY).
Vermaelen, T., 1981, Common stock repurchases and market signalling: An empirical study, Journal of Financial Economics 9, 139–183.
Wier, Peggy G., 1983, The costs of antimerger lawsuits: Evidence from the stock market, Journal of Financial Economics 11, this issue.
Williamson, Oliver E., 1975, Markets and hierarchies: Analysis and antitrust implications (Free Press, New York, NY).
Williamson, Oliver E., 1981, The modern corporation: Origins, evolution, attributes, Journal of Economic Literature 19, 1537–1568.
Wyser-Pratte, Guy P., 1982, Risk arbitrage II, Monograph 1982-3-4 (Salomon Brothers Center for the Study of Financial Institutions, New York University, New York, NY).

Part II
Insider Trading

[5]

An unorthodox view that discounts the harm and highlights the gain from what is generally taken for granted as being a bad practice.

In Defense of Insider Trading

By Henry G. Manne

In April 1965, when the Securities and Exchange Commission announced its action against executives of the Texas Gulf Sulphur Company for alleged violations of rules against insider trading, there was an outcry of public indignation against the defendants. It was as though men who were highly respected members of the community had suddenly been found out in heinous crime.

But this is only one more manifestation of a long and persistent trend. The main push came with the Pecora hearings in Congress in 1933–1934, where the activities of prominent executives who conceded playing some part in insider trading were characterized as "immoral," "unscrupulous," "unfair," a "betrayal of fiduciary duties," and a "vicious practice." [1] Since that time, leading academic figures, lawyers, businessmen, and spokesmen for the SEC, with almost boring uniformity, have castigated insider trading as being costly to shareholders and giving unfair and undeserved gains to insiders. The tone of most discussions on this subject suggests that there is no doubt whatever: insider trading is a sin, and the war against it is a holy one.

But, as in most holy wars, self-righteousness and hypocrisy may be the true order of the day. In the entire literature on insider trading there does not exist one careful analysis of the subject. Lawyers have been having a field day arguing about the meaning of words or the reach of the last case or any of a thousand technical and legal issues. Unfortunately, however, most lawyers do not have the skills to develop a careful economic analysis of the subject, and economists have offered no assistance. The tone of debate has remained essentially moralistic and question-begging. Logic has been totally lost to emotion.

It is very likely, however, that unless businessmen, commentators, and the courts wake up, far more than logic will be lost. For the current attack on insider trading may prove to be a fundamental attack on free capital markets and entrepreneurial capitalism. It would be a shame to lose the battle by default.

Careful analysis of insider trading requires consideration of at least three major questions:

(1) Who gains and who loses from insider trading? (We cannot assume that the shareowners who should be protected are necessarily the same people who are in danger of being hurt.)

(2) What are the long-run consequences of disallowing insider trading? (Even if some individuals may be hurt by it, the economy may be hurt more if we remove the incentive effect of such trading.)

(3) Can insider trading be prevented, and at what financial and social cost? (There are many indirect devices for trading in information, and they can be very subtle and hard to trace.)

AUTHOR'S NOTE: For fuller discussion and more technical details see my just-published book, *Insider Trading and the Stock Market* (New York, The Free Press, 1966).

[1] *Stock Exchange Practices, Hearings before the Committee on Banking and Currency*, U.S. Senate, 73rd Congress, 1st Session.

Full answers to these questions must await years of study and research, but we know quite a bit already and can confidently deduce quite a bit more.

This article constitutes at least a starting point for logical analysis of the subject. In particular, I shall argue that insider trading is the best, if not the only, method of adequately compensating corporate innovators, and I shall attempt to define and to answer objections to the practice of insider trading.

Gain & Loss

What, if any, advantages would flow to participants in the stock market if insider trading were effectively stopped? Here we come to one of the most astounding facts in this whole astounding business: the only stock market participants who are likely to benefit from a rule preventing insider trading are the short-term speculators and traders, not the long-term investors who are regularly stated to be the objects of the SEC's solicitude.

The initial error of most commentators is the assumption that the persons who sold to insiders before disclosure of important news would not have sold at all if the insiders were not in the market. Obviously this is absurd; the average seller has no way in the world of knowing the identity of his buyer. One of the great virtues of an organized securities market is its automaticity, which results in anonymity of traders. Publicly traded companies are quite different in this respect from small, closely held corporations, and the rules governing them should also be different.

If insiders are in the market, however, they represent additional buying power over what would prevail without them. So there must be some sellers in the market who can be said to sell only because of the insider's buying. But this is only the beginning of analysis. We need to know the identity of these additional sellers, and also we want to see if there is any benefit from the insider's trading activities that may counteract any harmful effects of this additional purchasing power.

Investors vs. Traders

To discover the identity of sellers who would not trade but for the insider's activities, we must first distinguish two types of shareholders — investors and traders. This distinction has certainly been overworked for many purposes, but it is of considerable value in the present analysis:

▼ Investors, the long-term shareholders, tend to select stocks based on so-called "fundamental" factors, such as earning potential, dividend history, growth prospects, or the reputation of management, to mention just a few. And they select stocks suitable for their own particular investment needs. They tend to sell either because their estimate of the fundamental factors proved wrong or because of some change in their personal circumstances or needs. They almost never buy or sell because of short-swing fluctuations in the price of a security.

▲ Short-swing traders, whether we call them "speculators" or not, may also trade on so-called "fundamental" factors. But many of them, unlike any of the true investors, also buy or sell simply because of recent changes in the price of a security. That is, they assume their ability to predict future price changes from previous changes in price and volume — so-called "technical" factors. And very many of these traders simply are gambling.

This is not the place to enter the debate on whether technical strategies can ever be used successfully, though a growing academic literature is casting grave doubts on the validity of technical factors as determinants of stock price movements. The importance of this trading for our purposes is that any price change is taken as a signal by the "technicians" in the market, or by the gamblers, to buy or sell. Consequently, as insiders cause a price rise by adding their buying power to the market, the selling necessary to complete the additional transactions will ordinarily be supplied by short-term traders. It cannot and should not be denied that the stock market provides the greatest competition for Las Vegas and the racetracks we have. This is not intended as criticism. But it is seriously disturbing to find the SEC pressing hard for a rule designed either to aid this group or to encourage their gambling proclivities.

In aggregate, the gamblers in a perfectly free stock market, with no inflation, are bound to lose money. Just as the house's cut in the gambling casino guarantees the long-term gambler a loss, so stockbrokerage commissions on each transaction must injure the steady stock trader who has no valid information. Furthermore, as we noticed previously, he often supplies the stock on which insiders profit. Thus he is matching wits with an expert in a game which does not pay off for amateurs. Perhaps the analogy to gambling against someone with loaded dice or marked cards is most apt.

How Much Harm?

Though statistically this is probably not significant, the long-term investor may turn out to be the individual who in fact sells to the insider. But since he is normally selling for reasons unrelated to the insider's trading, and would be selling in any event, he should be indifferent to the identity of his buyer. Actually, he may benefit from the insider's buying on good news, as the average price received may be higher with than without insider trading. For example:

> Let us assume that a stock is selling at $50, with undisclosed good news which will *ultimately* cause the stock to sell for $60, and that no factors other than the good news will affect the price.
>
> Suppose, further, that with insider trading the price of the shares rises *gradually* to $60. The average price at which shares sell during this period is somewhere in the neighborhood of $55 (more or less depending on the shape of the time-price curve). At $60, anyone who has held his shares will have received the full benefit of the new information whether it is disclosed to him or not. This advantage to the ultimate holder remains even if we effectively prevent insider trading.
>
> Without insider trading, however, the position of those who sell during the time required for the price to rise from $50 to $60 is radically altered. No longer do they receive an average price of $55. Assuming that the ultimate disclosure is made at the same time under either rule, they receive only $50 for their shares without insider trading. In short, they get less than they would with insider trading.

It may be argued that this overstates the direct advantages from insider trading. For, in fact, during the same relevant time period investors will be buying as well as selling, and — to take the same example — with insider trading they might buy at an average price of $55, while without it they would buy at an average price of $50. If the number of buyers among investors is the same as the number of sellers, then we are simply back where we started; the gains and losses cancel out (though not necessarily for the same individuals). It may be true, however, that a gradual price increase will cause fewer investment decisions to buy relative to decisions to sell than would be the case with an abrupt price change. (The difference, of course, is accounted for by other traders.) On balance, therefore, insider trading may still benefit investors.

Even if there is no appreciable net direct advantage or disadvantage to investors as a group from insider trading, it is likely that price fluctuations will not be so sharp, part of the excitement which attracts the gambler may be lost, and the occasionally valid "hot tip" will not pay off as much. Are not these all advantages, rather than disadvantages?

Wary Insiders

When it is further realized how rare significant insider trading must be, one wonders even more what all the shouting has been about. If insider trading does occur, insiders as a group trade in the stock market with greater certainty and success than do those not using fresh, reliable information. Accordingly, successful inside traders may tend to gamble in the stock market much less than all other traders, since they will more often have "sure things." This conservatism suggests that they have several likely attitudes toward their trading:

¶ The insider tends not to trade on information unless it will be very significant quantitatively. It must be of sufficient importance that the conservative trader, recognizing the natural uncertainties of the marketplace, will still trade.

¶ He must have some assurance that the information is not already or shortly to be in the hands of many other individuals; for if it is, he cannot expect to realize the full potential of his data.

¶ He will probably move very quickly to take his profit and get out of the market, since the longer he stays in, the more subject he will be to vagaries of the market which he can neither control nor know about in advance. Of course, the tax benefits for gains on assets held for six months influence him in the other direction, but an insider still has considerable incentive to buy and sell quickly.

Each of these phenomena reflects a recognition that the market is always full of uncertainties. A huge copper ore find may be followed closely by a collapse of world copper prices, and an important earnings increase may coincide with announcement of a tax hike. Thus even the most conservative insider can only deal in probabilities; and if he knows that he will regularly be privy to information, he will probably tend to trade only on that with the highest probability of allowing a gain.

Similarly, the longer stock is held, the greater

becomes the risk that other factors will develop and counteract his existing paper profits. Again conservatism will dictate speed, not greed. Only rarely will all the necessary conditions for effective, regular insider trading be met. Great developments, measured in stock price impact, do not happen very often in any company. And news of these occurrences is not always the exclusive property of a few insiders. Therefore really significant trading by insiders is probably not a very common occurrence.

Stimulus to Innovation

If this is all that could be said for or against insider trading, the matter would not be a very interesting one. But there is another and far more crucial facet to the issue, one which has not been noted in the existing literature. Basically, the argument is that profits from insider trading constitute the only effective compensation scheme for entrepreneurial services in large corporations.

Critical Distinction

I should begin this discussion with some explanation of what is meant by the "entrepreneurial function." The term is used here in a technical, economic sense, and the function differs in critical respects from that performed by managers:

Entrepreneur — An Innovator. Fundamentally the entrepreneur is a man who finds a new product or a new way to make or sell an old one. He may reorganize corporate administration, or he may be responsible for the merger of two companies. He may be a corporate promoter, or he may perform the job of selecting and guiding the managers. In short, he is the individual responsible for having or taking a new idea and causing it to be put into effect. A critical part of this definition is the "new idea," but there is no payoff unless the idea is put into effect successfully.

Since the value of an entrepreneur's contribution cannot be known until it has been made, there is rarely any way of appraising his services in advance. This is undoubtedly why early economists, including Adam Smith, did not see the entrepreneurial function as being distinct from the capitalist's function, for in the eighteenth century one was generally required to risk his own money to prove the value of his innovation. The return for successful innovation looks, superficially at least, like the return to the owner of capital.

Today, however, a sizable portion of economic literature, introduced principally by the late Joseph A. Schumpeter of Harvard University, has been built on the distinction between the entrepreneur and the capitalist, though it has not yet had a great impact on popular thinking.

Manager — A Technician. The management function is, in the pure sense, simply to administer a business along lines already determined. Though it may be extraordinarily complex and highly paid, the manager's job is basically that of a technician. As soon as he begins to reorganize the existing arrangement, then and only then is the executive performing an innovational or entrepreneurial activity, rather than a management function. Again the distinction between functions remains even though the same individual performs both. As Schumpeter commented, it is "just as rare for anyone always to remain an entrepreneur through the decades of his active life as it is for a businessman never to have a moment in which he is an entrepreneur, to however modest a degree." [2]

Reward for Performance

In return for performing its function, management receives its compensation, generally termed by economists the "wage." This wage is simply the market price for managerial skills. No one knowingly pays more or takes less. Similarly, the capitalist receives "interest," which, whatever the legal form might be called, is the economic return to him. It may be relatively certain, as in the case of bonds, or it may be very indefinite, as with speculative securities; but its economic nature remains the same. Although the degrees of risk may vary greatly, interest is the price that has to be paid for the use of money over time.

But in the sense that wages and interest are the market return for capital and management, there is no such thing as a market price for entrepreneurial skills. In fact, almost by definition, it is impossible to value entrepreneurial activities *before they have paid off in some other form*. Economic theorists do, however, have a word for the entrepreneurial return; it is termed "profit," although that particular usage of the word has not received popular acceptance. But, aside from having a word for it, we have little knowledge about the particular form that this "profit" may take, or even whether it can redound to the benefit of entrepreneurs in large corporations.

[2] Joseph Alois Schumpeter, *The Theory of Economic Development*, translated by Redvers Opie (Cambridge, Harvard University Press, 1934), p. 78.

Here it is important to turn once more to Schumpeter. Perhaps his greatest contribution to modern economic theory was the concept of dynamic competition. Schumpeter pointed out that where enterprise is allowed a free rein, no one can afford to stand still. His famous "perennial gale of creative destruction" is the process by which the most significant competition occurs. This is the competition created by the true entrepreneur, and it is a fierce thing.

Schumpeter thought that price competition, so loved by antitrusters, was effete indeed compared to the competitive effects of new products, new markets, and new ways of doing things. On this point he may well have been right. Price competition could probably be administered by pure managers, corporate bureaucrats, or today even by carefully programmed computers. But that kind of activity could never withstand the onslaught of the real entrepreneur.

Survival of Capitalism

For all his brilliance in developing the theory of entrepreneurship and dynamic competition, Schumpeter made a serious and well-known error concerning the American corporate system. This error occurred in his famous *Capitalism, Socialism and Democracy*, published in 1942.[3] Briefly, it was that the system of corporate capitalism simply could not survive. He believed that large corporations would become completely bureaucratized and management-oriented. He felt that innovation had been routinized, and the "romance of earlier commercial adventure" no longer characterized business leaders' activities. This routinization of innovation would first destroy the capitalist entrepreneurs as a class, and eventually capitalism would disappear for lack of an effective champion. "The true pacemakers of socialism," he said, "were not the intellectuals or agitators who preached it but the Vanderbilts, Carnegies, and Rockefellers."

It requires no argument to realize how wrong Schumpeter was in this prediction. For all their organization and bureaucratization, American corporations seem as dynamic, innovative, and entrepreneurial today as they have ever been. What, then, could explain such a gross misconception by one of the leading economic scholars of the century? The answer to this question seems to have eluded theoreticians up to now.

Closer examination of Schumpeter's arguments may explain his error. Schumpeter stated that any form of compensation for corporate executives other than salaries and bonuses was either "illegal or semi-illegal." Yet he realized that salary and bonuses were appropriate forms of compensation only for the pure management function. Entrepreneurs would require something much grander, though less certain. And since Schumpeter felt that this could not be made available to them in the large corporation, he assumed that they would disappear from the large corporate scene.

But he did not see the possibility of using insider information as an appropriate form of compensation for entrepreneurs in large corporations.

One cannot argue with Schumpeter's theory of what would happen to large corporations *if in fact* no entrepreneurs within them could receive an appropriate return. Government agencies and heavily regulated or protected industries are probably sufficient proof of the validity of this idea. On this basis the prediction for which Schumpeter has been frequently criticized could be closer to the mark than his critics have realized — that is, if misguided proposals to abolish our most effective system for rewarding entrepreneurs in large corporations (insider trading in one form or another) are adopted.

Compensation Not Enough

To provide an effective incentive, entrepreneurial compensation has to be available when the benefits are realized by the corporation, and it must vary with the value of the contribution. Since neither of these eventualities can ordinarily be predicted in advance, most existing compensation plans are inadequate for the task. Obviously, salary is inappropriate. The amount of salary has to be decided on in advance, it does not allow for distinguishing the manager who only manages from one who also innovates, and it is not flexible enough to reward particular contributions.

At first glance the bonus does seem to answer most of these objections. However, most bonuses today are formulated in advance and depend on total profits rather than individual contributions. Bonus plans are incentive devices, but they probably tend to generate managerial improvements, such as small cost-cutting, rather than radical innovations. The bonus plan, as opposed to the special bonus, will not serve the entrepreneur's purpose.

[3] New York, Harper & Brothers.

The special bonus can, of course, be used to reward great innovations, though there are legal restrictions if authorization is not established in advance. But the main drawback is that the true value of a particular contribution, in the form of higher profits, may not be known for many years. So there frequently are gross disparities in judgment between the bonus committee and the executive as to the latter's true worth. This misjudgment may become even more serious if the innovation has caused the price of the stock to rise but has not yet affected profits, though the stock price rise is precisely what the entrepreneur should be rewarded for.

In addition, the entrepreneurial type who is motivated by the possibility of "getting rich quick" probably does not like the idea of negotiating his reward after his contribution has been made. This distinction is like that between a patent system and a system of bonuses or government awards for inventions. Few will be found to argue that the latter system encourages as much invention as the former.

Stock options also add some incentive to efficiency for managers, but it is doubtful that they can serve the needs of the entrepreneur for massive reward for great innovations. The difficulty should be obvious. The number of shares to be optioned to various executives normally has to be determined in advance of any entrepreneurial innovation. If the options are granted after the innovation, they are the same as the special bonus, except that payment is made in the form of a free call on corporate stock rather than in the form of cash. Stock options undoubtedly add greatly to incentive, but they may still promise too little to entrepreneurial types with ambition, enthusiasm, and a large measure of self-confidence.

Incentives From Trading

On the other hand, free trading by insiders in a company's securities meets the objections mentioned for other compensation schemes and has special advantages of its own. Perhaps this can best be seen by comparing systems of compensation for patentable and nonpatentable innovations.

Basically the patent system is designed to allow inventors to receive an appropriate reward for successful innovations by preventing others from copying and participating in profits which we might say were not earned by them. The granting of a temporary monopoly to the patentee assures two goals: (1) it excludes the would-be interloper; (2) it provides the patentee with a substantial reward for his idea, although that reward will vary with the economic importance of the invention.

The patent system seems to work reasonably well, but only for patentable ideas. How can we guarantee a similar reward to inventors of nonpatentable ideas? In this area our legal system has been rather weak and ineffective; it has developed few really successful techniques for the protection of such ideas. Most businessmen recognize that secrecy and speed of marketing are the two principal devices for realizing substantial profits for their companies from nonpatentable innovations — secrecy to keep competitors away and speed because they cannot be kept away for long. But nothing in this scheme provides any protection or reward for the individual who has an important, nonpatentable idea which he personally is in no position to exploit.

For the man who has not founded his own business to exploit his idea — historically the traditional course for an entrepreneur — trading in the stock market on inside information provides a reward system, and is the only effective device available for the entrepreneur who is employed by a large corporation.

Insider trading allows any individual who works for a publicly traded corporation to play the entrepreneurial role, a very important advantage. Individuals can, in effect, sell their own ideas without the necessity of having large amounts of capital available. The increase in stock price, though not perfect, will provide as accurate a gauge of the value of the innovation as can be found, and it will leave little room for argument about an individual's worth.

Large corporations will be able to compete more effectively for entrepreneurial talent with closely owned companies, since they can now hold out the promise of very great rewards for the successful innovator. The image of corporate executives as gray bureaucrats can and should be erased. Large corporations can furnish as much romance, excitement, and opportunity for rapid economic and social advancement as any other avenues pursued today. But if corporations get hung up on foolish moralizing, such as characterizes most discussions of insider trading, they cannot hope to compete successfully or to survive the subtle attacks of government agencies.

If there really is an economic service or function that can be termed entrepreneurship, then we must have some way of compensating it. The cases are legion of new corporate managers bringing in fresh, imaginative, but often untested ideas. If these individuals were to be limited to the same compensation as their dull unimaginative, and overly conservative predecessors, what incentive would they have to innovate? Their salaries, bonuses, and pensions are usually secure, and few large companies face imminent bankruptcy. Their stock options and bonus plans will give some motivation to improve things, but not to take very great personal risks. For the true entrepreneur, the possibility of great riches will elicit more risk-taking activities and enterprise than will the possibility of smaller though more certain gain.

It might also be added that this promise attracts a different type of personality as well, one with which successful American businessmen have traditionally been proud to identify — the self-made, rags-to-riches, "Horatio Alger" hero. There is still room for such characters in the large modern corporation.

Objections Not Significant

There are some objections that can be raised to insider trading as a compensation device, although on balance they are not very significant.

Windfall Benefits. Here the argument goes that individuals would benefit fortuitously from good news which they have not produced. This does not seem too serious an objection, since innovators rarely receive the full value of their contribution anyway. With any nonpatentable invention, competitors flock in fast to copy and to claim entrepreneurial profits for themselves. Similarly, both stockholders and other executives will ordinarily share in the corporate entrepreneur's gains. When we view insider trading as an appropriate *form* of compensation rather than a device for accurately valuing innovations and paying a precise number of dollars, the windfall argument does not seem strong at all.

Unearned Returns. It may often appear that individuals who have not contributed anything to the corporation in years, if ever, will be regularly privy to inside information. But appearances may be deceiving. Frequently these individuals may be participating in an information exchange (to be discussed shortly), or perhaps an obligation is being met with valuable information rather than money.

One individual seldom has sole possession of information and so is unable to control its dissemination both within and outside his company, although insiders will have strong incentive to police the dissemination of information efficiently. But this does not mean that it will be economical to secure perfect policing, and therefore some leakage is bound to occur.

Trading on Bad News. Nor should the fact that profits can be made in the market by selling short on bad news deter us from adopting this theory of compensation. If the appropriate incentives and constraints are built into the modern corporation system, they will generate a desire to create good news, not bad.[4] And if this is so, the fact that one may incidentally profit from bad news should be of no more significance for this discussion than the fact that one may profit from good news which he did not personally produce.

Stock 'Manipulation.' Here the argument is that if insiders are allowed to trade freely, they will manipulate the affairs of the corporation so as to maximize their own trading profits rather than the company's earnings. There are many different forms to this argument, though critics of insider trading never clearly distinguish the different kinds of manipulation that are possible. Space does not allow detailed consideration of this matter, but some observations may be made:

- There are few incentives for manipulation of stock prices that conflict with the long-run interests of the corporation and its shareholders.
- Manipulation which takes the form only of changing the time at which disclosure is made is of no consequence to all outsider investors considered as a group.
- The grosser forms of manipulation can be dealt with quite effectively through less drastic techniques than preventing insider trading.

Regulatory Trends

The legal history of insider trading is one of constantly expanding regulation, by legislation, court decision, and SEC ruling.

Under Section 16(b) of the Securities Ex-

[4] For a full discussion of this point, see my article, "Mergers and the Market for Corporate Control," *Journal of Political Economy*, April 1965, p. 110.

change Act of 1934, profits resulting from any combination of a purchase and a sale of equity securities by an insider within a six-month period inure to the benefit of the corporation and may be claimed by any shareholder on behalf of the corporation in a simplified legal action. Monthly reporting of any changes in the holdings of officers, directors, and 10% shareholders is also required. The section applies to any corporation with $1 million in assets and 750 shareholders, but next year the latter figure drops to 500 shareholders.

SEC Hampered

There is no doubt that 16(b) constitutes, in the words of one of its key draftsmen, a "crude rule of thumb." Perhaps its very arbitrariness and its harshness are a measure of Congress' emotional response to the disclosures made during the Pecora hearings in 1933–1934.

But the SEC has long found that Section 16(b) rather severely constrains any broadside attack on the practice of insider trading. For one thing, it requires both a purchase and a sale, whereas considerable gain may be had simply from knowledgeable timing of long-term investments. Furthermore, both transactions must occur within a period of six months; if the sale at a profit occurs six months and one day after purchase, the section is inapplicable.

Perhaps most important, Section 16(b) only reaches trading by insiders of the particular company whose securities are involved. It does nothing about indirect techniques, although these are probably endemic in American business. Thus two individuals, each of whom is regularly privy to valuable information, may swap their knowledge and trade with impunity as far as 16(b) is concerned.

In the celebrated case of *Blau* v. *Lehman*,[5] the Supreme Court of the United States even refused to extend 16(b) liability for insider trading to a partnership when one of the partners was on the board of directors of the company involved and the partnership was trading in the stock. Of course, the partner's individual share of the profits was recoverable, but, without a demonstration that the firm "deputed" the partner to sit on the board for it or that the partner reported information back to the firm for trading purposes, the partnership could not be held to be a director under the 1934 act.

Interestingly, the Court recounted the legislative history of Section 16(b), noting that Congress had explicitly refused to adopt a broader provision covering "anyone . . . to whom unlawful disclosure" was made. The court concluded: "Congress might amend 16(b) if the Commission would present to it the policy arguments it has presented to us, but we think that Congress is the proper agency to change an interpretation of the Act unbroken since its passage, if the change is to be made."

Indirect Techniques

Note that only the simplest form of insider trading is specifically restricted by Section 16(b) of the Securities Exchange Act of 1934 and by shareholders' suits based on that law. It would be an unimaginative business community which would allow perhaps billions of dollars in stock market profits to sift through its hands like sand because direct trading is outlawed. The stakes are too large, and the alternative techniques are too easy.

Since direct exploitation of valuable information is ruled out, the next step is to find an indirect method of exchanging this valuable but unusable information for valuable and usable information. This may be done by a simple exchange of information. Undoubtedly many social relationships, such as club memberships, golf foursomes, and luncheon groups, provide opportunities for these mutually beneficial exchanges. There will always be some uncertainty in advice gained this way; but when the source is reliable, it is as different from the run-of-the-mine tip or the average broker's advice as gold is from clay.

But simple barter is never a very efficient exchange mechanism compared to using a medium of exchange like money. The parties may disagree on the value of their respective contributions; one may develop considerable information of value, while nothing important happens in the other's company; and neither can effectively control the further dissemination of information once it has been given out. The last point is especially important, since businessmen with property of great value should not be assumed to toss it away carelessly as they might a cigar wrapper.

To make this barter system function effectively, some sort of bank or clearinghouse operation is required. Here valuable information can be "deposited," and the ensuing credit drawn

[5] 368 U.S. 403 (1962).

on in the form of information about other companies when the depositor is in a legal and financial position to use it.

Clearly, the operator of the clearinghouse will have to be completely trustworthy, privy to fantastic amounts of very valuable information about many corporations and familiar with the roles played by the executives of these companies. The order may seem like a large one, but it is probably being filled regularly by familiar figures on the financial scene — the investment bankers. Some of the techniques used by investment banking houses in the operation of this information "bank" have long been evident but simply unidentified as such:

Boards of directors — The first and most obvious of these techniques is the control of one or more seats on various boards of directors. This may be used either as a method of allowing an individual to "draw" on his credits or to secure information for the common fund, as was alleged in *Blau* v. *Lehman*. But, as the SEC's Special Study of Securities Markets [6] suggested, bankers and brokers making markets in shares can get all the information they need without "deputing" anyone to sit on the board.

Priority lists — Another familiar device for operating an information bank is the preference or priority list. These lists simply designate certain individuals who are to be made privy to a specific bit of valuable information. This may be done either by disclosure of the information itself or simply by a recommendation to buy the stock. This method has the advantage of not requiring that the "information banker" also be the recipient's broker, but it has the disadvantage of causing a loss of control over further disclosures. It may also be too slow to be useful in some circumstances, though there are a number of variations on this technique which can improve its efficiency.

Discretionary accounts — Perhaps the most efficient device, at least since the outlawing of stock pools, is the so-called discretionary account. Here the information banker simply agrees to manage an investment fund of a stated amount. He may thus carefully control the value drawn from the common information fund, and there is no problem of policing the information since no disclosure is made. This device has considerable flexibility and can be used with a high degree of speed and precision. Furthermore, in its more complicated forms, it can thwart all but the most extreme methods of government policing.

[6] *Report of Special Study of Securities Markets of the S.E.C.*, House Document No. 95, 88th Congress, 1st Session, 1963.

The simplest approach to policing is basically that adopted by the 1934 act: find out who is engaged in insider trading. Reporting, as required by the act, is a first step. Other methods for discovering inside traders are possible. In addition to checking the identity of individuals who traded in particular securities just before important disclosures (which the SEC has done), a system of computerized cross-references might disclose the identity of individuals engaged in simple bartering.

But unpalatable as this should be to anyone sensitive to the right of privacy and the dangers of such governmental snooping, such policing techniques could still probably be thwarted by sophisticated uses of preference lists and discretionary accounts. As yet, the SEC has not argued forcefully for outlawing these practices or for separating the investment banking and brokerage functions, though these ideas have been advanced.

Fraud Rule

In spite of the Supreme Court's admonition not to expand the coverage of 16(b), the SEC has continued to try to develop a stronger weapon against insider trading through administrative acts. In 1942 it adopted what is now known as the "SEC fraud rule," Rule 10b-5, which, among other things, makes it illegal to issue an untrue or misleading statement, or omit a material fact in a statement, or commit any act of fraud or deceit in connection with the purchase or sale of a security. It purports to follow from Section 10(b) of the Securities and Exchange Act of 1934, though its operative terms are far broader than those of the act. In fact the important language is taken from Section 17 of the Securities Act of 1933, which applied only to sales of securities and was therefore useless in dealing with most insider trading.

Strangely enough, during the early development of 10b-5 as an insider trading provision, neither the SEC nor the most influential commentators saw it as very important. The general view was that the provision merely codified common law in the states, applied their doctrine in federal cases, and covered transactions in stocks listed on exchanges.

Whether this somewhat restrained view of 10b-5 was intended by the SEC or not, the courts began to use language strongly suggesting that the provision outlawed all forms of stock market trading with undisclosed information.

The holdings themselves could be and generally were, however, justified on other grounds, so the broader references were actually *obiter dicta*, or incidental opinions. Regarding insider trading, they necessarily implied the power of the SEC to promulgate a rule to that effect, but no reported decision ever examined and sustained the broad proposition that the SEC has the power to outlaw all insider trading under its rule-making authority.

The SEC's rule-making powers are much broader in connection with stockbrokers than for others trading in the market. So there can be little question of the propriety of its holding in *In the Matter of Cady, Roberts & Co.*,[7] written by Chairman William L. Cary in 1961. That opinion penalized brokers who sold stock for their own and discretionary accounts after a dividend was passed but before public disclosure of the news. The decision could have turned solely on the clear violation of a rule of the New York Stock Exchange regarding disclosure of dividend actions. But at no point did the opinion limit itself to brokers as active parties in insider trading. Its very broad language suggests that 10b-5 has come of age as a potent weapon in the war against insider trading.

Other Weapons

The SEC is presently in the process of shaping and developing another technique, more frightening and potentially more damaging than anything yet done. Instead of trying to discover the identity of inside traders after the fact, the SEC and the New York and American Stock Exchanges have sought to prevent insider trading by stopping all trading in a company's shares. At the moment, this technique can only be used when knowledge or rumors of important developments, combined with heavy trading in the stock, inform the SEC or the Stock Exchange of potential insider profiting.

But the SEC has other ways of getting word of impending developments. The monthly 8-K reports required to be filed with the Commission could be made to serve this purpose. Most 8-K reports at present contain little of value in this connection, but the rules could easily be changed. For example, the SEC currently has a proposal under consideration to require advance notice in the 8-K report of certain merger negotiations. It has also been recommended by one writer that 8-K's cover any important event, with management liable for any omissions that are made with "no reasonable basis."

Concluding Note

The insider trading scheme for compensating entrepreneurs is not a neat, one-for-one exchange arrangement. It may sometimes appear highly arbitrary. But it is probably the best scheme we can devise for compensating the entrepreneurial function in large corporations. There is undoubtedly much that we need to learn about how this scheme actually works in practice, but we know enough now to have serious reservations about the prevailing attitude on the subject.

The SEC has reflected, as well as helped to develop, this attitude toward insider trading. There is strong reason to believe that this has been a real disservice to the American shareholder. The public's indignation with the defendants at the outset of the *Texas Gulf Sulphur* case may well have been directed toward the wrong party in the action.

[7] Securities Exchange Act Reference No. 6668 (1961).

The share market of New York, or rather of the whole Union, in "the Street," as it is fondly named, is the most remarkable sight in the country after Niagara and the Yellowstone Geysers.

James Bryce, "Wall Street," *The American Commonwealth*, The Macmillan Company, 1888.

[6]

The Regulation of Insider Trading

Dennis W. Carlton* and Daniel R. Fischel**

Imagine two firms, A and B, which are identical in all respects except that, in its charter, firm A prohibits the trading of its shares based on inside (nonpublic) information. The firm requires insiders (employees) to report their trades, which a special committee or an independent accounting firm then checks to ensure compliance with the charter provision. Firm B, by contrast, neither prohibits insider trading nor requires reporting. Insiders openly trade shares of firm B and regularly earn positive abnormal returns. In competitive capital markets, which charter provision will survive?

Despite the deceptive simplicity of this question, it has no obvious answer.[1] The consensus, to the extent that any exists, appears to be that firm A's charter will survive because it eliminates various per-

* Professor of Economics, University of Chicago Law School.

** Professor of Law, Northwestern University Law School.

1. The literature on insider trading is too voluminous to cite in detail. The starting point for anyone interested in the subject is Henry Manne's brilliant book, *Insider Trading and the Stock Market,* which argues that insider trading is an efficient way to compensate entrepreneurs. *See* H. MANNE, INSIDER TRADING AND THE STOCK MARKET *passim* (1966) [hereinafter cited as H. MANNE, INSIDER TRADING AND THE STOCK MARKET]; *see also* Manne, *Economic Aspects of Required Disclosure Under Federal Securities Laws,* in WALL STREET IN TRANSITION: THE EMERGING SYSTEM AND ITS IMPACT ON THE ECONOMY 21 (1974); Manne, *Insider Trading and the Law Professors,* 23 VAND. L. REV. 547 (1970).

For more recent work, see Anderson, *Fraud, Fiduciaries, and Insider Trading,* 10 HOFSTRA L. REV. 341 (1982); Brudney, *Insiders, Outsiders, and Informational Advantages under the Federal Securities Laws,* 93 HARV. L. REV. 322 (1979); Dooley, *Enforcement of Insider Trading Restrictions,* 66 VA. L. REV. 1 (1980); Easterbrook, *Insider Trading, Secret Agents, Evidentiary Privileges, and the Production of Information,* 1981 SUP. CT. REV. 309 [hereinafter cited as Easterbrook, *Insider Trading*]; Easterbrook, *Insider Trading as an Agency Problem,* in THE AGENCY RELATIONSHIP — (J. Pratt & R. Zeckhauser eds.) (forthcoming); Haft, *The Effect of Insider Trading Rules on the Internal Efficiency of the Large Corporation,* 80 MICH. L. REV. 1051 (1982); Heller, Chiarella, *SEC Rule 14e-3, and* Dirks: *"Fairness" Versus Economic Theory,* 37 BUS. LAW. 517 (1982); Karjala, *Statutory Regulation of Insider Trading in Impersonal Markets,* 1982 DUKE L.J. 627; Levmore, *Securities and Secrets: Insider Trading and the Law of Contracts,* 68 VA. L. REV. 117 (1982); Scott, *Insider Trading: Rule 10b-5, Disclosure and Corporate Privacy,* 9 J. LEGAL STUD. 801 (1980); Wang, *Trading on Material Nonpublic Information On Impersonal Stock Markets: Who is Harmed, and Who Can Sue Whom Under SEC Rule 10b-5?,* 54 S. CAL. L. REV. 1217 (1981).

Economists also have become increasingly interested in insider trading. *See, e.g.,* Ross, *Disclosure Regulation in Financial Markets: Implications of Modern Finance Theory and Signaling Theory,* in ISSUES IN FINANCIAL REGULATION 177 (F. Edwards ed. 1979) [hereinafter cited as Ross, *Disclosure Regulation*]; Ross, *The Determination of Financial Structure: The Incentive-Signalling* ceived harmful effects of insider trading. Thus, investors would pay less for shares in B. The managers of B, in order to maximize the value of B shares, would have to adopt a similar charter provision.

As for these harmful effects, many believe that insider trading is "unfair" and undermines public confidence in capital markets.[2] Other critics have argued that insider trading creates perverse incentives by allowing corporate managers to profit on bad news as well as good,[3] encourages managers to invest in risky projects,[4] impedes corporate decisionmaking,[5] and tempts managers to delay public disclosure of valuable information.[6] Some also have argued that insider trading is an inefficient compensation scheme because, in effect, it compensates risk-averse managers with a benefit akin to lottery tickets.[7] Still others have claimed that insider trading allows insiders to divert part of the firm's earnings that would otherwise go to shareholders and therefore raises the firm's cost of capital.[8] Under this "insider trading is harmful to investors" hypothesis, competitive capital markets would force firm B to prohibit insider trading.

The difficulty with this hypothesis is that it appears to be contradicted by the actions of firms. Although no one has conducted rigorous empirical research in this area, it is generally believed that firms have made little, if any, attempt to prohibit insider trading, at least until very recently and then perhaps only as a response to regulation.[9] Today the area is federally regulated,[10] but the federal insider

Approach, 8 BELL J. ECON. 23 (1977); Mendelson, Book Review, 117 U. PA. L. REV. 470 (1969); R. Dye, Inside-Trading and Incentives (Feb. 1983) (unpublished working paper, University of Chicago Graduate School of Business) (on file with *Stanford Law Review*); R. Leftwich & R. Verrecchia, Insider Trading and Managers' Choice Among Risky Projects (Aug. 1981) (CRSP Working Paper No. 63, University of Chicago, Graduate School of Business) (on file with *Stanford Law Review*).

2. *See, e.g.,* Brudney, *supra* note 1, at 343-46; Karjala, *supra* note 1, at 629; Levmore, *supra* note 1, at 124-25; Schotland, *Unsafe at Any Price: A Reply to Manne,* Insider Trading and the Stock Market, 53 VA. L. REV. 1425, 1440-42 (1967).

3. *See, e.g.,* Levmore, *supra* note 1, at 149; Mendelson, *supra* note 1, at 489-90; Schotland, *supra* note 2, at 1451.

4. Easterbrook, *Insider Trading, supra* note 1, at 332; R. Leftwich & R. Verrecchia, *supra* note 1.

5. Haft, *supra* note 1, at 1053-64.

6. *See, e.g.,* Mendelson, *supra* note 1, at 489; Schotland, *supra* note 2, at 1448-49.

7. Easterbrook, *Insider Trading, supra* note 1, at 332; Scott, *supra* note 1, at 808.

8. Brudney, *supra* note 1, at 356; Mendelson, *supra* note 1, at 477-78.

9. *See* Dooley, *supra* note 1, at 44-45; Easterbrook, *Insider Trading, supra* note 1, at 333; *cf.* H. MANNE, INSIDER TRADING AND THE STOCK MARKET, *supra* note 1, at 1-2 (popular attitudes towards corporate morality did not until recently condemn insider trading); Wang, *supra* note 1, at 1245 (reasons why businessmen might not consider insider trading immoral). This general belief does not extend to specialized areas such as law firms or corporate printers.

10. Section 16 of the Securities Exchange Act of 1934, 15 U.S.C. § 78p (1976), was the

trading prohibitions are limited, have rarely been enforced, and have had little observable effect on insider trading.[11] Indeed, numerous empirical studies have demonstrated that insider trading is widespread and is highly profitable—insiders systematically outperform the market.[12] Critics of insider trading have offered no explanation for why firms have made so little attempt to prohibit insider trading.

Critics of insider trading also should predict that insiders who outperform the market reduce their compensation in labor markets. Just as a manager who is known to shirk or to make poor investment decisions will consequently command lower compensation, so should a manager who is known to trade on inside information and earn abnormal positive returns, as revealed by his reported trades.[13] Yet no evidence even suggests that managers who report profitable trades thereby decrease the value of their human capital.

---

first attempt to regulate insider trading. Section 16 applies only to directors, officers, and large shareholders. It requires these individuals to report all trading activity in the stock (or other financial instruments, like options) of their company, prohibits short selling, and requires disgorgement of any profit that results from holding a position less than 6 months. The prohibition was extended in 1968 by judicial construction of § 10(b) of the 1934 Act, 15 U.S.C. § 78j(b) (1976), to restrict individuals in possession of "material" information from trading. *See* note 90 *infra.* An earlier administrative decision of the SEC, Cady, Roberts & Co., 40 S.E.C. 907 (1961), was an important precursor to the 1968 extension of the laws against insider trading. We discuss the federal regulation of insider trading in more detail at notes 90–114 *infra* and accompanying text.

11. For an analysis of the lack of enforcement of insider trading prohibitions, see generally Dooley, *supra* note 1. This relative absence of enforcement may be changing with the recent crusade of the SEC against insider trading. It is too early to analyze this issue. On the limited nature of the prohibition, see note 10 *supra*; text accompanying notes 17–19 *infra.*

12. For empirical studies demonstrating that insiders systematically outperform the market, see Baesel & Stein, *The Value of Information: Inferences from the Profitability of Insider Trading,* 14 J. FIN. & QUANTITATIVE ANALYSIS 553 (1979); Finnerty, *Insiders and Market Efficiency,* 31 J. FIN. 1141 (1976); Jaffe, *The Effect of Regulation Changes on Insider Trading,* 5 BELL J. ECON. & MGMT. SCI. 93 (1974); Jaffe, *Special Information and Insider Trading,* 47 J. BUS. 410 (1974); Keown & Pinkerton, *Merger Announcements and Insider Trading Activity: An Empirical Investigation,* 36 J. FIN. 855 (1981); Lorie & Niederhoffer, *Predictive and Statistical Properties of Insider Trading,* 11 J.L. & ECON. 35 (1968); Penman, *Insider Trading and the Dissemination of Firms' Forecast Information,* 55 J. BUS. 479 (1982).

Because insider trading has continued to thrive despite regulation, firms still have incentives to minimize the practice if prohibition were in the best interests of investors. The absence of widespread private restrictive measures even today beyond what is required by regulation is therefore difficult to reconcile with the general perception that insider trading is harmful to investors.

13. This should follow even if the trades are not illegal under § 10(b) or § 16(b). The arguments of the critics of insider trading are dependent on the ability of insiders to earn abnormal positive returns, not on whether the trades are illegal. On the distinction between the legal and economic definitions of insider trading, see note 17 *infra* and accompanying text.

Also puzzling is the common law which, in the main, permitted insider trading.[14] Because capital is highly mobile, firms, in order to attract investors, have strong incentives to incorporate in states that have efficient corporation laws.[15] Because incorporations are profitable to the state, the states in turn have strong incentives to provide a set of legal rules that maximize shareholders' welfare. If eliminating insider trading produced gains, states that prohibit insider trading would have a comparative advantage over other states, and firms that incorporated in such states would have a comparative advantage over other firms. Yet no evidence suggests that this has occurred.

Similarly, insider trading in the capital markets of many other countries historically has been subject either to regulations that have not been enforced or to no regulation at all.[16] This phenomenon, like the absence of domestic private and state prohibitions, suggests that the question of the desirability of insider trading is far more complex than commonly assumed.

Finally, insider trading in this country, despite the widespread perception to the contrary, is generally permitted. A fundamental difference exists between the legal and economic definitions of insider trading. Insider trading in an economic sense is trading by parties who are better informed than their trading partners. Thus, insider trading in an economic sense includes all trades where information is asymmetric. This definition includes all trades, whether or not in securities, where one of the parties has superior information. By contrast, federal law has focused on purchases or sales by certain insiders within a 6-month period or on trading on the basis of "material"

---

14. The common law rules on insider trading are discussed in Freeman v. Decio, 584 F.2d 186, 191-95 (7th Cir. 1978); *see also* H. MANNE, INSIDER TRADING AND THE STOCK MARKET, *supra* note 1, at 17-26 (discussing the evolution of common law rules); Conant, *Duties of Disclosure of Corporate Insiders Who Purchase Shares,* 46 CORNELL L.Q. 53, 54-63 (1960).

15. For discussion of the significance of state corporation laws, see generally R. WINTER, GOVERNMENT AND THE CORPORATION (1978); Easterbrook & Fischel, *Voting in Corporate Law,* 26 J.L. & ECON. 395 (1983); Fischel, *The "Race to the Bottom" Revisited: Reflections on Recent Developments in Delaware's Corporation Law,* 76 NW. U.L. REV. 913 (1982).

16. *See generally* B. RIDER & H. FRENCH, THE REGULATION OF INSIDER TRADING (1979). In Japan, for example, insider trading is considered proper, and there has never been a reported case under the limited insider trading prohibition currently in effect. *Id.* at 361. Hong Kong first regulated insider trading in 1974, but this regulation has been repealed. *Id.* at 328. France has a narrow insider trading prohibition, but again, the practice is not considered immoral and "the total number of suits and administrative sanctions is nearly nil." *Id.* at 238. In the United Kingdom, there historically has been no regulation of insider trading, but the trend is towards regulation. *Id.* at 146, 445. This trend is too recent to analyze the level of enforcement.

information by a broader, more amorphous group of insiders or their tippees. Insider trading in an economic sense need not be illegal.[17] The law never has attempted to prohibit all trading by knowledgeable insiders.

For purposes of analyzing whether insider trading is beneficial or detrimental, nothing turns on whether a particular trade is illegal. In assessing the arguments for and against insider trading, therefore, we will focus on trading by managers or other employees in securities of their own firms based on superior knowledge regardless of whether the trade is illegal. We emphasize, however, that the arguments for and against insider trading may apply equally to trading by others.[18]

We attempt in this article to analyze critically the arguments in favor of prohibiting insider trading and to suggest why allowing the practice may be an efficient way to compensate corporate managers.[19] Part I demonstrates that the insider trading debate is really a debate about whether the firm, as a matter of contract, should be able to allocate property rights in valuable information to managers or to investors. We argue that the parties' self-interest will lead them to reach by private agreement the optimal allocation of what is simply one element of a compensation arrangement. We discuss in Part II several incentive and information effects which suggest that there may be gains from allocating property rights in valuable information to managers as opposed to investors. These gains may explain the lack of pervasive private, common law, and foreign and domestic restraints on insider trading. Part III analyzes some of the numerous objections to insider trading. The various legal rules regulating insider trading are critically analyzed in Part IV. Part V is a conclusion.

I. Insider Trading and the Coase Theorem

Critics of insider trading draw a sharp distinction between the proper legal response to insider trading and to other forms of managerial compensation. Salaries, bonuses, stock options, office size, vacation leave, secretarial support, and other terms of employment are all, it is generally assumed, properly left to private negotiation. Nobody would argue seriously that these terms and conditions of em-

17. *See* notes 94–100 *infra* and accompanying text.

18. *See* texts accompanying notes 56–57, 75–76, 96–102 *infra*.

19. We confine our discussion to publicly traded corporations and do not discuss small closely-held corporations or partnerships. The principle-agent problems in the latter groups of firms are likely to differ substantially from those in large publicly held corporations.

ployment should be set by government regulation—that a federal agency, for example, should monitor the amount of leisure time taken by corporate managers. Most would agree that these decisions are better made through negotiations between firms and managers, given the constraints of capital, product, and labor markets as well as the market for corporate control.[20] Although the negotiation and enforcement of these employment agreements are costly, these costs are presumptively lower than would be the case if negotiation and enforcement were handled by government regulators who are undisciplined by markets.[21]

Precisely the opposite presumptions have been applied with respect to insider trading. Most believe that existing government regulation is necessary and should be extended; virtually no one has considered the possibility, let alone has argued, that private negotiations between a firm and its employees can most efficiently determine whether insiders should be allowed to profit by trading on inside information.[22]

Does whatever difference that exists between profits from trading in shares and other forms of compensation warrant such different legal responses? It is no answer to argue that insider trading is unfair, constitutes theft, destroys investors' confidence, or compensates inefficiently. These characterizations just as aptly describe a hypothetical compensation scheme whereby managers pay themselves huge salaries and consume unlimited perquisites, regardless of their productivity. Government need not prohibit this type of compensation agreement because, given competitive markets, firms will have strong incentives to avoid such a scheme. The identical argument applies to insider trading: If it is bad, firms that allow insider trading will be at a competitive disadvantage compared with firms that curtail insider

20. These markets are discussed in more detail in Easterbrook & Fischel, *Corporate Control Transactions,* 91 YALE L.J. 698 (1982) [hereinafter cited as Easterbrook & Fischel, *Corporate Control Transactions*]; Easterbrook & Fischel, *The Proper Role of a Target's Management in Responding to a Tender Offer,* 94 HARV. L. REV. 1161 (1981).

21. Government enforcement of employment terms is not without precedent. Criminal penalties for theft are perhaps the best example. But such penalties probably are designed primarily for cases involving strangers, where there is no pre-existing contractual relationship. In any event, the main issue concerning the regulation of insider trading is not whether there should be public enforcement of a private prohibition, but whether there should be public enforcement even if there is no private prohibition. On the relationship between the regulation of insider trading and the penalties for theft, see text accompanying note 105 *infra.*

22. Only Manne has even suggested this argument. *See* H. MANNE, INSIDER TRADING AND THE STOCK MARKET, *supra* note 1, at 138–41.

trading.[23]

Coase's famous insight is quite relevant in this regard.[24] Whether insider trading is beneficial depends on whether the property right in information is more valuable to the firm's managers or to the firm's investors. In either case, the parties can engage in a value-maximizing exchange by allocating the property right in information to its highest-valuing user. If the critics of insider trading are correct, therefore, both the firm's investors and the firm's insiders could profit by banning insider trading, thereby allocating the property right in information to the firm's investors.

It is important to recognize that this mutual incentive to allocate the property right in information to its highest-valuing user does not depend on actual negotiations between insiders and investors. As long as investors understand the possibility of insider trading, both share price and managers' compensation will be higher if the efficient allocation is reached than if it is not.[25]

The preceding discussion assumes, of course, that transaction costs will not interfere with the optimal allocation of property rights. While the costs of negotiating contracts banning insider trading in the employer-employee situation appear to be low, some have argued that the costs of enforcing such contracts are high.[26] Firms must encourage managers to own shares, the argument runs, to induce them to act in shareholders' best interests. Once having permitted share ownership by managers, the firm, because it cannot separate proper from improper trades, cannot adequately enforce a rule against insider trading. These high enforcement costs render firms unable to prohibit insider trading, even if doing so would benefit all parties.

23. Given a sufficient amount of search by investors, firms will offer contract terms that investors desire even if a substantial percentage of other investors engage in no search. The shoppers, in effect, protect the nonshoppers. *See* Schwartz & Wilde, *Imperfect Information in Markets for Contract Terms: The Examples of Warranties and Security Interests,* — VA. L. REV. — (forthcoming Nov. 1983); Schwartz & Wilde, *Intervening in Markets on the Basis of Imperfect Information: A Legal and Economic Analysis,* 127 U. PA. L. REV. 630 (1979). In light of the constant efforts of investment analysts and other professional investors to outperform the market, it is obvious that the amount of search in securities markets is substantial.

24. Coase, *The Problem of Social Cost,* 3 J.L. & ECON. 1 (1960).

25. An analogy exists to the area of products liability, where firms have incentives to design products in a manner that minimizes the sum of production costs and consumers' expected accident losses. This suggests that regardless of legal liability rules, firms will reach efficient outcomes, as long as expected losses are known. *See* A. M. POLINSKY, AN INTRODUCTION TO LAW AND ECONOMICS 95–104 (1983); Hamada, *Liability Rules and Income Distribution in Product Liability,* 66 AM. ECON. REV. 228 (1976).

26. *See, e.g.,* Easterbrook, *Insider Trading, supra* note 1, at 334.

The only practical method to ban insider trading, the argument concludes, is public enforcement with large penalties.

This argument fails to consider that firms need not be able to enforce contracts prohibiting insider trading perfectly to benefit from entering into such contracts, if such contracts were in the interest of investors. The costs of including provisions in the corporate charter or in employment contracts banning insider trading and requiring reporting of all transactions in the firm's securities would be minimal. And it is reasonable to assume that such provisions would deter some, if not most, insider trading, particularly if they required an audit of schedule D of the manager's tax return and imposed sanctions such as liquidated damages, termination of employment, and forfeiture of benefits.[27] True, managers still might be able to engage in some insider trading or to communicate valuable information to friends or relatives. But the relevant point is that the gains from incomplete enforcement—under the hypothesis that insider trading is harmful to investors—would outweigh the negligible costs of contracting. Thus, the apparent absence of widespread use of such contracts cannot be explained by the difficulty of obtaining perfect enforcement. Rather, this absence suggests that such contracts are not efficient.[28]

Moreover, the argument overstates the problems with private enforcement because it assumes that managers must own shares to be induced to act in shareholders' best interests. There is no reason, however, why this must be the case. The strategy, presumably, is to ensure that managers have a stake in the venture so that they will profit from good performance and lose from bad performance. But this incentive effect in no way depends on the actual ownership of shares. Firms are perfectly free to base compensation on share performance and thus create incentives for managers to increase the value of their firms even if managers own no shares.[29] If managers

27. For discussion of the role of termination and forfeiture provisions in reducing the divergence of interest between managers and shareholders, see Lazear, *Why Is There Mandatory Retirement?*, 87 J. POL. ECON. 1261 (1979); Smith & Watts, *Incentive and Tax Effects of Executive Compensation Plans,* 7 AUSTL. J. MGMT. 139, 145–47 (1982).

28. An alternative explanation for the absence of such contracts is that a problem exists, but it is too small to worry about. If this were the case, of course, there would be no reason for federal regulation because there would be no significant problem to address.

29. *See* Diamond & Verrecchia, *Optimal Managerial Contracts and Equilibrium Security Prices,* 37 J. FIN. 275, 281–83 (1982). Contracts that base compensation on share performance would not be perfect substitutes for actual ownership of shares. First, the contract alternative raises the problem of forcing the manager to pay the firm for poor performance; a manager owning stock would suffer automatically when stock values drop. This problem increases as managers

are forbidden from owning shares, the problem of separating proper from improper trades disappears. Alternatively, firms could allow managers to own shares, but not trade them.[30] That firms generally do not eliminate insider trading by employing these alternative methods for controlling share ownership while linking managers' fortunes with those of the firm again suggests that the explanation for the absence of such prohibitions is that they are inefficient, not that they are unenforceable.[31]

The notion that the dispute concerning insider trading is really a dispute about which party more highly values a property right and that whatever bargain is reached can be enforced (albeit imperfectly) by the parties themselves undermines the case for regulatory prohibition of insider trading. Such a prohibition could be justified only if it were clear that the parties themselves had attempted to deter insider trading by contract and that the government had a comparative advantage in enforcing such contracts.[32] But the comparative advantage in enforcement is irrelevant without a showing that firms generally have attempted to limit insider trading by contract. Without such a showing, a regulatory prohibition will likely displace effi-

approach retirement because it becomes increasingly difficult to adjust compensation for future periods. For a discussion of how pensions can be used as a solution to this problem for managers nearing retirement, see Lazear, *supra* note 27. On the other hand, the contract alternative directly ties total compensation to stock performance rather than depending on the fortuitous elements of the amount of share ownership or general market movements. Second, the contract alternative may affect the market for corporate control. In any control fight, including a proxy fight, one natural contestant is the managerial group. Thus, optimal managerial contracts would have to allow some provision for the purchase of shares during control fights.

30. For a discussion of how such contracts might be written, see Levmore, *supra* note 1, at 129-32. Restricted and phantom stock plans that are used by some firms as incentive devices have the effect of allowing the ownership but not the trading of shares. *See* Smith & Watts, *supra* note 27; *see also* Miller & Scholes, *Executive Compensation, Taxes and Incentives,* in FINANCIAL ECONOMICS: ESSAYS IN HONOR OF PAUL COOTNER 179 (W. Sharpe & C. Cootner eds. 1982); C. Smith & R. Watts, The Structure of Executive Compensation Contracts and the Control of Management 23-25 (April 7, 1983) (unpublished manuscript) (on file with *Stanford Law Review*).

31. It is not possible to argue that federal regulations have eliminated the incentives for firms to ban insider trading because such trading is still widespread and profitable. *See* notes 11-12 *supra* and accompanying text.

32. Whether the government actually has a comparative advantage in enforcing contracts prohibiting insider trading is far from clear. *See* Dooley, *supra* note 1, at 46 ("[P]rivate firms have a decided advantage over the government in terms of the certainty and costs of enforcement."). Resolution of this issue would require a great deal of evidence that currently does not exist. Our point is that even if we assume that the government does have a comparative advantage in enforcing an insider trading prohibition, this alone does not justify enactment of the prohibition itself nor of a prohibition that firms cannot opt out of. *See* text accompanying notes 105-06 *infra*.

cient private arrangements with inefficient regulatory solutions, much in the same way that regulation of salaries, bonuses, office size, leisure time, and all other terms of employment would be inefficient.

Our conclusion that a regulatory prohibition of insider trading (which would involve a substantial extension of existing regulations) is unwarranted has relied heavily on the apparent lack of widespread attempts by firms to prohibit insider trading. Insider trading in an economic sense continues to be widespread. (Curiously, the proponents of regulation have failed to cite any evidence of private prohibitions to support their contention that firms desire to ban insider trading.) Of course, the allocation of the property right in valuable information to managers might not be optimal in all circumstances for every firm. But even if some firms would attempt to ban insider trading in the absence of regulation, other firms should nonetheless be able to opt out of the regulations if they so desire. No justification exists for precluding firms from contracting around a regulatory prohibition of insider trading.

II. Why Firms Might Want to Allocate the Property Rights in Valuable Information to Managers as Opposed to Shareholders

Thus far, we have argued that firms and managers are able to allocate property rights in valuable information by private negotiation. In this section, we explain why the parties might choose to allocate these property rights to managers and thus allow insider trading. Because unambiguous welfare statements can be very difficult to make even in simple economic models involving uncertainty, to expect any analysis to prove that insider trading is solely harmful or solely beneficial is unrealistic. The desirability of insider trading is ultimately an empirical question. Nevertheless, analyzing how insider trading affects information transmission and shapes incentives will enable us to understand better the consequences of different allocations of the property rights in valuable information.

A. *Information Effects*

The social gains from efficient capital markets are well known. The more accurately prices reflect information, the better prices guide capital investment in the economy. From the perspective of an individual firm, however, efficient capital markets are a public good, unless private, as opposed to social, gains accrue to the firm when the prices of its own securities convey accurate information. Why, then, does a firm disclose information about itself?

One reason is that disclosure can reduce wasteful expenditures on search and reduce investor uncertainty about the firm. This may make the firm more valuable to investors. Investors expend resources to identify overvalued or undervalued securities until the next dollar they spend on information no longer produces an additional dollar of return.[33] If the firm can produce information about itself at the lowest cost, disclosure of information by the firm will save resources by reducing the amount of expenditures on search and will lead to less investor uncertainty about the firm.

A second reason is that disclosure of information by the firm also may enable the firm's current investors to sell their shares to outsiders at a higher price, on average. If the firm discloses no information, outsiders may assume the worst and discount the price they are willing to pay for shares by a factor that reflects their uncertainty. Because every firm has an incentive to distinguish itself from those firms about which the worst is true, so that outsiders will pay a higher price for its shares, information will be produced.[34]

Finally, accurately priced securities will enable firms to observe more accurately when corporate managers are successful. Thus, markets for managerial services and for corporate control will function more effectively.[35] Also, the better managers will signal their quality by their willingness to tie a higher proportion of their compensation to stock performance. Accurate prices then enable these managers to receive the rewards for their superior performance. For these reasons, shareholders would want managers to disclose information about the value of the firm.

Complete disclosure, however, would not be optimal. Disclosure is costly, and at some point the costs will outweigh the benefits of increased disclosure. Moreover, in some cases, disclosure might destroy the information's value. It would not be in the investors' interest to disclose, for example, that a confidential study revealed the

33. For the classic statement of how the pursuit of trading profits can lead to excessive search, see Hirshleifer, *The Private and Social Value of Information and the Reward to Inventive Activity*, 61 AM. ECON. REV. 561 (1971); *cf.* Barzel, *Some Fallacies in the Interpretation of Information Costs*, 20 J.L. & ECON. 291 (1977) (demonstrating how markets find solutions to incentives to engage in excessive search).

34. Grossman, *The Informational Role of Warranties and Private Disclosure About Product Quality*, 24 J.L. & ECON. 461 (1981); Grossman & Hart, *Disclosure Laws and Takeover Bids*, 35 J. FIN. 323 (1980).

35. Fischel, *The Corporate Governance Movement*, 35 VAND. L. REV. 1259, 1278 (1982).

presence of valuable mineral ore deposits on land the firm intends to purchase.

Since the firm's shareholders value the ability to control information that flows to the stock market, they may also value insider trading because it gives the firm an additional method of communicating and controlling information. If insiders trade, the share price will move closer to what it would have been had the information been disclosed. How close will depend on the amount of "noise" surrounding the trade. The greater the ability of market participants to identify insider trading, the more information such trading will convey.[36] At the extreme, trading by insiders is as fully revealing as complete disclosure. But since insiders will limit the size of their positions because of risk aversion and will camouflage their trading to some degree, they convey less information by trading than that conveyed by (credible) full disclosure.

Several reasons explain why communicating information through insider trading may be of value to the firm. Through insider trading, a firm can convey information it could not feasibly announce publicly because an announcement would destroy the value of the information, would be too expensive, not believable, or—owing to the uncertainty of the information—would subject the firm to massive damage liability if it turned out ex post to be incorrect. Conversely, firms also could use insider trading to limit the amount of information to be reflected in price.[37] Controlling the number of traders who have access to information may be easier than controlling how much information gets announced over time. In other words, announcement of information need not be continuous, while trading on inside information can be.[38] Thus, insider trading gives firms a tool either to increase or to decrease the amount of information that is contained in share prices.[39]

---

36. *See* Plott & Sunder, *Efficiency of Experimental Security Markets with Insider Information: An Application of Rational-Expectations Models,* 90 J. POL. ECON. 663 (1982) (demonstration using simulation techniques that markets adjust very rapidly to inside information).

37. Complete disclosure might not be optimal if shareholders cannot diversify or insure the risks to which the disclosure exposes them. *See* Hirshleifer, *supra* note 33, at 567-69.

38. Disclosure of information could be made continuous by repeated announcements of probabilities of future states. Antifraud rules, however, constrain this technique. A firm, for example, could not announce that the probability of a new discovery is .52 if the discovery has already been made.

39. An alternative to insider trading to communicate information is for the firm itself to convey information by the purchase and sale of shares. The difficulty with this alternative is that there is little incentive for an employee to reveal information to the firm's trader.

B. *Efficiency Effects*

Because managers are agents whose actions cannot be monitored perfectly by their principals, managers have the ability and the incentive to take actions that are in their best interests but not necessarily in the best interests of the firm. Managers have incentives to divert more of the income stream generated by the firm's assets to themselves than they initially agreed upon. Alternatively, managers simply may not work hard. As a result of imperfect monitoring in the principal-agent relationship, managers also may be able to choose investment projects that are not optimal for the firm but that further the managers' interests. For example, a manager who is risk averse will be reluctant to take on high-payout, high-variance projects for fear that bankruptcy will occur or that poor performance will be attributed to him rather than to bad luck.

Markets limit the divergence of interest between managers and shareholders. Competition in product and capital markets limits the ability of managers to pursue actions that do not maximize the value of the firm. The market in corporate control also gives managers an incentive to maximize the value of the firm and simultaneously provides a mechanism for the removal of managers who perform poorly. Finally, given the market for managerial services, value-reducing behavior is constrained by managers' desires to increase the future value of their services to both current and prospective employers.

Because these markets do not work perfectly, however, they reduce rather than eliminate the divergence of interests between managers and shareholders. Since the costs of identifying and removing ineffective managers are positive, managers are able to engage in some shirking without fear of removal. But rational shareholders realize this and decrease the price they are willing to pay for shares accordingly. This in turn limits managers' compensation because the less shareholders are willing to pay for shares, the less managers will be able to charge for their services. Thus, both managers and shareholders have incentives to reach agreements ex ante that limit divergent behavior by managers: Such agreements increase the price shareholders are willing to pay for shares and hence the compensation managers are able to receive.[40]

A common scheme to make managers' interests conform more closely to those of the firm is to give them a stake in the firm. Indeed,

40. *See* Jensen & Meckling, *Theory of the Firm: Managerial Behavior, Agency Costs and Ownership Structure,* 3 J. FIN. ECON. 305 (1976).

recent research suggests that managers frequently own a higher percentage of the firm's shares than has been commonly assumed.[41] The risk aversion of managers, however, acts as a constraint on their willingness to invest a large percentage of their wealth, which includes their human capital, in one firm.[42] So long as a manager does not own the entire firm, some divergence of interest will remain.

As another possible solution to the agency cost problem, firms may write contracts that induce managers to take efficient actions.[43] Paying a worker [on] a piece rate rather than a fixed salary creates the correct incentives if the employer can more easily observe output than effort. But the principal may have difficulty in many cases in observing output directly— especially the output of managers. Even if output can be observed, it will typically depend on factors other than just one manager's performance, such as the efforts of other managers or random events such as developments in the relevant industry or in the economy as a whole.

Contracts that provide for periodic renegotiations ex post based on (imperfectly) observed effort and output are alternatives to contracts that ex ante tie compensation to output.[44] Such renegotiations are constrained by the difficulty of monitoring the effort and measuring the output of individual managers, and the bargaining process itself is costly. To reduce these costs, firms seek to minimize the number of renegotiations. But reduction in the number of renegotiations itself creates a cost. If renegotiations occur too infrequently, they are less likely to exert the proper incentives at any given time. The firm may solve this problem by having more frequent renegotiations, but in doing so it must incur the costs associated with renegotiation.[45]

Insider trading may present a solution to this cost-of-renegotiation dilemma. The unique advantage of insider trading is that it allows a manager to alter his compensation package in light of new knowledge, thereby avoiding continual renegotiation. The manager,

41. Demsetz, *The Structure of Ownership and the Theory of the Firm,* 26 J.L. & ECON. 375 (1983).

42. For ways in which shareholders can convince managers to hold a larger stake in the firm despite their risk aversion, see Beck & Zorn, *Managerial Incentives in a Stock Market Economy,* 37 J. FIN. 1151 (1982).

43. Fiduciary duties and voting rules in corporate law serve to minimize the costs of contracting and thus reduce agency costs. *See generally* Easterbrook & Fischel, *Corporate Control Transactions, supra* note 20; Easterbrook & Fischel, *supra* note 15.

44. *See* Fama, *Agency Problems and the Theory of the Firm,* 88 J. POL. ECON. 288 (1980).

45. For an extended discussion of the costs and benefits of salary renegotiations, see Smith & Watts, *supra* note 27, at 145-47.

in effect, "renegotiates" each time he trades. This in turn increases the manager's incentive to acquire and develop valuable information in the first place (as well as to invest in firm-specific human capital).[46] If a manager observes a possible valuable investment for the firm—such as a potential value-increasing merger or a possible new technology—he will be more inclined to pursue this opportunity if he is rewarded upon success.[47] Insider trading is one such reward. The alternative is to tell others of the opportunity, explain that it can be realized with extra effort, and hope to be compensated by some form of ex post settlement. The insider trading alternative reduces the uncertainty and cost of renegotiation and thus increases the incentives of managers to produce valuable information.[48] Moreover, because managers themselves determine the frequency of "renegotiations," they can tailor their compensation scheme to their particular attitudes towards risk.

A related advantage of insider trading is that it provides firms with valuable information concerning prospective managers. It is difficult for firms to identify those prospective managers who will work hard and not be overly risk averse in their choice of investment projects. Basing compensation in part on insider trading is one method for sorting superior from inferior managers. Because insider trading rewards those managers who create valuable information and are willing to take risks, managers who most prefer such compensation schemes may be those who are the least risk averse and the

46. Anthony Kronman has raised the question of whether regulatory attempts to curb insider trading can be justified by "the idea that inside information is more likely to be casually discovered rather than deliberately produced." Kronman, *Mistake, Disclosure, Information, and the Law of Contracts,* 7 J. LEGAL STUD. 1, 34 (1978). The difficulty with phrasing the question in this manner is the assumption that the valuable information already exists. Most valuable information must be deliberately produced before it can be casually acquired. As we have explained, a prohibition against insider trading that is enforced effectively would discourage the production of valuable information.

47. For a discussion of the importance of property rights in information to create incentives to produce information in the tender offer context, see Fischel, *Efficient Capital Market Theory, the Market for Corporate Control, and the Regulation of Cash Tender Offers,* 57 TEX. L. REV. 1 (1978); *see also* Kronman, *supra* note 46, at 9–18 (similar analysis with respect to law of contracts). For a more general discussion of the problem, see Easterbrook, *Insider Trading, supra* note 1.

48. The incentive effect associated with insider trading is likely to be more valuable in unregulated firms where the possibilities for realizing the benefits from value-increasing activities are greater. We predict, therefore, that insider trading is less common in regulated industries. *Cf.* Smith & Watts, *supra* note 27 (finding that incentive plans are more common in unregulated firms).

most capable.[49] Thus, with insider trading, self-selection minimizes the costs of screening potential managers, the monitoring costs created by risk-averse managers, and the opportunity costs resulting from suboptimal investment decisions.

Critics of insider trading correctly point out that compensation schemes that allow insider trading could backfire, particularly if short selling is permitted, since managers would have incentives to reduce the value of the firm. We think that the force of this argument has been exaggerated, a view which we develop in the next section. For present purposes, we wish to emphasize that allowing managers to profit by a decrease in the value of the firm may increase their incentive to *increase* the value of the firm. Insiders are worried about the value of their human capital. If a project succeeds, the insider's value as a manager is increased. But if the project fails, even if the investment was optimal ex ante, the manager will suffer a loss in the value of his human capital because he may be blamed for the failure (the usual monitoring problem).[50] To avoid this loss, managers will tend to accept investment projects that reduce volatility of cash flows even if they do not maximize the value of the firm. By permitting managers to sell short and thereby profit from investment projects that are optimal ex ante, even if they do not turn out well ex post, insider trading may induce managers to take on projects with a high expected return even if they are riskier.[51] The ability to profit by selling, therefore, as well as the ability to profit by buying, may reduce divergence of interests between managers and shareholders by causing managers to behave in a less risk-averse manner.

III. The Arguments Against Insider Trading

Critics have marshalled a wide array of arguments against insider trading. We do not attempt to analyze all of these arguments in detail, but rather focus on the major claims made by critics of insider trading. Nor is our purpose to demonstrate that none of the argu-

49. Recall that diversified investors do not want overly risk-averse managers running the firm.

50. The monitoring problem arises because the principal cannot perfectly observe the actions of the agent. The principal can observe the outcome, which depends only partially on the agent's actions. The principal has no choice but to infer that the agent was operating properly when outcomes are good and improperly when outcomes are bad.

51. *See* Demsetz, *Perfect Competition, Regulation, and the Stock Market*, in Economic Policy and the Regulation of Corporate Securities 1, 15 (H. Manne ed. 1969) ("If we wish decision makers who are risk averse to behave as if they are risk neutral, we may need to increase the reward they derive from successful decisions and reduce the penalty they suffer from unsuccessful decisions.").

ments against insider trading has any merit. But to show that insider trading would not be optimal in a world of perfect information is not a compelling argument for prohibiting insider trading in a world of costly monitoring and imperfect information. Whether the costs of insider trading outweigh the benefits is an empirical question. The apparent absence of widespread prohibitions of insider trading in employment contracts and corporate charters and the existence of common law rules permitting insider trading create a strong presumption that the practice may be beneficial in some circumstances. We argue in this section that the opponents of insider trading have not overcome this strong presumption.

A. *The Problems of Moral Hazard and Unbundling*

Many commentators have argued that insider trading is harmful because it creates a moral hazard by allowing insiders to profit on bad news.[52] At the extreme, they claim that allowing insiders to profit on bad information makes managers indifferent between working to make the firm prosperous and working to make it bankrupt. Another variant of this argument is that insider trading creates incentives for insiders to disseminate false information about the firm so that they can profit by buying and selling mispriced securities.[53] The moral hazard problem is related to the more general but less frequently recognized problem that insider trading allows insiders to unbundle or undo compensation agreements negotiated with the firm. The insider can undo the incentive effects of a stock ownership plan, for example, by selling an equivalent amount of stock. Banning insider trading would prevent insiders from undoing compensation agreements in this manner.

Prohibiting insider trading may be an overly blunt weapon to combat the problems of moral hazard and unbundling. These problems are most acute if short selling is permitted and therefore would be substantially eliminated if short selling, but not other forms of insider trading, were forbidden. Even limited to short selling, however, the argument is far from persuasive. First, short selling may have benefits, as discussed above, if it induces managers to invest in a way that maximizes the value of the firm.[54] Second, the problems themselves may be less severe than commonly assumed. Managers often work in teams and thus must first persuade one an-

52. *See* note 3 *supra* and accompanying text.

53. *See* Ross, *Disclosure Regulation, supra* note 1, at 185.

54. *See* notes 50-51 *supra* and accompanying text.

other that the firm should undertake a particular strategy. If a manager uncovers a good opportunity, his efforts will be magnified by the efforts of other managers and employees who themselves will profit by increasing the value of the firm because their own compensation is thereby increased. The same is not true for poor opportunities. Because each manager will be concerned with his own compensation, which will be tied to the performance of the firm, as well as his long run interest in his human capital, he will be unlikely to go along with a strategy that decreases the value of the firm. Thus, the ability of any one manager to pursue bad opportunities will be constrained because other managers and employees will attempt to maximize the firm's value. Collusion to decrease the value of the firm among managers in pursuit of trading profits is unlikely to succeed because, as in all cartels, each rational member will cheat insofar as the gains to a lone cheater from exposing others will exceed his gains from collusion.[55]

Moreover, the moral hazard and unbundling problems are potentially present in a wide variety of situations where existing insider trading rules do not apply, and casual empiricism suggests that the resulting costs are insignificant. For example, with respect to insider trading, the actions of a key executive of a firm do not differ in principle from those of a key supplier to the firm. If short selling creates a serious moral hazard for a key executive, it must also do so for a key supplier. An executive of the supplier could sell the firm's shares short with little fear of penalty from insider trading laws[56] and then, as long as damages for breach (including those to the supplier's reputation) were less than trading gains, profit from failing to deliver urgently needed materials to the firm.[57] But this possibility is not perceived as a problem, presumably because of the incentives of the supply executive and the supplier itself to develop a reputation as reliable and trustworthy for future commercial dealings. Precisely

55. *See* G. STIGLER, *A Theory of Oligopoly*, in THE ORGANIZATION OF INDUSTRY 39 (1968).

56. The supplier probably owes no fiduciary duty to the shareholders of another firm and has received no inside information from the firm. *See* Chiarella v. United States, 445 U.S. 222, 231-35 (1980).

57. We are using the concept of breach in a descriptive rather than a technical legal sense. If the breach is too blatant, the supplier might be liable for the full extent of the decrease in the value of the firm, thereby eliminating the gains from trading profits. Of course, this is also true for the insider who drives the firm into bankruptcy in order to profit from short selling. (The business judgment rule would not apply in this situation because of the obvious conflict of interest.) The point is that in both cases, a wide range of actions can be taken to decrease the value of the firm and yet avoid an action for damages.

the same is true for key executives of the firm, who have analogous reputational interests that provide incentives for them to maximize the value of their services.

Similarly, instead of selling their own firm short, key executives, by taking a long position in the securities of competitors whose income streams are highly correlated with the income stream of their own firm, can profit by taking actions unfavorable to their own firm.[58] No evidence suggests, however, that the availability of this practice seriously distorts the incentives of insiders to maximize the value of their firms.

In short, the perverse incentive effects that some attribute to insider trading would, for the same reasons, lurk in many practices that are currently unregulated. Given the lack of problems that short selling seems to have engendered (we are not aware of any empirical documentation in the economic literature pointing out the seriousness of these problems), it seems likely that the critics of insider trading have exaggerated the magnitude of the perverse incentives associated with short selling.

B. *Risky Investments*

A related argument made by Richard Leftwich and Robert Verrecchia[59] and Frank Easterbrook[60] is that insiders who trade have a perverse incentive to choose risky (high-variance) projects. Risky projects have a wider range of possible future outcomes, the argument runs, and thus increase the ability of insiders to obtain trading profits on the basis of their superior information. One response is that the incentive to choose riskier projects is not necessarily bad. Stock options increase in value as the volatility of the firm's cash flows increases[61] but no one ever has suggested persuasively that they are inefficient for this reason. On the contrary, the incentive to increase volatility may be one explanation for the existence of stock options. Because managers are risk averse, they, like bondholders, will tend to choose less risky projects even if the value of the firm is

58. Firms could limit the ability of managers to engage in this practice by acquiring other firms whose income streams are not highly correlated. Nobody has argued, however, that avoidance of insider trading is an explanation for conglomerate mergers.

59. *See* R. Leftwich & R. Verrecchia, *supra* note 1.

60. *See* Easterbrook, *Insider Trading, supra* note 1, at 332.

61. *See* Black & Scholes, *The Pricing of Options and Corporate Liabilities,* 81 J. POL. ECON. 637, 644 (1973).

not maximized.[62] An incentive device such as insider trading that, like a stock option, counters this tendency to choose less risky projects may promote shareholders' welfare.

If the claim is that insider trading causes managers to go to the opposite extreme and choose risky projects even at the expense of reducing the value of the firm, the argument and the responses are identical to the moral hazard argument.[63] The reality that managers must work in teams and the various incentives that managers have to maximize the value of their own services suggest that the temptation for managers to engage in value-decreasing activities for the purpose of trading profits may be quite limited. To the extent that some discretion remains, restrictions on insider trading may have little if any effect because of the managers' ability to achieve identical results by speculating in the securities of other firms whose income streams are highly correlated with that of their own firm.

C. *Insider Trading As an Inefficient Compensation Scheme*

Kenneth Scott and Frank Easterbrook have argued that to compensate managers by allowing them to trade on inside information is akin to compensating them with lottery tickets.[64] Because managers are risk averse, the argument runs, they gain less from receiving lottery tickets than the (risk-neutral) shareholders lose.[65] Thus, both managers and shareholders would be better off if such an inefficient compensation scheme were eliminated.

The first difficulty with this reasoning is that lottery tickets given every day are much more likely to be valued at their expected value than tickets given once a lifetime.[66] Thus, insider trading may be a less risky form of compensation scheme than commonly is assumed.

Second, and more importantly, the argument ignores the value of providing managers with contingent claims on the firm's income stream as a solution to the principal-agent problem. While share-

---

62. *See* Smith & Watts, *supra* note 27; *see also* Shavell, *Risk Sharing and Incentives in the Principal and Agent Relationship,* 10 BELL J. ECON. 55, 66 (1979).

63. *See* text accompanying notes 52–58 *supra.*

64. *See* note 7 *supra* and accompanying text.

65. Shareholdeis need not be risk neutral for this argument to apply. Many risk-averse shareholders, each holding only a small fraction of the firm in their optimal portfolio, will suffice.

66. This suggests that the expected value of trading profits will be less likely to be part of a compensation scheme where the relationship is short lived, the opportunities to trade are infrequent, and the stakes are large and highly uncertain (e.g., hiring an outside legal expert to investigate the legality of a proposed merger). *See* text accompanying note 95 *infra.*

holders could assume most risk by providing managers with career-long fixed claims on the firm's income stream, such a compensation scheme would not be optimal. As we have emphasized, a manager with a fixed claim on the firm's income stream would, like a bond-holder, tend to prefer projects that reduce variability of cash flows, even if the value of the firm is decreased. Low-risk projects ensure that the firm's cash flows will be sufficient to cover the managers' fixed claims and therefore give these claims greater value. But while the managers' fixed claims are more secure, the value of the residual claims of the shareholders may decrease.[67]

Contingent payments, whether in the form of bonuses, stock options, salary renegotiation, or insider trading, can tie managers' fortunes more closely to those of the firm. When used in lieu of salary, the expected value of these contingent payments is likely to exceed the expected value of salary because managers must be compensated for accepting this increased risk. But shareholders are not troubled by this possibility because they realize that contingent payments will lead to a larger pie of which both shareholders and managers will receive a larger slice.[68] Therefore, managers' risk aversion does not cause insider trading, any more than any other form of contingent payment, to be an inefficient compensation scheme.

Stephen Ross has proposed another variant of the inefficient-compensation-scheme hypothesis. Ross argues that the market for managerial services is not competitive, and as a result, managers are able to obtain contracts that allow insider trading. Insider trading enables managers to obtain higher compensation than they would receive if labor markets were competitive.[69] But there is no evidence to support the premise that labor markets are not competitive, and Ross suggests none. Moreover, Ross suggests no reason why, if labor markets really are not competitive, managers would use their monopoly power to trade on inside information rather than simply demanding a higher salary.

A final version of the argument that insider trading is an ineffi-

67. Managers with fixed claims do not share in the "upside" and so are indifferent to returns above their claims. Managers also have more wealth tied up in one firm and are less able to diversify. Shareholders, on the other hand, would prefer that project decisions be based on present value analysis, which assesses the combination of both risk and return.

68. This principle has limits. The increased expected value of contingent payments is worth paying only if there is a corresponding incentive effect. Thus, top managers are more likely to be paid a higher percentage of their total compensation in contingent claims than are janitors. *See* note 48 *supra*; text accompanying note 95 *infra*.

69. Ross, *Disclosure Regulation, supra* note 1, at 184, 193.

cient compensation device is that it works very imperfectly. Insiders, the argument runs, frequently will be compensated because of their fortuitous access to information rather than as a result of increased effort; even noninsiders such as janitors or secretaries will derive benefits from information.[70] At the extreme, the notion is that access to valuable information is substantially random. Again, however, there is no evidence in support of this position. Indeed, empirical evidence suggests that trading profits are positively correlated with position in the firms—the more important the position, the greater the trading profits.[71] This is not to suggest that access to valuable information will never be fortuitous. But to conclude that insider trading is an inefficient compensation scheme for this reason is a form of the Nirvana fallacy whereby existing arrangements are viewed as inferior to those that would prevail in a perfect world with zero information and transaction costs. No compensation scheme works perfectly. Managers may profit from a stock option plan, for example, because of an upturn in the market as a whole as opposed to their own productivity. The stock might have reached the same price without the stock option plan. But this possibility does not prove that stock option plans are inefficient. The relevant inquiry is not whether insider trading, stock options, or other forms of compensation work perfectly, but whether, in a world of imperfect compensation and costly monitoring, the same benefits can be obtained at lower cost from other imperfect types of compensation. Unless this can be shown, it is impossible to conclude that insider trading is an inefficient compensation scheme.

D. *Business Property*

Several commentators have stressed that insider trading should not be permitted in situations involving business property.[72] But this is simply another way of stating that insiders should not be allowed to appropriate a property right in information where the right has been allocated to the firm. It does not address the key question of why the firm and not the managers always should be allocated the property right in information. Obviously, if the firm chooses to allocate the information right to the managers and allows insider trad-

70. Levmore, *supra* note 1, at 149; Scott, *supra* note 1, at 809.

71. *See* H. Seyhun, Analysis of Market Response to Insider Trading Information (May 3, 1983) (unpublished manuscript) (on file with *Stanford Law Review*).

72. Easterbrook, *Insider Trading, supra* note 1, at 334; Scott, *supra* note 1, at 814-15, 817-18.

ing, then insider trading cannot be construed as a taking of business property.

E. *Timing of Disclosure*

Yet another argument made against insider trading is that it causes the disclosure of information to be delayed.[73] Like the other criticisms of insider trading, this one is a logical possibility, but has little empirical basis.[74] Our analysis demonstrates, moreover, that delaying disclosure of information may be beneficial in some situations. For example, some valuable information should be kept from competitors if it is to retain its value. Furthermore, the argument assumes that all information can be disclosed. But information such as revisions of probabilities of future states cannot necessarily be conveyed directly. In cases where disclosure otherwise would be either undesirable or impossible, insider trading gives firms an additional method for communicating information. Finally, insider trading in some cases may accelerate the speed of disclosure because the ability to profit is dependent on information reaching the market. Thus insiders, if allowed to trade, may have strong incentives to communicate information to the market.

F. *The Liquidity of the Stock Market*

Insider trading allows individuals to profit by trading on superior information. If transactions occur between uninformed and informed traders who are otherwise identical and if the uninformed know this, then the uninformed should realize that they could be better off not trading. In order to induce trade, something must prevent the uninformed from holding the "market" and not trading. Otherwise, markets for stock would become less liquid, and consequently, the people who have to trade for exogenous reasons (e.g., to pay for a child's tuition or to reallocate portfolios because of new inheritances) perforce would provide the profits for insider trading. Insider trading could be detrimental to the extent it reduces liquidity.

This problem raises the more general question of why the uninformed ever trade in individual stocks, a question to which theory provides no convincing answer.[75] Suffice it to say that no obvious

73. *See* note 6 *supra* and accompanying text.

74. *See* Dooley, *supra* note 1, at 34 (finding, after examining cases, that insider trading did not delay the public disclosure of information).

75. For a discussion of this problem, see Stiglitz, *Information and Capital Markets,* in Fi-

logic indicates that insider trading has any substantial effect on liquidity. If insiders could not trade, the gains to noninsiders from discovering nonpublic information would be higher and investors would have an incentive to expend resources to uncover such information. In fact, the only effect a ban on insider trading might have is that those with better access to information, such as brokers, would reap some of the gains from inside information. While this may be inefficient because brokers can become informed only at a higher cost, the informed-uninformed trader problem remains. Smart brokers, in other words, cause the same problem as smart insiders. Uninformed traders who know they are uninformed should not trade in either situation. That trade occurs suggests that traders either do not believe they are uninformed or realize that enough informed trading occurs for the prevailing prices to reflect most material information.[76]

G. *Fairness Arguments*

We have left for last the most common argument against insider trading—that it is unfair or immoral. The prevalence of this intui-

NANCIAL ECONOMICS: ESSAYS IN HONOR OF PAUL COOTNER 118 (W. Sharpe & C. Cootner eds. 1982).

76. Even if insider trading does reduce liquidity in the market for stock, firms, which would presumably bear the resulting costs, would try to prohibit insider trading. Such prohibitions would not be forthcoming only if the loss of liquidity imposed externalities—that is, if all firms whose stocks are traded on a particular exchange shared in the costs of any one firm allowing insider trading. The notion is that the exchange suffers when liquidity of any one stock is reduced. (The economic theory of market exchanges is still in its infancy. *See* Telser, *Why There Are Organized Futures Markets,* 24 J.L. & ECON. 1 (1982) (explaining existence of organized futures markets).) If true, this argument could provide grounds for prohibitions that firms could not opt out of. The prohibitions would come from stock exchanges themselves, as they compete with each other for optimal rules. Federal regulations would not be needed, unless the subpoena power of the state constitutes an enforcement advantage. Interestingly, some foreign stock exchanges (e.g., in the U.K.) have suggested guidelines governing insider trading. P. RIDER & H. FRENCH, *supra* note 16, at 166-70. Still, the notion that exchanges are harmed by insider trading is hard to square with the following facts: (1) the stock market was successful pre-1933 (before insider trading laws); (2) the stock market was successful pre-1960's (before judicial extension of insider trading laws); (3) the stock market is currently successful despite the existence of legal and perhaps illegal insider trading. A useful empirical study would be an analysis of the price of a seat on the New York Stock Exchange before and after judicial extension of Rule 10b-5 in SEC v. Texas Gulf Sulphur Co., 401 F.2d 833 (2d Cir. 1968) (en banc), *cert. denied,* 404 U.S. 1005 (1971).

Another externality related argument against insider trading is that the reduced liquidity of one stock could affect information about another stock. For example, if firms A and B compete, the price movements of firm A could reveal information about firm B (e.g., common industry demand). If stock of firm A is traded less frequently, information about firm B could be diminished. We are grateful to Ivan P'ng for this point. On the other hand, if insider trading causes the stock of firm A to be more informative, *see* text accompanying notes 33-39 *supra,* information about firm B could be increased.

tion is so powerful that many commentators have argued that insider trading should be prohibited even if it is efficient.[77] What is commonly left unsaid is how and why insider trading is unfair.[78]

Kenneth Scott has pointed out that if the existence of insider trading is known, as it surely is, outsiders will not be disadvantaged because the price they pay will reflect the risk of insider trading.[79] This is a useful insight and in some sense is a complete response to the claim that investors are exploited by insider trading. But the argument does not address the desirability of insider trading. If traders knew that a firm burned half of its assets, the price would fall and subsequent investors in the firm would have the same expected returns as any other asset of comparable risk. But the fact that investors would not be fooled does not mean that burning assets is a beneficial practice. On the contrary, firms that followed this strategy to a substantial degree, like firms that adopted inefficient compensation schemes, could not survive over time.

A more powerful response to the argument that insiders profit at the expense of outsiders is that if insider trading is a desirable compensation scheme, it benefits insiders and outsiders alike. Nobody would argue seriously that salaries, options, bonuses, and other compensation devices allow insiders to profit at the expense of outsiders because these sums otherwise would have gone to shareholders. Compensating managers in this fashion increases the size of the pie, and thus outsiders as well as insiders profit from the incentives managers are given to increase the value of the firm. Insider trading does not come "at the expense of" outsiders for precisely the same reason.[80]

Contrary to popular sentiment with respect to insider trading,

77. *See, e.g.*, Schotland, *supra* note 2, at 1439 ("Even if we found that unfettered insider trading would bring an economic gain, we might still forgo that gain in order to secure a stock market and intracorporate relationships that satisfy such noneconomic goals as fairness, just rewards and integrity.").

78. For an excellent discussion and refutation of the various forms of the fairness arguments in the context of insider trading, see Easterbrook, *Insider Trading*, *supra* note 1, at 323-30.

79. Scott, *supra* note 1, at 807-09.

80. Numerous commentators have argued that insider trading raises firms' cost of capital because insiders' gains are diverted from, and therefore come "at the expense of," outsiders. *See* Mendelson, *supra* note 1, at 477-78; note 8 *supra* and accompanying text. One fallacy in this argument is that it assumes the size of the pie is fixed. Under this logic, all forms of managerial compensation would raise firms' cost of capital because shareholders receive less than they otherwise would. Moreover, even if the size of the pie is fixed, the argument ignores that in a competitive labor market, the salary of a manager who cannot trade on inside information will be higher than that of a manager who can trade. The stockholder class as a

therefore, there is no tension between considerations of fairness and of efficiency. To say that insider trading is a desirable method of compensating corporate managers is to say that shareholders would voluntarily enter into contractual arrangements with insiders giving them property rights in valuable information. If insider trading is efficient, no independent notions of fairness suggest that it should be prohibited.

IV. Legal Rules Restricting Insider Trading

In this section, we analyze the common law and various state and federal rules governing insider trading. At the outset, we should note the fundamental difference between state and federal rules governing internal corporate relationships. States' ability to enact rules that reduce investors' welfare is limited by competition between states. If one state adopts inefficient rules, it is a simple matter for a firm to avoid them by reincorporating in another state. Therefore, state statutory and common law rules that survive over time, like private contractual arrangements, are presumptively welfare increasing. Not surprisingly, enabling statutes such as Delaware's, which allow private parties to structure their affairs with relative freedom, have demonstrated the greatest survival qualities.[81]

Analysis of federal rules yields exactly the opposite conclusion. Federal rules—whether pertaining to the amount of information produced, the types of issues on which shareholders are entitled to vote, or whether firms can structure compensation packages that include a property right in information—displace private arrangements and the competition between states. Although firms can avoid these rules by not incorporating or by "going private," they obviously would find these alternatives more costly than simply changing the state of incorporation. Federal rules governing insider trading or any other aspect of intracorporate activity, therefore, are not entitled to the same presumption of efficiency as are long-standing state rules.[82]

---

whole winds up paying the managers' compensation whether or not insider trading is ultimately part of the manager's compensation package.

81. *See* R. Winter, *supra* note 15, at 7–11; Fischel, *supra* note 15, at 921–23. For an empirical study demonstrating that reincorporation in Delaware increases shareholders' welfare, see Dodd & Leftwich, *The Market for Corporate Charters: "Unhealthy Competition" versus Federal Regulation,* 53 J. Bus. 259 (1980).

82. For a similar analysis with respect to legal rules governing voting, see Easterbrook & Fischel, *supra* note 15, at 418–19.

A. *Common Law Rules*

The general common law rule is that insider trading in publicly traded corporations is permitted.[83] Failure by an insider to disclose information before trading is not actionable. Neither the corporation nor an investor trading on the opposite side of a transaction to the insider has any legal remedies against the insider. This general common law rule has some exceptions. Some jurisdictions allowed suits against insiders for trading if the plaintiff could prove "special facts"—that his trade was induced by express or implied misrepresentations concerning the value of the securities or the identity of the purchaser.[84] Corporations also have been allowed to bring actions under the corporate opportunity doctrine against insiders who take advantage of their knowledge in ways that harm the firms' business.[85] For example, an employee who, upon learning of an impending land purchase or corporate repurchase plan, rushes out and purchases the land or shares in order to resell to the firm at a high price would be held to have usurped a corporate opportunity.

This general common law rule is consistent with our analysis. Because trading by insiders appears to be consistent with their contract with the firm, no action lies for the firm or for a shareholder on the firm's behalf.[86] If the insider (or someone acting on his behalf) makes misrepresentations about the value of the firm or his identity in convincing an uninformed outsider to sell, however, the informational effect of the trade that we have discussed above is lost. Indeed the trade, like other types of fraud, will move prices away from, rather than towards, the "correct" price, particularly if the trade is a face-to-face transaction as opposed to an impersonal one.[87] Moreover, the incentive effect created by allowing such trades would be to distort

83. *See, e.g.,* Goodwin v. Agassiz, 283 Mass. 358, 186 N.E. 659 (1933); *see also* note 14 *supra.*

84. *See, e.g.,* Strong v. Repide, 213 U.S. 419 (1909). These cases typically did not involve publicly traded corporations and thus are not technically exceptions to the general common law rule.

85. *See, e.g.,* Guth v. Loft, Inc., 23 Del. Ch. 255, 5 A.2d 503 (1939).

86. One well known case has held that there is such a cause of action. *See* Diamond v. Oreamuno, 24 N.Y.2d 494, 248 N.E.2d 910, 301 N.Y.S.2d 78 (1969). *Diamond,* however, is a clear departure from the common law rule and has not been followed by other courts. *See* Freeman v. Decio, 584 F.2d 186 (7th Cir. 1978); Schein v. Chasen, 519 F.2d 453 (2d Cir. 1975).

87. The price set by trading activity of different types of traders with different information protects the uninformed in impersonal exchanges in a way that is not present in face to face transactions. For an elaboration, see Fischel, *Use of Modern Finance Theory in Securities Fraud Cases Involving Actively Traded Securities,* 38 BUS. LAW. 1, 3–5 (1982).

information as opposed to producing new information. The "special facts" rule, therefore, is a recognition that trading by insiders need not be protected when such trading is not efficient.[88]

The rationale for applying the corporate opportunity doctrine to insider trading also seems clear. If actions based on insider information harm the firm, those actions will be prohibited. In the land case, the firm instead of buying land in a competitive market must now negotiate with the employee. Transaction costs have risen. Firms would prefer to ban such behavior and pay the employee through increased salary. Similarly, the purchase of a target's shares in advance of a takeover probably would be considered a usurpation of a corporate opportunity. The action bids up the price of the target firm's shares and thereby makes the corporate action more expensive. This reduces the value of the takeover to the firm.[89] Thus, fiduciary duties under common law ban nonconsensual use of inside information, whether through trading in shares or otherwise, where the precipitating event is so rare as not to justify an explicit contractual prohibition.

B. *Section 10(b) and Rule 10b-5*

Courts have recently interpreted section 10(b) of the Security Exchange Act of 1934 and Rule 10b-5, promulgated under the 1934 Act by the Securities and Exchange Commission, to require corporate insiders and tippees either to disclose material inside information or to refrain from trading.[90] Several aspects of this cause of action are analyzed below.

---

88. Because the "special facts" exception typically has been applied to firms with few shareholders as opposed to publicly traded firms, it may also be premised, at least implicitly, on the difference between the principal-agent problems presented by the two situations.

89. This problem can arise in other contexts. In one case, Brophy v. Cities Serv. Co., 31 Del. Ch. 241, 70 A.2d 5 (1949), an employee's purchase of his firm's shares in advance of an impending corporate repurchase program was deemed a breach of fiduciary duty. Just as in the takeover example, the insider's purchase of shares in this situation had the effect of making the firm's contemplated action (i.e. corporate repurchase of shares) more expensive. A complete analysis of the welfare consequences of the decision in this case would require a more satisfactory explanation of the purposes of a corporate repurchase than is currently available.

90. *See, e.g.,* SEC v. Texas Gulf Sulphur Co., 401 F.2d 833 (2d Cir. 1968) (en banc), *cert. denied,* 404 U.S. 1005 (1971). This judicial development is, in all probability, contrary to congressional intent. There is no evidence that in enacting § 10(b) Congress intended to prohibit insider trading. In inferring a private damage remedy under Rule 10b-5 for insider trading, courts have invented both the substantive prohibition and a remedy for its violation. For a more complete articulation of this argument, see Dooley, *supra* note 1, at 55–69; Easterbrook, *Insider Trading, supra* note 1, at 317–20.

1. *The disclose-or-abstain-from-trading rule.*

Proponents of insider trading regulation may argue that section 10(b) and Rule 10b-5, as interpreted, do not actually prohibit insiders from trading; these provisions simply give the insider the option of either disclosing the nonpublic information or refraining from trading. Despite this formulation of the rule in the alternative, however, the rule, if enforced, actually operates as an almost complete prohibition against trading.

In many cases, the insider may not be able to disclose the information. For example, the information might be valuable to competitors. Indeed, it is in precisely such situations that insider trading may provide firms with a valuable additional method of communicating information to the market.[91] Forcing disclosure thus removes the firms' ability to use insider trading as a tool of communication when it is most needed. The result is usually neither trading nor disclosure.

In those situations where disclosure is both possible and not harmful to the firm, the act of disclosure in an efficient market will eliminate the gains to insiders from trading. The insider is then better off not trading. This outcome is undesirable if, as we have argued, the possibility of profits from trading gives managers an incentive to maximize the value of the firm to the benefit of themselves and shareholders alike. The disclose-or-abstain-from-trading rule weakens this incentive device.

The adverse effect of the rule on incentives to acquire valuable information is also evident in the context of investment analysts. These individuals perform a valuable economic function in monitoring corporate conduct and contributing to the efficient pricing of securities, which in turn leads to more effective markets in capital, managerial services, and corporate control.[92] Analysts' incentives to collect information about different firms lie in their ability to sell the acquired information to others or to profit directly by trading themselves. If they are unable to capitalize on the value of the information in one of these ways, analysts obviously will have no incentive to invest resources to gather information in the first place.[93] This is pre-

91. *See* text accompanying notes 36-39 *supra.*

92. *See generally* Jensen & Meckling, *supra* note 40. It is impossible to make a welfare statement as to whether there are too many or too few investment analysts.

93. This point has been lost on the SEC, as illustrated by its prosecution of Raymond Dirks for his role as an investment analyst in uncovering one of the major corporate scandals in recent years. *See* Raymond L. Dirks, S.E.C. Release No. 17,480 (Jan. 26, 1981). The Supreme Court has recently held that Dirks did not act illegally because the insiders that gave him the information did not benefit, directly or indirectly, from tipping the information,

cisely the effect of the disclose-or-abstain-from-trading rule. As in the case of corporate insiders, therefore, applying the rule to analysts reduces the gains to beneficial economic activity and therefore decreases the frequency of its occurrence.

2. *The requirement of a trade on the basis of material inside information.*

The effect of Rule 10b-5 should not be exaggerated. The disclose-or-abstain-from-trading rule applies only if a defendant trades on the basis of "material" inside information such as knowledge of an oil discovery, impending merger, or major change in earnings. This ensures that section 10(b) and Rule 10b-5 will have a minimal impact on insiders' behavior.

Insiders, because of their superior access to information, do not need to trade in order to outperform the market. They simply can earn superior returns through careful selection of their initial purchases. Moreover, trades motivated by knowledge of "bombshell" events which are the substance of lawsuits are the aberration, not the rule. Far more common are trades that allow insiders to earn rates of return that are on average slightly in excess of the market as a whole on a risk-adjusted basis.[94] These trades, though based on "inside" information in an economic sense (i.e. knowledge of information not fully reflected in stock prices), are not subject to legal attack because the materiality requirement is not satisfied. Knowledge that one of the firm's top managers is dispirited because of family problems or because preliminary reports on a new technological

but rather acted out of a desire to expose the fraud. Dirks v. SEC, 103 S. Ct. 3255, 3261-66 (1983). The existence of benefit is a question of fact to be determined by courts. *Id.* at 3265. Because many cases will exist where providing information to analysts will result in some type of benefit to the insider, the Court's test will not, in all probability, significantly decrease the application of Rule 10b-5 to investment analysts.

The Court's reasoning in *Dirks* is dubious. The Court stated that the "benefit" test was premised on the "inherent unfairness" when one takes advantage of "information intended to be available only for a corporate purpose and not for the personal benefit of anyone." *Id.* at 3261. The Court assumed that the property right in valuable information is always "intended" to be allocated to shareholders as opposed to managers. As we have argued, however, no basis exists for this assumption. *See* note 101 *infra.* Application of the "benefit" test will also be difficult. It would appear to allow an employee to give tips to individuals in anger or spite as long as he doesn't "profit." (Presumably he gains something—why else would he decide to release the information?) Tips to strangers are legal but tips to relatives are not. For a fuller analysis of *Dirks, see* Fischel, *Insider Trading and Investment Analysts: An Economic Analysis of* Dirks v. Securities and Exchange Commission, 3 SUP. CT. ECON. REV. — (forthcoming 1984).

94. *See* studies collected in note 12 *supra.*

process show that costs are running much higher than expected are examples of valuable information that is almost surely not material in a legal sense.[95] As long as insiders are allowed to own and trade shares, therefore, Rule 10b-5 is likely to have a minimal deterrent effect on most of the insiders' desired trading activities.

An argument could be made, however, that the materiality requirement effectively limits the operation of Rule 10b-5 to those cases of insider trading where the trading is inefficient. Certain classes of individuals—lawyers, accountants, printers, and government officials—typically receive valuable information only after it has been produced. Because the positive incentive effects created by allowing these individuals to trade are likely to be trivial or nonexistent, the firm may want to ban such trading. Similarly, in rare cases involving bombshell events where the rewards are large and highly uncertain, the value of the uncertain trading profits to risk-averse managers (and others) will be very low compared to the expected value of the event. Here again, insider trading might be an inefficient compensation scheme. In both classes of cases, firms might want to ban insider trading, but because the precipitating event is so rare, it simply may not be worth the (small) cost of including the prohibition in the corporate charter. If the materiality requirement acts as a filter distinguishing these two classes of cases from the more typical but less dramatic cases where insiders earn positive abnormal returns, it may be beneficial.

But the absence of observed contractual prohibitions before and after regulation and the failure of the common law to develop along these lines cast some doubt on this hypothesis. It may be, for example, that the incentive effects created by insider trading are most needed in connection with bombshell events such as identifying potential takeover targets or developing new technologies. Moreover, a firm might want to allow some individuals but not others to trade on the basis of material information. Thus, a firm might want to allow the manager who identifies a possible merger to trade on this information but simultaneously to deny the attorney who is hired to investigate the legality of the proposed merger the same ability. The materiality requirement, because it denies firms the ability to make this choice, is probably inefficient. Applying the materiality stan-

95. For discussion of the distinction between the meaning of information in an economic sense and the legal definition of materiality, see Lorie, *Insider Trading: Rule 10b-5, Disclosure, and Corporate Privacy: A Comment,* 9 J. LEGAL STUD. 819, 820–21 (1980); *see also* Fischel, *supra* note 87, at 5–7; Heller, *supra* note 1, at 526–32.

dard only to those cases of clearly nonconsensual trading (i.e., purchasing shares of a potential target) would be more consistent with the common law.

3. *The requirement of fiduciary duty.*

The Supreme Court has drawn a sharp distinction between the ability of insiders and the ability of others, such as printers or government officials, to trade on the basis of nonpublic information.[96] Because insiders are employed by the firm and thus owe a fiduciary duty to investors, the Court has reasoned that insiders cannot trade on the basis of inside information. Outsiders owe no such duty, however, and thus can trade without violating section 10(b) or Rule 10b-5.[97]

The legal distinction between insiders and outsiders rests on a questionable basis. The difficulty with limiting the class of "insiders" to those within the firm is that long term contracts are often a substitute for horizontal or vertical integration.[98] Outside suppliers or outside counsel may have as much inside information and ability to affect the fortunes of the firm as employees.[99] Nor is invoking "fiduciary duties" helpful in resolving who should be allowed to trade on inside information. Fiduciary duties are standard-form contractual terms that govern agency relationships.[100] They allow the parties to avoid excessively lengthy and detailed agreements, thereby reducing the costs of contracting. But such duties should be imposed only as a constraint on conduct if there is very clear evidence that most parties would impose the identical constraint by contract if bargaining were costless. Otherwise, imposing fiduciary duties threatens to create regulatory constraints on private behavior in the name of standard-form contractual terms. For this reason, no basis exists for interpreting the

96. *See* Dirks v. SEC, 103 S. Ct. 3255, 3261 (1983); Chiarella v. United States, 445 U.S. 222, 225–35 (1980).

97. Outsiders that are tippees, however, appear to be in the same position as insiders. *See Dirks,* 103 S. Ct. at 3261; *Chiarella,* 445 U.S. at 230 n.12. The Court has also stated that some outsiders such as accountants or lawyers who receive information solely for corporate purposes "may become fiduciaries of the shareholders" and thus insiders. *Dirks,* 103 S. Ct. at 3261 n.14.

98. Coase, *The Nature of the Firm,* 4 ECONOMICA 386, 391–92 (1937).

99. Under current legal rules, for example, a supplier to a firm could not be liable for selling the shares of the firm short, but it could be liable if the supplier were vertically integrated into the firm. *See* text accompanying notes 56–57 *supra.*

100. For a more detailed discussion of the function of fiduciary duties, see Easterbrook & Fischel, *Corporate Control Transactions, supra* note 20, at 700–03.

fiduciary duty of corporate managers to prohibit insider trading if some firms prefer to allow it.

The relevant question is whether trading on inside information is consensual, not whether the trader is an insider or outsider. If insider trading is an efficient method for compensating corporate managers, it should be permitted without interference from judicial or legislative notions of fiduciary duties.[101] Conversely, if a firm that intended to make a tender offer would not enter into a contract with a printer of the offering documents allowing him to purchase shares in advance of the offer, it should be irrelevant whether the printer is an outsider or an employee of the firm or whether the shares purchased are those of the target or another firm. Purchase of the shares by the printer might cause the price the firm must pay to rise, making the offer more expensive and producing no offsetting efficiency gains from superior printing. The same is true for suppliers, accountants, lawyers, and others in analogous positions. Whether these individuals are within the firm is a matter of firm organization that should have no effect on the propriety of trading.[102]

4. *The proper plaintiff.*

Federal law creates both private and public enforcement devices against insider trading. Rule 10b-5, as interpreted, gives shareholders who bought and sold during the time insiders were trading standing to bring private damage suits.[103] The federal government also can bring injunctive and criminal actions.[104]

Both of these enforcement schemes are suspect. One of the themes we have emphasized is that the dispute concerning insider trading is really a dispute about how managerial contracts allocate the property right in valuable information. If this property right is allocated to the managers, neither shareholders nor the government

101. The danger of invoking fiduciary duties is illustrated by the Court's statement in Dirks v. SEC, 103 S. Ct. 3255 (1983), that the securities laws were designed "to eliminate the idea that use of inside information for personal advantage was a normal emolument of corporate office." *Id.* at 3261 n.10. The problem with this logic is obvious once it is realized that insider trading, like salary, can be part of a manager's compensation scheme.

102. Casual empiricism suggests that many outside law and accounting firms often have rules preventing employees from trading in the shares of their clients. This provides a good instance of firms preventing insider trading when the positive incentive effects are likely to be small.

103. *See, e.g.,* Elkind v. Liggett & Myers, Inc., 635 F.2d 156 (2d Cir. 1980).

104. *See, e.g.,* SEC v. Texas Gulf Sulphur Co., 401 F.2d 833 (2d Cir. 1968) (en banc), *cert. denied,* 404 U.S. 1005 (1971) (injunctive action); Chiarella v. United States, 445 U.S. 222 (1980) (criminal action).

should have a cause of action. In cases of nonconsensual trading, such as trading by a printer in advance of a tender offer, the firm should have a cause of action for breach of contract.

As in any common law breach of contract action involving a corporation and an employee, the proper plaintiff should be the corporation or, when appropriate, a shareholder bringing a derivative suit on its behalf. The shareholder should have no more right to bring a direct action for insider trading than to challenge directly a salary or bonus decision. If a derivative action is brought, however, it should make no difference whether the complaining shareholder traded at the same time as the insider or, for that matter, traded at all.

The alternative to private enforcement is public enforcement. Because the probability of detection in situations involving nonconsensual trading is less than one and because the gains from trading are potentially great, the argument could be made that public, possibly criminal, enforcement with high penalties is preferable to private enforcement.[105] Insider trading laws under this interpretation would, in effect, be no different than other antitheft prohibitions involving trade secrets or other valuable information. Several reasons, however, suggest that public enforcement by the federal government may be of dubious value.

First, firms themselves may be able to control undesirable use of insider information as well as, and at a lower cost than, the government. Firms have considerable ability to control the flow of valuable information. Confidential information about the firm is not widely circulated. Low level employees whose trading might not produce significant incentive effects may never be privy to any inside information about the firm. Printers who do receive valuable information commonly receive it in code. The firm can monitor the trading activities of individuals likely to have access to inside information with reporting requirements. Moreover, firms can enter into arrangements with stock exchanges or other entities to monitor unusual trading activity in their securities. The ability of firms to control the flow of information as well as trading based on this information suggests, in short, that nonconsensual trading may not present a significant problem so that public enforcement would produce only small benefits.

Second, public enforcement may entail substantial costs. Apart from the obvious costs of regulators' salaries, offices, and other per-

105. *See* Easterbrook, *Insider Trading, supra* note 1, at 334 (relying on Landes & Posner, *The Private Enforcement of Law,* 4 J. LEGAL STUD. 1 (1974)).

quisites, public enforcement with high penalties might deter a significant amount of beneficial, consensual insider trading, particularly because regulators, unlike firms, are not disciplined by markets. (This danger would be minimized, of course, if firms could trigger the insider trading prohibition in the same manner as they do other antitheft prohibitions.) Until greater evidence than is currently available shows that a problem actually exists, the case for public enforcement, particularly federal enforcement, has not been made.

The preferable course would be to allow competition among states, rather than federal fiat, to resolve the issue of the desirability of public enforcement of nonconsensual insider trading. If public enforcement, criminal or otherwise, is optimal, states have incentives to provide it. That states before and after federal regulation have not enacted public enforcement schemes directed against insider trading suggests that such schemes are not optimal.[106]

C. *Section 16*

Section 16 of the Securities Exchange Act of 1934 requires directors, officers, and large stockholders (owning over 10% of the firm) to report trades in equity securities of their firm on a monthly basis, provides the firm with a cause of action to recover any profits made from the purchase and sale of securities in a 6-month period, and prohibits short selling. Section 16 differs from section 10(b) and Rule 10b-5 in several major respects: (1) Section 16 does not require trading on inside information for an action to lie—any short term profits made by buying and selling are recoverable;[107] (2) its scope is limited to the 6-month period; (3) it makes only specific insiders liable; and (4) it allows only the firm to recover.

1. *Reporting requirements.*

Requiring insiders to report their trades allows investors to make more accurate inferences about insiders' compensation schedules. Moreover, requiring insiders to report their trades provides information to future managers about potential compensation that is avail-

106. Federal regulation of insider trading does not eliminate the incentives of states to adopt their own regulatory schemes. Because federal regulation does not appear to have affected either the frequency or the profitability of trading, *see* note 11 *supra* and accompanying text, states (as well as firms) have strong incentives to deter the practice if it is detrimental to investors.

107. This prophylactic effect of § 16 has been weakened by judicial decisions that find liability under § 16 only where there has been a showing of a "possibility for speculative abuse." *See* Kern County Land Co. v. Occidental Petroleum Corp., 411 U.S. 582, 601 (1973).

able. These benefits might be small, however, because of the difficulty of inferring information from trading profits when portfolio decisions may be governed by many factors. An additional benefit is that the information effect of the insiders' trades will be strengthened if trades are observable ex post. The cost of post-trade reporting requirements appears to be limited to the cost of implementing such requirements.

2. *The prohibition against short-swing trading.*

Section 16(b), which authorizes the corporation to recover short-swing profits, has the advantage of placing the cause of action with the corporation. The more basic question, however, is whether there should be a cause of action at all. If insider trading provides net benefits to the firm, why does it warrant different treatment when the buying and selling occurs within a 6-month period?

One possible response is that the prohibition of short-swing trading decreases the ability of insiders to manipulate stock prices (i.e., to move prices away from their equilibrium value).[108] Suppose that insiders knew that their purchases would cause the price of shares to rise. In this event, insiders could make capital gains by purchasing shares and then immediately reselling (or selling short) before the market became aware of the manipulation and settled back to its former level. Prohibiting the buying and selling of shares within a 6-month period reduces the ability of insiders to engage in this sort of practice. But the prohibition (assuming it is enforced) may also entail substantial costs. Both the incentive and information effects of insider trading are weakened if a substantial set of trades are prohibited. The prohibition of short-swing trading also has the effect of forcing managers to hold nondiversified portfolios for longer periods of time. This will necessitate raising their compensation from other sources. Moreover, the ability of insiders to manipulate stock prices should not be exaggerated. The reason the market price might rise if insiders purchase is that investors believe such purchases convey valuable information about the firm's prospects. Investors will believe this only if the message conveyed by the insiders' trades is borne out by an increase in the firm's earnings. Manipulation, in sum, is inherently a shortrun phenomenon. Insiders who mislead investors will have their future attempts to convey information discounted by the market. And managers will balance any shortrun gains against long-

108. *See* H. MANNE, INSIDER TRADING AND THE STOCK MARKET, *supra* note 1, at 30.

run losses resulting from their inability to communicate information and, more generally, from a decrease in the value of their human capital.[109] In light of the low probability that manipulation is a serious problem and of the costs of a general prohibition of all buying and selling of securities within a 6-month period, the problem might better be addressed on a case-by-case basis, as are other types of fraud.

3. *Prohibition against short sales.*

The moral hazard and unbundling problems,[110] as well as the possible incentive of insiders to increase the volatility of earnings,[111] are most acute when insiders are permitted to engage in short selling. Section 16's prohibition against short selling can be viewed as an attempt to limit these perceived adverse consequences of insider trading.[112]

For the reasons discussed above,[113] however, we are skeptical of the magnitude of these effects. Moreover, banning short selling is not without costs. Short selling may be a valuable method of communicating information about the firm's prospects. In addition, the ability to short sell may induce managers to make superior investment decisions. In this event, shareholders might not contract for a ban on short selling.[114] This may explain why the common law made no distinction between short selling and other forms of insider trading.

The effect of section 16 on shareholders' welfare, therefore, is ambiguous. The reporting requirements, the prohibition against short-swing trading, and the ban on short sales all have a plausible basis, but also impose costs. The relative magnitudes of the costs and benefits are unknown. But the apparent absence of widespread private contractual arrangements or state law rules embodying restrictions

109. For a similar argument that managers have little ability and incentive to use dividend policy to mislead investors, see Fischel, *The Law and Economics of Dividend Policy,* 67 VA. L. REV. 699 (1981).

110. *See* notes 52-58 *supra* and accompanying text.

111. *See* notes 59-63 *supra* and accompanying text.

112. Short selling is only a special case of selling by insiders who will frequently be substantial equity holders in the firm. While prohibiting short selling limits the gains on bad news, it by no means eliminates them. Mangers can sell their shares on bad news and then replace them at lower cost after the market reacts.

113. *See* notes 52-63 *supra* and accompanying text.

114. This is not to suggest, however, that there may not be implicit contracts forbidding short sales in some circumstances. If a manager were observed to take large net short positions consistently, for example, a cause for termination might exist.

like those in section 16 creates a presumption that the benefits of section 16 do not outweigh the costs.

V. Summary and Conclusion

The most important points to understand in order to assess the desirability of insider trading laws are as follows:

1. Both the common law and state law place few, if any, restraints on insider trading. Section 16 of the Securities Exchange Act of 1934 restricts the trading of a select few insiders. Since the 1960's, judicial construction of section 10(b) and Rule 10b-5 has attempted to restrict the trading of employees and tippees based on "material" information. The existing law places no restrictions on transactions involving shares of competitors or trading based on "nonmaterial" information. The empirical evidence suggests that the judicial reinterpretation of section 10(b) as a ban on insider trading has had no detectable effect on insiders' rates of return. The existing laws make an artificial distinction between insiders and outsiders even where the outsiders have dealings with the firm, and these laws fail to constrain the trading activities of "outsiders." Therefore, existing federal regulations ban only a small percentage of trades by individuals with superior information.

2. No evidence suggests that firms generally have attempted to prohibit insider trading or, after 1934, attempted to plug the large gaps in the federal bans against insider trading.

3. The recent articles in the economic literature as well as the older general criticisms that illustrate some possible inefficiencies associated with trading by insiders do not justify the current federal regulations, but rather would justify far broader restrictions on insider trading. Such broader restrictions seem inconsistent with the desires of firms as revealed through their own choices of contractual terms and corporate charter provisions and with the development of state and common law rules.

4. Firms have strong incentives to allocate property rights in valuable information to the highest-valuing user. The absence of widespread prohibitions on insider trading in employment agreements and corporate charters indicates that firms may, in some situations, want to allocate this property right to managers or other employees. We have suggested several information and efficiency effects of insider trading to explain why this might be the case.

5. Even if the property right in information is allocated to the firm, federal regulation of insider trading would be justifiable only if

the federal regulations could enforce contracts against insider trading at a lower cost than private firms or states. The evidence does not conclusively support (or refute) this conclusion.

6. Even if federal regulation is justified on the basis of low enforcement costs, firms should have the opportunity to opt out of the regulation in the absence of any showing of third party effects. Firms are the best judges of how to structure the terms of their employment contracts.

7. The one aspect of existing regulation of insider trading under section 10(b) and Rule 10b-5 that might be desirable is public enforcement of nonconsensual trading based on material information. Because the materiality requirement does not distinguish between consensual and nonconsensual trading, however, it is not efficient.

8. Arguments can also be made in favor of the various provisions of section 16(b). And because the firm is the proper plaintiff in cases brought under this section, the danger of deterring consensual trading is greatly reduced. But the absence of private restrictions and common law rules like those in section 16(b) casts doubt on its desirability.

Based on the available evidence (which admittedly is scanty in some places), it appears that the allocation of the valuable property right in information would be better left to private negotiations and common law development.

[7]

Northwestern University Law Review

Printed in U.S.A.
Vol. 80, No. 6

A COASIAN MODEL OF INSIDER TRADING

*David D. Haddock**
*Jonathan R. Macey***

I. Introduction

Coase's pioneering observation that contracting parties, absent transactions costs, will reach a Pareto efficient allocation of property rights seems to have particular force when applied to the dilemma of insider trading. In this Article we seek to bring Coase's insight to bear on the insider trading debate: We consider what intrafirm rule shareholders would select if they could decide for themselves whether to permit their insiders to trade on information not yet reflected in the price of their firm's shares. In the context of insider trading, the relevant parties—insiders and shareholders—are in privity of contract[1] because of the insiders' employment with the shareholders' firm. As we will see, the

---

* Associate Professor of Economics, Emory University. B.A., Oklahoma State University (1966); Ph.D., University of Chicago (1980). Research for this Article originated while Professor Haddock was a Research Fellow in Civil Liability at the Yale Law School.

** Associate Professor of Law, Emory University School of Law; Visiting Associate Professor of Law, University of Virginia Law School. B.A., Harvard University (1977); J.D., Yale University (1982).

We have received helpful comments on earlier versions of this Article from William J. Carney, Frank H. Easterbrook, Jens Fejo, Victor Goldberg, D. Bruce Johnsen, Barbara Klose-Ullmann, Roberta Romano, Cliff Smith, Peter Zweifel, and particularly Michael Dooley. We also have benefitted from comments received in presentations at the European Association of Law and Economics, at a Liberty Fund Conference on Insider Trading, and at the University of Munich.

1 For a publicly held firm, the preexisting contractual relationship that provides the basis for the privity of contract between shareholders and insiders manifests itself in the firm's articles of incorporation. In addition, the primary purpose of state corporate law is that it serves as a standard set of implied contract terms that free firms from the burden of stipulating these terms anew every time they transact. R. Posner, Economic Analysis of Law 296 (2d ed. 1977). Similarly, an individual firm is free to alter the terms of the state law standard form contract if (net of transactions costs) it finds that such an alteration is advantageous.

The above discussion is a straightforward application of the basic principle of corporate finance that a firm is a nexus of contractual relationships. Shareholders, like other participants in the corporate enterprise such as creditors and employees, define their relationship with the firm in contractual terms. Indeed, the very existence and survival of the corporate form of business organization can be explained by the gains associated with dividing the management and risk-bearing attributes of ownership into separate components through incorporation. *See* Fama, *Agency Problems and the Theory of the Firm*, 88 J. Pol. Econ. 288, 291-93 (1980)

As applied to insider trading, the fact that a firm's articles of incorporation represent a preexisting contractual relationship between shareholders and managers means that the transactions costs of inserting a prohibition on insider trading within the intrafirm corporate contract is de nature of this relationship acts as an incentive to both outside shareholders and insiders to allocate the right to trade on inside information to the group that values it most highly. We begin by assuming there are no transactions costs and, perhaps more importantly, no agency costs. In parts V and VI, we relax these assumptions.

Carlton and Fischel were the first to apply Coase's insight to insider trading.[2] Our analysis expands on theirs in three ways. First, we consider how a competitive market for managers affects shareholder demands for an intrafirm rule constraining insider trading. Next we examine the impacts of risk aversion and managerial preference for receiving income from insider trading as opposed to traditional forms of compensation. Finally, we consider the ramifications of both of these phenomena in light of the differing levels of information-processing ability among the shareholding population.

Perhaps the most disconcerting aspect of the current debate over the

minimis. *See* Carlton & Fischel, *The Regulation of Insider Trading*, 35 STAN. L. REV. 857, 863 (1983).

On the other hand, while the costs of writing a prohibition against insider trading into a firm's corporate charter may be quite low, the costs of *enforcing* such a provision are likely to be extremely high. This will be due, in large part, to the high costs of monitoring and detecting insider trading activity. *See* Easterbrook, *Insider Trading, Secret Agents, Evidentiary Privileges, and the Production of Information*, 1982 SUP. CT. REV. 309, 334 [hereinafter Easterbrook, *Insider Trading*]. But, as one of us has explained elsewhere, high enforcement costs and probable economies of scale in enforcement suggest only that firms who wish to ban insider trading may be willing to pay outsiders, such as the SEC or the New York Stock Exchange, to monitor and enforce an intrafirm prohibition on insider trading; they do not justify a general prohibition on insider trading. *See* Macey, *From Fairness to Contract: The New Direction of the Rules Against Insider Trading*, 13 HOFSTRA L. REV. 9, 59-63 (1984).

The final issue that must be considered when looking at insider trading from a contractual perspective is the question whether firms are so dominated by their managers that they will not insert prohibitions on insider trading into their corporate charters even if the net wealth of the firm would increase if they did so. As Carlton and Fischel have observed in precisely this context, in a competitive capital market the firm that does not provide shareholders with the highest rate of return will not survive. *See* Carlton & Fischel, *supra*, at 857. And a famous insight of Jensen and Meckling is that the original owner-entrepreneurs of a firm will bear the full costs of any avoidable anticipated divergence between the interests of public investors and managers because the investors will reduce the price they pay for the firm's stock in the initial public offering by the full amount of any anticipated divergence. Jensen & Meckling, *Theory of the Firm: Managerial Behavior, Agency Costs and Ownership Structure*, 3 J. FIN. ECON. 305 (1976).

In sum, if it is in the interests of the shareholders of particular firms that insider trading be banned or curtailed, it is highly likely that, over time, such bans or restrictions will appear in the charters of such firms. There is, of course, a contrary school of thought which suggests that managers systematically are able to rob shareholders of their invested wealth. *See, e.g.*, A. BERLE & G. MEANS, THE MODERN CORPORATION AND PRIVATE PROPERTY (1932); Eisenberg, *The Modernization of Corporate Law: An Essay for Bill Cary*, 37 U. MIAMI L. REV. 187 (1983). This school of thought has been discredited by the available empirical evidence. See Easterbrook, *Managers' Discretion and Investors' Welfare: Theories and Evidence*, 9 DEL. J. CORP. L. 540 (1984) [hereinafter Easterbrook, *Managers' Discretion*], for a masterful review of the competing hypotheses and the relevant evidence.

2 Carlton & Fischel, *supra* note 1, at 863.

propriety of insider trading is that the critics and supporters of the practice are talking past each other. Either side can generate examples that make it patently clear that theirs is the sensible view, but since their views are mutually inconsistent, it is logically impossible to reach a mutually satisfactory outcome. Instead, we focus here on the underlying attributes of the trading economy and the law that governs it. We discover situations in which insider trading is beneficial to firms, as well as situations in which it is harmful. More importantly, we discover that outside shareholders in publicly held firms can distinguish between these situations *ex ante* and therefore would be expected, in the absence of transactions costs, to draft contractual agreements that grant insider trading privileges to managers as part of their total compensation package.

We find that in firms in which shareholders are not second in line behind insiders to receive the information that results in trading profits, shareholders will benefit by striking a bargain with insiders that allows the insiders to trade in exchange for a reduction in their wages.[3] By contrast, in firms in which the insiders are risk averse and shareholders are the next-best information processors after insiders, a mutually beneficial bargain that *bars* insiders from trading would likely be struck between shareholders and insiders.[4] But even here, an externally imposed ban on insider trading seems unnecessary; we suggest instead that shareholders will demand that managers accede to a private contractual ban as a condition of employment. Thus, it is not surprising that each side of the debate can generate plausible scenarios to bolster its position.

Moreover it is not at all clear to us that the current enforcement apparatus of the Securities and Exchange Commission (SEC) is necessary to supplement in the common law courts the regime of private enforcement that would take place if a "Coasian" system of private contracting were permitted to exist.[5] While the SEC's present rules banning insider trading may well be supportable under certain theoretical conditions, the SEC's refusal to permit firms to opt out of its rules suggests to us that the ban is motivated by political rent seeking rather than a quest for economic efficiency.[6]

---

3 *See infra* text accompanying note 25.

4 *See infra* text accompanying notes 26-27.

5 As one of us has explained elsewhere, economies of scale in monitoring suggest that it may be efficient to have a single organization monitor and report on insider trading. But it does not follow that it is necessary to have the SEC conduct such monitoring and reporting since it already is being done by the organized stock exchanges and by the National Association of Securities Dealers (NASD). *See* Macey, *supra* note 1, at 58-63.

6 *See* Macey & Haddock, *Regulation on Demand: The Influence of Special Interest Groups on SEC Enforcement of Insider Trading Rules*, 30 J. L. & Econ.—(1987) (forthcoming).

II. The Effects of Insider Trading on Shareholders

We begin our analysis by examining the effects of several possible insider trading rules on the price of shares of a hypothetical firm. The effect on share prices of an event that alters the present value of a firm's future net income is indicated in the accompanying figures. (*See* Appendix A.) In Figure 1, the event has a positive impact on share prices; in Figure 2, a negative one.

The solid lines in Figures 1 and 2 track the movement in the price of the firm's stock over time if there is a perfectly enforced ban on trading by anyone who has an informational advantage over the current shareholder group. The dotted lines represent the movement in the share price if the ban on insider trading is not perfectly enforced and, thus, is only partially effective. This line reflects the expectation that some traders—most likely a combination of insiders and market professionals—will trade on the information before the shareholder group, either by violating the law or by legally acquiring news in advance of its official announcement through research and analysis. The dashed lines represent the price movement with insider trading legalized both by statute and by contract.

As shown by the solid lines in Figures 1 and 2, when insiders are effectively barred from trading, the price of the stock will remain at the preevent level until the event is announced. There is no informed trading which signals the market that something important has taken place or is about to take place. Outside shareholders will not alter their trading patterns, but will continue to make their usual adjustments to their portfolios as though nothing had happened. If the news is good, those outsiders who buy shares of the firm between the event and its announcement will be better off if there is an effective ban of insider trading. Any insider trading would have driven the stock price up more quickly, requiring the buying outsiders to pay more to acquire shares.

Just as buying outsiders are better off, *ceteris paribus*, if insiders are prohibited from trading when the news is good, selling outsiders are worse off because they do not obtain as much for their shares as they would have if insider trading were permitted.[7] This is ironic, since it is precisely these selling outsiders that the SEC and the courts maintain are harmed by insider trading.[8] Indeed, such selling outsiders are the only group permitted to bring a private cause of action under the SEC's rule 10b-5.[9]

---

7 Of course, outsiders who buy or sell before the event date or after the announcement date are totally unaffected by insider trading.

8 *See* Macey, *supra* note 1, at 24-30 (discussing theoretical underpinnings of current liability rules).

9 Blue Chip Stamps v. Manor Drug Stores, 421 U.S. 723 (1975). The securities law restrictions on insider trading derive from section 10(b) of the Securities Exchange Act of 1934, 15 U.S.C. § 78j(b) (1982), and the SEC's rule 10b-5, 17 C.F.R. § 240.10b-5 (1984), as well as from section

As Figure 2 indicates, if the news is bad, the situation is reversed. Selling by insiders will be expected to drive the price of the stock down more quickly, making it possible for buying outsiders to purchase at a lower price than otherwise. Outsiders who sell between the event and its announcement will be better off without insider trading because they can dispose of their shares at a higher price than if the price had been driven down more promptly by insider trading. But outsiders who buy during the interim period are worse off without insider trading because they pay a higher price for the firm's shares.

Thus, *ex ante*, outsiders can expect sometimes to gain and sometimes to lose if insiders are effectively prohibited from trading. The accompanying graphs thus indicate that, if we neglect the impact of insider trading on managerial salary and motivation, shareholders who hold a diversified stock portfolio and follow a "buy and hold" strategy are indifferent about whether the insiders of the firms in which they own shares are banned from trading.

If, for example, there is an event that causes a positive shock to the value of a firm, and an outsider happens to be selling his stock during the period between the event date and the date on which the event is publicly disclosed, the outsider is better off if insiders are trading (the insiders, of course, will be buying in expectation that the firm's share price will rise after the good news is announced) because the value of the firm's shares will be driven upward by such trading. On the other hand, shareholders who happen to be buying when the insiders are buying are made worse off because, as Figure 1 indicates, the price these shareholders must pay is now higher than it would have been in the absence of insider trading.

It is worth noting that the only diversified outside traders with standing to sue in cases of either upward or downward fluctuations are actually *helped* by insider trading. It is well established that plaintiffs in cases brought under rule 10b-5 must be actual purchasers or sellers. Purchasers can bring suit only against selling insiders and sellers can bring suit only against buying insiders.[10] *Ex ante*, because investors who hold diversified portfolios expect to buy when insiders are buying as often as

16(b) of the Securities Exchange Act of 1934, 15 U.S.C. § 78p(b) (1982). Rule 10b-5 was promulgated pursuant to the SEC's authority under section 10(b). Section 10(b) gives the SEC authority to prohibit "any manipulative or deceptive device or contrivance." *Id.* Rule 10b-5 states,

> It shall be unlawful for any person, directly or indirectly, by the use of any means or instrumentality of interstate commerce, or of the mails, or of any facility of any national securities exchange,
>
> (a) To employ any device, scheme, or artifice to defraud,
>
> (b) To make any untrue statement of a material fact or to omit to state a material fact necessary in order to make the statements made, in the light of the circumstances under which they were made, not misleading, or
>
> (c) To engage in any act, practice, or course of business which operates or would operate as a fraud or deceit upon any person, in connection with the purchase or sale of any security.

17 C.F.R. § 240.10b-5 (1984).

[10] *See supra* note 9.

they expect to sell when insiders are buying, such investors are unaffected in the long run by the nature of the rule against insider trading, unless they expect to bring suit to recoup their losses on some occasions while retaining their profits on other occasions. Similar remarks apply when insiders are trading. Consequently, the proponents of the rule against insider trading must be championing the interests of some group other than diversified investors. As we will see, this group inevitably will consist of those traders who will be the first to acquire the valuable information that would have formed the basis for the insiders' trading if they were allowed to trade.

At any moment, those whose trading is not a function of nonpublic information have an equal probability of being a winner or a loser, all else being equal. But all else is not equal. As discussed more fully below, the insiders are employed by these outside shareholders, and insiders will forgo some increment of fixed salary in exchange for the right to engage in insider trading. It is for this reason that the outside shareholders have an incentive to permit insiders to engage in insider trading: it will lower the firm's payroll expenditures.

Another reason why outsiders may be concerned with the insider trading rules is that such trading may affect the variance in a firm's share price. It may well be the case that insider trading will decrease the day-to-day variance in the share price because price adjustments become less abrupt. But, as others have suggested, it is also possible that permitting insiders to trade gives them an incentive to increase the variance in their firm's share price in order to create more trading opportunities.[11]

In reality, insider trading is not completely prohibited. Even under the present system of rules, market professionals with significant informational advantages over outsiders are permitted to trade at will. Furthermore, certain insiders find the potential for profit from insider trading so enticing that they break the law either by engaging in insider trading themselves or by selling the information to others. The results of this behavior are indicated by the dotted lines in Figures 1 and 2, which reflect stock price movements when partial insider trading occurs.

Since today a ban on insider trading is in place, and we observe some insiders being tried and convicted, we may assume that the legal restrictions are having some effect. As indicated by the dotted lines in Figures 1 and 2, the experience of outsiders when there is partial enforcement of rules against insider trading will fall somewhere between the extreme cases discussed above.[12] Any outsider who, on a given occasion, would have benefitted fortuitously from a total ban will benefit to a lesser

[11] R. Leftwich & R. Verrecchia, Insider Trading and Managers' Choice Among Risky Projects (Chicago Graduate School of Business, Working Paper No. 63, 1981).

[12] *See supra* text accompanying notes 7-9.

extent by a partial ban. Similarly, those hurt by a total ban are injured to a lesser extent by a partial ban.

III. Insider Trading: Efficiency and Fairness

As the figures referred to in the preceding section make clear, insiders can profit by trading in the shares of their company when they possess important company-related information. Empirical studies support this theoretical supposition.[13] If the information bodes well for the company, then the share price will rise once the public learns the good news. But insiders can profit by buying shares from those who are ignorant of the inside information and then selling the shares after the news has elevated the prices. Conversely, if the private information bodes ill for the firm, insiders can quickly dispose of any shares they are holding and then sell future obligations short at relatively high prices, "covering" those obligations at the new lower price after the anticipated publicity has driven the share price down.

The above scenarios are concise descriptions of the world of stock trading when insiders are permitted by law and contract to trade on inside information in their possession, or when proscriptions cannot be enforced. On first sight, these scenarios strike many observers as somehow "unfair"[14] because canny insiders seem constantly to be profiting at the expense of outsiders. Yet there is a rapidly growing literature which argues that insider trading is not unfair at all.[15]

This literature starts with the premise that, while outsiders do not have access to inside information, they do know the approximate extent

---

13 The following empirical studies observe that insiders receive greater-than-market rates of return from trading activity: Baesel & Stein, *The Value of Information: Inferences from the Profitability of Insider Trading*, 14 J. FIN. & QUANTITATIVE ANALYSIS 553 (1979); Finnerty, *Insiders and Market Efficiency*, 31 J. FIN. 1141 (1976); Jaffe, *The Effect of Regulation Changes on Insider Trading*, 5 BELL J. ECON. & MGMT. SCI. 93, 101-05 (1974); Jaffe, *Special Information and Insider Trading*, 47 J. BUS. 410 (1974); Keown & Pinkerton, *Merger Announcements and Insider Trading Activity: An Empirical Investigation*, 36 J. FIN. 855 (1981); Lorie & Niederhoffer, *Predictive and Statistical Properties of Insider Trading*, 11 J. L. & ECON. 35 (1968); Penman, *Insider Trading and the Dissemination of Firms' Forecast Information*, 55 J. BUS. 479 (1982).

14 *See, e.g.*, E. HERMAN, CORPORATE CONTROL, CORPORATE POWER 116 (1981); Ferber, *The Case Against Insider Trading: A Response To Professor Manne*, 23 VAND. L. REV. 621 (1970); Kaplan, Wolf v. Weinstein*: Another Chapter on Insider Trading*, 1963 SUP. CT. REV. 273; Levmore, *Securities and Secrets: Insider Trading and the Law of Contracts*, 68 VA. L. REV. 117 (1982); Loss, *The Fiduciary Concept as Applied to Trading by Corporate "Insiders" in the United States*, 33 MOD. L. REV. 34 (1970); Painter, *Rule 10b-5: The Recodification Thicket*, 45 ST. JOHN'S L. REV. 699, 714 (1971); Schotland, *Unsafe at Any Price: A Reply to Professor Manne*, 53 VA. L. REV. 1425 (1967); *see also* Easterbrook, *Insider Trading, supra* note 1, at 323-30 (articulating and rejecting various arguments against insider trading).

15 H. MANNE, INSIDER TRADING AND THE STOCK MARKET (1966); Carlton & Fischel, *supra* note 1; Macey, *supra* note 1, at 9; M. Moran, Insider Trading in the Stock Market: An Empirical Test of the Damage to Outsiders (Washington Univ. Center for the Study of Business, Working Paper No. 39, 1984).

to which insider trading is apt to occur in the shares of particular firms, of particular industries, and of the stock market in general. Although such outsiders do not know when the insider trading will occur, nor which way or by how much the share price will move when insider trading does occur, they do know that insider trading *will* occur. They also know that those outsiders who invest in an information search will not benefit from the trading, and may well lose, at least in the short run. Consequently, to compensate for expected trading losses due to insider trading, it is argued that outsiders offer lower prices for new issues and subsequent resales than they would if they knew insider trading was impossible. Conversely, if insider trading cannot be barred, insiders retain the ability to skim off a substantial portion of the value of future inside information, but they have to accept a lower share price from outsiders when the firm initially goes public, because of the expected future skimming. Thus, those who claim that insider trading is fair argue that because outsiders can anticipate insider trading, they make whatever adjustments are appropriate to retain a competitive rate of return on their portfolio.

Moreover, drawing on the seminal work of Henry Manne, those who argue that insider trading is fair also argue that it is efficient.[16] One thread of this efficiency argument posits that to the extent that a firm's good fortune emanates from the actions of insiders, the insiders' ability to capture a part of the benefit for themselves spurs them to greater efforts on behalf of the firm, since this will create greater opportunities for profitable trades with outsiders.[17] The efficiency argument supporting insider trading has been attacked on several fronts. One seemingly persuasive objection that has yet to be answered is that no one has shown that insider trading opportunities actually arise to any important extent from the efforts of those who ultimately capitalize on them.[18] If profitable inside information is a casually acquired windfall rather than being deliberately created by the insiders, then banning it, it is asserted, will have no long-run deleterious effects on shareholders.[19] To be true, such an assertion requires stronger assumptions than are usually articulated, as we now show. Specifically, the arguments on both sides must expand to encompass the effects on insider salaries from banning insider trading.

16 Carlton & Fischel, *supra* note 1, at 881-82 (no tension between considerations of fairness and efficiency); Easterbrook, *Insider Trading, supra* note 1, at 323-30 (refuting fairness arguments).

17 H. MANNE, *supra* note 15, at 166.

18 *See* Kronman, *Mistake, Disclosure, Information and the Law of Contracts*, 7 J. LEGAL STUD. 1, 34 n.83 (1978).

19 *Id. But see* Wang, *Trading on Material Nonpublic Information on Impersonal Stock Markets: Who Is Harmed and Who Can Sue Under SEC Rule 10b-5?*, 54 S. CAL. L. REV. 1217, 1225-26 (1981).

IV. A Dispersion of the Interests of Shareholders

Much of the literature in defense of insider trading misses the central point that there are important distinctions among the shareholding population of any particular firm. Specifically, many investors with small portfolios find it uneconomical to purchase the advice of market professionals. Even though these investors recognize that without such advice they cannot reasonably hope for trading profits because they are at a severe informational disadvantage with respect to their trading partners, such investors will follow a "buy and hold" strategy designed only to acquire dividend-earning assets and to redistribute consumption over their life cycle. Because they trade securities infrequently, they will be relatively insensitive to the bid-ask spread charged by market makers.

But other investors, notably (but not exclusively) the so-called "institutional investors," such as commercial banks, pension funds, mutual funds, and the like, hold portfolios that are sizable enough for them to purchase advice from market professionals. These investors trade relatively frequently in order to reap the trading profits that comprise the benefits of that advice. Even if these large investors do not seek trading profits, they may still trade frequently because of the stochastic nature of the flows of the assets they handle and because of the high opportunity costs of large idle cash balances. Such investors will be quite sensitive to the transactions costs associated with their active trading, which, of course, include the bid-ask spread.

Specialists and other market makers systematically profit from trades with outsiders. But they systematically lose to insiders who are trading on inside information. Because insiders can purchase shares anonymously through third parties, market professionals cannot discriminate in price by requiring higher trading fees from insiders. This results in increased costs in the form of widened bid-ask spreads in markets where insiders have frequent opportunities to trade on inside information.[20] Consequently, all traders bear a share of the increased costs to market makers that are associated with insider trading.[21]

If the legal regime changes from one in which insider trading is permitted to one in which it is effectively banned, market makers benefit in the short run because the resulting short-run decrease in the bid-ask spread will not equal the decreased trading losses to informed insiders. The way these decreased transactions costs will be shared between market makers and outsiders will depend on the relative elasticities of the supply of and the demand for brokerage services.

20 The following studies predict a positive relation between insider trading and market makers' bid-asked spreads. Bagehot, *The Only Game in Town*, 2 Fin. Analyst J. 2, 12-24 (1971); Copeland & Galai, *Information Effects on the Bid-Ask Spread*, 38 J. Fin. 1457 (1983); Seyhun, *Insiders' Profits, Costs of Trading, and Market Efficiency*, 16 J. Fin. Econ. 189 (1986).

21 *See* Benston & Hagerman, *Determinants of Bid-Asked Spreads in the Over-the-Counter Market*, 2 J. Fin. Econ. 353 (1974); Copeland & Galai, *supra* note 20.

Consequently, some of the more actively trading investors will prefer that insider trading be banned because when it is allowed the resulting increase in their brokerage costs exceeds their share of the salary-reduction[22] and incentive advantages provided by insider trading. Similarly, investors who rarely adjust their portfolios may prefer to permit insider trading, since their shares of the salary reduction and incentive effects exceed the increase in their brokerage costs. The less actively trading investors, however, are often disorganized, and the small scale of their holdings makes it unlikely that they will devote sufficient resources to educate themselves about this rather subtle advantage. In other words, the "rational ignorance" of the small investors permits actively trading investors and market professionals to form a nearly unopposed coalition seeking bans on insider trading.

V. Exogenous Shocks to a Firm's Value

Suppose that initially all of some firm's shares are owned by shareholders in holdings of equal size. Imagine that some event occurs that is beneficial to the firm, but totally unexpected. Moreover, the event is not caused by any human agent, either in the firm or outside of it, and the event clearly will never recur. In other words, the present realization of the event has no impact on expectations about the future.

If this event comes to the attention of the firm's managers before anyone else learns of it, the managers will profit if they can trade on the basis of their knowledge of this fortuitous event. Just as clearly, the managers will not profit if such insider trading is effectively prohibited by law. But the opportunity to profit from the hypothesized event remains, whether or not insiders trade.[23] The key question becomes who captures that benefit when insiders cannot.

Removing people from the upper tail of a distribution of knowledge leaves a distribution, albeit a truncated one. Those who remain in the upper tail of the truncated distribution that results when insiders are removed will reap the value of the firm's good fortune. Thus, the answer to the question above is not readily apparent, although it is clear that the answer is not "the public," if by that one means that the gains are spread around randomly throughout the set of all noninsiders.[24]

A. *With Market Professionals as the Next-Best Information Processors*

If, after the insiders are lopped off, the market professionals—brokers, exchange specialists, analysts, and the like—who are in the upper tail of the distribution are not the only present shareholders, then the

22 *See infra* text accompanying notes 25-27.

23 For a careful argument that valuable property is never left lying about, and that resources are consumed in establishing title, see Cheung, *A Theory of Price Control*, 17 J. L. & Econ. 53 (1974).

24 Macey & Haddock, *supra* note 6.

other shareholders will not capture the gains. The relatively more knowledgeable individuals who do comprise the upper tail will trade on the basis of their superior knowledge. If the news is good, the market professionals will buy shares immediately from the ignorant among the shareholders, and sell for higher prices once the knowledge becomes widespread. If the news is bad, then the market professionals will sell shares when they acquire the information, and will sell relatively high-priced future obligations to unsuspecting investors, covering after the stock price has fallen. In other words, when insiders cannot trade, something of exactly the same form as the banned insider trading will still occur, but the set of beneficiaries is altered.

But it is argued that if insider trading is prohibited managers will more quickly announce the firm's good fortune, since the managers no longer stand to gain from delay. That insiders need, or can even use, any significantly lengthened trading period to capitalize on their knowledge seems unlikely. There is competition among insiders for trading profits. In securities markets, orders are executed with electronic speed, so any insider failing to take quick advantage of advance knowledge will find that other insiders have beaten him to the market. No gains remain for the sluggish. Moreover, the delays that occur between the event and announcement, while useful to inside traders, frequently are required by the firm as it attempts to arrange for inputs or dispose of outputs before those prices are altered by the impeding announcement. Of course, this hints at one way an outsider can move himself up in the distribution of knowledge—stand near the managers (figuratively speaking) in order to hear valuable announcements more quickly.

B. With Shareholders as the Next-Best Information Processors

Consequently, if insider trading is banned, neither managers nor "the public" will capitalize on the firm's good fortune. Perhaps the beneficiaries will be market professionals, such as brokers, exchange specialists, and financial analysts, who have situated themselves so as to be able to hear news first. But perhaps after managers and the like are barred from trading, the next-best information processors will be the firm's present shareholders. This may result either because shareholders invest in industries with which they are particularly familiar or because they threaten managers with dismissal if the managers do not inform the shareholders first when new information comes to the managers' attention. In these cases the shareholders will be the beneficiaries of the firm's good fortune.

But, as we now demonstrate, if some of our constraints are relaxed, the shareholders will be at least partial beneficiaries even if the insiders are permitted to trade on inside information. By contrast, most shareholders will not benefit if insiders are barred from such trades, and market professionals or other outsiders can beat the shareholders to the information. At this stage of our analysis a simple arithmetic model is helpful in identifying the effects of insider trading.

C. An Arithmetic Model for Insider Trading

1. Risk-Neutral Insiders.—Suppose, as above, that the firm realizes a purely fortuitous event. This is the "hard case" for our argument. Suppose that shocks to the firm's value are random events drawn from a known, albeit uncontrollable, distribution. Finally, suppose that the firm's shareholders profit from inside information if insiders cannot. Assume initially that insider trading is effectively banned. Suppose that in the new period the present value of a firm's expected future net earnings per share is $1.30 with probability 0.1, $1.40 with probability 0.2, $1.50 with probability 0.4, $1.60 with probability 0.2, and $1.70 with probability 0.1. To keep computations simple, initially, assume that for each shareholder there is one insider, who with unitary probability is paid a salary of $10 per period. The circumstances outlined are shown by Table 1. (*See* Appendix B.)

The present value of the expected net earnings stream of a shareholder's holdings next period is $150, and, netting out intervening dividends, that also will be the present market value of his holdings if the shareholder is well diversified. The variance of the value of this typical shareholder's portfolio next period is $120, since the shareholders are the next-best information processors after the legally disabled insiders. The expected value of the insider's salary is $10, with a variance of zero.

Alternatively, suppose that insider trading is permitted. Whichever direction the security price moves, insiders gain, but the amount of gain is limited. If the news is positive, the insider will want to buy shares before the price reaches its new equilibrium. The very act of buying, however, will begin to elevate the share price. To anyone who observes the insider's trading behavior, these purchases will signal an increased probability of an impending announcement of good news,[25] although the precise nature of the news may well remain a mystery to the observer. Consequently, if the insider realizes that the share price is about to go from $1.50 to $1.70, he will not succeed in denying all of the gain to the present shareholders; as observers notice the insider's trading activity, they will increase their reservation prices.

---

[25] Insiders also trade for reasons other than discovery of new inside information, of course. Like anyone else, they trade to rebalance portfolios and because their consumption and income streams do not track each other precisely. Moreover, many insiders receive a stream of the firm's shares or options to purchase the firm's shares as a regular part of their income, and this requires sales to the extent a part of that stream is to be consumed. Consequently, observers have to discount their observations of insider behavior to take account of these other trading motivations, but that discounting is of no particular importance here, and will henceforth be ignored.

That observers do track and react to insider trading activity is documented in Givoly & Palmon, *Insider Trading and the Exploitation of Inside Information: Some Empirical Evidence*, 58 J. Bus. 69 (1985).

Suppose the insider captures one-half of the value of the change in share price. Then our typical shareholder's portfolio will net him only $160 next period, not $170, and $10 will go to the insider. For simplicity, suppose that the insider also nets $10 by selling shares short for prices above their impending equilibrium level if the share price is going to fall by 20 cents. Notice that the effect of an insider's short sales is not the mirror image of an insider's purchases. When the expected price change is positive, the insider *moderates* the shareholder's gain by reducing the shareholder's holdings. But when the expected price change is negative, the insider *exacerbates* the shareholder's losses by increasing the shareholder's holdings. It is as if the quantity of shares held in the economy increases when the insider sells short. This is analogous to increases in the money supply that occur when a party borrows money from a fractional reserve bank. Consequently, insider trading not only reduces the mean return to shareholders; it also skews the distribution and creates a longer downward than upward tail. This is reflected in the modifications to the entries of Table 1 that are shown in Table 2 (*see* Appendix C).

Notice that the expected value of the shareholder's portfolio next period, net of losses to insiders, seems to be $146, or $4 less than its value when insider trading was barred. If that were so, then the initial offering price for shares would not have been $150, but $146, reflecting the expected losses to insiders. But as we will see when we examine the insider's behavior more carefully, this is not the end of the story. The $4 that the shareholder expects to lose is an expected gain to the insider. Coupled with the insider's hypothesized $10 salary, his expected income next period increases to $14. Fourteen dollars of expected income (with $10 of it assured as salary) will attract more competition for the insider's job than $10 assured income alone. The increased competition will drive the insider's base salary down. In the unlikely event that the insider's closest substitute as a manager is risk neutral and productively indistinguishable from the present occupant of the position, the insider's salary will fall by exactly $4 to offset precisely the expected insider trading profits.

As a result, the cost to the firm of doing business has fallen by exactly $4 per shareholder. This means that the net income per shareholder increases because $4 in salary costs is no longer being incurred. Consequently, the present value of the shareholder's shares and the net value of his portfolio (as reflected in the second and third columns of Table 2) must be increased by $4, and the insider's salary and total income (as reflected in the fourth and sixth columns of Table 2) must be decreased by $4, as shown in Table 3 (*see* Appendix D). As Table 3 illustrates, under these assumptions the expected value of the shareholder's portfolio is $150, exactly as it was in Table 1. Under our present assumptions, insider trading has absolutely no impact on the expected net returns to shareholders and consequently has no impact on share price, because the insider trading profits are returned to shareholders indirectly through their reduced salary obligations to insiders.

2. *Risk-Averse Insiders.*—Now relax the assumption that insiders are risk neutral. Unlike shareholders, who can widely diversify their securities portfolios, employees usually cannot diversify their human capital to any comparable extent.[26] Consequently, it is likely that insiders will be risk averse. As seen by comparing Table 1 with Table 3, the variance in returns to both insiders and shareholders increases when insider trading is permitted. This variance represents increased risk. Because of aversion to this additional risk, insiders who are permitted to trade on inside information will not reduce their salary demands by the full $4 increase in expected income that otherwise would accompany a license to engage in insider trading.

Suppose the insider's salary is reduced by only $3. Since shareholders are assumed to be the second-best information processors for data of this firm, there is a mutually beneficial bargain to be struck between shareholders and insiders. For example, the insider's salary might be raised by $3.50 if the insider agrees not to trade on inside information. The insider is better off by 50 cents because the certainty equivalent[27] of his income has increased from $10 to $10.50. The shareholder's position also is improved even though his firm's salary obligation has increased by $3.50, because the shareholder's expected trading losses from insider trading is reduced by $4. The variance of the shareholder's returns falls also, although this is of minor interest if his portfolio is well diversified.

Our results are consistent with the notion that if someone gets negative utility from bearing risk, and nobody gets positive utility, it is inefficient to create situations in which the only effect is to increase the risk to be borne. When a firm's shareholders are the second-best assimilators of firm-specific information, it is plausible that a mutually beneficial arrangement will bar insiders from trading on insider information. But presumably such a bar can be accomplished by contract between the firm and the insider.[28]

---

26 Kraakman, *Corporate Liability Strategies and the Costs of Legal Controls*, 93 YALE L.J. 857, 864 (1984).

27 "A certainty equivalent is the immediate (certain) payment that a person would regard as having a value equal to that of a particular uncertain set of prospects. In other words, a person given a choice should be indifferent between any prospect and its certainty equivalent." G. GOETZ, LAW AND ECONOMICS: CASES AND MATERIALS 76 (1984).

28 Even if insider trading cannot be effectively barred by contract, it is unclear that the SEC is the best alternative prohibitive mechanism. But even if the SEC is the best alternative, it is unclear why firms cannot opt out of the SEC's ban whenever insiders or shareholders have different relative risk preferences or exposure than is true for the economy as a whole, or when the inside information is particularly likely to arise directly from desirable productive or innovative efforts by the insiders themselves. It seems clear that it is efficient for some entity, either the SEC, the exchanges, or the

D. The Shareholders' Choice

Given the nature of the shock to the firm's value we have discussed to this point, relaxing the assumption that a firm's shareholders are the second-best assimilators of firm-specific information makes it more likely that shareholders will want insiders to trade. If members of some other group, such as exchange specialists in the firm's stock, market analysts, or arbitrageurs, are better at assimilating firm-specific information than are the firm's own shareholders, the shareholders will lose the trading profits whether or not insiders can trade. The only difference is the identity of the parties to whom the trading profits go—insiders or market professionals. But permitting insiders to trade on inside information will reduce the insiders' salary demands by the certainty equivalent of the expected insider trading profits—that is, by the amount of the expected insider trading profits minus the relevant risk premium needed to compensate for the greater risk associated with an income stream derived from insider trading. Consequently, when insider trading is permitted, part of any windfall to the firm will still accrue to shareholders in the form of reduced salary obligations to insiders.

Subject to the qualifications below, when insiders are barred from trading, the shareholders receive nothing in exchange for the higher salaries they must pay their insiders in compensation for the lack of trading opportunities, unless these shareholders are also the next-best information processors of firm-specific information. For such shareholders a ban reduces incentives to invest in new productive capital. A ban also increases incentives for market professionals to invest in ways that speed the acquisition of firm-specific information. The latter investments constitute a waste of real resources because insiders obtain the same information in the course of their normal duties without having to expend resources searching for it, and they can transfer the information to the securities markets more promptly than do the professionals. When market professionals are the next-best information processors, from the shareholders' perspective a ban on insider trading is the equivalent of a rule requiring insiders to throw money out a window of the firm's corporate headquarters. The market professionals who happen to be passing by at the time the money flutters down certainly benefit. But shareholders who have other productive uses for their time have no chance of grabbing any of these funds and inevitably lose.

The investments undertaken by market professionals striving to ac-

---

common law courts to enforce implicit or explicit contracts barring insider trading when those contracts are voluntary agreements between a firm and its insiders.

Notice that we make no argument about what the default provision for insider trading should be; perhaps if no explicit agreement speaks to the matter, insider trading should be taken as prohibited. We doubt that the default provision matters very much. Instead, we ask why the legal system will not permit explicit agreements to allow insider trading within those firms that find such arrangement beneficial. We suggest an answer to this question in Macey & Haddock, *supra* note 6.

quire and act on firm-specific information are "rent-seeking" investments that transfer wealth rather than create it. But to the individual, the rent-seeking investments look like any other investment. Tullock and Posner have argued that such rent-seeking investments will be pursued until the rents transferred are exactly consumed by the investment required to transfer them.[29] This is a singularly bad bargain when the investments lead to no net productive benefit, particularly when the arrangement that leads to the rent-seeking investments actually delays the transmission of new information to the market.

In summary, then, when dealing with exogenous shocks we can imagine that a small number of firms may have a plurality of shareholders who are among the second-best processors of information about their firm. Such shareholders may well benefit if their firm bans insider trading. Many of the shareholders of other firms will be less astute observers of their company, and they will be better off paying lower wages to insiders in exchange for permitting the insiders to trade on inside information, since they will not benefit if insiders do not trade.

Those less astute observers of their company are apt to be those who hold relatively small individual portfolios. Consequently, they are less likely to make sufficient investments in information to understand the benefits they could receive if insider trading was permitted.[30] Such "rational ignorance" permits market professionals to form a coalition with more cognizant shareholders to obtain public financing for policing the ban on insider trading that each desires, although for different reasons.

VI. Endogenous Shocks to a Firm's Value

Many of the events that give rise to insider trading profits originate within the insider's firm, either through the insider's own efforts or through the efforts of others within the firm. Manne has argued that insiders should be permitted to trade on all such information.[31] An external observer rarely will be able to distinguish insider trading made possible by that insider's efforts from trading due to events arising from efforts of others within the firm, since corporate employees typically engage in collective efforts as part of widely dispersed teams. Nevertheless, it is clear that specific insiders often have a hand in creating the events, so permitting insiders to profit from them retrospectively increases the incentives to create such events prospectively.

Objections have been raised (and answered) that alternative reward mechanisms provide adequate incentives for insiders to seek shocks to a

29 Posner, *The Social Cost of Monopoly and Regulation*, 83 J. Pol. Econ. 807 (1975); Tullock, *The Welfare Costs of Tariffs, Monopolies and Theft*, 5 W. Econ. J. 224 (1967).

30 Stigler, *The Economics of Information*, 69 J. Pol. Econ. 213 (1961).

31 H. Manne, *supra* note 15, at 166.

firm's value.[32] We do not intend to inform that particular debate beyond noting that no one has responded to Carlton and Fischel's argument that firms should be permitted to opt out of an insider trading ban if the firm's shareholders believe that insider trading opportunities provide the best way to maximize the value of the firm's shares.

Other objections have been raised (and answered) that shocks can be either positive or negative; that negative shocks damage shareholders but profit insiders; that insiders can create negative shocks as easily, or even more easily, than positive ones; and that insider trading consequently should be barred in favor of mechanisms that reward only positive shocks.[33] Again, we do not propose to inform that debate. Rather, our goals in this section are to expand the Manne scenario on one boundary, but to limit it on another.

First, the tabular analysis above also applies here, to an extent. Viewed *ex ante*, insider trading profits do not lead in their entirety to an increase in the income of the insider. If there is competition to hold the insider's post, the potential for trading profits simply will transform a part of the insider's salary into piecemeal rewards. Competition for a post that places trading profits within the employee's grasp will drive the insider's fixed salary down because potential employees may seek shocks to firm value and take the consequent piecemeal rewards that follow. An alternative is for the insider to live the quiet life, and trade only on the opportunities accompanying exogenous shocks or endogenous shocks created by other insiders, and settle for the relatively low income that accompanies this strategy. Even if shareholders tolerate the latter behavior, they benefit partially from the unexploited potential trading profits of the insiders, for salary obligations are reduced by the competition for the insider's post. The rewards to any inside trader are overestimated if we consider only the value of the winnings and neglect the price paid for the opportunity to take the gamble.

But it also matters how the insider trades. If the insider buys shares of his own firm, he is stating implicitly that he expects an increase in the value of his firm, and consequently a benefit to the firm's other shareholders who hold their shares long enough. But if the insider purchases shares of a firm that is about to be acquired by the insider's firm, or if he takes a position in inputs because he knows his firm soon will require them for new production processes, he drives up those prices and by doing so increases the future costs of his own firm. The same increase in

32 *See* Barzel, *Some Fallacies in the Interpretation of Information Costs*, 20 J. L. & ECON. 291 (1977) (demonstrating how markets provide solutions to perverse incentives to engage in inefficient search for information); R. Leftwich & R. Verrecchia, *supra* note 11, at 1 (compensation schemes based on insider trading have perverse incentive effects).

33 *Id.*; *see also* Levmore, *supra* note 14, at 149; Mendelson, Book Review, 117 U. PA. L. REV. 470, 477-78 (1969) (reviewing H. MANNE, INSIDER TRADING AND THE STOCK MARKET (1966)); Schotland, *supra* note 14, at 1451.

costs will result if the insider buys his own firm's shares, but market professionals are able to deduce from that act the unexploited attractiveness of the target or the inputs.[34]

Notice again that although there may be situations in which shareholders will want employees to have insider trading rights because of incentive and salary-reduction effects, shareholders are *harmed* if parties unassociated with the firm trade on inside information because that cuts into the rewards that provide incentives for the firm's employees, and that, in turn, augments the insider's salary demands. Yet, as we discuss elsewhere, the SEC rules rarely are enforced against external parties such as market professionals, and when they are, the motivation for the enforcement seems more an effort to curtail chiseling on an exchange cartel than any effort to defend the interests of shareholders.[35]

VII. The Lack of Demand for an Intrafirm Ban on Insider Trading

A market professional who makes profits trading on a firm's stock will at least sometimes be a shareholder of that firm. In that case, the dividing line between particularly knowledgeable shareholders and market professionals is indistinct. Perhaps the paradigmatic knowledgeable shareholder would be one who relatively infrequently seeks gains by trading shares, and then only by trading the shares of a single firm with which he is particularly familiar. Perhaps a paradigmatic market professional is one who seeks gains daily by moving investments from security to security, and so from firm to firm. Consequently, the knowledgeable shareholder will want to ban insider trading by those insiders working for the single firm about which he is well informed. If the rest of his portfolio is nonspeculative, our knowledgeable shareholder will benefit if the ban is specific to the firm with which he is particularly familiar, holding the enforcement costs he bears constant. A paradigmatic market professional, however, will prefer that insider trading bans be widely applicable.

One might suppose that knowledgeable shareholders and market professionals would simply form a coalition to alter corporate charters, inserting directives which require employment contracts that forbid insider trading, thereby creating a private antiinsider trading right of action in the common law courts. That supposition would be problematic for several reasons. The most obvious is that the members of the coalition would have to bear a fair share of the costs of private enforcement, whereas SEC enforcement places the bulk of those costs on other shareholders. But a much more telling problem with the supposition is that

34 Macey, *supra* note 1 (describing how insider trading might have affected Texas Gulf Sulphur shareholders negatively).

35 Macey & Haddock, *supra* note 6.

banning insider trading through alteration of corporate charters would not benefit most market professionals.

Market professionals are gamblers. They gamble on the belief that they know more about the market than do other participants. When they learn they are facing insiders, the market professionals usually have already lost the gamble, but when they face uninformed outsiders, they usually win. If market professionals face only particularly knowledgeable shareholders, or fellow market professionals, then only the most knowledgeable among that group will win, at the expense of the less knowledgeable.

But if a firm bans insider trading by corporate charter, ultimately only knowledgeable shareholders and market professionals will be shareholders in that firm. Then the good professionals will drive out the bad until the firm becomes closely held by a few particularly knowledgeable individuals who control the firm but no longer gamble on it.

To see why this process operates as it does, remember that permitting insider trading confers benefits on ordinary shareholders by enabling the firm to reduce its salary obligations to insiders, and possibly by offering unique incentives for insiders to innovate and to assume risks for the benefit of the firm. Moreover, these benefits cost ordinary shareholders nothing because they will not receive trading profits regardless of the firm's insider trading rules. An insider trading ban, if effective, merely alters the identity of the party to whom the ordinary shareholders yield their trading profits. But because a firm's wage bill rises with the imposition of a ban, while the innovativeness of its employees falls, the performance of the firm will falter. Consequently, ordinary shareholders have an incentive to alter their portfolios in favor of firms that have no insider trading ban. But in these firms the market professionals cannot win because they must gamble against insiders. Consequently, although particularly knowledgeable shareholders may seek, and sometimes may obtain, a private contractual ban on insider trading, they will not be joined in this quest by market professionals unless corporate charters are to be altered across the board.

VIII. Conclusion

In this Article we developed what may be described as a Coasian model of insider trading to begin to answer the question whether rational, value-maximizing shareholders would agree to permit insiders to trade on the basis of the nonpublic information that routinely comes into their possession. Contrary to all of the existing literature—some of which argues that insider trading is always beneficial to shareholders, and the rest of which argues that it is always harmful—our answer is "it depends."

We posit that the most important questions for evaluating the desirability of insider trading from the shareholders' perspective are the following: (1) Are the insiders risk averse?; and (2) who stands in line after insiders as the second-best processors of information regarding the corporation?

If insiders are risk averse, they will be unwilling to give up salary equivalent to their expected insider trading profits in exchange for the privilege of inside trading. Then shareholders may decide to forbid insider trading when the shareholder group contains an unusually large number of investors who are particularly knowledgeable about the company. But unless shareholders are going to benefit somehow if insiders are prohibited from trading, they will perfer to permit insiders to trade and to share the trading gains in the form of lower wage rates for insider-managers.

Our analysis leads to the conclusion that the legal prohibition against insider trading prevents shareholders from reaching compensation agreements with the managers of their firms that would make both sides better off. Thus, while insider trading law might provide for centralized *monitoring* of insider activities, the per se prohibitions on insider trading reflected in the current law seem deleterious to ordinary shareholders. Indeed, if insider trading law were intended to benefit ordinary shareholders, the current law could remain largely intact but would permit corporations to opt out of its restrictions if they chose to do so.

APPENDIX A

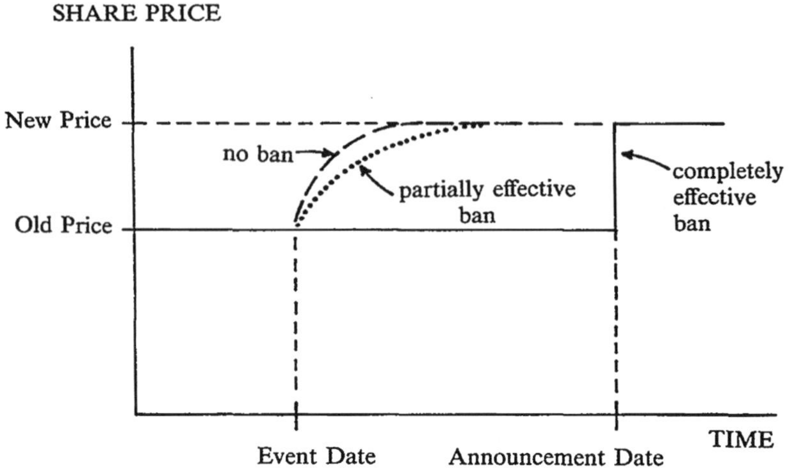

FIGURE 1: POSITIVE SHOCK TO FIRM VALUE

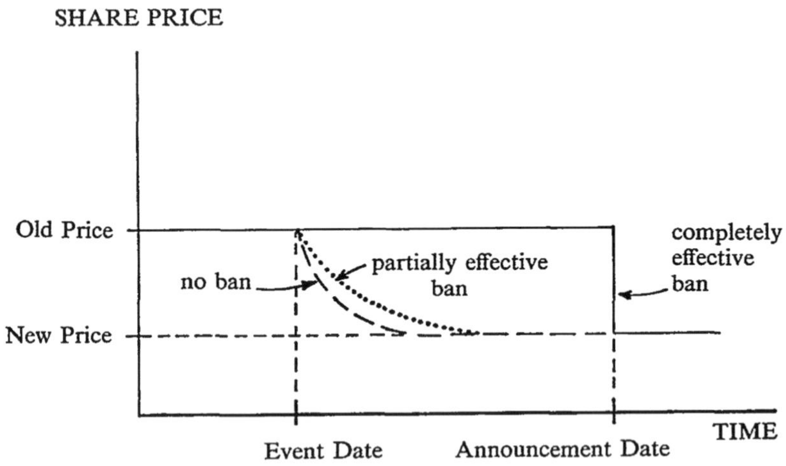

FIGURE 2: NEGATIVE SHOCK TO FIRM VALUE

APPENDIX B

TABLE 1

Probability	Present Value of 100 Shares Next Period		Insider's Income Next Period	
.1		$130		$10
.2		$140		$10
.4		$150		$10
.2		$160		$10
.1		$170		$10
	expected net value:	$150	expected net value:	$10
	variance:	$120	variance:	0

APPENDIX C

TABLE 2

(1) Probability	(2) Present Value of 100 Shares Next Period	(3) Net Value of Portfolio	(4) Insider's Salary	(5) Insider's Trading Profits	(6) Insider's Total Income
.1	$130	$120	$10	$10	$20
.2	$140	$135	$10	$ 5	$15
.4	$150	$150	$10	$ 0	$10
.2	$160	$155	$10	$ 5	$15
.1	$170	$160	$10	$10	$20
	expected net value:	$146		expected net value:	$14
	variance:	$134		variance:	$14

APPENDIX D

TABLE 3

(1) Probability	(2) Present Value of 100 Shares Next Period	(3) Net Value of Portfolio	(4) Insider's Salary	(5) Insider's Trading Profits	(6) Insider's Total Income
.1	$134	$124	$ 6	$10	$16
.2	$144	$139	$ 6	$ 5	$11
.4	$154	$154	$ 6	$ 0	$ 6
.2	$164	$159	$ 6	$ 5	$11
.1	$174	$164	$ 6	$10	$16
	expected net value:	$150		expected net value:	$10
	variance:	$134		variance:	$14

[8]

INSIDER TRADING AND CONTRACTING: A CRITICAL RESPONSE TO THE "CHICAGO SCHOOL"

JAMES D. COX*

American jurisprudence abhors insider trading[1] with a fervor reserved for those who scoff at motherhood, apple pie, and baseball. The commonly stated reasons for this reaction to insider trading are many and unpersuasive. The case law barely suggests why insider trading is harmful. The Supreme Court has condemned insider trading under the federal securities laws when the trading violates a fiduciary's obligations.[2] The Court did so, however, without revealing how such trading harms the corporation, threatens investors, or erodes the functioning of securities markets. Commentators have attempted to complete the opaque mosaic left by the Court's reasoning by advancing two theories. First, they argue that insider trading is unfair.[3] Second, they offer highly refined

* Professor of Law, Duke University School of Law. The author is grateful for the support of the E.T. Bost Research Professorship during the preparation of this article.

1. This article uses the term "insiders" to refer to those who hold managerial positions—corporate officers, directors, and middle managers—within the business organization. Recent enforcement practices have given insider trading a broader context by focusing on various types of professionals, from lawyers to investment bankers to printers. This article does not focus on these professional groups because with respect to such groups it is easy to justify the regulation of insider trading. These professionals usually trade using information that the client has generally taken great steps to keep secret. An early release of this information through the professional's trading unquestionably threatens the client's interest. *See, e.g.,* Power, *Litton Sues Levine, Shearson Lehman Over Itek Trading,* Wall St. J., Aug. 20, 1986, at 2, col. 3. The best evidence of this threat is the fact that the professional is swiftly dismissed when his employer discovers that he has abused the client's trust by trading on the client's information. On the other hand, there is no evidence that employers dismiss officers, directors, or even middle managers for insider trading. The free-market proponents argue that insider trading gives officers, directors, and managers an incentive to create events so that they can trade. The presence of these factors makes inquiry into the trading by officers, directors, and managers a more puzzling problem than is the case with respect to market professionals.

2. *See* Chiarella v. United States, 445 U.S. 222 (1980).

3. The most elusive complaint lodged against insider trading is that it is "unfair." This complaint has two distinct aspects. First, the insider is seen as having an unerodible advantage over others who cannot obtain the same information. Second, the information was produced not for the benefit of the inside trader, but rather as a result of the employer's quest for gain. *See* Brudney, *Insiders, Outsiders, and Informational Advantages Under the Federal Securities Laws,* 93 HARV. L. REV. 322, 356-57 (1979). The second point is an indispensable qualification of the first in characterizing trading as unfair, because the experience, intelligence, resources, or position of some investors will always give them superior insight into prospective market developments. For example, a brokerage house first makes its recommendations to its most important clients. Additionally, no one believes that it is "unfair" for an investor to purchase a security without disclosing his belief that the

arguments explaining how insider trading impacts the corporation's operation,[4] investor behavior,[5] and the allocational efficiency of capital markets.[6] The indeterminacy of these approaches is examined closely below.

Part I of this article criticizes the Supreme Court's contemporary justifications for regulating insider trading.[7] It develops the view that the

---

stock is a "bargain." Disclosure of such information would be dysfunctional because such disadvantages are inherent and necessary components of an exchange economy. *See* Hethrington, *Insider Trading and the Logic of the Law,* 1967 WIS. L. REV. 720, 725-30. Allowing the producer of information to prohibit another's use of that information is socially desirable in certain circumstances. *See* Barry, *The Economics of Outside Information and Rule 10b-5,* 129 U. PA. L. REV. 1307, 1323-28 (1981).

The concept of "unfairness" represents nothing more than a highly stylized line separating lawful and unlawful conduct. There are substantial "fairness" justifications for identifying investors who use an informational advantage for trading purposes. These include protecting the economic benefits that accompany both the production of the information and its private use by its producer. *See* Fleischer, Mundheim & Murphy, *An Initial Inquiry into the Responsibility to Disclose Market Information,* 121 U. PA. L. REV. 798, 808-09 (1973). The logic of the opposite side of this fairness argument, however, is not intuitively obvious. The need to encourage economically desirable conduct may justify one party's use of nonpublic information, but the same need does not necessarily proscribe a second person from using the same information, so long as the second person's use does not impair the first person's use. In fact, commentators who favor the legalization of insider trading have turned the fairness argument around by arguing that permitting insider trading provides incentives to undertake economically worthwhile activities. *See* Carlton & Fischel, *The Regulation of Insider Trading,* 35 STAN. L. REV. 857, 866-72 (1983). These free-market proponents have argued that information differs from most commodities in that one person's use of the information does not necessarily prevent another person from gaining equal or greater advantages from the same information. Thus, "unfairness" by itself is an insufficient basis to condemn insider trading. Professor Brudney, however, coupled "unfairness" arguments with concerns over whether insider trading harms market efficiency, impairs market integrity, induces manipulative practices, or increases the corporation's cost of capital. Brudney, *supra,* at 334-35, 356.

4. Relying on organizational behavior literature, Professor Haft has suggested that a laissez faire approach toward insider trading will promote information delays, manipulation of corporate releases, and intrafirm competition that is harmful to the corporation. *See* Haft, *The Effect of Insider Trading Rules on the Internal Efficiency of the Large Corporation,* 80 MICH. L. REV. 1051, 1051-64 (1982). Haft fails to consider an equally plausible middle ground: that market constraints prevent insiders from trading to an extent that their trading significantly harms the corporation. Professors Jensen and Meckling suggest that the market for managerial talent and corporate control operate as such preventative market constraints. *See* Jensen & Meckling, *Theory of the Firm: Managerial Behavior, Agency Costs and Ownership Structure,* 3 J. FIN. ECON. 305, 328-29 (1976). These market constraints on excessive insider trading are not, however, absolute under the Jensen and Meckling model. Professors Jensen and Meckling argue that a certain amount of managerial misbehavior is optimal. *Id.* at 345-51.

5. *See, e.g.,* Wang, *Trading on Material Nonpublic Information on Impersonal Stock Markets: Who is Harmed, and Who Can Sue Whom Under SEC Rule 10b-5?,* 54 S. CAL. L. REV. 1217, 1235-40 (1981) (arguing that insider trading either induces the unwitting investor to trade or preempts a price otherwise available to an outsider).

6. *See, e.g.,* Seligman, *The Reformation of Federal Securities Law Concerning Nonpublic Information,* 73 GEO. L.J. 1083, 1115-20 (1985) (investors prefer markets where managers have no hidden incentive to delay release of information and are otherwise compelled to disclose all material information prior to their private use of that information).

7. *See infra* notes 11-31 and accompanying text.

limitations that *Chiarella v. United States* and *Dirks v. SEC* impose on the disclose-or-abstain rule are completely artificial. Part II challenges the prevalent view that insider trading affects the market's allocational efficiency.[8] Accepting the assumption that insider trading leads to the manipulation of corporate disclosures, this article uses the capital market theory to demonstrate that insider trading harms neither the individual investor nor the market's allocational efficiency. Part III critically analyzes and takes exception to the emerging arguments of those commentators who contend that the present form of insider trading regulation is unjustified and that the law should allow corporations to license their agents to engage in insider trading.[9] Finally, in the wake of the exceptions taken to the Supreme Court and the commentators, Part IV provides a coherent justification for continuing the regulation of insider trading.[10]

I. The Supreme Court's Impact on Insider Trading

As originally formulated, the disclose-or-abstain rule prohibited trading by *anyone* on the basis of material nonpublic information.[11] The Court formulated the rule believing that the integrity and efficiency of securities markets would be eroded if investors were not confident that all market participants enjoyed the same access to inside information when trading.[12] For a while, this lofty mission guided the courts' holdings that the SEC,[13] the injured investor,[14] and the corporation in whose shares the defendant traded[15] enjoy significant rights against violators of

8. *See infra* notes 32-48 and accompanying text.

9. *See infra* notes 49-85 and accompanying text.

10. *See infra* notes 86-93 and accompanying text.

11. *See* SEC v. Texas Gulf Sulphur Co., 401 F.2d 833, 848 (2d Cir. 1968), *cert. denied,* 394 U.S. 976 (1969); Matter of Cady, Roberts & Co., 40 S.E.C. 907, 912 (1961).

12. *See Texas Gulf Sulphur,* 401 F.2d at 851-52.

13. *See id.* The deterrence value of requiring the insider and his tippee to merely disgorge profits earned before public disclosure of the information is inherently weak. Current enforcement techniques include criminal actions by the Department of Justice as well as civil sanctions by the SEC. The government can impose a fine up to $100,000, as well as a penalty up to three times the insider's profits. *See infra* note 56.

14. Private parties can recover only the insider's profits. *See, e.g.,* Elkind v. Liggett & Myers, Inc., 635 F.2d 156, 173 (2d Cir. 1980); *cf.* Fridrich v. Bradford, 542 F.2d 307, 322 & n.33 (6th Cir. 1976) (expressing support for rule that limits recovery to amount of insider's profits), *cert. denied,* 429 U.S. 1053 (1977). The disgorgement remedy does not include the gains the individual trading investors would have reaped had the insider disclosed the information before trading. This remedy is consistent with the thesis of this article—that investors are not harmed by insider trading.

15. The corporation's right to recover its fiduciary's profits depends on the willingness of the particular jurisdiction to assume that trading harms the corporation. In Diamond v. Oreamuno, 24 N.Y.2d 494, 499, 248 N.E.2d 910, 912-13, 301 N.Y.S.2d 78, 81-82 (1969), the New York Court of Appeals presumed that insider trading causes reputational injury to the corporation in all cases. In Freeman v. Decio, 584 F.2d 186, 191-96 (7th Cir. 1978), the United States Court of Appeals for the

the disclose-or-abstain rule. The utopian dream of information parity among investors was short-lived, however. Two Supreme Court decisions have revolutionized the rule's application, rendering the rationale underlying insider-trading regulation a dark mystery.

In *Chiarella v. United States,*[16] the Supreme Court held that the only persons subject to the disclose-or-abstain rule are those with a preexisting fiduciary relationship to the corporation in whose shares they trade. Chiarella, a markup man employed by Pandick Press, broke the secret code that his employer devised to conceal the identity of its clients and their takeover targets. On five occasions Chiarella purchased the target's shares before a takeover bid was announced. Justice Powell, writing for the majority, rejected the lower court's invocation of the so-called parity-of-information rule that "*[a]nyone*—corporate insider or not—who regularly receives material nonpublic information may not use that information to trade in securities without incurring an affirmative duty to disclose."[17] The Court held that Chiarella's fiduciary relationship was with Pandick Press and the bidder corporation. Chiarella did not have a duty to disclose or abstain because he did not have a fiduciary relationship with the target corporation in whose shares he traded.[18]

Later, in *Dirks v. SEC,*[19] the Court underscored the importance of a preexisting fiduciary relationship when it held that outsiders may freely trade on an insider's selective disclosure so long as the disclosure was not "improper."[20] Secrist, a former officer of Equity Funding of America, informed Dirks, an investment analyst, that Equity Funding's assets were fraudulently overstated. In the course of his aggressive investigation, Dirks shared Secrist's revelations with five investment advisers. These advisers caused their clients to liquidate more than sixteen million dollars worth of Equity Funding stock before the scandal was publicly disclosed. The *Dirks* Court easily could have held that since Secrist could not legally trade on the information, his tippees also could not trade. Instead, *Dirks* held that outsiders may freely trade on the insider's selective disclosure so long as that disclosure was not "improper."[21] According to the Court, a disclosure is improper if the insider tips a relative or expects

Seventh Circuit considered whether the corporation could have lawfully used the information. And in Schein v. Chasen, 313 So. 2d 739, 746 (Fla. 1975), the Florida Supreme Court stated that it would permit recovery only upon proof of actual harm to the corporation.

16. 445 U.S. 222, 233-34 (1980).

17. United States v. Chiarella, 588 F.2d 1358, 1365 (2d Cir. 1978), *rev'd,* 445 U.S. 222 (1980).

18. *Chiarella,* 445 U.S. at 232-33.

19. 463 U.S. 646 (1983).

20. *Id.* at 659-60.

21. *Id.*

to make a pecuniary gain from the selective disclosure.[22]

The threshold appeal of the Court's reasoning in *Dirks* lies in the fact that according analysts greater freedom furthers the efficient functioning of securities markets because it does not condemn the analyst to ferret out material nonpublic corporate information under a fear of violating the antifraud rule. This reasoning, however, has only a superficial appeal and fits the *Dirks* facts poorly. To be sure, the analyst and the corporate executive should be protected from draconian sanctions when the analyst, through persistence, has wrung an important selective disclosure from the executive and then made that disclosure generally available through a public medium. However, Dirks tipped his clients and attempted to give publicity to Equity Funding's fraudulent practices. In this respect, his gains were not all of the heart, but included earning commissions and establishing goodwill with the tipped clients.

Dirks's gains were no different than Merrill Lynch's gains garnered some years earlier in *Shapiro v. Merrill Lynch, Pierce, Fenner & Smith*.[23] As lead underwriter for Douglas Aircraft, Merrill Lynch learned that Douglas's inventories were going to be written down because of production delays caused by the Vietnam War. Merrill Lynch tipped several of its clients, thereby triggering a significant decline in Douglas Aircraft's stock before Douglas eventually announced the writedowns. There is little question that Merrill Lynch would have been beyond the *Dirks* protection. Under the *Dirks* view, Merrill Lynch would be an insider with disclose-or-abstain obligations similar to those of Secrist.[24] On the other hand, if Merrill Lynch had not been Douglas's underwriter and a Douglas officer had gratuitously informed Merrill Lynch of the pending writedown, Merrill Lynch's position would have been identical to that of Raymond Dirks. In each case, however, the analyst's private gains are at the expense of unsuspecting buyers. *Dirks* does not examine why duties under the disclose-or-abstain rule should depend upon the technical niceties of the analyst's position or the fact of a reward to an insider rather than upon some more useful insight into why employers prefer that trading and tipping by its insiders be circumscribed. Market efficiency is enhanced regardless of whether the analyst or other financial intermediary confers a benefit, financial or otherwise, upon the tipping insider. Moreover, it is quite reasonable to expect that a fiduciary's unauthorized premature disclosure could harm his employer's interests, regardless of whether he gains from that revelation. A further anomaly of *Dirks* is that state law, the source of all underlying fiduciary duties, does not re-

22. *Id.* at 663-64.

23. 495 F.2d 228 (3d Cir. 1974).

24. *Dirks*, 463 U.S. at 655 n.14.

quire a finding of personal gain as a prerequisite to establishing misconduct.[25] Nevertheless, *Chiarella* and *Dirks* emphasized reward to the insider, not harm to the employer.

Another development attributable to *Chiarella* is the so-called "misappropriation theory."[26] Under this theory, an employee who makes an unauthorized use of his employer's information by trading in another corporation's stock would appear to be violating Rule 10b-5's proscription of "any fraudulent scheme" by "any person" as well as reaping the kind of "undue trading advantage" that serves no "useful purpose" proscribed in the legislative history of the Exchange Act. Superficially, the misappropriation theory appears to be a natural analogue to *Chiarella* because it underscores the necessity for a fiduciary relationship to exist before the disclose-or-abstain rule applies. Certainly an employee's misuse of his employer's property, whether that property be tangible or intangible, is a clear example of fiduciary misconduct.[27] Moreover, the misappropriation theory is designed to protect the employer's property right to the information.[28]

25. *See generally* R. Clark, Corporate Law 147-50, 155-56 (1986) (unfairness in "self-dealing" transactions arises from harm to either corporation or stockholders; such self-dealing harms corporation because it creates investor uncertainty over frequency and magnitude of self-dealing, thereby increasing the corporation's cost of capital); Frankel, *Fiduciary Law,* 71 Calif. L. Rev. 795, 821-32 (1983) (nature and extent of fiduciary's obligations arises from entrusting party's natural expectations of how fiduciary will discharge powers entrusted to him). There are of course instances in which corporate fiduciaries are required to disgorge their gains as a prophylactic measure, even though the corporation or its shareholders have suffered no tangible harm. *See, e.g.,* Perlman v. Feldman, 219 F.2d 173, 178 (2d Cir. 1955). Even in these cases, the remedy as well as the duty are driven by a concern for protecting the stockholders or the corporation from potential harm.

26. *Chiarella,* 445 U.S. at 240-44 (Burger, C.J., dissenting).

27. Some commentators argue that the presence or absence of a fiduciary relationship should be irrelevant under the misappropriation theory. They reason that the antifraud rule should be no less inclusive than the common law in removing informational advantages gained tortiously or illegally. *See, e.g.,* Barry, *supra* note 3, at 1363. However, closer analysis reveals that the common law imposes no duty to disclose to one party when information has been purloined from another. The common law only provides a remedy to the information's creator against the misappropriator of that information. *See generally* G. Bower & A. Turner, The Law of Actionable Misrepresentation 103-08 (1974). The disclosure obligation under the Supreme Court's misappropriation theory thus has no common law parallel. Even common law copyright and design cases provide a remedy for only the information's creator; they exclude those who deal with the misappropriator. *Cf.* Tabor v. Hoffman, 118 N.Y. 30, 34, 23 N.E. 12, 13 (1889) (inventor selling machine without pattern retains exclusive property right in machine's pattern). Moreover, a nonemployee's use of a creator's information results in the imposition of a constructive trust only if the nonemployee knew he acquired the information through another's breach of fiduciary duty. *See* Ohio Oil Co. v. Sharp, 135 F.2d 303, 306 (10th Cir. 1943).

28. Some commentators have argued that in *Chiarella* and *Dirks* the Supreme Court intended to protect the corporation's "property interest" in the information. These commentators suggest that the Court's holdings should ultimately lead to recognizing the corporation's power to license insider trading. *See e.g.,* Macey, *From Fairness to Contract: The New Direction of the Rules Against Insider Trading,* 13 Hofstra L. Rev. 9, 39-47 (1984).

The misappropriation theory, even though a logical adjunct to the employer's expectations and the fiduciary obligations of its employees, resonates poorly with Rule 10b-5, the provision under which most parties prosecute insider trading cases.[29] In other contexts, Rule 10b-5 is devoted to protecting investors and securities markets from deceptive practices. For example, in *Santa Fe Industries v. Green* [30] the Supreme Court ruled that the antifraud rule did not apply when the complaint alleged no more than a breach of fiduciary duty or unfair dealings. The misappropriation theory, however, expands the antifraud rule to protect an employer's expectations that his employee will not use the employer's information for private gain. It is difficult to reconcile cases such as *Santa Fe Industries* with the misappropriation cases because the misappropriation cases emphasize the "unfairness" to the employment relationship,[31] regardless of the impact upon another's investment decision, and not deception and manipulation. More importantly, the Supreme Court's insider trading decisions have left in their wake only the empty concepts of "fiduciary," "improper disclosure," and "misappropriation." Neither these decisions nor subsequent lower court decisions consider the social benefits of regulating insider trading. The fact that such an aggressive level of regulation exists without a coherent, let alone articulated, philosophy of regulation is one of the most unsettling aspects of the federal securities laws.

29. In United States v. Newman, 664 F.2d 12 (2d Cir. 1981), the United States Court of Appeals for the Second Circuit attempted to bring the misappropriation theory within contemporary Rule 10b-5 jurisprudence by reasoning that injunctive relief is available under the antifraud rule even when the fraud did not give rise to a purchase or sale. As support, however, the court cited cases that either involved market manipulation affecting the share's value or conduct compelling the plaintiff to sell his stock. *See id.* at 17 (citing Crane Co. v. Westinghouse Air Brake Co., 419 F.2d 787, 798 (2d Cir. 1969); and Mutual Shares Corp. v. Genesco, Inc., 384 F.2d 540, 546-47 (2d Cir. 1967)). The court also invoked Superintendent of Ins. v. Bankers Life & Casualty Co., 404 U.S. 6 (1971), to reach fraudulent conduct affecting an employer. *Bankers Life,* however, upheld the application of Rule 10b-5 upon the plaintiff's allegation that the defendant had deceived the company's board of directors into selling their United States Treasury bonds. *Id.* at 8 n.1.

Investors who purchase from or sell to the misappropriating defendant lack standing to complain under the misappropriation theory because they are not the objects of the "fraud." *See* Moss v. Morgan Stanley, Inc., 719 F.2d 5, 16 (2d Cir. 1983), *cert. denied,* 465 U.S. 1025 (1984).

30. 430 U.S. 462, 476-77 (1977). The argument against the misappropriation theory is even stronger with respect to the antifraud provision of the Williams Act because the purpose of the Williams Act is to protect the shareholders of publicly traded corporations. *See* Schreiber v. Burlington N., Inc., 105 S. Ct. 2458, 2463 (1985).

31. *See, e.g.,* United States v. Carpenter, 1986 Fed. Sec. L. Rep. (CCH) ¶ 92,742, at 93,613 (2d Cir. 1986); SEC v. Materia, 745 F.2d 197, 201-02 (2d Cir. 1984), *cert. denied,* 105 S. Ct. 2112 (1985); United States v. Newman, 664 F.2d 12, 17 (2d Cir. 1981); SEC v. Musella, 578 F. Supp. 425, 437-38 (S.D.N.Y. 1984).

II. The Allocational Efficiency Argument

The grafting of the misappropriation theory to the antifraud provision is one of the Court's most truthful admissions in applying Rule 10b-5 to insider trading: the regulation of insider trading cannot be justified out of concern for protecting the unwary investor. Insider trading is at most a fortuity for the investor[32] because the investor is no worse off when the insider trades than when the insider does not trade.[33] The investor's decision to sell or purchase is unaffected by whether the insider is also secretly buying or selling shares in the open market. If the insider neither trades nor discloses his confidential material information, one can nevertheless expect the investor to pursue his trading plan. Sellers naturally are disadvantaged by the nondisclosure of good news, just as buyers are disadvantaged by the nondisclosure of bad news. These considerations, however, cast no light on why the insider's decision to trade should prompt disclosure. Therefore, the focus turns toward a concern greater than the individual investor's injury—namely, the operation of securities markets. Consequently, commentators have directed their attention to how insider trading affects the allocational efficiency of those markets.[34]

Commentators have spent a great deal of time speculating over how and why insider trading impairs the market's allocational efficiency, but there is very little evidence to support the conclusion that it does. Clearly it is a non sequitur to reason, as some commentators have,[35] that the market's operation is impeded because the market would learn about the information sooner if the insider did not trade. This reasoning overlooks the fact that there is no natural connection between the insider's trading and the delay of a corporate disclosure.[36] Certainly managers who have a direct and immediate gain awaiting their disclosure of corpo-

---

32. *See, e.g.*, Elkind v. Liggett & Myers, Inc., 635 F.2d 156, 172 (2d Cir. 1980); Fridrich v. Bradford, 542 F.2d 307, 321 (6th Cir. 1976), *cert. denied*, 429 U.S. 1053 (1977).

33. Some have suggested that the insider's trading does harm the outside investor by either preempting a price otherwise available to him or by inducing him to sell or purchase because of the increased activity in the stock. *See* Wang, *supra* note 5, at 1235. Neither harm is likely if the insider's trading is insignificant. Even if the insider's trading is significant, the harm in the preempted price situation is likely to be small; in the increased trading situation, the insider's trading causes the parallel trader to dispose of a dog or acquire a pearl.

34. *See* Scholtland, *Unsafe at any Price: A Reply to Manne, Insider Trading and the Stock Market*, 53 VA. L. REV. 1425, 1448-49 (1967); Mendelson, *The Economics Board of Insider Trading Reconsidered* (Book Review), 117 U. PA. L. REV. 470, 477-78 (1969) (reviewing H. MANNE, INSIDER TRADING AND THE STOCK MARKET (1966)); *cf.* Gilson & Kraakman, *The Mechanisms of Market Efficiency*, 70 VA. L. REV. 549, 631-35 (1984) (arguing that if insider trading is legalized, insiders should be required to disclose, at some point prior to trading, the identity and size of the intended trade).

35. *See* Scholtland, *supra* note 34, at 1448-49; Mendelson, *supra* note 34, at 489.

36. *See* Dooley, *Enforcement of Insider Trading Restrictions*, 66 VA. L. REV. 1, 34 (1980). Nevertheless, commentators cannot obtain a complete understanding of management's disclosure

rate information have a greater incentive to make the announcement than do managers who do not have a personal gain awaiting disclosure. On the other hand, if the insider must sacrifice his informational advantage before he trades, then not only is his incentive to trade removed, but also his incentive to make an earlier disclosure is dampened.[37]

The proponents of the disclose-or-abstain rule emphasize the need to regulate insider trading because they perceive the capital market's institutional integrity as the cornerstone of allocational efficiency.[38] Two questions test the accuracy of this view: How does insider trading erode the market's integrity? And how does such erosion impair allocational efficiency? The first question raises an issue that was addressed previously—whether there is a causal relationship between insider trading activity and the accuracy and timeliness of corporate disclosures. Proponents of the disclose-or-abstain rule believe that a perfectly laissez faire attitude toward insider trading would give an insider the leverage needed to manipulate the securities market to maximize his own trading agenda. Tardy corporate disclosures would be the most likely form of manipulation because the delay would give insiders and others the time needed to capture a greater share of the change in a firm's value. Ambiguous corporate disclosures and signals that are used to create market uncertainty are an even more ingenious form of manipulative trading practice. For example, insiders may use ambiguous announcements to enter the market and purchase their firm's securities at a lower price and to dispose of the stocks at a higher price following a later definitive disclosure. Insiders may even alter the timing of corporate activities for the sole purpose of creating intertemporal swings in the firm's value; they

incentives unless management's private trading practices are strictly regulated. *See* Trueman, *Motivating Management to Reveal Inside Information,* 38 J. FIN. 1253, 1254 (1983).

37. Professor Coffee has demonstrated that there is no inconsistency between mandatory disclosure and the prevalence of insider trading. *See* Coffee, *Market Failure and the Economic Case for a Mandatory Disclosure System,* 70 VA. L. REV. 717, 740 (1984). Insiders can comply with disclosure requirements and still enjoy a trading advantage if they act before the announcement has achieved its full effect. Moreover, the delays that occur are likely to be minimal. *See* Scott, *Insider Trading: Rule 10b-5, Disclosure and Corporate Privacy,* 9 J. LEGAL STUD. 801, 810 (1980). Finally, the disclose-or-abstain rule is likely to have little effect on management's tendency to delay releasing "bad news." *See* Givoly & Palmon, *Timeliness of Annual Earnings Announcement: Some Empirical Evidence,* 57 ACCT. REV. 486, 489-90 (1982); Patell & Wolfson, *Good News, Bad News, and the Intraday Timing of Corporate Disclosures,* 57 ACCT. REV. 509, 525 (1982). Some commentators hypothesize that upcoming audits, rather than the prospect of personal gain, drive management to disclose bad news. *See* Pastena & Ronen, *Some Hypotheses on the Pattern of Management's Informal Disclosures,* 17 J. ACCT. RES. 550, 551 (1979).

38. For general descriptions of how trading in the secondary securities markets affects the allocation of resources among competing productive uses, see Fama & Laffer, *Information and Capital Markets,* 44 J. BUS. 289 (1971); and Hirschleifer, *The Private and Social Value of Information and the Reward to Incentive Activity,* 61 AM. ECON. REV. 561 (1971).

thereby can reap the gains of their privileged positions by anticipating the direction of the stock's price movements. These and other disclosure horrors, referred to here as abusive insider-trading practices, are the subject of a great deal of conjecture in the literature. However, there is little empirical evidence on these abusive insider-trading practices.

If extensive evidence proved that abusive practices accompany insider trading, the courts could justify the regulation of insider trading as the most administrable response to curbing abusive insider-trading practices. Great uncertainty exists as to whether sound managerial judgment or the insider's hidden trading agenda drives an announcement's timing or its ambiguities, the initiation or delay of a corporate transaction, or the selection of a riskier project. Insider-trading regulation is a more administrable approach to these potential abusive insider-trading practices because it achieves two results by removing the corrupting incentive of insider-trading profits. First, regulation eliminates the highly problematic matter of proving that the manager's desire for private gain, rather than the corporate interest, motivated a disclosure, event, or project. Second, regulation focuses concern upon a single event—whether the defendant possessed and traded on confidential corporate information—which better lends itself to external analysis than does a subjective managerial business decision concerning corporate disclosures and operations. In this way, regulating insider trading eliminates the need to police a wide array of managerial misbehavior because it removes managerial incentives to engage in more serious wrongdoing.

It remains a matter of conjecture whether any, let alone a sufficient, connection exists between insider trading and the manipulation of corporate disclosures and events. Rather than leaving the question to be resolved more or less according to one's prejudices toward captains of industry, the remaining discussion in this part proceeds on the assumption that the above-described abuses would accompany the legalization of insider trading. Even with such an assumption, there is reason to doubt that the legalization of insider trading would harm the securities market's allocational efficiency.

Capital market theory offers a useful description of probable investor and manager behavior, if we assume that investors are concerned that the deregulation of insider trading will corrupt the timeliness and authenticity of the corporation's disclosures. Insider trading occurs randomly. Inside traders generally are not repeat players because all firms do not experience the kinds of financial developments that offer extraordinary returns to insiders who trade before disclosure occurs. Moreover, regardless of the legal environment, the varying moral compunctions experienced by different managers about the propriety of their use of confidential information also causes randomness. On the other hand, outside investors do not know ex ante which firms' managers possess inside information; nor do they know which firms' managers will trade before disclosing that information, or will engage in abusive insider-trading practices to heighten their trading profits. Due to these informational deficiencies, the rational investor will assume ex ante that each firm poses the same risk of abusive insider-trading practices as does the market as a whole and will accordingly discount the value of each firm by the average estimated agency cost of all firms.[39] Therefore, the risk of abusive insider-trading practices, even though random for the individual firm, becomes systematic due to the informational asymmetries that characterize public corporations. Because it is systematic, this risk cannot be reduced by diversification; an investor will merely ensure that his exposure to the harm is that of the market as a whole by adding more securities to his portfolio.

The ultimate contribution of capital market theory to the subject of insider trading is the support it gives to the emphasis on fiduciary relationships found in the Supreme Court's insider trading decisions. Capital market theory offers the compelling argument that insider trading harms the individual firm rather than the investor or the allocational efficiency of the securities markets. Insider trading does not harm investors because they can self-insure against abusive insider-trading practices by discounting all stocks by the average risk for all firms.[40] If an investor holds an efficient portfolio, the insider trading losses on one investment will be offset by the higher return of firms whose insiders do not trade. Over time, an investor can expect that his portfolio's insider trading losses will sum to zero.[41] On the other hand, the presence of abusive insider-trading

39. For a useful discussion of how buyers (i.e., investors) use various criteria to judge the quality of merchandisers, see Akerlof, *The Market for "Lemons": Quality Uncertainty and the Market Mechanism,* 84 Q.J. ECON. 488 (1970).

40. That such discounting occurs takes some steam out of the complaint that insider trading is unfair. The unfairness charge reflects an isolated evaluation of the insider's conduct after he has traded; if an ex ante assessment were made of the insider's right to trade which considered the investors' discounting, the unfairness charge would lose its force. *See* Scott, *supra* note 37, at 809.

41. In a related context, the author has questioned the free-market proponents' argument that it is desirable to have less demanding standards for managers, in part because owners may self-insure by holding an efficient portfolio. *See* Cox, *Compensation, Deterrence, and the Market as Boundaries for Derivative Suit Procedures,* 52 GEO. WASH. L. REV. 745, 752 (1985). Moreover, the free-market proponents must first establish not only what is wrong with the status quo, but also why investors should be driven to hold efficient portfolios. *See* Bebchuk, *The Case for Facilitating Competing Tender Offers: A Reply and Extension,* 35 STAN. L. REV. 23, 29-31 (1982). In any case, the nearly five-fold increase in the assets of mutual funds since 1980 evidences the recognition by the "little guy" that attachment to a larger investor, even for a fee, can compensate for a host of disadvantages. *See* Sebastian, *Many Small Investors Quit Picking Stocks, Shift to Mutual Funds,* Wall St. J., Feb. 7, 1986, at 1, col. 6.

practices increases each firm's cost of capital because investors discount all firm securities by the average risk of abusive trading practices. Therefore, many firms will seek to lower their cost of capital in order to reduce the discount applied to them by incurring nontrivial bonding, monitoring, and signaling costs designed both to deter their managers from abusive insider-trading practices and to signal effectively that their firm poses a lower risk of such practices.[42] In considering how to reduce its cost of capital, a firm will balance the marginal cost of each additional unit of bonding, monitoring, and signaling against the accompanying marginal benefits of reducing its managers' trading.[43] Therefore, no firm will ever be completely free from investor discounting for abusive insider-trading practices because it is not economical to stop insider trading at any cost.

Some firms may discourage their managers from trading while others may not; the overall effect is not to eliminate this component from each firm's systematic risk, but to reduce it for all firms. Taking a market perspective, the following question arises: What are the resulting social costs if many firms' managers do not seek to distinguish themselves as nontrading managers? Some believe this to be the case; indeed many corporations reveal no outward concern over insider trading at least insofar as they do not establish aggressive monitoring or bonding programs designed to discourage insider trading.[44] Because capital allocation occurs within the context of a comparative assessment among competing choices, any change that affects the cost of capital for all firms at the same rate will not affect the relative comparisons made by investors that

42. This multiperiod signaling model for insider trading is developed in Ross, *Disclosure Regulation in Financial Markets: Implications of Modern Finance Theory and Signaling Theory,* in ISSUES IN FINANCIAL REGULATION 177 (F. Edwards ed. 1979). *See also* Dooley, *supra* note 36, at 45-47.

43. *See* Jensen & Meckling, *supra* note 4, at 324-25.

44. Professor Mendelson was the first to argue that a firm experiencing insider trading will have a higher cost of capital. *See* Mendelson, *supra* note 34, at 477-78. If investors cannot identify which firms are experiencing insider trading, and if insider trading opportunities are randomly distributed across all firms, evidence that a particular firm is experiencing insider trading should not cause that firm's cost of capital to rise above that of other firms unless the market perceives that the particular firm has a higher-than-average likelihood of repeating the experience. If shareholders perceive that all firms have the same risk of insider trading, and firms do not signal, bond, or monitor to reduce the discount applied to them, the question arises whether an investor will favor other investment opportunities over the securities markets.

The resource question also arises when all stocks have an equal risk of abusive insider-trading practices. Assume that a firm is considering a project that offers a 9% return on investment. The lowest cost of capital for a firm of this risk classification is 9.1% in insider-trading markets. If insider-trading were regulated, the firm could offer a return of no greater than 9% to obtain the sums necessary for the investment. With insider trading legal, the firm cannot undertake the project without reducing its value, and the resources which would have been consumed in its undertaking will lie dormant or will be used in a venture of a different type.

drive the allocation of capital among the various investment choices.[45] If abusive insider-trading practices are assumed, and if firms continue not to signal their lower-than-average frequency of such practices, then the legalization of insider trading would equally affect the cost of capital for all firms. Therefore, investors will not discriminate between firms that produce computers and those that manufacture automobiles solely on the basis of insider-trading abuses, because investors see each firm as posing the same risk of such practices. Hence, legalization of insider trading, under this "lock-step" paradigm, would not adversely affect the allocational efficiency on an interfirm basis.

The rejoinder to the "lock-step" paradigm is that even though all firms' securities reflect ex ante the same risk of insider trading, insider trading affects resource allocation because investors are not limited to securities markets. In theory, investors have many investment alterna-

45. Theorists suggest that managers who do not engage in insider trading will seek to avoid any discounting of their firms' stock by distinguishing their firms from those firms whose managers do trade. Monitoring, bonding, and signaling are commonly hypothesized devices to overcome these asymmetries. Firms will undertake these acts, however, only up to the point at which their marginal costs equal their marginal gains. Professor Dooley searched for evidence of these devices, reasoning that their existence would corroborate investors' fears concerning the effects of abusive insider trading. Professor Dooley, however, focused only on whether firms directed monitoring, bonding, or signaling *solely* at their managers' trading activities. Finding no evidence of manager trading activities, Professor Dooley concluded that the case of investor malaise is overstated and that insider trading does not interfere with the allocational efficiency of securities markets. *See* Dooley, *supra* note 36, at 44-55.

Professor Dooley's findings are consistent with two conflicting hypotheses. A failure to find evidence of signaling, bonding, or monitoring supports the hypothesis that insider trading does not harm the individual firm's securities. It also supports the hypothesis that managers lack a compensation schedule that aligns their utility functions with the stockholders' interests. Absent an incentive to maximize the firm's value, managers will not use such devices to distinguish their firm from other firms.

Professor Dooley may not have looked at the correct indicia of signaling, monitoring, and contracting. He looked exclusively at arrangements that proscribed management insider trading. As noted earlier, investors may not fear the insider's trading itself as much as its collateral impact on discretionary actions, such as disclosure and stewardship practices. Abundant evidence shows that corporations employ numerous devices such as independent auditors and outside directors to minimize such agency costs. *See* Watts & Zimmerman, *Agency Problems, Auditing, and the Theory of the Firm: Some Evidence,* 26 J.L. & ECON. 613, 615 (1983) ("This evidence is consistent with the hypothesis that efficient, agency cost-minimizing contractual arrangements . . . include monitoring and is inconsistent with the explanation that independent corporate auditing is the consequence of companies or securities acts."). Express and implied liability under the federal securities laws for misleading corporate announcements can be viewed as externally imposed bonding. Furthermore, even voluntary disclosure practices serve to signal managerial qualities and insights. *See generally* Cox, *Insider Trading Regulation and the Production of Information: Theory and Evidence,* 64 WASH. U.L.Q. 475, 492-99 (1986). These factors neither support nor undermine Professor Dooley's conclusions because it is too difficult to ascertain whether their existence stems from the fears of investors concerning insider trading or from more sweeping concerns about managerial misbehavior. Professor Dooley's study is focused too narrowly because a relationship between such devices and trading abuses clearly would arise were insider trading legalized.

tives in markets where there are no informational asymmetries. For example, an investor fearing insider trading in equity securities may invest in government treasury bills, the closest available risk-free investment. Thus, while insider trading poses no allocational problems if investors were limited to corporate stocks and bonds, it does pose allocational problems if investors may freely withdraw from the corporate equity market and invest in different markets, instruments, or commodities.[46]

This analysis, however, contains two significant qualifications which in combination erode the prevalent belief that insider trading threatens allocational efficiency. First, it is hard to envision a passive investment that is not accompanied by serious informational asymmetries. Every investment entails either a direct managerial component or an external component that is connected to a managerial component. In either case, the managerial component provides its own opportunity for abusive insider-trading practices. For example, insider trading occurs even with the risk-free treasury bill; insiders have secretly traded in treasury bills on private knowledge concerning changes in the terms for new government offerings.[47] Second, not all investors can lawfully acquire alternative forms of investment. The most important investors, in terms of the market's allocational efficiency, are the institutional investors that dominate current capital markets; more importantly, these institutional investors are prisoners condemned by statute or charter to continue trading in markets characterized by insider trading.[48] Their sentence assures that the vast wealth they control, which today accounts for most of the trading volume on the exchanges, cannot be moved freely to areas where the risk of insider trading is lower. Because securities markets are the "only

46. Commentators believe that the potential for movement of funds across markets justifies disclosure requirements designed to reduce shareholder discounting. *See* Coffee, *supra* note 37, at 722 (mandatory disclosure system improves the allocational efficiency of the economy); Fox, *Shelf Registration, Integrated Disclosure, and Underwriter Due Diligence: An Economic Analysis,* 70 VA. L. REV. 1005, 1015-18 (1984) (developments in regulation of securities offerings that reduce trustworthiness of information have effect of raising cost of capital and reducing funds available for corporate expansion); Levmore, *Securities and Secrets: Insider Trading and the Law of Contracts,* 68 VA. L. REV. 117, 146 n.75 (1982) (discounting may cause investors to forgo purchasing securities).

47. *See In re* Blyth & Co., 43 S.E.C. 1037 (1969); *see also An Apparent Leak of GNP Statistics is Being Probed,* Wall St. J., Sept. 23, 1985, at 18, col. 3 (reporting Treasury bond futures price rise that occurred before release of Commerce Department information that caused interest rates to decline); *SEC Charges Navy Employee with Trading on Nonpublic Information About Contract,* 14 Sec. Reg. & L. Rep. (BNA) No. 16, at 682 (Apr. 23, 1982) (discussing case involving Department of Navy employee charged with purchasing stock of supplier before announcement of award of contract to supplier).

48. An excellent summary of the various portfolio restrictions imposed upon financial institutions appears in Clark, *The Soundness of Financial Intermediaries,* 86 YALE L.J. 1, 44 n.125 (1976). Institutional investors do spread their investments across many foreign securities markets. *See* Sesit, *U.S. Institutions Find Buying Foreign Stocks Can Be Very Profitable,* Wall St. J., June 3, 1986, at 1, col. 6. However, there is no reason to expect that insider trading does not exist in foreign markets.

game in town" for a significant portion of the institutional investor's fund, the comparative assessment among competing security choices would appear unaffected. Therefore, the impact of insider trading on allocational efficiency may be overstated. Insider trading may have an effect only at the margins and it may not impact interfirm comparisons; investors are likely to discount equally for this risk and insider-trading practices may not drive sufficient capital to other markets to adversely affect the operation of securities markets. For these reasons, if regulating insider trading serves some societal interest, that interest must be more than an interest in maintaining the allocational efficiency of securities markets.

III. Arguments Against Insider Trading Regulations

Commentators have recently advanced four arguments in support of the proposition that the present form of insider-trading regulation is unjustified and that the law should allow corporations to license their agents to engage in insider trading. First, they argue that there is no empirical evidence that insider trading is harmful. Second, they argue that insider trading promotes stock price changes. Third, they argue that insider trading creates managerial incentives by allowing managers to unilaterally alter their own compensation packages through insider trading. Finally, they argue that with deregulation, managers and stockholders would contract to license the managers to engage in insider trading because it would be to their mutual advantage to do so. Each of these positions is examined and dismissed below.

A. *The "It's An Empirical Question" Argument.*

Those who abandon hope that the courts will offer insight into what harm insider trading causes frequently turn to the law and economics literature, where insider trading has been a lively topic for scholarly debate for three decades. Professor Manne's celebrated book, *Insider Trading and the Stock Market,*[49] sharpened the issues in the debate over the purpose of insider trading regulation. Before the publication of his work, expressions such as "unfairness" and "conduct constituting a breach of fiduciary duty" used to justify insider-trading regulation.[50] Unfortunately, this treatment, like the Supreme Court's reasoning in *Chiarella,* conceals any thoughtful explanation why the defendant's conduct should be subject to such pejorative characterizations. Manne redefined and

49. H. Manne, Insider Trading and the Stock Market (1966).

50. *Id.* at 4-8.

clarified the debate by focusing on the costs and benefits of insider trading.

The perceived costs of insider trading are many. As discussed above,[51] some believe that the legalization of insider trading would corrupt the firm's disclosure practices and result in reports being delayed or otherwise manipulated to accommodate the manager's insider-trading designs. Managers who are not content to trade with the normal price changes that accompany the ebb and flow of their firm's individual performance may aggressively embrace high risk projects in order to induce even greater swings in the stock's price. Moreover, they may time corporate activities to enhance their short-term trading goals. In addition, with a complete laissez faire attitude toward insider trading, the manager can profit as easily from bad or good news. This two-way feature is troubling. One might see the manager's holding in his firm's stock as beneficial because it more closely identifies the manager's interests with those of the outside owners; however, the gap between the manager and the outside owners widens if the manager can profit regardless of the firm's performance. In sum, if these various insider trading abuses are perceived widely enough, they will erode investor confidence in American securities markets and increase the cost of capital for all firms.[52]

The free-market proponents react to this parade of horribles by employing the well-worn debating trick of framing the areas in contention around points on which they can prevail. For example, they baldly assert that insider trading is an empirical question.[53] They reason that if insider trading is harmful, there should be some empirical evidence supporting this position. On this front, their support lies in the few identifiable instances in which insider trading also led to manipulation of the corporation's disclosure or operating practices.[54] The scantness of this evidence, they argue, indicates an absence of any measureable investor malaise about insider trading.[55] Finding no evidence that insider trading

51. *See supra* note 38 and accompanying text.

52. *See* Brudney, *supra* note 3, at 356; Ross, *supra* note 42, at 182.

53. *See* Carlton & Fischel, *supra* note 3, at 873; Easterbrook, *Insider Trading, Secret Agents, Evidentiary Privileges, and the Production of Information,* 1981 SUP. CT. REV. 309, 338; Macey, *supra* note 28, at 34.

54. *See* Dooley, *supra* note 36, at 33-36.

55. Studies show that stocks that insiders actively trade do not have larger systematic risks than stocks that insiders seldom trade. *See* M. MORAN, INSIDER TRADING IN THE STOCK MARKET: AN EMPIRICAL TEST OF THE DAMAGE TO OUTSIDERS (Center for the Study of American Business Working Paper No. 89, 1984). There exists, of course, much anecdotal evidence to the contrary. *See Insider Trading Case Reinforces Belief that Small Investor is at a Disadvantage,* Wall St. J., May 20, 1986, at 2, col. 3; *SEC Chief, Seeking to Reassure Investors, Says Insider Trading Cases Are Limited,* Wall St. J., Nov. 17, 1981, at 16, col. 2.

causes widespread abuses or investor malaise, the free-market proponents score the debate points.

Rephrasing the debate to focus on raw economic and empirical questions not only guides the discourse to areas where the data favors the free-market view, but it also discretely manipulates the burden of persuasion. The free-market proponents' argument that regulation is an empirical question presumes that those who favor regulation must first support their position with empirical findings. This, of course, overlooks the fact that regulation is the status quo. Because regulation is the status quo, it is more appropriate that the free-market proponents should carry the burden of persuasion as to whether a change is necessary. The locus of the burden is of substantial importance because the free marketers' empirical evidence is consistent with two equally plausible, yet opposite, conclusions. Studies that report neither evidence of systematic abuse accompanying insider trading nor investor malaise over such conduct, on the one hand, support the free-market proponents' belief that insider trading is not harmful. On the other hand, these findings are equally consistent with the belief that the effects of insider-trading practices do not lend themselves to reliable empirical inquiry.

Several important factors suggest that the topic of abusive insider-trading practices does not lend itself to reliable empirical inquiry. Empiricists have difficulty in identifying the feared abuses, such as the insider trading itself. And when empiricists do isolate abuses, the connection with insider trading is at best speculative. So long as insider trading is criminally and civilly wrongful,[56] managers will not cooperate with the empiricist seeking to reveal trading or any other abusive conduct connected with trading. Thus, empiricists always will have difficulty establishing whether the insider's trading delayed or prompted a given activity or whether the delay or initiation occurred naturally and merely provided the manager an opportunity to trade.[57] Moreover, most types of abusive insider-trading practices involve discretionary manage-

56. *See* The Insider Trading Sanctions Act, 15 U.S.C. § 78u(d)(2)(A) (Supp. II 1984) (authorizing damages equivalent to three times the amount of insider trading profits); 15 U.S.C. § 78ff (Supp. II 1984) (possible criminal penalty of $100,000 fine and five years imprisonment); Racketeer Influenced and Corrupt Organizations Act, 8 U.S.C. § 1964(c) (1982) (authorizing treble damages and costs, including attorney fees, in private action).

57. Abundant evidence exists that insiders systematically trade on the eve of significant corporate announcements. *See* Elliott, Morse & Richardson, *The Association Between Insider Trading and Information Announcements,* 15 RAND J. ECON. 521, 529 (1984) (insiders pursue active strategy of buying before release of good news as well as passive strategy of not selling before release of such news); Keown & Pinkerton, *Merger Announcements and Insider Trading Activity: An Empirical Investigation,* 36 J. FIN. 855, 866 (1981) (approximately one-half of trading volume associated with merger announcements occurs before announcement is made); Penman, *Insider Trading and the Dissemination of Firms' Forecast Information,* 55 J. BUS. 479, 492 (1982) (impact of forecast an-

rial decisions for which there is an equally reasonable corporate interest that justifies a manager's decision to delay disclosure, to commence a business activity, or to report an event. Furthermore, so long as insider trading is prohibited, it will be impossible for the empiricist to observe managerial practices in a hypothesized free-market environment of no regulation. Hence, the impact of deregulating insider trading on a full array of managerial mores is beyond empirical evaluation within the current legally constrained environment.[58] Finally, investor malaise over inside trading may well affect stock valuations generally, but only at the margins. That is, an investor's discounting for insider trading, if it exists, is likely to be immeasureable because it is so insubstantial. However, even undetected discounting is inconsistent with the free marketers' thesis that insider trading does not cause an adverse reaction. Moreover, even slight discounting justifies an individual firm's questioning whether it can reduce its cost of capital relative to that of the market as a whole by proscribing trading by its insiders.

These alternate explanations for the "no empirically observable" discounting emphasize the importance of which school of thought carries the burden of proof. The empirical problems inherent in the insider-trading context will always produce a factual base which supports the free-market proponents' position, regardless of the substantive deficiencies of their views. In the end, empirical inquiry will always be unsatisfactory because the inherent secrecy involved with insider trading ensures that there will be no significant observable data.

B. *The Efficient Stock Price Change Argument.*

Without abandoning their position that the regulation of insider trading is an empirical question, the free-market proponents also argue for deregulation on nonempirical grounds. On this front, the free-market proponents employ Professor Manne's thesis that insider trading pro-

---

nouncement on stock prices is closely correlated with amount of insider trading occurring before announcement).

In some cases, managers have a legitimate corporate purpose for not disclosing an event. For example, in State Teachers Retirement Bd. v. Fluor Corp., 654 F.2d 843 (2d Cir. 1981), the purchaser instructed the seller to delay the announcement of a billion dollar contract for several days while financing could be arranged. During this time, insiders took liberal advantage of this external constraint on the firm's disclosure. *Id.* at 846-48. In other instances, the reason given for disclosure delay is much more suspect. *See, e.g.,* Elkind v. Liggett & Myers, Inc., 635 F.2d 156, 164 (2d Cir. 1980) (release delayed due to reluctance to correct overly optimistic financial projection). These problems justify the SEC's enforcement of the *firm's* disclosure duty when the firm's insiders are trading in its shares on the basis of material nonpublic corporate information. *See In re* Sharon Steel, [1981-1982 Transfer Binder] Fed. Sec. L. Rep. (CCH) ¶ 83,049, at 84,618 (D.D.C. Nov. 19, 1981).

58. *See supra* note 56 and accompanying text.

motes stock price changes[59] and stimulates managerial performance.[60] *SEC v. Texas Gulf Sulphur Co.*[61] illustrates their first point. In *Texas Gulf Sulphur,* a large discovery of copper and zinc near Timmins, Ontario was not disclosed for five months so that the corporation could quietly and cheaply acquire neighboring land. Extensive insider trading occurred in the months between the discovery and its ultimate disclosure.

Using Manne's thesis, the free-market proponents erroneously counsel that the corporate interest justifies such trading because the gentle nudging of the insiders' trading activity "smooths" the movement of the stock's price to its postdisclosure equilibrium, thereby averting sharp price changes upon announcement of the discovery.[62] To the extent insider trading influences a stock's price it benefits the insider's opposite trader who on good news gets a higher price, and on bad news purchases at a lower price, than he would get had the insider not traded. On the other hand, from the perspective of the insider's opposite, this is a poor second choice to the insider first disclosing his information. The insider's opposite is far better off with the price established by the insider's disclosure of the information than he is with a price that has been modestly nudged by the insider's secret trading.[63] In the case of the insider's nondisclosure of bad news, the opposite trader emerges owning a stock that has a lower price after disclosure than its purchase price; and in the case of good news, the insider's opposite emerges having sold the security for an amount substantially below its price following disclosure.

Certainly price changes will occur more quickly and efficiently through disclosure of the material nonpublic information than through the manager's use of personal resources and time to trade in his firm's stock. The insider's trading simply has too much "noise" associated with it to be an efficient substitute for a clarion corporate announcement.[64] For example, even with the extensive insider trading activities in *Texas Gulf Sulphur,* there was an extraordinary price change following the dis-

59. *See* H. MANNE, *supra* note 49, at 78-104.

60. *Id.* at 138-43.

61. 401 F.2d 833 (2d Cir. 1968), *cert. denied,* 404 U.S. 1005 (1971).

62. *See* Fischel, *Insider Trading and Investment Analysts: An Economic Analysis of* Dirks v. SEC, 13 HOFSTRA L. REV. 127, 133 (1984) (arguing that insider trading is a valuable and flexible method for communicating information to markets).

63. Of course, if the insider refrains from trading when there is no disclosure, the investor is no better off. These effects, however, are purely redistributive, and presumably the nondisclosure advances the goals of the firm. *See* Levmore, *supra* note 46, at 122, 132-37.

64. *See* Gilson & Kraakman, *supra* note 34, at 631. *See generally* Rose, *Tracking the Trades of Corporate Insiders Doesn't Always Give an Edge to Investors,* Wall St. J., Dec. 19, 1985, at 31, col. 4.

closure of the discovery.[65]

Cases in which there is a more modest change in the firm's fortunes are more appealing cases than *Texas Gulf Sulphur* for Manne's "nudging" thesis. For example, officers may early in a firm's third quarter possess nonpublic information that the firm has finally obtained control over the production costs for one of its many products while wholesale distributors are busy inquiring about two other product lines. The corporation does not disclose these facts because they are too tentative. Nevertheless, any investor selling during the period of nondisclosure would certainly benefit by whatever effects knowledge of these events will have on the market. Moreover, the officers, who, armed with knowledge of these facts, decide that it is not time to sell their firm's stock, have benefited by their use of inside information. These individuals obtain an advantage that insider-trading regulation makes available to them by proscribing only active trading conduct by the executives. Under these circumstances, an unwitting outsider may welcome the insider's trading if it provided even modest upward propulsion in the stock's price.

This scenario appears to be the better case for Manne's nudging thesis, because the combination of the tentativeness of the information and the relatively moderate magnitude of the ultimate event—a banner quarter—combine to make the insider's trading a more acceptable signal to the market insofar as such information is less likely to be disclosed through alternative means. These factors may suggest that under such circumstances insider trading can effect a significant portion of the price change appropriate for the information in hand. On the other hand, insiders will not gamble so much of their own monies on information about an event that remains inchoate. They may purchase, but not in sufficient quantities to move the stock or to cause any eye-catching "blip" in the stock's price. More importantly, any change in the stock's price related to events such as those described above is too easily associated with the efforts of outside analysts whose persistence and resourcefulness in prob-

65. On the first day of trading after Texas Gulf Sulphur's official announcement of the Ontario strike, the stock price increased almost 24%; it doubled within one month. *Texas Gulf Sulphur*, 401 F.2d at 847.

Professor Manne's response to such evidence confuses the issue and shows a misunderstanding of the difference between pre- and postannouncement stock price changes. He reasons that the stock market efficiently reflects new information because insider trading causes the stock to change almost instantaneously. Manne, *Insider Trading and the Law Professors*, 23 VAND. L. REV. 547, 561 n.43 (1970). Professor Manne overlooks the fact that if insider trading did have the benefits he identifies, there would not be any significant price or volume change associated with the corporate announcement itself. Contrary to Professor Manne's assertions, price changes do follow corporate announcements and this suggests that insider trading is not an efficient signal of nonpublic information. Moreover, evidence that markets rapidly reflect new information undermines Manne's thesis. *See* J. COX, FINANCIAL INFORMATION, ACCOUNTING AND THE LAW 186-87 (1980).

ing efforts within both the industry and the firm regularly detect such changes on a daily basis. Their investigation leads ultimately to the mobilization of resources that is more likely to account for stock changes associated with such developments. For these reasons, Manne's nudging thesis is not very compelling in even the best case scenario.

The free marketers' position that insider trading corrects the stock's price proves too much. If accepted, this position justifies massive trading and tipping to ensure that sufficient trading occurs to propel the stock to the equilibrium price appropriate for the nondisclosed information. Such widespread trading, however, compromises the corporate interest that justified nondisclosure in the first place. Therefore, all tips to outsiders must be on the basis of either ambiguous or misleading information so as to conceal the correct confidential information. Ambiguous or misleading statements, however, will not perfectly match the correct confidential information. Such surreptitious trading practices will therefore necessarily be inefficient in terms of prompting the price changes that are appropriate for the correct, albeit concealed, information. If we accept such ambiguous and misleading tipping practices as lawful devices that can be used to achieve an equilibrium market price prior to the disclosure of the correct information, it logically follows that the corporation should be able to announce a completely false event, so long as its magnitude is believed equal to that of the nondisclosed true event. This reasoning would have authorized Texas Gulf Sulphur to announce that a single core drilling in Peru revealed unusually large levels of uranium in November, 1963.

Fortunately for those of us who feel more secure with legal regimes that discourage manipulation and encourage full disclosure, we are spared this logical extension of Manne's "nudging" thesis. The savior in this case is, as we have seen, that Manne's thesis has no reliable support in either theory[66] or empirical data.[67]

---

66. The deficiencies of insider trading as either a signal or other mechanism to drive prices to the equilibrium appropriate for nondisclosed material information are described in Gilson & Kraakman, *supra* note 34, at 572-79. These deficiencies are exacerbated when the insider conceals his identity or otherwise hides his trading activities.

67. Empiricists have studied a variety of corporate announcements to determine the relationship between the amount of insider trading occurring prior to an announcement and the impact of the announcement on the stock's price. The evidence shows that systematic insider trading occurs prior to the announcement and that a significant change in the stock's price occurs with the actual announcement. This suggests that insider trading is not a completely efficient communicator of information.

C. *The Incentive Compensation Argument.*

Because the choice between disclosure and abstention entails two rather unburdensome options, one may wonder why the free-market proponents argue in favor of trading and nondisclosure, especially when disclosure is the most effective way to drive the security to its intrinsic value. The argument that insider trading is socially beneficial because it nudges a security's price to its appropriate equilibrium is so disingenuous that it suggests that the free marketers do not make it in good faith, but only use it as a transparent justification for some larger agenda. Their embrace of insider trading fulfills the free marketers' prescription for what "ails the American corporation"—managerial lethargy and risk aversion.[68] For these crippling afflictions, free marketers prescribe various managerial "self help" compensation arrangements,[69] one of which is insider trading.

To free-market proponents, managerial incentives are found first in compensation arrangements and second in competitive markets for managers and control. Compensation arrangements are intricate and must be reviewed and renegotiated periodically. Such negotiations, however, are time consuming and can involve the expenditure of nontrivial resources, especially for the large public corporation. The free-market proponents see insider trading as a means to avoid such periodic and wasteful negotiations, and propose that managers be licensed to alter unilaterally their own compensation packages through insider trading.[70] Like those who see children as always being responsible enough to decide how much of a sweet to consume before meals, the free-market proponents see managers as being responsible enough to accede only to the right amount of insider-trading profits. They further believe that managers who are free to trade will be stimulated to generate new information in order to provide themselves with further opportunities to gain by trading prior to disclosing the value-increasing event. The owners also benefit because such value-enhancing information means new developments, new markets, and other corporate events that increase the value of the firm.

The free-market proponents envision the manager's compensation package as having upside potential, even in a down market. They argue that managers should be free to gain from events that decrease as well as

68. *See* H. MANNE, *supra* note 49, at 578-79; Carlton & Fischel, *supra* note 3, at 861-66, 881; Macey, *supra* note 28, at 30-32.

69. Some would expand the manager's rewards beyond mere inside trading to include appropriating the corporation's business advantages and ultimately the owners' continuing interest in the firm. *See* Easterbrook & Fischel, *Corporate Control Transactions,* 91 YALE L.J. 698, 705-06 (1982).

70. *See* H. MANNE, *supra* note 49, at 138-41; Carlton & Fischel, *supra* note 3, at 870-71; Macey, *supra* note 28, at 39, 46, 57-58, 62-63.

increase the value of the firm. Permitting managers to profit on bad news, they argue, is necessary to overcome the manager's aversion to risk:[71] the manager will be more willing to embrace risky ventures if he is aware that a venture's failure can nevertheless be turned into his gain by selling short before announcing the failure. Licensing managers to trade on inside information provides a means to reward the manager who tried and failed. Insider trading, therefore, becomes a device for rewarding socially beneficial entrepreneurial risk-taking.

With such a perception of the potential benefits of insider trading, the proponents of the free-market view conclude that if managers and shareholders could costlessly contract, they would see that licensing managers to trade on inside information is in their mutual interest.[72] In this respect, the private contracting approach to insider trading is a natural adjunct to the free marketers' familiar refrain that the corporation is but a nexus of important contractual relations,[73] the most central being the one between owners and their managers. In this realm, managers and owners trade off costs and benefits. Therefore, stockholders will allow the insider to be compensated in a manner that will most likely stimulate entrepreneurial activity so that they can receive the benefits of heightened managerial effort and talent. These tradeoffs should nevertheless be judged by their relative costs and benefits. As explained below, the free-market proponents give insufficient attention to the costs of insider trading when weighing the assumed benefits.

First, the free-market proponents overlook the alternative dispositions that the firm could make with its inside information. For example, in a completely laissez faire environment, the firm could consider selling the information to one or more traders who could thereby reap the spread between what was paid to the firm to acquire the information and the gain derived by trading on the information's nondisclosure. Such marketing of the inside information has a leveraging effect of enhancing the wealth of remaining stockholders by appropriating more of the gain through the firm rather than the market. The firm's potential gains from such dispositions are considerable and could easily swamp those that the free-market proponents assert would accrue by licensing the firm's insid-

71. *See* Carlton & Fischel, *supra* note 3, at 873-76.

72. *See, e.g.*, Carlton & Fischel, *supra* note 3, at 871 (insider trading increases the manager's incentive to acquire and develop valuable information); H. MANNE, *supra* note 49, at 132-33 (arguing that if large corporations are to survive, a form of compensation must be devised that rewards individual entrepreneurial effort).

73. The seminal explication of this theory is found in Coase, *The Problem of Social Cost*, 3 J.L. & ECON. 1 (1960). Professor Coase rejects the argument that free marketers draw from his work because he assumes that parties possess perfect information before contracting. As discussed below, this is not possible with respect to insider trading.

ers to trade. To be sure, information is a public good in that selling it to one person does not prevent another's use of that information. But in the context of using corporate confidential information in capital markets there is a crowding-out effect, whereby one person's use can easily lead to another's indirect trading so that a later trader does not reap as great a market advantage from the same information. Therefore, a firm wishing to consider alternative dispositions of inside information could rightly see that such uses must foreclose trading by its managers. In any case, the free-market proponents should consider the benefits of the firm's alternative uses and dispositions of inside information in evaluating the dedication of inside information as a managerial prerequisite.

Second, the free-market proponents' belief that insider trading is necessary to increase entrepreneurial activity is vulnerable on many points. In several other areas of managerial behavior, the free-market proponents have counseled deregulation based on their unqualified belief that the competitive markets for managers and control pose a means to displace managers who are risk averse, inefficient, or who otherwise fail to maximize share values. In those areas, they believe the market offers sufficient stimuli for the managers to excel.[74] The free-market proponents, however, do not consider market-based forces when they promote insider trading as a necessary incentive for valuable entrepreneurial activity. As discussed above,[75] the free-market proponents prescribe insider trading as a device to overcome the manager's aversion to risk. However, managers who may profit equally from the corporation's gains as from its losses can be seen as neutral to whichever event occurs. Within such a compensation arrangement, the manager's incentives are hopelessly confused and certainly are not focused exclusively upon the stockholders' interest in maximizing the firm's value. Therefore, rather than

---

74. The free-market proponents generally favor deregulation in several areas of managerial behavior because competitive markets for managerial talent and corporate control efficiently displace managers who fail to maximize share values. In those areas, they believe that market forces will stimulate managers to excel. *See* Easterbrook & Fischel, *The Proper Role of a Target's Management in Responding to a Tender Offer,* 94 HARV. L. REV. 1161, 1173 (1981); Fischel, *The Corporate Governance Movement,* 35 VAND. L. REV. 1259, 1288 (1982); Fischel, *The Efficient Capital Market Theory, the Market for Control, and the Regulation of Cash Tender Offers,* 57 TEX. L. REV. 1, 7-8 (1978); Fischel & Bradley, *The Role of Liability Rules and the Derivative Suit in Corporate Law: A Theoretical and Empirical Analysis,* 71 CORNELL L. REV. 261, 275-76 (1985); Manne, *Mergers and the Market for Corporate Control,* 73 J. POL. ECON. 110, 118 (1965). To be sure, the corporate control and managerial talent markets are not perfect. The nature of team effort makes the managerial talent market a forgiving one, and it requires grand scale ineptitude to motivate a firm to displace another firm's incumbent management in order to acquire control. Commentators also believe that the derivative suit will provide an incentive for those managers whose inefficiencies and misbehavior have not reached the displacement level. *See, e.g.,* Anderson, *Conflicts of Interest: Efficiency, Fairness and Corporate Structure,* 25 UCLA L. REV. 738, 790-91 (1978).

75. *See supra* notes 70-71 and accompanying text.

driving managers to be risk preferring, the free-market proponents' solution enables managers to hedge on any decision and thereby become gain-neutral.

Third, the free-market proponents assert that an additional benefit of insider trading is that the compensation it produces is essentially self-established because it is contingent upon events largely within the managers' control. This argument's complete lack of novelty alone challenges its wisdom. Large public corporations today base a substantial percentage of managerial compensation upon bonus arrangements conditioned on some identifiable level of firm performance.[76] While the criteria by which the bonus level is identified are objective, a familiar criticism of executive bonus arrangements is that such criteria are within the control of the executives.[77] Because arrangements such as these already confer large financial rewards upon managers, it is extremely doubtful that those in the managerial ranks feel that they are seriously undercompen-

76. Earlier studies indicate that a significant portion of an executive's *contingent* compensation was tied to changes in the firm's stock value. *See* Easterbrook, *Managers' Discretion and Investors' Welfare: Theories and Evidence,* 9 DEL. J. CORP. L. 540, 559-61 (1984); Vagts, *Challenges to Executive Compensation: For the Markets or the Courts?,* 8 J. CORP. L. 231, 247-52 (1983). Management compensation practices changed when the bear market in the latter half of the 1970's placed a drag on management compensation. An ever increasing portion of the executive's total compensation package, the bonus, is tied to contingent events that are not based on the firm's stock value. One report placed the average bonus for chief executives at about 70% of annual salary. *See* Johnson, *Big Executive Bonuses Now Come With a Catch: Lots of Criticism,* Wall St. J., May 15, 1985, at 33, col. 4.

Professor Manne has a low opinion of these contemporary bonus plans. He does not base his opinion, however, on a close analysis of the way the plans operate. He believes a major deficiency in contingent bonus plans is that the people evaluating a manager's compensation level may not appraise the manager's talent as highly as the manager himself values it. *See* H. MANNE, *supra* note 49, at 141-43. Thus, rather than being free to set his own compensation through insider trading, the manager may have to dicker over his worth.

Professor Manne's criticism of contemporary contingent bonus plans contradicts the current free-market position that legal rules reflect the bargain that the parties would enter into if they could costlessly contract. Professor Manne's view ignores the fact that both parties to an executive compensation arrangement have found the terms of that arrangement to be appropriate.

77. To the extent that these bonuses depend on financial figures rather than market values, they are subject to manipulation within reasonable ranges. *See generally* J. COX, *supra* note 65, at 453-59 (dealing with overall corporate smoothing of reported income); Brindisi, *Why Executive Compensation Programs Go Wrong,* Wall St. J., June 14, 1982, at 20, col. 3 (executive compensation packages do not benefit shareholders equally). The ability to manipulate the bonus increases when performance is based on short time horizons. *See* Rappaport, *Don't Sell Stock Market Horizons Short,* Wall St. J., June 27, 1983, at 28, col. 3. Nevertheless, executive bonus arrangements more recently have begun to reflect a reward for gains directly connected to the executive's contributions. Moreover, these arrangements tie the rewards to gains within the firm over a three- to five-year period. *See* Bennett, *More Managers Find Salary, Bonus Are Tied Directly to Performance,* Wall St. J., Feb. 28, 1986, at 27, col. 5.

sated[78] and are clamoring for insider-trading profits as an incentive reward for further efforts. In this regard, it is significant that most insider-trading cases have not involved those whose entrepreneurial or other managerial efforts have produced the value-increasing event that was traded upon. Instead, the defendants have been outside directors, professionals, or clerks whose assistance was used to complete the transaction, not to create it.

In combination, these three complaints strike at the free-market proponents' thesis that inside trading will stimulate socially useful managerial and entrepreneurial activity. On reflection, the prevailing system of market-based penalties and performance-based reward mechanisms provides substantial incentives without the problem of gain-neutral managers or abusive insider-trading practices.[79] The argument that corporations should be allowed contractually to license their executives to trade on inside information contains an even more fundamental flaw: parties can not efficiently contract without reliable cost/benefit information. This flaw is closely examined in the following section.

D. *The Licensing Through Contracting Argument.*

The dominant constraint to the belief that parties will enter into mutually advantageous contractual arrangements is that they must know the consequences of their acts. It is essential, therefore, that parties know the costs and benefits of their actions if they are to negotiate a mutually advantageous contract.[80] Estimating costs and benefits is practical in a good many legal areas. For example, certain torts such as nuisances lend themselves to privately negotiated settlements because the

78. One survey shows that the average chief executive of a public corporation earns over $750,000 per year, and that the average outside director earns over $279,100 per year. HEIDRICK & STRUGGLES, DIRECTOR DATA 8 (1982).

79. Judge Easterbrook reports that managers of large corporations own an average of $150,000 of their firm's stock and that share values increase upon adoption of long-term compensation plans that increase management's ownership interest. Easterbrook, *supra* note 76, at 540, 558 (1984). This evidence supports the view that corporations can develop compensation plans without hidden costs which benefit stockholders.

80. In most contracting situations the parties do not know their respective costs and benefits because of numerous unpredictable variables over which they have no control. Nevertheless, estimates of the range of the possible outcomes are a necessary part of rational contracting. Such estimates do not reduce the parties' uncertainty over the ultimate benefits to be derived from their contract. However, numerous standard form terms in contracting owe their existence to the contribution they make toward reducing the parties' uncertainty over the expected costs and benefits. *See* Goetz & Scott, *Principles of Relational Contracts,* 67 VA. L. REV. 1089, 1095-110 (1981). In the case of contractual arrangements involving personal services, general fiduciary obligations are a substitute for the standard contracting form that may otherwise be used to reduce the parties' uncertainty over the level of performance. *Id.* at 1126-30. Even here, there is a balance of each party's respective costs and benefits. *Id.* at 1129.

parties can compare the plaintiff's nuisance damages to the defendant's abatement costs as well as the defendant's benefit from engaging in the nuisance activity.[81]

Unfortunately, it is not as easy to estimate the costs and benefits of insider trading, for the problem of quantification is substantial. In the case of insider trading, stockholders must not only be able to quantify the benefits—such as increased efficiency and more aggressive entrepreneurial activity—that they will receive from licensing managers to trade on confidential corporate information, but they also must know whether and by what amount these benefits will be accompanied by costs such as abusive insider-trading practices. Because so much of the activities of a business are team functions and frequently the result of forces beyond management's control, it is difficult to quantify the gains attributable to entrepreneurial activity generally, let alone the gains attributable to each individual manager's contribution toward these benefits.

Moreover, the costs of insider trading are open-ended. Minimally, insider-trading costs amount to a transfer of wealth to the inside trader from his opposite trader. In the case of good news, the insider can purchase shares in the market to the extent that his personal resources permit. A manager's gain, however, is not limited to the amount of personal wealth that he commits to trading. Options trading greatly expands the insider's trading gains and, hence, wealth transfers to the insider.[82] In the case of bad news, the accompanying welfare transfer is also immeasureable because the insider can engage in short trading.[83] In sum, the opposite trader's insider-trading costs are beyond quantification. Furthermore, hidden costs associated with various abusive insider-trading practices must also be taken into account. As discussed above, the existence and magnitude of such costs pose an insolvable problem, especially in the context of ex ante contracting.

To be sure, the parties may establish an arbitrary ceiling on the insider's gains; this approach, however, does not ensure that owners will believe it is in their interest to contract.[84] Even though the parties can

81. *See generally* R. POSNER, ECONOMIC ANALYSIS OF LAW 122-24 (2d ed. 1977).

82. In one instance, an AMAX director's son earned $427,000 in just 48 hours by purchasing an option for $3,125 on a tip from his father that AMAX would soon announce a merger with Standard Oil of California. *See* Longstreth, *SEC Battle against Insider Trading Is Worth the Effort,* Legal Times, May 10, 1982, at 16, col. 2.

83. Section 16 of the Securities Exchange Act, 15 U.S.C. § 78p(c) (1982), currently prohibits officers and directors from selling shares short. *See* Carlton & Fischel, *supra* note 3, at 893-94.

84. Both Professor Brudney and Professor Clark make the important point that the contract analogy is flawed because officers technically are not the agents or employees of the shareholders. Officers are appointed by directors who oversee the corporation's affairs. *See* Clark, *Agency Costs Versus Fiduciary Duties*, in PRINCIPALS AND AGENTS: THE STRUCTURE OF BUSINESS 55-58 (1985); Brudney, *Corporate Governance, Agency Costs, and the Rhetoric of Contract,* 85 COLUM. L. REV.

artificially establish a ceiling on the insider's trading profits, so that at least one dimension of the cost to owners is contained, there remains great uncertainty over whether the owners can reasonably expect benefits of an amount sufficient to justify these costs. Such a ceiling would likely have to reflect each insider's unique characteristics, including his personal indifference curve. This individual tailoring robs insider trading of its purported virtue of being a compensation mechanism that avoids costly contracting and monitoring. Moreover, a ceiling on insider trading would not contain the other costs associated with abusive insider-trading practices. The license to trade, even if trading is reasonably limited, can still provide ample incentives for costly manipulative practices. Finally, any ceiling arrangement is fraught with the substantial incentive for the manager to secretly trade so as to reap gains greater than those permitted by the contract's terms.[85]

The contract analogy simply fails to offer a workable format because its central condition—a capability on the part of the parties to reliably estimate their respective costs and benefits—cannot be satisfied in the case of insider trading. This does not mean, however, that the reference to contracting is futile or without significance. Quite to the contrary, the parties' likely contracting positions reveal that owners would not believe that it is in their best interest to license managers to trade.

IV. The Corporation's Interest in Regulation

Those who champion the view that stockholders will benefit by privately contracting for all matters of managerial discretion overlook the inherent institutional problems of the public corporation that impair the parties' incentives and ability to contract optimally. The separation of ownership from management problem is easier to overcome through contracting when there is a single owner than when there are large numbers of passive owners. The single owner will seek to reduce managerial shirking, self-dealing, and cheating so long as the costs of his efforts do

1403, 1428-30 (1985). This distinction, while an important one, does not completely dispose of the question. Shareholders do elect their directors, and, therefore, any concern over the officers' stewardship can impact the shareholders' decisions in nominating, voting for, or removing directors.

85. There is every reason to believe that managers will not find insider trading to be desirable if it results in an equal reduction in their fixed compensation. Risk averse managers will prefer a fixed salary of $100,000 over a fixed salary of $50,000 plus a 10% chance of $500,000 insider trading profits. The amount of potential insider trading profits needed to make the two types of compensation arrangements equivalent will differ in accordance with individual indifference curves. This makes it difficult to impose ex ante any meaningful ceilings on their trading profits because of the necessity to tailor each ceiling for the individual manager.

not exceed the expected benefits.[86] The contracting costs are greater for the public corporation because there are a greater number of units within the bargaining group. In addition, each stockholder receives only a proportionate share of the expected benefits. Both the presence of high costs and shared benefits discourage stockholders from privately contracting with their managers.[87] Stockholders will not expend their own resources to constrain managerial misbehavior because the passive stockholders will still receive a proportionate share of the resulting benefits; this free rider problem discourages any stockholder from taking action.[88] Alternatively, poor coordination among stockholders may result in a duplication of efforts, leading to excessive monitoring and contracting.[89]

For these reasons, the developed standardized rules, which may take the form of statutory directives or common law obligations, approximate the bargain that stockholders and managers would strike if they could contract at no cost. Free-market proponents view such externally developed rules as socially optimal substitutes for uneconomical private contracting.[90] Others might see this as too narrow a view of the role and content of fiduciary obligations. A middle ground between these two views is to reason that an arrangement which stockholders would never enter into if they could costlessly contract should not comprise an externally imposed fiduciary obligation. It is this point that is used below in rejecting the free-market proponents' belief that insider trading should be deregulated.

86. This is not to suggest that one or more owners do not need standardized obligations. It is not economical or practicable to specify all the details necessary to regulate the manager's behavior. Nor is it desirable that provisions common to such arrangements must constantly, like the wheel, be reinvented and renegotiated. Hence, the desirability of enactments such as the Uniform Partnership Act and of the development of generalized fiduciary obligations of agents has been recognized. *See* W. KLEIN, BUSINESS ORGANIZATION AND FINANCE 61-69 (1980).

87. *See* Anderson, *supra* note 74, at 778-81.

88. *Id.* at 778-80.

89. High communication costs for a large group of stockholders can cause coordination problems. These problems are exacerbated if time is of the essence. Thus, rational stockholders will enact measures to reduce their coordination costs and eliminate time pressures. One classic illustration is the imposition of a supermajority voting requirement before the firm can be acquired. *See* Carney, *Shareholder Coordination Costs, Shark Repellants, and Takeout Mergers: The Case Against Fiduciary Duties,* 1983 AM. B. FOUND. RES. J. 341, 374-78. Another illustration is the imposition of cumulative voting, *see* Anderson, *supra* note 74, at 779-80.

90. This is not to suggest that the characteristics of fiduciary standards will be identical to the characteristics of private contracting standards. *See* Clark, *supra* note 84, at 71-76 (faulting economists for overlooking important differences between the four identifying characteristics of fiduciary duties). Collectively, a large group of shareholders bargain for results that differ from those bargained for by a small number of individuals. Inquiry into stockholders' interests is, as Clark's own reasoning reveals, *id.* at 77-78, a useful beginning point. It seems more appropriate to say that externally developed rules *at a minimum* reflect what the parties would have provided for if they could have costlessly contracted.

A further consideration of the nature of externally imposed fiduciary obligations in the form of insider-trading rules is their collateral benefit of overcoming the natural bargaining advantage managers enjoy over remote owners.[91] If only private contracting existed, the manager's advantage would enable him to manipulate the terms of the agreement to his own benefit. This feature is particularly important in the area of insider trading. Management unquestionably has an incentive to acquire shareholders' stock at discounted prices by insider trading or leveraged buyouts. It is therefore in the manager's interest to manipulate the contract to earn the rewards of apparently complying with its provisions and at the same time secretly trading outside his established compensation schedule. For example, it is not surprising to find that while bonus arrangements recently have become the dominant part of managerial compensation packages, they generally are not measured by criteria which tie managers' gains to increases in shareholder wealth. For these reasons, private contracting arguments are better understood as suggesting that the foundations of externally imposed rules are minimally those requirements which the parties would have agreed to if they could have costlessly contracted.

As discussed above, there is no basis to believe that authorizing managers to engage in insider trading is in the shareholders' interest. Managers control the knowledge of such an arrangement and therefore have an incentive to overstate not only the total amount of the benefits, but also their contribution toward those benefits. Also, there is no reliable means by which the shareholders can satisfy themselves that an appropriate balance is maintained between those benefits and the attendant insider-trading costs. An external prohibition of insider trading can therefore be justified on the basis that stockholders have little to gain and much to lose by licensing their managers to trade on inside information. In this way the prevailing prohibition is consistent with what the parties would have privately agreed to were such negotiations practicable. That is, in place of a compensation device so ripe with informational asymmetries as insider trading, shareholders will rationally prefer unqualified openness for their managers' compensation arrangement. The prohibi-

91. *See* Anderson, *supra* note 74, at 781 (noting that managers have no interest in drafting contracts adverse to their own interest); Easterbrook & Fischel, *supra* note 69, at 702 (noting that managers will manipulate articles to their own advantage). Small investors tend to support charter provisions designed to discourage the takeover of the firm because they are not likely to have the incentive to scrutinize managements' true motives; institutional investors, on the other hand, usually disfavor such provisions. This indicates that managers may be taking undue advantage of the small stockholders. *See* Gilson, *The Case Against Shark Repellent Amendments: Structural Limitations on the Enabling Concept,* 34 STAN. L. REV. 775, 822-27 (1982).

tion of insider trading achieves this result.[92]

At least three reasons other than the uncertain costs and benefits of a free-market approach to insider trading also justify the insider trading prohibition. First, knowledge of an executive's compensation sources is indispensable for understanding what motivates his discretionary behavior. When an executive's compensation is tied to changes in the firm's value, or his renewal is conditioned upon achieving a stated performance level, investors are better assured that the manager will act in the shareholders' best interests than when compensation is not linked to an interest held by the shareholders. This knowledge also permits superiors to rely upon the same assumptions regarding their subordinates' activities. Investors and superiors can form these assumptions more easily when the compensation arrangement is free from the noise that insider trading creates by allowing managers to win with both good and bad news.

Second, an assessment of the manager's stewardship of the firm (an assessment dear to the hearts of free-market proponents as well as those who are not entirely comfortable with a free market) can occur only with full knowledge of both the executive's costs and his team's productivity.[93] Licensing managers to trade on inside information is similar to licensing managers to embezzle because in both cases the individual investor cannot assess the firm's return on its capital or the manager's compensation in light of his productivity. Therefore, shareholders expect a

92. My position that insider trading regulation is justifiable implies a rejection of the prevalent notion that investors have a private right of action for the manager's violation of the disclose-or-abstain rule. Recognition of a private right of action is of no consequence, though, because the private litigant has been a free rider to the detection and enforcement efforts of the SEC in insider trading cases. *See* Dooley, *supra* note 36, at 8-18.

Professor Macey has concluded that all insider trading regulation should be privatized. *See* Macey, *Too Strict a Crackdown Will Harm Markets,* Wall St. J., May 28, 1986, at 34, col. 4. This conclusion is not well-founded. The elaborate market surveillance devices that exist within various organizations as well as the increasing sophistication of order processing suggest that there are economies of scale in the enforcement of insider-trading rules. Just as one would certainly not deprive the corner gas station of local police protection, it is unreasonable to suggest that there is no role for public enforcement because employers will terminate their inside traders who are discovered. Moreover, the presence of distinct social and psychological barriers within the American corporation makes it doubtful that the corporation can clean its own stable. *See* Cox & Munsinger, *Bias in the Boardroom: Psychological Foundations and Legal Implications of Corporate Cohesion,* 48 LAW & CONTEMP. PROBS., Summer 1985, at 83, 83-108.

93. Some important insiders are not full-time employees, but outside directors and various professionals retained by the corporation for specialized projects. This group, however, has the weakest claim to any insider-trading prerogatives. Not among the "movers and shakers" championed by the free-market proponents, they are either highly compensated footmen (in the case of lawyers and accountants) or highly reliable monitors (in the case of directors) employed to curb management's misperception of the corporate interest. In either case, because an outsider's functions and compensation customarily are well understood, it is unfair for the outsider to secretly augment that compensation without prior consent.

regime that prohibits employment-derived earnings that are neither authorized nor fully disclosed. This is accomplished by prohibiting insider trading.

Third, shareholders expect the executive to concentrate on their welfare rather than his private investment agenda. The prohibition against insider trading is similar to the prohibition against a manager spending his time in the office developing his own interests; each prohibition stems from the shareholders' expectation that a manager is paid to look after the shareholders' welfare, not his own.

These three aspects of the employment relationship justify the continuation of insider trading regulation because employers, like consumers, have rationally based expectations about what they are purchasing when they hire managers or other professionals. Without a prior understanding between the firm and its insiders regarding the latter's trading prerogatives, the parties expect that the insider's compensation will be no more and no less than what their agreement provides. An insider unlawfully acquires gains by embezzling firm assets, deflecting a corporate opportunity, or using corporate information, because these matters are outside the employment contract. The parties could have raised these matters in their negotiations. Because owners, acting rationally, would see that licensing an insider to trade leaves nothing to be gained and a good deal to be lost, they will not license their insiders to trade. Therefore, the insider breaches his employment agreement when he trades.

The earlier discussed arguments of the free-market proponents—concerning empirical evidence, efficient price changes, and managerial incentives—independently fail to justify a laissez faire approach to insider trading. And, in light of the potential costs and questionable benefits of licensing managers to trade, the free-market proponents' notion of private contracting fails to justify deregulation. The irony for the free-market proponents' position concerning the desirability of private contracting is that the prohibition against insider trading is justified, not in spite of contract principles, but because of them.

[9]

Journal of Financial Economics 14 (1985) 71–100. North-Holland

BID, ASK AND TRANSACTION PRICES IN A SPECIALIST MARKET WITH HETEROGENEOUSLY INFORMED TRADERS*

Lawrence R. GLOSTEN

Northwestern University, and University of Chicago, Chicago, IL 60637, USA

Paul R. MILGROM

Yale University, New Haven, CT 06520, USA

Received August 1983, final version received September 1984

The presence of traders with superior information leads to a positive bid–ask spread even when the specialist is risk-neutral and makes zero expected profits. The resulting transaction prices convey information, and the expectation of the average spread squared times volume is bounded by a number that is independent of insider activity. The serial correlation of transaction price differences is a function of the proportion of the spread due to adverse selection. A bid–ask spread implies a divergence between observed returns and realizable returns. Observed returns are approximately realizable returns plus what the uninformed anticipate losing to the insiders.

1. Introduction

The usual economic view of markets is as a place where buyers and sellers come together and trade at a common price, the price at which supply equals demand. Securities exchanges are often singled out as excellent examples of markets that operate this way. In fact, however, trading on exchanges takes place over time, and some institutional arrangements are necessary to help match buyers and sellers whose orders arrive at different times. On exchanges like the New York Stock Exchange, the economic function of the specialists and the floor traders is that of middlemen: they hold the inventories that facilitate trade when trading occurs over time.

The problem of matching buyers with sellers is most acute in trading shares of small companies, where the volume of trade is relatively low. A common problem in this environment involves the number of insiders who trade in the shares relative to the total trading volume. Classical price theory, which has

*Milgrom's research was supported by National Science Foundation Grant IST-8208600. We wish to thank Rolf Banz, Dan Galai, Jay Ritter, Ravi Jagannathan, the participants in the University of Chicago Finance Workshop, the University of Michigan Finance Workshop and the participants in the University of Southern California conference on transaction prices for helpful comments. We also gratefully acknowledge comments by the editor, Clifford W. Smith, and two referees.

0304-405X/85/$3.30

little to say about the dynamics of matching buyers and sellers, offers few hints about the consequences of insider trading. It leaves unanswered such questions as: How completely do prices reflect insider information [Fama (1970)]? How large are insider profits? How does the specialist behave in this environment? How might the existence of insider trading alter the return characteristics of the stock?

A number of researchers have examined the optimal behavior of a specialist and how it leads to a bid–ask spread. The usual approach examines the management of inventory by a monopolist specialist, concentrating on the effect that inventory costs have on the bid–ask spread; e.g. Ohara and Oldfield (1982), Ho and Stoll (1981), Amihud and Mendelson (1980) and Garman (1976).

The approach taken in this paper is based on the idea that a bid–ask spread can be a purely informational phenomenon, occurring even when all the specialist's fixed and variable transactions costs (including his time, inventory costs, etc.) are zero and when competition forces the specialist's profit to zero. The core idea is that the specialist faces an adverse selection problem, since a customer agreeing to trade at the specialist's ask or bid price may be trading because he knows something that the specialist does not. In effect, then, the specialist must recoup the losses suffered in trades with the well informed by gains in trades with liquidity traders. These gains are achieved by setting a spread. This informational source of the spread has also been suggested by Bagehot (1971) and formally analyzed by Copeland and Galai (1983).

In this paper, we use a formal model to show how the spread arises from adverse selection. We analyze the determinants of the magnitude of the spread and investigate the informational properties of the transaction prices. We then show that, depending on how returns are measured, the information-based spread may cause realizable returns to be overestimated relative to the returns that are actually available to a trader without inside information.

Some of our results are restatements and generalizations, within the context of our model, of results presented in Copeland and Galai (1983). The major goal of this paper, however, is examination of some of the dynamic properties of the spread and transactions prices, with particular references to the question of how specialist markets process privately available information. Whereas Copeland and Galai assume that private information is revealed immediately after each trade, we allow there to be further trading until such time as information is revealed resolving the informational differences between insiders and the rest of the market. In this way, we can explicitly deal with questions related to the information contained in prices, the behavior of transaction prices and how the spread in turn responds to this market generated and other public information.

Our model posits a risk-neutral competitive specialist who faces no transactions costs (fixed or variable), that is, a specialist whose expected profit from each transaction is zero. We do not specify why the specialist should be competitive. It may be that he must compete for the right to conduct transactions with the floor traders or with another specialist in the same stock at another exchange. If any explicit model of Bertrand-style price competition among the market makers is to account for the zero profit condition, then one must assume that no single market maker can, by refusing to trade, ever cause a shortage of cash or securities to occur. The analogous assumption here is that the specialist has unlimited inventories of cash and securities with which to transact and the holding cost of these inventories is zero. All of this is subsumed in the assumption that the bid and ask prices at each trade are set to yield zero profits to the specialist.[1]

The model described and presented in section 2 is structured to emphasize the short-term price effects that may occur just after an event that gives an informational advantage to insiders. There is no discounting over this short period, and much of our focus is on how information is assimilated by the market, as reflected by the changing spread. In this model, prices exhibit a semi-strong form of efficiency: indeed, they may reflect slightly more information than was available to the specialist at the time he set the bid and ask prices. The explanation for this seemingly strange conclusion lies in the observation that the specialist does not set a single price. The ask price, for example, specifies what the price will be if the next customer is a buyer. Consequently, the ask price can be (and at equilibrium is) set using both the current information and the information that will be inferred if the next customer turns out to be a buyer.

There are five propositions established in section 2. We review them here in terms of the interpretations we intend, but the reader should be aware that the underlying assumptions vary slightly across the propositions, though the assumptions are mutually consistent.

The first of the five propositions simply asserts that the bid and ask prices straddle the price that would prevail if all traders had the same information as the specialist. This does not call for much comment; it is simply a mathematical affirmation of the logic of adverse selection.

The second proposition establishes that the prices at which transactions actually occur form a martingale. This result contradicts the idea that the negative serial correlation observed in microdata is a necessary consequence of the existence of spreads and the vibration of transactions between the bid and ask prices. Negative serial correlation does arise from spreads that cover the specialist's costs or that generate expected profits. In fact, the serial correlation coefficient of price changes can be used to determine the relative magnitudes of

[1] We shall see that this assumption results in the specialist sometimes accumulating large inventories of stock and sometimes large inventories of cash. It follows that if we were to recognize binding inventory constraints, we could not have a zero profit condition. Nevertheless, if the specialists' and floor traders' inventory carrying capacity were large enough, we anticipate that the expected profit from any given trade in a Bertrand model would be 'near to zero most of the time', so that our results are approximations of the results that would obtain.

these two sources of the spread – adverse selection and specialist costs or profits.

Proposition 3 gives a bound on the size of the spread that can arise from adverse selection. Specifically, the expected value of the squared average spread times volume has a uniform bound (independent of the pattern of trade) that is related to the variance of the underlying uncertainty. The proposition is proved using the observations that the variance of the price at each trade is roughly proportional to the squared spread, and the total variance of prices from trade to trade is bounded by the variance of the underlying value of the security. This proposition is less specific than one might hope, since it gives only a bound, rather than a precise order of magnitude, for the mean spread. As the example in section 3 makes clear, the mean spread depends on how the informed arrivals are distributed through the trading period, so one cannot make any headway on computing the mean spread from adverse selection without making strong assumptions about the unobservable arrival pattern of insiders.

The fourth proposition is that, over time, the value expectations of the specialist and the insiders tend to converge. This is our way of showing that insider information tends to be fully disseminated into the market prices.

The last proposition in section 2 investigates how the spread at a given trading date and with a given trading history responds to variations in the parameters of the model. The results accord well with what one might expect. Generally, ask prices increase and bid prices decrease if the insiders' information becomes better, or the insiders become more numerous relative to liquidity traders, or the elasticity of the expected supply and demand of a liquidity trader increases.

One of the interesting features of our model is that there can be occasions on which the market shuts down. Indeed, if the insiders' are too numerous or their information is too good relative to the elasticity of liquidity traders' supplies and demands, there will be no bid and ask prices at which trading can occur and the specialist can break even. Then, the equilibrium bid price is set so low and the ask price so high as to preclude any trade.[2] A situation like this feeds on itself. Insiders have information that results in a wide spread that precludes trade that prevents insiders from revealing their information through their trading behavior. Since trade itself brings information into the market, this shutting down of the market may worsen subsequent adverse selection problems and cause the next bid price to be lower and the next ask price to be higher than would otherwise be the case. Furthermore, a market, once closed, will stay closed until the insiders go away or their information is at least partly disseminated to market participants from some other information source.

Thus, the failure of a customer to trade may work an externality on future traders which is not accounted for by either the specialist or the current trader:

[2] We argue later that this cannot happen, however, if liquidity supply and demand are inelastic.

it deprives them of potentially valuable information. This opens the possibility that another way of arranging trade may exist which is Pareto superior to the competitive specialist system. The welfare loss we have described is at least partly due to the requirement that the specialist must break even on each trade. Everyone could be made beter off in our example if the specialist were required to make losses on some trades and permitted to recoup the losses on other trades. This might be accomplished in many ways, for example by allowing the specialist to have some monopoly power while requiring him to keep the difference between the bid and ask prices within some range. That similar restrictions are placed on market makers at some exchanges may not be entirely coincidental.

In section 3, we present an example to illustrate the model of section 2. We focus especially on how the proportion of insiders affects trading when enough trading occurs to allow essentially all inside information to be assimilated in the price. We also illustrate how an excess of insider trading can lead to a partial market breakdown.

Finally, in section 4, we examine a variation of the market model in which the uninformed traders expect a fixed positive return. The existence of a spread implies that, over any period, measured returns based on transactions prices tend to overstate the actual returns realizable by a liquidity trader. The reason for this is that the initial price, which may be either a bid or ask price, is on average lower than the ask price which the liquidity trader must pay. Similarly, the final price over the relevant period is on average higher than the bid price which the liquidity trader could expect to receive. We show that the measured return over a 'normal holding period' is approximately a normal return plus a return available only to insiders.

Thus, the bid–ask spread arising from adverse selection provides a possible route to explaining the small firm effect [Banz (1981)] and the ignored firm effect [Arbel and Strebel (1981)]. The evidence suggests that much of the excess returns on small firm investments occur in January. If the annual report for small firms tend to contain considerable new information and if insiders have early access to that information, then our analysis would predict that spreads are especially large in the period before the report is made public and presumably after the end of the firm's fiscal year. This combined with a 'required rate of return' assumption will lead to large measured returns but normal realizable returns. These returns should be observed in January for firms whose fiscal years coincide with the calendar year but in other months for firms with other fiscal years.[3]

[3]Blume and Stambaugh (1983) also show that the spread can lead to an upward bias in the measurement of expected returns due to the mismeasurement of 'true' prices. Our model may not be providing the whole story, since as Keim (1981) has noted, much of the excess January return occurs in the first few days of January – before insiders might be presumed to have accurate information. Also, Blume and Stambaugh do not measure a larger bias for January returns. This is consistent with a stationary spread, but is not necessarily inconsistent with our comments as Proposition 2 suggests.

We offer some concluding remarks and indicate possible directions for additional research in section 5.

2. The basic model

The market that we are modelling is a pure dealership market, i.e., the specialist performs no brokerage services, and in effect all orders are market orders. Trade occurs according to the following sequence of events. The specialist sets a bid and ask price with the interpretation that he is willing to sell one unit of stock at the ask and buy one unit of stock at the bid. An investor arrives at the market and is informed of the bid and ask at which time he is free to buy one unit at the ask or sell one unit at the bid or leave. The specialist is free to (and in general will) change the bid and ask at any time after an arriving investor has made a decision and before the next arrival of an investor. That is, if an arriving order leads to a trade, the trade takes place at the quoted bid or ask. After the trade, the specialist may revise the bid and ask.

The primary differences between the above description and the operation of the stock market are the limitation on the types of orders considered and the restriction to unit trades. In practice, an investor can submit a limit order and, by so doing, in effect compete directly with the specialist. To the extent that limit orders represent competition with the specialist, our assumption that the bid and ask are set competitively implicitly includes the possibility that investors can submit limit orders. However, there is a difference between limit orders and the quotes of the specialist in that limit orders typically have a prespecified lifetime (if unexecuted), whereas the specialist can change his bid and ask relatively freely. This fact implies that inclusion of limit orders may well alter the characteristics of transaction prices. We have not included limit orders because such a model should include investors optimally choosing the type of order to submit, and such detailed description of individual behavior is beyond the scope of this paper.

The assumption that only unit trades take place is restrictive, but it yields a corresponding benefit: It allows us to analyze a model that places no restrictions on the form of the traders' information. Of course, on the NYSE specialist quotes are valid for a specified number of units, and typically, the quotes are for only one unit (typically 100 shares). What we rule out is the specialist revising his quote for some other requested quantity. However, the fact that we put relatively few restrictions on the arrival process of traders makes this assumption somewhat less objectionable.

To examine the informational characteristics of such a market, we assume that there are informed investors and purely 'liquidity' traders. At some time T_0 in the future, some random dollar value V $[V \geq 0,\ \mathrm{var}(V) < \infty]$ per share will be realized, and the informed have information about this random variable V. Time T_0 may be interpreted as the time at which no trader has an informational advantage – just after an earnings announcement, for example. At that time, there will be agreement on the value of the firm and the informational differences between insiders and outsiders will be minimal. The informed may receive information about occurrences after time T_0, but this information will be public information at time T_0. This specification implies that there will be no informational asymmetries at time T_0, and hence it is meaningful to specify, exogeneously, the random value, V, which represents the consensus value of the stock given all public information.[4]

The informed receive information and place their orders. We do not rule out the possibility that any one informed investor may decide to submit several orders, each for a unit amount. The informed trader may be speculating based on private information or superior analysis, or he may simply have a 'liquidity' reason for trading, but in any event, his decision to buy, sell or leave is based on his information. We will refer to the informed traders as insiders though other interpretations are possible, for example, they may merely be individuals who are particularly skillful in processing public information.

To motivate the active participation of the uninformed traders in a model where everyone is rational, there must be some disparity of preferences or endownments across individuals. This disparity may arise from predictable life cycle needs or from less predictable events such as job promotions or unemployment, deaths or disabilities, or myriad other causes. We have chosen to suppress the details of the uninformed traders' motives from our formal model. Instead, we simply assign to each a time preference parameter which, together with his expectations, determines how much a trader is willing to pay to buy and to accept to sell a single unit of the stock. Specifically, all participants, informed, uninformed and the specialist, are risk-neutral. Each participant assigns random utility to shares of stock, x, and current consumption, c, as $\rho x V + c$, where ρ is a parameter of the individual investor's utility function representing his personal trade-off between current and future consumption derived from ownership of the asset. For the specialist, we take $\rho = 1$; this is just a normalization. Generally, a high ρ indicates a desire to invest for the future; a low ρ indicates a desire for current consumption. This 'liquidity parameter' could be the result of imperfect access to capital markets or it could represent differential subjective assessments of the distribution of the random variable V. The risk neutrality assumption implies that in order for there to be trade, there must be some variation in ρ across market participants, for otherwise the 'no trade theorem' of Milgrom and Stokey (1982) implies that the spread will be set large enough to preclude all trade. Since ρ is to be unknown to the specialist, and a pure preference parameter, we treat it as a

[4] This formulation is the usual one in the rational expectations models of a single market [for example, Grossman (1976)] and the proofs of our results use this formulation. A general equilibrium model would involve modeling the cash flows from the security and the consumption decisions of investors over an infinite horizon.

random variable independent of V and any information about V and independent across traders. We allow the possibility that ρ might follow a different distribution for the informed and the uninformed.

We assume that investors arrive one by one, randomly and anonymously at the specialist's post. For most of our analysis, the only restriction that we place on the arrival process is that there be only one arrival at any instant. Thus, the arrival process may depend on the history of trade. For example, the level of insider activity, and hence the nature of the arrival process might be a function of how much information has been made public relative to the information known by the insiders. All we require is that the specialist knows the probabilistic structure of the arrival process. For example, in response to private signals, there may be a bunching of insider orders (as seen by an omniscient observer). Our assumption that the specialist knows the probabilistic structure implies that he makes correct statistical inferences from observed data.

Investors, upon arriving at the market and hearing the bid and ask, maximize expected utility given their information to date. For uninformed investors, this information consists of all past transaction prices, the current bid and ask as well as any publicly available information. The informed also have access to the previous transaction price sequence, the current bid and ask, and all public announcements, but in addition they have been able to see some private signal. Formally, let H_t denote the information available publicly up to clock time t. If an uninformed investor arrives at time t, then his information, upon arrival, is H_t joined with the information generated by the quoted bid and ask. If an arrival at time t is informed, then his information includes both his private information, J_t, and the public information, H_t, and the information generated by the quoted bid and ask.[5] By including the specification of who is informed in the sample space, we can generally represent the information of an arrival at time t by F_t, a refinement of H_t which includes the information conveyed by the quoted bid and ask.

Putting the utility functions and information structures together, the optimal decision of an investor arriving at time t, given bid B and ask A is given by

$$\text{buy if } Z_t > A,$$

$$\text{sell if } Z_t < B,$$

where Z_t is given by

$$Z_t = \rho_t \mathrm{E}[V|F_t] = \rho_t(1-U_t)\mathrm{E}[V|H_t, J_t, A, B] + \rho_t U_t \mathrm{E}[V|H_t, A, B], \tag{1}$$

where U_t is one if the individual arriving at t is uninformed and zero otherwise.

[5] Note that since only one individual arrives at any time, we can identify an individual by specifying his time of arrival.

Given the above behavior of the market participants, the specialist chooses bid and ask prices. Let the information available to the specialist at time t be represented by S_t. Assuming anonymity, the specialist cannot know when the bid and ask prices are set whether the next customer will be an insider or an outsider. Given the investors' behavior, the information available to the specialist at time t, S_t, and bid and ask prices B and A, the specialist's expected profit from an arrival at time t is

$$\mathrm{E}\left[(A-V)I_{\{Z_t>A\}}+(V-B)I_{\{Z_t<B\}}|S_t\right], \tag{2}$$

where $I_{\{Z_t>A\}}$ and $I_{\{Z_t<B\}}$ are, respectively, the indicator functions of the events $\{Z_t>A\}$ and $\{Z_t<B\}$, i.e., $I_{\{Z_t>A\}}$ is one if the event $\{Z_t>A\}$ occurs; otherwise it is zero. The expression, (2), may be rewritten as

$$\begin{aligned}&(A-\mathrm{E}[V|S_t,Z_t>A])\mathrm{P}\{Z_t>A|S_t\}\\&-(B-\mathrm{E}[V|S_t,Z_t<B])\mathrm{P}\{Z_t<B|S_t\},\end{aligned} \tag{3}$$

where $\mathrm{E}[\cdot|\cdot]$ is the (conditional) expectation operator derived from the probability measure P.

The above holds as long as there are zero costs associated with all short positions in cash or stock. Our central assumption about the specialist is that he earns zero expected profits on each purchase and each sale, and he faces no transaction costs. To illustrate how competition might lead to such a description, suppose there are two specialists in this one stock. Both have the same information and face the same population. Suppose the first specialist sets an ask price A^1 so that $A^1>\mathrm{E}[V|S_t,Z_t>A^1]$. The second specialist will rationally undercut the first by choosing an ask $A^2<A^1$ and $A^2\geq\mathrm{E}[V|S_t,Z_t>A^2]$. The zero expected profit equilibrium at time t (if it exists) consists of a pair of functions A_t and B_t satisfying

$$\begin{aligned}A_t(\omega)&=\mathrm{E}[V|S_t,Z_t>A_t(\omega)](\omega),\\B_t(\omega)&=\mathrm{E}[V|S_t,Z_t<B_t(\omega)](\omega),\end{aligned} \tag{4}$$

where $Z_t=\rho_t\mathrm{E}[V|F_t]$ and A_t and B_t are measurable with respect to F_t (i.e., the customer knows the bid and ask prices).

General existence of such functions would be difficult to show, since it involves a 'rational expectations' type of fixed point condition. The definition is not vacuous, however, as the following examples show. If the specialist's information, S_t, is a finer partition than the information of the informed, then A_t and B_t will both be equal to the conditional mean of V given the information S_t. If, on the other hand, the specialist's information is the same as the publicly available information H_t, then A_t and B_t are given by

$$A_t = \inf\{a : a \geq \mathrm{E}[V|H_t, Z_t > a]\},$$
$$B_t = \sup\{b : b < \mathrm{E}[V|H_t, Z_t < b]\}. \tag{4'}$$

Our notion of equilibrium requires that the specialist not regret, ex post, any trade that he is obliged to make. For example, suppose that an investor arrives at time t and buys at the ask. After the trade, the information available to the specialist is S_t and the event that Z_t exceeded the ask. The specialist will update his expectation of V given this new bit of information, the probability that the trader was informed (given the past history) and the likelihood of a purchase given that he is informed. As long as the amount the specialist received was greater than or equal to this revised expectation, he does not regret the trade. Thus, the ask defined above is a reservation price. We assume that (unmodelled) competition drives the quoted ask to this reservation level.

This discussion of the equilibrium highlights an important interpretation of the bid and ask. The ask price is what the revised expectation of V will be if the specialist sells, and the bid is what the revised expectation will be if the specialist buys. Thus, once the bid and ask prices are specified, not only do we know that the possible transaction prices are, but we also know what the possible revised expectations of V are.

To insure that the customer's decision rule is formally well defined, and to illustrate the source of the spread, we must prove that at all times the ask exceeds the bid and, if insider trading actually occurs – or more precisely if it could occur – that the expectation of V lies strictly between the bid and ask. This proof and a later one rely on these two related facts from probability theory: (i) $\mathrm{E}[X|X > a] \geq \mathrm{E}[X]$ with a strict inequality when $0 < \mathrm{P}\{X > a\} < 1$, and (ii) $\mathrm{E}[X|X > a]$ is non-decreasing in a, being strictly increasing on any interval in the support of X.

Henceforth, we shall use E_t to denote conditional expectations given the common knowledge at time t, i.e., $\mathrm{E}_t[\cdot] = \mathrm{E}[\cdot|S_t \wedge H_t]$ where the 'meet' $S_t \wedge H_t$ denotes the events which are in both S_t and H_t. Notice that $A_t = \mathrm{E}_t[A_t]$ and $B_t = \mathrm{E}_t[B_t]$, since the bid and ask prices are common knowledge at time t. Also, our informal assumptions about ρ_t (that it conveys no information about V nor about an informed trader's opinions) can be adequately formalized by

(i) $\quad \mathrm{E}_t[V|F_t, \rho_t] = \mathrm{E}_t[V|F_t]$,

(ii) $\quad \mathrm{E}_t[\mathrm{E}_t[V|F_t]|\rho_t] = \mathrm{E}_t[V]$.

Proposition 1. Suppose equilibrium bid and ask prices exist satisfying the zero expected profit conditions:

$$A_t = \mathrm{E}[V|S_t, Z_t > A_t],$$

$$B_t = \mathrm{E}[V|S_t, Z_t < B_t].$$

Then the ask price is greater and the bid price is less than the expectation of V: $A_t \geq \mathrm{E}_t[V] \geq B_t$. *The inequalities are strict if adverse selection is possible, i.e., if*

$$\mathrm{P}\{Z_t > \mathrm{E}_t[V], \mathrm{E}_t[V|F_t] > \mathrm{E}_t[V]\} > 0,$$

$$\mathrm{P}\{Z_t < \mathrm{E}_t[V], \mathrm{E}_t[V|F_t] < \mathrm{E}_t[V]\} > 0.$$

Proof. We prove only the first inequality, since the proof of the second is similar. Also, for brevity, we omit the time subscripts. Let C be the event that the customer makes a purchase, i.e., the event that Z is greater than A,

$$C = \{Z > A\} = \{\mathrm{E}[V|F] > A/\rho\}.$$

Then, by definition, $A = \mathrm{E}[V|S, C]$ so

$$\begin{aligned} A &= \mathrm{E}[A|C] = \mathrm{E}[\mathrm{E}[V|S,C]|C] = \mathrm{E}[V|C] = \mathrm{E}[\mathrm{E}[V|C,\rho]|C] \\ &= \mathrm{E}[\mathrm{E}[\mathrm{E}[V|F,C,\rho]|C,\rho]|C] = \mathrm{E}[\mathrm{E}[\mathrm{E}[V|F,\rho]|C,\rho]|C] \\ &= \mathrm{E}[\mathrm{E}[\mathrm{E}[V|F]|C,\rho]|C] \geq \mathrm{E}[\mathrm{E}[\mathrm{E}[V|F]|\rho]|C] \\ &= \mathrm{E}[\mathrm{E}[V]|C] = \mathrm{E}[V]. \end{aligned}$$

If the additional condition stated in the proposition holds, then the inequality is strict. Q.E.D.

To stress again an interpretation of the bid and ask, it should be noted that in proving the reasonable proposition that the ask exceeds the bid, we have proved that it is necessarily the case that expectations of V are revised upward in response to specialist sales, and revised downward in response to specialist purchases. This is so, because the ask and bid are the revised expectations in the respective cases, and we have assumed that transaction prices are public information.

Define H_t^+ and S_t^+ to be, respectively, the information available to the uninformed and the specialist just after a trade at time t. These information sets include information about whether a trader has arrived at time t, whether he bought or sold, and the price at which trade occurred.

Let T_k be the times at which trades occur. The above discussion shows that the T_k are stopping times relative to $\{S_t^+\}$ and $\{H_t^+\}$, and hence we can define

S_k and H_k by $S_k = S_{T_k}^+$ and $H_k = H_{T_k}^+$. (Also, any process subscripted with a k will be understood to be the value of the process at time T_k.) If the kth trade takes place at the ask at time t, i..e, there is an arrival at time t and Z_t exceeds A_t, then the transaction price will be the ask price, which in this event is equal to the revised expectation of V given this event. Similarly, if there is a trade at the bid, the transaction price is the bid price which in this case is also the revised expectation of V given this (different) event. Mathematically, the transaction price is given by $A_k I_{\{Z_k > A_k\}} + B_k I_{\{Z_k < B_k\}}$. This is, by definition, equal to

$$\mathrm{E}\left[V|S_{T_k}, Z_{T_k} > A_{T_k}\right] I_{\{Z_{T_k} > A_{T_k}\}} + \mathrm{E}[V|S_{Tk}, Z_{Tk} < B_{Tk}] I_{\{Z_{T_k} < B_{T_k}\}}. \tag{5}$$

But (5) is just $\mathrm{E}[V|S_{T_k}^+] = \mathrm{E}[V|S_k]$. This observation allows us to write the kth transaction price as $p_k = \mathrm{E}[V|S_k]$, as long as k trades take place (i.e., as long as T_k is less than T_0). Thus, if N trades actually take place, then $p_1, \ldots, p_N$ are the prices at which trades occur. Notice, however, that p_{N+1} is also well defined, and represents some intermediate value between the bid and ask prices at the end of the trading period. If one thinks in terms of computing returns based on daily data, this use of an imaginary transactions price is not far from the way CRSP calculations are done for days in which there is no trade. The specification of H_t^+ from the preceding paragraph implies that p_k is measurable with respect to H_k which allows us to prove the following proposition:

Proposition 2. The sequence of transaction prices $\{p_k\}$ forms a martingale relative to the specialist's information, $\{S_k\}$, and the public information, $\{H_k\}$.

Proof. From (5), $p_k = \mathrm{E}[V|S_k]$. Thus,

$$\mathrm{E}[p_{k+1}|S_k] = \mathrm{E}[\mathrm{E}[V|S_{k+1}]|S_k] = \mathrm{E}[V|S_k] = p_k.$$

Since H_k is contained in S_k, and since p_k is measurable with respect to H_k, the sequence of transaction prices $\{p_k\}$ forms a martingale relative to $\{H_k\}$ as well. Q.E.D.

This result is slightly stronger than the usual statement of the semistrong form of the efficient markets hypothesis – prices form a martingale relative to all public information and the information known to the specialist. The assumed competition among equally informed specialists implies that there are no profit opportunities arising from the information known by the specialist. Furthermore, at the instant that a trade occurs and the price is announced, the specialist and all outsiders agree on the expected value of V, since $E[V|p_k] = E[V|E[V|S_k]] = E[V|S_k]$.

Another implication of Proposition 2 is that, in the environment that we have described, first differences of the transaction price process will be serially uncorrelated. This follows from the fact that the increments of a martingale are uncorrelated. Thus, spreads due only to adverse selection are qualitatively different from spreads due to specialist transactions costs, risk aversion or monopoly power. The latter sources of spread lead to negative serial correlation, while spreads due solely to adverse selection do not.

Further intuition into the nature of this result can be gained by considering an environment in which there is both asymmetric information and specialist transaction costs. Specifically, suppose every trade costs the specialist c dollars. The zero profit equilibrium bid and ask then satisfy

$$A = E[V|S_t, Z_t > A] + c,$$

$$B = E[V|S_t, Z_t < B] - c.$$

Following the development above [in (5)], transaction prices are then given by $p_k = E[V|S_k] + Q_k c$ where Q_k is one if the kth transaction involved the specialist selling at the ask, and is minus one if the specialist purchased at the bid. Under the assumption that $E[Q_{k+1}|H_t] = E[Q_k|H_t]$ for all $t < T_k$ where T_k is the time of the kth transaction, it is easy to show that transaction price changes will exhibit negative serial correlation.

To indicate how the negative serial correlation depends upon the relative magnitudes of the spread due to adverse selection and the spread due to the costs of transacting, suppose that the probabilities of a buy and a sell are equal so that $E[Q_k|H_t] = 0$ for $t < T_k$. Let Ψ be the part of the spread due to adverse selection,

$$\Psi = E[V|S_t, Z_t > A] - E[V|S_t, Z_t < B];$$

hence the total spread is $\Psi + 2c$. Some straightforward calculations show that the covariance of adjacent price changes is given by: $-\frac{1}{2}c\Psi - c^2$. The calculation is similar to the one in Roll (1984). We obtain a different result because Roll implicitly assumes that no part of the spread is due to adverse selection. If, as here, the spread is due in part to adverse selection, then a specialist sell, for example, leads to an upward revision of expections and hence future prices are not independent of the current transaction as Roll assumes.

The variance of the price change is given by the following: $\theta^2 + (\Psi/2)^2 + c\Psi + 2c^2$, where θ^2 is the variance of public information arriving exogenously between trades.[6] Let β be the proportion of the spread due to transaction costs; i.e., $\beta = 2c/(\Psi + 2c)$. Then the correlation coefficient, R, is given by the following:

$$R = -\beta/(\delta + \beta^2), \tag{6}$$

where $\delta = 1 + (2\theta/(\Psi + 2c))^2$. The correlation coefficient thus moves toward zero if the proportion of the spread due to informational asymmetries increases. We can invert (6) to get the proportional of the spread due to trading costs as a function of the correlation coefficient and δ (a measure of how much public information arrives relative to the spread),

$$\beta = \left(-1 + (1 - 4\delta R^2)^{1/2}\right)/2R. \tag{7}$$

Unfortunately, (7) alone does not define a useful statistic since in general δ will not be known. It does suggest the possibility that transaction data might be used to find a measure of informational assymetry.

In the introduction, we described the theoretical possibility that markets might close down entirely, with the bid price being set so low and the ask price so high as to discourage any trade. This problem is identical to the famous lemons problem of Akerlof (1970), in which adverse selection can destroy the market. For the next proposition to make sense, it must also be possible for markets to function well without suffering such a breakdown. The conditions that determine the functioning of markets depend in part on the supply and demand elasticities of uninformed traders. The expected demand when the ask price is A and the common knowledge value expectation is E is given by $1 - G(A/E)$, where G is the distribution function for an uninformed trader's preference parameter ρ. Similarly, the expected uninformed supply at a bid price of B is $G(B/E)$. If uninformed demand and supply is inelastic, then the closing of markets due to adverse selection can never occur. To prove this, it suffices to note that as A is raised, the expected losses suffered by the specialist to the informed decline and approach zero, while his expected profits from the

[6] The variance calculation is accomplished by dividing the change in expectations between the kth trade and the $(k+1)$st trade into the change in expectations as a result of public information arriving between the two trades and the information contained in the $(k+1)$st trade and noting that these are uncorrelated. The change in expectations squared as a result of the $(k+1)$st trade is one fourth of the spread due to adverse selection squared since a buy and sell are equally likely. Furthermore, Q^2 is identically one, and finally, $\mathrm{E}[Q_k \mathrm{E}[V|H_k]] = 1/2\Psi$. All other expectations are zero.

uninformed are positive and rising. Hence, the specialist's total profits from selling must be positive for some finite A. A symmetric argument applies to the bid price B.

We now turn our attention to the properties of the bid and ask prices when trading does not break down. Imagine performing the following experiment. Every time there is a transaction, record the bid and ask that prevailed just prior to the trade. Do this for a unit of time, and denote the number of trades observed by N. The following proposition shows that if trade is reasonably balanced (i.e., the probability of a purchase given that a trade occurred is bounded away from zero and one) then the expectation of the number of trades times the average spread squared is bounded by a number that is independent of the pattern of trade.[7]

Proposition 3. Define

$$1/\gamma_k = \mathrm{P}\{Z_k > A_k|S_{T_k}\}\mathrm{P}\{Z_k < B_k|S_{T_k}\},$$

and let γ^* be the mean value of γ_j over the $N+1$ observations; i.e., $\gamma^* = \sum^{N+1}\gamma_k/(N+1)$ (if $N+1$ trades do not occur prior to T_0, put $\gamma_{N+1}=4$). Further, define Ψ_N to be the average spread over N trades, i.e.,

$$\Psi_N = \sum^{N}(A_k - B_k)/N.$$

Then,

$$\mathrm{E}[(N/(N+1))\Psi_N^2 N/\gamma^*] \leq \mathrm{var}(V).$$

In particular, if there is a number γ such that $\mathrm{P}\{\gamma^* < \gamma\} = 1$, then

$$\mathrm{E}[(N/(N+1))N\Psi_N^2] \leq \mathrm{var}(V)\gamma,$$

and hence, if N is almost surely positive, the expected value of the volume times average spread squared is bounded by a number that is independent of the pattern of trade,

$$\mathrm{E}[N\Psi_N^2] \leq 2\,\mathrm{var}(V)\gamma.$$

Proof. Since p_{N+1} is a conditional expectation of V, the variance of V

[7]We remind the reader that we are returning to an environment in which there are no costs associated with trade, and the specialist earns a zero profit on average.

exceeds the variance of p_{N+1}. Taking p_0 to be E[V], we have

$$\operatorname{var}(p_{N+1}) = \operatorname{var}\left(\sum^{N+1}(p_k - p_{k-1})\right) = \mathrm{E}\left[\left(\sum^{N+1}(p_k - p_{k-1})\right)^2\right]$$

$$= \mathrm{E}\left[\sum^{N+1}(p_k - p_{k-1})^2\right]$$

$$+ 2\mathrm{E}\left[\sum_k^{N+1}\sum_i^{k-1}(p_k - p_{k-1})(p_k - p_{i-1})\right]$$

$$= \mathrm{E}\left[\sum^{\infty}(p_k - p_{k-1})^2 I_{\{k-1\le N\}}\right]$$

$$+ 2\mathrm{E}\left[\sum^{\infty}\sum^{k-1}(p_k - p_{k-1})(p_i - p_{i-1}) I_{\{k-1\le N\}}\right].$$

Since the transaction price sequence forms a square integrable martingale, we can move the expectation inside the summation in each case. In the second term, condition first on H_{k-1}. Since the increments of a martingale are uncorrelated and have mean zero, the second expectation is zero.

Define e_k by

$$e_k = \mathrm{E}\left[(p_k - p_{k-1})^2 | H_{k-1}, A_k, B_k, \gamma_k\right].$$

Thus, we have

$$\operatorname{var}(V) \ge \mathrm{E}\left[\sum^{N+1} e_k\right].$$

Some algebraic manipulation shows that $e_k \ge (A_k - B_k)^2/\gamma_k$ (see footnote 6), and hence for any N,

$$\sum^{N+1}(e_k\gamma_k)^{1/2} \ge \sum^{N+1}(A_k - B_k)^2.$$

By the Cauchy–Schwarz inequality, $\sum^{N+1} e_k \ge (\sum^{N+1} A_k - B_k)^2/\gamma^*(N+1)$, and thus,

$$\operatorname{var}(V) \ge \mathrm{E}\left[\left(\sum^{N} A_k - B_k\right)^2 \Big/ (N+1)\gamma^*\right] = \mathrm{E}\left[(N/(N+1))N\Psi_N^2/\gamma^*\right].$$

If $\gamma^* \leq \gamma$ a.s., then

$$E[(N/(N+1))N\Psi_N^2] \leq \text{var}(V)\gamma.$$

If N is positive a.s., then $N/(N+1)$ is greater than or equal to $\frac{1}{2}$, so $E[N\Psi_N^2] \leq 2\,\text{var}(V)\gamma$. Q.E.D.

Since the bound in Proposition 3 is independent of the pattern of trade (given that N is a.s. at least one and $\gamma^* < \gamma$) the proposition suggests a relation between average volume and average spread. Loosely speaking, markets in which there is, on average, large volume will have small average spreads and vice versa. This is consistent with the usual explanation of the relation between spreads and volume which focuses on the specialist's need to recoup fixed costs from the market participants. However, the fixed cost explanation implies that the average spread will be proportional to one over average volume, while proposition 3 suggests that the average spread will be proportional to one over the root of average volume.

It should be clear from the above proof, that the conclusion of the proposition is true when N is some deterministic number of trades. In this case, the proposition states that the average spread squared tends to decline for large N. Indeed, if T_0 is very large relative to the interarrival times of traders, so that N can be very large, the proposition implies that the spread will go to zero a.s.

Within our model, the fact that spreads decline with the number of trades reflects the assimilation by the market of the insiders' information. This leads eventually (if there are sufficiently many trades) to an approximate consensus expectation of value (V) in the market. Proposition 4 offers a formal statement of that tendency toward consensus.

Proposition 4. If trade is reasonably balanced in the sense of Proposition 3, i.e., the probability of a purchase is bounded away from zero and one, then the expectations of the specialist and the traders converge as the number of trades increases, i.e., $E[V|S_k] - E[V|F_k]$ *converges to zero in probability (where* F_k *is the information of the* kth *trader to arrive).*

Proof. We use the notation and results of Proposition 1 and two general facts from probability theory cited earlier. The suppressed time subscript is now $t = T_k$.

$$A = E[V|C] = E[E[V|F,\rho]|C] = E[E[V|F]|E[V|F] > A/\rho]$$

$$> E[E[V|F]|E[V|F] > E[V]/\rho].$$

Define D by

$$D = E[V|F] - E[V].$$

Then,

$$A - \mathrm{E}[V] \geq \mathrm{E}[D|D > \mathrm{E}[V](1-\rho)/\rho].$$

By the Chebyshev inequality,

$$\begin{aligned}\mathrm{E}[D|D > \mathrm{E}[V](1-\rho)/\rho] &\geq \varepsilon \mathrm{P}\{D \geq \varepsilon | D > \mathrm{E}[V](1-\rho)/\rho\} \\ &\geq \mathrm{P}\{D \geq \varepsilon\}\varepsilon.\end{aligned}$$

By Propositions 1 and 3, $A_t - \mathrm{E}_t[V]$ converges almost surely to zero, so $\mathrm{P}\{D_t \geq \varepsilon\}$ must also converge to zero for all positive ε. A similar argument using bid prices shows that $\mathrm{P}\{D_t \leq -\varepsilon\}$ goes to zero. Thus, $\mathrm{E}_k[V|F_k] - \mathrm{E}_k[V]$ converges in probability to zero. Also, $\mathrm{E}_k[V|S_k] = \mathrm{E}_k[V]$ (both are equal to A_k if the customer buys and B_k if he sells). Q.E.D.

As the consensus described in Proposition 4 emerges, there comes to be a balance between expected supply and expected demand:

Corollary 1. The specialist's inventory of stocks tends to a driftless stochastic process; i.e.,

$$\lim \mathrm{P}\{Z_k < B_k|H_k\} - \mathrm{P}\{Z_k > A_k|H_k\} = 0.$$

Proof. Using the results of the Proposition 4, let $\hat{p}$ be the limit of $\mathrm{E}[V|S_k]$ and let $\hat{Z} = \rho\hat{p}$. Then,

$$\begin{aligned}\lim(\mathrm{P}\{Z_k < B_k|H_k\} - \mathrm{P}\{Z_k > A_k|H_k\}) &= \mathrm{P}\{\hat{Z} < \hat{p}|\hat{S}\} - \mathrm{P}\{\hat{Z} > \hat{p}|\hat{S}\} \\ &= \mathrm{P}\{\rho < 1\} - \mathrm{P}\{\rho > 1\} = 0,\end{aligned}$$

where $\hat{S}$ is the specialist's limiting information. Q.E.D.

That the specialist's inventory will not drift on average is only true in the limit. To see why inventories might drift, suppose that the insiders may have early access to information about a takeover attempt which would be favorable for stockholders of the firm, but is generally considered unlikely to transpire. There is then an asymmetry in the adverse selection problem faced by the specialist; active buying by insiders might be considered quite informative while active selling would convey less information. In this case, the ask price might include a premium (over the share's expected value) that is larger than the corresponding discount in the bid price. An expected inventory accumulation might result. The fact that there may be an inventory build-up is largely an artifact of our assumption of risk neutrality on the part of the specialist. As

Ho and Stoll (1981) and Ohara and Oldfield (1982) have demonstrated a risk-averse specialist will adjust the level and/or the magnitude of the spread to avoid inventory build-ups. The corollary indicates that the accumulation of inventory will not be too extreme even in the risk-neutral case because eventually, supply and demand will be approximately equal.

We now turn to our analysis of the determinants of the size of the spread. For this analysis, it is useful to distinguish sharply between insiders and liquidity traders, so we assume that insiders have no liquidity motive ($\rho = 1$). We also assume that the specialist has only public information; i.e., $S_t = H_t$. Proposition 5 provides proof of results also reported in Copeland and Galai (1983, p. 1463).

Proposition 5. For any given time t, the ask price A_t increases and the bid price B_t decreases when, other things being equal,

(i) *the insiders's information at time t becomes better (i.e., finer),*
(ii) *the ratio of informed to uninformed arrival rates at t is increased, or*
(iii) *the elasticity of uninformed supply and demand at time t increases.*

Proof. If there is an arrival at time t, we can express the reservation price Z_t by

$$Z_t = (1 - U_t)\mathrm{E}[V|H_t, J_t] + U_t\rho_t\mathrm{E}[V|H_t],$$

where [as in (1) above] U_t is one if an arrival at t is uninformed and zero otherwise, and J_t is the information of an insider if an insider arrives at t (for the succeeding discussion, time subscripts have been dropped to simplify the notation). Define M by $M = \mathrm{E}[V|J]$ where J is the information set of an arriving insider, and let G be the distribution function of the liquidity parameter (and let g be its density). Denote demand and supply elasticities of the uninformed by e_{D} and e_{S}. Then e_{D} and e_{S} are given by

$$e_{\mathrm{D}} = Ag(A/\mathrm{E}[V])/\mathrm{E}[V](1 - G(A/\mathrm{E}[V])),$$

$$e_{\mathrm{S}} = Bg(B/\mathrm{E}[V])/\mathrm{E}[V]G(B/\mathrm{E}[V]).$$

Recalling [from (4a)] that A and B, the ask and bid, are the smallest a and largest b satisfying

$$a \geq \mathrm{E}[V|Z > a], \qquad b \leq \mathrm{E}[V|Z < b],$$

then, for ask price A and bid price B,

$$A\mathrm{P}\{Z > A\} - \mathrm{E}\left[VI_{\{Z > A\}}\right] \geq 0,$$

$$\mathrm{E}\left[VI_{\{Z < B\}}\right] - B\mathrm{P}\{Z < B\} \geq 0.$$

The left sides can be expanded to

$$\mathrm{E}\big[(1-U)(A-M)I_{\{M>A\}}+UAg(A/\mathrm{E}[V])(A/\mathrm{E}[V]-1)/e_{\mathrm{D}}\big]$$

$$=\mathrm{E}\big[\phi(A,U,M,e_{\mathrm{D}})\big],$$

$$\mathrm{E}\big[(1-U)(M-B)I_{\{M<B\}}+UBg(B/\mathrm{E}[V])(1-B/\mathrm{E}[V])/e_{\mathrm{S}}\big]$$

$$=\mathrm{E}\big[\psi(B,U,M,e_{\mathrm{S}})\big].$$

The functions $\phi(\cdot)$ and $\psi(\cdot)$ are concave in M and increasing in U. Also, $\phi(\cdot)$ is decreasing in e_{D} and $\psi(\cdot)$ is decreasing in e_{S}.

For (i), let A' and B' be the ask and bid prices associated with insider information J' and define M' by $M'=\mathrm{E}[V|J']$ where J' is finer than J. For (ii), let A'' and B'' be the ask and bid prices when the arrival of uninformed is governed by U'', where $U''(\omega)\leq U(\omega)$. For (iii), let A''' and B''' be the ask and bid prices when the demand and supply elasticities are e_{D}''' and e_{S}''' respectively with $e_i'''>e_i$ for $i=\mathrm{D,S}$.

If J' is finer than J, then $M=\mathrm{E}[M'|J]$. This and Jensen's inequality allow us to conclude:

$$\mathrm{E}\big[\phi(A',U,M,e_{\mathrm{D}})\big]\geq\mathrm{E}\big[\phi(A',U,M',e_{\mathrm{D}})\big].$$

Since ϕ is increasing in U, and $U''\leq U$,

$$\mathrm{E}\big[\phi(A'',U,M,e_{\mathrm{D}})\big]\geq\mathrm{E}\big[\phi(A'',U'',M,e_{\mathrm{D}})\big].$$

Also, since ϕ is decreasing in e_{D},

$$\mathrm{E}\big[\phi(A''',U,M,e_{\mathrm{D}})\big]\geq\mathrm{E}\big[\phi(A''',U,M,e_{\mathrm{D}}''')\big].$$

[Similar inequalities hold for the function $\psi(\cdot)$.] By the definitions of A', A'' and A''' the right-hand sides are all non-negative. But, $A=\inf\{a|\mathrm{E}[\phi(a,U,M,e_{\mathrm{D}})]\geq 0\}$, so A', A'' and A''' all exceed A. The same argument will prove the corresponding bid inequalities. Q.E.D.

Intuitively, the adverse selection problem is worse the greater the fraction of informed traders and the better their information. The specialist is forced to set a higher spread if there are more informed or if they have better information, in order to avoid losses. On the other hand, the greater the desire of the uninformed to trade (measured by the elasticities), the easier is the specialist able to make back his losses to informed traders. The zero-profit condition then results in a smaller spread.

Alternatively, Proposition 5 can be interpreted as an analysis of the determinants of the specialist's updating of his expectations. That the spread is small when the probability that the next arrival is informed is small implies that when this probability is small, updated expectations in response to trade will differ only slightly from the prior expectations. Similarly, when uninformed demand and supply is very inelastic, trade leads to relatively small revisions in expectations.

This proposition also suggests a lagged statistical relation between volume and the spread. Specifically, suppose the level of insider activity is positively related to volume. When the specialist sees unexpectedly high volume, he will revise upward his estimate of the probability of an insider arrival and increase the spread accordingly. Thus, this proposition would suggest a positive correlation between past volume and current spread.

It is easy to make the mistake of interpreting Proposition 5 as a comparative equilibrium result. What the proposition says is that *other things equal*, including the past history of trade, certain changes have determinate effects on the size of the spread. Since the history of trade after the time when insiders gain their information is endogenous and depends on the same parameters as those studied in the proposition, the proposition has a comparative equilibrium interpretation only for the time just after the insiders have become informed. For example, an increase in the frequency of insider arrivals has the immediate effect of increasing the spread. However, as long as trade continues, the increase in insider activity means more information will be conveyed by transaction prices. This in turn may mean that spreads in the future will be smaller because the informational differences between insiders and outsiders will be decreased. This intuition is indicated in the proof of Proposition 3. Recall that there we showed that the expected average spread squared times the volume is bounded by a number that is independent of the level of insider activity. Thus, if spreads increase now, they must be reduced later on as long as there is sufficient trading activity. We pursue this intuition in the following examples.

3. An example

To illustrate the theory of section 2, we present two simple examples. The examples show how bid and ask prices are determined, how the proportion of insiders affects the spread and the informativeness of prices, and how market breakdown can occur.

Suppose that the stock can have either of two values, $V=1$ or $V=11$, and that the higher value has prior probability π. The expectation of V is then $E=11\pi+1(1-\pi)$.

Insiders in this example have perfect information about the value of V and have preference parameters $\rho=1$. Liquidity traders have only public information. We shall consider two distributions of the liquidity traders' preference parameters ρ: the case where ρ equals 0 or ∞, each with probability one-half, which is the case of perfectly inelastic liquidity supply and demand, and the case where ρ is uniformly distributed on $(0,2)$. No information arrives exogenously during the trading period.

The inelastic demand case serves as an interesting benchmark. The uniform case is richer in the range of phenomena that can arise. In particular, it allows the logical possibility that markets may shut down on one side (trader's buying at the ask) but not the other, since the liquidity trader's demand is elastic at high prices but their supply has unitary elasticity at all prices.

Let the proportion of insiders in the trading population be designated by the parameter α. For these examples, we assume that insiders arrive independently of their realization of information, and hence the *a priori* probability that any particular trader is an insider is α.

It is clear that with our standing assumptions and in the absence of adverse selection the price would be the expected value E. Suppose that the ask price is set at A (where $A < 11$) and that the next trader is an insider who wants to buy at that price. Then the specialist will lose $11 - A$ to the insider. The event just described will occur with probability $\alpha\pi$, since the event that the buyer is an insider is independent of the value of V. The probability that a liquidity trader will buy at an ask price of A is precisely the probability that the preference parameter ρ exceeds A/E, which in the inelastic case is 0.5 and in the uniform case is $1 - A/(2E)$. So the specialist's break-even condition in the inelastic case is the linear equation (in A),

$$\alpha\pi(11 - A) = 0.5(1 - \alpha)(A - E), \tag{8}$$

and in the uniform case is the quadratic equation,

$$\alpha\pi(11 - A) = (1 - \alpha)[1 - A/(2E)](A - E), \tag{9}$$

provided $A \leq 2E$. The smaller root of the quadratic equation is the relevant one here, since the ask price is the *lowest* price at which the specialist breaks even.

A similar argument shows that the bid price for the inelastic case solves the linear equation

$$\alpha(1 - \pi)(B - 1) = 0.5(1 - \alpha)(E - B), \tag{10}$$

while the bid price for the uniform case is the larger root of the quadratic equation

$$\alpha(1 - \pi)(B - 1) = (1 - \alpha)[B/(2E)](E - B). \tag{11}$$

We have described how the specialist in this model determines a bid and ask price as a function of the parameter α and his beliefs π. To complete the description of his dynamic behavior, it only remains to show how π changes as a result of market behavior. We let π^+ denote the posterior beliefs of the specialist after a trade has just occurred. These posterior beliefs also serve as the prior beliefs for determining the bid and ask prices for the next trader. π^+ is determined from Bayes' Theorem using the formula

$$[\pi^+/(1-\pi^+)] = [\pi/(1-\pi)] \; Factor,$$

where *Factor* is the likelihood ratio whose numerator is the probability of the trader's action given that $V = 11$ and whose denominator is the probability of the action given $V = 1$. Note that *Factor* may depend on the action taken, the bid price, the ask price, π and α, as well as on the model used – uniform or inelastic.

For any given model and any value of the parameter α, the endogenous variable π determines the expected value E, the bid and ask prices B and A, the spread, the probability that the next trader will buy or sell, etc. Then, from the formula for π^+ above, it is clear that the stochastic process of values of π over time is a Markov process; given the current value of π, its future distribution is independent of its history. Moreover, since π_k is a conditional probability given all information up to time T_k, the Markov process is a martingale. In addition, in the inelastic case, $\log(\pi_k(1-\pi_0)/\pi_0(1-\pi_k))/\log(1+\alpha)/(1-\alpha)$ is, given V, a random walk whose value is the accumulated excess of purchases over sales by arriving customers.

Let us say that "nearly all of the insider information has been assimilated in the prices" when we reach the point where $\pi/(1-\pi) < 1/Odds$ when V is low or $\pi/(1-\pi) > Odds$ when V is high. For the case of perfectly inelastic demand, one can show[8] that the expected number of trades that must take place before nearly all information is revealed is approximately[9]

$$\frac{\log(Odds) + (1-\pi_0)\log(\pi_0/(1-\pi_0))}{\alpha\log((1+\alpha)/(1-\alpha))}. \tag{12}$$

For small values of α, (12) is approximately proportioned to $1/\alpha^2$. Also for small values of α and for any π, the size of the spread determined in (8) and (10) is approximately proportional to α. Thus, the effect of doubling α from, say, 0.1 to 0.2 is roughtly to double the spread at each level of π and to divide by four the time taken until nearly all insider information has been assimilated in prices.

[8] The proof uses Wald's lemma separately for the cases $V = 1$ and $V = 11$.

[9] The expression is approximate because $(\log(Odds) - \log(\pi_0/(1-(\pi_0)))/\log((1+\alpha)/(1-\alpha))$ and $(\log(Odds) + \log(\pi_0/(1-\pi_0)))/\log((1+\alpha)/(1-\alpha))$ may not both be integral.

Of course, the spread after nearly all insider information has been assimilated is nearly zero. So, if enough trading occurs in the period of interest to assimilate information for either value of α, then the expected average spread over the period for the case $\alpha = 0.1$ would be about twice that for the case $\alpha = 0.2$, but the expected squared total spread would be about the same for both cases. Thus, given plenty of trading volume, one can make strong statements about the expected squared total spread without knowing anything about the fraction of insiders α, but statements about the expected mean spread require that extra information. This formal analysis is example specific, but it does accord nicely with Proposition 3, which derives a bound on the expectation of spread squared times volume which is independent of the proportion or arrival pattern of insiders.

When α is small, simulation results for the uniform case are not dissimilar from those for the inelastic case. This is as might be expected, since for small α the ratios A/E and B/E which enter into the break-even equations are approximately equal to 1. Substituting 1 for these ratios yields precisely the equations of the inelastic case.

As α grows larger, however, the spread can become so large as to deter most, and eventually all, potential liquidity buyers. In the numerical example at hand, if $\alpha = 0.3$, then there is no ask price at which the specialist can break even [as evidenced by the fact that the discriminant of the quadratic equation for A, (9), is negative].

In this example, there is still a bid price at which both insiders and liquidity traders will trade and the specialist will break even. It is a feature of our example that the demand function of liquidity traders is quite elastic for high ask prices but the supply function has unitary elasticity. For such cases, as we noted in the previous section, market breakdown (on the supply side) can never occur.

Of course, by choosing ρ, the liquidity parameter, to be uniformly distributed on $(0.5, 1.5)$, one can create an example in which both sides of the market break down for large values of α and intermediate values of the prior expectation. When a market breakdown does occur in this model, since we have assumed stationarity and no exogenous flow of information, the problem will persist. The market will remain closed indefinitely. As we observed in the introduction, this possibility strongly suggests that the trading institution we have been describing is not socially optimal.

4. A model with discounting

The model discussed in the previous section is based on a particular normalization of reservation prices that was mathematically convenient. This normalization took the form of the specialist having a ρ of one, while the median of the ρ's of the traders was one. Another normalization that is of economic interest is the following: the reservation price of an individual arriving at time t is Z_t^* given by $Z_t^* = \exp(r_t(T_0 - t))Z_t$ where Z_t is as defined in the previous section, and T_0 is the time of the informational event. The parameter r_t may arise from other unmodeled market opportunities and depends only on time, not on any personal characteristics. The zero profit condition for the specialist now becomes a zero excess return condition and may be stated as (if solutions exists):

$$A_t^* = \exp(-r_t(T_0 - t))\mathrm{E}[V|S_t^*, Z_t^* > A_t^*],$$
$$B_t^* = \exp(-r_t(T_0 - t))\mathrm{E}[V|S_t^*, Z_t^* < B_t^*]. \tag{13}$$

Since the market now being described is merely a renormalization of the one described in section 2, it is straightforward to show that A_t^* and B_t^* are given by $A_t^* = \exp(-r_t(T_0 - t))A_t$; $B_t^* = \exp(-r_t(T_0 - t))B_t$, where A_t and B_t satisfy (as above)

$$A_t = \mathrm{E}[V|S_t, Z_t > A_t], \qquad B_t = \mathrm{E}[V|S_t, Z_t < B_t].$$

To insure that outsiders have an incentive to be involved in the market, the following hypothesis is offered. Let τ be a holding period. The expected gross holding period return of someone buying at time t and holding for τ periods of time is $\mathrm{E}_t[B_{t+\tau}^*]/A_t^*$. It is assumed that at any time t, $\mathrm{E}_t[B_{t+\tau}^*]/A_t^* = \mathrm{e}^{i\tau}$, where i is an exogenously given rate of return. Although this is implicitly a hypothesis about the exogenous variables, it is stated in terms of market parameters and appears to be testable. The variable i might be taken to be a required return consistent with the risk of the stock. The important limitation such a condition imposes on the data is that i be unrelated to the magnitude of the spread and constant through time. In effect, this assumption defines r_t.[10] Since $B_{t+\tau}^*$ is a function of $r_{t+\tau}$ and A_t^* is a function of r_t, a terminal condition and the above expected holding period return condition will define r_t. The proof of the following proposition is tedious, and is relegated to an appendix.

Proposition 6. Let the expected realizable return of an uninformed trader over the normal holding period be i, i.e., $\mathrm{E}_t[B_{t+\tau}^*/A_t^*] = \mathrm{e}^{i\tau}$ for all t. Assume that after the informational event at T_0, V becomes known so that for $t \in [T_0 - \tau, T_0]$,

[10]Stoll and Whaley (1983) have shown that transactions costs including the bid–ask spread may explain part of the small firm effect. Their analysis makes use of a 'holding period' such as specified here.

$B^*_{t+\tau} = Ve^{-i(T_0-t-\tau)}$ (i.e., $r_{t+\tau} = i$ for $t \in [T_0-\tau, T_0]$). Then r_t, the discount rate at t, is the normal return i plus a premium,

$$r_t = i + (n+1)/(T_0 - t)\log(k_t),$$

where

$$\frac{1}{k_t} = \left\{ \mathrm{E}_t \left[\frac{B_{t+\tau}}{A_t} \frac{B_{t+2\tau}}{A_{t+\tau}} \cdots \frac{B_{t+(n+1)\tau}}{A_{t+n\tau}} \right] \right\}^{1/(n+1)} \le 1,$$

and

$$t + n\tau \in [T_0 - \tau, T_0).$$

The discount rate applied at time t, r_t, has a particularly interesting interpretation. Notice that $(1/k_t)$ is the expected geometric mean gross return per τ units of time earned by an investor that follows a strategy of buying and selling every τ periods of time in a market with no discounting. The log of this is thus the continuously compounded expected return from such a strategy. Obviously, such a return is negative. Recall from the definition of A_t and B_t that the specialists sets the bid and ask so that on average what he loses to the informed is made up by what he gains from the uninformed liquidity traders. Thus, $(n+1)/(T_0-t)\log(k_t)$ (a positive number) is, in return (per unit time) terms, what the uninformed on average lose to the informed. Thus, r_t represents the expected holding period return, i, plus the return that the uninformed anticipate losing to the informed. Note that r_t depends upon the holding period τ. In particular, $n+1$ in Proposition 6 is approximately $(T_0-t)/\tau$, and hence r_t is approximately $i + (1/\tau)\log(k_t)$.

The above proposition, with i specified exogenously, closes the model in the sense that Z^*_t, A^*_t, B^*_t are now specified. The resulting price process will be $\{p^*_t\}$ with $p^*_t = e^{-r_t(T_0-t)}p_t$ where p_t is as specified in section 2. The observed holding period return will be $p^*_{t+\tau}/p^*_t$. If $T_0 - t$ is large relative to τ, then r_t and $r_{t+\tau}$ will be approximately equal, in which case $p^*_{t+\tau}/p^*_t$ will be on average approximately equal to $e^{r_t\tau}$. The observed returns will be larger than i, the hypothesized holding period return, since $p^*_{t+\tau} \ge B^*_{t+\tau}$ and $p^*_t \le A^*_t$, and hence $p^*_{t+\tau}/p^*_t \ge B^*_{t+\tau}/A^*_{t+\tau}$, which is equal to $e^{i\tau}$ in expectation. That is, returns calculated by observing transaction prices will always be at least as large as the returns that one could realize by buying at time t and selling at time $t+\tau$.

On the other hand, it is easy to see that the existence of a bid–ask spread is less important the longer is the investment horizon. Intuitively, this spread can be amortized over a larger number of periods. To see this, the expected value of the return that can be realized long-term is

$$\mathrm{E}_t\left[\left(\frac{V}{A_t^*}\right)\right] = \mathrm{E}_t\left[\left(\frac{p_t^*}{A_t^*}\frac{p_{t+\tau}^*}{p_t^*}\cdots\frac{p_{t+n\tau}^*}{p_{t+(n-1)\tau}^*}\frac{V}{p_{t+n\tau}^*}\right)\right]$$

$$= \mathrm{E}_t\left[\left(\frac{p_t^*}{A_t^*}\right)\left(\frac{p_{t+\tau}^*}{p_t^*}\cdots\frac{p_{t+n\tau}^*}{p_{t+(n-1)\tau}^*}\frac{V}{p_{t+n\tau}^*}\right)\right]$$

$$= \mathrm{E}_t\left[\left(\frac{p_t}{A_t}\right)\left(\frac{p_{t+\tau}^*}{p_t^*}\cdots\frac{p_{t+n\tau}^*}{p_{t+(n-1)\tau}^*}\frac{V}{p_{t+n\tau}^*}\right)\right]. \tag{14}$$

Since $p_t \leq A_t$, the above expected return is less than the observed return. If $T_0 - t$ is large, however, then $(p_t/A_t)^{1/T_0 - t}$ will be close to one, and the long-term per period mean return will be close to the observed (from the transaction price sequence) per period return.

These observations may provide some insight into such 'anomalies' as the 'small firm effect' and the 'ignored firm effect'. In both cases it may be reasonable to conjecture that informational differences between market participants may be significant. In the case of the small firm effect, it may be the case that insiders hold a larger proportion of the stock. As the results in section 2 show, this will indicate (other things equal) a larger spread earlier in the period of time when there are informational asymmetries, and hence a larger divergence between r_t and i. In the latter case, the lack of public reporting on a firm may imply that there is a larger informational difference between insiders and outsiders. This will also mean a larger spread and hence a greater difference between r_t and i. The above results suggest that the measured 'excess returns' are not realizable in a short-run basis. Rather, the spread, which represents the expected loss of the uninformed to the informed, leaves an outsider with a 'normal' rate of return. In the long run, returns will indeed be larger on average, but these higher returns can only be realized by buying and holding.

5. Conclusion

We have analyzed a model of a securities market in which the arrival of traders over time is accommodated by a specialist. Adverse selection, by itself, can account for the existence of a spread between the ask and bid prices, and the average magnitude of the spread depends on many parameters, including the exogenous arrival patterns of insiders and liquidity traders, the elasticity of supply and demand among liquidity traders, and the quality of the information held by insiders. Furthermore, the transaction prices are informative, and hence spreads tend to decline with trade.

We do not claim that adverse selection is the sole source of the bid–ask spread. Even if there were free entry into the specialist and floor trading business, the expected profit of a specialist need not be zero – or even constant – from trade to trade. Free entry and risk neutrality can only imply that the expected profit of a new entrant, net of inventory holding costs, the opportunity cost of the entrant's time, etc. must be zero [Phillips and Smith (1980)].[11] However, the spread from such sources has a qualitatively different effect on the serial correlation of price changes, and the correlation coefficient can be used to determine the relative magnitudes of the sources of the spread. Moreover, the average spread from sources other than informational asymmetries declines as one over the average volume of trade, whereas the average spread from adverse selection need only decline as one over the square root of the average volume of trade.

The spread can be important both because of its welfare implications, which we have hinted at but not fully analyzed in this paper, and because it offers a potential explanation of the measured excess returns on small firms just after their fiscal year ends. To the extent that these fiscal year ends differ from the tax years of investors in small firms, this explanation is distinguishable from explanations based on the tax consequences of investing.

Appendix: Proof of Proposition 6

First consider $t \in [T_0 - \tau, T_0)$. Then

$$\mathrm{E}_t[B^*_{t+\tau}/A^*_t] = \mathrm{e}^{-i(T_0 - t - \tau)}(\mathrm{E}_t[B_{t+\tau}]/\mathrm{e}^{-r_t(T_0 - t)}A_t) = \mathrm{e}^{i\tau}.$$

That is,

$$r_t = i + \log\left[\left(\frac{1}{\mathrm{E}_t[B_{t+\tau}]/A_t}\right)^{T_0 - t}\right].$$

For $t + \tau < T_0$, and $t + n\tau \in [T_0 - \tau, T_0)$, suppose

$$r_{t+\tau} = i + (n/(T_0 - t - \tau))\log(k_{t+\tau}).$$

Then,

$$\mathrm{e}^{i\tau} = \frac{\mathrm{E}_t[\exp(-(i + (n/(T_0 - t - \tau))\log(k_{t+\tau}))(T_0 - t - \tau))B_{t+\tau}]}{A_t\exp(-r_t(T_0 - t))},$$

[11]It is hard to reconcile free entry and risk-averse specialists without also including transactions costs. Risk aversion of the specialists would also contribute to the spread [Ho and Stoll (1981)].

and

$$r_t = i + \frac{1}{T_0 - t}\log\left(\frac{A_t}{\mathrm{E}_t[B_{t+\tau}/k^n_{t+\tau}]}\right)$$

$$= i + \log\left[\left(\frac{1}{\mathrm{E}_t[B_{t+\tau}/A_t k^n_{t+\tau}]}\right)^{1/T_0 - t}\right].$$

Now,

$$\mathrm{E}_t\left[\frac{B_{t+\tau}}{A_t}\left(\frac{1}{k_{t+\tau}}\right)^n\right] = \mathrm{E}_t\left[\frac{B_{t+\tau}}{A_t}\mathrm{E}_{t+\tau}\left[\frac{B_{t+2\tau}}{A_{t+\tau}}\cdots\frac{B_{t+(n+1)\tau}}{A_{t+n\tau}}\right]\right]$$

$$= \mathrm{E}_t\left[\frac{B_{t+\tau}}{A_t}\frac{B_{t+2\tau}}{A_{t+\tau}}\cdots\frac{B_{t+(n+1)\tau}}{A_{t+n\tau}}\right]$$

$$= (1/k_t)^{n+1} \leq 1,$$

since

$$\mathrm{E}_{t+(k+1)\tau}\left[\frac{B_{t+(k+1)\tau}}{A_{t+k\tau}}\right] \leq \mathrm{E}_{t+k\tau}\left[\frac{P_{t+(k+1)\tau}}{A_{t+k\tau}}\right] = \frac{P_{t+k\tau}}{A_{t+k\tau}} \leq 1.$$

Thus, $r_t = i + ((n+1)/(T_0 - t))\log(k_t)$. The (backwards) induction argument shows that r_t is as claimed. Q.E.D.

References

Akerlof, G.A., 1970, The market for 'lemons', qualitative uncertainty and the market mechanism, Quarterly Journal of Economics 84, 488–500.

Arbel, Avner and Paul Strebel, 1981, Neglected firm effect and the inadequacy of the capital asset pricing model, Unpublished working paper no. 81-08 (State University of New York at Binghamton, Binghamton, NY).

Amihud, Yakov and Haim Mendelson, 1980, Dealership market, Journal of Financial Economics 8, 31–53.

Bagehot, Walter (pseud.), 1971, The only game in town, Financial Analysts Journal 22, 12–14.

Banz, Rolf, 1981, On the relationship between return and market value of common stocks, Journal of Financial Economics 9, 3–18.

Blume, Marshall E. and Robert F. Stambaugh, 1983, Biases in computed returns: An application to the size effect, Journal of Financial Economics 12, 387–404.

Copeland, Thomas and Dan Galai, 1983, Information effects on the bid ask spread, Journal of Finance 38, 1457–1469.

Fama, Eugene F., 1970, Efficient capital markets: A review of theory and empirical work, Journal of Finance 25, 383–417.

Garman, Mark B., 1976, Market microstructure, Journal of Financial Economics 3, 257–275.

Grossman, Sanford, 1976, On the efficiency of competitive stock markets when traders have diverse information, Journal of Finance 31, 573–585.

Ho, Thomas and Hans R. Stoll, 1981, Optimal dealer pricing under transactions and return uncertainty, Journal of Financial Economics 9, 47–73.

Keim, Donald B., 1983, Size related anomalies and stock return seasonality: Further empirical evidence, Journal of Financial Economics 12, 13–32.

Milgrom, Paul R. and Nancy Stokey, 1982, Information, trade and common knowledge, Journal of Economic Theory 26, 17–27.

Ohara, Maureen and George Oldfield, 1982, Microeconomics of market making, Working paper (Graduate School of Business, Cornell University, Ithaca, NY).

Phillips, Susan M. and Clifford W. Smith, Jr., 1980, Trading costs for listed options: The implications for market efficiency, Journal of Financial Economics 12, 179–201.

Roll, Richard, 1984, A simple measure of the effective bid/ask spread in an efficient market, Journal of Finance 39, 1127–1139.

Stoll, Hans R. and Robert E. Whaley, 1983, Transactions costs and the small firm effect, Journal of Financial Economics 12, 57–79.

Part III
Behavioral Finance

[10]

Journal of Financial Economics 104 (2012) 272–287

Contents lists available at SciVerse ScienceDirect

Journal of Financial Economics

journal homepage: www.elsevier.com/locate/jfec

Global, local, and contagious investor sentiment ☆

Malcolm Baker [a], Jeffrey Wurgler [b,*], Yu Yuan [c]

[a] Harvard Business School and NBER, Baker Library 261, Boston, MA 02163, USA
[b] NYU Stern School of Business and NBER, 44 West 4th Street, Suite 9-190, New York, NY 10012, USA
[c] Wharton School of Business, University of Pennsylvania, 3620 Locust Walk, Suite 2300, Philadelphia, PA 19104, USA

ARTICLE INFO

Article history:
Received 1 September 2010
Received in revised form
6 September 2011
Accepted 4 October 2011
Available online 10 November 2011

JEL classification:
G11
G12
G14
G15
G17

Keywords:
Sentiment
Return predictability

ABSTRACT

We construct investor sentiment indices for six major stock markets and decompose them into one global and six local indices. In a validation test, we find that relative sentiment is correlated with the relative prices of dual-listed companies. Global sentiment is a contrarian predictor of country-level returns. Both global and local sentiment are contrarian predictors of the time-series of cross-sectional returns within markets: When sentiment is high, future returns are low on relatively difficult to arbitrage and difficult to value stocks. Private capital flows appear to be one mechanism by which sentiment spreads across markets and forms global sentiment.

1. Introduction

We investigate the effect of global and local components of investor sentiment on major stock markets, at the level of both the country average and the time-series of the cross-section. We also consider whether and how sentiment spreads across markets. We find evidence that investor sentiment plays a significant role in international market volatility and generates return predictability of a form consistent with corrections of overreaction.

Our quantitative sentiment indices follow six stock markets: Canada, France, Germany, Japan, the United Kingdom, and the United States. We construct indices of "total" investor sentiment for each country by forming the first principal component of several time-series proxies for sentiment. We decompose the six total sentiment indices into a single "global" index and six "local" indices. The data are annual from 1980 to 2005 and drawn from several international sources. Sentiment is intrinsically difficult to measure precisely (and if there was an unambiguous, real-time measure, even the mediocre investor would be able to recalibrate himself and in the process, reduce or eliminate the information content in the measure) so we begin with an index validation test.

Our validation test is based on dual-listed shares. These so-called Siamese twins are pairs of securities that claim equal cash flows but trade in different markets and

☆ We thank Alexander Ljungqvist, Jay Ritter, and EUROFIDAI for providing data. We thank our two referees, David Hirshleifer and Paolo Pasquariello, as well as Rob Engle, Byoung-Hyoun Hwang, Karen Lewis, Mujtaba Mian, Geoff Tate, and seminar participants at the AFA, China International Conference in Finance, New York University, Rutgers, Temple University, and University of Iowa for helpful comments. We thank EUROFIDAI, Alexander Ljungqvist, and Jay Ritter for data. Baker gratefully acknowledges financial support from the Division of Research of Harvard Business School, and Yuan gratefully acknowledges financial support from Weiss Center for International Financial Research and University of Iowa.

* Corresponding author. Tel.: +1 212 598 9968; fax: +1 212 995 4233.
E-mail addresses: mbaker@hbs.edu (M. Baker), jwurgler@stern.nyu.edu (J. Wurgler), yuanyu@wharton.upenn.edu (Y. Yuan).

0304-405X/$ - see front matter
doi:10.1016/j.jfineco.2011.11.002

sometimes at substantially different prices. The large price deviations have not been explained in the context of rational markets with realistic frictions, let alone frictionless and efficient markets. We document that twins' relative prices are positively related to the relative local sentiment indices of their respective markets. This provides a relatively clean experiment that supports the empirical validity of our indices. We are not aware of other sentiment indices that have been validated by a more convincing method.

We then ask how sentiment affects international stock markets. The basic supposition is that if sentiment drives prices too far, we may observe corrections in the form of return predictability. We start with regressions to predict market returns, pooling six markets together for power in our short sample. We find that total sentiment, and particularly the global component of total sentiment, is a contrarian predictor of country-level market returns. These results are similar for both value- and equal-weighted market returns and for non-U.S. markets.

Next we examine the effect of sentiment on the time-series of cross-sectional returns. Baker and Wurgler (2006, 2007) predict that broad waves of sentiment will have greater effects on hard to arbitrage and hard to value stocks; these stocks will exhibit high "sentiment beta" (see, e.g., Glushkov, 2005). Confirming this hypothesis, we find that when a country's total sentiment is high, future returns are relatively low for its small, high return volatility, growth, and distressed stocks. These results are also apparent in the non-U.S. sample. The local component of sentiment affects the cross-section considerably more than it does the time-series market return. This result is intuitive. Many global investors are looking for diversification and simply invest in index funds rather than select specific international stocks. In addition, local investors have an overwhelming home bias toward their local market, as in, e.g., French and Poterba (1991), and can trade at lower costs than international investors. They, and their sentiment, therefore should be expected to have a disproportionate effect on the pricing of the cross-section.

Our final investigation considers whether sentiment is contagious across countries. Given the importance of global sentiment in our results, this is an important question. We use the absolute value of U.S. capital flows with the other five sample countries to obtain cross-sectional variation in the extent of integration between these markets. We find that not only do local and global sentiment predict the cross-section of those countries' returns, but so does U.S. sentiment in those countries linked with the United States by significant capital flows. This evidence suggests that capital flows are a key mechanism through which global sentiment develops and propagates, but there are surely others, including word-of-mouth and the media.

Our study contributes to a growing literature studying the role of investor sentiment. In addition to the papers above, Brown and Cliff (2004), Lemmon and Portniaguina (2006), Qiu and Welch (2004), and other papers have found evidence for a role of investor sentiment in U.S. stock market returns. Brown, Goetzmann, Hiraki, Shiraishi, and Watanabe (2005) study U.S. and Japanese flows into bull and bear funds. Yu and Yuan (2011) argue that the tradeoff between risk and expected return applies only in low sentiment periods; Stambaugh, Yu, and Yuan (in press) argue that sentiment's predictive power is concentrated in high-sentiment periods and in stocks in short legs. Baker and Wurgler (forthcoming) investigate how sentiment connects the cross-section of stock returns and government bonds, while Bekaert, Baele, and Inghelbrecht (2010) discuss sentiment and the time-series relationships between government bond and stock market returns. Papers arguing that sentiment affects aggregate financing patterns include Baker and Wurgler (2000), Henderson, Jegadeesh, and Weisbach (2006), and Kim and Weisbach (2008).

To summarize, we make several contributions to this literature. First, this paper is the first to investigate the role of sentiment within and across international equity markets. We construct usable indices of total, global, and country-specific sentiment for six markets. Second, we conduct a validation exercise with Siamese twins; most of the sentiment literature is unable to provide any validation exercise. Third, we study the effects of sentiment at the index level, where we find significant predictability relationships, perhaps because the panel of countries provides more power than a single U.S. time-series. Fourth, we provide the first extensive study of the international time-series of the cross-section of stock returns, and in particular, we find that the U.S. results by Baker and Wurgler (2006) translate to other markets. Fifth, we provide some initial evidence about how global sentiment develops and propagates.

Section 2 explains the method of construction of the sentiment indices. Section 3 describes the validation test. Section 4 uses sentiment to predict the time-series of market returns, and Section 5 considers the time-series of the cross-section of returns. Section 6 investigates sentiment contagion. Section 7 concludes.

2. Total, global, and local sentiment indices

2.1. Basic approach

Our method for estimating international markets' sentiment builds on Baker and Wurgler's (2006) strategy for U.S. sentiment. We employ a number of sentiment proxies that we hypothesize contain some component of investor sentiment and some component of non-sentiment-related idiosyncratic variation. To remove the latter, we first orthogonalize the raw sentiment proxies to a variety of macro series. Each market's "total" sentiment is then estimated as the first principal component of those orthogonalized sentiment proxies. A single "global" sentiment series is then estimated as the first principal component of these total sentiment series. Finally, each market's "local" sentiment is estimated as the residual of its total sentiment regressed on global sentiment.

2.2. Sentiment proxies: motivation and data

We are constrained by the availability of international sentiment proxies and cannot employ all those that the predominantly U.S. investor sentiment literature has examined. We also elect to use the same four proxies for all six international markets, as much as possible, although an argument could be made that the principal components methodology outlined above should be able to tolerate different proxies for different markets.

The first proxy is a quantity that we refer to as the volatility premium and simply identifies times when valuations on high idiosyncratic volatility stocks are high or low relative to valuations on low idiosyncratic volatility stocks. This is by analogy to Baker and Wurgler's (2004) use of the U.S. dividend premium, which, as the relative valuation of dividend- and non-dividend-paying stocks, is highly related (inversely) to the U.S. volatility premium.[1]

The motivation for this variable derives from the theoretical prediction that sentiment has its strongest effects on hard to value and hard to arbitrage stocks. Obviously, all else equal, these are stocks that noise traders can plausibly defend extreme values for, as befits their current optimism or pessimism. One example is Koski, Rice, and Tarhouni (2008) who show that volatility attracts day traders. More generally, the proportion of individual ownership is increasing in volatility (Sias, 1996).[2]

Somewhat less obviously, volatile stocks are, all else equal, also particularly unattractive to arbitrageurs, which in turn redoubles the potential for those stocks to be affected by noise trader sentiment. Volatile stocks are inherently riskier to trade—volatility brings with it fundamental and arbitrage risk, as in Pontiff (1996) and Wurgler and Zhuravskaya (2002), and they are associated with noise trader risk, as just mentioned. Volatile stocks also tend to be costlier to trade. Bid-ask spreads are wider due to the probability of informed trading (Glosten and Milgrom, 1985) and higher inventory costs (Ho and Stoll, 1980). Price impact beyond spreads is larger (Chan and Lakonishok, 1997). Short-sales costs are higher because upward price movements generate more frequent margin calls (Mitchell, Pulvino, and Stafford, 2002; Bali, Scherbina, and Tang, 2011) and because the rebate rate is higher (Diether, 2008), which may reflect the fact that the supply of borrowed shares is influenced by institutional ownership, which is negatively correlated with volatility (Sias, 1996).

The volatility premium (*PVOL*) is the yearend log of the ratio of the value-weighted average market-to-book ratio of high volatility stocks to that of low volatility stocks. High (low) volatility denotes one of the top (bottom) three deciles of the variance of the previous year's monthly returns, where decile breakpoints are determined country by country.[3] Total volatility is defined as the standard deviation of the trailing 12 months of monthly returns, and to control for any association with beta and a confusion with priced risks, we compute the volatility premium based only on beta-adjusted idiosyncratic volatility (for simplicity, however, we will continue to refer to this variable as the volatility premium). This variable was available for all years and all countries. On average in our sample, the market-to-book ratio of high volatility stocks has been higher than that of low volatility stocks, but in each country this relationship has been reversed within our time period.

The second and third proxies we employ are derived from initial public offering (IPO) data. They are the total volume of IPOs and their initial, first-day returns (sometimes called underpricing). The theoretical motivation for using the volume of IPOs is simply that insiders and long-run shareholders have strong incentives to time the equity market for when valuations are greatest, which is presumably when sentiment is highest. Low long-run returns to IPOs have been noted by Stigler (1964), Ritter (1991), and Loughran, Ritter, and Rydqvist (1994), which is ex post evidence of successful market timing relative to a market index. But issuers need not care that much whether their firm's misvaluation is due to firm-specific or marketwide factors; consistent with that notion, equity issues as a fraction of total new issues forecast low market returns as well (Baker and Wurgler, 2000). The worst future returns occur for IPOs and equity issues from "hot market" cohorts with high total issuance volume.

It has been widely noted that the initial returns on IPOs increase in hot markets. In the United States in 1999, for example, there were 477 IPOs and the *average* raw first-day return was 70%. And in Japan that year, the average first-day return was 137%! It is implausible that these figures reflect just adverse selection premiums, for example. If anything, the anecdotal evidence suggests that the issues with the highest first-day returns were in the greatest demand. Ritter (1998) sums up our motivation for these two sentiment proxies: "rational explanations for hot markets are difficult to come by" (p. 10).

The number of IPOs (*NIPO*) is the log of the total number of IPOs that year. The initial returns on IPOs (*RIPO*) are the average initial (most often, first-day) return on that year's offerings. The returns are equal-weighted across firms. The data were obtained from a variety of sources. We were able to find both variables for the full sample with the exception of France for 1980 through 1982 and Germany for 2003 through 2005. In the United States, the annual number of IPOs has ranged from 64 to 953 in the sample period, and the average first-day return on IPOs has ranged from around 7% to a high of 70% (exponentiate the Min and Max values from Table 2), as noted above. Most other countries have also seen high variation in these quantities.[4]

[1] We cannot form the dividend premium in some markets because dividends are relatively uncommon and, in some countries, dividends do not appear to be viewed by local investors as connoting "stability" in the way they historically have for U.S. investors.

[2] We will later describe, and control for, a non-sentiment association between valuations and volatility based on Pastor and Veronesi (2003).

[3] We follow Fama and French (1993), who use the top three deciles and bottom three deciles for factor construction.

[4] An important question is whether IPO market measures have the same meaning in bank-oriented countries (in our sample, France, Germany, and Japan) as they do in market-oriented countries. The survey of international IPO market studies in Loughran, Ritter, and Rydqvist (1994) does not indicate any obvious differences in dimensions of particular interest, including mean IPO underpricing; the relationships between IPO volume, market returns, and future gross national product (GNP) growth; and mean abnormal returns on IPOs.

Table 1
Data sources.

Country	Item	Period	Data source
Panel A: Volatility premium (*PVOL*)			
All countries	Stock return	1980–2005	Datastream (http://www.datastream.com/default.htm)
	Market value	1980–2005	Datastream
	Book value	1980–2005	Worldscope (http://www.thomsonreuters.com/)
Panel B: IPO volume (*NIPO*)			
Japan, U.K., and U.S.	*NIPO*	1980–2005	Updated version of Loughran et al. (1994) (http://bear.cba.ufl.edu/ritter/Int2008.pdf)
Canada	*NIPO*	1980–1983	Jog and Riding (1987) via updated version of Loughran et al. (1994)
		1984–1991	Jog and Srivastava (1994) via updated version of Loughran et al. (1994)
		1992–2005	Updated version of Loughran et al. (1994)
France	*NIPO*	1983–2005	Updated version of Loughran et al. (1994)
Germany	*NIPO*	1980–2002	Alexander Ljungqvist
Panel C: IPO First-day returns (*RIPO*)			
Japan, U.K., and U.S.	*RIPO*	1980–2005	Updated version of Loughran et al. (1994)
Canada	*RIPO*	1980–1983	Jog and Riding (1987) via updated version of Loughran et al. (1994)
		1984–1991	Jog and Srivastava (1994) via updated version of Loughran et al. (1994)
		1992–2005	Updated version of Loughran et al. (1994)
France	*RIPO*	1983–1998	Updated version of Loughran et al. (1994)
		1999–2005	Dealogic via updated version of Loughran et al. (1994)
Germany	*RIPO*	1980–2002	Alexander Ljungqvist
Panel D: Turnover (*TURN*)			
Canada; U.K.; and U.S.	Dollar volume	1980–2005	Datastream
France	Dollar volume	1980–2005	EUROFIDAI (http://www.eurofidai.org/)
Japan	Dollar volume	1980–1989	Global Financial Data (https://www.globalfinancialdata.com/)
		1990–2005	Datastream
Canada; Japan; U.K.; and U.S.	Market value	1980–2005	Datastream
France	Market value	1980–2005	EUROFIDAI

Data sources for proxies for sentiment from 1980 to 2005. The first proxy (*PVOL*) is the log ratio of the equal-weighted average market-to-book ratios of stocks with high idiosyncratic volatility (top three deciles) and stocks with low idiosyncratic volatility (bottom three deciles). The second proxy (*NIPO*) is the log number of initial public offerings over the year. The third proxy (*RIPO*) is the average first-day returns of initial public offerings in the year. The fourth proxy (*TURN*) is detrended log turnover over the year.

The fourth sentiment proxy is market turnover. Commentators on speculative episodes such as Bagehot (1873) and Kindleberger (1978) have noted that high trading volume in the overpriced asset is a pattern that goes back to the tulip bubble. Cochrane (2002) states that "the association of price and volume is a generic feature of the historical 'bubbles'" (p. 17). Lamont and Thaler (2003) examine tech stock carve-outs and find that the relatively overpriced IPO subsidiaries have an average turnover rate of 38% *per day* over the first 20 days of trading (not including the first day), which is more than five times that of parent turnover. There was much greater volume in Internet relative to non-Internet stocks between 1998 and 2000 (Ofek and Richardson, 2003). In a cleaner test, Mei, Scheinkman, and Xiong (2009) find a correlation between trading and price differentials in fundamentally identical Chinese A–B shares. Smith, Suchanek, and Williams (1988) find experimental evidence that bubbles are associated with high turnover. Subsequent research indicates that this correlation is robust to the introduction of trading fees, short-sales constraints, and the use of business professionals as test subjects.

There is also ample theory to connect sentiment and trading volume. Any greater-fool theory of rational bubbles (Harrison and Kreps, 1978) or models of positive feedback trading by informed investors essentially requires that those who believe the asset is overvalued be able to trade it away before the mispricing corrects (De Long, Shleifer, Summers, and Waldmann, 1990b). Uninformed fund managers can churn bubbles to confuse their clients into thinking they are informed (Allen and Gorton, 1993). Baker and Stein (2004) point out that when shorting is relatively costly, sentimental investors are more likely to trade when they are optimistic, and overall volume goes up. Scheinkman and Xiong (2003) provide a complementary argument based on overconfidence for using turnover as a proxy for sentiment. So, as with the other three measures, we expect a positive relationship between the observed proxy and underlying sentiment.

Market turnover (*TURN*) is the log of total market turnover, i.e., total dollar volume over the year divided by total capitalization at the end of the prior year. We detrend this with an up-to-five-year moving average. We could obtain market-level turnover statistics for all markets but Germany. We detrend because all markets except Japan display a positive trend in turnover.[5]

Overall, we used roughly a dozen primary data sources to construct these proxies. They are listed in Table 1 and summary statistics are given by country in Table 2.

[5] For Canada, France, and the United States, the data are obtained from a single source. For Japan and the United Kingdom, the data from two different sources were combined to provide long series from 1980 to 2005. To make the series from different sources consistent, we multiply the later series by constants to render it to have the same standard deviations with the early series in the overlapping periods.

Table 2
Total investor sentiment, 1980–2005.

					Correlations with $SENT_c^{Total}$		Loadings	Correlations with sentiment components			*p*-values		
	Mean	SD	Min	Max	$SENT_c^{Total}$	*p*-value		*PVOL*	*NIPO*	*RIPO*	*PVOL*	*NIPO*	*RIPO*
Panel A: Canada													
PVOL	0.70	0.42	0.05	1.82	0.65	(0.00)	0.36	1.00			(.)		
NIPO	2.70	0.83	1.61	4.26	0.13	(0.54)	0.07	−0.23	1.00		(0.27)	(.)	
RIPO	0.07	0.06	−0.04	0.24	0.90	(0.00)	0.49	0.50	0.04	1.00	(0.01)	(0.86)	(.)
TURN	0.21	0.30	−0.35	1.03	0.75	(0.00)	0.41	0.15	0.29	0.54	(0.47)	(0.15)	(0.00)
Panel B: France													
PVOL	0.28	0.57	−0.36	2.11	0.12	(0.58)	0.06	1.00			(.)		
NIPO	3.39	0.73	1.61	4.69	0.84	(0.00)	0.42	0.34	1.00		(0.12)	(.)	
RIPO	0.11	0.07	0.02	0.26	0.66	(0.00)	0.33	−0.21	0.26	1.00	(0.35)	(0.23)	(.)
TURN	0.16	0.30	−0.59	0.62	0.91	(0.00)	0.46	−0.03	0.67	0.50	(0.89)	(0.00)	(0.02)
Panel C: Germany													
PVOL	0.19	0.44	−0.74	1.23	0.62	(0.00)	0.31	1.00			(.)		
NIPO	3.02	0.85	1.79	5.12	0.90	(0.00)	0.45	0.35	1.00		(0.10)	(.)	
RIPO	0.12	0.12	−0.00	0.43	0.89	(0.00)	0.45	0.34	0.75	1.00	(0.11)	(0.00)	(.)
Panel D: Japan													
PVOL	0.57	0.40	−0.65	1.46	0.91	(0.00)	0.40	1.00			(.)		
NIPO	4.34	0.73	2.64	5.14	0.45	(0.02)	0.20	0.38	1.00		(0.06)	(.)	
RIPO	0.31	0.22	0.07	0.86	0.79	(0.00)	0.35	0.67	0.02	1.00	(0.00)	(0.93)	(.)
TURN	−0.05	1.97	−5.88	2.65	0.80	(0.00)	0.35	0.57	0.27	0.48	(0.00)	(0.19)	(0.01)
Panel E: U.K.													
PVOL	0.20	0.44	−0.77	0.94	0.67	(0.00)	0.36	1.00			(.)		
NIPO	4.41	0.69	2.56	5.43	0.64	(0.00)	0.34	0.23	1.00		(0.26)	(.)	
RIPO	0.16	0.12	0.06	0.61	0.50	(0.01)	0.27	0.00	0.15	1.00	(0.98)	(0.45)	(.)
TURN	0.88	1.17	−0.81	3.63	0.87	(0.00)	0.47	0.49	0.37	0.37	(0.01)	(0.06)	(0.06)
Panel F: U.S.													
PVOL	0.17	0.48	−1.29	1.25	0.74	(0.00)	0.35	1.00			(.)		
NIPO	5.83	0.75	4.16	6.86	0.54	(0.00)	0.26	0.06	1.00		(0.76)	(.)	
RIPO	0.17	0.11	0.07	0.53	0.71	(0.00)	0.34	0.48	0.14	1.00	(0.01)	(0.48)	(.)
TURN	0.22	0.26	−0.28	0.68	0.86	(0.00)	0.41	0.51	0.52	0.40	(0.01)	(0.01)	(0.04)

Means, standard deviations, and correlations for proxies for sentiment. The first proxy (*PVOL*) is the log ratio of the equal-weighted average market-to-book ratios of stocks with high idiosyncratic volatility (top three deciles) and stocks with low idiosyncratic volatility (bottom three deciles). The second proxy (*NIPO*) is the log number of initial public offerings over the year. The third proxy (*RIPO*) is the average first-day returns of initial public offerings in the year. The fourth proxy (*TURN*) is detrended log turnover over the year. Total investor sentiment, $SENT_c^{Total}$, is the first principal component of four time-series proxies for sentiment for the given country.

Finally, to remove information about expected returns that may be contained in our sentiment proxies that is not related to sentiment, we follow Baker and Wurgler (2006) and orthogonalize each proxy to six macro series. These are consumption growth (Breeden, 1979), from the Penn World Tables, and industrial production growth (Chen, Roll, and Ross, 1986), inflation (Fama and Schwert, 1977; Chen, Roll, and Ross, 1986), employment growth (Santos and Veronesi, 2006), the short-term rate (Fama and Schwert, 1977), and the term premium (Keim and Stambaugh, 1986; Fama and French, 1989), from the Organisation for Economic Co-operation and Development (OECD).

The macro series turn out to explain comparatively little of the variation in the sentiment proxies. Consequently, the correlation between the orthogonalized and raw proxies is, on average across the four proxies, 0.88. It is comforting that macro series that contain a great deal of contemporaneous and forward-looking information about economic fundamentals are, even in combination, so unrelated to our proxies. Admittedly, however, it is impossible to rule out that an as-yet undiscovered risk factor drives all of the various relationships between the sentiment proxies and expected returns that we find later.

2.3. Total sentiment indices

The total sentiment index coefficients for each country are reported in the loadings column of Table 2. The index coefficients are estimated using the first principal component of each of the macro-orthogonalized sentiment proxies. The resulting indices are linear functions of the within-country standardized values of the proxies and thus have mean zero:

$$SENT^{Total}_{Canada,t} = 0.36PVOL_t + 0.07NIPO_t + 0.49RIPO_t + 0.41TURN_t, \quad (1)$$

$$SENT^{Total}_{France,t} = 0.06PVOL_t + 0.42NIPO_t + 0.33RIPO_t + 0.46TURN_t, \quad (2)$$

$$SENT^{Total}_{Germany,t} = 0.31PVOL_t + 0.45NIPO_t + 0.45RIPO_t, \quad (3)$$

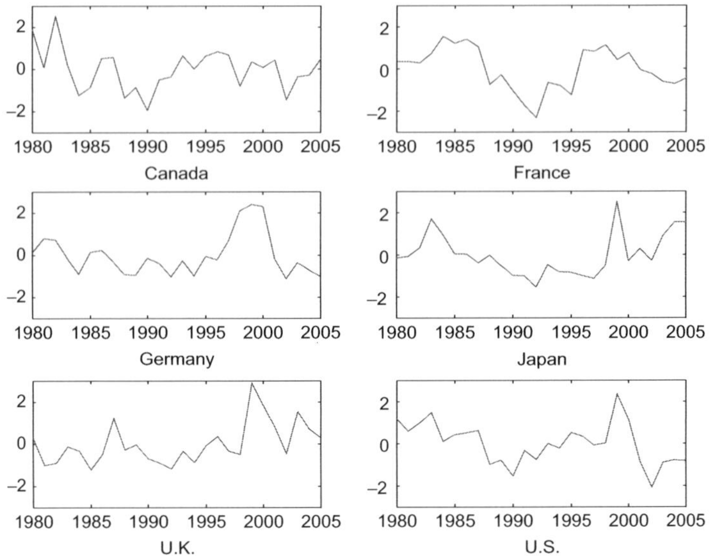

Fig. 1. Total investor sentiment, 1980–2005. Total investor sentiment, $SENT_c^{Total}$, is the first principal component of four time-series proxies for sentiment for the given country. The first proxy (*PVOL*) is the log ratio of the equal-weighted average market-to-book ratios of stocks with high idiosyncratic volatility (top three deciles) and stocks with low idiosyncratic volatility (bottom three deciles). The second proxy (*NIPO*) is the log number of initial public offerings over the year. The third proxy (*RIPO*) is the average first-day returns of initial public offerings in the year. The fourth proxy (*TURN*) is detrended log turnover over the year. Prior to forming the first principal component, the proxies are orthogonalized with respect to consumption growth, industry production growth, employment growth, the short-term interest rate, inflation, and the term premium.

$$SENT_{Japan,t}^{Total} = 0.40PVOL_t + 0.20NIPO_t + 0.35RIPO_t + 0.35TURN_t, \tag{4}$$

$$SENT_{UK,t}^{Total} = 0.36PVOL_t + 0.34NIPO_t + 0.27RIPO_t + 0.47TURN_t, \tag{5}$$

$$SENT_{US,t}^{Total} = 0.35PVOL_t + 0.26NIPO_t + 0.34RIPO_t + 0.41TURN_t, \tag{6}$$

where the country subscripts on the proxies have been suppressed.[6] The fraction of variance explained by the first principal components are, in order of the countries listed above, 38%, 40%, 48%, 37%, 37%, and 42%, and in each country there is at least one eigenvalue that exceeds unity. These figures resemble the 49% reported in Baker and Wurgler (2006) for a six-factor index of U.S. sentiment.

We standardize the total sentiment indices and plot them in Fig. 1. A prominent feature is the Internet bubble of the late 1990s and its subsequent crash; this is clearly represented not only in the United States but in at least three other countries. These results serve as a reminder that Germany's Neuer Markt, France's Nouveau Marche, and London's TECHMark—only the last of which still exists—were overseas cousins of the more familiar Nasdaq in both composition and performance.[7]

A feature that we will return to when we discuss empirical hypotheses is mean-reversion of the sentiment indices. For now, we just mention the facts. The first-order autocorrelations of *changes* in the indices are −0.423 (Canada), −0.163 (France), 0.092 (Germany), −0.373 (Japan), −0.287 (UK), and −0.138 (US). The second-order autocorrelations of changes are 0.036 (Canada), 0.028 (France), −0.222 (Germany), 0.034 (Japan), −0.311 (UK), and −0.219 (US). Thus, only changes in Germany's index have a positive first-order autocorrelation, and this is ultimately outweighed by its larger negative second-order autocorrelation. This feature of the German index is suggested in a close look at Fig. 1: whereas a few other countries experienced one-year sentiment spikes around the Internet bubble, German sentiment, as measured by our indices, stayed at a peak for one or two years more.

2.4. Global and local sentiment indices

We separate the total sentiment indices into one global and six local components. The global index is the

[6] French IPO data for 1980–1982 and Germany IPO data for 2003–2005 were not available. For each country, we fit their total sentiment indices to the other other five countries' indices in the period of overlap, and then used the predicted value to fill the missing data points.

[7] Other examples include the Italian Nuovo Mercato, the Nordic New Market, and approximately ten other European markets that opened between 1996 and 2001.

Table 3
Global and local investor sentiment, 1980–2005. Global sentiment ($SENT^{Global}$) is the first principal component of the total sentiment indices ($SENT_c^{Total}$) in the six countries. Local sentiment ($SENT_c^{Local}$) is the residual from the regression: $SENT_c^{Total} = b_c\, SENT^{Global} + SENT_c^{Local}$, for each country.

Panel A: Total and global sentiment

	Correlations with $SENT^{Global}$		Loading	Correlations among $SENT_c^{Total}$ indices						*p*-values					
	Global	*p*-value		Canada	France	Germany	Japan	U.K.	U.S.	Canada	France	Germany	Japan	U.K.	U.S.
Canada	0.57	(0.00)	0.20	1.00						(.)					
France	0.66	(0.00)	0.23	0.20	1.00					(0.34)	(.)				
Germany	0.76	(0.00)	0.27	0.26	0.45	1.00				(0.19)	(0.02)	(.)			
Japan	0.55	(0.00)	0.20	0.10	0.28	0.15	1.00			(0.63)	(0.16)	(0.45)	(.)		
U.K.	0.63	(0.00)	0.23	0.18	0.19	0.40	0.53	1.00		(0.39)	(0.35)	(0.04)	(0.01)	(.)	
U.S.	0.88	(0.00)	0.31	0.60	0.51	0.66	0.33	0.34	1.00	(0.00)	(0.01)	(0.00)	(0.10)	(0.09)	(.)

Panel B: Local sentiment

	Correlations among $SENT_c^{Local}$ indices						*p*-values					
	Canada	France	Germany	Japan	U.K.	U.S.	Canada	France	Germany	Japan	U.K.	U.S.
Canada	1.00						(.)					
France	−0.28	1.00					(0.16)	(.)				
Germany	−0.31	−0.10	1.00				(0.12)	(0.64)	(.)			
Japan	−0.31	−0.12	−0.48	1.00			(0.12)	(0.56)	(0.01)	(.)		
U.K.	−0.28	−0.37	−0.14	0.29	1.00		(0.16)	(0.06)	(0.48)	(0.15)	(.)	
U.S.	0.25	−0.18	−0.02	−0.37	−0.55	1.00	(0.21)	(0.37)	(0.90)	(0.06)	(0.00)	(.)

first principal component of the six total indices. The loadings are reported in Table 3 as

$$SENT_t^{Global} = 0.20SENT_{Canada,t}^{Total} + 0.23SENT_{France,t}^{Total} + 0.27SENT_{Germany,t}^{Total} + 0.20SENT_{Japan,t}^{Total} + 0.23SENT_{UK,t}^{Total} + 0.31SENT_{US,t}^{Total}. \quad (7)$$

The United States is widely considered the world's bellwether market. Consistent with this position, the United States' total sentiment index exhibits a high degree of commonality with other countries' indices and receives the highest loading in the global index.

The standardized version of the global index is plotted in Fig. 2. Not surprisingly, Fig. 2 indicates that global sentiment rose steadily through the mid-1990s, peaked in 1999 and 2000, and then dropped by a few standard deviations within three years. Before entering the Internet bubble, global sentiment had declined from the late 1980s to the early 1990s.

Local indices are defined as the components of the total indices orthogonal to the global index. That is, we regress the total sentiment indices on the global index in each country and define local indices as the residuals. We standardize these and plot them in Fig. 2.

Qualitative interpretations of the indices involve a large degree of conjecture as well as an understanding of historical market conditions. Proper interpretation of the local indices, in particular, requires a grasp of both global and market conditions, as well as some caution given the unavoidable noise in the estimates. With these qualifications in mind, one can speculate on some of the variation in the U.S. local index. The index reaches high levels in the early 1980s, perhaps reflecting speculative activity in biotech and natural resources shares that was concentrated in the United States. The index declines somewhat following the 1987 crash, but not dramatically, reflecting the fact that the crash was a global phenomenon (Roll, 1988).

Perhaps because the technological advances of the Internet were concentrated in the United States, the local index suggests that the sentiment associated with the bubble may have materialized there (and in Canada) first. Interestingly, while the U.S. total sentiment was high at the bubble's peak, it was not uniquely high relative to other countries in the sample. However, U.S.-specific sentiment did decline to an unusual degree with the crash, most likely reflecting the combination of the crash and the terrorist attacks on September 11, 2001.

3. Validation with Siamese twins

3.1. The Siamese twins

The existing investor sentiment literature rarely provides any external validation test for its proxies. In this paper we attempt to do somewhat better, because an experiment exists in the international context that does not exist in the U.S. context. Specifically, we connect our sentiment indices to the international violations of the law of one price observed in dual-listed companies. Dual-listed companies, often termed "Siamese twins," are literally textbook violations of arbitrage (see, e.g., Bodie, Kane, and Marcus, 2008).

More background will help to motivate this validation exercise. A twin pair comprises two companies which are incorporated in different countries and whose shares trade locally in those countries but, frequently as a result of a merger, have contractually agreed to operate their business as one and divide its cash flows to shareholders in a fixed ratio. There are around a dozen such company pairs as of the time of this writing, but the pair of Royal Dutch (traded mainly in the United States and the

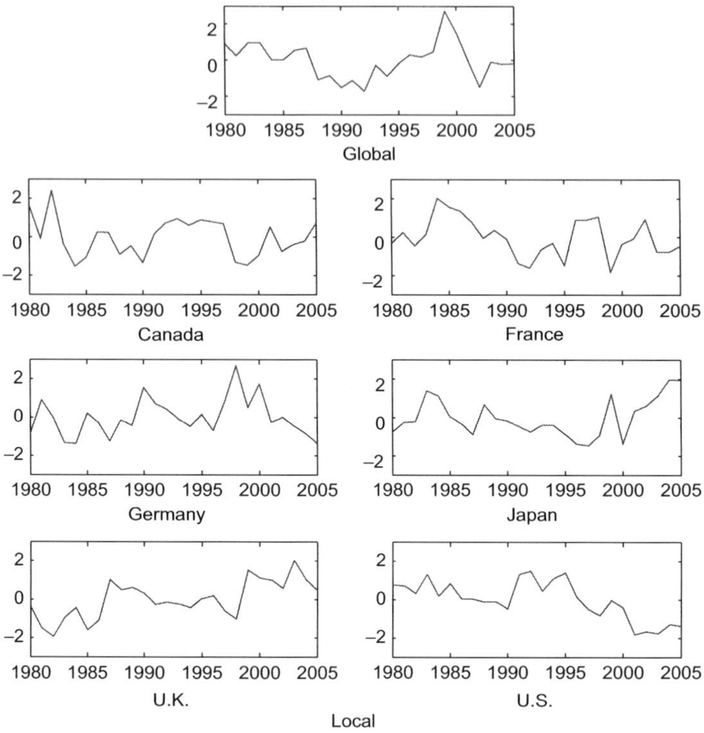

Fig. 2. Global and local investor sentiment, 1980–2005. Global sentiment ($SENT^{Global}$) is the first principal component of the total sentiment indices ($SENT_c^{Total}$) in the six countries. Local sentiment ($SENT_c^{Total}$) is the residual from the regression: $SENT_c^{Total} = b_c SENT^{Global} + SENT_c^{Local}$, for each country.

Netherlands) and Shell Transport (traded mainly in the United Kingdom) is still the best-known example, despite their recent unification.

For the Royal Dutch-Shell pair, as determined by a 1907 alliance, all cash flows, adjusting for corporate tax considerations and control rights, are split in the proportion 60:40. However, as shown by Rosenthal and Young (1990), Froot and Dabora (1999), and De Jong, Rosenthal, and Van Dijk (2009), the Siamese twins, among the largest and most liquid securities in the world, trade at prices that differ from the fixed cash flow ratio, and often by considerable amounts. For example, in our sample period, deviations from parity of more than 50 cents on the dollar—from −35% to +17%—are observed. De Jong, Rosenthal, and Van Dijk (2009) report that such deviations are observed in all Siamese twin pairs to a greater or lesser degree.

Froot and Dabora (1999) provide a comprehensive examination of structural reasons why these price gaps may occur. They consider six explanations in depth: "discretionary uses of dividend income by parent companies; differences in parent expenditures; voting rights issues; currency fluctuations; ex-dividend-date timing issues; and tax-induced investor heterogeneity. Only that latter hypothesis can explain some (but not all) of the facts." Shleifer (2000) further points out that any fixed structural or differences-in-risk explanation would have trouble explaining how the deviation from parity changes sign over time: "there is no story in which the cash flows of one stock are subjected to a different fundamental risk than the cash flows of the other" (p. 31).[8] He and others conclude that the deviation exists and persists because arbitrageurs fear noise trader risk, i.e., the risk that noise trader sentiment drives the mispricing to get worse before it gets better.[9,10]

[8] Shleifer (2000) and Bodie, Kane, and Marcus (2008) also point out that this is a cleaner demonstration of the violation of the law of one price than the closed-end fund discount, which does involve management fees and other structural features.

[9] Lowenstein (2000) reports that Long Term Capital Management bet $2.3 billion on Royal Dutch-Shell alone, illustrating that it was viewed as a mispricing by sophisticated investors, and lost almost $200 million on the trade, illustrating noise trader risk. See De Jong, Rosenthal, and Van Dijk (2009) for a detailed examination of the risks and return of dual-listed company arbitrage.

[10] On July 9, 2002, Royal Dutch was removed from the Standard and Poor (S&P) 500 Index along with several other non-U.S. firms. What was a Royal Dutch premium became a discount in a matter of days, as index

With our putative sentiment measures we are able to examine this explanation more directly. To the extent that it is borne out in the data, it supports the joint hypothesis that our sentiment indices are valid and that the drivers of the Siamese twins' price gaps include differential investor sentiment. Note that this joint hypothesis is the principal limitation of this exercise. It could be true that the twins' discount does not reflect relative sentiment, but some other unidentified economic force that is driving both the discount and our indices. This resembles the standard joint hypothesis problem that arises in tests of market efficiency: to test market efficiency, one must take a stand on the market's model of expected returns (Fama, 1970). But in the case of the Siamese twins, this argument has considerably less force. As Shleifer (2000) points out, given the unique features of the experiment, "the Fama (1970) critique is irrelevant" (p. 31).

In summary, after more than 20 years of research on the Siamese twins, we could find no paper that finds or even asserts the existence of such a hidden explanation. Those who do advance specific explanations generally assert that noise trader risk is what allows the deviation to exist and persist. As such, the validation test would seem informative. At the very least, it provides a better test than any yet presented in the sentiment literature.

3.2. Data and results

We obtain the relative prices of Siamese twin pairs from 1981 through 2002 from Mathias Van Dijk (http://mathijsavandijk.com/dual-listed-companies). Three pairs of twins have both companies in our sample markets and provide 51 annual observations. They all involve the United States and United Kingdom. Fig. 1 indicates that our sentiment measures in these countries are highly correlated, which reduces the power of the test and thus the ability to document a connection with the Siamese twins.[11]

The sentiment indices include both changes or return-like components, such as first-day returns on IPOs and perhaps detrended turnover, and level components, like the volatility premium. We therefore compare them to both changes in and levels of twin relative prices. We use annual observations on the yearend log price ratio, scaled such that a value of zero represents theoretical parity, and compare the changes and levels to the prevailing difference between U.S. sentiment and U.K. sentiment. The specifications are:

$$\Delta dev_{i,t} = a + b(SENT^*_{US,t} - SENT^*_{UK,t}) + c\Delta dev_{i,t-1} + u_{i,t} \quad (8)$$

and

$$dev_{i,t} = a + b(SENT^*_{US,t} - SENT^*_{UK,t}) + c\,dev_{i,t-1} + u_{i,t}, \quad (9)$$

where i denotes one of the three twin pairs. We use the asterisk superscript because we test both total and local sentiment indices. We control for the lagged relative price level because it is empirically quite persistent; because the sentiment indices are not measured without error; and because both sentiment indices have been standardized, removing any differences in means or scales. The change in the deviation is not very persistent, so its inclusion in the first specification is not material.

Table 4 indicates that the relative level of investor sentiment has a significant relationship to the relative level and changes of twins' prices. Given the sample size and low power of this test, the magnitude of the coefficient is surprisingly statistically significant and economically important. The standard deviation of the change of the log price ratio is 9.38%, while the standard deviation of the total sentiment gap is 0.992, so a one-standard-deviation change in the latter is associated with a change in the log price ratio swift of $4.43\% \times 0.992 = 4.39\%$, or approximately half of a standard deviation. Note that we report two-sided p-values, based on clustered standard errors, by convention, although our hypothesis is one-sided. We has also conducted Stambaugh (1986) corrections and added control variables with little statistical or economic change in the results.

The results provide some extra support that a sentiment interpretation of our indices is reasonable. To repeat, we aknowledge that this interpretation is conditional on this test having largely resolved the joint hypothesis problem. If, as Shleifer (2000) and others

Table 4
Time series regressions for Siamese twins. The dependent variable is the change or level of the annual log deviation of the relative price of three pairs of Siamese twins trading in the U.S. and the U.K. between 1981 and 2002. The independent variables are the difference between total (or local) sentiment. Clustered p-values are in braces.

	N	Constant	$SENTdiff \times 10^2$	Δdev_{t-1}	R^2
Panel A: Deviation change					
$\Delta dev_{i,t} = a + b(SENT^*_{US,t} - SENT^*_{UK,t}) + c\Delta dev_{i,t-1} + u_{i,t}$					
Total sentiment	48	0.01	**4.43**	−0.21	36%
		[0.36]	**[0.00]**	[0.17]	
Local sentiment	48	0.01	**2.42**	−0.11	29%
		[0.54]	**[0.00]**	[0.44]	
Panel B: Deviation level					
$dev_{i,t} = a + b(SENT^*_{US,t} - SENT^*_{UK,t}) + c\,dev_{i,t-1} + u_{i,t}$					
Total sentiment	51	0.01	**2.40**	0.82	74%
		[0.35]	**[0.02]**	[0.00]	
Local sentiment	51	0.01	**1.29**	0.81	72%
		[0.40]	**[0.09]**	[0.00]	

(*footnote continued*)
funds and benchmark-sensitive investors sold Royal Dutch over this period. Royal Dutch dropped by 25% between the announcement and the effective date. Shell fell too, as arbitrage maintained relative prices, but only by 17%. Both prices rebounded in the following weeks, but the deviation in prices did not revert to its previous level. Unilever, operating in a very different sector, had the same pattern of returns in its twin shares. This case study illustrates that the Siamese twin deviations capture index level differences in nonfundamental demand. While this particular demand shock had nothing to do with country-level sentiment, it proves the point that country-level relative demand for broad baskets of stocks would be apparent in Siamese twin deviations.

[11] Royal Dutch (U.S.) and Shell Transport (U.K.) from 1981 through 2002; Smithkline Beecham H shares (U.S.) and Smithkline Beecham E shares (U.K.) from 1990 through 1996; and Unilever NV (U.S.) and Unilever PLC (U.K.) from 1981 through 2002.

argue, that is the case, then in addition to supporting the indices, the results also provide further evidence that they are right that noise trader sentiment-driven mispricing helps to explain why the Siamese twins deviate so far from parity. With a joint hypothesis, it is all or nothing. We conclude that the exercise does, at a minimum, provide a more compelling validation test for a sentiment index than any in the literature.

4. Sentiment and market-level returns

4.1. Prior evidence, hypotheses, and market-level data

Baker and Wurgler (2006) provide an anecdotal history of investor sentiment in the United States since the early 1960s. They note the electronics boom in the early 1960s, the growth stocks boom in the late 1960s, the Nifty Fifty preference of the early 1970s, various industry-specific bubbles through the late 1970s through the mid-1980s, and the Internet bubble. We shall not attempt to catalog other (asserted) stock market bubbles and sentiment-driven variation for each of our non-U.S. markets, although this is a worthy task.

The empirical literature has employed sentiment-type measures as contrarian market-level return predictors only sporadically and mainly in the U.S. context. Kothari and Shanken (1997) discuss the predictability of the aggregate book-to-market ratio for annual U.S. market returns. They propose a sentiment-type explanation based on evidence of predictably negative risk premiums, which is inconsistent with market efficiency since rational risk premiums must be positive. Baker and Wurgler (2000) adopt this approach using the equity share in total equity and debt issues and find results consistent with Kothari and Shanken; they, too, find periods of predictably negative market returns. Henderson, Jegadeesh, and Weisbach (2006) extend this evidence to financing patterns in international markets. Baker and Wurgler (2007) find some evidence that an index similar to that estimated here predicts market-level U.S. returns, while Brown and Cliff (2004) do not find evidence of predictability.

The general impression from the time-series predictability literature, not just that involving sentiment, is that there are few if any variables that strongly reject the null of no predictability. Our panel of six countries has more power to reject the null of no market return predictability than returns from the United States alone (Ang and Bekaert, 2007), although due to cross-correlation, this amounts to fewer than six independent observations per period.

Motivated by the prior sentiment literature using U.S. data, we hypothesize that our sentiment indices are contrarian predictors of international index-level returns. As in the cross-sectional literature that derives predictability implications from cross-sectional limits to arbitrage, contrarian predictability at the market level can arise from at least two mechanisms. One is that arbitrageurs are essentially sidelined in extreme periods by noise trader risk (De Long, Shleifer, Summers, and Waldmann, 1990a; Shleifer and Vishny, 1997)—the variability of investor sentiment—and prices correct when noise traders' own beliefs correct, perhaps because the noise traders are confronted by realizations of economic fundamentals.

A second mechanism behind predictability is that noise traders' beliefs and hence mispricing stabilize at an extreme level, perhaps because they are fully invested, at which arbitrageurs find the expected returns so great that they outweigh the noise trader risk. They, too, wait for the facts to materialize, and as this happens in the expected direction, which it does on average if the arbitrageurs are correct, they are willing to become more and more heavily invested, pushing the aggregate demand curve and restoring fundamental value.

It is not easy to distinguish between these mechanisms, and we do not attempt to do so here. Earlier we showed that our total sentiment series exhibited mean-reversion over the horizon of one or two years. This is consistent with an explanation for predictability involving reversion in noise trader beliefs. Regarding the reason for this change, Baker and Wurgler (2006), where sentiment indices predict the time-series of the cross-section of earnings announcement returns—high sentiment forecasts lower earnings announcement returns on hard to value and hard to arbitrage stocks.[12] This is consistent with an information-based mechanism, but it cannot determine the extent to which this information is changing noise trader beliefs or confirming to arbitrageurs that they can be more aggressive.

We collect monthly market return data from Datastream, which cover the stocks from the largest exchange in each country except in the United States. For the United States, it covers the union of the NYSE, Amex, and Nasdaq. We gather both value-weighted and equal-weighted indexes; the difference in predictive effects between these will foreshadow the results in the time-series of the cross-section to come later.

4.2. Predicting market returns

We pool monthly returns from 1981 to 2006 for our countries and regress the monthly market returns for country c in year t on its beginning-of-year investor sentiment index value (i.e., the value prevailing as of the end of the previous year, which we shall call $t-1$ in an abuse of monthly and yearly notation):

$$R_{MKT,c,t} = a + dSENT^{Total}_{c,t-1} + u_{c,t}, \tag{10}$$

and

$$R_{MKT,c,t} = b + eSENT^{Global}_{t-1} + fSENT^{Local}_{c,t-1} + u_{c,t}. \tag{11}$$

Because of the cross-correlation in returns, our significance tests use month-clustered standard errors.

Table 5 indicates that total investor sentiment serves as a statistically significant contrarian predictor of market returns across these six markets.[13] The economic

[12] We do not attempt this test here because of the low quality of international earnings announcement dates data.

[13] Once again, we report two-sided p-values per convention, though the sign of all theoretical predictions in the paper is unambiguous and thus the statistical hypotheses are, in fact, one-sided.

Table 5

Time series regressions for country-level index returns, 1981–2006. Regressions of monthly country-level value- and equal-weighted index returns on previous yearend $SENT_c^{Total}$ (in Eq. (1)), or on previous yearend $SENT^{Global}$and previous yearend $SENT_c^{Local}$ (in Eq. (2)). In Panel A, the sample includes monthly country-level index returns from 1981 to 2006 in six countries. In Panel B, the sample excludes U.S. data. The first column shows the results from Eq. (1), and the second and third columns show the results from Eq. (2). Clustered *p*-values are in braces.

$$R_{MKT,C,t} = a + dSENT_{c,t-1}^{Total} + u_{c,t} \quad (1)$$

$$R_{MKT,C,t} = b + eSENT_{t-1}^{Global} + fSENT_{c,t-1}^{Local} + u_{c,t} \quad (2)$$

	$SENT_{c,t-1}^{Total}$			$SENT_{t-1}^{Global}$		$SENT_{c,t-1}^{Local}$		
	d	$p(d)$	R^2	e	$p(e)$	f	$p(f)$	R^2
Panel A: Including U.S.								
VW	−0.29	[0.08]	0.3%	−0.45	[0.05]	0.03	[0.68]	0.7%
EW	−0.36	[0.04]	0.4%	−0.47	[0.05]	−0.07	[0.48]	0.8%
Panel B: Excluding U.S.								
VW	−0.27	[0.10]	0.2%	−0.44	[0.06]	0.01	[0.91]	0.6%
EW	−0.33	[0.05]	0.4%	−0.45	[0.05]	−0.06	[0.57]	0.7%

significance of the effect is nontrivial. All sentiment indices are standardized, so a one-standard-deviation increase in a country's total investor sentiment index is associated with 3.5 percentage points per year (29 basis points per month) lower value-weighted market returns and 4.3 percentage points (36 basis points per month) lower equal-weighted returns. The stronger equal-weighted results presumably reflect smaller stocks being harder to value (due to spottier information and less certain prospects) and to arbitrage (due to generally greater costs and risks). This logic is developed a bit further in the next section, which focuses solely on cross-sectional tests.

Interestingly, the country-level results are mainly driven by global sentiment. A one-standard-deviation increase in the global sentiment index is associated with 5.4 percentage points per year (45 basis points per month) lower value-weighted market returns and 5.6 percentage points (47 basis points per month) lower equal-weighted market returns. This conclusion also does not depend on including the United States in the sample, and it raises the important issue of cross-country sentiment contagion. We consider this below. For now, Table 5 represents new evidence that sentiment affects markets around the world, not just in the United States where it has been most extensively studied.

We performed but do not report a number of additional robustness tests for the results in Table 5 that were prompted by referee suggestions. None of the following had a major effect on these results: excluding Germany, for which we are missing a few years of sentiment data; controlling for the lagged dividend yield (see, e.g., Shiller, 1984; Campbell and Shiller, 1988; Fama and French, 1988, and others) and the short-term interest rate (Fama and Schwert, 1977); excluding turnover from the sentiment proxy set; excluding the idiosyncratic volatility premium from the proxy set; using a total volatility premium rather than an idiosyncratic volatility premium; using an idiosyncratic volatility premium where idiosyncratic volatility is first orthogonalized to firm age, to control for a Pastor and Veronesi (2003) effect in which valuations depend on uncertainty about firm profitability that changes over time.

Finally, in unreported results we tested whether the U.S.-the U.K. Siamese twin premium predicts relative market returns on those two markets, consistent with the presumption of our validation approach that it reflects sentiment. We find that a one-standard-deviation higher deviation from twin parity predicts a −7.2% relative equal-weighted market return (Newey-West two-sided *p*-value of 0.07) and a −4.0% relative value-weighted return (Newey-West two-sided *p*-value of 0.12) in the coming year. The economic magnitude is nontrivial and the statistical significance is not unimpressive given the 22-year sample period and single time-series.

5. Sentiment and the cross-section of returns

5.1. Prior evidence, hypotheses, and firm-level data

The literature on predicting the time-series of the cross-section of expected stock returns is fairly small and uses only U.S. data, often with a focus on investor sentiment. Brown and Cliff (2004), Lemmon and Portniaguina (2006), and most extensively, Baker and Wurgler (2006) investigate the ability of sentiment to explain the time-series of the cross-section. Brown and Cliff (2004) find little connection using their sentiment measures, and Lemmon and Portniaguina (2006) find stronger evidence of sentiment as a contrarian predictor of small stocks and low institutional ownership stocks but not value or momentum portfolios. Qiu and Welch (2004) also use sentiment to predict small stocks. Also, from a non-sentiment perspective, Ghosh and Constantinides (2011) develop a predictor based on economic regimes.

Baker and Wurgler (2006) find robust predictability of the time-series of the cross-section using a U.S. index similar to that used here. Their stronger results may indicate more informative sentiment proxies and/or sharper cross-sectional predictions. In particular, they observe that sentiment should have relatively stronger effects on stocks that are hard to arbitrage—those that arbitrageurs find relatively costly or risky to trade against mispricings. For a recent survey of the theoretical literature on limits to arbitrage, see Gromb and Vayanos (2010); a large empirical literature documents cross-sectional variation in frictions such as short-selling costs, transaction costs and asymmetric information, arbitrage risk, and noise trader risk. These frictions lead certain stocks' aggregate demand curves to be more downward sloping and thus their prices more sensitive to sentiment-driven demand shifts. Second and perhaps more novel, Baker and Wurgler (2006) observe that sentiment should have relatively stronger effects on stocks that are hard or highly subjective to value properly. Both extremely high or low valuations on such stocks can be plausibly defended by sentimental investors, as befits their current sentiment.

The basic empirical prediction of all this is that sentiment may serve as a contrarian predictor of "high sentiment beta" portfolios. Again, as discussed above, contrarian predictability can arise from corrections in noise traders' own beliefs, consistent with the negative autocorrelations of changes in the sentiment indices, or eventual pressure from arbitrageurs, who become more aggressive as earnings realizations confirm mispricing. Baker and Wurgler (2006) find that sentiment indices predict the time-series of the cross-section of U.S. earnings announcement returns, consistent with an information-based mechanism.

Conveniently, several key stock portfolios are classifiable as either relatively easy to arbitrage and easy to value or as relatively hard to arbitrage and hard to value, making this prediction straightforward to test.[14] Examples of stock portfolios with high sentiment beta characteristics are small, high volatility, non-dividend paying, unprofitable, distressed, or extreme growth portfolios; their complement portfolios are lower, perhaps even negative sentiment beta.

An interesting subtlety is how to capture growth and distress characteristics using value or sales growth portfolios. Baker and Wurgler (2006) find that the effects of sentiment on these portfolios are roughly U-shaped. Very high book-to-market or very low (negative) sales growth can be associated with distress; very low book-to-market can be associated with extreme growth, as is very high sales growth. In other words, when sorting stocks along value or sales growth dimensions, high sentiment beta stocks commonly reside in the extreme high and low deciles where staid, low sentiment beta stocks are typically found in the middle. We account for this U-shape in our tests.[15]

Our cross-sectional portfolios are formed based on four firm or stock characteristics that are easy to gather for each market: firm size, total risk, book-to-market equity ratio, and sales growth. Returns and market capitalization are from Datastream. Book equity values (item WC05476) and annual sales (item WC05508) are from Worldscope. We exclude observations with negative book equity. Total risk is the volatility of monthly total returns over the prior year. Decile breakpoints vary by country-year. Returns are equal-weighted within each decile portfolio.

5.2. *Predicting the time-series of the cross-section*

Simple two-way sorts are presented in Table 6. We sort stocks across years according to whether the level of their total sentiment index is positive or negative. The basic predictions are borne out. The top volatility decile stocks earn 134 basis points per month lower returns when the year starts in a high-sentiment state, consistent with a correction of sentiment-driven overpricing. This return difference cumulates to 16.1 percentage points over the year. High-sentiment periods also portend 100 basis points per month lower returns on the smallest capitalization portfolio, another large effect. As hypothesized, the effect of sentiment is much smaller on low volatility stocks or large stocks, their being relatively easy to arbitrage and value.

As mentioned above, we predict a somewhat U-shaped effect of sentiment on book-to-market and sales growth portfolios. This is borne out to a greater extent in the sales growth than the book-to-market portfolios. In the sales growth portfolios, the bottom decile earns 69 less basis points per month coming out of high-sentiment periods, and the top decile earns 107 basis points less, whereas the differences in the middle deciles (12 and 18 basis points in portfolios five and six) are typically smaller. Cumulated over the year, the differences between the extreme and middle deciles are meaningful, though not as strong as the volatility and capitalization results. In unreported results, we exclude the United States and the results are similar.

Next, we move to time-series regressions to predict long-short portfolios. This provides a simpler setting in which to conduct hypothesis tests and also allows us to look at the separate effects of global and local sentiment. The basic regression models are:

$$R_{X_{it}=long,c,t} - R_{X_{it}=short,c,t} = a + dSENT^{Total}_{c,t-1} + u_{c,t}, \tag{12}$$

and

$$R_{X_{it}=long,c,t} - R_{X_{it}=short,c,t} = b + eSENT^{Global}_{t-1} + fSENT^{Local}_{c,t-1} + u_{c,t}. \tag{13}$$

Again, the significance tests incorporate month-clustered standard errors.

The total sentiment column in Table 7 is highly consistent with the results from the sorts. In five out of six hypothesis tests, the effect of total sentiment is statistically significant with the expected sign. The remaining long-short portfolio, which sorts on distress by using high value against medium value, is of the expected negative sign. The economic significance of the effects implied here is naturally similar to that from the sorts, with the effects for the volatility portfolios again

[14] Notably, momentum does not fall clearly in either set.

[15] Not accounting for this nonmonotonicity in sentiment beta may explain why some prior research found no clear connection between sentiment and value portfolios.

Table 6

Two-way sorts: Total sentiment and firm characteristics, 1981 to 2006. For each month, we form ten portfolios according to the total risk (σ), firm size (ME), book-to-market ratio (*BE/ME*), and sales growth (*GS*). We report equal-weighted portfolio returns over months where total sentiment ($SENT_c^{Total}$) from the previous yearend is higher than within-country median, lower than within-country median, and the difference between the two averages. The sample includes monthly country-level portfolio returns from 1981 to 2006 in the six countries.

	$SENT_{t-1}^{Total}$	Decile										Overall		
		1	**2**	**3**	**4**	**5**	**6**	**7**	**8**	**9**	**10**	**10-1**	**10-5**	**5-1**
σ	High	0.86	1.07	1.13	1.18	1.14	1.15	1.07	0.89	0.69	0.63	−0.23	−0.52	0.29
	Low	0.87	1.04	1.16	1.33	1.45	1.59	1.57	1.69	1.86	1.97	1.09	0.52	0.58
	Difference	−0.01	0.03	−0.03	−0.14	−0.30	−0.44	−0.50	−0.81	−1.17	−1.34	−1.32	−1.04	−0.29
ME	High	1.83	1.34	1.01	0.84	0.81	0.81	0.84	0.87	0.91	0.95	−0.88	0.15	−1.03
	Low	2.83	2.06	1.69	1.52	1.46	1.33	1.20	1.19	1.15	1.19	−1.64	−0.26	−1.37
	Difference	−1.00	−0.72	−0.69	−0.68	−0.65	−0.52	−0.36	−0.32	−0.24	−0.24	0.76	0.41	0.35
BE/ME	High	0.93	0.88	0.86	1.00	1.04	1.05	1.08	1.18	1.27	1.50	0.57	0.46	0.11
	Low	1.86	1.53	1.44	1.43	1.37	1.49	1.51	1.48	1.60	2.08	0.22	0.72	−0.50
	Difference	−0.93	−0.65	−0.58	−0.43	−0.32	−0.44	−0.43	−0.29	−0.33	−0.58	0.35	−0.26	0.61
GS	High	0.77	0.96	1.05	1.21	1.30	1.32	1.33	1.28	1.19	0.97	0.20	−0.33	0.53
	Low	1.45	1.33	1.39	1.37	1.41	1.50	1.63	1.61	1.77	2.03	0.58	0.62	−0.04
	Difference	−0.69	−0.36	−0.34	−0.16	−0.12	−0.18	−0.30	−0.33	−0.59	−1.07	−0.38	−0.95	0.57

Table 7

Time series regressions for cross-sectional returns, 1981–2006. Regressions of long-short equal-weighted portfolio returns on previous yearend $SENT_c^{Total}$ (in Eq. (1)), or on previous yearend $SENT^{Global}$ and previous yearend $SENT_c^{Local}$ (in Eq. (2)). The first column shows the results from Eq. (1), and the second and third columns show the results from Eq. (2). The sample includes monthly country-level portfolio returns from 1981 to 2006 in the six countries. The long-short portfolios are formed based on firm characteristics (*X*): firm size (*ME*), total risk (σ), book-to-market ratio (*BE/ME*), and sales growth (*GS*). High includes the top two deciles; low includes the bottom two deciles; medium includes the middle two deciles. Clustered *p*-values are in braces:

$$R_{X_{it}=long,c,t} - R_{X_{it}=short,c,t} = a + dSENT_{c,t-1}^{Total} + u_{c,t} \quad (1)$$

$$R_{X_{it}=long,c,t} - R_{X_{it}=short,c,t} = b + eSENT_{t-1}^{Global} + fSENT_{c,t-1}^{Local} + u_{c,t} \quad (2)$$

		$SENT_{c,t-1}^{Total}$			$SENT_{t-1}^{Global}$		$SENT_{c,t-1}^{Local}$		
		d	*p(d)*	R^2	*e*	*p(e)*	*f*	*p(f)*	R^2
Panel A: Size and risk									
σ	High-Low	−0.73	[0.00]	1.8%	−0.82	[0.00]	−0.27	[0.08]	2.4%
ME	SMB	−0.24	[0.05]	0.2%	−0.21	[0.04]	−0.17	[0.30]	0.3%
Panel B: Growth opportunities									
BE/ME	Low-Medium	−0.32	[0.00]	0.9%	−0.23	[0.03]	−0.20	[0.00]	0.8%
GS	High-Medium	−0.40	[0.00]	1.7%	−0.29	[0.03]	−0.25	[0.03]	1.5%
Panel C: Distress									
BE/ME	High-Medium	−0.03	[0.80]	0.0%	−0.09	[0.52]	0.03	[0.64]	0.1%
GS	Low-Medium	−0.20	[0.03]	0.5%	−0.13	[0.15]	−0.15	[0.09]	0.5%
Panel D: Size and risk, excluding U.S.									
σ	High-Low	−0.65	[0.00]	1.5%	−0.76	[0.00]	−0.25	[0.12]	2.3%
ME	SMB	−0.22	[0.04]	0.2%	−0.23	[0.05]	−0.12	[0.52]	0.3%
Panel E: Growth opportunities, excluding U.S.									
BE/ME	Low-Medium	−0.28	[0.00]	0.7%	−0.16	[0.13]	−0.23	[0.00]	0.7%
GS	High-Medium	−0.37	[0.01]	1.5%	−0.22	[0.17]	−0.28	[0.01]	1.4%
Panel F: Distress, excluding U.S.									
BE/ME	High-Medium	0.01	[0.89]	0.0%	−0.07	[0.58]	0.07	[0.24]	0.1%
GS	Low-Medium	−0.17	[0.05]	0.5%	−0.08	[0.35]	−0.16	[0.04]	0.5%

being largest. Sorting on volatility leads to particularly clear contrasts on both arbitrage risk and valuation ambiguity dimensions. Excluding the United States leads to similar results.

The influence of local sentiment is much more prominent in the cross-section. With the exception of the volatility portfolios, where global sentiment remains three times as important as local sentiment, local and global sentiment are roughly equally important. Also, local sentiment tends to be more statistically significant in specifications where global sentiment is not, at least in part, because it includes cross-sectional variation.

The greater effect of local sentiment on the cross-sectional results is intuitive. Global investors have less information on individual companies and face higher transaction costs. Many global investors are simply looking for diversification, and this is available at lowest cost through a market-tracking investment such as an index fund or Exchange-Traded Fund. More in a sentiment vein, local investors are more likely to act on rumors or develop unusual beliefs about specific local stocks. They also have a comparative trading cost advantage. All this, and given the very strong home bias (French and Poterba, 1991), leads to the prediction that local sentiment will have greater effects in the local cross-section.

We conducted but do not report various robustness exercises for the results in Tables 6 and 7. We find that controlling for the Fama and French (1993) factors tends to attenuate statistical significance but the qualitative results are similar. In a sense, this is not really a robustness test, because some attenuation is predicted under our hypotheses: for example, controlling for small and medium enterprises (SMBs) or market return minus risk-free return ($Rm-Rf$) amounts to controlling for effects that we predict and show in Tables 5 and 7, and reduces the variation in sentiment that is orthogonal to the independent variables. We also repeat exercises that we performed to investigate the robustness of the market-level preditability patterns: excluding Germany; excluding turnover from the sentiment proxy set; excluding the idiosyncratic volatility premium from the proxy set; using a total volatility premium rather than an idiosyncratic volatility premium; using an idiosyncratic volatility premium where idiosyncratic volatility is first orthogonalized to firm age. None of these variants made a noteworthy difference to the results.

6. Sentiment contagion

Our results suggest that both global and local sentiment affect stock prices. When global and local sentiment are high, future local stock returns are low, and particularly so for stocks predicted to have high sentiment betas. The local sentiment effects extend the evidence from the United States on sentiment and the cross-section of stock returns. The effect of global sentiment suggests a more novel mechanism: sentiment may be contagious.

There are two sources of contagion. One possibility is that investors in one country are optimistic (for example) about investment prospects in another and bid up the shares of that particular country. Using our measures, this will be captured by local sentiment. Local sentiment rises with the local volatility premium, the local number of IPOs, the local first-day return on IPOs, and the local rate of share turnover. These are local measures, but they reflect capital market activity, which in principle can come from foreign as well as local investors. The evidence in Klibanoff, Lamont, and Wizman (1998) and Hwang (2011), who examine the pricing of closed-end funds, is suggestive of this channel.

Another possibility is that investors in one country, say, e.g., the United States, are simply optimistic and this leads to a shift into risky assets more broadly, including international equities. United States sentiment will then affect prices in another target country, above and beyond local sentiment, provided that our measure of local sentiment is not absolutely complete, as it surely is not, and provided that there is a robust flow of private capital from the United States into the target.

To be specific, what we care about is the round-trip flow of capital, both from the United States to another country in our sample and back to the United States. Countries with high absolute flows, we hypothesize, will be subject to sentiment propagation. High U.S. sentiment will predict negative future returns to a greater extent if capital flows from the United States are high. Low U.S. sentiment will predict positive future returns to a greater extent if capital flows back to the United States are high. This pattern suggests using the interaction of the absolute value of flows with sentiment to predict future returns.

We test this hypothesis in Table 8. We regress future returns of long-short portfolios formed on size, volatility, growth, and distress in the five countries excluding the United States on lagged sentiment in the local country, as before. But we now include U.S. sentiment, and more interestingly, U.S. sentiment interacted with capital flows from the United States to each of the five other countries

$$R_{X_{it}=high,c,t} - R_{X_{it}=low,c,t} = a + bSENT_{c,t-1}^{Total} + cSENT_{US,t-1}^{Total} + d\left|Flow_{US\leftrightarrow c,t-1}\right| + eSENT_{US,t-1}^{Total}\left|Flow_{US\leftrightarrow c,t-1}\right| + u_{c,t}. \tag{14}$$

The data on capital flows come from the Treasury Bulletin and are normalized by the market value of the foreign stock market. In every case where the effect of sentiment of the local country is statistically significant, there is also a strong and conditional effect of U.S. sentiment. Provided the capital flows between the United States and Canada, to take an example, are high in absolute value, then U.S. sentiment has the same effect on hard to value and to arbitrage Canadian stocks as Canadian sentiment. The results are consistent with private capital flows being a mechanism that spreads sentiment across markets.

There are, of course, other mechanisms to spread sentiment. One is social influence, i.e., word-of-mouth sharing of positive investment experiences. Shiller (1984) discusses this mechanism, and Hirshleifer (2009) models how the bias toward sharing positive information leads to the spread of investing, particularly in volatile, hard to value stocks. Kaustia and Knüpfer (in press) show that high stock returns of local peers in Finland encourage additional stock market participation. Hong, Kubik, and Stein (2004) find that mutual fund managers in the same city exhibit common trading patterns. Brown, Ivkovic, Smith, and Weisbenner (2008) find that stock market participation depends on that of neighbors. Strictly speaking, this evidence pertains to the spread of sentiment

Table 8
Time series regressions for sentiment contagion, 1981–2006. The dependent variable is the long-short equal-weighted portfolio return from five countries: Canada, France, Germany, Japan, and the U.K. $|Flow_{US\leftrightarrow c,t-1}|$ is the absolute value of the normalized capital flow between U.S. and the other five countries. It is normalized by the market value of the foreign stock market. The long-short portfolios are formed based on firm characteristics (X): firm size (ME), total risk (σ), book-to-market ratio (BE/ME), and sales growth (GS). High includes the top two deciles; low includes the bottom two deciles; medium includes the middle two deciles. Clustered p-values are in braces.

$$R_{X_{it}=long,c,t}-R_{X_{it}=short,c,t}=a+bSENT^{Total}_{c,t-1}+cSENT^{Total}_{US,t-1}+d|Flow_{US\leftrightarrow c,t-1}|+eSENT^{Total}_{US,t-1}\times|Flow_{US\leftrightarrow c,t-1}|+u_t$$

		Constant	$SENT^{Total}_{c,t-1}$	$SENT^{Total}_{US,t-1}$	$\lvert Flow_{US\leftrightarrow c,t-1}\rvert$	$SENT^{Total}_{US,t-1}\times\lvert Flow_{US\leftrightarrow c,t-1}\rvert$	R^2
Panel A: Size and risk							
σ	High-Low	−0.38	−0.41	−0.07	0.06	**−0.45**	3.6%
		[0.31]	[0.03]	[0.86]	[0.01]	**[0.02]**	
ME	SMB	0.23	−0.20	0.24	0.58	**−0.40**	1.6%
		[0.37]	[0.30]	[0.24]	[0.01]	**[0.01]**	
Panel B: Growth opportunities							
BE/ME	Low-Medium	0.01	−0.30	0.29	0.11	**−0.18**	0.8%
		[0.95]	[0.01]	[0.07]	[0.34]	**[0.12]**	
GS	High-Medium	0.25	−0.29	0.11	−0.01	**−0.13**	1.5%
		[0.29]	[0.07]	[0.49]	[0.81]	**[0.09]**	
Panel C: Distress							
BE/ME	High-Medium	0.11	0.05	−0.20	0.17	**0.03**	0.6%
		[0.52]	[0.62]	[0.32]	[0.08]	**[0.76]**	
GS	Low-Medium	−0.21	−0.14	0.29	−0.02	**−0.19**	0.9%
		[0.11]	[0.11]	[0.01]	[0.80]	**[0.00]**	

within a geographic area. The effects tail off with the distance between actors.

Technology and mass-media can reduce the effects of distance and represent another distinct mechanism by which sentiment can spread, potentially across borders, in the absence of direct investment. Shiller (1984) discusses this as well. Tetlock (2007) shows a causal effect of business news on stock returns, for instance, and Antweiler and Frank (2004) try to connect them to the conversations of Internet chat rooms.

7. Conclusion

We summarize by reviewing the main contributions of the paper. The first is to construct practical indices of investor sentiment for six major stock markets and global markets as a whole; prior literature and available sentiment indices focus on the United States. Specifically, we construct sentiment indices for Canada, France, Germany, Japan, the United Kingdom, and the United States, and from these total sentiment indices we extract one global and six local, or country-specific, indices. Second, we connect these indices to Siamese twins' share prices, providing a degree of external validation that the existing sentiment literature does not.

The third and fourth contributions of the paper are to document that investor sentiment affects the time-series of international market-level returns as well as the time-series of the cross-section of international stock returns. We find that global sentiment is a statistically and economically significant contrarian predictor of market returns. Both global and local components of sentiment help to predict the time-series of the cross-section; namely, they predict the returns on high sentiment-beta portfolios such as those including high volatility stocks or stocks of small, distressed, and growth companies. Our paper appears to be the first to study the international time-series of the cross-section of stock returns, and the results indicate that the U.S. results of Baker and Wurgler (2006) extend to the international context. All of these results are directionally consistent with theoretical predictions.

Our fifth contribution is to investigate how global sentiment emerges and propagates. We find evidence that it emerges at least in part because sentiment is contagious across markets, and at least one of the mechanisms at play is international capital flows. Ours is a simple investigation of the contagion question; there is considerable scope for further research on investor sentiment within and across international markets.

References

Allen, F., Gorton, G., 1993. Churning bubbles. Review of Economic Studies 60, 813–836.

Ang, A., Bekaert, G., 2007. Stock return predictability: is it there? Review of Financial Studies 20, 651–707

Antweiler, W., Frank, M.Z., 2004. Is all that talk just noise? The information content of Internet stock message boards. Journal of Finance 59, 1259–1294.

Bagehot, W., 1873. Lombard Street: A Description of the Money Market. Henry S. King and Co., London.

Bali, T.G., Scherbina, A., Tang, Y., 2011. Unusual News Events and the Cross-section of Stock Returns. Unpublished working paper, City University of New York Baruch, University of California–Davis, and Fordham University.

Baker, M., Stein, J., 2004. Market liquidity as a sentiment indicator. Journal of Financial Markets 7, 271–299.

Baker, M., Wurgler, J., 2000. The equity share in new issues and aggregate stock returns. Journal of Finance 55, 2219–2257.

Baker, M., Wurgler, J., 2004. A catering theory of dividends. Journal of Finance 59, 1125–1165.

Baker, M., Wurgler, J., 2006. Investor sentiment and the cross-section of stock returns. Journal of Finance 61, 1645–1680.

Baker, M., Wurgler, J., 2007. Investor sentiment in the stock market. Journal of Economic Perspectives 21, 129–151.

Baker, M., Wurgler, J. Comovement and Predictability Relationships between Bonds and the Cross-section of Stocks. Review of Asset Pricing Studies. Forthcoming.
Bekaert, G., Baele, L., Inghelbrecht, K., 2010. The determinants of stock and bond return comovements. Review of Financial Studies 23, 2374–2428.
Bodie, Z., Kane, A., Marcus, A.J., 2008. Investments, eighth ed. McGraw-Hill/Irwin, New York.
Breeden, D.T., 1979. An intertemporal asset pricing model with stochastic consumption and investment opportunities. Journal of Financial Economics 7, 265–296.
Brown, G.W., Cliff, M.T., 2004. Investor sentiment and the near-term stock market. Journal of Empirical Finance 11, 1–27.
Brown, J., Ivković, Z., Smith, P., Weisbenner, S., 2008. Neighbors matter: causal community effects and stock market participation. Journal of Finance 63, 1509–1531.
Brown, S.J., Goetzmann, W.N., Hiraki, T., Shiraishi, N., Watanabe, M., 2005. Investor Sentiment in Japanese and U.S. Daily Mutual Fund Flows. Unpublished working paper, Kwansei Gakuin University, New York University, Rikkyo University, and Yale School of Business.
Campbell, J.Y., Shiller, R.J., 1988. The dividend-price ratio and expectations of future dividends and discount factors. Review of Financial Studies 1, 195–227.
Chan, L., Lakonishok, J., 1997. Institutional equity trading costs: NYSE versus Nasdaq. Journal of Finance 52, 713–735.
Chen, N., Roll, R., Ross, S.A., 1986. Economic forces and the stock market. Journal of Business 59, 383–403.
Cochrane, J.H., 2002. Stocks as Money: Convenience Yield and the Tech-stock Bubble. Unpublished working paper, University of Chicago.
De Jong, A., Rosenthal, L., Van Dijk, M.A., 2009. The risk and return of arbitrage in dual-listed companies. Review of Finance 13, 495–520.
De Long, B.J., Shleifer, A., Summers, L.H., Waldmann, R., 1990a. Noise trader risk in financial markets. Journal of Political Economy 98, 703–738.
De Long, B.J., Shleifer, A., Summers, L.H., Waldmann, R., 1990b. Positive feedback investment strategies and destabilizing rational speculation. Journal of Finance 45, 379–395.
Diether, K.B., 2008. Short Selling, Timing and Profitability. Unpublished working paper, The Ohio State University.
Fama, E.F., 1970. Efficient capital markets: a review of theory and empirical work. Journal of Finance 25, 383–417.
Fama, E.F., French, K.R., 1988. Dividend yields and expected stock returns. Journal of Financial Economics 22, 3–25.
Fama, E.F., French, K.R., 1989. Business conditions and expected returns on stocks and bonds. Journal of Financial Economics 25, 23–49.
Fama, E.F., French, K.R., 1993. Common risk factors in the returns on stocks and bonds. Journal of Financial Economics 33, 3–56.
Fama, E.F., Schwert, G.W., 1977. Asset returns and inflation. Journal of Financial Economics 5, 115–146.
French, K.R., Poterba, J.M., 1991. Investor diversification and international equity markets. American Economic Review 81, 222–226.
Froot, K.A., Dabora, E.M., 1999. How are stock prices affected by the location of trade? Journal of Financial Economics 53, 189–216
Ghosh, A., Constantinides, G.M., 2011. The Predictability of Returns with Regime Shifts in Consumption and Dividend Growth. Unpublished working paper, University of Chicago.
Glosten, L.R., Milgrom, P.R., 1985. Bid, ask and transaction prices in a specialist market with heterogeneously informed traders. Journal of Financial Economics 100, 14–71.
Glushkov, D., 2005. Sentiment Betas. Unpublished working paper, University of Texas, Austin.
Gromb, D., Vayanos, D., 2010. Limits of arbitrage: the state of the theory. Annual Review of Financial Economics 2, 251–275.
Harrison, J.M., Kreps, D., 1978. Speculative investor behavior in a stock market with heterogeneous expectations. Quarterly Journal of Economics 89, 323–336.
Henderson, B.J., Jegadeesh, N., Weisbach, M.S., 2006. World markets for raising new capital. Journal of Financial Economics 82, 63–101.
Hirshleifer, D., 2009. Self-enhancing Transmission Bias and Active Investing. Unpublished working paper, University of California, Irvine.
Ho, T., Stoll, H., 1980. On dealer markets under competition. Journal of Finance 35, 259–267.
Hong, H., Kubik, J.D., Stein, J.C., 2004. Social interaction and stock-market participation. Journal of Finance 59, 137–163.
Hwang, B., 2011. Country-specific sentiment and security prices. Journal of Financial Economics 100, 382–401.
Jog, V.M., Riding, A.L., 1987. Underpricing in Canadian IPOs. Financial Analysts Journal 43, 48–54.
Jog, V.M., Srivastava, A., 1994. Underpricing in Canadian IPOs, 1971–1992—an update. FINECO 4, 81–87.
Kaustia, M., Knüpfer, S. Peer performance and stock market entry. Journal of Financial Economics, doi:10.1016/j.jfineco.2011.01.010. In press.
Keim, D., Stambaugh, R.F., 1986. Predicting returns in the stock and bond markets. Journal of Financial Economics 17, 357–390.
Kim, W., Weisbach, M., 2008. Motivations for public equity offers. Journal of Financial Economics 87, 281–307.
Kindleberger, C.P., 1978. Manias, Panics, and Crashes: A History of Financial Crises. Basic Books, New York.
Klibanoff, P., Lamont, O., Wizman, T., 1998. Investor reaction to salient news in country closed-end funds. Journal of Finance 53, 673–699.
Koski, J.L., Rice, E., Tarhouni, A., 2008. Day Trading and Volatility: Evidence from Message Board Postings in 2002 vs. 1999. Unpublished working paper, University of Washington.
Kothari, S.P., Shanken, J.A., 1997. Book-to-market, dividend yield, and expected market returns: a time-series analysis. Journal of Financial Economics 44, 169–203.
Lamont, O., Thaler, R., 2003. Can the market add and subtract? Mispricing in tech stock carve-outs. Journal of Political Economy 111, 227–268.
Lemmon, M., Portniaguina, E., 2006. Consumer confidence and asset prices: some empirical evidence. Review of Financial Studies 19, 1499–1529.
Loughran, T., Ritter, J.R., Rydqvist, K., 1994. Initial public offerings: international insights. Pacific-Basin Finance Journal 2, 165–199.
Lowenstein, R., 2000. When Genius Failed: The Rise and Fall of Long-Term Capital Management. Random House, New York.
Mei, J., Scheinkman, J., Xiong, W., 2009. Speculative trading and stock prices: evidence from Chinese A-B share premia. Annals of Economics and Finance 10, 225–255.
Mitchell, M.L., Pulvino, T.C., Stafford, E., 2002. Limited arbitrage in equity markets. Journal of Finance 57, 551–584.
Ofek, E., Richardson, M., 2003. DotCom mania: the rise and fall of Internet stock prices. Journal of Finance 58, 1113–1137.
Pastor, L., Veronesi, P., 2003. Stock valuation and learning about profitability. Journal of Finance 58, 1749–1789.
Pontiff, J., 1996. Costly arbitrage: evidence from closed-end funds. Quarterly Journal of Economics 111, 1135–1151.
Qiu, L., Welch, I., 2004. Investor Sentiment Measures. Unpublished working paper, Brown University.
Ritter, J., 1991. The long-run performance of initial public offerings. Journal of Finance 46, 3–27.
Ritter, J., 1998. Initial public offerings. Contemporary Finance Digest 2, 5–30.
Roll, R., 1988. The international crash of October 1987. Financial Analysts Journal 44, 19–35.
Rosenthal, L., Young, C., 1990. The seemingly anomalous price behavior of Royal Dutch/Shell and Unilever N.V./PLC. Journal of Financial Economics 26, 123–141.
Santos, T., Veronesi, P., 2006. Labor income and predictable stock returns. Review of Financial Studies 19, 1–44.
Scheinkman, J., Xiong, W., 2003. Overconfidence and speculative bubbles. Journal of Political Economy 111, 1183–1219.
Shiller, R.J., 1984. Stock prices and social dynamics. Brookings Papers on Economic Activity 15, 457–510.
Shleifer, A., 2000. Inefficient Markets: An Introduction to Behavioral Finance. Oxford University Press, New York.
Shleifer, A., Vishny, R.W., 1997. The limits of arbitrage. Journal of Finance 52, 35–55.
Sias, R., 1996. Volatility and the institutional investor. Financial Analysts Journal 52, 13–20.
Smith, V., Suchanek, G., Williams, A., 1988. Bubbles, crashes, and endogenous expectations in experimental spot asset markets. Econometrica 56, 1119–1153.
Stambaugh, R.F., 1986. Bias in Regressions with Lagged Stochastic Regressors. Unpublished working paper, University of Chicago.
Stambaugh, R.F., Yu, J., Yuan, Y. The short of it: investor sentiment and anomalies. Journal of Financial Economics, doi:10.1016/j.jfineco.2011.12.001. In press.
Stigler, G.J., 1964. Public regulation of the securities markets. Journal of Business 37, 117–142.
Tetlock, P., 2007. Giving content to investor sentiment. Journal of Finance 62, 1139–1168.
Wurgler, J., Zhuravskaya, E., 2002. Does arbitrage flatten demand curves for stocks? Journal of Business 75, 583–608
Yu, J., Yuan, Y., 2011. Investor sentiment and the mean–variance relation. Journal of Financial Economics 100, 367–381.

[11]

THE JOURNAL OF FINANCE • VOL. LVI, NO. 4 • AUGUST 2001

Investor Psychology and Asset Pricing

DAVID HIRSHLEIFER*

ABSTRACT

The basic paradigm of asset pricing is in vibrant flux. The purely rational approach is being subsumed by a broader approach based upon the psychology of investors. In this approach, security expected returns are determined by both *risk* and *misvaluation*. This survey sketches a framework for understanding decision biases, evaluates the a priori arguments and the capital market evidence bearing on the importance of investor psychology for security prices, and reviews recent models.

The best plan is...to profit by the folly of others.
— Pliny the Elder, from John Bartlett, comp.
Familiar Quotations, 9th ed. 1901.

IN THE MUDDLED DAYS BEFORE THE RISE of modern finance, some otherwise-reputable economists, such as Adam Smith, Irving Fisher, John Maynard Keynes, and Harry Markowitz, thought that individual psychology affects prices.[1] What if the creators of asset-pricing theory had followed this thread? Picture a school of sociologists at the University of Chicago proposing the *Deficient Markets Hypothesis*: that prices inaccurately reflect all available information. A brilliant Stanford psychologist, call him Bill Blunte, invents the *Deranged Anticipation and Perception Model* (or *DAPM*), in which proxies for market misvaluation are used to predict security returns. Imagine the euphoria when researchers discovered that these mispricing proxies (such

* Hirshleifer is from the Fisher College of Business, The Ohio State University. This survey was written for presentation at the American Finance Association Annual Meetings in New Orleans, January, 2001. I especially thank the editor, George Constantinides, for valuable comments and suggestions. I also thank Franklin Allen, the discussant, Nicholas Barberis, Robert Bloomfield, Michael Brennan, Markus Brunnermeier, Joshua Coval, Kent Daniel, Ming Dong, Jack Hirshleifer, Harrison Hong, Soeren Hvidkjaer, Ravi Jagannathan, Narasimhan Jegadeesh, Andrew Karolyi, Charles Lee, Seongyeon Lim, Deborah Lucas, Rajnish Mehra, Norbert Schwarz, Jayanta Sen, Tyler Shumway, René Stulz, Avanidhar Subrahmanyam, Siew Hong Teoh, Sheridan Titman, Yue Wang, Ivo Welch, and participants of the Dice Finance Seminar at Ohio State University for very helpful discussions and comments.

[1] Smith analyzed how the "overweening conceit" of mankind caused labor to be underpriced in more enterprising pursuits. Young workers do not arbitrage away pay differentials because they are prone to overestimate their ability to succeed. Fisher wrote a book on money illusion; in *The Theory of Interest* ((1930), pp. 493–494) he argued that nominal interest rates systematically fail to adjust sufficiently for inflation, and explained savings behavior in relation to self-control, foresight, and habits. Keynes (1936) famously commented on animal spirits in stock markets. Markowitz (1952) proposed that people focus on gains and losses relative to reference points, and that this helps explain the pricing of insurance and lotteries.

as book/market, earnings/price, and past returns), and mood indicators such as amount of sunlight, turned out to be strong predictors of future returns. At this point, it would seem that the deficient markets hypothesis was the best-confirmed theory in the social sciences.

To be sure, dissatisfied practitioners would have complained that it is harder to actually make money than ivory tower theorists claim. One can even imagine some academic heretics documenting rapid short-term stock market responses to news arrival in event studies, and arguing that security return predictability results from rational premia for bearing risk. Would the old guard surrender easily? Not when they could appeal to intertemporal versions of the DAPM, in which mispricing is only corrected slowly. In such a setting, short-window event studies cannot uncover the market's inefficient response to new information. More generally, given the strong theoretical underpinnings of market inefficiency, the rebels would probably have an uphill fight.

This alternative history suggests that the traditional view that financial economists have had about the rationality of asset prices was not as inevitable as it may seem. Despite many empirical studies, scholarly viewpoints on the rationality of asset pricing have not converged. This is probably a result of strong prior beliefs on both sides. On one side, strong priors are reflected in the methodological claim that we should adhere to rational explanations unless the evidence compels rejection, and in the use of the term "risk premium" interchangeably with "mean return in excess of the risk-free rate." For those on the opposite side, risk often comes quite late in the list of possible explanations for return predictability.

Often advocates of one approach or the other have cast the first stone out the door of their own glass house. There is, in fact, a notable parallelism among objections to the two approaches, illustrated in corresponding fashion in Table I. (Lining up each objection with its counterpart does not imply parity in the *validity* of the arguments.)

This survey assesses the theory and evidence regarding investor psychology as a determinant of asset prices. This issue is at the heart of a grand debate in finance spanning the last two decades. In the last few years, financial economists have grown more receptive to imperfect rational explanations. Over time I believe that the purely rational paradigm will be subsumed by a broader psychological paradigm that includes full rationality as a significant special case.

Two superb recent presentations of the asset pricing field (Campbell (2000) and Cochrane (2000)) emphasize objective external sources of risk. As Campbell puts it (p. 1516), "... asset pricing is concerned with the sources of risk and the economic forces that determine the rewards for bearing risk." For Cochrane (p. 455), "The central task of financial economics is to figure out what are the real risks that drive asset prices and expected returns."

In contrast, I argue here that the central task of asset pricing is to examine how expected returns are related to *risk* and to *investor misvaluation*. Campbell's survey emphasizes the stability of the finance paradigm over the last two decades. I will argue that the basic paradigm of asset pricing is in vigorous and productive flux.

Table I

Common Objections to the Psychological Approach to Asset Pricing and Parallel Objections to the Fully Rational Approach

Objection to Psychological Approach	Objection to Fully Rational Approach
Alleged psychological biases are arbitrary.	Rationality in finance theory requires impossible powers of calculation.
Experiments that generate alleged psychological biases are not meaningful.	The evidence we possess does not support rational behavior.
It is too easy to go theory fishing for psychological biases to match data ex post.	It is too easy to go theory fishing for factor structures and market imperfections to match data ex post.
Rational traders should arbitrage away mispricing.	Irrational traders should arbitrage away efficient pricing.
Rational investors will make better decisions and get richer.	Irrational investors will bear more risk and get richer.
Confused investors will learn their way to good decisions.	Accurate investors will learn their way to bad decisions.
Apparent return predictability is spurious, so psychological models of predictability are misguided.	Apparent return predictability is spurious, so rational models of predictability are misguided.

Figure 1 illustrates static asset pricing (analogous to the CAPM) when investors misvalue assets and securities. Returns are increasing with risk (measured here by CAPM beta) and with current market undervaluation of the asset. There are several potential noisy proxies for the degree of underpricing, such as price-containing variables (e.g., book/market, market value, earnings/price), measures of public mood (e.g., the weather), or actions possibly taken to exploit mispricing (e.g., recent occurrence of a stock repurchase or insider purchases). Risk and mispricing effects do not necessarily take such a simple linearly separable form (see the models described in Section IV), but it is still useful to keep the two notions conceptually distinct.

This picture is only a starting point. Just as the static risk effects of the CAPM have been generalized to intertemporal asset pricing, so the dynamic behavior of mispricing must be accounted for as well. After decades of study, the sources of risk premia in purely rational dynamic models are well understood. In contrast, dynamic psychology-based asset-pricing theory is in its infancy.

In the remainder of the introduction, I discuss market forces that can maintain or eliminate mispricing, and why we cannot dismiss mispricing on conceptual grounds. Section I of the survey presents relevant psychological biases and argues that many of the important biases grow naturally from just a few deep roots. Section II summarizes evidence on capital market and investor behavior regarding the importance of risk and misvaluation effects. Section III presents asset-pricing theories based on imperfect rationality. Section IV concludes with further directions for research.

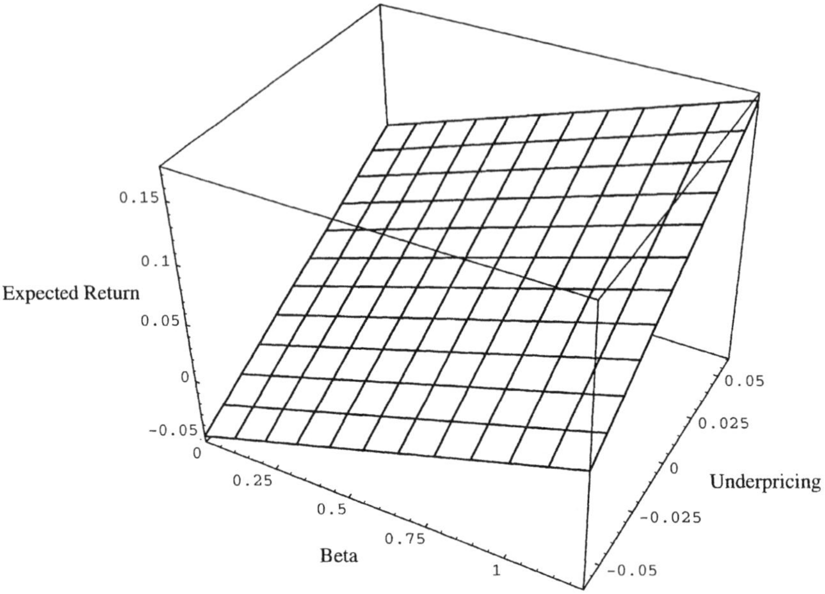

Figure 1. The Security Market Plane. Graph of security return against risk, as measured by beta, and underpricing (positive or negative).

To think about whether mispricing is viable, consider the traditional argument for rational price setting. In this account, smart traders spot dollar bills lying on the ground and grab them, which does away with mispricing. Setting aside the dynamics of wealth momentarily, the arbitrage story is incomplete in two ways. First, equilibrium prices reflect a weighted average of the beliefs of the rational and irrational traders.[2] So long as each group has significant risk-bearing capacity, both influence prices significantly. Arbitrage is a double-edged blade: Just as rational investors arbitrage away inefficient pricing, foolish traders arbitrage away efficient pricing. Second, in some respects, *all* investors may be imperfectly rational. Even in the Olympics, no one runs at the speed of light; some cognitive tasks are just too hard for any of us.

The traditional argument further asserts that wealth flows from foolish to wise investors. This point carries considerable weight. Suppose that some rational individuals are immune from bias, and that all markets are liquid. Suppose that terminal dividends obey a linear factor model with K systematic and N idiosyncratic payoff components (I will call these systematic and idiosyncratic "factors"). An irrational investor on average trades and loses on

[2] See, for example, Figlewski (1978), Shiller (1984), DeLong et al. (1990a), Campbell and Kyle (1993), and Shefrin and Statman (1994).

every factor that he misvalues. If the number of factors $N + K$ is large, and if a nontrivial fraction of them are substantially mispriced, then, on average, irrational investors lose a very large amount of money almost surely. Soon superior rationality will prevail.

Thus, as long as some investors are rational and markets are perfect, there can be substantial mispricing in only a small fraction of the $N + K$ factors. If $N \gg K$, then some or all of the systematic factors can be substantially mispriced, but only a small fraction of the N idiosyncratic components can be (see Daniel, Hirshleifer, and Subrahmanyam (2001a)).

On the other hand, people are likely to be more prone to bias in valuing securities for which information is sparse. This suggests that misperceptions are strongest in the dusty, idiosyncratic corners of the market place. One way to reconcile both intuitions is to recognize that there are biases that almost no one is immune to. In this case, there can be widespread idiosyncratic mispricing which only becomes apparent ex post.

Although misperceptions are probably most severe when information is sparse and arrives slowly, there is no reason to think that confusion is confined purely to idiosyncratic factors. Market timers trade based on what they perceive to be superior information about the market or about industry plays such as high-tech. Investors (whether wisely or not) purchase macroeconomic forecasts. So if investors sometimes misinterpret information, they will make systematic as well as idiosyncratic errors. Indeed, to the extent that misperceptions are conveyed through social processes, mistakes may be greatest for systematic factors along with a few well-known securities.

The fact that several empirical patterns of predictability are strongest in small (presumably less liquid) firms suggests that illiquid markets may be less efficient. This is less obvious than it sounds—the findings may result from the sparser information available about small, illiquid firms. Since arbitrage is double-edged, holding wealth constant, there is no presumption that liquidity immediately reduces mispricing. It does, however, speed the flow of wealth between smart and foolish traders, which may in the long run do so.[3]

It is often suggested that the expertise of hedge funds or investment banks will improve arbitrage enough to eliminate any significant mispricing. This works if foolish investors are wise enough to delegate to sound managers. However, intermediaries have incentives to serve or exploit the irrationalities of potential clients. It is not obvious that layering agency over folly improves decisions.[4] So misvaluation does not require that there be frictions

[3] Liquidity makes it easier for smart traders to arbitrage away mispricing, but also easier for foolish traders to arbitrage away efficient pricing. Barber and Odean (1999) find that traders who switch to online brokerages trade more aggressively yet subsequently perform poorly—their greater liquidity encouraged bad trades.

[4] Furthermore, regardless of whether there are intermediaries, it is exactly when a security or sector becomes more mispriced that smarter investors become poorer. This weakens rational arbitrage (and strengthens irrational anti-arbitrage) in an untimely way (Shleifer and Vishny (1997) and Kyle and Xiong (2000)).

or special impediments to fundraising by smart players. Such frictions, however, can slow the flow of wealth between smart and foolish smart traders, perhaps allowing mispricing to persist longer.

When substantial mispricing is limited to a few factors and residuals, less rational investors do not necessarily lose on average to wiser ones. Investors who underestimate risk take larger long positions in risky assets, and thereby achieve higher expected returns (DeLong et al. (1990a, 1991)). It could further be argued that trading pressure by irrational investors induces cross-sectional return predictability; that these investors thereby lose money; but that on average they make up their losses by bearing more aggregate market risk. However, if overconfident investors irrationally overbuy the market, this should result in a *low* expected return. This does not jibe well with the equity premium puzzle of Mehra and Prescott (1985).

There are other means by which imperfectly rational individuals can earn high expected returns. Overconfident investors who buy and sell aggressively in response to valid private information signals may exploit liquidity traders more profitably than rational investors (Hirshleifer and Luo (2001)). In an imperfectly competitive securities market, overconfident traders can benefit by intimidating competing informed traders (Kyle and Wang (1997)).[5] Overconfident individuals are also likely to overinvest in acquiring private information, at the expense of leisure.[6]

However, what evidence we have suggests that aggressively trading individual investors do badly.[7] Despite the ingenious explanations for profitable foolishness, it is quite plausible that, in fact, fools and their money are soon parted. Even if so, a misperception that derives from a fundamental human psychological trait can remain important for asset prices in the long term. There are two related reasons.

First, wealth is reshuffled in the process of generational succession. Second, in the process of getting rich, individuals can learn to be less rational. For example, biased self-attribution (Section I.B) causes individuals to attribute successes to their own qualities and failures to chance. As a result, losses by overconfident individuals can be offset by the rising confidence of the nouveau riche (see Daniel, Hirshleifer, and Subrahmanyam (1998) and Gervais and Odean (2001)).

It is challenging to find a source of risk to explain rationally the magnitude of cross-sectional predictability (see Section II). The challenge for the mispricing theory is to explain how irrational investors can remain important while hemorrhaging a great deal of cash. The disappearance of the size

[5] See also Benos (1998), Wang (1998), and Fischer and Verrecchia (1999)).

[6] Other means by which the imperfectly rational can do well or poorly have been described as well; see Blume and Easley (1982, 1990, 2000), Palomino (1996), Luo (1998), and Sandroni (2000).

[7] See Barber and Odean (1999, 2000a, 2000b) and Odean (1999). However, most of the theoretical models imply that only investors with moderate overconfidence will do well. The data may be picking up the poor performance of the extremely overconfident.

effect in the mid-1980s and the inconsistency of the value effect in the last few years is suggestive.[8]

There is a further problem. Having detected a return pattern statistically, it is hard for an investor to know whether *other* investors have yet detected and acted upon it. In 1984, how could an investor be sure whether other investors were overexploiting the size effect (Daniel and Titman (1999))? This uncertainty suggests that sometimes patterns of mispricing will be arbitraged away too slowly, and other times will overshoot. Conceivably the long life of the momentum effect has resulted from arbitrageurs each mistakenly fearing that others have started to trade aggressively. As Yogi Berra commented about a popular restaurant, "No one goes there any more because it's too crowded."

The other possible reason for persistent mispricing is that some relevant pieces of public information are ignored or misused by everyone. This can occur either because the signals are obscurely located or because our shared model of the world is just not sophisticated enough to make their relevance clear. A pricing error of this sort may disappear once a smart econometrician identifies it.

It is impossible to be comprehensive on a topic of this scope. Several important topics have been discussed in greater depth elsewhere.[9] My focus is on the psychology of imperfect rationality, not psychological determinants of rational risk aversion or time preference. My benchmark for comparison throughout is the traditional asset-pricing paradigm; I do not cover market imperfections, nor models of rational bubbles.

I. Judgment and Decision Biases

This section describes some psychological effects that are potentially relevant for securities markets, with hints at possible explanations based upon adaptiveness.[10] Economists have traditionally been skeptical of the varied array of seemingly arbitrary biases offered by experimental psychology. The empirical findings gain credence if we can understand what causes them. I argue here that these patterns generally derive from common roots.

[8] The U.S. small firm effect was strongly positive every year during 1974 to 1983, and then was negative for six out of the next seven years; the two closing years of the millennium, which followed the publication of an important paper on "...Good News for Value Stocks" (La Porta et al. (1997)) were the worst years for value stocks since 1928, though 2000 was better.

[9] I generally focus on asset market regularities involving a time horizon of at least a month, and do not consider seasonalities (for recent evidence see Hawawini, Keim, and Ziemba (2000)). Several surveys examine the equity premium puzzle in greater depth (see, e.g., Kocherlakota (1996), Campbell (1999, 2000), and Mehra and Prescott (2001)). Experiments in psychology and economics are surveyed in Camerer (1995, 1998), Bossaerts (2000), and Hertwig and Ortmann (2001).

[10] See also the surveys of Camerer (1995), DeBondt and Thaler (1995), Rabin (1998), and Shiller (1999). There are also important literatures that build "fast and frugal" heuristics based upon ex ante considerations (Gigerenzer, Todd, and ABC-Group (1999)), and that model the decision consequences of bounds on rationality (Conlisk (1996)).

Since time and cognitive resources are limited, we cannot analyze the data the environment provides us with optimally. Instead, natural selection has designed minds that implement rules-of-thumb ("algorithms," "heuristics," or "mental modules") selectively to a subset of cues (see Simon (1956)). Such heuristics are effective when applied to appropriate problems. But their inevitable biases can become flagrant when used outside their ideal domain of applicability.

Economists often argue that errors are independent across individuals, and therefore cancel out in equilibrium. However, people share similar heuristics, those that worked well in our evolutionary past. So on the whole, we should be subject to similar biases. Systematic biases (common to most people, and predictable based upon the nature of the decision problem) have been confirmed in a vast literature in experimental psychology.

There is much debate about exactly how good a job heuristics do. While psychologists such as Daniel Kahneman and Amos Tversky have made clear that heuristics can play a positive role, in the last decade, evolutionary (Darwinian) psychologists have strongly emphasized the adaptiveness of cognitive processes. In many cases biases diminish but do not vanish when probabilities are reexpressed as numerical frequencies,[11] and when problems are posed in visual formats. However, there is no guarantee that financial decision problems will be presented to individuals in a manner that favors the most accurate decisions.

The modern environment differs greatly from the prehistoric environment of evolutionary adaption for which human cognitive mechanisms were designed by natural selection. Modern humans deal with new abstractions such as securities, money, impersonal markets, probabilities, and government and with temptations such as easy access to fats and sugars, gambling casinos, and real-time Internet trading.

The general fact that cognitive resource constraints force the use of heuristics to make decisions I will call *heuristic simplification.* (For cognitive resource constraints, read limited attention, processing power, and memory.) A second source of bias arises indirectly from cognitive constraints. This is that natural selection probably did not design human minds solely to make good decisions. Trivers (1985, 1991) discusses evidence that people cannot perfectly control indicators of their true internal states. This creates selection for the ability to read subtle cues such as facial expression, eye contact, posture, tone of voice, and speech tempo to infer the mental states of other individuals. In Trivers' self-deception theory, individuals are designed to think they are better (smarter, stronger, better friends) than they really are. Truly believing this helps the individual fool others about these qualities. A third source of bias is that we are subject to emotions that can overpower reason. An evolutionary rationale for a lack of self-control is that emotions such as love and rage can act as mechanisms that allow credible commitment or

[11] See Tversky and Kahneman (1983), Gigerenzer (1991), Gigerenzer et al. (1996), Gigerenzer and Hoffrage (1995), Cosmides and Tooby (1996), and Kahneman and Tversky (1996).

threat toward potential allies and enemies (Hirshleifer (1987); see also Frank (1988), Nesse (2001)).

I argue that heuristic simplification, self-deception, and emotional loss of control provide a unified explanation for most known judgment and decision biases. This framework can provide guidance as to which biases identified in experiments represent general mechanisms, and which are conditional side-effects.[12]

Why don't people simply learn their way out of biased judgments? To some extent they do. One barrier is that learning is just too hard. The other barrier arises from self-deception. Individuals who think they are already competent may be slow to adjust their decision procedures (e.g., Einhorn and Hogarth (1978)).

Much of the evidence described here derives from experiments by economists and psychologists; their methods are somewhat different. Financial economists are familiar with criticisms of psychological experiments: that the stakes are low, that subjects have little experience with the experimental setting, that there is weak incentive to pay attention or tell the truth, and that publication depends on finding an effect. What may not be as familiar is that there is data addressing these issues. On the whole, training and increasing rewards and number of repetitions often reduces, but does not eliminate, biases. Lessons learned through repetition often do not carry over well across seemingly similar tasks. The well-known biases have been subjected to replication.[13] Many (though not all) of the cognitive biases are stronger for individuals with low cognitive ability or skills than for those with high ability or skills, consistent with biases being genuine errors (see Stanovich and West (2000)).

Subsections I.A and I.B consider individual biases organized by proposed causes (heuristic simplification and self-deception). Subsection I.C considers emotion and self-control, Subsection I.D discusses social interactions, and Subsection I.E discusses modeling alternatives to expected utility theory and to Bayesian updating.

A. *Heuristic Simplification*

A.1. *Attention / Memory / Ease-of-Processing Effects*

Limited attention, memory, and processing capacities force a focus on subsets of available information. Unconscious associations also create selective focus. In many studies, priming subjects with (possibly irrelevant) verbal information triggers associations that influence judgments (see, e.g., Gilovich (1981) and Higgins (1996)).

[12] Explanations based upon cognitive adaptiveness are subject to the objection that it is too easy to come up with "just-so" stories that fit the data ex post. However, my goal here is not to make the case that the evidence supports the adaptiveness approach (see Barkow, Cosmides, and Tooby (1992)). Rather, my point is that it is hard to make sense out of biases without a conceptual framework. Adaptiveness is about the only one we have.

[13] See, for example, Camerer (1995), Rabin (1998), and Hertwig and Ortmann (2001).

Selective triggering of associations causes *salience and availability effects* (e.g., Kahneman and Tversky (1973)). An information signal is salient if it has characteristics (e.g., differing from the background or from a past state) that are good at hooking our attention or at creating associations that facilitate recall. In the *availability heuristic* (Tversky and Kahneman (1973)), items that are easier to recall are judged to be more common. This generally makes sense, since things that are more common are noticed or reported more often, making them easier to remember. Shiller (2000b) suggested that the ease with which regular Web users can think of examples relating to the Internet revolution encouraged the market boom of the late 1990s.

One reason people are influenced by the format of decision problems is that they cannot perfectly retrieve relevant information from memory (Tversky and Kahneman (1973) and Pennington and Hastie (1988)). People underweight the probabilities of contingencies that are not explicitly available for consideration (Fischhoff, Slovic, and Lichtenstein (1978)). This suggests a kind of overconfidence (see Subsection I.B), and apparent market overreaction when unforeseen contingencies do occur.

According to *self-perception theory* (see Bem (1972), p. 2), "Individuals come to know their own attitudes, emotions and internal states by inferring them from observations of their own behavior and circumstances in which they occur." The need to infer can result from memory loss or from simple lack of access to unconscious internal states. A tendency to form *habits* can be an optimal mechanism to address memory loss, reflecting an implicit self-perception that actions taken before probably had a good reason (Hirshleifer and Welch (2000)). Habits also economize on thinking. Habits, including the habitual adherence to self-imposed *rules* can also play a role in self-regulation strategies (e.g., consume only out of dividends, not principal; see Thaler and Shefrin (1981) and Shefrin and Statman (1984)).

The *halo effect* causes someone who likes one outstanding characteristic of an individual to extend this favorable evaluation to the individual's other characteristics (Nisbett and Wilson (1977a)). An analogous misattribution bias could potentially cause stock market mispricing. In an efficient market, a stock being good in terms of growth prospects says nothing about its prospects for future risk-adjusted returns (which are on average zero). If people mistakenly extend their favorable evaluation of a stock's earnings prospects to its return prospects, growth stocks will be overpriced (see Lakonishok, Shleifer, and Vishny (1994) and Shefrin and Statman (1995)).

There are ease-of-processing effects analogous to the effects of ease of retrieval. For example, *the illusion of truth* is the finding that people are more inclined to accept the truth of a statement that is easy to process (see, e.g., Reber and Schwarz (1999)). Familiar signal combinations (e.g., yellow with banana) are easier to perceive than unfamiliar ones (Bruner, Postman, and Rodrigues (1951)). There is a strong and robust *mere exposure effect* in which exposure to an unreinforced stimulus tends to make people like it more (see, e.g., Bornstein and D'Agostino (1992) and Moreland and Beach (1992)). The basis for this heuristic may be that what is familiar, being understood better, is often less risky. However, this can be taken too far, as when people prefer to bet on a matter about which they know more than another equivalent gamble (Heath and Tversky (1991)). People also like similarity in choice of friends and mates (Berscheid and Reis (1998)). According to evolutionary psychology, people prefer familiar and similar individuals because these were indicators of genetic relatedness (e.g., Trivers (1985)). These biases suggest a tendency to prefer local investments (see also Huberman (1999)).

A literature in psychology has examined how subjects learn by observation over time to predict a variable that is stochastically related to multiple cues (see, e.g., Kruschke and Johansen (1999)). A pervasive finding is that animals and people do not achieve correct understanding of the correlation structure. Instead, *cue competition* occurs: salient cues weaken the effects of less salient ones, and the presence of irrelevant cues causes subjects to use relevant cues and base rates (unconditional frequencies) less. There is also learned utilization of irrelevant cues. Cue competition raises interesting questions about how information flooding through the Internet will affect misvaluation.

The learned usage of irrelevant cues comes close to *magical thinking*, the belief in relations between causally unrelated actions or events (as with astrology and other superstitions). A type of magical thinking called the *illusion of control* consists of the belief that a person can favorably influence unrelated chance events. A possible example is that people value lottery ticket numbers they select more than randomly assigned ones (Langer (1975)).

A.2. Narrow Framing/Mental Accounting/Reference Effects

Narrow framing (see Kahneman and Lovallo (1993) and Read, Loewenstein, and Rabin (1999)) involves analyzing problems in too isolated a fashion. This makes excellent sense when time and cognitive resources are limited. Many problems can be compartmentalized safely. An implication is that the form of presentation of logically identical decision problems, such as the highlighting of a different reference for comparison of outcomes can have large *framing effects* on choices (Tversky and Kahneman (1981, 1986)). Optimizing with respect to a problem-specific *reference point*, and having a direct preference over deviations (instead of over total consumption) economizes on thinking. *Money illusion* is another documented example of sensitivity to irrelevant description features (Shafir, Diamond, and Tversky (1997)).

By using different presentations or procedures, experimenters can elicit *preference reversals*. Faced with a choice between a binary lottery with a high probability but relatively low maximum payoff, versus another with lower probability and higher maximum payoff, subjects often tend to prefer the high probability lottery, yet place a higher valuation on the high-maximum-payoff lottery![14] There are also *context effects* in which the presence of a nonselected choice alternative affects which alternative is selected.

[14] Lichtenstein and Slovic (1971), Grether and Plott (1979), and Tversky, Slovic, and Kahneman (1990).

Mental accounting (Thaler (1985)) is a kind of narrow framing that involves keeping track of gains and losses related to decisions in separate mental accounts, and to reexamine each account only intermittently when action relevant. Mental accounting may explain the *disposition effect* (Shefrin and Statman (1985)), an excessive propensity to hold on to securities that have declined in value and to sell winners. Having observation of gains and losses trigger pleasant or unpleasant feelings seems a sensible mental design to motivate profitable actions. Such a mechanism may, however, be sidetracked when the individual avoids *recognizing* losses. Self-deception theory reinforces this argument, because a loss is an indicator of low decision ability, and a self-deceiver maintains self-esteem by avoiding recognition of such indicators.

Related arguments can explain the *house money effect* (Thaler and Johnson (1990))—a greater willingness to gamble with money that was recently won. The unpleasantness of a loss of recently won money may be diluted by aggregating it with the earlier gain.

Anchoring (Tversky and Kahneman (1974)) is the phenomenon that people tend to be unduly influenced in their assessment of some quantity by arbitrary quantities mentioned in the statement of the problem, even when the quantities are clearly uninformative. Some recent authors offer and test possible explanations in which the process of evaluating the anchor makes anchor-consistent arguments more accessible.[15]

According to expected utility theory, utility derives solely from the probability distribution of payoffs resulting from a choice. However, people seem to be *regret averse* in their choices (e.g., Josephs et al. (1996) and Ritov (1996)). They seem to be concerned not just that a choice may lead to low consumption, but that consumption may be *lower than the outcome provided by an alternative choice*.

An efficient heuristic method of comparing decision alternatives may be to line up and compare possible outcomes by state of the world (rather than evaluating the expected utility of each alternative separately and then comparing). Thus, having feelings be triggered by comparison of outcomes may be an effective mechanism for motivating good choices. Regret avoidance may also reflect a self-deception mechanism designed to protect self-esteem about decision-making ability (Josephs et al. (1996)).

Regret is stronger for decisions that involve action rather than passivity (Kahneman and Tversky (1982)), an effect sometimes called the *omission bias* (Ritov and Baron (1990)). Regret aversion can explain the *endowment effect*, a preference for people to hold on to what they have rather than exchange for a better alternative, as with the refusal of individuals to swap a lottery ticket for an equivalent one plus cash.[16] The *status quo bias* (Samuelson and Zeckhauser (1988)) involves preferring the choice designated as the default or status quo among a list of alternatives.

[15] Chapman and Johnson (1999) and Mussweiler and Strack (1999).

[16] See Knez, Smith, and Williams (1985), Kahneman, Knetsch, and Thaler (1991), and Bar-Hillel and Neter (1996).

Loss aversion is the phenomenon that people tend to be averse even to very small risks relative to a reference point, suggesting a kink in the utility function. This may result from the cognitive efficiency of mentally discretizing continuous variables, as reflected in the use of terms like "gain," "break even," and "loss," which make the distinction between a gain and loss more salient.

A.3. The Representativeness Heuristic

The *representativeness heuristic* (Kahneman and Tversky (1973), Tversky and Kahneman (1974), and Grether (1980)) involves assessing the probability of a state of the world based on the degree to which the evidence is perceived as similar to or typical of the state of the world. Similarity can be viewed as an indicator of the conditional probability of the evidence given the state of the world versus other states. However, a Bayesian also takes into account heavily the prior probability of the outcomes, whereas people tend to underweight statements about unconditional population frequencies in performing conditional updating—*base-rate underweighting*. Furthermore, people's perceptions of how "representative" a piece of evidence is of a state of the world may match its conditional probability poorly. For example, people tend to rely too heavily on small samples (the "law of small numbers") and rely too little on large samples, inadequately discount for the regression phenomenon, and discount inadequately for selection bias in the generation or reporting of evidence.[17] Representativeness effects have been detected in experimental markets (see Camerer (1995), Section II.C.4.)

The idea that a sample should resemble the population is often correct, especially in a large unbiased independent sample. The preceding errors amount to applying an inference too weakly within its realm of validity (large sample size) and too strongly beyond its realm of validity (small sample size). This is a natural consequence of the trade-offs involved with the design of an efficient heuristic. The resulting errors are not random: here, the error is predictable based on the sample size. The law of small numbers suggests that newly popular theories about the market drawn from recent investment experience may cause overreaction.

Misunderstanding of how randomness works can also cause a phenomenon of *gambler's fallacy*. This is the belief that, in an independent sample, the recent occurrence of one outcome increases the odds that the next outcome will differ. In fact, people avoid betting on a lottery number that was a winner sometime over the preceding few days (Clotfelter and Cook (1993)).

On the other hand, use of the representativeness heuristic can cause trend chasing, because people are too ready to believe that trends have systematic causes. Statisticians refer to the *clustering illusion*, wherein people perceive random clusters as reflecting a causal pattern. People mistakenly believe in

[17] See, for example, Tversky and Kahneman (1971); Kahneman and Tversky (1973); Nisbett and Ross (1980), Ch. 4, and references therein; Griffin and Tversky (1992); and Brenner, Koehler, and Tversky (1996b).

"hot hands" among sports players even when actual performance is very close to serially independent (Gilovich, Vallone, and Tversky (1985)). In an experimental market, consistent with gambler's fallacy, Andreassen and Kraus (1990) find that when exogenous prices fluctuate modestly, subjects buy on dips and sell on rises. However, when a trend appears, subjects do less of this tracking and possibly switch to chasing trends. There is further evidence from experiments and from surveys that real estate and stock market investors extrapolate trends in forecasting price movements.[18]

A.4. Belief Updating: Combining Effects

Edwards (1968) identified the phenomenon of *conservatism*, that under appropriate circumstances individuals do not change their beliefs as much as would a rational Bayesian in the face of new evidence. The more useful the evidence, the greater the shortfall between actual updating and rational updating.

Having a framework for assessing biases can help when they seem to conflict. For example, conservatism implies underweighting of new evidence. Yet, if we view prior beliefs as a base rate, conservatism would seem to contradict base-rate underweighting. Perhaps conservatism is a consequence of anchoring upon an initial probability estimate. Yet, the representativeness heuristic predicts that people will extrapolate *too strongly* from patterns in small samples, and salience bias also causes people to overreact to certain kinds of information. Which bias do we believe?

To resolve conflicts like this requires a focus on underlying causes, and how they will operate in a particular setting. For example, self-deception can cause conservatism in a stable environment, because an individual who has explicitly adopted a belief may be reluctant to admit to himself that he made a mistake. On the other hand, if the environment is volatile, there may be no dishonor in recognizing that different beliefs are called for.

One explanation for conservatism is that processing new information and updating beliefs is costly. There is evidence that information that is presented in a cognitively costly form is weighed less: information that is abstract and statistical, such as sample size and probabilistic base-rate information. Furthermore, people may overreact to information that is easily processed, that is, scenarios and concrete examples.

The costly-processing argument can be extended to explain base-rate underweighting. If an individual underweights new information received about population frequencies (base rates), then base rate underweighting is really a form of conservatism. Indeed, base rates are underweighted less when they are presented in more salient form or in a fashion which emphasizes their causal relation to the decision problem (see Koehler (1996)). This costly-processing-of-new-information argument does not suggest that an individual will underweight his preexisting internalized prior belief. On the other hand,

[18] See Shiller (1988), Case and Shiller (1990), and DeBondt (1993).

if base-rate underweighting is a consequence of the use of the representativeness heuristic, there *should* be underweighting of priors.

Griffin and Tversky (1992) suggest that base-rate underweighting and conservatism, interpreted as under- versus overreaction to signals, can be understood as results of excessive reliance on the *strength* of information signals and underreliance on the *weight* of information signals. The strength of an information realization is how "extreme" the evidence is (in some sense) and the weight of evidence is its reliability or precision. For example, a large sample of conditionally i.i.d. signals has high weight. But if the preponderance of favorable over unfavorable signals is modest, it has low strength. Conservatism arises when people rely too little on high-weight evidence such as a long sample, and base-rate neglect when people rely too heavily on high-strength evidence such as a few signals all in one direction.

In summary, different experimental settings can lead to under- or overreliance on new signals; people seem to make judgments differently in different situations (see Grether (1992) and Payne, Bettman, and Johnson (1992)). Given the different possible effects, invoking the name of a bias does not provide compelling support for assuming under- or overreaction in a financial model. Further support can be provided by comparing the economic decision environment of the model with the specific experimental decision setting in which the bias was documented, and especially by running new experiments that match closely the decision environment in the financial model.

Most studies of price forecasts find bias that is predictable using current observables. For example, forecasts are often found to be adaptive, that is, they respond partially to past forecast errors.[19] Such biases are potentially consistent either with Bayesian learning with an unknown distribution or with overconfidence. Experimental studies involving a fixed distribution generally also yield biases, and forecasts are adaptive in most forecast experiments involving endogenously determined prices as well (see Camerer (1995), Section II.E). Consistent with overconfidence, forecasters seem to put too little weight on the known forecasts of other forecasters (Batchelor and Dua (1992)).

Analyst forecasts of earnings are overoptimistic at long time horizons and pessimistic at short horizons (e.g., Richardson, Teoh, and Wysocki (1999)). Such biases may come from misperceptions or from agency incentives. However, we would normally expect rational agents to provide at least a positive incremental value in their forecasting activities. There is conflicting evidence as to whether stock market analysts' forecasts of earnings do better or worse than a time-series forecast (see the review of Kothari (2000)). A large literature shows that real-world decision makers such as Ph.D. admission committees or doctors do not predict outcomes as well as mechanical decision rules based on simple linear combinations of objective input measures

[19] See the discussions in Lovell (1986) and Williams (1987), but see also Keane and Runkle (1990). There is a similar finding for survey forecasts of macroeconomic variables (e.g., Aggarwal, Mohanty, and Song (1995)).

(see Camerer (1991)). This suggests that the rise of arbitrage based upon modern statistical analysis in securities markets will indeed reduce mispricing.

B. Self-Deception

The self-deception theory implies *overconfidence*, a very well-documented bias (as reviewed, e.g., in Odean (1998b)).[20] An extensive literature on calibration shows that people believe their knowledge is more accurate than it really is.[21] For example, their predictions of probabilities of events are too extreme (too high relative to the true frequency when they think the event probably will occur, too low when they think it will not). The confidence intervals they provide for quantities are too narrow, for example, 98 percent confidence intervals contain the true quantity only 60 percent of the time (Alpert and Raiffa (1982)). Experts are well-calibrated in some contexts but not others (see Camerer (1995) pp. 592–593). Experts can be more prone to overconfidence than nonexperts when predictability is low and evidence is ambiguous (Griffin and Tversky (1992)). Overconfidence is greater for challenging judgment tasks, and individuals tend to be more overconfident when feedback on their information or decisions is deferred or inconclusive.[22]

Overconfidence is sometimes reversed for very easy items (Lichtenstein and Fischhoff (1977)).[23] Overconfidence implies *overoptimism* about the individual's ability to succeed in his endeavors. Such optimism has been found in a number of different settings (Miller and Ross (1975)). Men tend to be more overconfident than women, though the size of the difference depends on whether the task is perceived to be masculine or feminine.[24]

Since people fail more often than they expect to, rational learning over time would tend to eliminate overconfidence. So for self-deception to succeed, nature must provide mechanisms that bias the learning process. This is consistent with self-enhancing *biased self-attribution*. People tend to attribute good outcomes to their own abilities and bad outcomes to external

[20] Hirshleifer and Hirshleifer (2001) model equilibrium self-deception and observer inferences based upon Trivers' approach. Bernardo and Welch (2000) provide an alternative theory of overconfidence based upon group informational benefits.

[21] See, for example, Lichtenstein, Fischhoff, and Phillips (1982), Yates (1990), Keren (1991), and McClelland and Bolger (1994).

[22] Fischhoff et al. (1977), Einhorn (1980), Lichtenstein et al. (1982), Yates (1990), and Griffin and Tversky (1992).

[23] This is not surprising on mechanical grounds; in the extreme case of perfect decision accuracy, it is possible to be under- but not overconfident about accuracy. It has been suggested that apparent overconfidence could be an artifact of the choice of questions that are not a "representative sample of the knowledge domain" (e.g., Gigerenzer, Hoffrage, and Kleinbolting (1991)), but overconfidence remains when questions are randomly selected from the knowledge domain, and has been documented in many practical choice settings (Griffin and Tversky (1992), Brenner et al. (1996a), and Soll (1996)).

[24] Deaux and Emswiller (1974), Lenney (1977), and Lundeberg, Fox, and Puncochar (1994).

circumstances.[25] Overconfidence and biased self-attribution are static and dynamic counterparts; self-attribution causes individuals to learn to be overconfident rather than converging to an accurate self-assessment.

Self-deception also explains why there are *action-induced attitude changes* of the sort that motivate the theory of *cognitive dissonance*.[26] In one experiment, people who chose between two products downgraded their assessments of the one they did not pick. In another, women who had to exert greater effort to gain entry to a group subsequently liked the group more. In other experiments, people who were induced with mild incentives or by request to express opinions became more sympathetic to those opinions. A tendency to be excessively attached to activities for which one has expended resources, the *sunk cost effect*, has been confirmed in several contexts (Arkes and Blumer (1985)). The self-deception theory suggests that a tendency to adjust attitudes to match past actions is a mechanism designed to persuade the individual that he is a skillful decision maker (see also Nel, Helmreich, and Aronson (1969) and Steele and Liu (1983)).

Similar reasoning can explain *hindsight bias* (e.g., Hawkins and Hastie (1990))—it helps our self-esteem to think we "knew it all along"; and the phenomenon of *rationalization*—constructing a plausible ex post rationale for past choices helps an individual feel better about his decision competence. People are very ready to devise and apparently believe their explanations for alleged facts about the world as well as themselves.[27]

People tend to interpret ambiguous evidence in a fashion consistent with their own prior beliefs. They give careful scrutiny to inconsistent facts and explain them as due to luck or faulty data gathering (see Gilovich (1991) Chap. 4). This *confirmatory bias* can help maintain self-esteem, consistent with self-deception. Exposure to evidence should tend to cause rational Bayesians with differing beliefs to converge, whereas the attitudes of experimental subjects exposed to mixed evidence tend to become more polarized (e.g., Lord, Ross, and Lepper (1979) and Isenberg (1986)). Forsythe et al. (1992) find that individuals more subject to this confirmation bias lose money in an experimental market to those who are less subject to it. Confirmatory bias may cause some investors to stick to unsuccessful trading strategies, causing mispricing to persist.

Some general biases toward confirmation of hypotheses do not rely on self-deception. In evaluating hypotheses assigned by the experimenter about the relation of two kinds of variables (e.g., studying the night before an exam, and getting a good grade), a large literature finds that people put too much weight on confirming evidence. This involves focusing on cases in which

[25] Langer and Roth (1975), Miller and Ross (1975), Fischhoff (1982), and Taylor and Brown (1988).

[26] Festinger and Carlsmith (1959), Cooper and Fazio (1984), and Harmon-Jones and Mills (1999, Ch. 1).

[27] See, for example, Nisbett and Wilson (1977b), and Ross et al. (1977b), Gazzaniga (1988) pp. 12–14.

both study and a good grade occurred, and neglecting other information (cases in which one but not the other occurred).[28] It has been argued that such a bias is an efficient shortcut in many contexts (Klayman and Ha (1987)).

People are also biased toward *seeking* confirmatory information. In the famous Wason task experiments (Wason (1966)), subjects were asked to turn over cards to evaluate a hypothesis. They often turned over cards which potentially could provide instances consistent with the hypothesis, and often left unturned cards that could conclusively reject the hypothesis. A possible explanation is that positive cases are easier to process cognitively. There is evidence that people are more influenced by the information reflected in the occurrence of an event than the nonoccurrence.[29]

C. Emotions and Self-Control

Emotions probably play a role in such traditionally rational considerations as time and risk preference, and in most or all of the effects described earlier. I discuss some further aspects of emotion here.

C.1. Distaste for Ambiguity

Choices are influenced by the structure of gambles above and beyond the overall probability distribution of consumption outcomes that the gambles provide. The Ellsberg paradoxes (Ellsberg (1961)) suggested that people are *averse to ambiguity*, causing irrational choices. Ambiguity aversion has been confirmed in market experimental settings. It seems to reflect a more general tendency for emotions such as fear to affect risky choices (see Peters and Slovic (1996)). As suggested by Camerer (1995), ambiguity aversion may increase risk premia unduly when new financial markets are introduced, because of the layering of uncertainty about both the structure of the economic environment and about resulting outcomes. A possible explanation for ambiguity aversion is that the obvious absence of an identifiable parameter of the decision problem may often be associated with higher risk and the possibility of hostile manipulation. This justifies a focus on missing information, but such a heuristic can go astray when there is no hostile manipulation. In a related vein, the evidence of Heath and Tversky (1991) indicates that, holding probabilities constant, people prefer gambles that give them a sense of understanding or competence.

C.2. Mood, Feelings and Decisions

Risk aversion, regret aversion, and loss aversion may reflect a calculated avoidance of unpleasant future feelings. However, mood and emotions felt today affect people's perceptions of and choices with respect to risk (see, e.g.,

[28] See, for example, Jenkins and Ward (1965), Crocker (1982), and Fischhoff and Beyth-Marom (1983).

[29] For example, Newman, Wolff, and Hearst (1980), and Nisbett and Ross (1980).

Mann (1992)). For example, sales of State of Ohio lottery tickets were found to increase in the days following a football victory by Ohio State University (Arkes, Herren, and Isen (1988)). More generally, people who are in good moods are more optimistic in their choices and judgments than those in bad moods (see, e.g., Wright and Bower (1992)). Bad moods are associated with more detailed and critical strategies of evaluating information (Petty, Gleicher, and Baker (1991)). The influence of mood and emotion on purchase plans and the effects of advertising have been studied by marketing researchers as well.[30] Bodily sensations and cognitive experience (e.g., the ease and fluency of perception or recall) also affect the decision-making process (see, e.g., the survey of Schwarz and Skurnik (2001)).

Affective states (feelings or moods) contain information that individuals can use to draw inferences about the environment.[31] However, people often attribute arousal or feelings to the wrong source, leading to incorrect judgments or *misattribution biases* (see, e.g., Ross (1977)). For example, people feel happier on sunny days than on rainy days, but priming them by asking them about the weather affects their judgment of how happy they are (Schwarz and Clore (1983)). Mood states tend to affect relatively abstract judgments more than specific ones about which people have concrete information.[32] This suggests, for example, that if the weather in New York puts stock market traders in a bad mood, their pessimism may concern long-term market growth prospects rather than whether the Fed is going to lower interest rates next week.

C.3. Time Preference and Self-Control

The conventional representation of decisions over time has an additively separable utility function with exogenous, declining exponential weights. However, evidence from psychology suggests that discount rates change with circumstances. Deferring consumption involves self-control, and is therefore related to mood and feelings. There is evidence that discount rates are sometimes remarkably high, that gains are discounted more heavily than losses, that small magnitudes are discounted more heavily than large, that the framing of a choice as a delay versus an advance has a large effect on decisions, that time preference differs greatly in different decision domains (e.g., money versus health), and that visceral influences such as pain or hunger affect intertemporal choices.[33]

The exponential specification is time consistent. However, experimental studies suggest that people and nonhuman animals are *time-inconsistent*. Specifically, they tend to discount a deferral of consumption from date t to

[30] Cohen and Areni (1991), Erevelles (1998), and Mano (1999), and Barone, Miniard, and Romeo (2000).

[31] See for example, Wilson and Schooler (1991), and Clore, Schwarz, and Conway (1994).

[32] Clore et al. (1994) and Forgas (1995).

[33] See, for example, the discussions of Loewenstein and Prelec (1992), Loewenstein (1996, 2000), and Chapman (1998).

$t + 1$ more heavily as date t approaches, consistent, for example, with a hyperbolic form for discount rates.[34] This causes choice reversals even when no new information arrives. *Hyperbolic discounting* has been disputed.[35] Nevertheless, recent economic studies have applied time-inconsistent discounting to a wide range of issues including savings, liquidity premia, and the equity premium puzzle.[36]

D. Social Interactions

Financial economists have borrowed more from the psychology of the individual than from social psychology. Financial theorists have examined how information is transmitted by prices, volume, or corporate actions. However, person-to-person and media contagion of ideas and behavior also seems important. People tend to conform with the judgments and behaviors of others, as documented in the famous length-estimation experiments of Asch (1956). A meta-analysis of 133 related studies (Bond and Smith (1996)) confirmed the *conformity effect*, which is, however, history and culture dependent. There are rational informational reasons to learn by observing the actions of others.[37] However, a fully descriptive analysis will have to encompass imperfect rationality (see, e.g., Ellison and Fudenberg (1995)).

Conversation is critical in the contagion of popular ideas about financial markets, as emphasized by Shiller (2000a).[38] In a survey of individual investors, Shiller and Pound (1989) found that almost all of the investors who recently purchased a stock had their attention drawn to it through direct interpersonal communication. The influence of conversation on trading may arise from individuals' overconfidence about their ability to distinguish pertinent information from noise or propaganda; examples of large price movements triggered by Internet chat comes to mind.

As discussed by Shiller (1999), owing to limited attention, people tend to pay much more attention to ideas or facts that are reinforced by conversation, ritual, and symbols. In consequence, culture becomes an important determinant of behavior, and expression of ideas can be self-reinforcing. Kuran and Sunstein (1999) describe the process of belief formation as leading to "availability cascades," wherein an expressed perception is perceived to be more plausible as a consequence of its increased availability in public discourse.

[34] See Ainslie (1975), Thaler (1981), Loewenstein and Prelec (1992), and Kirby and Herrnstein (1995).

[35] See Mulligan (1996), Fernandez-Villaverde and Mukherji (2000), and Rubinstein (2000).

[36] See Laibson (1997), O'Donoghue and Rabin (1999), Luttmer and Mariotti (2000), and Harris and Laibson (2001).

[37] See, for example, Banerjee (1992) and Bikhchandani, Hirshleifer, and Welch (1992); on the possibility of informational cascades in securities markets, see Avery and Zemsky (1998) and Lee (1998).

[38] See the conversational learning models of Banerjee and Fudenberg (1999) and Cao and Hirshleifer (2000).

Conversation pools information surprisingly poorly. Groups of people tend to talk much more about information signals that they already share than individual-specific signals (Stasser, Taylor, and Hanna (1989)). As a result, groups sometimes fail to detect patterns that are discernable by combining individual-specific signals (Stasser and Titus (1985)). Environmental pressures such as crowding and unusual circumstances cause group members to experience "cognitive overload," and rigid thinking (adherence to habitual behaviors; see Argote, Turner, and Fichman (1988)).

When communicating information, people tend to *sharpen* and *level*, that is, emphasize what they construe to be the main point, and deemphasize qualifying details that might confuse this point. This is necessary for clarity given cognitive constraints (Anderson (1932) and Allport and Postman (1947)), but tends to cause listener beliefs to move to extremes. A closely related point is that causes tend to be oversimplified, distorting listener beliefs. There are also systematic message distortions related to a desire to be entertaining or to manipulate the listener (see Gilovich (1991), Chap. 6). These facts point to the need for analysis of conversation and rumors in securities markets.

The *fundamental attribution error* (Ross (1977)) is the tendency for individuals to underestimate the importance of external circumstances and overestimate the importance of disposition in determining the behavior of others. In a financial context, such a bias might cause observers of a repurchase to conclude that the CEO dislikes holding excess cash rather than that the CEO is responding to market undervaluation of the stock. This would suggest market underreaction to corporate events.

People mistakenly believe that others share their beliefs more than they really do, the *false consensus effect* (e.g., Ross, Green, and House (1977a); Welch (2000) reports a false consensus effect among financial economists about the equity premium). Self-deception may encourage this by making the individual reluctant to consider the possibility that he is making a deviant error. False consensus may also result from availability (since like-minded people tend to associate together). The *curse of knowledge* (Camerer, Loewenstein, and Weber (1989)) is a tendency to think that others who are less informed are more similar in their beliefs to the observer than they really are.

E. Modeling Alternatives to Expected Utility and to Bayesian Updating

Expected utility theory has dominated financial modeling because it captures rational decision making elegantly. However, the paradoxes of Allais (1953) and subsequent confirmations showed systematic violations of expected utility; people seem to be influenced by "irrelevant alternatives." Further violations have multiplied. Evidence of systematic preference reversals suggests that choice may not be well described by maximization of a utility function at all. A less radical departure from the traditional approaches is to consider alternative objectives (Camerer (1995, 1998) provides an in-depth treatment). Camerer discusses generalizations that involve functional forms on probability weightings and utility functions, in some cases explicitly derived from modified axioms of choice.

In *prospect theory* (Kahneman and Tversky (1979) and Tversky and Kahneman (1992)), individuals maximize a weighted sum of "values" (analogous to utilities), where the weights are functions of probabilities (instead of true probabilities). Extremely low probabilities are treated as impossibilities, and extremely high probabilities as certainties. In contrast, very (but not extremely) low probabilities are overestimated, and very (but not extremely) high probabilities are overestimated. For intermediate probabilities, the weighting function increases with a slope less than one. The value function is kinked at the "reference point" (loss aversion).[39] The value function is concave to the right of the reference point and convex to the left, reflecting risk aversion among gambles that involve only gains and risk seeking among gambles involving only losses.

The advantage of this approach is that it can capture many of the known patterns of individual choice under risk, as well as financial regularities (see, e.g., Camerer (1998) and Shiller (1999)). Indeed, Camerer (1998) argues that a form of prospect theory fits the data better than either expected utility theory or the other generalizations that have been proposed.

Several other generalizations of time-additively separable expected utility have been applied to asset pricing issues, especially the equity premium puzzle. Epstein and Zin (1989) developed a class of intertemporal utility functions that allow for nonadditivity and nonexpected utility behavior. *Priming* is a phenomenon in which exposure to a stimulus affects a subject's later response to further presentation of the same or a related stimulus. Evidence of priming effects does not tell us how people react to repeated consumption choices (self-administered stimuli of a sort), but is broadly suggestive that past consumption levels may influence how people respond to future consumption levels. Such dependence is reflected in habit formation preferences (Sundaresan (1989) and Constantinides (1990)), in which the utility derived from current consumption also depends on a habitual level of consumption.

Gilboa and Schmeidler (1995) offer a *case-based decision theory* which, unlike expected utility theory, is not based on evaluating outcomes and their probabilities. A case is a menu of decision options. Choices are evaluated based on outcomes of past choices and how similar those choices are to those in the current menu.

The evidence on heuristics and biases also suggests that Bayesian updating is not fully descriptive of human behavior. However, Bayes theorem is nonarbitrary, which is a useful discipline for modeling. Some recent models describe updating based on self-attribution bias and confirmatory bias.[40]

[39] First-order risk averse preferences (Epstein and Zin (1990)), like loss aversion, involve a utility function that depends on a reference point, and in which there is nontrivial aversion even to small risks. In the case of disappointment aversion (Gul (1991)), investors weigh outcomes that are worse than the certainty-equivalent outcome more heavily than favorable outcomes.

[40] See Daniel et al. (1998), Rabin and Schrag (1999), Rabin (2000), Gervais and Odean (2001), and Yariv (2001).

II. Evidence of Risk and Mispricing Effects

I classify the evidence bearing on asset mispricing into five categories: (1) return predictability; (2) the equity premium puzzle; (3) evidence as to whether firms take actions *in response* to mispricing; (4) whether firms take actions in order to *create* mispricing; and (5) evidence of investment errors.[41] My emphasis here is on findings that have received confirmation over time and location. However, such consistency is not a prerequisite for a pattern to be interesting. If widespread and fairly stable patterns of mispricing exist, then almost surely transient and situation-specific ones do too.

A. *Predictability of Security Returns*

Return predictability research is haunted by the specter of data mining. Some of the patterns described here are probably just vagaries of chance. However, predictability is a generic prediction of modern asset-pricing theories. So cautious skepticism rather than profound suspicion is called for.

Most of the patterns of return predictability summarized here have dual (and duelling) explanations based on either risk premia or mispricing. Empirical papers on predictability often interpret psychological explanations naively. Several authors interpret evidence that factor loadings or aggregate conditioning variables can capture predictability as counter to the psychological approach. But the psychological approach recognizes that investors should care about factor risk. To attribute a return pattern to *rational* factor pricing requires not just a finding that factors matter, but measurement of whether expected returns are commensurate with the relevant risks. Furthermore, the psychological approach predicts that factors, not just residuals, will be mispriced. The conditioning variables and the variables used to identify factors, such as aggregate dividend yield, the term premium, the default premium, book/market, and size, are very natural proxies for factor misvaluation, as will be discussed.

A.1. Predictability Based Upon Factor Risk Measures

I focus here on CAPM beta and the factor loadings of Fama and French (1993). A positive univariate relation of beta with expected returns is found in most studies, but depends on the country, time period, empirical implementation, and form of the CAPM being tested.[42] Beta has incremental

[41] This topic is vast; for recent reviews of different aspects of the evidence pertaining to mispricing, see Fama (1991, 1998), Kothari (2000), Daniel, Hirshleifer and Teoh (2001), and Lee (2001). I do not discuss actions by outsiders such as mutual funds to exploit predictability.

[42] See, for example, Black, Jensen, and Scholes (1972), Fama and MacBeth (1973), Solnik (1974), Harvey (1989), Fama and French (1992), Handa, Kothari, and Wasley (1993), Kothari, Shanken, and Sloan (1995), Kim (1997), Heston, Rouwenhorst, and Wessels (1999), Rouwenhorst (1999), Kothari and Shanken (2000), and Bossaerts (2000).

power to predict future returns after controlling for market value and/or fundamental/price ratios in some studies but not others.[43]

A.2. Predictability Based Upon Price and Benchmark Value Measures

A natural way to identify mispricing is to compare an asset's price to a related value measure. A remarkably consistent empirical pattern is that almost any such pairing that researchers try predicts future returns in the right direction—the "cheap" security on average appreciates relative to a risk-adjusted benchmark, or relative to an "expensive" security. Efficient market fans will conclude, however, that the security is cheap because it is riskier, and that the risk adjustment is misspecified.[44]

In several cases, the market value of a parent firm has been substantially less than one of its parts, and managers undertook transactions apparently suitable for exploiting the overpricing of a division.[45] Closed end funds often trade at discounts and premia relative to net asset value; these discounts predict future small stock returns.[46] Securities that are virtually perfect substitutes are sometimes traded at different prices by different clienteles (Rosenthal and Young (1990) and Froot and Dabora (1999)).

A short-term yield provides a value benchmark for a long-term bond. Discrepancies between long- and short-term yields positively predict the holding period returns on long-term bonds.[47] Bonds denominated in different currencies provide mutual benchmarks. Investing in a country's bonds that have recently become cheaper (higher nominal yield) relative to another country's bonds on average earns higher returns—the forward premium puzzle (see, e.g., Engel (1996)).

Stock benchmarks include fundamental measures such as book value, earnings, or even a constant (for the size effect). Cross-sectionally, equity-price-related variables (e.g., 1/price, book/market, earnings/price, debt/equity) predict high stock returns in the United States and many other countries, even after controlling for beta.[48] For the stock market as a whole, high fundamental/price ratios (dividend yield or book/market) predict future in-

[43] See, for example, Fama and French (1992, 1996a), Handa et al. (1993), Kothari et al. (1995), Jagannathan and Wang (1996), Kim (1997), Knez and Ready (1997), Heston et al. (1999), and Kothari and Shanken (2000).

[44] This insight has been applied to stocks by Ball (1978), Keim (1988), and Berk (1995).

[45] Schill and Zhou (1999), Cornell and Liu (2000), and Lamont and Thaler (2000).

[46] See Swaminathan (1996) and Neal and Wheatley (1998). Bodurtha, Kim, and Lee (1995) find that U.S. traded closed-end country fund premia and discounts are often large, and comove primarily because of their common sensitivity to the U.S. market. Country fund premia predict returns on U.S. size-ranked portfolios and fund stock returns.

[47] Shiller, Campbell, and Schoenholtz (1983), Mankiw and Summers (1984), Mankiw (1986), Fama and Bliss (1987), Campbell and Shiller (1991), Bekaert, Hodrick, and Marshall (1997b), and Cochrane (2000) Section 20.1.

[48] See, for example, Stattman (1980), Banz (1981), Basu (1983), Rosenberg, Reid, and Lanstein (1985), DeBondt and Thaler (1987), Bhandari (1988), Chan, Hamao, and Lakonishok (1991), Fama and French (1992, 1998), Davis (1994), Heston, Rouwenhorst, and Wessels (1995), Haugen and Baker (1996), Jagannathan, Kubota, and Takehara (1998), Rouwenhorst (1999), Davis, Fama, and French (2000), Hawawini and Keim (2000), and Daniel, Titman, and Wei (2001).

dex returns in the United States and internationally in several, though not all, studies.[49] A better predictor of cross-sectional and aggregate returns can be formed by normalizing price with earnings-based indices of fundamental value.[50] Market returns are also predictable based on term and default spreads.[51]

Size and value portfolios are associated with a factor or factors distinct from the stock market portfolio.[52] The loadings on three factors based on size, value, and the market predict the returns on portfolios sorted on various characteristics, but do not explain short-term momentum; a global two-factor model predicts international returns (Fama and French (1996b, 1998)).

Several studies report very high Sharpe ratios achievable based on cross-sectional value effects,[53] a point reinforced by low international correlations of some size and value strategies (Hawawini and Keim (1995)). This raises the question of whether the implied variability of marginal utility across states under rational asset pricing is implausibly high (see Hansen and Jagannathan (1991)). Chen (2000) finds that book/market and momentum-based portfolios do not contain enough information about future returns on aggregate wealth to be strongly priced as state variables in a Merton ICAPM.

Fama and French (1995) suggest that size and book/market factors may be correlated with harms suffered by individuals when firms are distressed. Differing conclusions have been drawn about the association of size and book/market with distress.[54] The book/market effect remains strong after controlling for distress (Griffin and Lemon (2001)). The voluntary allocation by employees of personal retirement funds into shares of their own firms (Benartzi (1997)) opposes the distress–risk hypothesis.

Conclusions differ as to whether "characteristics" (size, book/market) or factor loadings do a better job predicting returns.[55] Perhaps the most compelling evidence for expectational errors is that, after portfolios are formed, growth stocks on average respond very negatively to subsequent earnings announcements for several years, and value stocks do not (La Porta et al. (1997) and Skinner and Sloan (2000)).

[49] See Campbell and Shiller (1988a), Fama and French (1988a), Hodrick (1992), Pesaran and Timmermann (1995), Kothari and Shanken (1997), Pontiff and Schall (1998), Bossaerts and Hillion (1999), Goyal and Welch (1999), Lewellen and Shanken (2000), and Goetzmann, Ibbotson, and Peng (2001).

[50] See Abarbanell and Bushee (1998), Frankel and Lee (1998, 2001), Chang, Chen, and Dong (1999), and Lee, Myers, and Swaminathan (1999).

[51] See Keim and Stambaugh (1986), Campbell (1987), and Fama and French (1989).

[52] See Fama and French (1993, 1995), and Liew and Vassalou (2000). This of course does not guarantee that the loadings on these factors are priced separately from market beta; for example, under the CAPM they would not be.

[53] Brennan, Chordia, and Subrahmanyam (1998), Lakonishok et al. (1994), and MacKinlay (1995).

[54] Chan and Chen (1991), Shumway (1996), Chen and Zhang (1998), and Dichev (1998).

[55] See Daniel and Titman (1997), Jagannathan et al. (1998), Lewellen (1999), Davis et al. (2000), and Daniel et al. (2001).

A.3. Predictability Based Upon Past Returns: Momentum and Reversal

In many asset and security classes internationally, there is positive short-lag autocorrelation and negative long-lag autocorrelation.[56] Cross-sectionally, U.S., European, and emerging market stocks that have done very well in the recent past (about 3 to 12 months) tend to do well over the next month.[57] Long term reversals in the cross section are documented by DeBondt and Thaler (1985).[58] Momentum is stronger in small firms, growth firms, firms with low analyst following, and in the security-specific (nonmarket) component of stock returns.[59] Volume interacts with momentum in predicting future returns, suggesting a possible cycle of overreaction and correction (Lee and Swaminathan (2000b)). Chordia and Shivakumar (2000) report that momentum profits can be captured based on security sensitivities to a few aggregate variables (see also Ahn, Conrad, and Dittmar (2000)). Lewellen (2000) provides evidence of negative autocorrelation and cross-serial correlation in industry and size portfolios, consistent with negative market autocorrelation during the study's time period.[60]

Past winners earn substantially higher returns than do past losers at the dates of quarterly earnings announcements occurring in the seven months following portfolio formation.[61] This is surprising from a rational risk perspective, because high momentum firms should become less leveraged and *less* risky. Also, firms with extremely low returns over the several months are having trouble, so the distress factor view of value effects suggests that negative momentum firms should earn *high* future returns.

A.4. Predictability Based Upon Public Versus Private News Events

Several event studies have documented abnormal returns subsequent to the event date. One explanation, *event selection*, is that a firm's decision

[56] See Fama and French (1988b), Poterba and Summers (1988), Case and Shiller (1990), Cutler, Poterba, and Summers (1991), Gyourko and Keim (1992), Barkham and Geltner (1995), Richards (1997), Balvers, Wu, and Gilliland (2000), Chan, Hameed, and Tong (2000), and Ng and Fu (2000). On methodological and robustness issues for stocks, see Kim, Nelson, and Startz (1988), Richardson and Stock (1989), Jegadeesh (1991), Richardson and Smith (1994), and Carmel and Young (1997). There is also a literature on whether stock returns are excessively volatile relative to dividend variability (Shiller (1979, 1981), LeRoy and Porter (1981), Kleidon (1986), Marsh and Merton (1986), Campbell and Shiller (1988a, 1988b), and West (1988). This is equivalent to the issue of whether there is excessive long-run reversal in stock prices (see Cochrane (1991)), since any overreaction must increase volatility.

[57] Jegadeesh and Titman (1993), Rouwenhorst (1998, 1999).

[58] On methodological issues and the robustness of this finding, see Chan (1988), Ball and Kothari (1989), Chopra, Lakonishok, and Ritter (1992), and Ball, Kothari, and Shanken (1995).

[59] See Jegadeesh and Titman (1993), Daniel and Titman (1999), Grinblatt and Moskowitz (1999), Hong, Lim, and Stein (2000), and Grundy and Martin (2001). Both industry and non-industry components of momentum help predict future returns (Moskowitz and Grinblatt (1999) and Grundy and Martin (2001)).

[60] A given serial covariance structure is potentially subject to very different causal interpretations. Jegadeesh and Titman (1995) provide a decomposition that distinguishes factors from residuals, and therefore lends itself to a distinction between factor versus residual autocorrelation.

[61] Jegadeesh and Titman (1993); see also Chan, Jegadeesh, and Lakonishok (1996).

whether and when to engage in the event depends on whether there is market misvaluation. A second possibility, *manipulation*, is that around the time of the action, the firm reconfigures other information reported to investors in order to induce misvaluation.

There is evidence suggesting that both selection and manipulation occur. Regarding selection, a remarkable pattern emerges from studies of discretionary corporate events (actions chosen by management or other potentially informed parties). The average abnormal stock return in the three to five years subsequent to the event has the same sign as the event-date stock price reaction. I call this regularity *postevent return continuation*.[62]

The evidence that has appeared since this postevent return continuation hypothesis was proposed by Daniel et al. (1998) has generally been supportive over new time periods and events. There has been little study of postevent performance for events that are not taken at the discretion of management or analysts with incentives to react to mispricing. However, Cornett et al. (1998) find that there is postevent continuation when bank stocks issue equity, *except* when equity issuance is forced by reserve requirements.

Fama (1998) argues that these return patterns are sensitive to empirical methodology. Several recent studies have concluded that there is limited or no underperformance of new issue firms.[63] However, some recent methods minimize the power to detect misvaluation effects (Loughran and Ritter (2000)). Jegadeesh (1999) reports large post-SEO underperformance even relative to several (excessively) stringent return benchmarks.

The argument that post-IPO underperformance is eliminated by an appropriate benchmark is counterintuitive, because it amounts to saying that IPO firms have unusually *low* risk. Risk reduction may justify a low re-

[62] Events for which this has been found include stock splits (Grinblatt, Masulis, and Titman (1984), Ikenberry, Rankine, and Stice (1996), Desai and Jain (1997b), and Ikenberry and Ramnath (2000)); tender offer and open market repurchases (Lakonishok and Vermaelen (1990) and Ikenberry, Lakonishok, and Vermaelen (1995, 2000)); equity carveouts (Vijh (1999)); spinoffs (Cusatis, Miles, and Woolridge (1993) and Desai and Jain (1997a)); accounting write-offs (Bartov, Lindahl, and Ricks (1998)); analyst earnings forecast revisions (Chan et al. (1996) and Lin (2000a, 2000b)); analyst stock recommendations (Groth et al. (1979), Bjerring, Lakonishok, and Vermaelen (1983), Elton, Gruber, and Gultekin (1984), Womack (1996), Michaely and Womack (1999), Krische and Lee (2000), and Barber et al. (2001)); dividend initiations (Michaely, Thaler, and Womack (1995) and Boehme and Sorescu (2000)); dividend omissions (Michaely et al. (1995)); seasoned issues of debt (Spiess and Affleck-Graves (1999)); seasoned issues of common stock (Loughran and Ritter (1995), Spiess and Affleck-Graves (1995), Cornett et al. (1998), Teoh et al. (1998b), Jegadeesh (1999), Foerster and Karolyi (2000), but see Kang, Kim, and Stulz (1999)); public announcement of previous insider trades (Rozeff and Zaman (1988) and Seyhun (1988)); and venture capital share distributions (Gompers and Lerner (1998)). The hypothesis has not been tested for IPOs since we do not observe the price reaction to the announcement that an IPO will occur. The pattern does not hold for exchange listing (McConnell and Sanger (1987), Dharan and Ikenberry (1995), and Foerster and Karolyi (1999)) and private placements (Hertzel et al. (1999)), which may involve informed discretion on the part of the buying as well as the selling party.

[63] See Brav, Geczy, and Gompers (2000), Eckbo and Norli (2000), Eckbo, Masulis, and Norli (2000), Gompers and Lerner (2000), and Mitchell and Stafford (2000).

turn benchmark for SEO firms, but risk increases would seem to imply a higher benchmark after debt issues or bond rating downgrades, making the underperformance after these events[64] even stronger. Poor postdowngrade performance also opposes the distress-risk-factor theory of return predictability. New issue firms perform especially badly at subsequent earnings announcement dates, which is hard to interpret as a negative risk premium.[65]

Irrelevant, redundant, or old news affects security prices when presented saliently.[66] These demonstrable examples of mispricing suggest that less blatant mispricing may occur routinely. Little of stock price or orange juice futures price variability has been explained empirically by relevant public news.[67] Historical crashes and speculative episodes are often hard to explain in terms of fundamental news.[68] Allen (2001) provides examples suggesting that bubbles have major economic consequences, and argues that agency problems among financial institutions may cause bubbles.

Several studies explore fundamental trends and subsequent returns. Cash or earnings surprises are followed by positive abnormal returns in the short run, and perhaps negative abnormal returns in the long run.[69] Investors also seem to extrapolate fundamentals in options and in football betting markets (Avery and Chevalier (1999) and Poteshman (2001)).

A.5. Predictability Based Upon Mood Proxies

Environmental factors that influence mood are correlated with stock price movements. Kamstra, Kramer, and Levy (2000a) find that a deterministic variable, changes to and from daylight saving time, disrupts sleep patterns, and is related to stock returns.[70] A stochastic variable, cloud cover in the city of a country's major stock exchange, is associated with low daily stock index returns in a joint test of 26 national exchanges as well as in the United States (Hirshleifer and Shumway (2001) and Saunders (1993)).

[64] Spiess and Affleck-Graves (1999) and Dichev and Piotroski (2001).

[65] Jegadeesh (1999) and Denis and Sarin (2000); see also Ikenberry and Ramnath (2000).

[66] Ashton (1976), Ho and Michaely (1988), Hand (1990, 1991), Rau and Vermaelen (1998), Andrade (1999), Avery and Chevalier (1999), Klibanoff, Lamont, and Wizman (1999), Cooper, Dimitrov, and Rau (2000), Huberman and Regev (2001), and Rashes (2001).

[67] Roll (1984, 1988), Cutler, Poterba, and Summers (1989), and Fair (2000).

[68] See, for example, Cutler et al. (1989), Seyhun (1990), Shiller (2000b) Ch. 4; for a mainly rational perspective on the Dutch tulip bulb boom, see Garber (1989).

[69] On short run postearnings announcement drift, see, for example, Bernard and Thomas (1989, 1990). For poor long-lag performance, see DeBondt and Thaler (1987), Lakonishok et al. (1994), Lee and Swaminathan (2000a), but see also DeChow and Sloan (1997), and Daniel and Titman (2000).

[70] Kamstra, Kramer, and Levi (2000b) examine the relation of another deterministic variable, seasonal shifts in length of day, to returns in several countries.

B. Equity Premium and Risk-free Rate Puzzles

The equity premium puzzle[71] is that U.S. equity market returns are high relative to risk, implying high levels of risk aversion and so a low elasticity of intertemporal substitution in consumption. This in turn implies very high real interest rates to induce individuals to accept lower consumption now than in the future (consistent with historical growth in consumption; see Weil (1989)).

C. Actions Possibly Taken in Response to Mispricing

Corporations buy and sell shares in a way that is correlated with possible measures of market mispricing.[72] The amount of financing and repurchase varies widely over time in an industry-specific way. Merger bids, which often rely on equity financing, are also prone to booms and quiet periods by industry. New closed-end funds are started in those years when seasoned funds trade at small discounts or at premia relative to net asset value (Lee, Shleifer, and Thaler (1991)), and tend to be issued at a premium (plus commission) before reverting to a discount in the aftermarket (Peavy (1990)).

D. Actions Possibly Taken to Create Misvaluation

Firms sometimes make accounting adjustments (accruals) to boost their earnings relative to actual cash flow. These adjustments are publicly disclosed in firms' financial statements. When accruals are abnormally high, stocks on average subsequently experience poor return performance.[73] Managers boost accruals at the time of new IPO and seasoned equity issues (Teoh et al. (1998a, 1998b)). Greater earnings management in IPOs and in SEOs are associated with more optimistic errors in analyst earnings forecasts, and with more adverse subsequent long-run abnormal stock returns.[74]

Managers adjust earnings to meet threshold levels such as zero, past levels, and levels forecast by analysts (DeGeorge, Patel, and Zeckhauser (1999)). Possibly under the influence of management, stock analysts on average "walk down" their forecasts from overly optimistic levels at long horizons to pessimistic forecasts that firms are likely to beat by year-end (Richardson et al. (1999)).

[71] See Shiller (1982), Hansen and Singleton (1983), Mehra and Prescott (1985), and Hansen and Jagannathan (1991). Purely rational explanations have been offered based upon learning (Brennan and Xia (2001)), luck (Fama and French (2000)), selection bias in the focus of academic attention (Brown, Goetzmann, and Ross (1995)), borrowing constraints (e.g., Constantinides, Donaldson, and Mehra (2000)), and non-stock-market income shocks (e.g., Constantinides and Duffie (1996) and Heaton and Lucas (1996)).

[72] See, for example, Jindra (2000), D'Mello and Shrof (2000), and Dittmar (2000); Korajczyk, Lucas, and McDonald (1991) provide a possible rational explanation for this phenomenon.

[73] See Sloan (1997), Teoh, Welch, and Wong (1998a), Teoh et al. (1998b), and Chan, Jegadeesh, and Lakonishok (2000).

[74] See Teoh et al. (1998a, 1998b) and Teoh and Wong (2001).

E. Quality of Information Aggregation

In contrast with early classic work on experimental markets, the thrust of much experimental market research in the late 1980s and 1990s is that in only a slightly more complicated environment, information is not aggregated efficiently (see, e.g., the survey of Libby, Bloomfield, and Nelson (2001) and Sunder (1995)). Presumably this is because confounding effects make it harder for investors to disentangle the reasons behind the trades of others (see, e.g., Bloomfield (1996)).

F. Investor Behavior

Portfolio theory suggests that (apart from transaction costs) everyone should participate in all security markets. But even now, many investors neglect major asset classes. Nonparticipation may derive from salience bias, or from mere exposure (familiarity) effects. Investors are subject to a strong bias toward investing in stocks based in their home country and in their local region.[75] Employees invest heavily in their own firm's stock and perceive it to have low risk (Huberman (1999)). The degree to which they invest in their employer's stock does not predict the stock's future returns (Benartzi (1997)). There is also experimental evidence that investors sometimes fail to form efficient portfolios and violate two-fund separation.[76]

Several, though not all, studies of investor behavior in natural and experimental markets report evidence consistent with a disposition effect—a greater readiness to realize gains than losses.[77] Certain groups of investors change their behaviors in parallel ("herding"), in some cases engaging in momentum (or positive feedback) trading and in other cases in contrarian trading.[78] Similar behavior is not irrational per se, but some groups of investors do poorly.

People (especially males) seem to trade too aggressively, incurring higher transactions costs without higher returns.[79] Furthermore, traders in experimental markets do not place enough weight on the information and actions of others (Bloomfield, Libby, and Nelson (1999)). Both findings are consistent with overconfidence. In experimental markets, as in psychological ex-

[75] See, for example, Cooper and Kaplanis (1994), Tesar and Werner (1995), Kang and Stulz (1997), Coval and Moskowitz (1999), Huberman (1999), Lewis (1999), and Grinblatt and Keloharju (2001a).

[76] Kroll, Levy, and Rapoport (1988a, 1988b), Kroll and Levy (1992), and Bossaerts, Plott, and Zame (2000).

[77] See, for example, Shefrin and Statman (1985), Ferris, Haugen, and Makhija (1988), Odean (1998a), Weber and Camerer (2000), and Grinblatt and Keloharju (2001b); but see also Ranguelova (2000).

[78] See Lakonishok, Shleifer, and Vishny (1992), Grinblatt, Titman, and Wermers (1995), Choe, Kho, and Stulz (1999), Nofsinger and Sias (1999), Wermers (1999), and Grinblatt and Keloharju (2000).

[79] See Odean (1999) and Barber and Odean (2000a, 2000b).

periments, investors and prices are more prone to overreacting to unreliable than to reliable information.[80]

Investors not infrequently make flagrant errors, such as failing to exercise in-the-money options at expiration, and apparently failing to exploit arbitrage opportunities (Longstaff, Santa-Clara, and Schwartz (1999) and Rietz (1998)). In retirement fund contribution decisions, there is evidence that people are strongly subject to status quo bias, diversify naively by dividing their contributions evenly among the options offered, and appear to naively extrapolate past return performance.[81]

III. Asset-pricing Theories Based on Investor Psychology

A. *The Origins of Psychology-based Asset Pricing*

The evidence in the preceding section presents challenging puzzles to be explained. It is natural to consider whether failures of rationality explain these patterns. As mentioned in footnote 1, for many years, economists theorized without apology about the effects of imperfect rationality. Upon its ascendancy, there were critics of the fully rational paradigm. The most fully developed critiques and alternative approaches arose from the work of Herbert Simon and colleagues at Carnegie Mellon University, and from experimental psychologists such as Daniel Kahneman and Amos Tversky. Simon offered a theory of bounded rationality, in which limited calculating power and the complexity of decision problems prevent fully rational decisions. Simon (1955) proposed that instead individuals engage in "satisficing," the choice of solutions that are good enough. These ideas were further developed to explore organizational slack, the supoptimal use of resources by firms (see Cyert and March 1963).

Bounded rationality implies a need for simple heuristics for making decisions, suggesting that computational simulation of heuristic agents may be a fruitful line of inquiry for finance. The costliness of evaluating contingencies suggests that the market may undervalue complex securities, and that imperfect rationality affects the introduction and success of new securities. Simon also studied the optimal design of cognitive mechanisms given resource contraints. This design stance toward the human mind provides a way of thinking about the source of biases identified in psychological experimental studies.

The experimental psychology literature (see Section I) attempts to identify and describe heuristics and biases. Researchers from this intellectual lineage recognize that heuristics are designed to be adaptive, but the focus is on identifying the conditions that can cause heuristics to work poorly. The experimental psychology evidence has been applied more directly in finance

[80] See Bloomfield et al. (2000, 2001).

[81] See Benartzi (1997), Madrian and Shea (2000), and Benartzi and Thaler (2001).

than have general notions of bounded rationality, because a priori reasoning about the effects of cognitive design constraints remains speculative until empirically confirmed. However, as argued in Section I, the design stance remains important because it helps researchers evaluate alternative heuristics that are potentially consistent with the experimental findings.

The application of psychological evidence to problems in economics was led by Richard Thaler and colleagues starting in the 1980s. Psychological ideas relating to overreaction stimulated the collection of empirical evidence on stock price serial correlation and volatility (see Section II). The 1986 publication of Fischer Black's (1986) AFA presidential address on "Noise," and the 1987 stock market crash further increased academic interest in imperfectly rational trading.

Some pioneering analytic models captured imperfect rationality in asset markets by including mechanistic traders who either make pure noise trades, or positive feedback trades in which new purchases are an increasing function of past price moves.[82] This was an efficient way to illustrate some crucial insights about survival, arbitrage, and pricing. However, in full generality, the mechanistic modeling approach is very elastic. If noise trades can be arbitrarily correlated with other economic variables, *any* return pattern can be explained. The economic content of mechanistic trader models comes from the choice of assumptions on trades to reflect facts about psychology or trading. In the hope of being more accurately predictive, recent research has explicitly modeled how decision making occurs in a way that reflects psychological biases.

In a specific investment setting, it can be hard to judge which documented psychological bias is relevant. This creates an extra degree of freedom for model-mining not present in the purely rational approach. Thus, even more than for purely rational theories, a psychological theory becomes more persuasive if it explains a *range* of empirical patterns in different contexts, and generates new implications.

The next subsection starts with models of the simple statics of mispricing and correction. Models of dynamics follow in Subsection III.C. A static setting can address how risk and mispricing determine the cross section of expected returns. Mispricing proxies capture long-term misvaluation and correction. Models of dynamics can describe intertemporal patterns, such as a shift from underreacting to overreacting to a stream of news, or a pattern of overreacting and then overreacting even more. Thus, dynamic analyses can address patterns of short- versus long-term return autocorrelations. Subsection III.D discusses how to empirically distinguish psychology-based pricing theories.

B. Static Asset Pricing

I consider static models based upon either limited attention/participation, or overconfidence. Merton (1987) analyzed the cross section of security re-

[82] See Frankel and Froot (1986, 1990), Cutler et al. (1990), and DeLong et al. (1990a, 1990b).

turns in a static asset-pricing model with exogenous nonparticipation. Such nonparticipation can be viewed as reflecting limited attention, preference for the familiar, and salience effects. The key implication of the model is that neglected stocks earn abnormally high expected returns.

Some recent static analyses of psychology and security returns are based on investor overconfidence. Financial analysts and investors differ in their skill at acquiring information through means such as interviewing management, analyzing financial statements, and Internet chat. An investor who overestimates his ability to do so will underestimate his errors in forecasting value. Thus, as in Kyle and Wang (1997), in these models an overconfident investor overestimates the precision of his information signals.

Odean (1998b) studies the statics of overconfidence when there is a single risky security. When price-taking investors think the signal is more accurate than it really is, the market price overreacts to the signal. Eventually, when the true state of the world resolves, the price corrects. This pattern of overreaction and reversal causes excess price volatility, and negative long-run return autocorrelation.

Instead of a general tendency to overestimate signal precision, in Daniel et al. (1998), investors are only overconfident about private information signals. This reflects the notion that an investor's self-esteem is tied to his own ability to acquire useful information. Individuals receive a private signal, and subsequently update based on an inconclusive public signal. In the static version of the model, investor confidence is fixed. Managers may selectively undertake good news activities such as a stock split or repurchase at least partly in response to market undervaluation of the firm, and other activities such as new issue when the firm is overvalued.

Since investors overreact to private signals, returns on private information arrival dates tend to reverse. In contrast, for selective public events, the model implies postevent continuation of stock returns: selective events associated with positive (negative) average event-date reactions are also associated with positive (negative) average postevent long-run abnormal returns. Intuitively, when the firm (or another party) takes a public action in opposition to overconfident mispricing, the market corrects only partially in the short run.

In a model with multiple securities, Daniel et al. (2001a) provide an analog to the CAPM when investors are overconfident. Security terminal cash flows satisfy a linear factor model, and each investor observes signals about the factors and the idiosyncratic component of security payoffs. Risk-averse investors form what they perceive to be mean-variance efficient portfolios. Overconfident individuals trade with risk-averse arbitrageurs who form rational beliefs. A security's equilibrium expected return is linearly increasing in the security's beta with the market, and the security's current mispricing. Variables containing market price are proxies for the security's misvaluation. For example, a fundamental/price ratio such as book/market is driven down when favorable news drives a stock up. Since there is overreaction, this is when the stock is overvalued. Thus, a high fundamental/price ratio predicts high future returns. Aggregate value measures such as the market dividend yield or book/market positively predict future market returns.

A fundamental/price ratio (e.g., high book/market) tends to be high if either risk is high or if the market has overreacted to a highly adverse signal. In either case, price on average rises. Since high book/market reflects both mispricing and risk, whereas beta reflects only risk, book/market tends to be a better predictor of returns. These two sources of predictive power are unequal. Beta helps disentangle these cases, so beta and book/market are joint predictors of future returns.

However, when overconfidence becomes very strong, and if the proxy for the unconditional expected value (e.g., book value) is perfect, then the incremental ability of beta to predict future returns vanishes. The fundamental/price ratio dominates beta even though risk is priced. This is an extreme case, but it helps explain why empirical findings on the incremental effect of beta have been weak and inconsistent. The model also implies that in univariate regressions, beta should predict future returns. The model further describes the tradeoffs in constructing optimal price-related proxies for misvaluation.

Daniel, Hirshleifer, and Subrahmanyam (2001b) extend the Daniel et al. (2001a) model to examine regressions of future returns on both book/market and HML loadings (Subsection II.A.2). They find that in an imperfectly rational model, either characteristics (e.g., book/market) or covariances (e.g., HML loadings) can be stronger predictors of future returns.

C. Dynamic Asset Pricing

Static models provide simple generalizations of the insights of the CAPM that can encompass the effect of risk as well as mispricing. However, a static approach has no hope of capturing the distinction between short-term continuation and long-term reversals. In both static and dynamic models, long-run reversal occurs when there is an overreaction to an impulse such as the arrival of good news. In a dynamic setting, short-run positive autocorrelation is consistent with long-run reversal so long as the process of overreaction and correction is sufficiently smooth. Such smoothness implies that when an impulse sets price rising, it will probably rise some more; that on average the last up-move to the peak of the impulse response function is not followed by a precipitous drop; and when the price is falling, it tends to fall some more. In contrast, a long-lag autocorrelation tends to associate positive returns during the overreaction process with negative returns arising during the correction process. The subsections that follow describe the effects of *pure* (independent) noise trading, mechanistic models based on correlated trading (positive feedback), the effects of mistaken beliefs, and the effects of alternative preferences.

C.1. Pure Noise Trading

Pure noise trading and positive feedback trading cause overreaction, and hence negative autocorrelations in long-run returns. When a stock rises too high, it needs to correct back down. Equivalently, this overreaction causes excess volatility in returns. Furthermore, Campbell and Kyle (1993) show that overreaction can cause aggregate stock market value measures such as dividend yield to predict future market returns, so that contrarian investment strategies are on average profitable.

DeLong et al. (1990a) model the consequences of unpredictable random trades. Two securities pay identical, riskless dividends. The price of one asset is exogenously fixed. The other asset is risky because pure noise trades cause stochastic mispricing. Rational arbitrageurs with exogenous short time horizons limit their arbitrage trades for fear that the mispricing will get worse before it gets better. On average the risky asset trades at a discount, the risk premium demanded by the rational investors.

The noise-trading approach provides an explanation for the existence and behavior of closed-end fund discounts and their correlations with stock returns. According to DeLong et al. (1990a), noise traders buy and sell closed-end funds in a correlated fashion, causing discounts or premia relative to net asset value to fluctuate. The mispricing risk this creates makes these funds less attractive to rational investors, so on average there is a discount. This theory implies that fund discounts move together based on a systematic noise-trading factor; such comovement exists (e.g., Lee et al. (1991)). The theory also explains why such funds are created: to exploit optimistic noise traders.

Lee et al. (1991) suggest that shifts in fund discounts reflect shifts in noise-trader sentiment toward all small stocks. This is consistent with their evidence that narrowing of closed-end fund discounts is associated contemporaneously with high small stock returns. This implies that discounts predict small stock returns (see Section II). If discounts were a consequence of *pure* noise trading, they would be uncorrelated with future fundamentals, such as accounting performance. Swaminathan (1996) finds that at lags of greater than one year, high discounts predict both low future accounting profits and high future stock returns. This is consistent with fund investors overreacting to genuine information.

The comovement in small stock returns documented in Fama and French (1993) may come from correlated imperfectly rational trades (see Shleifer (2000), p. 20). The DeLong et al. (1990a) approach then suggests that small stocks, including closed-end fund shares, will earn high expected returns in compensation for their high mispricing risk. Alternatively, low market-value stocks may earn high returns because a stock's low market value on average derives partly from its being undervalued (see, e.g., Daniel et al. (2001a)). The U.S. small firm effect has been weak or absent in the last 15 years, yet closed-end fund discounts remain.

C.2. Positive Feedback Trading

Positive feedback trading has several possible motivations, one being that investors form expectations of future prices by extrapolating trends (a topic covered in the next subsubsection). DeLong et al. (1990b) offer a model with a risky asset and risk-free cash, in which information arrives sequentially. The exogenous date 2 demand of the positive feedback traders is linearly increasing in the preceding price trend. Foreseeing this, rational speculators buy into price trends, exaggerating trends, and overshooting. As a result there is excess volatility, and long-term negative autocorrelations in returns.

In Cutler et al. (1990), there are two types of imperfectly rational traders, positive feedback traders, and fundamental traders who ignore price and trade based upon a signal about the security's payoff. Some fundamental traders observe this signal with a lag. This lag creates price trends which are profitably exploited by feedback traders. The gradual process of overshooting and correction induces both short-lag positive autocorrelation and long-lag negative autocorrelation.

More recent models with endogenous decisions have found things akin to pure noise trading—a limiting case of overconfidence, and positive feedback trading. But endogenously derived positive feedback is conditional and statistical, which seems more realistic than the older models. For reasons of both descriptiveness and predictiveness, explicit modeling of the psychology of investors is likely to supersede the mechanistic approach (except in otherwise-intractable applications).

C.3. Mistaken Beliefs

One explanation for return predictability is that investors set prices based on mistaken expectations.[83] This subsection first considers dynamics when irrational individuals share the same biases (either overconfidence, or representativeness and conservatism). I then consider the interaction of multiple trader types with different biases.

C.3.1. The Dynamics of Biased Attribution and Overconfidence. Two recent papers provide models with a single risky security that reflect the fact that people learn about their own abilities in a biased, self-promoting fashion. In these models, investors do not know the precision of their private information signals, which reflects their information-gathering ability. They learn about their precision through time by observing whether later public news confirms or disconfirms their previous signal. The analyses assume the dynamic complement of overconfidence, biased self-attribution. When an investor receives confirming news, his confidence in his precision rises too much, and when there is disconfirming news, his confidence declines too little.

In Daniel et al. (1998), the impulse response function to a favorable initial shock, the private information signal, is hump-shaped. Price on average rises further as public information arrives, because confidence about the private signal on average grows. Eventually, however, accumulating evidence forces investors back to a more reasonable self-perception. This smooth hump-shaped impulse response implies positive short-lag and negative long-lag

[83] Shefrin and Statman (1994) analyze the general effect of mistaken beliefs on equilibrium prices in securities markets. They predict that when prices are inefficient, mispricing is related to a "beta correction"; it has not been obvious how to test this.

return autocorrelations. Daniel et al. (1998) also numerically simulate the correlation of a public information surprise (such as favorable accounting performance) with future returns with self-attribution bias. At short lags, this correlation is positive, but at long lags, the correlation can be negative (see Section II.A.4).

Gervais and Odean (2001) provide a model that accommodates analytical solution for the learning process under biased self-attribution. As traders become overconfident, trading volume and market return volatility increase. Since equity is in positive net supply, the model also predicts that trading volume will be higher after market rises than market falls, consistent with Statman and Thorley (1998).[84]

C.3.2. The Dynamics of Representativeness and Conservatism. Barberis, Shleifer, and Vishny (1998) offer an explanation for under- and overreactions based on a model in which actual earnings for a risky asset follow a random walk, but investors do not understand this. They mistakenly believe that the earnings process stochastically fluctuates between a regime with mean-reverting earnings, and a regime with expected earnings growth.

If recent earning changes reverse, investors erroneously believe the firm is in a mean-reverting state, and underreact to recent news, consistent with conservatism (Section I.A.4). If investors see a sequence of growing earnings, they tend to conclude (wrongly) that the firm is in a growth regime, and overextrapolate trends, which is arguably reminiscent of representativeness (Section I.A.3). Overreaction to a long enough trend implies subsequent low returns during the process of correction. Thus, there can be long-term overreaction and correction, implying negative long-lag return autocorrelation. Yet the average response to an initial impulse can be smooth, implying positive short lag autocorrelation. Similarly, the model can accommodate a positive short-term correlation between the asset return and an earnings change, and a negative long-term correlation. If sporadic events such as dividend initiations are viewed as isolated from earnings patterns, a single-event version of the model implies, under appropriate parameter values, underreaction.

Cross-sectional effects (such as a value effect) are simulated with earnings that are independently distributed across stocks. This implies a nearly risk-free arbitrage opportunity for a rational investor who buys and sells stocks based on return predictors. Such arbitrage would be risky in a setting where investors update their beliefs about systematic factors in earnings trends or reversals. The psychological literature on multiple cue learning (Section I.A) may provide guidance for such a model.

[84] The implication of attribution/overconfidence models for whether there should be something akin to a disposition effect (holding winners, selling losers) is not obvious. When a stock is first becoming a winner, rational arbitrageurs who foresee further price rises should drive the price up even higher than the overconfident think is justified. This encourages the overconfident to sell, consistent with the disposition effect. However, for a stock that has been a winner for some time, the arbitrageurs will sell to the overconfident as the price peaks. Other recent models of momentum and reversal have similar opposing effects.

C.3.3. Interactions Among Traders with Different Biases. Hong and Stein (1999) analyze a market in which, as in Cutler et al. (1990), some traders react sluggishly, and others trade based on positive feedback. Each group of traders is risk averse, and is able to process only a subset of available information. Information about the liquidating dividend dribbles into the hands of different groups of news watchers. News watchers condition on their own private signals but ignore market prices, causing underreaction.

Momentum traders, in contrast, condition on the cumulative price change over the last k periods. Each trader takes a fixed position for a given number of periods. Momentum traders exploit the underreaction of news watchers by buying in response to price increases. This accelerates the reaction to news, but also causes overshooting. The smoothness of the overreaction process causes positive short-lag and negative long-lag autocorrelation. Slower information diffusion tends to launch a more powerful overreaction, leading to more negative long-lag autocorrelations.

C.3.4. Other Errors in the Dynamics of Beliefs. Although it is impossible to be comprehensive, I briefly mention some other approaches to the dynamics of beliefs.[85] Shefrin (1997) discusses how base rate underweighting may shed light on the anomalous behavior of implied volatilities in options markets. Cecchetti, Lam, and Mark (1999) model the equity premium puzzle and related issues as arising from a combination of errors, including underestimation of the persistence of high- versus low-consumption growth regimes. They describe a rule-of-thumb calculation method that lead to such errors, but do not address whether other rule-of-thumb methods would imply the opposite error.

Informal arguments about money illusion affecting prices have been offered by several authors.[86] Investors subject to money illusion may discount real cash flows at nominal interest rates, causing overdiscounting during high-inflation (growing inflation?) periods. They also may fail to take into account that higher inflation reduces the real value of a firm's debt. Ritter and Warr (2001) provide evidence suggesting that inflation illusion contributed to the 1982 to 1999 bull market.

C.4. Alternative Preferences

Psychological evidence does not support the traditional assumption of time-additive expected utility. Theorists, often motivated more by puzzling securities price evidence than by psychological evidence, have offered models based upon alternative preferences. Alternative preference models can address the equity premium puzzle, the interest rate puzzle, and excess stock market volatility in at least two ways. First, by breaking the link between

[85] Kurz (1997) describes his theory of endogenous uncertainty and rational belief equilibrium, which focuses on sets of beliefs that cannot be reliably contradicted by existing data. However, Bayesian updating has greater appeal as a theory of rational decisions.

[86] Fisher (1928), Modigliani and Cohn (1979), Sharpe (1999), and Ritter and Warr (2001).

risk aversion and the intertemporal elasticity of substitution, a high equity risk premium (which demands high aversion to risk) can be reconciled with low interest rates (which demand reasonably high intertemporal elasticity of substitution). Second, by allowing risk aversion to vary stochastically, stock price volatility can be increased relative to consumption variability.

Several papers address the equity premium and risk-free rate puzzles applying habit-forming preferences.[87] Constantinides (1990) shows that habit formation (Subsection I.E) reconciles a high equity premium with realistic consumption smoothness and growth, and moderate levels of risk aversion. Campbell and Cochrane (1999) and Chan and Kogan (2000) find that habit preferences that involve a Veblen-like concern for consumption of others imply stochastic risk aversion, which can reconcile a variety of facts about first and second moments of returns and consumption.

Several papers apply aspects of prospect theory and first-order risk averse preferences.[88] Benartzi and Thaler (1995) consider investors who make a sequence of myopic single-period portfolio decisions. Consistent with loss-aversion, investors care about changes in wealth or consumption relative to a reference point that shifts from decision to decision, and their value function is kinked at the reference point. Investors, therefore, are highly averse to risks of short-term losses in stocks relative to bonds.

Shumway (1998) extends this approach to explain the cross section of expected returns as well as the market expected return. Consistent with prospect theory, he assumes a modified power utility function that implies risk aversion over gains and risk seeking over losses. The reference point is a zero market return. In consequence, small market returns cause relatively large changes in the stochastic discount factor. In equilibrium, stock prices are a linear function of the stock's upside beta and its downside beta.

Empirically, Shumway (1998) finds that the model does quite well in fitting both the equity premium puzzle and the cross section of security returns. He suggests that the high premium on equity results from loss aversion, which causes marginal utility to vary more with slightly negative market returns. This tends to magnify the effect of stocks' downside risk relative to that of bonds.

Barberis et al. (2001) offer a model based upon a combination of loss aversion, and the "house money" effect of Thaler and Johnson (1990), the tendency for individuals who have experienced recent gains to be less averse to risky gambles. To capture loss aversion, they assume a piecewise linear value function that is steeper among losses than among gains relative to the reference point. After the good news of a high dividend, individuals become more risk tolerant. Stochastic variation in risk aversion increases the vola-

[87] See, for example, Sundaresan (1989), Abel (1990), Constantinides (1990), Ferson and Constantinides (1991), Heaton (1995), Boldrin, Christiano, and Fisher (1997), and Campbell and Cochrane (1999).

[88] See Ang, Bekaert, and Liu (2000), Barberis, Huang, and Santos (2001), Barberis and Huang (2000), Bekaert, Hodrick, and Marshall (1997a), Benartzi and Thaler (1995), Epstein and Zin (1990, 1991, 1993), Gomes (2000), and Shumway (1998).

tility of returns relative to dividends. These fluctuations in risk aversion tend to reverse, causing predictability in stock returns. The high return variability raises the equity risk premium even without high aversion to consumption risk, and is therefore consistent with a reasonably low risk-free rate.

Barberis and Huang (2000), like Shumway (1998), examine the dynamics of loss aversion with many risky securities. Barberis and Huang (2000) consider two kinds of mental accounting. Under individual stock accounting, investors care about total consumption, but are also loss averse over individual stock movements. In the other, portfolio accounting, individuals are loss averse with respect to movements in their total stock portfolio.

Investors are also subject to the house money effect. Using plausible parameter values, under individual stock accounting, the typical individual stock has a high expected excess return, and its returns are variable relative to dividend variability. The cross section of returns is predictable using measures of size, value, and whether the firm was a winner or loser over the last three years. The model implies an even higher equity premium than Barberis et al. (2001) because investors are loss-averse with respect to the residual risk of individual stock movements.

In a broadly similar spirit, Epstein and Zin (1993) examine a first-order risk averse setting and report that the case of disappointment averse preferences fit the data well (see also Epstein and Zin (1990)). Bekaert et al. (1997a) find that first-order risk aversion can explain predictability in U.S. and Japan equity, bond, and foreign exchange markets better than the expected utility model, but not enough to match the data. Ang et al. (2000) find that a high U.S. equity premium is consistent with reasonable parameters of disappointment averse preferences.

A rather different approach from applications of loss-averse or first-order risk averse preferences focuses on aversion to ambiguity (Subsection I.C.1) and a consequent taste for robustness.[89] A robust decision rule is one that does well in the face of model uncertainty when Nature chooses the most adverse possible model in response to the individual's choice. Tornell (2000) provides a model based upon agents who choose robust forecasting techniques to explain high equity returns, predictability, and excess volatility.

Even slight stochastic shifts in preferences can substantially increase the volatility of stock prices relative to the variability of consumption (Allen and Gale (1994), Kraus and Sagi (2000), and Mehra and Sah (2000)). The psychological evidence that visceral factors affect decisions are consistent with such variability.

C.5. Evolving Populations

A promising field for exploration uses evolutionary simulation of the interactions of agents in financial markets. In the last five years, physicists have begun to do research on financial markets, some calling their field *econo-*

[89] See, for example, Hansen, Sargent, and Tallarini (1999) and Maenhout (2000).

physics (see Farmer (1999)). Some of the recent models by physicists make such radical mechanistic assumptions about investor behavior and market structure that the resulting insights seem unlikely to generalize. Fortunately, a very promising strand of evolutionary literature explores the populations of traders who are imperfectly rational but do learn and make endogenous decisions. Freed from the constraints of analytical tractability, modelers are able to explore a wider space of economic settings.

An evolutionary approach could address the argument that even though individuals are imperfectly rational, as they learn from their trading outcomes, the system will progress toward the fully rational equilibrium rapidly. I conjecture that a simple tropism among traders towards actions that generate higher investment profits will not converge to the ICAPM quickly. Even with a long history of evidence, it is hard for a trader to figure out whether a trading strategy has done well after adjusting for risk unless he understands risk, and the income and substitution effects of Merton ICAPM hedging are, I conjecture, too subtle for most individual or even sophisticated institutional investors.

Some brief recent surveys of the computational field include Farmer (1999), Farmer and Lo (1999), and Lebaron (2000a). Some recent findings are that long-horizon investors frequently do not drive shorter-horizon investors out of financial markets, and that populations of long- and short-horizon agents can create patterns of volatility and volume similar to actual empirical patterns (Lebaron (2000b, 2000c)).

D. Empirically Distinguishing Pricing Theories

The effects described in different psychological pricing theories need not be mutually exclusive, but it is useful to examine how their predictions differ. My focus is on value, momentum, and event-based effects.

D.1. Distinguishing Explanations for Size and Value Effects

Several past authors have pointed out that long-run overreaction will induce cross-sectional value effects. Two recent models derive cross-sectional value and size effects when securities are subject to systematic and idiosyncratic influences (Barberis and Huang (2000) and Daniel et al. (2001a)).

Daniel et al. (2001a) provides no help in explaining the equity premium puzzle. The Barberis and Huang (2000) theory does address the equity premium and associated puzzles because people who do individual-stock accounting are averse to the high residual risk of stocks. Thus, a further implication of Barberis and Huang (2000) is that residual risk is cross-sectionally priced (Brennan (2001)). Furthermore, in contrast with the Merton (1987) limited participation theory, the Barberis and Huang (2000) theory seems to imply that, ceteris paribus, greater participation by individual investors will increase the premium for residual risk.

Daniel et al. (2001a) offer further implications, largely untested, concerning the cross-sectional dispersion in fundamental/price ratios, and the ability of current volume to predict future return volatility. Another implication is that as confidence exogenously varies over time, the dispersion in security fundamental/price ratios varies together with the ability of such ratios to predict future returns. Cohen, Polk, and Vuolteenaho (2000) confirm such a relationship between the book/market "value spread" and the profitability of value trading strategies.

In Daniel et al. (2001a), mispricing is present in a small number of factors. The importance of idiosyncratic effects in the Barberis and Huang (2000) theory suggests that rational arbitrageurs should take strong contrarian positions and earn large expected profits. More broadly, the strong flow of wealth in the Barberis and Huang (2000) theory suggests that mispricing effects should be more transitory than in Daniel et al. (2001a). Barberis and Huang (2000) also point out that the rise of mutual and pension fund stock investments should have led to less individual stock accounting, and is, therefore, consistent with a weakening in size and value effects.

There is psychological evidence that overconfidence is strongest when information signals are less precise and when feedback is inconclusive (e.g., Einhorn (1980) and Griffin and Tversky (1992)). Thus, Daniel et al. (2001a) predicts that fundamental/price ratios should forecast risk-adjusted returns more strongly for businesses that are hard to value (e.g., R&D-intensive firms comprised largely of intangible assets). Chan, Lakonishok, and Sougiannis (1999) subsequently report evidence consistent with such a pattern.

Neither Barberis and Huang (2000) nor Daniel et al. (2001a) capture momentum. The absence of a unified model that directly captures the two most conspicuous cross-sectional effects, value and momentum, is an obvious gap in the literature. The results of Daniel et al. (1998) and of Barberis et al. (1998) suggest that unified explanations may be possible based upon either overconfidence, or upon misperceptions of regime-shifting.

D.2. Distinguishing Explanations for Postevent Continuation

The Daniel et al. (1998) analysis of postevent continuation differs from the Barberis et al. (1998) model in predicting continuation only for selective events taken by a party such as management or an analyst in response to market mispricing. The support for this from one type of event (see Subsection II.A.4 at footnote 62) is intriguing. Event studies on other low-discretion events (such as regulatory announcements, input supply shocks, or output demand shocks) provide an attractive direction for further testing.

The Barberis et al. (1998) model is based upon public information. The Daniel et al. (1998) model implies negative long-run return autocorrelation associated with private information arrival, and positive long-run return autocorrelation associated with public signals. This is consistent with evidence of Daniel and Titman (2000). Daniel et al. (1998) further predict that postevent continuation will be strongest in stocks about which investors have poor information (often illiquid or smaller stocks). Daniel et al. (1998) also offer several untested predictions about the occurrence of and price patterns around corporate events, and about volatility at the time of private versus public signals.

D.3. Distinguishing Explanations for Momentum and Reversal

Analytically, the three recent models of how mistaken beliefs cause momentum and reversals (Barberis et al. (1998), Daniel et al. (1998), and Hong and Stein (1999)) all generate an impulse response function to a new information signal in which there is a gradual rise in the average reaction to a positive signal and a gradual average process of correction.

In all these models, the misperceptions that drive momentum are also the drivers of long-term reversal. These models therefore imply that if there is some market segmentation, then those sets of assets with largest momentum effects should also have the largest reversal effects; international testing would be of interest. It is interesting that much of the empirical evidence of return predictability, including both momentum and reversal, is stronger in small firms (see Fama (1998) and Loughran and Ritter (2000)). Barberis et al. (1998) and Daniel et al. (1998), but not Hong and Stein (1999), further imply that those countries or sets of securities with strongest momentum effects should also have strongest post-earnings-announcement drift.

More generally, greater uncertainty about a set of stocks, and a lack of accurate feedback about their fundamentals, leaves more room for psychological biases. At the extreme, it is relatively hard to misperceive an asset that is nearly risk-free. Thus, the misvaluation effects of almost any mistaken-beliefs model should be strongest among firms about which there is high uncertainty/poor information (cash flow variance is one possible proxy). Furthermore, in Daniel et al. (1998) and Hong and Stein (1999), greater information asymmetry strengthens the predicted effects; the adverse selection component of the bid-ask spread is a possible proxy. Barberis et al. (1998) does not have implications based on information asymmetry. Firm size, analyst following, and dispersion in analyst forecasts are potential proxies for information asymmetry, but they also may proxy for mere uncertainty. Thus, evidence that small firms (internationally) and firms with low analyst following have greater momentum is consistent with, but does not sharply distinguish, the three models.

Barberis et al. (1998) predict overreaction to trends, which can also occur in Daniel et al. (1998), but it is not obvious that the Daniel et al. (1998) implication extends to zero net supply securities. Thus, the evidence of Poteshman (2001) of daily underreaction and multiple-day overreaction of option prices to shifts in volatility supports Barberis et al. (1998) (at a very different time horizon).

Bloomfield and Hales (2001) directly test the Barberis et al. (1998) theory that people misperceive random walks to be shifts between continuation and reversal regimes by examining predictions by MBA-student experimental subjects. Consistent with Barberis et al. (1998), subjects overreacted to changes preceded by sequences of continuations, and underreacted to changes preceded by many reversals. However, people on average tended to expect continuation, whereas a perceived tilt toward reversal is needed to obtain postearnings announcement drift and postevent return continuation.

Another testing approach is to find data sets in which the trades of irrational traders versus rational arbitrageurs can be identified.[90] Coval and Shumway (2000) analyze a rich database to describe how the positions of futures market-makers change following recent trading success. Another suggestion has been to view market orders as irrational and limit orders as rational (Hvidkjaer (2000)). However, it does not seem clear why this would be the case based upon these theories, and empirically it is limit order traders who lose money in the short run (Chordia, Roll, and Subrahmanyam (2000)). Further progress on these issues calls for explicit modeling of psychology and microstructure.

IV. Conclusion

Man is neither infinite in faculties, nor in apprehension like a god. Nor is human fallibility shed at the doorstep of the stock exchange. Psychology-based asset-pricing theory has promise of capturing this reality, though at this point we are at an early stage.

Financial economists have grown more receptive to entertaining psychological explanations. One sign of this is the popularity of utility functions that seem to violate time consistency or the rationality axioms of expected utility in recent literature on the equity premium and risk-free rate puzzles. Some of these preferences could be endogenized as reduced form summaries of rational settings with market frictions, but this does not seem to be a high research priority even among fans of the full-rationality approach.

In Section I, I tried to give some hint of the wealth of psychological findings, many utterly unexploited, that can inform financial modeling. Subsection III.D offered hints for empirical work to distinguish alternative psychology-based pricing theories. I now mention a few other possible theoretical and empirical directions.

1. So far few psychology-based asset-pricing models allow for both risk aversion and multiple risky securities. It will be useful to explore the dynamics of mistaken beliefs when there is a cross section of securities, to address such issues as volume as a predictor of returns, and the effects of different rates of overreaction and correction for factors and residuals.
2. Pricing models based upon loss- and disappointment-aversion can be viewed as reflecting a concern about future feelings. But more directly, the effect of currently experienced emotions on current prices merits analysis.

[90] Conjecturally, Daniel, Hirshleifer, and Subrahmanyam (1998) implies that rational arbitrageurs buy after good news (foreseeing further overreaction). Overconfident traders sell (because the arbs drive prices up even higher than justified based on current overconfident beliefs). Some period of time after the favorable impulse, the arbs tend to sell out to the overconfident, and to go short. Anticipation by arbs of overreaction should generate similar trading patterns in Barberis et al. (1998); in the Hong and Stein (1999) setting, the behavior of irrational traders is more complex.

3. It is often not obvious how to translate preexisting evidence from psychological experiments into assumptions about investors in real financial settings. Routine experimental testing of the assumptions and conclusions of asset-pricing theories is needed to guide modeling.
4. We lack a quantified set of capital budgeting and risk-management procedures that reflect mispricing and are ready for practitioners to apply (but see Stein (1996)).
5. The great missing chapter in asset-pricing theory, I believe, is a model of the social process by which people form and transmit ideas about markets and securities. In addition to studying what influences individuals' valuations, an appealing direction is to study how attention is focused on certain groups of stocks, and the effects of resulting swings in participation. A different empirical direction is to analyze the specific content of widespread, erroneous investor theories to identify ways of predicting returns. Robert Shiller has discussed and documented investor theories, belief transmission, and effects on pricing (e.g., Shiller (1984, 1990, 2000c); see also the analysis of DeMarzo, Vayanos, and Zwiebel (2000)). This research has blazed a path upon which further work will follow.

My list of further directions is necessarily idiosyncratic. In an area that is just coming of age, many new prospects are open. This is an exciting time for the field of asset pricing.

REFERENCES

Abarbanell, J. S., and B. J. Bushee, 1998, Abnormal returns to a fundamental strategy, *Accounting Review* 73, 19–45.

Abel, A. B., 1990, Asset prices under habit formation and catching up with the Joneses, *American Economic Review* 80, 38–42.

Aggarwal, R., S. Mohanty, and F. Song, 1995, Are survey forecasts of macroeconomic variables rational?, *Journal of Business* 68, 99–119.

Ahn, D.-H., J. S. Conrad, and R. F. Dittmar, 2000, Risk adjustment and trading strategies, Working paper, University of North Carolina at Chapel Hill.

Ainslie, G., 1975, Specious reward: A behavioral theory of impulsiveness and impulse control, *Psychological Bulletin* 82, 463–496.

Allais, M., 1953, La psychologie de l'home rationnel devant le risque: critique des postulats et axiomes de l'cole amricaine, *Econometrica* 21, 503–546.

Allen, F., 2001, Do financial institutions matter? *Journal of Finance* 56, 1165–1175.

Allen, F., and D. Gale, 1994, Limited market participation and volatility of asset prices, *American Economic Review* 84, 933–955.

Allport, G. W., and L. J. Postman, 1947, *The Psychology of Rumor* (Holt, New York).

Alpert, M., and H. Raiffa, 1982, A progress report on the training of probability assessors, in Daniel Kahneman, Paul Slovic, and Amos Tversky, ed.: *Judgement Under Uncertainty: Heuristics and Biases* (Cambridge University Press, Cambridge).

Anderson, T. W., 1932, *Remembering: A Study in Experimental and Social Psychology* (Cambridge University Press, London, York).

Andrade, G. M., 1999, *Do appearances matter? The impact of eps accretion and dilution on stock prices*, Working paper, Harvard University.

Andreassen, P. B., and S. J. Kraus, 1990, Judgemental extrapolation and the salience of change, *Journal of Forecasting* 9, 347–372.

Ang, A., G. Bekaert, and J. Liu, 2000, Why stocks may disappoint, Working paper, Columbia Business School.

Argote, L., M. Turner, and M. Fichman, 1988, To centralize or not to centralize: The effects of uncertainty and threat on group structure and performance, *Organizational Behavior* 42, 1–17.

Arkes, H., L. Herren, and A. Isen, 1988, The role of potential loss in the influence of affect on risk-taking behavior, *Organizational Behavior and Human Decision Processes* 66, 228–236.

Arkes, H. R., and C. Blumer, 1985, The psychology of sunk costs, *Organizational Behavior and Human Decision Processes* 35, 124–140.

Asch, S., 1956, Studies of independence and conformity: A minority of one against a unanimous majority, *Psychological Monographs* 70 Whole No. 416.

Ashton, R. H., 1976, Cognitive changes induced by accounting changes: Experimental evidence on the functional fixation hypothesis, *Journal of Accounting Research* 14, 1.

Avery, C., and J. Chevalier, 1999, Identifying investor sentiment from price paths: The case of football betting, *Journal of Business* 72, 493–521.

Avery, C., and P. Zemsky, 1998, Multi-dimensional uncertainty and herd behavior in financial markets, *American Economic Review* 88, 724–748.

Ball, R., 1978, Anomalies in relationships between securities' yields and yield-surrogates, *Journal of Financial Economics* 6, 103–126.

Ball, R., and S. P. Kothari, 1989, Non-stationary expected returns: Implications for tests of market efficiency and serial correlations of returns, *Journal of Financial Economics* 25, 51–74.

Ball, R., S. P. Kothari, and J. Shanken, 1995, Problems in measuring portfolio performance: An application to contrarian investment strategies, *Journal of Financial Economics* 38, 79–107.

Balvers, R., Y. Wu, and E. Gilliland, 2000, Mean reversion across national stock markets and parametric contrarian investment strategies, *Journal of Finance* 55, 745–772.

Banerjee, A., 1992, A simple model of herd behavior, *Quarterly Journal of Economics* 107, 797–817.

Banerjee, A., and D. Fudenberg, 1999, Word-of-mouth communication and social learning, Working paper, Harvard University.

Banz, R. W., 1981, The relationship between return and the market value of common stocks, *Journal of Financial and Quantitative Analysis* 14, 421–441.

Bar-Hillel, M., and E. Neter, 1996, Why are people reluctant to exchange lottery tickets? *Journal of Personality and Social Psychology* 70, 17–27.

Barber, B., R. Lehavy, M. McNichols, and B. Trueman, 2001, Can investors profit from the prophets? Consensus analyst recommendations and stock returns, *Journal of Finance* 56, 531–563.

Barber, B., and T. Odean, 1999, Online investors: Do the slow die first? University of California–Davis.

Barber, B., and T. Odean, 2000a, Boys will be boys: Gender, overconfidence, and common stock investment, *Quarterly Journal of Economics*, forthcoming.

Barber, B., and T. Odean, 2000b, Trading is hazardous to your wealth: The common stock investment performance of individual investors, *Journal of Finance* 55, 773–806.

Barberis, N., and M. Huang, 2000, Mental accounting, loss aversion, and individual stock returns, Manuscript, University of Chicago.

Barberis, N., M. Huang, and J. Santos, 2001, Prospect theory and asset prices, *Quarterly Journal of Economics* 116:1, 1–53.

Barberis, N., A. Shleifer, and R. Vishny, 1998, A model of investor sentiment, *Journal of Financial Economics* 49, 307–343.

Barkham, R., and D. Geltner, 1995, Price discovery in American and British property markets, *Real Estate Economics* 23, 21–44.

Barkow, J. H., L. Cosmides, and J. Tooby, 1992, *The Adapted Mind: Evolutionary Psychology and the Generation of Culture* (Oxford University Press, New York).

Barone, M., P. Miniard, and J. Romeo, 2000, The influence of positive mood on brand extension evaluations, *Journal of Consumer Research* 26, 386–400.

Bartov, E., F. W. Lindahl, and W. E. Ricks, 1998, Stock price behavior around announcements of writeoffs, *Review of Accounting Studies* 3, 327–346.

Basu, S., 1983, The relationship between earnings yield, market value, and return for NYSE common stocks: Further evidence, *Journal of Financial Economics* 12, 126–156.
Batchelor, R., and P. Dua, 1992, Conservatism and consensus-seeking among economic forecasters, *Journal of Forecasting* 11, 169–181.
Bekaert, G., R. J. Hodrick, and D. Marshall, 1997a, The implications of first-order risk aversion for asset market risk premiums, *Journal of Monetary Economics* 40, 3–39.
Bekaert, G., R. J. Hodrick, and D. Marshall, 1997b, 'Peso problem' explanations for term structure anomalies, NBER Working Paper No. W6147.
Bem, D. J., 1972, Self-perception theory, in L. Berkowitz, ed.: *Advances in Experimental Social Psychology* (Academic Press, New York).
Benartzi, S., 2001, Excessive extrapolation and the allocation of 401(k) accounts to company stock, *Journal of Finance* 56:5.
Benartzi, S., and R. Thaler, 1995, Myopic loss aversion and the equity premium puzzle, *Quarterly Journal of Economics* 110, 75–92.
Benartzi, S., and R. H. Thaler, 2001, Naive diversification strategies in retirement saving plans, *American Economic Review* 91:1, 79–98.
Benos, A., 1998, Aggressiveness and survival of overconfident traders, *Journal of Financial Markets* 1, 353–383.
Berk, J., 1995, A critique of size related anomalies, *Review of Financial Studies* 8, 275–286.
Bernard, V. L., and J. K. Thomas, 1989, Post-earnings-announcement drift: Delayed price response or risk premium? *Journal of Accounting Research*, Supplement 27, 1–48.
Bernard, V. L., and J. K. Thomas, 1990, Evidence that stock prices do not fully reflect the implications of current earnings for future earnings, *Journal of Accounting and Economics* 13, 305–340.
Bernardo, A., and I. Welch, 2000, On the evolution of overconfidence and entrepreneurs, Working paper #9-97, UCLA.
Berscheid, E., and H. Reis, 1998, Attraction and close relationships, in S. Fiske, D. Gilbert, and G. Lindzey, eds.: *The Handbook of Social Psychology*, 4th edition (McGraw Hill, New York).
Bhandari, L. C., 1988, Debt/equity ratios and expected common stock returns: Empirical evidence, *Journal of Finance* 43, 507–528.
Bikhchandani, S., D. Hirshleifer, and I. Welch, 1992, A theory of fads, fashion, custom, and cultural change as informational cascades, *Journal of Political Economy* 100, 992–1026.
Bjerring, J. H., J. Lakonishok, and T. Vermaelen, 1983, Stock prices and financial analysts' recommendations, *Journal of Finance* 38, 187–204.
Black, F., 1986, Noise, *Journal of Finance* 41, 529–543.
Black, F., M. Jensen, and M. Scholes, 1972, The capital asset pricing model: Some empirical tests, in Michael C. Jensen, ed.: *Studies in the Theory of Capital Markets* (Praeger, New York).
Bloomfield, R., 1996, Quotes, prices and estimates of value in a laboratory market, *Journal of Finance* 51, 1791–1808.
Bloomfield, R., and J. Hales, 2001, Predicting the next step of a random walk: Experimental evidence of regime-shifting biases, Johnson School, Cornell University.
Bloomfield, R., J. Hales, R. Libby, and M. Nelson, 2001, The effect of information, strength and weight on behavior in financial markets, *Organizational Behavior and Human Decision Processes*, forthcoming.
Bloomfield, R., R. Libby, and M. Nelson, 1999, Confidence and the welfare of less-informed investors, *Accounting, Organization and Society* 24, 623–647.
Bloomfield, R., R. Libby, and M. Nelson, 2000, Underreactions, overreactions and moderated confidence, *Journal of Financial Markets* 3, 113–137.
Blume, L., and D. Easley, 1982, Learning to be rational, *Journal of Economic Theory* 26, 340–351.
Blume, L., and D. Easley, 1990, Evolution and market behavior, *Journal of Economic Theory* 58, 9–40.
Blume, L. E., and D. Easley, 2000, If you're so smart, why aren't you rich? Belief selection in complete and incomplete markets, Working paper, Cornell University.
Bodurtha, J., D.-S. Kim, and C. M. C. Lee, 1995, Closed-end country funds and U.S. market sentiment, *Review of Financial Studies* 8, 879–918.

Boehme, R., and S. M. Sorescu, 2000, Seven decades of long term abnormal return persistence: The case of dividend initiations and resumptions, Working paper, University of Houston.

Boldrin, M., L. Christiano, and J. Fisher, 1995, Asset pricing lessons for modeling business cycles, NBER Working Paper No. 5262.

Bond, R., and P. Smith, 1996, Culture and conformity: A meta-analysis of studies using Aschs (1952b, 1956) line judgement task, *Psychological Bulletin* 119, 111–137.

Bornstein, R., and P. D'Agostino, 1992, Stimulus recognition and the mere exposure effect, *Journal of Personality and Social Psychology* 63, 545–552.

Bossaerts, P., 2000, Experiments with financial markets: Implications for asset pricing theory, Working paper, Cal Tech.

Bossaerts, P., and P. Hillion, 1999, Implementing statistical criteria to select return forecasting models: What do we learn? *Review of Financial Studies* 12, 405–428.

Bossaerts, P., C. Plott, and W. Zame, 2000, Prices and allocations in financial markets: Theory and evidence, Working paper, Cal Tech.

Brav, A., C. Geczy, and P. A. Gompers, 2000, Is the abnormal return following equity issuances anomalous? *Journal of Financial Economics* 56, 209–249.

Brennan, M., 2001, Mental accounting, loss aversion, and individual stock returns: Discussion, Working paper, Anderson Graduate School of Management, UCLA.

Brennan, M., T. Chordia, and A. Subrahmanyam, 1998, Alternative factor specifications, security characteristics and the cross section of expected stock returns, *Journal of Financial Economics* 49, 345–373.

Brennan, M., and Y. Xia, 2001, Stock price volatility and the equity premium, *Journal of Monetary Economics,* forthcoming.

Brenner, L. A., D. J. Koehler, V. Liberman, and A. Tversky, 1996a, Overconfidence in probability and frequency judgments: A critical examination, *Organizational Behavior and Human Decision Processes* 65, 212–219.

Brenner, L. A., D. J. Koehler, and A. Tversky, 1996b, On the evaluation of one-sided evidence, *Journal of Behavioral Decision Making* 9, 59–70.

Brown, S. J., W. N. Goetzmann, and S. A. Ross, 1995, Survival, *Journal of Finance* 50, 853–873.

Bruner, J., L. Postman, and J. Rodrigues, 1951, Expectations and the perception of color, *American Journal of Psychology* 64, 216–227.

Camerer, C., 1995, Individual decision making, in John H. Kagel, and Alvin E. Roth, ed.: *The Handbook of Experimental Economics* (Princeton University Press, Princeton NJ).

Camerer, C. F., 1991, The process-performance paradox in expert judgment: How can experts know so much and predict so badly? in K. A. Ericsson, and J. Smith, eds.: *Towards a General Theory of Expertise: Prospects and Limits* (Cambridge University Press, New York).

Camerer, C. F., 1998, Bounded rationality in individual decision making, *Experimental Economics* 1, 163–183.

Camerer, C. F., G. Loewenstein, and M. Weber, 1989, The curse of knowledge in economic settings: An experimental analysis, *Journal of Political Economy* 97, 1232–1254.

Campbell, J., 1999, Asset prices, consumption, and the business cycle, in John B. Taylor, and Michael Woodford, eds.: *Handbook of Macroeconomics* (North Holland, Amsterdam).

Campbell, J. Y., 1987, Stock returns and the term structure, *Journal of Financial Economics* 18, 373–399.

Campbell, J. Y., 2000, Asset pricing at the millennium, *Journal of Finance* 55, 1515–1567.

Campbell, J. Y., and J. H. Cochrane, 1999, By force of habit: A consumption based explanation of aggregate stock market behavior, *Journal of Political Economy* 107, 205–251.

Campbell, J. Y., and A. S. Kyle, 1993, Smart money, noise trading, and stock price behaviour, *Review of Economic Studies* 60, 1–34.

Campbell, J. Y., and R. J. Shiller, 1988a, The dividend-price ratio and expectations of future dividends and discount factors, *Review of Financial Studies* 1, 195–228.

Campbell, J. Y., and R. J. Shiller, 1988b, Stock prices, earnings, and expected dividends, *Journal of Finance* 43, 661–676.

Campbell, J. Y., and R. J. Shiller, 1991, Yield spreads and interest rates: A bird's eye view, *Review of Economic Studies* 58, 495–514.

Cao, H. H., and D. Hirshleifer, 2000, Conversation, learning and informational cascades, Working paper, Ohio State University.
Carmel, J. P., and M. Young, 1997, Long horizon mean reversion in the stock market: The postwar years, Working paper, University of Michigan.
Case, K. E., and R. Shiller, 1990, The behavior of home buyers in boom and post-boom markets, *New England Economic Review* 80, 29–46.
Cecchetti, S. G., P.-S. Lam, and N. C. Mark, 1999, Asset pricing with distorted beliefs: Are equity returns 'too good to be true?' *American Economic Review* 90, 787–805.
Chan, K., 1988, On the contrarian investment strategy, *Journal of Business* 61, 147–163.
Chan, K., and N.-F. Chen, 1991, Structural and return characteristics of small and large firms, *Journal of Finance* 46, 1467–1484.
Chan, K., A. Hameed, and W. Tong, 2000, Profitability of momentum strategies in the international equity markets, *Journal of Financial and Quantitative Analysis* 35, 153–172.
Chan, K., N. Jegadeesh, and J. Lakonishok, 2000, Earnings quality and stock returns: The evidence from accruals, Working paper, University of Illinois.
Chan, L., Y. Hamao, and J. Lakonishok, 1991, Fundamental and stock returns in Japan, *Journal of Finance* 46, 1739–1764.
Chan, L. K., N. Jegadeesh, and J. Lakonishok, 1996, Momentum strategies, *Journal of Finance* 51, 1681–1714.
Chan, L. K., J. Lakonishok, and T. Sougiannis, 1999, The stock market valuation of research and development expenditures, NBER Working Paper #7223.
Chan, Y. L., and L. Kogan, 2000, Catching up with the Joneses: Heterogeneous preferences and the dynamics of asset prices, Wharton School #14-00.
Chang, C., Z. Chen, and M. Dong, 1999, Investing with a stock valuation model, Working paper, Ohio State University and Yale University.
Chapman, G. B., 1998, Sooner or later: The psychology of intertemporal choice, in Douglas L. Medin, eds.: *The Psychology of Learning and Motivation* (Academic Press, San Diego, CA).
Chapman, G. B., and E. J. Johnson, 1999, Anchoring, activation, and the construction of values, *Organizational Behavior and Human Decision Processes* 79, 115–153.
Chen, J., 2000, Can the intertemporal CAPM explain the cross section of stock returns? Working paper, Stanford University.
Chen, N.-F., and F. Zhang, 1998, Risk and return of value stocks, *Journal of Business* 71, 501–535.
Choe, H., B.-C. Kho, and R. M. Stulz, 1999, Do foreign investors destabilize stock markets? the Korean experience in 1997, *Journal of Financial Economics* 54, 227–264.
Chopra, N., J. Lakonishok, and J. R. Ritter, 1992, Measuring abnormal performance: Do stocks overreact? *Journal of Financial Economics* 31, 235–268.
Chordia, T., R. Roll, and A. Subrahmanyam, 2000, Order imbalance, liquidity, and market returns, Working paper, UCLA.
Chordia, T., and L. Shivakumar, 2000, Momentum, business cycle and time varying expected returns, Working paper, Emory University.
Clore, G. L., N. Schwarz, and M. Conway, 1994, Affective causes and consequences of social information processing, in Robert S. Wyer, Jr. and Thomas K. Srull, eds.: *Handbook of Social Cognition*, 2nd edition (Lawrence Erlbaum, Hillsdale, NJ).
Clotfelter, C. T., and P. J. Cook, 1993, The 'gambler's fallacy' in lottery play, *Management Science* 39, 93–95.
Cochrane, J. H., 1991, Volatility tests and efficient markets: Review essay, *Journal of Monetary Economics* 27, 463–485.
Cochrane, J. H., 2000, *Asset Pricing* (Princeton University Press, Princeton, NJ).
Cohen, J. B., and C. S. Areni, 1991, Affect and consumer behavior, in Thomas S. Robertson, and Harold H. Kassarjian, eds.: *Handbook of Consumer Behavior* (Prentice-Hall, Englewood Cliffs, NJ).
Cohen, R. B., C. K. Polk, and T. Vuolteenaho, 2000, The value spread, Working paper, University of Chicago.
Conlisk, J., 1996, Why bounded rationality? *Journal of Economic Literature* 34, 669–700.

Constantinides, G. M., 1990, Habit formation: A resolution of the equity premium puzzle, *Journal of Political Economy* 98, 519–543.
Constantinides, G. M., J. B. Donaldson, and R. Mehra, 2000, Junior can't borrow: A new perspective on the equity premium puzzle, Working paper, Columbia University.
Constantinides, G. M., and D. Duffie, 1996, Asset pricing with heterogeneous consumers, *Journal of Political Economy* 104, 219–240.
Cooper, I., and E. Kaplanis, 1994, Home bias in equity portfolios, inflation hedging, and international capital market equilibrium, *Review of Financial Studies* 7, 45–60.
Cooper, J., and R. H. Fazio, 1984, A new look at dissonance theory, in L. Berkowitz, ed.: *Advances in Experimental Social Psychology* (Academic Press, Orlando, FL).
Cooper, M. J., O. Dimitrov, and P. R. Rau, 2001, A rose.com by any other name, *Journal of Finance*, forthcoming.
Cornell, B., and Q. Liu, 2000, The parent company puzzle: When is the whole worth less than one of its parts? Anderson School Working paper #7-00, UCLA.
Cornett, M. M., H. Mehran, and H. Tehranian, 1998, Are financial markets overly optimistic about the prospects of firms that issue equity? Evidence from voluntary versus involuntary equity issuance by banks, *Journal of Finance* 53, 2139–2159.
Cosmides, L., and J. Tooby, 1996, Are humans good intuitive statisticians after all? Rethinking some conclusions from the literature on judgment under uncertainty, *Cognition* 58, 1–73.
Coval, J. D., and T. J. Moskowitz, 1999, Home bias at home: Local equity preference in domestic portfolios, *Journal of Finance* 54, 145–166.
Coval, J. D., and T. Shumway, 2000, Do behavioral biases affect prices? Working paper, University of Michigan Business School.
Crocker, J., 1982, Biased questions in judgement of covariation studies, *Personality and Social Psychology Bulletin* 8, 214–220.
Cusatis, P., J. Miles, and J. Woolridge, 1993, Restructuring through spinoffs: The stock market evidence, *Journal of Financial Economics* 33, 293–311.
Cutler, D. M., J. M. Poterba, and L. H. Summers, 1989, What moves stock prices? *Journal of Portfolio Management* 15, 4–12.
Cutler, D. M., J. M. Poterba, and L. H. Summers, 1990, Speculative dynamics and the role of feedback traders, *American Economic Review* 80, 63–68.
Cutler, D. M., J. M. Poterba, and L. H. Summers, 1991, Speculative dynamics, *Review of Economic Studies* 58, 529–546.
Cyert, R. M., and J. G. March, 1963, A Behavioral Theory of the Firm (Prentice Hall, Englewood Cliffs, NJ).
Daniel, K., D. Hirshleifer, and S. H. Teoh, 2001, Investor psychology in capital markets: Evidence and policy implications, Working paper, Ohio State University.
Daniel, K. D., D. Hirshleifer, and A. Subrahmanyam, 1998, Investor psychology and security market under- and overreactions, *Journal of Finance* 53, 1839–1886.
Daniel, K. D., D. Hirshleifer, and A. Subrahmanyam, 2001a, Mispricing, covariance risk, and the cross section of security returns, *Journal of Finance* 56, 921–965.
Daniel, K. D., D. Hirshleifer, and A. Subrahmanyam, 2001b, Discriminating between efficient and inefficient markets theories of cross-sectional return predictability, Working paper, Northwestern University.
Daniel, K. D., and S. Titman, 1997, Evidence on the characteristics of cross-sectional variation in common stock returns, *Journal of Finance* 52, 1–33.
Daniel, K. D., and S. Titman, 1999, Market efficiency in an irrational world, *Financial Analysts' Journal* 55, 28–40.
Daniel, K. D., and S. Titman, 2001, Market reactions to tangible and intangible information, Working paper, Kellogg School.
Daniel, K. D., S. Titman, and J. Wei, 2001, Explaining the cross section of stock returns in Japan: Factors or characteristics? *Journal of Finance* 56, 743–756.
Davis, J., E. F. Fama, and K. R. French, 2000, Characteristics, covariances, and average returns: 1929–1997, *Journal of Finance* 55, 389–406.
Davis, J. L., 1994, The cross-section of realized stock returns: The pre-COMPUSTAT evidence, *Journal of Finance* 50, 1579–1593.

Deaux, K., and T. Emswiller, 1974, Explanations for successful performance on sex-linked tasks: What is skill for the male is luck for the female, *Journal of Personality and Social Psychology* 29, 80–85.

DeBondt, W. F. M., 1993, Betting on trends: Intuitive forecasts of financial risk and return, *International Journal of Forecasting* 9, 355–371.

DeBondt, W. F. M., and R. H. Thaler, 1985, Does the stock market overreact? *Journal of Finance* 40, 793–808.

DeBondt, W. F. M., and R. H. Thaler, 1987, Further evidence on investor overreaction and stock market seasonality, *Journal of Finance* 42, 557–581.

DeBondt, W. F. M., and R. H. Thaler, 1995, Financial decision-making in markets and firms: A behavioral perspective, in Robert A. Jarrow, Voijslav Maksimovic, and William T. Ziemba, eds.: *Finance, Handbooks in Operations Research and Management Science* (North Holland, Amsterdam).

DeChow, P. M., and R. G. Sloan, 1997, Returns to contrarian investment strategies: Tests of naive expectations hypotheses, *Journal of Financial Economics* 41, 3–27.

DeGeorge, F., J. Patel, and R. Zeckhauser, 1999, Earnings manipulation to exceed thresholds, *Journal of Business* 71, 1–34.

DeLong, J. B., A. Shleifer, L. Summers, and R. J. Waldmann, 1990a, Noise trader risk in financial markets, *Journal of Political Economy* 98, 703–738.

DeLong, J. B., A. Shleifer, L. Summers, and R. J. Waldmann, 1990b, Positive feedback investment strategies and destabilizing rational speculation, *Journal of Finance* 45, 375–395.

DeLong, J. B., A. Shleifer, L. Summers, and R. J. Waldmann, 1991, The survival of noise traders in financial markets, *Journal of Business* 64, 1–20.

DeMarzo, P., D. Vayanos, and J. Zwiebel, 2000, A near-rational model of persuasion—with implications for financial markets, Working paper, Stanford University.

Denis, D., and A. Sarin, 2001, Is the market surprised by poor earnings realizations following seasoned equity offerings? *Journal of Financial and Quantitative Analysis*, forthcoming.

Desai, H., and P. C. Jain, 1997a, Firm performance and focus—long-run stock market performance following spinoffs, *Journal of Financial Economics* 54, 75–101.

Desai, H., and P. C. Jain, 1997b, Long-run common stock returns following stock splits and reverse splits, *Journal of Business* 70, 409–434.

Dharan, B. G., and D. Ikenberry, 1995, The long-run negative drift of post-listing stock returns, *Journal of Finance* 50, 1547–1574.

Dichev, I., 1998, Is the risk of bankruptcy a systematic risk? *Journal of Finance* 53, 1131–1147.

Dichev, I., and J. Piotroski, 2001, The long-run stock returns following bond ratings changes, *Journal of Finance* 56, 173–203.

Dittmar, A. K., 2000, Why do firms repurchase stock? *Journal of Business* 73, 321–356.

D'Mello, R., and P. K. Shrof, 2000, Equity undervaluation and decisions related to repurchase tender offers: An empirical investigation, *Journal of Finance* 55, 2399–2424.

Eckbo, B. E., R. W. Masulis, and O. Norli, 2000, Seasoned public offerings: Resolution of the 'new issues puzzle,' *Journal of Financial Economics* 56, 251–291.

Eckbo, B. E., and O. Norli, 2000, Leverage, liquidity, and long-run IPO returns, Working paper, Dartmouth College.

Edwards, W., 1968, Conservatism in human information processing, in B. Kleinmutz, ed.: *Formal Representation of Human Judgement* (Wiley, New York).

Einhorn, H. J., 1980, Overconfidence in judgment, *New Directions for Methodology of Social and Behavioral Science* 4, 1–16.

Einhorn, H. J., and R. Hogarth, 1978, Confidence in judgement: Persistence in the illusion of validity, *Psychological Review* 85, 395–416.

Ellison, G., and D. Fudenberg, 1995, Word of mouth communication and social learning, *Quarterly Journal of Economics* 110, 93–126.

Ellsberg, D., 1961, Risk, ambiguity, and the savage axioms, *Quarterly Journal of Economics* 75, 643–699.

Elton, E. J., M. J. Gruber, and M. N. Gultekin, 1984, Professional expectations: Accuracy and diagnosis of errors, *Journal of Financial and Quantitative Analysis* 19, 351–363.

Engel, R., 1996, The forward discount anomaly and the risk premium: A survey of recent evidence, *Journal of Empirical Finance* 3, 123–192.
Epstein, L., and S. Zin, 1989, Substitution, risk aversion, and the temporal behavior of consumption growth and asset returns I: A theoretical framework, *Econometrica* 57, 937–969.
Epstein, L., and S. Zin, 1990, 'First-order' risk aversion and the equity premium puzzle, *Journal of Monetary Economics* 26, 387–407.
Epstein, L., and S. Zin, 1991, Substitution, risk aversion, and the temporal behavior of consumption growth and asset returns II: An empirical analysis, *Journal of Political Economy* 99, 263–286.
Epstein, L., and S. Zin, 1993, The independence axiom and asset returns, Carnegie Mellon University.
Erevelles, S., 1998, The role of affect in marketing, *Journal of Business Research* 42, 199–215.
Fair, R., 2000, Events that shook the market, Working paper, Yale University.
Fama, E. F., 1991, Efficient capital markets II, *Journal of Finance* 46, 1575–1643.
Fama, E. F., 1998, Market efficiency, long-term returns and behavioral finance, *Journal of Financial Economics* 49, 283–306.
Fama, E. F., and R. R. Bliss, 1987, The information in long-maturity forward rates, *The American Economic Review* 77, 680–692.
Fama, E. F., and K. R. French, 1988a, Dividend yields and expected stock returns, *Journal of Financial Economics* 22, 3–25.
Fama, E. F., and K. R. French, 1988b, Permanent and temporary components of stock prices, *Journal of Political Economy* 96, 246–273.
Fama, E. F., and K. R. French, 1989, Business conditions and expected returns on stocks and bonds, *Journal of Financial Economics* 25, 23–49.
Fama, E. F., and K. R. French, 1992, The cross-section of expected stock returns, *Journal of Finance* 47, 427–465.
Fama, E. F., and K. R. French, 1993, Common risk factors in the returns on stocks and bonds, *Journal of Financial Economics* 33, 3–56.
Fama, E. F., and K. R. French, 1995, Size and book-to-market factors in earnings and returns, *Journal of Finance* 50, 131–156.
Fama, E. F., and K. R. French, 1996a, The CAPM is wanted, dead or alive, *Journal of Finance* 51, 1947–1958.
Fama, E. F., and K. R. French, 1996b, Multifactor explanations of asset pricing anomalies, *Journal of Finance* 51, 55–84.
Fama, E. F., and K. R. French, 1998, Value versus growth: The international evidence, *Journal of Finance* 53, 1975–1999.
Fama, E. F., and K. R. French, 2000, The equity premium, Working paper, University of Chicago.
Fama, E. F., and J. MacBeth, 1973, Risk, return and equilibrium: Empirical tests, *Journal of Political Economy* 81, 607–636.
Farmer, J. D., 1999, Physicists attempt to scale the ivory towers of finance, *Computing in Science and Engineering* 1, 26–39.
Farmer, J. D., and A. W. Lo, 1999, Frontiers of finance: Evolution and efficient markets, *Proceedings of the National Academy of Sciences* 96, 9991–9992.
Fernandez-Villaverde, J., and A. Mukherji, 2000, Can we really observe hyperbolic discounting? Working paper, University of Minnesota.
Ferris, S. P., R. A. Haugen, and A. K. Makhija, 1988, Predicting contemporary volume with historic volume at differential price levels: Evidence supporting the disposition effect, *Journal of Finance* 43, 677–697.
Ferson, W. E., and G. M. Constantinides, 1991, Habit persistence and durability in aggregate consumption; empirical tests, *Journal of Financial Economics* 29, 199–240.
Festinger, L., and J. M. Carlsmith, 1959, Cognitive consequences of forced compliance, *Journal of Abnormal and Social Psychology* 58, 203–211.
Figlewski, S., 1978, Market 'efficiency' in a market with heterogeneous information, *Journal of Political Economy* 86, 581–597.
Fischer, P., and R. Verrecchia, 1999, Public information and heuristic trade, *Journal of Accounting and Economics* 27:1, 89–124.

Fischhoff, B., and R. Beyth-Marom, 1983, Hypothesis evaluation from a bayesian perspective, *Psychological Review* 90, 239–260.

Fischhoff, B., P. Slovic, and S. Lichtenstein, 1977, Knowing with certainty: The appropriateness of extreme confidence, *Journal of Experimental Psychology* 3, 552–564.

Fischhoff, B., P. Slovic, and S. Lichtenstein, 1978, Fault trees: Sensitivity of estimated failure probabilities to problem representation, *Journal of Experimental Psychology: Human Perception and Performance* 4, 330–334.

Fischhoff, B., 1982, For those condemned to study the past: Heuristics and biases in hindsight, in Daniel Kahneman, Paul Slovic, and Amos Tversky, eds.: *Judgement under Uncertainty: Heuristics and Biases* (Cambridge University Press, Cambridge).

Fisher, I., 1928, *The Money Illusion* (Adelphi Company, New York).

Fisher, I., 1930, *The Theory of Interest* (MacMillan, New York).

Foerster, S. R., and G. A. Karolyi, 1999, The effects of market segmentation and investor recognition on asset prices: Evidence from foreign stocks listing in the United States, *Journal of Finance* 54, 981–1013.

Foerster, S. R., and G. A. Karolyi, 2000, The long-run performance of global equity offerings, *Journal of Financial and Quantitative Analysis* 35, 499–528.

Forgas, J. P., 1995, Mood and judgment: The affect infusion model (aim), *Psychological Bulletin* 117, 39–66.

Forsythe, R., F. Nelson, G. Neumann, and J. Wright, 1992, Anatomy of an experimental political stock market, *American Economic Review* 82, 1142–1161.

Frank, R. 1988. *Passions Within Reason: The Strategic Role of the Emotions.* (Norton, New York).

Frankel, J. A., and K. A. Froot, 1986, Understanding the US dollar in the eighties: The expectations of chartists and fundamentalists, *Economic Record*, Supp. 62, 24–38.

Frankel, J. A., and K. A. Froot, 1990, Chartists, fundamentalists, and trading in the foreign exchange market, *American Economic Review* 80, 181–185.

Frankel, R., and C. Lee, 1998, Accounting valuation, market expectation, and the book-to-market effect, *Journal of Accounting and Economics* 25:3, 283–321.

Frankel, R., and C. Lee, 2001, Accounting diversity and international valuation, *Journal of Accounting and Economics*, forthcoming.

Froot, K., and E. Dabora, 1999, How are stock prices affected by the location of trade? *Journal of Financial Economics* 53, 189–216.

Garber, P., 1989, Tulipmania, *Journal of Political Economy* 97, 535–560.

Gazzaniga, M. S., 1988, *Mind Matters: How Mind and Brain Interact to Create our Conscious Lives* (Houghton Miffin, Boston).

Gervais, S., and T. Odean, 2001, Learning to be overconfident, *Review of Financial Studies* 14, 1–27.

Gigerenzer, G., 1991, How to make cognitive illusions disappear: Beyond 'heuristics and biases,' in W. Stroche and M. Hewstone, eds.: *European Review of Social Psychology* (Wiley, New York).

Gigerenzer, G., and U. Hoffrage, 1995, How to improve Bayesian reasoning without instruction: Frequency formats, *Psychological Review* 102, 684–704.

Gigerenzer, G., U. Hoffrage, and H. Kleinbolting, 1991, Probabilistic mental models: A Brunswikian theory of confidence, *Psychological Review* 98, 506–528.

Gigerenzer, G., U. Hoffrage, and H. Kleinbolting, 1996, On narrow norms and vague heuristics: A reply to Kahneman and Tversky, *Psychological Review* 103, 592–596.

Gigerenzer, G., P. Todd, and ABC-Group, 1999, *Simple Heuristics that Make Us Smart* (Oxford University Press, New York).

Gilboa, I., and D. Schmeidler, 1995, Case-based decision theory, *Quarterly Journal of Economics* 110, 605–639.

Gilovich, T. R., 1981, Seeing the past in the present: The effect of associations to familiar events on judgments and decisions, *Journal of Personality and Social Psychology* 40, 797–808.

Gilovich, T. R., 1991, *How We Know What Isn't So: The Fallibility of Human Reason in Everyday Life* (Free Press, New York).

Gilovich, T. R., R. Vallone, and A. Tversky, 1985, The hot hand in basketball: On the misperception of random sequences, *Cognitive Psychology* 17, 592–596.

Goetzmann, W. N., R. G. Ibbotson, and L. Peng, 2001, A new historical database for the NYSE 1815 to 1925: Performance and predictability, *Journal of Financial Markets* 4, 1–32.

Gomes, F., 2000, Loss aversion and the demand for risky assets, Working paper, London Business School.

Gompers, P., and J. Lerner, 1998, Venture capital distributions: Short-run and long-run reactions, *Journal of Finance* 53, 2161–2183.

Gompers, P., and J. Lerner, 2000, The really long-run performance of initial public offerings: The pre-Nasdaq evidence, Working paper, Harvard University.

Goyal, A., and I. Welch, 1999, The myth of predictability: Does the dividend yield forecast the equity premium? Working paper, UCLA.

Grether, D. M., 1980, Bayes' rule as a descriptive model: The representativeness heuristic, *Quarterly Journal of Economics* 95, 537–557.

Grether, D. M., 1992, Testing Bayes rule and the representativeness heuristic: Some experimental evidence, *Journal of Economic Behavior and Organization* 17, 31–57.

Grether, D. M., and C. R. Plott, 1979, Economic theory of choice and the preference reversal phenomenon, *American Economic Review* 69, 623–638.

Griffin, D., and A. Tversky, 1992, The weighing of evidence and the determinants of overconfidence, *Cognitive Psychology* 24, 411–435.

Griffin, J. M., and M. L. Lemon, 2001, Does book-to-market equity proxy for distress or overreacton? Working paper, University of Arizona.

Grinblatt, M., and M. Keloharju, 2000, The investment behavior and performance of various investor types: A study of Finland's unique data set, *Journal of Financial Economics* 55, 43–67.

Grinblatt, M., and M. Keloharju, 2001a, How distance, language, and culture influence stockholdings and trades, *Journal of Finance* 56, 1053–1073.

Grinblatt, M., and M. Keloharju, 2001b, What makes investors trade? *Journal of Finance* 56, 589–616.

Grinblatt, M., R. W. Masulis, and S. Titman, 1984, The valuation effects of stock splits and stock dividends, *Journal of Financial Economics* 13, 97–112.

Grinblatt, M., and T. Moskowitz, 1999, The cross-section of expected returns and its relation to past returns: New evidence, Working paper #24-99, UCLA.

Grinblatt, M., S. Titman, and R. Wermers, 1995, Momentum investment strategies, portfolio performance, and herding: A study of mutual fund behavior, *American Economic Review* 85, 1088–1105.

Groth, J. C., W. G. Lewellen, G. C. Scharbaum, and R. C. Lease, 1979, An analysis of brokerage house securities recommendations, *Financial Analysts' Journal* 35, 32–40.

Grundy, B., and J. S. Martin, 2001, Understanding the nature of the risks and the source of the rewards to momentum investing, *Review of Financial Studies* 14, 29–78.

Gul, F., 1991, A theory of disappointment aversion, *Econometrica* 59, 667–686.

Gyourko, J., and D. B. Keim, 1992, What does the stock market tell us about real estate returns? *Journal of the American Real Estate and Urban Economics Association* 20, 457–485.

Hand, J. R. M., 1990, A test of the extended functional fixation hypothesis, *Accounting Review* 65, 740–763.

Hand, J. R. M., 1991, Extended functional fixation and security returns around earnings announcements: A reply to Ball and Kothari, *Accounting Review* 66, 739–746.

Handa, P., S. P. Kothari, and C. Wasley, 1993, Sensitivity of multivariate tests of the capital asset-pricing model to the return measurement interval, *Journal of Finance* 48, 1543–1551.

Hansen, L., T. J. Sargent, and T. D. Tallarini, 1999, Robust permanent income and pricing, *Review of Economic Studies* 66, 873–907.

Hansen, L. P., and R. Jagannathan, 1991, Implications of security market data for models of dynamic economies, *Journal of Political Economy* 99, 225–262.

Hansen, L. P., and K. J. Singleton, 1983, Stochastic consumption, risk aversion, and the temporal behavior of asset returns, *Journal of Political Economy* 91, 249–265.

Harmon-Jones, E., and J. Mills, 1999, An introduction to cognitive dissonance theory and an overview of current perspectives on the theory, in Eddie Harmon-Jones and Judson Mills, eds.: *Cognitive Dissonance: Progress on a Pivotal Theory in Social Psychology* (American Psychological Association, Washington, DC).

Harris, C., and D. Laibson, 2001, Dynamic choices of hyperbolic consumers, *Econometrica*, forthcoming.

Harvey, C., 1989, The world price of covariance risk, *Journal of Finance* 46, 111–157.

Haugen, R. A., and N. L. Baker, 1996, Commonality in the determinants of expected stock returns, *Journal of Financial Economics* 41, 401–439.

Hawawini, G., and D. B. Keim, 1995, On the predictability of common stock returns: World-Wide evidence, in Robert A. Jarrow, Voijslav Maksimovic, and William T. Ziemba, eds.: *Finance, Handbooks in Operations Research and Management Science* (North Holland, Amsterdam).

Hawawini, G., and D. B. Keim, 2000, The cross section of common stock returns: A review of the evidence and some new findings, in Gabriel Hawawini, Donald B. Keim, and William T. Ziemba, eds.: *Security Market Imperfections in World Wide Equity Markets* (Cambridge University Press, Cambridge, UK).

Hawawini, G., D. B. Keim, and W. T. Ziemba, 2000, *Security Market Imperfections in World Wide Equity Markets* (Cambridge University Press, Cambridge, UK).

Hawkins, S. A., and R. Hastie, 1990, Hindsight: Biased judgements of past events after the outcomes are known, *Psychological Bulletin* 107, 311–327.

Heath, C., and A. Tversky, 1991, Preferences and beliefs: Ambiguity and competence in choice under uncertainty, *Journal of Risk and Uncertainty* 4, 5–28.

Heaton, J. C., 1995, An empirical investigation of asset pricing with temporally dependent preference specifications, *Econometrica* 63, 681–717.

Heaton, J. C., and D. J. Lucas, 1996, Evaluating the effects of incomplete markets on risk-sharing and asset pricing, *Journal of Political Economy* 104, 443–487.

Hertwig, R., and A. Ortmann, 2001, Experimental practices in economics: A challenge for psychologists? *Behavioral and Brain Sciences* 24, forthcoming.

Hertzel, M., M. L. Lemmon, J. S. Linck, and L. Rees, 1999, Long-run performance following private placements of equity, Working paper, University of Rochester.

Heston, S. L., K. G. Rouwenhorst, and R. E. Wessels, 1995, The structure of international stock returns and the integration of capital markets, *Journal of Empirical Finance* 2, 173–197.

Heston, S. L., K. G. Rouwenhorst, and R. E. Wessels, 1999, The role of beta and size in the cross-section of European stock returns, *European Financial Management* 4, 4–28.

Higgins, E., 1996, Knowledge activation: Accessibility, applicability, and salience, in E. T. Higgins, and A. W. Kruglanski, eds.: *Social Psychology: Handbook of Basic Principles* (Guilford, New York).

Hirshleifer, D., and J. Hirshleifer, 2001, An adaptive theory of self-deception, Working paper, Ohio State University.

Hirshleifer, D., and G. Y. Luo, 2001, On the survival of overconfident traders in a competitive security market, *Journal of Financial Markets* 4, 73–84.

Hirshleifer, D., and T. Shumway, 2001, Good day sunshine: Stock returns and the weather, Working paper 2001-3, Ohio State University.

Hirshleifer, D., and I. Welch, 2000, An economic approach to the psychology of change: Amnesia, inertia, and impulsiveness, Working paper, Ohio State University.

Hirshleifer, J. (1987). On the emotions as guarantors of threats and promises, in J. Dupre, ed.: *The Latest on the Best: Essays on Evolution and Optimality* (MIT Press, Cambridge, MA).

Ho, T., and R. Michaely, 1988, Information quality and market efficiency, *Journal of Financial and Quantitative Analysis* 5, 357–386.

Hodrick, R. J., 1992, Dividend yields and expected stock returns: Alternative procedures for inference and measurement, *Review of Financial Studies* 5, 357–386.

Hong, H., T. Lim, and J. Stein, 2000, Bad news travels slowly: Size, analyst coverage and the profitability of momentum strategies, *Journal of Finance* 55, 265–295.

Hong, H., and J. C. Stein, 1999, A unified theory of underreaction, momentum trading and overreaction in asset markets, *Journal of Finance* 54, 2143–2184.

Huberman, G., 1999, Familiarity breeds investment, Working paper 97-04, Columbia University.

Huberman, G., and T. Regev, 2001, Contagious speculation and a cure for cancer, *Journal of Finance* 56, 387–396.

Hvidkjaer, S., 2000, A trade-based analysis of momentum, Working paper, Johnson School of Management.

Ikenberry, D., J. Lakonishok, and T. Vermaelen, 1995, Market underreaction to open market share repurchases, *Journal of Financial Economics* 39, 181–208.

Ikenberry, D., J. Lakonishok, and T. Vermaelen, 2000, Stock repurchases in Canada: Performance and strategic trading, *Journal of Finance* 55, 2373–2397.

Ikenberry, D., and S. Ramnath, 2000, Underreaction, Working paper, Rice University.

Ikenberry, D., G. Rankine, and E. K. Stice, 1996, What do stock splits really signal? *Journal of Financial and Quantitative Analysis* 31, 357–375.

Isenberg, D. J., 1986, Group polarization: A critical review and meta-analysis, *Journal of Personality and Social Psychology* 50, 1141–1151.

Jagannathan, R., K. Kubota, and H. Takehara, 1998, Relationship between labor-income risk and average return: Empirical evidence from the Japanese stock market, *Journal of Business* 71, 319–348.

Jagannathan, R., and Z. Wang, 1996, The CAPM is alive and well, *Journal of Finance* 51, 3–53.

Jegadeesh, N., 1991, Seasonality in stock price mean reversion: Evidence from the U.S. and the U.K., *Journal of Finance* 46, 1427–1444.

Jegadeesh, N., 1999, Long-run performance of seasoned equity offerings: Benchmark errors and biases in expectations, Working paper, University of Illinois.

Jegadeesh, N., and S. Titman, 1993, Returns to buying winners and selling losers: Implications for stock market efficiency, *Journal of Finance* 48, 65–91.

Jegadeesh, N., and S. Titman, 1995, Overreaction, delayed reaction, and contrarian profits, *Review of Financial Studies* 8, 973–999.

Jenkins, H. M., and W. C. Ward, 1965, Judgement of contingency between responses and outcomes, *Psychological Monographs* 79, 1–17.

Jindra, J., 2000, Seasoned equity offerings, overvaluation and timing, Working paper, Ohio State University.

Josephs, R., R. P. Larrick, C. M. Steele, and R. E. Nisbett, 1996, Protecting the self from the negative consequences of risky decisions, *Journal of Personality and Social Psychology* 62, 26–37.

Kahneman, D., J. L. Knetsch, and R. H. Thaler, 1991, The endowment effect, loss aversion, and status quo bias: Anomalies, *Journal of Economic Perspectives* 5, 193–206.

Kahneman, D., and D. Lovallo, 1993, Timid choices and bold forecasts: A cognitive perspective on risk taking, *Management Science* 39, 17–31.

Kahneman, D., and A. Tversky, 1973, On the psychology of prediction, *Psychological Review* 80, 237–251.

Kahneman, D., and A. Tversky, 1979, Prospect theory: An analysis of decision under risk, *Econometrica* 47, 263–291.

Kahneman, D., and A. Tversky, 1982, The psychology of preferences, *Scientific American* 246, 160–173.

Kahneman, D., and A. Tversky, 1996, On the reality of cognitive illusions: A reply to Gigerenzer's critique, *Psychological Review* 103, 582–591.

Kamstra, M. J., L. A. Kramer, and M. D. Levi, 2000a, Losing sleep at the market: The daylight-savings anomaly, *American Economic Review* 12, 1005–1000.

Kamstra, M. J., L. A. Kramer, and M. D. Levi, 2000b, Winter blues: Seasonal affective disorder (SAD), the January effect, and stock market returns, Working paper, University of British Columbia.

Kang, J.-K., Y.-C. Kim, and R. M. Stulz, 1999, The underreaction hypothesis and the new issue puzzle: Evidence from Japan, *Review of Financial Studies* 12, 519–534.

Kang, J.-K., and R. M. Stulz, 1997, Why is there a home bias? An analysis of foreign portfolio equity ownership in Japan, *Journal of Financial Economics* 46, 3–28.

Keane, M. P., and D. E. Runkle, 1990, Testing the rationality of price forecasts: New evidence from panel data, *American Economic Review* 80, 714–735.

Keim, D. B., 1988, Stock market regularities: A synthesis of the evidence and explanations, in Elroy Dimson, ed.: *Stock Market Anomalies* (Cambridge University Press, Cambridge).

Keim, D. B., and R. F. Stambaugh, 1986, Predicting returns in the stock and bond markets, *Journal of Financial Economics* 17, 357–390.

Keren, G., 1991, Calibration and probability judgments: Conceptual and methodological issues, *Acta Psychologica* 77, 217–273.

Keynes, J. M., 1936, *The General Theory of Employment, Interest and Money* (Macmillan, London).

Kim, D., 1997, A reexamination of firm size, book-to-market, and earnings price in the cross-section of expected stock returns, *Journal of Financial and Quantitative Analysis* 32, 463–489.

Kim, M.-J., C. R. Nelson, and R. Startz, 1988, Mean reversion in stock prices? A reappraisal of the empirical evidence, *Review of Economic Studies* 58, 551–528.

Kirby, K., and R. J. Herrnstein, 1995, Preference reversals due to myopic discounting of delayed reward, *Psychological Science* 6, 83–89.

Klayman, J., and Y. Ha, 1987, Confirmation, disconfirmation and information in hypothesis testing, *Psychological Review* 94, 211–228.

Kleidon, A. W., 1986, Anomalies in financial economics: Blueprint for change? *Journal of Business* 59, S469–S499.

Klibanoff, P., O. Lamont, and T. A. Wizman, 1999, Investor reaction to salient news in closed-end country funds, *Journal of Finance* 53, 673–699.

Knez, P., V. L. Smith, and A. Williams, 1985, Individual rationality, market rationality, and value estimation, *American Economic Review Papers and Proceedings* 52, 397–402.

Knez, P. J., and M. J. Ready, 1997, On the robustness of size and book-to-market in cross-sectional regressions, *Journal of Finance* 52, 1355–1382.

Kocherlakota, N. R., 1996, The equity premium: It's still a puzzle, *Journal of Economic Literature* 34, 42–71.

Koehler, J. J., 1996, The base rate fallacy reconsidered: Normative, descriptive and methodological challenges, *Behavioral and Brain Sciences* 19, 1–53.

Korajczyk, R. A., D. J. Lucas, and R. L. McDonald, 1991, The effect of information releases on the pricing and timing of equity issues, *Review of Financial Studies* 4, 685–708.

Kothari, S., 2000, Capital market research in accounting, Working paper, MIT.

Kothari, S., and J. Shanken, 1997, Book-to-market, dividend yield, and expected market returns: A time-series analysis, *Journal of Financial Economics* 44, 169–203.

Kothari, S., and J. Shanken, 2000, Beta and book-to-market: Is the glass half full or half empty? in Donald B. Keim and William T. Ziemba, eds.: *Security Market Imperfections in World Wide Equity Markets* (Cambridge University Press, Cambridge).

Kothari, S., J. Shanken, and R. Sloan, 1995, Another look at the cross-section of expected returns, *Journal of Finance* 50, 185–224.

Kraus, A., and J. S. Sagi, 2000, Inter-temporal flexibility preferences, Working paper, University of California, Berkeley.

Krische, S. D., and C. M. Lee, 2000, The information content of analyst stock recommendations, Working paper, Simon Fraser University.

Kroll, Y., and H. Levy, 1992, Further tests of the separation theorem and the capital asset pricing model, *American Economic Review* 82, 664–670.

Kroll, Y., H. Levy, and A. Rapoport, 1988a, Experimental tests of the mean-variance model for portfolio selection, *Organizational Behavior and Human Decision Processes* 42, 388–410.

Kroll, Y., H. Levy, and A. Rapoport, 1988b, Experimental tests of the separation theorem and the capital asset pricing model, *American Economic Review* 78, 500–519.

Kruschke, J. K., and M. K. Johansen, 1999, A model of probabilistic category learning, *Journal of Experimental Psychology: Learning, Memory, and Cognition* 25, 1083–1119.

Kuran, T., and C. Sunstein, 1999, Availability cascades and risk regulation, *Stanford Law Review* 51, 683–768.

Kurz, M., 1997, *Endogenous Economic Fluctuations* (Springer Verlag, New York).

Kyle, A., and F. A. Wang, 1997, Speculation duopoly with agreement to disagree: Can overconfidence survive the market test? *Journal of Finance* 52, 2073–2090.

Kyle, A., and W. Xiong, 2000, Contagion as a wealth effect, Working paper, Duke University.
La Porta, R., J. Lakonishok, A. Shleifer, and R. W. Vishny, 1997, Good news for value stocks: Further evidence on market efficiency, *Journal of Finance* 52, 859–874.
Laibson, D., 1997, Golden eggs and hyperbolic discounting, *Quarterly Journal of Economics* 112, 443–477.
Lakonishok, J., A. Shleifer, and R. W. Vishny, 1992, The impact of institutional trading on stock prices, *Journal of Financial Economics* 32, 23–43.
Lakonishok, J., A. Shleifer, and R. W. Vishny, 1994, Contrarian investment, extrapolation and risk, *Journal of Finance* 49, 1541–1578.
Lakonishok, J., and T. Vermaelen, 1990, Anomalous price behavior around repurchase tender offers, *Journal of Finance* 45, 455–477.
Lamont, O., and R. Thaler, 2000, Can the market add and subtract? Mispricing in tech stock carveouts, Working paper, University of Chicago.
Langer, E. J., 1975, The illusion of control, *Journal of Personality and Social Psychology* 32, 311–328.
Langer, E. J., and J. Roth, 1975, Heads I win, tails it's chance: The illusion of control as a function of the sequence of outcomes in a purely chance task, *Journal of Personality and Social Psychology* 32, 951–955.
LeBaron, B., 2000a, Agent-based computational finance: Suggested readings and early research, *Journal of Economic Dynamics and Control* 24, 679–702.
LeBaron, B., 2000b, Evolution and time horizons in an agent-based stock market, Working paper, Brandeis University and NBER.
LeBaron, B., 2000c, Evolving long run investors in a short run world, Working paper, Brandeis University and NBER.
Lee, C., 2001, Market efficiency and accounting research, *Journal of Accounting and Economics*, forthcoming.
Lee, C., A. Shleifer, and R. Thaler, 1991, Investor sentiment and the closed-end fund puzzle, *Journal of Finance* 46, 75–109.
Lee, C. M., J. Myers, and B. Swaminathan, 1999, What is the intrinsic value of the Dow? *Journal of Finance* 54, 1693–1741.
Lee, C. M., and B. Swaminathan, 2000a, Do stock prices overreact to earnings news? Working paper, Cornell University.
Lee, C. M., and B. Swaminathan, 2000b, Price momentum and trading volume, *Journal of Finance* 55, 2017–2069.
Lee, I. H., 1998, Market crashes and informational avalanches, *Review of Economic Studies* 65, 741–759.
Lenney, E., 1977, Women's self-confidence in achievement settings, *Psychological Bulletin* 84, 1–13.
LeRoy, S. F., and R. D. Porter, 1981, Stock price volatility: A test based on implied variance bounds, *Econometrica* 49, 97–113.
Lewellen, J., 1999, The time-series relations among expected return, risk, and book-to-market, *Journal of Financial Economics* 54, 5–43.
Lewellen, J., 2000, Momentum profits and the autocorrelation of returns, Working Paper, University of Rochester.
Lewellen, J., and J. Shanken, 2000, Market efficiency, rational expectations, and estimation risk, Working Paper, University of Rochester.
Lewis, K. K., 1999, Trying to explain home bias in equities and consumption, *Journal of Economic Literature* 37, 571–608.
Libby, R., R. Bloomfield, and M. Nelson, 2001, Experimental research in financial accounting, Working paper, Cornell University.
Lichtenstein, S., and B. Fischhoff, 1977, Do those who know more also know more about how much they know? *Organizational Behavior and Human Performance* 20, 159–183.
Lichtenstein, S., B. Fischhoff, and L. Phillips, 1982, Calibration of probabilities: The state of the art to 1980, in Daniel Kahneman, Paul Slovic, and Amos Tversky, eds.: *Judgement under Uncertainty: Heuristics and Biases* (Cambridge University Press, Cambridge).

Lichtenstein, S., and P. Slovic, 1971, Reversals of preference between bids and choices in gambling decisions, *Journal of Experimental Psychology* 89, 46–56.

Liew, J., and M. Vassalou, 2000, Can book-to-market, size and momentum be risk factors that predict economic growth? *Journal of Financial Economics* 57, 221–245.

Lin, P., 2000a, Analyst forecast error and the profitability of earnings revisions strategies: Evidence from U.S. and U.K. equity markets, Working paper, University of Washington, Seattle.

Lin, P., 2000b, Earnings revisions strategies in the U.S., U.K., and Japan, Working paper, University of Washington, Seattle.

Loewenstein, G., and D. Prelec, 1992, Anomalies in intertemporal choice: Evidence and an interpretation, *Quarterly Journal of Economics* 107, 573–597.

Loewenstein, G. F., 1996, Out of control: Visceral influences on behavior, *Organizational Behavior and Human Decision Processes* 65, 272–292.

Loewenstein, G. F., 2000, Emotions in economic theory and economic behavior, *American Economic Review* 65, 426–432.

Longstaff, F. A., P. Santa-Clara, and E. Schwartz, 1999, Throwing away a billion dollars: The cost of suboptimal exercise strategies in the swaptions market, Anderson School Working paper #8-00, UCLA.

Lord, C. G., L. Ross, and M. R. Lepper, 1979, Biased assimilation and attitude polarization: The effects of prior theories on subsequently considered evidence, *Journal of Personality and Social Psychology* 37, 2098–2109.

Loughran, T., and J. Ritter, 1995, The new issues puzzle, *Journal of Finance* 50, 23–52.

Loughran, T., and J. Ritter, 2000, Uniformly least powerful tests of market efficiency, *Journal of Financial Economics* 55, 361–389.

Lovell, M. C., 1986, Tests of the rational expectations hypothesis, *American Economic Review* 76, 110–124.

Lundeberg, M. A., P. W. Fox, and J. Puncochar, 1994, Highly confident but wrong: Gender differences and similarities in confidence judgements, *Journal of Educational Psychology* 86, 114–121.

Luo, G. Y., 1998, Market efficiency and natural selection in a commodity futures market, *Review of Financial Studies* 11, 647–674.

Luttmer, E. G. J., and T. Mariotti, 2000, Subjective discounting in an exchange economy, Working paper, London School of Economics.

MacKinlay, A. C., 1995, Multifactor models do not explain deviations from the CAPM, *Journal of Financial Economics* 38, 3–28.

Madrian, B., and D. Shea, 2000, The power of suggestion: Inertia in 401(k) participation and savings behavior, NBER working paper 7682.

Maenhout, P. J., 2000, Robust portfolio rules and asset pricing, Working paper, Harvard University.

Mankiw, N. G., 1986, The term structure of interest rates revisited, *Brookings Papers Economic Activity* 1, 61–110.

Mankiw, N. G., and L. H. Summers, 1984, Do long-term interest rates overreact to short-term interest rates? *Brookings Papers Economic Activity* 1, 223–242.

Mann, L., 1992, Stress, affect, and risk taking, in J. Frank Yates, ed.: *Risk-taking Behavior* (Wiley, Chichester).

Mano, H., 1999, The influence of pre-existing negative affect on store purchase intentions, *Journal of Retailing* 75, 149–172.

Markowitz, H. M., 1952, The utility of wealth, *Journal Political Economy* 60, 151–158.

Marsh, T. A., and R. C. Merton, 1986, Dividend variability and variance bounds tests for the rationality of stock market prices, *American Economic Review* 76, 483–498.

McClelland, A., and F. Bolger, 1994, The calibration of subjective probabilities: Theories and models 1980–1993, in George Wright and Peter Ayton, eds.: *Subjective Probability* (Wiley, Chichester).

McConnell, J. J., and G. C. Sanger, 1987, The puzzle in post-listing common stock returns, *Journal of Finance* 42, 119–140.

Mehra, R., and E. Prescott, 1985, The equity premium: A puzzle, *Journal of Monetary Economics* 15, 145–161.

Mehra, R., and E. Prescott, 2001, The equity premium puzzle in retrospect, in G.M. Constantinides, M. Harris, and R. Stulz, eds.: *Handbook of the Economics of Finance* (North Holland, Amsterdam).

Mehra, R., and R. Sah, 2000, Mood fluctuations, projection bias and volatility in equity prices, Working paper, University of California, Santa Barbara.

Merton, R. C., 1987, A simple model of capital market equilibrium with incomplete information, *Journal of Finance* 42, 483–510.

Michaely, R., R. H. Thaler, and K. L. Womack, 1995, Price reactions to dividend initiations and omissions: Overreaction or drift? *Journal of Finance* 50, 573–608.

Michaely, R., and K. Womack, 1999, Conflict of interest and the credibility of underwriter analyst recommendations, *Review of Financial Studies* 12, 573–608.

Miller, D. T., and M. Ross, 1975, Self-serving bias in attribution of causality: Fact or fiction? *Psychological Bulletin* 82, 213–225.

Mitchell, M., and E. Stafford, 2000, Managerial decisions and long-term stock price performance, *Journal of Business* 73, 287–320.

Modigliani, F., and R. Cohn, 1979, Inflation, rational valuation, and the market, *Financial Analyst Journal* 35:2, 24–44.

Moreland, R. L., and R. Beach, 1992, Exposure effects in the classroom: The development of affinity among students, *Journal of Experimental Social Psychology* 28, 255–276.

Moskowitz, T. J., and M. Grinblatt, 1999, Do industries explain momentum? *Journal of Finance* 54, 1249–1290.

Mulligan, C. B., 1996, A logical economist's argument against hyperbolic discounting, Working paper, University of Chicago.

Mussweiler, T., and F. Strack, 1999, Hypothesis-consistent testing and semantic priming in the anchoring paradigm: A selective accessibility model, *Journal of Experimental Social Psychology* 35, 136–164.

Neal, R., and S. M. Wheatley, 1998, Do measures of investor sentiment predict returns?, *Journal of Financial and Quantitative Analysis* 33, 523–547.

Nel, E., R. Helmreich, and E. Aronson, 1969, Opinion change in the advocate as a function of the persuasibility of his audience: A clarification of the meaning of dissonance, *Journal of Personality and Social Psychology* 12, 117–124.

Nesse, R. 2001, Commitment in the clinic, in R. Nesse, ed.: *The Evolution of Subjective Commitment* (Russell Sage Press, New York).

Newman, J., W. Wolff, and E. Hearst, 1980, The feature-positive effect in adult human subjects, *Journal of Experimental Psychology: Human Learning and Memory* 6, 630–650.

Ng, L. K., and Y. Fu, 2000, Market efficiency and return statistics: Evidence from real estate and stock markets using a present-value approach, Working paper, University of Wisconsin.

Nisbett, R., and L. Ross, 1980, *Human Inference: Strategies and Shortcomings of Social Judgment* (Prentice-Hall, Englewood Cliffs, NJ).

Nisbett, R. E., and T. D. Wilson, 1977a, The halo effect: Evidence for unconscious alteration of judgments, *Journal of Personality and Social Psychology* 35, 250–256.

Nisbett, R. E., and T. D. Wilson, 1977b, Telling more than we can know: Verbal reports on mental processes, *Psychological Review* 84, 231–259.

Nofsinger, J. R., and R. W. Sias, 1999, Herding and feedback trading by institutional and individual investors, *Journal of Finance* 54, 2263–2295.

Odean, T., 1998a, Are investors reluctant to realize their losses? *Journal of Finance* 53, 1775–1798.

Odean, T., 1998b, Volume, volatility, price and profit when all traders are above average, *Journal of Finance* 53, 1887–1934.

Odean, T., 1999, Do investors trade too much? *American Economic Review* 89, 1279–1298.

O'Donoghue, T., and M. Rabin, 1999, Doing it now or later, *American Economics Review* 89, 103–124.

Palomino, F., 1996, Noise trading in small markets, *Journal of Finance* 51, 1537–1550.

Payne, J. W., J. R. Bettman, and E. J. Johnson, 1992, Behavioral decision research: A constructive processing perspective, *Annual Review of Psychology* 43, 87–131.

Peavy, J. W., 1990, Returns on initial public offerings of closed-end funds, *Review of Financial Studies* 3, 695–708.

Pennington, N., and R. Hastie, 1988, Explanation-based decision making: Effects of memory structure on judgment, *Journal of Experimental Psychology: Learning, Memory, and Cognition* 14, 521–533.

Pesaran, M. H., and A. Timmermann, 1995, Predictability of stock returns: Robustness and economic significance, *Journal of Finance* 50, 1201–1228.

Peters, E., and P. Slovic, 1996, The role of affect and worldviews as orienting dispositions in the perception and acceptance of nuclear power, *Journal of Applied Social Psychology* 26, 1427–1453.

Petty, R. E., F. Gleicher, and S. M. Baker, 1991, Multiple roles for affect in persuasion, in J. Forgas, ed.: *Emotion and Social Judgments* (Pergamon, Oxford).

Pontiff, J., and L. D. Schall, 1998, Book-to-market ratios as predictors of market returns, *Journal of Financial Economics* 49, 141–160.

Poterba, J. M., and L. H. Summers, 1988, Mean reversion in stock returns: Evidence and implications, *Journal of Financial Economics* 22, 27–59.

Poteshman, A., 2001, Underreaction, overreaction, and increasing misreaction to information in the options market, *Journal of Finance* 56, 851–876.

Rabin, M., 1998, Psychology and economics, *Journal of Economic Literature* 36, 11–46.

Rabin, M., 2000, Inference by believers in the law of small numbers, Working paper, University of California, Berkeley.

Rabin, M., and J. Schrag, 1999, First impressions matter: A model of confirmatory bias, *Quarterly Journal of Economics* 94, 37–82.

Ranguelova, E., 2000, Disposition effect and firm size: New evidence on individual investor trading activity, Working paper, Harvard University.

Rashes, M. S., 2001, Massively confused investors making conspicuously ignorant choices (mci–mcic), *Journal of Finance* 56:5.

Rau, P. R., and T. Vermaelen, 1998, Glamour, value and the post-acquisition performance of acquiring firms, *Journal of Financial Economics* 49, 223–253.

Read, D., G. Loewenstein, and M. Rabin, 1999, Choice bracketing, *Journal of Risk and Uncertainty* 19, 171–197.

Reber, R., and N. Schwarz, 1999, Effects of perceptual fluency on judgments of truth, *Consciousness and Cognition* 8, 338–342.

Richards, A. J., 1997, Winner-loser reversals in national stock market indices: Can they be explained? *Journal of Finance* 52, 2129–2144.

Richardson, M., and T. Smith, 1994, A unified approach to testing for serial correlation in stock returns, *Journal of Business* 67, 371–399.

Richardson, M., and J. H. Stock, 1989, Drawing inferences from statistics based on multiyear asset returns, *Journal of Financial Economics* 25, 323–348.

Richardson, S., S. H. Teoh, and P. D. Wysocki, 1999, Tracking analysts' forecasts over the annual earnings horizon: Are analysts' forecasts optimistic or pessimistic? Working paper, Ohio State University.

Rietz, T. A., 1998, Enforcing arbitrage restrictions in experimental asset markets, Working paper, University of Iowa.

Ritov, I., 1996, Probability of regret: Anticipation of uncertainty resolution in choice, *Organizational Behavior and Human Decision Processes* 66, 228–236.

Ritov, I., and J. Baron, 1990, Reluctance to vaccinate: Omission bias and ambiguity, *Journal of Behavioral Decision Making* 3, 263–277.

Ritter, J. R., and R. S. Warr, 2001, The decline of inflation and the bull market of 1982 to 1999, Working paper, University of Florida.

Roll, R. W., 1984, Orange juice and weather, *American Economic Review* 74, 861–880.

Roll, R. W., 1988, r^2, *Journal of Finance* 43, 541–566.

Rosenberg, B., K. Reid, and R. Lanstein, 1985, Persuasive evidence of market inefficiency, *Journal of Portfolio Management* 11, 9–17.

Rosenthal, L., and C. Young, 1990, The seemingly anomalous price behavior of Royal Dutch Shell and Unilever NV/PLC, *Journal of Financial Economics* 26, 123–141.

Ross, L., 1977, The intuitive psychologist and his shortcomings: Distortions in the attribution process, in L. Berkowitz, ed.: *Advances in Experimental Social Psychology* (Academic Press, New York, NY).

Ross, L., D. Green, and P. House, 1977a, The "false consensus effect": An egocentric bias in social perception and attribution processes, *Journal of Experimental Social Psychology* 13, 279–301.

Ross, L., M. R. Lepper, F. Strack, and J. Steinmetz, 1977, Social explanation and social expectation: Effects of real and hypothetical explanations on subjective likelihood, *Journal of Personality and Social Psychology* 35, 817–829.

Rouwenhorst, K. G., 1998, International momentum strategies, *Journal of Finance* 53, 267–284.

Rouwenhorst, K. G., 1999, Local return factors and turnover in emerging stock markets, *Journal of Finance* 54, 1439–1464.

Rozeff, M. S., and M. A. Zaman, 1988, Market efficiency and insider trading: New evidence, *Journal of Business* 61, 25–44.

Rubinstein, A., 2000, Is it 'economics and psychology'?: The case of hyperbolic discounting, Working paper, Princeton University Economics Department.

Samuelson, W., and R. Zeckhauser, 1988, Status-quo bias in decision making, *Journal of Risk and Uncertainty* 1, 7–59.

Sandroni, A., 2000, Do markets favor agents able to make accurate predictions? *Econometrica* 68, 1303–1342.

Saunders, E. M. J., 1993, Stock prices and Wall Street weather, *American Economic Review* 83, 1337–1345.

Schill, M. J., and C. Zhou, 1999, Pricing an emerging industry: Evidence from internet subsidiary carve-outs, Working paper, University of California, Riverside.

Schwarz, N., and G. L. Clore, 1983, Mood, misattribution, and judgments of well-being: Informative and directive functions of affective states, *Journal of Personality and Social Psychology* 45, 513–523.

Schwarz, N., and I. Skurnik, 2001, Feeling and thinking: Implications for problem solving, in Janet Davidson, and Robert Sternberg, eds.: *The Nature of Problem Solving* (Cambridge University Press, Cambridge).

Seyhun, H. N., 1988, The information content of aggregate insider trading, *Journal of Business* 61, 1–24.

Seyhun, H. N., 1990, Overreaction or fundamentals: Some lessons from insiders' response to the market crash of 1987, *Journal of Finance* 45, 1303–1331.

Shaffr, E., P. Diamond, and A. Tversky, 1997, Money illusion, *Quarterly Journal of Economics* 112, 341–374.

Sharpe, S. A., 1999, Stock prices, expected returns, and inflation, Board of Governors of the Federal Reserve System, Finance and Economics Discussion Series no. 1999-2.

Shefrin, H., 1997, Behavioral option pricing, Working paper, Santa Clara University.

Shefrin, H., and M. Statman, 1984, Explaining investor preference for cash dividends, *Journal of Financial Economics* 13:2, 253–282.

Shefrin, H., and M. Statman, 1985, The disposition to sell winners too early and ride losers too long: Theory and evidence, *Journal of Finance* 40, 777–790.

Shefrin, H., and M. Statman, 1994, Behavioral capital asset pricing theory, *Journal of Financial and Quantitative Analysis* 29, 323–349.

Shefrin, H., and M. Statman, 1995, Making sense of beta, size, and book-to-market, *Journal of Portfolio Management* 21:2, 323–349.

Shiller, R. J., 1979, The volatility of long term interest rates and expectations models of the term structure, *Journal of Political Economy* 87, 1190–1219.

Shiller, R. J., 1981, Do stock prices move too much to be justified by subsequent changes in dividends? *American Economic Review* 71, 421–498.

Shiller, R. J., 1982, Consumption, asset markets, and macroeconomic fluctuations, *Carnegie Rochester Conference Series on Public Policy* 17, 203–238.

Shiller, R. J., 1984, Stock prices and social dynamics, *Brookings Papers on Economic Activity Review* 2, 457–498.

Shiller, R. J., 1988, Portfolio insurance and other investor factors in the 1987 stock market crash, *NBER Macroeconomics Annual* pp. 287–296.

Shiller, R. J., 1990, Speculative prices and popular models, *Journal of Economic Perspectives* 4, 55–65.

Shiller, R. J., 1999, Human behavior and the efficiency of the financial system, in J. Taylor, and M. Woodford, eds.: *Handbook of Macroeconomics* (Elsevier, Amsterdam).

Shiller, R. J., 2000a, Conversation, information, and herd behavior, *American Economic Review* 85, 181–185.

Shiller, R. J., 2000b, *Irrational Exuberance* (Princeton University Press).

Shiller, R. J., 2000c, Measuring bubble expectations and investor confidence, *Journal of Psychology and Financial Markets* 1, 49–60.

Shiller, R. J., J. Y. Campbell, and K. L. Schoenholtz, 1983, Forward rates and future policy: Interpreting the term structure of interest rates, *Brookings Papers on Economic Activity* 1, 173–217.

Shiller, R. J., and J. Pound, 1989, Survey evidence on the diffusion of interest and information among investors, *Journal of Economic Behavior and Organization* 12, 46–66.

Shleifer, A., 2000, *Inefficient Markets: An Introduction to Behavioral Finance* (Oxford University Press, Oxford).

Shleifer, A., and R. Vishny, 1997, The limits to arbitrage, *Journal of Finance* 52, 35–55.

Shumway, T., 1996, Size, overreaction, and book-to-market effects as default premia, Working paper, University of Michigan Business School.

Shumway, T., 1998, Explaining returns with loss aversion, Mimeo, University of Michigan.

Simon, H. A., 1955, A behavioral model of rational choice, *Quarterly Journal of Economics* 69, 99–118.

Simon, H. A., 1956, Rational choice and the structure of environments, *Psychological Review* 63, 129–138.

Skinner, D. J., and R. G. Sloan, 2000, Earnings surprises, growth expectations, and stock returns or don't let an earnings torpedo sink your portfolio, Working paper, University of Michigan.

Sloan, R., 1997, Do stock prices fully reflect information in accruals and cash flows about future earnings? *Accounting Review* 71:3, 289–315.

Soll, J. B., 1996, Determinants of overconfidence and miscalibration: The roles of random error and ecological structure, *Organizational Behavior and Human Decision Processes* 65, 117–137.

Solnik, B., 1974, International pricing of risk: An empirical investigation of the world capital markets, *Journal of Finance* 29, 48–54.

Spiess, D. K., and J. Affeck-Graves, 1995, Underperformance in long-run stock returns following seasoned equity offerings, *Journal of Financial Economics* 38, 243–268.

Spiess, D. K., and J. Affeck-Graves, 1999, The long-run performance of stock returns following debt offers, *Journal of Financial Economics* 54, 45–73.

Stanovich, K. E., and R. F. West, 2000, Individual differences in reasoning: Implications for the rationality debate? *Brain and Behavioral Sciences* 22.

Stasser, G., L. Taylor, and C. Hanna, 1989, Information sampling in structured and unstructured discussions of three- and six-person groups, *Journal of Personality and Social Psychology* 57, 67–78.

Stasser, G., and W. Titus, 1985, Pooling of unshared information in group decision making: Biased information sampling during discussion, *Journal of Personality and Social Psychology* 48, 1467–1478.

Statman, M., and S. Thorley, 1998, Overconfidence and trading volume, Working paper, Santa Clara University.

Stattman, D., 1980, Book values and stock returns, *The Chicago MBA: A Journal of Selected Papers* 4, 25–45.

Steele, C., and T. Liu, 1983, Dissonance processes as self-affirmation, *Journal of Personality and Social Psychology* 45, 393–397.

Stein, J., 1996, Rational capital budgeting in an irrational world, *Journal of Business* 69, 429–455.

Sundaresan, S. M., 1989, Intertemporally dependent preferences and the volatility of consumption and wealth, *Review of Financial Studies* 2, 73–89.

Sunder, S., 1995, Experimental asset markets: A survey, in John H. Kagel, and Alvin E. Roth, eds.: *The Handbook of Experimental Economics* (Princeton University Press, Princeton, NJ).

Swaminathan, B., 1996, Time-varying expected small firm returns and closed-end fund discounts, *Review of Financial Studies* 9, 845–888.

Taylor, S. E., and J. D. Brown, 1988, Illusion and well-being: A social psychological perspective on mental health, *Psychological Bulletin* 103, 193–210.

Teoh, S. H., I. Welch, and T. J. Wong, 1998a, Earnings management and the long-term market performance of initial public offerings, *Journal of Finance* 53, 1935–1974.

Teoh, S. H., I. Welch, and T. J. Wong, 1998b, Earnings management and the underperformance of seasoned equity offerings, *Journal of Financial Economics* 50, 63–99.

Teoh, S. H., and T. J. Wong, 2001, Analysts' credulity about reported earnings and overoptimism in new equity issues, *Review of Financial Studies*, forthcoming.

Tesar, L., and I. M. Werner, 1995, Home bias and high turnover, *Journal of International Money and Finance* 14:4, 467–492.

Thaler, R., 1981, Some empirical evidence on dynamic inconsistency, *Economic Letter* 8, 201–207.

Thaler, R., and E. J. Johnson, 1990, Gambling with the house money and trying to break even: The effects of prior outcomes on risky choice, *Management Science* 36, 643–660.

Thaler, R. H., 1985, Mental accounting and consumer choice, *Marketing Science* 4, 199–214.

Thaler, R. H., and H. M. Shefrin, 1981, An economic theory of self-control, *Journal of Political Economy* 89, 392–406.

Tornell, A., 2000, Robust-h_8 forecasting and asset pricing anomalies, NBER Working Paper 7753.

Trivers, R., 1985, *Social Evolution* (Benjamin/Cummings, Menlo Park).

Trivers, R., 1991, Deceit and self-deception, in R. Robinson, and L. Tiger, eds.: *Man and Beast Revisited* (Smithsonian Press, Washington DC).

Tversky, A., and D. Kahneman, 1971, Belief in the law of small numbers, *Psychological Bulletin* 76, 105–110.

Tversky, A., and D. Kahneman, 1973, Availability: A heuristic for judging frequency and probability, *Cognitive Psychology* 5, 207–232.

Tversky, A., and D. Kahneman, 1974, Judgment under uncertainty: Heuristics and biases, *Science* 185, 1124–1131.

Tversky, A., and D. Kahneman, 1981, The framing of decisions and the psychology of choice, *Science* 211, 453—458.

Tversky, A., and D. Kahneman, 1983, Extensional versus intuitive reasoning: The conjunction fallacy in probability judgment, *Psychological Review* 90, 293–315.

Tversky, A., and D. Kahneman, 1986, Rational choice and the framing of decisions, *Journal of Business* 59, S252–S278.

Tversky, A., and D. Kahneman, 1992, Advances in prospect theory: Cumulative representation of uncertainty, *Journal of Risk and Uncertainty* 5, 297–323.

Tversky, A., P. Slovic, and D. Kahneman, 1990, The causes of preference reversal, *American Economic Review* 80, 204–217.

Vijh, A. M., 1999, Long-term returns from equity carveouts, *Journal of Financial Economics* 51, 273–308.

Wang, F. A., 1998, Strategic trading, asymmetric information and heterogeneous prior beliefs, *Journal of Financial Markets* 1, 321–352.

Wason, P. C., 1966, Reasoning, in B. M. Foss, ed.: *New Horizons in Psychology* (Penguin, Harmondsworth, Middlesex, UK).

Weber, M., and C. Camerer, 2000, The disposition effect in securities trading: An experimental analysis, *Journal of Economic Behavior and Organization* 33, 167–184.

Weil, P., 1989, The equity premium puzzle and the risk-free rate puzzle, *Journal of Monetary Economics* 24, 401–421.

Welch, I., 2000, Views of financial economists on the equity premium and on professional controversies, *Journal of Business* 73, 501–537.

Wermers, R., 1999, Mutual fund herding and the impact on stock prices, *Journal of Finance* 54, 581–622.

West, K. D., 1988, Dividend innovations and stock price volatility, *Econometrica* 56, 37–61.

Williams, A. W., 1987, The formation of price forecasts in experimental markets, *Journal of Money, Credit, and Banking* 19, 1–18.

Wilson, T. D., and J. Schooler, 1991, Thinking too much: Introspection can reduce the quality of preferences and decisions, *Journal of Personality and Social Psychology* 60, 181–192.

Womack, K. L., 1996, Do brokerage analysts' recommendations have investment value? *Journal of Finance* 51, 137–168.

Wright, W. F., and G. H. Bower, 1992, Mood effects on subjective probability assessment, *Organizational Behavior and Human Decision Processes* 52, 276–291.

Yariv, L., 2001, I'll see it when I believe it—A simple model of confirmatory bias and cognitive dissonance, Mimeo, Harvard University.

Yates, J. F., 1990, *Judgement and Decision Making* (Prentice Hall, Englewood Cliffs, NJ).

[12]

Journal of Economic Perspectives—Volume 17, Number 1—Winter 2003—Pages 83–104

From Efficient Markets Theory to Behavioral Finance

Robert J. Shiller

Academic finance has evolved a long way from the days when the efficient markets theory was widely considered to be proved beyond doubt. Behavioral finance—that is, finance from a broader social science perspective including psychology and sociology—is now one of the most vital research programs, and it stands in sharp contradiction to much of efficient markets theory.

The efficient markets theory reached its height of dominance in academic circles around the 1970s. At that time, the rational expectations revolution in economic theory was in its first blush of enthusiasm, a fresh new idea that occupied the center of attention. The idea that speculative asset prices such as stock prices always incorporate the best information about fundamental values and that prices change only because of good, sensible information meshed very well with theoretical trends of the time. Prominent finance models of the 1970s related speculative asset prices to economic fundamentals, using rational expectations to tie together finance and the entire economy in one elegant theory. For example, Robert Merton published "An Intertemporal Capital Asset Pricing Model" in 1973, which showed how to generalize the capital asset pricing model to a comprehensive intertemporal general equilibrium model. Robert Lucas published "Asset Prices in an Exchange Economy" in 1978, which showed that in a rational expectations general equilibrium, rational asset prices may have a forecastable element that is related to the forecastability of consumption. Douglas Breeden published his theory of "consumption betas" in 1979, where a stock's beta (which measures the sensitivity of its return compared to some index) was determined by the correlation

■ *Robert J. Shiller is the Stanley B. Resor Professor of Economics and also affiliated with the Cowles Foundation and the International Center for Finance, Yale University, New Haven, Connecticut. He is a Research Associate at the National Bureau of Economic Research, Cambridge, Massachusetts. His e-mail address is ⟨robert.shiller@yale.edu⟩.*

of the stock's return with per capita consumption. These were exciting theoretical advances at the time. In 1973, the first edition of Burton Malkiel's acclaimed book, *A Random Walk Down Wall Street,* appeared, which conveyed this excitement to a wider audience.

In the decade of the 1970s, I was a graduate student writing a Ph.D. dissertation on rational expectations models and an assistant and associate professor, and I was mostly caught up in the excitement of the time. One could easily wish that these models were true descriptions of the world around us, for it would then be a wonderful advance for our profession. We would have powerful tools to study and to quantify the financial world around us.

Wishful thinking can dominate much of the work of a profession for a decade, but not indefinitely. The 1970s already saw the beginnings of some disquiet over these models and a tendency to push them somewhat aside in favor of a more eclectic way of thinking about financial markets and the economy. Browsing today again through finance journals from the 1970s, one sees some beginnings of reports of anomalies that didn't seem likely to square with the efficient markets theory, even if they were not presented as significant evidence against the theory. For example, Eugene Fama's 1970 article, "Efficient Capital Markets: A Review of Empirical Work," while highly enthusiastic in its conclusions for market efficiency, did report some anomalies like slight serial dependencies in stock market returns, though with the tone of pointing out how small the anomalies were.

The 1980s and Excess Volatility

From my perspective, the 1980s were a time of important academic discussion of the consistency of the efficient markets model for the aggregate stock market with econometric evidence about the time series properties of prices, dividends and earnings. Of particular concern was whether these stocks show excess volatility relative to what would be predicted by the efficient markets model.

The anomalies that had been discovered might be considered at worst small departures from the fundamental truth of market efficiency, but if most of the volatility in the stock market was unexplained, it would call into question the basic underpinnings of the entire efficient markets theory. The anomaly represented by the notion of excess volatility seems to be much more troubling for efficiency markets theory than some other financial anomalies, such as the January effect or the day-of-the-week effect.[1] The volatility anomaly is much deeper than those represented by price stickiness or *tatonnement* or even by exchange-rate overshooting. The evidence regarding excess volatility seems, to some observers at least, to imply that changes in prices occur for no fundamental reason at all, that they occur because of such things as "sunspots" or "animal spirits" or just mass psychology.

The efficient markets model can be stated as asserting that the price P_t of a

[1] A good discussion of the major anomalies, and the evidence for them, is in Siegel (2002).

share (or of a portfolio of shares representing an index) equals the mathematical expectation, conditional on all information available at the time, of the present value P_t^* of actual subsequent dividends accruing to that share (or portfolio of shares). P_t^* is not known at time t and has to be forecasted. Efficient markets say that price equals the optimal forecast of it.

Different forms of the efficient markets model differ in the choice of the discount rate in the present value, but the general efficient markets model can be written just as $P_t = E_t P_t^*$, where E_t refers to mathematical expectation conditional on public information available at time t. This equation asserts that any surprising movements in the stock market must have at their origin some new information about the fundamental value P_t^*.

It follows from the efficient markets model that $P_t^* = P_t + U_t$, where U_t is a forecast error. The forecast error U_t must be uncorrelated with any information variable available at time t, otherwise the forecast would not be optimal; it would not be taking into account all information. Since the price P_t itself is information at time t, P_t and U_t must be uncorrelated with each other. Since the variance of the sum of two uncorrelated variables is the sum of their variances, it follows that the variance of P_t^* must equal the variance of P_t plus the variance of U_t, and hence, since the variance of U_t cannot be negative, that the variance of P_t^* must be greater than or equal to that of P_t.

Thus, the fundamental principle of optimal forecasting is that the forecast must be less variable than the variable forecasted. Any forecaster whose forecast consistently varies through time more than the variable forecasted is making a serious error, because then high forecasts would themselves tend to indicate forecast positive errors, and low forecasts indicate negative errors. The maximum possible variance of the forecast is the variance of the variable forecasted, and this can occur only if the forecaster has perfect foresight and the forecasts correlate perfectly with the variable forecasted.

If one computes for each year since 1871 the present value subsequent to that year of the real dividends paid on the Standard & Poor's Composite Stock Price Index, discounted by a constant real discount rate equal to the geometric average real return 1871–2002 on the same Standard & Poor Index, one finds that the present value, if plotted through time, behaves remarkably like a stable trend.[2] In contrast, the Standard & Poor's Composite Stock Price Index gyrates wildly up and down around this trend. Figure 1 illustrates these patterns.

How, then, can we take it as received doctrine that, according to the simplest efficient markets theory, the stock price represents the optimal forecast of this present value, the price responding only to objective information about it? I argued in Shiller (1981), as did also Stephen LeRoy and Richard Porter (1981), that the stability of the present value through time suggests that there is excess volatility in

[2] The present value, constant discount rate, is computed for each year t as $p^*_{const,t} = \Sigma_{\tau=t+1}^{\infty} \rho^{(\tau-t)} D_\tau$, where ρ is a constant discount factor, and D_t is the real dividend at time t. An assumption was made about real dividends after 2002. See note to Figure 1.

Figure 1
Real Stock Prices and Present Values of Subsequent Real Dividends
(annual data)

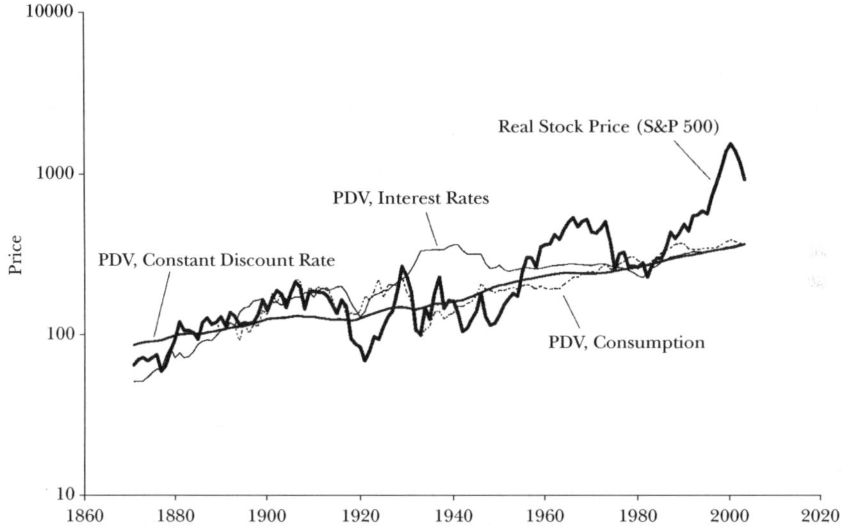

Notes: The heaviest line is the Standard & Poor 500 Index for January of year shown. The less-heavy line is the present value for each year of subsequent real dividends accruing to the index discounted by the geometric-average real return for the entire sample, 6.61 percent. Dividends after 2002 were assumed equal to the 2002 dividend times 1.25 (to correct for recent lower dividend payout) and growing at the geometric-average historical growth rate for dividends, 1.11 percent. The thin line is the present value for each year of subsequent real dividends discounted by one-year interest rates plus a risk premium equal to the geometric average real return on the market minus the geometric average real one-year interest rate. The dashed line is the present value for each year of subsequent real dividends discounted by marginal rates of substitution in consumption for a representative individual with a coefficient of relative risk aversion of 3 who consumes the real *per capita* nondurable and service consumption from the U. S. National Income and Product Accounts. Real values were computed from nominal values by dividing by the consumer price index (CPI-U since 1913, linked to the Warren and Pearson producer price index before 1913) and rescaling to January 2003 = 100. Some of the very latest observations of underlying series were estimated based on data available as of this writing; for example, the consumer price index for January 2003 was estimated based on data from previous months. Source data are available on ⟨http://www.econ.yale.edu/~shiller⟩, and the further descriptions of some of the data are in Shiller (1989). See also footnotes 1, 5 and 6.

the aggregate stock market, relative to the present value implied by the efficient markets model. Our work launched a remarkable amount of controversy, from which I will recall here just a few highlights.

The principal issue regarding our original work on excess volatility was in regard to thinking about the stationarity of dividends and stock prices. My own work in the early 1980s had followed a tradition in the finance literature of assuming that dividends fluctuated around a known trend.[3] However, one might also argue, as do Marsh and Merton (1986), that dividends need not stay close to a trend and that even if earnings followed a trend, share issuance or repurchase could make dividends depart from a trend indefinitely. In addition, if business managers use dividends to provide a smoothed flow of payouts from their businesses, then the stock prices might be expected to shift more rapidly than dividends. Marsh and Merton argued that such dividend smoothing could make stock prices unstationary in such a way that in finite samples prices appear more volatile than the present values.

Thus, the challenge became how to construct a test for expected volatility that modeled dividends and stock prices in a more general way. As such tests were developed, they tended to confirm the overall hypothesis that stock prices had more volatility than an efficient markets hypothesis could explain. For example, West (1988) derived an inequality that the variance of *innovations* (that is, surprises) in stock prices must be less than or equal to the variance of the *innovations* in the forecasted present value of dividends based on a subset of information available to the market. This inequality is quite general: it holds even when dividends and stock prices have infinite variances so long as the variance of the innovation (the unexpected change) in these is finite. Using long-term annual data on stock prices, West found that the variance of innovations in stock prices was four to 20 times its theoretical upper bound.[4] John Campbell and I (1988) recast the time series model in terms of a cointegrated model of real prices and real dividends, while also relaxing other assumptions about the time series, and again found evidence of excess volatility.[5] Campbell (1991) provided a variance decomposition for stock returns that indicated that most of the variability of the aggregate stock market conveyed information about future returns, rather than about future dividends.

Another contested issue regarding the early work on excess volatility questioned the assumption of the early work that the efficient markets model was best conveyed through an expected present value model in which the real discount rate is constant through time. The assumption of a constant discount rate over time can only be considered a first step, for the theory suggests more complex relationships.

[3] It should be pointed out that dividend payouts as a fraction of earnings have shown a gradual downtrend over the period since 1871 and that dividend payouts have increasingly been substituted by share repurchases. Net share repurchases reached approximately 1 percent of shares outstanding by the late 1990s. However, share repurchases do not invalidate the theoretical model that stock prices should equal the present value of dividends. See Cole, Helwege and Laster (1996).

[4] In more technical terms, this argument is over whether dividends could be viewed as a stationary series. The discussion was often phrased in terms of the "unit root" property of the time series, where a unit root refers to notion that when a variable is regressed on its own lags, the characteristic equation of the difference equation has a root on the unit circle. West (1988) can be viewed as a way of addressing the unit root issue. In our 1988 paper, Campbell and I handled nonstationarity by using a vector autoregressive model including the log dividend-price ratio and the change in log dividends as elements.

[5] Barsky and De Long (1993), however, later showed that if one assumes that real dividends must be *twice* differenced to induce stationarity (so that dividends are even more unstationary in the sense that dividend *growth rates*, not just levels, are unstationary), then the efficient markets model looks rather more consistent with the data.

One such efficient markets model makes the discount rate correspond to interest rates. The line in Figure 1 labeled "PDV, Interest Rates" illustrates this concept.[6] However, allowing time-varying interest rates in the present value formula does little to support the efficient markets model. The actual price is still more volatile than the present value, especially for the latest half century. Moreover, what changes through time there are in the present value bear little resemblance to the changes through time in the stock prices. Note for example that the present value is extremely high throughout the depression years of the 1930s, not low as was the actual stock market. The present value is high then because real interest rates were at extreme lows after 1933, into the early 1950s, and since real dividends really did not fall much after 1929. After 1929, real Standard & Poor's dividends fell to around 1925 levels for just a few years, 1933–1935 and 1938, but, contrary to popular impressions, were generally higher in the 1930s than they were in the 1920s.[7]

An alternative approach to the possibility of varying real discount rates looks at the intertemporal marginal rate of substitution for consumption, which is shown in Figure 1 with the line labeled "PDV, Consumption."[8] The models of efficient financial markets from the 1970s like Merton (1973), Lucas (1978) and Breeden (1979) concluded that stock prices are the expected present value of future dividends discounted using marginal rates of substitution of consumption, and in these models the equations for stock returns were derived in the context of a model maximizing the utility of consumption. Grossman and Shiller (1981) produced a plot of that present value since 1881, using Standard & Poor dividend data and using aggregate consumption data to compute the marginal rates of substitution as discount factors, and this plot is updated here, and this is what is shown in Figure 1. We

[6] The present value, discounted by interest rates, is a plot for each year t of

$$P^*_{r,t} = \sum_{\tau=t}^{2002} \prod_{j=0}^{\tau} 1/(1 + r_{t+j} + \phi)D_\tau + \prod_{j=t}^{2002} 1/(1 + r_{t+j} + \phi)P^*_{const,2003}.$$

See note to Figure 1.

[7] Campbell and I (1989) recast the argument in terms of a vector autoregressive model of real stock prices, real interest rates and real dividends, in which each of these variables was regressed on lags of itself and lags of the other variables. We found that the dividend-price ratio not only shows excess volatility, but shows very little correlation with the dividend divided by the forecast of the present value of future dividends.

[8] The present value, consumption discounted, is a plot for each year t of

$$P^*_{c,t} = \sum_{\tau=t+1}^{2002} (C_t/C_\tau)^3 D_\tau + (C_t/C_{2003})^3 P^*_{const,2003},$$

where C_t is real *per capita* real consumption at time t. This expression is inspired by Lucas (1978) and derived in Grossman and Shiller (1981) assuming a coefficient of relative risk aversion of 3. See note to Figure 1.

found, as can also be seen here in Figure 1, that the present value of dividends as discounted in this model had only a tenuous relation to actual stock prices, and did not appear volatile enough to justify the price movements unless we pushed the coefficient of relative risk aversion to ridiculously high levels, higher than the value of three that was used for the plot.

Grossman and Shiller (1981) stressed that there were some similarities between the present value and the actual real price, notably the present value peaks in 1929 and bottoms out in 1933, close to the actual peak and trough of the market. But the present value does this because consumption peaked in 1929 and then dropped very sharply, bottoming out in 1933, and the present value takes account of this, as if people had perfect foresight of the coming depression. But in fact it appears very unlikely that people saw this outcome in 1929, and if they did not, then the efficient model does not predict that the actual real price should have tracked the present value over this period.

Actually, the consumption discount model, while it may show some comovements at times with actual stock prices, does not work well because it does not justify the volatility of stock prices. I showed (1982) that the theoretical model implies a lower bound on the volatility of the marginal rate of substitution, a bound which is with the U.S. data much higher than could be observed unless risk aversion were implausibly high. Hansen and Jagannathan later generalized this lower bound and elaborated on its implications, and today the apparent violation of this "Hansen-Jagannathan lower bound" is regarded as an important anomaly in finance.[9]

Some very recent research has emphasized that, even though the aggregate stock market appears to be wildly inefficient, individual stock prices do show some correspondence to efficient markets theory. That is, while the present value model for the aggregate stock market seems unsupported by the data, there is some evidence that *cross-sectional* variations in stock prices relative to accounting measures show some relation to the present value model. Paul Samuelson some years ago posited that the stock market is "micro efficient but macro inefficient," since there is considerable predictable variation across firms in their predictable future paths of dividends but little predictable variation in aggregate dividends. Hence, Samuelson asserted, movements among individual stocks make more sense than do movements in the market as a whole. There is now evidence to back up this assertion.

Vuolteenaho (2002) showed, using vector-autoregressive methods, that the ratio of book-to-market-value of U.S. firms explains a substantial fraction of changes in future firms' earnings. Cohen, Polk and Vuolteenaho (2002) concluded that 75 to 80 percent of the variation across firms in their book-to-market ratios can be explained in terms of future variation in profits. Jung and Shiller (2002) show that, cross-sectionally, for U.S. stocks that have been continually traded since 1926, the price-dividend ratio is a strong forecaster of the present value of future dividend

[9] See, for example, John Cochrane's (2001) book *Asset Pricing*, which surveys this literature. Much of the older literature is summarized in my 1989 book *Market Volatility*.

changes. So, dividend-price ratios on individual stocks do serve as forecasts of long-term future changes in their future dividends, as efficient markets assert.

This does not mean that there are not substantial bubbles in individual stock prices, but that the predictable variation across firms in dividends has often been so large as to largely swamp out the effect of the bubbles. A lot of this predictable variation across firms takes the form of firms' paying zero dividends for many years and investors correctly perceiving that eventually dividends will be coming, and of firms in very bad shape with investors correctly perceiving they will not be paying substantial dividends much longer. When it comes to individual stocks, such predictable variations, and their effects on price, are often far larger than the bubble component of stock prices.

There is a clear sense that the level of volatility of the overall stock market cannot be well explained with any variant of the efficient markets model in which stock prices are formed by looking at the present discounted value of future returns. There are many ways to tinker with the discount rates in the present value formulas, and someday someone may find some definition of discount rates that produces a present value series that "fits" the actual price better than any of the series shown in Figure 1.[10] But it is unlikely that they will do so convincingly, given the failure of our efforts to date to capture the volatility of stock prices. To justify the volatility in terms of such changes in the discount rates, one will have to argue that investors also had a great deal of information about changes in the factors influencing these future discount rates.

After all the efforts to defend the efficient markets theory, there is still every reason to think that, while markets are not totally crazy, they contain quite substantial noise, so substantial that it dominates the movements in the aggregate market. The efficient markets model, for the aggregate stock market, has still never been supported by any study effectively linking stock market fluctuations with subsequent fundamentals. By the end of the 1980s, the restless minds of many academic researchers had turned to other theories.

The Blossoming of Behavioral Finance

In the 1990s, a lot of the focus of academic discussion shifted away from these econometric analyses of time series on prices, dividends and earnings toward developing models of human psychology as it relates to financial markets. The field of behavioral finance developed. Researchers had seen too many anomalies, too

[10] Other factors are considered by McGrattan and Prescott (2001), who emphasize tax rate changes, and Siegel (2002), who considers not only tax rate changes but also changes in the volatility of the economy, changes in the inflation rate, and changes in transactions costs. Neither of these studies shows a "fit" between present value and prices over the long sample, however. Notably, the factors they use do not go through sudden changes at the time of the stock market booms and crashes surrounding 1929 and 2000.

little inspiration that our theoretical models captured important fluctuations. An extensive body of empirical work, summarized in Campbell, Lo and MacKinlay's 1996 book *The Econometrics of Financial Markets*, laid the foundation for a revolution in finance.

Richard Thaler and I started our National Bureau of Economic Research conference series on behavioral finance in 1991, extending workshops that Thaler had organized at the Russell Sage Foundation a few years earlier.[11] Many other workshops and seminars on behavioral finance followed. There is so much going on in the field that it is impossible to summarize in a short space. Here, I will illustrate the progress of behavioral finance with two salient examples from recent research: feedback models and obstacles to smart money. For overall surveys of the field of behavioral finance, the interested reader might begin with Hersh Shefrin's *Beyond Greed and Fear: Understanding Behavioral Finance and the Psychology of Investing* (2000) or Andrei Shleifer's *Inefficient Markets* (2000). There are also some new books of collected papers in behavioral finance, including a three-volume set, *Behavioral Finance*, edited by Hersh Shefrin (2001), and *Advances in Behavioral Finance II*, edited by Richard H. Thaler (2003).

Feedback Models

One of the oldest theories about financial markets, expressed long ago in newspapers and magazines rather than scholarly journals, is, if translated into academic words, a price-to-price feedback theory. When speculative prices go up, creating successes for some investors, this may attract public attention, promote word-of-mouth enthusiasm, and heighten expectations for further price increases. The talk attracts attention to "new era" theories and "popular models" that justify the price increases.[12] This process in turn increases investor demand and thus generates another round of price increases. If the feedback is not interrupted, it may produce after many rounds a speculative "bubble," in which high expectations for further price increases support very high current prices. The high prices are ultimately not sustainable, since they are high only because of expectations of further price increases, and so the bubble eventually bursts, and prices come falling down. The feedback that propelled the bubble carries the seeds of its own destruction, and so the end of the bubble may be unrelated to news stories about fundamentals. The same feedback may also produce a negative bubble, downward price movements propelling further downward price movements, promoting word-of-mouth pessimism, until the market reaches an unsustainably low level.

Such a feedback theory is very old. As long ago as 1841, Charles MacKay in his

[11] For a list of our programs since 1991, with links to authors' websites, see ⟨http://cowles.econ.yale.edu/behfin⟩.

[12] Descriptions of new era theories attending various speculative bubbles are described in my book (2000). Popular models that accompanied the stock market crash of 1987, the real estate bubbles peaking around 1990 and various initial public offering booms are discussed in my paper in this journal (1990).

influential book *Memoirs of Extraordinary Popular Delusions* described the famous tulipmania in Holland in the 1630s, a speculative bubble in tulip flower bulbs, with words that suggest feedback and the ultimate results of the feedback (pp. 118–119):

> Many individuals grew suddenly rich. A golden bait hung temptingly out before the people, and one after another, they rushed to the tulip marts, like flies around a honey-pot . . . . At last, however, the more prudent began to see that this folly could not last forever. Rich people no longer bought the flowers to keep them in their gardens, but to sell them again at cent per cent profit. It was seen that somebody must lose fearfully in the end. As this conviction spread, prices fell, and never rose again.[13]

The feedback theory seems to be even much older than this. Note of such feedback, and the role of word-of-mouth communications in promoting it, was in fact made at the time of the tulipmania itself. One anonymous observer publishing in 1637 (the year of the peak of the tulipmania) gives a fictional account of a conversation between two people, Gaergoedt and Waermondt, that illustrates this author's impression of the word-of-mouth communications of that time:

> Gaergoedt: "You can hardly make a return of 10% with the money that you invest in your occupation [as a weaver], but with the tulip trade, you can make returns of 10%, 100%, yes, even 1000%.
> Waermondt: " . . . . But tell me, should I believe you?"
> Gaergoedt: "I will tell you again, what I just said."
> Waermondt: "But I fear that, since I would only start now, it's too late, because now the tulips are very expensive, and I fear that I'll be hit with the spit rod, before tasting the roast."
> Gaergoedt: "It's never too late to make a profit, you make money while sleeping. I've been away from home for four or five days, and I came home just last night, but now I know that the tulips I have have increased in value by three or four thousand guilder; where do you have profits like that from other goods?"
> Waermondt: "I am perplexed when I hear you talking like that, I don't know what to do; has anybody become rich with this trade?"
> Gaergoedt: "What kind of question is this? Look at all the gardeners that used to wear white-gray outfits, and now they're wearing new clothes. Many weavers, that used to wear patched up clothes, that they had a hard time putting

[13] Garber questions MacKay's facts about the tulipmania in his 1990 article in this journal and in his book *Famous First Bubbles*. For example, the crash was not absolutely final; Garber documents very high tulip prices in 1643. The actual course of the bubble is ambiguous, as all contracts were suspended by the states of Holland in 1637 just after the peak, and no price data are available from that date.

> on, now wear the glitteriest clothes. Yes, many who trade in tulips are riding a horse, have a carriage or a wagon, and during winter, an ice carriage, ..."[14]

Casual observations over the years since then are plentiful evidence that such talk, provoking a sense of relative futility of one's day-to-day work and envy of the financial successes of others, and including some vacuous answer to doubts that the price rise may be over, is effective in overcoming rational doubts among some substantial number of people and tends to bring successive rounds of them into the market.

In my book *Irrational Exuberance*, published (with some luck) at the very peak of the stock market bubble in March 2000, I argued that very much the same feedback, transmitted by word-of-mouth as well as the media, was at work in producing the bubble we were seeing then. I further argued that the natural self-limiting behavior of bubbles, and the possibility of downward feedback after the bubble was over, suggested a dangerous outlook for stocks in the future.

One might well also presume that such simple feedback, if it operates so dramatically in events like the tulip bubble or the stock market boom until 2000, ought often to recur at a smaller scale and to play an important if lesser role in more normal day-to-day movements in speculative prices. Feedback models, in the form of difference equations, can of course produce complicated dynamics. The feedback may be an essential source of much of the apparently inexplicable "randomness" that we see in financial market prices.

But the feedback theory is very hard to find expressed in finance or economics textbooks, even today. Since the theory has appeared mostly in popular discourse, and not in the textbooks, one might well infer that it has long been discredited by solid academic research. In fact, academic research has until recently hardly addressed the feedback model.

The presence of such feedback is supported by some experimental evidence. Psychologists Andreassen and Kraus (1988) found that when people are shown real historical stock prices in sequence (and which they knew were real stock prices) and invited to trade in a simulated market that displays these prices, they tended to behave as if they extrapolate past price changes when the prices appear to exhibit a trend relative to period-to-period variability. Smith, Suchanek and Williams (1988) were able to create experimental markets that generated bubbles that are consistent with feedback trading. Marimon, Spear and Sunder (1993) showed experiments in which repeating bubbles were generated if subjects were preconditioned by past experience to form expectations of bubbles.

The presence of such feedback is also supported by research in cognitive psychology, which shows that human judgments of the probability of future events show systematic biases. For example, psychologists Tversky and Kahneman have shown that judgments tend to be made using a representativeness heuristic,

[14] Anonymous (1637). Bjorn Tuypens translated this passage.

whereby people try to predict by seeking the closest match to past patterns, without attention to the observed probability of matching the pattern. For example, when asked to guess the occupations of people whose personality and interests are described to them, subjects tended to guess the occupation that seemed to match the description as closely as possible, without regard to the rarity of the occupation. Rational subjects would have chosen humdrum and unexceptional occupations more because more people are in these occupations. (Kahneman and Tversky, 1974). By the same principle, people may tend to match stock price patterns into salient categories such as dramatic and persistent price trends, thus leading to feedback dynamics, even if these categories may be rarely seen in fundamental underlying factors.

Daniel, Hirschleifer and Subramanyam (1999) have shown that the psychological principle of "biased self-attribution" can also promote feedback. Biased self-attribution, identified by psychologist Daryl Bem (1965), is a pattern of human behavior whereby individuals attribute events that confirm the validity of their actions to their own high ability and attribute events that disconfirm their actions to bad luck or sabotage. Upon reading the above passage from the time of the tulipmania, one easily imagines that Gaergoedt is basking in self-esteem and relishing the telling of the story. Many readers today can probably easily recall similar conversations, and similar ego-involvement by the spreaders of the word, in the 1990s. Such human interactions, the essential cause of speculative bubbles, appear to recur across centuries and across countries: they reflect fundamental parameters of human behavior.

There is also evidence supportive of feedback from natural experiments, which may be more convincing than the lab experiments when they occur in real time, with real money, with real social networks and associated interpersonal support and emotions, with real and visceral envy of friends' investment successes, and with communications-media presence. Ponzi schemes may be thought of as representing such natural experiments. A Ponzi scheme (or pyramid scheme or money circulation scheme) involves a superficially plausible but unverifiable story about how money is made for investors and the fraudulent creation of high returns for initial investors by giving them the money invested by subsequent investors. Initial investor response to the scheme tends to be weak, but as the rounds of high returns generates excitement, the story becomes increasingly believable and enticing to investors. These schemes are often very successful in generating extraordinary enthusiasms among some investors. We have seen some spectacular Ponzi schemes recently in countries that do not have effective regulation and surveillance to prevent them. A number of Ponzi schemes in Albania 1996–1997 were so large that total liabilities reached half a year's GDP; their collapse brought on a period of anarchy and civil war in which 2000 people were killed (Jarvis, 1999). Real world stock-market speculative bubbles, I argued in my 2000 book *Irrational Exuberance*, resemble Ponzi schemes in the sense that some "new era" story becomes attached to the bubble and acquires increasing plausibility and investor enthusiasm as the market continues to achieve high returns. Given the obvious success of Ponzi schemes when they are not stopped by the law, we would need a good reason to think that analogous phenomena of speculative bubbles are not also likely.

The stock market boom that ended in early 2000 is another relevant episode. According to my survey data, now expressed in the form of stock market confidence indexes produced by the Yale School of Management and available at ⟨http://icf.som.yale.edu/confidence.index⟩, the confidence of individual investors that the stock market will go up in the next year, and will rebound from any drop, rose dramatically 1989–2000. As in the tulipmania centuries before, there was a focusing of public attention and talk on the speculative market and a proliferation of wishful-thinking theories about a "new era" that would propel the stock market on a course that, while uneven, is relentlessly upward, theories that were spread by word of mouth as well as the media.

It is widely thought that there is a problem with the feedback theories: the theories would seem to imply that speculative price changes are strongly serially correlated through time, that prices show strong momentum, continuing uniformly in one direction day after day. This seems inconsistent with the evidence that stock prices are approximately a random walk.

But simple feedback models do not imply strong serial correlation, as I stressed in Shiller (1990). There, I presented a model of the demand for a speculative asset as equaling a *distributed lag* with exponentially declining weights on past price changes through time (the distributed lag representing feedback distributed over time), plus other factors that affect demand. The model asserts that people react gradually to price changes over months or years, not just to yesterday's price change. A history of price increases over the last year may encourage buying today even if yesterday's price change was down. Also, the model recognizes that there are other shocks, besides feedback, influencing price.

In such a model, a disturbance in some demand factor other than feedback can in certain cases be amplified, at least for a time, because it changes the price and thus affects future prices through the distributed lag.[15] However, unless we know something about the other factors that drive demand, such a distributed lag model does not imply anything at all about the serial correlation properties of speculative price changes. The feedback model does not imply that there is much serial correlation in day-to-day stock price changes, since the noise in the other factors feeds directly into short-run changes, and the effect on today's price of lagged other factors operates at a low frequency that is essentially unrelated to day-to-day changes and has effects that can be observed only from its cumulative effect after a long period of time.

Thus, the approximate random walk character of stock prices is not evidence

[15] The feedback model is $p_t = c \int_{-\infty}^{t} e^{-\gamma(t-\tau)}\, dp_\tau + \pi_t$, $0 < c < 1$, $0 < \gamma$. Here, p_t is price at time t, and π_t is the combined effect of other factors on demand. It follows that $p_t = \pi_t + (c/(1-c))(\pi_t - \overline{\pi}_t)$, where $\overline{\pi}_t = (\gamma/(1-c)) \int_{-\infty}^{t} e^{-(\gamma/(1-c))(t-\tau)} \pi_\tau d\tau$ is a weighted average of lagged π. See Shiller (1990, p. 60). Such a model does not imply that price behaves smoothly through time: price can look much like a random walk if, for example, π_t is a random walk.

against feedback. Moreover, even if feedback did imply some momentum, we can also note that the random walk character of stock prices is really not fully supported by the evidence anyway, and that in fact there has been more than a little momentum to stock prices. Jegadeesh and Titman (1993) found that winning stocks, stocks that showed exceptionally high six-month returns, beat losing stocks, stocks that showed exceptionally low six-month returns, by 12 percent over the following year. In contrast, over longer periods of time this momentum seems to reverse itself. De Bondt and Thaler (1985) find that over the period 1926 to 1982, stocks represented on the Center for Research in Security Prices data set of the University of Chicago whose returns had been in the top decile across firms over three years (thus, "winner" stocks) tended to show negative cumulative returns in the succeeding three years. They also found that "loser" stocks whose returns had been in the bottom decile over the prior three years tended to show positive returns over the succeeding three years. Thus, there is a tendency for stock prices to continue in the same direction over intervals of six months to a year, but to reverse themselves over longer intervals. Campbell, Lo and Mackinlay (1996) document this fact carefully.[16] A pattern like this is certainly consistent with some combination of feedback effects and other demand factors driving the stock market largely independently of fundamentals.

Smart Money vs. Ordinary Investors

Theoretical models of efficient financial markets that represent everyone as rational optimizers can be no more than metaphors for the world around us. Nothing could be more absurd than to claim that *everyone* knows how to solve complex stochastic optimization models. For these theoretical models to have any relevance to the stock market, it must somehow be the case that a smaller element of "smart money" or the "marginal trader" can offset the foolishness of many investors and make the markets efficient.

The efficient markets theory, as it is commonly expressed, asserts that when irrational optimists buy a stock, smart money sells, and when irrational pessimists sell a stock, smart money buys, thereby eliminating the effect of the irrational traders on market price. But finance theory does not necessarily imply that smart money succeeds in fully offsetting the impact of ordinary investors. In recent years, research in behavioral finance has shed some important light on the implications of the presence of these two classes of investors for theory and also on some characteristics of the people in the two classes.

From a theoretical point of view, it is far from clear that smart money has the power to drive market prices to fundamental values. For example, in one model with both feedback traders and smart money, the smart money tended to *amplify*, rather than diminish, the effect of feedback traders, by buying in ahead of the

[16] Grinblatt and Han (2001) have argued that this tendency of stock prices to show momentum for a while and then reverse themselves might be related to the phenomenon that investors tend to hold on to losers and sell winners (Statman and Shefrin, 1985; Odean, 1998).

feedback traders in anticipation of the price increases they will cause (De Long, Shleifer, Summers and Waldman, 1990b). In a related model, rational, expected-utility-maximizing smart money never chooses to offset all of the effects of irrational investors because they are rationally concerned about the risk generated by the irrational investors and do not want to assume the risk that their completely offsetting these other investors would entail (De Long, Shleifer, Summers and Waldman, 1990b).[17]

Often, speculative bubbles appear to be common to investments of a certain "style," and the bubbles may not include many other investments. For example, the stock market bubble that peaked in the year 2000 was strongest in tech stocks or Nasdaq stocks. Barberis and Shleifer (2002) present a model in which feedback traders' demand for investments within a particular style is related to a distributed lag on past returns of that style class. By their budget constraint, when feedback traders are enticed by one style, they must move out of competing styles. The smart money are rational utility maximizers. Barberis and Shleifer present a numerical implementation of their model and find that smart money did not fully offset the effects of the feedback traders. Style classes go through periods of boom and bust amplified by the feedback.

Goetzmann and Massa (1999) provided some direct evidence that it is reasonable to suppose that there are two distinct classes of investors: feedback traders who follow trends and the smart money who move the other way. Fidelity Investments provided them with two years of daily account information for 91,000 investors in a Standard and Poor's 500 index fund. Goetzmann and Massa were able to sort these investors into two groups based on how they react to daily price changes. There were both momentum investors, who habitually bought more after prices were rising, and contrarian investors, or smart money, who habitually sold after prices were rising. Individual investors tended to stay as one or the other, rarely shifted between the two categories.

Recent research has focused on an important obstacle to smart money's offsetting the effects of irrational investors. The smart money can always buy the stock, but if the smart money no longer owns the stock and finds it difficult to short the stock, then the smart money may be unable to sell the stock. Some stocks could be in a situation where zealots have bought into a stock so much that only zealots own shares, and trade is only among zealots, and so the zealots alone determine the price of the stock. The smart money who know that the stock is priced ridiculously high may well use up all the easily available shortable shares and then will be standing on the sidelines, unable to short more shares and profit from their knowledge. Miller (1977) pointed out this flaw in the argument for market efficiency, and his paper has been discussed ever since.

It seems incontrovertible that in some cases stocks have been held primarily by zealots and that short sellers have found it very difficult to short. One example is the

[17] Shleifer and Summers (1990) present a nice summary of these themes in this journal.

3Com sale of Palm near the peak of the stock market bubble (Lamont and Thaler, 2001). In March 2000, 3Com, a profitable provider of network systems and services, sold to the general public via an initial public offering 5 percent of its subsidiary Palm, a maker of handheld computers. 3Com announced at the same time that the rest of Palm would follow later. The price that these first Palm shares obtained in the market was so high, when compared with the price of the 3Com shares, that if one subtracts the implied value of the remaining 95 percent of Palm from the 3Com market value, one finds that the non-Palm part of 3Com had a *negative* value. Since the worst possible price for 3Com after the Palm sale was completed would be zero, there was thus a strong incentive for investors to short Palm and buy 3Com. But, the interest cost of borrowing Palm shares reached 35 percent by July 2000, putting a damper on the advantage to exploiting the mispricing.[18] Even an investor who knew for certain that the Palm shares would fall substantially may have been unable to make a profit from this knowledge. The zealots had won with Palm and had control over its price, for the time being.

The Palm example is an unusual anomaly. Shorting stocks only rarely becomes so costly. But the example proves the principle. The question is: How important are obstacles to smart money's selling in causing stocks to deviate from fundamental value?

Of course, in reality, the distinction between zealots and smart money is not always sharp. Instead, there are sometimes all gradations in between, especially since the objective evidence about the fundamental value of individual stocks is always somewhat ambiguous. If selling short is difficult, a number of individual stocks could become overpriced. It would also appear possible that major segments of the stock market, say the Nasdaq in 1999, or even the entire stock market, could wind up owned by, if not zealots, at least relatively optimistic people. Short-sale constraints could be a fatal flaw in the basic efficient markets theory.

The problem with evaluating Miller's (1977) theory that a lack of short selling can cause financial anomalies like overpricing and bubbles is that there has been little or no data on which stocks are difficult to short. There are long time series data series on "short interest," which is the total number of shares that are shorted. Figlewski (1981) found that high levels of short interest for individual stocks predicts low subsequent returns for them, a direction that would be predicted by Miller's theory. But the predictability was weak. On the other hand, differences in short interest across stocks do not have an unambiguous connection with difficulty of shorting. Stocks differ from each other in terms of the fraction of shares that are in accounts that are shortable. Differences across stocks in short interest can also reflect different demand for shorting for hedging needs. Thus, there is a significant

[18] Put option prices on Palm also began to reflect the negative opinions and became so expensive that the usual relation between options prices and stock price, the so-called "put-call parity," failed to hold. One must remember that options markets are derivative markets that clear separately from stock markets, and overpriced puts have no direct impact on the supply and demand for stock unless arbitrageurs can exploit the overpricing by shorting the stock.

errors-in-variables problem when using short interest as an indicator of the cost of shorting.

Some recent papers have sought to detect the presence of barriers that might limit short sales indirectly by observing the differences of opinion that can have an impact on price if there is a difficulty shorting stocks. Without observing barriers to shorting stocks directly, we can still infer that when differences of opinion are high about a stock, it is more likely that short-sale restrictions will be binding for that stock, and thus that the more pessimistic investors will not prevent the stock from becoming overpriced and hence subject to lower subsequent returns.

Scherbina (2000) measured differences of opinion by calculating the dispersion of analysts' earnings forecasts. She found that stocks with a high dispersion of analysts' forecasts had lower subsequent returns, and she linked the low returns to the resolution of the uncertainty. Chen, Hong and Stein (2000) measured difference of opinion by a breadth of ownership measure derived from a database on mutual fund portfolios. The breadth variable for each quarter is the ratio of the number of mutual funds that hold a long position in the stock to the total number of mutual funds for that quarter. They find that firms in the top decile by breadth of ownership outperformed those in the bottom decile by 4.95 percent per annum after adjusting for various other factors.

What we would really like to have to test the importance of short sales restrictions on stock pricing is some evidence on the cost of shorting. If those stocks that have become very costly to short tend to have poor subsequent returns, then we will have more direct confirmation of Miller's (1977) theory. There is surprisingly little available information about the cost of shorting individual stocks. Such data have not been available for economic research until recently. A number of recent unpublished papers have assembled data on the cost of shorting individual stocks, but these papers have assembled data for no more than a year around 2000.

Recently, Jones and Lamont (2001) discovered an old source of data on the cost of shorting stocks. In the 1920s and 1930s in the United States, there used to be a "loan crowd" on the floor of the New York Stock Exchange, where one could lend or borrow shares, and the interest rates at which shares were loaned were reported in the *Wall Street Journal*. Jones and Lamont assembled time series of the interest rates charged on loans of stocks from 1926 to 1933, eight years of data on an average of 80 actively-traded stocks. They found that, after controlling for size, over this period the stocks that were more expensive to short tended to be more highly priced (in terms of market-to-book ratios), consistent with the Miller (1977) theory. Moreover, they found that the more expensive-to-short stocks had lower subsequent returns on average, again consistent with the Miller theory. Of course, their data span only eight years from a remote period in history, and so their relevance to today's markets might be questioned.

Why has there not been more data on the cost of shorting? Why did the loan crowd on the New York Stock Exchange disappear and the loan rates in the *Wall Street Journal* with it? Perhaps after the crash of 1929 the widespread hostility to short sellers (who were widely held responsible for the crash) forced the market to go underground. Jones and Lamont (2001) document a consistent pattern of political opposition to short sellers after 1929 and point out that J. Edgar Hoover, the head of the Federal Bureau of Investigation, was quoted as saying that he would investigate a conspiracy to keep stock prices low. By 1933, the rates shown on the loan list become all zeros, and the *Wall Street Journal* stopped publishing the loan list in 1934.

Fortunately, this long drought of data on the cost of shorting stocks may be over, and stocks should become easier to short. In 2002, a consortium of financial institutions established an electronic market for borrowing and lending stocks online via a new firm, EquiLend, LLC. The new securities lending platform at ⟨http://www.equilend.com⟩ exceeded $11 billion in transactions in its first two weeks, and daily availability posting exceed $1 trillion.

But the true cost of shorting stocks is probably much higher than the explicit interest cost of borrowing the shares, because of the psychological cost that inhibits short selling. Most investors, even some very smart investors, have probably never even considered shorting shares. Shorting shares is widely reputed to involve some substantial risks and nuisances. For example, the short-seller always stands the risk that the ultimate owner of the shares will want to sell the shares, at which time the short-seller is forced to return the shares. This detail may be little more than a nuisance, for the short seller can likely borrow them again from another lender, but it may figure largely in potential short-sellers' minds.

A more important consideration that may weigh on short sellers' minds is the unlimited loss potential that short sales entail. When an investor buys a stock, the potential loss is no greater than the original investment. But when an investor shorts a stock, the potential losses can greatly exceed the original investment. An investor can always terminate these losses by covering the shorts, but this action typically brings considerable psychological anguish. Deciding to cover one's shorts and get out of a short position after losses is psychologically difficult, given the evidence on the pain of regret. Kahneman and Tversky's prospect theory (1979) suggests that individuals are far more upset by losses than they are pleased by equivalent gains; in fact, individuals are so upset by losses that they will even take great risks with the hope of avoiding any losses at all. The effects of this pain of regret have been shown to result in a tendency of investors in stocks to avoid selling losers, but the same pain of regret ought to cause short sellers to want to avoid covering their shorts in a losing situation. People prefer to avoid putting themselves in situations that might confront them with psychologically difficult decisions in the future.

The stock market that we have today always limits the liability of investors. As Moss (2002) has documented, the idea that all publicly traded stocks should have limited liability for their investors was the result of experimenting with different kinds of stockholder liability in the United States in the early nineteenth century and the discovery of the psychological attractiveness of limited liability stocks. The debates in the early nineteenth century were concerned with the balancing of the agency costs of limited liability, which encourages businesses to take greater risks, against the benefits in terms of peace of mind to investors. Various alternatives were considered or experimented with, including unlimited liability, unlimited proportional liability (where individual investors in a company are limited to their proportionate share of the company's losses according to their share in the company), and double liability (where individual investors are accountable for the capital subscribed once again). By around 1830, it was apparent from experiments in New York and surrounding states that investors found it very appealing that they could put money down to buy a stock today, and from that day forward face no further losses beyond what they already put down. It allowed them, once having purchased a stock, to concentrate their emotions on the small probability of the stock doing extremely well, rather on the small probability that someone would come after them for more money. People have always been very attracted to lottery tickets, and the invention of limited liability, Moss concludes, turned stock investments psychologically into something a lot like lottery tickets. By the same theory, then, investors will not find shorting stocks very attractive.

Remarkably few shares are in fact sold short. According to New York Stock Exchange data, from 1977 to 2000 year-end short interest ranged from 0.14 percent to 1.91 percent of all shares. According to Dechow, Hutton, Muelbroek and Stone (2001), less than 2 percent of all stocks had short interest greater than 5 percent of shares outstanding 1976–1983. Given the obviously large difference of opinion about and difference of public attention to different stocks, it is hard to see how such a small amount of short selling could offset the effect on stock price of the extra demand of investors who develop an irrational fixation on certain stocks.

Conclusion

The collaboration between finance and other social sciences that has become known as behavioral finance has led to a profound deepening of our knowledge of financial markets. In judging the impact of behavioral finance to date, it is important to apply the right standards. Of course, we do not expect such research to provide a method to make a lot of money off of financial market inefficiency very fast and reliably. We should not expect market efficiency to be so egregiously wrong that immediate profits should be continually available. But market efficiency can be egregiously wrong in other senses. For example, efficient markets theory may lead to drastically incorrect interpretations of events such as major stock market bubbles.

In his review of the literature on behavioral finance, Eugene Fama (1998) found fault for two basic reasons. The first was that the anomalies that were discovered tended to appear to be as often underreaction by investors as overreaction. The second was that the anomalies tended to disappear, either as time passed or as methodology of the studies improved. His first criticism reflects an incorrect view of the psychological underpinnings of behavioral finance. Since there is no fundamental psychological principle that people tend always to overreact or always to underreact, it is no surprise that research on financial anomalies does not reveal such a principle either. His second criticism is also weak. It is the nature of scholarly research, at the frontier, in all disciplines, that initial claims of important discoveries are often knocked down by later research. The most basic anomaly, of excess volatility, seems hardly to have been knocked down, and it is in fact graphically reinforced by the experience of the past few years in the stock markets of the world. Moreover, the mere fact that anomalies sometimes disappear or switch signs with time is no evidence that the markets are fully rational. That is also what we would expect to see happen even in highly irrational markets. (It would seem peculiar to argue that irrational markets should display regular and lasting patterns!) Even the basic relation suggested by market inefficiency, that stocks whose price is bid up by investors will tend to go back down later, and stocks that are underpriced by investors will tend to go up later, is not a relation that can be easily tested or that should hold in all time periods. The fundamental value of stocks is hard to measure, and, moreover, if speculative bubbles (either positive bubbles or negative bubbles) last a long time, then even this fundamental relation may not be observed except in very long sample periods.

In further research, it is important to bear in mind the demonstrated weaknesses of efficient markets theory and maintain an eclectic approach. While theoretical models of efficient markets have their place as illustrations or characterizations of an ideal world, we cannot maintain them in their pure form as accurate descriptors of actual markets.

Indeed, we have to distance ourselves from the presumption that financial markets always work well and that price changes always reflect genuine information. Evidence from behavioral finance helps us to understand, for example, that the recent worldwide stock market boom, and then crash after 2000, had its origins in human foibles and arbitrary feedback relations and must have generated a real and substantial misallocation of resources. The challenge for economists is to make this reality a better part of their models.

References

Andreassen, Paul and Stephen Kraus. 1988. "Judgmental Prediction by Extrapolation." Unpublished paper, Department of Psychology, Harvard University.

Anonymous. 1637. *Samen-spraeck tusschen Waermondt ende Gaergoedt nopende de opkomste ende ondergangh van flora.* Haerlem: Adriaen Roman, reprinted in *Economisch Historisch Jaarboek.* 1926, 12:20–43, pp. 28–29.

Barberis, Nicholas and Andrei Shleifer. 2000. "Style Investing." NBER Working Paper No. w8039.

Barsky, Robert and J. Bradford De Long. 1993. "Why Does the Stock Market Fluctuate?" *Quarterly Journal of Economics.* May, 108, pp. 291–311.

Bem, Daryl J. 1965. "An Experimental Analysis of Self-Persuasion." *Journal of Experimental Social Psychology.* 1, pp.199–218.

Breeden, Douglas T. 1979. "An Intertemporal

Asset Pricing Model with Stochastic Consumption and Investment Opportunities." *Journal of Financial Economics.* 7:2, pp. 265–96.

Campbell, John Y. 1991. "A Variance Decomposition for Stock Returns." *Economic Journal.* March, 101:405, pp. 157–79.

Campbell, John Y. and Robert J. Shiller. 1988. "Stock Prices, Earnings, and Expected Dividends." *Journal of Finance.* July, 43:3, pp. 661–76.

Campbell, John Y. and Robert J. Shiller. 1989. "The Dividend-Price Ratio and Expectations of Future Dividends and Discount Factors." *Review of Financial Studies.* 1:3, pp. 195–228.

Campbell, John Y., Andrew W. Lo and A. Craig MacKinlay. 1996. *The Econometrics of Financial Markets.* Princeton: Princeton University Press.

Chen, Joseph, Harrison Hong and Jeremy C. Stein. 2000. "Breadth of Ownership and Stock Returns." Unpublished paper, Stanford University.

Cochrane, John H. 2001. *Asset Pricing.* Princeton: Princeton University Press.

Cohen, Randolph, Christopher Polk and Tuomo Vuolteenaho. 2002. "The Value Spread." Unpublished paper, Harvard Business School. Forthcoming, *Journal of Finance.*

Cole, Kevin, Jean Helwege and David Laster. 1996. "Stock Market Valuation Indicators: Is This Time Different?" *Financial Analysts Journal.* May/June, pp. 56–64.

Daniel, Kent, David Hirshleifer and Avanidhar Subramanyam. 1998. "Investor Psychology and Security Market Under- and Overreactions." *Journal of Finance.* December, 53:6, pp. 1839–885.

De Bondt, Werner F. M. and Richard H. Thaler. 1985."Does the Stock Market Overreact?" *Journal of Finance.* July, 40:3, pp. 793–805.

De Long, J. Bradford, Andrei Shleifer, Lawrence H. Summers and Robert J. Waldmann. 1990a. "Noise Trader Risk in Financial Markets." *Journal of Political Economy.* August, 98:4, pp. 703–38.

De Long, J. Bradford, Andrei Shleifer, Lawrence H. Summers and Robert J. Waldmann. 1990b. "Positive Feedback Investment Strategies and Destabilizing Rational Speculation." *Journal of Finance.* June, 45:2, pp. 379–95.

Dechow, Patricia M., Amy P. Hutton, Lisa Muelbroek and Richard G. Stone. 2001. "Short-Selling, Fundamental Analysis and Stock Returns." *Journal of Financial Economics.* Forthcoming.

Fama, Eugene F. 1970. "Efficient Capital Markets: A Review of Empirical Work." *Journal of Finance.* May, 25:2, pp. 383–417.

Fama, Eugene F. 1991. "Efficient Capital Markets: II." *Journal of Finance.* December, 46:5, pp. 1575–617.

Fama, Eugene F. 1998. "Market Efficiency, Long-Term Returns, and Behavioral Finance." *Journal of Financial Economics.* September, 49:3, pp. 283–306.

Figlewski, Stephen. 1981. "The Informational Effects of Restrictions on Short Sales: Some Empirical Evidence." *Journal of Financial and Quantitative Analysis.* November, 16:4, pp. 463–76.

Figlewski, Stephen and Gwendolyn P. Webb. 1993. "Options, Short Sales, and Market Completeness." *Journal of Finance.* June, 48:2, pp. 761–77.

Garber, Peter M. 1990. "Famous First Bubbles." *Journal of Economic Perspectives.* Spring, 4:2, pp. 35–54.

Garber, Peter M. 2000. *Famous First Bubbles.* Cambridge: MIT Press.

Goetzmann, William N. and Massimo Massa. 1999. "Daily Momentum and Contrarian Behavior of Index Fund Investors." Unpublished paper, Yale University.

Grinblatt, Mark and Bing Han. 2001. "The Disposition Effect and Momentum." Unpublished paper, Anderson School, UCLA.

Grossman, Sanford J. and Robert J. Shiller. 1981. "The Determinants of the Variability of Stock Market Prices." *American Economic Review.* May, 71:2, pp. 222–27.

Hansen, Lars P. and Ravi Jagannathan. 1991. "Implications of Security Market Data for Models of Dynamic Economies." *Journal of Political Economy.* April, 99:2, pp. 225–62.

Jarvis, Chris. 1999. "The Rise and Fall of the Pyramid Schemes in Albania." International Monetary Fund Working Paper No. 99-98.

Jegadeesh, Narasimhan and Sheridan Titman. 1993. "Returns to Buying Winners and Selling Losers: Implications for Stock Market Efficiency." *Journal of Finance.* March, 48:1, pp. 65–91.

Jones, Charles M. and Owen A. Lamont. 2001."Short-Sale Constraints and Stock Returns." NBER Working Paper No. 8494.

Jung, Jeeman and Robert J. Shiller. 2002. "One Simple Test of Samuelson's Dictum for the Stock Market." NBER Working Paper No. w9348.

Kahneman, Daniel and Amos Tversky. 1979. "Prospect Theory: An Analysis of Decision Under Risk." *Econometrica.* March, 47:2, pp. 263–92.

Lamont, Owen A. and Richard H. Thaler. 2001. "Can the Market Add and Subtract? Mispricing in Stock Market Carve-Outs." National Bureau of Economic Research Working Paper

No. 8302, 2000. Forthcoming, *Journal of Political Economy*.

LeRoy, Stephen F. and Richard D. Porter. 1981. "The Present-Value Relation: Tests Based on Implied Variance Bounds." *Econometrica*. May, 49:3, pp. 97–113.

Lucas, Robert E. 1978. "Asset Prices in an Exchange Economy." *Econometrica*. November, 46:6, pp. 1429–445.

MacKay, Charles. 1996. "Memoirs of Extraordinary Popular Delusions," 1841, in *Extraordinary Popular Delusions and the Madness of Crowds and Confusión de Confusiones*. Martin Fridson, ed. New York: John Wiley.

Malkiel, Burton G. 1973. *A Random Walk Down Wall Street*. New York: W. W. Norton.

Marimon, Ramon, Stephen E. Spear and Shyam Sunder. 1993. "Expectationally Driven Market Volatility: An Experimental Study." *Journal of Economic Theory*. October, 61:1, pp. 74–103.

Marsh, Terry A. and Robert C. Merton. 1986. "Dividend Variability and Variance Bounds Tests for the Rationality of Stock Market Prices." *American Economic Review*. June, 76:3, pp. 483–98.

McGrattan, Ellen R. and Edward C. Prescott. 2001. "Taxes, Regulation, and Asset Prices." Unpublished paper, Federal Reserve Bank of Minneapolis.

Merton, Robert C. 1973. "An Intertemporal Capital Asset Pricing Model." *Econometrica*. September, 41:5, pp. 867–87.

Miller, Edward M. 1977. "Risk, Uncertainty and Divergence of Opinion." *Journal of Finance*. September, 32:4, pp. 1151–168.

Moss, David A. 2002. *When All Else Fails: Government as the Ultimate Risk Manager*. Cambridge, Mass.: Harvard University Press.

Odean, Terrance. 1998. "Are Investors Reluctant to Realize their Losses?" *Journal of Finance*. October, 53:5, pp. 1775–798.

Samuelson, Paul A. 1998. "Summing Up on Business Cycles: Opening Address," in *Beyond Shocks: What Causes Business Cycles*. Jeffrey C. Fuhrer and Scott Schuh, eds. Boston: Federal Reserve Bank of Boston, pp. 33–36.

Scherbina, Anna. 2000. "Stock Prices and Differences in Opinion: Empirical Evidence that Prices Reflect Optimism." Unpublished paper, Northwestern University.

Shefrin, Hersh. 2000. *Beyond Greed and Fear: Understanding Behavioral Finance and the Psychology of Investing*. Boston, Mass.: Harvard Business School Press.

Shefrin, Hersh. 2001. *Behavioral Finance (The International Library of Critical Writings in Financial Economics), Volumes I through IV*. Cheltenham, U.K.: Edward Elgar.

Shiller, Robert J. 1982. "Consumption, Asset Markets and Macroeconomic Fluctuations." *Carnegie-Rochester Conference Series on Public Policy*. Autumn, 17, pp. 203–38.

Shiller, Robert J. 1989. *Market Volatility*. Cambridge, Mass.: MIT Press.

Shiller, Robert J. 1990a. "Speculative Prices and Popular Models." *Journal of Economic Perspectives*. Spring, 4:2, pp. 55–65.

Shiller, Robert J. 1990b. "Market Volatility and Investor Behavior." *American Economic Review*. May, 80:2, pp. 58–62.

Shiller, Robert J. 2000a. *Irrational Exuberance*. Princeton, N.J.: Princeton University Press.

Shiller, Robert J. 2000b. "Measuring Bubble Expectations and Investor Confidence." *Journal of Psychology and Financial Markets*. 1:1, pp. 49–60.

Shiller, Robert J. 2002. "Bubbles, Human Judgment, and Expert Opinion." *Financial Analysts Journal*. 58, pp. 18–26.

Shleifer, Andrei. 2000. *Inefficient Markets*. Oxford: Oxford University Press.

Shielfer, Andrei and Lawrence Summers. 1990. "The Noise-Trader Approach to Finance." *Journal of Economic Perspectives*. Spring, 4:2 pp. 19–33.

Siegel, Jeremy J. 2002. *Stocks for the Long Run*. Third Edition. New York: McGraw-Hill.

Smith, Vernon, Gerry Suchanek and Arlington Williams. 1988. "Bubbles, Crashes, and Endogenous Expectations in Experimental Spot Asset Markets." *Econometrica*. September, 56:5, pp. 1119–153.

Statman, Meir and Hersh Shefrin. 1985. "The Disposition to Sell Winners Too Early and Ride Losers Too Long: Theory and Evidence." *Journal of Finance*. July, 40:3, pp. 777–90.

Thaler, Richard. 2003. *Advances in Behavioral Finance II*. New York: Russell Sage.

Tversky, Amos and Daniel Kahneman. 1974. "Judgment under Uncertainty: Heuristics and Biases." *Science*. 185:4157, pp. 1124–31.

Vuolteenaho, Tuomo. "What Drives Firm-Level Stock Returns?" *Journal of Finance*. February, 57:1, pp. 233–64.

West, Kenneth D. 1988. "Dividend Innovations and Stock Price Volatility." *Econometrica*. January, 56:1, pp. 36–71.

[13]

ARTICLES

BEHAVIORAL ECONOMICS AND THE SEC

Stephen J. Choi* & A.C. Pritchard**

---

* Professor of Law, University of California, Berkeley (Boalt Hall).

** Professor of Law, University of Michigan Law School. The authors thank Jennifer Arlen, Mitu Gulati, Andrew Guzman, Kim Krawiec, Jim Krier, Donald Langevoort, Ronald Mann, Un Kyung Park, Jeff Rachlinski, and participants at the University of Michigan Law School Fawley Lunch, the Washington University, St. Louis School of Law Faculty Workshop, the Georgetown University Law Center Sloan Workshop, the University of North Carolina School of Law Faculty Workshop,the American Law and Economics Association Annual Meeting and the Columbia University Law and Economics seminar for helpful comments. Pritchard acknowledges the generous financial support of the Cook Fund of the University of Michigan Law School.

INTRODUCTION

Not all investors are rational. Quite apart from the obvious examples of credulity in the face of the latest Ponzi scheme, there is no shortage of evidence that many investors' decisions are influenced by systematic biases that impair their abilities to maximize their investment returns.[1] For example, investors will often hold onto poorly performing stocks longer than warranted, hoping to recoup their losses.[2] Other investors will engage in speculative trading, dissipating their returns by paying larger commissions than more passive investors.[3] And we are not just talking about widows and orphans here. There is evidence that supposedly sophisticated institutional investors—mutual funds, pension funds, insurance companies—suffer from similar biases that impair their decisions.[4] These biases are not merely isolated quirks, rather, they are consistent, deep-rooted, and systematic behavioral patterns. Apparently even the considerable sums at stake in the securities markets are not enough to induce market participants to overcome these cognitive defects on a consistent basis.

Not surprisingly, these findings of scholars working at the intersection of psychology and economics have recently found their way into legal scholarship. This burgeoning trend has come to be called "behavioral law and

1. For a useful survey, see David A. Hirshleifer, *Investor Psychology and Asset Pricing*, 56 J. FIN. 1533 (2001).

2. *See* Terrence Odean, *Are Investors Reluctant to Realize Their Losses?*, 53 J. FIN. 1775 (1998) (finding that investors were more willing to sell winning positions than losing ones, despite tax advantages); Hersh Shefrin & Meir Statman, *The Disposition To Sell Winners Too Early and Ride Losers Too Long: Theory and Evidence*, 40 J. FIN. 777, 788 (1985) (developing a behavioral model of loss aversion due to, among others, "mental accounting, regret aversion, and self-control" and providing evidence that tax considerations alone cannot explain patterns of loss realization).

3. *See* Brad M. Barber & Terrence Odean, *Trading is Hazardous to Your Wealth: The Common Stock Investment Performance of Individual Investors*, 55 J. FIN. 773 (2000) (finding that more active traders tend to have lower returns); Terrence Odean, *Do Investors Trade Too Much?*, 89 AM. ECON. REV. 1279 (1999) (providing evidence that the trading volume on the part of those with discount brokerage accounts is excessive in the sense that the returns from such trades do not outweigh the transaction costs). Odean, indeed, provides evidence that the trading returns for those with discount brokerage accounts are negative irrespective of transaction costs. *See id.* at 1283-84.

4. *See infra* notes 74-94 and accompanying text (discussing the behavioral biases afflicting securities market institutions).

economics."[5] Behavioral law and economics is defined primarily by what it rejects: the rational actor model that is the fundamental premise of conventional law and economics. The rational actor model postulates that individuals shrewdly calculate the course of action that will maximize their wealth and utility.[6] This presumption is bolstered in market settings, where economically minded commentators commonly assume that the most rational will dominate in competition with those less cognitively able.

In the context of the securities markets the rational actor model has considerably less Darwinian implications than one might suppose. Under the Efficient Capital Market Hypothesis,[7] the "smart" money will set prices and through the process of arbitrage will swamp the influence of the poorly informed or foolish. Even the unsophisticated therefore can rely on market efficiency to ensure that the price he pays for a security will be "fair." More importantly, the unsophisticated can accomplish their investment goals by passively tracking the overall market without evaluating individual companies and the securities that they issue.[8] Far from weeding out unsophisticated investors, the overwhelming influence of smart money actually indirectly protects the interests of the poorly informed, as evidenced by the burgeoning popularity of index funds.[9]

The more provocative implication of the efficient market hypothesis is that government regulation of financial intermediaries and companies' financial disclosures may be unnecessary and potentially wasteful. Investors will price legal protections—or the lack thereof—when valuing securities. If financial intermediaries do not give credible assurances that they will not abuse their customers' trust, investors will not entrust them with their investment dollars. And if companies do not give credible assurances that they will disclose truthfully the information that investors rely upon to value securities, those companies will pay substantial risk premia (thereby compensating investors for the risk of fraud) or be unable to sell their securities altogether. We confess to

5. *See, e.g.*, BEHAVIORAL LAW & ECONOMICS (Cass R. Sunstein ed., 2000).

6. *See* Richard A. Posner, *The Economic Approach to Law*, 53 TEX. L. REV. 757, 761 (1973) ("The basis of an economic approach to law is the assumption that the people involved with the legal system act as rational maximizers of their satisfactions.").

7. *See* Eugene F. Fama, *Efficient Capital Markets: A Review of Theory and Empirical Work*, 25 J. FIN. 383 (1970) (providing a survey of theoretical implications of efficient markets and empirical testing of the efficient markets hypothesis).

8. Some finance theorists argue that markets are not efficient due to the presence of "noise traders" who trade not based on information but rather due to liquidity needs. *See, e.g.*, J. Bradford De Long, Andrei Shleifer, Lawrence H. Summers & Robert J. Waldmann, *Noise Trader Risk in Financial Markets*, 98 J. POL. ECON. 703, 713, 717 (1990).

9. The authors share this faith: Our retirement savings are indexed. Of course, the popularity of index funds may reflect regret aversion as investors are more likely to regret poor investments when they are actively involved in making those choices. *See* Daniel Kahneman & Amos Tversky, *The Psychology of Preferences*, 246 SCI. AM. 160 (1982) (finding that individuals suffered greater regret from decisions involving action rather than inaction).

having penned a few lines of this sort ourselves in prior work.[10]

Adherents to behavioral law and economics are not so sanguine about investors' capacity to fend for themselves. They argue that arbitrage will not drive irrationality from the market but instead may fuel it: "Arbitrage is a double-edged blade: Just as rational investors arbitrage away inefficient pricing, foolish traders arbitrage away efficient pricing."[11] If mispricing is a persistent phenomenon, the behavioralists fear that investors left to the mercies of unscrupulous brokers and corporate executives will be systematically fleeced. Rejecting the laissez-faire normative outlook that underlies much law and economics scholarship, the behavioral economics school generally subscribes to an "anti-antipaternalism."[12] As any high school English teacher no doubt could translate, this means a belief in the benefit of "paternalism."[13] In the context of the securities regulation, this faith has a quite tangible object of worship: the Securities and Exchange Commission (SEC).

Several commentators use the evidence of cognitive defects among investors to justify preserving and expanding the role of the SEC.[14] In the

10. *See, e.g.*, Stephen J. Choi, *Promoting Issuer Choice in Securities Regulation*, 41 VA. J. INT'L L. 815 (2001); Stephen J. Choi & Andrew T. Guzman, *Portable Reciprocity: Rethinking the International Reach of Securities Regulation*, 71 S. CAL. L. REV. 903 (1998); A.C. Pritchard, *Markets as Monitors: A Proposal to Replace Class Actions with Exchanges as Securities Fraud Monitors*, 85 VA. L. REV. 925 (1999).

11. Hirshleifer, *supra* note 1, at 1536. Moreover, arbitrage is costly, which may limit its effect on correcting mispricing. *See, e.g.*, Andrei Shleifer & Robert W. Vishny, *The Limits of Arbitrage*, 52 J. FIN. 35 (1997) (discussing possible anomalies in the financial markets and why arbitrage fails to counter such anomalies).

12. Cass R. Sunstein, *Looking Forward: Behavioral Analysis of Law*, 64 U. CHI. L. REV. 1175, 1178 (1997) (noting that his "anti-antipaternalism" view does not necessarily lead to paternalism, but nonetheless requires that "objections to paternalism should be empirical and pragmatic, having to do with the possibility of education and likely failures of government response, rather than a priori in nature").

13. It is hard to ignore the ideological tenor of this work. *See, e.g.*, Donald C. Langevoort, *Are Judges Motivated to Create "Good" Securities Fraud Doctrine?*, 51 EMORY L.J. 309, 318 (2002) ("Political conservatives are especially inclined to discount psychological excuses and project onto the world an unrealistic level of intentionality.") (citing Philip Tetlock, *Cognitive Biases and Organizational Correctives: Do Both Disease and Cure Depend on the Politics of the Beholder?*, 45 ADMIN. SCI. Q. 293 (2000)); *see also* Stephen M. Bainbridge, *Mandatory Disclosure: A Behavioral Analysis*, 68 U. CINN. L. REV. 1023, 1027 (2000) ("[I]t seems probable that behavior economics increasingly will be invoked by those who favor government intervention precisely because behavioral economics offers a new line of argument in favor of regulating private conduct."); Philip E. Tetlock & Barbara A. Mellers, *The Great Rationality Debate*, 13 PSYCHOL. SCI. 94, 97 (2002) ("It should not be surprising that Kahneman and Tversky's research program is more enthusiastically embraced by economists on the left, who have long doubted that markets are infallibly self-correcting and suspected that people sometimes need to be protected from themselves, than by economists on the laissez-faire right, who worry about what kind of 'micro' case is not being manufactured for new meddlesome forms of government intervention.").

14. *See* Lawrence A. Cunningham, *Behavioral Finance and Investor Governance*, 59 WASH. & LEE L. REV. 767 (2002) (proposing to reform various aspects of securities

absence of government regulation, greedy promoters will step into the void to prey on the cognitive defects of investors. Particular scorn is directed toward proposals to substitute market regulation for SEC oversight.[15] Market participants, the argument goes, will not precommit to regulatory protections to win the trust of investors but will instead manipulate investors' biases systematically to enrich themselves.[16] Competition cannot be relied upon to promote investor welfare because of the systematic nature of the biases. The small investor cannot count on the smart money to demand fair treatment for all investors—the smart money suffers from the same set of biases. Only government intervention can protect investors from their own cognitive defects.

While we think the magnitude of investor biases is open to question,[17] we focus on a different question here: If cognitive defects are pervasive, will intervention help? Even well-intentioned and fully rational regulators may find it difficult to solve the problem of cognitive illusions among investors. Disclosure, the prevailing regulatory strategy in the securities markets, may not protect investors if cognitive biases prevent them from rationally incorporating the information disclosed into their investment decisions. More fundamentally, if everyone suffers from cognitive defects, doesn't that also include the commissioners and staff of the SEC?

Regulators may respond that their expertise shields them from some cognitive illusions. The work of behavioral economists, however, shows that experts may fall prey to their own set of biases.[18] Moreover, regulators do not face the same competitive pressures that investors and other securities market participants do.[19] Those competitive forces may help mitigate behavioral biases

---

regulation to take into account insights from behavioral finance); Robert Prentice, *Whither Securities Regulation? Some Behavioral Observations Regarding Proposals for its Future*, 51 DUKE L.J. 1397, 1400 (2001) (stating his belief that "that American securities regulation is the optimal system for governing capital markets").

15. *See* Prentice, *supra* note 14 (casting scorn on both Choi and Pritchard's prior market-based proposals); *see also* Donald C. Langevoort, *Taming the Animal Spirits of the Stock Markets: A Behavioral Approach to Securities Regulation*, 97 NW. U. L. REV. 135, 153 (2003) ("Behavioral finance can be invoked as a counterweight, to demonstrate the costs and risks of [deregulatory] proposals under an arguably more realistic view of how markets behave.") [hereinafter Langevoort, *Taming the Animal Spirits*].

16. Donald C. Langevoort, *Selling Hope, Selling Risk: Some Lessons for Law from Behavioral Economics About Stockbrokers and Sophisticated Customers*, 84 CAL. L. REV. 627, 648-67 (1996) (detailing how brokers may manipulate both individual and institutional investor biases for the brokers' own opportunistic ends) [hereinafter Langevoort, *Selling Hope*].

17. We address some of these magnitude questions *infra* Part I.C.

18. We discuss the biases facing "expert" SEC regulators *infra* Part II.

19. *See* Kent Daniel, David Hirshleifer & Siew Hong Teoh, Investor Psychology in Capital Markets: Evidence and Policy Implications 3 (Aug. 3, 2001), (unpublished manuscript, on file with the Stanford Law Review), *available at* http://papers.ssrn.com/sol3/papers.cfm?abstract_id=278848 ("Individual political participants are not immune to the biases and self-interest exhibited in private settings. . . . Indeed, the economic incentives of officials to overcome their biases in evaluating

among investors and securities professionals (at the very least forcing out of the market those with the greatest levels of cognitive difficulties). Regulators, by contrast, generally enjoy monopolies in their field, which immunizes them from the stringent constraints of the market that might force corrections in decision making flaws. If biases are universal, do regulators suffer more or less from those biases than investors? Markets deal harshly with fools; our cynical side worries that government affords a safe haven.

Not all commentators applying behavioral insights to securities regulations call unquestioningly for government intervention to correct for market-based biases. The possibility of regulator biases has led some to question the wisdom of regulation as a solution for market-based biases.[20] For those attempting to take into account regulator behavioral biases, the question nonetheless remains: How should policymakers weigh investors' behavioral biases against those affecting regulators? Obviously perfect regulation trumps an imperfect market. But we do not face this choice. Instead, we propose a framework for assessing regulation to correct for market biases. A cautious approach is warranted in this area because regulators themselves typically make the decision whether to intervene in the market. Overconfidence (or more mundane public choice reasons) may cause regulators to ignore their own behavioral limitations and push toward excessive intervention. Regulatory intervention to correct for biases also poses the very real danger of regulatory mistake. Once in place, new regulatory protections often take a life of their own, so even if regulations are ill conceived, they become difficult to displace. The market corrects its mistakes; regulators frequently resist doing so. Indeed, focusing on the behavioral problems of investors without also addressing the problems among regulators may lead to a perverse result. Investors—to the extent they are capable of learning and adjusting to cognitive limitations through feedback in the market—may come to rely (mistakenly) on regulators to protect them from

---

fundamental value are likely to be weaker than the incentives of market participants. So government efforts to correct market perceptions are likely to waste resources and increase *ex ante* uncertainty.").

20. *See* Jennifer Arlen, *The Future of Behavioral Economic Analysis of Law*, 51 VAND. L. REV. 1765, 1769 (1998) ("Proposals designed to address biases generally entail the intervention of judges, legislators, or bureaucrats who are also subject to various biases. The very power of the behavioralist critique—that even educated people exhibit certain biases—thus undercuts efforts to redress such biases."); Bainbridge, *supra* note 13, at 1057-58 ("[L]egislators and regulators are no less subject to bounded rationality and other cognitive biases than any other decisionmakers."); Donald C. Langevoort, *Behavioral Theories of Judgment and Decision Making in Legal Scholarship: A Literature Review*, 51 VAND. L. REV. 1499, 1519 (1998) ("Less attention has been devoted to whether courts or regulators are likely to be biased along the lines suggested in the behavioral literature, perhaps because bureaucratic activity seems more organizational than individual."). For a more general account of the behavioral biases affecting government officials, see Jeffrey J. Rachlinski & Cynthia R. Farina, *New Theories of the Regulatory State: Cognitive Psychology and Optimal Government Design*, 87 CORNELL L. REV. 549 (2002) (discussing the role expertise has in both reducing cognitive errors in some ways and increasing errors in others).

themselves,[21] diminishing the market's ability to overcome behavioral biases on its own. We therefore argue that regulations designed to remove investment choices from individual decisionmaking require very strong justification. Other forms of regulatory interventions disrupt markets less. So, for example, we are more open to regulations intended to assist investors in overcoming their behavioral biases. Investor education might be one such intervention.

Part I summarizes some of the cognitive defects found by psychologists and reviews the evidence that these defects affect the financial markets. Part II applies the insights of behavioral economics to the SEC (and other regulators). Part III sets forth a framework for comparing SEC and market-based responses to cognitive biases. A short conclusion summarizes our main points.

I. The Behavioral Approach to Securities Regulation

Some call behavioral law and economics the growth stock of legal academia,[22] a contention borne out by the increasing number of articles employing the behavioral approach.[23] A common theme runs through this literature: It is simply wrong to assume that people act rationally with every decision.[24] In this Part we (A) discuss biases in the context of investors; (B) discuss alternative explanations for investor behavior (including a preference for speculation); and (C) comment on the possible magnitude of behavioral biases among investors.

A. *Investor Biases*

What biases plague human decisionmaking? Psychologists have identified a long list, including the hindsight bias,[25] the (flawed) reliance on heuristics[26]

---

21. Indeed, investors may themselves become overconfident in the ability of regulators to provide airtight protections, leading to perhaps even greater investor losses. *See* Langevoort, *Taming the Animal Spirits*, *supra* note 15, at 175 (citing Henry T.C. Hu, *Faith and Magic: Investor Beliefs and Government Neutrality*, 78 TEX. L. REV. 777 (2000)).

22. *See* Kent Greenfield, *Using Behavioral Economics to Show the Power and Efficiency of Corporate Law as Regulatory Tool*, 35 U.C. DAVIS L. REV. 581, 583 (2002) ("If one could invest in areas of legal scholarship, 'behavioral law and economics' (BLE) would be a growth stock.").

23. As a crude test, we performed a Westlaw search among law review articles for the word "behavioral" in the title. There were 14 articles listing 2001 as the publication year compared with only 6 listing 1997.

24. It is hard to quarrel with this proposition; rational choice economists have always conceded that this fundamental assumption was a crude, albeit useful, simplification. *See* MILTON FRIEDMAN, *The Methodology of Positive Economics*, *in* ESSAYS IN POSITIVE ECONOMICS 3-43 (1953).

25. The hindsight bias describes the tendency to place too great a weight on events that actually did occur in the past (rather than events that might have occurred but did not) in predicting the probability of events. *See* Baruch Fischhoff, *Hindsight Is Not Equal to Foresight: The Effect of Outcome Knowledge on Judgment Under Uncertainty*, 1 J.

(including the availability heuristic),[27] the presence of overconfidence and overoptimism,[28] the endowment effect (and other framing related biases),[29] and

EXPERIMENTAL PSYCHOL: HUM. PERCEPTION & PERFORMANCE 288, 288 (1975) (discussing evidence of the hindsight bias). Similarly, people tend to give too little weight to large samples and too much weight to small samples in drawing inferences on the characteristics of an overall population. *See, e.g.*, Amos Tversky & Daniel Kahneman, *Belief in the Law of Small Numbers*, *in* JUDGMENT UNDER UNCERTAINTY: HEURISTICS AND BIASES 23-24 (Daniel Kahneman, Paul Slovik & Amos Tversky eds., 1982) ("[P]eople view a sample randomly drawn from a population as highly representative, that is, similar to the population in all essential characteristics. Consequently, they expect any two samples drawn from a particular population to be more similar to one another and to the population than sampling theory predicts . . . ."); Amos Tversky & Daniel Kahneman, *Judgment Under Uncertainty: Heuristics and Biases*, 185 SCI. 1124, 1124-31 (1974) [hereinafter Tversky & Kahneman, *Judgment Under Uncertainty*].

26. People may use heuristic shortcuts to manage large quantities of information (operating under bounded rationality). Heuristics, of course, are not always inaccurate. Indeed, their survival over time provides some evidence that heuristics provide a cost-effective way of arriving at an answer that generally will be correct. In specific situations, however, heuristics may lead users astray. For example, people are more willing to accept the truth of a statement that is easy to understand (the "illusion of truth"). *See* Rolf Reber & Norbert Schwarz, *Effects of Perceptual Fluency on Judgments of Truth*, 8 CONSCIOUSNESS & COGNITION 338 (1999) (providing empirical evidence that "any variable that increases experienced ease of processing is also likely to increase judgments of truth"). Once heuristics become entrenched, people may be unable to discern when a heuristic is inappropriate for a particular situation.

27. Under the availability heuristic, people place undue weight on recent events and other readily available information. The availability heuristic may lead people to discount excessively the possibility of losses from high magnitude but low probability risks if such a loss has not occurred recently. Conversely, immediately after a loss does occur (for example, an earthquake in San Francisco or a financial meltdown at Enron), people may exaggerate the probability of future loss. *See* Tversky & Kahneman, *Judgment Under Uncertainty*, *supra* note 25, at 1127-28 (describing the availability heuristic).

28. Experts, in particular, may also develop a sense of overconfidence, leading to a countervailing increase in errors. *See* Dale Griffin & Amos Tversky, *The Weighing of Evidence and the Determinants of Confidence*, 24 COGNITIVE PSYCHOL. 411 (1992). Experience may or may not help increase analyst forecast accuracy. *Compare* John Jacob, Thomas Z. Lys & Margaret A Neale, *Expertise in Forecasting Performance of Security Analysts*, 28 J. ACCT. & ECON. 51 (1999) (providing evidence that analyst forecast accuracy does not increase with experience), *with* Michael B. Mikhail, Beverly R. Walther & Richard Willis, *The Development of Expertise: Do Security Analysts Improve their Performance with Experience?*, 35 J. ACCT. RES. 131 (1997) (finding a statistically significant decline in analyst forecast errors as their firm-specific experience increases). Overconfidence does not necessarily correlate with less wealthy investors. In investment markets, success itself may lead traders to develop overconfidence. *See* Simon Gervais & Terrance Odean, *Learning To Become Overconfident*, 14 REV. FIN. STUD. 1, 2 (2001) ("Overconfidence does not make traders wealthy, but the process of becoming wealthy *can* make traders overconfident."). Overoptimism is a closely related bias. *See* MAX H. BAZERMAN, JUDGMENT IN MANAGERIAL DECISION MAKING 37-39 (3d ed. 1994); Neil D. Weinstein, *Unrealistic Optimism About Future Life Events*, 39 J. PERSONALITY & SOC. PSYCHOL. 806 (1980). Some amount of overoptimism, of course, can be useful. *See* Jeffrey J. Rachlinski, *The "New" Law and Psychology: A Reply to Critics, Skeptics, and Cautious Supporters*, 85 CORNELL L. REV. 739, 760 (2000) (noting that "[p]sychologists have shown, for example, that only clinically depressed people make accurate predictions about their likelihood of success").

the confirmation bias.[30] Several commentators have attempted to categorize the

---

29. The endowment effect describes the greater value that people place on things presently in their possession. *See* Richard H. Thaler, *Toward a Positive Theory of Consumer Choice*, 1 J. ECON. BEHAV. & ORG. 39 (1980) (setting forth the endowment effect theory). People frequently demand more to sell an item than they would be willing to pay for the same item. *See* Daniel Kahneman, Jack L. Knetsch & Richard H. Thaler, *Experimental Tests of the Endowment Effect and the Coase Theorem*, 98 J. POL. ECON. 1325 (1990) (providing evidence from an experimental setting that the endowment effect persists even when parties are given the opportunity to learn). In other words, the framing of the question (whether to buy or sell the same item) may affect the valuation of an item. The magnitude of the endowment effect, however, may vary with the context. Jennifer Arlen, Matt Spitzer, and Eric Talley have shown that framing a relationship as an agency appears to reduce the overall impact of the endowment effect for the agent-decisionmaker. *See* Jennifer Arlen, Matthew Spitzer & Eric Talley, *Endowment Effects Within Corporate Agency Relationships*, 31 J. LEG. STUD. 1, 31 (2002) (noting that their results "are largely consistent with the hypothesis that situating subjects in an agency context mutes the endowment effect because the subjects focus on the exchange value of the entitlements for trade."); *see also* Russell Korobkin, *The Endowment Effect and Legal Analysis*, 97 NW. U. L. Rev. 1227, 1238 (2003) (noting that the endowment effect is reduced for products with close market substitutes) (citing Jason F. Shogren, Seung Y. Shin, Dermot J. Hayes & James B. Kliebenstein, *Resolving Differences in Willingness to Pay and Willingness to Accept*, 84 AM. ECON. REV. 255, 259-64 (1994)). Securities, of course, would be a paradigm of such a good. *See* RICHARD A. BREALEY & STEWART C. MYERS, PRINCIPLES OF CORPORATE FINANCE 345 (5th ed. 1996).

Endowment effects are related to loss aversion, which describes the phenomenon of people valuing the avoidance of a loss much higher than an improvement of the same magnitude over their current position. *See* Amos Tversky & Daniel Kahneman, *Loss Aversion and Riskless Choice: A Reference-Dependent Model*, 106 Q.J. ECON. 1039 (1991) (providing a model of consumer choice where the value of gains and losses depends on a person's reference point); Daniel Kahneman & Amos Tversky, *Prospect Theory: An Analsyis of Decision Under Risk*, 47 ECONOMETRICA 263 (1979) (noting that the tendency of people to overweight certain outcomes and underweight probabilistic outcomes may lead people to accept overly high risks in the hopes of avoiding a certain loss). Loss aversion informs people's notions of fairness: People are more offended by shifts away from the norms in transactions that result in harm to consumers and workers than by failures to improve the terms of trade for those individuals. *See* Daniel Kahneman, Jack L. Knetsch & Richard H. Thaler, *Fairness as a Constraint on Profit Seeking: Entitlements in the Market*, 76 AM. ECON. REV. 728 (1985); Daniel Kahneman, Jack L. Knetsch & Richard H. Thaler, *Fairness and the Assumptions of Economics*, 59 J. BUS. S285 (1986). People may have a general bias toward the status quo. *See* William Samuelson & Richard Zeckhauser, *Status Quo Bias in Decision Making*, 1 J. RISK & UNCERTAINTY 7 (1988).

30. The confirmation bias induces people to confirm prior decisions regardless of whether the decisions were correct when made. *See, e.g.*, Robert Forsythe, Forrest Nelson, George R. Neumann & Jack Wright, *Anatomy of an Experimental Political Stock Market*, 82 AM. ECON. REV. 1142 (1992); Charles G. Lord, Lee Ross & Mark R. Lepper, *Biased Assimilation and Attitude Polarization: The Effects of Prior Theories on Subsequently Considered Evidence*, 37 J. PERSONALITY & SOC. PSYCHOL. 2098 (1979). For example, suppose an individual makes an ill-advised decision to purchase an expensive convertible to drive himself to work. Even after discovering that the costs of such a car in the Michigan winter far outweigh the benefits, the person may then invent new perceived benefits (such as how good Frank Sinatra sounds on the swell stereo) to justify the purchase. And he may fail to recognize some of the costs attributable to the car, such as his daughter's increased number of colds from sitting in the back seat of this drafty vehicle. *See* Langevoort, *Taming*

biases.[31] Despite efforts at categorization, no underlying theory behind why we operate under biases has emerged.[32] Instead of a theory, behavioral economics relies on a hodgepodge of evidence showing the ineffectiveness of human decisionmaking in various circumstances (often in a controlled, laboratory setting).[33] Many questions therefore remain unanswered including: (a) how can

---

the Animal Spirits, *supra* note 15, at 142 ("Once a person voluntarily commits to an idea or course of action, there is a strong motivation to resist evidence that it was ill-chosen."). Pritchard has just recently made this ill-advised choice and has not yet born the adverse consequences requiring rationalization. His unfortunate daughter will just have to bundle up come winter.

31. Christine Jolls, Cass Sunstein, and Richard Thaler ("JST") classify behavioral biases according to the qualification that the behavioral bias imposes on the rational man assumption: bounded rationality, bounded willpower, and bounded self-interest. *See* Christine Jolls, Cass Sunstein & Richard Thaler, *A Behavioral Approach to Law and Economics*, 50 STAN. L. REV. 1471, 1476-80 (1998) (noting that "[e]ach of these bounds represents a significant way in which most people depart from the standard economic model"). While useful descriptively, JST's grouping does not move us forward in determining biases' underlying causes. JST offer no theory of how we process information. Rather, JST simply group empirically similar phenomena together (based on their impact on the rational man assumption). One could similarly group birds and airplanes together (both can fly) without explaining how birds and airplanes remain airborne.

Jeffrey Rachlinski classifies behavioral biases based on their source within the human brain's information processing apparatus. *See* Rachlinski, *supra* note 28, at 750-52. Rachlinski identifies three categories of biases: (1) overoptimism, the fact that people act as if their abilities and memory are limitless when in fact there are limits; (2) heuristics, short-cuts that people use without being aware of them; and (3) people's tendency to react to things in a relative way (rather than an absolute way) in making decisions. *See id.* Rachlinski's division sheds light on the origins of behavioral biases. Our brains' tendencies to act without limits, take short cuts, and interpret phenomena in a relative manner lead to systematic behavioral biases. Rachlinski's division, nonetheless fails to explain why our brains in fact process information in this manner.

Yet other ways of organizing the myriad biases are possible. *See* Hal R. Arkes, *Costs and Benefits of Judgment Errors: Implications for Debiasing*, 110 PSYCHOL. BULL. 486, 486-87 (1991) (dividing behavioral biases into strategy, associational, and psychophysically based errors and contending that the benefits obtained from the biases generally outweigh the costs of the biases).

32. *See* Bainbridge, *supra* note 13, at 1035 ("To date, behavioral economics has not (and may not ever) develop a single theory that explains or predicts the full range of human behavior, as rational choice theory claims to do. Instead, it offers a pragmatic collection of 'situation-specific mini-theories useful in the analysis of discrete legal problems.'"); Richard A. Posner, *Rational Choice, Behavioral Economics, and the Law*, 50 STAN. L. REV. 1551, 1560-61 (1998) (contending that proponents of behavioral economics "have no theory, but merely a set of challenges to the theory-builders, who in the relevant instances are rational-choice economists and, I am about to suggest, evolutionary biologists").

33. *See* Jon D. Hanson & Douglas A. Kysar, *Taking Behavioralism Seriously: The Problem of Market Manipulation*, 74 N.Y.U. L. REV. 630, 715 (1999) (noting that "behavioral research remains a somewhat haphazard collection of seemingly unrelated cognitive quirks. . . . Drawing legal conclusions for a topic like consumer risk perception then becomes primarily a game of 'who has the most anomalies wins'"). Whether these experimental results can be duplicated in business settings is open to question. *See* Arlen et al., *supra* note 29 (providing an experimental test for the importance of endowment effect for individuals situated in an agency relationship and finding little evidence of the effect). For a

we measure the magnitude of the various bounded aspects of rationality and (b) what effect will particular regulatory reforms have in overcoming people's bounded nature (if this is even a desirable policy goal).[34] How do we ameliorate such biases if we don't understand their origins or how they respond to various policy levers? The lack of a developed theory is not so much a fault of the behavioral school as it is a sign that the school is still in its infancy.[35] Nonetheless, it does suggest that legal scholars should use behavioral economics with caution.[36]

Despite these gaps, various legal scholars have taken insights from behavioral law and economics and applied them to the securities markets.[37] Some have written, for example, that investors often act with overconfidence in their investment abilities.[38] Investing encompasses a wide range of choices, including the type of risk an investor is willing to bear, the class of financial product (for example, bonds versus equity) in which the investor will place his money, and within that class, which instruments provide the best return for a

---

comment on the value of the experimental data, see Gregory Mitchell, *Why Law and Economics' Perfect Rationality Should Not Be Traded for Behavioral Law and Economics' Equal Incompetence*, 91 GEO. L.J. 67, 72 (2002) ("Behavioral law and economics bases its model of bounded rationality on a very limited set of empirical data and draws unsupportable conclusions about human nature from this partial data set.").

34. And what if some of the biases are countervailing, effectively canceling each other out? *See* Hanson & Kysar, *supra* note 33, at 689 ("Kahneman and Tversky's decisionmaker may be subject to conflicting biases. For instance, the endowment effect may cause one to want to retain an asset that is dropping in market value while the maxim of loss aversion counsels abandonment.").

35. *See* Rachlinski, *supra* note 28, at 752 ("Because the field is still new, [behavioral decision theory] sometimes appears to be a loose collection of aberrations, but researchers in the field are working toward developing general theories of human judgment and choice."). *But see* Posner, *supra* note 32, at 1552 (arguing that "behavioral economics is . . . antitheoretical"). Posner provides an evolutionary biology explanation of the source of at least some seemingly irrational forms of behavior. *See id.* at 1561-64. Posner theorizes that much of what is irrational today would have been perfectly rational in a prelaw society where people tended to live (and stay isolated with) a small group of close relatives and were motivated out of desire to see as many of their genes as possible move on to the next generation. Thus, altruism makes sense when the recipients of such kindness tended to be close genetic relatives. *See id.* at 1561.

36. *See* Mitchell, *supra* note 33, at 127 (arguing that "legal scholars who have no training in the social sciences or who have only a superficial understanding of behavioral decision theory should refrain from the unaided application of behavioral decision theory to the law"). Rachlinski is similarly critical of "[l]egal scholars who use [behavioral decision theory because they] have unfortunately presented the field as if it had little or no order, logic, underlying theory, or limiting principles." Rachlinski, *supra* note 28, at 750.

37. The tendency to rush toward regulatory solutions when it comes to behavioral problems in the capital markets is not one shared among all commentators taking the behavioral economics approach. *See supra* note 20 and accompanying text.

38. As one example, Robert Prentice worries that investors will be overconfident in their abilities as traders, a problem exacerbated by the illusion of control, leading them to ignore the statistical evidence that active traders tend to trail market averages. *See* Prentice, *supra* note 14, at 1459-60.

given risk level.[39] Commentators have argued that investors often do not recognize how difficult these choices are and instead rely on a belief that their innate abilities will lead to a good investment result.[40] The large number of day traders as the bull market peaked in the late 1990s supports the overconfidence hypothesis.[41] Empirical work, moreover, has found that male traders, particularly younger men, trade more frequently than other groups of traders.[42] More trading led to lower returns for these overconfident young men.[43] Similarly risky behavior can be seen in the heavy investments that people make in their employers' stock, an obvious mistake from the perspective of diversification.[44] Overoptimism implies that investors may neglect disclosure provisions intended to protect them from poor investments.

More generally, investors are often simply poor judges of probabilities.[45] Investors may suffer from the availability heuristic, unduly emphasizing recent events. Investors may underweigh low probability, high magnitude risks if no obvious examples of the risk have recently been brought to their attention. On the flip side, once a big event happens—such as the Enron scandal—investors may overreact, emphasizing the risk of fraud unduly.[46] Immediately after the Enron and WorldCom scandals in the United States, the net volume of money flowing into mutual funds actually turned negative for a period of time, even though the holders of diversified mutual funds are unlikely to suffer any significant reduction in their returns from fraud at any particular company.[47]

39. This last decision may not be all that important, given that "the capital asset pricing model[] collapses the investment choice into one attribute—the security's sensitivity to changes in the expected rate of return on the market portfolio (the stock beta)." Roberta Romano, *A Comment on Information Overload, Cognitive Illusions, and Their Implications for Public Policy*, 59 S. CAL. L. REV. 313, 325 (1986).

40. *See, e.g.*, Jonathan Clements, *The Stock Market Isn't as Bad as You Think: The Right Moves for Tough Times*, WALL ST. J., Sept. 11, 2002, at D1 (noting that "[o]verconfident investors also attributed those gains to their own investment savvy, leading them to become even bolder in their investment bets").

41. *See* Aaron Elstein, *Yes, Day Traders Still Exist, They Just Keep a Lower Profile*, WALL ST. J., Oct. 17, 2002, at D4 (estimating 400,000 people engaged in day trading at the height of the bull market).

42. *See* Brad Barber & Terrence Odean, *Boys Will be Boys: Gender, Overconfidence, and Common Stock Investment*, 116 Q.J. ECON. 261 (2001) (providing evidence based on a sample of 35,000 households that men trade 45% more than women and experience lower returns).

43. *See id.*

44. *See* Gur Huberman, Familiarity Breeds Investment (1999) (unpublished manuscript, on file with the Stanford Law Review), *available at* http://papers.ssrn.com/sol3/papers.cfm?abstract_id=199314 (providing evidence that investors tend to overly concentrate their portfolio investments in familiar companies).

45. *See* Hirshleifer, *supra* note 1, at 1545-46.

46. *See* Peter Klibanoff, Owen Lamony & Thierry A. Wizman, *Investor Reaction to Salient News in Closed-end Country Funds*, 53 J. FIN. 673 (1999) (finding that investors react more strongly to events reported in the *New York Times*).

47. *See* Shaheen Pasha, *Redemptions Aren't Lone Villain*, WALL ST. J., Aug. 7, 2002, at D13 (reporting that "investors pulled a net $28.47 billion from stock funds in July, beating

Framing effects may also impair investor decisionmaking. When investors' stocks have lost value, they may hold onto the stocks longer than warranted in hope of reversing the losses.[48] Conversely, investors that make large investment gains may not value the gains as highly, taking on added risk with their gains (treating the gains much like "house" money in a casino).[49]

Investors, like everyone else, need to be able to live with their decisions. Commentators have argued that investors will often experience cognitive dissonance, rationalizing their prior investment decision no matter how poor the returns.[50] Such cognitive dissonance may then lead investors to delay selling poor investments. Biases that discourage selling may deter investors from the rational strategy of realizing losses for tax purposes at the earliest opportunity. The need to maintain self-esteem may prevent investors from learning from their mistakes, attributing their failures to chance rather than their own decisionmaking limitations.[51] Successes, of course, will be attributed to investment skill.[52]

Investors may also fail to process all relevant information on a particular security, employing heuristics and satisficing.[53] Rather than read a voluminous prospectus, an investor may rely simply on the identity of the managing underwriters, applying a heuristic that well-known underwriters often equate to lower risk offerings.[54] Even well-known underwriters, of course, cannot

---

even the $23.6 billion in withdrawals that . . .were made in September following the terrorist attacks").

48. *See* Shefrin & Statman, *supra* note 2, at 785-88 (reporting evidence that investors sell gain stock too quickly and hold on to loss stock too long compared to the optimal holding period from a tax perspective).

49. *See, e.g.*, Clements, *supra* note 40, at D1 (noting that "[t]his increased appetite for risk was further bolstered by the 'house money' effect. Like casino gamblers who get lucky early in the evening, investors made so much money that they felt they could take a few extra chances. After all, even if they lost a little, they would still have handsome profits."); *see also* Nicholas Barberis & Ming Huang, *Mental Accounting, Loss Aversion and Individual Stock Returns*, 56 J. FIN. 1247 (2001) (arguing that investors are loss averse with regard to individual stocks as well as their overall portfolio); Nicholas Barberis, Ming Huang & Tano Santos, *Prospect Theory and Asset Prices*, 66 Q.J. ECON. 1 (2001) (arguing that risk aversion will be reduced after the revelation of good news that increases the price of a stock); Richard Thaler & E.J. Johnson, *Gambling with the House Money and Trying to Break Even: The Effects of Prior Outcomes on Risky Choice*, 36 MGMT. SCI. 199 (1990) (finding that people are more willing to take on risks with money that was recently won).

50. *See* Langevoort, *Selling Hope*, *supra* note 16, at 659-60.

51. *See id.* at 639.

52. *See id.*

53. *See* Herbert A. Simon, *A Behavioral Model of Rational Choice*, 69 Q.J. ECON. 99 (1955) (postulating a rational choice model under which actors have limited knowledge and ability); *see also supra* notes 26-27 (citing sources on heuristics).

54. Some truth, of course, may attach to the underwriter-quality heuristic. *See* Richard B. Carter, Frederick H. Dark & Ajai K. Singh, *Underwriter Reputation, Initial Returns, and the Long-Run Performance of IPO Stocks*, 53 J. FIN. 285 (1998) (providing updated list of the Carter-Manaster rankings of underwriters); Richard B. Carter & Steven Manaster, *Initial Public Offerings and Underwriter Reputation*, 45 J. FIN. 1045, 1056-66 (1990) (developing a

guarantee against fraud, so investors following such a heuristic may underestimate their true risk of encountering fraud.

Investors may also fall prey to fads. During the Internet frenzy, firms that announced that they were changing their name to include "dot.com" experienced abnormal returns, regardless of whether the announcement coincided with a change in business plan.[55] After the Internet bubble popped, companies eliminating "dot.com" from their names also enjoyed abnormal returns.[56]

After perusing the growing behavioral finance literature, we wonder how investors are able to make any positive return from the market. Indeed, one proponent of the behavioral approach to finance, Robert Prentice, has observed that reading the literature may leave one with the impression that investors are "dunderheaded."[57] Prentice quickly qualifies this impression with the notation that "not all heuristics and biases apply at all times and in all settings to all investors,"[58] but he fails to offer any guidance on when biases do in fact apply. We—and policymakers who must make regulatory choices—are left to guess.

B. *Biases or Preferences?*

In order to evaluate investors' rationality, we must first consider a more fundamental question: Why do investors invest? The commonsense answer from the rational actor framework is that individuals use investments to smooth their incomes to match their consumption patterns.[59] Dollars are saved in high-income years so that consumption can be maintained in low-income years, (for example, retirement) or heavy expenditure years (for example, sending the children to college). Unfortunately, the data reflect substantial deviations from this model.[60] Most conspicuously, investors trade much more frequently than

ranking of underwriters based on their position on an offering "tombstone" announcement and finding that higher ranking underwriters correlate with lower risk offerings). Nonetheless, the question remains whether investors can accurately assess the precise risk of fraud even with a high reputation underwriter.

55. *See* Michael J. Cooper, Orlin Dimitrov & P. Raghavendra Rau, *A Rose.com by Any Other Name*, 56 J. FIN. 2371 (2001) (finding a 74% positive cumulative abnormal return for companies adding "dot.com" to their name regardless of the companies actual involvement with the Internet).

56. *See* Ken Brown, *For Dot-Coms, New Names Are Good for a Pop*, WALL ST. J., DEC. 18, 2002, at C1 (reporting results of follow-up study by Cooper et al.).

57. *See* Prentice, *supra* note 14, at 1489.

58. *Id.*

59. This intuition is closely related to the life cycle hypothesis, under which consumers attempt to smooth out their consumption over their lifetime. *See* MILTON FRIEDMAN, A THEORY OF THE CONSUMPTION FUNCTION (1957).

60. *See* W.F.M. Debondt & R.H. Thaler, *Financial Decision-Making in Markets and Firms: A Behavioral Perspective*, *in* 9 FINANCE HANDBOOKS IN OPERATIONS RESEARCH AND MANGAGEMENT SCIENCE 385-410 (R.A. Jarrow, V. Maksimovic & W.T. Ziembe, eds., 1995).

would be required to satisfy liquidity needs and adjust their portfolios to match their risk preferences. What explains all this trading?

The behavioralists, as related above, provide one explanation—overconfidence in one's own abilities. An alternative explanation is that many investors view the stock market as a substitute for gambling.[61] Many middle class individuals—who view lotteries as a foolish waste of money—may be engaged in similar behavior with their investments. They are pursuing the "next Microsoft," hoping against the odds that they will become rich enough to leave their everyday jobs and lifestyles behind. At bottom, we suspect, is a utility function that favors a remote chance of striking it rich over the slow but steady gains from buying and holding a well-diversified portfolio.[62] We do not share this speculative preference for our own investments,[63] but we cannot dismiss it as irrational.[64]

If regulators seek to protect investors from themselves and those who would prey on their weaknesses, regulators must first identify the specific ailments afflicting investors. Regulations designed to address behavioral biases may not help investors with speculative preferences. Indeed, these investors may enjoy their speculative investments. If so, it is hardly obvious that government should interfere with this preference, particularly if investors resent the interference. Moreover, investors may all have some level of speculative preference and suffer from some cognitive defects, but it seems more plausible that the magnitude of such effects varies. Some segment of investors may seek to maximize their return (given the risk).[65] Other investors may act equally rationally but with a greater (and perhaps unwise) preference to engage in speculation. And still other investors face behavioral biases that impair their ability to process information and make decisions. Different regulatory

61. *See* Lynn A. Stout, *Are Stock Markets Costly Casinos? Disagreement, Market Failure, and Securities Regulation*, 81 VA. L. REV. 611, 613-67 (1995) (contending that trading volume often represents speculative trades on the part of investors with heterogeneous expectations on the value of companies).

62. Ed McCaffery discusses this theory in the context of lotteries. *See* Edward J. McCaffery, *Why People Play Lotteries and Why It Matters*, 1994 WIS. L. REV. 71; *see also* Theresa A. Gabaldon, *John Law, with a Tulip, in the South Seas: Gambling and the Regulation of Euphoric Market Transactions*, 26 J. CORP. L. 225 (2001) (drawing parallels between gambling and speculative trading).

63. Both Choi and Pritchard put all their investment dollars into index funds. It's very boring.

64. Behavioral biases, of course, may feed the speculative instinct. The salience of Bill Gate's success may obscure the much greater probability that a start-up venture will fail; the illusion of control in investing may lead these speculative investors to be overconfident of their chances of success; self-justification may cause them to attribute their past investment successes to skill while attributing their investment failures to chance. Nonetheless, the urge to speculate cannot be dismissed as entirely the product of bias.

65. Warren Buffett might be the paradigm of this approach. In 1997 the *Cardozo Law Review* held a symposium in honor of Warren Buffett. *See* Lawrence A. Cunningham, *Introduction to the Warren Buffett Symposium Papers*, 19 CARDOZO L. REV. 221 (1997) (surveying the symposium papers).

responses might be needed for these varying characteristics among investors.[66]

C. *The Questionable Importance of Biases*

Conceding that some biases are genuine cognitive errors with a significant effect on behavior, the behavioralist school must still address at least three possible responses to their critique of the financial markets. First, some behavioral biases may counteract each other. Prentice notes that "people tend to ignore low probability risks" and this may cause investors to underestimate the probability of fraud under a market regulatory regime.[67] Setting aside Prentice's prediction of rampant fraud under such a regime, more troubling is his omission of the other bias in calculations of probability—the tendency for people to *overestimate* the probability of salient risks. For example, people wildly overestimate the risks of flying because plane crashes are newsworthy. Car crashes are much more common but far less salient. If recent press coverage is any indicator, fraud is more like plane crashes than car crashes. If anything, investors are likely to exaggerate the likelihood of fraud given its salience. Prentice argues, however, that "[d]ue to the availability heuristic, investors bombarded with advertisements about the reliability of a brokerage firm are likely to believe them despite numerous problems with the company's true actions."[68] But the availability heuristic is affected by the salience of the information presented. Newspaper headlines reporting securities industry scandals seem much more salient than the industry's commercials.[69] A believer in the availability heuristic might well predict that investors (upon reading about Enron, WorldCom, Tyco, and so on) would overestimate the risks of fraud. Predicting which effect will dominate is a hazardous business.[70]

The second point: Not all investors are dunderheads! While a range of behavioral biases may exist in the general population, self-selection affects the level of biases in a particular profession. Richard Posner has observed that those with an oversized sense of fairness will not choose to enter highly competitive professions.[71] Similarly, those with poor investment

66. For a proposal to shift the focus of securities regulation from issuers to investors see Stephen J. Choi, *Regulating Investors Not Issuers: A Market-Based Proposal*, 88 CAL. L. REV. 279 (2000).

67. *See* Prentice, *supra* note 14, at 1482.

68. *Id.* at 1431-32.

69. *See* Michael Orey & Milo Geyelin, *Lawyers Find Jury Pools Polluted by Antibusiness Biases*, WALL ST. J., Aug. 12, 2002, at B1 (reporting that lawyers selecting jurors find considerable distrust of business ethics in the wake of recent high-profile scandals).

70. More self-interested policymakers may then abuse the malleability of behavioral biases, framing their favored regulatory programs in a way to take advantage of the public's biases.

71. *See* Posner, *supra* note 32, at 1570 ("People who are unusually 'fair' will avoid (or, again, be forced out of) roughhouse activities—including highly competitive businesses, trial

decisionmaking skills may opt out of the capital markets altogether. This is not to say that biases are eliminated (especially as new investors arrive daily to the market), but they may be less significant than in the general population. Moreover, if behavioral biases vary across investors, perhaps regulations could be tailored to address the needs of the specific groups of investors while letting market forces work in other areas.[72] This strategy, however, carries risks; if investors are unaware of their biases, they may resent being categorized with the cognitively challenged.

The third point builds on the second. Institutions have emerged to aid individuals with poor decisionmaking skills. Investors can purchase financial expertise by investing through an intermediary. Intermediaries may not be subject to cognitive biases to the same degree as people making decisions for themselves; detachment may enhance decisionmaking.[73] Mutual funds help investors choose investments in addition to providing low cost diversification. Financial planners assist investors in developing an appropriate portfolio of investments. Brokers also provide investment advice to their clients. The prevalence of these institutions suggests that overconfidence among investors may be a relatively isolated phenomenon.

Donald Langevoort points out, however, that institutions themselves (more precisely, people who work for institutions) may also suffer from behavioral biases.[74] Even institutional investors suffer from loss aversion. Money managers that fail to meet a perceived benchmark, for example, may take overly risky positions in an attempt to "catch up."[75] Money managers may also

---

lawyering, and the academic rat race.").

72. *See* Choi, *supra* note 66 (proposing a system of investor-focused regulation).

73. *See* James D. Marshall, Jack L. Knetsch & J. A. Sinden, *Agents' Evaluations and the Disparity in Measures of Economic Loss*, 7 J. ECON. BEHAV. & ORG. 115 (1986) (finding no endowment effect for subjects placed in the role of advisors); Michael J. Roszkowski & Glenn E. Snelbecker, *Effect of Framing on Measures of Risk Tolerance: Financial Planners Are Not Immune*, 19 J. BEHAV. ECON. 237, 245 (1990) ("The bad news is that financial planners are prone to the same framing bias that occurs with the population-at-large . . . . The 'good' news conveyed by our results is that financial planners seem to be more cautious in how they handle their client's money than their own money."). *But see* Russell Korobkin, *The Status Quo Bias and Contract Default Rules*, 83 CORNELL L. REV. 608 (1998) (finding status quo bias among law students asked to negotiate contracts for hypothetical clients).

74. *See* Langevoort, *Selling Hope*, *supra* note 16, at 641-48. Prentice argues in a similar vein that institutional investors will be unable to protect themselves because "[a]s with most other behavioral foibles, the availability heuristic affects professional investors as well as amateurs, perhaps even more." Prentice, *supra* note 14, at 1432; *see also* Hirshleifer, *supra* note 1, at 1537 ("It is not obvious that layering agency over folly improves decisions."). For a useful survey of research findings relating to the use of financial accounting, see Robert Libby, Robert Bloomfield & Mark W. Nelson, Experimental Research in Financial Accounting (2001) (unpublished manuscript, on file with the Stanford Law Review), *available at* http://papers.ssrn.com/sol3/papers.cfm?abstract_id=261860.

75. *See* Langevoort, *Selling Hope*, *supra* note 16, at 643 ("A string of losses can cause the agent to assume more risk simply to get back to even, especially if failure to do so might result in termination and severe reputational penalty.").

discount small, low probability risks, and act overconfidently.[76] They are also subject to framing effects: For instance, analysts give more favorable earnings forecasts to firms that lowball preannouncements of earnings.[77] Anchoring and overoptimism also seem to be at work: Analysts underreact to unfavorable information but overreact to favorable information.[78] They also appear to discount evidence of earnings management.[79] Auditors may provide little check on earnings management if their biases cause them to favor their clients' views.[80]

Worse yet, instead of leading investors away from their behavioral biases, financial professionals may prey upon investors' behavioral quirks.[81] Brokers may realize that cognitive dissonance may cause investors to ratify even unsound decisions once they are made.[82] Having placed their trust in their

76. *See* Don A. Moore, Terri R. Kurtzberg, Craig R. Fox & Max H. Bazerman, *Positive Illusions and Forecasting Errors in Mutual Fund Investment Decisions*, 79 ORG. BEHAV. & HUM. DECISION PROCESSES 95 (1999) (reporting on an experiment involving the portfolio allocation decisions of 80 business school students and finding that the students consistently overestimated the future and past performance of their investments).

77. *See* Hun-Tong Tan, Robert Libby & James E. Hunton, Analysts' Reactions to Earnings Pre-Announcement Strategies (2000) (unpublished manuscript, on file with the Stanford Law Review), *available at* http://papers.ssrn.com/sol3/papers.cfm?abstract_id=186929 (reporting evidence that firms receive a greater upward revision of future earnings from analysts when the firms understate positive news).

78. *See* John C. Easterwood & Stacey R. Nutt, *Inefficiency in Analysts' Earnings Forecasts: Systematic Misreaction or Systematic Optimism?*, 54 J. FIN. 1777 (1999) (contending that analyst tendencies to underreact to negative information and overreact to positive information is consistent with systematic optimism in the reaction of analysts to information). This effect, however, appears to be mitigated by experience. *See* Michael B. Mikhail, Beverly R. Walther & Richard H. Willis, *The Effect of Experience on Security Analyst Underreaction*, 35 J. ACCOUNT. & ECON. 101 (2003) (finding that analysts underreact less to prior earnings information as they gain experience).

79. *See* Siew Hong Teoh & T.J. Wong, *Why New Issues and High Accrual Firms Underperform: The Role of Analysts' Credulity*, 15 REV. FIN. STUD. 869 (2001). Of course, other reasons may explain the failure of analysts to provide accurate investment advice. Analysts, for example, may purposefully skew their opinions toward management in return for indirect compensation in the form of high investment banking fees. For a more detailed discussion of analyst corruption as well as possible solutions, see Stephen Choi & Jill Fisch, *How to Fix Wall Street: A Voucher Financing Proposal*, YALE L. J. (forthcoming 2003).

80. *See* Max H. Bazerman, George Loewenstein & Don A. Moore, *Why Good Accountants Do Bad Audits*, HARV. BUS. REV. Nov. 2002, at 87, 100 (discussing how familiarity, discounting, and escalation may bias auditors toward taking a more lenient approach to a client's accounting irregularities).

81. *See* Elaine A. Welle, *Freedom of Contract and the Securities Laws: Opting Out of Securities Regulation by Private Agreement*, 56 WASH. & LEE L. REV. 519, 581 (1999) (arguing that permitting contractual waiver of the securities laws "would permit securities-industry professionals . . . to use cognitive distortions to solicit waivers at a time when an investor is most vulnerable. Rather than encouraging these Faustian bargains, we should be protecting investors from such predatory conduct").

82. *See* Langevoort, *Selling Hope*, *supra* note 16, at 660 ("The customer . . . has ample means to rationalize short-run poor performance of an individual investment as something other than the product of bad advice and bad decisions.").

brokers, investors may give them substantial leeway.[83] Opportunistic brokers, may then steer investors toward poor or inappropriate investments.[84] Investors also may choose poorly among available investments: Flows into mutual funds tend to follow funds that have enjoyed extraordinary performance.[85] While this strategy has intuitive appeal, that performance does not persist.[86] As Kent Daniel and his colleagues point out, "The fact that vast amounts of invested wealth are placed in funds that appear to be wasting resources on active management does not support the view that investors are good at choosing funds, nor that funds make good choices on behalf of investors."[87] And the amount being wasted on active management is not chump change: One estimate suggests that mutual fund investors spend more than $10 billion per year on fees for active mutual fund management.[88]

Organizational culture within institutions may exacerbate behavioral problems. Writing more generally about the possibility of cognitive dissonance in corporate entities, Langevoort poses the question of why managers in a corporation may lie even when the gain from deception is small, such as when the corporation is not ıssuing securities and the managers are not engaged in insider trading.[89] Langevoort argues that group cognitive dissonance may lead to corporate lying. An entity's culture, for example, may foster overoptimism, which may lead managers (perhaps unwittingly) to mislead investors about future profitability.[90] Managers may also fall prey to a confirmation bias, causing them to misrepresent the viability of previously adopted strategies.[91]

83. *See* Donald C. Langevoort, *Ego, Human Behavior, and Law*, 81 VA. L. REV. 853, 879 (1995) ("Having committed to a particular expert . . . investors feel a strong tendency to bolster their choice.") [hereinafter Langevoort, *Ego*].

84. *See* Langevoort, *Selling Hope, supra* note 16, at 661.

85. *See* Erik R. Sirri & Peter Tufano, *Costly Search and Mutual Fund Flows*, 53 J. FIN. 1589 (1998) (finding that consumers invest disproportionately more in funds which performed well in the prior period).

86. *See* Mark M. Carhart, *On Persistence in Mutual Fund Performance*, 52 J. FIN. 57 (1997) (finding evidence that persistence in mutual fund performance is not due to investment skill on the part of fund managers but instead are mostly explained by common factors in stock returns as well as differences fund expense levels). *Cf.* Mark Grinblatt, Sheridan Titman & Russ Wermers, *Momentum Investment Strategies, Portfolio Performance, and Herding: A Study of Mutual Fund Behavior*, 85 AM. ECON. REV. 1088 (1995) (reporting evidence that simple trading rules—such as momentum trading and herding with other mutual funds—as opposed to superior information at least partially explains higher mutual fund performance).

87. Daniel et al., *supra* note 19, at 32.

88. *See id.* at 43; *see also* GREGORY BAER & GARY GENSLER, THE GREAT MUTUAL FUND TRAP (2002) (amassing evidence that actively managed mutual funds overwhelmingly trail the returns of the overall market while taking on greater amounts of risk).

89. *See* Donald C. Langevoort, *Organized Illusions: A Behavioral Theory of Why Corporations Mislead Stock Market Investors (and Cause Other Social Harms)*, 146 U. PA. L. REV. 101 (1997) [hereinafter Langevoort, *Organized Illusions*].

90. *See id.* at 139-40.

91. *See id.* at 142-43.

Managers suffering from bounded rationality may ignore danger signals, causing the firm to withhold important information from the public.[92] Langevoort argues that competition will not necessarily weed out organizations suffering from group cognitive dissonance because the same overoptimism that leads to the misrepresentations may also promote morale and productivity.[93] Naïve optimism may enhance the bottom line. In addition, biases toward the status quo and ignoring small danger signs may make it easier to handle vast information flows.[94] The alternative of attempting to process rationally all available information could lead to organizational paralysis.

Institutions do suffer from behavioral biases. Nevertheless, just as not all investors are "dunderheads," institutions will not suffer from behavioral biases equally. If institutions can overcome some biases that plague investors then institutions can improve the functioning of the capital markets. Moreover, while some amount of biases may be beneficial for institutions and therefore resistant to competitive pressures (such as overoptimism), such biases will have limited impact on investor welfare. Institutional-based biases that have large negative impacts on investors will impair profitability, making those institutions vulnerable to competition from other institutions. There is also evidence that incentives—if sufficiently large—can ameliorate some biases.[95] For example, pricing anomalies tend to disappear once they have been identified.[96] Even if institutions persist with some low level of biases, the question remains whether regulation—by inevitably fallible regulators—can improve investor welfare. If investors act irrationally, will intervention help?

II. BEHAVIORAL BIASES WITHIN THE SEC

For argument's sake, we accept the premise that behavioral problems exist in the financial markets, that both investors and the institutions that assist them suffer from these biases, and that they are problematic in their scope and magnitude. Even accepting these points, however, those who believe strongly in cognitive biases among investors must explain why similar biases do not also

92. *See id.* at 147.

93. *See id.* at 155.

94. *See id.* at 152.

95. *See* Vernon L. Smith & James M. Walker, *Monetary Rewards and Decision Cost in Experimental Economics*, 31 ECON. INQUIRY 245 (1993) (reporting results of experimental studies showing that incentives can improve decisionmaking). *But see* Dan N. Stone & David A. Ziebart, *A Model of Financial Incentive Effects in Decision Making*, 61 ORG. BEHAV. & HUM. DECISION PROCESSES 250, 259 (1995) ("[I]t seems plausible that financial incentives may help prevent decision errors that arise from insufficient attention, but may exacerbate those that arise from faulty intuition or task misperception. Further, in contradiction to arguments made by some economists, very high incentives may potentially *decrease* (not increase) decision quality by increasing negative affect.") (citations omitted).

96. *See* Hirshleifer, *supra* note 1, at 1538-39 (citing "the disappearance of the size effect" and a lack of persistence for the value effect).

affect regulators. Behavioralists must account for cognitive biases among regulators (and the likelihood that such biases are often greater in magnitude than those facing investors).[97]

Applying the insights from behavioral economics, we catalog a series of biases that SEC officials may face. Organizations may evolve and adapt to minimize the impact of biases.[98] Nevertheless, just as such biases may persist within professional institutions, they may cling stubbornly to SEC regulators. This possibility is heightened by the fact that the SEC does not face competition, which may whittle down biases within private organizations. Moreover, biases specific to groups of regulators are also possible in ways that do not afflict individual investors.

A. *Cataloging the Biases at the SEC*

It is impossible to compile a comprehensive list of biases that may affect SEC officials. Indeed, we freely concede that, as with other attempts to apply behavioral insights to the law, our account is necessarily ad hoc. Nonetheless, we find evidence of many of the biases identified by the behavioralists in the SEC's regulatory positions. Other explanations are possible for SEC policy decisions, including public choice accounts.[99] We believe that a behavioral analysis can complement and enrich the public choice story.[100]

1. *Bounded search.*

Bounded search at the SEC may blind regulators to possible alternatives to regulation.[101] The SEC is not known for regulatory creativity, often attempting to tackle difficult problems of corporate governance with measures invariably

97. *See* Daniel et al., *supra* note 19, at 53 (arguing that "the case for laissez faire rests most persuasively not on extreme information efficiency of private markets, but on the comparative information and resource inefficiency of the political process"); Posner, *supra* note 32, at 1575 ("The expert, too, is behavioral man. Behavioral man behaves in unpredictable ways. Dare we vest responsibility for curing irrationality in the irrational?").

98. *See generally* Chip Heath, Richard P. Larrick & Joshua Klayman, *Cognitive Repairs: How Organizational Practices Can Compensate for Individual Shortcomings*, 20 RES. ORG. BEHAV. 1 (1998) (compiling different techniques for overcoming the effects of heuristics and biases).

99. *See, e.g.*, Jonathan R. Macey, *Administrative Agency Obsolescence and Interest Group Formation: A Case Study of the SEC at Sixty*, 15 CARDOZO L. REV. 909 (1994).

100. *See* Jolls et al., *supra* note 31, at 1543 ("Availability entrepreneurs in the private sector can heighten the demand for regulation, and public sector availability entrepreneurs can take advantage of, and heighten, this effect, by advocating anecdote-driven policy. Thus public choice accounts of legislation can work productively with behavioral accounts; there is a good deal of synergy between behavioral mechanisms and interest group leaders, many of whom are amateur (or professional?) behavioral economists.").

101. *See* Heath et al., *supra* note 98, at 9-10 (discussing the tendency of individuals to unduly constrict search for solutions to problems).

derived from some variant of disclosure. Disclosure traditionally has been justified as a means of exposing potentially problematic activities. Justice Louis Brandeis' oft-quoted phrase that "sunlight . . . is the best disinfectant" provides a succinct summary of the philosophy behind disclosure.[102] Once investors (and others) can see such activities clearly, then market participants are less likely to engage in opportunistic behavior in the first place. Managers considering a self-dealing transaction, for example, may choose not to do so when related-party transactions must be disclosed.[103] In addition to ferreting out agency costs, disclosure may assist rational investors in allocating their investment dollars, leading to better use of capital and more accurate securities prices.

For behavioralists, the single-minded focus of the SEC on disclosure presents a puzzle. We doubt that disclosure is the optimal regulatory strategy if most investors suffer from cognitive biases. Disclosure may be ineffective in educating investors who suffer from biases in decisionmaking.[104] Investors suffering from an overconfidence bias, for example, may ignore the warning signs from disclosure. Similarly, it is unclear how disclosure can overcome the cognitive dissonance of people who have made a poor investment choice in the past. Investors with intractable loss aversion will continue holding a losing position in hopes of reversing their losses without regard to disclosure. And what disclosure will help them avoid ratifying their poor investment choices as "good" decisions? Finally, investment decisions may be driven in substantial part by the conversations that investors have had most recently. Disclosure may do little to influence investment decisions based on "tips" or fads.[105]

The SEC's fixation with disclosure can also be seen in its efforts to protect investors from fraud in the wake of the Enron and WorldCom scandals. In response, the SEC proposed requiring corporate chief executive officers to certify corporate financial statements annually. Congress, anxious to be seen "doing something," followed this proposal with legislation enacting the CEO certification requirement into law.[106] Investors plagued with overconfidence,

102. LOUIS D. BRANDEIS, OTHER PEOPLE'S MONEY 92 (1913).

103. *See* Paul G. Mahoney, *Mandatory Disclosure as a Solution to Agency Problems*, 62 U. CHI. L. REV. 1047 (1995) (contending that mandatory disclosure works to deter managers from engaging in opportunistic behavior at the expense of shareholders).

104. *See* Langevoort, *Ego*, *supra* note 83, at 880 ("[W]e can readily see why the law's prized warnings and disclosure will so often have relatively little practical effect, especially if they are formalized into boilerplate. Investors and consumers want to think the warnings are meant for someone else, not them.").

105. *See* Robert J. Shiller & John Pound, *Survey Evidence on the Diffusion of Interest and Information Among Investors*, 12 J. ECON. BEHAV. & ORG. 46 (1989).

106. *See* Sarbanes-Oxley Act of 2002 § 302(a), 15 U.S.C. § 7241(a) (2002) (Corporate Responsibility For Financial Reports). The Sarbanes-Oxley Act also requires a similar certification from corporate Chief Financial Officers (CFOs). *See id.* Both the CEO and the CFO must attest to the "appropriateness of the financial statements and disclosures contained in the periodic report, and that those financial statements and disclosures fairly present, in all material respects, the operations and financial condition of the issuer." *Id.*

however, may fail to appreciate the risks posed by companies for which the CEO has failed to provide an unqualified certification. On the other hand, investors may place too much weight on a salient recent certification, ignoring (under the influence of the availability heuristic) more distant evidence of wrongdoing and other risks posed by corporate management. And certification will not overcome framing effects, including loss aversion by investors.[107] Given these behavioral difficulties with disclosure as a regulatory tool, the SEC's continued reliance on disclosure suggests an unduly narrow search within the SEC.

Perhaps disclosure's continued allure for the SEC stems from its being a "compromise" solution, midway between doing nothing and regulating substantive conduct.[108] In part, the SEC's regulatory strategy reflects the broad grants of authority to the agency to mandate corporate disclosures under the 1933 and 1934 Acts.[109] Alternatives to disclosure generally would require the SEC to seek statutory authorization from Congress. To get that authority, however, would almost certainly require the SEC to make an empirical showing to justify the need for a new regulatory tool. Even though it relies on disclosure as the cure-all for the maladies of securities markets, the SEC has done surprisingly little to investigate the impact that disclosure has on those markets.[110] The agency instead prefers to remain above the grubbiness of empirical data, preferring to ground its policy prescriptions in "investor confidence."[111] Significantly, the SEC avoids any meaningful definition of investor confidence, thereby avoiding the possibility of empirical contradiction.

2. *Bounded rationality.*

The SEC receives vast amounts of information: registration statements from companies making public offerings, periodic filings for public companies,

107. More troublingly, disclosure may exacerbate some agency costs. In recent experimental work, Cain et al. found that advisors whose compensation was tied to how high their clients' estimates were, made even *more* biased estimates if their conflict was disclosed to their client-estimator. Worse yet, disclosure did not cause the estimators to discount the advice provided by their conflicted advisor. *See* DAYLIAN CAIN, DON MOORE & GEORGE LOEWENSTEIN, THE DIRT ON COMING CLEAN: THE PERVERSE EFFECTS OF CONFLICTS AND THEIR DISCLOSURE (Carnegie-Mellon Univ., Working Paper 2002).

108. *See* Langevoort, *supra* note 20, at 1504-05 (arguing that "the relative preference as between two options may be unduly affected by the availability of alternatives, particularly if they involve compromise possibilities").

109. The SEC's campaign to mandate "one share, one vote" in the 1980s ran afoul of this limitation. *See* Bus. Roundtable v. SEC, 905 F.2d 406 (D.C. Cir. 1990).

110. *See* Langevoort, *Taming the Animal Spirits*, *supra* note 15, at 173 ("[T]he Commission has never studied investor behavior deeply enough to say—publicly at least—what percentage of investors read or understand these documents, or what influence the fundamental analysis-oriented disclosure has on their investment decisions.").

111. *See infra* note 165 and accompanying text (citing the SEC's uncritical use of "investor confidence" to support the recently promulgated Regulation FD).

as well as the myriad filings for secondary market transactions;[112] yet more information comes from the various securities exchanges on the functioning of the markets.[113] Through its enforcement work, the SEC also receives almost daily intelligence on the latest ingenious frauds against investors. When the SEC engages in rulemaking, it is often deluged with a large number of comment letters on its proposed rules.[114] Finally, securities lawyers and law professors provide a steady stream of commentary (like this Article) on topics ranging from specific regulatory provisions to the overall nature of the securities regulatory system.

Devising new regulations is costly, requiring analysis of complicated economic phenomena. Market participants are likely to know far more about these phenomena than regulators.[115] It is no surprise, therefore, that regulators often develop tunnel vision, sticking to known regulatory schemes. The SEC's inability to assess all market risks and prioritize among them (due to the bounded capabilities of the agency staff and commissioners) may help explain the SEC's difficulties in grappling with problems in the financial markets.

Agenda setting provides one possible example of bounded rationality within the SEC. Instead of formulating a cohesive regulatory agenda, the SEC is generally reactive in its policymaking. Immediately prior to the Enron scandal, CEO certification of financial statements was nowhere to be found on the SEC list of policy initiatives. It was hardly news that CEOs sometimes fudge the numbers, occasionally on a grand scale.[116] Nonetheless, CEO certification (and other aspects of the Sarbanes-Oxley Act) would not have been adopted without the external pressure to react to a supposed crisis.[117]

Only rarely does the SEC proactively review its overall regulatory scheme.

---

112. The SEC makes available many of the SEC filings (under the EDGAR disclosure system) at its website located at www.sec.gov (last visited Oct. 2, 2003).

113. The New York Stock Exchange, for example, provides various data on the NYSE market at http://www.nyse.com/marketinfo/marketinfo.html (last visited Oct. 2, 2003).

114. For example, the Concept Release proposing Regulation FD provoked 6,000 comment letters. *See* Selective Disclosure and Insider Trading, Securities Act Release No. 33-7881, Fed. Sec. L. Rep. (CCH) ¶ 51716, at 51717 (Aug. 15, 2000).

115. *Cf.* Henry T.C. Hu, *Misunderstood Derivatives: The Causes of Informational Failure and the Promise of Regulatory Incrementalism*, 102 YALE L.J. 1457, 1499 (1993) ("[R]egulators may have trouble tapping into the informal information networks accessible to bankers. The personnel movement that causes information flow is unlikely to occur between the government and industry because, among other things, the salary differentials are awesome.").

116. For an example of fraud prior to Enron, one need only look to Sunbeam Inc. and former CEO "Chainsaw Al" Dunlap who was removed as CEO in 1998 after allegations of financial fraud. *See* Kelly Greene, *Dunlap Agrees to Settle Suit over Sunbeam*, WALL ST. J., Jan. 15, 2002, at A3.

117. Historical evidence exists that waves of securities regulation typically follow financial market collapses. *See* Stuart Banner, *What Causes New Securities Regulation? 300 Years of Evidence*, 75 WASH. U. L.Q. 849, 850 (1997) (contending that over the past 300 years the major pieces of securities related regulation came about following a large and sustained price collapse in the stock market).

Even then, the agency often fails to follow up the review with substantive policy initiatives. For several years, the SEC engaged in an ambitious review of the transaction focus of the Securities Act's regulation of public offerings.[118] A comprehensive study in the 1990s under the guidance of then-commissioner Steven Wallman recommended moving toward a company registration system of regulation.[119] The rulemaking proposal that followed, however, was a series of half-measures that were greeted with hostility by the securities industry and corporate bar.[120] We are still waiting for a comprehensive overhaul of the public offering process, the basic structure of which dates to the 1930s.

3. *Availability, hindsight, and fundamental attribution biases.*

Closely related to bounded rationality are the heuristics that regulators use to manage the deluge of information and problems stemming from the financial markets. Like investors, regulators suffer from the availability heuristic, focusing too much attention on recent and immediately available information. Regulators may also be too quick to see a pattern in a series of events that are in fact random.[121] A handful of salient accounting scandals may be construed as a corporate governance crisis.[122] SEC regulators may also suffer from hindsight, placing too much weight on the probability of past events that actually occurred (relative to those that did not). Finally, the fundamental attribution bias may lead SEC investigators to overestimate the influence of perceived disposition (for example, fraud-prone) in explaining a person's behavior while overlooking the influence of the person's particular circumstances in any given situation.[123] Once the SEC has determined someone

118. For a discussion of the transaction focus of the current securities regime, see Stephen J. Choi, *Company Registration: Toward a Status-Based Antifraud Regime*, 64 U. CHI. L. REV. 567, 604-15 (1997).

119. *See* SECURITIES AND EXCHANGE COMMISSION, ADVISORY COMMITTEE ON THE CAPITAL FORMATION AND REGULATORY PROCESSES REPORT (1996), *available at* http://www.sec.gov/news/studies.shtml.

120. *See* The Regulation of Securities Offerings, Exchange Act. Release No. 33-7606, 63 SEC Docket 835 (Nov. 3, 1998); Exchange Act Release No. 34-40632, 68 SEC Docket 853 (Nov. 17, 1998).

121. *Cf.* Thomas Gilovich, Robert Vallone, & Amos Tversky, *The Hot Hand in Basketball: On the Misperception of Random Sequences*, 17 COGNITIVE PSYCHOL. 295 (1985) (contending that perceived "hot hand" streaks of success are in fact random).

122. Lucian Bebchuk and Oren Bar-Gill, for example, motivate a theoretical paper on the incentives of managers and companies to engage in fraud with the observation that the number of accounting restatements has increased from 49 per year through most of the 1990s to 156 per year by 2000. *See* Lucian Ayre Bebchuk & Oren Bar-Gill, Misreporting Corporate Performance (2002) (unpublished manuscript, on file with the Stanford Law Review), *at* http://papers.ssrn.com/sol3/papers.cfm?abstract_id=354141. As a percentage of the number of total filings made by the over 16,000 public reporting companies, however, the increase is miniscule.

123. See Justin Kruger & Thomas Gilovich, Naïve Cynicism in Everyday Theories of Responsibility Assessment: On Biased Assumptions of Bias, 76 J. PERSONALITY & SOC.

is not trustworthy, the inclination will be to look for fraud, rather than an innocent mistake, regardless of the particular situation. And rarely will the SEC receive the feedback of having to test its theories in court. Most enforcement actions will be settled because defendants will not want to risk the potentially ruinous collateral estoppel effect of having a fraud judgment entered against them.[124]

Each of these biases is exacerbated by the political imperative to respond to the latest headlines. Analyst independence only became a priority when the New York state attorney general revealed incriminating internal emails from Merrill Lynch.[125] Only after Enron and WorldCom moved accounting from the business page to the front page was auditor independence a compelling need. The SEC (and many others) readily assumed that the small number of companies implicated in these scandals reflected a broader pattern, a statistically very dubious proposition (following the "law" of small numbers).[126] Notwithstanding this dubious empirical foundation, once this story took hold alternative explanations were pushed aside.[127] Just as curious as the (over)-reaction to the Enron scandal was the lack of reform effort prior to the scandal. The Enron scandal provided no new information. The SEC and indeed most investors have long known that analyst ratings are skewed toward optimism and that auditors often provide nonauditing services to their clients.[128]

Of course, one could argue that the SEC's preoccupation with scandals stems from political pressure that also reflects the availability heuristic. The fact that Congress itself may act under the availability heuristic, however, is

---

PSYCHOL. 743 (1999); Langevoort, supra note 20, at 1504; see also Donald C. Langevoort, Monitoring: The Behavior Economics of Inducing Agents' Compliance with Legal Rules, 2002 COLUM. BUS. L. REV. 71, 89 ("My suspicion, however, is that concealed compliance wrongdoing by agents is only occasionally the product of inherently bad moral dispositions. More often, a morally normal person gets caught in a situation that leads gradually to increasingly bad choices. Here, we revisit the fundamental attribution bias: the idea that observers underestimate in others the influence of situational factors, and overestimate character.").

124. *See* Rachlinski & Farina, *supra* note 20, at 559 ("Experience accompanied by feedback allows experts to identify situations in which they are using inappropriate heuristics or are trapped by misleading schema.").

125. *See* Cheryl Winokur Munk, *Merrill Changes Stock-Research Rating Process*, WALL ST. J., June 10, 2002, at C16.

126. *See supra* note 25 (discussing the tendency of people to put too much weight on small samples).

127. *See* Clifford R. Mynatt, Michael E. Doherty & William Dragan, *Information Relevance, Working Memory, and the Consideration of Alternative*, 46A Q.J. EXPERIMENTAL PSYCHOL. 759 (1993) (finding that subjects who had developed a plausible hypothesis were less able to recognize alternatives).

128. *See* Steven D. Jones, *Heard in the Northwest: Region's Rare 'Sell' Ratings Apply to Burgers, Machinery and a Thrift*, WALL ST. J. NW, at 2, 1999 WL-WSJ 24923975 (noting that "of 833 opinions in place on the 135 stocks last week [of companies located in the Northwest United States], there was a 'strong sell' on only one").

hardly cause for comfort. Combining availability with the political imperative to "do something" creates a high likelihood of regulatory overreaction.[129] Such a bias within Congress, combined with biases at the SEC, further reduces the likelihood that the regulatory scheme will protect investors in a cost-effective fashion.

4. *Framing effects.*

How a particular question is framed may determine whether and how SEC officials respond. Framing effects may lead the SEC to fight vigorously to avoid a possible loss (in terms of investor welfare or the SEC's own authority). On the other hand, the SEC may be less interested in advancing investor welfare beyond the present status quo.[130]

The indifference of the SEC to various areas of securities regulation absent a large loss to investors suggests not only bounded rationality (and the related availability heuristic and hindsight bias) but also the importance of loss aversion. Many regulatory initiatives by the SEC have been launched shortly after either a large loss to investors or the threat of diminished authority for the SEC.[131] The SEC and Congress have been galvanized to action recently with the collapse of stock prices in the technology and telecom sectors and the allegations of accounting malfeasance that followed.[132] The threatened loss of issuers and investors to overseas markets spurred the passage of Regulation S and Rule 144A in 1990.[133] On the other hand, absent a threat to the SEC's authority or to investors, the SEC has typically remained complacent.

One could argue that this regulatory approach makes sense—put out fires and "don't fix what ain't broken." The impact on regulations is uncertain. Moreover, it may be costly to experiment with new regulations without the

129. For evidence that the urge to "do something" is highest immediately following a drop in the financial markets, see Banner, *supra* note 117, at 850.

130. *See* Steven M.H. Wallman, *Competition, Innovation, and Regulation in the Securities Markets*, 53 BUS. LAW. 341, 346 (1998) ("Frequently, criticism is leveled at regulators' concrete failure to protect someone who is hurt, rather than for precluding something new or experimental that might—although no one is sure—have led to a better world.").

131. *See* Banner, *supra* note 117, at 850.

132. *See* Charles Gasparino & Tom Hamburger, *Congress Broadens Probe of Enron Fall To Wall Street Firms*, WALL ST. J., Mar. 7, 2002, at C1 (reporting Congressional investigation into "analysts who continued to recommend Enron's stock last fall as the company careened toward bankruptcy").

133. *See* Resale of Restricted Securities, Securities Act Release No. 6862 [1989-1990 Transfer Binder] Fed. Sec. L. Rep. (CCH) ¶ 80,637, at 80,639 (Apr. 23, 1990); *see also* Josh Futterman, *Evasion and Flowback in the Regulation S Era: Strengthening U.S. Investor Protection While Promoting U.S. Corporate Offshore Offerings*, 18 FORDHAM INT'L L.J. 806, 840-41 (1995) ("Prior to the adoption of Regulation S, some members of the U.S. investment industry maintained that, due to U.S. restrictions on offshore securities offerings, U.S. issuers were at a disadvantage to their overseas counterparts in the offshore markets.").

threat of a perceived and immediate loss to investors. But this generalization cannot always be true. Sometimes rationalizing regulation, such as the proposal for company registration,[134] may benefit both issuers and investors. The continued bias toward reactive reform to the securities laws may represent at least partially a framing-effects-related bias toward the status quo.[135]

5. *Overconfidence.*

SEC regulators may be overconfident in their policy prescriptions, leading to errors and regulatory overreaching. Indeed, the specialized expertise claimed by the SEC may inflate the confidence with which regulators make decisions. Experts tend to be overly optimistic in assessing their own decisionmaking ability.[136] As Dale Griffin and Amos Tversky put it, experts are "often wrong but rarely in doubt."[137]

Examples of SEC overconfidence in its ability to regulate the securities markets come readily to mind. The SEC's ambitious plan to integrate the stock exchanges and the over-the-counter market into a unified national market system is widely regarded as a failure, some twenty-five years after the proposal was first adopted.[138] Likewise, the SEC consistently has argued that U.S. style securities regulation is superior to other regulatory regimes around the world, a position more awkward to sustain after Enron and WorldCom. The SEC, for instance, has insisted on the superiority of GAAP over international accounting standards, despite a dearth of empirical evidence to support the assertion.[139]

Insider trading provides another conspicuous example of SEC overconfidence in regulation. Bolstered by the strong performance of the U.S. capital markets in the 1980s and 1990s, the SEC aggressively exported U.S. style insider trading prohibitions across the world. In large part due to the SEC's efforts, many countries adopted formal prohibitions against insider trading in the 1980s and 1990s.[140] The SEC hoped that insider trading

134. *See supra* note 119 and accompanying text.

135. *See* Rachlinski & Farina, *supra* note 20, at 605 ("If those affected by a regulatory program 'endow' the status quo, the status will likely remain in place.").

136. *See* Griffin & Tversky, *supra* note 28, at 411, 427, 430.

137. *Id.* at 412.

138. *See* Jonathan R. Macey & David D. Haddock, *Shirking at the SEC: The Failure of the National Market System*, 1985 U. ILL. L. REV. 315 (contending that special interest group influences on the SEC make the success of the national market system unlikely).

139. *See* Christian Leuz, *IAS Versus US GAAP: Information Asymmetry-Based Evidence from Germany's New Market*, 41 J. ACCT. RES. 445 (2003) (finding no differences between firms following IAS and those following GAAP for a series of measures of information asymmetry).

140. *See* Harvey L. Pitt & David B. Hardison, *Games Without Frontiers: Trends in the International Response to Insider Trading*, 55 L. & CONTEMP. PROBS., Autumn 1992, at 199, 204–06.

prohibitions would become accepted (and enforced) in other countries as they are in the United States. Despite the presence of formal insider trading bans, few countries have ever enforced their insider trading prohibitions.[141] At the end of 1998, 87 countries with stock exchanges prohibited insider trading, but only 38 countries had enforced their prohibitions even once.[142] In our view, this campaign by the SEC reflects undue optimism in the power of the law to change behavior.

The SEC's regulatory turf battles with the CFTC may also stem from overconfidence. The United States allocates regulatory responsibility for "securities"[143] to the SEC and responsibility for regulating "commodities" and "futures" to the Commodities and Futures Trading Commission (CFTC).[144] The SEC and CFTC have squabbled over their respective authorities where the jurisdictional lines are unclear. These turf battles have occurred not only between the regulatory agencies, but also within Congress, with the Commerce Committee siding with the SEC and the Agricultural Committee siding with the CFTC. This competition between the agencies generally has produced substantial lobbying costs and distraction without any evidence of improvement for investors.[145] Although a straightforward public choice explanation rooted in regulators' desires to amass their own power explains this turf battle quite well, a pervasive overconfidence in the SEC's own regulatory abilities compared with the CFTC's (and vice versa) may have exacerbated the ongoing rift.[146]

141. *See* Utpal Bhattacharya & Hazem Daouk, *The World Price of Insider Trading*, 57 J. FIN. 75, 80-84, 88-90 (2002) (reporting that prior to 1990 only 9 of 34 countries with prohibitions on insider trading have ever enforced their prohibitions).

142. *See id.*

143. *See* 15 U.S.C. § 77b(1) (1994) (providing a definition of "security" for the Securities Act of 1933); 15 U.S.C. § 78c(a)(10) (1994) (providing a definition of "security" under the Securities Exchange Act of 1934).

144. A futures contract is a standardized agreement under which a buyer agrees to purchase a specific quantity of a particular commodity at a specified date in the future at a fixed price.

145. Indeed, SEC officials during the 1970s feared that the definition of the term "commodity" could even encompass ordinary securities. Former SEC Chairman Roderick Hills noted in 1975 that "it is relatively easy to suggest that the most basic examples of what is unambiguously a security, such as a share of GM or AT&T, are literally within the definition of a 'commodity' . . . ." Letter from SEC Chairman Roderick M. Hills to CFTC Chairman William T. Bagley [1975-1977 Transfer Binder] Comm. Fut. L. Rep. (CCH) ¶ 20,117 (Nov. 13, 1975). The SEC's battle with the CFTC culminated in the Shad-Johnson Accord of 1982. *See* Sanford A. Fine, *Back to the (Single Stock) Future: The New Regulatory Framework Governing Single-Stock Futures Trading*, 54 ADMIN. L. REV. 513, 520-22 (2002).

146. *See* Arlen, *supra* note 20, at 1776 ("This self-serving tendency may even grow stronger when groups predictably attempt to maximize the *difference* between themselves and another group.") (emphasis added).

6. *Confirmation bias.*

Regulators at the SEC may suffer from a confirmation bias.[147] Once regulations are on the books, regulators may feel the need to justify their worth instead of critically evaluating their effects. Evidence that does not discredit regulation unambiguously will be ignored.[148] And the confirmation bias will be more pronounced if the evidence is more complex and subject to conflicting inferences, a fair characterization of most regulatory problems in the securities markets.[149] Self-justification is exacerbated when decisionmakers are held

147. *See* Joshua Klayman, *Varieties of Confirmation Bias*, 32 PSYCHOL. LEARNING & MOTIVATION 385 (1995) (describing different ways in which the confirmation bias can affect decisions). If the behavioral economists are right about the pervasiveness of cognitive biases, perhaps we should not be surprised that the writing of even behavioral economists is infected by the biases. *See* Mitchell, *supra* note 33, at 73 n.9 ("The behavioral law and economics scholars exhibit a pessimism bias in their work: they tend to ignore or discount research findings contrary to their view of legal decision-makers as afflicted by numerous judgmental biases and decision-making errors, while simultaneously interpreting ambiguous research findings as supportive of their pessimistic view of human rationality.") (internal quotations omitted). For example, Robert Prentice reports the existence of a confirmation bias, which causes "trained scientists [to] judge research reports that agree with their views to be of higher quality than those that disagree." Robert A. Prentice, *The Case of The Irrational Auditor: A Behavioral Insight Into Securities Fraud Litigation*, 95 NW. U. L. REV. 133, 146 (2000) (citing Jonathan J. Koehler, *The Influence of Prior Beliefs on Scientific Judgments of Evidence Quality*, 56 ORG. BEHAV. & HUM. DECISION PROCESSES 28, 47 (1993)). Prentice then goes on to downplay the significance of studies finding that auditors paid more attention to disconfirming than confirming evidence, praising a study that supports his thesis of a confirmation bias.

One might defer more to Prentice's interpretation of the empirical evidence if errors of statistical inference were not so prevalent in his work. For example, Prentice identifies a "rising tide of insider trading lawsuits involving accountant defendants." *Id.* at 189. The basis for this claim, however, is a string cite of seventeen SEC enforcement actions over a period of *twenty-five years*. *Id.* at 189 n.314. This is obviously too small a sample from which to draw any meaningful inferences. More fundamentally, one cannot infer anything about a change of the behavior of accountants over time because of "the rising tide of insider trading lawsuits" generally over that time. The SEC will almost certainly find more insider trading by accountants if it devotes more resources to prosecuting insider trading, as it did during this period even if accountants are not engaging in more insider trading. Changes in the number of suits against accountants tells us nothing about the behavior of accountants if we do not control for the amount of insider trading enforcement resources generally. Similarly, Prentice claims that accounting fraud violations "tend not to be niggling," based on a study of SEC enforcement actions. *See id.* at 201 n.390 (citing Ehsan H. Feroz, Kyungjoo Park & Victor S. Pastena, *The Financial and Market Effects of the SEC's Accounting and Auditing Enforcement Releases*, 29 J. ACCT. RES. 107, 114 (Supp. 1991)). SEC enforcement actions cannot tell us anything about the *average* magnitude of accounting violations because the size of a violation is a factor that the SEC relies upon in deciding which cases to prosecute.

148. *See* Langevoort, *Organized Illusions*, *supra* note 89, at 137 ("Ambiguous information tends to be dismissed as unmanageable.").

149. Jon D. Hanson & Douglas A. Kysar, *Taking Behavioralism Seriously: The Problem of Market Manipulation*, 74 N.Y.U. L. REV. 630, 648 n.60 (1999) (collecting studies).

accountable in public settings.[150] Such self-justification can obstruct any change in the status quo.

The SEC in particular is prone to the self-justification bias because the SEC can always point to the depth and liquidity of the U.S. securities markets to justify its regulatory efforts. It is difficult to argue with success. But this self-congratulation ignores the status of the U.S. securities markets as the deepest and most liquid in the world *before* the SEC was created.[151] In fact, the liquidity of the U.S. markets gives SEC regulators large leeway to make mistakes and reduce overall investor value before investors would depart for other markets.[152] SEC regulators that focus on the success of the U.S. securities markets therefore may become "locked in," making future changes to regulations difficult.[153]

150. *See* Langevoort, *Organized Illusions*, *supra* note 89, at 142 ("[O]nce executives have committed to a course of action, their subsequent survey of information is strongly biased to bolster their choice—especially when their choice is public, and they can be held accountable for their decisions.").

151. U.S. markets were more liquid than their European counterparts before the securities laws were adopted in the United States and the adoption of those laws had no apparent effect on liquidity. Prentice incorrectly claims that the regulation by the SEC "led directly to a large increase in investor participation in the stock markets." Prentice, *supra* note 14, at1420 (citing JOEL SELIGMAN, THE TRANSFORMATION OF WALL STREET 561-62 (rev. ed. 1995)). In fact, the Exchange Act was a resounding failure at restoring investor confidence—the volume of trading remained below 1929 levels for another three decades. *See* ROBERT SOBEL, N.Y.S.E.: A HISTORY OF NEW YORK STOCK EXCHANGE 1935-1975 303 (1975) (finding that the average daily trading volume in 1955 was 1.7 million shares below 1929 averages). Further, the passage of the Exchange Act—with its strong antimanipulation provisions—resulted in significant declines in NYSE and AMEX seat values. *See* G. William Schwert, *Public Regulation of National Securities Exchanges: A Test of the Capture Hypothesis*, 8 BELL J. ECON. 128, 134 (1977) (providing evidence that the average seat price on the NYSE and AMEX fell 50% during the month when Congress first considered the Securities and Exchange Act). Reduction in seat values is not the result one would have expected from government regulation intended to "restore investor confidence," i.e., willingness to trade over the exchanges. Part of this decline in seat values may be attributable to the SEC's open hostility at the time to the goal of liquidity. *See* RALPH F. DE BEDTS, THE NEW DEAL'S SEC: THE FORMATIVE YEARS 158 (1964) (discussing criticisms of liquidity by former SEC Chairman William O. Douglas and in staff reports). In this regard, it is worth noting that institutional investors—who should have been a primary beneficiary of regulation—were critical of the Exchange Act. *See* C. John Kuhn, *The Securities Act and Its Effect upon the Institutional Investor*, 4 L. & CONTEMP. PROBS. 80, 85 (1937) ("[I]t is the consensus of opinion among trained security buyers that regulations [under the Exchange Act] . . . have a restrictive effect upon markets outweighing the benefits gained.").

152. To put it another way, the liquidity of the U.S. securities markets is tied together with the U.S. securities regulatory regime. One of us has recommended undoing this tie to increase competitive pressure on securities regulators. *See, e.g.*, Choi & Guzman, *supra* note 10, at 918.

153. A similar problem may afflict the SEC's supporters. Prentice spends a substantial portion of his article documenting the existence of fraud in the securities markets (*see* Prentice, *supra* note 14, at 1415-26) "even with seventy years of regulation on the books." *Id.* at 1458 n.286. The continuing existence of fraud is a startling revelation, but it is not at all clear how the prevalence of securities fraud under the SEC's watch counsels in favor of

The SEC is also reluctant to concede weaknesses in its policy positions. For many years, the SEC prohibited forward-looking ("soft") information disclosures in SEC filings.[154] This position persisted despite evidence that investors, when making an investment decision, often care most about the future prospects of a company and their implications for future cash flows to investors.[155] Although the SEC finally adopted a limited safe harbor for forward-looking disclosures in 1979,[156] its reach is narrow and the agency continues to limit such disclosures, in some cases prohibiting forward-looking disclosures under its gun-jumping rules for companies planning a public offering.[157] When Congress enacted the Private Securities Litigation Reform Act of 1995, which contained a statutory forward-looking information safe harbor, the SEC pushed for a long list of transactions that would be excluded from the safe harbor.[158] And it has yet to exercise the exemptive authority provided by Congress in that law to expand the safe harbors.

The confirmation bias (and the SEC's overconfidence in its prior policies) can be seen in the path dependence in the SEC's regulations. As originally enacted in the 1933 and 1934 Acts, the securities laws provided separate disclosure standards for companies making public offerings and those whose securities simply trade on the secondary markets. For several decades thereafter, commentators recognized the need to unify disclosure standards.[159] Disclosures have the same relevance to investors whether they are purchasing in a public offering or on the secondary market. The SEC did not seriously consider revamping the scheme until the 1960s, ultimately adopting the present integrated disclosure system.[160] Even that, however, falls short of a full-fledged

retaining the SEC rather than considering a market alternative.

154. *See* Edmund W. Kitch, *The Theory and Practice of Securities Disclosure*, 61 BROOK. L. REV. 763, 777-87 (1995); *see also* Disclosure of Projections of Future Economic Performance, Securities Act Release No. 5362, [1972-1973 Transfer Binder] Fed. Sec. L. Rep. (CCH) ¶ 79,211 (Feb. 2, 1973).

155. *See, e.g.*, Homer Kripke, *Can the SEC Make Disclosure Policy Meaningful?*, J. PORTFOLIO MGMT., Summer 1976, at 32, 35-37.

156. *See* 17 C.F.R. § 240.3b-6 (1997), originally promulgated in Safe Harbor Rule for Projections, Exchange Act Release No. 33-6084 (June 25, 1979), available in 1979 WL 16388; 17 C.F.R. § 230.175 (1997).

157. *See* Guidelines for the Release of Information by Issuers Whose Securities Are in Registration, SEC Release No. 5180, 1 Fed. Sec. L. Rptr. (CCH) ¶ 3056 (Aug. 16, 1971) (warning that "care should be exercised so that, for example, predictions, projections, forecasts, estimates and opinions concerning value are not given with respect to such things, among others, as sales and earnings and value of the issuers' securities").

158. *See, e.g.*, Noelle Matteson, *Private Securities Litigation Reform Act of 1995: Do Issuers Still Get Soaked in the Safe Harbor?*, 27 GOLDEN GATE U. L. REV. 527, 548 n.139 (1997).

159. The seminal article making the case for integrated securities disclosure is Milton H. Cohen, *"Truth in Securities" Revisited*, 79 HARV. L. REV. 1340 (1966).

160. *See* Adoption of Integrated Disclosure System, Securities Act Release No. 6383, 47 Fed Reg 11,380 (Mar 16, 1982).

scheme of company disclosure.[161]

The SEC also tends to believe that investors view the world the same way that it does. The false consensus effect is the "widespread and stubborn illusion . . . that others share one's own attitudes and behaviors to a greater extent than they really do."[162] Closely related, the SEC may engage in self-serving inferences, choosing to view investors in the light most supportive of the need and importance of the SEC.[163] The SEC's insistence that investor attitudes mirror views among SEC commissioners and staff may lead the agency toward ill-advised regulations. The SEC often uncritically states that it seeks to protect investors—and in particular, that absent the SEC's efforts, investor confidence in the market will deteriorate. Rarely, however, does the SEC verify that its assumptions are correct. The SEC instead simply asserts that investor confidence demands its latest regulatory intervention. The recently promulgated Regulation FD, prohibiting selective disclosures from companies, is just such an example.[164] The SEC argued (with no empirical basis) that the practice of selective disclosure to analysts was undermining investor confidence.[165] A new regulatory burden was imposed on issuers with little or no evidence that it would produce countervailing benefits for investors.[166]

7. *Groupthink.*

Cognitive biases within the SEC are magnified by pervasive organizational "groupthink." Groupthink occurs when individuals come to identify with the organization and accept its mission uncritically due to their perceived membership in the group.[167] Once a commitment has been made, group

161. *See supra* note 119 and accompanying text.

162. Langevoort, *Ego*, *supra* note 83, at 859 (citing Gary Marks & Norman Miller, *Ten Years of Research on the False-Consensus Effect: An Empirical and Theoretical Review*, 102 PSYCHOL. BULL. 72 (1987)).

163. Donald Langevoort describes self-serving inferences as follows:

> Self-serving inferences arise when there is a reasonably high level of ambiguity surrounding a situation. With that kind of cognitive freedom, the mind tends to form stronger-than-justifiable inferences in the direction of a person's self-interest. More simply, people see as correct what is more properly described as convenient. Having rationalized their inferences, people feel little guilt in acting upon them.

Donald C. Langevoort, *When Lawyers and Law Firms Invest In Their Corporate Clients' Stock*, 80 WASH. U. L.Q. 569, 574 (2002).

164. 17 C.F.R. § 243 (2000) (Regulation FD).

165. *See* Selective Disclosure and Insider Trading, Securities Act Release No. 33-7881, 65 Fed. Reg. 51,716, 51,716 (Aug. 15, 2000) ("We believe that the practice of selective disclosure leads to a loss of investor confidence in the integrity of our capital markets.").

166. On a related note, Donald Langevoort has argued that the case for Regulation FD is at best uncertain from the viewpoint of behavioral economics. *See* Langevoort, *Taming the Animal Spirits*, *supra* note 15, at 165-75.

167. *See* IRVING L. JANIS, VICTIMS OF GROUPTHINK (1972); *see also* James D. Cox & Harry L. Munsinger, *Bias in the Boardroom: Psychological Foundations and Legal Implications of Corporate Cohesion*, 48 L. & CONTEMP. PROBS., Summer 1985, at 83, 99-

members will downplay feedback that is inconsistent with that position in order to minimize tensions within the group.[168] Although an individual may assess a particular decision critically, members of a group defer to the consensus. Groupthink will also tend to reduce the range of hypotheses that an organization considers when faced with a problem.[169]

The SEC is known for its strong organizational culture. Often praised as hard-working and dedicated, the mission of "investor protection" is taken to heart by virtually all SEC staffers.[170] This tendency is no doubt reinforced by self-selection among those seeking SEC employment.[171] The type of people who choose to become regulators and enforcement officials may have a heightened sense of justice and fairness. Such traits may lead regulators to work hard for relatively low pay. Such a culture helps maintain morale and focuses SEC staffers on the task of regulating the capital markets.

Despite these benefits, the strong investor protection culture within the SEC may also lead to groupthink. Homogeneous groups like the self-selected SEC staffers are particularly susceptible to the confirmation bias[172] and are perhaps more likely to engage in self-serving inferences (to the extent that all the staffers have a homogeneous interest).[173] Once the SEC has committed to a policy initiative through a rulemaking proposal—thereby tentatively committing to the "group"—feedback on the proposal may get less weight than it would have if the information had been solicited before the SEC fixated upon a specific proposal.

Groupthink may also manifest itself in the SEC's single-minded focus on

---

108 (applying analysis to decisions by corporate boards); Robert J. Haft, *Business Decisions by the New Board: Behavioral Science and Corporate Law*, 80 MICH. L. REV. 1, 37-49 (1981) (same).

168. *See* Langevoort, *Ego*, *supra* note 83, at 874.

169. *See* Heath et al., *supra* note 98, at 20 ("Often, organizations ensure that individuals weigh information effectively by forcing them to interact with others who might weigh the information differently.").

170. In a speech delivered while he was Chairman of the SEC, Arthur Levitt, summarized the SEC's mission:

> Investor protection is our legal mandate.
>
> Investor protection is our moral responsibility.
>
> Investor protection is my top personal priority.

Arthur Levitt, *A Question of Integrity: Promoting Investor Confidence by Fighting Insider Trading*, 12(4) INSIGHTS 17, 18 (1998). Pritchard, a former senior counsel at the SEC, can attest from personal experience that this attitude is widely shared among the staff.

171. *Cf.* Rachlinski & Farina, *supra* note 20, at 579-80 ("Those who seek work at an agency charged with responsibility for the environment probably have strong views about the appropriate goals and means of environmental regulation. Consequently, agencies can become myopically focused on their missions.").

172. *See* Stefan Schulz-Hardt, Dieter Frey, Carsten Lüthgens & Serge Moscovici, *Biased Information Search in Group Decision Making*, 78 J. PERSONALITY & SOC. PSYCHOL. 655 (2000) (describing tendency for like-minded individuals to exacerbate the confirmation bias).

173. *See supra* note 163 (describing self-serving inferences).

investor protection. When a decision can be placed on a normative scale, such as more or less investor protection, group decision dynamics will push the group toward a polar end of the scale.[174] At the SEC, the systematic tendency will be to settle on outcomes that promise more investor protection. Many investors may be able to protect themselves, but the SEC usually focuses on the stereotypical "widows and orphans" in crafting protections.

Perhaps due to groupthink, overconfidence, the confirmation bias, self-serving inferences, loss aversion, or some combination of these biases, the SEC assumes that it knows what investors consider "fair" in the capital markets.[175] To take one example, the SEC has for years contended that insider trading is "unfair" and that, if not prohibited, the practice will cause investors to lose confidence in the markets.[176] But why is it unfair if investors discount for the risk of insider trading and thereby pay a lower price for their securities? Perhaps an independent and unchangeable norm exists that insider trading is unfair. Or perhaps investors lack the ability to fully discount for the risk of insider trading and failing to prohibit such activities will dry up market liquidity. This possibility seems unlikely, however, given the commonly acknowledged prevalence of insider trading before the SEC became serious about enforcement in the 1980s. Market liquidity coexisted peacefully with notorious insider trading, as it continues to do in many countries.[177] Our task here is not to defend insider trading.[178] We only point out that the SEC has accepted uncritically the premise of unfairness without investigation and has

174. *See* Mark Seidenfeld, *Cognitive Loafing, Social Conformity, and Judicial Review of Agency Rulemaking*, 87 CORNELL L. REV. 486, 535 (2002 ("When the outcome of a decision can be placed on a normative scale, such as being risky rather than safe, liberal rather than conservative, or certain rather than uncertain, then the dynamics of group decisionmaking can actually increase the tendency of the group to choose an outcome that is on one end of the scale rather than in the middle."); *see also* Cass R. Sunstein, *Deliberative Trouble? Why Groups Go to Extremes*, 110 YALE L.J. 71 (2000) (canvassing evidence on group polarization).

175. *See* Jeffrey M. Laderman, William B. Glaberson, Gene G. Marcial, Peter Philipps & John N. Frank, *The Epidemic of Insider Trading*, BUS. WK., Apr. 29, 1985, at 78 (quoting former SEC Chairman Arthur Levitt as stating, "If the investor thinks he's not getting a fair shake, he's not going to invest, and that is going to hurt capital investment in the long run.").

176. *See, e.g.*, Brief for the United States, United States v. O'Hagan, 521 U.S. 642 (1997) (No. 96-842). Full disclosure: Pritchard, then a lawyer at the SEC, helped write this brief. For a criticism of the confidence-in-the-market argument, see Stephen M. Bainbridge, *Incorporating State Law Fiduciary Law Duties into the Federal Insider Trading Prohibition*, 52 WASH. & LEE L. REV. 1189, 1241-45 (1995).

177. *See* Bhattacharya & Daouk, *supra* note 141 (providing evidence that enforcement of insider trading laws is relatively infrequent outside the United States).

178. For such a defense, see HENRY G. MANNE, INSIDER TRADING AND THE STOCK MARKET (1966). For criticisms, see, for example, Robert J. Haft, *The Effect of Insider Trading Rules on the Internal Efficiency of the Large Corporation*, 80 MICH. L. REV. 1051, 1051-64 (1982); Saul Levmore, *Securities and Secrets: Insider Trading and the Law of Contracts*, 68 VA. L. REV. 117, 149 (1982) (arguing that insiders may structure a corporation's transactions to profit from insider trading); Kenneth E. Scott, *Insider Trading: Rule 10b-5, Disclosure and Corporate Privacy*, 9 J. LEGAL STUD. 801, 810-11 (1980).

ignored evidence that insider trading does not impair investor confidence.

B. *Corrective Mechanisms*

Corrective measures may help to overcome the behavioral biases of regulators. If you explain framing effects to a person and then immediately ask how they value avoiding the loss of a coffee mug compared with gaining a coffee mug, the person is less prone to framing.[179] This example shows that structural mechanisms can reduce behavioral biases. For our purposes, the relevant questions are: Which mechanisms would work for the SEC and are these mechanisms cost-justified? We review below possible antidotes to cognitive biases within the SEC.

1. *Internal organization.*

Organizations can structure themselves to reduce the impact of behavioral biases. Absent intervention, "experts may myopically focus on issues within their area of expertise and thereby fail to recognize that a decision would benefit from accessing other bodies of knowledge or ways of thinking."[180] Organizations can call on multiple decisionmakers with different types of expertise to reduce the risk that heuristics will be applied without consideration of context.[181] The staff of the SEC is organized into multiple divisions, and most regulatory proposals will be reviewed by more than one division. At a minimum, the general counsel's office will comment on any proposal before the commissioners approve it. This structure requires the division proposing a regulatory initiative to defend its assumptions and may allow for creative alternatives.[182]

The process by which commissioners approve staff proposals suggests another means by which organizations can reduce cognitive bias: hierarchical review. Forcing decisionmakers to justify their decision may reduce some cognitive problems, as with judicial and political oversight. In the SEC, this takes the form of the commissioners reviewing the proposals that typically originate with the agency staff. In this way, the expert commissioners scrutinize the work of the experts on the staff. And the mandate of political balance among the commissioners provides some assurance that proposals will be subjected to diverse viewpoints.[183] Of course, the efficacy of this review will

179. *See* Arlen et al., *supra* note 29 (providing evidence on the importance of context in determining the magnitude of framing effects).

180. Rachlinski & Farina, *supra* note 20, at 560.

181. *See* Heath et al., *supra* note 98.

182. *See* Rachlinski & Farina, *supra* note 20, at 561 (arguing that placing experts into separate groups helps avoid "escalating commitment" to a proposal).

183. The Exchange Act provides for five commissioners at the head of the SEC. No more than three of the five commissioners may be from the same political party. *See* 15

be undermined if political considerations or cronyism, rather than merit and intellectual diversity, drive the selection of commissioners.

Despite the promise of organizational structure, the effects of behavioral biases are unlikely to be eliminated completely. Although organizational structure may reduce some biases, it may introduce countervailing biases. Assigning different tasks to different divisions may help increase diversity of perspectives, but contribution to a group product may reduce individuals' incentives to engage fully in making the decision.[184] Individual effort will be further reduced if the decisionmaker only has authority to make recommendations, rather than making the ultimate decision.[185] So, although review by SEC commissioners may bring accountability to the SEC staff, it comes at the cost of reducing the engagement of the staff in the initial decision. Moreover, the thoroughness of review by the commissioners will be limited by the fact that each commissioner has only one vote and that vote will rarely be decisive. The power of any individual commissioner will be further diluted by the practice of the SEC staff of not vetting proposals with commissioners until the time for final approval. At that point, scrutiny from the commissioners may have little impact.[186]

The lack of a unified theory of behavioral biases makes it unclear what effect organizational structure will have on the magnitude of the biases.[187] Does introducing experts from different fields appreciably reduce the tendencies of specific experts to act with overconfidence and to misapply heuristics learned in one field more generally to other fields? We simply do not know the answers to these questions.

2. *Judicial review.*

Behavioral decision theory commentators have argued that judicial review can ameliorate the behavioral biases of regulators. This makes intuitive sense; not surprisingly, as Jeffrey Rachlinski writes, "cognitive biases are easier to spot in others than in oneself."[188] Mark Seidenfeld contends that review—even

U.S.C. § 78(d) (2003).

184. *See* Seidenfeld, *supra* note 174, at 510-11.

185. *See id.* at 511.

186. In addition, to the extent the commissioners and the SEC's staff share a common preference (for example, the expansion of the SEC's authority), the self-serving inferences of commissioners will become magnified when commissioners are called upon to endorse equally self-serving judgments made by the staff. *See* Kristina A. Diekmann, Steven M. Samuels, Lee Ross & Max H. Bazerman, *Self-Interest and Fairness in Problems of Resource Allocation: Allocators Versus Recipients*, 72 J. PERSONALITY & SOC. PSYCHOL. 1061 (1997).

187. *See supra* notes 31-36 and accompanying text (discussing the lack of any unified theory explaining behavioral biases).

188. Jeffrey J. Rachlinski, *Heuristics and Biases in the Courts: Ignorance or Adaptation?*, 79 OR. L. REV. 61, 65-66 (2000).

by a nonexpert judiciary—may reduce the biases of expert regulators.[189] Regulators who anticipate review by an unknown audience will tend to take greater care in arriving at their decisions. In creating a written record, regulators will look at more diverse information sets if a written record is required.[190] This may mitigate the biasing effects of the availability heuristic. Being forced to consider alternatives and counterarguments is a useful antidote to overconfidence.[191] Biases related to the conviction of regulators in their positions (for example, overconfidence and overoptimism biases) can be reduced if regulators are forced to list the weaknesses in their position.[192] The potential for review will also discourage regulators from relying on heuristics because they must justify their decisions in writing to nonexperts.

Judicial review, however, will not eliminate regulatory biases and it may introduce others. Regulators subject to review may take advantage of their expertise and information advantages over the court and downplay their positions' weaknesses. The subject matter under review may be sufficiently complex that judges simply cannot determine the exact nature of the reasoning. If a lack of judicial expertise is a serious problem, judicial oversight may have little effect on regulators' decisions, thus doing little to overcome cognitive biases among regulators. Judicial review is also likely to exacerbate regulators' confirmation bias (resulting in a "circle the wagons" effect as regulators defend their past regulatory positions).[193] Judges, moreover, may face their own behavioral biases.[194]

3. *Political oversight*

The SEC is not the only regulator of the securities markets. Congress and the President have considerable influence over the capital markets both directly, through legislation and the nomination processes, and indirectly, through budgetary and other pressure on the SEC. While the SEC has sought to expand its authority, Congress has worked, on occasion, to reduce the regulatory burdens of regulation. For example, the 1995 Private Securities Litigation Reform Act reduced the cost to issuers of defending securities fraud class actions.[195]

Political oversight, however, is no panacea for behavioral biases among regulators. Politicians themselves may face their own behavioral biases, and

---

189. *See* Seidenfeld, *supra* note 174, at 508-26.

190. *See id.* at 516 ("Individuals who are accountable to an audience with unknown views are significantly more self-critical while making their decisions.").

191. *See* Rachlinski & Farina, *supra* note 20, at 588.

192. *See* Linda Babcock, George Loewenstein & Samuel Issacharoff, *Creating Convergence: Debiasing Biased Litigants*, 22 L. & SOC. INQUIRY 913, 920 (1997).

193. *See* Seidenfeld, *supra* note 174, at 524.

194. For a discussion of judicial biases, see *infra* Part III.A.2.

195. 15 U.S.C. §§ 78u-4(b)(1), (2) (2003).

there is no reason to think that the politicians' biases are any less than those facing regulators.[196] Before the Enron scandal broke, Capitol Hill was silent on the roles that auditors and analysts play as gatekeepers in the securities markets. After the scandal, politicians were baying for regulatory reform. This shift on the part of lawmakers could represent a rational response to new information, but we doubt it. More likely, it is a symptom of the availability heuristic at work.[197] Indeed, opportunistic politicians may take advantage of the biases of the electorate, playing up recent instances of fraud to gain electoral support.

Scandal driven reform followed by political neglect has been a recurring pattern in the securities markets. Congress passed the Glass-Steagall Act in the Great Depression in response to scandals in the banking industry. While scandals may be needed to focus dispersed lawmakers' collective will, they often result in overreaction,[198] particularly if political entrepreneurs succeed in framing the issue in a way that resonates with the electorate.[199] "Fraud led to the market crash that wiped out your savings!" is easier to sell to voters who weigh losses more heavily than gains than "[e]xcessive regulations will reduce your investment gains by one-half of one percent per year!" Once in place, legislation often takes on a life of its own. It took Congress over six decades to get around to repealing the Glass-Steagall Act.[200] Legislators may accept the wisdom of prior legislation uncritically, operating under a confirmation bias. And industry participants may be quiescent if regulation serves as a barrier to entry.[201] Without any recent information of equal salience (nonscandals tend

---

196. *See* Rachlinski & Farina, *supra* note 20, at 572:

> Members [of Congress] seem vulnerable to the cognitive illusions that typically go unrecognized and unremediated by lay decisionmakers: being more attuned to potential harm than to foregone benefits (framing effects); overestimating the prevalence of events that are easy to remember (the availability heuristic); and disregarding the prevalence of an event altogether in evaluating its importance (the representativeness heuristic).

197. *See* Roger G. Noll & James E. Krier, *Some Implications of Cognitive Psychology for Risk Regulation*, 19 J. LEGAL STUD. 747, 762 (1990) ("[I]mmediately following a widely publicized disaster, citizens will place unusually great demands on their government to take action against recurrence, but as attention subsides, so too will the demand for action.").

198. *See* Banner, *supra* note 117, at 850 (contending that over the past 300 years most of the major pieces of securities related regulation came about following a large and sustained price collapse in the stock market).

199. *See* Noll & Krier, *supra* note 197, at 769 ("[A]deptness at characterizing issues can go a long way in determining the policy preferences expressed by the electorate.").

200. See Gramm-Leach-Bliley Act, Pub. L. No. 106-102, 113 Stat. 1338 (1999).

201. Roger Noll and Jim Krier argue that this will often be a conscious political strategy:

> [T]he best political strategy might be to enact rather rigorous and explicitly specified policy targets but set up a process of implementation that provides distributive benefits to participants in the process. An example would be a cumbersome process for setting industry standards, combined with differentially more rigorous standards for new sources of risk than for old ones—so that the costs to industry of the tough standards will be offset (perhaps more than offset) by barriers to competitive entry.

Noll & Krier, *supra* note 197, at 774-75. The 1933 Act provides an obvious example of this not to generate newspaper headlines) no impetus will exist to remove the protective legislation.[202]

Congressional review will also lead the SEC to skew deliberation to make rules easier to justify to committee chairs and their staffs. If rules are proposed to satisfy political demands, legislative oversight will induce greater justification for those rules, but it is unlikely to generate more thoughtful consideration on the part of regulators.[203] Because the SEC staff will be aware of the preferences of important members of congressional committees, the staff will tailor regulatory rules to conform to those preferences.[204] To the extent congressional committees suffer from their own biases or are motivated out of public choice concerns, the SEC's incentive to tailor rules toward the interests of such committees may not improve investor welfare.

C. *Other Explanations for Regulatory Failure at the SEC*

Other theories may explain the SEC's policy decisions, such as public choice explanations that rely on the rational actor model.[205] SEC regulators may push new regulations not because they are caught in heuristic traps but because more regulation equates with an increased role for the SEC. Likewise, SEC regulators may fight the CFTC for jurisdiction and otherwise expand the

strategy in the context of securities regulation. *See* Paul G. Mahoney, *The Political Economy of the Securities Act of 1933*, 30 J. LEGAL STUD. 1 (2001) (contending that the "technical" provisions of the 1933 Act limiting disclosure of a pending public offering prior to the filing of a registration statement with the SEC worked "to protect high-prestige wholesale investment banks, and the retail dealers who sold on their behalf, from competition by integrated wholesale/retail investment banks that gained market share in the late 1920s").

202. Congress' inertia may be an inevitable byproduct of an institution designed to ameliorate the instability inherent in majority voting schemes. *See* Noll & Krier, *supra* note 197, at 761 (arguing that "political institutions designed to combat the inherent instability of majority-rule democracy also attenuate the responsiveness of policy to changes in citizen preferences. Hence, if citizens exhibit intertemporal inconsistencies in preferences regarding risk regulation, modifications in policy are unlikely fully to reflect these changes in preferences.").

203. *See* Seidenfeld, *supra* note 174, at 515. The utility of political review will be further undermined by the fact that it is likely to be based on the outcome rather than the process by which the agency arrived at the rule, leading to an increase in biases in agency decisionmaking. *See id.* at 517 ("For accountability to be beneficial, a decisionmaker must perceive that the evaluation of her decision will be based on the process that she used to reach the decision, rather than on the outcome of the decision."). Seidenfeld notes that studies exist indicating that those who are judged based on the outcome of a decision rather than their decisionmaking process systematically are biased by sunk costs. *See id.*

204. *See* Mark Seidenfeld, *The Psychology of Accountability and Political Review of Agency Rules*, 51 DUKE L.J. 1059, 1078 (2001) ("Given the threat of cuts in appropriations or statutory limitations on agency authority, agencies have a strong incentive to conform their actions to be at least acceptable to the committee chair and a majority of committee members.").

205. *See generally* Macey, *supra* note 99 (providing a public choice explanation for the SEC's continued existence despite its obsolescence).

SEC's domain beyond the United States not because of overconfidence, but because SEC regulators want to maximize their authority.[206] But even if behavioral biases do not affect regulators, the fact that the SEC (or Congress) may engage in wrongheaded decisions for reasons other than cognitive bias is cold comfort for those who would rely on regulators to cure behavioral biases among investors.

Public choice and behavioral theories frequently complement each other. Self-interested regulators may point to behavioral biases among investors to expand regulatory protections for investors and the requisite agency resources to provide such protections.[207] The fact that regulators may be motivated to expand their own prestige and future compensation does not make them any less susceptible to behavioral biases. Indeed, cognitive illusions may magnify the harm caused by the more self-interested regulators. Regulators do not fit neatly into either the opportunistic or completely selfless boxes—a range of motivations exists. Within this range, cognitive biases may encourage regulators to equate self-interest and the public interest. An overoptimistic regulator, for example, may be able to delude himself into believing that a regulatory change, which coincidentally increases the prestige and power of the regulator's position, also benefits the market.[208] Former SEC Chairman Harvey Pitt's effort to elevate his position to cabinet level in the wake of a series of accounting scandals in 2002 affords a salient example of this tendency.[209] Reducing the cognitive dissonance between benefiting oneself and benefiting investors may help SEC regulators sleep easier, but it does not help investors. Similarly, an SEC regulator may convince himself that a particular regulation that happens to benefit a powerful securities industry group (which may be a source of future employment for the regulator) also is good for the market. Self-persuasion will be that much easier if the industry group can threaten credibly to create trouble with the SEC's overseers on Capitol Hill. Although we cannot identify the precise motivation behind the actions of the SEC and its staff, it does not follow from the existence of behavioral biases that more regulation is the solution.

---

206. *See supra* text accompanying notes 143-46 (describing the conflict between the SEC and the CFTC).

207. Indeed, regulators may attempt to take advantage of the public's behavioral biases to push forward self-interested regulatory programs. *See* Jonathan R. Macey, *Cynicism and Trust in Politics and Constitutional Theory*, 87 CORNELL L. REV. 280, 299 (2002) ("[P]eople will tend to either underestimate a relatively high-probability risk, or to overestimate a relatively low-probability risk. This cognitive bias permits opportunistic politicians and interest groups to exploit rationally ignorant citizens by convincing them that costly, draconian legislation is necessary to address low-probability risks.") (footnote omitted).

208. *See supra* note 163 and accompanying text (discussing the self-serving inferences affecting the SEC).

209. *See* Stephen Labaton, *S.E.C. Chief Draws Ridicule in Quest for Higher Status*, N.Y. TIMES, July 25, 2002, at C9.

III. ASSESSING REGULATION TO CORRECT BIASES

The behavioralist critique of investor decision making unfortunately yields few answers. Investors may act irrationally in their decision making. Investors also may trade excessively due to a speculative preference. It is difficult to construct a response to cognitive biases among investors (and other market participants) absent a theory of why we have behavioral biases.[210] A case has been made that behavioral phenomena may affect the capital markets. But how prevalent are the phenomena? Can people correct for their own biases? And if so how? If behavioral biases are simply hardwired into our brains, then no amount of effort may be able to change them. Disclosure alone, the principal regulatory response, fails to address the needs of investors operating under a dense cloud of behavioral illusions. Moreover, regulators themselves face cognitive problems of their own. Given these uncertainties, the biases of regulators, and the costs of regulation, the cure may be worse than the disease.

One response to this uncertainty would be to ignore investors' behavioral biases altogether and structure regulation on the basis of the rational actor model. We think that is an unlikely outcome,[211] so we instead provide a framework for assessing regulatory responses to behavioral biases. Perhaps more important than measuring the magnitude of biases among investors and regulators is deciding *who* will weigh these biases against one another (and under what burden) in determining: (a) whether a regulatory response is warranted, and (b) how to structure regulatory decision making to reduce biases within the regulatory agency (using, for example, judicial review or internal organizational controls). Ultimately the SEC (or some other regulatory decisionmaker) must determine whether to promulgate new regulations aimed at remedying investors' cognitive biases.

Significantly, the very decision on the part of the regulator whether to intervene to remedy market-based behavioral biases is itself subject to behavioral biases. Regulators focusing on market-based biases may ignore their own biases, leading to potentially ill-suited responses to behavioral biases. Recall that experts may suffer from larger overoptimism and heuristic biases when applying their expertise in areas outside their primary area.[212] Few SEC commissioners or staffers are likely to be experts in investor psychology. Such

210. *See* Donald C. Langevoort, *Monitoring: The Behavioral Economics of Corporate Compliance with Law*, 2002 COLUM. BUS. L. REV. 71, 74 ("I cannot quantify the net impact of these kinds of errors, which limits the precise policy lessons we can draw from the analysis."); Mitchell, *supra* note 33, at 131 ("As currently conceptualized, legal decision theory is nothing more than a mess of overgeneralizations about how people exhibit this or that bias or anomaly under largely unspecified conditions.").

211. This belief is in part due to the recent wave of articles focusing on behavioral biases among investors. *See* sources cited *supra* notes 13-14.

212. *See* Griffin & Tversky, *supra* note 28, at 430 (arguing that "experts who have rich models of the system in question are more likely to exhibit overconfidence than lay people who have a very limited understanding of these systems").

regulators may systematically opt for a regulatory solution to the presence of market behavioral biases. Moreover, while market biases continually face the pressure of competition, behavioral biases among regulators may go unchecked if regulators enjoy monopoly authority. Newly installed regulations often take on a life of their own, leading to more intrusive regulations over time; regulations to correct cognitive errors are unlikely to be an exception.

Should regulators take an active stand against behavioral biases, moreover, investors may become overly optimistic that they are fully protected against their own foibles and therefore reduce their own vigilance against behavioral biases. Any such intervention to correct for behavioral biases will have gaps, however, and overoptimistic (or perhaps overly trusting) investors may suffer even more harm.[213]

Before starting down the road toward a regulatory response, therefore, we propose a framework for assessing regulation to correct market-based cognitive biases. Our framework varies along two dimensions: (1) the type of regulator, and (2) the form of behavioral intervention contemplated. On the first dimension, we argue that monopolistic regulators should face a stronger presumption against intervention than regulators facing competition. On the second dimension, some forms of regulation interfere more directly with the autonomy of market participants and therefore should overcome a correspondingly higher presumption against intervention.

We do not attempt here to specify the details of how our framework would be implemented in practice. In certain cases, implementing the framework may involve court review of agency decisions using the appropriate presumption against behavioral bias-targeted intervention. Some policymakers, however, such as Congress, are not realistically subject to any review. In those cases, our presumptions are simply cautions for policymakers to heed before attempting to address behavioral biases. We also do not address how behavioral biases at the SEC should affect review of the SEC's efforts to deal with more traditional problems in the securities markets, such as fraud motivated by greed. Regulators (and courts) are well acquainted with fraud in the financial markets and the effectiveness of regulatory solutions against fraud.[214] While biases may afflict all forms of SEC decision making, regulator biases have their greatest impact when regulators are focused on how to deal with uncertain and amorphous issues—such as interventions to correct market-based biases. In an

213. *Cf.* W. KIP VISCUSI, FATAL TRADEOFFS: PUBLIC AND PRIVATE RESPONSIBILITIES FOR RISK 234-42 (1992) (describing the lulling effect).

214. Of course, even in well-known areas, regulators may abuse their authority to expand regulation unnecessarily. *See, e.g.*, Macey, *supra* note 99 (providing a public choice critique of the SEC). Some biases, such as overconfidence, may affect regulators regardless of their experience with a particular type of intervention. An argument therefore exists that our presumption approach should apply to all regulatory interventions on the part of the SEC. We are focused here, however, on interventions to correct behavioral biases, and we leave the possibility of a more general set of presumptions for another paper.

area of heightened uncertainty, the SEC's tendency to act out of a confirmation bias, with overconfidence, and following self-serving inferences may become accentuated. We define three levels of presumptions:

Presumption	**Standard**
Strong Presumption	Highest likelihood of net benefits of regulation and no less restrictive alternative
Intermediate Presumption	Substantial likelihood of net benefits of regulation and no less restrictive alternative
Weak Presumption	A likelihood of net benefits of regulation

While the precise level of each presumption is somewhat arbitrary, the notion that different forms of regulations to correct market-based biases require varying levels of justification is not. We turn now to a more detailed description of the two dimensions along which we set our presumptions against regulation targeting behavioral biases.

A. *Regulatory Decisionmakers*

In this section we discuss how the framework for assessing regulatory intervention should vary for (1) monopolistic and centralized regulators such as the SEC; (2) federal courts; (3) regulators facing competition from other sources of regulatory protections for investors (including market-based regulators such as securities exchanges).

1. *Monopolistic regulators.*

We posit that regulatory decisionmakers with monopoly authority—such as the SEC with respect to most domestic securities regulation—should have to overcome a strong presumption against intervention to correct cognitive biases. The SEC should be required to demonstrate a high likelihood of net benefits from the regulation as well as no less restrictive alternative.

Why impose such a strong presumption against intervention by the SEC and similar monopolistic regulators? Simply put, market forces are unlikely to correct the biases affecting monopolistic regulators. Without competitive pressure, biases may flourish. Just as a lack of competition gives regulators the ability to slack or direct rents from regulation to themselves, monopolistic regulators may also satisfice, employ flawed heuristics, and suffer from other cognitive biases with minimal feedback and no direct penalties. To be sure, extremely poor regulation may eventually produce a market backlash if investors exit the capital markets. But there remains considerable leeway for behavioral flaws to go uncorrected within the SEC.[215]

The SEC is not an unconstrained monopolist. Congress controls the SEC through its power over the agency's purse strings. In addition, Congress may legislate changes in the SEC's mission and any other aspect of the current securities regulatory regime through legislation. Courts also review SEC decisions. As we have discussed above, however, neither congressional oversight nor court review can correct all (or even most) biases among regulators. More significantly, the current interplay between Congress, the courts, and the SEC is not subject to significant competitive pressure. If investors do not have a choice of regulatory regime, the checks and balances represented by judicial and congressional oversight of the SEC may not be the most cost-effective means of curtailing the influence of cognitive bias on regulation. Congress, the SEC, and perhaps even judges may bend to political pressure (especially from concentrated interest groups). This interplay of political forces is not necessarily focused on investor welfare but, instead, may reflect both the interests and biases of specific groups. Judicial review and congressional oversight do not dissuade us from recommending a strong presumption against intervention by the SEC to correct market-based behavioral biases.

The combination of behavioral biases and public choice motivations of SEC regulators may also generate a one-way ratchet effect: Regulations are easy to promulgate but difficult to remove. Overconfidence may fuel self-interest to push the SEC to implement new regulations. Once new regulations are in place, the confirmation bias may lead SEC regulators to then further "buy in" to the usefulness of such regulations. Why question the status quo, which has proven so effective in the past? Feedback tending to show that regulations are imposing costs in excess of benefits will be downplayed because of the SEC's confidence in its regulatory abilities.

Various interest groups may conform their businesses to the regulatory status quo; some groups (such as attorneys, accountants, and investment bankers) may derive additional revenue from the market barriers erected by the regulations. Moreover, even poorly conceived regulations may benefit a small number of investors. Removing such regulations may produce a net social benefit by reducing costs for the overall pool of investors. Nevertheless, the minority of investors that benefit from the regulations may suffer very visible and concentrated losses, spurring regulators and Congress (operating under the availability heuristic) to preserve such regulations. The widely dispersed, and thus less observable, potential benefits from reducing regulatory costs will tend to be ignored. The SEC therefore has strong incentives to add, but few incentives to pare, regulations. Because imposing regulations is often a one-way street, monopolistic regulators should bear a heavy burden in

215. In part this is due to the fundamental strength and liquidity of the U.S. markets. *See supra* note 152 and accompanying text.

demonstrating the need to start down the street in the first place.

Further supporting the strong presumption against monopolistic regulators is the risk that heavy-handed regulatory interventions designed to address behavioral flaws may backfire.[216] While flawed, the present regulatory regime (which generally ignores investors' behavioral biases) does a reasonable job of protecting investors. The daunting task of weeding out behavioral anomalies among investors and securities professionals may inadvertently reduce the value of the present regime.

2. *The courts.*

Courts, in addition to reviewing SEC decisions, also directly implement statutory and regulatory provisions through their interpretations. For example, courts play the leading role in interpreting "materiality."[217] Although judges suffer from their own behavioral biases, we nevertheless propose only an intermediate standard for evaluating judge-made law intended to deal with investors' behavioral biases. Proponents would have to demonstrate to a judge (or judges on appeal reviewing a lower court decision) substantial evidence that the remedy chosen advances the interests of investors while not burdening the markets more than necessary.[218]

We support an intermediate presumption for several reasons. First, decentralized judge-made law poses less danger to the market than does the SEC's centralized decisions. Although SEC regulators may seek to expand their regulatory authority and prestige, judges are unlikely to share this motivation. Judges may seek to maximize their own welfare, but for many judges self-interest does not translate into greater regulatory intervention into the securities markets. The judge writing an opinion will typically be limited in his involvement to the specific case and will not reap any benefits ex post from greater regulatory intervention. Judges, therefore, are much less likely than the SEC to interpret the securities laws to expand their authority through unnecessary interference with the markets. Second, judges do not suffer from the groupthink that plagues SEC regulators. Dispersed and independent judges, unlike SEC regulators, will have heterogeneous views on how to handle securities markets problems. Judging can be a lonely job, but it does encourage judges to think for themselves.[219] Finally, the opinions of judges are subject to

216. Investors, for example, may come to believe that they are more protected than they really are due to the overconfidence bias. *See supra* note 213 and accompanying text.

217. *See, e.g.*, TSC Indus., Inc. v. Northway, Inc., 426 U.S. 438 (1976) (defining materiality for proxies).

218. As we discuss below, we do not provide an explicit plan on how to impose such a presumption on courts. At a minimum, courts could voluntarily adopt such an approach to behavioral-bias-oriented remedies.

219. There is evidence, however, that judges may systematically decide cases along ideological lines. *See* Richard L. Revesz, *Environmental Regulation, Ideology, and the D.C.*

some measure of feedback. Federal district and circuit court judges face the possibility of appellate review.[220] While monopolistic regulators may also face eventual court review, review of lower court opinions often occurs more frequently (and sooner in time).[221] Moreover, unlike monopolistic regulators, lower court judges benefit from seeing how other judges handle similar behavioral issues, which encourages an open-minded approach. Indirectly, judges compete with one another to have their views cited in the opinions of other judges. Large numbers of citations lead to greater prestige for the judges.[222]

Disclosure demonstrates the comparative advantage of courts in responding to market behavioral biases. If investors have bounded rationality, more disclosure simply makes the matter worse. The SEC, however, presently pays no attention to the problem of limited investor attention. The SEC has virtually ignored the problem of too much disclosure.[223] Every crisis of confidence in

Circuit, 83 VA. L. REV. 1717 (1997) (providing evidence from a sample of environmental law-related cases that judicial decisions in the D.C. Circuit are significantly correlated with the political party of the President who nominated particular judges); *see also* Tracey E. George, *The Dynamics and Determinants of the Decision to Grant En Banc Review*, 74 WASH. L. REV. 213, 238-39 nn.128-30 (1999) (collecting studies). *But see* Joseph A. Grundfest & A.C. Pritchard, *Statutes with Multiple Personality Disorders: The Value of Ambiguity in Statutory Design and Interpretation*, 54 STAN. L. REV. 627 (2002) (finding little evidence of a political pattern in judicial interpretations of the "strong inference" provision of the Private Securities Litigation Reform Act).

220. We would also impose an intermediate presumption on appeal against judge-fashioned remedies targeting behavioral biases.

221. The large grant of authority to the SEC to engage in regulatory rulemaking under the securities laws limits the extent of possible judicial review of SEC rulemaking. *See, e.g.*, Securities Act § 19(a), 15 U.S.C. § 77s(a) (1994) ("The Commission shall have authority from time to time to make, amend, and rescind such rules and regulations as may be necessary to carry out the provisions of [the Act]. . . ."); Exchange Act § 23, 15 U.S.C. § 78w (1994). Additionally, aggrieved parties face a general requirement that parties exhaust administrative remedies before seeking judicial review. For an overview of the exhaustion doctrine, see Rebecca L. Donnellan, *The Exhaustion Doctrine Should Not Be a Doctrine with Exceptions*, 103 W. VA. L. REV. 361 (2001) (discussing among other things the many exceptions to the exhaustion doctrine). Note that Section 9 of the Securities Act and Section 25 of the Exchange Act explicitly authorize parties aggrieved by a SEC order to seek review at a circuit court. *See* Securities Act § 9, 15 U.S.C. § 77i (1994); Exchange Act § 25, 15 U.S.C. § 78y (1994).

222. It is unclear, nonetheless, how many judges in fact will actively compete over citations. Only a few "superstar" judges may in fact capture the lion share of citations (making it not worthwhile for nonsuperstar judges to even get into the competition). *See, e.g.*, Stephen M. Bainbridge & G. Mitu Gulati, *How Do Judges Maximize? (The Same Way Everybody Else Does—Boundedly): Rules of Thumb in Securities Fraud Opinions*, 51 EMORY L.J. 83, 108-09 (2002). For a proposal to induce more competition among circuit court judges, see Stephen J. Choi & G. Mitu Gulati, *A Tournament of Judges?*, 92 CAL. L. REV. (forthcoming 2004).

223. *See* Roberta Romano, *A Comment on Information Overload, Cognitive Illusions, and Their Implications for Public Policy*, 59 S. CAL. L. REV. 313, 324 (1986) ("[A]lthough mandated disclosure to protect investors is a long-standing, albeit widely debated, policy of corporate law, the perils of information overload are virtually unnoticed in the field.").

the securities markets is met with a raft of new disclosure requirements (coincidentally expanding the SEC's authority); seldom, if ever, does the agency subtract from the laundry list of disclosure requirements. Enron, for example, led to a new set of disclosures for special purpose entities, but no reduction in required disclosure in other areas.[224] Is everything supposed to be important to the average investor? In contrast to the SEC's approach, the materiality standards devised by courts reflect the cognitive limitations facing investors. In announcing the materiality standard, the Supreme Court worried that a lower standard might cause management "to bury the shareholders in an avalanche of trivial information—a result that is hardly conducive to informed decisionmaking."[225] The SEC has shown no such restraint.

Despite the advantage of judges relative to the SEC, we think good arguments support an intermediate presumption against regulatory intervention by judges to correct cognitive biases. Dispersed nonexpert judges may lack expertise in evaluating intervention; while perhaps better motivated and less prone toward overconfidence than the SEC, the lack of expertise still leaves judicial regulation of the securities market prone to error. Judges may also face their own set of behavioral biases.[226] While self-interested judges may not maximize regulatory authority, they may instead opt for simple heuristic-like rules to get cases off their dockets.[227] Judges may prefer to dispose of cases quickly, particularly if securities law cases are a disfavored class due to their complexity or other reasons. Judges that generate quick and simple heuristics to dispose of such cases will tend to have their rules cited more often than judges who rely on standards that look to the totality of the facts and circumstances. While heuristics may cut down on decisionmaking costs, they may not produce a rule of law that provides the most cost-effective protection for investors and the capital markets. To the extent heuristics are both over and underinclusive, judge-made securities opinions aimed at investor behavioral biases may produce error-prone rules. Judges may also get caught up in framing effects. Decisions posed as a question of whether to avoid a loss to investors may result in different judicial decisions compared with decisions posed as a question of

224. *See* Proposed Rule: Disclosure in Management's Discussion and Analysis About Off-Balance Sheet Arrangements, Contractual Obligations and Contingent Liabilities and Commitments, 67 Fed. Reg. 68054-01 (proposed Nov. 8, 2002) (to be codified at 17 C.F.R. pts. 228, 229, 249).

225. TSC Indus., Inc. v. Northway, Inc., 426 U.S. 438, 448-49 (1976); *see also* Kohn v. Am. Metal Climax, Inc., 322 F. Supp. 1331 (E.D. Pa. 1970), *modified*, 458 F.2d 255 (3d Cir. 1972) (stating the buried facts doctrine of materiality).

226. *See* Rachlinski & Farina, *supra* note 20, at 577 ("From the psychological perspective, the courts are probably the institution least well-suited to making policy decisions that avoid cognitive traps.").

227. Bainbridge & Gulati, *supra* note 222, at 100-05; *see* Hillary A. Sale, *Judging Heuristics*, 35 U.C. DAVIS L. REV. 903 (2002). Donald C. Langevoort's response can be found in Donald Langevoort, *Are Judges Motivated To Create "Good" Securities Fraud Doctrine?*, 51 EMORY L.J. 309 (2002).

whether to increase overall investor welfare.[228]

228. Robert Prentice's writing unintentionally exemplifies the risk of error by judges who would interpret the securities laws from the perspective of behavioral law and economics. Taking on a "judging" role himself in second guessing courts, Prentice has written about the "irrational auditor" who jeopardizes a firm's reputation by signing off on misleading financial statements. *See* Prentice, *supra* note 147. Prentice argues at length that behavioral law and economics demonstrates the likelihood that auditors will succumb to this seemingly irrational risk to their firm's reputation. Prentice is responding to Judge Frank Easterbrook's dicta, in dismissing a securities fraud complaint against an accounting firm, that it would have been irrational for the firm and its auditors to jeopardize their reputations through complicity in an alleged fraud by the firm's client. *See id.* at 135-36 (citing DiLeo v. Ernst & Young, 901 F.2d 624 (7th Cir. 1990)). Capital markets share Easterbrook's intuition: Stock price reactions are stronger to earnings reports for firms with Big 8 (now Big 4) auditors. *See* Siew Hong Teoh & T.J. Wong, *Perceived Auditor Quality and the Earnings Response Coefficient*, 68 ACCT. REV. 346 (1993).

Prentice's attack is based on a misreading of Easterbrook's decision, apparently the result of Prentice failing to recognize the application of one of the principal cognitive biases upon which he relies (the base rate fallacy). Easterbrook's dismissal of the complaint was based not on blind faith that people do not act irrationally but rather the plaintiffs' failure to provide any evidence that irrational acts had occurred. Easterbrook argues:

> People sometimes act irrationally, but indulging ready inferences of irrationality would too easily allow the inference that ordinary business reverses are fraud. One who believes that another has behaved irrationally has to make a strong case. The complaint does not come close. *It does not identify any of E & W's auditors or explain what that person might have had to gain from covering up Continental's wrongs.*

DiLeo, 901 F.2d at 629 (emphasis added) (citations omitted). Easterbrook dismisses the complaint, not because of an irrebuttable presumption of rationality, but because the plaintiffs have alleged no facts to rebut that presumption. The complaint alleged no facts about the accounting firm that would distinguish it from any other accounting firm whose client suffered a business reversal. *C.f.* Jeffrey N. Gordon, *What Enron Means for the Management and Control of the Modern Business Corporation: Some Initial Reflections*, 69 U. CHI. L. REV. 1233, 1239 (2002) (providing account of how auditors at Arthur Andersen were compromised in the Enron audit). Far from ignoring the risk of cognitive bias, Easterbrook imposes a rule that avoids the temptation to fall into the base rate fallacy. Most business reversals are just business reversals. The overall rate of fraud by corporations is very low, and the percentage of those frauds in which the auditors participate is lower still. Prentice acknowledges these facts, but fails to recognize their significance for Easterbrook's approach. *See* Prentice, *supra* note 147 ("[I]n the general run of things, there is no reason to suspect that auditors are auditing fraudulently or recklessly, any more than there is reason to believe that drivers are driving recklessly. Most audits are completed competently, just as most car trips are."). The temptation—when faced by the salient evidence of huge losses that typically prompt securities fraud suits—is to ignore this very low base rate in assessing whether there has been fraud. *See id.* at 158-59 (discussing representativeness heuristic). That temptation is enhanced by the "hindsight bias"; the auditors "must have known" of the fraud when it was being committed in light of the subsequently revealed evidence. *See* Baruch Fischhoff, *For Those Condemned to Study the Past: Heuristics and Biases in Hindsight*, *in* JUDGMENT AND UNCERTAINTY: HEURISTICS AND BIASES 335, 341 (Daniel Kahneman, Paul Slovic & Amos Tversky eds., 1982) (*quoted in* Jeffrey J. Rachlinski, *A Positive Psychological Theory of Judging in Hindsight*, 65 U. CHI. L. REV. 571, 572 (1998)) ("In hindsight, people consistently exaggerate what could have been anticipated in foresight. They not only tend to view what has happened as having been inevitable but also to view it as having appeared 'relatively inevitable' before it happened. People believe that others should have been able to anticipate events much better than was actually the case."). The "very high barrier," *see* Prentice, *supra* note 147, at 138, erected by Easterbrook simply

Finally, judge-made law may suffer from its own form of the one-way ratchet effect. Judges may be less likely to intrude on the market than SEC officials, but once judges take behavioral biases into account, the force of precedent may lead other judges addressing similar issues to adopt the same position in subsequent cases. Judges face little competitive pressure to overcome their cognitive failings.[229] Without the disciplining effect of a potential loss of market share or other feedback, we doubt that judges will learn to overcome their cognitive failings. Market participants also will adjust their behavior to take into account new judge-made securities law. Consider a judicial opinion that defines materiality to reflect the disclosure needs of behaviorally challenged investors. Investors, once aware of this change, may be less skeptical in interpreting information (given the added protection of antifraud liability), which may then leave them more exposed to fraud. Subsequent judges may then find even prior, ill-advised changes to the definition of materiality now justified given the reduced vigilance of investors. Because of the effect of precedent and the practical difficulties of reversing past judicial opinions, we favor an intermediate presumption against allowing judges to take investor behavioral biases into account in their decisions.

3. *Competitive regulators.*

Our current regime, under which competition counters the behavioral biases of investors, but not those of regulators, is not preordained. One could, instead, subject securities regulation to the forces of market competition.[230] Securities regulators faced with competition would have less latitude to ignore their own behavioral biases. Regulators that failed to organize their institutional structure to reduce the impact of such biases would lose companies and investors to competing jurisdictions.[231] For this reason, we propose that

requires the plaintiff to offer *some* evidence that this case differs from the overwhelming percentage of nonfraud cases represented by the base rate. That approach makes perfect sense from the perspective of behavioral economics. Prentice's selective use of cognitive defects is, at a minimum, a warning that judges must handle the insights of behavioral economics with care. In the absence of an organizing theory of cognitive bias, particular biases can be invoked to support or criticize almost any judicial decision.

229. *See* Jeffrey J. Rachlinski, *supra* note 189, at 64 ("Civil engineers who build faulty buildings will quickly find themselves without clients, but courts are public resources that do not face true competitive pressures. Judges surely have some incentives to make good law and avoid illusions of judgment, but they lack the incentives that other institutions face.") (footnote omitted).

230. *See, e.g.*, Choi & Guzman, *supra* note 10; Roberta Romano, *Empowering Investors: A Market Approach to Securities Regulation*, 107 YALE L.J. 2359 (1998).

231. *See* Arlen, *supra* note 20, at 1782 ("[I]n some circumstances, high quality firms may have an incentive to encourage consumers to focus on the risks associated with low quality products."). The one area that the SEC does face competition—listings by foreign issuers—does reflect the influence of market pressures. Foreign issuers are relieved of a number of the more onerous requirements imposed on domestic public companies. *See*

regulators facing substantial competition from other regulators must overcome only a weak presumption against intervention. Under this weak presumption, regulators need only show a likelihood of net benefits when intervening to correct behavioral biases.[232]

The global capital markets have already moved toward greater competition. Investors today can choose where to place their money, including most prominently the NYSE, the London Stock Exchange, the Deutsche Börse, and the Tokyo Stock Exchange.[233] To the extent behavioral biases reduce the value of one of these securities markets, competition provides a large incentive for regulators to implement reforms to reduce such biases. The lack of any obvious responses to behavioral biases by these competing securities exchanges calls into question the magnitude of such biases. The choice present in the global capital markets, nevertheless, is somewhat limited. Investors cannot invest on

---

Securities Exchange Act Rule 3a12-3(b), 17 C.F.R. § 240.3a12-3 (2003) (exempting foreign issuers from insider trading restrictions and proxy rules). Policies deemed essential to investor protection when applied to domestic companies are mysteriously nonessential when applied to foreign companies. Regulation FD, for example, applies only to domestic issuers. *But see* Merritt B. Fox, *Regulation FD and Foreign Issuers: Globalization's Strains and Opportunities*, 41 VA. J. INT'L L. 653 (2001) (arguing that Regulation FD's exemption for foreign issuers is justified). And American markets are already feeling the effect of the reaction by Congress and the SEC to Enron, WorldCom, and other accounting scandals. Foreign companies that were considering U.S. listings have decided against it; some foreign issuers may decide to withdraw from the American market rather than comply with these new regulations. *See Porsche Won't List Shares in the U.S.*, WALL ST. J., Oct. 17, 2002, at C16 ("A factor in Porsche's decision was the new U.S. rule demanding that chief executives and chief financial officers of U.S.-listed companies attest to the accuracy of their financial results."). Perhaps for this reason, the SEC's proposed rules on audit committee requirements pursuant to the Sarbanes-Oxley Act, while not completely exempting foreign issuers, provide for a number of specific exemptions. *See* Standards Relating to Listed Company Audit Committees, 68 Fed. Reg. 2638-01 (proposed Jan. 17, 2003) (to be codified at 17 C.F.R. pts. 228, 229, 240, 249, 274).

232. Despite the current dearth of competition, some adherents of the behavioralist school seem oblivious to the possibility that the existing regulatory structure is anything less than perfect. Robert Prentice, for example, claims: "*If* issuers and brokers opt into a relatively full measure of public regulation, then investor regulation really would not accomplish much. It would not save any money or create any meaningful efficiencies. Issuers, for example, would continue to bear the expense of full disclosure and antifraud liability." Prentice, *supra* note 14, at 1408. Prentice implicitly assumes that even in a system of full choice everyone would view the present regime as "optimal." Every regulation is the best in this best of all possible regulated worlds. If the SEC faced competition, is it realistic to expect that the SEC would not change *any* of its policies? The available evidence from markets in which government and private entities compete to provide a service contradicts this assumption. To take a familiar example, it is difficult to believe that government institutions of higher learning are not affected by competition from private universities. Our personal experience at state universities is that the policies of private universities are a very real constraint on the (in)efficiencies of our schools.

233. For a discussion on the growing competition among global securities exchanges, see John C. Coffee, Jr., *Racing Towards the Top?: The Impact of Cross-Listings and Stock Market Competition on International Corporate Governance*, 102 COLUM. L. REV. 1757 (2002).

the NYSE without automatically coming under the protection of the U.S. securities laws.[234] For investors and issuers desiring access to the U.S. capital markets, the SEC still enjoys a regulatory monopoly.

Under what conditions will regulatory competition enhance investor welfare (the so-called "race to the top")? On the one hand, rational and fully informed investors will incorporate the value to investors of an issuer's selection of a particular regulatory regime into the company's stock price. Issuers will then have an incentive to opt into regimes offering value-increasing investor protections. On the other hand, investors that operate under extreme levels of behavioral biases may miscalculate the value of competing sets of regulatory protections. If so, competition may not improve investor welfare.

Nonetheless, even when behavioral biases affect investors, different investors may be more or less affected by such biases. Larger institutional investors may have enough self-awareness of their own susceptibility to behavioral biases to appreciate a regime that protects them against such biases.[235] For example, an institution may realize that its managers may suffer from overconfidence, the availability heuristic, and so on. If a regulatory regime truly solves these problems, the institution may protect itself from the foibles of its own agents by adopting a policy of investing only in companies opting into a protective regime (or discounting companies that do not). To the

234. For a discussion of the current tie between securities markets and the securities regulatory regime, see Choi & Guzman, *supra* note 10, at 918.

235. And the endowment effect suggests that investors will be reluctant to cede protections that they currently enjoy, even if they would have been unwilling to pay the price to obtain the protections in the first instance. *See* Jack L. Knetsch & J.A. Sinden, *Willingness to Pay and Compensation Demanded: Experimental Evidence of an Unexpected Disparity in Measures of Value*, 99 Q.J. ECON. 507 (1984) (reporting results from a series of experiments showing that people demand more in compensation for a loss compared with their willingness to pay for an equivalent-sized gain). If so, even the cognitively challenged may then free ride off the selectiveness of more informed and rational investors. On the other side of the equation, executives of firms choosing a listing are likely to underestimate their probability of being sanctioned by a regulator (to the extent that only a low probability of being sanctioned exists). *See* Weinstein, *supra* note 28, at 810 (finding that people underestimate their probability of being sued); *see also* Christine Jolls, *Behavioral Economics Analysis of Redistributive Legal Rules*, 51 VAND. L. REV. 1653, 1663 (1998) ("It is difficult to come up with examples of events giving rise to individual liability the probability of which is likely to be overestimated rather than . . . underestimated."). (Of course, they may periodically overestimate after recent salient examples of enforcement.) This tendency to underestimate personal risks is particularly pronounced for events that are perceived to be within the individual's control. *See* Peter Harris, *Sufficient Grounds for Optimism?: The Relationship Between Perceived Controllability and Optimistic Bias*, 15 J. SOC. & CLINICAL PSYCHOL. 9 (1996). Consequently, corporate managers will perceive little risk to selecting regulatory regimes with the most vigorously enforced standards. Investors, by contrast, will be less likely to be overoptimistic in their chances of avoiding fraud, which is largely beyond their ability to control. If so, cognitive biases may help fuel a "race to the top," or even overshooting the top. Of course, this argument may be all wrong. Without knowing the extent of biases or how they interact, predictions of how policies will work in practice are little more than guesswork.

extent that large institutional investors' decisions are incorporated into the stock market price, smaller investors may free ride on the price since it incorporates information about the value of behavioral protections provided through a particular regulatory regime.

Even without any conscious recognition of behavioral biases, institutional and individual investors will flock to regimes offering higher overall returns (for a given level of risk). If behavioral biases reduce returns then investors eventually will abandon such regimes and search for alternatives offering higher returns. Issuers seeking the capital of those investors will then follow suit. For example, suppose the NYSE mandates a minimal trading delay, which reduces the effect of behavioral biases, increasing overall returns for investors.[236] Assume that NASDAQ does not adopt such a delay. Even without knowledge of the precise mechanisms by which returns are increased, investors generally will shift to companies trading on the NYSE, as returns increase (leading more companies to list on the NYSE, thereby increasing overall trading volume and the profitability of NYSE member brokers).

The market, of course, may not behave so efficiently; the example of a trading delay above is unlikely as long as exchanges' profitability is tied to trading volume.[237] Or maybe the market will be unable to overcome pervasive behavioral biases affecting the estimation of institutional investors of their own biases or difficulties that investors face in comparing returns across markets. Such inefficiencies are plausible; the recent performance of the U.S. stock market supports the possibility of stock bubbles.[238] Some market participants may attempt to take systematic advantage of the behavioral biases of the less sophisticated (and opt into regimes facilitating such opportunistic behavior). And to the extent new (and behaviorally naïve) investors constantly enter the market, opportunistic participants may have a steady pool of investors upon which to prey. In the long run, bubbles burst. Eventually, investors may become suspicious of a particular regulatory regime fostering opportunism. But, during this "long run," many investors may in fact lose large sums of money.

To reduce the possibility of only a "long run" adjustment, the government could rely on a hybrid between government oversight and market-based regulators, including existing self-regulatory organizations. Securities

236. For a discussion of trading delays and their role in reducing behavioral biases, see *infra* Part III.B.3.

237. Trading delays, like any other transaction cost, are likely to reduce the overall number of trades, an unattractive outcome for the exchanges. *See* Adam C. Pritchard, *Self-Regulation and Securities Markets*, 26 REGULATION 32 (2003).

238. Certainly the belief that a stock market bubble existed toward the end of the 1990s is prevalent in the financial press. *See* Dennis K. Berman, Julia Angwin & Chip Cummins, *Tricks of the Trade: As Market Bubble Neared End, Bogus Swaps Provided a Lift*, WALL ST. J., Dec. 23, 2002, at A1; Ianthe Jeanne Dugan, *Fingers Point at New Jersey Fund: Pension Operation Racks Up Huge Losses Since Bubble Burst, Prompting Suits and Shake-up*, WALL ST. J., Dec. 19, 2002, at C1.

exchanges, for example, already have incentives to implement investor-related protections.[239] To the extent investors are better protected when investing in firms that trade on a particular exchange, the exchange (and its members) will earn greater revenues in the form of listing fees as well as commissions on trading volume.[240] Just as a securities exchange can protect rational investors (who may lack information or expertise to protect themselves), exchanges can also provide protections for behaviorally challenged investors. Exchanges may also have more expertise than more distant regulators in determining the types and magnitudes of biases affecting investors.[241]

The SEC may then enhance the competition among exchanges, monitoring the regulation provided by private exchanges.[242] As under the current self-regulatory organization (SRO) regime,[243] we see value in having exchanges justify their proposed regulations to the SEC. Requiring private exchanges to submit to SEC review may lead the exchanges to avoid many possible behavioral biases themselves.[244] If private regulators must justify their actions, they will be less likely to employ shortcut heuristics. Spelling out the case for new private regulations may also help expose over-reliance on salient information and combat overconfidence. Moreover, the SEC, with its expertise, may prove a better monitor than the judiciary or Congress. An independent SEC may also avoid cognitive dissonance lock-in effects in reviewing private regulatory actions adopted by exchanges and other SROs.

The SEC therefore may have a limited role to play in providing a safety net for regulatory competition, protecting against the fear that behavioral biases may lead issuers to select ever-decreasing levels of investor protection. Moreover, placing the SEC in a secondary position of monitoring exchange-provided protections lessens the risk that the SEC will use its monopoly power

239. *See* Paul G. Mahoney, *The Exchange as Regulator*, 83 VA. L. REV. 1453 (1997); Pritchard, *supra* note 10, at 925.

240. *But see* Stephen Craig Pirrong, *The Self-Regulation of Commodity Exchanges: The Case of Market Manipulation*, 38 J.L. & ECON. 141 (1995) (arguing that exchanges will have suboptimal incentives to combat market manipulation because it may increase trading volume).

241. Prentice argues that investors did not bargain for the right level of disclosure before the passage of the federal securities laws. *See* Prentice, *supra* note 14, at 1453. But as Prentice acknowledges, there is no evidence that investors demanded more regulation than the NYSE provided. Nonetheless, Prentice claims to know that investors failed to bargain for the correct level of disclosure. He does not explain, however, how he knows what the right level is. Regardless, the more relevant question than what the NYSE did in the nineteenth century is what would the NYSE be doing today if the SEC had not been invented?

242. *See* Pritchard, *supra* note 10.

243. *See* Securities Exchange Act of 1934 § 19, 15 U.S.C.§ 78s (2003). The SEC has the power to approve, disapprove, or modify SRO rules as it "deems necessary or appropriate to insure the fair administration of the self-regulatory organization" among other things. 15 U.S.C. § 78s(c) (2003).

244. *See generally* Jennifer S. Lerner & Philip E. Tetlock, *Accounting for the Effects of Accountability*, 125 PSYCHOL. BULL. 255 (1999) (surveying evidence on the effects of accountability on decisionmaking).

to push forward unwarranted protections (or protections designed to expand the SEC's own authority). Once limited to reviewing regulations (rather than imposing its own regulations), the SEC's confirmation bias will be reduced. Overconfidence will also play less of a role in SEC review to the extent that the SEC itself does not initially generate exchange-based regulatory initiatives (or become involved in their implementation).[245]

When behavioral biases pervade the market, competition may not fully weed them out. Nonetheless, even possibly imperfect competition may better address behavioral biases than would a monopolistic regulator. While the possibility of a "race to the bottom" theoretically exists (fueled perhaps by opportunistic issuers and other market participants seeking to exploit behaviorally challenged investors), we believe that the presence of more rational investors (and a pricing mechanism to transmit their choices to others), as well as the ongoing desire of investors to seek markets with higher returns, reduces the downside likelihood of a "race to the bottom." Moreover, without the threat of competition, we cannot know if biases are inevitable or merely an excuse for poor regulatory decisionmaking.[246] Indeed, competition may lead regulatory regimes seeking to attract investors to adopt those oversight mechanisms (including judicial review and legislative oversight) that provide the most cost-effective means of reducing biases among regulators. Competition would provide greater assurance that judicial review and legislative oversight reduce regulator biases to the net benefit of investor welfare.[247]

---

245. Significantly, we focus on the SEC's authority to review exchange-based decisions. We are less supportive of the SEC's power to modify unilaterally exchange rules (including adding new rules), which empowers the SEC to force exchanges to adopt SEC initiatives. *See* Securities Exchange Act of 1933 § 19, 15 U.S.C. § 78s (2003). This authority opens the backdoor for the SEC to use exchanges to forward its own mandatory regulatory agenda subject to the behavioral biases plaguing regulators without any tempering from competition.

246. The possibility of regulatory competition may not eliminate all biases within regulators. As with private securities market institutions, organizational illusions will remain within regulators. *See supra* text accompanying notes 74-94 (discussing the behavioral biases afflicting securities market institutions). Nonetheless, those biases that persist will be those that make the regulators more effective. For example, overconfidence and groupthink may, to some extent, help make the SEC a cohesive body with high morale. As with private organizations, the competitive environment then necessarily limits the impact of such biases. Where overconfidence and groupthink are so extensive as to reduce the value of the SEC's provided regulations to investors in a competitive environment, investors will switch to the regulatory protections of a competing supplier.

247. Despite our analysis, some may remain unconvinced of the value of regulatory competition in reducing the influence of behavioral biases on regulators. Those skeptical of competition, therefore, may wish to adopt a greater presumption against regulatory intervention targeting behavioral biases (including possible intermediate or strict levels of presumptions against intervention). Our central point, however, is that those who question the ability of even competitive regulators to effectively counteract investors' biases should also question the ability of monopolistic regulators (cushioned against any form of competitive pressure) to do so, lending support for our strict presumption against

B. *Forms of Regulatory Intervention*

Behaviorally challenged regulators present the distinct risk of ill-advised intervention to correct investor behavioral biases. Moreover, the same behaviorally challenged regulators may refuse to recognize their errors, compounding the costs to investors over time. The form of regulatory intervention, in turn, has considerable influence on the overall cost of potential regulatory error. The presumption against regulatory intervention should correspondingly vary with the magnitude of potential error.

In this section we canvass three forms of intervention: (1) regulations that restrict the range of available investments, directly supplanting market decisionmakers; (2) regulations that adjust existing securities regulatory provisions in ways that may indirectly supplant the market (through excessive regulatory costs leading to fewer investment choices); and (3) regulations that influence investors' decisions, but only minimally restrict their available choices.

1. *Restricting investment options.*

We contend that regulators seeking to supplant the market in order to correct behavioral biases should bear the burden of overcoming a strong presumption against regulation. Such market-supplanting interventions should be supported by evidence demonstrating a high likelihood of net benefits of the regulations and the lack of any less restrictive alternative, thereby minimizing potential errors.

For those convinced of the severity of behavioral biases among investors, depriving investors of certain investment options has obvious appeal. The most extreme version of this approach is merit regulation (surprisingly ignored by adherents of the behavioral approach) under which regulators simply remove "undesirable" investments from the market altogether.[248] Put simply, if investors lack the ability to make good investment decisions then why not have regulators make this decision for investors?

Behavioral economics, if taken seriously, would seem to point to merit regulation. Will behavioral economics take us back to the quasi-socialist interventionism advocated by William O. Douglas and his fellow travelers?[249] Given the well-known defects of merit regulation, this agenda seems unlikely

intervention for relatively monopolistic regulators.

248. Note that it is unclear what exactly constitutes "undesirable" investments. High risk investments are not necessarily undesirable if they provide a correspondingly high return.

249. *See* William O. Douglas, *Protecting the Investor*, 23 YALE REV. 521, 524 (1934) (bemoaning the lack of merit regulation in the Securities Act: most investors have neither "the time, money, nor intelligence to assimilate the mass of information in the registration statement").

to gather steam.[250] Merit regulation founders on the problem facing any central planner in a complex economy: Even expert regulators cannot begin to assign relative values to every single investment. Throw in the element of change in a dynamic economy and the problem becomes overwhelming. Indeed, the limits of regulators attempting merit regulation can be viewed as one of bounded rationality. Decentralized market actors following the "invisible hand" bring much greater aggregate processing power and localized knowledge to bear in determining the proper allocation of capital and other resources to meet people's preferences.[251] No single regulatory body, no matter how expert, can hope to match the capacity to value securities of greed-driven market participants.[252] The worldwide collapse of socialism leaves little room for debate on the superiority of decentralized markets over central planners. Taken to its logical extreme, behavioral economics offers the questionable benefit of North Korean-style efficiency to our financial markets.

Perhaps we are unduly pessimistic; less invasive regulatory options are available. One example would be precluding trading in the (worthless) shares of bankrupt companies.[253] Regulators also could require certain investors to invest through market intermediaries.[254] Regulators could similarly restrict the choices available to unsophisticated investors to a subset of the investment opportunities in the market. This strategy has already been implemented in part. For nonaccredited individual investors, for example, few (if any) opportunities exist to invest in securities of firms that choose not to register their securities in a public offering.[255] Nonetheless, any issuer may overcome this barrier by registering its securities offering with the SEC and making the required disclosures, thereby gaining access to *all* investors.[256] Proponents of the view that investors suffer from behavioral biases may wonder whether the disclosure

250. *See* Rutherford B. Campbell, Jr., *An Open Attack on the Nonsense of Blue Sky Regulation*, 10 J. CORP. L. 553, 563-67 (1985) (criticizing state blue sky merit regulation); Mark A. Sargent, *A Future for Blue Sky Law*, 62 U. CIN. L. REV. 471 (1993) (chronicling the demise of merit regulation).

251. *See* 1 ADAM SMITH, AN INQUIRY INTO THE NATURE AND CAUSES OF THE WEALTH OF NATIONS 456 (R.H. Campbell, A.S. Skinner & W.B. Todd eds., Liberty Classics 1981) (1776).

252. Ivan Boesky during the 1980s actively pushed the notion that "greed is good." *See* DOUGLAS FRANTZ, LEVINE & CO.: WALL STREET'S INSIDER TRADING SCANDAL 145 (1987) (noting that Boesky stated at a UC Berkeley Business School graduation that "Greed is all right, by the way. I want you to know that. I think greed is healthy. You can be greedy and still feel good about yourself.").

253. *See* Marc Hopkins, *Shares of Distressed Firms Still Sell*, WALL ST. J., Jan. 22, 2003, at B4 (discussing active trading in shares of bankrupt companies even after companies have disclosed that common stock will be wiped out in reorganization).

254. *See* Choi, *supra* note 66, at 290-96.

255. *See infra* notes 260-62 and accompanying text (describing private placements).

256. Public registration involves, among other things, the creation and filing of a registration statement with the SEC. For a description of the registration process, see JAMES D. COX, ROBERT W. HILLMAN & DONALD C. LANGEVOORT, SECURITIES REGULATION: CASES AND MATERIALS 211-321 (2d ed. 1997).

required for a public offering in fact addresses the needs of the behaviorally challenged.[257] Those who doubt the value of disclosure in rectifying behavioral biases among investors may instead wish to cabin the securities choices available to investors with higher levels of behavioral biases.

Although potentially the most effective means of addressing behavioral biases among investors, regulations designed to supplant market decisionmakers also pose the greatest risk of error. To begin, it may be difficult to sort the investors who need to be protected from themselves from those who should be given free rein in devising their investment strategies. Competitive pressures may suffice for investors who act completely rationally and seek to maximize their overall investment return (given their preference for risk). On the other hand, policymakers might improve overall investor welfare by limiting securities transactions if they were confident that they were curtailing primarily speculatively motivated trades.[258] This response, of course, assumes that policy intervention to discourage such trades is justified.[259]

How do we distinguish investors recklessly speculating from those prudently rebalancing their portfolios based on fundamental analysis of company prospects? These trades all look alike as they come across the ticker. How can we sort these rational traders from those investors wracked with cognitive illusions, loss aversion tendencies, and the availability heuristic? Regulators who cannot make such distinctions run the risk of providing unneeded and costly regulatory protections for many investors who do not want or need them.

The problem of partitioning investors is not new. The private placement exemption under the securities laws allows investors who can "fend for themselves" more latitude to invest in relatively less-regulated private placement offerings.[260] Even in this well-trodden field, controversy exists on how to determine if an investor qualifies as sophisticated.[261] Determining which investors may suffer from behavioral biases poses an even more

257. *See supra* Part II.B (questioning the ability of disclosure to correct for behavioral biases).

258. *See* Stout, *supra* note 61 (contending that many investors engage in wasteful, speculative trades).

259. *See supra* Part I.B (discussing the possibility that some investors have preferences for speculation in their investments and noting that the argument to hinder such preferences is far from clear).

260. SEC v. Ralston Purina Co., 346 U.S. 119, 125 (1953) (introducing the concept of investors being able to "fend for themselves" in interpreting the scope of § 4(2)'s exemption from the Securities Act's registration requirements under § 5). A safe harbor for private placements is provided under Regulation D of the Securities Act. *See* 17 C.F.R. §§ 230.501-508 (2003).

261. *See* C. Edward Fletcher, III, *Sophisticated Investors Under the Federal Securities Laws*, 1988 DUKE L.J. 1081; Howard M. Friedman, *On Being Rich, Accredited, and Undiversified: The Lacunae in Contemporary Securities Regulation*, 47 OKLA. L. REV. 291 (1994); *see also* Choi, *supra* note 66, at 310-18 (proposing both mandatory and voluntary licensing schemes to distinguish among investors).

daunting task. Because no unifying theory explains why we suffer from behavioral biases, we cannot predict which investors suffer from biases, nor can we gauge the magnitude of these biases. Generalizations are possible. Expert investors, for example, may suffer from fewer availability and framing biases. Their experience and training "allow" them to "see" such biases and avoid them. For example, Wall Street veterans warn newcomers "Don't confuse brains and a bull market," a reminder about the risks of self-serving justification and failure to pay heed to the base rate of investment success.[262] On the other hand, experts may suffer more from overoptimism and heuristics when applying their expertise in areas outside their primary area.[263] Without some underlying theory of biases, we cannot say whether the magnitude of biases afflicting experts is greater (or lesser) than the biases of ordinary investors. Absent the ability to distinguish among investors, crafting regulatory responses to behavioral biases becomes a guessing game.[264]

One response might be that all investors are equally behaviorally challenged and thus equally in need of regulatory intervention.[265] Alternatively, one might contend that, as a normative matter, we should target our regulatory efforts to protect those least cognitively able. Distinguishing among investors then becomes a nonissue (as all regulatory protections focus on the least able regardless of the actual sophistication of particular investors). We think that this response ignores a number of potential costs.

First, even inexperienced and cognitively challenged investors are capable of learning. Once freed of the responsibility and discipline of making investment decisions, investors lose the feedback mechanism that facilitates such learning. Indeed, some investors may come to believe (overoptimistically) that regulatory protections fully insulate them from investment risks. When this is not true (and even merit regulation cannot eliminate all investment risks) investors with overconfidence in the power of regulation will then take even less care and may face a greater risk of facing large financial losses as a result.

Second, supplanting markets limits the ability of investors to ameliorate the effects of ill-conceived forms of regulation, leading to higher error costs. Merit regulation and other means of restricting choices curtail investment options in the United States. As an alternative, U.S. investors and issuers may attempt to engage in capital market transactions outside the United States. Both U.S. issuers and investors, however, face higher transaction costs in finding overseas

262. Heath et al., *supra* note 98, at 1, 6 (citation omitted).

263. Griffin & Tversky, *supra* note 28, at 430 (showing that experts tend to be more overconfident in their predictions than laypeople).

264. *Cf.* Choi, supra note 66, at 310-19 (advancing proposals to distinguish investors based on licensing exams and to allow investors some degree of choice in their own self-classification).

265. *See* Prentice, *supra* note 14, at 1450 ("[M]any if not most investors, even with more information, will be unable to adequately protect themselves under [an issuer choice regime].").

markets in which to transact, plus the potential for foreign securities regulations that conflict with the demands of U.S. regulatory requirements.

Finally, regulations that remove choice from investors also risk the one-way ratchet effect. Markets work, but not if regulation chokes them. Once regulations supplant the market, investors' decisionmaking skills may atrophy. Intermediaries that aid investors may exit the market. If regulations leave investors incapable of protecting themselves and thwart institutions that could help, regulatory protections that were originally unwarranted may become essential. Before regulators trigger this self-fulfilling scenario of investor dependency, regulators should overcome a strong presumption against interventions that remove choice.

2. *Adjusting existing securities regulation.*

Regulators may account for behavioral biases in other ways. In particular, regulators may adjust the contours of existing regulatory provisions to counteract cognitive illusions. While intervention of this sort will not eliminate investment options completely, it may hinder (greatly) such choices. We propose that intervention into the contours of existing securities regulation, to correct for behavioral biases, must overcome a medium presumption under which regulators must show a substantial likelihood of net benefits.

While current securities regulations cover many facets of the securities markets, here we discuss three: the definition of materiality, antifraud liability, and the gun-jumping rules for registered public offerings. Disclosure forms the central focus of most of the federal securities laws. In a public offering, issuers must put together a registration statement for filing with the SEC and must distribute a statutory prospectus widely to the securities market as part of the offering.[266] Most publicly traded issuers also must comply with periodic disclosure filing requirements.[267] From a behavioral perspective, however, disclosure risks confusing investors already suffering from bounded rationality, availability, and hindsight.

---

266. *See* COX ET AL., *supra* note 256, at 211-321.

267. The Exchange Act imposes periodic information reporting requirements for certain issuers, commonly known as "Exchange Act reporting companies." Companies listed on a national securities exchange as well as companies whose total assets exceed $10 million and have a class of equity security (other than an exempted security) held of record by more than 500 shareholders, among others, must register and comply with the SEC's periodic information disclosure requirements, and must register the securities under the Exchange Act and thereby come under the periodic reporting requirements of § 13(a). *See* Securities Exchange Act of 1934 §§ 12(b), 12(g), 13(a), 15 U.S.C. §§ 78l(b), 78l(g), 78m(a) (2003); *see also* 17 C.F.R. § 240.12g-1 (2003) (raising asset requirement to $10 million). These required periodic information filings include annual Form 10-K, quarterly Form 10-Q, and occasional Form 8-K documents. *See* 15 U.S.C. § 78m(a) (2003); 17 C.F.R. § 240.13a-1 (2003) (providing rules on periodic disclosure requirements of Exchange Act registered companies); 17 C.F.R. § 249.310 (2003) (Exchange Act Form 10-K); 17 C.F.R. § 249.308 (2003) (Exchange Act Form 8-K); 17 C.F.R. § 249.308a (2003) (Exchange Act Form 10-Q).

This risk of confusion calls into question the threshold materiality requirement used throughout the securities laws' disclosure provisions.[268] Current securities regulations take an objective approach, defining materiality in terms of what information a reasonable investor would want in light of the total mix of information presently available in the market.[269] If many investors suffer from behavioral biases, the "reasonable" investor becomes more difficult to identify. But how would we alter the standard? If investors are easily led astray by overoptimism, then perhaps a broader definition of materiality is required. For example, the definition might be expanded to include "puffery" that could trigger overoptimism.[270] On the other hand, bounded rationality implies that investors will have limited attention spans—requiring more disclosure may cause them to ignore more important information.[271] Indeed, armed with an overconfident sense of his ability to digest mountains of disclosure, an investor may miss important aspects of disclosure.[272] Bounded rationality may therefore lead one to recommend a *narrower* concept of materiality for securities disclosure to reduce the amount of information given to investors.[273]

Adjusting information disclosure to ameliorate behavioral biases of investors is a difficult and error-prone task. Moreover, limiting information flows for the benefit of the behaviorally challenged will undermine the ability of more rational investors to value securities accurately. The result could be diminished securities market efficiency. Reduced market efficiency may then increase the risk to investors of putting money into new securities offerings, raising the cost of capital and thereby constricting the range of available

---

268. Rule 408 of the Securities Act, for example, provides: "In addition to the information expressly required to be included in a registration statement, there shall be added such further material information, if any, as may be necessary to make the required statements, in the light of the circumstances under which they are made, not misleading." 17 C.F.R. § 230.408 (2003).

269. *See* TSC Indus. v. Northway Inc., 426 U.S. 438, 449 (1976).

270. Many courts today exclude puffery from the definition of materiality. *See* Eisenstadt v. Centel Corp., 113 F.3d 738, 746 (7th Cir. 1997); *see also* Jennifer O'Hare, *The Resurrection of the Dodo: The Unfortunate Re-emergence of the Puffery Defense in Private Securities Fraud Actions*, 59 OHIO ST. L.J. 1697, 1697 (1998) (arguing that "courts have misused the puffery defense and have improperly insulated companies from civil liability for their misrepresentations").

271. Robert Prentice notes "that investors typically do not read disclosure documents when investing in securities." Prentice, *supra* note 14, at 1456; *see also* DAVID A. HIRSHLEIFER, SONYA SEONGYEON LIM & SIEW HONG TEOH, DISCLOSURE TO A CREDULOUS AUDIENCE: THE ROLE OF LIMITED ATTENTION (Dice Ctr., Working Paper No. 2002-3, 2002), *available at* http://papers.ssrn.com/sol3/papers.cfm?abstract_id=344160 (modeling the impact of limited attention on the part of investors on the incentives of firms to disclose information).

272. *See* Daniel et al., *supra* note 19, at 60 ("Greater disclosure is not an unalloyed virtue, because investors can lose the forest for the trees.").

273. This narrower conception is embodied today within the buried facts doctrine. *See supra* note 225 and accompanying text.

investment opportunities for investors.

Closely related to disclosure are the various antifraud provisions of the securities laws.[274] Stringent antifraud provisions (and accompanying private and public enforcement) help ensure that the disclosures made to investors are truthful and accurate. Even if investors cannot process information rationally, the threat of private litigation and public enforcement may deter fraud and opportunistic behavior. As with disclosure, materiality forms a key component of antifraud liability.[275] Regulators attempting to expand the definition of materiality to take into account the range of behavioral biases may fail to gauge accurately the extent of such biases. Expanding the materiality concept may also lead to more frivolous lawsuits, thereby impairing the value of antifraud liability as a deterrent against fraud.[276] Firms may also reduce their disclosures in an effort to avoid their exposure to fraud suits. Both frivolous suits and reduced disclosure will raise the cost of capital, once again resulting in fewer investment opportunities for investors.[277]

Another concern with altering antifraud standards to accommodate cognitive biases is that corporate managers and accountants may not engage in fraud consciously. Fraud traditionally requires scienter. Misleading information, however, may be the byproduct of the cognitive failings of managers and accountants and their organizations. The tendency toward

274. For an overview of the antifraud provisions of the U.S. securities laws, see COX ET AL., *supra* note 256, at 589-649, 681-774.

275. Rule 10b-5 makes it unlawful for any person "to make any untrue statement of a material fact or to omit to state a material fact necessary in order to make the statements made, in the light of the circumstances under which they were made, not misleading . . . ." (assuming the other requirements of Rule 10b-5 are met). Securities Exchange Act Rule 10b-5, 17 C.F.R. § 240.10b-5 (2003).

276. For a summary of the frivolous lawsuit literature, see James Bohn & Stephen Choi, *Fraud in the New-Issues Market: Empirical Evidence on Securities Class Actions*, 144 U. PA. L. REV. 903, 918-23 (1996).

277. Another complication for strategies to alter the materiality standard to correct behavioral biases is that many biases may vary in intensity and impact with the market context. *See, e.g.*, Arlen et al., *supra* note 29, at 33 (reporting evidence that the endowment effect varies by context). Reported instances of fraud, for example, may be particularly salient information for investors attempting to gauge market risks. Investors suffering from the availability heuristic, however, will draw inappropriate inferences from the revelation of fraud. When an Enron-type situation is disclosed, investors may overreact, withdrawing too much money from the markets. Conversely, when no major frauds have been disclosed recently, investors may be too sanguine about their investments. Regulators attempting to correct for such fluctuations in the views of investors may be tempted to change the antifraud and disclosure regimes to accommodate this variation. Materiality, for example, could be expanded to cover a wider range of information in times when investor confidence is low to induce more capital flow into the market. Such constant accommodation, however, is an enormous task—and therefore subject to a much greater degree of error (and possible investor confusion as the standards for antifraud liability change). On the other hand, the fraud regime may in fact already vary implicitly on the salience of recent fraud without any intervention by regulators, if highly publicized fraud makes jurors more willing to impose liability on businesses. *See* Orey & Geyelin, *supra* note 69.

overoptimism may result in a cascade of only optimistic information from the bottom of a corporate hierarchy to the top, magnifying the positive aspects of information flows perhaps to the point of becoming materially misleading.[278] But if corporate managers and accountants are themselves led by their own cognitive defects to mislead investors, what can antifraud liability do about it?[279] Presumably a person is not intentionally misleading anyone if he is making false statements under the influence of a cognitive defect (for example, due to irrational overoptimism).[280] Even recklessness would seem a stretch: If cognitive defects, such as irrational optimism, are pervasive, then a false statement that resulted from such a defect could not be an extreme departure from the standard of ordinary care because ordinary care would arguably encompass the cognitive defect. Changing the standard of antifraud liability to strict liability is no answer. Cognitive defects may be extremely difficult to overcome, in which case liability would serve little purpose in changing behavior.[281] Expanding liability for misstatements would simply transfer money from corporations and their managers to investors and lawyers, with no reduction in fraud. The net result would be to increase the cost of investment. If anything, the lessons of the behavioralists may favor protecting defendants by raising the standards for establishing liability.[282] Overconfident plaintiffs' lawyers may be bringing suits with little chance of success,[283] and corporate defendants may be overestimating the risk of liability given the salience of the occasional large verdict in this area, such as the recent $3 billion payout by Cendant.[284] If such is the case, then the net result could very well be a general

278. *See* Langevoort, *Organized Illusions*, *supra* note 89, at 120-22 (stating that "[t]he difficulty, of course, is that if material information must pass through a number of relay points in a hierarchy, the message can change (and lose accuracy) in the process").

279. *Cf.* Bainbridge, *supra* note 13, at 1057 n.165 ("Managerial decisionmaking biases will not disappear simply because the state adopts a mandatory disclosure regime.").

280. *See* Langevoort, *Taming the Animal Spirits*, *supra* note 15, at 158 ("If we are seriously interested in deterring corporate deception, then fraud liability should not turn on conscious awareness by the specific senior executives responsible for corporate communications of the misleading nature of their misstatements or omissions.").

281. *Cf.* Sale, *supra* note 227, at 919 ("People facing high-risk situations, are more likely to gamble on a risky outcome than to accept the loss upfront. 'Rational' or not, their commitment to the situation escalates, sunk costs dominate, and the ability to pull back and reexamine the situation is diminished.").

282. *Cf.* Langevoort, *Organized Illusions*, *supra* note 89, at 162 (pointing out that the "puffery" doctrine allows courts "to weed out—without the need for fact-intensive discovery into corporate state of mind—the kinds of cases where optimistic bias, rather than intentional deceit, is particularly likely to have driven the allegedly misleading disclosure").

283. *See* Langevoort, *Ego*, *supra* note 83, at 862-63 ("But as often as not, I suspect, lawyers bringing low-merit suits have an honest but nonetheless self-serving assessment of those merits. Once committed to the claims, they are motivated to consider them legitimate, if not clear-cut winners.").

284. *See* Jolls et al., *supra* note 31, at 1525 ("In a case in which the threat of being found liable is highly salient, individuals may tend to *overestimate* the likelihood of being sanctioned.") (emphasis added).

chilling of corporate speech.

The "gun-jumping" rules are another area that might be reconsidered. Companies going public must go through a tightly controlled process when making a public offering. Under the gun-jumping rules, companies must avoid "conditioning" the market during the period prior to the filing of the registration statement with the SEC.[285] The behavioralist critique might suggest even more stringent limitations on preoffering disclosures by companies to curtail the tendency of investors to go into a "frenzy" over an upcoming public offering. If investors are prone to overconfidence and overoptimism, even the most routine disclosures could generate an overly enthusiastic response and thereby condition the market. Taking behavioral law and economics into account, therefore, could further reduce the disclosure of material information during the quiet period. The reduction of information again may have negative effects on overall market efficiency, raising the cost of capital and restricting investment choices for investors.

In sum, regulatory adjustments to materiality, antifraud, and the gun-jumping rules to address behavioral biases may do as much harm as good to the market. Moreover, many of the regulatory responses may perversely result in higher costs generally for investors and issuers, reducing the number of investment options available for investors.[286] For these reasons, regulators should show a substantial likelihood of net benefits before adjusting the contours of current securities regulations to correct cognitive biases.

3. *Influencing investors.*

Regulators might instead modify the decisionmaking environment for investors. Efforts to improve investors' decisions should only overcome a weak presumption, requiring a showing of the likelihood of net benefits. To be sure, even these milder interventions to correct cognitive errors pose risks. If "debiasing" investors proves ineffective, we worry that little stands in the way of regulators moving incrementally toward more interventionist and costly approaches.

If the greatest harm from cognitive biases and speculation stems from investors investing too quickly and trading too much, perhaps regulators should

285. *See* Guidelines for the Release of Information by Issuers Whose Securities Are in Registration, Release No. 5180, 1 Fed. Sec. L. Rep. (CCH) at 3056 (Aug. 16, 1971) (listing rationale of gun-jumping rules to stop the conditioning of the market).

286. As with interventions that displace the market, overly strict regulations may cause market participants to adjust in ways that further entrench those regulations. Regulating to accommodate biases may undermine the efforts of investors to learn and adjust for their biases, making otherwise unnecessary regulatory interventions indispensable. Reducing mandatory disclosure to take into account behavioral biases may generate new norms in the market around this lower level of disclosure. Expanding the definition of "conditioning" the market under the gun-jumping rules may similarly affect market norms, reducing the pressure to undo even ill-conceived regulations.

simply discourage trading. One path to encouraging a more "rational" decisionmaking environment would be to impose trading delays on investors.[287] With a trading delay, investors would have more time to contemplate their decision. Investors might recognize their behavioral biases during that "cooling off" period and thereby engage in more rational decisionmaking.[288] Trading delays do pose the risk of increasing transaction costs for investors. Investors that profit from the ability to trade instantly on new information may bear particularly high costs from trading delays (thus discouraging investments in obtaining timely information). Nevertheless, short trading delays do not preclude investors from constructing their chosen portfolio. The market may also react to lessen the cost of delays imposed on trading decisions. Investors who need to trade for long term planning purposes, such as tax considerations or tuition bills, may simply initiate their trades sooner than they otherwise would.

Trading delays, however, are not a panacea. Trading delays may encourage impatience instead of diminishing overconfidence. Moreover, it is unclear whether trading delays will generate more informed decisionmaking or simply higher transaction costs.[289] If people are incapable of recognizing their own biases, they may experience considerable disutility from intervention intended to correct those biases. Worse yet, if we succeed in discouraging people from speculative trading and/or discourage investors with behavioral biases from trading, do we also run the risk of discouraging them from participating in the stock market entirely? The speculator might be better off if he traded less, but would he be better off with his money in a passbook savings account? Perhaps a little speculation is needed to encourage investment over consumption. And the liquidity produced by speculative trading does lower execution costs for investors who need to trade for liquidity reasons. Discouraging speculation could force investors into black market alternatives, such as offshore accounts that allowed them to trade more often.

287. For a discussion on the ability of trading delays (preceded by information disclosure) to reduce the advantage of informed traders in the markets, see Ian Ayres & Stephen Choi, *Internalizing Outsider Trading*, 101 MICH. L. REV. 313, 394-401 (2002).

288. Alternatively, regulators may deter overly optimistic investors from engaging in excessive trades through a trading tax. *See, e.g.*, Joseph E. Stiglitz, *Using Tax Policy to Curb Speculative Short-Term Trading*, 3 J. FIN. SERV. RES. 101 (1989) (making the case for taxing speculative securities transactions); Lawrence H. Summers & Victoria P. Summers, *When Financial Markets Work Too Well: A Cautious Case for a Securities Transaction Tax*, 3 J. FIN. SERV. RES. 261 (1989) (same). *But see* Joseph A. Grundfest & John B. Shoven, *Adverse Implications of a Securities Transactions Excise Tax*, 6 J. ACCT. AUDITING & FIN. 409 (1991) (arguing against a tax on securities transactions).

289. Others have put forth recommendations for "debiasing" human decisionmakers in the jury context (with respect in particular to the hindsight bias). *See* Hal R. Arkes, *Principles in Judgment/Decision Making Research Pertinent to Legal Proceedings*, 7 BEHAV. SCI. & L. 429, 450-51 (1989). These attempts, however, have not met with much success. *See, e.g.*, Kim A. Kamin & Jeffrey J. Rachlinski, *Ex Post Not Ex Ante: Determining Liability in Hindsight*, 19 L. & HUM. BEHAV. 89, 99 (1995).

Education can also influence investors' decisions. Perhaps disclosure—particularly if focused on relative investment performance—can educate investors and thereby reduce the overall level of irrationality in the securities markets.[290] Learning and feedback may also help to diminish the impact of cognitive biases.[291] Studies in other areas of cognition have shown that participants, when told to consider the perspective of other parties or to consider the likelihood of alternative outcomes, have mitigated the effect of certain biases.[292] Of course, little can help the intractably irrational. But investors need not be free of cognitive biases, just aware of their own deficiencies. Regulators could educate investors and train them to avoid behavioral pitfalls.

Despite the positive arguments in favor of minimal intervention to educate and caution investors to correct for behavioral biases, we still argue for a weak presumption against their use. The silence of the SEC on the well-documented advantages of passive investing for the small investor is deafening. We have little confidence that the SEC will soon see the light and begin to discourage small investors from picking their own stocks, thereby incurring the wrath (and lobbying clout) of the investment industry. A more likely scenario is educational interventions to promote "more rational" active investing.

A weak presumption discourages regulatory interventions that serve little useful purpose. Some of the biases identified by behavioral scholars appear to be beyond regulatory intervention. For example, commentators have cited the tendency for stock prices to go up on sunny days in New York and decline on

290. *See* James Fanto, *We're All Capitalists Now: The Importance, Nature, Provision and Regulation of Investor Education*, 49 CASE W. RES. L. REV. 105 (1998) (arguing for the importance of investor education on saving, investing, and financial fraud); *see also* PETER SEDLMEIER, IMPROVING STATISTICAL REASONING: THEORETICAL MODELS AND PRACTICAL IMPLICATIONS (1999) (reporting evidence on the effectiveness of training in statistical reasoning). *But see* Henry T.C. Hu, *Faith and Magic: Investor Beliefs and Government Neutrality*, 78 TEX. L. REV. 777, 840-42 (2000) (criticizing the SEC's educational efforts).

291. *See* Mitchell, *supra* note 33, at 31-40 (summarizing studies showing the ability of learning to improve decisionmaking).

292. *See* Linda Babcock & George Loewenstein, *Explaining Bargaining Impasse: The Role of Self-Serving Biases*, 11 J. ECON. PERSP. 109, 115 (1997) (noting that having disputants write down arguments convincingly for their opponent's side reduced the discrepancy in expectations of the two sides in dispute); D. Jordan Lowe & Philip M.J. Reckers, *The Effects of Hindsight Bias on Jurors' Evaluations of Auditor Decisions*, 25 DECISION SCI. 401, 401-14 (finding evidence that having jurors consider alternative possible outcomes reduces the hindsight bias). Nonetheless, a question remains whether people can self-correct for biases even when aware of their biases. *See id.* at 115 (noting that in their experiment on parties in dispute "being informed of the bias had no effect on the discrepancy of the parties' expectations, nor on the likelihood of settlement"); *see also* Neal R. Feigenson, *Accidents as Melodrama*, 43 N.Y.L. SCH. L. REV. 741, 781 n.131 (1999-2000) (explaining that "jurors cannot simply debias themselves from being influenced by deep-seated habits of thought. Even if they are aware of those habits of thought, they may lack the motivation or the tools to correct properly for what they perceive to be a bias in their thinking").

overcast days.[293] Should we therefore close the markets on cloudy days? As far as we know, the SEC has no policies for modifying the weather in New York. This amusing example raises a broader point. Finance professors apparently have the time and inclination to do the data mining necessary to identify such anomalies. Financial professionals may do likewise. Arbitrage may then eventually eliminate the impact of behavioral biases on stock market prices (although new anomalies may emerge).[294] But whether or not arbitrage eliminates behavioral biases, many of the anomalies discovered are beyond the power of regulation—public or private—to affect.[295] Market actors may or may not respond to these anomalies once they are identified. The question then becomes whether we should lose sleep over them either way. A minimal presumption against intervention screens out regulations intended to solve problems that are not worth worrying about.

Proponents of bounded rationality may also worry that additional information, even in the form of education about biases, may further confuse investors. Investors already suffering from information overload may overreact to information on their own biases, perhaps leading them to withdraw from capital markets altogether.

We also question whether investor education will have much impact. On the one hand, investor education provides little risk of regulatory error—many investors may simply ignore erroneous or extraneous information. But investors may also ignore even useful educational materials on cognitive biases. The feature that makes investor education low risk also reduces its effectiveness in ameliorating biases. Perhaps investors suffer from such overconfidence that education will not dissuade them from making their own investment decisions. Overconfident investors may (if they bother to read educational materials) still believe that they are too "expert" to be overconfident. We have no doubt that day traders display overconfidence and overoptimism.[296] But if their speculative preference is sufficiently strong, passive alternatives that would

293. *See* Prentice, *supra* note 14, at 1410 (citing David Hirshleifer & Tyler Shumway, *Good Day Sunshine: Stock Returns and Weather*, 58 J. FIN (forthcoming 2003)); *see also* M.J. Kamstra, L.A. Kramer & M.D. Levi, *Losing Sleep at the Market: The Daylight-Savings Anomaly*, 12 AM. ECON. REV. 1005 (2000) (finding a relation between the switch to daylight savings time and stock returns).

294. Indeed, at least one prominent behavioral economist has recently taken to managing his own fund designed to take advantage of the behavioral quirks of other investors. Richard Thaler is a partner at Fuller & Thaler Asset Management Inc. Thaler's fund manages $1.4 billion in assets. Thaler describes his fund's approach as follows: "'We just try to forecast the errors of others.'" Mara Der Hovanesian, *Don't Just Analyze the Market, Analyze the Investor*, BUS. WK., May 21, 2001, at 124.

295. Prentice also notes the salience of a given company may affect investment decisions. *See* Prentice, *supra* note 14, at 1470. Once again, it is impossible to point to anything that the SEC has done to address this "problem" or any explanation of how any regulator could counteract this.

296. The market downturn appears to have trimmed their numbers. *See* Aaron Elstein, *supra* note 41, at D4 (reporting a drop in full-time day traders from 20,000 to 7,500).

curb their penchant for trading are unlikely to appeal to them. And then again, maybe they will. Lacking a theory of biases, it's hard to make predictions concerning the effect of policy proposals on investor behavior.

Even if investor education is effective at reducing biases, regulators may not be the best source of that education. Sometimes nothing can substitute for hard experience. An investor that consistently underperforms a salient and easily accessible benchmark such as the S&P 500 index may eventually rethink his strategy. Investors unable to make such adjustments may choose instead to hire expertise—by purchasing index funds, investing through active mutual funds, and investing only in companies with known reputations that trade on nationally recognized exchanges (such as the NYSE). The "dumb money" (such as this Article's authors) does just fine with its investments, once the futility of trying to beat the market is recognized.

Mutual funds and investment advisors will also compete to educate the less-than-rational about their behavioral problems to obtain the business of even more investors. In fact, financial intermediaries, such as Fidelity, are attempting to educate their investors about the risks that cognitive biases pose for their investment decisionmaking.[297] The financial press also covers these issues.[298] To be sure, intermediaries that promote active trading are unlikely to disseminate empirical research that shows the unlikelihood of beating the market. Other intermediaries, however, who promote passive alternatives will have strong incentives to convince people of their behavioral fallibilities.

As Langevoort and others have pointed out, however, institutions may face their own behavioral biases.[299] Money managers may manage funds in a way that leads to herding with other money managers.[300] To the extent that managers fear sanctions for poor performance (for example, losing one's job) more than they seek rewards for beating the average (for example, a higher salary), money managers may stick close to the crowd of other managers.[301]

---

297. *See* Russ Banham, *Mind Over Matter*, FIDELITY OUTLOOK, Aug. 2002, at 14 (explaining how cognitive biases can impair investment returns and how to avoid them).

298. *See, e.g.*, Holman W. Jenkins, *How Could They Have Done It?*, WALL ST. J., Aug. 28, 2002, at A15 (applying behavioral decision theory to meltdown of Enron); Mary Rowland, Nobel Winner Unearths 5 Common Investing Mistakes, (Nov. 4, 2002), *at* http://moneycentral.msn.com (reporting common investment mistakes identified by Nobel prize winner Daniel Kahneman).

299. *See supra* notes 74-94 and accompanying text.

300. *See, e.g.*, David Scharfstein & Jeremy Stein, *Herd Behavior and Investment*, 80 AM. ECON. REV. 465 (1990); Russ Wermers, *Mutual Fund Herding and the Impact on Stock Prices*, 54 J. FIN. 581 (1999); *see also* DAVID HIRSHLEIFER & SIEW HONG TEOH, HERD BEHAVIOR AND CASCADING IN CAPITAL MARKETS: A REVIEW AND SYNTHESIS, (Working Paper, 2001), *available at* http://papers.ssrn.com/sol3/papers.cfm?abstract_id=296081 (surveying empirical evidence on herding behavior by professional investors).

301. *See* Judith Chevailier & Glenn Ellison, *Career Concerns of Mutual Fund Managers*, 114 Q.J. ECON. 389, 390-91 (1999) (reporting from their study of 453 portfolio managers from the early 1990s that "we find that a young manager is more likely to be terminated if his fund's sector weightings or unsystematic risk level deviates considerably

And we cannot expect the investment industry to advise small investors to make a wholesale conversion to passive investment strategies. Where are the trading commissions and management fees in that?

Nonetheless, if the overall performance of funds exceeds the performance of individual investors (although they may still trail the market averages after expenses), mutual funds enhance investor welfare. The popularity of such funds demonstrates that at least some investors prefer to delegate investment decisionmaking to intermediaries with greater expertise. And some funds are immune from the cognitive defects of money managers. In particular, index funds provide an obvious alternative for investors seeking to avoid investment mistakes. The pioneer in bringing this strategy to investors, Vanguard, now boasts that one of its index funds is the largest mutual fund in the United States.[302]

In sum, once the language of behavioral bias becomes common, it is only a short step to more interventionist responses to correct such biases.[303] Given the dangers of such responses, we think caution should apply even to limited forms of debiasing efforts. While we see plausible arguments for why carefully targeted education may benefit investors, we still think that even such limited intervention should be justified by a showing of a likelihood of net benefit.

C. *Applying the Framework*

We limit our presumptions to changes to the existing securities regulatory regime. Some of the present securities regulatory regime, of course, may already take into account investors with cognitive limitations and biases. For example, the buried fact doctrine of materiality addresses the bounded rationality under which investors operate.[304] Applying our presumptions to existing law nonetheless may result in overly large amounts of uncertainty (as to what laws and regulations will fail to overcome the presumptions). The existing regime also works reasonably well, and we favor a conservative approach to guard against potential harmful changes to that regime.

Our framework for assessing regulatory responses to cognitive biases focuses on two relevant factors: the identity of the regulatory decisionmaker and the type of regulatory intervention. Our sliding scale approach is necessarily incomplete. Other types of regulatory intervention to address perceived behavioral biases among investors are undoubtedly possible. We argue that a presumption of some form should exist against all regulatory

---

from the mean of the fund's objective group. Young managers may thus have an incentive to herd . . . .").

302. Information on Vanguard can be found at http://www.vanguard.com (last visited Oct. 2, 2003).

303. Even small interventions in the market to correct for behavioral biases may condition both regulators and the market to take into account behavioral biases.

304. *See supra* note 225 and accompanying text.

interventions to counteract cognitive biases. Regulators suffer from their own set of behavioral biases. Given the imprecise (and often contradictory) ways behavioral biases may affect investors, the possibility of mistake is high. Moreover, the costs of such mistakes are significant given the difficulty of undoing regulations once they are put in place.

In applying the framework, care must be taken in balancing the two identified factors. Only the strongest evidence can justify efforts by a monopolistic SEC to remove investment choices altogether. At the other end of the scale, initiatives by private securities exchanges (in competition with one another) to educate investors about behavioral biases raise minimal concerns. A harder choice exists when the SEC attempts to educate investors. And, attempts by a securities exchange to supplant market decisionmakers present a similarly difficult question. The risks of misguided and costly interventions to correct cognitive biases are reduced in both situations and correspondingly less justification should be required for such actions.

Ultimately, the notion of a framework for assessing regulatory interventions to address cognitive biases must rely on some institution to apply the presumptions. At a minimum, agencies and courts (as well as Congress) should take caution in intervening to correct market behavioral biases, potentially self-imposing our framework and providing some record of how regulatory proposals meet the applicable presumption. Commentators proposing policy changes should also take caution in attempting to remedy market cognitive biases through regulatory intervention. For certain situations, courts may apply the varying presumptions in reviewing agency regulations as well as lower court decisions targeting market behavioral biases. Courts have their own set of biases, but our proposal does not ask reviewing courts to revisit de novo the decision on how to deal with investor biases. Rather, such courts only must judge whether the regulatory decisionmaker in question has met its burden of proof to overcome the relevant presumption.[305]

One possible criticism of our proposal is that regulators determined to fashion regulatory remedies targeting behavioral biases may do so without stating that such biases are the basis for intervention. It is unclear, however, why regulators would in fact desire to disguise their motivations. At least some well-intentioned regulators should welcome the ability to provide rationales if only to ensure (or disprove) whether in fact they are taking the correct regulatory actions in a highly uncertain area. To be sure, not all regulators are so candid. Regulators may seek to expand their regulatory authority and prestige. But they may do so already without invoking behavioral biases. To

305. Of course, courts may also face the decision directly as to what to do about a perceived behavioral bias (including, for example, whether the definition of materiality should encompass investor cognitive defects). In such a situation, we have argued that courts should face their own intermediate presumption against intervention to correct the bias. *See supra* Part III.A.2. Such a presumption should be both self-imposed by the initial, deciding lower court as well as applied by a higher level court reviewing the lower court.

the extent regulators have already exhausted nonbehavioral justifications to expand their regulatory authority, turning to these same justifications (even if simply as a disguise for a behavioral bias-related justification) will not gain the regulators any additional benefit. It is also possible that a well-intentioned regulator may be overconfident in his or her own ability and correspondingly distrustful of the ability of outsiders to know the best solution for behavioral biases. Such a regulator may seek to disguise regulations targeting behavioral biases. Additional barriers nonetheless exist against these backdoor attempts. First, regulators must point to some rationale. And to the extent that other rationales (including, for example, justifications that assume rational investors) do not support a desired regulatory policy (such as merit regulation) then regulators will lack the ability to push the reform forward. Second, reviewing institutions (such as courts) may come to question overly vague rationales (such as "investor confidence") regarding them as simple facades for behavioral bias motivated regulation.

CONCLUSION

Questioning the assumption that investors act rationally with their investments is an emerging trend in securities regulation scholarship. This trend is likely to accelerate with the recent award of the Nobel Prize in Economics to Daniel Kahneman, a pioneer in bringing psychology to the study of economic behavior.[306] The evidence that investors suffer from cognitive failings is impressive. Investors satisfice and employ flawed heuristics. Investors may also experience endowment effects, valuing a loss much greater than a corresponding gain. Cognitive dissonance may then affect investors, leading them to confirm the value of even poorly made decisions. Commentators have seized upon the evidence that investors act with limited cognitive capacity to justify regulatory intervention.

Given the array of biases presented, readers themselves may apply the availability heuristic, placing too much weight on what can go wrong in investing rather than weighing the overall evidence related to the ability of investors.[307] And evidence exists in fact that the securities markets in part already have internalized and responded to the presence of behavioral biases. Very few investors participate in active day trading, and increasing numbers of investors put their savings into passive low cost and tax efficient index funds.

We find the insights of behavioral theory provocative. It is unclear, however, what regulatory response is both necessary and plausible. Disclosure is the primary tool of the present U.S. securities regulatory regime. Yet

306. *See* Jon E. Hilsenrath, *Nobel Winners For Economics Are New Breed*, WALL ST. J., Oct. 10, 2002, at B1.

307. *See* Jay J.J. Christensen-Szalanski & Lee Roy Beach, *The Citation Bias: Fad and Fashion in Judgment and Decision Literature*, 39 AM. PSYCHOLOGIST 75 (1984) (arguing that behavioral literature may unduly emphasize evidence of nonrational decisionmaking).

disclosure is unlikely to help investors suffering from overconfidence, loss aversion, and cognitive dissonance. One could imagine a more interventionist regime, such as merit regulation. But merit regulation comes with a much larger set of problems. The specter of regulators centrally planning investment decisions does not bode well for the allocation of investment capital to its highest valued uses.

Less intrusive regulatory alternatives carry their own risks. Regulators are vulnerable to a wide range of behavioral contagion. Regulators may suffer from overconfidence and process information with only bounded rationality. Heuristics play a large role in how regulators make decisions. Even with expertise, regulators may misapply heuristics across the spectrum of different regulatory problems. Regulators may also suffer from confirmation bias, supporting prior regulatory decisions whatever the wisdom of the decisions.

And in groups the decisionmaking of regulators may decline rather than improve. On the one hand, groups and organizational structures may help alleviate some of the mistakes that derive from individually biased decisions. Studies of group decisionmaking provide evidence that the total can indeed be greater than the sum of individuals in enhancing the accuracy of decisions. But cognitive illusions may grip entire groups. Groupthink may also lead to an uncritical acceptance of regulatory decisions.

If both investors and regulators operate under the influence of behavioral biases, the value of regulation in correcting these biases comes into question. If regulators are not well equipped to determine whether regulation will counteract the biases facing investors, regulation may well do more harm than good. Worse still, SEC regulators may suffer greater behavioral biases than securities market participants. Investors that perform poorly will either learn (and perhaps put their money into an index fund or otherwise hire expertise) or exit the market. Private institutions face similar market pressures to serve the interests of their client-investors or perish. Although some types of biases may give institutions a competitive edge, the magnitude of such biases is limited by the cost that they impose on investors. The market may not function perfectly, but regulators under the present regime face no such pressures. To the extent regulators themselves make the decision whether to intervene into markets, the risk of ill-conceived intervention is even more acute. We therefore propose a framework for assessing regulatory interventions to correct for behavioral biases.

The appropriate presumption against regulation varies with the type of regulator and form of regulation. Certain types of regulators, including private securities exchanges and other competitive regulators, and certain forms of intervention, including investor education, pose a much lower risk of error. Despite their behavioral biases, regulators may have a role to play in channeling market forces toward achieving the best level of investor protection. In addition to serving as a source of investor education, regulators may oversee competition among private regulators such as exchanges to help counteract behavioral biases within the exchanges. While competition will weed out some biases, having to answer to monitoring regulators may further weed out biases among self-regulatory organizations.

We offer only tentative solutions to the problem of behavioral biases among securities regulators. The insights of behavioral law and economics are limited by the lack of a general theory to explain why the human mind results in behavioral biases in decisionmaking. Without such a theory, assessing possible methods for ameliorating such biases is a murky task at best. It is considerably clearer that focusing on biases among investors, while ignoring equivalent or worse biases among regulators, will lead to excessive regulatory intervention. Our contribution in this Article is to balance the behavioral critique of investors with one of regulators.

Part IV
Regulatory Design

[14]

Article

Empowering Investors: A Market Approach to Securities Regulation

Roberta Romano†

---

† Allen Duffy/Class of 1960 Professor of Law, Yale Law School. I have benefited from comments from Barry Adler, Anne Alstott, Yakov Amihud, Ian Ayres, Lucian Bebchuk, Boris Bittker, John Coates, Boris Feldman, Jill Fisch, Merritt Fox, Henry Hansmann, Howell Jackson, Marcel Kahan, Ehud Kamar, Michael Klausner, Alvin Klevorick, Paul Mahoney, Geoffrey Miller, Richard Painter, Peter Schuck, Alan Schwartz, Joel Seligman, Linda Silberman, Erik Sirri, Michael Solimine, and participants at the University of California at San Diego Political Science Department Law and Behavioral Studies Seminar; a seminar at the Commissione Nazionale per le Società e la Borsa (CONSOB), Rome; the Harvard Law School Seminar in Law and Economics; the Max-Planck-Institut, Hamburg Symposium on Comparative Corporate Governance; the New York University Center for Law and Business Law and Finance Seminar; the Stanford Law School Law and Economics Workshop; and the Yale Law School Faculty Workshop.

The U.S. securities laws have repeatedly been assailed as burdensome or ineffective. Reform efforts have conversely been attacked for undermining an effective mechanism by which shareholders can discipline management. Moreover, even reformers have been dissatisfied with the effectiveness of their product. For example, after enacting the Private Securities Litigation Reform Act of 1995,[1] members of Congress became concerned that their efforts to rein in frivolous private lawsuits under the federal securities laws were being circumvented by state court filings and introduced legislation to preempt such action.[2] There is some validity to their concern: In a report to President Clinton on the impact of the 1995 Act, the Securities and Exchange Commission (SEC) cited preliminary studies indicating a decrease in federal court filings and an increase in state court filings.[3]

This Article contends that the current legislative approach to securities regulation is mistaken and that preemption is not the solution to frivolous lawsuits. It advocates instead a market-oriented approach of competitive federalism that would expand, not reduce, the role of the states in securities regulation. It thereby would fundamentally reconceptualize our regulatory approach and is at odds with both sides of the debate over the 1995 Act, each of which has sought to use national laws as a weapon to beat down its opponent's position by monopolizing the regulatory field.

The market approach to securities regulation advocated in this Article takes as its paradigm the successful experience of the U.S. states in corporate law, in which the fifty states and the District of Columbia compete for the business of corporate charters. There is a substantial literature on this particular manifestation of U.S. federalism indicating that shareholders have benefited from the federal system of corporate law by its production of corporate codes that, for the most part, maximize share value.[4] This Article proposes extending the competition among states for corporate charters to two of the three principal components of federal securities regulation: the registration of securities and the related continuous disclosure regime for issuers; and the antifraud provisions that police that system. The third component, the regulation of market professionals, is not included in the proposed reform. The

1. Pub. L. No. 104-67, 109 Stat. 737 (codified at 15 U.S.C.A. § 77 (West 1997)).

2. *See* Securities Litigation Improvement Act of 1997, H.R. 1653, 105th Cong.; Securities Litigation Uniform Standards Act, H.R. 1689, 105th Cong. (1997).

3. *See* U.S. SEC. & EXCH. COMM'N, REPORT TO THE PRESIDENT AND THE CONGRESS ON THE FIRST YEAR OF PRACTICE UNDER THE PRIVATE SECURITIES LITIGATION REFORM ACT OF 1995, pt. IV, at 22, pt. VII, at 72 (1997) (summarizing a study by National Economic Research Associates of securities litigation filings after the Act). Joseph Grundfest and Michael Perino also document a shift to state court filings. *See* JOSEPH A. GRUNDFEST & MICHAEL A. PERINO, SECURITIES LITIGATION REFORM: THE FIRST YEAR'S EXPERIENCE (Stanford Law School, John M. Olin Program in Law & Econ. Working Paper No. 140, 1997). More recent data, however, suggest a reversal of this trend, with state filings declining and federal filings increasing in the first half of 1997. *See 1995 Private Securities Litigation Reform Act: Federal Securities Class Action Filings Rise as State Filings Fall, NERA Finds*, 29 Sec. Reg. & L. Rep. (BNA) 1001 (July 18, 1997).

4. *See generally* ROBERTA ROMANO, THE GENIUS OF AMERICAN CORPORATE LAW (1993).

proposed market approach can be implemented by modifying the federal securities laws in favor of a menu approach to securities regulation under which firms elect whether to be covered by federal law or by the securities law of a specified state, such as their state of incorporation.

Under a system of competitive federalism for securities regulation, only one sovereign would have jurisdiction over all transactions in the securities of a corporation that involve the issuer or its agents and investors. The aim is to replicate for the securities setting the benefits produced by state competition for corporate charters—a responsive legal regime that has tended to maximize share value—and thereby eliminate the frustration experienced at efforts to reform the national regime. As a competitive legal market supplants a monopolist federal agency in the fashioning of regulation, it would produce rules more aligned with the preferences of investors, whose decisions drive the capital market.

Competitive federalism for U.S. securities regulation also has important implications for international securities regulation. The jurisdictional principle applicable to domestic securities transactions is equally applicable to international securities transactions: Foreign issuers selling shares in the United States could opt out of the federal securities laws and choose those of another nation, such as their country of incorporation, or those of a U.S. state, to govern transactions in their securities in the United States. The federal securities laws would also, of course, not apply to transactions by U.S. investors abroad in the shares of firms that opt for a non-U.S. securities domicile. Under this approach, U.S. law would apply only to corporations affirmatively opting to be covered by U.S. law, whether they be U.S.- or non-U.S.-based firms. It therefore would put an end to the ever-expanding extraterritorial reach of U.S. securities regulation, which currently extends to transactions abroad involving foreign firms, as long as there are any U.S. shareholders or U.S. effects.[5]

Stemming the trend of extraterritorial application of U.S. law will not harm U.S. investors because they have, in fact, often been disadvantaged by the expansion of U.S. securities jurisdiction. For example, to avoid the application of U.S. law, foreign firms have frequently explicitly excluded U.S. investors from takeover offers, and such investors have thus missed out on bid premiums.[6] In addition, adoption of the market approach would facilitate foreign firms' access to capital, as they would be able to issue securities in the United States without complying with U.S. disclosure and accounting rules that differ substantially from their home rules, a requirement that has been a

5. For a discussion of SEC and court efforts at extraterritorial coverage in the context of securities regulation of takeover bids, see Arthur R. Pinto, *The Internationalization of the Hostile Takeover Market: Its Implications for Choice of Law in Corporate and Securities Law*, 16 BROOK. J. INT'L L. 55 (1990).

6. *See id.* at 66-76.

significant deterrent to listings.[7] This consequence of the proposed modification of U.S. law would also benefit U.S. investors, who would no longer incur the higher transaction costs of purchasing shares abroad in order to make direct investments in foreign firms.

The market approach to securities regulation is a natural extension of the literature on state competition for corporate charters, and commentators, recognizing the possibility of this extension, have occasionally mentioned it as an alternative to the current system of securities regulation.[8] Advancing those earlier suggestions, this Article makes a systematic case for competitive federalism by articulating the rationales for the approach and by crafting the mechanics of its implementation. The position advocated in this Article—elimination of the exclusive mandatory character of most of the federal securities laws—may seem on first impression to many readers surprising, if not unrealistic or worse. In my judgment, a compelling case can be made on the substantive merits of the proposal.

There may be an understandable desire to discount the need for the proposal because of the vibrancy of U.S. capital markets and the calls for piecemeal reform rather than comprehensive revamping of the current regime by issuers and investors. This would be a mistake. While U.S. capital markets are the largest and most liquid in the world, it is incorrect to attribute this fact to the federal regime. U.S. capital markets were the largest and most liquid global markets at the turn of the century,[9] before the federal regime was established, and their share of global capitalization has declined markedly over the past two decades,[10] facts at odds with the contention that the current federal regime is the reason for the depth of U.S. capital markets. The absence of calls for comprehensive reform is a function of a lack of imagination, rather than evidence that the current regulatory apparatus does not produce

---

7. *See* Franklin R. Edwards, *SEC Requirements for Trading of Foreign Securities on U.S. Exchanges*, *in* MODERNIZING U.S. SECURITIES REGULATION: ECONOMIC AND LEGAL PERSPECTIVES 57, 57-58 (Kenneth Lehn & Robert W. Kamphuis, Jr. eds., 1992) [hereinafter MODERNIZING U.S. SECURITIES REGULATION].

8. *See, e.g.*, ROMANO, *supra* note 4, at 99-100, 107-08; Jonathan R. Macey, *Administrative Agency Obsolescence and Interest Group Formation: A Case Study of the SEC at Sixty*, 15 CARDOZO L. REV. 909, 935-36 (1994); JEFFREY G. MACINTOSH, INTERNATIONAL SECURITIES REGULATION: OF COMPETITION, COOPERATION, CONVERGENCE, AND CARTELIZATION 31-32 (University of Toronto Faculty of Law, Law & Econ. Working Paper WPS-48, 1996).

9. *See* R.C. MICHIE, THE LONDON AND NEW YORK STOCK EXCHANGES 1850-1914, at 34 (1987) (arguing that the New York exchange gained preeminence among world's security markets from World War I).

10. *See* BRUNO SOLNIK, INTERNATIONAL INVESTMENTS 168 exh.6.1 (3d ed. 1996) (reporting that the U.S. share of global capitalization dropped from 57% to 36% between 1974 and 1994). With the recent market boom, the U.S. share rose to 41% in 1996. *See* IBBOTSON ASSOCS., AI/RI GLOBAL PORTFOLIO INTENSIVE CLASSROOM PROGRAM 1997, at Day 1-16 (1997) (citing *Developed Markets*, MORGAN STANLEY CAPITAL INT'L EAFE AND WORLD PERSPECTIVE (Morgan Stanley Capital Int'l, New York, N.Y.), Jan. 1996, at 5; IFC EMERGING MARKET DATA BASE MONTHLY REVIEW OF EMERGING STOCK MARKETS 8 (n.d.)).

deadweight losses.[11] Blind adherence to the securities regulation status quo imposes real costs on investors and firms, and there is a better solution.

Some may conclude that the proposal does not go far enough, and that all government interference in capital markets, whether federal or state, should be abolished. I believe that the intermediate position advocated in this Article is a more sensible public policy than eliminating all government involvement. This is because state competition does not foreclose the possibility of deregulation should that be desired by investors: A state could adopt a securities regime that delegates regulatory authority over issuers to stock exchanges, just as the current federal regime delegates regulatory authority for market professionals to the stock exchanges and National Association of Securities Dealers (NASD). State competition permits experimentation with purely private regulatory arrangements, while retaining a mechanism to reverse course easily—migration to states that do not adopt such an approach—which is not present in a purely private regime. On a more pragmatic level, there is a more immediate point to the Article: to caution against the current impetus to extend the federal government's monopoly over securities regulation. Instead of supplanting state securities regulation, Congress should rationalize it by legislatively altering the multijurisdictional, transactional basis of state regulatory authority to an issuer-domicile basis.

The argument proceeds as follows. In Part I, a market-based approach to U.S. securities regulation is outlined, and the mandatory federal system is critiqued. The rationale for excluding from the proposal the third component of the federal securities regime, the regulation of market professionals, and comparisons with alternative market-oriented reforms, such as regulation by exchanges, are also provided. Part II discusses the details for implementing the proposal, including changing the current choice-of-law rule for securities transactions from one that focuses on the site of the transaction to an issuer-based approach analogous to the internal affairs rule applied in corporate law, and conditioning opting out of the federal regime upon compliance with two procedural requirements. The requirements, which seek to ensure the integrity of the investor decisions that drive the regulatory competition, are the disclosure of the issuer's securities domicile at the time of a security purchase and a shareholder vote to effectuate a change in securities domicile. Finally, Part III extends the proposal to international securities regulation.

11. Issuers have focused their efforts on removing regulatory authority from the states to the federal level because they have not recognized the possibility of removing the source of the state-level problems of plaintiff forum shopping and burdensome registration requirements. Such problems could be solved by altering the state jurisdictional rule of investor domicile to that proposed in this Article, under which only one state, chosen by the issuer as its securities domicile, would have jurisdiction over all transactions in the firm's securities.

I. COMPETITIVE FEDERALISM: A MARKET APPROACH TO SECURITIES REGULATION

Although both the states and the federal government regulate securities transactions, the current regulatory arrangements are a far cry from competitive federalism. The federal securities regime, consisting of the Securities Act of 1933[12] and the Securities Exchange Act of 1934,[13] applies to all publicly traded firms and is a mandatory system of disclosure regulation, bolstered by antifraud provisions. While the federal laws do not preempt all state regulation,[14] states cannot lower the regulatory standards applicable to firms covered by the federal regime because its requirements are mandatory. They have also been prevented from raising regulatory standards on some occasions.[15] As a consequence, the states have essentially abandoned the regulation of public firms to the SEC. In the proposed system of competitive federalism, state and federal regulators would stand on an equal regulatory footing, and firms would be able to choose the applicable regulatory regime.

A. *The Essence of Competitive Federalism*

A market approach to U.S. securities regulation requires two significant departures from current law. First, a public corporation's coverage under the national securities laws must be optional rather than mandatory. Second, the securities transactions of a corporation that elects not to be covered by the federal securities laws are to be regulated by the corporation's selected domicile for securities regulation. This approach is premised on the idea that competition among sovereigns—here the fifty states, the District of Columbia, and the federal government (represented primarily by the SEC)—in the production of securities laws would benefit investors in public corporations by facilitating the adoption of regulation aligned with investors' preferences, as has been true of the competitive production of corporation codes. The motivation for the proposal is that no government entity can know better than market participants what regulations are in their interest, particularly as firms' requirements are continually changing with shifting financial market conditions. Competing regulators would make fewer policy mistakes than a

---

12. 15 U.S.C.A. §§ 77a to -bbbb (West 1997).

13. *Id.* §§ 78a to -mm.

14. Although both statutes originally expressly reserved the rights of states to regulate securities, the 1933 Act was amended in 1996 to preempt state regulation of the registration of publicly traded securities. *See* National Securities Markets Improvement Act of 1996, Pub. L. No. 104-290, § 102, 110 Stat. 3416, 3417-20 (codified at 15 U.S.C.A § 77r).

15. *See, e.g.*, Edgar v. MITE Corp., 457 U.S. 624, 640-46 (1982) (invalidating a state takeover regulation that was more extensive than the federal regulation as a burden on interstate commerce). Only a plurality of the Court in *MITE* held that the takeover statute was preempted by the federal act. *See id.* at 634-40.

monopolistic regulator as competition harnesses the incentives of the market to regulatory institutions.

Regulatory competition is desirable because when the choice of investments includes variation in legal regimes, promoters of firms will find that they can obtain a lower cost of capital by choosing the regime that investors prefer. For example, as long as investors are informed of the governing legal regime, if promoters choose a regime that exculpates them from fraud, investors will either not invest in the firm at all or will require a higher return on the investment (that is, pay less for the security), just as bondholders charge higher interest rates to firms bearing greater risk of principal nonrepayment.[16] Investors set the price because financial capital is highly mobile and financial markets are highly competitive; the set of investment opportunities is extensive, and with the use of derivatives, virtually limitless. It is plausible to assume that investors are informed about liability rules given the sophistication of the institutional investors who comprise the majority of stock market investors and whose actions determine market prices on which uninformed investors can rely.[17] Promoters thus will bear the cost of operating under a legal regime inimical to investor interests, and they will

---

16. *See* FRANK H. EASTERBROOK & DANIEL R. FISCHEL, THE ECONOMIC STRUCTURE OF CORPORATE LAW 17-21 (1991) (discussing how entrepreneurs choose terms that enhance investors' expected returns in order to increase securities prices); Ralph K. Winter, Jr., *State Law, Shareholder Protection, and the Theory of the Corporation*, 6 J. LEGAL STUD. 251, 275-76 (1977) (arguing that securities of firms incorporated in states with codes unfavorable to shareholders will be unattractive investments).

17. In 1995, for example, institutional investors—pension funds, insurance companies, mutual funds, and bank-managed investment funds—held 50% of total equity in the United States, including 57.2% of the largest 1000 firms, *see* CAROLYN K. BRANCATO, INSTITUTIONAL INVESTORS AND CORPORATE GOVERNANCE 19-20 (1997), compared to less than 10% of total equity in 1950, *see* NEW YORK STOCK EXCH., FACT BOOK 1995 DATA 57 (1996), and 46.6% of the top 1000 firms in 1987, *see* BRANCATO, *supra*, at 20. Although there are formal models of informationally inefficient capital markets (markets with, for instance, speculative bubbles) that depend on the existence of irrational, uninformed traders termed "noise traders," these models provide no theory that can predict when irrational pricing will occur and are simply unrealistic with regard to market behavior. Namely, informed investors and arbitrageurs will trade against the irrational individuals, preserving market efficiency, as the noise traders experience significant losses and stop trading. For the development of this critique, see MILTON FRIEDMAN, *The Case for Flexible Exchange Rates*, *in* ESSAYS IN POSITIVE ECONOMICS 157 (1953); Eugene F. Fama, *The Behavior of Stock-Market Prices*, 38 J. BUS. 34, 37-39 (1965); and Paul A. Samuelson, *The "Fallacy" of Maximizing the Geometric Mean in Long Sequences of Investing or Gambling*, 68 PROC. NAT'L ACAD. SCI. 2493 (1971). Modelers of inefficient markets have been unable to amend the models to respond to these criticisms. For example, in models where noise traders affect price, they cannot be shown to survive over time (and thus to affect prices in the long run), *see* J. Bradford De Long et al., *Noise Trader Risk in Financial Markets*, 98 J. POL. ECON. 703, 713, 717 (1990), but in the models in which noise traders can "survive" over time (i.e., they do not go bankrupt from their irrational trading), their misperceptions do not affect prices (i.e., the model is unsolvable if they are allowed to affect prices), *see* J. Bradford De Long et al., *The Survival of Noise Traders in Financial Markets*, 64 J. BUS. 1, 2 (1991). In addition, more generalized versions of models in which noise traders can affect prices have multiple equilibria, including the classical (efficient pricing) equilibrium. In such models, the noisy (inefficient pricing) equilibria require very strong and unrealistic assumptions concerning noise traders, such as their ability to hold infinite positions. *See* Ravi Bhushan et al., *Do Noise Traders "Create Their Own Space?"*, 32 J. FIN. & QUANTITATIVE ANALYSIS 25, 28 (1997). There is, however, one context in which unsophisticated investors are not protected by the actions of institutional investors (that is, they cannot rely on prices set by informed investors): their relations with brokers. This provides another reason for excluding the regulation of brokers from the proposal. *See infra* notes 27-29 and accompanying text.

therefore select the regime that maximizes the joint welfare of promoters and investors.

The analytical point concerning the ability of capital markets to assess legal regimes and consequently the beneficial effect of competition is confirmed by empirical research in the bond indenture and corporate law contexts: Creditor protection provisions in bond indentures are positively priced,[18] and firms experience statistically significant positive changes in stock prices upon changing their incorporation state.[19] The entrepreneurial motivation to reduce capital costs that operates in a competitive legal system mitigates the otherwise core problem for a government regulator of identifying what regulation will benefit investors in capital markets.

Federal intervention in capital markets in the 1930s was justified by a contention that securities markets operate poorly on two dimensions: First, they fail to protect investors from stock price manipulation and fraud; and second, they produce an inadequate level of corporate disclosure because the benefits of information concerning a firm cannot be appropriated solely by the firm that bears the cost of the information's production (that is, corporate information is a public good).[20] Analytically, a demonstration that there are information externalities necessitating government intervention depends on the mix of informed and uninformed investors.[21] But a theoretical need for government regulation to prevent a market failure is not equivalent to a need for a monopolist regulator. The premise of competitive federalism is that if, for example, corporate information would be underproduced to investors'

18. *See, e.g.*, Robert E. Chatfield & R. Charles Moyer, *"Putting" Away Bond Risk: An Empirical Examination of the Value of the Put Option on Bonds*, FIN. MGMT., Summer 1986, at 26, 31-32; Leland Crabbe, *Event Risk: An Analysis of Losses to Bondholders and "Super Poison Put" Bond Covenants*, 46 J. FIN. 689, 690 (1991); Richard J. Kish & Miles Livingston, *Estimating the Value of Call Options on Corporate Bonds*, J. APPLIED CORP. FIN., Fall 1993, at 95, 97.

19. *See* Roberta Romano, *Law as a Product: Some Pieces of the Incorporation Puzzle*, 1 J.L. ECON. & ORG. 225, 271 (1985); Jianghong Wang, Performance of Reincorporated Firms 14-18, 21 (Nov. 17, 1995) (unpublished manuscript, on file with the *Yale Law Journal*).

20. *See* EASTERBROOK & FISCHEL, *supra* note 16, at 277 (explaining the antifraud rationale); Joel Seligman, *The Historical Need for a Mandatory Corporate Disclosure System*, 9 J. CORP. L. 1, 9 (1983) (discussing the optimal disclosure level rationale). The economic theory underlying the argument concerning information production is ambiguous, however: Capital markets can overproduce information as well as underproduce it. The informational efficiency of capital markets implies that only the first investor to obtain private information about a firm is likely to realize the value of the information through trading, and this creates an incentive for investors to engage in costly duplicative efforts at information production (that is, overproduction) in a race to be first. *See* Jack Hirshleifer, *The Private and Social Value of Information and the Reward to Inventive Activity*, 61 AM. ECON. REV. 561, 565-66 (1971). From this perspective, mandatory disclosure could be beneficial by reducing the amount of privately produced information.

21. The formal models indicate that information will not be underproduced if the proportion of investors who are informed (that is, capable of understanding the significance of nondisclosure) is not too low. *See* MICHAEL J. FISHMAN & KATHLEEN M. HAGERTY, MANDATORY VS. VOLUNTARY DISCLOSURE IN MARKETS WITH INFORMED AND UNINFORMED CUSTOMERS 17 (Department of Fin., Kellogg Graduate Sch. of Management, Northwestern Univ. Paper No. 233, 1997); Ronald A. Dye, Investor Sophistication and Voluntary Disclosures 18 (1997) (unpublished manuscript, on file with the *Yale Law Journal*). As these papers show, if all investors are informed, no information externality exists—investors draw negative inferences from nondisclosure, forcing firms to reveal both good and bad information. *See* FISHMAN & HAGERTY, *supra*, at 1-2; Dye, *supra*, at 1.

detriment in an unregulated market, then there would be a demand for, matched by a supply of, mandated disclosure regulation in a regime of state competition for securities regulation, just as in the monopolist SEC system.

A third rationale more recently offered for federal intervention is a refinement of the public good rationale. This rationale identifies the information problem as involving information that would benefit an issuer's competitors as well as investors.[22] According to this theory, because competitors can use such information to compete more effectively with the issuer and thereby diminish the issuer's profitability, investors as well as firms would not wish to reveal such information, even though it would improve investors' ability to evaluate firms. Such an externality would render mandatory disclosure rules necessary. It can be shown analytically, however, that even in the case of such third-party externalities, mandatory disclosure is not always optimal compared to voluntary disclosure, and it would in all likelihood be extremely difficult for a regulator to determine when mandatory disclosure is optimal.[23] But putting aside the theoretical uncertainty of the need for a mandatory regime, even this third-party externality argument does not require an exclusive federal regulator. The majority of investors hold portfolios, not single shares of stock, and therefore, unlike the issuer, they will internalize the externality if they make the disclosure decision. That is, they will desire a regime requiring the information's disclosure because, by definition of a positive externality, the expected gain on their shares in competitors will offset the loss on their shares in the issuer.

Because the antifraud rationale does not depend on the presence of an externality for government action, it presents even less of an objection to a system of competitive federalism than the mandatory disclosure rationale: It is silly to contend that investors will choose regimes that encourage fraud. Joel Seligman states that a federal antifraud law was needed in the 1930s because state securities laws did not reach out-of-state sellers.[24] Whatever the merit of the argument at that time, it is not applicable to modern jurisdictional doctrines and is therefore not relevant to today's policy discussions.[25]

---

22. *See* EASTERBROOK & FISCHEL, *supra* note 16, at 290-91.

23. *See* Ronald A. Dye, *Mandatory Versus Voluntary Disclosures: The Cases of Financial and Real Externalities*, 65 ACCT. REV. 1, 15-16, 18-19 (1990) (providing a formal model indicating that divergence between voluntary and mandatory disclosure depends on information—specifically, detailed a priori knowledge of the covariances of firms' returns—that regulators are unlikely to obtain).

24. *See* Seligman, *supra* note 20, at 21.

25. Frank Easterbrook and Daniel Fischel suggest an analogous reason for a federal law: the efficiency of enforcing all claims involving a particular transaction in one case. *See* EASTERBROOK & FISCHEL, *supra* note 16, at 285. The choice-of-law reform discussed *infra* Part II, which adopts the issuer-based jurisdictional approach of corporate law for state securities regulation, can resolve this concern: As is true of shareholder class action claims for fiduciary breach, all securities claims can be consolidated into one court action, with one law applying, that of the issuer's securities domicile. This reform also resolves Easterbrook and Fischel's other explanation for why state competition would not work in the securities context: The potential to exploit out-of-state shareholders with rules favoring in-state shareholders given the multistate jurisdictional rules based on shareholder residence, *see id.* at 300-01, would disappear because

Moreover, if there was concern in the 1930s over the states' capacities to handle securities fraud cases, this is no longer a serious issue. Given the overlapping nature of the current antifraud regime, the states have developed active securities law enforcement divisions and coordinating capacities to deal with interstate fraud.[26]

The federal securities regime regarding the regulation of securities markets and market professionals who broker transactions between investors and issuers is excluded from the proposed market approach.[27] Brokers are excluded because the domicile choices of their employing organizations are not subject to the same capital market forces that prod regulatory competition to adopt rules preferred by investors as are issuers. The owners of broker-dealers, whose preferences would dictate the choice of securities regime, are not the customers whose interests the securities regime seeks to protect.[28] Unless the interests of broker-owners and customers are identical on this dimension (that is, share value is maximized under the securities regime customers prefer), the owners may not choose the regime that customers desire.

Reputational concerns in the competition for customers surely affect brokerage firms' incentives regarding the choice of regime. But reputation provides lower-powered incentives here than in the case of issuers because there are many potential conflicts of interest between broker-owners and customers over the desirable rules.[29] This scenario is different from the choice

the reform would result in only one state's law governing all shareholders' transactions, regardless of the shareholder's residence.

26. *See, e.g.*, Mark A. Sargent, *A Future for Blue Sky Law*, 62 U. CIN. L. REV. 471, 504-05 (1993). A recent example illustrates the vigor of state enforcement activity. The New York state prosecutor's criminal enforcement action against an insider trading on material information was undercut by the federal government: The U.S. attorney seized the case and struck a plea bargain with the defendant after the state prosecutor had developed the case and obtained an indictment. *See Morgenthau v. White*, N.Y. TIMES, Dec. 6, 1997, at A18. The states have also agreed to coordinate regulation of electronic offerings on the Internet. *See* John C. Coffee, Jr., *Brave New World?: The Impact(s) of the Internet on Modern Securities Regulation*, 52 BUS. LAW. 1195, 1231-32 (1997). Indeed, the Internet is likely to facilitate state enforcement efforts, as it has for the SEC, as state securities regulator websites will offer a ready means for communication of complaints by nonresident investors. *See Microcap Fraud, Staffing Issues Top Enforcement Agenda*, 29 Sec. Reg. & L. Rep. (BNA) 1773 (Dec. 19, 1997) (reporting the statement of SEC Enforcement Division Director William McLucas that the Internet has made it easier for people to get in touch with the SEC concerning complaints, as well as for the agency to "run down" people engaged in misconduct because their electronic interactions with investors leave identifying trails).

27. Trading by such professionals that would fall under current antifraud provisions and is not related to their relationship with a customer, such as trading on inside information in violation of section 10(b) of the Securities Exchange Act, 15 U.S.C. § 78j (1994), *see* United States v. O'Hagan, 117 S. Ct. 2199 (1997), *is* included in the proposal (as is any such activity conducted by any non-issuer-affiliated third party).

28. This is also true for investment advisers, who are regulated under the Investment Advisers Act of 1940, 15 U.S.C. § 80b-1 to -18a.

29. Brokers that are also dealers have multiple revenue sources, which can create conflicts of interest in trading policies. *See, e.g.*, E.F. Hutton & Co., Exchange Act Release No. 34-25,887, 41 SEC Dock. 473 (July 6, 1988) (finding a conflict between market-making activities and brokerage activities regarding customer limit orders although dividing on the appropriate practice). After the *E.F. Hutton* decision, the NASD revised its rules to eliminate the conflict by according priority to customer limit orders, which was subsequently approved by the SEC. *See* Exchange Act Release No. 34,279, 59 Fed. Reg. 34,883 (1994) (approving the rule). In addition, although competition should restrain the conflict between brokerage firms

of securities regime by the owners of issuers, because the issuer-related provisions of the securities laws concern precisely the relation between issuers and owners. A further consequence of this distinction between the regulation of issuers and brokers is that brokerage customers who are not informed of the relevant securities regime may not be protected by the presence of informed investors in the market. In contrast, uninformed stockholders benefit from informed investors' evaluation of issuers as it is revealed in stock prices.

There is one change that must be made in the regulation of market professionals, however, to maintain the integrity of the market approach to securities regulation for issuers. In order to prevent the SEC from being able surreptitiously to regulate issuers not subject to its jurisdiction, the small subset of SEC regulations that relate market professionals' conduct to substantive SEC regulation of issuers, such as the requirement that brokers and dealers obtain issuers' periodic SEC filings before providing quotations,[30] will have to be modified to refer to the substantive law of the issuer's domicile. Such a reform would not undermine the SEC's responsibility to oversee market professionals. Given that none of the SEC's substantive issuer disclosure requirements are drafted with its market professional oversight responsibilities in view, where states require a different or reduced set of issuer disclosures than the SEC, such information would also be adequate for the SEC's oversight purposes, as competition would produce the level of issuer disclosure deemed cost-effective by investors.

Whether exchanges should be included in the proposed regulatory reform is more complicated. Exchanges are also not investor-owned corporations; they are not-for-profit organizations controlled by member trading firms. They are, however, exposed to incentive-aligning market forces. Competition for trading across exchanges tends to align exchange members' regulatory choices with investors' preferences, to the extent that trading volume is maximized under trading rules preferred by investors. If there is a conflict between rules maximizing trading volume and investor welfare, the market will not provide exchanges with high-powered incentives.

There is disagreement in the literature over whether there is a conflict between increased trading volume and the trading rules preferred by investors,[31] but the severity of any such conflict is likely to be small and controllable. For example, Yakov Amihud and Haim Mendelson, who believe

---

and customers over trading costs, the securities industry recently reached a substantial settlement in litigation charging dealer collusion over bid-ask spreads in the over-the-counter market. *See* Patrick McGeehan, *Settlement of Nasdaq Suit To Hit Some Firms Harder*, WALL ST. J., Dec. 24, 1997, at C1.

30. *See* 17 C.F.R. § 240.15c2-11 (1997).

31. *Compare* Yakov Amihud & Haim Mendelson, *A New Approach to the Regulation of Trading Across Securities Markets*, 71 N.Y.U. L. REV. 1411, 1434-42 (1996) (emphasizing the conflict between exchange and investor preferences), *with* Daniel R. Fischel, *Organized Exchanges and the Regulation of Dual Class Common Stock*, 54 U. CHI. L. REV. 119, 123-25 (1987) (emphasizing the compatibility of exchange and investor preferences).

there is a conflict, contend that if issuers, rather than exchanges, controlled the listing decision, the incentive problem regarding exchanges' choice of trading rules would be eliminated.[32]

There is, moreover, a further, pragmatic reason to exclude exchanges from the proposal that is independent of the debate over exchanges' incentives: to target the proposal where it will do the most good. In contrast to corporate issuers, exchanges are self-regulating under the federal securities scheme. Rather than specify regulatory requirements for exchanges and their members, federal law delegates regulatory authority to the exchanges themselves, subject to oversight by the SEC. The benefits from regulatory competition would thus be far more attenuated for exchanges than for issuers.[33] Even more important than in the context of market professionals, there is a critical change that must be made to the existing regulatory regime for exchanges to integrate successfully the exchanges' continued oversight by the SEC with a competitive regime for issuers. The SEC's authority over exchanges must be statutorily limited to non-issuer-related matters, such as trading rules. Otherwise, the agency would be able to undermine the market approach by introducing mandatory rules for issuers in the form of exchange requirements that preempt competing state regimes.

Finally, mutual funds, which are regulated by the SEC under the Investment Company Act of 1940,[34] a regime that entails far more than disclosure requirements, present a more complicated regulatory context. Some funds could easily come under the proposal—the mutual funds that are subject to the same investor-driven market forces as corporate issuers because their owners are their customers, the objects of securities regulation. There is, however, a potentially important difference between these funds and issuers: The most informed investors in the stock market, large institutions, hold securities directly and typically do not invest in mutual funds that are held by individual investors. Thus, for competitive federalism to work for mutual fund registration, there must be a sufficient number of individual investors in mutual fund shares who are informed about the legal regimes governing their shares such that their regulatory preferences will govern fund domicile outcomes. Under such circumstances—a set of informed fund investors—the overall

32. *See* Amihud & Mendelson, *supra* note 31, at 1442-46.

33. This is not to say that the SEC's oversight of exchange rules has unambiguously benefited investors. It has not. For example, the SEC supported the anticompetitive fixed commission rule of the New York Stock Exchange (NYSE) for many years, *see* SUSAN M. PHILLIPS & J. RICHARD ZECHER, THE SEC AND THE PUBLIC INTEREST 53-89 (1981), and the benefit to investors from the SEC's commitment to developing multiple markets in NYSE stocks has been questioned, *see* Amihud & Mendelson, *supra* note 31, at 1454. Rather, it is simply to acknowledge that there is a need for priorities and that the SEC's exclusive jurisdiction over issuers is a source of greater harm to investors than is its oversight of exchange rules because, in contrast to its policies toward issuers, the SEC has not successfully imposed uniformity on all exchange rules and practices. *See, e.g.*, Macey, *supra* note 8, at 937-38 (discussing the SEC's failed effort through Rule 19c-4 to impose a one-share one-vote requirement on all exchanges)

34. 15 U.S.C. § 80a-1 to -64 (1994).

mechanics of competitive federalism for investment companies would follow the mechanics for issuers.

Many funds are not, however, customer-owned. For these funds, potential incentive-alignment concerns regarding owner and customer interests would be present, as they are in the broker and exchange contexts. The competitiveness of the mutual fund industry suggests that funds would have incentives to ensure that investors are informed about the benefits of their domiciles, as compared to those of competitors, just as funds advertise their rates today. Moreover, the fast-developing access to information concerning securities regulation on the Internet suggests that the probability that competition would work in this context is quite high.[35] But given the absence of research that pertains to this issue, the alignment of regime choice across fund owners and customers is not assured. Accordingly, this Article does not provide a detailed proposal to implement a market approach to mutual fund regulation.

B. *Is Abandoning a Mandatory Federal Securities Law Justified?*

This section first reviews the empirical literature that has sought to measure the impact of the federal securities regime on investors. The analysis rests on contemporary empirical studies because the historical "evidence" of market abuses whose revelation congressional investigators orchestrated during the hearings preceding the creation of the federal regime as part of the New Deal agenda has been shown to be inaccurate.[36] The hearings were held for the purpose of furthering a political end (federal regulation of the stock market), and the statistical techniques used by modern researchers were not available to researchers in the 1930s to develop the case for or against regulation. Even today, little empirical evidence suggests that the federal regime has affirmatively benefited investors. To develop an educated prediction of what the counterfactual (a competitive securities regime) would produce, this section then reviews the empirical evidence on investor welfare of the next best thing—state competition for corporate charters. It compares favorably.

The difficulty of discerning an affirmative impact on investors from the federal regime detailed in this section supports abandoning its exclusivity. While it does not prove the counterfactual—that state competition would be better—the near total absence of measurable benefits from the federal regulatory apparatus surely undermines blind adherence to the status quo. Under regulatory competition, lawmakers have incentives to replace regimes

35. *See, e.g.*, *Technology Issues Priorities for SEC in '98, Barbash States*, 29 Sec. Reg. & L. Rep. (BNA) 1720 (Dec. 12, 1997) (summarizing the SEC Division of Investment Management Director's prediction that Web sites containing major securities laws from regulators around the world will be available to investors by the end of 1998).

36. *See* HAROLD BIERMAN, JR., THE GREAT MYTHS OF 1929 AND THE LESSONS TO BE LEARNED 133-46 (1991); *see also infra* text accompanying notes 72-74.

that do not measurably support their objectives with those that do. In a competitive regulatory system, undesirable mandatory policies cannot be maintained over time, because they are not enforceable: Firms will migrate to the regulatory regime that does not impose such mandates.

The competitively produced state corporation codes, in contrast to the federal securities laws, consist primarily of enabling provisions that reduce the cost of business by providing firms and investors with a standardized contractual form to govern their relationships. Thus, to the extent the empirical literature suggests that federal securities laws have been fashioned from a set of misguided premises, adoption of the market approach to securities regulation will weed out inefficiencies in the federal regime, by permitting capital market participants to establish a new regulatory equilibrium with a mix of enabling and mandatory provisions, if that is what investors prefer.

1. *Empirical Evidence on the Rationales for Federal Securities Regulation*

a. *Mandatory Disclosure*

There is little tangible proof of the claim that corporate information is "underproduced" in the absence of mandatory disclosure, or that the benefits to investors from information that firms would not produce in the absence of mandatory disclosure actually outweigh their costs. For instance, before the enactment of the federal securities laws in the 1930s, public corporations voluntarily disclosed financial statements, typically under a stock exchange listing requirement, that contained substantially all of the information subsequently required under the federal laws. In an important and still underappreciated study, George Benston found that the only major mandated item that was not reported by a significant set of firms prior to the 1934 legislation was sales. Comparing the pre- and post-legislation stock returns of the firms for which the legislation was relevant (firms that had not previously reported their sales, which were 38% of New York Stock Exchange (NYSE)-listed corporations) with those for which it was not (the remaining 62% of NYSE corporations that had disclosed sales information), he found no significant price effect from the new mandated disclosure.[37]

37. *See* George J. Benston, *Required Disclosure and the Stock Market: An Evaluation of the Securities Exchange Act of 1934*, 63 AM. ECON. REV. 132, 144-45 (1973) [hereinafter Benston, *Evaluation*]. *see also* George Benston, *An Appraisal of the Costs and Benefits of Government-Required Disclosure: SEC and FTC Requirements*, LAW & CONTEMP. PROBS., Summer 1977, at 30, 51-52 [hereinafter Benston, *Appraisal*]. Joel Seligman criticizes the significance of this finding, *see* Seligman, *supra* note 20, at 16-17, but his objections, which follow those of Irwin Friend and Randolph Westerfield, *see* Irwin Friend & Randolph Westerfield, *Required Disclosure and the Stock Market: Comment*, 65 AM. ECON. REV 467 (1975), actually reinforce Benston's conclusions. For example, in criticism of Benston's finding of no stock price effect of the SEC's disclosure requirements, Seligman cites more recent studies showing that the data in SEC filings

Benston's finding, upon reflection, should not be surprising: Because firms need capital and investors need information, firms have powerful incentives to disclose information if they are to compete successfully for funds against alternative investment opportunities. Consistent with this explanation, studies have found that the quantity and quality of publicly traded firms' voluntary disclosures (such as earnings forecasts) are positively correlated with the issuance of securities[38] and with information asymmetry in the market for the firm's stock (that is, managers release information voluntarily when there is greater information asymmetry, as measured by the stock price's bid-ask spread),[39] and negatively related to the cost of capital (that is, increased voluntary disclosure reduces firms' cost of capital).[40] In addition, European firms listing in London typically comply with the higher United Kingdom disclosure requirements rather than with the lower ones of their home countries, although they need not comply with U.K. rules under the European Community disclosure directives.[41] A further datum relevant to the issue of

---

affect stock prices in an effort to prove that the SEC's mandated disclosure program is of value to investors. *See* Seligman, *supra* note 20, at 16. But it is not the SEC's disclosure requirements that are affecting stock value in these studies, because they have not added any new items into the information mix already disclosed: The information examined in the studies Seligman cites, earnings, was disclosed, as Benston demonstrates, even prior to the creation of the SEC and would continue to be disclosed if there were no SEC. *See* Benston, *Evaluation*, *supra*, at 135-36. Seligman acknowledges this point by adding that the issue is whether the SEC compels information that otherwise would not have been voluntarily disclosed, rather than where the item is disclosed (SEC report or otherwise). *See* Seligman, *supra* note 20, at 16. But the studies he cites, *see id.* at 16 n.48, do not bear upon this issue. Seligman also objects to Benston's test because it did not adequately distinguish between disclosure and nondisclosure firms, as all the firms in his sample disclosed earnings. But this is precisely Benston's point: The SEC's mandated disclosure added only one item—sales—that had not been disclosed by NYSE firms, and release of the new information under its requirement had no effect on the stock prices of those firms that previously had not been disclosing sales. *See* Benston, *Evaluation*, *supra*, at 141-42.

38. *See, e.g.*, Richard Frankel et al., *Discretionary Disclosure and External Financing*, 70 ACCT. REV. 135, 141 (1995) (finding that firms are significantly more likely to forecast earnings if they access capital markets over the sample period); Mark Lang & Russell Lundholm, *Cross-Sectional Determinants of Analyst Ratings of Corporate Disclosures*, 31 J. ACCT. RES. 246, 265-69 (1993) (finding that a firm's Financial Analyst Federation disclosure quality rating increases with security issuance); William Ruland et al., *Factors Associated with the Disclosure of Managers' Forecasts*, 65 ACCT. REV. 710, 720 (1990) (finding that firms reporting forecasts are more likely to issue new capital); *cf.* Frederick D.S. Choi, *Financial Disclosure and Entry to the European Capital Market*, 11 J. ACCT. RES. 159, 168-70 (1973) (finding that firms entering the Eurobond market increase disclosure).

39. *See* CAROL A. MARQUARDT & CHRISTINE I. WIEDMAN, VOLUNTARY DISCLOSURE, INFORMATION ASYMMETRY, AND INSIDER SELLING THROUGH SECONDARY EQUITY OFFERINGS 16, 19-20, 22 (John M. Olin School of Business, Washington Univ. Working Paper No. 97-05, 1997) (finding that, in secondary offerings, managers act as if reduced information asymmetry is correlated with reduced cost of capital, such that their participation in an offering explains the frequency of voluntary disclosure); Maribeth Coller & Teri Lombardi Yohn, *Management Forecasts and Information Asymmetry: An Examination of Bid-Ask Spreads*, 35 J. ACCT. RES. 181 (1997) (finding that firms with increasing bid-ask spreads release forecasts to reduce spread).

40. *See* Christine A. Botosan, *Disclosure Level and the Cost of Equity Capital*, 72 ACCT. REV. 323, 344, 346 (1997) (showing that voluntary disclosure in the annual report significantly explains the cost of capital of firms with small analyst followings).

41. *See* HAL S. SCOTT & PHILIP A. WELLONS, INTERNATIONAL FINANCE: TRANSACTIONS, POLICY, AND REGULATION 314 (3d ed. 1996) (citing references concerning Danish and French firms' compliance with United Kingdom standards); G.K. Meek & S.J. Gray, *Globalization of Stock Markets and Foreign Listing Requirements: Voluntary Disclosures by Continental European Companies Listed on the London*

information production is the fact that European stock markets are no less efficient than U.S. stock markets even though the European accounting and disclosure regimes require the revelation of considerably less information than does the SEC.[42]

There is, accordingly, ample evidence that firms voluntarily disclose significant amounts of information beyond that mandated by securities regulators. It is difficult to prove what, if any item, among required disclosures is of less value to investors than items voluntarily disclosed, but the great variety in content across disclosure regimes—a recent study identified one hundred SEC disclosure items deemed excessive compared to international standards[43]—suggests that a number of mandates are not cost effective. Although the estimates are extremely crude and conservative, Susan M. Phillips and J. Richard Zecher calculated in 1975 that the termination of the SEC's mandatory periodic disclosure programs would reduce corporate disclosure costs by at least $213 million.[44] These data make it plain that regulators do not have superior knowledge concerning what information investors need (otherwise firms would not on occasion disclose more than required), which bolsters the desirability of regulatory competition, as it will reduce regulatory mistakes.

In a detailed defense of federal legislation, Seligman challenges Benston's findings with data compiled by the SEC during the 1940s and 1950s in order to expand its jurisdiction, data which indicate that small firms not subject to the federal securities laws disclosed less information than the SEC required of its larger-sized registrants.[45] In particular, Seligman notes that the SEC reported that most of the small firms did not disclose management compensation or insider transactions in proxy statements and that some firms did not furnish income statements or provided inadequate accounting information, compared to SEC requirements, in their balance sheets.[46] But these data do not provide proof of the efficacy of the federal securities regime. The failure to provide voluntarily the information that the SEC mandates does

---

Stock Exchange, 20 J. INT'L BUS. STUD. 315 (1989) (reviewing a sample of European companies trading in London).

42. *See* GABRIEL HAWAWINI, EUROPEAN EQUITY MARKETS: PRICE, BEHAVIOR AND EFFICIENCY (1984); William J. Baumol & Burton G. Malkiel, *Redundant Regulation of Foreign Security Trading and U.S. Competitiveness*, *in* MODERNIZING U.S. SECURITIES REGULATION, *supra* note 7, at 39, 46-50; Edwards, *supra* note 7, at 64-66.

43. *See* Frederick D.S. Choi, *Financial Reporting Requirements for Non-U.S. Registrants: International Market Perspectives*, 6 FIN. MARKETS INSTITUTIONS & INSTRUMENTS 23, 29 (1997). There are also significant differences in the securities disclosure regimes of emerging markets, where we might expect a need for substantial disclosure to encourage foreign investment. *See* Shahrokh M. Saudagaran & Joselito G. Diga, *Financial Reporting in Emerging Capital Markets: Characteristics and Policy Issues*, ACCT. HORIZONS, June 1997, at 41.

44. *See* PHILLIPS & ZECHER, *supra* note 33, at 49-51. Their estimate of the extra costs imposed in the 1975 new issue market was $193 million. *See id.* at 51.

45. *See* Seligman, *supra* note 20, at 36-39.

46. *See id.* at 36.

not demonstrate that such disclosure enhances investor welfare. It does so only with an additional assumption—that the SEC, and not the firms, has made the correct cost-benefit calculation.

To address the issue of the adequacy of the differential level of disclosure by nonregistrants, we need to know the answers to the following questions: Were financial analysts and shareholders unable to value firms accurately under the more limited voluntary disclosures? If so, did they underpay or overpay for the shares (that is, did promoters and insiders bear the cost of the allegedly inadequate disclosure, or did the outside investors)? It would be difficult to make such judgments directly, although a finding of significant changes in stock prices upon firms' increased disclosures under SEC requirements would be probative on the issue.

There is no study of which I am aware that examines the effect of the 1965 extension of the continuing disclosure requirements to small firms. But there was no significant increase in stock prices after enactment of the 1933 Act for new issue registration,[47] a finding that strongly suggests that the new federal regime had, at best, no effect on investor welfare. If the 1933 Act did not increase stock prices of covered firms, it is unlikely that the 1965

47. *See* George J. Stigler, *Public Regulation of Securities Markets*, 37 J. BUS. 117, 120-21 (1964) (finding that SEC registration requirements had no effect on returns); *see also* Gregg A. Jarrell, *The Economic Effects of Federal Regulation of the Market for New Securities Issues*, 24 J.L. & ECON. 613, 645, 666 (1981) (reaching the same conclusion by examining returns over five years from issuance); Carol J. Simon, *The Effect of the 1933 Securities Act on Investor Information and the Performance of New Issues*, 79 AM. ECON. REV. 295, 305 (1989) (finding no effect on returns of NYSE and seasoned regional exchange issues). Simon did find that one subsample of firms, unseasoned issues traded on regional exchanges, had greater returns after the enactment of the Act (they were overpriced before the Act), *see* Simon, *supra*, at 305-06, but this subsample performed significantly worse in all periods than the other new issues in the study, *see id.* at 308. Irwin Friend and Edward S. Herman, in a study on which Seligman relies heavily, criticized Stigler's interpretation of his data because, although not statistically significant, post-Act issues had higher returns than pre-Act issues, and because there was a significant positive return after four years. *See* Irwin Friend & Edward S. Herman, *The S.E.C. Through a Glass Darkly*, 37 J. BUS. 382, 391 (1964). These criticisms do not, however, impeach Stigler's findings. The length of the interval over which they find a stock price effect—four years—is so long that it is impossible to attribute the price change to the legislation. Friend and Herman also do not provide a theory explaining why the 1933 Act should improve a new issue's returns only four years after its issuance. Not only is such a result inconsistent with a relatively efficient stock market, but we would also expect mandated disclosure to have the greatest impact over the shorter interval of Stigler's study, as short-term performance would be more predictable than long-term performance from financial disclosures. Nor do Friend and Herman explain why statistically insignificant findings should be given any evidentiary weight, counter to conventional social scientific practice. Further damaging to Friend and Herman's critique is the confirmation of Stigler's basic results by the more recent studies of Jarrell and Simon. A study of existing stocks, rather than new issues, finds that the 1933 Act had a negative price impact, which the author attributes to the Act's restrictions on accounting procedures, which may have adversely affected the firms' ability to comply with debt covenants that were based on accounting numbers. *See* Chee W. Chow, *The Impacts of Accounting Regulation on Bondholder and Shareholder Wealth: The Case of the Securities Acts*, 58 ACCT. REV. 485, 489, 502, 507 (1983). Chow expected to find a wealth transfer from shareholders to bondholders given the accounting covenants hypothesis, but he was unable to identify such an effect. Because the sample stocks were not new issues (to which the 1933 Act applied), it is difficult to interpret the study's results without knowing whether these firms planned to issue new securities in the future. A further difference, which is a serious shortcoming, between this study and the others is that, in contrast to the other studies, it did not adjust stock returns for market movements, which may account for the results. *See id.* at 503.

extension of the Act did so, for the absence of a price increase after 1933 suggests that the market elicited the right level of disclosure. A similar conclusion can be drawn from studies of a more specific instance of SEC-mandated disclosure—the requirement that large corporations disclose the current replacement cost of inventories, plant, and equipment. Researchers found no stock price effect when firms disclosed the newly mandated replacement cost information, suggesting that investors did not find the SEC's mandated disclosure useful for valuing firms.[48]

The variance of stock returns, however, decreased after the enactment of the 1933 Act.[49] A plausible interpretation is that the legislation simply forced riskier investments off the market.[50] Consistent with this explanation, after the 1933 Act there was a decrease in the proportion of outstanding new issues of common stock compared to debt, and there was a dramatic increase in private placements of debt concentrated among bonds of higher risk.[51] Such a result—reduction in the investment opportunity set—does not obviously benefit investors, who merely require higher compensation for riskier securities, while in all likelihood it reduces social welfare by restricting the availability of financing for the riskiest ventures.

The finding of a decrease in return variance has also been interpreted as indicating that the disclosure mandated by the Act enabled investors to form more accurate price predictions.[52] Even this alternative explanation does not, however, demonstrate that the Act benefited investors. A core tenet of modern finance theory is that investors are compensated for bearing market risk, and it was firm-specific risk and not market risk that was measured to have decreased with the 1933 Act. In this regard, it is not surprising that there is no stock price effect: A reduction in own-return variance (that is, more accurate stock prices) is of no value to diversified investors. Consequently, commentators who point to the return variance reduction as evidence affirming the efficacy of the 1933 Act are mistaken; investors benefit only from reductions in risk that is priced.

Seligman provides a further datum in support of the contention that the SEC's mandatory disclosure program benefits investors: From 1955 to 1971, "approximately two percent of the registration statements filed with the SEC were withdrawn after receipt of an SEC letter of comment [seeking additional

48. *See* ROSS L. WATTS & JEROLD L. ZIMMERMAN, POSITIVE ACCOUNTING THEORY 174 & n.9 (1986) (citing studies).

49. *See* Jarrell, *supra* note 47, at 646; Simon, *supra* note 47, at 309; Stigler, *supra* note 47, at 122.

50. *See* Jarrell, *supra* note 47, at 648-49, 668; Stigler, *supra* note 47, at 122. Seha Tinic offers a further gloss on this explanation, finding that the kind of securities that underwriters were willing to offer changed to larger, less risky issues after enactment of the 1933 Act because the underwriters were fearful of their legal liability under the Act. *See* Seha M. Tinic, *Anatomy of Initial Public Offerings of Common Stock*, 43 J. FIN. 789, 813 (1988).

51. *See* Jarrell, *supra* note 47, at 661, 664, 667, 669.

52. *See* Seligman, *supra* note 20, at 10; Simon, *supra* note 47, at 313.

disclosures] or . . . [an SEC] stop order."[53] This datum does not, however, indicate that the SEC's program aided investors. The key datum, which is not knowable, is whether, had those withdrawn issues been marketed as planned, investors would have overpaid for the issue or otherwise been defrauded concerning the firms' value. Emphasis on registration withdrawal data presupposes gross investor stupidity by assuming that an investor reading a prospectus that SEC staff thought deficient would not similarly recognize the deficiency and discount the share price. Why assume that the analytical ability of the SEC staff is superior to that of financial analysts or investors? Such an assumption simply does not square with what we know.

One reason for the surreal character of the arguments based on historical data that are raised in support of the federal regime is that capital markets have changed dramatically since the securities laws were adopted. The institutional investors who dominate today's markets have far greater ability, as well as financial incentives, to process information and price securities than does the SEC staff.[54] Institutional investors' pricing determinations better protect unsophisticated investors than any of the SEC's mandated disclosure requirements because, given the efficiency of U.S. capital markets in information aggregation, and the fact that securities sell for one price, institutional investors cannot use their superior information-processing ability to extract wealth systematically from uninformed investors, particularly those long-term investors who follow a buy-and-hold strategy.[55] The federal regime has not adapted well to this changed context. The interests of sophisticated and unsophisticated investors in the choice of securities regime will not diverge for the issuer-investor relations that come under the regime of competitive federalism proposed by this Article, and will, in fact, be better served by the new regulatory arrangement.

One particularly egregious example of the SEC's problematic disclosure policies will serve to underscore the point that it would be a profound mistake to presume that the SEC gets things right. The SEC prohibited for decades the disclosure of projected earnings. Such information, however, is far more valuable to investors than the accounting information the SEC required,

---

53. Seligman, *supra* note 20, at 43.

54. This discrepancy in expertise is evident in recent rulemaking activity by the SEC. By abandoning its usual approach of standardized disclosure requirements in its new rule requiring disclosure of the market risk of derivative securities, the SEC implicitly acknowledged that it is, and will always be, woefully behind market participants in understanding and developing the most accurate valuation techniques for these complex instruments. *See* Disclosure of Accounting Policies for Derivative Financial Instruments and Derivative Commodity Instruments and Disclosure of Quantitative and Qualitative Information About Market Risk Inherent in Derivative Financial Instruments, Other Financial Instruments, and Derivative Commodity Instruments, Exchange Act Release No. 33-7386, 62 Fed. Reg. 6044, 6048 n.45, 6057 (1997) (to be codified at 17 C.F.R. pts. 210, 228, 229, 239, 240, 249) [hereinafter SEC Derivatives Disclosure] (explaining why the rule permits choice of quantitative disclosure methods, including model parameters).

55. For a recent review of the research on market efficiency, see Eugene F. Fama, *Efficient Capital Markets: II*, 46 J. FIN. 1575, 1600-02 (1991).

because stock value is a function of future cash flows not historical data.[56] The SEC modified its position in 1979 to permit the disclosure of projections within a safe harbor rule,[57] but even today the agency's approach is still quite guarded when it comes to such disclosures. For instance, when Congress recently legislated a safe harbor from civil liability for forecasts, the SEC was responsible for the extended list of transactions excluded from the safe harbor provision.[58]

The SEC's historic concern was that projections were more susceptible to abuse than accounting data. This concern was premised on a bizarre view of investor decisionmaking, that investors believe all figures are "written on stone" and do not discount managers' optimism and therefore have to be protected from all but "verifiable" information (namely, historical cost).[59] This approach has made SEC disclosure documents of limited value for investment decisionmaking and was the subject of sustained criticisms throughout the 1970s. Ironically, the SEC's approach particularly disadvantaged public investors by closing off their ability to obtain information on projected earnings, as firms would not make public earnings forecasts for fear of liability, although they would provide them to analysts and other professionals.[60]

The 1979 modification did not substantially increase public forecasts, given firms' liability concerns,[61] and was clearly outmoded for modern markets populated by institutional investors. Congress therefore sought to increase the disclosure of forecasts in the 1995 securities reform legislation by explicitly creating a safe harbor from civil liability for the release of forecasts.[62] Whether the legislation will have the intended effect is not yet ascertainable, but some early indications suggest that the new law is having minimal impact on the disclosure of projections.[63] The restrictions on the applicability of the

---

56. *See, e.g.*, Homer Kripke, *Can the SEC Make Disclosure Policy Meaningful?*, J. PORTFOLIO MGMT., Summer 1976, at 32, 35-37.

57. *See* 17 C.F.R. § 240.3b-6 (1997), *originally promulgated in* Safe Harbor Rule for Projections, Exchange Act Release No. 33-6084 (June 25, 1979), *available in* 1979 WL 16388; 17 C.F.R. § 230.175 (1997).

58. *See, e.g.*, Noelle Matteson, Comment, *Private Securities Litigation Reform Act of 1995: Do Issuers Still Get Soaked in the Safe Harbor?*, 27 GOLDEN GATE U. L. REV. 527, 548 n.139 (1997) (citing sources indicating that the SEC supported the provision only after Congress agreed to the SEC's proposed transaction exclusions).

59. Kripke, *supra* note 56, at 40.

60. *See* Homer Kripke, *The SEC, the Accountants, Some Myths and Some Realities*, 45 N.Y.U. L. REV. 1151, 1199 (1970).

61. *See* Safe Harbor for Forward-Looking Statements, Exchange Act Release No. 33-7101, 59 Fed. Reg. 52,723, 52,728-29 (Oct. 19, 1994), *available in* 1994 WL 562021, at *7-8.

62. *See* Private Securities Litigation Reform Act of 1995, Pub. L. No. 104-67, § 102, 109 Stat. 737, 749-56 (codified at 15 U.S.C.A. §§ 77z-2, 78u-5 (West 1997)).

63. *See, e.g.*, *Panelists Dispute Reform Law's Impact on Private Class Securities Fraud Litigation*, 29 Sec. Reg. & L. Rep. (BNA) 1134 (Aug. 15, 1997); Matteson, *supra* note 58, at 550-51. A recent study, however, finds that forecasts by a sample of high technology firms increased after the Act. *See* Marilyn Johnson et al., The Impact of Securities Litigation Reform on the Disclosure of Forward-Looking Information by High Technology Firms (Jan. 2, 1998) (unpublished manuscript, on file with the *Yale Law*

safe harbor so vigorously advanced by the SEC surely enhance the likelihood that the statute's impact will be limited, and they serve as a useful reminder of how difficult it is for a monopolist government agency to alter course and implement significant policy changes.

This illustration of utterly misguided SEC disclosure mandates makes plain that an SEC disclosure initiative does not itself provide evidence that the market is inadequately producing relevant information and, consequently, should not be privileged by assuming that the agency is always (or even more often than not) right. It indicates quite the opposite, that the SEC may not possess even a rudimentary understanding of, much less a superior capacity over anyone else to identify, what information investors require for decisionmaking. Such regulatory mistakes would be far less likely with competition: Investors would be able to reveal their preference for particular information by bidding up the price of firms subject to a regime in which they could make forecasts, compared to firms subject to one that prohibits such disclosures.

b. *Mandatory Disclosure Involving Third-Party Externalities*

Proponents of the third-party externality rationale have not specified what information requirements the rationale justifies, let alone whether that information is the focus of SEC disclosure requirements. In fact, such information is at times explicitly excluded from the SEC's mandated disclosure.[64] It is thus difficult to use empirical studies of SEC mandates as tools for investigating this rationale compared to the more general information underproduction rationale. One area that might be seen as an instance of mandated disclosure designed to assist third parties is the segment or line-of-business financial reporting requirements promulgated by the SEC in 1969.[65] These requirements mandated separate disclosure of both profits and revenues of firms' different business product lines. Such disclosure could enable rival firms to discern more precisely firms' costs, facilitating competitive strategies. The results of studies investigating whether the additional information disclosed under the segment-reporting requirements benefited investors essentially duplicate the results of the studies of the 1933 Act. They report no significant change in stock price and an increased consensus among financial statement users concerning predicted earnings, but are in disagreement over

Journal).

64. *See, e.g.*, Regulation S-K, Item 101, 17 C.F.R. § 229.101(c)(ii) (1997) (providing that an issuer is not required to disclose narrative information concerning new business lines and products "the disclosure of which would affect adversely the registrant's competitive position").

65. *See* Adoption of Amendments to Forms S-1, S-7 and 10, Exchange Act Release No. 4988 (July 14, 1969), *available in* 1969 S.E.C. LEXIS 709.

whether there was a significant change in firms' market risk from the increased disclosure.[66]

The absence of any consistent discernible effect on firm value of the line-of-business disclosures is consistent with Edmund Kitch's contention that the SEC's segment-reporting requirements do not lead to disclosure of information of competitive value because of the discretion necessarily afforded management, under the disclosure rules, in the allocation of costs and grouping of activities.[67] If Kitch's analysis is correct and proprietary information is not effectively disclosed by line-of-business reporting, then it is not an example of a disclosure mandate that mitigates third-party externalities. Kitch further contends that it is virtually impossible in practice to implement a disclosure regime that includes proprietary information—either firms will not meaningfully disclose information that can benefit their competitors, or they will delist to avoid such disclosure.[68] This contention, supported by the empirical research on segment reporting, highlights an essential weakness of the third-party externality rationale for the federal regime of mandatory disclosure: A theory that cannot be implemented effectively cannot serve as the basis for public policy.

c. *Antifraud Provisions*

The federal antifraud laws have not been a focus of as much empirical research as the federal disclosure regime.[69] But even here there is little evidence indicating that federal, as opposed to state, securities laws are necessary to protect investors from fraud and manipulation. In truth, the data that would be probative of the efficacy of the federal antifraud regime have not

66. *See, e.g.*, Bipin B. Ajinkya, *An Empirical Evaluation of Line-of-Business Reporting*, 18 J. ACCT. RES. 343, 357-59 (1980) (reporting no effect on returns and increased consensus in probability assessments); Daniel W. Collins & Richard R. Simonds, *SEC Line-of-Business Disclosure and Market Risk Adjustments*, 17 J. ACCT. RES. 352, 372-73, 378-80 (1979) (noting change in market risk); Bertrand Horwitz & Richard Kolodny, *Line of Business Reporting and Security Prices: An Analysis of an SEC Disclosure Rule*, 8 BELL J. ECON. 234, 239, 241-42, 246 (1977) (reporting no effect on market risk or on returns). *See generally* Rosanne M. Mohr, *The Segmental Reporting Issue: A Review of Empirical Research*, 2 J. ACCT. LITERATURE 39, 45-52, 56-62 (1983) (reviewing the literature and concluding that there was no effect on returns, some improvement in analyst forecasts, increased consensus, and mixed evidence concerning whether market risk shifted).

67. *See* Edmund W. Kitch, *The Theory and Practice of Securities Disclosure*, 61 BROOK. L. REV 763, 858 (1995).

68. *See id.* at 874.

69. If disclosure reduces the frequency of fraud and fraudulent issues are generally of high risk, then one explanation of the finding that the 1933 Act reduced the variance of stock returns could be that the 1933 Act eliminated fraudulent issues. *See* Jarrell, *supra* note 47, at 649. Jarrell sought to test this hypothesis by examining the performance of pre-SEC new issues but excluding from the pre-1934 sample the firms that would have been screened out by the SEC's regulation (the riskiest issues) had the Act been in effect in the earlier years. *See id.* at 650. He found that the screened sample performed no better than the entire pre-SEC sample. *See id.* Jarrell concludes that the reduction in variance after the Act is not due to effective deterrence of fraud, because high variance is not connected to poor performance in the unregulated period. *See id.*

been compiled. Because all states had antifraud statutes prior to the adoption of the federal securities laws, and only Nevada did not have an administrative entity to investigate securities fraud at that time,[70] an investigation of whether reported instances of investor fraud decreased after the enactment of federal securities laws would be a useful step in determining the efficacy of the federal regime. The difficulty, however, of establishing a preenactment baseline rate (given differences in enforcement regimes across states, for example), probably would make the task infeasible. Other probative research would examine whether securities issued outside of the SEC's jurisdiction (intrastate issues of small firms, state and local government securities, or foreign issues) have higher frequencies of fraud and price manipulation than SEC-registered securities, although, again, developing good estimates of comparative base-rate frequencies would be quite difficult.

Seligman cites SEC testimony to Congress in the 1940s and a 1963 SEC study as part of the agency's twenty-year effort to expand its jurisdiction over small firms, indicating that the SEC initiated more fraud investigations against issues exempt from federal registration requirements than against those that were registered.[71] These data are of little import. First, we do not know whether the SEC allocated more resources to investigating exempt issues than to investigating registered issues, an altogether plausible possibility given the SEC's agenda at the time, the extension of its disclosure requirements to small firms exempt from its regulation. Such an enforcement policy would make it impossible to draw any conclusion concerning relative rates of fraud from the data. And, of course, the initiation of an investigation does not mean that fraud actually occurred. Second, it is important to ascertain the level of state antifraud activity against such issuers to determine whether federal intervention was necessary. Third, even if one accepted Seligman's contention that massive securities frauds went undeterred by the states and necessitated the enactment of the federal laws, it is important to determine whether fraud occurred more frequently in small rather than large firms. Such a finding would indicate that the lower rate of fraud investigations for firms covered by the 1933 Act would not be a function of the mandatory disclosure regime, but of the population's lower underlying occurrence rate.

But the evidence supporting the contention that rampant fraud necessitated the federal laws is itself quite thin. After reviewing the legislative record and other sources, Benston concludes, in contrast to Seligman, that there is scant evidence of fraudulent financial statements prior to the 1934 Act.[72] Harold Bierman has also reviewed the evidence concerning stock market fraud and manipulation prior to the 1929 crash, scrutinizing in particular the sensational

70. *See* EASTERBROOK & FISCHEL, *supra* note 16, at 277.
71. *See* Seligman, *supra* note 20, at 34-35.
72. *See* Benston, *Evaluation*, *supra* note 37, at 135.

charges raised against several prominent financiers in the Pecora hearings that led to the federal securities legislation. He concludes that the hearings and the attempted prosecutions in their aftermath did not uncover fraudulent or dishonest behavior on Wall Street and that the amount of manipulation in the 1920s was "surprisingly small."[73] More important, a recent empirical study of the operation of stock pools that were a principal focus of the congressional investigation leading to the enactment of the federal securities laws found no evidence that the pools manipulated stock prices.[74]

In short, a fair reading of the empirical literature on the effects of the federal securities laws points to an expansive regulatory apparatus with no empirical validation for its most fundamental objectives. The SEC appears to be a regulatory edifice without foundation. A competitive regulatory system would put such a characterization to the test, as firms would be able to seek out the securities regime that investors prefer.

2. *Empirical Evidence on Corporate Charter Competition*

The most prudent approach to the considerable data reviewed in the previous subsection, which cast doubt on the efficacy of the federal securities regime, is to replace the monopolist federal regulator with regulatory competition. This is, of course, the gist of the market approach embedded in a system of competitive federalism. To find fault with a market approach one must maintain that a competitive regulatory setting will do a worse job than the federal monopolist in achieving the investor-protection goals of securities regulation. For such a contention to be correct, a further assumption is required, that the states will engage in a "race for the bottom" and enact rules that favor promoter-issuers over investors.[75] This assumption cannot be directly tested because there is at present no competitive regime for securities laws; besides the national mandates, the governing regime is fixed by the investor's residence or place of sale. But there is a competitive regime for corporate charters. The most important data bearing on the question whether the federal securities regime should be eliminated is, consequently, the research on the impact on shareholder welfare of state competition for charters. This research indicates convincingly, in my judgment, that investors are at a minimum not harmed from the competition and, in all likelihood, benefit from changes in corporate domicile to states such as Delaware, the leading incorporation state.

---

73. BIERMAN, *supra* note 36, at 133-45.

74. *See* Paul G. Mahoney, *The Stock Pools and the Securities Exchange Act*, J. FIN. ECON. (forthcoming 1999) (manuscript at 38, on file with the *Yale Law Journal*).

75. Seligman, for example, asserts that there is a need for mandatory national securities laws "because of the history of state corporate law 'chartermongering.'" Seligman, *supra* note 20, at 53-54.

There have been six event studies of the effect of state competition on shareholder wealth. The wealth effect is measured by the stock price reaction to a domicile change. Measured over a variety of time periods and sample firms, these studies find either a significant positive stock price effect or no significant price effect upon reincorporation.[76] No study observes a negative stock price effect. The empirical research on state competition undermines the race-for-the-bottom argument against eliminating the federal securities monopoly by demonstrating that choice of jurisdiction does not leave investors defenseless against unscrupulous promoters.[77]

The race-for-the-bottom view of state competition is no longer the consensus view of scholars in the debate over the efficacy of state competition

76. *See* Michael Bradley & Cindy A. Schipani, *The Relevance of the Duty of Care Standard in Corporate Governance*, 75 IOWA L. REV. 1, 66-67 (1989) (significant positive returns on the event date and approximately one month before); Peter Dodd & Richard Leftwich, *The Market for Corporate Charters: "Unhealthy Competition" Versus Federal Regulation*, 53 J. BUS. 259, 272-75 (1980) (significant positive returns two years before the event date); Allen Hyman, *The Delaware Controversy—The Legal Debate*, 4 DEL. J. CORP. L. 368, 385 (1979) (positive returns four days before the event date); Jeffry Netter & Annette Poulsen, *State Corporation Laws and Shareholders: The Recent Experience*, 18 FIN. MGMT. 29, 35-37 (1989) (positive returns roughly one month around the event date that were significant at the 10% level only); Romano, *supra* note 19, at 270-71 (significant positive returns at three-day, one-week and one-month intervals around the event date); Wang, *supra* note 19, at 14-18, 21 (significant positive returns for the full sample over a three-day event interval and significant positive returns for Delaware firms over 40 days before the event date and over a three-day interval if the shareholder meeting date is used as the event date).

77. In an attempt to explain away the non-negative stock price effects of reincorporation, Lucian Bebchuk asserts that stock price studies are not probative of whether state competition benefits shareholders because state competition may produce some provisions that are harmful to shareholders even if the overall package of provisions is not. *See* Lucian Arye Bebchuk, *Federalism and the Corporation: The Desirable Limits on State Competition in Corporate Law*, 105 HARV. L. REV. 1435, 1449-50 (1992). This is not a particularly damaging contention against competition and in favor of a federal monopolist for several reasons. First, it is the net wealth effect of a code on investors that is important, and that effect is positive for state corporate law. Second, because state corporation codes are enabling statutes, firms can avoid any such harmful provisions by customizing their charters or bylaws. *See infra* text accompanying note 82 (discussing numerous firms' opting out of the Pennsylvania takeover statute). Indeed, Bebchuk does not identify specific mandatory (hence unavoidable) provisions in state codes that he believes benefit managers over shareholders. Third, Bebchuk offers no support for the prediction that a federal corporation code would contain fewer harmful provisions than state codes. An examination of the lobbying process in the corporate context indicates that the differences between federal and state politics are, in fact, minimal. *See infra* notes 84-89 and accompanying text. Bebchuk offers two other speculations to refute the validity of the empirical research, but they are incorrect. His contention (offered to explain insignificant price effects of reincorporation) that both the original and the destination state's laws are equally harmful to shareholders, *see* Bebchuk, *supra*, at 1449-50, is not borne out by the evidence. Not only do some studies find significant positive results, *see supra* note 76, but more important, the legal regimes of the destination states differ significantly from those of the states of origin: The destination states are more responsive to reincorporating firms' demands than the originating states in enacting code innovations; and reincorporating firms perceive significant differences between the legal regimes of the two states and offer them as a reason for moving, *see* Romano, *supra* note 19, at 246-47, 258-60. Bebchuk's other contention (offered to explain positive stock price effects) that any price effects of reincorporation are due to changes in the firm's business accompanying or anticipated by the move rather than a reflection of investors' assessment of the new regime, *see* Bebchuk, *supra*, at 1449, while plausible, is not supported by the data. I tested for significant differences in abnormal returns across reincorporating firms grouped according to such potentially confounding transactions, where some transactions would be hypothesized to be negative and others positive, for shareholder wealth, and found none. *See* Romano, *supra* note 19, at 272. This finding is strong evidence that the positive price effects for the full sample in my study were due to investors' positive assessments of the domicile change and not of the accompanying or anticipated transactions.

for corporate charters precisely because its advocates cannot provide tangible proof that competition is, in general, harmful to investors. There is no reason to expect state competition to operate differently for securities law than it does for corporate law. The informational efficiency of capital markets and the dominant presence of institutional investors in such markets ensure that the content of legal regimes will be impounded in the cost of capital, whether they concern only corporate governance or include securities transactions. Accordingly, if mandatory securities rules benefit shareholders, notwithstanding the absence of empirical support in their favor, then competitive federalism will produce mandatory rules as well.

This is not to say that state competition is perfect. In the 1980s, when hostile takeovers emerged as a mechanism for changing control and, correlatively, for replacing incumbent management, the vast majority of states enacted laws that attempted to lower the probability of a hostile takeover. Because shareholders receive substantial premiums in hostile takeovers, most commentators hypothesized that the objective of these statutes was not to enhance shareholder welfare, but to entrench management.[78] Indeed, some antitakeover statutes made explicit their non-shareholder-wealth-maximization objectives. Such laws, referred to as "other constituency statutes," permit management to consider interests other than those of shareholders (that is, factors besides the offered price) in deciding whether to oppose a bid.[79]

Consistent with the view that restricting hostile takeovers is not beneficial to shareholders, the enactment of antitakeover laws produced negative or statistically insignificant stock price reactions.[80] Delaware, with the largest

78. *See, e.g.*, EASTERBROOK & FISCHEL, *supra* note 16, at 220-22. Some commentators contended, however, that takeover defenses benefited shareholders by solving a coordination problem created by dispersed stock ownership and thereby enabling managers to negotiate higher bid prices. *See, e.g.*, Lucian Arye Bebchuk, *The Sole Owner Standard for Takeover Policy*, 17 J. LEGAL STUD. 197 (1988); William J. Carney, *Shareholder Coordination Costs, Shark Repellents, and Takeout Mergers: The Case Against Fiduciary Duties*, 1983 AM. B. FOUND. RES. J. 341.

79. For an analysis of these statutes, see Roberta Romano, *What Is the Value of Other Constituency Statutes to Shareholders?*, 43 U. TORONTO L.J. 533 (1993). I found these statutes had no significant stock price effect on the specific legislative event dates and within two-day event intervals. *See id.* at 537. John C. Alexander et al., however, found a significant negative price effect (for firms without poison pills or antitakeover charter amendments) for two of the statutes that I examined when a longer event interval of two days before and three days after was used, and for a third statute, enacted by Indiana in 1989, that was improperly included in their sample because Indiana had had an other-constituency statute in effect since 1986. *See* John C. Alexander et al., *Nonshareholder Constituency Statutes and Shareholder Wealth. A Note*, 21 J. BANKING & FIN. 417, 427 (1997). In fact, I found a negative effect for the earlier Indiana statute, *see* Romano, *supra*, at 539, but it is not a "clean" statute in that it was passed with another antitakeover provision. I did not find any difference for firms with or without defensive tactics in place, but the sample was not subdivided by firm characteristics for each state statute separately, and therefore the results cannot be compared. In addition, my sample consisted of larger firms, as it was constructed solely from NYSE listings while Alexander et al. include firms traded on the American Stock Exchange and NASD's Automated Quotation System (NASDAQ). Because at least one study has found that it is small firms that experience negative price effects from takeover statutes, *see* M. Andrew Fields & Janet M. Todd, *Firm Size, Antitakeover Charter Amendments, and the Effect of State Antitakeover Legislation*, 21 MANAGERIAL FIN. 35 (1995), the difference in the studies' samples may explain the difference in the results.

80. The most comprehensive study, which finds a small but significant negative stock price effect, is

stake in the chartering business, stands out, however, as an anomaly in the takeover statute legislative process. In contrast to its position as an innovator in corporation code provisions, in the takeover context Delaware was a laggard behind other states, and its regulation is considerably less restrictive of bids.[81] More important, charter competition limits the extent to which states can restrict takeovers: When Pennsylvania enacted what was considered to be a draconian statute, a majority of firms opted out of its coverage because of demands made by their investors, who raised the prospect of selling their shares and reinvesting in firms incorporated in states with no statutes or less restrictive statutes, such as California and Delaware.[82] Consequently, other states did not adopt the Pennsylvania statute.[83]

There is also no evidence that a monopolist-regulator enforcing one national corporation law would produce better takeover regulation than the states. Quite to the contrary, in all likelihood a monopolist regulator would make the situation worse. The political dynamics of takeover regulation at the state level would be unchanged at the national level. The groups that are influential in state politics outside of Delaware—local firm managers—are as influential in Washington. They provide, for instance, the bulk of the witnesses testifying for takeover regulation.[84] In addition, members of Congress whose districts included hostile takeover targets were the principal advocates for antitakeover legislation,[85] just as states with hostile targets were the enactors of similar protective legislation.[86] Moreover, the congressional legislation on takeovers enacted under the securities laws, the Williams Act,[87] paralleling the state statutes, favors incumbent managers over bidders by delaying bids, and the overwhelming majority of bills introduced concerning federal takeover regulation since the Williams Act have sought to make hostile bids more difficult.[88]

Jonathan M. Karpoff & Paul H. Malatesta, *The Wealth Effects of Second-Generation State Takeover Legislation*, 25 J. FIN. ECON. 291 (1989), which assesses 40 statutes. ROMANO, *supra* note 4, at 60-69, reviews the empirical research on takeover statutes and shareholder wealth.

81. Correspondingly, in contrast to the antitakeover statutes of other states, the Delaware statute did not have a negative stock price effect. *See* John S. Jahera, Jr. & William Pugh, *State Takeover Legislation: The Case of Delaware*, 7 J.L. ECON. & ORG. 410, 416-19 (1991) (finding insignificant or positive returns over eight two-day event intervals); Karpoff & Malatesta, *supra* note 80, at 315 (finding an insignificant price effect over a two-day event interval).

82. *See* ROMANO, *supra* note 4, at 68-69.

83. *See id.* at 70.

84. *See* Roberta Romano, *The Future of Hostile Takeovers: Legislation and Public Opinion*, 57 U. CIN. L. REV. 457, 485 (1988). Only witnesses employed by the government participated in a greater number of takeover legislation hearings than corporate managers. *See id.*

85. *See id.* at 482-84; Kenneth Lehn & James W. Jones, The Legislative Politics of Hostile Corporate Takeovers (1987) (unpublished manuscript, on file with the *Yale Law Journal*).

86. *See* Henry N. Butler, *Corporation-Specific Anti-Takeover Statutes and the Market for Corporate Charters*, 1988 WIS. L. REV. 365 *passim*; Romano, *supra* note 84, at 461.

87. Pub. L. No. 90-439, 82 Stat. 454 (1968) (amending Securities Exchange Act of 1934 § 14(d), (e), 15 U.S.C. § 78n(d), (e) (1994)).

88. *See* Romano, *supra* note 84, at 470-74.

With only a national law, there would be no safety valve offered by a competing jurisdiction (such as California and Delaware in the current federal system of corporate law) to constrain takeover legislation, and a legislative or judicial mistake would be more difficult to reverse, as Congress moves considerably more slowly than state legislatures.[89] As the experience with state takeover laws indicates, although in the short run there will be deviations from the optimum in a federal system, in the longer run competitive pressure is exerted when states make mistakes, as in the example of firms opting out of Pennsylvania's takeover statute. Such pressure is absent in an exclusive one-regulator system.

The empirical literature concerning the efficacy of state competition for corporate charters has been my focus of analysis, not only because an assessment of the efficacy of charter competition underlies the arguments for and against the market approach to securities regulation, but also because economic theory provides limited guidance concerning whether a monopolist will provide the optimal degree of product quality, variety, or innovation, issues of importance in the regulatory context. Whether a monopolist's choice of quality is socially optimal depends on the difference between the marginal and average consumers' willingness to pay for quality, as is true of price-taking competitors; whether the monopolist will undersupply quality compared to the competitive market depends on the elasticity of demand.[90] There is a similar ambiguity concerning whether a monopolist will produce too few or too many products; the answer again depends on the elasticities of demand and whether the goods in question are substitutes.[91]

Extending the theory of monopolistic firms to regulators, William P. Albrecht et al. present a model in which competing regulators, in contrast to a monopolist (or to collusive regulators), provide efficient regulation when the

89. *See* ROMANO, *supra* note 4, at 48-49. This explains why Congress did not amend the Williams Act to restrict takeovers further in the 1980s. Over the course of its lengthy deliberative process on takeover legislation, the Supreme Court upheld state takeover regulation, *see* CTS Corp v. Dynamics Corp of Am., 481 U.S. 69, 94 (1987), and firms redirected their lobbying efforts from Congress to the states, which could provide a target with relief more quickly than Congress, *see* sources cited *supra* note 86

90. In other words, while a social planner would set quality by the average consumer's valuation because she looks at all consumers' welfare, the monopolist, concerned with profits and not social surplus, sets quality by the marginal consumer's valuation because the price increase for higher quality can be passed on to all inframarginal consumers. As the marginal consumer is not likely to be representative of the population, the monopolist's product quality choice will differ from that of the social planner (i.e., it will undersupply quality if the average valuation exceeds the marginal valuation) The bias in quality introduced by the monopolist can be identified only if output will be the same in both cases, this is generally not the case because a monopolist tends to produce less output for a given quality *See* JEAN TIROLE, THE THEORY OF INDUSTRIAL ORGANIZATION 100-02 (1988)

91. When the monopolist can produce only one product because the monopolist cannot appropriate the net consumer surplus from introducing a new product design, there may be too few products under monopoly compared to the social optimum; when the monopolist can offer multiple products that are substitutes, it may introduce "too many" products compared to the social optimum because if it charges an above-marginal price for one good it can create demand for a second good, which would not exist if the first good was competitively priced. *See id.* at 104-05. The analysis concerning the monopolist's choice for product diversity is substantially the same as that for product innovation

goods regulated are substitutes.[92] Although it is most plausible to conceptualize the products in the securities regulation context as substitutes, as all states' securities codes are available to all firms, if different states' laws are appropriate for specific types of firms and diversified investors desire to hold such firms in fixed proportions, the products could be conceptualized as complements. Lacking information on demand elasticities for securities laws, Albrecht et al.'s model is only suggestive of the benefits of the policy advocated in this Article, and we must rely instead on the best available empirical evidence, the evidence from state competition for corporate charters. Charter competition has not resulted in product differentiation across states (that is, corporate law regimes are substitutes),[93] and investors have benefited from the competition. These data are consistent with the existence of substantial benefits for investors from opening securities regulation up to competition as well.

C. *How Would State Competition for Securities Regulation Work?*

For states to compete in the production of specific laws, a state must receive some benefit from the activity. In the corporate law setting, the benefit is financial: States collect franchise tax revenues from locally incorporated firms. Over the past thirty years, the franchise tax revenue collected by Delaware, which is the leading incorporation state despite having few local corporations, averaged 16.7% of its total tax revenue (see Appendix Table 1). This revenue greatly exceeds what Delaware spends on its corporate law system.[94] If the regulation of securities transactions depended on the incorporation state as well, the incentive to obtain franchise tax revenues would increase, as there would be more dimensions on which a state could serve its corporate clientele. That is, a state could increase the number of incorporations, and hence its franchise tax revenues, by offering a desirable securities regime as well as a desirable corporation code.

An additional potential revenue source for states competing over securities regulation is filing fees, which accompany the registration of a public offering

92. *See* William P. Albrecht et al., *Regulatory Regimes: The Interdependence of Rules and Regulatory Structure*, *in* THE INDUSTRIAL ORGANIZATION AND REGULATION OF THE SECURITIES INDUSTRY 9, 27 (Andrew W. Lo ed., 1996).

93. *See* ROMANO, *supra* note 4, at 45-48.

94. The figures in Appendix Table 1 provide a conservative estimate of the profitability of Delaware's chartering business because they overstate its expenditures by including, in addition to the appropriations for the Division of Corporations in the Office of the Secretary of State, which administers the corporate registration process, the total appropriations for the Chancery Court and Delaware Supreme Court, which hear corporate law cases at trial and on appeal, respectively, although such cases are a fraction of their caseload. For example, only 30% of Chancery Court cases are corporate law cases. *See Chancery Court High Stakes in Delaware*, NAT'L L.J., Feb. 13, 1984, at 32. In addition, the outlays for the Division of Corporations were separately itemized only after 1972; for the years before 1972, the table includes the entire appropriation for the Secretary's Office, although in the subsequent years the ratio of the budget for the Division to the budget for the Office was slightly under 80%.

of securities. These fees can be substantial, as indicated in Appendix Table 2, which reproduces the fees collected by the SEC over the past thirty years for the registration of securities and various other filings.[95] Since 1983, the SEC's fee collections have been more than 100%, often more than 200%, of its gross outlays.[96] As a monopolist, the SEC has been able to charge a higher fee for registration than could competitive states, but competition need not drive such fees to zero. Delaware, for instance, charges higher incorporation fees than other states and is still the leading incorporation state—a phenomenon indicating that firms are willing to pay a premium for a superior legal product.[97]

Securities transaction taxes could be a further source of revenue, as they would accrue to the securities-regulating state, but the competitiveness of capital markets has constrained states from imposing substantial taxes on share transfers. The trend in European countries, for example, has been to reduce or eliminate securities transaction taxes because of competition for stock exchange business.[98] Annual securities domicile franchise fees, analogous to incorporation franchise fees, would be preferable to securities transaction taxes as a revenue source, however, because they are assessed per firm, rather than according to individual trades, and will thus not adversely affect liquidity by deterring particular transactions.

The financial incentives generating state charter competition have resulted in a race that has tended to the top in corporate law. This result suggests that it would be beneficial for investors to create similar financial incentives for states in the securities law context. Presently, however, states have little of value to offer firms in return for the payment of securities "franchise" taxes. State securities case law is not as extensive as that for corporate law because

95. The bulk of the SEC's fee revenue comes from securities' registration. For example, in 1996, securities registered under the 1933 Act accounted for 75% of the agency's fee revenue, and transactions of covered exchange-listed securities comprised a further 17%. *See SEC 1996 Annual Report* (visited Jan 5, 1998) <http://www.sec.gov/asec/annrep96/polas.htm>. The figures for fees collected in the 1960s-1970s include the fees from the registration of exchanges and brokers as well as securities. *See, e.g.*, 33 SEC ANN. REP. 149 (1967) (figures for 1965-1967); 36 SEC ANN. REP. 210 (1970) (figures for 1968-1970).

96. *See* CONGRESSIONAL BUDGET OFFICE, 104TH CONG., 1ST SESS., MEMORANDUM ON GROWTH OF FEDERAL USER CHARGES: AN UPDATE (Comm. Print 1995). The SEC's revenue is so great that for many years it sought to be self-financing. Congress initially refused its request, preferring to retain a system in which the fees from SEC filings entered into general revenues and the SEC was allocated a budget far lower than the revenues it produced. In 1996, however, Congress enacted legislation reducing SEC fees over time so that eventually the SEC will collect no more in fees than it costs to run the agency. *See* National Securities Markets Improvement Act of 1996, Pub. L. No. 104-290, §§ 402-405, 110 Stat. 3416, 3441-44 (codified at 15 U.S.C.A. §§ 78a, 77f(b), 78ee (West 1997)). That statute also restricted states' ability to charge filing fees for the registration of securities traded on national exchanges, at the same time as it preempted their ability to regulate such issues' registrations. *See id.* § 102(a), 102(c)(2)(D), 110 Stat. at 3417, 3420 (codified at 15 U.S.C.A. § 77r). The change in securities regime advocated in this Article would reword this restriction, to permit the securities domicile alone to charge such fees. The domicile would be a state, foreign country, or the SEC, depending on the issuer's selection.

97. *See* Romano, *supra* note 19, at 257.

98. *See* Colin Jamieson, *Stamp Duties in the European Community: Harmonisation by Abolition?*, 1991 BRIT. TAX REV. 318, 318-19.

until recently the national securities laws have occupied the field, given expansive interpretations of the federal antifraud provisions by the SEC and courts and the desirability of using federal courts.[99] State securities law is not a complete void, however, because some litigants began turning to state actions in the aftermath of the Supreme Court's restrictive interpretations, beginning in the 1970s, of the federal antifraud provisions.[100] This trend is expected to increase given Congress's recent tightening of procedural requirements for federal securities actions,[101] unless Congress enacts the proposed preemption bills.[102]

The relative dearth of a developed body of securities case law places states at a distinct disadvantage in competing for corporations with the federal government in terms of substantive securities regulation. In choosing their statutory domicile, corporations place a premium on the presence of comprehensive case law because a stock of precedents facilitates business planning: Firms can structure transactions to minimize the possibility of liability.[103] States can, however, compensate for the problem of meager judicial precedents by formally incorporating federal court decisions interpreting the national laws, through either legislation or judicial action, to the extent that the state's statutory language tracks the national laws. This approach is not novel and has, in fact, been adopted in the corporate law context: It facilitated the replacement of New Jersey as the leading incorporation state by Delaware when corporations sought an alternative statutory domicile after a lame-duck Governor Woodrow Wilson and the Progressive Party majority in the New Jersey legislature drastically revised the corporation code. Delaware's judiciary had incorporated New Jersey precedents in interpreting its code, which was modeled on the former New Jersey statute.[104] Moreover, a state such as Delaware, with a specialized corporate

99. *See, e.g.*, THOMAS L. HAZEN, THE LAW OF SECURITIES REGULATION 769, 773 (3d ed. 1996) (discussing the courts' expansion of statutory scope). While the 1934 Act provides the federal courts with exclusive jurisdiction for 1934 Act violations, *see* 15 U.S.C. § 78aa (1994), the 1933 Act does not, *see* 15 U.S.C. § 77v, and plaintiffs can bring claims under state securities laws for conduct that would be a 1934 Act violation. Nevertheless, the preponderance of securities lawsuits are brought in federal court. *See* GRUNDFEST & PERINO, *supra* note 3, at 3-9 (discussing filing trends in securities legislation).

100. *See, e.g.*, Santa Fe Indus. v. Green, 430 U.S. 462, 474-77 (1977) (holding that a breach of fiduciary duty was not a violation of federal securities law); Ernst & Ernst v. Hochfelder, 425 U.S. 185, 201 (1976) (requiring scienter for liability under federal securities fraud statutes).

101. For an overview of the advantages to investors of bringing securities claims in state rather than federal courts, see Marc I. Steinberg, *The Emergence of State Securities Laws: Partly Sunny Skies for Investors*, 62 U. CIN. L. REV. 395, 418-27 (1993). Grundfest and Perino note the incentives created by the 1995 Reform Act for plaintiffs to use state courts. *See* GRUNDFEST & PERINO, *supra* note 3, at 39.

102. *See* sources cited *supra* note 2.

103. *See* ROMANO, *supra* note 4, at 32-34 (discussing how firms reincorporate to reduce litigation costs); Romano, *supra* note 19, at 249-51 (same).

104. *See* Wilmington City Ry. v. People's Ry., 47 A. 245, 251 (Del. Ch. 1900). For a more recent example of this approach, see *Santa Fe Hills Golf & Country Club v. Safehi Realty Co.*, 349 S.W.2d 27, 34-35 (Mo. 1961).

law court, can compensate for the dearth of precedents by offering litigants the prospect of far greater judicial expertise than the federal courts.

The limited experience of states with securities regulation is one important reason for maintaining a federal government option—at a minimum as a transitional mechanism—in the context of creating competitive federalism for securities law in contrast to corporate law, for which there is no analogous federal code in the United States. It is, however, probable that opening securities regulation up to state competition would enhance Delaware's dominant position as an incorporation state. This is because, to the extent that the national securities laws have been accurately taken to task for requiring costly and excessive disclosure and fostering frivolous antifraud litigation, Delaware, in all likelihood, would offer a securities regime that mitigates these problems.

Delaware's fiscal prosperity depends to a significant extent upon providing rules that reduce firms' costs of doing business. As a small state, it would not have indigenous income sources to replace the substantial revenue it derives from the franchise tax were it to lose incorporations to a state more responsive to business needs. This motivation is a key to Delaware's chartering market success: Delaware's reliance on franchise tax revenues serves as a commitment device to ensure firms that it will continue to enact legislation that firms desire (statutes that maintain share values as new business conditions warrant code revision).[105] Such a commitment device is critical to the production of corporate charters because a corporate charter is a relational contract, extending over many years during which unforeseen contingencies are likely to arise. Such uncertainty makes it difficult for contracting parties to specify in advance their obligations, and, as performance is not simultaneous, the possibility of opportunistic breach is increased. In particular, firms select their domicile and pay franchise taxes based on the extant legal regime and run the risk that as business conditions change thereafter, the state will not adapt its code (or will repeal key provisions to firms' disadvantage). The opportunism problem of relational contracting is exacerbated when one of the contracting parties is the state, given its role as the enforcer of contracts through the court system.

Delaware has surmounted the commitment problem by investing in assets that have no value outside of the chartering market, thereby guaranteeing to firms that it will continue to be responsive in its code after they incorporate. These assets include its specialized corporate court system and a reputation for responsiveness dependent on its high ratio of franchise taxes to total tax revenues. To the extent that Delaware can gain further franchise revenues from crafting a responsive securities regime, the same factors will operate in the

105. For the details of the argument, see ROMANO, *supra* note 4, at 38; and Romano, *supra* note 19, at 240-42.

securities, as in the chartering, context, and Delaware will have stronger incentives than the SEC to find the desirable regulatory balance.

D. *Regulatory Innovation and Competition: Variety and Uniformity in State Securities Laws*

A more traditionally articulated benefit of federalism that is integrally related to the incentive effects of competition is that it permits experimentation in legal rules, as states implement different solutions to specific problems. This, in fact, occurs in the corporate chartering context. Successful corporate law innovations diffuse rapidly across the states.[106] For instance, to address a perceived crisis in directors' and officers' liability insurance in the mid-1980s, states enacted a variety of statutory approaches, including permitting firms to cap or eliminate monetary liability of outside directors for negligence and changing the fiduciary duty standard of care from negligence to willful misconduct or recklessness.[107] Within a few years, the vast majority of states copied Delaware's approach, permitting charter amendments to eliminate liability.[108]

There is, however, far greater variation in state approaches to securities regulation than to corporate law, which has tended to uniformity in key default provisions through the diffusion of statutory innovations.[109] For example, some states have merit review regimes, which condition securities' registration on their meeting a standard of investment worthiness or merit, while the majority of states employ a disclosure approach, similar to the federal securities laws.[110] The distinction across state securities regimes is not, after all, entirely clear-cut, because merit review for compliance with the investment standard can take the form of requiring greater disclosure of aspects of an issue viewed with disfavor by the regulator, rather than denial of registration.[111]

106. *See* William J. Carney, *Federalism and Corporate Law: A Non-Delaware View of the Results of Competition*, *in* INTERNATIONAL REGULATORY COMPETITION AND COORDINATION: PERSPECTIVES ON ECONOMIC REGULATION IN EUROPE AND THE UNITED STATES 153, 172-74 (Joseph McCahery et al. eds., 1996); Romano, *supra* note 19, at 233-35.

107. *See* Roberta Romano, *Corporate Governance in the Aftermath of the Insurance Crisis*, 39 EMORY L.J. 1155, 1160-61 (1990).

108. *See id.*; *see also* Carney, *supra* note 106, at 167. Firms that reincorporated in Delaware to take advantage of the limited liability statute experienced positive returns, while event studies of the enactment of Delaware's limited liability statute, and of firms' charter amendments to opt into the statute, do not pick up a significant (positive or negative) price effect. *See* ROMANO, *supra* note 4, at 19-24.

109. *See* Carney, *supra* note 106, at 165, 174-75; Romano, *supra* note 19, at 235.

110. *See* Ad Hoc Subcomm. on Merit Regulation of the State Regulation of Sec. Comm. of the Am. Bar Ass'n, *Report on State Merit Regulation of Securities Offerings*, 41 BUS. LAW. 785, 790 (1986) [hereinafter ABA Report]. Variation in states' approaches to securities regulation dates from the initiation of state securities laws at the turn of the century, when only a subset of the states adopted merit regulation modeled after Kansas's pioneering blue sky law (another name for state securities laws), which predated the federal legislation. *See* Jonathan R. Macey & Geoffrey P. Miller, *Origin of the Blue Sky Laws*, 70 TEX. L. REV. 347, 377-80 (1991).

111. *See* ABA Report, *supra* note 110, at 823.

In addition, the import of the difference is limited because only a subset of securities are subject to state regulation; nationally traded shares are excluded, and individual exemptions are often granted.[112] Investors can also avoid a home state's merit review regime: If a security is not registered in their state, they can acquire it in an unsolicited secondary market transaction rather than in the initial public offering.[113]

The absence of competition in the securities field probably accounts for the greater variation in regulatory approach across the states than in corporate law.[114] But the limited applicability of the states' registration regimes is undoubtedly also a factor, for where the vast majority of investors prefer a particular regime, competition will produce incentives for regulators to choose that regime. Accordingly, if the variation in securities regulation is due, for instance, to regulators' preference for merit review differing from that of investors, in a competitive system merit regulation would not survive. In fact, even in the absence of regulatory competition, merit regulation has been on the decline, for, in addition to the expanding number of exemptions from coverage under merit regimes, several important states, such as Illinois, eliminated their merit review provisions in the 1980s.[115]

The empirical research on state securities laws does not provide much support for merit regulation. Studies find that securities sold in non-merit-review states have higher returns and greater risk than those sold in merit review states;[116] while this result is what merit regulators set out to accomplish, there is no evidence that the reduction in risk is desirable. Specifically, there is no evidence that securities risk is positively correlated with fraud, that investments in non-merit-review states are subject to more

112. *See id.* at 796 (describing exemptions for issues traded on national exchanges or registered with the SEC); Kevin G. Salwen, *State Laws Are Often Overkill, Some Say*, WALL ST. J., July 20, 1987, at 35 (describing individual exemptions). Of course, these issues are not exempt from the states' antifraud statutes.

113. *See* UNIF. SEC. ACT § 402(b)(3), 7B U.L.A. 601 (1985) (providing an unsolicited offer exemption for securities resales).

114. Saul Levmore offers two explanations of variety in legal rules that suggest that differences would remain across securities regimes even in the presence of competition. Variety exists because the rules "do not much matter or . . . raise issues about which reasonable people (even in the same culture) could disagree." Saul Levmore, *Variety and Uniformity in the Treatment of the Good-Faith Purchaser*, 16 J. LEGAL STUD. 43, 44 (1987). If reasonable people can disagree over which securities regime best safeguards investors against fraud and low-quality investments, competition would not eliminate merit regulation but rather would preserve it, as investors (and hence firms) self-selected across states, choosing the regime that they considered preferable for protecting their financial interest. In addition, if the adoption of either merit review or disclosure regulation does not differentially affect the level of investor fraud, then the choice of regime would not matter and variety could be preserved, although, as Levmore notes, the commercial needs of a national market would press toward uniformity despite the inconsequential effect of variety. *See id.* at 60.

115. *See, e.g.*, ABA Report, *supra* note 110, at 786 (reporting that Illinois and Louisiana abandoned merit review in 1983 and 1985, respectively).

116. *See* DAVID J. BROPHY & JOSEPH A. VERGA, THE INFLUENCE OF MERIT REGULATION ON THE RETURN PERFORMANCE OF INITIAL PUBLIC OFFERINGS (University of Michigan Sch of Bus. Admin. Working Paper 91-19, 1991) (reviewing other studies and presenting new data).

instances of fraud than those registered in merit review states, or that investors residing in merit review states are more risk-averse, uninformed, or financially unsophisticated than those in non-merit states. The absence of a showing of significant benefits to investors from merit regulation suggests that opening state securities regulation up to competition would hasten its demise.

The probability that competition will hasten the demise of merit regulation is important because it sheds light on a potential concern over abandoning the mandatory federal system: Would investors be harmed by a subsequent loss of standardized disclosure across firms governed potentially by fifty-plus regimes? Competitive federalism does not necessarily increase variation in the legal regime. State charter competition has, in fact, produced substantial uniformity across corporate codes, preserving variety in its enabling approach to rules, an approach that permits firms to customize their charters if the default provisions of the statutes are not suitable.[117] This situation is likely to be true for competitive disclosure regimes, as the most desirable disclosure standards would diffuse across the states.

More important, the most significant area of standardization, firms' financial reporting, would still be controlled by the private sector under the Financial Accounting Standards Board (FASB), and thus be consistent across firms complying with its rules. States could require compliance with FASB standards to assist firms' needs for uniformity,[118] or stock exchanges could perform a standardizing function, as they did prior to the enactment of the federal regime, by requiring listing firms to comply with FASB or their own disclosure requirements. Even without such requirements, most firms would comply with most FASB standards voluntarily to reduce their cost of capital, just as firms at times disclose information beyond that required by regulators today.[119] It is important to note that although the SEC does not exercise any statutory control over the FASB, it has authority to promulgate accounting rules,[120] and it has thereby exerted significant influence over FASB by the threat that it would adopt its own standards if FASB would not act.[121] Because the market approach eliminates the SEC's prescription of accounting rules for any firms other than those voluntarily submitting to its jurisdiction, its power to influence FASB standards would be greatly reduced under the proposal.

117. *See* ROMANO, *supra* note 4, at 1.

118. In fact, most states currently recognize FASB as the accounting standards-setter through their regulation of public accountants. State accounting boards, which license public accountants, control accountants' activities by identifying sources of generally accepted accounting principles (GAAP) and enforcing compliance with such principles through ethics regulations, which typically recognize the FASB as the authority on GAAP. *See* PAUL B.W. MILLER ET AL., THE FASB: THE PEOPLE, THE PROCESS, AND THE POLITICS 22 (3d ed. 1994).

119. *See supra* notes 38-41 and accompanying text.

120. *See* 15 U.S.C. § 78m (1994).

121. *See* PELHAM GORE, THE FASB CONCEPTUAL FRAMEWORK PROJECT 1973-1985, at 18, 22 (1992).

When competition is introduced into securities regulation, specific rules will undoubtedly develop that differ from those imposed by the SEC, even under state disclosure regimes, as states experiment to find the regime most attractive to registering firms. This could be accomplished by two routes: enactment of substantively different rules from SEC rules; or application to securities laws of the enabling approach taken by corporate law, in which state securities laws (which may or may not be the same as SEC rules) would operate as default rules from which firms could opt out if they so chose. Where a majority of firms opt out of a default, the state obtains information concerning the appropriateness of that rule, and eventually the rule is revised by that state or another state that obtains new registrations (and hence increased revenue) by enacting the more desirable default.[122] Analogous to the states' offering of special statutes for small firms, referred to as close corporation statutes, in the chartering context, with competitive securities regulation, a state could further offer firms a menu of regimes from which to choose (such as the choice of an extensive disclosure regime, a more limited disclosure regime, and a merit review regime).

If the SEC's rules are optimal, as its supporters contend, then either firms will not opt out of SEC coverage or they will opt into state securities regimes that are identical to the SEC's regime. But if all states simply mimicked the SEC's rules, the benefits from enacting the market approach would be reduced: Although needed regime revisions would be more speedily undertaken as a state regulator would act more quickly than the SEC to update its code to meet investor preferences, investors would bear increased transaction costs under competition; firms would have to inform investors, or investors would otherwise have to learn, of the firms' securities domicile choice. The absence of empirical support for the rationales underlying federal regulation, important instances of misguided SEC disclosure policy, and persistent concerns voiced over frivolous litigation suggest, however, that the particulars of securities regulation under competition will differ significantly from the present federal regime.

E. *Alternative Market-Oriented Proposals*

There are two alternatives to the competitive federalism approach to securities regulation advocated in this Article that are also market-oriented: eliminating the mandatory features of the federal regime by converting the federal securities laws into default provisions from which firms could opt out,

122. An example of a default rule change in state corporation codes is the default for preemptive rights. In the earliest corporation codes, shareholders had these rights unless a firm expressly opted out of them in its charter, whereas in modern codes these rights exist only if the firm expressly includes them in its charter. *See* Samuel Arsht & Walter Stapleton, *Delaware's New General Corporation Law: Substantive Changes*, 23 BUS. LAW. 75, 76-77 (1967).

analogous to the enabling form of corporation codes; and replacing the government regulatory apparatus with a private, exchange-based regulatory regime.[123] Both of these alternatives harness market-based incentives to the regulatory system. Neither is precluded by this Article's multiple-regulator approach.

1. *A Federal Default Regime*

In a federal default regime, firms that did not wish to be governed by particular SEC rules or statutory provisions could specify alternative provisions in their corporate charters or bylaws (or in the indenture contracts for debt securities). Congress would either specify itself, or delegate to the SEC to determine, which securities regulations, if any, a firm must opt out of by a charter, as opposed to bylaw, amendment.[124] A default system would clearly be more desirable than the present one-size-fits-all regime, which is difficult to change because consensus must be developed among all participants regarding a new rule, even if their needs are quite different. For example, the SEC has been surveying registrants with a view to updating its rules regulating shareholder proxy proposals, and on the question whether to retain the current voting thresholds for a proposal's resubmission, ten corporate respondents produced eight different threshold proposals.[125] A lack of consensus among firms on such a matter is of far lesser import under a default system because firms can obtain the threshold level most appropriate for their shareholder configuration by provision in their charter or bylaws.

Under an enabling approach, if a default rule is suboptimal (that is, the rule's compliance costs outweigh benefits to investors), the majority of firms will elect not to be subject to the rule. Assuming the SEC became informed of firms' choices, perhaps by a requirement that firms file securities "charters" with the agency so that it could track deviations from the defaults, this market response would feed back into the SEC's decisionmaking process, leading it to readjust its beliefs concerning what regulation was most appropriate and, ultimately, to alter the default rule to one more compatible with investors' needs, just as would occur with state competition. There would also be a potential benefit compared to state competition for securities regulation: Transaction costs would be reduced because investors would not have to determine which regime governs their transactions. But if the SEC is not attentive in updating its defaults, there would be little savings in transaction

123. *See* ROMANO, *supra* note 4, at 107.

124. The difference between charter and bylaw amendment is that state corporation codes require shareholder approval of changes to the charter, but not to the bylaws. *See, e.g.*, DEL. CODE ANN. tit. 8, § 109 (1996) (bylaw amendment); *id.* § 242(b) (charter amendment).

125. *See Some of Surveyed Firms Show Consensus on "Cracker Barrel," Other Issues*, 29 Sec. Reg. & L. Rep. (BNA) 567, 569 (Apr. 25, 1997).

costs, because investors would have to identify whether a firm were operating under particular outdated SEC defaults or its own alternatives.

An enabling national regime would be preferable to the current mandatory one, but, in my judgment, a competitive system of securities regulation is even more preferable. State competition would not preclude a national enabling regime, as the federal government could adopt an enabling regime in competition with the states, as may any or all states. But state competition would provide an additional benefit over a federal enabling regime: There would be a straightforward mechanism by which regulators learn of firms' adoption of statutory defaults. Under regulatory competition, there would be some variety in defaults across states, even if key innovations diffuse over time across the states, as has occurred in the corporate law context. This phenomenon would accelerate regulators' identification of the rules most desired by investors, as more firms would register in the states with the more desirable default rules. This would also reduce investors' transaction costs of learning whether a firm has customized an outdated default.

A further benefit of state competition compared to a federal enabling regime would be a more rapid updating of undesirable defaults because of financial incentives. A state such as Delaware would be considerably more attentive to the need to reduce the transaction costs generated by obsolete defaults than the SEC, because of the state's financial dependence on the relevant franchise taxes. Because firms have no alternative regulator in the monopolist enabling regime, the SEC is not exposed to the same code-updating incentives as would be experienced by states—declining revenues due to declining registrations.[126] The pressure experienced by the SEC from global competition, whether under an enabling statute or the mandatory regime currently in effect, is quite weak because resort solely to foreign capital markets for financing is not a viable option for publicly traded U.S. firms. The best evidence that global competition is not as effective a motivator for the SEC as direct domestic regulatory competition comes from the regulation of derivative securities. In the derivatives regulatory context, where the SEC has exclusive jurisdiction over the derivatives disclosures of publicly traded domestic companies, it has been minimally responsive to issuers' concerns

126. A regulatory monopoly affords the SEC the opportunity to implement policies favoring the interests of financial market professionals rather than investors. *See, e.g.*, PHILLIPS & ZECHER, *supra* note 33, at 22-23 (discussing disclosure policies); David D. Haddock & Jonathan R. Macey, *Regulation on Demand: A Private Interest Model, with an Application to Insider Trading Regulation*, 30 J.L. & ECON. 311, 318-30 (1987) (discussing insider-trading regulation). Market professionals benefit from receiving free information from firms under the SEC's mandatory disclosure policies, and from the absence in the market of more informed traders under the insider-trading prohibition. Regulatory capture by market professionals would be more difficult under the market approach to securities regulation because corporations would opt for the regime more congenial to investors, as the providers of capital direct their funds to firms in those regimes; correspondingly, regulators sensitive to the number of corporations subject to their jurisdiction would adapt their rules to the preferences of investors, rather than to those of market professionals.

about regulatory costs and competitiveness.[127] Where the SEC competes with the Commodity Futures Trading Commission (CFTC) for jurisdiction, however, it has shifted from an initial position of opposing equity derivative products to one encouraging and promoting innovation by its regulatees, stock exchanges, to facilitate their competition against the futures exchanges regulated by the CFTC.[128]

A final potential benefit of state competition compared to an enabling national regime turns on whether any mandatory rules are desirable in the securities context, for instance, to facilitate a firm's credible commitment to investors that it will not engage in opportunistic behavior by altering a securities default to one offering less protection after the investments are made.[129] Mandatory rules could not be effectuated satisfactorily under a national enabling approach. For if the national enabling regime consisted of a mix of defaults and mandatory provisions, then we would be left with the problem endemic in the current monopolist-regulator setup: There would be no

127. *See* SEC Derivatives Disclosure, *supra* note 54, at 6054-62 (describing minor changes made in response to comment letters on the proposal and presenting a superficial cost-benefit analysis of the proposal).

128. *See* Roberta Romano, *The Political Dynamics of Derivative Securities Regulation*, 14 YALE J. ON REG. 279, 354-59 (1997) (discussing the shift in the SEC's approach to product innovation). Some might attempt to characterize the SEC's loosening of its holding period for the resale of restricted (unregistered) securities under Rule 144, *see* Revision of Holding Period Requirements in Rules 144 and 145, 62 Fed. Reg. 9242 (1997) (to be codified at 17 C.F.R. pt. 230), as evidence of the SEC's responsiveness to competitive pressures, since the reform is a recognition by the agency that compliance costs were too high for small businesses, *see id.* at 9243-44. In my opinion, this action does not provide evidence that the SEC is particularly responsive to competitive pressure. The holding period revision took almost two years to be adopted. Delaware, by contrast, responds to corporate complaints much more quickly. *See* Romano, *supra* note 107, at 1160 (discussing the enactment of a limited liability statute within one year of an insurance crisis and a controversial judicial opinion). Moreover, the change has had no effect on the disclosure obligations of the public companies that are the focus of this Article's proposal, as it is directed at easing 1933 Act offering requirements for small firms and not at easing the continuing reporting obligations of the 1934 Act. The 1934 Act disclosure obligations have, in contrast to the SEC's moves to limit 1933 Act coverage, significantly increased over time, as the SEC has come to view the 1934 Act as the centerpiece of its regulatory authority rather than the 1933 Act, in a policy referred to as "integrated disclosure." *See, e.g.*, DAVID L. RATNER & THOMAS L. HAZEN, SECURITIES REGULATION 129-34 (5th ed. 1996). Finally, and most important, the SEC has sought to eliminate competition and establish its regime internationally, by identifying harmonization of regulatory standards as a central goal of its policy toward international securities regulation. *See* Policy Statement of the Securities and Exchange Commission on Regulation of International Securities Markets, Exchange Act Release No. 6807, 53 Fed. Reg. 46,963, 46,963 (1988) (stating that regulators should "seek to minimize differences between systems"). Although the SEC's policy statement also asserted that regulators should be "sensitive to cultural differences and national sovereignty concerns," *id.*, this is belied by the SEC's implementation of the policy at home, where it requires foreign firms to reconcile their financial statements with GAAP in order to list in the United States, *see infra* notes 190-191 and accompanying text.

129. Jeffrey Gordon has advanced this argument in the corporate law context. *See* Jeffrey N. Gordon, *The Mandatory Structure of Corporate Law*, 89 COLUM. L. REV. 1549, 1573-75 (1989). I remain skeptical, however, of a justification for mandatory rules involving promoters' needs for a commitment device concerning the stability of the initial domicile choice. *See* Roberta Romano, *Answering the Wrong Question: The Tenuous Case for Mandatory Corporate Laws*, 89 COLUM. L. REV. 1599 (1989) (responding to Gordon's argument). A shareholder vote would be required for a change in securities domicile, as it is for a change in incorporation state, *see infra* Subsection II.B.2, and, accordingly, the need for mandatory rules as a commitment device would be minimal because the successful occurrence of an opportunistic relocation would be extremely remote.

mechanism to check whether the mandatory provisions were, in fact, the ones that investors would voluntarily choose. Multiple regulators would permit mandatory provisions without the consequent costs, as such provisions could vary across jurisdictions, and information would therefore be provided concerning which provisions were desirable through the registration decisions of firms.

2. *Regulation by Exchanges*

A more decidedly deregulatory approach would be to leave securities regulation to the stock exchanges on which firms list.[130] In such a regime, exchange-listing conditions would include the substantive content of securities laws, such as periodic disclosure requirements. Exchanges can solve free rider problems concerning information production encountered by individual firms, as well as coordination problems presented by investors' need for standardized disclosure. Thus exchanges could replace the government as the solution to a securities market failure. Indeed, much of the disclosure predating the 1934 Act discussed by Benston was an NYSE listing requirement.[131] Moreover, multiple exchanges compete for listings. To the extent that maximizing trading volume is a function of listings, exchanges would be subject to the same incentives as states competing for charters, leading them to adopt listing requirements preferred by investors (or to shares discounted accordingly).[132]

As with a national default regime, an exchange-based regime would be likely to save transaction costs compared to state competition, because investors are directly informed of which regime applies when they trade shares.[133] But there could still be a regulatory role for the states in an exchange-regulated system. Although the over-the-counter market for the largest stocks, NASD's Automated Quotation System (NASDAQ), is a sufficiently developed regulatory organization capable of offering its own securities regime, if the NASDAQ regime were poorly suited for the smallest

130. For a recent article advocating this approach, see Paul G. Mahoney, *The Exchange as Regulator*, 83 VA. L. REV. 1453 (1997).

131. *See* Benston, *Evaluation*, *supra* note 37, at 133. Paul Mahoney provides a detailed description of the NYSE's pre-SEC disclosure requirements. *See* Mahoney, *supra* note 130, at 1466.

132. *See* Fischel, *supra* note 31, at 125; Mahoney, *supra* note 130, at 1459. Amihud and Mendelson argue that exchanges would provide trading rules that benefit investors only if firms, and not exchanges, choose where a security is listed (in the context of multiple listing of shares or the trading of derivative securities). *See* Amihud & Mendelson, *supra* note 31, at 1442-46. The issues of interest here, however, involve issuer-shareholder transactions and not trading rules. The concerns of Amihud and Mendelson and other critics of exchange self-regulation (which focus on exchanges' mismatched incentives regarding trading rules that can exploit investors, *see, e.g.*, Mahoney, *supra* note 130, at 1462-63), are thus not relevant to the discussion.

133. The transaction cost savings would obviously be reduced if a firm's shares were traded on more than one exchange. Even if the secondary exchange were to adopt a regime that recognized the primary exchange's rules as governing all issuer shares regardless of transaction location, investors still would have to know which exchange was the primary one.

firms traded over-the-counter ("bulletin board" and "pink sheet" issues), it might be more cost-effective for a state, rather than for the firms' market makers to organize and operate a separate securities regime.

State regulation would, however, offer some decided benefits over stock exchange regulation: a more effective mechanism of private dispute resolution for securities suits against issuers, and a public enforcement system, should the deterrent effect of criminal prosecution for securities law violations be a necessary complement to civil liability. Class action litigation is not well-suited for private arbitration,[134] and it is not surprising that arbitration programs currently administered by exchanges resolve individual complaints against brokers, not class complaints against issuers. As a consequence, even when courts have permitted classwide arbitration, they have retained substantial judicial involvement, including the initial determination of the certifiability of the class and review of the settlement.[135] Thus, state or federal courts would be required to enforce the exchanges' regulatory regime. This creates two difficulties. First, the use of tribunals not operated by exchanges externalizes the cost of their legal proceedings, which is a disadvantage from a social welfare, as opposed to investor, perspective. With state securities regulation, the fees the states earn in the registration process would defray the costs of administering securities cases.

Second, regulatory competition is most effective when the sovereign's jurisdiction includes both the court and the legislature. Canada, for instance, has not developed a vigorous charter competition across the provinces in large part because the provincial governments do not control the adjudication of corporate law disputes; securities administrators (of any province) and the national supreme court share that authority with the incorporation province.[136] This renders it impossible for a province to guarantee a responsive legal regime to prospective incorporators, because a securities administrator can impose obligations on firms countermanding provincial laws. A similar difficulty would be experienced by exchanges that were unable to

134. The hybrid use of courts and arbitrators in class arbitration suggests some of the difficulties. *See, e.g.*, Keating v. Superior Court, 645 P.2d 1192, 1214-18 (Cal. 1982) (Richardson, J., dissenting) (describing problems with class arbitration). For a discussion of these and other difficulties by proponents of arbitration, see G. Richard Shell, *Arbitration and Corporate Governance*, 67 N.C. L. REV. 517, 551, 553-55, 561 (1989); and Note, *Classwide Arbitration: Efficient Adjudication or Procedural Quagmire?*, 67 VA. L. REV. 787, 799, 805-06 (1981).

135. *See Keating*, 645 P.2d at 1209-10 (holding that judicial involvement in class arbitration includes determination of certification and notice to class, supervision of the adequacy of counsel, and dismissal or settlement, and remanding to the trial court to determine the feasibility of the class); Lewis v. Prudential Bache Sec., 235 Cal. Rptr. 69, 75-76 (Ct. App. 1986) (finding class arbitration feasible, and leaving to the trial court the determination of all issues necessary to certify the class and to provide proper notice); Izzi v. Mesquite Country Club, 231 Cal. Rptr. 315, 322 & n.6 (Ct. App. 1986) (remanding to the trial court to determine certifiability of the arbitration class and noting the preferability of court determination of any class action problems involving notice and discovery). None of the cases permitting classwide arbitration has involved securities law claims.

136. *See* Ronald J. Daniels, *Should Provinces Compete? The Case for a Competitive Corporate Law Market*, 36 MCGILL L.J. 130, 182-84 (1991).

adjudicate all of the disputes arising under their securities regimes. This problem is, in fact, raised in a weaker form even under the competitive federalism proposal advocated in this Article, for unless firms adopt forum clauses specifying that all securities claims are to be adjudicated in courts of their securities domicile, investors would be able to file in non-domicile courts. Although these courts would apply the law of the domicile, they might lack the expertise to adjudicate disputes as effectively as the domicile.[137] In sum, regulation by exchanges will at best be a dual regulatory system, with much of the enforcement of exchange rules performed by the government.[138]

It is important to note that state competition for securities regulation would not preclude exchange-based regulation. A state could, for instance, adopt a securities regime only for non-exchange-traded corporations, or enact no mandatory disclosure requirements at all, thereby leaving the determination of such requirements to exchanges. Because such an outcome would be within the realm of possible outcomes under competitive federalism, the prudent approach to regulatory policy reform would be to implement incremental experimentation: Replace the current monopolist regulator with state competition and permit the competitive process to reach the judgment that an exchange-based securities regime provides a set of rules as good as or more optimal than those provided by the states.

II. Implementing the Market Approach to Securities Regulation

Operationalizing a market approach to securities regulation for issuers requires two legislative reforms. The first and more straightforward reform is to make the federal securities laws optional. This could be achieved by an act of Congress. Alternatively, the SEC could cede its exclusive authority over public corporations under its newly granted exemptive power.[139] This solution is, however, akin to asking the agency to put itself out of business, behavior that would be decidedly out of character for an agency that has historically sought to increase, not to decrease, its jurisdictional scope.[140] In addition, an act of Congress expressly eliminating the SEC's exclusive regulatory authority over publicly traded firms is the preferable course of action because the statute creating the SEC's exemptive authority also preempted the states from applying registration requirements to nationally

137. *See infra* Section II.A; Subsection III.A.2.

138. *Cf.* Mahoney, *supra* note 130, at 1498-99 (discussing the need for government assistance in deterring exchange-regulation fraud).

139. *See* National Securities Markets Improvement Act of 1996, Pub. L. No. 104-290, § 105, 110 Stat. 3416, 3423 (codified at 15 U.S.C.A. §§ 77z-3, 78mm (West 1997)).

140. For an analysis of the SEC's failed effort to expand its jurisdiction to include derivative securities, see Romano, *supra* note 128, at 355-80.

traded securities.[141] The facial inconsistency between using the exemption to increase state authority when Congress was otherwise reducing state authority would provide opponents of the market approach to securities regulation reform the opportunity to use litigation to delay, if not defeat, its implementation.

The second major policy reform, adapting the choice-of-law rule governing securities transactions (site of sale) to one compatible with competition (issuer domicile), could be more complicated to accomplish because it would entail coordination by the states to adopt a new rule. It would therefore be more expedient for the congressional legislation making the federal regime optional also to institute the requisite change in choice of law, and this Article advocates such an approach. But because Congress has not typically legislated choice-of-law rules, this part of the Article not only explains the requisite change, but also justifies its adoption and critiques the reigning conflicts approach.

Two additional requirements for the successful implementation of the proposal are also discussed in this part: disclosure of the securities domicile to the purchaser of a security at the time of the purchase and a shareholder vote to accomplish a change in securities domicile. These refinements would ensure that the new market-oriented regime meets the stated goal of the federal securities laws: investor protection.

A. *An Internal Affairs Approach to the Choice-of-Law Rule for Securities Transactions*

With a market approach to securities regulation, only one sovereign's law can apply to an issuer's securities transactions. This means that only one state's securities law would govern securities transactions when the SEC option is not invoked. Similarly, when the SEC regulatory option were selected, it would preempt all state securities regulation, including antifraud provisions. The state with legislative jurisdiction[142] must be connected to the issuer to ensure that state competition operates properly—that one state's law governs and that it is the state chosen by the issuer. This would necessitate recrafting the reigning choice-of-law approach, which follows the site of the securities transaction and not the issuer's domicile.

---

141. *See* National Securities Markets Improvement Act § 102, 110 Stat. at 3417 (codified at 15 U.S.C.A. § 77r).

142. I adopt here terminology more commonly used in the international, as opposed to domestic, law setting: Legislative or prescriptive jurisdiction is "the authority of a state to make its laws applicable to particular conduct, relationships or status" (whether or not that state is the forum state), GARY B. BORN, INTERNATIONAL CIVIL LITIGATION IN UNITED STATES COURTS 491 (3d ed. 1996), as distinct from judicial jurisdiction, the power of a court to adjudicate a dispute, which, for U.S. courts, requires both personal jurisdiction and subject matter jurisdiction, *see id.* at 1-2. The federal securities laws confer both prescriptive and subject matter jurisdiction on federal courts.

1. *Applicability of the Internal Affairs Approach to Securities Transactions*

The prevailing choice-of-law approach to securities transactions is codified in provisions of the Uniform Securities Act: The applicable law is that of the site of the transaction, which is the state in which either the offer or the acceptance to buy the security takes place.[143] More than one state can claim legislative jurisdiction over a transaction under this approach, and the state whose law governs is not connected to the issuer.

The present choice-of-law rule, under which the securities law varies across a firm's stockholders based on where they purchased their shares, has a number of undesirable consequences for a legal system. These include lack of uniform treatment across similarly situated individuals and unpredictable standards of conduct for issuers, given the possible application of fifty-one (state and D.C.) statutes. These difficulties are, in fact, on occasion presented as the reason for the federal securities laws in cases involving the states' overlapping jurisdiction with the federal regime, such as the regulation of broker-dealers.[144] In the corporation code setting, the operational problems created by an absence of uniformity and predictability due to multistate shareholders are eliminated because the choice-of-law rule recognized by all of the states fixes one state's law, that of the incorporation state, as governing all shareholders' claims. This choice-of-law rule is referred to as the "internal affairs doctrine," because the subject matter of corporate law is characterized as the internal affairs of the corporation.[145]

The rationale for application of the internal affairs rule to corporate law disputes is equally applicable to the choice of law for securities transactions. In particular, choice-of-law commentators justify the internal affairs doctrine by the need for uniform treatment of shareholders. For example:

> It would be intolerable for different holders of the same issue of stock to have different sets of rights and duties by reason of their stockholdings, perhaps according to the laws of the various places at which they acquired their stock. Unity of treatment is desirable, and the only single law by which it can be achieved is that of the corporation's domicile.[146]

143. *See* UNIF. SEC. ACT § 414, 7B U.L.A. 672 (1985); *see also, e.g.*, CAL. CORP. CODE § 25008 (Deering 1997) (codifying section 414).

144. *See, e.g.*, Orman v. Charles Schwab & Co., 676 N.E.2d 241, 246 (Ill. App. Ct. 1996) (refusing to apply state law to claims against a broker because such application would frustrate, if not destroy, the goal of federal uniformity, and stating that "if uniformity is not to prevail, neither rule 10b-10 nor the SEC would serve any function or purpose in regulating disclosure").

145. *See* RESTATEMENT (SECOND) OF CONFLICTS OF LAW § 302 (1971).

146. ROBERT A. LEFLAR ET AL., AMERICAN CONFLICTS LAW 700 (4th ed. 1986). For a similar analysis by a choice-of-law scholar who specializes in corporate law issues, see P. John Kozyris, *Some Observations on State Regulation of Multistate Takeovers—Controlling Choice of Law Through the Commerce Clause*, 14 DEL. J. CORP. L. 499, 509-11 (1989).

The *Restatement (Second) of Conflicts of Law* similarly stresses as the rationale for preserving the internal affairs rule the need for "[u]niform treatment of directors, officers and shareholders . . . which can only be attained by having [their] rights and liabilities . . . governed by a single law."[147] The Supreme Court has also followed this approach in considering whether state takeover laws violate the Commerce Clause. The Court's validation of such statutes depends critically on a state's exclusive legislative jurisdiction as the incorporation state (that is, on the internal affairs rule), which avoids the impermissible risk of a corporation's encountering "inconsistent regulation by different States."[148]

Application of the internal affairs rule to securities transactions should go further than covering litigation arising from initial public offerings under state registration requirements and should include secondary market trading. Fraud claims against an issuer should be uniformly adjudicated across investors. It is even more troubling to differentiate fraud claims from corporate internal affairs than to differentiate securities registration requirements from corporate law. There is no plausible rationale for distinguishing a fiduciary standard of conduct to govern an officer's or director's judgment concerning a corporate transaction, such as payment of a dividend or undertaking a merger, from that officer's or director's judgment concerning disclosure about the firm's performance in a public document. Nor is there a rationale for permitting the differentiation of such standards across shareholders. Yet choice-of-law rules establish the application of one state's (the incorporation state's) standard to fiduciary duties in corporate law but leave the latter decision on disclosure to vary with the investor's domicile, even though a duty of full and fair disclosure is at the heart of the fiduciary duties of state corporate law. Such intellectual incoherence concerning fiduciary conduct is the fallout of current choice-of-law doctrine.

The bizarre possibility of fiduciary standards differing across shareholders according to their residence (or other location of their stock purchase or sale) has not yet been the focus of legislators' or commentators' attention because there have not been many cases involving conflicting fiduciary standards: The vast majority of securities claims are brought in federal court and settled.[149] In particular, the problem of certifying a class when the standard of liability depends on the shareholder's domicile or investment contract situs has not been raised with any frequency in the securities context, in contrast to the mass tort product liability context.[150] If securities cases are filed increasingly in

---

147. RESTATEMENT (SECOND) OF CONFLICTS OF LAW § 302 cmt. e.

148. CTS Corp. v. Dynamics Corp. of Am., 481 U.S. 69, 89 (1987). For an analysis of the relation of the *CTS* decision to the corporate choice-of-law rule, see Kozyris, *supra* note 146, *passim*.

149. *See* Vincent E. O'Brien, *A Study of Class Action Securities Fraud Cases 1988-1996*, at 4 (visited Dec. 28, 1997) <http://www.lecg.com/study2.htm#att>; *see also* GRUNDFEST & PERINO, *supra* note 3, at 9, 31.

150. *Cf.* Amchem Prods., Inc. v. Windsor, 117 S. Ct. 2231, 2249-50 (1997) (affirming the appellate court's rejection of an asbestos class action settlement for failing to meet statutory class requirements, and suggesting that the predominance of common issues that is a problem in mass tort litigation may not be

state, rather than federal, courts, whether in response to the 1995 securities litigation reform[151] or for other reasons, such as a more amenable settlement process,[152] then the class certification issue will take on a pressing importance. Beyond accomplishing this Article's immediate aim of empowering investors by creating a competitive regulatory regime, extending the internal affairs rule to state securities fraud claims would have the salutary effect of disposing of a thorny substantive law problem of varying liability standards, thereby ensuring that a class could be certified.

An additional salutary effect of following an internal affairs approach to securities regulation would be eliminating the potential problem of under-enforcement with multiple potential regulators. Without such an approach, ambiguity in regulatory responsibility can lead to regulatory free riding, as each regulator expects another regulator to be responsible. This is an increasing possibility with the expansion of Internet trading.[153] The internal affairs rule specifies precisely one regulator, the issuer's securities domicile, thereby removing the free-riding problem.

2. *Flaws in the Reigning Choice-of-Law Approach to Securities Transactions*

Conflict-of-law scholars typically rationalize the disparate choice-of-law approach to securities law that insulates state regulation of transactions in foreign corporations' shares from application of the internal affairs rule by contending that individual securities transactions do not implicate concerns

---

a problem in securities fraud). In a small number of securities cases, the courts have referred to the class certification issue in passing and largely ignored it when certifying the federal class, adding, on occasion, the proviso that the class could be decertified or divided up at a later date if individual state law issues presented a problem. *See, e.g.*, Lubin v. Sybedon Corp., 688 F. Supp. 1425, 1460-61 (S.D. Cal. 1988) (holding that for purposes of the state securities claim, the federal class, if certified, would need to be divided into subclasses of California and non-California investors); Weinberger v. Jackson, 102 F.R.D. 839, 847 (N.D. Cal. 1984) (certifying a class despite the assertion that a need for individual determinations of state law applicable to members' claims would overwhelm the commonality of the class, by finding the assertion of a conflicts problem premature as the defendants did not show that there was a true conflict among states' interests). Moreover, when the federal suit thereafter settled, there was either no mention of the individual state law determination issue, *see, e.g.*, Weinberger v. Jackson, No. C-89-2301-CAL, 1991 U.S. Dist. LEXIS 3938 (N.D. Cal. Mar. 19, 1991), or the federal class was certified without any mention of the need to subdivide it for the state claims, *see, e.g.*, *In re* U.S. Grant Hotel Assoc. Sec. Litig., 740 F. Supp. 1460, 1464 (S.D. Cal. 1990) (declaring settlement of the *Lubin v. Sybedon Corp.* litigation). *Matsushita Electric Industrial Co. v. Epstein*, 116 S. Ct. 873 (1996), in which a state court settlement disposed of federal securities claims, did not raise the multijurisdictional issue, because the state class action was a corporate law claim for breach of fiduciary duty and thus only one state's law applied to the class members. *See id.* at 882.

151. *See supra* notes 1-3 and accompanying text (discussing the impact of the 1995 Act on filings).

152. *See* Marcel Kahan & Linda Silberman, Matsushita *and Beyond: The Role of State Courts in Class Actions Involving Exclusive Federal Claims*, 1996 SUP. CT. REV. 219, 234-48 (discussing use of state courts to settle federal claims).

153. *Cf.* Clay Harris, *European Regulators Probe Defunct 'Virtual' Brokerage*, FIN. TIMES, Dec. 22, 1997, at 16 (reporting that an Internet broker that sold U.S. over-the-counter shares globally was being investigated by four nations' regulators after operations ceased).

about uniformity.[154] The explanation advanced for the distinction has two prongs: (1) In stock transactions, the individual purchasers are not yet shareholders (i.e., not members of the "corporate community") and therefore the transaction can be characterized as having purely local effect, which is said to give the buyer's domicile state an interest in regulation more significant than that of the issuer's state; and (2) a corporation can avoid a state's regulation by not selling its shares in that state, and thus need not be subject to inconsistent regulations.[155] The choice-of-law distinction between corporate and securities law is a legerdemain, but it has a certain practicality: It is more feasible for a corporation to issue fifty different disclosure statements to accompany the registration of securities than it is to operate with fifty different policies on dividend payouts and voting rights.

The flaw in the choice-of-law analysis that distinguishes corporate and securities laws is, however, easy enough to identify. The common shares of a corporation are the same in whatever state they are sold, and it is arbitrary to apply different criteria to transactions in the same securities simply because of differences in purchasers' residences. Indeed, securities litigation between investors and issuers is not individualized litigation: Management's defective disclosures are not differentially or personally directed at particular investors in the anonymity of modern capital markets, and the composition of the class of affected shareholders (those who entered into transactions in the relevant interval) is therefore fortuitous. In short, neither the prospective feature of the shareholder relation for a buyer of new securities nor the voluntary choice of selling securities in particular states can be characterized as individualizing the multiparty context of the corporate contract sufficiently to overcome the desirability of regulatory uniformity across security transactions for the issuer, as well as for investors, as they bear the increased cost of compliance with a panoply of regimes.

The demand for uniform and consistent treatment across investors is, in fact, recognized by the states' voluntary refusal to exercise regulatory authority over the securities of interstate (exchange-traded) corporations. The shift in legal regime from mandatory to optional federal coverage would not alter the desirability of this approach. Just as the federal law has trumped securities choice-of-law analysis under the exemptive policy of the state statutes, where a public corporation has chosen a specific state over the SEC as its securities regulator, registration requirements should be governed by that state's law.

Moreover, the limitation of a court's exercise of local legislative jurisdiction by a contract's choice-of-law clause's selection of a foreign state

154. *See, e.g.*, RESTATEMENT (SECOND) OF CONFLICTS OF LAW § 302 cmt. e (1971); Kozyris, *supra* note 146, at 520-21.

155. *See* Kozyris, *supra* note 146, at 521.

is well-established.[156] Although there are specific circumstances when courts refuse to enforce such provisions—when there are defects in contract clause formation, such as when the contracts are unconscionable adhesion contracts, or when the contracts contravene the public policy of the state that would otherwise exert legislative jurisdiction[157]—they are not relevant for securities law transactions. First, given the multiplicity of investment choices, securities transactions are not adhesion contracts. In addition, the proposed notice requirement concerning which state's law applies[158] would render highly improbable the possibility that an investor's agreement to a choice-of-law clause was fraudulently obtained. Second, securities transactions specifying the governing law of a state other than the buyer's state are also not contracts in contravention of public policy, the enforcement of which would deprive the plaintiff of an adequate remedy. Even in the remote possibility that the chosen securities domicile had no securities regulation at all, the absence of an appropriate remedy would not be an issue because a defrauded purchaser could still pursue a complaint under that state's common law fraud and fiduciary doctrines.[159]

The conventional conflicts-of-law objection to application of an internal-affairs-type doctrine to securities transactions, which is captured by the public policy exception to choice-of-law clause enforcement and to requirements that the chosen state have a reasonable connection to the transaction or the parties, is that the investor's domiciliary state has a more important "interest" in a securities dispute than the issuer's domicile.[160] The policy concern that is confusedly asserted as a state's "interest" in this instance is that the issuer's state will not provide an adequately protective regulatory regime against fraudulent sales practices because the buyers (or a majority of them) are not its citizens. This concern is founded, however, on a mistaken premise: The research on state competition for charters indicates that states that compete

156. *See, e.g.*, BORN, *supra* note 142, at 654-55 (stating that the contemporary approach in U S law regards choice-of-law provisions as presumptively enforceable). LEFLAR ET AL., *supra* note 146, at 415-19 (noting that authorities generally both approve of the right of parties to determine themselves what law governs contracts and prefer this basis for contract choice of law (citing RESTATEMENT (SECOND) OF CONFLICTS OF LAW § 187)).

157. *See, e.g.*, BORN, *supra* note 142, at 655, 661; LEFLAR ET AL., *supra* note 146, at 416-17, *cf* The Bremen v. Zapata Off-Shore Co., 407 U.S. 1, 12-13, 15-16 (1972) (expressing similar concerns in enforcing a choice-of-forum clause).

158. *See* discussion *infra* Subsection II.B.1.

159. *See* Roby v. Corporation of Lloyd's, 996 F.2d 1353, 1365-66 (2d Cir 1993) (upholding a United Kingdom choice-of-law contract provision over federal securities law claims, while noting the adequacy of remedies in English law). The adequacy-of-the-remedy prong of the Supreme Court's exemptions from upholding contractual choice-of-law clauses has been raised in securities law cases because the federal securities laws prohibit waiver of compliance. *See* 15 U.S C §§ 77n, 78cc(a) (1994) Were the federal statutes optional, the anti-waiver provisions would not apply to firms opting out of the federal regime, and the argument against enforcing a choice-of-law clause would be even more attenuated than it is at present

160. *See* LEFLAR ET AL., *supra* note 146, at 417 n.18 (discussing the relationship between the "reasonable relation" requirement and the public policy limitation on choice-of-law clauses under the Uniform Commercial Code).

successfully for corporate charters do not enact regimes that diminish investors' wealth.[161] Investors would benefit from an internal affairs rule for securities regulation as well because, as occurs in the chartering market, investors' preferences drive the regulatory competition. In addition, the proposed requirement that disclosure of securities domicile must be provided upon stock purchase[162] would eliminate the concern of the buyer's state that its citizens were inadequately protected: Domicile notice would ensure that buyers were informed of which state's regime is applicable. If the regime of the issuer's state were less favorable to investors than that of the buyer's state, the investor would pay less for the shares or not purchase them in the first place. Consequently, a requirement of physical connection to the state to make contracting parties' choice of law effective makes absolutely no sense in the securities context.[163]

3. *Which State Should Be the Securities Domicile?*

There are three plausible candidates for the single state whose rules govern a firm's securities transactions in place of the SEC: (1) a state chosen specifically for securities regulation by the issuer; (2) the issuer's incorporation state; and (3) the issuer's principal place of business. The first approach would be implemented through a choice-of-law clause in the corporation's charter (and noticed on the security). It would create, in effect, a statutory domicile for securities law. Under a choice-of-law clause approach, the choice of securities domicile could vary across a firm's financial instruments, as well as differ from the firm's statutory domicile (its incorporation state). The other two approaches operate automatically by the firm's choice of statutory domicile or headquarters site and hence would not require independent action by the corporation to effect a securities domicile choice, unless that choice were the SEC.

The least desirable securities domicile approach is to choose the state of principal place of business. This is because a physical presence requirement introduces friction into state competition. When physical and human capital must be relocated in order to effect a change in legal regime, a firm's decision to move to a more preferable securities domicile is considerably, if not prohibitively, more expensive than when such a relocation can be accomplished by means of a paper filing. Few firms would change domicile

161. *See supra* Subsection I.B.2.

162. *See* discussion *infra* Subsection II.B.1.

163. The *Restatement*, *see* RESTATEMENT (SECOND) OF CONFLICTS OF LAW § 187 cmt. f (1971), the Uniform Commercial Code, *see* U.C.C. § 1-105 (1996), and many states, *see, e.g.*, N.Y. GEN. OBLIG. LAW § 5-1401 (Consol. Supp. 1997), recognize that geographic contacts may be unnecessary for parties' effective choice. *See, e.g.*, LEFLAR ET AL., *supra* note 146, at 417-18 (discussing the implications of the New York provision).

to take advantage of incremental legal improvements under such a domicile approach compared to the other two approaches and, correspondingly, the incentives of states to provide securities codes responsive to investor preferences would be sharply diminished. The difference between the domicile choice of incorporation state (statutory domicile) and state of physical presence (referred to as the "*siège réel*," the corporation's real or effective seat, in some European nations) in corporate law is, in fact, a principal reason for the absence of charter competition across the nations of the European Union compared to U.S. states.[164]

Whether the most desirable approach for fostering competition over securities regulation is the choice-of-law clause or the incorporation state approach depends, in large part, on whether there are synergies from one state's administering both the corporate and securities law regimes. This is because the incorporation state approach harnesses the in-place apparatus of charter competition to the securities context. In general, such synergies should be substantial because corporate law expertise readily transfers to securities law. For instance, with one state's law adjudicating both corporate and securities issues, the standard for directors' and officers' fiduciary duties, including disclosure obligations, would be harmonized.[165] More specifically, all litigation relating to conduct during hostile takeovers would be governed by one state's law. In addition, all legal issues concerning shareholder meetings would be subject to the same legal regime, eliminating the considerable confusion surrounding the SEC's rules regulating shareholder proxy proposals, which simultaneously look to state corporate law's allocation of authority between shareholders and managers and effectively ignore it.[166] Where the synergies of an incorporation state securities domicile include the expertise of the judiciary, a firm could adopt a forum clause to ensure that securities claims are filed in the incorporation state.[167]

---

164. *See* ROMANO, *supra* note 4, at 132-33.

165. Indeed, two Supreme Court cases interpreting the federal securities law illustrate the difficulties created by the two regimes' being distinct. In *Basic Inc. v. Levinson*, 485 U.S. 224, 232-34 (1988), while imposing disclosure duties on managers regarding merger negotiations, the Court rejected as a valid concern the acquirer's desire for secrecy when nondisclosure for such reasons would not obviously be a breach of fiduciary duty at state law. In *Virginia Bankshares, Inc. v. Sandberg*, 501 U.S. 1083, 1102-06 (1991), a case involving proxy statement misstatements, the Court did not find the requisite causation for a private right of action under section 14(a) of the 1934 Act, 15 U.S.C. § 78n(a) (1994), where the complaining shareholders' votes were not required by state law to authorize the action subject to the proxy solicitation. The Court left open the question whether there would be sufficient causation if the shareholders lost a state remedy otherwise available because of the misstatement. *See Virginia Bankshares*, 501 U.S. at 1107-08.

166. *Compare* 17 C.F.R. § 240.14a-8(c)(1) & (7) (1997) (stating that firms can exclude proposals that are "not a proper subject for action by security holders" and involving "ordinary business operations"), *with* Adoption of Amendments Relating to Proposals by Security Holders, Exchange Act Release No. 12999, 41 Fed. Reg. 52,994 (1976) (permitting, where the subject is not proper for shareholder action, proposals couched in precatory language because recommendations to the board are not improper actions at state law, and permitting proposals involving ordinary business, such as employment practices, where they implicate social policy).

167. Such clauses are presumptively enforced at federal common law and by most states. *See* Carnival Cruise Lines, Inc. v. Shute, 499 U.S. 585, 593-95 (1991); Michael E. Solimine, *Forum-Selection Clauses*

But even if the substantive law synergies were limited in number, there is a further benefit associated with the incorporation state approach. Litigation costs would be reduced because the significance of line-drawing over whether a dispute implicates securities or corporate law is reduced, as the same sovereign's rules would apply in either scenario.

Although the arguments supporting the choice of incorporation state as the securities domicile appear to be compelling, there are countervailing considerations that militate against mandating such an approach rather than leaving the choice of domicile up to the issuer (the choice-of-law clause approach). First and most important, the choice-of-law clause approach obviates the need to guess whether the potential synergies of one regime for corporate and securities law are substantial—market participants' domicile choices would provide the information. It is therefore most consistent with the market approach to securities regulation. Second, given the variety of securities issued by firms, it is possible that states would specialize in different securities, and consequently, that firms could benefit from being able to select different domiciles for different issues. This is particularly relevant for debt securities, where there are no regulatory synergies with the incorporation state because corporate law deals solely with manager-shareholder relations.[168] Third, permitting a self-standing securities domicile might enhance state competition, as a state could decide to compete more vigorously for securities issues than for corporate charters and thus prevent Delaware from being able to slouch on the securities regime it offers because of its success in obtaining incorporations.

4. *Adapting the Securities Law Choice-of-Law Regime to the Market Approach*

Choice-of-law rules are generally creatures of judicial, rather than legislative, determination. But statutes may codify choice-of-law rules. For instance, some states have enacted the Uniform Securities Act's choice-of-law provisions, which select the most common judge-made choice, the state where the securities are offered for sale.[169] In addition, some states have adopted

---

and the Privatization of Procedure, 25 CORNELL INT'L L.J. 51, 63, 69 (1992).

168. *See, e.g.*, Revlon, Inc. v. MacAndrews & Forbes Holdings, Inc., 506 A.2d 173, 182 (Del. 1985) (finding that a board breached its fiduciary duty to shareholders by engaging in a takeover defensive tactic that protected noteholders, whose rights are a matter of contract); Harff v. Kekorian, 324 A.2d 215, 219-20 (Del. Ch. 1974) (stating that bondholders cannot bring a derivative suit), *rev'd on other grounds*, 347 A.2d 133, 134 (Del. 1975). A corporate code would be relevant for a bond contract only when a corporation is close to insolvency, for at that point some states might hold that the board's fiduciary duty encompasses creditors. *See* Credit Lyonnais Bank Nederland, N.V. v. Pathe Communications Corp., No. 12150, 1991 Del. Ch. LEXIS 215, at *108 (Del. Ch. Dec. 30, 1991) (suggesting that a board's duty shifts away from shareholders when the company enters the "vicinity of insolvency").

169. *See, e.g.*, CAL. CORP. CODE § 25008 (West 1997) (codifying UNIF. SEC. ACT. § 414, 7B U.L.A. 672 (1985)).

choice-of-law clause statutes, which guarantee enforcement of contractual choice-of-law provisions regardless of standard conflicts rules, such as whether the contracting parties have any relationship to the state.[170] Coordinated statutory action by the states altering the site-of-sale rule to an issuer securities domicile rule, such as by amendment to the Uniform Securities Act, would be a more expeditious route than reliance on judicial action for implementing the new domicile choice-of-law approach.

An even more efficacious alternative than coordinated state statutory action would be for Congress to legislate the mandatory application of the issuer domicile approach as the securities transactions choice-of-law rule in the statute rendering the federal securities regime optional. Although Congress has not mandated choice-of-law rules, it could do so under its Commerce Clause and Article IV powers.[171] Congressional action is the preferred mechanism for implementing the securities domicile choice-of-law rule, whether the incorporation state or choice-of-law clause approach is chosen, because it is the most expeditious method for achieving that end, as it does not require coordination by fifty state courts or legislatures.

Coordination can occur—the universal recognition of the internal affairs approach to corporate law is a prime example—but it takes time. For instance, most states enforce forum selection clauses; this sea change from an earlier era when such clauses were considered presumptively invalid has occurred by a mix of state legislative and judicial action, exemplifying a policy of reciprocity (that is, the states recognize residents' contracts to litigate in another state) rather than conscious coordination through adoption of a uniform act.[172] But, while the gradual shift to acceptance has been led by Supreme Court decisions upholding such clauses in federal cases over the past two decades,[173] there are still some states that do not enforce them.[174] If there is a similar pattern in the securities context as in the recognition of forum selection clauses—increasing acceptance of the concept of securities domicile with an

170. *See, e.g.*, DEL. CODE ANN. tit. 6, § 2708(c)(ii) (1993) (requiring a $100,000 minimum contractual amount); N.Y. GEN. OBLIG. LAW § 5-1401 (Consol. Supp. 1997) (requiring a $250,000 minimum contractual amount).

171. *See* LEFLAR ET AL., *supra* note 146, at 6. They note:

> [A]ssuming that the local law of a particular American state permits one of its courts to act in a given instance, the only authority which can effectively say that the court may not apply the law that it chooses is that of the federal government, under the powers delegated to it by the Federal Constitution.

Id. Although there is a well-established judicial tradition upholding forum clauses in commercial contexts, including securities transactions, *see, e.g.*, Scherk v. Alberto-Culver Co., 417 U.S. 506, 519-20 (1974); The Bremen v. Zapata Off-Shore Co., 407 U.S. 1, 18-19 (1972), to the extent there might be a question whether firms opting out of the federal regime can also opt out of the federal court system, the congressional legislation establishing the market approach should specify that federal courts are to enforce forum clauses selecting a state court.

172. *See* Solimine, *supra* note 167, at 75-76.

173. *See* cases cited *supra* note 171.

174. *See* Solimine, *supra* note 167, at 55, 63 & n.84 ("[A]t least four states explicitly reject . . . such clauses.").

outstanding small number of holdouts after many years—making the federal securities regime optional would not engender successful competition in securities regulation, at a minimum in the short run, because the incentives of issuers, investors, and regulators are not aligned when the law of the issuer's selected domicile does not govern all securities transactions.

Congressional enactment of a securities domicile conflicts rule would shortcut such an evolutionary process by immediately implementing all states' adherence to the securities domicile choice-of-law approach, and would thereby preserve the advantages of the market approach. It is, perhaps, ironic that the byproduct of federal intervention in the states' securities choice-of-law rulemaking would be a greatly invigorated competitive federalism.[175]

B. *Refinements to the Implementation of the Market Approach*

To ensure that the investor protection goal of the federal securities laws functions smoothly under the market approach, the congressional legislation that would render the federal regime optional and would fix an issuer domicile approach to the states' securities choice-of-law rule should contain two additional statutory mandates. These statutory requirements would establish investor safeguards at two critical transactional junctures, one occurring at the individual investor level and the other at the aggregate firm level. The first requirement is disclosure of the applicable legal regime (the firm's securities

175. Bruce Hay has criticized adopting a non-buyer-state approach to products liability litigation, contending that state competition in choice-of-law rules is a more promising alternative approach to substantive law competition regarding such torts. *See* Bruce L. Hay, *Conflicts of Law and State Competition in the Product Liability System*, 80 GEO. L.J. 617, 617 (1992). He asserts that states' policies of choice-of-law rules and substantive laws are inversely correlated. Thus, when states can follow a choice-of-law rule favorable to their citizen-plaintiffs under what is referred to in choice-of-law as the "governmental interests" approach, they can adopt pro-manufacturer substantive laws to protect in-state firms without harming in-state consumers. He concludes that this scenario indicates that competition over choice-of-law rules would produce the optimal level of substantive products liability law, because it would enable states to favor consumers in the choice-of-law rule and manufacturers in the substantive law. *See id.* at 651-52.

Hay's analysis is, however, mistaken. The governmental interest approach looks to the state's substantive policy to determine a state's "interest" in a lawsuit. If a state's law favored defendant-manufacturers, then a court applying the governmental interest standard would not be able to find that the state has expressed an interest in protecting its citizen-plaintiffs. It would therefore not be able to choose a pro-plaintiff state's law to govern the dispute, as Hay expects. As a consequence, Hay's crucial assumption, that the policy underlying a state's choice-of-law rule would be the inverse of the state's substantive law, is incorrect; the two policies must be positively correlated. Hence, competition in choice-of-law rules cannot substitute for substantive law competition in the products liability setting of concern to Hay, nor in any other substantive law setting. The operation of conflicts-of-law interest analysis prevents opportunistic choices of inconsistent substantive policies and choice-of-law rules. States can, of course, compete on both choice-of-law and substantive dimensions, but the choice-of-law rule that benefits investors in the securities context, an issuer securities domicile rule, is straightforward because it fosters substantive competition, which advantages investors since their preferences dictate the competitive outcome. States would thus have an incentive to choose the issuer domicile conflicts rule. But to achieve the full benefits from competition, one state's use of the internal affairs rule must be recognized by all the other states to assure that one state's law governs all of a firm's transactions with investors. This means that the same choice-of-law rule must be uniformly applied as the choice-of-law rule across the states. Over time, states would probably do so. *See supra* text accompanying notes 172-174.

domicile) at the time an investor acquires a security; the second is a vote of the affected security holders in order to accomplish a change in securities domicile.[176]

1. *Disclosure of the Applicable Securities Regime*

For state competition to function properly, investors must know what regime will apply to a particular security.[177] The domicile disclosure requirement would ensure that this condition holds. To accomplish this notice function, the securities domicile should be indicated on the instrument (stock certificate or note), just as corporate law requires that restrictions on share transferability, to be effective, must be noticed on the stock certificate.[178] But because investors rarely receive a financial instrument even after purchase (most stock investments transfer electronically and remain physically held by the clearinghouse depositary), a further mode of notice is essential. The most plausible additional means of domicile disclosure would entail a two-pronged approach, directed at both brokers and firms. First, brokers should be required to inform prospective buyers of the securities domicile at the time of purchase (or short sale). As federal broker regulation would not be transferred from the SEC under the proposed approach, such a requirement could easily be implemented by agency regulation.

Second, and more important, issuers should be required to disclose their securities domicile at the time of initial public offerings as a condition of opting out of the federal regime. The required disclosure should be permitted to take a variety of forms. Where the issuer's domicile requires use of a prospectus to sell securities, the federal requirement should be satisfied by indicating the domicile in that offering document. Where there is no prospectus

176. Albert Breton's theory of competitive federalism offers a rationale for requiring such provisions, even though competitive securities regimes would most likely adopt the disclosure and voting requirements on their own, as a means to ensure the vitality of competition. Breton maintains that a central government can play a useful role in stabilizing competitive federalism by monitoring state activity to prevent collusion or "races to the bottom" that would undermine the benefits of competition. *See* ALBERT BRETON, COMPETITIVE GOVERNMENTS: AN ECONOMIC THEORY OF POLITICS AND PUBLIC FINANCE 251 (1996). The two statutory requirements would obviate the need for the central government to monitor actively the competition over securities regimes. But because a race for the bottom will not occur in the securities context, given the dynamics of capital markets exemplified by the corporate charter market, it is not obvious that monitoring by the central government is necessary in this context.

177. Of course, not every investor needs to know a stock's domicile; the informed investors set the price. This is the meaning of an efficient market. The best available evidence indicates that the U.S. stock market is efficient regarding publicly available information, which includes an issuer's securities domicile. *See* Fama, *supra* note 55, at 1577, 1607 (stating that event studies, which test the "adjustment of prices to public announcements," provide the "cleanest evidence on market efficiency"). For general models of information aggregation through prices with heterogeneously informed investors, see Alan Schwartz & Louis Wilde, *Competitive Equilibria in Markets for Heterogeneous Search Goods Under Imperfect Information: A Theoretical Analysis with Policy Implications*, 13 BELL J. ECON. 181 (1982); and sources cited *supra* note 21.

178. *See, e.g.*, DEL. CODE ANN. tit. 8, § 202(a) (1996).

or other offering document requirement, the issuer should have to inform the prospective buyer of the securities domicile in writing, an obligation that could be satisfied by the issuer's contracting with the underwriting syndicate to provide the information in writing to prospective purchasers. In addition, for public offerings of a firm whose securities are already traded and whose securities domicile imposes periodic reporting requirements, disclosing securities domicile in the required documents should satisfy the issuer's federal notice requirement as long as such reports are matters of public record (i.e., filed with a state office) and thus available to prospective purchasers. Where a domicile imposes no periodic reporting requirements, voluntary disclosure of securities domicile in a public document available on a continuing periodic basis (such as in an annual financial report or proxy statement sent to shareholders for the annual meeting to elect directors, in the corporate charter on file with the Secretary of State, or in a publicly available record kept by the stock exchange on which the shares trade) should also satisfy the federal disclosure requirement. These latter forms of disclosure would also suffice for any issuer responsibility regarding domicile notice to investors who acquire securities in secondary trading markets.

Domicile disclosure would not be a costly requirement for issuers under any of the possible mechanisms that have been outlined. It would also not be costly for brokers to identify an issuer's securities domicile to prospective purchasers. But mandating disclosure of securities domicile at the time of a securities purchase is not clearly necessary to protect investors: Markets will price significant differences in securities regimes, as sophisticated investors obtain domicile information prior to their purchases, even were domicile disclosure not mandated. But, given the historical application of the federal regime to all securities, mandated domicile disclosure would go a considerable distance toward mitigating the relatively remote possibility of less sophisticated investors' not knowing that the federal regime might no longer apply. Because such confusion is most likely to occur in the initial years following the adoption of the market approach, the domicile disclosure requirement could be enacted as a sunset provision, expiring, for example, three years after the statute's effective date. For securities trading in markets where unsophisticated investors are predominant, such as penny stocks, the domicile disclosure requirement could be retained beyond such a transition period, as a protective measure for such investors.

The domicile disclosure requirement would not mandate disclosure of the substantive content of the relevant regime. Firms could, of course, provide such information to investors in their domicile disclosure, but the statutory requirement would leave acquisition of such details to investors. To the extent there might be concern that unsophisticated investors might mistakenly assume that all state regimes contain similar protections and could thereby be duped into buying penny stocks registered under a regime that institutional investors shun, a written disclaimer could be required at the time of such securities' acquisition, in addition to the domicile disclosure, that would inform investors, in large print, that "their rights under the securities laws may differ significantly across the states." Alternatively, a requirement could be fashioned to disclose the details of a regime's significant differences. I am reluctant to advocate such an approach given the costly line-drawing questions it is likely to entail. It would, at minimum, require careful drafting to specify the norm against which differences are to be measured, such as the rules of a majority of the states, the old federal regime, and so forth. The prospect of litigation over the fulfillment of the domicile disclosure requirement under such an alternative leads me to opt for the more generic disclaimer approach, should any disclosure beyond the domicile be required.

2. *Security Holder Approval of Securities Domicile Changes*

A different set of concerns regarding the securities domicile choice is implicated when an issuer determines to change its securities domicile midstream than is implicated when a shareholder purchases a security with a given domicile. Namely, the price the investor paid for its shares will not reflect the value of the new domicile (unless the change was anticipated at the time of purchase). This is of concern if corporate insiders can behave opportunistically and move to a securities domicile that requires less disclosure or has a lower securities fraud standard than the original regime. Such a move could shift value away from the public to insiders' shares, assuming, of course, that outside investors did not anticipate such opportunistic behavior and paid less for the more protective domicile in the first place.

Insider opportunism regarding domicile choice could be mitigated by requiring the voting approval of the affected security holders before a domicile change can be effected.[179] As in the corporate law context, the federal statute would create a minimum default for the required vote of a simple majority. Firms wishing to operate under a higher, supermajority voting requirement would therefore be able to do so. The most practical means of implementing a supermajority voting requirement would be for the corporation to include such a rule in its corporate charter (and, if commitment to such a voting rule was of concern, to subject its repeal to an analogous supermajority vote). States could also establish higher voting minimum defaults in their securities codes. A supermajority voting default to accomplish changes in securities domicile, however, would not be desirable from the global perspective of competitive federalism: When exit from a regime is too difficult, the signals

179. A change in incorporation state (the firm's statutory domicile) requires a shareholder vote because it is effected by a merger of the corporation into a subsidiary incorporated in the new domicile state. Under all state corporation codes, a merger requires shareholder approval. *See, e.g., id.* §§ 251-252.

from migration patterns concerning firms' preferred provisions are weakened, and the beneficial effects of competition stymied.

A majority voting requirement for securities domicile changes could ultimately aid insiders. In the absence of a voting requirement, it is possible that investors would expect value-diminishing moves to occur and pay less for their shares initially. The presence of a voting requirement would commit insiders to proposing a domicile change only when the new regime increases firm value, rather than when the regime disproportionately benefits their own shares, and, as a consequence, investors would not discount shares for opportunistic midstream domicile changes. To the extent that promoters value such a precommitment device, a federal voting requirement may well be unnecessary because competitive state codes would include such a requirement. Nevertheless, placing the requirement in the federal statute would create a more robust commitment device because, as an integral part of the regulatory regime, it would be difficult to rescind. It is, for example, more difficult to change congressional than state legislation.

Some commentators contend that shareholder voting is not an effective safeguard against insider opportunism because it is irrational for shareholders to vote—that is, an individual shareholder's cost of becoming informed in order to vote his or her interest outweighs the pro rata benefit he or she will receive from a correct outcome.[180] This contention, in my judgment, is vastly overblown.[181] In a capital market dominated by institutional investors holding portfolios of stock, issues are repeatedly raised across portfolio firms, reducing information costs significantly on any one vote. Moreover, the preferences of these informed voters—institutional investors—regarding securities regimes would not conflict with those of uninformed individual investors. This is because the vast majority of institutional investors, whose choices would determine the regime, do not possess private information or great skill at obtaining such information, and they would accordingly not benefit from a regime that minimizes firms' public disclosures.[182] It is possible that some

180. *See, e.g.*, Gordon, *supra* note 129, at 1575.

181. In particular, it can be shown that, under plausible assumptions concerning the breakdown of stock ownership among insiders, outside blockholders, and dispersed investors, a rational strategy for an uninformed shareholder concerned about the possibility of opportunism would not be the strategy of always supporting management with "yes" votes, the strategy emphasized by commentators critical of shareholder voting, but rather a mixed strategy of voting randomly against management's proposals, or a strategy of not voting at all, leaving the decision to the informed voters. Both of these latter strategies are better than always voting "no," as well as always voting "yes." *See* Romano, *supra* note 129, at 1607-10.

182. Mutual funds, for instance, do not outperform the stock market. *See, e.g.*, STEPHEN A. ROSS ET AL., CORPORATE FINANCE 348 (4th ed. 1996). This fact shows that these institutions do not have access to, or a comparative advantage in processing, private information, and there is little reason to think this circumstance would change with the switch to a competitive regime. The criticism leveled at relational investing, in which institutional investors engage in active monitoring of managers, that such investors may obtain private benefits that generate a conflict between their and other shareholders' interests, thereby reducing the value of their activism, *see* Jill E. Fisch, *Relationship Investing: Will It Happen? Will It Work?*, 55 OHIO ST. L.J. 1009, 1040-41 (1994); Edward B. Rock, *Controlling the Dark Side of Relational Investing*, 15 CARDOZO L. REV. 987, 989 (1994), is not applicable in our context. The posited private

institutional investors possess a superior ability to process public information; such investors would support a high level of disclosure, as that furthers their competitive advantage.

A probative example of this congruence in interest between institutional and individual investors regarding disclosure policy concerns the issues sold to institutional investors under Rule 144A, which exempts such issues from federal registration and hence the prospectus disclosure requirements of the 1933 Act.[183] These issues have come to include disclosures equivalent to those required in the prospectuses of registered public offerings.[184] Although the reason for this phenomenon could be underwriter concern over liability (the 1934 antifraud provisions still apply to such offerings[185]), it suggests that institutional investors find issuer disclosure more cost-effective than reliance on private information collection.

Voting rights in corporate law are often accompanied by appraisal (dissenters') rights—the right of dissenters to be cashed out of the firm at a price set by a court under statutory guidance.[186] Appraisal rights mitigate adverse outcomes from uninformed voting: Informed shareholders can dissent and, under the statutory standard, obtain the cash value of their shares equal to the value "exclusive" of the transaction that was the subject of the vote.[187] Thus, for a value-diminishing transaction such as an unfavorable domicile shift, the share's appraisal value would be the stock price before any adverse effect from the market's assessment of the value in the new domicile (the outcome of the vote). Such rights could be mandated for dissenters to a domicile change. Appraisal rights, however, come with costs, such as the potential for an unwanted cash drain if many shareholders exercise their rights, the hold-up power that comes from shareholders' exercising such rights against a non-value-decreasing proposal, and imprecise valuation of the dissenters' shares that may over- or undercompensate them.

---

benefits of such investors arise most frequently from the institutions' holding preferred securities, *see, e.g.*, Rock, *supra*, at 1022, but preferred stockholders do not select the regime for common stock. More important, the number of institutions that are able to attain such preferred relational positions is quite small (there are few outside investors equal to Warren Buffett whom managements are willing to trust with the rights of relational positions), and thus they will not be the marginal investor whose tastes dictate regime choices. Accordingly, the possibility of a divergence between institutional and retail investors' preferred securities regime is remote.

183. *See* 17 C.F.R. § 230.144A note (1997).

184. *See* Luis F. Moreno Trevino, *Access to U.S. Capital Markets for Foreign Issuers: Rule 144A Private Placements*, 16 HOUS. J. INT'L L. 159, 195 (1993).

185. *See* 17 C.F.R. § 230.144A (Preliminary Notes).

186. *See, e.g.*, DEL. CODE ANN. tit. 8, § 262 (1996) (providing appraisal rights in conjunction with mergers, which require shareholder approval); MODEL BUS. CORP. ACT § 13.02 (1992) (providing appraisal rights in conjunction with mergers, asset sales, amendments of articles of incorporation that materially and adversely affect shares by specified impact, and any actions taken pursuant to a shareholder vote where charter, bylaws, or board resolution provide for such rights).

187. *E.g.*, DEL. CODE. ANN. tit. 8, § 262(h) (providing that for merger dissenters entitled to appraisal, the court should determine "fair value exclusive of any element of value arising from" the merger).

There has not been empirical research examining cross-sectionally the functioning of appraisal rights for charter amendments. Such research could provide information concerning how frequently such rights are used, what the stock price reaction is to amendments when the rights are used, and whether charter amendment proposals and voting outcomes differ systematically across firms when such rights are present. In states where appraisal rights are not statutorily provided for dissenters to charter amendments, firms do not appear to include such rights in their charters.[188] A plausible inference from such behavior is that appraisal costs outweigh the benefits; either they are an inadequate remedy for opportunistic amendments or insiders rarely propose opportunistic charter amendments. Indeed, if midstream opportunism were rampant, institutional investors would become aware of the practice, and promoters would have incentives—higher share prices—to bind themselves against engaging in opportunistic charter amendment by providing appraisal rights for such votes or otherwise locking in initial charter provisions. Accordingly, rather than have Congress mandate dissenters' rights in the securities domicile context, their presence should be left to the decisions of securities domiciles, which can legislate such rights, and issuers, which can place such rights in their charters or bylaws if domiciles do not mandate them.

III. The Regulation of Foreign (Non-U.S.) Issuers

The desirability of regulatory competition does not stop at national borders, for the same incentives are at work in a global setting: Financial capital is as mobile across nations as it is across U.S. states, and capital providers will require higher returns from investments governed by regimes less protective of their interests, prodding firms to seek out the securities regime preferred by investors in order to reduce their cost of capital.[189] The market approach to securities regulation advocated in this Article should, accordingly, apply equally to U.S. and non-U.S. issuers of securities.

---

188. In the course of over a decade of research requiring examination of hundreds of corporate charters, I have not come across such a provision.

189. Although investors favor their home countries in their portfolio allocations, *see* Kenneth French & James Poterba, *Investor Diversification and International Equity Markets*, 81 Am. Econ. Rev. 222, 222 (1991), cross-border flows of capital have dramatically increased over time and are expected to continue to do so, *see* Alan C. Shapiro, Multinational Financial Management 403-04 (4th ed. 1991). As financial markets have been deregulated globally, international market capitalizations have increased, and the benefits of international diversification are becoming widely recognized. *See* Solnik, *supra* note 10, at v-vi. For concise reviews in the legal literature of such investment trends, see MacIntosh, *supra* note 8, at 6-10; and Merritt Fox, *Securities Disclosure in a Globalizing Market: Who Should Regulate Whom?*, 95 Mich. L. Rev. 2498, 2523-25 (1997).

A. *Applying the Market Approach to Non-U.S. Issuers*

1. *The Market Approach*

Under the market approach to securities regulation, the issuer's securities domicile controls for all securities sold in the United States, whether that domicile is a U.S. state or a foreign nation. This would be a dramatic turnabout from the SEC's current practice, which assumes jurisdiction over all transactions occurring in the United States, and until recently, asserted jurisdiction over foreign transactions involving U.S. citizens,[190] analogous to the states' choice-of-law rule for securities transactions that looks to the sale location or purchaser domicile.

The SEC's territorial approach to jurisdiction prevents foreign issuers who are in compliance with their home states' disclosure requirements (which are less extensive than the SEC's) from listing on U.S. stock exchanges. The principal reason that the vast majority of non-U.S. firms who could qualify for exchange trading do not list in the United States is that their disclosure costs would significantly increase, particularly with respect to accounting data, as they would have to comply with the SEC's regime.[191] Although the precise cost of reconciliation with U.S. generally accepted accounting principles (GAAP) is not publicly available, James Fanto and Roberta Karmel report that given compliance costs, companies find a U.S. listing worthwhile only if large amounts of equity capital (over $300 million) are required.[192] Other data suggestive of the costliness of reconciliation are that the London Stock Exchange lists five times the number of foreign firms that the NYSE lists,[193] and that, after the SEC extended its reporting requirements to foreign firms trading on the NASDAQ, the number of such listings declined by almost thirty percent over the following seven years (after having tripled over the seven years prior to the change).[194]

---

190. *See* Registration of Foreign Offerings by Domestic Issuers, Exchange Act Release No. 33-4708, 29 Fed. Reg. 9828, 9828 (1964) (stating that requirements of the 1933 Act are "intended to protect American investors"); *see also* Stephen J. Choi & Andrew T. Guzman, *The Dangerous Extraterritoriality of American Securities Law*, 17 NW. J. INT'L L. & BUS 207, 221 (1997) (discussing the SEC's adoption of Regulation S, governing overseas transactions, which changed the regulatory emphasis from "the protection of U.S. investors, wherever they may be located, to the protection of American capital markets")

191. *See* James L. Cochrane, *Are U.S. Regulatory Requirements for Foreign Firms Appropriate?*, 17 FORDHAM INT'L L.J. S58, S61 (1994) (noting that there are "2,000 foreign companies eligible to go on [NYSE's] list . . . were it not for SEC regulations"); James A Fanto & Roberta S Karmel, *A Report on the Attitudes of Foreign Companies Regarding a U.S. Listing*, 3 STAN. J.L. BUS & FIN 51, 70 (1997)

192. *See* Fanto & Karmel, *supra* note 191, at 71. William Baumol and Burton Malkiel point out that beyond the time and expense entailed in the translation process for GAAP reconciliation, there are difficulties arising from the fact that GAAP requirements are not adapted to the "circumstances of the foreign firm," such as the fact that GAAP rules are tailored to U.S. corporate tax rules, which vary significantly from other nations' taxation. Baumol & Malkiel, *supra* note 42, at 41

193. *See* Baumol & Malkiel, *supra* note 42, at 41.

194. *See* Edwards, *supra* note 7, at 63.

The market approach would open up U.S. markets to non-U.S. issuers. This is a policy shift that would not only make U.S. securities regulation more respectful of other nations' policy decisions by reaffirming a norm of international comity, but would also benefit U.S. investors. They would no longer have to incur the substantial costs of purchasing shares on foreign exchanges, as they have been doing in increasing numbers to invest directly in non-U.S. corporations.[195]

Under the market approach, foreign firms (firms not incorporated in the United States) would be able to choose their securities domicile for U.S. trading purposes, and therefore would not need to comply with SEC disclosure requirements in order to trade in the United States. This result has some precedent: The Multijurisdictional Disclosure System (MDS) adopted by the SEC and the Ontario and Quebec Securities Commissions in 1991 enables Canadian firms to trade in the United States by complying with Canadian disclosure requirements, although they must reconcile their financial data with GAAP.[196] Canada is the only nation with which the SEC has entered into such an agreement, however, because its disclosure requirements are similar to U.S. requirements.[197] In addition, the SEC has itself relaxed its disclosure requirements for non-U.S. firms, including eliminating certain nonfinancial items such as management compensation and related party transactions.[198] The market approach expands the SEC's MDS without requiring that disclosure regimes be harmonized with the SEC rules or GAAP reconciliation. But it goes still further than these precedents: It would render inapplicable to such issuers the antifraud provisions of the federal securities laws (unless they opt for SEC regulation), in contrast to the MDS, which retains U.S. antifraud liability for Canadian firms. If all nations adopt the market approach, then all of a firm's shareholders would be subject to the same securities regime, wherever they purchased their shares, and there would be uniform treatment of investors, as occurs in the corporate law context. Rather than harmonization of national securities regimes, the universal application of the market approach should be the goal of international securities regulation.

The SEC was unwilling to extend the multijurisdictional accord globally to nations with lower levels of disclosure than it requires because, in its view, investors in U.S. markets would not be adequately protected if firms traded without releasing all of the information that SEC and U.S. accounting standards mandate. There is, however, an absence of evidence that the lower levels of disclosure in other nations adversely affect investors. Studies of price

195. *See id.* at 58-59, 63-64.

196. *See* Multijurisdictional Disclosure and Modifications to the Current Registration and Reporting System for Canadian Issuers, Exchange Act Release No. 6902, 56 Fed. Reg. 30,036 (July 1, 1991).

197. *See* RICHARD W. JENNINGS ET AL., SECURITIES REGULATION: CASES AND MATERIALS 1581 (7th ed. 1992).

198. *See* Fanto & Karmel, *supra* note 191, at 56.

reactions to foreign issuers' release of information reconciling their financial reports with GAAP do not consistently find any effects, leading a number of economists to conclude that the SEC's requirement that foreign firms' disclosures conform to GAAP is of no benefit to investors.[199] In addition, despite the lower level of disclosure required, foreign markets are not less efficient than U.S. markets.[200] Finally, differences in accounting systems do not appear to provide less information about firms' financial situations of importance to investors; for instance, although German accounting is considerably less rigorous than GAAP, the information it discloses provides as good a probability estimate of a German firm's bankruptcy as GAAP information does for U.S. firms.[201]

If the lower level of disclosure of other nations were, in fact, of concern to U.S. investors or adversely affected investments, investors would discount the shares of foreign firms or not invest in them in the first place. Because of such a reaction, many firms would voluntarily reveal more information than required by their home state, albeit less than the SEC would have required, under the market approach.[202] An increase in U.S. listings of non-U.S. issuers that were covered by less extensive disclosure regimes than the SEC requires would not, therefore, be harmful to investors and would instead lower the transaction costs entailed in direct foreign investment. To the extent that foreign firms chose to list in the United States—to come under the more stringent SEC disclosure requirements or to subject themselves to the more extensive U.S. liability regime—as a credible commitment to signal their quality to investors and thereby to reduce their cost of capital,[203] they could, of course, continue to do so under the market approach. The credibility of such firms' commitment to the U.S. regime could be sustained further by their placing a supermajority voting rule in their corporate charter in order to change their securities domicile.[204]

199. *See, e.g.*, Baumol & Malkiel, *supra* note 42, at 46-50; Edwards, *supra* note 7, at 65-66 (noting, however, that more studies must be done before definite conclusions can be reached).

200. *See supra* text accompanying note 42.

201. *See* Jorg Baetge, The Role of Disclosure and Auditing as Affecting Corporate Governance, Presentation at the Symposium on Comparative Corporate Governance at the Max-Planck-Institut, Hamburg, Germany (May 16, 1997).

202. Firms currently respond to such incentives. *See supra* text accompanying notes 38-41.

203. For signaling explanations of foreign firm listings in the United States, see C. Sherman Cheung & Jason Lee, *Disclosure Environment and Listing on Foreign Stock Exchanges*, 19 J. BANKING & FIN. 347 (1995); Oren Fuerst, A Theoretical Analysis of the Investor Protection Regulations: Argument for Global Listing of Stocks (Feb. 17, 1998) (unpublished manuscript, on file with the *Yale Law Journal*); and Edward B. Rock, Mandatory Disclosure as Credible Commitment: Going Public, Opting In, Opting Out, and Globalization (1998) (unpublished manuscript, on file with the *Yale Law Journal*).

204. To the extent that the SEC requirement for deregistration of fewer than 300 shareholders, *see* Rock, *supra* note 203, at 11-13 (discussing exit routes under SEC rules), would no longer be applicable under the market regime because it would impede effective jurisdictional competition, firms could duplicate such an exit barrier by placing a similarly worded provision in their charters. Where the firm's home nation does not recognize a domicile approach and the firm is listed both domestically and in the United States, the firm could craft a supermajority charter amendment limited to the choice of domicile for U.S.-traded shares. In the common case in which the foreign firm uses depositary receipts for its U.S. issue, *see*

The securities domicile choice of foreign firms available under the market approach might be limited in practice to a firm's home country (assuming it does not choose the SEC), in contrast to U.S. firms' choices, because their home countries' choice-of-law rules might not recognize the legislative jurisdiction of a nation that is not the site of the securities transaction. For example, regarding corporate law domicile, many nations do not recognize a statutory domicile and follow instead a physical presence or "seat" rule.[205] If those nations were to follow this principle for securities domicile as well, then non-U.S. firms would have no securities domicile choice but their home country (or the United States as the site of the transaction). But even if the domicile choice were circumscribed because of home country practices, the number of foreign firms listed on U.S. exchanges would markedly increase under the market approach because it would eliminate the need for such firms to undertake costly expenditures to comply with the SEC's disclosure regime, such as the GAAP reconciliation.

2. *Securities Litigation Involving Non-U.S. Issuers*

There is a potential problem for U.S. investors who invest in firms subject to a non-U.S. securities regime should they need to seek redress for a securities law violation. Namely, the collective action problem inherent in any type of shareholder litigation—the cost of pursuing a lawsuit exceeds a shareholder's pro rata share of any recovery but not the aggregate award[206]—would be exacerbated by requiring prosecution of a claim in a foreign forum, both because of the expense and because of the absence of mechanisms for aggregating claims in many countries.

U.S. investors would, of course, discount the shares of foreign firms against which they could never exercise their rights under foreign securities laws or would avoid such securities entirely. Foreign firms might therefore find it in their self-interest to ensure that U.S. investors could prosecute securities claims in U.S. courts. The institutional mechanism for obtaining a foreign corporation's consent to a U.S. court's jurisdiction would not be difficult to construct: The issuer could provide such a written consent in the documentation accompanying the sale of stock to a U.S. investor. In addition,

---

generally Joseph Velli, *American Depositary Receipts: An Overview*, 17 FORDHAM INT'L L.J. S38 (1994) (providing an overview of the depositary receipts market), it might be possible for the firm to place a provision in the service contract entered into with the sponsor of the receipts (which the sponsor would enforce) either prohibiting a domicile change or requiring a supermajority vote of the American depositary receipt holders to effect such a change.

205. *See* ROMANO, *supra* note 4, at 132 (noting that, with the exception of the United Kingdom and the Netherlands, European nations follow the real seat rule).

206. *See generally* John C. Coffee, Jr., *The Unfaithful Champion: The Plaintiff as Monitor in Shareholder Litigation*, LAW & CONTEMP. PROBS., Summer 1985, at 5 (discussing the collective action problem in shareholder litigation).

U.S. stock exchanges competing for business could require issuers' consent to jurisdiction in the United States as a listing requirement, if they thought that such a rule would enhance the value of listed shares and thereby increase trading interest.

There is, however, a question whether U.S. courts would accept jurisdiction as a forum state over a securities dispute between investors and an issuer that is subject to foreign (non-U.S.) securities law. Traditionally, in international litigation, securities law has been treated as a species of public law, over which local courts have either declined to exercise jurisdiction or accepted jurisdiction but applied their own substantive law. The distinction between public and private law is arcane, and has largely been undone by the Supreme Court in the securities context through its validation of arbitration clauses to resolve securities law disputes, reversing the prior convention that considered arbitration inappropriate for public, as opposed to private, law subjects.[207] Accordingly, in keeping with the contemporary trend merging the jurisdictional approach in public and private law areas, it would be appropriate for U.S. courts to apply private law jurisdictional principles to international securities transactions.[208] In the private law setting, forum selection clauses are presumptively enforceable,[209] and the exceptions to this presumption—defects in contract formation, unreasonableness, and public policy,[210] as well as the *forum non conveniens* doctrine—have no relevance for our context: The foreign defendant will have consented to a U.S. forum, federal policy will have expressly authorized foreign legislative jurisdiction, and the plaintiff-investor's local domicile and purchase would provide sufficient "contact" with a U.S. forum to render the local forum's retention of jurisdiction both feasible and desirable.

While U.S. jurisdiction would be readily attainable, a more important question is whether a U.S. court should exercise jurisdiction at all, or, to put it another way, is it desirable from the perspective of regulatory competition for foreign firms to choose a U.S. forum for securities suits? The adjudication of securities disputes by non-domicile courts could undermine the effectiveness of competition, as the legislating state does not control the interpretation of its laws. The problem would not be as severe as it is for Canadian provinces competing for corporate charters because the U.S. courts would be attempting in good faith to apply the domicile's law, whereas Canadian securities administrators intentionally apply their own governance standards rather than

207. *See* Rodriguez v. Shearson/Am. Express, Inc., 490 U.S. 477 (1989); Shearson/Am Express, Inc v. McMahon, 482 U.S. 220 (1987); Scherk v. Alberto-Culver Co., 417 U.S 506 (1974) (overruling Wilko v. Swan, 346 U.S. 427 (1953)).

208. The Supreme Court's forum selection clause jurisprudence has especially emphasized the needs of parties engaged in international commercial transactions when sustaining parties' contractual choices *See, e.g.*, The Bremen v. Zapata Off-Shore Co., 407 U.S. 1, 8-18 (1972).

209. *See id.* at 17-18; *see also supra* note 167 and accompanying text.

210. *See* BORN, *supra* note 142, at 395.

the law of the domicile province.[211] But the difficulty here is not solely a matter of substantive law interpretation.[212] The U.S. approach that adopts the procedural rules of the forum can have a significant impact on substantive outcomes because, in addition to class action mechanisms to aggregate individual claims not prevalent in other countries, U.S. procedure—including rules on discovery, pleading requirements, contingent fees, and the absence of a "loser pays" cost rule—are far more favorable to plaintiffs than those of foreign courts.[213]

A powerful competing consideration in favor of a U.S. forum and against the substantive concerns raised by a non-domicile adjudicator is the significant inconvenience for a U.S. investor to prosecute a securities claim abroad. The balancing of the factors regarding the appropriateness of a U.S. forum is a calculation that is best undertaken by the foreign issuer, rather than by Congress or regulators. As long as investors were informed of the issuer's choice-of-law and choice-of-forum selections, they would be able to price their ability to obtain relief for securities violations, and issuers would respond accordingly, trading off U.S. forum protections that facilitate securities litigation and affect the cost of capital with the substantive advantages of a foreign forum.

B. *Comparison with Other Reform Proposals*

The outcome of applying the market approach to non-U.S. issuers—that their shares will be able to trade in U.S. markets under a non-U.S. securities regime—is certainly not a novel idea. Several commentators have advocated

211. *See* Daniels, *supra* note 136, at 182-84; *see also supra* text accompanying note 136.

212. Under current law, U.S. courts have imposed U.S. standards on foreign issuers instead of applying non-U.S. law in their role as a forum court, in a misguided attempt to protect U.S. investors. *See, e.g.*, Consolidated Gold Fields PLC v. Minorco, S.A., 871 F.2d 252 (2d Cir.), *modified*, 890 F.2d 569 (2d Cir. 1989) (applying U.S. law to a takeover contest between foreign firms where the bid permitted U.S. residents to tender only if they did so from outside the United States); Leasco Data Processing Equip. Corp. v. Maxwell, 468 F.2d 1326 (2d Cir. 1972) (applying U.S. law to a purchase of stock in a British corporation by a U.S. corporation on the London Stock Exchange). The danger of such conduct's continuing under the proposed regime is probably low, given that Congress will have expressly authorized the applicability of non-U.S. law to the transactions.

213. *See* BORN, *supra* note 142, at 4. The critical differences in litigation procedures could lead some foreign issuers to consider an alternative approach to the selection of a convenient forum for disputes, such as the use of an international arbitration clause. But it is problematic whether investors would place sufficient value on this approach to make it worthwhile for the issuer to offer arbitration, unless some features of U.S. litigation practices are retained in the arbitration agreement, such as the use of representative actions. Although arbitration is less costly than litigation to pursue an individual claim, the profitability of most securities cases comes from the ability of an attorney to aggregate claims. Despite potential difficulties in claim aggregation, in the international securities context there is a significant advantage to arbitration over litigation that may make it highly attractive to U.S. investors: It is easier to enforce arbitration awards worldwide because virtually all nations (including the United States) are signatories to the United Nations Convention recognizing arbitration awards, while there is no global treaty concerning the enforcement of judgments. *See* ANDREAS F. LOWENFELD, INTERNATIONAL LITIGATION AND ARBITRATION 332 (1993).

reform of the SEC's approach to foreign issuers to enable such issuers' shares to trade in U.S. markets without coming under the SEC's regulatory regime (or its more onerous components, such as GAAP reconciliation).[214] Some commentators have simply called for an end to the extraterritorial application of U.S. securities laws. Depending on the particular concern of the commentator, the solutions have been to permit foreign firms to list on U.S. exchanges, or, more narrowly, to permit U.S. investors to participate in foreign firms' takeovers, without having U.S. law apply,[215] or to advocate a strict territorial (site-of-sale) approach, regardless of the shareholders' ultimate residence or firms' domicile.[216] While these proposals resolve the most

214. *See, e.g.*, Cochrane, *supra* note 191, at S61, S63-65, Fox, *supra* note 189, at 2582; Merritt Fox, The Political Economy of Statutory Reach: U.S. Disclosure Rules in a Globalizing Market for Securities 14-15 (1997) (unpublished manuscript, on file with the *Yale Law Journal*).

215. *See, e.g.*, Cochrane, *supra* note 191, at S61, S63-65 (criticizing applicability of SEC disclosure requirements for NYSE listing); Jill E. Fisch, *Imprudent Power: Reconsidering U.S. Regulation of Foreign Tender Offers*, 87 NW. U. L. REV. 523, 573-74 (1993) (criticizing applicability of the Williams Act); Pinto, *supra* note 5, at 73 (same).

216. *See, e.g.*, Choi & Guzman, *supra* note 190, at 241 (reviewing possible jurisdictional rules, including site of sale and firms' choice of domicile, and concluding, "This [strict rule of territorial jurisdiction based on the connection the transaction has with the capital markets of the country] is the rule we advocate"); Stephen J. Choi & Andrew T. Guzman, *National Laws, International Money: Regulation in a Global Capital Market*, 65 FORDHAM L. REV. 1855, 1895 (1997) [hereinafter Choi & Guzman, *National Laws*] ("[W]e propose a clear and simple rule: all transactions that occur through an exchange or organized market should be considered within the exclusive jurisdictional reach of the country within which the exchange or organized market operates."). In a recent paper, Choi and Guzman's position has evolved from advocating a strict territorial (site-of-sale) approach to an approach similar to this Article's issuer securities domicile approach. *See* Stephen J. Choi & Andrew T. Guzman, *Portable Reciprocity: Rethinking the International Reach of Securities Regulation*, 71 S. CAL. L. REV. (forthcoming July 1998).

Choi and Guzman seek to encourage regulatory competition across nations because they believe that different rules are appropriate for different issuers and investors. One reason for their refusal in their earlier articles to advocate the logical implication of regulatory competition, an issuer domicile rather than site-of-sale approach, was that they finessed the question whether regulatory competition is for the "top" or "bottom" with respect to investor protection. They asserted that the question was complicated and did not need to be resolved because different rules were appropriate for different clienteles. *See, e.g.*, Choi & Guzman, *National Laws*, *supra*, at 1876. This is an unsatisfactory position because, if the competitive race to diversity produced laws disadvantageous to investors (that is, it was a race for the "bottom"), there would be no demand for such differentiated regimes. Notwithstanding their contention, it only makes sense to advocate a policy of regulatory diversity if the competition results in regimes that benefit investors (that is, it is a race for the top).

The inconsistency in Choi and Guzman's initial position becomes more apparent when they sidestep the implications of a policy of regulatory competition for domestic regulation. Relying on the existing practice of a monopolist SEC, they contend that either investors and issuers within a single nation have homogeneous preferences regarding securities regulation or domestic markets do not value diversity produced by competition, and conclude that the desirability of international regulatory competition is distinguishable from the domestic context. *See id.* at 1882-83. Their justification of local regulatory monopolies stems from a mistaken understanding of the dynamics of competitive federalism: Competition can lead to uniformity as well as diversity in substantive law. Moreover, uniformity produced by regulatory competition is more likely to be of benefit to investors than uniformity derived from a noncompetitive regime. *See* Carney, *supra* note 106, at 169-72 (comparing uniform corporate law produced competitively in the U.S. with that produced by noncompetitive European harmonization process). There is, finally, little evidence that diverse securities regimes are appropriate for U.S. and non-U.S. multinationals, or for U.S. investors holding such firms, notwithstanding Choi and Guzman's conjecture. Similar product diversity arguments were hypothesized to explain the benefits of state charter competition, yet the data do not support such claims. *See* ROMANO, *supra* note 4, at 45-48. There is, then, simply no theoretical or empirical basis for distinguishing between domestic and international securities regulatory competition.

egregious problems in the extraterritorial application of U.S. law, to the extent that they are more restrictive than the domicile approach advocated in this Article—by limiting their reach to the takeover context or by choosing the site of sale, which issuers cannot control as easily as domicile—they are suboptimal when international issues are considered within the broader context of fostering competitive securities regulation.

In a more comprehensive effort to rationalize international securities regulation, Merritt Fox contends that an issuer nationality rule (physical presence domicile) is the rule that maximizes social welfare.[217] Although the substantive policy outcomes of Fox's proposal and of this Article may not be significantly different—that is, non-U.S. issuers trading on a U.S. exchange are likely to choose their home countries' securities regimes under the market approach—the rationales are fundamentally at odds. This is because Fox assumes that international regulatory competition would lead to a "race for the bottom" regarding disclosure requirements. Fox provides two reasons for this projected outcome: Firms would not voluntarily produce the desirable level of financial information because of third-party externality concerns; and U.S. stock exchanges' interest in increased listings would dominate the regulatory process, resulting in a lowering of disclosure requirements to enable them to compete for listings against foreign markets.[218] Fox therefore advocates a physical presence rule to stymie such regulatory competition. Not only would firms have to change their nationality in order to change regulators, which is a costly undertaking, but also exchanges would no longer have an incentive to lobby for lower local securities standards in order to increase foreign listings, as listing decisions would be independent of the regulatory regime of the stock exchange's location.

This Article's proposal for shifting to an issuer-domicile-based rule is premised on an assessment of competition that is the precise opposite of Fox's. As discussed earlier,[219] neither of Fox's rationales depicting destructive competition holds up to scrutiny. The need to internalize third-party externalities is a tenuous rationale for securities regulation, and such externalities are not, in any event, likely to account for the items of mandatory disclosure pursued by the SEC or the differences across national regimes. More important, there is no reason to assume that firms would list on the exchange with the lowest level of disclosure requirements. Rather, they would choose the one whose requirements lower their cost of capital, which will not be the exchange operating under the least amount of disclosure because investors place affirmative value on information. The supporting evidence against the race-for-the-bottom thesis, as already noted, is that firms the world over

217. *See* Fox, *supra* note 189, at 2580-83; Fox, *supra* note 214, at 14-15.
218. *See, e.g.*, Fox, *supra* note 214, at 34-35.
219. *See supra* Section I.B.

voluntarily release more information than their securities regulators require in order to raise capital, with the best example being the European firms listing in London, which voluntarily choose to meet higher local disclosure requirements.[220]

Finally, it should also be noted that Fox's concern regarding the political process in a competitive regulatory setting—the incentives of stock exchanges to lobby for lowered disclosure—is not relevant under the market approach. Whether the securities domicile is statutory, contractual, or Fox's proposed domicile of physical presence, the location of the stock exchange would not determine the issuer's securities regime; the issuer's securities domicile would. Accordingly, while Fox's proposed regulatory reform is compatible with the approach in this Article, the rationales could not be much farther apart.

IV. CONCLUSION

This Article has advocated fundamental reform of the current strategy toward securities regulation by implementing a regulatory approach of competitive federalism, under which firms select their securities regulator from among the fifty states and the District of Columbia, the SEC, or other nations. Competitive federalism harnesses the high-powered incentives of markets to the regulatory state in order to produce regulatory arrangements compatible with investors' preferences. This is because firms will locate in the domicile whose regime investors prefer in order to reduce their cost of capital, and states have financial incentives (such as incorporation and registration fees) to adapt their securities regimes to firms' locational decisions. This prediction of securities market participants' and regulators' responses to competition is well-grounded: There is a substantial literature examining the workings of competitive federalism in the corporate charter setting that indicates that such regulatory competition does not harm, and in all likelihood benefits, investors.

To establish competitive federalism in the securities law context, the current choice-of-law rule for securities transactions must be altered to follow the issuer's securities domicile rather than the securities' site of sale. In addition, two procedural safeguards would be required of firms opting out of federal regulation: domicile disclosure upon securities purchases and a security-

220. *See supra* text accompanying notes 38-41. One study of foreign stock exchange listings found an inverse relation between listings and disclosure requirements, but the exchanges with the lowest level of disclosure did not have the most foreign listings (although the United States, with the highest disclosure level, did have the fewest foreign listings); more important, the inverse relation was not significant when domestic and foreign exchange disclosure levels were compared. *See* Shahrokh M. Saudagaran & Gary C. Biddle, *Financial Disclosure Levels and Foreign Stock Exchange Listing Decisions*, *in* INTERNATIONAL CAPITAL MARKETS IN A WORLD OF ACCOUNTING DIFFERENCES 159, 181, 184 (Frederick D.S. Choi & Richard M. Levich eds., 1994). That is, the data do not support the race-for-the-bottom hypothesis that the probability of a firm listing on a given foreign exchange is inversely related to the exchange's disclosure level when its disclosure level is higher than the disclosure level of the firm's domestic exchange *See id*

holder vote to effectuate a domicile change. These requirements ensure that informed investor preferences drive the regulatory competition. When competition is introduced, SEC rules and regulations that are not cost-effective or are otherwise detrimental to investors will be replaced by competing regulators with rules investors prefer, as the domicile choices of capital market participants establish a new regulatory equilibrium.

The mandatory federal securities regime has been in place for over sixty years, but the theoretical support for it is thin, and there is no empirical evidence indicating that it is effective in achieving its stated objectives. In fact, there is a developing literature pointing in the opposite direction. At a minimum, this literature suggests that the securities status quo should no longer be privileged, and that it should instead be opened up to market forces by means of competitive federalism. Corporation codes have benefited from precisely such competition. Although the current legislative trend in Congress, supported by both the proponents and opponents of the existing regulatory regime, is to seek to monopolize even further securities regulation at the federal level, this Article maintains that it would be far better public policy to expand, not restrain, state regulatory involvement. As long as only one state's law, chosen by the issuer, controls the regulation of a firm's securities transactions, regulatory competition will emerge, and there are compelling reasons to prefer such a regulatory arrangement to the mandatory federal regime.

APPENDIX

TABLE 1. DELAWARE'S REVENUE FROM CORPORATE CHARTERS

YEAR	FRANCHISE TAXES ($000)	% OF TOTAL TAX COLLECTED	APPROPRIATIONS ($000)
1966	14,091	10.9	492
1967	17,615	12.6	517
1968	21,414	14.8	606
1969	20,572	13.1	645
1970	43,924	22.5	722
1971	55,212	24.9	836
1972	49,129	19.1	697
1973	50,777	17.1	699
1974	57,073	18.5	984
1975	55,030	16.4	1051
1976	67,887	18.9	1208
1977	57,949	14.8	1255
1978	60,509	13.5	1385
1979	63,046	12.8	1482
1980	66,738	12.9	1899
1981	70,942	12.9	2230
1982	76,591	12.9	2448
1983	80,031	12.5	2847
1984	92,270	12.9	2721
1985	121,057	14.8	3242
1986	132,816	15.0	3809
1987	152,152	15.4	4746
1988	180,583	17.7	4719
1989	195,862	17.3	4873
1990	200,201	17.7	6398
1991	203,868	17.5	6953
1992	297,004	22.1	6591
1993	284,839	21.3	6831
1994	307,008	21.3	7980
1995	336,348	21.2	7104
1996	350,035	20.7	9462

Sources: U.S. BUREAU OF THE CENSUS, STATE GOVERNMENT TAX COLLECTIONS (1966-1996); 55-70 Del. Laws (1965-1995). Appropriations for Delaware's chartering business consist of state outlays, for the fiscal year ending June 30, on the Division of Corporations in the Office of the Secretary of State and on the Supreme and Chancery Courts.

TABLE 2. THE SEC'S FINANCING

YEAR	APPROPRIATION ($000)	FEES COLLECTED ($000)	% FEES TO APPROPRIATION
1966	16,442	6608	40
1967	17,550	9706	55
1968	17,730	14,623	82
1969	18,624	21,996	118
1970	21,905	15,526	71
1971	23,615	16,374	69
1972	26,817	19,000	71
1973	30,293	22,000	73
1974	36,227	22,000	60
1975	44,427	24,000	54
1976	49,000*	26,000	53
1977	56,270	29,000	52
1978	62,475	26,100	42
1979	67,100	33,000	47
1980	72,739	48,000	66
1981	80,200	65,300	81
1982	83,306	78,200	94
1983	86,690	98,600	110
1984	94,000	121,000	129
1985	106,382	144,000	135
1986	106,323	215,000	202
1987	114,500	263,700	230
1988	135,221	250,000	185
1989	142,640	214,000	150
1990**	166,633	232,000	139
1991	189,083	259,000	137
1992	225,792	406,000	180
1993	253,235	517,000	204
1994	259,000	593,000	229
1995	267,000	559,000	209
1996	297,400	774,000	260

* This figure excludes supplemental appropriations of over $13 million for the transitional quarter, accommodating change in the fiscal year.

** Since 1990, SEC appropriations acts increased registration fees by 0.01% of the offering's dollar value, with the increase offsetting the SEC's costs rather than going into general revenues.

Sources: SECURITIES AND EXCHANGE COMMISSION, ANNUAL REPORTS (1966-1996). Fees collected for 1972-1977 were obtained from Henry I. Hoffman, Assistant Comptroller of the SEC.

[15]

VICARIOUS LIABILITY FOR FRAUD ON SECURITIES MARKETS: THEORY AND EVIDENCE

*Jennifer H. Arlen**
*William J. Carney***

This article examines the efficiency of vicarious liability for Fraud on the Market. Standard analysis of vicarious liability argues that this rule is efficient. Professors Arlen and Carney argue, however, that in Fraud on the Market cases vicarious liability does not serve the goals of optimal deterrence or optimal risk spreading, nor does it promote optimal loss spreading.

Breaking with traditional vicarious liability literature, the authors examine monitoring costs in detail, and posit a model that predicts that Fraud on the Market generally occurs when agents fear themselves to be in their last period of employment. An empirical study of Fraud on the Market cases demonstrates that these frauds generally are the product of last period agency costs.

The article also shows who pays for securities fraud under a rule of vicarious liability. The empirical study shows that an issuer's potential liability for the fraud of its agents is enormous, representing a substantial share of the equity of the firm. Imposing liability on the firm results in a large wealth transfer from one group of innocent investors to another similar group. Because this transfer neither deters fraud nor spreads losses, it performs no useful social function. The authors conclude that a rule of agent liability, supplemented with criminal enforcement, is preferable.

---

* *Associate Professor of Law, Emory University. B.A. 1982, Harvard University; J.D. 1986, Ph.D. (Economics) 1992, New York University.* *This author would like to acknowledge the financial assistance of the John M. Olin Program at the University of California at Berkeley School of Law.*

** *Charles Howard Candler Professor of Law, Emory University. B.A. 1959, LL.B. 1962, Yale University.*

The authors wish to acknowledge the helpful comments of Barry Adler, Ian Ayres, Theodor Baums, Bernard Black, Richard Craswell, David Haddock, Andrew Kull, Fred McChesney, Geoffrey Miller, Roberto Pardolesi, Manuel Utset, Frank Vandall, and participants at faculty workshops at Boston University School of Law, Emory University School of Law, Georgetown Law Center, and Northwestern University School of Law, as well as at the Second Annual Meeting of the American Law and Economics Association and the Eighth Annual Conference of the European Association of Law and Economics. In addition, we would like to acknowledge the helpful and resourceful research assistance of Cherie King, Leah McCarty, and Susan Dignan.

I. Introduction

United States securities laws nearly always hold a corporation liable for fraudulent statements regarding its securities made to the market by its agents in the course of their employment. Although this use of enterprise liability[1] for "Fraud on the Market"[2] subjects corporations to the risk of extraordinary liability, few American commentators have questioned it.[3] Most American scholars, it appears, assume that the economic arguments made in favor of enterprise liability in the torts context are equally valid when applied to Fraud on the Market cases. These arguments are that: (1) enterprise liability better serves the goal of optimal deterrence than does agent liability;[4] (2) enterprise liability optimally spreads the risk of liability between the firm and its agents;[5] and (3) enterprise liability optimally allocates the losses to the firm rather than to the victims.[6]

Although these arguments may be valid in the context of conventional torts cases, they cannot be assumed to apply to Fraud on the Market cases. Fraud on the Market differs from standard torts in several important respects. In the standard torts case, the goal is not to prevent all harms, but rather is to induce the actor to take the optimal level of care. By contrast, Fraud on the Market is optimally deterred when agents are induced to refrain from fraud altogether;[7] consequently, overdeterrence is not an issue.[8] In the standard tort case, the wrongful agent generally injures only third parties. By contrast, in Fraud on the Market cases the wrongful agent generally injures the principal as well

1. The term enterprise liability is used throughout this article to refer to corporate liability for acts of its agents. The term, therefore, encompasses both direct corporate liability for acts of senior management deemed to be those of the corporation and vicarious corporate liability for acts of agents.

2. Fraud on the Market cases are securities fraud actions filed under § 10(b) of the Securities Exchange Act of 1934, 15 U.S.C. § 78j(b) (1988), for fraudulent statements regarding a firm's securities made to the market by agents of the firm, generally in circumstances where the firm neither purchased nor sold the affected securities. *See infra* text accompanying notes 23-35.

3. Scholars' failure to question this rule is particularly remarkable because it contrasts with the rule in Germany (and perhaps elsewhere in Europe), under which a corporation is shielded from liability for its agents' fraudulent statements about the value of its securities.

4. *E.g.*, Steven Shavell, An Economic Analysis of Accidents 170-72 (1987); Lewis A. Kornhauser, *An Economic Analysis of the Choice Between Enterprise and Personal Liability for Accidents*, 70 Cal. L. Rev. 1345 (1982); Alan O. Sykes, *The Economics of Vicarious Liability*, 93 Yale L.J. 1231 (1984) [hereinafter Sykes II]; Alan O. Sykes, *An Efficiency Analysis of Vicarious Liability Under the Law of Agency*, 91 Yale L.J. 168 (1981) [hereinafter Sykes I]; *see* Frank H. Easterbrook & Daniel R. Fischel, *Optimal Damages in Securities Cases*, 52 U. Chi. L. Rev. 611, 619 (1985).

5. Reinier H. Kraakman, *Corporate Liability Strategies and the Costs of Legal Controls*, 93 Yale L.J. 857 (1984); Sykes II, *supra* note 4; *see* Easterbrook & Fischel, *supra* note 4, at 640-41.

6. John J. Musewicz, *Vicarious Employer Liability and Section 10(b): In Defense of the Common Law*, 50 Geo. Wash. L. Rev. 754, 794-97 (1982).

7. *See infra* text accompanying notes 69-73 and note 73.

8. This statement assumes low error costs in enforcing antifraud rules. We assume that fraud is readily differentiated from negligent nondisclosure or misstatement by the requirement of scienter—a knowledge of falsehood or a reckless disregard for the truth. *See* Ernst & Ernst v. Hochfelder, 425 U.S. 185, *reh'g denied*, 425 U.S. 986 (1976); *see also infra* notes 72 and 129.

because shareholders of the firm are among those defrauded. Moreover, conventional analysis of enterprise liability for torts usually assumes that the principal and agents have an ongoing relationship. By contrast, Fraud on the Market usually occurs when agents fear themselves to be in their last period of employment.[9] Thus, the firm's ability to sanction wrongful agents is considerably less than assumed by conventional analysis.

Finally, conventional analysis of enterprise liability oversimplifies the principal-agent problem, viewing the principal as a single owner-manager of a firm who hires agents to perform various tasks on his behalf.[10] The principal also decides what measures the firm will take to deter wrongful acts by the agents. As applied to Fraud on the Market cases (as well as to many torts) this analysis is incomplete. Fraud on the Market cases involve publicly held firms in which the owners of the firm, the "principal," often are a group of widely dispersed shareholders. These shareholders face collective action problems because they are too numerous to manage the firm and to monitor its agents themselves. They therefore hire agents (directors) to manage it for them. These directors, not the firm's owners, decide how the firm will deter wrongful acts by its agents.[11] Under enterprise liability these directors may not impose optimal sanctions on the firm's agents. This possibility introduces an additional level of agency costs that conventional analysis of enterprise liability ignores. This additional level of agency costs is particularly important in Fraud on the Market cases, because Fraud on the Market is generally committed by some of the very directors and senior officers hired to manage the firm and to deter fraud.

Accordingly, we cannot assume that it is efficient to hold corporations liable for Fraud on the Market simply because prior economic analysis of enterprise liability suggests that this rule is efficient in other tort contexts. We must reexamine the arguments made in favor of enterprise liability for standard torts to determine whether the rule is efficient when applied to Fraud on the Market cases. To do this, however, we must know something about who commits Fraud on the Market and why.

In this article we examine the economic arguments for enterprise liability for Fraud on the Market cases and present the first empirical analysis of these cases. Fraud on the Market involves false or misleading statements made to financial markets involving actively traded securities, in circumstances where market prices are expected to reflect the misinformation.[12] We focus on this type of securities fraud because it illus-

---

9. *See infra* text accompanying notes 53-58 and part IV.

10. *E.g.*, Easterbrook & Fischel, *supra* note 4 (recognizing that this is a simplifying assumption); Kornhauser, *supra* note 4; Sykes II, *supra* note 4; Sykes I, *supra* note 4.

11. We employ an economic definition of agency and thus treat both officers and directors as agents. By contrast, under a legal definition of agency, some states hold that directors are not agents because directors control the corporation, rather than being subject to its control.

12. The Supreme Court has approved the application of the "Fraud on the Market" doctrine

trates most starkly the agency cost problems present in many securities fraud cases.[13] Moreover, the unusually large potential liability in these cases warrants their being given special consideration. Finally, it raises serious questions about the proper interpretation of the control person provisions of the federal securities laws.

The analysis in this article proceeds as follows. In part II we present the law on enterprise liability for Fraud on the Market. In part III we employ economic theory to examine who commits Fraud on the Market and why. We predict that Fraud on the Market generally will be committed by officers and directors seeking to conceal from the market, and from the firm's shareholders, that the firm is ailing in an attempt to save their jobs and their investments in the firm. In other words, Fraud on the Market is a product of agency costs between owners and managers in circumstances where the managers fear themselves to be in their last period of employment. The types of fraud at issue in *Texas Gulf Sulphur*[14] and *Basic v. Levinson*,[15] which involved concealing good news, are, therefore, the exceptions, not the rule, according to our hypothesis.[16]

Using our last period hypothesis, we then examine whether the standard economic arguments in favor of enterprise liability apply to Fraud on the Market cases. We find that enterprise liability for Fraud on the Market is not better able to deter Fraud on the Market than is agent liability. In fact, agent liability probably achieves superior deterrence. We also show that administrative costs are probably higher under enterprise liability. In addition, we show that enterprise liability for Fraud on the Market cannot be justified as promoting optimal risk spreading. Moreover, we show that enterprise liability results in large wealth transfers from one group of innocent investors to another that are inconsistent with the goal of optimal loss spreading. These wealth transfers are subjected to a substantial deduction for litigation costs, a deadweight loss that only benefits attorneys. Finally, we show that the goal of "just compensation" cannot justify enterprise liability because the burden of the liability falls primarily on innocent shareholders. In order to achieve effective deterrence, sanctions must be imposed on the agents who face the temptation to commit fraud. Because of the agent insolvency problem,

---

to create a presumption of reliance on the part of all investors who trade after a false statement to the public markets. Basic, Inc. v. Levinson, 485 U.S. 224, 241-47 (1988); *see also infra* text accompanying notes 23-35.

13. Fraud on the Market involves publicly held corporations, which rarely are owned predominantly by management. Where management owns a majority of the stock in a corporation, ownership and control are effectively unified, and the agency cost problems we consider here do not appear.

14. SEC v. Texas Gulf Sulphur Co., 401 F.2d 833 (2d Cir. 1968), *cert. denied*, 394 U.S. 976 (1969).

15. 485 U.S. 224.

16. *See infra* Table 1 (less than nine percent of the Fraud on the Market cases involved attempts to conceal good news). In both *Texas Gulf Sulphur* and *Basic*, the extent of the defendants' obligations to disclose were unclear prior to these decisions. No such problems exist in the garden variety types of fraud studied here. *See infra* text accompanying notes 150-53.

we conclude that agent liability supplemented with criminal enforcement is probably the superior rule.

In part IV we present an empirical analysis of Fraud on the Market cases to determine whether the evidence supports our hypothesis that Fraud on the Market is the product of last period agency costs. The evidence reveals that Fraud on the Market typically is committed by corporate officers, apparently without consent of the board of directors or major shareholders. In addition, we find that fraud generally results from attempts by officers and directors to present an artificially favorable financial picture under circumstances which are consistent with our last period hypothesis. Finally, we examine the size of the potential damage claims under a rule of enterprise liability. We discover that on average the magnitude of potential claims in Fraud on the Market class actions is so great that, in many cases, the use of enterprise liability could wipe out nearly all shareholder equity. Under enterprise liability a substantial portion of this loss is borne by innocent shareholders. A comparison of the relative size of the average potential plaintiff class (measured in number of shares held by this class) with the firm's outstanding shares at the time liability is imposed demonstrates that, generally, enterprise liability does not spread losses.

II. Enterprise Liability for Fraud on the Market

A. *Enterprise Liability Defined*

Both the Securities Act of 1933 and the Securities Exchange Act of 1934 provide for control person liability.[17] Under these statutes a person in control of another is liable for the other's fraud unless he acted in good faith. Because employers are always "in control" of employees acting within the scope of their employment, control person liability for wrongful statements of corporate officers would seem to be available in almost all Fraud on the Market cases.[18] But the employer is not liable if it acted in good faith. The employer, therefore, will not be liable if it neither knew of the agent's wrongful act nor had reasonable ground to know of it after taking reasonable precautions under the circumstances.[19]

On its face it would appear that, except for employers actively involved in the securities industry (e.g., broker-dealers), most innocent issuers should be able to meet this good faith standard where a disloyal

17. Securities Act of 1933, § 15, 15 U.S.C. § 77o (1988), and Securities Exchange Act of 1934, § 20(a), 15 U.S.C. § 78t (1988).

18. *Cf.* SEC v. Geon Indus., 531 F.2d 39 (2d Cir. 1976); SEC v. Management Dynamics, 515 F.2d 801 (2d Cir. 1975). Some claim that controlling person liability is narrower than we suggest. This is not relevant to our analysis, however, because respondeat superior applies to most securities fraud actions. *See infra* text accompanying note 22.

19. *Cf.* Thomas Hazen, The Law of Securities Regulation § 10.14, at 460 (2d ed. 1990) (suggesting that control person liability requires "not only that the defendant be a control person of the primary violator but also that the defendant was a culpable participant in the illegal activity").

agent committed fraud to conceal his own failures.[20] The effectiveness of this defense, however, is illusory for several reasons. First, Section 11 of the Securities Act of 1933 imposes absolute liability on an issuer for false statements in a registration statement; no defenses are available.[21] Second, notwithstanding that "controlling person" liability is governed by statute, most courts of appeal now hold that the common law doctrine of respondeat superior applies to securities fraud actions.[22] Accordingly, enterprises can be held liable, regardless of good faith, if an agent's fraudulent statements occurred within the scope of his employment. Finally, many decisions simply treat the corporation itself as the person uttering the fraudulent statements and hold it liable for false statements made in its name, such as those in required filings with the SEC. We treat all of these methods for holding a corporation liable as examples of "enterprise liability."

B. A Description of Fraud on the Market Cases

It is well established under Rule 10b-5 that material false statements about securities are actionable in suits brought by injured buyers or sellers (as the case may be).[23] To prevail in such an action the plaintiff must prove that the statement was false or misleading, that it was made with scienter (either knowledge of the falsity of the statement or a reckless disregard for the truth),[24] that it involved a material fact, and that the plaintiff relied on it to his detriment when he bought or sold the affected

20. Courts seem to have imposed a presumption that broker-dealers are on notice of the greater temptations facing their employees, thereby imposing on broker-dealers a higher duty of care to monitor for fraud in order to invoke the good faith defense. *Cf.* Zweig v. Hearst Corp., 521 F.2d 1129 (9th Cir.), *cert. denied*, 423 U.S. 1025 (1975).

21. 15 U.S.C. § 77k (1988).

22. Hollinger v. Titan Capital Corp., 914 F.2d 1564, 1576-77 (9th Cir. 1990), *cert. denied*, 111 S. Ct. 1621 (1991); Commerford v. Olson, 794 F.2d 1319 (8th Cir. 1986); *In re* Atlantic Financial Mgt., Inc., 784 F.2d 29, 32-35 (1st Cir. 1986); Marbury Management, Inc. v. Kohn, 629 F.2d 705 (2d Cir. 1980), *cert. denied*, 449 U.S. 1011 (1981); Kerbs v. Fall River Indus., 502 F.2d 731, 740-41 (10th Cir. 1974); Fey v. Walston & Co., 493 F.2d 1036, 1051-53 (7th Cir. 1974); Lewis v. Walston & Co., 487 F.2d 617, 623-24 (5th Cir. 1973); Armstrong, Jones & Co. v. SEC, 421 F.2d 359, 361-62 (6th Cir.), *cert. denied*, 398 U.S. 958 (1970); Johns Hopkins Univ. v. Hutton, 422 F.2d 1124, 1130 (4th Cir. 1970); *contra* Rochez Bros. v. Rhoades, 527 F.2d 880 (3d Cir. 1975); *but see* Sharp v. Coopers & Lybrand, 649 F.2d 175 (3d Cir. 1981) (exception where defendant has a "stringent duty" to supervise employees); Carpenter v. Harris, Upham & Co., 594 F.2d 388 (4th Cir.), *cert. denied*, 444 U.S. 868 (1979). For a discussion of this recent trend towards the use of respondeat superior see Christopher York, Comment, *Vicarious Liability of Controlling Persons: Respondeat Superior and the Securities Acts—A Reversible Consensus in the Circuits*, 42 EMORY L.J. (forthcoming 1993); *see also* William J. Fitzpatrick & Ronald T. Carman, *Respondeat Superior and the Federal Securities Laws: A Round Peg in a Square Hole*, 12 HOFSTRA L. REV. 1 (1983) (arguing that respondeat superior is inapplicable to § 10(b) claims).

23. Superintendent of Ins. v. Bankers Life & Cas. Co., 404 U.S. 6, 13 n.9 (1971). Investors who relied on the fraudulent statement to their detriment but who neither purchased nor sold stock during the period of the fraud do not have standing to sue. Blue Chip Stamps v. Manor Drug Stores, 421 U.S. 723, 731 (1975).

24. Ernst & Ernst v. Hochfelder, 425 U.S. 185 (1976). Although the Supreme Court has not ruled on whether the scienter requirement can be met by showing recklessness, every court of appeals that has considered the issue has ruled that recklessness will suffice.

security.[25] In most instances, these requirements do not vary substantially from the requirements of common law fraud.

Fraud on the Market cases generally involve false or misleading statements about a firm made to the market by corporate officials. These statements may take the form of a fraudulent registration statement for a new issue, some other filing with the SEC, public statements by officers, or a press release. If credible, the fraudulent statement will affect the market price of a company's shares exactly as would a true statement. In efficient markets a credible fraudulent favorable statement will either cause the price to rise or retard a price decline.[26] Until revelation of truthful information about the matter, the stock's price will reflect the fraudulent "news" about the issuer. This means that all persons trading in the stock between the announcement of the fraudulent information and the disclosure of the truth will trade at prices affected by the fraud. Whether they actually read or heard the fraudulent statement does not matter; the price they pay or receive will reflect the fraudulent information.[27]

Defendants in Fraud on the Market cases generally did not engage in securities transactions, but instead were alleged to be legally responsible for the false statements.[28] Section 10(b)'s prohibition of fraudulent statements "in connection with" the purchase or sale of securities applies to nearly all statements about companies with traded securities and certainly to any statements made in a sufficiently public manner to affect traders' beliefs about the value of a security.[29]

Fraud on the Market cases usually proceed as class action suits brought by those who traded to their detriment during the period of the

25. Basic, Inc. v. Levinson, 485 U.S. 224, 231-32, 243 (1988); Huddleston v. Herman & MacLean, 640 F.2d 534, 543 (5th Cir. 1981), *rev'd on other grounds*, 459 U.S. 375 (1983); *accord* Zlotnick v. TIE Communications, 836 F.2d 818, 821 (3d Cir. 1988); Rousseff v. E. F. Hutton Co., 843 F.2d 1326, 1329 (11th Cir. 1988); Peil v. Speiser, 806 F.2d 1154, 1160 (3d Cir. 1986); Dupuy v. Dupuy, 551 F.2d 1005, 1014 (5th Cir. 1977), *cert. denied*, 434 U.S. 911 (1977).

26. A false negative statement will either retard a price increase or cause the price to fall. False negative statements rarely occur, however. Our analysis of Fraud on the Market cases revealed that less than nine percent of the cases involved allegations of false negative signals about issuers, and these can generally be explained by conflicts of interest faced by managers and control shareholders in leveraged buyouts and takeouts of minority shareholders. *See infra* Table 1. We found one inexplicable case alleging a shift of earnings from a present to a future period, and one case alleging an attempt to depress a stock price so that an insider could purchase stock cheaply.

27. In all likelihood the truth will leak to some traders prior to the public revelation of the truth. Thus on the date of the fraud the stock price will fully reflect the false value of the information, but at some later date part of this value will be dissipated by informed traders. For purposes of simplification we ignore this phenomenon in this article. The problem is considered at length in Bradford Cornell & R. Gregory Morgan, *Using Finance Theory to Measure Damages in Fraud on the Market Cases*, 37 UCLA L. REV. 883, 889-97 (1990).

28. A handful of Fraud on the Market cases do involve insider trading by agents, however. *See infra* Table 2 (only 3.3% of frauds that concealed bad news were committed to enable insiders to sell their securities).

29. *See, e.g.*, SEC v. Texas Gulf Sulphur Co., 401 F.2d 833, 860 (2d Cir. 1968).

fraud.[30] In order to prevail in such an action, plaintiff class members must prove that they relied to their detriment on the fraudulent statements. Proof of reliance is an individual matter for each trader, and could have presented an insurmountable difficulty for a class action on behalf of all traders.[31] Courts eliminated this barrier for class plaintiffs, however, by creating a presumption of reliance in Fraud on the Market cases.[32] This presumption involves an economically correct assumption that in efficient markets stock prices are affected promptly by announcements of material information, true or false, about an issuer.[33] It then assumes that individual investors act as if the stock's price reflects all publicly available information, and that all stock prices are "fair" with respect to each other, in the sense that, as a result of active trading in the shares, stock prices reflect unbiased estimates of similar returns for similar risks.[34] The Supreme Court described the presumption as meaning that investors are entitled to rely on the integrity of the market price under these circumstances.[35] As a practical matter, this means that the plaintiff class does not need to prove that each class member read or heard the false statement before trading in the stock, but only that the trade took place after the false information was announced and before the truth was revealed.

C. Incidence of Liability

The presumption of reliance in Fraud on the Market cases has facilitated class actions on behalf of thousands of investors involving trading

30. This is not to say that individual investors never bring Fraud on the Market actions. A few do. The vast majority, however, are brought as class actions.

31. Basic, Inc. v. Levinson, 485 U.S. 224, 243 (1988) (citing Ernst & Ernst v. Hochfelder, 425 U.S. 185, 206 (1976)); *see also* Lipton v. Documation, Inc., 734 F.2d 740, 742 (11th Cir. 1984), *cert. denied*, 469 U.S. 1132 (1985). This problem does not exist under § 11 of the Securities Act of 1933 because reliance is only required if the issuer has made generally available an earnings statement covering at least 12 months beginning after the effective date of the registration statement under § 11(a)(5).

32. *Basic*, 485 U.S. at 245-47; Blackie v. Barrack, 524 F.2d 891, 906 (9th Cir. 1975), *cert. denied*, 429 U.S. 816 (1976).

33. *Basic*, 485 U.S. at 246 n.24. We exclude from this discussion those cases where presumptions of reliance have been afforded in initial offerings, either public or private, on other rationales. *See, e.g.*, Shores v. Sklar, 647 F.2d 462 (5th Cir. 1981) (en banc), *cert. denied*, 459 U.S. 1102 (1983). For a criticism of those cases, see Barbara Black, *Fraud on the Market: A Criticism of Dispensing With Reliance Requirements in Certain Open Market Transactions*, 62 N.C. L. REV. 435, 452-53 (1984); William J. Carney, *The Limits of the Fraud on the Market Doctrine*, 44 BUS. LAW. 1259 (1989); Daniel R. Fischel, *The Use of Modern Finance Theory in Securities Fraud Cases Involving Actively Traded Securities*, 38 BUS. LAW. 1, 12 (1982); Robert N. Rapp, *Rule 10b-5 and "Fraud on the Market"—Heavy Seas Meet Tranquil Shores*, 39 WASH. & LEE L. REV. 861, 886-87 (1982); Note, *The Fraud-on-the-Market Theory*, 95 HARV. L. REV. 1143, 1158 (1982).

34. The plurality opinion in *Basic* cited empirical studies suggesting that "the market price of shares traded on well-developed markets reflects all publicly available information, and, hence, any material misrepresentations." 485 U.S. at 246. It stated that " '[t]he market is acting as the unpaid agent of the investor, informing him that, given all the information available to it, the value of the stock is worth the market price.' " 485 U.S. at 244 (quoting *In re* LTV Sec. Litig., 88 F.R.D. 134, 143 (N.D. Tex. 1980)).

35. *Id.* at 247.

in millions of shares. The dollar amounts in dispute are correspondingly large. Under traditional tort theories, plaintiffs are entitled to their "out-of-pocket" damages—for example, the difference between the price the victim paid and the value received in a purchase transaction.[36] In Fraud on the Market cases, liability runs to all those who traded at a price affected by the fraud, regardless of the defendant's trading activity.

Plaintiffs in these cases generally utilize enterprise liability to sue the corporation; they sue the agents accused of the fraud significantly less frequently.[37] A Fraud on the Market action against a corporation threatens it with extraordinary liability, with some disturbing consequences.[38] Revelation of the fraud, and of the corporation's prospective liability, has an immediate impact on the price of the issuing corporation's stock: the price adjusts to reflect both the truth previously concealed by the fraud and the corporation's expected liability for the fraud.[39] Those who are shareholders at the time the fraud is revealed bear the cost of this price adjustment.[40]

In most cases, these shareholders are no more culpable than are the plaintiffs.[41] When fraud involves an attempt to conceal "bad news" about the firm, the only shareholders who benefit from the fraud are those who sold shares before the truth was revealed. But under enterprise liability these fortunate shareholders bear none of the costs of liability.[42] Enterprise liability, therefore, imposes most of the cost of fraud on

36. *See generally* HAZEN, *supra* note 19, § 13.7, at 714-15; Robert B. Thompson, *The Measure of Recovery Under Rule 10b-5: A Restitution Alternative to Tort Damages*, 37 VAND. L. REV. 349, 356-57 (1984). Both authors note that other measures of damages have been employed by some courts, but these differences are not critical to our analysis.

37. *See infra* note 171 and *infra* text accompanying notes 171-74.

38. *See infra* part IV(D).

39. *See generally* Daniel R. Fischel & Michael Bradley, *The Role of Liability Rules and the Derivative Suit in Corporate Law: A Theoretical and Empirical Analysis*, 71 CORNELL L. REV. 261 (1986) (examining the impact on stock prices of announcements of derivative suits).

40. *See* Easterbrook & Fischel, *supra* note 4, at 638-39.

41. Judge Friendly alluded to the problem in his concurring opinion in *Texas Gulf Sulphur*, when he stated that "[t]he consequences of holding that negligence . . . may impose civil liability on the corporation are frightening . . . . '[A]ny remedy imposed against the issuer itself is indirectly imposed on all holders of the common stock, usually the most important segment of the total category of investors intended to be protected.' " SEC v. Texas Gulf Sulfur Co., 401 F.2d 833, 866-67 (2d Cir. 1968) (Friendly, J., concurring) (quoting Milton Cohen, *Truth in Securities Revisited*, 79 HARV. L. REV. 1340, 1370 (1967)). Similarly, the importance of the stockholders' identity in derivative actions was recognized in Perlman v. Feldmann, 219 F.2d 173 (2d Cir.), *cert. denied*, 349 U.S. 952 (1955), where a control premium paid by a buyer of a control block was recovered from the seller for the benefit of the "corporation." The court recognized that because the buyer was the largest shareholder, awarding the recovery to the corporation would reward the buyer and reduce its acquisition cost, rather than provide a reward to the public shareholders. *Id.* at 178. In *Basic*, Justice White, dissenting in part, complained about the length of the class period, the size of the potential class, and concluded:

> And who will pay the judgments won in such actions? I suspect that all too often the majority's rule will "lead to large judgments, payable in the last analysis by innocent investors, for the benefit of speculators and their lawyers." *Cf.* SEC v. Texas Gulf Sulphur Co., 401 F.2d 833, 867 (2nd Cir. 1968) (en banc) (Friendly, J., concurring) . . . .

Basic, Inc. v. Levinson, 485 U.S. 224, 262 (1988).

42. Enterprise liability imposes costs on a shareholder who benefits from the fraud only when

shareholders who were not responsible for, and received no benefit, from the fraud. Moreover, some of the shareholders who bear the cost of liability may themselves be victims of the fraud if they were dissuaded from selling their shares by false positive news about the company. Yet, under the securities laws these shareholders do not have standing to sue.[43] Accordingly, the effect of enterprise liability is to make these shareholders bear some of the costs of the fraud to others, in addition to bearing the full cost of the fraud to themselves. Finally, in some cases it would be possible for most of the plaintiff class to be shareholders of the issuer at the time of suit. In these cases, payment of damages to the injured class is virtually equivalent to a dividend or a partial liquidation.[44] The result in any case is no more than a wealth transfer from one group of diversified investors to another, with a substantial deduction for litigation costs, a result no investor would prefer ex ante. The only persons receiving a net benefit from enterprise liability under these circumstances would be the attorneys for both parties.[45]

III. The Efficiency of Enterprise Liability

Although the preceding analysis of the incidence of enterprise liability for Fraud on the Market suggests that the rule is unjust, its use nevertheless might be desirable were the rule efficient.[46] Conventional analysis of enterprise liability in the torts context presents three economic justifications for holding enterprises liable instead of relying on only agent liability: (1) enterprise liability is better able to deter fraud by agents than is agent liability;[47] (2) enterprise liability efficiently spreads the risk of liability between the firm and its agents;[48] and (3) enterprise liability efficiently allocates the risk of loss to the firm rather than to the victims.[49] The issue presented is whether any of these arguments justify the use of enterprise liability in Fraud on the Market cases. To address this issue we must first determine who commits Fraud on the Market and why.

---

he sells a portion of his shares, retaining the rest until the fraud is revealed. Even then his liability may not equal the benefit he receives.

43. Blue Chip Stamps v. Manor Drug Stores, 421 U.S. 723 (1975).

44. Easterbrook & Fischel, *supra* note 4, at 639.

45. *Cf.* Jonathan R. Macey & Geoffrey P. Miller, *The Plaintiffs' Attorney's Role in Class Actions and Derivative Litigation: Economic Analysis and Recommendations for Reform*, 58 U. CHI. L. REV. 1 (1991) (arguing that the interests of entrepreneurial attorneys in small-claim class actions may diverge from those of the members of the plaintiff class).

46. Because the efficiency of enterprise liability is our primary concern, the present analysis ignores the unjust enrichment resulting from random wealth transfers among investors occasioned by vicarious liability for Fraud on the Market. *See infra* part III(B)(4).

47. *See, e.g.*, SHAVELL, *supra* note 4; Kornhauser, *supra* note 4; Sykes II, *supra* note 4; Sykes I, *supra* note 4.

48. Easterbrook & Fischel, *supra* note 4, at 640-41; Kraakman, *supra* note 5; Sykes II, *supra* note 4.

49. Musewicz, *supra* note 6.

A. Expected Characteristics of Fraud on the Market

Our hypothesis is that managers of ailing firms commit Fraud on the Market in an attempt to save their jobs, by using the period of the fraud to turn the firm around. Our reasons for reaching this conclusion are as follows.

We expect that securities fraud is a tort (and a crime) that is peculiarly susceptible to ultimate detection when committed by agents of publicly held corporations. The credibility of false positive statements about a company's sales or profits, for example, can be sustained only so long as a firm remains financially viable and suffers no business reverses that will reveal the fraud. Consequently, fraud generally will remain undetected only if either later events make earlier false statements come true, or the firm's subsequent operating results are so positive that no one appears to have been harmed by an earlier false positive statement, and thus there are no visible damages. Such fortuitous occurrences are unlikely. To constitute actionable fraud the misstatement must be "material," involving facts sufficiently important to affect the market price of the firm's stock. Only a very fortuitous subsequent turn of events would be able to conceal such large lies. Fraud is thus, at best, an extremely risky strategy. Further, because Fraud on the Market involves false statements made in a public way by company officials to a market populated by large, well-informed investors, ultimate detection of individual wrongdoers should be relatively certain.

We expect that corporate agents commit Fraud on the Market in order to serve their own interests, and not simply to benefit the corporation's existing shareholders. We do not believe that shareholders want agents to commit fraud. Corporations relying on public markets for sources of future financing expect to be repeat players in securities markets; consequently, they would find the long-term costs of Fraud on the Market far higher than any short-term payoffs.[50] Furthermore, uninformed shareholders acting on false information are as likely to be injured as they are to benefit from such frauds. Fraud on the Market is therefore likely to be the act of the firm's agents, generally undertaken without actual authority of the board of directors or the shareholders in the legal sense. Fraud is, in short, an aspect of agency costs.[51] Accordingly, we expect that Fraud on the Market by publicly traded companies usually does not result from a formal corporate decision, either at the

50. Moreover, even shareholders of firms that may fail (firms in a "last period") are not likely to want their agents to commit fraud because each shareholder runs the risk of being a victim of a policy that encourages fraud; lulled by the fraud, the shareholder may retain stock that might otherwise have sold at a higher price. *See infra* text accompanying notes 59-62. Furthermore, diversified shareholders will prefer no fraud in securities markets, because they are equally likely to be victims or beneficiaries.

51. For the seminal discussion of agency costs, see Michael Jensen & William Meckling, *The Theory of the Firm: Managerial Behavior, Agency Costs and Ownership Structure*, 3 J. FIN. ECON. 305 (1976).

board or shareholder level.[52]

We also predict that firm agents commit Fraud on the Market only under unusual circumstances. For most agents, the expected costs of committing Fraud on the Market are very high and the expected benefits are low. Agents benefit from Fraud on the Market only to the extent that they benefit from higher firm share prices. A manager of a healthy firm generally will not benefit substantially from fraud even if he owns shares in the firm, because the passage of time is likely to reveal that the manager's fraudulent positive statements were false, at which point the stock price will fall, and the manager's paper gains will vanish.[53] By contrast, the costs of committing fraud are extremely high—with sanctions ranging from termination of employment and civil liability to potential criminal liability. In Fraud on the Market cases, the threat of termination of employment is a particularly effective sanction. Fraudulent statements usually are issued by, or at the direction of, senior managers, who would forfeit considerable firm specific human capital if they were fired. Additionally, some of these agents may be earning quasi rents, representing deferred compensation from earlier periods (such as stock options and other plans that reward long-term performance) that also would be lost were the agent fired.[54] Under ordinary conditions, therefore, managers have strong incentives to behave honestly when dealing with securities markets.

Because of these risks an agent generally will not commit Fraud on the Market so long as his future employment seems assured.[55] When the firm is ailing, however, an agent's expectations of future employment no longer serve as a constraint on behavior.[56] In this situation a manager

52. We recognize that corporate policy generally is determined by agents of the corporation, not by the shareholders. Accordingly, the conclusion that agents commit fraud to serve their own interests, not those of shareholders, does not eliminate the possibility that fraud might result from a board decision.

53. Of course, the manager might benefit more directly by selling his stock before the fraud is revealed. This is not "pure" Fraud on the Market, however, but rather Fraud on the Market and insider trading. We define "pure" Fraud on the Market cases as those where a Fraud on the Market action is the only available remedy. In this article we only consider pure Fraud on the Market cases because a separate sanction exists for insider trading, and also most Fraud on the Market cases involve pure Fraud on the Market. *See infra* Table 2 (only three frauds intended to conceal bad news about the firm involved insider trading).

54. Appropriable quasi rents are the difference between an investment in specific capital and its salvage value. Benjamin Klein, Robert Crawford & Armen Alchian, *Vertical Integration, Appropriable Rents, and the Competitive Contracting Process*, 21 J.L. & ECON. 297, 298 (1978). For a discussion of the specific capital invested by senior managers in firms, see William J. Carney, *Controlling Management Opportunism in the Market for Corporate Control: An Agency Cost Model*, 1988 WIS. L. REV. 385, 418-20. *See generally* Robert Topel, *Specific Capital, Mobility, and Wages: Wages Rise with Job Senority*, 99 J. POL. ECON. 145 (1991).

55. *But cf. supra* note 53.

56. *See generally* Lynn M. LoPucki & William C. Whitford, *Bargaining Over Equity's Share in the Bankruptcy of Large, Publicly Held Companies*, 139 U. PA. L. REV. 125 (1990) (managers usually lose their jobs in bankruptcy reorganizations); Susan Rose-Ackerman, *Risk Taking and Ruin: Bankruptcy and Investment Choice*, 20 J. LEGAL STUD. 277 (1991) (managers risk losing their jobs if a firm goes bankrupt and will take actions that do not necessarily maximize expected firm profits in order to avoid this possibility).

may view securities fraud as a positive net present value project. Aside from criminal liability, in a last period the expected costs of fraud (civil liability[57] and job loss) are minimal, while the expected benefits of fraud may have increased. As remote as the prospects for success may seem, these benefits include possible preservation of employment as well as the value of the manager's assets related to the firm's stock, if by committing fraud he is able to buy sufficient time to turn the ailing firm around.[58]

It might appear that, contrary to the prior discussion, managers' incentives to save the firm align their interests with those of shareholders. Generally, however, this is not the case. First, managers may fear themselves to be in a last period when the firm itself is not in a last period—for example, when a previously healthy firm is ailing as a result of bad management decisions, but can expect an eventual, although not immediate, recovery if policies (and managers) are changed. In these circumstances, managers may perceive a personal benefit from committing fraud when shareholders would not. Additionally, even in a last period situation for the firm, committing a successful (undetected) Fraud on the Market to avoid bankruptcy usually benefits a manager more than the average shareholder. Managers have most of their wealth tied to their corporate employer in the form of quasi rents,[59] which they lose if the firm goes bankrupt. Shareholders, by contrast, are fully diversified and have not invested a substantial portion of their wealth in any one firm.[60] To avoid bankruptcy, managers are willing to act inconsistently with the shareholders' goal of maximizing expected firm profits.[61] Finally, diversified shareholders are as likely to be victims of fraud as they are to be its beneficiaries. Accordingly, shareholders usually cannot anticipate any net benefit from allowing managers to commit Fraud on the Market in a last period situation and as a general rule prefer securities markets that are free from fraud.[62]

---

57. The primary assets that a manager risks in the event of civil liability are assets derived from his wage income and his stock-related investments in the firm, yet both are also at risk should the firm fail. *See supra* note 56. Accordingly, a manager facing a last period of employment is not likely to view civil liability as as great a threat as will a manager of a healthy firm.

58. *Cf.* Kraakman, *supra* note 5, at 866 n.25 (Under enterprise liability, "managers who face imminent replacement—due, for example, to poor performance—may take 'irrational' legal risks on behalf of the firm because they have nothing to lose by doing so."). If the firm's financial situation does improve, the manager probably need not fear being held liable for securities fraud: private plaintiffs have little, if any, claim to damages if the firm's share price goes up (or falls very little) after revelation of the fraud and therefore are unlikely to sue. Similarly, in this situation, there will be little to cause government enforcement officials to investigate whether there was fraud.

59. *See supra* note 54 and accompanying text.

60. Furthermore, shareholders in firms that undergo bankruptcy reorganization often retain some of their initial investment should the firm become successful after emerging from reorganization. *See* Jonathan R. Macey, *Agency Theory and the Criminal Liability of Organizations*, 71 B.U. L. REV. 315, 326-27 (1991).

61. *See generally* Rose-Ackerman, *supra* note 56.

62. This is not to say that shareholders never benefit from Fraud on the Market. Because creditors bear most of the costs of failure, under some circumstances shareholders may prefer that managers undertake fraud to buy time for a recovery, regardless of the low probability of success. This possibility does not undermine our agency cost argument, however, because shareholders of

B. Enterprise Liability in a Last Period Context

Given our last period hypothesis, we now examine whether using enterprise liability to govern Fraud on the Market cases is efficient.[63]

We assume in our model that under enterprise liability the corporation pays the entire judgment, even though generally both enterprise and agent liability are available simultaneously.[64] In other words, we view the question of whether enterprise liability is efficient as equivalent to whether substituting exclusive enterprise liability for agent liability is efficient.[65] This view of the issue is consistent with both the prior literature on enterprise liability,[66] and our findings in part IV that (1) under our present system of joint enterprise and agent liability plaintiffs invariably sue corporate issuers,[67] and (2) that because Fraud on the Market cases almost always settle out of court, agents who are sued may avail themselves of indemnification agreements with the issuer and liability insurance coverage.[68]

1. Efficient Deterrence

The central aim of the securities laws is to deter fraud.[69] Therefore,

---

publicly held firms are in no better position to encourage such fraud than they are to prevent it. Moreover, it is impossible to encourage just "beneficial" types of Fraud on the Market without also encouraging unwanted last period frauds. Finally, to the extent that shareholders diversify by purchasing corporate bonds, these frauds are at best a zero sum game for them. But see the argument of Professors Macey and Miller, *infra* note 73, that shareholders would prefer fraud if it is necessary to preserve the value of certain deals for the firm.

63. In this part we assume that frauds generally involve attempts either to conceal bad news about a firm or attempts to overinflate good news, generally in a possible last period context. In theory, of course, frauds also can involve attempts to conceal good news about a firm. For the reasons we have previously stated, we expect that there will be few such cases: agents generally benefit from a more valuable firm and a higher stock price. This hypothesis is supported by the evidence in *infra* part IV.

64. Both § 15 of the Securities Act of 1933, 15 U.S.C. § 77o (1988), and § 20(a) of the Securities Exchange Act of 1934, *id.* § 78t(a), expressly provide for joint and several liability for control persons.

65. We recognize, of course, that under enterprise liability the corporation will be able to shift some of this cost onto the agents.

66. *See* Kornhauser, *supra* note 4, at 1347, 1357 (arguing that enterprise and agent liability should be treated as alternatives because enterprises rarely exercise their rights to indemnification); Renier Kraakman, *The Econonic Functions of Corporate Liability*, *in* CORPORATE GOVERNANCE AND DIRECTORS' LIABILITIES 178, 179-80 (Klaus Hopt & Gunther Teubner eds., 1985); Sykes II, *supra* note 4; *see also* Shavell, *supra* note 4, at 172-75. By contrast, in the criminal context, enterprise and agent liability should be treated as simultaneous, not alternative, sanctions. *See* JENNIFER H. ARLEN, OPTIMUM CRIMINAL SANCTIONS FOR CORPORATIONS (Emory Univ. Law & Economics Working Paper No. 36, 1992). This is because—in contrast with civil liability where full satisfaction of a judgment against one defendant precludes a plaintiff from seeking recovery from the other defendants—the magnitude of the criminal sanction imposed on the agent does not affect the magnitude of the criminal sanction that can be imposed on the enterprise. The government can, and does, therefore, seek to impose full sanctions on both the enterprise and its agents.

67. *See infra* Table 6. Issuers are only omitted as defendants where protected from suit by bankruptcy or Chapter 11 reorganization proceedings.

68. *See infra* notes 85 and 182.

69. Easterbrook & Fischel, *supra* note 4, at 613; *see* Frank H. Easterbrook & Daniel R. Fischel, *Mandatory Disclosure and the Protection of Investors*, 70 VA. L. REV. 669, 693-94 (1984). The claim that the securities laws are intended primarily to deter fraud, not to compensate all injured

the desirability of a rule imposing enterprise liability for Fraud on the Market depends primarily on whether it deters fraud better than agent liability. Efficient deterrence depends on the nature of the harmful activity. When the harmful activity produces social benefits, the efficient level of the harmful activity is often positive. By contrast, when the harm-producing activity yields no social benefits, efficient deterrence is achieved when agents refrain from the activity altogether, assuming no serious risk of court error.[70]

Fraud on the Market produces substantial social costs[71] and yields no social benefit. Agents can avoid committing fraud at zero cost by simply refraining from intentional material misstatements.[72] Nor does

---

victims, finds support in the fact that Congress did not provide an express cause of action for violations of § 10(b). In addition, the Supreme Court in *Blue Chip Stamps* restricted standing to actual purchasers and sellers, despite the fact that, as the Court recognized, this would leave many who were injured by the fraud without a remedy. Blue Chip Stamps v. Manor Drug Stores, 421 U.S. 723, 754 (1975). In fact, numerous judicial statements repeat that the securities laws were not intended to provide a scheme of investor's insurance. Basic, Inc. v. Levinson, 485 U.S. 224, 252 (1988) (White, J., dissenting); Freeman v. Laventhol & Horwath, 915 F.2d 193, 198 (6th Cir. 1990); Grigsby v. CMI Corp., 765 F.2d 1369, 1376 (9th Cir. 1985); T.J. Raney & Sons, Inc. v. Fort Cobb, Okla. Fuel Auth., 717 F.2d 1330, 1333 (10th Cir. 1983); List v. Fashion Park, Inc., 340 F.2d 457, 463 (2d Cir.), *cert. denied*, 382 U.S. 811 (1965). Moreover, as we later observe, even if just compensation is a goal of the securities laws, it is not served by vicarious liability for Fraud on the Market because this rule transfers wealth from one innocent group of investors to another. *See infra* text accompanying note 135, 185-99.

70. Easterbrook & Fischel, *supra* note 4, at 621-22; *see* Fred S. McChesney, *Desperately Shunning Science?*, 71 B.U. L. REV. 281 (1991); Fred S. McChesney, *Boxed In: Economists and the Social Value of Crime*, — INT'L REV. L. & ECON. (forthcoming 1993) [hereinafter *Boxed In*]; George J. Stigler, *The Optimum Enforcement of Laws*, 78 J. POL. ECON. 526, 527 (1970); Gordon Tullock, *The Welfare Costs of Tariffs, Monopolies and Theft*, 5 W. ECON. J. 224, 228 (1967). This statement is subject to the qualification that where enforcement is costly, the second-best optimal amount of fraud (and other wrongs) may be greater than zero. *See* Michael R. Darby & Edi Karni, *Free Competition and the Optimal Amount of Fraud*, 16 J.L. & ECON. 67, 83-86 (1973); Stigler, *supra*. Costly enforcement, however, does not undermine our conclusion that optimal damages exceeds the present value of the agent's net compensation from the firm. Within certain limits, the optimal solution to the problem of costly enforcement is to reduce substantially the probability of detection and dramatically increase the sanction above the optimal sanction when enforcement is costless, in order to economize on enforcement costs. *See* Louis Kaplow, *The Optimal Probability and Magnitude of Fines for Acts that Definitely are Undesirable*, 12 INT'L REV. L. & ECON. 3, 5 (1992); Nicholas Stern, *On the Economic Theory of Policy Towards Crime*, *in* ECONOMIC MODELS OF CRIMINAL BEHAVIOR 123-52 (John M. Heineke ed., 1978); *see also* A. Mitchell Polinsky & Steven Shavell, *The Optimal Tradeoff Between the Probability and Magnitude of Fines*, 69 AMER. ECON. REV. 880 (1979) (examining optimal fines for crimes that produce social benefits).

71. The social costs of securities fraud include the costs to shareholders of information verification and the costs to society of the misallocation of resources between equity and other investments resulting from the discount for fraud. Subsequent litigation, to the extent that it fails to deter fraud, imposes its own deadweight losses. Finally, in the case of public offerings, fraud also results in a misallocation of resources between firms.

72. Securities fraud requires a showing of scienter. Accordingly, liability is not based on the negligent failure to discover information, but rather requires that the defendants knew (or recklessly disregarded) the truth. Moreover, fraud requires a misstatement (or an omission that makes another statement misleading). A mere error in judgment about whether to disclose additional facts needed to make a statement not misleading is not sufficient. Ernst & Ernst v. Hochfelder, 425 U.S. 185 (1976).

We acknowledge, however, the argument that managers may be overdeterred from engaging in corporate speech by a liability system designed to eliminate fraud. The solution to this problem is to strengthen the scienter requirement, not to reduce liability for fraud. Moreover, overdeterrence is society benefit in any other way from a deliberate attempt to induce investors to allocate capital to a firm to which they would not allocate it otherwise.[73] Fraud on the Market therefore should be deterred completely.

This presents the issue: Which rule, enterprise liability or agent liability, is better able to deter fraud? The Coase Theorem implies that if transaction costs are negligible, the assignment of liability between the enterprise and the agent should not affect the efficiency of the outcome (here, the amount of fraud).[74] To illustrate, assume, solely for purposes of this example, that agents and firms are risk neutral. In this situation, under agent liability the agent will bear directly the cost of all liability, which will induce the agent to refrain from engaging in fraud. Under enterprise liability the firm will be directly liable to plaintiffs, but will transfer the entire burden of liability to the responsible agent, once again providing the agent with the incentive to refrain from fraud.[75] The argu-

---

less of a concern in fraud cases (particularly where the firm is concealing bad news) because the social value of the grey region separating the legal from the illegal is dubious. *See* Kraakman, *supra* note 5, at 868 n.28. Thus we believe error costs associated with enforcement of antifraud rules involved in Fraud on the Market cases should be low, excluding cases involving public offerings, where § 11 of the Securities Act of 1933, 15 U.S.C. § 77k (1988), imposes a due diligence standard on defendants other than the issuer.

73. *See infra* Table 1 (91.3% of the cases for which we have information on the nature of the fraud involved attempts to conceal bad news). Fraud on the Market imposes costs on society by distorting capital markets, *see supra* note 71, without creating any mitigating social benefits. It is no more costly to reveal the truth than to reveal a lie, and therefore the fraud does not result in any cost savings. In fact, a deliberate lie is probably more costly for society than is the truth because the lying agents will expend resources to hide the truth; furthermore, the possibility of fraud creates incentives for shareholders and others to investigate both valid and invalid claims to determine their validity. *See* Easterbrook & Fischel, *supra* note 4, at 622.

Nevertheless, Professors Macey and Miller argue that fraud may be necessary to protect some transactions, such as mergers, that might be thwarted by premature disclosure. Jonathan R. Macey & Geoffrey P. Miller, *Good Finance, Bad Economics: An Analysis of the Fraud-on-the-Market Theory*, 42 STAN. L. REV. 1059 (1990). These authors assume, incorrectly, that the only way to avoid disclosure of merger negotiations is to lie. Justice Blackmun rejected that argument in his plurality opinion in *Basic*: "To be actionable, of course, a statement must also be misleading. Silence, absent a duty to disclose, is not misleading under Rule 10b-5." *Basic*, 485 U.S. at 239 n.17. Since his pronouncement, many firms have officially adopted "no comment" policies that require corporate officials to announce that not commenting on rumors about firm activity is corporate policy. This removes any possible signal from the "no comment" response, if "no comment" is used consistently by the firm. Moreover, fraud cannot be justified as an attempt to reduce information costs because here, as in the other cases, those committing the fraud invariably incurred the investigative costs necessary to obtain the beneficial information and also incurred disclosure costs in committing and concealing the fraud. Our differences with Macey and Miller notwithstanding, we acknowledge the ongoing debate on whether fraud should be permitted in some circumstances. *See, e.g.*, Ian Ayres, *Back to* Basics: *Regulating How Corporations Speak to the Market*, 77 VA. L. REV. 945 (1991); Marcel Kahan, *Games, Lies, and Securities Fraud*, 67 N.Y.U. L. REV. (forthcoming 1992). The outcome of this debate does not affect the conclusions of this article, however. Our argument regarding the relative efficiency of enterprise and agent liability does not depend on our conclusion that fraud should be deterred absolutely.

74. *See* Kornhauser, *supra* note 4, at 1347-48; Sykes II, *supra* note 4, at 1239-41 (citing Ronald H. Coase, *The Problem of Social Cost*, 3 J.L. & ECON. 1 (1960)). This conclusion holds even when the enterprise is only able to condition the agent's wage on whether the wrong occurred, and not on how much care the agent took to avoid it. Kornhauser, *supra* note 4, at 1358.

75. In a perfect world in which agents and firms are risk averse, enterprise liability and agent liability also are equally effective at inducing optimal risk spreading.

ment for enterprise liability, therefore, focuses on various real-world imperfections that are thought to make enterprise liability the superior rule.

a. Judgment Proof Agents

Probably the most important argument in favor of enterprise liability is that agent liability will not deter fraud efficiently if damage awards exceed the responsible agent's wealth, because judgment proof agents do not bear the full cost of the sanction and thus will not avoid all fraud.[76] The problem of judgment proof agents is a very real concern in Fraud on the Market cases. To deter fraud completely, the damage award must remove all the gains to the agent from committing fraud. Therefore, the damage award imposed on the agent must equal the agent's expected gain from the fraud divided by the probability that the agent will be found liable.[77] We have suggested that relatively senior members of management typically commit Fraud on the Market in order to protect their positions. Accordingly, the optimal damage award equals the net present value of the agent's expected compensation, including deferred compensation from stock and stock benefits (net of the compensation he will earn in his alternative employment), divided by the probability that he will be found liable. It is, in other words, a function of the expected net present value to the agent of being employed by this firm (including stock and stock-related profits).[78] We expect that agents apprehended for fraud usually will be judgment proof, because the firm's value (and thus the agent's wealth and ability to satisfy the optimal damage award) declines dramatically when the fraud is revealed.[79]

The likelihood of judgment proof agents implies that agent liability will not deter fraud completely, but it does not demonstrate that enterprise liability is the superior rule. Enterprise liability is a superior solution to the judgment proof problem only if: (1) the principal can impose greater ex post sanctions on its agents than can the courts; (2) the principal is better able to apprehend guilty agents than are private plaintiffs; or (3) the principal is better able to deter fraud ex ante. We consider each of these possibilities in turn.

76. *See* Sykes I, *supra* note 4, at 168 (arguing that the law of vicarious liability exists primarily to deal with the problem of judgment proof agents).

77. Robert Cooter, *Prices and Sanctions*, 84 COLUM. L. REV. 1523 (1985); David D. Haddock, Fred McChesney & Menahem Spiegal, *An Ordinary Economic Rationale for Extraordinary Legal Sanctions*, 78 CAL. L. REV. 1 (1990); *see* Jennifer H. Arlen, *Why the Commission's Proposal is not Good Economics*, 3 FED. SENT. REP. 138 (1990); McChesney, *Boxed In*, *supra* note 70; *see also* Easterbrook & Fischel, *supra* note 4, at 622.

78. In those few cases where agents commit fraud in order to benefit directly from trading on inside information, *see supra* note 53, damage awards should include an amount equal to the benefit to the insiders of these trades divided by the probability that the agent will be found liable for the fraud.

79. Moreover, agents apprehended for fraud also may lose their jobs, and consequently a substantial portion of their capital (human and financial).

b. Ex Post Monetary Sanctions

Scholars analyzing vicarious liability for standard torts and crimes argue that judgment proof agents are less of a concern under enterprise liability than under agent liability because the firm can impose greater sanctions on its agents than can the courts. Specifically, these scholars argue that firms can solve the agent insolvency problem by paying those managers in a position to commit fraud a wage sufficiently in excess of the "market wage"[80] that the cost to a manager of the wage reduction that occurs if he is caught committing fraud equals the optimum damage award.[81]

Whatever may be the merits of this argument as applied to standard torts and crimes,[82] it does not hold in Fraud on the Market cases. Because the optimum damage award for Fraud on the Market is a multiple of the agent's expected net compensation from being employed by the firm,[83] any increase in an agent's wage results in an equivalent increase in the optimum damage award, leaving the judgment proof status of the agent unchanged. In the Fraud on the Market context, therefore, the firm is in no better position to sanction the responsible agents than are shareholder-victims. Although under enterprise liability the firm can affect a responsible agent's future income stream by firing him and also affect his wealth by suing for indemnification, under agent liability shareholder-victims can have the same impact on the agent's wealth, as well as on his future income stream, by obtaining a judgment against him.[84]

Of course, the presence of indemnification agreements and director

80. A "market wage" is the wage that the manager normally would earn in the market given his contribution to the firm (i.e., given the marginal product of his labor). An "above-market wage" is any wage in excess of this amount.

81. *See* Gary S. Becker & George J. Stigler, *Law Enforcement, Malfeasance, and Compensation of Enforcers*, 3 J. LEGAL STUD. 1, 6 (1974); *see also* Kornhauser, *supra* note 4, at 1362-66.

82. There is a problem with this argument even as applied to standard torts and crimes: paying managers above market wages is itself inefficient because it distorts the labor market by inducing agents to flock to the jobs that pay these wages, thereby creating an excess supply of workers for these jobs. *See* Becker & Stigler, *supra* note 81, at 9; B. Curtis Eaton & William White, *Agent Compensation and the Limits of Bonding*, 20 ECON. INQUIRY 330, 331 (1982). This excess supply of workers would force firms (and thus society) to employ nonmarket factors to select between workers. *Id.* Moreover, this labor market problem cannot be solved by requiring employees to bid for these lucrative jobs. *Cf.* Becker & Stigler, *supra* note 81. Firms usually need their managers to have specialized skills, and often firm-specific human capital. It is likely that the supply of qualified agents with sufficient wealth to pay the optimum "entry fee" on these jobs is less than the demand, in which case the bidding system will not eliminate the economic rents from these jobs, and the labor market will remain distorted. Eaton & White, *supra*. Moreover, agents may not be willing to pay such fees if they fear that they may be fired even though they have not committed fraud, thus losing the entry fee without obtaining the expected financial benefit from the job. *Id.* at 341-42.

83. *See supra* text accompanying note 78.

84. Both corporate employers and shareholders can affect an agent's future income stream by suing for damages for Fraud on the Market because an agent probably cannot obtain a discharge in bankruptcy for this debt. There is no discharge for a debt incurred by fraud while acting in a fiduciary capacity. 11 U.S.C. § 523(a)(4) (1988). Whether this rule extends to liability for Fraud on the Market, however, is not established. Moreover, even under agent liability, revelation of the fraud often will result in the firm being sent into bankruptcy proceedings, *see infra* text accompanying note 166, in which case the wrongful agents will lose their jobs, as well as their deferred compensation

and officer (D&O) liability insurance may diminish the deterrent effect of monetary sanctions.[85] This problem applies equally to agent liability and enterprise liability, however. Moreover, for reasons discussed below, D&O insurance well may strengthen the case for agent liability.[86]

Accordingly, one cannot justify resort to enterprise liability for Fraud on the Market by citing firms' superior ability to impose monetary sanctions on agents ex post. In fact, the deterrent effect of the available monetary sanctions under agent liability may exceed the effect of enterprise liability. If, as appears likely, agents are stigmatized more by civil judgments than they are by sanctions imposed privately by firms,[87] agent liability may exert a greater deterrent force on agents than will enterprise liability.[88] Moreover, the judgment proof problem can be eliminated completely by supplementing civil agent liability with nonmonetary criminal sanctions.[89]

c. Are Firms Superior Enforcers?

Even if firms are unable to impose greater monetary sanctions on agents than the courts, enterprise liability still may be the superior rule when agents are judgment proof, if firms are better situated than the courts and private plaintiffs to identify and sanction wrongdoers once fraud has occurred. If the probability that the firm will impose a sanc-

---

and the value of their stock-related assets. *See supra* note 56. In addition, some firms will fire managers found liable for Fraud on the Market in order to preserve the firm's reputation.

85. Top corporate officers likely to be charged with fraud usually have indemnification agreements or liability insurance coverage that covers liability for torts. Janet C. Alexander, *Do the Merits Matter? A Study of Settlements in Securities Class Actions*, 43 STAN. L. REV. 497, 550-57 (1991) (94% of public companies have directors and officers liability insurance (citing WYATT CO., 1989 DIRECTORS AND OFFICERS LIABILITY SURVEY 42 (1989)); Kraakman, *supra* note 5. Typical liability policies and indemnification provisions exclude losses based on a director or officer's liability for having acted dishonestly. Joseph Hinsey, *The New Lloyd's Policy Form for Directors and Officers Liability Insurance—An Analysis*, 33 BUS. LAW. 1961, 1970-71 (1978); *see also* PRACTICING LAW INST., DIRECTORS' AND OFFICERS' LIABILITY 640-55 (1986); Clifford Holderness, *Liability Insurers as Corporate Monitors*, 10 INT'L REV. L. & ECON. 115, 117 (1990); Dale A. Oesterle, *Limits on a Corporation's Protection of Its Directors and Officers from Personal Liability*, 1983 WIS. L. REV. 513, 549-50. Managers, however, often settle these cases, partly in order to avail themselves of indemnification provisions and director and officer insurance.

86. *See infra text* accompanying notes 102-07.

87. Although the reputational cost to managers of civil judgments has not been measured, John Lott has found that white collar criminals face substantially higher collateral penalties (in the form of lost licenses and the loss of legitimate income after returning to the work force) than their poorer counterparts. John R. Lott, Jr., *The Effect of Conviction on the Legitimate Income of Criminals*, 34 ECON. LETTERS 381, 381-85 (1990); *see* John R. Lott, Jr., *An Attempt At Measuring the Total Monetary Penalty From Drug Convictions: The Importance of Individual Reputation*, 21 J. LEGAL STUD. 159 (1992).

Similarly, a successful action by investors against an agent may increase the chances that the SEC will proceed against the agent with an administrative or injunctive proceeding. Being subject to administrative or injunctive orders with respect to securities fraud may result in the agent being barred from utilizing certain exemptions under the securities laws, *see, e.g.*, 17 C.F.R. §§ 230.262(b), 505(b)(iii), and from serving as an investment advisor, *see* 15 U.S.C. § 80b-3(e) (1988).

88. *See* Kornhauser, *supra* note 4, at 1369-70.

89. *See generally* Steven Shavell, *Criminal Law and the Optimal Use of Nonmonetary Sanctions as a Deterrent*, 85 COLUM. L. REV. 1232 (1985).

tion on a fraudulent agent exceeds the probability that the agent will be found liable for damages in an action by victims, then the optimal sanction under enterprise liability[90] (benefit of fraud/probability of sanction) is lower than the optimal damage award under agent liability (benefit of fraud/probability of liability). Because fewer agents will be judgment proof under the lower sanction required by a rule of enterprise liability, proponents argue that this rule will deter more agents from committing fraud.[91]

This claim as to the superiority of enterprise liability contains two separate arguments: (1) that firms are better able than plaintiffs and courts to identify the agents who committed the fraud; and (2) that firms are at least as likely as private plaintiffs to sanction responsible agents once discovered. Both of these claims fail in the context of Fraud on the Market cases.

Standard torts cases often involve multiple, and intersecting, wrongful *failures* to act. Thus, concluding that firms are in a superior position to determine which agents are responsible for the tort is reasonable.[92] By contrast, Fraud on the Market cases involve affirmative wrongful public acts that frequently are in writing and attributed to signatories or a named spokesperson, so the identity of the wrongdoer is readily ascertainable by plaintiffs, as well as by the enterprise.[93] Plaintiffs can determine which agents are responsible for the fraud by examining the firm's records to determine which agents must approve SEC filings and press releases and the lines of command leading to these documents. Indeed, SEC filings must be signed in compliance with regulations, and press releases frequently are attributed to a particular individual. Although the ostensible attribution of such documents well may fail to identify the ultimate wrongdoer, it provides the victims the same starting point for investigation that it gives the firm's board of directors. Accordingly, there is little reason to believe that firms are better able than plaintiffs to determine which agents are responsible for the fraud.

There is a second problem with the argument that firms are in a superior position to sanction wrongdoers. Plaintiffs are more likely to proceed against a wrongful agent under agent liability than are firms under enterprise liability. In a perfect Coasean world of zero transaction

90. By "optimal sanction under enterprise liability" we mean the amount of liability that the enterprise must shift to the agent (for example, in the form of lower wages) in order to deter fraud optimally.

91. This is because under enterprise liability fewer agents will be judgment proof.

92. *See* Kornhauser, *supra* note 4, at 1370. For example, when an accident could have been avoided had any one of a number of agents acted differently, the firm will often be in a better position than the victim to determine which agent should have acted otherwise, and thus which agent is responsible for the harm.

93. In this respect Fraud on the Market differs from most other cases of corporate crime, where some argue that the responsibility for the crime is so diffused that it is difficult to determine which individuals were actually responsible for the action. CHRISTOPHER D. STONE, WHERE THE LAW ENDS 58-59 (1975).

costs, firms pass liability for securities fraud on to the responsible agents. Securities laws, however, preclude firms from doing this: the SEC and some courts have taken the position that it is against public policy for one codefendant to seek indemnification from another where both have been held liable in a securities fraud action.[94] Enterprises thus may be barred from seeking indemnification from agents in cases where wrongful knowledge is sufficiently widespread among directors or responsible officers that it is imputed to the enterprise. Moreover, under enterprise liability a firm's board of directors may hesitate to impose sanctions on a wrongful agent while litigation is pending for fear that to do so would amount to a corporate admission that the corporation itself was liable for the fraud. Under these circumstances a prudent board well might defer action against an employee until after corporate liability is determined or the matter settled, if not forego the opportunity altogether.[95]

Finally, agency cost problems may cause a publicly held firm to refrain from sanctioning wrongful agents. A substantial portion of Fraud on the Market cases involve alleged frauds committed by senior management, often Chief Executive Officers (CEOs). The decision whether the firm should sanction these agents generally is made by the board of directors, not the shareholders. Although shareholders may want to sanction the responsible agents, the board may be reluctant to do so for a variety of reasons, in addition to the disinclination to admit corporate liability mentioned above.[96] For example, only the board can weigh the costs to the firm resulting from the fraud against the advantages of retaining a manager. Moreover, some observers suggest that structural bias in favor of colleagues may influence many board members to go easy on top managers.[97] The problem is exacerbated when a majority of the directors are either insiders of the firm or outside directors who owe their positions on the board to the senior managers implicated in the fraud.[98] Inside directors also may be inclined to go easy on the obvious wrongdoer in ex-

94. Globus v. Law Research Serv., 418 F.2d 1276 (2d Cir. 1969), *cert. denied*, 397 U.S. 913 (1970). The SEC's hostile policy toward indemnification is expressed in Regulation S-K, Items 702, 510 and 512. Besides requiring full disclosure of indemnification arrangements, Item 512(i) provides that the SEC will not accelerate the effective date of a registration statement (a critical step in most public offerings) unless the registrant undertakes to submit to a court a determination of whether indemnification is against public policy. Should acceleration not be sought, the registration statement must nevertheless include a disclosure that the registrant has been informed that "in the opinion of the Securities and Exchange Commission such indemnification is against public policy as expressed in the Act and is therefore unenforceable." Regulation S-K, Item 510.

95. The agent may benefit substantially from this period of delay because during this period he will continue to collect his salary and can cash in on his stock options.

96. Conventional analysis of enterprise liability generally has ignored this additional level of agency costs.

97. *See generally* James Cox & Harry Munsinger, *Bias in the Boardroom: Psychological Foundations and Legal Implications of Corporate Cohesion*, 48 LAW & CONTEMP. PROBS., 83 (1985).

98. Should the firm become insolvent, the new board of directors may fire the guilty manager. Yet this sanction has no particular deterrent effect because the manager no doubt would be fired in any event should the firm become insolvent. *See* LoPucki & Whitford, *supra* note 56; Rose-Ackerman, *supra* note 56. Also, firms held liable for securities fraud face the SEC's public policy objections when seeking indemnification. *See supra* note 94 and accompanying text.

change for his not implicating them.[99] So long as the board follows proper procedures, any decision it makes not to proceed against individual officers will be insulated by the Business Judgment Rule, and collective action problems generally will preclude shareholders from effectively pressuring the board to sanction wrongful agents.[100]

By contrast, under agent liability victims have every reason to proceed against solvent wrongful agents. The senior managers of publicly held firms who commit Fraud on the Market usually are wealthy and may have sufficient assets to make a suit worthwhile (at least to the plaintiffs' lawyers)—although they probably will not have sufficient assets to satisfy the full optimum judgment.[101] The presence of D&O insurance also increases the likelihood that managers will be able to satisfy the judgment. Because most Fraud on the Market cases settle, managers may be able to avail themselves of this insurance coverage.

In fact, D&O insurance provides an additional argument for agent liability. Agent liability for Fraud on the Market provides insurance companies with an incentive to monitor managers to deter fraud.[102] Although we question the efficacy of any ex ante monitoring,[103] to the extent that such monitoring is possible, insurance companies are in a better position to do so than are shareholders or firm managers: an insurance company does not face the collective action problems plaguing shareholders and does not suffer from the agency cost problems associated with managers' efforts to monitor each other.[104] Moreover, agent liability coupled with D&O insurance increases the likelihood that wrongful managers will be sanctioned. Under D&O insurance policies, managers are not covered if they acted dishonestly or committed willful violations of the law.[105] Accordingly, under agent liability insurance companies will investigate to determine whether the agent indeed committed a fraud, even if the case settles.[106] Moreover, this investigation is likely to have an additional deterrent effect: should the wrongful officer seek employment with another firm, the insurance company may be reluctant to insure him.[107]

99. *See* Christopher D. Stone, *The Place of Enterprise Liability in the Control of Corporate Conduct*, 90 YALE L.J. 1, 30 (1980).

100. John Coffee, *Corporate Crime and Punishment: A Non-Chicago View of the Economics of Criminal Sanctions*, 17 AM. CRIM. L. REV. 419, 469 (1980) (available empirical evidence does not support claim that firms subject to criminal fines discipline responsible employees). Notwithstanding agency costs, some firms hoping to be repeat players in financial markets may fire wrongful agents in order to protect their reputations. This pressure on firms to fire wrongful agents is market driven, however, and thus should operate with equal force under enterprise liability and agent liability.

101. *See supra* text accompanying notes 76-79.

102. *See* Holderness, *supra* note 85.

103. *See infra* text accompanying notes 116-20.

104. *See supra* text accompanying notes 96-100; *see infra* text accompanying notes 116-20.

105. *See supra* note 85.

106. *See* Holderness, *supra* note 85, at 121-22.

107. *See id.* at 122-23. Moreover, other insurance companies may learn of the agent's wrongful conduct because an insurance company is less likely to suppress information revealed during an investigation than is the firm. *Id.* at 123.

Because of limitations on D&O insurance coverage, however, many agents will be judgment proof and thus fewer Fraud on the Market actions will be brought under agent liability than under enterprise liability.[108] This, in and of itself, is not an argument against agent liability. The reduction in lawsuits should not impair the deterrent effect of the securities laws, because firms generally are unable or unwilling to sanction wrongful agents where plaintiffs proceed and prevail under enterprise liability.[109] Nor does enterprise liability lead to effective firm monitoring of agents.[110] Accordingly, because enterprise liability has virtually no additional deterrent effect, any reduction in lawsuits associated with agent liability hardly reduces the deterrent effect of the securities laws. In fact, a reduction in lawsuits well may argue in favor of agent liability. Given the enormous litigation costs associated with Fraud on the Market cases, and the difficulty of using enterprise liability to deter these last period frauds, society well may be better off trading the marginal increase in frauds associated with fewer lawsuits for the tremendous decrease in socially wasteful litigation costs resulting from a switch to agent liability.[111]

Accordingly, in contrast to the conventional wisdom, in Fraud on the Market cases enforcement concerns appear to weigh in favor of imposing liability directly on agents and not on firms.

d. Incentives To Screen for Honest Agents

Although the preceding analysis suggests that firms are not in a better position than the courts to sanction agents ex post, enterprise liability nevertheless might be preferable to agent liability if, as some have argued, enterprise liability provides firms with superior incentives to screen its prospective agents for honesty.[112]

Although shareholders bear the burden of enterprise liability when agents are insolvent, it is their agents, either directors or officers, who

108. *See* Alexander, *supra* note 85 (finding that, in the small sample of cases studied, plaintiffs' lawyers bring securities fraud actions if the settlement value equals or exceeds five million dollars).

109. *See supra* text accompanying notes 96-100 (discussing reasons why firms may not proceed against wrongful agents).

110. *See infra* text accompanying notes 116-20 (firms are not likely to be able to deter fraud by monitoring agents).

111. *Cf.* Roberta Romano, *Corporate Governance in the Aftermath of the Insurance Crisis*, 39 EMORY L.J. 1155, 1167-68, 1183 (1990) (eliminating duty of care suits may be desirable because they result in enormous litigation costs and have little deterrent effect). This benefit of agent liability includes the reduction in meritless suits that would accompany a switch from joint agent and enterprise liability to a system of pure agent liability. *See infra* text accompanying note 124.

112. In fact, some scholars argue that under agent liability firms may have an incentive to hire agents who are inclined to commit fraud because the firms will get the benefits from the fraud but bear none of the costs. *See* RICHARD POSNER, AN ECONOMIC ANALYSIS OF LAW 398 (3d ed. 1988) (making this argument in favor of corporate criminal liability). We reject this argument because shareholders see themselves (and the firms in which they invest) as repeat players in capital markets—shareholders because some day they will want either to buy or sell more shares in the firm, and the firms because the cost of future capital will depend on the firm's reputation for integrity in its dealings in capital markets. *See infra* note 115.

must decide whether and to what extent to screen other potential agents for honesty. Screening imposes direct costs on these agents, involving both time and effort to obtain and analyze information on the willingness of prospective employees to commit fraud. Accordingly, we must determine the extent to which directors and officers benefit from screening for honest colleagues and subordinates under enterprise liability and agent liability.

Outside directors' compensation generally is not tied to firm profits; thus they benefit from screening only to the extent that it reduces their expected personal liability for fraud, which is minimal in the absence of scienter. Enterprise liability, therefore, usually does not provide them with additional incentives to screen agents. Officers' compensation generally is tied to firm profits, however. They benefit both from higher firm profits that increase their own compensation and from reduced exposure to personal liability or discipline for fraud. When agents are judgment proof, fraud has a greater impact on firm profits under enterprise liability than it does under agent liability.[113] Accordingly, the benefits to managers of screening are theoretically higher under a rule of enterprise liability.

These additional benefits are likely to be small, however, and usually are exceeded by the costs that additional screening imposes on managers. Screening for agents willing to commit fraud is costly and is unlikely to identify potential wrongdoers. Identifying the flagrantly dishonest may not be so difficult.[114] But Fraud on the Market (in our hypothesis) is caused by top corporate officials, and only under extreme circumstances. An agent realistically cannot be tested for a propensity to commit this kind of fraud until he has held high corporate office under conditions where Fraud on the Market is likely—i.e., conditions where the firm is failing or where the manager has failed. Managers of failed firms, however, are rarely candidates for other such positions of responsibility; persons promoted from within organizations generally have succeeded at their previous responsibilities and thus have had no occasion to cover up huge failures. Accordingly, we do not believe that enterprise liability will result in superior screening to avoid hiring agents willing to commit Fraud on the Market.[115]

e. Ex Ante Monitoring

Proponents of enterprise liability argue that this rule creates supe-

113. This is because the firm bears the burden of all liability in excess of its wrongful agents' wealth under enterprise liability, but not under agent liability.

114. We note that firms already have incentives to screen for the flagrantly dishonest, in order to avoid hiring those likely to commit fraud against the firm itself. These incentives are not likely to be noticeably higher under enterprise liability because Fraud on the Market appears to occur quite infrequently.

115. *Cf.* Macey, *supra* note 60, at 325 (abandoning criminal enterprise liability will not lead shareholders to hire managers willing to commit crimes in part because shareholders will not be able to identify managers who have predisposition for engaging in criminal acts).

rior incentives to monitor current employees to prevent them from committing Fraud on the Market. This argument assumes either that firm owners (the shareholders) can monitor at relatively low cost, or that enterprise liability creates superior incentives for top level managers to monitor lower level employees and each other, and that they can do so effectively. The first assumption does not hold in Fraud on the Market cases because widely dispersed owners of publicly held firms face serious collective action problems.[116] Indeed, nonshareholder investors who may be victimized by Fraud on the Market are just as competent as shareholders to monitor, if both groups hold diversified portfolios. Moreover, should some shareholders be able to monitor, agent liability provides them with an incentive to do so—in order to avoid being a victim of fraud.

As for the second assumption, we acknowledge that enterprise liability may provide managers with greater incentives to monitor, if their compensation is tied to firm profits.[117] Nevertheless, we do not expect to find greater monitoring under enterprise liability because managers' incentives to monitor each other for Fraud on the Market decline dramatically in the very circumstance in which such fraud is most likely to occur: when the firm is at serious risk of failing. Under our last period hypothesis, Fraud on the Market usually results from the efforts of a few desperate managers to hide the fact that the corporation is ailing or has done sufficiently badly relative to reasonable expectations that senior managers can expect to be replaced. In this last period situation, even honest managers have relatively little to gain from preventing other managers from committing Fraud on the Market. If a manager prohibits fraud that would cover up the firm's difficulties, the firm may fail, and she will lose her job. If she permits fraud, however, there are two possible outcomes. First, the fraud may be discovered, in which case the firm may fail, the manager will lose her job, and be no worse off than if the fraud had not occurred. Alternatively, the fraud may succeed, in which case the manager's job and firm-specific investments will be salvaged. Additionally, enterprise liability is unlikely to result in increased monitoring in last periods because the senior managers in charge of monitoring are the very people most likely to commit Fraud on the Market. They also control the access of firm agents to the news media and the SEC.[118]

Furthermore, even if senior managers are inclined to monitor each

116. *See* ADOLPH BERLE & GARDINER MEANS, THE MODERN CORPORATION AND PRIVATE PROPERTY (1932). For a thoughtful analysis of the legal rules that render even large shareholders passive, see Bernard S. Black, *Agents Watching Agents: The Promise of Institutional Investor Voice*, 39 UCLA L. REV. 811 (1992); Bernard S. Black, *Shareholder Passivity Reexamined*, 89 MICH. L. REV. 520 (1990).

117. *See supra* note 113 and accompanying text. Under agent liability, firms will establish some procedures to monitor for fraud because ex ante firms and managers view themselves as repeat players in capital markets where reputational capital has value.

118. Nor can we rely on widely dispersed shareholders to pressure management into incurring

other and lower level employees for fraud, there is little evidence that they can do so effectively. Fraud usually is committed by the people in control of the relevant information; checking the veracity of this information will be nearly impossible.[119] Accordingly, we do not expect enterprise liability to result in greater monitoring for Fraud on the Market than agent liability.[120] We therefore conclude that the presence of judgment proof agents does not justify enterprise liability for Fraud on the Market.

f. Administrative Costs

A final argument in favor of enterprise liability is that administrative costs of collecting judgments are lower under this rule because: (1) collecting from many agents is more expensive than collecting from a firm; and (2) collecting from any given agent is more expensive than collecting from a firm because locating sufficient assets may be more difficult. Enterprise liability reduces administrative costs of collection, proponents argue, by providing the plaintiff with a single, and likely more solvent, defendant.[121]

This argument is not valid. Enterprise liability exerts the requisite deterrent effect on agents only if the firm shifts its liability to the wrongful agents. By shifting liability, the firm, and thus society, incurs the very administrative costs that victims would bear under a rule of agent liability.[122] Ironically, enterprise liability actually increases the administrative

---

these monitoring costs. Shareholders cannot monitor directly, and collective action problems generally preclude shareholders from inducing management to engage in optimal monitoring.

119. *Cf.* Barry D. Baysinger, *Organization Theory and the Criminal Liability of Organizations*, 71 B.U. L. REV. 341 (1991) (noting the difficulty that top level managers have in affecting the criminal behavior of their subordinates).

We note that the SEC faced severe difficulties in enforcing the monitoring duty imposed by the Foreign Corrupt Practices Act, Pub. L. No. 95-213, 91 Stat. 1494 (1977) (amending 15 U.S.C. § 78m(b)(2)(B) (1977)). In 1979, the SEC proposed that management disclose its opinion of whether internal accounting controls provide reasonable assurance that specified objectives were met, and describe any material weaknesses of such controls that independent accountants communicated to management. SEC Securities Exchange Act Release No. 15,772, [1979 Transfer Binder] Fed. Sec. L. Rep. (CCH) ¶ 82,063 (Apr. 30, 1979). The SEC abandoned that attempt, SEC Securities Exchange Act Release No. 16,877, 557 Sec. Reg. & L. Rep. (BNA), No. 34, at H-1 (June 6, 1980), and undertook a case by case ex post approach to determining what amount of monitoring was insufficient. *See* William J. Carney, *Section 4.01 of the American Law Institute's Corporate Governance Project: Restatement or Misstatement?*, 66 WASH. U. L.Q. 239, 262 n.119 (1988). Similarly, the SEC abandoned attempts to establish monitoring rules under the controlling person provisions of the securities laws.

Additionally, registered broker dealers have long been required to monitor registered representatives when dealing with customers. NAT'L ASS'N SEC. DEALERS, RULES OF FAIR PRACTICE, art. III, § 27, NASD Manual (CCH) ¶ 2177 (1992). The continued flow of litigation involving claims of fraud by these representatives demonstrates the difficulties of monitoring, even in these routine, repetitive situations.

120. In fact, enterprise liability may produce inefficient incentives to monitor if plaintiffs may use the firm's monitoring evidence to help them prove fraud. *See* Arlen, *supra* note 66; CYRUS CHU & YINGYI QIAN, VICARIOUS LIABILITY UNDER A NEGLIGENCE RULE (Stanford Univ. Working Paper No. 92, 1992).

121. *See* Kornhauser, *supra* note 4; Stone, *supra* note 99, at 29.

122. Although the firm can impose some sanctions on the agents cheaply—by firing them—to

costs of collection, by adding the cost of the shareholders' suit against the firm to the cost of the actions against the wrongful agents.

Moreover, while agent insolvency presents a genuine difficulty, firms may be judgment proof as well. If, as our analysis predicts, agents commit fraud because they fear that the firm is in danger of failing, then we should expect many of these firms to be insolvent as well. In these cases, it will be as difficult to collect from the enterprise as from the agent, and plaintiffs will seek other solvent defendants.[123]

An additional administrative cost concern favors the use of agent liability. The current availability of both enterprise and agent liability appears to increase litigation costs substantially by leading to unjust suits against the corporation. Under the current system, plaintiffs have incentives to bring nuisance suits against both the enterprise and its managers, with the intention of dropping the action against the managers in exchange for a settlement by the firm. Managers have a strong incentive to settle because they may not be covered by D&O insurance if they proceed to trial and lose.[124]

2. *Managerial Risk Shifting*

Some who agree that deterrence arguments do not support enterprise liability nevertheless advocate enterprise liability on the grounds that it increases social welfare by shifting the risk of liability from managers, who are risk averse, to shareholders, who are risk neutral.[125] Shareholders can easily purchase fully diversified portfolios, and thus are effectively risk neutral and wish their firms to behave similarly. Managers, by contrast, are not fully diversified because they generally have a substantial portion of their human capital, and a considerable portion of their wealth, invested in their corporate employer.[126] The cost of a given amount of liability, therefore, will be greater for risk averse managers than it will be for the risk neutral shareholders. Accordingly, it is argued that enterprise liability is preferable to agent liability because managers faced with agent liability will be overly cautious.[127]

---

impose sufficient sanctions to deter fraud, the firm would have to sue to recover additional amounts. *See supra* text accompanying note 78 (optimum sanctions are a multiple of the agent's expected net present value of being employed by the firm, including stock and stock-related profits).

123. We observe that in many cases plaintiffs proceed against third parties, such as accounting firms. *See infra* text accompanying note 179. Part of the explanation for this appears to be that defendant enterprises frequently are insolvent. Our study shows that at least 24% of these firms were involved in bankruptcy reorganization proceedings subsequent to the revelation of the fraud. *See infra* text accompanying note 166.

124. *See* Stone, *supra* note 99, at 30 n.119; *cf.* Alexander, *supra* note 85 (most securities fraud actions settle regardless of the merits).

125. *E.g.*, Easterbrook & Fischel, *supra* note 4, at 640-41; *see* Sykes II, *supra* note 4, at 1235-36.

126. *See* Jennifer H. Arlen, *Should Defendants' Wealth Matter?*, 21 J. LEGAL STUD. 413 (1992); Carney, *supra* note 54, at 418-20; Easterbrook & Fischel, *supra* note 4, at 641; Macey, *supra* note 60; Rose-Ackerman, *supra* note 56.

127. Easterbrook & Fischel, *supra* note 4, at 641; *see* Sykes II, *supra* note 4, at 1236. This argument implicitly assumes the presence of transactions costs (or agency costs, *see supra* text accompanying notes 97-98), that operate to make an agent's expected liability less under agent liability

Although this argument may have some merit when applied to torts cases, it is not valid in the context of Fraud on the Market. In standard torts cases, the optimal level of accidents is not zero. The risk shifting argument, therefore, is a claim that the cost to society of those "optimal" accidents that do occur should be as low as possible. This is achieved by placing the burden of these accidents on the party who is the superior risk bearer—the shareholders. By contrast, the optimal level of Fraud on the Market is zero.[128] If damage awards are optimal, risk spreading is not a concern because fraud will not occur.[129]

Of course, fraud does occur, both because actual damage awards are not optimal and because agents expect to be judgment proof. The solution to the problem of suboptimal damage awards, however, is to reform the damage rules under agent liability, not to employ enterprise liability. The solution to the judgment proof agent problem is not to shift the risk of liability from agents to enterprises and their shareholders, but rather to increase the cost to agents of committing fraud, for example, by employing nonmonetary criminal sanctions in addition to agent civil liability. Shifting costs from agents in a misplaced attempt to improve risk spreading simply impairs the ability of the securities laws to serve their main goal of deterrence.[130]

3. Loss Spreading

Some scholars argue that enterprise liability for torts is appropriate because it shifts the risk of harm off the victim and onto the firm, which can spread the cost of the unfunded liability[131] among its shareholders. These scholars argue that this shifting is desirable because the aggregate

than under enterprise liability. For, under the Coase Theorem, absent transactions costs, agents' expected liability should be the same under the two rules.

128. *See supra* text accompanying notes 69-73. As noted previously, this conclusion excludes monitoring and enforcement costs. *See supra* note 70 and *infra* note 130.

129. Because securities fraud claims require a showing of scienter, we have far less reason to be concerned that courts will impose liability erroneously than we do under the negligence standard generally employed in standard torts cases. *See supra* note 72. Again, we exclude the negligence standard of § 11 of the Securities Act, which applies only to registered offerings, from this analysis. We also have little reason to fear that agents will engage in fraudulent disclosures not knowing they are illegal because senior managers of publicly held firms are likely to be well advised about securities fraud rules.

130. This conclusion also holds when costly enforcement is taken into account. When enforcement is costly and individuals are risk averse, a probability of detection sufficient to deter all individuals may be optimal, *see* Kaplow, *supra* note 70, at 6, in which case, shifting liability from agents to enterprises clearly is not desirable. Moreover, in circumstances where the optimal amount of the wrongful activity is not zero because of enforcement costs, the solution to the problem of risk averse agents is not to shift liability from the agent, but rather it is to decrease the sanction below the optimum sanction when the probability of detection is negligible and to increase the probability of detection. *See id.*

The risk spreading argument for enterprise liability for Fraud on the Market is particularly unpersuasive once one recognizes that such liability may bankrupt firms, injuring creditors and employees. Like managers, employees are risk averse and not diversified. *See* Kraakman, *supra* note 66, at 195.

131. The unfunded liability is the amount of liability that exceeds the amount that the firm can collect from the wrongful agents.

burden to shareholders of bearing a small financial loss is less than the victims' burden of each bearing a large loss.[132]

There are several problems with this argument, both in general and as applied to Fraud on the Market cases. First, we must be wary of grounding the imposition of liability on loss shifting arguments because nothing in the loss spreading argument limits its application. This argument could be used, for example, to support a rule under which the decision whether to hold a defendant liable for an accident depends solely on the relative burden of liability to the plaintiff and defendant and not on whether the defendant had anything to do with the plaintiff's losses.[133]

Moreover, the loss spreading argument is invalid in the context of Fraud on the Market cases. Victims of Fraud on the Market are usually fully diversified investors, as are the shareholders who ultimately bear the costs under a rule of enterprise liability. Because both types of investors are effectively risk neutral, shifting the losses from one group of investors to the other produces no welfare gain.

The argument for loss spreading also fails even if both groups of investors are risk averse. Because of the high volume of shares traded on the national stock exchanges, the number of shares in the potential plaintiff class is likely to exceed the number of shares held by the defendant shareholders.[134] Accordingly, it is likely that the number of victims exceeds the number of the defendant firm's shareholders, in which case the loss spreading argument implies that losses should remain with the victims.

4. *Just Compensation*

Some scholars defend enterprise liability on the grounds that it provides superior compensation to victims when agents are judgment proof. We concede that victims are likely to recover larger judgments under enterprise liability. Although compensating victims may be a laudable goal, enterprise liability does not serve the goal of just compensation because it simply replaces one group of innocent victims with another: those who were shareholders when the fraud was revealed. Moreover, enterprise liability does not even effect a one-to-one transfer between innocent victims: a large percentage of the plaintiffs' recovery goes to their lawyers. Finally, enterprise liability may injure innocent people in addition to shareholders. For example, employees are injured if enterprise liability sends a firm into bankruptcy or causes it to lay off employees.[135]

132. Musewicz, *supra* note 6, at 794-97. This argument implicitly assumes that agent liability will not adequately shift the risks from victims because the agents are likely to be judgment proof.

133. Sykes I, *supra* note 4, at 172.

134. *See infra* text accompanying notes 185-98, and *infra* note 189.

135. *See* John Coffee, *No Soul to Damn, No Body to Kick: An Unscandalized Inquiry into the Problem of Corporate Punishment*, 79 MICH. L. REV. 386, 401 (1981); Kraakman, *supra* note 66, at 195.

C. Summary

We conclude that enterprise liability should not be applied to Fraud on the Market cases.[136] The last period nature of the agency problems involved and the additional agency costs that plague efforts by publicly held corporations to monitor and sanction senior managers render the conventional analysis of enterprise liability inapplicable to Fraud on the Market cases. In contrast, we find that there is little reason to believe that enterprise liability is the superior rule from the standpoint of deterrence, and there are many reasons to suspect the contrary. The deterrent effect of the available monetary sanctions under agent liability probably exceeds the deterrent effect of enterprise liability because a civil judgment against an agent hurts his reputation more than does a sanction imposed by the firm in private.[137] Moreover, the threat that sanctions will be imposed appears to be greater under agent liability. Agent liability places the responsibility of sanctioning wrongful agents with the victims, who have no reason not to proceed against them and have every reason to proceed. Enterprise liability, by contrast, places the responsibility of proceeding against the wrongful agents with the firm, and thus with the very agents (and their close associates) most likely to have committed fraud. Moreover, agent liability in effect enlists insurance companies as corporate monitors and disciplinarians, thereby eliminating the agency costs associated with firm managers monitoring and disciplining each other. Furthermore, the judgment proof problem under agent liability can be completely eliminated if, in addition to civil liability, the government imposes sufficient nonmonetary criminal penalties on agents, such as imprisonment.[138] Finally, we find that administrative costs probably are lower under agent liability.

In addition to the deterrence arguments favoring agent liability, an interest in loss spreading also favors the use of this rule. Moreover, justice concerns favor replacing enterprise liability with agent liability because enterprise liability for Fraud on the Market results in liability being imposed on innocent investors, some of whom are victims of the fraud not entitled to compensation under the securities laws.[139]

IV. The Evidence

Our conclusion that agent liability for Fraud on the Market is the

136. Our conclusion that enterprise liability is inferior applies most directly to the frauds designed to conceal bad news, which were the focus of our analysis. Our analysis also applies to some "good news" frauds, however: specifically, hostile takeovers where managers are fighting to keep their jobs. These two types of fraud should account for virtually all pure Fraud on the Market cases. Now that the Supreme Court has clarified the law governing disclosure of merger negotiations, *see* Basic, Inc. v. Levinson, 485 U.S. 224 (1988), we do not expect to see many of these "good news" cases in the future. Unresolved questions of materiality may generate some litigation in the short run, however.

137. *See supra* text accompanying note 87.

138. *See* Kraakman, *supra* note 5.

139. *See supra* text accompanying notes 41-45.

superior rule depends heavily on our last period hypothesis. Accordingly, we now present an empirical analysis of Fraud on the Market cases to demonstrate that the evidence supports our hypothesis.

A. The Data Base

We examined all cases in the LEXIS database, "Fedsec" library, "cases" file, under the heading "fraud w/2 market" between 1975 and mid-1990.[140] This period was chosen because the Fraud on the Market doctrine, which relaxed the reliance requirement when securities are publicly traded, was first announced in 1975.[141] Most of the decisions involved preliminary rulings on issues such as class certification, appropriateness of class representatives, motions to dismiss, or motions for summary judgment. Few involved final judgments on the merits, because generally Fraud on the Market cases are either dismissed at a preliminary stage or settled.[142] Thus our data base consisted largely of allegations rather than proven charges. Nevertheless, given the fact that relatively few Fraud on the Market cases proceed to trial, we do not believe a superior set of cases exists to examine civil liability rules for securities fraud.[143] We assume that the set of cases brought is an unbiased set of actual frauds found in securities markets; that is, that plaintiffs do not have incentives to bring groundless charges more frequently with respect to any particular type of activity.[144]

We limited our review to allegations of issuer fraud in companies not engaged in securities offerings unless it appeared that a registration statement merely continued a fraud begun at an earlier date. We also excluded cases involving public offerings for several reasons.[145] First, our purpose in this article is to examine fraud on secondary trading markets. In addition, as the courts are beginning to recognize, the Fraud on

140. In relying on LEXIS for our data, we limited ourselves to cases with published opinions. We do not believe that this biases our sample, however. The issue of bias depends on whether the complaints that produce published opinions are more or less likely than the total population of Fraud on the Market complaints to be cases in which our last period hypothesis is correct. We do not see any reason to expect bias. First, Fraud on the Market cases proceed as class actions, which generate numerous procedural motions likely to lead to published opinions. Therefore, we expect that a relatively high percentage of Fraud on the Market complaints produce published opinions. Moreover, there is nothing in either the decision of whether to file such a procedural motion or the decision of whether to publish an opinion that is likely to bias the sample for or against frauds committed in a last period situation.

141. Blackie v. Barrack, 524 F.2d 891 (9th Cir. 1975).

142. *See infra* note 182.

143. SEC enforcement actions may provide more detail about actual, as opposed to alleged, wrongdoing. They do not, however, provide information about the potential impact of civil liability rules.

144. The one exception is fraud in the context of takeovers, where litigation may be used strategically rather than to vindicate rights of investors. We excluded these cases from our analysis for the reasons presented *infra* text accompanying notes 150-53.

145. We also excluded cases involving commodities fraud where Fraud on the Market cases were cited in support of analogous arguments. Other cases found with our LEXIS search did not involve Fraud on the Market, although our search technique included them in the set of cases retrieved.

the Market doctrine cannot legitimately be applied to initial public offering (IPO) cases.[146] Moreover, IPOs do not represent the typical model of a publicly held corporation with widely dispersed shareholders, because at the time of the alleged fraud these firms are typically closely held and do not experience the same agency costs as publicly held firms. Finally, liability rules governing registered offerings differ significantly from those governing public statements or SEC filings by officials of publicly held companies.[147] Section 11 liability under the Securities Act extends to a wide variety of participants (and even some who are not active participants) in the offering and imposes liability on the basis of negligence, rather than scienter.[148] For reasons we have previously discussed, the analysis of enterprise liability for negligent torts differs significantly from that for intentional torts such as fraud.[149]

We also excluded cases involving allegations of fraud in the context of mergers and hostile takeovers. Until recently, disclosure rules when a target firm was negotiating with a prospective merger partner were poorly specified.[150] It appears that many of the "frauds" that occurred prior to the Supreme Court's ruling in *Basic* were not fraud in the standard sense of the word but rather resulted from confusion over the legal standard governing disclosure in the merger negotiation context. As for hostile takeovers, fraud charges are a standard part of the arsenal of the contestants, regardless of their merits.[151] Therefore, we were not comfortable relying on allegations of fraud in takeover battles to provide any valuable information about what frauds are actually committed. Moreover, excluding these cases should not bias our results because target

146. *See* Carney, *supra* note 33. The courts of appeal are divided on this extension. Harris v. Union Elec. Co., 787 F.2d 366 (8th Cir.), *cert. denied*, 479 U.S. 823 (1986) (approving the extension); T.J. Raney & Sons v. Fort Cobb, Okla. Irrigation Fuel Auth., 717 F.2d 1330 (10th Cir. 1983), *cert. denied*, 479 U.S. 1065 (1984); Shores v. Sklar, 647 F.2d 462 (5th Cir. 1981) (en banc), *cert. denied*, 459 U.S. 1102 (1983); Arthur Young & Co. v. United States District Court, 549 F.2d 686 (9th Cir.), *cert. denied*, 434 U.S. 829 (1977). *Contra* Vervaecke v. Chiles, Heider & Co., 578 F.2d 713 (8th Cir. 1978) (rejecting the extension). The Eleventh Circuit appeared ready to reconsider its extension of the doctrine in Ross v. Bank South, N.A., 837 F.2d 980 (11th Cir.), *opinion vacated and reh'g granted en banc*, 848 F.2d 1132 (11th Cir. 1988), but ultimately decided the case on other grounds, Ross v. Bank South, N.A., 885 F.2d 723 (11th Cir. 1989) (en banc).

147. We recognize that many of these offerings were unregistered, largely because they involved offerings of tax-free industrial revenue bonds issued by municipalities. These offerings present special agency problems because the municipal officials have weak incentives to monitor project sponsors for fraud. These offerings also are not an appropriate subject for application of the Fraud on the Market doctrine. Carney, *supra* note 33.

148. Securities Act of 1933, § 11, 15 U.S.C. § 77k (1991). Liability is extended to what Kraakman calls "gatekeepers"—professionals, such as underwriters and accountants (and occasionally lawyers) whose participation is required to complete the registration process. Kraakman, *supra* note 5.

149. *See supra* text accompanying notes 7-11.

150. These rules were clarified in Basic, Inc. v. Levinson, 485 U.S. 224 (1988), although some critics might argue that the materiality standard chosen by the Court is less clear than the bright line "agreement in principle" test argued for by *Basic*.

151. *See generally* Herbert Wachtell, *Special Tender Offer Litigation Tactics*, 32 BUS. LAW. 1433 (1977) (describing litigation as a tool to affect attitudes of arbitragers, to delay the other side, or to protect target employee morale).

managers' incentives to commit fraud in takeover cases result from similar last period concerns to those operating in other Fraud on the Market cases (because quasi rents are at stake),[152] although the probability of prompt detection of fraud in takeover cases is much higher.[153]

Ultimately, we had a base of 111 reported decisions. Because of limited statements of the facts in some of the opinions, the set of cases examined for specific questions usually was less than 111. All of the complaints examined alleged liability under Section 10(b) and Rule 10b-5, the general antifraud provisions of the Securities Exchange Act under which the Fraud on the Market doctrine developed. Five complaints also made claims under the similar language of Section 17(a) of the Securities Act.[154] Three cases alleged claims under Section 18 of the Securities Exchange Act, which is surprising in view of the reliance requirement imposed by that section.[155]

In addition to the reported opinions, we examined Moody's Industrials, Standard & Poor's Reports, and SEC filings for information about the number of outstanding shares of each company; the Dow Jones Historical Stock Quote Reporter Service for information about trading volumes during the period of alleged frauds; and reports of the New York Stock Exchange, American Stock Exchange, and the over-the-counter stock markets for daily prices. To render the research project manageable, we used monthly trading volumes rather than daily trading volumes, including both the month of the alleged fraudulent or misleading statement and the month of the revelation of the fraud. This overstates the trading volume during the period of the fraud somewhat.[156] The extent of overstatement is mitigated by the average length of the interval between the alleged fraud and its revelation. We adjusted stock prices to account for market movements but did not account for the Beta of individual securities; we assumed that our set was representative of a market portfolio, in part because many of the securities are thinly traded in the over-the-counter market. In addition, we employed the Dow Jones Industrial Average rather than broader measures of the market. In view of the large magnitude of price changes found, we do not believe that these departures from standard event study methodology would affect the directions of price movements, although the magnitudes may be affected somewhat.[157]

---

152. *See* Kenneth J. Martin & John J. McConnell, *Corporate Performance, Corporate Takeovers, and Management Turnover*, 46 J. FIN. 671 (1991) (turnover rate for top managers of target firms significantly increases following completion of a tender offer-takeover).

153. *See* Carney, *supra* note 54.

154. Securities Act of 1933, § 17(a), 15 U.S.C. § 77q(a) (1991). The relatively small number of such claims is explained both by the fact that § 17(a) covers only fraudulent sales and not purchases, and by the fact that the circuits are divided over whether implied rights of action exist under § 17(a). *See* cases collected in HAZEN, *supra* note 19, § 13.13.

155. 15 U.S.C. § 78r (1991).

156. Where the revelation occurred in the first several days of a month we excluded that month's trading volumes from the count in order to achieve somewhat greater accuracy.

157. *See generally* Stephen J. Brown & Jerold B. Warner, *Using Daily Stock Returns: The Case*

Although our data base contains a considerable amount of information, we were unable to answer a number of important questions. For example, in most instances we were unable to learn the amount of damages claimed. Most complaints do not appear to request a specific amount of damages, probably because the size of the plaintiff class and the prices paid by individual class members are unknown at the time of suit. In most cases, subsequent reports by issuers of these claims in their 10-K filings do not mention the amount requested. As a result, we have only a small amount of information about damage claims. Moreover, we were unable to determine how much successful plaintiffs actually receive in most cases because these cases generally settle before trial if the plaintiffs survive preliminary challenges to certification of the class, motions to dismiss, and motions for summary judgment.[158]

B. Is Fraud a Consequence of Last Period Agency Costs?

Previously we postulated that most fraud on securities markets is committed by desperate agents who fear that they are in a last period of employment. To test this last period agency cost hypothesis, we first examined the data to determine whether: (1) Fraud on the Market generally results from attempts to put the firm in a false favorable light, rather than attempts to conceal good news about the firm; (2) the frauds were sufficiently serious to suggest that accurate pictures of the firms would reveal that they were ailing (and thus that the senior managers would have reason to fear getting fired); and (3) the duration of the frauds were sufficiently short that agents would be unlikely to commit Fraud on the Market unless they were desperate from facing a last period situation.

To determine the nature of the frauds committed, we categorized the types of alleged fraud on the basis of whether the fraudulent information provided a false positive or false negative signal about the company, and whether it was in the context of a securities offering (not an IPO) or a disclosure in the ordinary course of business, whether an SEC filing, a proxy statement, or a press release. Our results are contained in Table 1.

We were unable to classify the type of fraud in eight of the reported cases, and therefore the relevant set contains only 103 cases. As we expected, only a small percentage of the frauds in these cases (8.7%) involved attempts to understate the value of securities. In the vast majority

---

of Event Studies, 14 J. FIN. ECON. 1 (1985); Eugene Fama et al., *The Adjustment of Stock Prices to New Information*, 10 INT'L ECON. REV. 1 (1969); G. William Schwert, *Using Financial Data to Measure Effects of Regulation*, 24 J.L. & ECON. 121 (1981). Many of our companies were traded over the counter and, thus, are not represented in the Center for Research in Securities Prices' tapes, or in standard Beta reference books. They are thinly traded in some cases, in markets that can be expected to be of relatively weak efficiency. While we recognize that the assumptions that the Dow Jones Industrial Average is an acceptable proxy for overall market averages and that our study sample has a Beta of one are strong ones, we do not believe more refined methods would alter our conclusions.

158. Data on class action settlements could be obtained, at considerable expense, by examining court records across the country. We are unaware of any published reports of these settlements.

of cases (91.3%), managers were accused of providing false favorable information to the market.[159] Moreover, 89.3% of the cases involved fraud in the context of regular reports and press releases to investors. These frauds clearly hurt current shareholders by lulling them with false assurances to retain their shares.[160] These cases thus support our agency cost hypothesis.

As for the 8.7% of the cases in which managers understated the value of the securities, closer examination of these cases reveals that typically they involve managers and control shareholders who were alleged to have a conflict of interest because they were attempting to buy out the public shareholders at an unfairly low price. There are other remedies for these kinds of fraud, which typically hold the wrongdoers directly liable for their profits.[161] Accordingly, the evidence supports our assertion in the preceding part that pure Fraud on the Market cases[162] should be viewed as resulting from agents' attempts to provide the market with a falsely favorable picture of the firm.

Establishing that managers usually are motivated by last period concerns, however, requires additional analysis. Table 2 attempts to break down the false positive announcements in more detail. Approximately 67.7% of these cases clearly involve potential last period situations: 50.5% of the cases involved false positive statements designed to conceal declines in earnings, while another 17.2% of the frauds were designed to conceal bad news about the issuer. An additional 20.4% of the cases involved false optimistic statements of business developments and projections. We believe that most of these cases were also attempts to conceal bad news, as evidenced by the dramatic stock price declines reported in Table 3.

Moreover, the exaggerations of earnings or claims of positive business developments involved in these cases appear to be extremely serious, as predicted by our last period hypothesis. In order to determine the magnitude of the alleged frauds, we examined the movement of stock prices resulting from revelation of the fraud. Table 3 presents the average price declines from the date of the announcement of the fraudulent news (the "announcement date") to ten days after the revelation of the fraud. A ten-day window allowed sufficient time for revelations to be reflected in stock prices, even where stocks were thinly traded. Both announcement dates and revelation dates were taken from judicial opinions.[163] Firms that announced false positive news to the market experienced an overall 42.6% drop in stock prices when the truth was revealed. Firms that concealed bad news experienced even larger losses

159. *See infra* Table 1.

160. *See infra* Table 2.

161. For example, these defendants may be charged with breach of fiduciary duties under state law.

162. *See supra* note 53.

163. *See supra* text accompanying note 157.

(47.8%). Although there is no way to separate the amount of the decline attributable to the revelation of the truth from the amount of the decline attributable to anticipated liability for fraud,[164] the magnitude of the price changes revealed in Table 3 are sufficiently great to indicate that, even if there were no liability, revelation of the truth would have caused a significant decline in the firm's value.[165] This finding is consistent with our hypothesis that the fraud was intended to conceal that the firm was ailing. Moreover, 24.3% of the firms saw the inside of bankruptcy courts, which further supports our last period hypothesis. In many other cases newspaper accounts contain reports of financial difficulties and speculation about the likelihood of bankruptcy.[166]

In sum, the evidence reveals that two types of fraud predominate in Fraud on the Market actions: false positive financial statements to conceal declines in earnings[167] and omission of bad news in SEC filings and public statements.[168] Table 2 reveals that concealing adverse business developments was the most common source of fraud charges, followed by concealing self-dealing and illegal acts. Table 3 shows that stock prices declined an average of 43.6% when bad news was revealed. These results are consistent with our last period agency cost hypothesis.

We find further support for our last period hypothesis from an examination of the duration of the frauds committed. Previously we hypothesized that agents are unlikely to commit fraud unless they are desperate because fraud is usually detectable over time and therefore is very risky. As a result, we concluded that fraud is likely to appear to be a viable option only for a manager of a failing company who thinks that he can turn the company around and perhaps obtain new financing in the intervening period.

The cases support this claim that fraud is highly risky. We obviously do not have any data on frauds which were undetected. Examining the data on detected[169] frauds, however, reveals that some frauds were discovered in less than a month, the median period before discovery was twelve months, and the average period was 16.3 months.[170] The longest

164. At least one event study suggests that the anticipated impact of announcement of the filing of a derivative action is quite small. *See* Fischel & Bradley, *supra* note 39.

165. Although we have very little data on actual judgments and settlements in Fraud on the Market cases, the data we do have reveals that the average expected value of a judgment and settlement is 11.2% of the market value of the firm. *See infra* Table 8. This suggests that approximately 75% of the decline in the value of the equity is attributable to the revelation of the bad news about the firm.

166. Our hypothesis that agents commit fraud when they fear themselves to be in a last period of employment is consistent with, but does not require, evidence that the firm itself is in its last period. Senior managers may fear that they will be fired if the firm's finances decline substantially, even though the firm itself may not yet be in a last period situation.

167. *See infra* Table 2.

168. *See infra* Table 1. These two categories overlap substantially. The overlapping cases have been included in Table 1, while those that do not overlap have been set out separately in Table 5.

169. This analysis is based on the 61 cases in which we were able to determine when the fraud was detected.

170. *But cf.* Basic, Inc. v. Levinson, 485 U.S. 224, 260 (1988) (White, J., dissenting in part)

period was six years. Only 11% of the frauds went undiscovered for three years or longer. These results are consistent with our claim that fraud is a product of last period concerns. A manager of a healthy firm anticipating a continuing relationship with capital markets could not expect to obtain much benefit from an increase in the firm's share price occurring for so short a time. A year or so, however, might be enough time to enable the manager of an ailing firm to save the firm—for example, by deferring adverse creditor actions or by obtaining new financing.

C. *Is Fraud a Corporate Policy or an Agency Problem?*

Previously we hypothesized that although enterprises are sued for fraud,[171] senior managers generally commit fraud in order to benefit themselves; fraud is not committed at the behest of, or in order to serve, the shareholders.[172] The evidence presented above is consistent with this hypothesis. To obtain further support for this hypothesis, we examined the cases to determine (1) whether the agents sued for fraud usually are senior managers, as opposed to lower level employees, and (2) whether there is any evidence that fraud is the product of corporate policy, as opposed to being committed by agents acting on their own behalf.

Table 4 displays the identity of the persons named as defendants in the cases involving financial statements allegedly concealing declines in earnings. In the forty-seven cases of financial fraud by issuers to conceal earnings declines, 91% of the complaints named defendants in addition to the issuer. These defendants were never employees below the officer level. Indeed, officers were named in 80.9% of these complaints, while accountants were named in 59.6% of the complaints; major shareholders were named in five cases (10.6%).[173] We believe that this evidence supports the desperate manager hypothesis, with managers named as defendants in 80.9% of all complaints. It is not surprising that the next most frequent category of individual defendants includes outsiders—the "other" category—which is dominated by accounting firms as defendants.

Table 5 describes the nineteen cases of omission or concealment of bad news about issuers and concealment of self-dealing, not included in Table 4. Table 5 reveals a somewhat different pattern for these "other type of bad news" frauds. Officers were named defendants in 63.2% of these cases. In 36.8% of these cases, however, no one other than the

---

(asserting that the 11-month fraud period in that case was "virtually without precedent in prior fraud-on-the-market cases.").

171. We found no cases where agents were sued but the firm was not. As Table 6, *infra*, reveals, generally both the firm and its agents are sued.

172. *See supra* text accompanying notes 50-52.

173. This finding that in some cases major shareholders are named in addition to senior managers is not inconsistent with our hypothesis that agents do not commit fraud in order to benefit the firm's owners. There is no evidence in these cases that the major shareholders were acting on behalf of the other shareholders, and there is every reason to suspect the contrary.

issuer was named. Although this is somewhat troubling, under enterprise liability plaintiffs have weak incentives to add individual defendants if the defendant enterprise is solvent. Major shareholders were named in only one case (5.3%). The "others" category contains two complaints against accountants (10.5%), one against a company controlled by corporate insiders, and one claim against a securities broker—a random assortment of alleged participants in wrongdoing.

Table 6 examines the total relevant set of Fraud on the Market cases (109 cases). We found that officers were named in 71.6% of the cases and major shareholders in 18.3%.[174] Persons outside the firm, primarily accountants, were named in 41.3% of the complaints.[175]

We next examined whether the evidence is consistent with our hypothesis that the wrongful agents were acting on their own behalf and not on behalf of the firm. Because it is not possible to test agents' motivation directly, we examined the validity of an alternative hypothesis: Fraud results from either a formal corporate policy or a decision made at the board level in publicly held corporations, rather than from decisions of individual agents.[176] To evaluate this alternative hypothesis, we examined how often outside directors were sued. We focused on outside directors because Fraud on the Market generally requires the issuance of a statement or filing by someone with actual or apparent authority to speak for the corporation. An outside director can authorize such a statement only to the extent that it is the product of board action. Accordingly, we generally expected to find outside directors joined as defendants only if they were alleged to have participated in the fraud in their capacity as board members.[177] Thus, we expected to find outside directors sued when the fraud resulted from board action—i.e., corporate policy—instead of simply from acts of individual agents.

We believe that board involvement in the fraud is unlikely for several reasons. The outside members of the board generally will not participate in fraud unless someone—for example, the shareholders—have provided powerful financial incentives for them to do so. Outside directors have less at stake if the firm were to fail, because they earn most of

174. *See infra* Table 6. In 20% of the cases the issuer was named as a defendant when no individuals were named, suggesting the strength of the presumption of vicarious liability.

175. These are our best estimates because of the inadequate descriptions of the defendants in many reported decisions.

176. We recognize that a finding that fraud results from board action would not rule out the possibility that fraud is the product of agency costs, because board members may act to serve themselves, not the shareholders. We nevertheless consider whether the board is involved, however, because lack of board involvement suggests that the shareholders (as a group) did not pressure the firm's agents to commit fraud: if the shareholders wanted the firm to commit fraud, they would be best able to achieve this goal by exercising the influence they have over the board of directors. Moreover, generally we do not expect to see outside members of the board participating in fraud unless someone—for example, the shareholders—have pressured them to do so. *See infra* text accompanying note 178.

177. We assume that plaintiffs attorneys engage in some preliminary investigation before filing suit.

their income outside the firm. Indeed, because their reputational capital may be threatened by association with fraudulent activities, outside directors have incentives to deter, rather than to encourage, fraud. Finally, it would be difficult for dispersed shareholders to communicate effectively to the board their desire that the firm commit fraud.[178]

The results of our case analysis are consistent with our expectations and are presented in Table 6. Based on our set of 109 cases, we found that outside directors were named in only 39.4% of the cases at most, and in as few as 28.4%. Of the forty-three cases listed in Table 6, we are certain that thirty-one actually involved outside directors (28.4%), and the reported decisions are ambiguous in the remaining twelve cases. These cases involving outside directors appear to constitute the only ones where formal corporate action could be said to be alleged, at least in the sense that the full board of directors was alleged to have approved or known of the action taken.

We suspect, however, that the 28.4% of the cases in which outside directors certainly were sued overestimates the percentage of cases in which the board of directors actually participated in the fraud, and these cases are therefore analyzed in more detail in Table 7. Few of these thirty-one cases in which outside directors were definitely sued contain allegations of specific knowledge by directors. Moreover, in many cases the description of the alleged fraud seems to focus on the wrongdoing of an individual officer or major shareholder to such an extent that it is extremely unlikely that the outside directors could have known of the fraud, and one wonders why the plaintiffs thought these directors were involved. As for the other cases, in virtually all of them, little indicates board involvement in the fraudulent disclosures. This is best illustrated by the seventeen cases involving false financial statements (54.8%),[179] 76% of which name accountants as defendants. The board employs accountants to serve as outside monitors of the integrity of the firm's financial reporting systems. Normally, information about difficulties with these systems flows from the accountants to the audit committee of the board, typically composed of outside directors. Formal action by the board of directors authorizing publication of financial statements is not required. Therefore, the fact that outside directors were sued does not imply that the frauds involved formal board authorization, or even knowledge, of the alleged fraud. Rather, it suggests that controls instituted by the board were thwarted by disloyal agents. As for the 29% of the cases involving conflicts of interest,[180] even if all of these cases involved formal board decisions to commit fraud, they comprise only ten of 111 cases, or 9% of all cases. Moreover, the board action in these

178. Where there is a single dominant shareholder, however, this difficulty disappears. This may explain the presence of large shareholder defendants in some Fraud on the Market cases. These complaints generally involve additional charges of conflicts of interest by these shareholders.

179. *See infra* Table 7.

180. *See infra* Table 7.

cases probably was in furtherance of personal, not shareholder, interests. Accordingly, these frauds cannot properly be treated as acts of the corporate principal.[181] We conclude that Fraud on the Market is not usually the product of corporate policy but rather results from acts of individual agents.[182]

In conclusion, the evidence presented above reveals that Fraud on the Market is a risky short-term strategy engaged in by senior managers, without the approval of either the board of directors or a majority of the shareholders. Almost all of these frauds were designed to deceive the market and current shareholders into believing that the firm's financial situation was better than it was. Most frauds involved attempts to conceal declines in earnings or other bad news. The dramatic decline in share prices following the revelation of the frauds demonstrates the seriousness of the cover-ups involved. These facts, combined with the observation that most Fraud on the Market cases did not involve managerial self-dealing,[183] support our last period agency cost hypothesis, and thus our conclusion in part III that agent liability, combined with criminal sanctions, is better able to deter Fraud on the Market than enterprise liability.

D. The Incidence of Fraud on the Market Liability

We now test our conclusion regarding enterprise liability as a vehicle for loss distribution by examining the monetary impact of Fraud on the Market suits on firms and their shareholders. Specifically, we examine both the magnitude of the potential wealth transfer resulting from a judgment against the firm, and whether this transfer can be justified as promoting loss spreading.

We have relatively few judgments and settlements to report because most of the reported cases involve the preliminary procedural issues of class certification or defendants' motions for summary judgment. The few dispositions we have report only payments by corporate principals,

---

181. *See supra* note 176. Presumably these frauds were pursued to further the goals of a dominant shareholder that were in conflict with the interests of other shareholders. *Cf.* William J. Carney, *The Theory of the Firm: Investor Coordination Costs, Control Premiums and Capital Structure*, 65 WASH. U. L.Q. 1 (1987) (describing the nature of conflicts that arise among coinvestors).

182. Although the evidence supports our hypothesis that individual agents commit fraud without actual authority to do so, there are few judgments against officers, employees, and directors. This is explained by the prevalence of settlements in securities fraud litigation. *See* Alexander, *supra* note 85 (all class actions involving initial public offerings resolved by settlement); Barbara A. Banoff & Benjamin S. Du Val, *The Class Action as a Mechanism for Enforcing the Federal Securities Laws: An Empirical Study of the Burdens Imposed*, 31 WAYNE L. REV. 1, 57-59 (1984) (only 2% of securities fraud class actions filed in Southern District of New York went to trial, while 48% of cases that were not class or derivative actions were tried); John E. Kennedy, *Securities Class and Derivative Actions in the United States District Court for the Northern District of Texas: An Empirical Study*, 14 HOUS. L. REV. 769, 811 (1977) (83% of the 54 class and derivative securities actions filed in U.S. District Court in Dallas settled).

183. If most of these cases resulted from managerial self-dealing, this would provide an alternative to our last period hypothesis as to why managers commit Fraud on the Market.

and none by corporate agents, with one possible exception. Table 8 reveals judgments and settlements that range from .01% to 39% of the market value of the firm's equity when the fraud was revealed,[184] with an average of 11.2%. The largest amount was $100 million and the smallest was $1 million. Thus these observed settlements and judgments had a very substantial impact on shareholder wealth, although a sample of six firms is too small a sample from which to generalize.

Because we had little information on judgments and settlements, we sought to use information on the amount of damages sought by plaintiffs. This proved even more difficult because only two of the reported decisions described the amounts sought. Table 9 sets forth plaintiffs' damage award requests in two cases: these were 35% and 60% of the market value of the firm's equity. Generally, complaints do not contain requests for recovery of specific monetary damages; Fraud on the Market cases are class actions and the plaintiffs, at the time the suit is filed, do not know the size of the class or the potential damages for each class member. Instead, plaintiffs leave this matter open for subsequent determination by the court.

Because so few of the reported cases reveal either the amount claimed or the amount awarded, we estimated the potential impact of securities fraud actions on shareholders by examining the sixty-two cases for which we had data on the volume of securities traded between announcement and revelation dates. We assumed that the number of shares purchased or sold by potential members of the plaintiff class was represented by the number of shares traded between the date of the fraud and the revelation date.[185] We further assumed that all those who were shareholders when the fraud was revealed would bear the expected liability.[186]

Because of the high turnover of the float of publicly traded securities, if a fraud is perpetrated for any significant period of time, the number of shares bought by the plaintiff class may be quite large compared to the total number of shares outstanding. The average trading volume was 199% of outstanding shares; in the median case trading volume equalled 131% of the number of outstanding shares in the firm. The large difference between the median and mean results from a handful of cases where trading volumes exceeded 400% of the number of outstand-

184. Our measure of the market value of firms' equity is based on month-end market prices at the close of the month after revelation of the fraud.

185. Some cases indicate the number of class members, but as a general rule reported decisions do not give this information. We did not attempt the costly task of determining the number of shareholders from shareholder lists because this information is not particularly revealing since so many shares are held in nominee names by a few nominee corporations.

186. Because our trading data was processed manually, it is not as precise as we would wish. We used monthly trading volumes rather than daily volumes. We included the month of the announcement and the month of the revelation, which overstates trading volume somewhat. We corrected for this in some cases by excluding the month in which the fraud was revealed where the revelation occurred in the first several days of the month.

ing shares, including two cases in which trading volumes exceeded 1000%. Volumes ranged from trivial—.003% in one case—to more than twelve times outstanding shares in another. In over one-third of the cases trading volume was more than double the number of shares outstanding.

Given the dearth of evidence about the size of damage claims, we estimated the potential damage awards by taking the stock price decline from the date of the fraud to the revelation date, adjusting this price decline to the market, and then multiplying the resulting number by the number of shares traded during the relevant period.[187] We used this measure on the theory that the stock price decline measures the damages caused by the fraud, although we recognize that it also includes the impact of the revelation of other bad news about the firm. An average decline of 47.8% in cases where bad news has been concealed, multiplied by the average trading volume of 199%, yields potential damages that represent 95% of the market value of the firm after the revelation date.[188] If we use the average decline of 43.3% in all Fraud on the Market cases, and multiply it by 199%, the potential damages are 86% of the entire market value of the firm.[189] The potential liability is thus enormous.

Whether imposing this liability on the enterprise promotes loss spreading depends on whether the number of victim shareholders exceeds the number of firm shareholders at the time the fraud is revealed.[190] Although we were unable to determine the number of plaintiff and defendant shareholders, we were able to determine the potential number of plaintiff and defendant shares. Based on the volume of shares traded during the fraud, on average the number of potential plaintiff shares is nearly twice as large as the number of outstanding shares (defendant shares); in the median case trading volume equalled 131% of the number of outstanding shares in the firm. Although we suspect that this analysis overestimates the relative size of the plaintiff and defendant

187. These prices were adjusted to the market using the Dow Jones Industrial Average, as described above. *See supra* text accompanying note 157. We did not use the price decline for the period of 10 days following the revelation date, because it appeared that in many cases considerable leakage of the bad news occurred prior to the revelation date. Despite the length of the test periods, we believe that the presence of other bad news about firms generally should be offset by good news in a portfolio of this size, so that the price declines are primarily, if not exclusively, attributable to the bad news concealed by the fraud, and to the news of the fraud itself.

188. *See infra* Table 3.

189. *See infra* Table 3. We recognize that these numbers may overstate the magnitude of the firm's expected liability. The volume of shares traded during the fraud will exceed the number of shares represented by the plaintiff class if many members both purchased and sold during the period of the fraud, and the price did not fall during that period. In this case, these shareholders would not have been injured by the fraud. It is important to note, however, that the number of shares represented by the plaintiff class can exceed the firm's outstanding shares at the time of revelation if the firm's stock price declined during the period between the fraud and its revelation. In this case the shareholders who sold during the period of the fraud can sue for damages, as can those who purchased stock from these shareholders (if the stock price continued to fall).

190. The loss spreading issue depends on the number of shareholders at the time the fraud is revealed, and not the number at the time the firm's liability is established, because when the fraud is revealed, the market price of the stock will fall to reflect the firm's expected liability.

classes,[191] our evidence suggests that in general plaintiff shares outnumber defendant shares.[192] Consequently, enterprise liability for Fraud on the Market usually shifts losses from a larger group onto a smaller group, thus concentrating losses instead of spreading them.[193] Accordingly, if we wish to spread losses, agent liability, which, in the event of agent insolvency leaves the plaintiffs bearing most of the losses, is the superior rule.

We were surprised by the relationship between the average number of shares traded during the period of the fraud and the outstanding shares because it suggests a huge potential wealth transfer from revelation-date shareholders to the members of the plaintiff class.[194] The surprisingly large potential wealth transfers result from the liquidity of American securities markets, the relatively high trading volumes observed in these companies, and the length of time the fraud typically went undetected.[195] Judicial opinions almost invariably ignore this wealth transfer phenomenon.[196]

In addition, if a significant number of these cases result in either judgments for the plaintiff class or substantial settlements, the result is a transfer of wealth from existing shareholders in the firm at the revelation date to former shareholders who may have held shares representing more than the total outstanding shares of the firm.[197] In publicly held companies this would mean that a small group of passive investors would partially compensate a large group of similarly situated investors, when in fact, both groups are without fault.[198] Accordingly, enterprise liability is inconsistent with the goal of loss distribution.

Moreover, the primary victims in the plaintiff class may be those who bought while the fraud was in effect and remained as shareholders after the revelation date. Therefore, under enterprise liability some existing shareholders are compensated at the expense of the remaining

191. *See supra* note 189.

192. The number of shares represented by the plaintiff class can exceed the number of shares outstanding when the fraud is revealed. *See supra* note 189.

193. The loss relevant to this analysis is the unfunded liability. *See supra* note 131.

194. *See, e.g.*, the comments of Judge Friendly (quoted *supra* note 41) in SEC v. Texas Gulf Sulphur Co., 401 F.2d 833, 866-67 (2d Cir. 1968). This brings to mind the comments of Professor David Ruder on the first class actions involving a Fraud on the Market—the *Texas Gulf Sulphur* case in 1968. Ruder noted that if liability were imposed on the company from the date it failed to disclose valuable inside information until the revelation date, damages would have been approximately $390,000,000 or $150,000,000 more than the net worth of Texas Gulf. Even if liability were limited to the period from a misleading press release on April 12, 1964, until revelation of the true state of affairs on April 16, damages could amount to $84,000,000, still a substantial portion of the shareholder's entire equity. David S. Ruder, Texas Gulf Sulphur—*The Second Round: Privity and State of Mind in Rule 10b-5 Purchase and Sale Cases*, 63 NW. U. L. REV. 423, 428-29 (1968).

195. As we pointed out earlier, the median period before discovery was 12 months, while the average was 16.3 months. *See supra* text accompanying note 170.

196. *But see supra* note 41.

197. *See supra* note 189.

198. Compensation would be partial because some of the plaintiffs also will be current shareholders, and thus will bear a pro rata share of the cost of the damage award.

shareholders, but as plaintiffs bear part of the cost of their own judgment. Where virtually all of the firm's shares are owned by the plaintiffs, the result is, as we have mentioned, essentially equivalent to a distribution in complete or partial liquidation.[199] The only true winners in this situation are the lawyers.

V. Conclusion

United States securities laws enable injured shareholders to recover enormous sums from a firm for Fraud on the Market committed by the firm's agents in the course of their employment. In recent years courts have undermined a firm's ability to defend against such actions by permitting plaintiffs to employ the doctrine of respondeat superior in securities fraud cases, thus removing good faith as a defense. Enterprise liability for Fraud on the Market, however, is unwarranted. Fraud on the Market generally is committed by senior managers attempting to save their jobs, not trying to serve shareholders. Yet, enterprise liability allows plaintiffs to ignore the assets of these responsible agents and to proceed instead against the pool of assets held by the firm for the benefit of innocent shareholders, many of whom also were victims of the fraud. This use of enterprise liability cannot be defended on the ground that it promotes optimal deterrence; in fact, enterprise liability appears more likely to shelter individual wrongdoers from liability than to deter them. Neither risk spreading nor loss distribution arguments justify this rule. Rather, it appears that a rule of agent liability, combined with criminal liability, is the superior approach.

The switch towards agent liability is more easily accomplished than it might first appear. Courts could adopt in effect a rule of agent liability simply by rejecting the use of respondeat superior for Fraud on the Market and allowing corporate defendants to employ the good faith defense of the control person provisions of the securities acts. In this way issuers would be liable when fraud was a corporate policy designed to benefit shareholders, but would not be liable when fraud was initiated to serve agents' own ends.

199. *See supra* text accompanying note 44.

TABLE 1
TYPES OF FRAUD ALLEGED

Type of Fraud	Number	Percentage
Hiding Bad News:		
False positive statements in SEC filings & press releases	71	64
Omission of bad news in securities offerings	2	1.8
Omission of bad news in SEC filings & press releases	21	18.9
Hiding Good News:		
Omission of good news in securities offerings	1	1
Omission of good news in SEC filings & press releases	3	2.7
False negative statements in SEC filings & press releases	4	3.6
False negative statements in securities offering	1	1
*Unclassified**	8	7.2
Total	111	100.2**

* In some cases the decisions did not provide information about the nature of the fraud, while others involved denials of merger negotiations prior to the clarification of the law in *Basic, Inc.* One involved the only known payment of "hushmail."
** This totals 100.2% because of rounding.

TABLE 2
TYPES OF FALSE POSITIVE STATEMENTS ALLEGED

Type of Fraud	Number	Percentage*
False Positive Statements by Issuers in SEC Filings & Press Releases:		
Statements to conceal declines in earnings	47	50.5
Optimistic statements of business developments	13	14.0
Projections of sales and earnings	3	3.2
False projections until insiders can sell out	3	3.2
False positive statements by management in proxy fight	1	1.1
False financial statements	4	4.3
Omission of Bad News in SEC Filings & Press Releases:		
Omission of adverse business developments	13	14.0
Concealment of bad news until insiders can sell out	3	3.2
Concealment of self-dealing and illegal acts	5	5.4
Third Party Frauds:		
Against issuers for assisting insiders' manipulation	1	1.1
Total	93	

* Percentages exceed 100% because there were multiple claims in some cases.

TABLE 3
AVERAGE STOCK PRICE DECLINE 10 DAYS AFTER MONTH OF REVELATION OF FRAUD

Type of Fraud	**Number Cases**	**Average Percent Decline***
False Positive Statements by Issuers in SEC Filings & Press Releases:		
Statements to conceal declines in earnings	21	42.6
Optimistic statements of business developments	12	43.7
Projections of sales and earnings	2	47.2
False projections until insiders can sell out	1	18.5
Total False Positive Statements	36	42.6
Omission of Bad News in SEC Filings & Press Releases:		
Omission of adverse business developments	7	47.4
Concealment of bad news until insiders can sell out	1	30.2
Concealment of self-dealing and illegal acts	1	68.3
Total Omissions	9	47.8
Average Stock Price Decline		43.3

* Stock prices were adjusted to account for market movements using the Dow Jones Industrial Average.

TABLE 4
DEFENDANTS IN CASES INVOLVING FINANCIAL STATEMENTS ALLEGED TO CONCEAL DECLINES IN EARNINGS

Defendants	Number of Cases	Percentage
Officers	38	80.9
No one other than issuer	4	8.5
No one other than issuer and third parties outside firm	3	6.4
Nonofficer employees	0	
Outside directors	14	29.8
Major shareholders	5	10.6
Others (accountants, brokers, attorneys, etc.)	28	59.6

TABLE 5
DEFENDANTS IN CASES INVOLVING ALLEGATIONS OF OMISSIONS OF ADVERSE BUSINESS DEVELOPMENTS AND CONCEALMENT OF ILLEGAL OR SELF-DEALING ACTS

Defendants	Number of Cases	Percentage*
No one other than issuer	7	36.8
No one other than issuer and third parties outside firm	0	
Officers	12	63.2
Nonofficer employees	0	
Outside directors	2	10.5
Major shareholders	1	5.3
Others (accountants, brokers, etc.)	4	21.3

* Percentages exceed 100% because multiple defendants were named in many cases.

TABLE 6
DEFENDANTS NAMED IN FRAUD ON THE MARKET CASES

Defendants	Number of Cases	Percentage of Total Cases*
Issuer	88**	80.7
No one other than issuer	21	19.3
No one other than issuer and third parties outside firm	3	2.8
Officers of issuers	78	71.6
Nonofficer employees	2	1.8
Outside directors	43***	39.4
Major shareholders	20	18.3
Others (accountants, brokers, attorneys, etc.)	45	41.3

* Percentages exceed 100% because multiple defendants were named in many cases.
** In at least nine cases (8.2%) the issuer was not named a defendant because it was involved in bankruptcy proceedings. Because we found that approximately 25% of the issuers were bankrupt, it seems likely that bankruptcy explains the absence of the issuer as a defendant in most of these cases.
*** Twelve of these cases may involve inside rather than outside directors, but the reports do not allow us to discriminate.

TABLE 7
TYPES OF CASES IN WHICH OUTSIDE DIRECTORS WERE SUED

Type of Charges	Number of Cases	Percentage
False financial statements	17	54.8
Concealment of conflicts of interest	9	29.0
No information	2	6.4
General fraud allegations	3	9.7

TABLE 8
SETTLEMENTS AND JUDGMENTS REPORTED

Issuer	Amount of Judgment/Settlement ($000)	Market Value of Company ($000)	Award as Percent of Market Value
Apple Computer	100,000	1,323,153	7.6
Pepsico	22,000	3,947,527	0.6
Comserv	4,000	10,314	38.8
Dorchester Gas	1,037		
Saxon Corp.	20,000		
Warner Communications	10,300	3,739,375	0.3
Cenco, Inc.	19,250	96,250	20.0
Union Carbide	31,730	2,308,444	1.4
Ferrovanadium Corp.	1,000		

TABLE 9
AMOUNTS OF DAMAGES SOUGHT BY PLAINTIFFS

Issuer	Market Value of Company ($000)	Amount Claimed ($000)	Claim as Percent of Market Value
Alpha Industries	106,099	37,482	35.3
Hospital Corp. of America	2,472,764	1,500,000	60.7

Part V
The Role of Shareholders

[16]

COLUMBIA LAW REVIEW

VOL. 91 OCTOBER 1991 NO. 6

LIQUIDITY VERSUS CONTROL: THE INSTITUTIONAL INVESTOR AS CORPORATE MONITOR

John C. Coffee, Jr. *

Table of Contents

* Adolf A. Berle Professor of Law, Columbia University Law School. The author acknowledges the helpful comments of Bernard Black, Deborah DeMott, Merritt Fox, Ronald Gilson, Louis Lowenstein, Mark Ramseyer, Edward Rock, Mark Roe, Robert Thompson, and Ms. Rebecca Simmons, Columbia Law School, Class of 1991.

INTRODUCTION

Within academia, paradigm shifts occur regularly, some more important than others. As the takeover wave of the 1980s ebbs,[1] a significant shift now appears to be in progress in the way the public corporation is understood. Above all, the new thinking emphasizes that political forces shaped the modern corporation. While the old paradigm saw the structure of the corporation as the product of a Darwinian competition in which the most efficient design emerged victorious,[2]

1. The rate of takeovers and other acquisitions has declined significantly and continues to decline. During the first quarter of 1991, merger and acquisition activity declined 18% over the corresponding quarter in the preceding year and hit an eleven year low. See Mergers at an 11-year Low, N.Y. Times, Apr. 18, 1991, at D10. The reasons for this decline are various: The drying up of the junk bond market; restrictive state antitakeover legislation, see infra note 5 and accompanying text; and judicial decisions that have accepted preemptive defensive tactics by target management. See, e.g., Paramount Communications Inc. v. Time Inc., 571 A.2d 1140 (Del. 1989). This decline in takeover activity, particularly as a result of restrictive state legislation, has supplied the impetus, in my judgment, for scholars to consider the thesis that politics, more than economics, shaped the modern American corporation.

2. What I am terming the "old paradigm" of the public corporation rests on two basic structural pillars: (1) the view of the public corporation as a private and largely contractual undertaking and thus devoid of much "public law" significance, see, e.g., Frank H. Easterbrook & Daniel R. Fischel, The Corporate Contract, 89 Colum. L. Rev. 1416 (1989), and (2) the view that the separation of ownership and control is both inevitable and efficient. The separation of ownership and control was first identified by Adolf A. Berle and Gardiner C. Means in their path-breaking book, The Modern Corporation and Private Property (1932). Recent theorists have argued that this separation is efficient because it allows entrepreneurs to obtain capital from risk-neutral shareholders who, because they are diversified, can accept business risks that would deter undiversi-

this new perspective sees political forces as constraining that evolutionary process and possibly foreclosing the adoption of a superior organizational form. Thus, my colleague Professor Mark Roe has argued that the Berle/Means corporation, in which ownership and control are separated, was not "an inevitably natural consequence" of the economic and technological forces that shaped modern capitalism, but rather was an adaptation to political forces that limited the scale, scope, and power of financial institutions.[3] Absent these politically imposed constraints, he suggests, the evolution of the modern corporation might have resulted in the emergence of a very different dominant organizational form, one more nearly resembling the Japanese or German industrial system in which financial institutions are the major shareholders of, and closely monitor, industrial corporations.[4]

Perhaps it should not be surprising that this new focus on political constraints has surfaced just as the combination of state antitakeover statutes and adverse judicial decisions has largely succeeded in eclipsing the hostile takeover as a mechanism of corporate accountability.[5] During the late 1980s, political constraints seemed puny in comparison to the power of the market to drive corporate control transactions, but today the political vulnerability of the takeover movement is obvious. Still, there is an irony to the assertion that political forces crippled the potential monitoring capacity of financial institutions. Academics are raising the claim at the same time that (1) Congress is proposing to repeal or substantially relax the Glass-Steagall Act, which separates commercial from investment banking, and to amend related legislation that restricts interstate branching,[6] and (2) the SEC is proposing to re-

fied shareholder/managers. The new focus on the political forces shaping the modern corporation chiefly challenges this second pillar of the current orthodoxy, but in time, a public choice perspective, applied rigorously, could challenge the first pillar as well.

3. Mark J. Roe, A Political Theory of American Corporate Finance, 91 Colum. L. Rev. 10 (1991) [hereinafter Roe, Political Theory]; see Mark J. Roe, Political and Legal Restraints on Ownership and Control of Public Companies, 27 J. Fin. Econ. 7 (1990). Even before Professor Roe, the thesis that financial institutions had been regulated into passivity in their role as shareholders had been advanced (at least in an abbreviated fashion) by Michael Jensen. See Michael C. Jensen, Eclipse of the Public Corporation, Harv. Bus. Rev., Sept.–Oct. 1989, at 61, 65–66.

4. Roe, Political Theory, supra note 3, at 59–62. Professor Roe is careful not to argue that control of corporations by financial institutions is necessarily desirable, but he does conclude that the "[f]oreign experience provides strong evidence that" such a pattern would have developed, absent regulation. Id. at 60. This Article disagrees.

5. The 1980s saw 34 states pass over 65 statutes restricting corporate takeovers. These are examined and categorized in Jonathan M. Karpoff & Paul H. Malatesta, The Wealth Effects of Second-Generation State Takeover Legislation, 25 J. Fin. Econ. 291 (1989). See also Roberta Romano, The Future of Hostile Takeovers: Legislation and Public Opinion, 57 U. Cin. L. Rev. 457 (1988) (arguing that such legislation chiefly benefitted the managements of target corporations).

6. What legislative modifications, if any, of the Glass-Steagall Act will ultimately pass Congress remains uncertain, but as of mid-1991, each of the Administration, House, and Senate bills would eliminate most of the barriers to commercial banks own-

lax its proxy rules to facilitate shareholder collective action, particularly by institutional shareholders.[7] If the public at large has a concern about financial institutions today, it is not their strength, but their weakness, that worries them. To the extent that the public perceives banks as reckless, unstable, or infirm, it may still favor their paternalistic regulation, but the populist image of a domineering J.P. Morgan seems to have been forever erased from the public's mind by the recent wave of insolvencies.

Without challenging the historical accuracy of the thesis that political and ideological forces inhibited the growth of financial monitoring in the United States, this Article doubts that this thesis takes us very far. In particular, its contemporary relevance is undercut by the fact that most of the barriers that confined commercial banks to limited sectors of the economy appear to be facing a demolition that is as sudden and complete as the collapse of the Berlin Wall. More importantly, even if the new theorists are correct in their view that, but for political constraints, U.S. financial institutions could have developed into efficient corporate monitors—much as they believe that they have in Japan, Germany and elsewhere[8]—that this scenario raises two major questions that their political history of institutional development alone cannot adequately answer: (1) Is a similar system of corporate monitoring

---

ing securities affiliates and to interstate branching. See Stephen Labaton, Riegle Offers a Third Bill on Banking, N.Y. Times, July 17, 1991, at D6. In June, 1991, the House Banking Committee approved legislation that would permit the expansion of banks into both the securities and insurance fields. See Stephen Labaton, House Panel Approves Sweeping New Bank Rules, N.Y. Times, June 29, 1991, at A35. To the extent that restrictions on commercial banks' ability to engage in interstate banking or investment banking was the primary evidence relied upon to prove that political forces constrained the development of financial monitoring in the United States, see supra note 3 and accompanying text, this political theory seems to have limited predictive power.

7. In June, 1991, the SEC proposed to amend its proxy rules under § 14(a) of the Securities Exchange Act of 1934 to facilitate inter-shareholder communications and to reduce the costs of compliance for persons engaged in a proxy solicitation. See Regulation of Securityholder Communications, Exchange Act Release No. 29,315, 56 Fed. Reg. 28,987 (June 25, 1991). This proposed relaxation of the proxy rules was in response to a request made by the California Public Employees Retirement System (CalPERS) that their impact on institutional investors be reexamined. See infra note 46 and accompanying text. In light of the SEC's apparent willingness to relax at least some regulations that burden institutional investors, the overregulation thesis again loses some of its contemporary force.

8. In addition to Professor Roe, I would list Professors Bernard Black of Columbia, Ronald Gilson and Joseph Grundfest of Stanford, and Reinier Kraakman of Harvard as among those academics who have most notably advanced the overregulation thesis that the monitoring capacity of institutional investors has been inhibited by excessive regulation. See sources cited infra notes 10–13 and accompanying text. I should indicate that I do not disagree with them that there has been some overregulation which should be relaxed, but I believe other factors—most notably conflicts of interest, a preference for liquidity, and collective action problems—deserve greater weight in any theory of institutional investor behavior. As a result, deregulation alone is not an adequate policy response.

through institutional investors necessarily efficient or desirable? and (2) In the absence of political constraints, would other causes have impeded the development of a system of institutional monitoring within the United States?

These questions will be the focus of this Article. Although those dissatisfied with the current state of shareholder power in American corporate governance may find foreign models of corporate governance more attractive, the danger in such comparisons is the "grass-is-always-greener" fallacy: one can easily idealize foreign systems and see only their benefits and not their costs. Monitoring by financial institutions does not necessarily mean net gains for other shareholders, but may improve only the position of the monitoring financial institution. Similarly, assigning primary causal significance to political constraints may lead to overlooking deeper and more fundamental reasons why financial monitoring has not developed in the United States. Put simply, the agents controlling institutional investors have considerable reason to remain "rationally apathetic" about corporate governance and little reason to become active participants. Why? Various reasons will be advanced, but one stands out that will be the centerpiece of this Article: a trade-off exists and must be recognized between liquidity and control. Investors that want liquidity may hesitate to accept control.

This assertion—that a preference for liquidity chills the willingness of institutional investors to participate in the control of major corporations—may sound heretical. With only a few exceptions,[9] both practitioners and academics have shared the assumption that institutions are on the verge of becoming active monitors. On the one hand, proponents of the overregulation thesis have argued that SEC and banking regulation has hobbled institutional investors, resulting in high agency costs, weak capital market discipline, and managerial entrenchment. Former SEC Commissioner Joseph Grundfest aptly synthesized the views of these critics in a striking paragraph in a recent article:

> America seems not to trust her capitalists. For more than half a century, state and federal governments have limited investors' influence over the governance of publicly traded corporations. Investors' ability to monitor corporate performance, and to control assets that they ultimately own, has been subordinated to the interests of other constituencies, most notably corporate management.[10]

9. The leading exception to this generalization is an incisive recent article by Professor Edward Rock. See Edward B. Rock, The Logic and (Uncertain) Significance of Institutional Shareholder Activism, 79 Geo. L. J. 445 (1991).

10. Joseph A. Grundfest, Subordination of American Capital, 27 J. Fin. Econ. 89, 89–90 (1990).

In a similar vein, John Pound[11] and Bernard Black[12] have separately examined the legal rules and regulatory policies governing shareholder voting and have reported that this body of law, which was long thought to protect the shareholder's franchise, often operates to frustrate its effective exercise. Other scholars have taken a more activist stance and proposed specific courses of action by which institutional investors can directly influence substandard corporate managements.[13] All these new critics tend to favor deregulation of financial institutions so that they can serve as more effective corporate monitors. For many of these critics, the relationship between financial institutions and corporate managements in the German and Japanese economies provides the relevant model.[14]

On the other hand, defenders of corporate management seem equally convinced that, unless their power is checked, institutional investors will soon dominate corporate managements.[15] As a result, they have advanced a very different set of policy proposals, which seek to subject institutional investors to greater oversight. Typically, these proposals have portrayed institutional investors not as highly constrained and overly regulated entities, but as financial adolescents, recklessly preoccupied with short-term profit maximization. One example is the 1989 Report of the New York State Task Force on Pension Fund Investment, which recommended that public pension funds be subjected to greater legislative control and guidance.[16] Others have

11. John Pound, Proxy Voting and the SEC: Democratic Ideals Versus Market Efficiency (paper presented at the Structure and Governance of Enterprise Conference, March 29–31, 1990, Kennedy School of Government, Harvard University) (unpublished manuscript, on file with the Columbia Law Review). Similarly, Professors Lucian Bebchuk and Marcel Kahan have argued that the state law rules on expense reimbursement unduly favor incumbents over challengers. See Lucian Ayre Bebchuk & Marcel Kahan, A Framework for Analyzing Legal Policy Toward Proxy Contests, 78 Cal. L. Rev. 1071 (1990).

12. Bernard S. Black, Shareholder Passivity Reexamined, 89 Mich. L. Rev. 520 (1990).

13. Ronald J. Gilson & Reinier Kraakman, Reinventing the Outside Director: An Agenda for Institutional Investors, 43 Stan. L. Rev. 863 (1991).

14. This is particularly true in the case of Professor Roe. See Roe, Political Theory, supra note 3, at 59–62. See also Gilson & Kraakman, supra note 13, at 876; David P. Hale, Learning from Germany and Japan, Wall St. J., Feb. 4, 1991, at A10 (suggesting that until early in this century, American banks, such as the Morgan Bank, played such a monitoring role). Actually, both sides in the current debate cite the Japanese and German models to support their contentions. See Martin Lipton & Steven A. Rosenblum, A New System of Corporate Governance: The Quinquennial Election of Directors, 58 U. Chi. L. Rev. 187, 218–22 (1991).

15. See infra notes 16–20 and accompanying text.

16. New York State Task Force on Pension Fund Investments, Our Money's Worth: The Report of the Governor's Task Force on Pension Fund Investment (1989). Another even more ominous signal for institutional investors was the passage in 1990 of a Pennsylvania statute under which institutional investors could be forced to disgorge their profits on the sale of a Pennsylvania-chartered corporation's stock, if they participated in a control group. See infra notes 187–189 and accompanying text. For the

made similar suggestions that (1) pension funds "pass through" their votes to their constituents,[17] (2) corporate managements reassert control over their pension fund investment and voting policies,[18] and (3) institutions invest in stocks principally through vehicles that are allied with corporate management.[19] Alarmed by the power and what they perceive as the short-term mentality of institutional investors, Martin Lipton and Steven Rosenblum have suggested an even more sweeping change: abolition of the annual election of directors in favor of a quinquennial election.[20] In short, two polar views of the institutional investor compete for supremacy today: (1) the academic view of financial institutions as Prometheus chained to the rock by outmoded regulations that serve only to entrench and insulate incumbent managements, and (2) corporate management's image of these same institutions as frenzied gamblers in a financial casino, each competing to outdo the other in short-term performance. Both sides in this debate share the common assumption that, for better or worse, institutional investors would soon dominate corporate managements in the absence of political constraints.

This Article disagrees with that assumption. It will argue that the primary explanation for institutional passivity is not overregulation, but the insufficiency of existing incentives to motivate institutional money managers to monitor. Although proponents of institutional activism have analyzed at length the potential ability of institutional investors to hold corporate managers accountable, they have largely ignored the question of who holds institutional money managers accountable. The problem of who will guard the guardian is a timeless one, but it is particularly complicated when the proposed guardian is the institutional investor. Not only do the same problems of agency cost arise at the institutional investor level, but there are persuasive reasons for believing that some institutional investors are less accountable to their "owners" than are corporate managements to their shareholders. Put simply, the usual mechanisms of corporate accountability are either unavailable or largely compromised at the institutional level.[21] This con-

fullest statement of the view that Wall Street's influence forces corporate managers to focus on the short-term, see Louis Lowenstein, What's Wrong with Wall Street: Short-term Gain and the Absentee Shareholder 1, 5–6, 9, 56–63, 76 (1988); Robert H. Hayes & William J. Abernathy, Managing Our Way to Economic Decline, Harv. Bus. Rev., July–Aug. 1980, at 67, 68–70.

17. George H. Cain, Corporate Participation, Nat'l L. J., Sept. 10, 1990, at 13.

18. A recent trend toward such reassertion of voting control has been reported. See Pension Fund Sponsors Urged to Retain Control of Proxy Voting, 22 Sec. Reg. & L. Rep. (BNA) No. 26, at 979 (June 29, 1990).

19. See Ira M. Millstein, On the Making of Pension Funds as "Patient Capitalists," Directors & Boards, Winter 1990, at 11, 14 (recommending that institutional investors take guidance from corporate management because of their greater knowledge of corporate governance and greater commitment to corporate performance).

20. Lipton & Rosenblum, supra note 14, at 224 & n.53.

21. The point is obvious but fundamental: while corporate managements are sub-

clusion does not deny that there has been overregulation of institutional investors, but it suggests its impact may have been overstated by the new critics. More importantly, this perspective implies that deregulation alone is an inadequate policy response. If the diagnosis that rational apathy will continue to prevail at the institutional level is accurate, then the law must intervene to correct the market's failure by creating adequate incentives for institutional managers to monitor.

This Article will therefore explore possible strategies by which agency costs can be reduced at this second level in order that institutional investors will more effectively monitor corporate managements. But the larger problem of the institutional investor's role in corporate governance cannot be telescoped simply into one of reducing agency costs at the fund manager level. Rather, the nature of that role is itself problematic. In one key respect, American institutional investors are unlike both individual shareholders in the United States and the financial monitors in Japan and Germany. Potentially, American institutional investors have the capacity to unite liquidity and control. Although institutional investors do not appear to have achieved such a

---

ject to the disciplinary threat of hostile takeovers, proxy fights, and other corporate control transactions, the managements of most institutional investors are not. Only in the case of the closed-end mutual fund is a takeover even conceivable, and actual instances of such takeovers are virtually unknown. Other forms of capital market discipline are also lacking: while banks and other creditors can pressure corporate managements that are underperforming, pension funds are immune from similar capital market pressures because they are creditors, not debtors. In the case of defined benefit pension plans (but not defined contribution plans), the corporate sponsor does have an incentive to remove a substandard investment manager (in order to reduce the future contribution it must make), but management of the corporate sponsor is itself subject to a conflict of interest on the issue of whether it wishes its pension managers to engage in active shareholder monitoring of corporate managements. To the extent that corporate managers prefer to forego the benefits to their corporation resulting from more active monitoring by pension fund managers in return for an implicit system that ensures the job security of corporation managers, pension managers today have little reason to resist them. Indeed, an investment manager who acquires a reputation as an active monitor may cease to be given pension fund accounts. See infra notes 181–184 and accompanying text.

On a more abstract level, two other problems suggest that agency costs will be higher at the institutional investor level than at the corporate management level. First, the problem of collective action is potentially more severe at the institutional investor level than at the corporate level. Not only are the beneficiaries of a pension fund (to use the example of the largest, most important institutional investor) as dispersed as the shareholders in a large corporation, but there is no analogue in the pension fund context to the large shareholder in the public corporation who may be willing to undertake monitoring and similar expenditures that benefit other shareholders. See infra note 23. Second, one of the basic techniques in corporate governance for aligning managerial and shareholder preferences is the use of executive compensation devices, such as the stock option, that give managers an incentive to maximize value for shareholders. See Michael C. Jensen & Kevin J. Murphy, CEO Incentives—It's Not How Much You Pay, But How, Harv. Bus. Rev. May–June 1990, at 138, 139–40. For reasons discussed later, such executive compensation formulas are less used and more difficult to design for institutional investors. See infra notes 336–347 and accompanying text.

union in any modern industrial economy to date, it is within reach in the United States in the near future—if institutional investors are "unleashed."

Thus, we return to a major concern of this Article: is such a union of liquidity and control desirable? Do we want the institutional monitor to have the same ability to exit the firm costlessly as does the individual shareholder? Would the institutional monitor who possessed such liquidity undertake the often costly burden of monitoring? These are difficult questions, but the choices are not limited to a simple yes or no. Rather, public policy could choose any of a number of possible positions along a continuum that runs from allowing investors to combine liquidity and control to requiring an election between them. This Article will seek to evaluate some of the risks and related considerations that should be weighed in making any choice.

To point to the dangers in uniting liquidity and control is not to reject, however, the claim that overregulation of institutional investors is both possible and undesirable. In fact, three distinct hypotheses can explain the passivity of institutional investors: (1) an "interest group" story that views regulation chilling institutional investor participation in corporate governance as the product of low-visibility political coalitions between management and other groups;[22] (2) a collective action story that views the costs of organizing dispersed investors to be sufficiently high as to make them rationally apathetic about participation in corporate governance;[23] and (3) a public interest story suggesting that pub-

22. Essentially, commentators such as Jensen, Pound, Roe, Black, and Grundfest, tell such a story (although they do not deny that collective action problems also exist). See supra notes 3, 8–13. State antitakeover legislation seems easily explained on this basis. See Romano, supra note 5, at 458–65.

23. This form of explanation begins with the work of Mancur Olson and focuses on the problems of dispersed shareholders in organizing to take action that is in their collective interest. See Mancur Olson, The Logic of Collective Action: Public Goods and the Theory of Groups 55–56 (2d ed. 1971). See also Russell Hardin, Collective Action (1982). Professor Rock relies on essentially such an argument to explain institutional passivity. See Rock, supra note 9, at 453–63. To define the collective action problem, it is useful to distinguish it from the problem of agency costs. Agency costs arise because the interests of shareholders and managers can conflict (over salary, corporate policy or whatever); thus, both shareholders and managers must undertake some costs to minimize these conflicts of interest through monitoring and bonding expenditures, and some losses will in any event remain because their prevention is too costly. The sum of these costs and the residual loss is called "agency costs." See Michael C. Jensen & William H. Meckling, Theory of the Firm: Managerial Behavior, Agency Costs and Ownership Structure, 3 J. Fin. Econ. 305, 308–10 (1976). In contrast, the collective action problem arises as soon as there is more than one owner. Corporate monitoring is an example of what economists call a collective good; that is, it benefits all shareholders whether or not they pay for it. See Robert C. Clark, Corporate Law § 9.5, at 389–400 (1986). Rationally, shareholders would prefer to "free ride" on the efforts of others than to subscribe to their pro rata share of the costs of corporate monitoring. Large shareholders will, however, subscribe to these costs to the extent that their share of the expected payoff exceeds the costs they must incur, thus permitting smaller shareholders

lic-regarding legislation and administrative rules have long and wisely resisted the union of liquidity and control. Although recent critics have focused on the first explanation, this Article will stress the second and third. None of these explanations is necessarily inconsistent with the others, but the latter two have received less attention, as economic theorists, always suspicious of regulation, have tended to view the regulation of financial institutions as intended to entrench corporate managements.

Yet there are demonstrable problems with the simple overregulation story. In fact, a close comparative analysis demonstrates that the actual limitations placed by American law on financial institutions as investors are not significantly more restrictive than, for example, the applicable laws in Japan and certain other comparable economies.[24] Nor is it at all clear that in an unregulated legal environment, financial institutions will necessarily develop into corporate monitors.[25] Thus, the assumption that—but for regulatory and political constraints—American financial institutions would have evolved into controlling shareholders, as German and Japanese banks have arguably done, seems shaky.[26]

Equally important, the overregulation thesis simply overlooks the liquidity/control trade-off. Only once the uniqueness of the American context is understood can one assess intelligently this Article's claim that the union of liquidity and control would be socially undesirable. Both the German and Japanese economies (as do many others) depend on internal capital markets, as opposed to the external capital markets

to free ride on their monitoring efforts. For example, if expenditures by shareholders of $1,000,000 would yield benefits of $2,000,000, it would not be rational for a 25% shareholder to expend $1,000,000, because it would benefit only to the extent of $500,000. But if the gains to shareholders exceed $4,000,000, then the 25% shareholder will rationally expend $1,000,000 (and thereby confer a benefit on the dispersed, but "free riding," small shareholders). The key implication of a collective action analysis is that shareholder resistance to managerial actions that are adverse to their welfare will often be underfunded, because of the difficulty in taxing the "free riders."

24. See infra notes 58–63, 129 and accompanying text.

25. Although unconstrained by legal restrictions, banks in the United Kingdom have not developed into active corporate monitors, and institutional investors seldom hold more than 1%–2% of the stock of any individual corporation. See infra notes 143–147 and accompanying text. Even in Germany, where institutional investors are little regulated, they do not own a higher percentage of equity securities in individual corporations than current U.S. law would permit a bank holding company to own. See infra notes 99–102 and accompanying text.

26. One qualification here is necessary: federalism did restrict the growth of financial institutions in the United States. Because each state could charter banks and prevent the entry of out-of-state competition, the result was a highly fragmented financial industry in which even leading institutions could not grow to the same scale as Japanese and German banks. Federalism is not, however, a regulatory constraint that can be explained under an interest group theory that gives corporate management a central role, because use of the corporate form arose well after the adoption of the U.S. Constitution.

that characterize the United States and the United Kingdom.[27] In such internal capital markets, industrial firms obtain the bulk of their capital from a very limited number of capital suppliers in direct negotiations. In consequence, these capital suppliers have both greater leverage and less liquidity than do institutional investors in the United States. To some degree, this system of internal capital markets may be breaking down with the growth of an international capital market that will give all large firms access to public capital markets. But the critical point is that institutional investors in the United States have a degree of liquidity that their European and Japanese counterparts largely lack. At present, any attempt by institutional investors in the United States to exercise control over corporate managements will entail a probable sacrifice of this liquidity, which may be an unacceptable cost to them. Put more generally, when faced with the choice, U.S. institutional investors have traditionally preferred liquidity to control. This empirical observation leads in turn to a broader, normative contention: *liquidity and control are antithetical*. American law has said clearly and consistently since at least the 1930s that those who exercise control should not enjoy liquidity and vice versa.[28] Ultimately, this Article will defend the proposition that the separation of liquidity and control is not only a cause of institutional passivity, but to some degree should be. In short, those institutions that most desire liquidity would make poor monitors.

Nor should this contention seem surprising: most other industrial societies seem to have reached a similar resolution (either by legal rule or by business adaptation). From a comparative perspective, advanced industrial economies can be classified along a continuum ranging from those, such as Japan and Germany, that permit financial institutions to control corporate managements, but effectively deny them liquidity, to those that inhibit institutional control, but maximize their liquidity. On such a continuum, the dominant American organizational form—the Berle/Means public corporation—represents the latter pole: investors have only limited ability to control management, but near-perfect li-

---

27. One recent survey finds that in Germany there are only 497 German corporations listed on the eight German stock exchanges, and of these "not more than 100" lacked a controlling shareholder. Similarly, in France, only "around 460" corporations (out of nearly 135,000 stock corporations chartered in France) were listed on the Paris Stock Exchange. This same pattern holds true also in Belgium, which has 35,000 stock corporations, but only 190 listed on the Brussels Stock Exchange. See Klaus J. Hopt, Takeover and Other General Bids in European Law 4 (paper delivered at conference sponsored by University of Ghent on May 30, 1991) (on file with the Columbia Law Review). In sharp contrast, there are some 2450 British corporations listed on the London Stock Exchange, even though the British economy is much smaller than that of either Germany or France. Id.

The point here is that because relatively few German or French corporations are publicly traded (and even those firms typically have a controlling stockholder or stockholder group), financial institutions that hold a substantial equity stake in these firms lack liquidity by definition.

28. See infra notes 221–223, 247–267 and accompanying text.

quidity in deep and relatively stable financial markets. The oft-repeated "Wall Street Rule" expressed the basic equilibrium that until recently prevailed: dissatisfied investors could sell, but they could not effectively challenge management.[29]

The tension between liquidity and control can also explain why the historic passivity of the institutional investor is declining. Today, the press reports on an almost daily basis that institutional investors are displaying a new activism.[30] Clearly, some institutions—most typically, public pension funds—sponsor shareholder proposals, lobby state legislatures, and, in a few cases, support insurgents in proxy contests.[31] What explains this new activism? On a theoretical level, the trade-off between liquidity and control is simply a context-specific application of Albert O. Hirschman's famous generalization that the members of any organization face a choice between "exit" and "voice."[32] If an easy, low-cost "exit" is possible (such as that provided by securities markets), the members will rationally have little interest in exercising a more costly "voice." But if "exit" is blocked, the members will become more interested in exercising a "voice" in governance decisions. From this perspective, the new activism of American institutional investors can be explained as the product of "voice" becoming less costly, because of the growth in institutional ownership of securities and the resulting increased capacity for collective action, while "exit" has become more difficult, because institutional investors, who increasingly own large unmarketable blocks, must accept substantial price discounts in order to

29. The basic notion underlying the "Wall Street Rule" was that institutions should support and vote with management—or sell their shares. Some trace the origins of this informal rule of behavior to guidelines developed in the 1940s by the American Bankers Association. See Pension and Welfare Benefits Administration, U.S. Department of Labor, Proxy Project Report 1 (1989) (on file with the Columbia Law Review).

30. See, e.g., Brett D. Fromson, The Big Owners Roar, Fortune, July 30, 1990, at 66; Debbie Galant, Putting New Muscle into Proxy Voting, Institutional Investor, Feb. 1990, at 161; Sanford L. Jacobs, Big Holders Resolve to Flex Their Muscles, Wall St. J., Feb. 28, 1989, at C1; Roberta S. Karmel, CalPERS Versus the Business Roundtable, N.Y.L.J., Feb. 21, 1991, at 3; David Pauly, Wall Street's New Musclemen, Newsweek, June 5, 1989, at 46; Anise C. Wallace, Institution's Proxy Power Grows, N.Y. Times, July 5, 1988, at D1.

31. The most activist institutions tend to be either state or municipal pension funds (which I shall refer to as "public funds") that may be pursuing an agenda that enhances the political reputations of the public officials controlling them or small private "pools" of capital assembled from foreign investors. See infra note 53 and accompanying text. Such "private" investment companies appear to behave very differently from the much larger mutual funds that are open to the ordinary investor, and they strive to maintain a reputation as "friendly" long-term investors. See Diana B. Henriques, Fidelity's Secret Agent Man, N.Y. Times, Jan. 27, 1991, § 3 (Business), at 1. For a review of institutional involvement in recent proxy contests, see Black, supra note 12, at 570–75. For data on the relative size of private and public pension funds, see infra note 42.

32. Albert O. Hirschman, Exit, Voice, and Loyalty: Responses to Decline in Firms, Organizations, and States (1970).

liquidate these blocks.[33] These trends toward greater "voice" and lesser "exit" seem likely to continue for institutional investors.[34] As a result, greater institutional activism is predictable, even in the face of a static legal environment.

The trade-off between "exit" and "voice" also suggests a regulatory strategy: restrict "exit" to encourage "voice." Undoubtedly, such a policy could be carried too far and might at some point induce institutional investors to prefer alternative investments to equity securities. Still, the new critics of regulation have not recognized the reverse side of this coin: simplified "exit" may mean less "voice." At a minimum then, a strategy for deregulation should accord a priority to relaxing those rules that inhibit "voice," while exercising considerable caution before making "exit" easier.[35] In other words, rather than "unleashing" institutional investors en masse, the more sensible policy may be a selective one: deregulate first those institutions most likely to exercise "voice" rather than seek "exit."

This Article is divided into four parts. Part I surveys the relationship of financial institutions to corporate managements in several advanced industrial economies, particularly Germany and Japan. It finds that (1) ownership and other legal restrictions similar to those now said to hobble U.S. financial institutions also exist in many of these countries, but generally have had only a modest impact; (2) the relative control of financial institutions over industrial corporations appears to be declining in both Japan and Germany as successful corporate managements exploit international capital markets or retain cash flow in order to escape close monitoring and the conflicts posed by bank ownership;[36] and (3) in those economies where financial institutions do dominate corporate managements, the industrial structure is organized around internal capital markets,[37] thus making the "exit" option un-

33. For the conclusion that pension funds "cannot dispose of large blocks of stock easily" and face increasing illiquidity as their holdings grow, see Millstein, supra note 19, at 15. In addition, exit is less attractive because institutions have come to realize that they cannot outperform the market (at least without accepting additional risk). This is the central insight of the Efficient Capital Market Hypothesis, and based on it many institutions have turned to "indexed" investing, which implies a buy-and-hold policy. See infra notes 236–239 and accompanying text.

34. See infra notes 236–243 and accompanying text.

35. There may also be other diseconomies associated with uniting liquidity and control. An earlier era used the pejorative term "pools" to describe loose associations among large investors, which were thought to be able to manipulate securities prices. Prevention of such manipulation was a major focus of the Securities Exchange Act of 1934. See infra notes 221–223 and accompanying text.

36. See infra notes 79–83, 108–116 and accompanying text.

37. The term "internal capital market" has been widely used to refer to the allocation of capital within a large conglomerate through bureaucratic decision-making centralized in the office of the chief executive. In theory, senior management redirects cash flows received from its subsidiaries and divisions to those having the best future prospects. See Oliver E. Williamson, Markets and Hierarchies: Analysis and Antitrust Impli-

available. The contrast between internal capital markets in Japan and Germany and the more developed external capital market in the United States casts considerable doubt on whether foreign economies provide relevant models for future regulatory reform within the United States. Part II assesses the extra-legal factors that have retarded participation by institutional investors in corporate governance in the United States and concludes that a strategy of deregulation is likely to produce only modest results. Part III considers the potential diseconomies that might follow if deregulation were to permit investors to combine liquidity and control. Finally, Part IV asks how regulation might encourage the development of institutional monitoring, particularly in light of the rise of "indexed" investing.[38] Indexed investors, who may hold securities in a thousand or more corporations, have largely abandoned "exit," but also find the exercise of "voice" infeasible because their extensive holdings exceed their capacity to monitor. Part IV therefore suggests that new mechanisms must be created to make monitoring both feasible and mandatory. Although Part IV is not necessarily optimistic about the prospect of active institutional monitoring developing in the near future, it does outline the legal prerequisites necessary before indexed or other widely diversified institutional investors are likely to play an active monitoring role: First, "excessive" diversification must be discouraged; second, investment management services should be "unbundled" from monitoring services, so that a true market in the latter can develop; and, finally, incentive compensation formulas that align the interests of the institutional money manager, as agent, with those of its principal and thus encourage monitoring should be authorized and implemented. This may sound like a visionary, rather than realistic, scenario for reform. Perhaps it is, but it is less idealized than the expectation that, in the absence of such changes, institutional investors will naturally behave like individual shareholders who hold large equity stakes.

I. A Comparative Examination of the Institutional Investor

Part I briefly examines the position of institutional investors in the United States and contrasts it with that of similar institutions in other developed economies. Part I begins with the United States and then

cations 143–48 (1975). The term has also been used by others to apply to allocation decisions made within a larger group or network of firms (such as the Japanese *keiretsu*, see infra notes 65–76 and accompanying text) or between a firm and its principal shareholder and creditor. See John Cable, Capital Market Information and Industrial Performance: The Role of West German Banks, 95 Econ. J. 118 (1985). This Article uses the term in that latter sense to distinguish an "internal capital market" from an "external market" in which the firm has access to many active suppliers of capital.

38. "Indexed" investing refers to a passive investment strategy whereby an investor holds a portfolio of securities that serves as a proxy for the market as a whole (such as the Standard & Poor's 500). Such investors seek not to beat the market, but to match it. See infra notes 236–244 and accompanying text.

moves from internal capital market economies, such as Japan and Germany, to the purest example of an external market economy, Great Britain. Midway along this continuum are Sweden and Canada. Despite active stock markets in these nations, the rise of institutional ownership has produced defensive responses by corporate managements that effectively prevent the union of liquidity and control. Necessarily, this Part's treatment of each country is incomplete and, in some respects, cursory. The intent, however, is (1) to contrast the essentially internal capital markets that characterize Germany and Japan with the external capital market in the United States, and (2) to note the institutions and practices that have developed in those other countries that have external capital markets in order to mediate conflicts between institutional investors and corporate managements.

A. *The United States*

As a result of Columbia University's Institutional Investor Project,[39] reliable statistical data on institutional ownership is now available. This data demonstrates that the percentage of equity in United States corporations held by institutional investors has skyrocketed, particularly during the last decade.[40] In 1950, institutional investors owned only 8% of the equity in United States corporations. By 1980, this level had risen to 33%, and by 1988, it had reached 45%.[41] Institutional ownership is disproportionately heavy at the upper end of corporate America. Among the top one hundred American corporations in terms of stock market value, the level of institutional ownership is now at 53%.[42] Among some of the largest and best-known corporations, the percentage of institutional ownership nearly swallows the market, for example: General Motors Corp. (82%), Mobil Corp. (74%), Citicorp (70%), Amoco (86%), and Eli Lilly & Co. (71%).[43]

39. The Institutional Investor Project is under the auspices of the Center for Law and Economic Studies at the Columbia University School of Law.

40. See Carolyn Kay Brancato & Patrick A. Gaughan, The Growth of Institutional Investors in U.S. Capital Markets (Nov. 1988). This study has been partially updated as of 1990. See Carolyn Kay Brancato, The Pivotal Role of Institutional Investors in Capital Markets, *in* Institutional Investing: The Challenges and Responsibilities of the 21st Century 3, 17–19 (Arnold W. Sametz ed., 1991) [hereinafter Brancato, Pivotal Role of Institutional Investors]. As Professor Black has pointed out, the definition of institution used in the Brancato study is incomplete, because it excludes investment banks, bank holding companies, and certain trustees. See Black, supra note 12, at 567 n.168. Thus, institutional ownership is probably even slightly higher than these numbers reveal.

41. See William Taylor, Can Big Owners Make a Big Difference?, Harv. Bus. Rev., Sept.–Oct. 1990, at 70 (citing Brancato data).

42. See Carolyn Kay Brancato, The Momentum of the Big Investor, Directors & Boards, Winter 1990, at 38 [hereinafter Brancato, Big Investor]; Brancato, Pivotal Role of Institutional Investors, supra note 40, at 21. Perhaps more importantly, 29.6% of the companies in this top 1000 had institutional ownership levels above 60%. Id.

43. Brancato, Big Investor, supra note 42, at 39 (table listing percentage of institutional ownership of top fifty U.S. corporations). An earlier study by Professor Conard

The level of institutional ownership looks even greater from the perspective of the institutions themselves. As my colleague Professor Bernard Black has calculated, the thirteen largest institutions each held, on average, over 1% of the United States stock market at the end of 1989 and together the top fifty institutions owned 27%.[44] Many institutions now own 2–3% of the stock of a single company, he reports, and some hold over 5%. Calculating the data a different way, another colleague, Professor Louis Lowenstein, has examined the Form 13F filings made by institutional investors with the SEC and found that for the average corporation listed in the Standard & Poor's 500, "it takes just twenty institutional holders to account for 34% of the outstanding stock."[45] On this basis, it is entirely possible that twenty or fewer institutions could hold de facto control of a major industrial corporation without any individual institution acquiring so large a block as necessarily to impair its liquidity. Viewed in these terms, it may appear that the union of control and liquidity has already occurred.

Yet if one looks only at the size of institutional holdings, one may commit the classic mistake of confusing an ox for a bull. Although public pension funds are "bulls" who often engage in aggressive, outspoken criticism of corporate management, they constitute only a modest minority of institutional investors.[46] Most other institutional investors seem closer to "oxen," because they have shown little willingness to oppose corporate managements or even to support dissidents in proxy

shows institutional ownership levels in publicly traded securities reaching up to 90%. Thirty companies in a sample of 100 randomly chosen exchange-listed firms had institutional ownership levels over 60%, and sixty had levels over 40%. See Alfred F. Conard, Beyond Managerialism: Investor Capitalism?, 22 U. Mich. J.L. Ref. 117, 132 (1989).

44. Professor Black's calculations match institutional ownership against the Wilshire 5000 Index. See The Institutional Investor 300: Ranking America's Top Money Managers, Institutional Investor, July 1990, at 137, 173. The Wilshire 5000 Index was at $3.42 trillion as of December 31, 1989. See Black, supra note 12, at 567–68 & n.170.

45. See Louis Lowenstein, Sense and Nonsense in Corporate Finance (forthcoming 1991) (manuscript at ch. 11, p. 3, on file with the Columbia Law Review). In truth, this calculation might understate the level of institutional ownership because it considers only institutional investors and only those required to file Form 13F. Thus excluded are individual owners and smaller institutions. Under Rule 13f-1, 17 C.F.R. § 240.13f-1 (1991), "institutional investment managers" having investment discretion over at least $100 million in certain defined equity securities must file Form 13F quarterly.

46. By some estimates, pension funds now hold as much as 40% of all equities. See Jay O. Light, The Privatization of Equity, Harv. Bus. Rev. Sept.–Oct. 1989, at 62–63. However, of the total assets controlled by pension funds, it is generally estimated that corporate pension funds control one half; public pension funds, one third; and the balance is held by union pension funds and funds of non-profit entities. See Letter from Richard Koppes, General Counsel, CalPERS, to Linda C. Quinn, Director, Division of Corporation Finance, Securities and Exchange Commission 3 (Nov. 3, 1989) (on file with the Columbia Law Review) [hereinafter, CalPERS Letter]. CalPERS is an abbreviation for the California Public Employees' Retirement System. See also, America's Shareholders Break into the Boardroom, The Economist, Apr. 29, 1989, at 75 (public pension funds control $600 million of the $2 trillion in assets controlled by all pension funds).

contests.[47] Indeed, some evidence suggests that a high level of institutional ownership correlates with greater managerial success in proxy contests.[48] Even the most enthusiastic proponents of institutional shareholder activism recognize that institutional investors historically have not opposed corporate management, but usually have supported them against insurgents.[49] Despite recurrent press stories about the activism of institutional investors,[50] most antitakeover amendments still pass,[51] and surveys show that institutions support management proposals between 59% and 74% of the time.[52] What is clearest, however, is that, within the United States, different institutions behave differently: public pension funds and, to a lesser degree, mutual funds and endowments appear "pressure resistant" and frequently vote against management, but banks and insurance companies seldom are willing to oppose management.[53] The reasons for these differences are assessed later,[54] but even those institutions that are described as the most "pressure resistant" appear eager to project themselves as "friendly" long-term investors.[55] The bottom line to date then is that while some institutions have become more assertive in the limited context of takeover defensive tactics, their activism has not spread beyond this special arena nor led them to seek participation in corporate governance generally.[56]

47. Recently, there has even been a decline in proxy fights for corporate control. From 41 contests in 1989, the number fell to 35 in 1990, and only 12 were under way by mid-March 1991. See Leslie Wayne, Behind the Drop in Proxy Fights, N.Y. Times, Mar. 19, 1991, at D10. See also With M&A in the Doldrums, Proxy Fights Plummet, Corp. Control Alert, May 1991, at 1 (noting 15 proxy contests under way at mid-year).

48. See John Pound, Proxy Contests and the Efficiency of Shareholder Oversight, 20 J. Fin. Econ. 237, 256–60 (1988). Pound's study relies on data from the early 1980s, which may be out of date. See Black, supra note 12, at 606.

49. See Gilson & Kraakman, supra note 13, at 892–93 ("Not only have institutional investors failed to oppose management's candidates for the board with their own nominees, but many institutions have even voted with management in proxy fights, including the Texaco and Lockheed contests. . . .").

50. See supra note 30.

51. See Jeffrey W. Biersach, Voting by Institutional Investors on Corporate Governance Issues in the 1990 Proxy Season 13 (IRRC). Admittedly, the margin by which they pass is slim, and managements do not propose amendments they think likely to fail.

52. See Karen Van Nuys, Managerial Incentives and Shareholder Approval: Evidence from the 1988 Proxy Season 5–8 (U. Rochester Working Paper 1990) (on file with the Columbia Law Review).

53. See James A. Brickley, et al., Ownership Structure and Voting on Antitakeover Amendments, 20 J. Fin. Econ. 267, 276–79 (1988); Biersach, supra note 51, at 3, 10.

54. See infra notes 180–191 and accompanying text.

55. For such an evaluation of the Fidelity group of mutual funds, see Henriques, supra note 31, at 10.

56. For example, only in extremely rare occasions have institutional investors sought to elect representatives to corporate boards. See id. at 10 (discussing general reluctance of Fidelity group to have representation on corporate boards). Indeed, in one recent case in which an executive of a major institutional investor agreed to serve as an insurgent group's nominee for election to the USX board, his employer appears to

B. *Japan*

To understand the relationship between financial institutions and industrial corporations in Japan, some history is necessary. During the early decades of the twentieth century, the *zaibatsu*—family-owned, bank-centered holding companies—expanded through both vertical integration and diversifying acquisitions. These institutions have been described as "the world's first multinational conglomerates."[57] By the eve of World War II, they held most corporate equity and debt in Japan. During the occupation of Japan, the American authorities liquidated the *zaibatsu*, expecting that American-style public corporations would evolve in their absence.[58] As part of this effort to decentralize economic power, a Japanese equivalent of the Glass-Steagall Act, which separates commercial and investment banking in the United States,[59] was imposed on Japan. Under section 65 of Japan's Securities and Exchange Act of 1948,[60] a Japanese bank may not engage in investment banking, and under section 11 of Japan's Anti-Monopoly Act,[61] a Japanese bank may not own more than five percent of the stock of any domestic corporation.[62] Ironically, these restrictions were even more clearly intended to prevent the concentration of economic power than

---

have been angered. See Quirk's Role in Icahn Proxy Fight Lands them in Hot Water With Prim Board, Vol. XV Money Mgmt. Letter (No. 25) Dec. 10, 1990 at 1.

CalPERS is probably the leading exception to this generalization. As of late 1989, it reported that it had sponsored 28 shareholder proposals, and it has sought to reform the proxy rules. See Letter from Dale M. Hanson, Chief Executive Officer of CalPERS to Linda C. Quinn, Director, Division of Corporation Finance, Securities and Exchange Commission 1 (Nov. 3, 1989) (on file with the Columbia Law Review) [hereinafter CalPERS Letters]. Yet, even CalPERS has not sought to fund or sponsor proxy contests for the election of directors.

57. Aron Viner, Inside Japanese Financial Markets 1 (1988). For a fuller discussion of the *zaibatsu*, see Rodney Clark, The Japanese Company 41–44 (1979).

58. During the post-World War II occupation of Japan, the American authorities required that the equity in the constituent members of the *zaibatsu* conglomerates be sold to Japanese individuals. As a result, on the reopening of the Japanese stock markets in the late 1940s, individuals held more than 69% of the outstanding shares in Japanese corporations. Viner, supra note 57, at 55.

59. The Glass-Steagall Act, 48 Stat. 184 (1933), codified at 12 U.S.C. §§ 24, 78, 377, 378 (1988), consists of four sections of the Banking Act of 1933 (§§ 16, 20, 21, and 32). Under § 21, 12 U.S.C. § 378, individuals and organizations engaged in investment banking may not receive deposits. Correspondingly, § 16, 12 U.S.C. § 24, bars a bank that is a member of the Federal Reserve System from dealing in or underwriting securities.

60. *Shoken torihikiho* (Securities Exchange Act), § 65, Law No. 25 of 1948.

61. *Shiteki dokusen no kinshi oyobi kosei torihiki no kakuho ni kansuru horitsu* (An act regarding the prohibition of private monopolies and the maintenance of fair trade), § 11(a), Law No. 54 of 1947 [hereinafter Anti-Monopoly Act].

62. Originally, the Anti-Monopoly Act placed the maximum level at 10%, but this was reduced to 5% in 1977. Banks were given until December, 1987, to divest excess holdings. See J. Mark Ramseyer, Legal Rules in Repeated Deals: Banking in the Shadow of Defection in Japan, 20 J. Legal Stud. 91, 99 n.21 (1991). I am grateful for the assistance of Professor Haruhiko Katagi of Hiroshima University for explaining the Japa-

were the restrictions imposed on American banking institutions, which today prevent an American bank holding company from owning more than five percent of the voting stock of any nonbanking company.[63]

Yet, in Japan, these restrictions failed. Because the American occupational authorities underestimated the power and centrality of the banks within the *zaibatsu* confederations, they did not insist on the liquidation of these institutions, and this omission eventually resulted in the reemergence of a looser regrouping of the former *zaibatsu* interests.[64] These successor coalitions became known as "*keiretsu*."[65] The internal structure of the *keiretsu* varies with the industry or the relationship upon which the coalition is based, but typically each consists of a diversified confederation of companies clustered around a "main bank" that provides loans to the members of the group as their chief source of financing. Although the main bank in the *keiretsu* is usually both a major shareholder and the principal creditor of the members of its constellation of companies,[66] its position is clearly distinguishable from that of the parent company in a large American conglomerate, because the main bank—the putative "parent" in the *keiretsu*—is in turn owned by its subsidiaries and affiliates. It is probably more accurate to think of the *keiretsu* as a miniature common market in which each member generally relies on the others as its principal trading partners, preferring them to external sources as suppliers, customers, and creditors.

The legal force knitting together this structure is a system of inter-

---

nese law to me. Under § 11, an insurance company may own up to 10% of a domestic Japanese corporation.

63. See Bank Holding Company Act of 1956, §§ 4(c)(6)–(7), 12 U.S.C. §§ 1843(c)(6)–(7) (1988). Indeed, under this statute, bank holding companies have been authorized to own up to 25% of the nonvoting stock of a nonbanking corporation. See Pauline B. Heller, Federal Bank Holding Company Law § 4.03(2)(a), at 4–60.9 (1989).

64. Viner, supra note 57, at 55–56.

65. There are today six major *keiretsu* groups in Japan. Three of these (Mitsui, Mitsubishi, and Sumitomo) are descended from former *zaibatsu*, while the other three are newer groups that have formed around major banks (Fuyo-Fuji, Dai-Ichi Kangyo, and Sanwa). The number of firms within a group varies widely, from the Sumitomo group's 16 to the Dai-Ichi Kangyo group's 57. See William G. Ouchi, The M-Form Society, app. at 290–91 (1984). The word "*keiretsu*" is derived from the words "*kei*" meaning "faction or group" and "*retsu*" meaning "arranged in order." See Viner, supra note 57, at 2. For a more detailed examination of the internal structure of a *keiretsu*, see Hiroshi Okumura, Interfirm Relations in an Enterprise Group: The Case of Mitsubishi *in* Kazuo Sato & Yasuo Hoshino, The Anatomy of Japanese Business, 166–75 (1984) (describing relations among 120 "principal allied companies" and over 300 subsidiaries of Mitsubishi group).

66. A recent study reports that, on average, a Japanese company's largest debtholder owned 6.2% of the company's equity; that the five largest debtholders owned 18.2% of the equity; and that out of 133 companies surveyed, the largest debtholder was the largest shareholder in 57 cases or was a member of the same *keiretsu* as the largest shareholder in an additional 67 cases. See Stephen D. Prowse, Institutional Investment Patterns and Corporate Financial Behavior in the United States and Japan, 27 J. Fin. Econ. 43, 46–47 (1990).

locking cross-ownership under which each constituent company owns from 0.5 to 3% of the equity in each other member in the *keiretsu*, thereby effectively locking control within the group.[67] Originally, these reciprocal stock acquisitions were financed through loans provided by the main bank in the combine, and each member in the *keiretsu* understands that it may not dispose of the shares it owns in other members of the group.[68] It is estimated that between 65% and 70% of the stock in all listed companies on the Tokyo Stock Exchange is now held in such interlocked cross-ownership.[69] Indeed, because the stock held by the members of the *keiretsu* is illiquid, the float on many Japanese stocks is extremely thin and is held almost exclusively by individual investors.[70] Over the years, the percentage of individual share ownership of all listed companies on Japanese stock exchanges has declined steadily, from 70% during the early days of the occupation to 22% today.[71]

In terms of this Article's focus on the trade-off between liquidity and control, the Japanese system seems based on an implicit understanding that liquidity is unavailable to those who participate in control. That is, individual investors and certain other non-controlling institutional investors do enjoy reasonable liquidity (albeit in a volatile market), but they have no hope of acquiring control or exercising significant influence over management.

Still, this explanation leaves the role of the main bank in the *keiretsu* ambiguous. Clearly, its role is pivotal, but who is it allied with? Several scenarios are plausible. First, the main bank could be providing consulting and monitoring services that benefit the minority shareholders and for which the latter reward the main bank by granting it preference in servicing the corporations' financial needs (possibly at above market interest rates or fees). Such a deal might well be in the minority shareholders' interests, depending on how generous the above market terms were, because it would reduce agency costs at the corporate manage-

67. Id. at 56. A 1983 study found that the average shareholding of any single group member in other group members is down to 1.78% of each company's outstanding stock, with each company holding stock in an average of half of all the other companies in the group. See Ouchi, supra note 65, at 291.

68. Viner, supra note 57, at 56. Of course, explicit agreements not to resell are unnecessary. A member of a *keiretsu* that sold stock in its fellow members could both lose its principal trading partners and customers and alienate a group holding the majority of its stock. Thus, its management would become vulnerable to ouster.

69. Viner estimates that 65% of the stock is held by other *keiretsu* members. Id. at 56. A more recent estimate is 70%. See Steven Barber, A Close Circle of Friends, Institutional Investor, Feb. 1991, at 35 (citing Robert Zielinski & Nigel Holloway, Unequal Equities: Power and Risk in Japan's Stock Market (1990)).

70. Again, estimates vary. Viner estimates that "only an average 30 percent of the total float of shares in listed companies is traded." Viner, supra note 57, at 328. A more recent estimate is 22%. See Barber, supra note 69, at 35. This may help explain the high volatility that has long characterized the Japanese stock market.

71. See Barber, supra note 69, at 35. For an earlier estimate that it had fallen to 25% as of 1985, see Viner, supra note 57, at 100–01.

ment level. A second possibility is that the main bank could ally itself less with minority shareholders than with the incumbent management and receive above-market fees and interest for protecting them. A third interpretation postulates still another quid pro quo: the main bank lends to the corporate borrower at an attractive rate in return for the latter's agreement to support the bank's share price by purchasing the bank's securities in the secondary market.[72] From this perspective, the main bank is less a financial monitor than a co-conspirator in stock manipulation. Still, whatever the scenario offered, only an implicit contract exists between the participants, and the main bank may on occasion defect and switch sides. Thus, whatever coalitions exist may to a degree be unstable.

Interestingly, although Japanese scholars have not framed the question of the main bank's role in terms this blunt, they have recognized the possibility that the main bank protects managerial interests more than shareholder interests. For example, one of the most popular explanations within Japan for the development of the *keiretsu* form of organization was that it protected wage differentials under which employees of *keiretsu* member firms received substantially higher wages than employees of smaller, independent firms.[73] In a stockholder-controlled firm, employees presumably would be less able to escape the market's disciplinary effect on their wage rates. To the extent that this explanation of above market wages is valid, the main bank seems less an efficient monitor for its fellow shareholders than an ally of the incumbent management.[74]

Another well-known theory asserts that the main bank provides a substitute for the bankruptcy and corporate reorganization procedures that have developed in the United States to reduce bankruptcy losses.[75]

---

72. See Marshall Auerback, Japan Inc.'s Days Are Numbered, Wall St. J., Sept. 3, 1991 at A18. By the of 1989, the free float in most Japanese bank stocks had fallen to as low as 8% of the total market capitalization, thus permitting price-earnings ratios to soar to "stratospheric multiples of 70, 80 or even 160." Id. Because of special accounting rules, a high stock price enabled Japanese banks to engage in riskier lending activities, in which non-Japanese banks could not engage. With the 1989 stock market crash in Japan (in which the Nikkei Stock Averages fell a total of 42%), Japanese corporate borrowers found bank credit more difficult to obtain and in return, with less liquid funds, were less able to support the price of their main banks. Auerback suggests that the gradual unwinding of this reciprocal agreement "adds up to a death knell for Japan's cross-shareholding structure." Id. At a minimum, it suggests that a large equity stakeholder need not necessarily be an efficient financial monitor, but may have other incentives.

73. See Okumura, supra note 65, at 175–76. Another theory was that it permitted the enterprise to engage in riskier activities. Id. at 176.

74. It can be argued that the *keiretsu* members pay above-market wages to induce their employees to invest in firm-specific human capital. Yet this argument seems implausible in the Japanese context, where full-time employees typically have life tenure. That is, employers both inside and outside the *keiretsu* have the same incentive to induce lifetime employees to invest in the acquisition of firm-specific human capital.

75. Okumura, supra note 65, at 177 ("Bankruptcy and the Corporation Reorganiza-

Assume that the main bank in the *keiretsu* is committed to bailing out any failing member, and, in return, is permitted to charge an above market interest rate on its loans to member firms. Who benefits most from such an arrangement? In economic terms, such a relationship is best described as an "implicit insurance contract."[76] In the words of one expert, "The main-bank/corporate-borrower relation can be viewed in terms of the firm paying insurance premiums to the bank in normal times in the expectation of receiving assistance in times of corporate downturn."[77] Yet would rational shareholders wish to pay such a premium to obtain this insurance? The answer is probably no, because shareholders can diversify to protect themselves from losses and so would not want expensive insurance purchased from banks at the price of above-market interest rates.[78] The logical answer, then, is that this implicit insurance contract chiefly benefits the management of the borrower and the main bank, at the other shareholders' expense.

For some, this managerialist theory is implausible. They instead view the *keiretsu* as a continuation of a traditional Japanese form of organization, one that reflects Japan's social character with its much-noted emphasis on cooperation and a desire for stability. But of all possible theories about the *keiretsu*, this is the most tenuous. The surprising fact—to Westerners—is that Japanese firms regularly switch their main banks and smaller Japanese firms even switch their affiliations between *keiretsu* groups.[79] So much for the picture of unchanging stability. As in the West, corporations quickly gravitate to the cheapest supplier of capital and seek to limit their dependence on any one firm.

How effective is the *keiretsu* as a monitoring system? In general, bank monitoring in Japan appears to be relatively slack and focused largely on the danger of insolvency or sustained unprofitability. Such a finding is consistent with the view that the *keiretsu* serves the interests of management more than shareholders. Interestingly, contemporary accounts stress that the stronger, more successful Japanese corporations have largely escaped bank control.[80] Professor Ramseyer notes that once the Euromarket developed as an alternative source of credit, "Jap-

tion Law are, in fact, being used by big enterprises as weapons for enterprise affiliation.").

76. See Ramseyer, supra note 62, at 111.

77. Id. at 111–12 (quoting Australian economist and Japanese scholar Paul Sheard, Main Banks and Internal Capital Markets in Japan, 157 Shoken Keizai 255 (1986)).

78. This is Professor Ramseyer's conclusion also. See id. at 112 n.66.

79. Ramseyer notes that over a five year period, 15% of a sample of the firms listed on the Tokyo Stock Exchange switched their main bank affiliation, and over a ten year period, as many as 33% may have. Id. at 98 n.18. Moreover, in the electric machinery industry, one-fifth of the subcontractors changed their affiliation with their general contractor each year. Id.

80. See James C. Abegglen & George Stalk, Jr., Kaisha, The Japanese Corporation 189 (1985) ("The conclusion is that dependence on a bank is no more to the liking of Japanese management than management in other countries, and for leading Japanese companies no longer a significant issue."). Strong firms can spread their borrowings

anese firms deserted the banks in droves."[81] Absent a crisis, direct involvement by the main bank in the management of a member of the *keiretsu* is rare today. Only when a member firm in the *keiretsu* becomes financially distressed or otherwise embarrasses its colleagues does the main bank step in and reorganize the firm. In such a case, the main bank typically will insert its own executives into positions of control and even temporarily assume a direct management role in order to avert bankruptcy.[82]

In sharp contrast to American institutional investors, the Japanese main bank seems relatively unconcerned about maximizing the current share value of the members of its *keiretsu*. Japanese corporations historically have paid dividends equal only to approximately ten percent of the par value of their stock,[83] and dividend yields as a percentage of the market value of shares are much lower, usually between one and two percent of market value.[84] These figures would be extraordinarily low for most U.S. corporations. More importantly, they may suggest that Japanese firms are pursuing an inefficient empire-building policy that hoards "free cash flow" that might be more efficiently paid out to shareholders.[85] Indeed, during the 1980s, as Japanese corporations escaped their dependence on their main banks, their debt/equity ratios fell significantly.[86] Such a pattern in the United States might attract a

between several banks "to ensure that no one bank will exert undue influence on the corporation." Id. at 166 (discussing Hitachi).

81. Ramseyer, supra note 62, at 98. Professor Ramseyer also finds that Japanese firms have recently developed multiple banking relationships to reduce their former dependence on their main bank. See id. at 107–08.

82. See Abegglen & Stalk, supra note 80, at 166–67. In a recent example, the Sumitomo Bank Ltd. sent in its own managers to rescue Itoman & Co., "a heavily indebted trading company closely affiliated with the bank," which was on the brink of bankruptcy. See Masayoshi Kanabayashi & Marcus W. Brauchli, Sumitomo to Send Managers to Help Troubled Itoman, Wall St. J., Nov. 19, 1990, at A11. Eventually, Sumitomo, which held less than 5% of Itoman, forced the ouster of the latter's president, a former Sumitomo employee whom the bank had lent to Itoman to oversee its rehabilitation after a prior financial crisis. See James Sterngold, Ouster of Realty Leader Jolts Corporate Japan, N.Y. Times, Jan. 26, 1991, at 32.

83. See Abegglen & Stalk, supra note 80, at 169.

84. Id. at 184.

85. "Free cash flow" basically refers to income after debt service and the acceptance of investment projects having a positive net present value (using the firm's cost of capital as the discount rate). See Michael C. Jensen, Agency Costs of Free Cash-Flow, Corporate Finance, and Takeovers, 76 Am. Econ. Rev. 323 (1986). When a firm undertakes an investment project that has a negative net present value (that is, an expected rate of return below its cost of capital), it will reduce the market price of its shares. In short, proceeds for which the firm lacks an attractive investment use should be paid out to shareholders as dividends, but a firm that seeks to maximize growth, rather than shareholder value, will hoard such cash flow. Professor Jensen argues that the excessive retention of free cash flow was a major cause of the takeover and LBO waves in the United States of the 1980s. See id. at 328–29.

86. See Ramseyer, supra note 62, at 97 n.16 (ratio of new capital borrowed from financial intermediaries fell from 74.3% in 1960s to 60.4% in 1980s).

hostile takeover (at least until recently), because unused borrowing capacity can fund shareholder distributions or can finance a takeover. But hostile raids are virtually unknown in Japan, where, after all, the majority of the stock is locked up in friendly hands. Nonetheless, dissatisfaction among Japanese institutional investors with low dividend yields has recently become open and public, as Japanese insurance companies in particular have criticized corporations with low dividend payouts.[87]

In this light, the Japanese model of financial monitoring is less clearly a more efficient organizational form and may represent a mechanism for managerial entrenchment. The foregoing description suggests an industrial structure in which agency costs are high, as above-market wages are prevalent and substantial insurance payments are made to protect against an insolvency risk that concerns managers more than investors. Indeed, the very structure of the *keiretsu* seems designed to ensure weak monitoring. Because the main bank holds an ownership level that is below five percent by definition, it must secure the consent of its fellow *keiretsu* members before it can take disciplinary action or remove senior management. Yet these other members share a common interest in restricting main bank interventions in the internal affairs of each member to occasions in which the demonstrated delinquency of a member firm threatens the *keiretsu* as a whole.

The evidence on the *keiretsu*, however, is not clear-cut. Rational economic motives can also explain why the main bank that dominates the *keiretsu* tolerates managerial slack in its member firms. From an efficiency-oriented perspective, one can hypothesize that the deliberate use of minority public ownership permits some capital market discipline. The advantage of minority ownership is that the members of the *keiretsu* are not all lumped together on an aggregate basis. Instead, if one firm has better prospects or a superior track record, the market can price its publicly traded shares at a premium. Such market signaling may affect the allocation of capital within the group or indicate the need for outside intervention. Alternatively, Professor Masahiko Aoki, a noted Japanese economist, has argued that the relatively weak control exercised by banks over industrial corporations in Japan is efficient because it complements the internal organizational character of the Japanese firm.[88] One hard fact supports either theory: At least prior to Japan's 1989 stock market decline, Japanese shareholders enjoyed a

87. See Chiharu Okajima & John Taylor, Tokyo Stock Slide Triggers Shareholder Rebellion, IRRC Global Shareholder, Autumn 1990, at 5. The veiled threat made by some of these insurance companies was that unless payouts increased they might sell their holdings in the lowest paying firms. Such concentrated selling might collapse the firm's stock price. Insurance companies appear to be the one institution in the Japanese markets that parallels an American institutional investor.

88. See Masahiko Aoki, Toward an Economic Model of the Japanese Firm, 28 J. Econ. Lit. 1, 14–18 (1990).

very high annual after-tax market rate of return.[89] Nonetheless, one may well ask whether the *keiretsu* system was responsible for this rate of return or, rather, whether the rate of return was responsible for shareholder tolerance for the *keiretsu* system. In any event, the irony is that if the Japanese *keiretsu* system is efficient, it seems to work well only within its special context and, according to Aoki, largely because it relies on a relatively passive and deferential style of monitoring.

Still, even if accepted, these arguments do not necessarily imply that the main bank is an efficient corporate monitor. Because the bank's position as a debtholder may outweigh its position as an equity holder, which cannot exceed five percent, it may be risk averse and want cash hoarded within the firm paid out as dividends. Or, it may use its controlling position to exact above-market interest rates on the loans it makes to member firms in its *keiretsu*,[90] and may tolerate a managerial preference for empire-building in return. Clearly, this hypothesis suggests not optimal monitoring but a conflict between the interests of the main bank and the minority shareholders in the firm. For this Article's purposes, the basic point is that a substantial investor's willingness to incur significant monitoring expenses does not necessarily imply that it will act in the interest of the minority shareholders. Rather, it may behave opportunistically, such as by charging above-market interest rates. In short, a system that relies on institutional investors as monitors could simply substitute a new set of agency cost problems for the traditional problem of managerial opportunism.[91]

Some observers believe that the *keiretsu* mode of organization is gradually disappearing in Japan. They report that few of the most successful Japanese multinational corporations over the last several decades have been members of traditional *keiretsu*.[92] More importantly,

---

89. See id. at 15 (after-tax annual market rate of return from 1963 to 1986 was 11.7%). Recent developments, however, raise the possibility that this extraordinarily high rate of return may have been partially the product of systematic stock market manipulation. Twenty-one Japanese securities firms have admitted paying at least $1.3 billion to cover trading losses of major clients. See James Sterngold, Regulation, Japan Style, N.Y. Times, Sept. 9, 1991, at D1, D2. Such a de facto investor insurance system could easily result in stock prices and price-earning ratios that are not sustainable over the long term. For other evidence of manipulation, see Auerback, supra note 72.

90. Such a possibility has also been noted by Professor Aoki. See Masahiko Aoki, Shareholders' Non-Unanimity on Investment Financing: Banks vs. Individual Investors, *in* The Economic Analysis of the Japanese Firm 193 (Masahiko Aoki ed., 1984).

91. Put simply, while a large shareholder can perform effective monitoring that benefits all shareholders, there is no logical reason for it to perform such a service gratuitously. If it can demand a side payment (such as above-market interest rates or an obligation on the borrower's part to support the bank's stock price, see supra note 72 and accompanying text) in which the minority does not share, in return for tolerating some slack, it has little reason to decline such an exchange. The Japanese experience is at least consistent with such a story.

92. See Abegglen & Stalk, supra note 80, at 189–90 (listing among others, Toyota, Hino, and Suzuki in vehicles; Hitachi, Sharp, Sanyo, Matsushita, and Sony in electronics; Fuji, Canon, Ricoh, and Seiko in cameras and films as among those recently emergent

these observers note that the period of tightest control of Japanese corporations by financial institutions was during the 1950s and 1960s when Japan was still recovering from World War II and capital was scarce.[93] By the mid-1980s, they note, the roles had reversed:

> With greatly increased liquidity in the Japanese economy, and with stronger company balance sheets, this system has changed. Banks must now solicit attractive borrowers, and find themselves providing funds to the weaker companies, in which their powers remain considerable. The most successful of Japan's companies . . . are hardly under bank control. The leading companies have little debt, and they can choose their bank sources.[94]

In short, the control of financial institutions is strong in times of capital scarcity, but weak otherwise. As discussed later, the same characterization can be applied to the relationship between Germany's "universal banks" and its industrial corporations. The rise of an international capital market may spell the end for financial monitors in internal capital markets.[95]

C. *Germany*

Even more than in Japan, German corporations depend upon their banking system for access to all forms of external finance.[96] The German stock markets are used by relatively few German corporations (402 as of 1988), and even these firms obtain only a small proportion of their capital by issuing exchange-listed securities.[97] Of the German firms that do trade in the public market, fewer than one hundred lack a con-

---

firms that were not group members or bank dependent). Some of these firms have, however, begun to form their own groups that mimic the *keiretsu*. Id. For a similar view that the *keiretsu* system is breaking down (but for different reasons), see Auerback, supra note 72.

93. Abegglen & Stalk, supra note 80, at 188–89.

94. Id. at 189.

95. See infra notes 108–116 and accompanying text.

96. See John Cable, Capital Market Information and Industrial Performance: The Role of West German Banks, 95 Econ. J. 118, 119 (1985). Bank borrowing is the largest single external source of capital (20% of total enterprise funds), and banks also handle most new issues of marketable securities, placing substantial proportions of them with their customers. See id.

97. A 1989 study conducted by Coopers & Lybrand for the British Department of Trade and Industry provides the best comparative data on the size of the European stock markets and the role of institutional investors in them. It found: "Germany's stock markets have never been a significant factor in the equity raising process as companies have traditionally relied upon long term loans from their primary banks as the major source of finance." See 2 Department of Trade and Industry, Barriers To Takeovers in The European Community 16 (1989) [hereinafter, Coopers & Lybrand Report]. Whereas the U.K. had 1804 publicly traded domestic corporations listed on its stock exchanges as of the end of 1988, Germany had only 402. 2 id. at 26. Another revealing statistic is that the total capitalization of the London Stock Market in 1988 was 587.6 billion (in European Currency Units), as compared to 205.8 billion for Germany, 190.4

trolling shareholder or shareholder group.[98] In short, investors who pursue liquidity have little chance at participating in control.

Unlike the Japanese banks, German banks are merchant banks that handle both commercial banking and securities underwriting. Yet, bank domination of German industrial corporations does not result from outright ownership, because German banks in fact own under 5% of the stock of the largest one hundred German corporations.[99] Rather, control is effectively held by the major German banks because they provide the country's stockbrokerage services, and shares in German corporations are generally deposited by their owners with the banks, which can vote the shares on behalf of their owners.[100] As a practical matter, the German proxy voting system produces a functional analogue to the Japanese *keiretsu*. Because of it, German banks exercise nearly 34% of the total voting power in the top one hundred German corporations and over 50% of the total voting power in the ten largest companies.[101] Once again, we encounter a puzzle: despite the absence of legal restrictions, German banks own no more stock on a percentage basis than do Japanese banks—or than U.S. bank holding companies

billion for France, and 115.6 billion for Italy. 1 id. at 9. Thus, the U.K. market capitalization exceeds the total of the next three largest markets.

Institutional investors other than banks appear to play a relatively insignificant role in corporate finance in Germany, and fund managers are particularly unimportant. The Coopers & Lybrand Report sets forth the following breakdown of funds under discretionary management as of 1986: U.K. (580 billion pounds); France (148 billion pounds); the Netherlands (147 billion pounds); West Germany (142 billion pounds). 1 id. at 11.

98. See Hopt, supra note 27, at 4. The Coopers & Lybrand Report estimates that the combined holdings of the two largest classes of institutional investors in Germany (banks and insurance companies) accounted for 21% of the ownership of publicly held German corporations as of the end of 1988. 2 Coopers & Lybrand Report, supra note 97, at 26. No other class of institutional investor had significant holdings. Hence the overall level of institutional ownership of German corporations is around half that in the United States.

99. Cable, supra note 96, at 120. No legal restriction requires German banks to hold ownership to this level. Recently, this percentage has fallen to around 3.2% in the case of exchange listed firms. See infra note 112 and accompanying text.

Interestingly, German banks do not appear to provide much new equity finance for their corporate clients. The Coopers & Lybrand Report finds that in 1987 financial institutions across Europe provided new equity finance according to the following breakdown: France ($15 billion); Italy ($2.8 billion); the Netherlands ($0.7 billion); United Kingdom ($21.6 billion); West Germany ($5.5 billion). 1 Coopers & Lybrand Report, supra note 97, at 13. In short, British banks (at least in 1987) provided nearly four times as much equity finance as did their much larger German rivals. Instead, German banks appear to provide primarily debt finance to their clients. Possibly, this is a consequence of the limited liquidity available to banks in the German economy or of the desire of those holding control not to dilute their control position.

100. See 2 Coopers & Lybrand Report, supra note 97, at 13–14.

101. See Cable, supra note 96, at 120. Based on this voting power, German banks hold 9.8% (through their officers and agents) of the total seats on the supervisory boards of the one hundred largest German companies. Id. at 119.

are permitted to own.[102]

Bank supervision of corporate managements in Germany has been described as close and intensive. One observer reports that:

> Through the exercise of voting rights the big banks greatly influence hirings and firings in West German corporations' executive bodies, the supervisory boards; as well as on managing boards. They have a voice in all fundamental business decisions.[103]

This greater interest in "voice" seems easily explainable in terms of this Article's framework of analysis: because German banks lack liquidity, as a result of the relatively undeveloped state of the German stock markets, they are compelled to exercise "voice." Commentators characterize the relationships between the three major German banks and their corporate clientele as "very close and stable" and note that the problem of "[s]hort-termism" does not arise.[104]

How effective is the German system of monitoring? The available empirical evidence indeed suggests that it does benefit minority shareholders. One recent statistical study of the largest German corporations finds a "significant, positive relationship between the degree of bank involvement in leading industrial companies and their financial performance."[105] Regression analysis suggests that these results are not explainable simply in terms of the market power or credit advantages that these corporations obtain from their banking associations.[106] Rather, the explanation that works best to explain the German data is that bank monitoring reduces agency and information costs applicable to these corporations and results in their exhibiting "greater conformity to cost-minimising, profit-oriented goals."[107]

Still, even if the German system works well, it may be rapidly changing. The balance of power between German financial institutions and German industrial corporations seems to be shifting in the latter's favor. During the 1970s and 1980s, large German corporations (the *Aktiengesellschaften*) appear to have escaped their former dependence on the universal banks as a source of debt capital.[108] Debt/equity ratios shifted correspondingly, but, even more importantly, the development

---

102. See supra note 63 and accompanying text.

103. Hermann H. Kallfass, The American Corporation and The Institutional Investor: Are There Lessons From Abroad?, 1988 Colum. Bus. L. Rev. 775, 783.

104. Id. at 790. See also 2 Coopers & Lybrand Report, supra note 97, at 14 ("banks' representatives [on the board] are not viewed suspiciously . . . but are gladly welcomed").

105. Cable, supra note 96, at 130 (study of 48 leading German corporations).

106. See id. at 129–30.

107. Id. at 121.

108. The share of bank credits and loans in the overall capital position of the *Aktiengesellschaften* fell from 16.9% in 1974 to 6.6% in 1984. In the chemical sector, it fell from 18.4% to 4.0%, and in the electronics sector from 16.3% to 2.8%. See Josef Esser, Bank Power in West Germany Revised, 13 W. Eur. Pol. 17, 23 (1990).

of international capital markets allowed German industrial corporations to select their creditors and hence escape their traditional monitors.[109] Between 1976 and 1986, the number of German corporations in which the universal banks jointly held a 10% or greater equity stake fell from 129 to 86,[110] and by the end of 1986, this aggregate ownership amounted to only 0.7% of the capital of all German non-banking firms (down from 1.3% ten years earlier).[111] Among German firms having a stock exchange listing, the average equity stake held by German banks similarly fell from 4.5% to 3.2%.[112] Furthermore, the representation of German banks on the supervisory boards of the hundred largest firms fell to 7% of the board members by 1989.[113] At least one close observer reports that management had succeeded "in usurping the controlling function of the supervisory boards."[114]

Even more striking has been the behavior of Germany's leading universal bank, Deutsche Bank, which has voluntarily begun to relinquish its chairmanships on the supervisory boards of German corporations.[115] Why should it abandon the chairmanship of these boards, when by all accounts the chairman wields the greatest influence and performs the principal monitoring role on the supervisory board? A partial answer is that the Deutsche Bank repeatedly found itself caught in conflicts of interest. With the appearance of an incipient merger and acquisition movement in Germany, some have speculated that Deutsche Bank wanted to avoid entanglements with corporations that might prevent it from financing, or engaging in, such takeovers.[116] Still, a more general explanation is possible that focuses on the declining profitability to Deutsche Bank from monitoring: Deutsche Bank's

---

109. See id. at 23–24.

110. Id. at 25.

111. Id.

112. Id. The Coopers & Lybrand Report finds that German bank ownership in all public companies fell from 10% in 1987 to 9% in 1988, and attributes this decline partly to public criticism of bank domination of German industry. See 2 Coopers & Lybrand Report, supra note 97, at 13.

113. Esser, supra note 108, at 26. It is also noteworthy that employee representatives and union leaders must constitute half the directors on the supervisory board of German corporations with more than 2,000 employees. See Julian Franks & Colin Mayer, Capital Markets and Corporate Control: A Study of France, Germany and the UK, 5 Econ. Pol'y 191, 205–06 (1990) (noting that such representation blocks frequent control changes and takeovers). Hence, the German system of co-determination under which labor and capital share control of the supervisory board may make the role of financial institutions a desirable counter-weight to labor's powerful position in the boardroom. At the least, co-determination implies that the German system is very different from that in the United States.

114. Esser, supra note 108, at 27. German corporations have two boards: an exclusively outside or "supervisory" board (the *Aufsichtsrat*) and the managing or executive board (the *Vorstand*). The domination of the *Vorstand*, which is chosen by the *Aufsichtsrat*, means that insiders are running the corporation.

115. See New Dreams at Deutsche Bank, Economist, June 22, 1991 at 79, 80.

116. See id. at 80.

disengagement from the supervisory boards it formerly chaired may be a direct consequence of the greater reliance of German corporations on international capital markets. Monitoring is often costly, including both the direct costs of supervision and the indirect opportunity costs of lost business which conflicts of interest required the Deutsche Bank to forgo. In the past, the German universal banks may have been compensated for their monitoring services by virtue of the near monopoly position they held as the sole or primary provider of capital market services to German corporations. As an international capital market brought competition and a lower cost of capital to German corporations, however, it also made monitoring less profitable for the German universal banks. In short, unless shareholders can compensate an institutional monitor (either through above-market interest rates or some other means), the amount of monitoring provided may decline.

D. *Intermediate Cases: Sweden and Canada*

Sweden and Canada provide interesting case studies because each reveals the adaptive responses to which corporations can resort when they are exposed to direct monitoring by institutional investors in a developed external capital market. The Swedish economy has both a well-developed stock market[117] and a high level of takeover activity.[118] As in the United States, there has been a dramatic recent increase in the level of institutional ownership. Between the 1960s and 1988, individual ownership of stock in Sweden fell from roughly 70% to 23%.[119] The balance of the stock in Swedish corporations is held by a diverse group of institutional investors, with investment companies and insurance companies constituting the largest categories.[120]

Yet another trend is equally noticeable in Sweden: over the same period that institutional ownership has risen, stock has become concentrated in the hands of small control groups assembled by management or the firm's founders. In 1978, the largest single owner of a Swedish

117. In 1985, the Swedish Government authorized the Minister of Industry to appoint a parliamentary commission to study stock ownership and control. The Commission on Stock Ownership and Efficiency submitted its report in 1988. An English-language summary of that report has been prepared. See Rolf Skog & Mats Isaksson, Ownership and Control in the Swedish Business Sector (Institutional Investor Project, Columbia University School of Law, 1989). It reports that, of the 200 "major" companies in the private sector in Sweden, approximately half were listed on the Stockholm Stock Exchange. Id. at 3. These companies "accounted for about 90% of the total number of employees in the 200 private sector companies." Id.

118. Of the 90 major companies listed on the Stockholm Stock Exchange in 1978, 40 were taken over by other companies by August, 1988, with three-fourths of these transactions occurring after 1983. See id. at 16. Skog and Isaksson do not indicate whether these takeovers were "friendly" or "hostile"; however, they do note that in 29 cases a change in company control occurred.

119. Id. at 5.

120. As of year-end 1985, Swedish stockholders fell into the following categories:

"major" company accounted on average for 20% of the equity; by 1985, this figure had risen to 29%. The five largest shareholders together held 41% of the equity in 1978, but 56% by 1985.[121]

These figures actually understate the degree to which control of Swedish corporations has been locked up in a very small group of controlling shareholders. Under Swedish law, corporations may issue two classes of common stock with different voting rights.[122] Thus, ownership of equity does not imply equivalent voting rights. When one looks instead at the concentration of the voting stock, one finds that in 1978 the largest single holder averaged 27% of the voting stock, but this figure had risen to 39% by 1985.[123] Similarly, the top five shareholders combined averaged 48% of the voting power in 1978, but 66% by 1985.[124] Once an additional adjustment is made for stock held by affiliated companies, the largest owner's share of the voting power rose from 34% in 1978 to 47% in 1985, and the top five owners' voting power together rose from 51% in 1978 to 69% in 1985.[125]

In short, the typical Swedish firm has either a single shareholder or a closely affiliated group which clearly holds control. More importantly, this trend toward consolidation of control occurred concomitantly with the rise of institutional ownership. Thus, at least viewed from a distance, Swedish institutional investors may have liquidity, but apparently not control.

A closer look at the transition in Sweden reveals that control has been insulated from capital market discipline by a variety of less visible measures as well. First, Sweden has developed a system of cross-ownership and circular ownership of stock that closely resembles the

Category of Owner	Percentage of Total Stock Market Value
Individuals	25%
Mutual funds	1%
Payroll investment and national investment funds	5%
Listed investment and holding companies	16%
Non-listed investment and holding companies	3%
Insurance companies	11%
Pension and employee investment funds	4%
Listed non-financial companies	9%
Non-listed nonfinancial companies	2%
Foundations	9%
National and local governments	2%
Other institutional owners	5%
Foreign owners	8%
	100%

Id. at 12.

121. See id. at 13.

122. See id.

123. Id.

124. Id.

125. Id. at 13–14.

Japanese pattern.[126] Frequently, Company *A* owns stock in Company *B*, which owns stock in Company *C*, which owns stock in Company *A*. A Swedish Parliamentary Commission found the levels of such reciprocal ownership varied from 2% to almost 50% and averaged 14%.[127] Second, dual-class voting schemes have come into increasing use over the last decade. By 1985, 75% of major companies had adopted such a scheme.[128] Obviously, both devices—cross-ownership and dual-class voting stock—are means by which management or a controlling family can entrench itself. Finally, Sweden restricts the voting power that investment funds, insurance companies, and pension funds may possess in any single company.[129]

In terms of this Article's analysis, Sweden's significance lies in the separation it has effected between liquidity and control. Institutional investors appear to dominate the stock market in Sweden, but they do not control individual companies. The high rate of takeover activity in Sweden shows that control can pass to other nonfinancial corporations, but institutional investors appear to have accepted liquidity in lieu of control.

The Canadian experience resembles Sweden's. Much like the United States and Great Britain, Canada has an active stock market and takeovers are common. But, unlike either country, Canada has experienced a recent and rapid concentration of stock ownership in the hands of controlling shareholders. A Royal Commission on Corporate Concentration reported in 1978 that of Canada's 100 largest nonfinancial corporations, 48% were either wholly owned (usually by a foreign corporation) or were controlled by a majority stockholder.[130] This breakdown appears to have understated the level of control because it overlooked those firms subject to minority control through a de facto controlling shareholder.[131] A later 1985 study found that nine Cana-

126. In a summary of cross- and circular ownership among Swedish listed companies in 1988, the Swedish Parliamentary Commission found 26 cases of cross-ownership out of fewer than 100 listed firms. See id. at 19. For a description of the Japanese practice, see supra notes 65–95 and accompanying text.

127. Skog & Isaksson, supra note 117, at 19.

128. Id. at 13.

129. Even more than in the case of Japan, Swedish law places strict ownership limits on the amount of stock that insurance companies, investment funds, and pensions may own in an individual corporation. A Swedish insurance company may not hold more than 5% of the voting stock in any single company. Id. at 9. A similar rule applies to investment funds. Id. at 8. Pension funds are restricted to either 8% or 10%, depending on the particular type of fund. Id. at 10. These are the largest classes of institutional investors in Sweden, where banks do not appear to play an active role in corporate monitoring. See table supra note 120.

130. See Report of The Royal Commission on Corporate Concentration 288–89 (1978).

131. For criticisms of the Royal Commission's Report on this ground, see Wallace Clement, An Exercise in Legitimation: Ownership and Control in The Report of the Royal Commission on Corporate Concentration *in* Perspectives on The Royal Commis-

dian families held control over 46% of the top 300 companies traded on the Toronto Stock Exchange.[132] Even more recent data shows that only 20 of Canada's 400 largest public corporations are widely held, and some 380 have a single shareholder with at least a 15% holding (and in 374 of these, a conglomerate or family holds between 25% and 30% of the stock).[133] The Canadian experience thus resembles the Swedish, but with the difference that the vehicle holding control is not typically another non-financial corporation, but a family dynasty.[134]

E. *United Kingdom*

The British capital markets match those of the United States in being extremely active and well-developed.[135] Institutional ownership is increasing, and has long been higher in the U.K. than in the U.S.[136] Thus, the United Kingdom comes closest to an economy that offers investors both liquidity and control. Still, there are other significant differences between the U.K. and the U.S. that militate against the uniting of liquidity and control in British markets. First, it is estimated that the major pension funds hold 60% of the equity in U.K. corporations,[137] whereas the corresponding U.S. figure is only 20.4%.[138] Although British pension funds can be active and substantial shareholders, and indeed in one recent case have even launched a successful takeover,[139] observers report that they are in general long-term holders who do not need "the overnight liquidity of the stock market."[140] This is logical because, unlike mutual funds, pension funds do not face shareholder redemptions; nor are they engaged in an active competition for investors' funds. Moreover, there are structural differences between the typ-

---

sion on Corporate Concentration 215, 220–21 (Paul K. Gorecki & W.T. Stanbury eds., 1979).

132. See Deborah A. DeMott, Comparative Dimensions of Takeover Regulation, *in* Knights, Raiders and Targets: The Impact of the Hostile Takeover 398, 400 (John C. Coffee, Jr. et al. eds., 1988).

133. See Diane Francis, Controlling Interest: Who Owns Canada? 4 (1986).

134. See id. By comparison, in the United States only 75 of the companies in the Standard & Poor's index have a 15% shareholder. See id.

135. See Jonathan Charkham, The American Corporation and the Institutional Investor: Are There Lessons from Abroad?—Hands Across the Sea, 1988 Colum. Bus. L. Rev. 765, 765.

136. British institutional ownership rose from 47% in 1975 to over 63% today. See Taylor, supra note 41, at 70. British households own less than 20% of British equities. See id. Currently, institutional investors own approximately 45% of publicly owned corporate equity in the United States. See supra note 41 and accompanying text.

137. See Charkham, supra note 135, at 770.

138. See Brancato, Pivotal Role of Institutional Investors, supra note 40, at 18, 20 (presenting data from 1986).

139. See Stephen Clark, Taking a Big Bite, Institutional Investor, Aug. 1990, at 68 (noting successful takeover by British Coal Pension Funds of Globe Investment Trusts).

140. Leonard J. Hollie, Europe Has Appetite for Venture Capital, Pensions & Investments, Apr. 30, 1990, at 22 (quoting Alan Patricof, president of Patricof Associates, Inc., a New York investment banking and consulting firm).

ical U.K. pension fund and its U.S. equivalent. U.K. funds typically invest more heavily in long-term, illiquid assets, including real estate and foreign stocks.[141] British funds also tend to do most of their investing through "in-house staffs,"[142] while the normal U.S. practice is for the funds to allocate the management of their assets among several investment advisers, thereby effectively staging a competition among them. Arguably, the use of internal money managers and the absence of competition in the U.K. may reduce the pressure for short-term performance.

Another fact about British institutional investors is more striking: although unrestricted by legal constraints, individual institutional investors seldom hold more than one to two percent of the stock of any corporation.[143] Why not? The most plausible explanation for this self-imposed limitation is that larger-sized blocks would render them illiquid. Institutional investors often share the same views and thus trade in a herd-like manner.[144] Because British pension funds make up a disproportionate amount of the British financial markets, a fund that held a large block of stock might find it necessary to accept a substantial block discount. In this light, a decision to limit holdings to a low percentage of each issuer's outstanding stock reflects the preference of British institutions for liquidity over control.

Because Britain has long had a level of institutional ownership that exceeds the current U.S. level,[145] its experience with the growth of institutional ownership may foreshadow future changes and trends within the U.S. corporate environment. British institutional investors tend to act collectively through umbrella institutions when dealing with corporate managements. Four "Industry Associations"—covering pension funds, insurance companies, unit trusts, and investment companies, respectively—have developed, in part to share the expenses and political burden of confronting and opposing individual corporate managements.[146] When an emergency situation arises—such as a takeover de-

141. See Barry B. Burr, British Lead In Investing Abroad, Pensions & Investments, July 23, 1990, at 14. Some 81.4% of the assets in the typical British pension fund are allocated to stocks, as contrasted to 45.1% for the 200 largest U.S. pension funds. See id.

142. Id.

143. See W. A. Thomas, The Big Bang 18 (1986).

144. Thomas concludes that because institutional investors in Britain tend to hold an "identity of view" (that is, they tend to trade the same way at the same time) the liquidity of the British equity market has been diminished. See id. at 18. This could, in turn, explain why institutions restrict themselves to small stakes of under 2%.

145. In 1975, British institutions owned 45% of all British equities, which is about equal to the current U.S. level of institutional ownership. Today, British institutions own over 63%. See supra note 136.

146. See Louis Lowenstein & Ira M. Millstein, The American Corporation and the Institutional Investor: Are There Lessons from Abroad?—Introduction, 1988 Colum. Bus. L. Rev. 739, 748 (quoting Robert Monks, former chief executive of Institutional Shareholder Services, Inc.).

fense—the four associations will form a "case committee" to deal with the particular corporate management.[147] In addition, the Bank of England plays a behind-the-scenes mediating role when tensions arise between dissatisfied institutional investors and corporate managements that appear to have been underperforming.[148] This collective strategy is in sharp contrast to the classic Wall Street Rule, under which dissatisfied institutions dump their shares into the market and move on. Arguably, this pattern shows that (1) institutional investors will exercise greater "voice" when their ability to "exit" is diminished, and (2) to exercise "voice," some protective mechanism must evolve that spares them from head-on, one-to-one confrontations with corporate managements.

F. *An Initial Summary*

Three fundamentally different kinds of relationships between institutional investors and corporate managements can be posited based on the foregoing survey. The first is the internal capital market. For the present at least, the external capital markets that typify the United States and the United Kingdom remain unique. In other major economies—most notably Japan and Germany—the allocation of capital to corporate users is determined principally by internal capital markets. These internal capital markets maximize the monitoring power of financial institutions, but the monitoring process remains relatively consensual, not hostile, and the trip wire for external intervention tends to be the approach of insolvency, not the failure to maximize stock price. Moreover, financial institutions undertake external intervention gradually and generally as a last resort. Even when it occurs, disruption is carefully minimized, and control eventually returns to internal management, after, perhaps, the replacement of the most senior level of the incumbent management.[149] By contrast, monitoring in external capital markets often involves hostile contests for corporate control that are

147. See id. Further research is needed on the role played by these industry associations. They may also serve to dissuade individual members from liquidating their holdings.

148. See Taylor, supra note 41, at 80.

149. As Professor Aoki observes, within the Japanese firm, bank monitoring follows a gradual progression from first raising questions to later intervening as a shareholder, to, finally, removing the senior executives, but even then, typically replacing them from within the firm:

> If the profit of a company starts to decline, the main bank is able to detect the problem at a rather early stage through information gained from the management of commercial accounts, short-term credits, long-term personal contacts with top management of the company and its business partners, and so on, because of its special position. Tacit and explicit pressure for the internal overhaul of management would be initiated in exchange for various types of rescue operations as noted before. If bad states continue, the main bank may decide to take over management through the governance structure of the company. . . . Recent experiences indicate, however, that banks do not change the

triggered simply by a share discount.[150] Typically, such discipline results in the substitution of an entire external management team for the incumbent senior management.

The second form of relationship begins with the deterioration of the first. Reliance on internal capital markets is diminishing with the growth of a single international capital market. In both Japan and Germany, there is evidence that corporate managers are gradually escaping the control of a single financial monitor by moving to diversify their credit sources. As this happens, the independence of financial monitors is increasingly compromised because they must begin to market their services to corporate managements against active competition. In turn, as profits erode, financial monitors may begin to cut back on those monitoring services for which they feel inadequately compensated. From this perspective, the days of internal capital markets may be numbered. Unless special means can be found to compensate them for their monitoring services, financial monitors, such as the German universal banks, may survive only under circumstances of capital scarcity—such as post-war Europe and Japan—where they hold control over access to capital.

The third relationship is less stable: as financial monitors—such as the German universal banks or the Japanese main banks—face increasing competition, they may begin to strike new alliances.[151] If they cannot offer their clients lower cost capital than can the international markets, they can provide management with other services that may justify special compensation, such as protection from hostile takeovers. To describe this scenario is also to recognize that financial monitors need not ally inherently with minority shareholders.

The rise of the institutional investor to a controlling position is by no means inevitable. Defensive alliances are also possible between corporate managements and other shareholders. As the Canadian and Swedish experiences show, even in economies with external capital markets, structural defenses can evolve that insulate managements from the full impact of capital market discipline. In other major economies, the level of public ownership remains simply too small to enable institutional investors to discipline corporate management.[152]

> fundamental nature of internal management, but rather hand over top management after recuperation to internally promoted employees . . . .

Aoki, supra note 88, at 15.

150. For a detailed discussion of the view that takeovers are motivated by a margin (or "share discount") between a firm's liquidation value and its stock market value, see Reinier Kraakman, Taking Discounts Seriously: The Implications of 'Discounted' Share Prices as an Acquisition Motive, 88 Colum. L. Rev. 891 (1988).

151. On the general subject of shifting alliances within the public corporation and defections among allies unable to reach enforceable agreements, see John C. Coffee, Jr., Unstable Coalitions: Corporate Governance as a Multi-Player Game, 78 Geo. L.J. 1495 (1990).

152. The Coopers & Lybrand Report finds that of over 200 listed companies in

The foregoing survey places us in a position to evaluate the historic passivity of American institutional investors. Although the new critics attribute this passivity to overregulation, this brief survey casts substantial doubt on the overregulation thesis. At least five fundamental objections can be made to the overregulation story as the primary explanation for shareholder passivity.

First, the claim that American banks were uniquely subject to regulation seems puzzling given that Japanese banks are subject to effectively the same five percent limitation on voting stock ownership.[153]

Italy, only seven have over 50% of their shares in public hands. 1 Coopers & Lybrand Report, supra note 97, at 22. It estimates that in France over half of the 200 largest companies are "family controlled." Id. In addition, government shareholdings and cross-shareholdings also minimize the possibility of takeovers and institutional investor influence in France. Others provide a similar assessment of the thinness of the French capital markets. See Gareth P. Dyas & Heinz T. Thanheiser, The Emerging European Enterprise: Strategy and Structure in French and German Industry 169–71 (1976). According to Dyas and Thanheiser, the financial markets in France "are described by all observers as extremely 'narrow.' " Id. at 170. They conclude that "this is ascribable, in part, to the preponderance of the state as lender and borrower of available funds." Id. Only around 460 French corporations trade on the Paris Stock Exchange (out of some 135,000 stock corporations incorporated in France), and the remainder would appear to be financed largely through internal capital markets. See Hopt, supra note 27, at 4. See also Franks & Mayer, supra note 113, at 208–09 (noting government involvement as a shareholder in French corporations as a barrier to takeovers and control changes).

153. The National Bank Act does not authorize banks to own stocks directly. See 12 U.S.C. § 24 (1988). However, until the Glass-Steagall Act of 1933, banks could easily outflank this prohibition by investing through securities affiliates. See Roe, Political Theory, supra note 3, at 17. While the Glass-Steagall Act precluded commercial banks from having an affiliation with firms "dealing" in securities, it did not directly prohibit banks from being owned by a parent company that simply owned securities, either directly or through an affiliate. See supra note 59. For a variety of reasons, bank holding companies appeared during the 1950s, and because they were not covered by the National Bank Act, they were effectively unregulated. In response, Congress enacted the Bank Holding Company Act of 1956, which generally precluded a bank holding company from owning more than 5% of the voting stock of a nonbanking company. See 12 U.S.C. §§ 1843(c)(6)–(7) (1988). Effectively, this means that virtually any major bank may legally acquire up to 5% of the voting stock of an industrial corporation through a parent or securities affiliate. See supra note 63. In addition, bank trust departments, which are not restricted in stock ownership by the prohibition on bank ownership, may invest up to 10% of their funds in the stock of a single corporation. See 12 C.F.R. § 9.18(b)(9)(ii) (1991). Alone, this provision would allow a bank with a large trust department to exercise control over corporations of substantial size (although fiduciary requirements would necessitate diversification). Finally, the Bank Holding Company Act permits banks to acquire businesses whose activities are "so closely related to banking . . . as to be a proper incident thereto." 12 U.S.C. § 1843(c)(8) (1988). Recently, bank regulators have expanded the category of activities falling within this exception. See American Land Title Ass'n v. Board of Governors of the Fed. Reserve Sys., 892 F.2d 1059 (D.C. Cir. 1989).

One commentator observes that the "most dramatic shift in bank regulation over the last decade has been the extent to which banks have been permitted to diversify their activities and investments." Helen A. Garten, Regulatory Growing Pains: A Perspective on Bank Regulation in a Deregulatory Age, 57 Fordham L. Rev. 501, 529 (1989). In

Similar limitations on stock ownership exist in other countries as well.[154]

Second, in other economies—for example, Germany and Great Britain—in which substantive limitations on bank ownership of equity securities have not existed, financial institutions still have not exceeded this same five percent level.[155] Perhaps the need to diversify investments limits banks in these countries, or perhaps other factors—such as the need for liquidity, possible conflicts of interest, or fear of business or political reprisals—cause them to halt ownership of voting stock at this low level. Alternatively, banks may just not view equity ownership as a business at which they have a comparative advantage.

Third, even within the United States, banks generally have not exploited the statutory powers they do possess to own and hold equity securities—possibly because they have not found such ownership to be particularly profitable.[156] Although nonbanking activities of bank holding companies were virtually unregulated until the passage of the Bank Holding Company Act of 1956, banks made little use of these powers.[157] After the Act's passage, real constraints were placed on the ability of bank holding companies to make acquisitions, but even the

combination, these exceptions to the general prohibition on bank ownership of corporate stock potentially overwhelm the rule and permit a single bank to exercise a significant influence over most corporations. But extra-legal factors seem to prevent this from happening. See infra note 156.

154. In Sweden, for example, insurance companies may not own more than 5% of the voting stock of any company. The largest Swedish insurance company owns 2% of more than 100 listed Swedish companies. See Skog & Isaksson, supra note 117, at 9. In contrast, American banks have not utilized their legal capacity to buy stocks.

155. German banks today own 3.2% of the voting stock of the 100 largest major German corporations. See supra notes 99, 112. British banks own even less of the stock of British industrial companies. See E. Gerald Corrigan, Reforming the U.S. Financial System: An International Perspective, FRBNY Quarterly Review, Spring, 1990, at 1, 2 (noting that "bank holding of shares of commercial firms is far less common" in Britain than in Germany). British institutional investors tend to hold in the 1%–2% range. See Thomas, supra note 143, at 18.

156. As noted earlier, see supra note 153, although national banks may not directly own equity securities for their own account, bank holding companies may hold up to 5% of the voting stock of a non-banking corporation. One explanation for why banks have failed to exploit this power (and why they did not diversify before 1956 when the Bank Holding Company Act was passed) is that they have found diversification to be only marginally profitable. See Garten, supra note 153, at 519, 557. Professor Garten concludes: "[T]he evidence suggests that bank holding company management of nonbanking subsidiaries has not been very successful . . . ." Id. at 557. If so, perhaps banks do not make particularly efficient monitors either.

157. Professor Garten notes that the "relative importance of [bank] holding companies actually declined between 1936 and 1956." Id. at 519 (footnote omitted). Indeed, between 1930 and 1939, only 34 nonbank subsidiaries were formed or acquired by bank holding companies, and between 1950 and 1959 only 290 nonbank subsidiaries were formed or acquired. Id. at 519 n.85. As Garten notes, a logical explanation for this reluctance to diversify into nonbanking activities is that bank holding companies found such acquisitions to be less profitable than their traditional activities. See id. at 519.

substantial powers that remain are not exploited. Today, Citicorp, the largest U.S. banking institution with total assets of over $200 billion, holds only about $1 billion in equities.[158] Even when U.S. banks do take equity stakes in U.S. corporations, they do so indirectly, for example, through leveraged buyout ("LBO") funds.[159] Perhaps the use of a buyout fund vehicle enables the banks to obtain greater diversification, and thus reduces the risk of equity ownership, or perhaps, as some observers have suggested, the motive for the equity investment was not the investment itself, but the lucrative fees received by the banks for financing the LBO.[160] Whatever the reason, it is difficult to assign a causal relationship to legal restrictions on ownership when American financial institutions historically have not used, and today continue not to use, the considerable discretion that the law gives them.

A fourth problem with the claim that U.S. institutional investors were regulated into passivity is that this explanation lacks a meaningful benchmark for comparison. From a comparative perspective, one can point to countervailing examples in which U.S. law is more protective of institutional investors' freedom of action. For example, the German co-determination law gives half the seats on the supervisory board to labor and employee representatives, thereby effectively precluding takeovers and limiting shareholder control.[161] Another example is ERISA's requirement that pension funds be adequately funded and structured as free-standing legal entities.[162] In many European countries, there is no such requirement, and often there is no separate pension fund, only a legal claim held by the pensioner against the general

158. See, e.g., Black, supra note 12, at 552. Other U.S. banks own considerably less. See Robert Guenther, Bankers Trust Leads Way for Major Banks in Investment Banking, Wall St. J., Dec. 5, 1989 at A1, A14. Again, this limited ownership may reflect the limited profitability of such activities. See supra note 156.

159. See Anise C. Wallace, Banks With Stakes in Borrowers Are in Spotlight, N.Y. Times, July 4, 1990, at 47 (discussing equity investments by major banks in buyout fund run by Kohlberg, Kravis & Roberts). The key fact about an LBO fund, however, is that the general partner (such as KKR) and not the bank investor plays the principal monitoring role.

160. See id. (estimating that banks have collected $350 million in fees for financing buyouts arranged by Kohlberg, Kravis & Roberts and $150 million in such fees during 1988 alone). Under this interpretation, the banks invested in buyout funds as a form of "relationship-building" (as one bank official acknowledged) in order to "win some of the lucrative lending business generated by" these transactions. Id.

161. For a discussion of the impact of this requirement, see Franks & Mayer, supra note 113, at 205–07.

162. Section 402(a) of ERISA requires that every employee benefit plan be established and maintained pursuant to a written instrument. 29 U.S.C. § 1102(a)(1) (1988). This trust requirement is supplemented by section 403(a) of ERISA, which requires that all assets of an employee benefit plan be held in trust by one or more trustees. 29 U.S.C. § 1103(a) (1988). In effect, the corporate sponsor may not hold the assets out of whose earnings the pension is to be paid. Such a "funded" scheme is in contrast to "pay-as-you-go" pension systems, which do not require a separate fund. See John Creedy, State Pensions in Britain 13–14 (1982).

assets of the employing corporation.[163] This arrangement effectively eliminates the pension fund as an *entire class* of institutional investor and over the long run necessarily reduces the level of institutional ownership of corporate stock. A third example is the legal rule in Britain and Canada that may require a person acquiring a controlling position in a corporation to offer to buy out all the remaining minority shareholders.[164] Such a rule may chill institutional activism far more than the basically disclosure-oriented rules imposed on institutional investors who seek to exercise control in the United States. In short, legal restrictions on financial institutions and other institutional investors exist in most industrial economies that could support the thesis that political coalitions in those countries had conspired to hobble those institutions. For overregulation to be meaningful as an explanation of institutional passivity, it must be shown at a minimum that U.S. institutional investors suffer from more overregulation than similar institutions elsewhere. This showing has not yet been made.

A fifth problem with the overregulation story is historical. A premise of this story is that the Glass-Steagall Act, and the consequent separation of commercial and investment banking, precluded financial institutions within the United States from evolving into corporate monitors in a manner that would have paralleled the German universal banks or the Japanese main banks. However, the historical evidence suggests that well before the Glass-Steagall Act, the largest, most powerful American financial institutions had already begun to retreat from an active monitoring role. In his monumental history of the Morgan Bank, Ron Chernow reports on developments within the Morgan Bank during the 1920s:

> Gradually, if imperceptibly, the banker was becoming less a corporate partner and more a professional, a disinterested intermediary . . . . In [Pierpont Morgan's] day, weak companies needed to lean on strong bankers. But by the 1920s, a Standard Oil of New Jersey or a U.S. Steel had a stability compara-

163. Indeed, in most European countries, private pension plans are a rarity, with "the vast majority of an individual's pension [coming] through the social security system." Eric Short, First Steps on a Very Long Journey Towards a Single Market, Fin. Times, May 3, 1990, Pension Fund Investment Section, at 5. While separate pension funds are common in the United Kingdom, both Germany and France currently rely on alternative systems that do not give rise to pension funds as institutional investors. See Margaret Price, EC Funds Get Ready: New Rules to Liberalize Pension Investing, Pensions & Investments, Aug. 20, 1990, at 1, 38.

164. British takeover law discourages partial bids and under some circumstances requires a corporation that has assembled a substantial (but still a minority) percentage of a firm's stock to make a mandatory bid for all the remaining shares. Such a mandatory bid requirement obviously increases the costs of acquiring control. See DeMott, supra note 132, at 408–09 (City Takeover Code requires persons acting in concert who assemble 30% or more of voting securities to make mandatory buyout bid for remaining shares at highest price paid by them within last twelve months).

ble to that of the House of Morgan itself.[165]

As Chernow observes, the bankers' power was at its zenith "when capital markets were limited, with few financial intermediaries to tap them."[166] Yet, as capital markets developed and became "globally integrated," competition reduced the power of the Wall Street banker.[167] Much this same process—of gradual "emancipation" of industrial corporations from bank influence—seems to be occurring in Germany and Japan today.[168] Their slower development may be the product of the longer survival of internal capital markets in those countries or the result of the instability and chaos following World War II, which may have made association with a bank more important to financially strained corporations in a war-ravaged economy. The irony here is that, rather than Germany and Japan serving as a model for future industrial development in the United States, the reverse may be gradually happening, as international capital markets gradually supersede internal capital markets. Predictions are speculative, but the internationalization of the capital markets does seem to weaken banker control.[169]

II. The Extra-Legal Causes of Shareholder Passivity

Without denying that the overregulation of institutional investors may partially account for shareholder passivity, this Article suggests that extra-legal causes contribute more to an explanation of why insti-

---

165. Ron Chernow, The House of Morgan: An American Banking Dynasty and the Rise of Modern Finance 258 (1990).

166. Id. at 486. It is far from clear that even during this era Morgan bankers were monitoring the corporations on whose boards they sat to assure that management maximized value for shareholders. Rather, because the basic business of the Morgan Bank was bond sales, its own rational incentives were to protect its creditor clients by encouraging the retention of free cash flow within the corporation. Also, a seat on the client's board is an obvious way for an investment bank to protect its business from the competitive efforts of rival investment banking firms and to market its own services.

167. Id. ("Gradually Wall Street bankers would lose their unique place in world finance.").

168. See supra notes 92–95, 108–116 and accompanying text.

169. One last possibility should be noted. Arguably, the impact of the legal differences to which institutional investors in different countries are subject can be overemphasized. Thus, an alternative standard might be to compare the percentages of listed companies in different countries that have majority or controlling shareholders. Such a comparison clearly suggests that the U.S. economy has comparatively fewer such shareholders who might make effective monitors. Of the 5240 firms on national stock exchanges in the United States in 1984, 663 (or 12.7%) had majority shareholders. See, e.g., Clifford G. Holderness & Dennis P. Sheehan, The Role of Majority Shareholders in Publicly Held Corporations, 20 J. Fin. Econ. 317, 321 (1988). In contrast, over 48% of Canadian firms had majority shareholders. See DeMott, supra note 132, at 425 n.12; supra note 130 and accompanying text. A comparable level of Swedish firms had such shareholders. See Skog & Isaksson, supra note 117, at 14. But what does this comparison ultimately show? Does it imply that U.S. investors were somehow deterred by legal or other forces from acquiring control or simply that they preferred liquidity to control? This is the basic chicken-or-egg question that confounds the overregulation thesis.

tutional investors have not yet exerted a greater "voice" in corporate governance.[170] From this perspective, institutional investors cannot be characterized as a Gulliver tied down by Lilliputian bureaucrats; if anything, they more resemble spectators at the Roman Colosseum, content with bread and circuses and unwilling to organize for political reform as long as the game continues.

Neither metaphor, however, captures adequately the nature of the extra-legal barriers to institutional activism. These barriers are diverse and have little in common, except that they would remain even if deregulation reduced the legal barriers to collective shareholder action.

A. *Liquidity and Thin Equity*

Some institutions need liquidity more than others. For institutions requiring liquidity, taking a large control position is unacceptable if such a stake would be illiquid. Mutual funds, banks, and insurance companies fall into this class of institutions, chiefly because their shareholders, depositors, or policyholders can withdraw their funds on short notice.[171] Not surprisingly, the latter two have been characterized as the institutions most unlikely to oppose corporate managements.[172] This problem is most acute in the case of "open end" mutual funds, which must stand ready to redeem on a daily basis the shares of customers who wish to sell. Thus, most mutual funds are active traders and would hesitate to make any investment the liquidation of which would require a significant block discount. In addition, because mutual funds compete for customers' funds based on their asserted ability to

170. The term "extra-legal" requires a word of definition. This Article uses it to refer to practices, norms, or conventions that have not historically been considered unlawful (even though potentially such practices could be made unlawful). Thus, if institutional money managers wish to avoid acquiring a reputation as "activist" shareholders for fear that it will cost them future pension fund accounts, this factor would be considered an extra-legal one (even if a visionary might imagine a legal regime under which such reputations could not be considered).

171. Traditionally, insurance companies have not been grouped with mutual funds, because their payout to customers is actuarially predictable. However, they are also subject to panic surges in policyholder redemptions and withdrawals. Recently, three insurance companies—Mutual Benefit Life Insurance Co., Monarch Life Insurance Company, and First Capital Life Insurance Company—were taken over by state regulators in the wake of policyholder panics about their firm's solvency. See Eric N. Berg, Rater to Add Policyholder Panic Factor, N.Y. Times, Aug. 2, 1991, at D1. Hence, the need to assure policyholders of their solvency may inhibit insurance companies as well from investing in illiquid investments.

172. This is the view of professional proxy solicitors. See Could Girard Have Won the Proxy Fight?, Corp. Control Alert, Sept. 1990, at 11 (Joseph Morrow of proxy solicitor Morrow & Co. describing insurers and bank affiliated positions as "the two groups most likely to support management").

outperform their competitors,[173] they need to be able to report the current market value of their investments. The resulting focus on short-term performance is inconsistent with holding a collection of illiquid blocks. As a result, so long as mutual funds face a market in which investors will continually, and with little notice, shift their funds from one fund to another or will withdraw their funds to purchase other non-capital market investments, preservation of maximum liquidity must remain a high priority for the rational mutual fund manager.

Banks and, to a lesser extent, insurance companies face a more important obstacle: Structurally, they have very thin equity compared with that of industrial corporations. For example, among the largest commercial banks, the proportion of equity capital to total assets has steadily fallen from 60% during the early nineteenth century, to 20% at the turn of this century, to below 10% since the early 1950s, and to under 5% since the mid-1970s.[174] The significance of this point comes into clearer focus when we consider the balance sheet of a hypothetical bank with $1 billion in assets and equity of under $50 million. If it held even 20% of its assets (or $200 million) in the form of equity securities and the stock market declined by 25% over a period of, say, two months, the bank's equity would be wiped out, and the bank would be, at least technically, insolvent. In short, highly leveraged but regulated entities, such as banks or insurance companies, lack the capacity to hold

173. Whether in fact they can outperform the market or their competitors is an entirely different question. See infra note 192 and accompanying text.

The foregoing analysis does not consider the "indexed" mutual fund, which is not an active trader and which is discussed at infra notes 236–244 and accompanying text.

174. See Yair E. Orgler & Benjamin Wolkowitz, Bank Capital 3 (1976). For all national banks as a group, the ratio of shareholders' equity to total assets was 5.8% in 1983. See Federal Deposit Insurance Corporation, Bank Operating Statistics: 1983, Table 1, at 2. This definition of equity includes both undistributed earned surplus and reserves for contingencies and other capital reserves.

For the ten largest banks in the United States in 1988, the ratios of total equity capital to total assets were as follows:

Bank	Total Assets	Total Equity Capital	Percentage
	(In Millions)		
Citibank	150,241.0	8,168.0	5.4
Bank of America	82,912.0	3,611.0	4.4
Chase Manhattan	77,542.5	4,372.9	5.6
Morgan Guaranty	71,227.8	4,020.1	5.6
Bankers Trust Co.	55,349.9	2,889.1	5.2
Manufacturer's Hanover	54,210.0	2,546.0	4.7
Chemical Bank	50,933.0	2,488.0	4.9
Security Pacific National Bank	48,920.5	2,216.6	4.5
Wells Fargo Bank	43,732.1	2,576.5	5.9
First National Bank of Chicago	35,172.7	1,302.2	3.7

This table was derived from data on total assets and equity capital obtained from Sheshunoff Information Services Inc., 1000 Largest U.S. Banks: 1989, at II.1 (1989).

volatile investments, such as equity securities, as a significant portion of their investment portfolios. While this volatility problem may explain why bank holding companies appear not to hold equity securities up to the ceiling now permitted by the Bank Holding Company Act,[175] it also undermines the claim that regulatory constraints are the decisive factor in the passivity of these financial institutions. Further complicating the volatility problem is the prevailing practice among financial regulators to write down the value of marketable securities in determining a regulated firm's legal capital.[176] Thus, if banks could directly own equity securities, regulators would predictably apply more or less the same "haircuts" to these investments as they now apply to the securities portfolios of broker-dealers.[177]

The need for liquidity is based on more than simply the necessity of assuring customers that their investments can be repaid or redeemed on request. In fact, some institutions do not promise their customers ready liquidity, and thus they potentially could hold more illiquid equity stakes. But these firms—closed-end mutual funds, holding companies, and natural resource companies—typically trade at significant discounts below their asset liquidation value.[178] Thus, for some institutions, the real risk in holding illiquid assets for the long-term is that they thereby incur a substantial discount in their share value, which could in turn invite a hostile takeover by those investors seeking to arbitrage the difference between the firm's market value and its underly-

175. See supra notes 156–160 and accompanying text.

176. Brokers and dealers registered under the Securities Exchange Act of 1934 are subject to the "net capital" rule. See Rule 15c3-1, 17 C.F.R. § 240.15c3-1 (1991) ("Net Capital Requirements for Brokers or Dealers"). This rule requires "securities haircuts" under which all securities must be reduced in value by a specified percentage for purposes of calculating a firm's capital. See Rule 15c3-1(c)(2)(vi) ("Securities Haircuts"). The haircut for common stock is 30% plus an additional 15% in some circumstances. See Rule 15c3-1(c)(2)(vi)(J). Although national banks may not currently own equity securities, see 12 U.S.C. § 24 (1988), they are subject to similar regulation by the Comptroller of the Currency, which restricts the "investment securities" that they may hold. See 12 C.F.R. § 1.7 (1991). In addition, the Comptroller requires that specified ratios be maintained between "risk-weighted assets" and total capital. See 12 C.F.R. Part 3, App. A, § 4(a)(1) (1991). It seems likely, then, that if equity securities could be owned by national banks, financial regulators would require write-downs at least as severe as now mandated by the SEC for broker-dealers.

177. Investment banks own relatively little stock in comparison to other institutional investors, see Black, supra note 12, at 603, in part for this reason. Other commentators do not even consider investment banks in their tabulation of institutional ownership of equity assets. See, e.g., Brancato, Pivotal Role of Institutional Investors, supra note 40, at 13–17.

178. See Kraakman, supra note 150 at 901–08. Professor Kraakman notes that "discounts on seasoned funds of 20% or more, persisting for five years or longer, have been common . . . ." Id. at 903. This tendency, he suggests, may explain the phenomenon of "bust-up" takeovers. For earlier observations to a similar effect, see John C. Coffee, Jr., Shareholders Versus Managers: The Strain in the Corporate Web, 85 Mich. L. Rev. 1 (1986).

ing asset value. Obviously, this danger poses no threat to pension funds (which have a uniquely low need for liquidity), but it would present a substantial barrier for other institutions, such as merchant banks, if deregulation were to permit commercial and investment banking activities to be combined.

B. *Conflicts of Interest*

Because conflicts of interest have been fully and ably discussed by others,[179] they will only be briefly treated here. Generally, commentators report that banks and insurance companies are the institutions least willing to oppose corporate managements.[180] Usually, the reason given for their reluctance is fear that their firm will lose business—either of the specific firm whose management they have opposed or of the corporate community generally if the investor is perceived as an "activist." Private pension funds are subject to a related form of pressure in that corporate managements can, and do, instruct the professional investment management firms, to which voting and investment discretion usually are delegated, as to how to vote in a proxy contest.[181] Moreover, trustees of private pension funds often are corporate employees or agents who report to senior management and predictably share their attitudes toward institutional activism.[182]

Even if regulations adopted under ERISA prohibited such influence, their efficacy is doubtful for two reasons. First, corporate managements have the legal power to reclaim voting discretion over the portfolio's assets. To some extent, this power is now being exercised;[183] and, once reclaimed, corporate managements predictably will

179. The leading works are James E. Heard & Howard D. Sherman, Conflicts of Interest in The Proxy Voting System (IRRC 1987) and John Brooks, Corporate Pension Fund Asset Management, *in* Abuse on Wall Street: Conflicts of Interest in the Securities Markets 224 (Twentieth Century Fund ed., 1980). See also Black, supra note 12, at 595–608 (arguing that conflicts of interest may prevent significant monitoring by institutional investors); Rock, supra note 9, at 469–72 (same).

180. See supra note 53 and accompanying text; infra notes 181–191 and accompanying text.

181. A 1987 survey by the magazine Institutional Investor found that half of all corporate pension officers considered it "appropriate" to advise pension money managers how to vote and that money managers almost uniformly followed any such advice that was given; only 6.8% of them claimed to have resisted. See Pensionforum: Taking the Offensive, Institutional Investor, Dec. 1987, at 101. More recently, the Department of Labor has begun to question such pressure, but low visibility practices are extremely hard to detect or discourage. See Black, supra note 12, at 553–56.

182. See Nell Minow, One Man's Pension Trustee is Another's CEO, Wall St. J., Apr. 23, 1987, § 1, at 32. More generally, see John H. Langbein & Daniel Fischel, ERISA's Fundamental Contradiction: The Exclusive Benefit Rule, 55 U. Chi. L. Rev. 1105, 1126–28 (1988) (discussing the perils of the nonneutral fiduciary).

183. Professor Black reports that as the Labor Department has begun to scrutinize corporate pressure on professional pension money managers, more companies are choosing to retain (or reclaim) voting discretion, while delegating to the professional

support each other in the expectation that a Golden Rule of Deference may someday benefit them. Only public pension funds and mutual funds are relatively free from such pressure and, not surprisingly, they are the most likely to oppose management's proposals. Second, even if active retaliation were forbidden so that corporate managements could not terminate or withdraw voting discretion from an institutional money manager who supported dissidents, there would remain the problem of reputation. Money managers are in active competition for new pension accounts. If a reputation as an "activist" inhibits one's ability to obtain new accounts, then money managers will predictably shun behavior that could give them that reputation—even if reprisals by existing pension accounts could somehow be strictly forbidden.[184]

Real as the problem of conflicts of interest is, its magnitude can be debated. For institutional investors that are substantial shareholders in a company, the gains to be made from improved corporate performance seem likely to exceed the potential losses from business that moves elsewhere. Thus, as the scale of institutional holdings grows, the expected gains from activism should increasingly outweigh the losses. Still, "exit" remains a rational strategy to the extent that reputational damage could follow from active involvement in a proxy fight or similar contest. It may be difficult ex ante, to estimate the likelihood or severity of the reputational injury that a specific corporate contest could threaten. Moreover, even if the gains from improved corporate governance were large, these gains should be available at many firms, while specific conflicts are likely to exist only with respect to a few firms for any individual investor. Hence, it may make sense for an institutional investor to flee proxy or other control fights when the corporation can credibly threaten retaliation. So long as the "exit" option is available, the rational institutional investor can make its decision on an ex post basis—in effect, casting its vote with the dissidents only after it has first evaluated the potential downside in terms of the threats management can make. In turn, this gives corporate managements a greater incentive to use threats of business retaliation. Once again, however, the bottom line is that the "exit" option weakens institutional "voice."

C. *Political Retaliation*

Institutional activism may trigger political repercussions. The

manager only investment discretion over the portfolio's assets. See Black, supra note 12, at 598 ("Often, the conscious purpose is to ensure promanager votes.").

184. Based on a series of interviews with pension fund managers, two anthropologists working with Columbia University's Institutional Investor Project report that fund managers "are reluctant to do anything which attracts any sort of attention." See John M. Conley & William M. O'Barr, The Culture of Capital: An Anthropological Investigation of Institutional Investment 31 (1991) (unpublished manuscript, on file with the Columbia Law Review).

1989 report of the New York State Task Force on Pension Fund Investment, which recommended restrictive legislation barring pension fund involvement in takeovers, was one ominous signal.[185] The recent attempt by California Governor Pete Wilson to oust the CalPERS board and take direct control over that particularly active pension fund may be a similar signal, or it may just reflect the covetous desire with which public officials battling deficits eye cash-rich pension funds.[186] At a minimum, however, it suggests that the traditional independence and insularity of pension funds is not inevitable.

Probably the clearest example of legislative pressure aimed at institutional investors is the recent Pennsylvania antigreenmail statute.[187] This statute requires institutions to disgorge any profits if they acquire, either individually or as a group, a twenty percent stake in a Pennsylvania-chartered company and sell their shares at a profit within eighteen months thereafter.[188] Even more chilling to institutional activism, the Pennsylvania statute apparently also would be triggered if investors formed a "control" group to elect directors. Although such statutes are clearly "legal" restraints, the extra-legal threat is that continued activism could bring additional restrictions. For institutions, the real object lesson is supplied by the success of corporate managements in securing the passage of antitakeover legislation in over forty-two states during the 1980s.[189] Whether corporate managements would be as successful in challenging pension funds as corporate raiders is debatable, but the risk may be substantial enough to discourage some institutional investors.

D. *Soft Information*

Institutional investors who oppose management risk cutting themselves off from the flow of soft information that management provides to "friendly" securities analysts and institutions.[190] The magnitude of this problem is difficult to assess, but there is anecdotal evidence that securities analysts who issue negative reports about a company may be

185. See supra note 16 and accompanying text.

186. See Robert J. McCartney & Kathleen Day, California Governor Seeks Control of Pension Fund; Plan Would Cut Benefits of State's Retirees, Wash. Post, June 18, 1991, at C1, C3. Although Governor Wilson partially backed down in the face of an outcry from pensioners who did not want to subsidize the state's deficit, other governors and legislatures have recently hinted at similar plans. See Michelle Osborn, Politicians Coveting Pension Funds, USA Today, July 3, 1991, at 4B.

187. 15 Pa. Cons. Stat. Ann. §§ 2573–2575 (Purdun Supp. 1991).

188. The disgorgement rule does not apply to shares bought more than two years prior to the acquisition of a 20% stake. See id. § 2575(2).

189. See 42 States Currently Have Antitakeover Laws, ABA Group Told, 22 Sec. Reg. & Law Rep. (BNA) 1216 (Aug. 17, 1990).

190. This threat has been acknowledged by many commentators. See, e.g., Black, supra note 12, at 602. Mutual funds are thought to be the most susceptible to it because they are very active traders.

denied further information.[191]

In terms of this Article's framework, the trade-off between "exit" and "voice" is once again posed here. Soft information is desired by institutions that trade actively in order to outperform the market—in effect by dumping shares if the information provided to it suggests a downturn in earnings that the market has not yet anticipated. To be sure, the ability of institutions to outperform the market is questionable—although those in possession of truly material, nonpublic information have certainly been able to profit even in an efficient market.[192] In any event, institutions in a highly competitive market, such as mutual funds, fear less that they will underperform the market than that by passing up such information they may underperform the other institutions with whom they are in direct competition. In contrast, for long-term holders, such as indexed funds and some pension funds, the value of soft information is minimal because it benefits only active traders, not those who effectively hold the market in their portfolios. For these larger holders, the probable block discounts they might suffer on the disposition of their substantial holdings are likely to be greater than the gains or losses from active trading.

E. *"Short-Termism"*

The benefits of improved corporate governance do not immediately translate into enhanced share value. The election of a few independent directors or the granting of greater "voice" to institutional investors will seldom, if ever, make an unprofitable company profitable in the short-run.[193] Indeed, the introduction of dissident directors

191. See Debbie Galant, The Hazards of Negative Research Reports, Institutional Investor, July, 1990 at 73.

192. Considerable doubt exists that mutual funds can outperform the market (at the same level of risk). See Michael C. Jensen, The Performance of Mutual Funds in the Period 1945-1964, 23 J. Fin. 389 (1968) (finding mutual fund returns to be no better than that of a passive investor holding a market portfolio). More recent research, however, has found that mutual funds earned significant abnormal returns (although transaction costs largely consumed these gains). See Norman E. Mains, Risk, The Pricing of Capital Assets, and the Evaluation of Investment Portfolios: Comment, 50 J. Bus. 371, 384 (1977); see also Jeffrey N. Gordon & Lewis A. Kornhauser, Efficient Markets, Costly Information, and Securities Research, 60 N.Y.U. L. Rev. 761, 839–41 (1985) (questioning the relevance of performance comparisons between mutual funds and the Capital Asset Pricing Model). It should be emphasized that a finding that mutual funds do outperform the market is not inconsistent with the standard "semi-strong" version of the Efficient Capital Market Hypothesis, because mutual funds may have access to nonpublic information through the medium of securities analysts. See id. at 839 n.209.

193. Some may question whether institutional ownership and monitoring has any observable impact on share value. Obviously, investors that are skeptical about the financial payoff from reforms will not support them, and frankly the available evidence is scanty. Some studies have found that the market responds positively to the appointment of outside directors. See Stuart Rosenstein & Jeffrey G. Wyatt, Outside Directors, Board of Independence and Shareholder Wealth, 26 J. Fin. Econ. 175 (1990). Yet, because management usually selects outside directors, this finding does not imply that mecha-

onto a board may even result in an interim period of disruption, uncertainty, and decreased profitability. Thus, for the short-term trader who expects to hold a stock only for a few months, the long-term benefits of improved governance and increased accountability mean little, while the costs of financing shareholder opposition remain real.

Reliance on the timing differences between long-term benefits and short-term costs to account for passivity is incomplete, however, in the absence of some explanation of why institutional money managers need to focus on the short-term. The most plausible answer focuses on agency costs at the institutional level. Many institutional investors are in head-to-head competition for investor funds, mutual funds being the most obvious example. If their profitability lags even for a quarter, some investors may withdraw their funds and move them to a competing firm.[194] Other institutions, such as pension funds, are not subject to this same pressure, but other internal pressures for performance may be equally intense. For example, pension funds use a variety of external money managers and regularly replace those whose market performance lags behind that of their peers.[195] Thus, so long as pro-

---

nisms for the appointment of outside directors selected by institutional investors, see Gilson & Kraakman, supra note 13, would have a similar impact. Some inferential evidence is available that firms with a concentrated institutional ownership are less subject to managerial retention of free cash flow. See John J. McConnell & Henri Servaes, Additional Evidence on Equity Ownership and Corporate Value, 27 J. Fin. Econ. 595 (1990) (finding that firms with high institutional ownership have a higher Tobin's Q, the ratio of stock market value to the replacement cost of tangible assets). Still, as Professor Rock has pointed out to me, this relationship may imply that institutional investors invest in such firms, not that their presence causes the firm to have a higher Tobin's Q. Moreover, no correlation has yet been found between firm profitability (according to reported accounting profits) and institutional ownership. See Harold Demsetz & Kenneth Lehn, The Structure of Corporate Ownership: Causes and Consequences, 93 J. Pol. Econ. 1155 (1985). In contrast, studies of the correlation between the board of director's ownership and firm Tobin's Q have suggested a positive relationship between board ownership and profitability. See Randall Morck, et al., Management Ownership and Market Valuation: An Empirical Analysis, 20 J. Fin. Econ. 293 (1988). In short, managerial and individual owner control may matter, but the evidence that institutional control relates to profitability has not yet been presented. Absent such evidence, some sophisticated observers may believe that corporate governance issues have little impact on share value, unless they foreshadow a takeover bid.

194. Numerous commentators have raised the same point that the competition among money managers leads each to seek "a short-term premium for a portfolio stock," even though they recognize that stockholders would profit more from a buy and hold policy. See Lipton & Rosenblum, supra note 14, at 207 (citing other authorities); see also Michael L. Dertouzos et al., Made in America: Regaining the Productive Edge 62 (1989) (main criterion for evaluating fund managers is current value of portfolio).

195. A recent survey of pension funds and other money managers found that over 90% reviewed the performance of the outside money managers they employed at least quarterly. Only 5.6% relied on semiannual review, and only 3% on annual review. See Pensionforum: Dismay Over Short-termism, Institutional Investor, Mar. 1991, at 139. Although underperforming managers were not replaced immediately (three years being the typical period before replacement for below-market performance was likely), the pressure of such constant reviews is the critical variable.

fessional money managers are held accountable in terms of their monthly or quarterly performance and the benefits of improved corporate governance do not accrue over this same period, they obviously will be reluctant to expend funds or incur costs that do not affect their current competitive standing vis-a-vis their peers. Moreover, in any competition, there are inevitably laggards. For example, if a pension fund uses four external money managers, the one whose performance has most lagged can expect replacement unless it catches up. In such an environment, short-term performance matters greatly for the money manager, as agent, even if it is a secondary concern for the pension fund, as principal. In essence, this is a moral hazard problem, because the laggard manager has an incentive both to gamble and cut costs recklessly. As a result, agency problems at the institutional level can frustrate efforts to correct agency cost problems at the corporate level, even if institutional shareholders own sufficiently large blocks to be able to resolve their collective action problems.

F. *Agent Apathy*

Even if institutional investors have an interest in corporate governance issues, it does not necessarily follow that their agents will share their concerns. What could explain such a disparity in attitudes? The short answer is a combination of a lack of incentives for the agent to monitor plus an inability on the part of the principal to detect such shirking by the agent. This explanation becomes more plausible when one learns that the federal securities laws greatly restrict the ability of an investment adviser to receive incentive compensation based on capital appreciation in the fund it manages.[196] If an investment manager is compensated simply on the basis of an annual fee equal to a declining percentage of the fund it manages (that is, 1/3 of 1% of the first $500 million, 1/4 of 1% of the next $250 million, etc.), it may have insufficient incentive to engage in monitoring so long as it bears the monitoring costs, while the fund's beneficiaries receive the benefit. Yet, exactly this structure prevails in mutual funds[197] and, to a lesser extent, in pension funds.[198] Of course, successful monitoring may attract new clients and

196. See Investment Advisers Act of 1940 § 205(1), 15 U.S.C. § 80b-5(1) (1988). See infra notes 336-347 and accompanying text for a fuller explanation of these limitations and the SEC rules implementing them.

197. Typically, the investment adviser bears the fund's administrative costs and charges an annual fee based on the fund's assets under its management to compensate it. For examples of such a fee structure, see Krinsk v. Fund Asset Management, 875 F.2d 404, 407 (2d Cir. 1989); Gartenberg v. Merrill Lynch Asset Management, 694 F.2d 923, 926 (2d Cir. 1982); Galfand v. Chestnut Corp., 545 F.2d 807, 810 (2d Cir. 1976). Obviously, such a fee structure gives the investment manager a strong incentive to economize on the administrative and operating costs that it bears.

198. The largest indexed money manager charges its clients, including many pension funds, an annual service charge of two basis points a year. See infra note 244 and accompanying text. Clearly, this will not cover much monitoring.

increased assets into the fund, thus partially solving the problem. But this depends on whether the difference between real versus merely formalistic monitoring by the agent is immediately observable by the principal. If it is not, even successful monitoring will not necessarily attract new business in the form of increased funds for the agent to manage. The bottom line is that, in the absence of incentive compensation, agents may be rationally indifferent about monitoring and will thus do only the minimum required of them by the law.

G. *Managerial Manipulation of Agenda*

Management's most effective tactic in securing shareholder approval of an antitakeover proposal has been its ability to link a disfavored proposal to a "sweetener," such as a recapitalization with a large dividend or a stock buyback.[199] For those investors who are focused on the short-term, the gain from the "sweetener" exceeds the loss on the other linked transaction, and so they vote in favor of both. Although the "sweetener" may leave the shareholder better off than if no inducement for its acquiescence were paid, this tactic still reduces the expected payoff from shareholder activism. It thus aggravates the traditional collective action problem.[200]

Obviously, agenda manipulation is a problem that only regulation, and not deregulation, can address.[201] Still, this tactic of "bundling" issues again implicates the trade-off between "exit" and "voice." Shareholders who rely on the "exit" option seem more likely to vote approval in such a case, expecting to receive the sweetener and then sell their shares. However, for longer-term investors, who effectively hold the market in their portfolios, such linkages are distasteful because in effect management is "bribing" shareholders into passivity with corporate funds that already belong to the shareholders. Thus, if share-

---

199. For a fuller discussion of this theme, see Black, supra note 12, at 592–94. Black gives as an example the 1987 proxy statement of Holiday Corporation, which asked shareholders to vote on a single proposal to (i) declare a massive special dividend, (ii) grant very large stock options to management, and (iii) adopt a "capped voting" antitakeover charter amendment that prevented new shareholders from voting more than 10% of the corporation's stock. Id. at 593. On the general theory of agenda manipulation, see Michael E. Levine & Charles R. Plott, Agenda Influence and its Implications, 63 Va. L. Rev. 561 (1977).

200. See supra note 23. The inevitable existence of free riders (i.e., shareholders who will not contribute to the costs of collective coordination and resistance) implies that the expected payoff from the proposed course of action must exceed its aggregate costs by a corresponding margin. The more the payoff is reduced, the less likely it becomes that large shareholders will fund the costs of coordination (such as by financing a proxy solicitation).

201. SEC Rule 14a-4(a) does contain a potential limitation on linking unrelated matters by seemingly requiring a separate vote on "each matter or group of related matters." See 17 C.F.R. § 240.14a-4(a) (1991). CalPERS has proposed tightening this vague limitation to prevent some forms of agenda manipulation. See CalPERS Letter, supra note 56, at 11. The feasibility of these proposals is beyond this Article's scope.

holders perceive themselves as long-term holders who are locked into the market, the rational course of action may more often be to reject the bribe and seek eventually to secure the distribution of the excess corporate funds, or "free cash flow," by exercising "voice."

H. *Summary*

Some institutional investors need liquidity. Whether this need derives from "thin equity," the need to meet potential redemptions, a fear of their own stock being discounted, or other factors, it seems to be the common denominator that also explains why even unregulated British and German banks actually acquire only modest to intermediate stakes in their clients.[202]

If we also assume that for the foreseeable future some institutions will remain active traders with a high turnover in their portfolios, these two factors—the inability to take large positions and an active trading style—explain why they will show only a limited interest in corporate governance issues, except possibly those related to takeovers. Put simply, money managers are rationally apathetic because the expected gains from most such governance issues are small, deferred, and received by investors, while the costs are potentially large, immediate, and borne by money managers. This problem is compounded because the competitive pressures on institutional money managers give them little reason to focus on the long-term. To address this imbalance one must either induce institutional investors to hold larger stakes or to hold even modest stakes for a longer term, over which the expected gains from improved governance would materialize. Additionally, the compensation formulas used to reward money managers ought to create incentives for monitoring. In the absence of these conditions, however, the reasons for shareholder passivity would remain, even if the current legal obstacles to the exercise of shareholder "voice" were greatly reduced.

Where does this analysis lead? It is by no means intended to justify existing legal rules that chill shareholder "voice," but to take us back to the essential trade-off between liquidity and control. The more significant these legal and extra-legal obstacles are judged to be, the more likely it becomes that institutional investors will stand and fight only if their "exit" option is made less available or less attractive.

III. The Potential Costs of Uniting Liquidity and Control

To this point, this Article has argued only that a trade-off between liquidity and control characterizes most major industrial economies. Thus, the famous generalization of Berle and Means that the modern

202. As noted earlier, German banks own less than 5% of the top one hundred German corporations and British institutional investors seldom exceed 2% ownership in any individual corporation. See supra notes 99, 143 and accompanying text.

public corporation produced the separation of ownership and control can be translated into the deeper and more accurate statement that public shareholders in the modern corporation purchased liquidity at the cost of control.[203] Still, the state of the world described by Berle and Means may already be in flux. With institutional ownership of corporate equity nearing the fifty percent level and some of the largest U.S. corporations already having over three quarters of their stock owned by institutions, it is easily imaginable that, absent legal restrictions, a dozen or so institutional investors could form a group overnight that would hold effective control of a giant U.S. corporation.

To be sure, today there are substantial legal obstacles to the formation of such a control group, and commentators have begun to debate the scope and purpose of existing regulations.[204] However, such a debate cannot sensibly begin with the regulations themselves; rather, it should start by identifying the potential harms that regulation should address. This Part will assess five potential problems with relying on institutional monitoring to end the separation of ownership and control. In each case, it will suggest that the problem lies less in institutional monitoring itself than in its combination with easy liquidity.

A. *The Exiting Monitor*

The first and most obvious problem with institutions as monitors is that they are watchdogs whose every incentive is to flee at the first sign of trouble. This is where the liquidity/control trade-off is the most acute. A traditional controlling shareholder, owning perhaps thirty percent or more of a corporation's voting stock, necessarily realizes that its investment is illiquid, even though a deep and active market exists. Any attempt by it to dispose of a substantial portion of its stock in the market is likely to be perceived by the market as a bail-out and to be greeted by a collapse in the stock price, as sophisticated market professionals infer from this disposition that the controlling shareholder has received nonpublic, but material, adverse information.[205]

The same is not necessarily true for a loose association of institutional investors, numbering perhaps between ten and twenty, who

203. For a similar observation, see Walter Werner, Corporation Law in Search of its Future, 81 Colum. L. Rev. 1611, 1662–63 (1981). Martin Lipton has more recently argued that stockholders "view the corporation more as the holder of a betting slip views a racehorse." See Lipton & Rosenblum, supra note 14, at 194 (citation omitted).

204. For a partial review of these obstacles, see infra notes 246–287 and accompanying text. Some commentators have expressed doubt that these obstacles are substantial enough to deter institutional monitoring. See Gilson & Kraakman, supra note 13, at 894–905. This Article does not directly analyze that debate, although it does suggest that extra-legal forces may be more important to some institutional investors.

205. For the finding that the market does distinguish between block sales by insiders and block sales by institutional investors and penalizes the former more heavily, see Myron S. Scholes, The Market for Securities: Substitution versus Price Pressure and the Effects of Information on Share Prices, 45 J. Bus. 179 (1972).

might collectively own a controlling block. Because they own smaller blocks on an individual basis—say, one to three percent each—and because they have lesser visibility, they may be able to liquidate their positions on learning of adverse developments, without alerting the market. For such investors, the choice is between seeking to reverse the company's decline in fortune and seeking to beat the market's recognition of that decline. Of course, this use of material, nonpublic information by a controlling investor may violate the insider trading laws. Yet, while this may be formally true, institutional investors are in a marginally safer position under these laws than the traditional controlling shareholder. Typically, they will have no employee on the board; nor will they necessarily be in direct contact with corporate officers. Confidential information will reach them through indirect leakages, usually through security analysts. Moreover, the information on which they act typically will be soft information; not hard, specific data, but looser general impressions and a premonitory feel for future trends. In short, bail-outs seem both relatively more feasible and marginally less vulnerable as a legal matter when institutional investors constitute the control group.

Even if institutional investors cannot exit before the market's perception of the problem, there are other reasons why they might prefer to flee than fight. Conflicts of interest or fear of reputational loss (either at the institutional level or, more likely, at the level of their money manager agents) could motivate such a decision. Put simply, while the ten percent stakeholder can be expected to fight, the one percent holder is apt to be a "sunshine patriot" unwilling to remain on duty during the corporation's winter of discontent.

B. *The Market-Dominated Monitor*

In all likelihood, the principal impact of institutional investors as large shareholders will be to make corporate management more sensitive to the market's judgment. This development will yield greater efficiency only to the extent that the market can make a better informed or less biased judgment than can the corporation's own management. Often, the market can. Yet, because management inherently has access to nonpublic information that the market lacks, it is impossible to conclude that the market's judgment will always be superior. Even in an efficient market, those possessing "inside" information are capable of outperforming the market.[206] Thus, institutional investors may tend to

206. Under the standard "semi-strong" version of the Efficient Capital Markets Hypothesis, one assumes only that the market has incorporated all publicly available information into the share price, not that nonpublic information is reflected. Thus, those in possession of such information, as management typically is, can make a better judgment of the firm's value than can the market. For a fuller explanation of efficient market theory, see Ronald J. Gilson & Reinier H. Kraakman, The Mechanisms of Market Efficiency, 70 Va. L. Rev. 549, 554–92 (1984).

follow the herd, enforcing the generic judgments and conventional wisdom of the market, but thereby chilling entrepreneurial managers who believe they perceive opportunities that the market has missed.[207]

One answer to this claim is that if a management team truly knows more than the market, it has every incentive to explain and defend its judgment by persuading the consensus of securities analysts on whom the market, and institutional investors, rely. Still, there is a problem with this answer: Such an explanation may release confidential, proprietary information. Suppose, for example, that at a time when the market believes that American companies should cease to produce a particular technology because they cannot outcompete Japanese firms that seemingly have a comparative advantage, one lone American firm bucks the market's judgment and seeks to expand its activities in this area. If this firm is heavily owned by institutions, this deviant behavior likely will encounter institutional resistance.

What happens next? Possibly, the corporation's management can explain to the market why its new technology can outperform all existing products made by the competition. But to be credible, this claim must be corroborated. At this point, if the corporation reveals to its institutional investors, or to the market generally, its basis for believing its new technology to be superior, it may effectively release—directly or indirectly—proprietary information, thereby benefitting its competitors. Conversely, if it just asserts the superiority of its new technology, its position may not be credible to market-sensitive institutional investors. The paradox is a familiar one: it is often difficult to value proprietary information without revealing it and thereby sacrificing its proprietary value.

Although corporate management has long faced the prospect that an unsympathetic market would discount its share price if it bucked the conventional wisdom, management could withstand this pressure in the past, either because public shareholders were too disorganized to mount effective opposition or because the controlling shareholders, such as a family group, would have participated in the decision, or at least could have it explained and justified to them in confidence. Again, the difference between a traditional controlling shareholder and a loose association of institutional investors is significant here. It is one thing to disclose confidential plans and data to a single majority shareholder or a close-knit family group, and quite another to explain the same information to the community of securities analysts on whom institutional investors rely. In the latter case, information leakage is likely.

This problem is not insurmountable. Institutional investors could

207. For the hypothesis that institutional shareholders are susceptible to herd behavior, see David S. Scharfstein & Jeremy C. Stein, Herd Behavior and Investment, Am. Econ. Rev., June 1990, at 465.

rely on professional directors selected by them to evaluate management's plans and projections, without proprietary information leaking to the public.[208] Yet, this course would require institutional investors to accept some market penalty during the period when the market was skeptical of management's plans. Many institutional investors might be willing to pay this price, but others would not because of their need for liquidity. For this latter group, the ideal position is to be a low-profile member of a loose investors' association that has access to nonpublic information and projections, and to choose "exit" when that information suggests a future market decline in the firm's stock price. In short, such actively trading investors make poor monitors because they are unwilling to pursue long-run policies that may elicit a short-run market discount.

C. *The Risk-Preferring Monitor*

Standard finance theory recognizes that the shareholder in a highly leveraged firm will prefer a higher-risk course of action than would the same shareholder in a less leveraged firm.[209] Because in such a firm most of the loss will be borne by creditors, while most of the gain will go to the shareholders, shareholders might rationally prefer a high-risk investment with a low probability of success to another investment with a projected lower return but a much higher probability of success—even though these shareholders would have the opposite preference if they were the suppliers of all the capital for the project. Based on this analysis, some commentators have contended that the Japanese/German model, under which the same banking institution provides both debt and equity capital to the firm, has significant efficiency advantages.[210] Monitors who hold both debt and equity need not be "excessively risk-prone" because their attitude will reflect their weighted average position as both creditors and shareholders.[211] Stephen

208. Such an institutional arrangement has been carefully spelled out by other recent commentators. See Gilson & Kraakman, supra note 13. They assume (as do I) that institutional investors must delegate to outside professionals the actual responsibility for monitoring.

209. This has been a central insight of standard finance theory. See Michael C. Jensen & William H. Meckling, Theory of the Firm: Managerial Behavior, Agency Costs and Ownership Structure, 3 J. Fin. Econ. 305, 334 (1976) (noting that managers in a leveraged firm will have an incentive to accept projects having a high payoff but low risk of success because the shareholders capture the gain and creditors suffer the loss). While Jensen and Meckling ignore that managers may have firm-specific human capital at risk that may dissuade them from accepting such risks, their analysis works well for institutional investors.

Of course, this problem is mitigated if institutional investors also hold the debt securities of the firms in whose equity securities they invest. See Prowse, supra note 66, at 46–48 (discussing Japanese pattern). Still, no reason is apparent why U.S. institutions would undertake on their own to diversify on such a matched basis.

210. See Prowse, supra note 66, at 51–52.

211. See Aoki, supra note 88, at 16 (citing Phillipe Aghion & Patrick Bolton, An

Prowse has reasoned that allowing financial institutions to serve as both creditors and shareholders should minimize agency costs.[212]

The immediate point, however, is that the legal restrictions in the United States that inhibit banks and insurance companies from owning stock should logically produce monitoring by other institutional investors of a very different character than prevails in Japan or Germany. Rather than being neutral monitors, American institutional investors have a logical incentive, at least in the case of leveraged companies, to prefer risky strategies that may transfer wealth from debtholders to shareholders. To be sure, managers may have the opposing tendency to be excessively risk averse because they have undiversifiable human capital and other wealth locked into the firm.[213] Ultimately, it is hard to determine how this tension between risk-averse managers and potentially risk-preferring institutions will be resolved. However, it stands in sharp contrast to an earlier era when the incentives of the controlling shareholders tended to match those of management because the bulk of their wealth was typically invested in the firm so that they could not be risk neutral.

D. *The Disruptive Monitor*

A substantial economic literature has described contracting within the firm as based on "implicit contracts."[214] Because managers and other employees should be risk averse, while diversified shareholders should be risk neutral, this literature argues that the two sides maximize their respective interests by entering into employment contracts under which employees trade off some portion of the wages they could demand in return for employment stability. One aspect of this system of implicit contracting is that it defers a considerable portion of the managers' expected aggregate compensation until the end of their careers.[215] But, such implicit contracts are vulnerable if there is a hostile change of control because the new owners can in effect renege on this implicit agreement and withhold the deferred compensation.[216]

"Incomplete Contract" Approach to Bankruptcy and the Financial Structure of the Firm (M.I.T. Dept. of Economics Working Paper No. 484, 1988)).

212. See Prowse, supra note 66.

213. See Coffee, supra note 178 at 17–19.

214. For a general review of this literature, see Sherwin Rosen, Implicit Contracts: A Survey, 23 J. Econ. Literature 1144 (1985); see also Costas Azariadis & Joseph E. Stiglitz, Implicit Contracts and Fixed Price Equilibria, 98 Q.J. Econ. 1 (Supp. 1983) (appraising current state of theory of implicit contracts).

215. Deferred compensation is a protection against both shirking and managerial departures. This theory assumes that the manager's value to the firm is often difficult to estimate until a subsequent period; thus, deferred compensation acts as a bonding device to reduce the need for costly monitoring.

216. For a fuller statement of this theme as a rationale for hostile takeovers, see Charles R. Knoeber, Golden Parachutes, Shark Repellents, and Hostile Tender Offers, Am. Econ. Rev., Mar. 1986, at 155, 159–61.

This same point can be made in more overtly political terms. Professor William Simon has argued that a tradition of "economic republicanism" in the United States has long been hostile to "speculators and intermediaries" because "they introduce a community-threatening liquidity to investments."[217] Fear of such destabilizing changes may well explain the recent wildfire-like passage of antitakeover statutes in the majority of states.[218]

From either an implicit contract standpoint or this community-oriented perspective, liquidity is disquieting because it implies instability. Thus, the future power of institutional investors presents many of the same issues as did the hostile takeover. Potentially, pools of institutional investors could form and re-form. Particularly because they arrive on the scene at an interim point in the corporation's existence, they are unlikely to feel bound by prior implicit wage and employment arrangements between the corporation and its employees and managers. Thus, they may disrupt the implicit contract by pressuring senior management to reduce employment and compensation levels. Some empirical support exists for this proposition, with one study finding the level of deferred compensation to be higher in firms with low shareholder concentration.[219] Arguably, managers may be less willing to rely on implicit contracts as institutional ownership increases.

E. *The Opportunistic Monitor*

Institutional investors should not be mistaken for financial saints. Their representatives on a board will not automatically represent all shareholders; to the extent that conflicts among shareholders exist, board members who are institutional employees or agents may favor the interests of their employers.[220] For example, because mutual funds are often affiliated with investment banking firms, it is not unimaginable that mutual fund representatives on boards might pursue the interests of their investment banking firm sponsors, favoring transactions that generated fees for them. Pension funds have less obvious conflicts, but to the extent that they are dominated by their own corporate managements, they could logically pursue a policy of reciprocal deference to their host management. Individuals may also act opportunistically, using their influence to obtain corporate office or perquisites. Indeed,

217. See William H. Simon, Contract Versus Politics in Corporation Doctrine, *in* The Politics of Law 387, 397 (David Kairys ed., 1990).

218. See supra notes 187–189 and accompanying text.

219. See Gerald Garvey & Noel Gaston, Delegation, the Role of Managerial Discretion As a Bonding Device, and the Enforcement of Implicit Contracts, 9 Advances in Econometrics (forthcoming 1991) (manuscript at 2, 20, 25, on file with the Columbia Law Review).

220. I am here referring to directors who are directly affiliated with institutional investors and not to the professional director proposal advocated by others. See Gilson & Kraakman, supra note 13, at 885–88.

although public pension funds probably have the fewest potential conflicts, their own employees are also probably the least monitored, giving them a vast range for discretionary decision-making.

Finally, there is the overriding danger of market manipulation. Unlike risk averse corporate managers, who tend to favor steady earnings and stock price growth, institutional investors who possess de facto control can benefit from volatile swings in stock price and could manipulate corporate affairs to create profitable trading opportunities.[221] The enactment of the Securities Exchange Act of 1934 was motivated to a considerable degree by Congressional dissatisfaction with the behavior of "notorious market pools,"[222] which were essentially trading syndicates formed by large investors to manipulate stock prices. Absent restrictions on liquidity, the growth of institutional ownership creates the preconditions under which such pools could reappear.[223]

F. *The Unaccountable Monitor*

Public pension funds have been the most active of institutional investors, but they may also be the least accountable to their own beneficiaries. A state or municipal pension fund covers an enormous number of employees, and therefore substantial collective action problems would be obvious, even if the beneficiary had some recourse other than litigation. But unlike the corporate pension fund, there is no corporate sponsor looking over the public pension fund trustee's shoulder and seeking to economize on its own contribution. Instead, the public pension fund offers an attractive vehicle by which political leaders, or would-be candidates, can present themselves to the public. The more prominent the role of public pension funds becomes, the greater will be the political allure of such office. The result is a special agency problem: political leaders as pension fund trustees are subject to strong constituency pressures that can conflict with their obligation to maximize value for their beneficiaries. In fairness, this problem has not yet materialized in the United States,[224] but its eventual appearance seems

221. See Steve Thel, The Genius of Section 16: Regulating the Management of Publicly Held Companies, 42 Hastings L.J. 391, 399 (1991) (arguing that the Congressional purpose underlying § 16(b) of the Securities Exchange Act of 1934 was not to prevent insider trading, but to eliminate the incentive for the manipulation of corporate affairs to produce stock price fluctuations).

222. Id. at 439–40.

223. Recently adopted rules under § 16(b) may reduce this danger, but do not eliminate it. See infra notes 256–258 and accompanying text.

224. Others have already warned of this danger. See Leo Herzel, Are Institutional Investors A Likely Substitute for the Takeover Market?, *in* Institutional Investing: The Challenges and Responsibilities of the 21st Century 128, 134 (Arnold W. Sansetz ed., 1991); Deborah J. Martin, The Public Piggy Bank Goes To Market: Public Pension Fund Investment In Common Stock and Fund Trustees' Social Agenda (1991) (unpublished manuscript on file with the Columbia Law Review). Mr. Herzel points to an English case in which the Bishop of Oxford sued the Church Commissioners of the Church of Eng-

certain.

G. *Summary*

This Article does not contend that institutional monitoring is undesirable. To the contrary, the benefits seem likely to outweigh the costs by a substantial margin. The point here, however, is that monitoring is not a neutral phenomenon; all monitors have characteristic biases. The substitution of institutional investors for previous monitors, such as family groups, carries with it the risks that new agency costs will be substituted for old ones. Chief among these risks are the following: (1) the new monitors will be more prone to bail out when crises loom; (2) a volatile market will interfere with long-term planning; (3) under some circumstances, the new monitors will have a higher tolerance for risk than society as a whole deems desirable; and (4) implicit contracts will be disrupted. These risks are simply that: Risks, not certainties. Part IV will next discuss how they can be mitigated and, in that light, how the "unleashing" of the institutional investor should proceed.

IV. Shaping the Institutional Monitor: The Role of Regulation

If one sought to define the optimal corporate monitor, what criteria would one select? Three factors seem to stand out: (1) the institutional monitor should be reasonably free from conflicts of interest so that its evaluation of corporate management will not be biased by the opportunity to earn fees or income not equally available to other shareholders; (2) its stake in the corporation should be large enough to justify the expenditure of significant monitoring costs; and (3) its preferred investment horizon should be sufficiently long so that it has an interest in improved corporate governance, even when no immediate value-maximizing transaction, such as a takeover or LBO, is in the offing. Based on these three criteria—the absence of conflicts of interest, a substantial stake, and a long-term horizon—the relative superiority of the pension fund over other institutional investors seems clear. First, unlike banks or insurance companies, the pension fund has no other opportunities to earn fees or income from the corporation.[225]

land to compel them to invest the Church's portfolio in greater accordance with the Church's religious and moral beliefs. Herzel, supra, at 137 n.9. Similarly, public pension funds face a tension between social investing and shareholder returns. See Martin, supra, at 1–2. Arguably, there could be "collusive" arrangements in some cases by which corporate managements agreed to pursue social goals in return for the fund's agreement to vote to maintain them in office. For the present, however, these remain speculative possibilities.

225. For a recent instance in which fee income may have driven decisions by banks to invest in corporate equity, see Wallace, supra note 159 (discussing fee income received by banks from LBO lending and its influence on their decision to invest in

Second, it is increasingly likely to hold a substantial stake in the corporations in which it invests; but because it cannot make a takeover bid, there is less prospect for a conflict arising between its interests and those of smaller shareholders.[226] Third, it characteristically has a lower turnover rate on its stock portfolio than most other institutional investors and so has a relatively longer investment horizon.[227]

Because pension funds represent the largest, and still growing, category of institutional investor, their relative superiority to other institutions in terms of these criteria may seem fortunate. However, pension funds are hardly immune from pressure,[228] and some commentators believe there is an unresolvable fundamental tension between the legal responsibilities of pension managers to their beneficiaries and their actual subservience to senior corporate officials.[229] At a minimum, most commentators recognize that senior corporate management wants its pension managers to vote for management and against insurgent shareholders.[230] While overt pressure on pension managers may no longer be permissible,[231] only obtuse money managers will fail to detect their client's or superior's sympathies and the corresponding impact on their self-interest.

Although the conflict of interest problem has been duly noted by a number of commentators, two more serious obstacles to active institutional monitoring have received less attention. First, many institutions—pension funds in particular—are so widely diversified, holding literally a thousand or more stocks, that it is simply beyond their realis-

---

Kohlberg, Kravis & Roberts buyout fund). In contrast, ERISA requires that pension managers make all decisions "for the exclusive purpose of [] providing benefits to participants and their beneficiaries." 29 U.S.C. § 1104(a)(1)(A)-(A)(i) (1988). But see infra notes 228-233 and accompanying text (discussing other conflicting interests that affect pension managers).

226. No U.S. pension fund has ever made a takeover bid, and such a substantial investment would probably run afoul of ERISA's diversification requirement. See 29 C.F.R. § 2550.404a-1 (1990). See also Donovan v. Bierwirth, 680 F.2d 263 (2d Cir. 1982) (in a takeover bid, trustees who are also corporate officers have a duty to resign when their positions as trustees conflict with their positions as corporate officers).

227. One recent study of turnover rates found the annual turnover rate for pension funds to be 61%, while it was 76% for mutual funds and 51% for college and university endowments. See Stephen A. Berkowitz & Dennis E. Logue, The Portfolio Turnover Explosion Explained, J. of Portfolio Mgmt., Spring 1987, at 38, 40.

228. For examples of such pressure, see Joe Kolman, The Proxy Pressure on Pension Managers, Institutional Investor, July 1985, at 145-47; Minow, supra note 172, at 32. Black, supra note 12, at 596-98; Rock, supra note 9, at 469-71.

229. See Daniel Fischel & John H. Langbein, ERISA's Fundamental Contradiction: The Exclusive Benefit Rule, 55 U. Chi. L. Rev. 1105, 1126-28 (1988).

230. See Black, supra note 12, at 596-97; Rock, supra note 9, at 469-70.

231. Beginning in 1988, the U.S. Labor Department has campaigned to reform pension voting practices and has issued a series of interpretations requiring plan fiduciaries to vote shares held by the plan or supervise those with voting discretion. See Black, supra note 12, at 597 (noting that subtler pressures still remain possible); Rock, supra note 9, at 476-78.

tic monitoring capacity to make any meaningful evaluation of the competence of the management at individual firms or of the likely impact of proposals raised by other shareholders of those firms.[232] Second, institutional money managers are typically compensated based on formulas that leave them rationally indifferent to shareholder voting decisions.[233]

It is debatable whether these problems can be overcome, and the trend toward global diversification suggests that both will be aggravated. Without expressing either optimism or pessimism, this Part will chart the structural changes that would be necessary to achieve effective monitoring through institutional investors.

Three basic proposals will be considered: (1) an *unbundling* strategy which would shift proxy voting decisions from institutional money managers to specialized proxy advisers, who would be encouraged to develop and sell their expertise to institutional investors; pension fiduciaries would be required either to use these services or to demonstrate a sufficient in-house capacity to internalize voting decisions; (2) a *restricted diversification* strategy which would discourage institutional investors from diversifying beyond the limits of their monitoring capacity; and (3) an *incentive compensation* strategy which would reward money managers for voting decisions that increased their portfolio's value. The first strategy addresses the informational overload on the institution, while the second and third increase the expected payoff from monitoring to the institution and its agents, respectively. As discussed below, these strategies can also be linked.

Such a combined strategy would require some deregulation, but not a broad "unleashing" of institutional investors that freed them from all existing constraints under the federal securities laws. Rather, because "voice" and "exit" are competing options for the investor, reforms that increase the availability of "exit" by enhancing the liquidity of institutional investors could chill "voice," namely, their willingness to participate in corporate governance. Thus, relaxation of "exit" regulations should selectively focus on both: (1) whether the investors thus aided will still have an incentive to exercise an increasingly costly "voice" in corporate governance,[234] and (2) whether relaxed "exit" will

232. The problem is most acute with respect to "indexed" funds that follow a passive investment strategy. See infra notes 236–245 and accompanying text. The problem is not, however, limited to the indexed funds. For a similar, if more pessimistic, view, see Lipton & Rosenblum, supra note 14, at 206.

233. See infra notes 336–347 and accompanying text.

234. By "costly," I mean to cover both financial and nonfinancial costs. Current estimates place the direct financial cost of a proxy campaign in opposition to management at between $2 million and $15 million, depending upon the size of the corporation and the specific proposal. See Proxy Contests: Oasis for Dissidents—or a Mirage? Corp. Control Alert, May 1990, at 1, 10 [hereinafter Proxy Contests]. Undoubtedly, legal reforms can reduce these costs, but any campaign to elect directors or dismantle antitakeover charter provisions is likely to encounter managerial resistance and entail

give the wrong investors an incentive to participate in control groups in order to manipulate corporate affairs to benefit from stock volatility.[235]

A. *The Decline of "Exit"*

Although commentary about institutional investors customarily distinguishes among them in terms of their legal status (e.g., pension funds, mutual funds, or insurance companies), a more important distinction may lie in their differing investment philosophies. Today, it is estimated that nearly one-third of all equity investments held by institutional funds are "indexed"[236]—that is, they are invested in a portfolio of securities that is intended to represent an accurate proxy for the stock market as a whole. Such passive investing seeks not to beat the market, but to duplicate its movements, and, as a result, such investors tend to hold for the long-term.[237] In this Article's terminology, such indexed investors have essentially abandoned their "exit" option and have become long-term holders. This decision was motivated by their perception that an active trading strategy did not enable them to outperform the market, but only increased the brokerage and other costs they bore.[238]

Demographic forces indicate that pension funds will hold a progressively larger percentage of all equity securities and may account for forty percent of the equity ownership of U.S. corporations by the year

considerable costs. Nonfinancial costs, such as business reprisals, are harder to quantify, but may be more significant.

235. See supra notes 221–223 and accompanying text.

236. A survey by Financial Executives Institute of pension plans found 34% of the equity investments held by the surveyed plans were indexed. See David M. Walker, The Increasing Role of Pension Plans in the Capital Markets and in Corporate Governance Matters, *in* Institutional Investing: The Challenges and Responsibilities of the 21st Century 34, 36 (Arnold W. Sametz ed., 1991). The New York Stock Exchange has reported that "analysts estimate that between $200 billion and $300 billion—or about 30 percent—of institutional assets are held in portfolios that replicate or mirror a market index." NYSE Press Release, Panel Recommends Initiatives Aimed at Reducing Volatility, Enhancing Investor Confidence, June 12, 1990. Public pension funds are particularly "indexed." For example, it has been estimated that of the $40 billion in equities held by the three principal New York pension funds covering state and local employees, "$30 billion are in indexed portfolios." Taylor, supra note 41, at 72.

237. For example, CalPERS has an average holding period of between six and ten years for each security in its portfolio and an annual turnover rate of approximately 10%. See Gilson & Kraakman, supra note 13, at 863. CalPERS is apparently moving to the point where it will be 85% indexed during 1991. See Stephen Clark, Why Dale Hanson Won't Go Away, Institutional Investor, Apr. 1990, at 80. A recent survey by the Financial Executives Institute found that the average turnover rates for pension funds are falling. For actively managed equity portfolios, the average turnover rate declined from 66% in 1987 to 47% in 1989, and for passively managed portfolios, the turnover rate declined from 24% in 1987 to 13% in 1989. See Walker, supra note 236, at 36.

238. As Professors Gilson and Kraakman accurately observe, these institutional investors have essentially accepted the Efficient Capital Market Hypothesis. See Gilson & Kraakman, supra note 13, at 865–67.

2000.[239] As both pension funds and mutual funds switch to an indexed strategy, indexed investing eventually will account for a significant fraction of all equity investment. Necessarily, however, a ceiling will be reached on the percentage of the total market for which indexed investors account. If all, or nearly all, institutional investors were to adopt passive trading strategies, there would simply be no market—or at least not an efficient one. Economic theory suggests that if indexed investing were to become the predominant strategy for institutions, other investors would be enabled to pursue more profitable trading strategies.[240] Thus, there seems considerable reason to believe that institutional investors will divide along a continuum whose poles are represented by (1) indexed investors and others who follow basically long-term trading strategies and (2) active traders who may find that the growth of indexed trading increases the opportunities available for profitable short-term trading.

Among fund managers, there is already a wide divergence in trading styles, as shown by their different turnover rates.[241] Recognition of this diversity should be the starting point for a sensible public policy analysis of the institutional investor, because different institutions are likely to behave very differently as corporate monitors. Having abandoned "exit," indexed investors present little risk of bail-outs or the misuse of inside information. Sharing a long-term perspective, they have less reason to be interested in obtaining short-term gains by disrupting implicit contracts. In contrast, active traders seem more likely to exert pressure for management decisions and strategies that will in-

239. For this estimate by the Pension and Welfare Benefits Administration, see Pension and Welfare Benefits Admin., U.S. Dep't of Labor, Proxy Project Report, Mar. 2, 1989, at 1.

240. See Sanford J. Grossman & Joseph E. Stiglitz, On the Impossibility of Informationally Efficient Markets, 70 Am. Econ. Rev. 393 (1980) (concluding that there will be an equilibrium level of disequilibrium because the market cannot stay efficient without some incentive to search for new information).

241. See Walker, supra note 236, at 36 (noting that in 1989 actively managed equity portfolios of pension plans had an average turnover rate of 47%, while passively managed portfolios of the same institutions averaged only 13%). Another recent survey of turnover rates by Institutional Investor reported the following range of rates among responding fund managers:

Turnover Rate	Percentage of Funds
25% or below	26.3%
26 to 50%	41.6%
51 to 75%	21.8%
76 to 100%	8.2%
101 to 150%	1.7%
151 to 200%	0.3%

See Pensionforum: Dismay Over Short-Termism, Institutional Investor, Mar. 1991, at 139. Fifty-six percent of the surveyed funds also reported that their turnover rates were unchanged as compared to five years ago, but of the 24% that did have a lower turnover rate, the majority attributed the decline to "a shift in assets into index funds." Id. at 139.

crease the volatility of the corporation's securities, which, to a degree, they can anticipate because of their privileged position as quasi-insiders. Accordingly, as a normative matter, deregulation of the restrictions on institutional ownership, and particularly those regulating "exit," should go further and faster in the case of the indexed investor.

Although indexed investors are typically long-term and substantial holders, it does not follow from this that they will be active monitors. The problem is that indexed funds are typically managed by external money managers who have little incentive to monitor. Rather, having abandoned any attempt to outperform the market, they compete by reducing their costs in order to be the lowest-cost provider of "indexing" services.[242] Obviously, a money manager intent on radical cost economizing has little interest in undertaking costly monitoring activities. The extent of this problem is revealed by a question aptly posed by my colleague, Professor Louis Lowenstein. He reports that Wells Fargo Institutional Trust, the leading index fund manager, has nearly $60 billion invested in indexed equity funds for its clients, of which $40 billion is in its S&P 500 index,[243] and that it holds perhaps 5000 different stocks in these funds. Yet, because of the competitive nature of the indexing industry, it charges fees as low as two basis points a year. Thus, he asks: "How much monitoring do we get for two basis points?"[244]

The only logical answer is that one gets very little monitoring for such a price. But if capital markets are competitive, why do not other competitors offer more meaningful monitoring services and charge a higher fee? The most likely answer involves a combination of the corporate manager's desire for an implicit and reciprocal system of self-protective passivity, under which corporate sponsors dissuade their money managers from supporting shareholder activism and the fear of money mangers that if they acquire a reputation for activism they will be less able to attract additional pension fund accounts. Under this combination of factors, even if all corporate sponsors do not seek to chill active monitoring by money managers, the latter still fear acquiring an adverse reputation and so seek a low profile. The result resembles an implicit contract: money managers are free to use their own discretion in making investment decisions, but not in the case of voting decisions, because the latter more clearly threaten executive job stability.

242. This point has been well made by Professor Rock. See Rock, supra note 9, at 474.

243. Lowenstein, supra note 45, at 33–34.

244. Id. at 33. A basis point is 1% of 1%. Thus, two basis points charged annually on a $1,000,000 fund would amount to $200 a year. The director of proxy voting at Wells Fargo described their voting practices to Professor Lowenstein as follows: "[S]ince we invest by formula, we vote by formula." Id. at 34. In my view use of such a formula reflects simply an attempt to minimize costs while achieving minimal compliance with the Department of Labor's guidelines.

Finally, there is a third factor: Most pension funds have only a skeleton in-house staff, which then hires several external money managers.[245] Both investment and voting decisions are then delegated to the external managers, and the function of the in-house staff is basically to evaluate the performance of these fund managers. To such an in-house staff, a manager who expends funds or time on proxy voting may seem to be overcharging, particularly given the likely delay between voting and any resulting increase in share value.

What then is the answer? Clearly, a small in-house staff is even less able to monitor the managements of the 500 firms in the S&P 500 or to follow other corporations on a world-wide basis as pension funds increasingly diversify their holdings on a global basis. Inevitably, a serious reform program must consider whether some level of portfolio diversification is "excessive" because it is inconsistent with a capacity to monitor even minimally the firms held in the portfolio. Because such a reform would undoubtedly be controversial, it seems best to consider first several less drastic measures.

B. *The Regulation of "Exit"*

What gains could be realized simply by relaxing existing regulatory barriers to institutional activism? Much of the federal securities laws and many state statutes can be grouped into two categories: (1) legal rules that regulate "voice," and (2) legal rules that regulate "exit." In the former category, for example, are those rules that apply to shareholder communications[246] or that require disclosure of plans and intentions once certain ownership thresholds are crossed.[247] Much commentary has recently recommended revision of the federal proxy rules and state corporate law to reduce the costs of proxy contests to insurgents.[248] Recently, the SEC has proposed relaxing significantly the proxy rules as they would apply to shareholder communications among institutional investors.[249] Highly desirable as the SEC's proposed reforms are, this Article doubts that either they or the reforms proposed by academic commentators would, if adopted, "unleash" in-

245. See Black, supra note 12, at 596 (describing this relationship as "the most common pattern").

246. The proxy rules are contained in Rules 14a-1 to 14b-2, 17 C.F.R. §§ 240.14a-1 to 14b-2 (1991). For a discussion of their impact on the organization of shareholder groups seeking to oppose management, see Black, supra note 12, at 536–42. But see infra note 249 and accompanying text (discussing proposed relaxation of proxy rules).

247. See Securities Exchange Act of 1934, § 13(d), 15 U.S.C. § 78m(d) (1988); Rules 13d-1 to 13d-7, 17 C.F.R. §§ 240.13d-1 to 13d-7 (1991).

248. See supra text accompanying notes 10–14. See also Floyd Norris, A Debate Grows Over Proxy Rules, N.Y. Times, Dec. 18, 1990, at D8 (reporting the Business Roundtable's opposition to rule revisions).

249. Regulation of Securityholders Communications, Exchange Act Release No. 29,315, 56 Fed. Reg. 28,987 (June 17, 1991) (to be codified at 17 C.F.R. § 240). For a discussion of this Release, see infra text accompanying notes 290–292.

stitutional investors.[250] In contrast, "exit" regulation, which focuses on the disposition of securities by persons holding control, has received less attention but may be more effective in inducing institutional investors to join and participate in control groups. Among the legal rules that fall into this category are the following:

1. *The Securities Act of 1933.* — An individual or a group that possesses control of a company is deemed an "affiliate" and is therefore restricted in its ability to resell any of its shares and may resell only pursuant to a registration statement or an exemption from registration.[251] As a practical matter, the only feasible means by which an affiliate can dispose of shares in a publicly held company at the market price is pursuant to Rule 144, which imposes both volume and sometimes holding period restrictions on affiliates.[252] Thus, the acquisition of "control" by an institutional investor, or a group of them, implies at least some restrictions on liquidity before resale is likely to be economically feasible.

2. *Section 16(b) of the Securities Exchange Act of 1934.* — Any gain that an officer, director, or ten percent beneficial holder of any class of an equity security of a "reporting" company receives on purchases or sales that occur within six months of any earlier sale or purchase must be disgorged to the corporation.[253] Although long thought of as a prohibition on insider trading, the better, and original, rationale for this extraordinarily prophylactic rule against "short-swing" trading profits is that it is necessary to deter manipulative behavior by corporate insiders.[254] Effectively, this threat of a six-month period of illiquidity deters most institutional holders from crossing the ten percent threshold.[255]

The potential reach of section 16(b) as it applies to institutional

250. See supra notes 10–14, 153–169 and accompanying text.

251. Under § 2(11) of the Securities Act of 1933, 15 U.S.C. § 77(b)(11) (1988), a person who acquires shares from a "control" person becomes an "underwriter" who also cannot sell shares in the issuer without registering the shares with the SEC or obtaining an exemption from registration. "Control" is defined very broadly in Rule 405 to mean the "possession, direct or indirect, of the power to direct or cause the direction of the management and policies of a person . . . ." 17 C.F.R. § 230.405 (1991). Rule 144 does provide a practical exemption from the registration requirement for affiliates, but under Rule 144(a)(1), an affiliate of an issuer is defined as one who "controls . . . or is under common control with, such issuer." 17 C.F.R. § 230.144(a)(1) (1991). Thus, if an institutional investor joins a control group, its ability to resell even the shares acquired in the open market is significantly restricted.

252. See 17 C.F.R. § 230.144(e)(1) (1991). A controlling shareholder may also make a "private sale" to another sophisticated person or institution, but typically such a sale will be at a significant discount to reflect the fact that the shares remain "restricted." In the future, Rule 144A may liberalize these restrictions, but at present it does not apply to publicly traded securities.

253. See Securities Exchange Act of 1934, § 16(b), 15 U.S.C. § 78p(b) (1988).

254. See Thel, supra note 221, at 393–401. Professor Thel distinguishes this rationale from the frequently stated rationale that § 16(b) prevents the misuse of nonpublic information, a function that § 16(b) accomplishes only imperfectly.

255. See Black, supra note 12, at 568.

investors is uncertain because current law is conspicuously imprecise as about when members of a loose association of institutional investors become subject to it. For example, assume such a group seeks to elect a slate of directors to a corporate board. Potentially, this group either (1) could be deemed to be "constructive" directors if any candidate on their slate is elected, under a legal doctrine based on "deputization theory,"[256] or (2) could have their individual holdings aggregated and thus be considered a single beneficial ten percent holder for purposes of section 16(b). To date, the SEC has declined to define when support of, or solicitation for, a directorial candidate will trigger this "deputization theory" under which an institution, or group of institutions, becomes a constructive director for section 16(b) purposes.[257] The SEC has, however, indicated that if investors form a "voting group" that requires disclosure under the Williams Act and if this group collectively controls ten percent or more of a class of equity securities, then it will be deemed subject to section 16(a).[258] As a result, an institution that solicits proxies may be deemed the beneficial owner of the shares corresponding to the proxies it receives. Alternatively, by participating in discussions with other institutions, the solicited institutions could be found to have entered into a voting group. Under either theory, insti-

256. Some decisions suggest that an institution or group that has "deputized" an agent or employee to serve on a corporate board will be deemed to be a constructive director for purposes of § 16(b), regardless of whether its holdings exceed 10%. See Feder v. Martin Marietta Corp., 406 F.2d 260 (2d Cir. 1969); Lowry v. Howmet Corp., 424 F. Supp. 461 (S.D.N.Y. 1977).

257. See Ownership Reports and Trading, Exchange Act Release No. 26,333, [1988-1989 Transfer Binder] Fed. Sec. L. Rep. (CCH) ¶ 84,343, at 89,602 (Dec. 2, 1988) ("fact-intensive analysis" necessary to resolve issue).

258. 15 U.S.C. § 78p(a) (1988). As part of its comprehensive revision of the rules under § 16(b) of the Exchange Act, the SEC adopted Rule 16a-1 in early 1991. This Rule defines the term "beneficial owner" for purposes of determining whether a person or group holds more than 10% of any class of equity securities to "mean any person who is deemed a beneficial holder pursuant to section 13(d) of the Act and the rules thereunder." See Rule 16a-1(a)(1), 17 C.F.R. § 240.16a-1(a)(1) (1991). However, Rule 16a-1 then exempts shares held by institutions that are eligible to file beneficial ownership reports on Form 13G that are held for clients in a fiduciary capacity in the ordinary course of business, "as long as such shares are acquired by such institutions or persons without the purpose or effect of changing or influencing control of the issuer. . . ." Id. Although this language does discourage institutional investor participation in a voting group (at least one intent on "influencing control" of the issuer), its overall impact is not great, because this definition applies only to § 16(a) and not § 16(b). For purposes of § 16(b), the term "beneficial ownership" is defined by Rule 16a-1(a) (2), 17 C.F.R. § 240.16a-1(a) (2) (1991), which requires that the investor "has or shares a direct or indirect pecuniary interest in the equity securities." The scope of the term "indirect pecuniary interest" is uncertain. Does it arise when a group of investors would be able to command a control premium for their shares that they could not expect to obtain on an individual basis? For the SEC release explaining the concept of "beneficial ownership" and "indirect pecuniary interest," see Ownership Reports and Trading by Officers, Directors and Principal Securities Holders, Exchange Act Release No. 28,869 [1990-1991 Transfer Binder] Fed. Sec. L. Rep. (CCH) ¶ 84,709 (Feb. 8, 1991).

tutions may become subject to section 16(a), even though they have agreed to pad their holdings and each holds well under the ten percent threshold. The consequence is at least a mild disincentive that may chill institutions from co-operating in solicitation support for a candidate for director.

3. *Insider Trading Liability.* — An institution with an employee or agent on a corporate board also becomes potentially liable if it trades while it is in constructive possession of material nonpublic information.[259] In principle, the mere possession of such information within the corporate enterprise may be sufficient to create liability, even though those making the trading decision did not use it or have access to it.[260] As a practical matter, this prospect of vicarious liability for information possessed by an employee or agent may force the institution to accept illiquidity if it allows an officer to sit on the corporate board of an issuer in which it holds an equity stake.[261] Thus, to maintain liquidity, the institution must delegate its monitoring role to an outside agent, with whom it must have only limited contacts.[262]

C. *The Deregulation of "Exit": What Rules Are Desirable?*

Life would no doubt be simpler for the institutional investor if the foregoing rules were relaxed.[263] But the cost of such relaxation might be to tolerate some low-visibility forms of insider trading and stock market manipulation. No reason is apparent why the antifraud purposes of the federal securities laws should be any less applicable to the behavior of institutional investors than that of any other group. In this light, what forms of "exit" deregulation could curb unnecessary over-

259. The institution could be liable for compensatory damages to contemporaneous traders and to the SEC for a civil penalty of up to three times its profit. See Securities Exchange Act of 1934, §§ 20(a), 21(a), 15 U.S.C. §§ 78t(a), 78u(a) (1988).

260. The SEC's long-standing position has been that mere possession of material information is sufficient to create liability, and the plaintiff need not show that the information was actually used in the investment decision. See Louis Loss & Joel Seligman, Securities Regulation, at 3503–04 (3d ed. 1991). Where a "Chinese Wall" has been erected to bar the person making the trading decision from access to the information, a different result may follow, but the discussion in the text assumes that no such structural protection has been implemented. Indeed, it is generally infeasible if a senior officer of the institutional investor were to sit on the corporate board.

261. Again, this statement must be qualified to the extent that a "Chinese Wall" can be erected to cordon off the officer on the corporate board from investment decision-making at the institutional investor. However, most institutional investors have relatively "thin" in-house staffs, and most senior officers are involved in investment decision-making. Hence, the feasibility of this option seems doubtful.

262. In essence, this is the proposal for outside professional directors made by Gilson and Kraakman. See Gilson & Kraakman, supra note 13, at 884–88.

263. Other commentators believe the overreach of the § 13(d) rules could potentially pose an equally serious problem. See Gilson & Kraakman, supra note 13, at 896–901. I do not, because § 13(d) requires only disclosure, not illiquidity. Nonetheless, I acknowledge that the case they make for defining its scope more precisely is persuasive.

reach without imperiling important policies of the federal securities laws? The following very marginal changes could encourage those investors that this Article suggests have the greatest potential to become optimal monitors—namely, indexed investors—to participate in corporate governance. Collectively, they would encourage such investors to hold larger stakes and engage in more open discussions among themselves about corporate governance issues.

1. *A Section 16(b) Safe Harbor.* — Today, with the uncertainty that exists over when a "voting group" will be treated as a single beneficial owner,[264] section 16(b) has newly emerged as an obstacle to institutional activism. Although indexed investors are basically passive investors, they still must engage in constant trading in order to adjust their portfolios. As a result, section 16(b) unnecessarily inhibits these investors who have no interest in manipulation or insider trading. Yet, the SEC has broad authority to create exemptions under section 16(b) and has regularly utilized this authority.[265] In principle, a variety of solutions could work: (1) "deputization theory" could be curtailed so that it would not create liability for institutions where they neither employed nor paid the director alleged to be their "deputy" (but only solicited proxies for such person); (2) "deputization theory" could be clarified so that it would not apply to a campaign to elect only a minority of the directors;[266] (3) trades made by indexed investors simply to adjust their portfolios in line with a stock index could be exempted from section 16(b); or (4) the concept of beneficial ownership could be redefined to exclude investors who have reached an understanding that amounts to a "voting group" for purposes of electing directors, but do not otherwise have control over, or an agency relationship with, those who are to be elected. The few decisions that have addressed what constitutes a "deputy" sufficient to trigger section 16(b) liability for its controlling principal have generally involved senior officers or directors of one corporation who were delegated the task of serving on the board of another.[267] Thus, a court could still rule, consistent with prior

264. See supra notes 256–258 and accompanying text.

265. The last sentence of § 16(b) authorizes the Commission to adopt rules and regulations to exempt transactions "not comprehended within the purpose of this subsection." 15 U.S.C. § 78p(b) (1988). See, e.g., Rules 16a-4 to 16a-11, 17 C.F.R. §§ 240.16a-4 to 16a-11 (1991) (exempting various classes of transactions).

266. This position has been advanced by Professors Gilson and Kraakman. See Gilson & Kraakman, supra note 13, at 902–03. As discussed in the text, I am not optimistic about its chances of adoption.

267. In Feder v. Martin Marietta Corp., 406 F.2d 260, 264–66 (2d Cir. 1969), the deputy was the president of one corporation who served on the other's board at the direction of his own corporation. In Lowey v. Howmet Corp., 424 F. Supp. 461, 463–64 (S.D.N.Y. 1977), Felix Rohatyn, a director of Howmet, was allegedly deputized by Howmet to represent its interests on the board of Pfizer Incorporated. Finding the issue to require a detailed factual analysis, the court denied motions made by both sides for summary judgment. In contrast, institutional investors are unlikely to use either their own officers or directors as their representatives on the corporate boards of portfolio

precedents, that merely favoring or even soliciting proxies for a candidate does not make such a candidate into one's agent or "deputy." Rather, some economic or other special relationship with the principal should be necessary.

In the absence of such a judicial statement, however, the simplest, narrowest reform would be administratively to exempt from section 16(b) trading transactions that are undertaken simply to maintain an indexed portfolio.[268] At a stroke, this solves the section 16(b) problem for the indexed investor, who buys for the long-term, but recurrently needs to adjust its portfolio.[269] The rationale for such an exemption is that the motive for such trading transactions is so clear and innocent that any presumption of misuse of inside information is rebutted. To implement such a rule, the indexed investor seeking to rely on it could be required to file in advance a description of its indexing strategy, and still would be required to report all trading transactions. Above all, however, such a rule creates a greater incentive for the long-term holder to play a monitoring role than it does for the active trader.

In contrast, a policy such as that proposed by Professors Gilson and Kraakman, which would exempt a transaction from section 16(b)

---

companies, in part because of the need to maintain a "Chinese Wall" to protect against insider trading liability. In Exchange Act Release No. 28,869 [1990–1991 Transfer Binder], Fed. Sec. L. Rep. (CCH) ¶ 84,709 (Feb. 8, 1991), the Commission declined to adopt a rule expressly codifying or clarifying "deputization theory," but instead indicated that that doctrine's development "will be left to case law." Id. at 81,251 n.27.

268. Such an exemption is far from fanciful. In its newly adopted Rule 16a-1, the SEC exempts from the definition of "derivative securities" "interests in broad-based index options, broad-based index futures and broad-based publicly traded market baskets of stocks approved for trading by the appropriate federal governmental authority." See 17 C.F.R. 240.16a-1(c)(4) (1991). See also Exchange Act Release No. 28,869, supra note 267, at 81,264 (streamlining the compliance requirements under § 16 of the Securities Exchange Act of 1934 with respect to derivative securities, employee benefit plans, and trusts administered by insider trustees). This exemption does help the institutional investors that own shares themselves rather than derivative securities (such as options, futures, or baskets), but conceptually the rationale that justifies exempting trading in indexes through derivative securities should also exempt transactions in the underlying securities. In both cases the underlying justification for the exemption is that transactions by indexed investors create little potential for abuse.

269. Indexed investors may need to trade for a variety of reasons. First, stocks are continually added to, and subtracted from, the S&P 500 and other indexes. Second, indexes differ, and under some ("equal weighted" indexes) the user invests equivalent dollar amounts in each stock in the index. In such a case, if an individual stock appreciates (or declines significantly), it will bear a disproportionate relationship to the portfolio as a whole, and the indexed investor would need to sell some shares (or buy more shares) to maintain a properly diversified portfolio. Third, investors may often decide to index only a portion of their portfolio (say, 50%) and, if they revise this percentage (up or down), sales or purchases will be necessary. Finally, the assets under the institutional investor's control may change, necessitating sales or purchases. For example, a mutual fund may experience a significant number of redemptions during a market downturn. The key point about all these trading transactions is that the indexed investor is not making individual, firm-specific trading decisions.

simply because the investor group seeks to elect only a minority of the board,[270] reflects a misunderstanding of the purpose of section 16(b). Section 16(b) is concerned not with control, but with the formation of "pools" and access to inside information.[271] An investor group controlling a minority of the board clearly can amount to such a "pool" and can possess such access, even if it lacks control.

2. *Redefining Control*. — An investor or investor group that possesses "control" faces two problems: (1) it cannot sell its shares, absent registration or an exemption,[272] and (2) a "controlling" shareholder is prima facie liable for federal securities law violations committed by the "controlled" corporation, unless an affirmative defense of non-negligence can be established.[273] The term "control" is defined very broadly by SEC rules,[274] and under this definition, the power to elect even a minority of the board could well constitute control. Indeed, the SEC's staff has taken the position that a ten percent holding creates "a rebuttable presumption of control, especially if such holdings are combined with . . . membership on the board."[275] If so, institutional investors who join a "control" group potentially face the worst of all possible combinations: illiquidity and liability.

What exemptions from this definition of control make sense for the institutional investor? First, with respect to the illiquidity problem, it would sensibly parallel this Article's earlier suggestion that portfolio adjustments by an indexed investor should not be considered transactions within the scope of section 16(b) to exempt these same portfolio modifications from the concept of "distribution" under the Securities Act of 1933.[276] The practical significance of this proposal is limited,

270. See Gilson & Kraakman, supra note 13, at 903.

271. See Thel, supra note 221, at 417 ("Section 16(b) was intended to deter affiliates from trading except on the basis of long-term (almost permanent) investment decisions."). An exemption for indexed transactions is consistent with this purpose.

272. See supra notes 251–252 and accompanying text. "Private" sales can, of course, be made to other institutional investors, but these sales are typically made at a discount and thus force the seller to sacrifice the advantage of liquidity. In addition, affiliates may resell securities under Rule 144 that are not "restricted securities" without any holding period, but these sales are subject to a volume restriction. See Rule 144(e). 17 C.F.R. § 230.144(e)(1) (1991).

273. See Securities Act of 1933, § 15, 15 U.S.C. § 77o (1988); Securities Exchange Act of 1934, § 20, 15 U.S.C. § 78t (1988). On the significance of this danger to institutional investors, see Conard, supra note 43, at 159.

274. See Securities Act Rule 405, 17 C.F.R. § 230.405 (1991); Exchange Act Rule 12b-2, 17 C.F.R. § 240.12b-2 (1991). For the content of Rule 405, see supra note 251.

275. See A.A. Sommer, Jr., Who's In Control?—S.E.C., 21 Bus. Law. 559, 568 (1966); Raymond A. Enstam & Harry P. Kamen, Control and the Institutional Investor, 23 Bus. Law. 289, 315 (1968). More recently, the SEC has acknowledged the "widely held belief that the ownership of 20% . . . voting power in a widely held company in most instances constitutes control." Approval of Proposed Rule Change Relating to Shareholder Approval Policy, Exchange Act Release No. 34-27,035, 54 Fed. Reg. 30,490 (July 14, 1989).

276. See Securities Act of 1933, § 2(11), 15 U.S.C. § 77b(11) (1988). The term

however, because Rule 144 already permits an affiliate to sell up to the greater of one percent of the class or the average weekly trading volume of the security every three months.[277] Nonetheless, Rule 144 could, and should, be extended expressly to permit indexed investors who have a "control" relationship to the corporation to sell, regardless of volume, provided that their disposition was undertaken as part of a portfolio modification consistent with an indexed strategy previously filed with the SEC.[278] Thus, the indexed investor would face no significant increase in illiquidity, even if it wished to dispose of more than one percent of the class and was a member of a control group.

"Controlling person" liability presents a more serious problem for institutional investors who are considering whether to join a collective effort to influence corporate management.[279] Here, the best answer is explicit rule-making by the SEC to tighten its overly expansive definition of "control." Some have argued that a group formed to elect only a minority of the board should not be considered a "control group."[280] Doctrinally, this argument faces an uphill battle, given a tradition of SEC interpretation to the contrary.[281] Moreover, it is not at all clear that directors who are representatives of institutional investors will necessarily be in the minority on any given decision. More typically, the board will act as a group and reach a consensus. Thus, a narrower and more doctrinally feasible route to the same protective safe harbor might be for the SEC to promulgate rules that indicate that merely agreeing on voting decisions without soliciting proxies does not make

---

"distribution" is never defined by the Securities Act, but it is understood to be the process by which securities flow from the company through an underwriter or a controlling person to the public. One who participates in such a "distribution" is deemed to be a statutory underwriter, who cannot sell without registration or an available exemption. See 15 U.S.C. § 77(d), (f) (1988). Even an indirect participation in a "distribution" of securities makes one a statutory underwriter. See SEC v. Chinese Consol. Benevolent Ass'n, 120 F.2d 738, 740–41 (2d Cir. 1941). Criminal liability for engaging in an unregistered distribution is also possible. See United States v. Wolfson, 405 F.2d 779, 782–83 (2d Cir. 1968).

277. See Securities Act Rule 144(e), 17 C.F.R. § 230.144(e) (1991). This 1% volume limit assumes, however, that the securities are not "restricted securities" that were acquired in a private placement.

278. This proposal does not extend to "restricted securities," which are issued in a transaction or series of transactions not involving a public offering. See Rule 144(a)(3), 17 C.F.R. § 230.144(a)(3) (1991). "Restricted securities" must be held for a two-year holding period. See Rule 144(d)(1), 17 C.F.R. § 230.144(d)(1) (1991). This Article is concerned only with the impact of Rule 144 on "free" stock that has been purchased by a person having "control." Rule 144 subjects such "affiliates" to special volume restrictions regardless of their holding period. See Rule 144(e) and (k), 17 C.F.R. §§ 230.144(e), (k) (1991).

279. Professor Conard has argued that this is the principal regulatory barrier to active institutional participation in corporate governance. See Conard, supra note 43, at 158–59.

280. See Gilson & Kraakman, supra note 13, at 902.

281. See supra notes 274–275 and accompanying text.

one a "controlling person" where one would otherwise not possess control.[282]

Similarly, SEC rules could also specifically extend and apply the affirmative defense that the federal securities laws provide to a controlling person so that it would clearly protect the institutional investor who lacks actual knowledge but does have a nonemployee representative on the corporate board.[283] Under the Securities Act of 1933, a controlling person is not liable for securities law violations committed by the corporation that it nominally controls if it "had no knowledge of or reasonable ground to believe in the existence of the facts by reason of which the liability of the controlled person is alleged to exist."[284] The same principle, expressed in slightly different words, is also contained in the Securities Exchange Act of 1934.[285] Yet, some decisions have held that a controlling person has a duty to supervise.[286] Such a duty is simply beyond the monitoring capacity of the typical pension fund, with its usually small, in-house staff. Thus, a safe harbor exemptive rule could be adopted by the SEC to protect institutional investors by establishing "bright line" standards for them. For example, such a rule might appropriately provide that shareholders should not be deemed to have "knowledge of or reasonable grounds to believe in the existence of the facts by reason of which the liability of the controlled person is alleged" if the investor lacked actual knowledge, had no direct employee or paid agent on the board, and had taken reasonable precautions by establishing a "Chinese Wall" between itself and any

282. Where the agreement related to the election of directors, such a definition would need to indicate that there could be no agency relation between the institution and the director. It could add, however, that support for an unaffiliated candidate did not make that candidate an agent. Thus, this proposal is not inconsistent with the Gilson and Kraakman idea that directors should be dependent on institutions. See Gilson & Kraakman, supra note 13, at 880–82.

283. There are several precedents for such a safe harbor defense. Under § 11(b) of the Securities Act of 1933, see 15 U.S.C. § 77k(b) (1988), Rule 176 sets forth criteria to guide courts in interpreting the "due diligence" defense. See 17 C.F.R. § 230.176 (1991). See also Rule 175, 17 C.F.R. § 230.175 (1991) (statements on behalf of issuer not deemed fraudulent if made on a reasonable basis and in good faith).

284. See Securities Act of 1933, § 15, 15 U.S.C. § 77o (1988).

285. Section 20(a) of the Securities Exchange Act of 1934 requires that "the controlling person acted in good faith and did not directly or indirectly induce the act or acts constituting the violation or cause of action." See 15 U.S.C § 78t (1988).

286. Compare SEC v. First Sec. Co., 507 F.2d 417, 421 (7th Cir. 1974) (brokerage firm liable for fraud committed by its officer on escrow investors) with Zweig v. Hearst Corp., 521 F.2d 1129 (9th Cir. 1975) (newspaper liable for "touting" columns written by one of its columnists). These decisions generally have involved corporations who were supervising their own employees. Courts have been more lenient with outside directors. See Burgess v. Premier Corp., 727 F.2d 826 (9th Cir. 1984) (where director was not involved in day-to-day operation of corporation, he was not a controlling person). A fortiori, courts should be even more lenient with an outside investor group holding less than a majority of the shares and electing less than a majority of the board.

implicit representative on the controlled corporation's board.[287]

There is a trade-off to such a defense; to invoke it, the institutional investor would have to delegate its monitoring role to a representative—i.e., the director it sponsored—with whom it could have only limited contacts. Yet, such a separation is probably made necessary in any event by the potential for insider trading liability, and thus there is little marginal cost to this standard.

In sum, what would be the net impact of the foregoing proposed reforms? It is difficult to predict more than a modest increase in activism if they were implemented alone. Thus, the real point here is that any program of deregulation that is consistent with the basic assumptions of securities regulation will not have much impact and will certainly not "unleash" institutional investors. At bottom, institutional passivity is primarily a product of: (1) a preference for liquidity over control, and (2) agency problems that leave money managers without sufficient incentives to be concerned about voting. The foregoing proposals deal only with the former problem, but the next section addresses the latter.

D. *The Reregulation of "Voice"*

Many recent commentators have proposed the relaxation of those SEC rules that limit institutional "voice."[288] In response to this criticism, and in particular to a series of detailed proposals made by CalPERS,[289] the SEC has proposed a bold, sensible, and far-reaching program of deregulation in order that its proxy rules not inhibit intershareholder communication.[290] The proposal most relevant to institutional holders would exempt solicitations by any "disinterested" person who is not seeking to obtain authority to vote proxies.[291] Thus, institutional investors could freely communicate and recommend opposition to a management proposal (so long as they did not solicit proxies).

The SEC's proposals would largely remove the chill on shareholder communications that the current proxy rules create.[292] But,

287. The relevance of such a "Chinese Wall" here is not that it rebuts the possession of indirect control, but that it demonstrates the absence of "reasonable grounds" to know of the facts giving rise to the asserted liability.

288. See supra notes 10–14, 48 and accompanying text.

289. See CalPERS Letter, supra note 56.

290. Regulation of Securityholder Communications, Exchange Act Release No. 29,315, 56 Fed. Reg. 28,987 (June 17, 1991).

291. Release No. 29,315 sets forth a proposed Rule 14a-2(b)(1) that would exempt a "disinterested" person's communications from the obligation to file a proxy statement. The definition of "disinterested" requires that the person not have as "material economic interest" in the solicitation (other than as a securityholder) and not seek a proxy or related authority. No exemption is given from the anti-fraud rules relevant to proxy solicitations.

292. Under current rules, the term "solicitation" includes any request for, or any

they respond less adequately to the problem of rational apathy. The basic dilemma is that most institutional investors, and particularly those agents that run them, have insufficient interest in exercising "voice." This is true particularly for the indexed investors that this Article has argued have an unrecognized potential to serve as corporate monitors. Although these investors have less need for liquidity and are typically less affected by conflicts of interest, their interest in "voice" is limited by two basic constraints: First, investors following an indexed investment strategy typically hold a highly diversified portfolio in which no single stock is likely to amount to more than a small percentage of the portfolio.[293] This fact implies both an informational overload problem and a low expected payoff from involvement with issues at any single corporation in the portfolio. Second, the competitive strategy of external money managers who provide indexing services is to cut costs and engage in price competition.[294] As a result, the real policy challenge is not how to deregulate but, rather, how to motivate the rational institutional investor *and* its agents to engage in costly monitoring. The following proposals address this challenge.

1. *Making Monitoring Mandatory*. — As a starting point, let us assume that indexed investors are disinclined to be active monitors. After all, a primary purpose of indexing is to economize on transaction costs, and participating in proxy fights is certainly costly. Still, because institutions hold for the long-term, such investors are more likely to reap the benefits of improved corporate governance than are shorter-term traders whose portfolios turn over regularly. Also, because indexed investors hold shares in numerous companies, they seem more able to exploit economies of scale in reaching voting decisions and coordinating to oppose management, a factor that one commentator has argued should reduce the costs of active monitoring to an acceptable level.[295] Finally, the largest institutional investors may hold a two or

request not to execute a proxy, or any "other communication to security holders under circumstances reasonably calculated to result in the procurement, withholding or revocation of a proxy." See Rule 14a-1(l), 17 C.F.R. § 240.14a-1(l)(iii) (1991). Rule 14a-2(b)(1) then exempts "solicitations" of ten or fewer persons. See 17 C.F.R. § 240.14a-2(b)(1) (1991). Thus, an institutional investor could contact up to ten other institutions today while staying within this safe harbor. But even in this case, it is not clear whether persons solicited in turn by the ten or fewer persons originally so solicited would count against this limit on the theory that it was a "group" conducting the solicitation.

293. See Lowenstein, supra note 45, at 33–34; see also text accompanying supra note 243 (noting that the largest indexed money manager supervises a portfolio of 5000 stocks for its clients). Also, as institutional investors increasingly diversify on a global basis, they will invest in multiple indexes (i.e., an S&P index for U.S. investments, and equivalent indexes for European and Asian investments).

294. See supra notes 243–244 and accompanying text; see also Rock, supra note 9, at 474 (arguing that since all indexed fund managers hypothetically produce the same gain or loss, the key to competition is to be the lowest cost producer, which provides disincentives for engaging in costly corporate governance activities).

295. See Black, supra note 12, at 588–91. Some corporate issues will recur regu-

three percent stake in the corporations in their index.[296] At this level of investment, any improvement in corporate governance that translates into improved financial performance can justify the expenditure of substantial costs. If monitoring is then rational for the institution but does not occur, the most logical diagnosis is that an agency problem exists.

If so, one answer might be regulatory initiatives that require the agent to engage in costly monitoring that it would prefer to avoid. Beginning in the mid-1980s, the U.S. Department of Labor tried this approach, warning ERISA fiduciaries that participation in corporate governance is not optional.[297] Basically, the Labor Department has required that pension plans and their investment managers vote their shares in proxy contests, rather than abstain, and has mandated that they establish procedures to ensure that their vote is informed. The doctrinal basis for this position is the Labor Department's view that voting rights are a pension plan asset that must be exercised "solely in the interests of . . . and for the exclusive purpose of providing benefits to participants and beneficiaries."[298] Finally, the Labor Department requires that, in voting, investment managers must act prudently and in the exclusive interest of plan participants.[299] As a normative statement of fiduciary responsibilities, the Department of Labor's recent pronouncements on proxy voting by investment managers cannot be faulted. But the effect upon money managers, particularly money managers handling indexed accounts, may only be to require the creation of formalized procedures and voting guidelines that are largely window dressing.[300]

What other steps could motivate pension plan fiduciaries to take monitoring more seriously? Put simply, for monitoring to work, some agent in the process must see monitoring as in its self-interest. One means to this end would be to create and make mandatory a new professional—the proxy adviser. Actually, such a professional already exists, and the market for its services is growing.[301] Intelligent regulation

---

larly: poison pills, staggered boards, reincorporation decisions, etc. An investor with a large portfolio can formulate a general policy on these issues and also will be better able to evaluate relevant factual distinctions.

296. See Black, supra note 12, at 568.

297. For an overview, see Rock, supra note 9, at 477–78.

298. In 1988, the Labor Department made this ruling in a well-known letter to Avon Products, Inc. Letter from Deputy Assistant Secretary of Labor, Alan Lebowitz, to Helmuth Fandl, Avon Products, Inc., 15 Pens. Rep. (BNA) No. 9, at 391, 392 n.4 (Feb. 23, 1988) [hereinafter Avon Products Letter]. See also Black, supra note 12, at 554 & n.116 (citing Avon Products Letter).

299. See Labor Department Opinion Letter on Proxy Voting, 17 Pens. Rep. (BNA), No. 5, at 244, 244–46 (Jan. 23, 1990) (letter from Alan Lebowitz to Robert Monks, Institutional Shareholder Services, Inc.).

300. See Lowenstein, supra note 45, at 34 (comment of largest indexed money manager that it votes "by formula").

301. Among the groups specializing in providing voting advice are: Investor Re-

could further increase the demand for such services, both in terms of providing voting advice and monitoring those investment managers who hold voting discretion. Today, the Department of Labor's rulings require the pension plan's trustees to monitor "the activities of the investment manager" to whom voting discretion is delegated.[302] Thus, there is both a duty to vote, which in the typical case of external investment management will fall on the investment manager to whom discretion over the portfolio is given, *and* a duty to monitor voting, which chiefly will fall on the pension plan's trustees. These standards however, do not adequately answer the important question: What steps must a pension plan take to ensure that voting decisions will be given adequate and disinterested attention by professional managers? In effect, there is a duty of care imposed on the pension plan's trustees to supervise the voting performance of its investment managers. Yet, not only is the content of this duty uncertain, but the internal staff of most pension plans is simply not equipped to undertake a detailed evaluation of hundreds, perhaps thousands, of individual voting decisions. Thus, professional assistance is required. The simplest way to fulfill this duty is to rely on a qualified expert—namely, the professional proxy adviser.

2. *Creating a Market for Monitoring Services.* — The problem with the foregoing proposal is not in showing that a need for such a professional exists but in demonstrating that a market for its services can be created. Three distinct steps seem appropriate:

a. *"Unbundling" Prices.* — Today, investment managers generally charge a single price for their services; in the case of index fund managers, this price is low because the investment management services provided are minimal.[303] What then would be the impact of requiring these managers to unbundle their services and quote separate prices for investment management and proxy voting advice?[304] In all likelihood, their charge for proxy voting advice would be low to nominal because these firms seem to follow simple voting formulas.[305] Yet, it is also clear that one gets what one pays for, and a nominal charge thus reflects only nominal service. If nominal prices are charged, the bur-

---

sponsibility Research Center (IRRC); Institutional Shareholder Services (founded in 1985 by Robert Monks); and The Analysis Group (started in 1988). See Release No. 29,315, supra note 290, at 28,987; Rock, supra note 9, at 479–81; Black, supra note 12, at 573. I do not mean to suggest that the pension plan must wholly delegate its voting discretion to such an organization. It could also hire such a firm in an advisory capacity.

302. See Labor Department Opinion Letter, supra note 299, at 245–46.

303. Professor Lowenstein suggests that the annual fee may be as low as two basis points. See Lowenstein, supra note 45, at 34.

304. The same investment adviser or investment banking firm could provide both investment and voting services. The point is not to add a new agent, standing alone, but to break out and distinguish the separable and entirely distinct task of monitoring from that of investment advice and stock picking. Of course, where the same firm provides both voting and investment services, it could not monitor itself, and the trustees of the fund would have to satisfy this obligation.

305. See supra note 244 and accompanying text.

den would then fall on the pension plan's fiduciaries to justify how they could expect to receive adequate service for a trivial charge. If higher prices are charged, true competition can develop.

In part, this strategy seeks to embarrass pension fiduciaries by highlighting the inadequacy of existing advice. Companies that did not hire such an advisor could be placed under special scrutiny and asked to justify how their skeletal, in-house staff expected to monitor all the voting decisions before them. Still, the larger point is that the first step toward the creation of an actual market for professional services is to prevent those services from being provided on a tie-in basis. Instead, ERISA regulations should require that they be specifically contracted for. This would allow new entrants to quote potentially competitive rates. The next step would be to specify through regulation what the minimum content of those services should include: for example, specific review of the proxy statements, record-keeping, and an articulated basis for the decision to vote for or against a specific proposal or slate of candidates. To be sure, such rule-making would be unpopular with corporate sponsors to the extent that it raises the administrative cost of the pension fund, but the inescapable fact is that monitoring is costly. In reality, most firms today are buying only investment advice and not voting advice.

b. *Restricted Diversification.* — An even more controversial and more important step toward implementing a serious system of institutional monitoring would be to restrict portfolio diversification, including indexing, to a level consistent with the institution's ability to monitor. In theory, a diversified portfolio can be assembled with as few as 15 stocks,[306] and 95% of the value of diversification can be achieved with a portfolio of only 20 stocks.[307] Clearly, indexing does not require the purchase of all of the Standard & Poor's 500, and "excess" diversification is thus wasteful because it raises the transaction costs, both in terms of unnecessary securities transactions and unnecessary monitoring.[308] Although it may be impossible for any investment manager to monitor 500 stocks, even a medium-sized institution could monitor 25 to 50. The impact of any rule restricting "excess" diversification would also increase the size of the stake that institutions would typically hold in individual companies because, other factors being held constant, the same total investment would be invested by the same institutions in fewer companies. Thus, the expected payoff from improved corporate

306. See James H. Lorie et al., The Stock Market: Theories and Evidence 85 (2d ed. 1985).

307. See Richard A. Brealey & Stewart C. Myers, Principles of Corporate Finance 156 (3d ed. 1988). In addition, 99% of the value of diversification can be achieved based on a 100 stock portfolio. Id.

308. One reason for "excess" diversification might be the excess brokerage commissions that integrated broker-dealer firms receive when the portfolios they handle diversify based on the S&P 500 index.

governance would be higher, and institutions would rationally spend more on researching and lobbying corporate governance issues.

Potentially, such a restricted diversification rule would also create an incentive for institutions to hire professional proxy advisers in order to help them justify that their monitoring capacity was consistent with their preference for a larger portfolio. The proposed rule would not prevent a pension fund from exceeding the 20 or 100 stock levels at which 95% or 99%, respectively, of the value of diversification can be achieved. Rather, it would only require such a fund to prove that its monitoring capacity enabled it to follow a larger portfolio adequately. In short, this strategy would have two goals: (1) by restricting "excess diversification," pension funds would be required to hold larger stakes in fewer companies, and (2) by recognizing the use of proxy advisers as a basis for demonstrating adequate monitoring capacity, the growth of a new and necessary industry would be encouraged.

Simple as this proposal sounds, it faces two serious obstacles, one structural and one legal. First, if one were seriously to insist that institutions limit their investments to stakes in some small number of companies (for example, 50 or 100), the result would be that large institutions, such as CalPERS, would be compelled to hold huge blocks, possibly 30% stakes or more, and only in very large companies, simply to invest that portion of their portfolios currently invested in the entire market. Because the net result would be to institutionalize the equivalent of the German universal banking system overnight, it is clearly unrealistic to think that such a sweeping change could be imposed on the corporate world in the absence of any strong political consensus for change. Thus, modifications are necessary. One possibility would be to place a safety valve on this proposal: for example, a 3–5% permissive cap could be incorporated, so that institutions would not be deemed to be "excessively" diversified as long as the stakes they held in corporations were within this range. The result still creates large enough holdings to justify close monitoring.

Another alternative would be to apply the restricted diversification standard in terms of individual fund managers. Thus, a large pension fund might have five fund managers handling different portfolios, each of which would be restricted to a maximum number of stocks consistent with effective monitoring. The net result is to give the individual fund manager (who might be limited to holding, say, 20 stocks) a strong incentive to monitor, because its impact could be far greater on the performance of such a limited portfolio.

The second obstacle is created by ERISA, which mandates a unique and economically unsophisticated form of diversification. Under section 1104a of the ERISA statute, a fiduciary must "diversify[] . . . so as to minimize the risk of large losses, unless . . . it is clearly prudent not to do so."[309] This language focuses the fiduciary's attention not on the net losses to the portfolio, but on the risk of individual losses of sizable magnitude.[310] As a result, concentrated ownership is dangerous in terms of the trustee's exposure to liability.[311] To be sure, a 100 stock portfolio, or even a 50 stock portfolio, may actually satisfy this special diversification standard, but a risk-averse trustee may think otherwise. Here then, a change in regulatory attitude does seem necessary in order to implement this proposal. Indeed, given the obvious controversy that mandating a "restricted diversification" policy would arouse, the most practical first step is to relax this unnecessary rule that today seems to require excessive diversification.

If investment managers were free to diversify on the basis of a smaller portfolio, then the final proposal that this Article will make—namely, that incentive compensation be more generally permitted[312]—might itself be sufficient to cause investment managers to focus on monitoring as a means of creating value for their clients and themselves.

c. *Retention of Voting Discretion*. — The decision of a pension fund to delegate investment discretion, while retaining or reclaiming voting discretion, is inherently questionable, particularly in the case of an indexed investor. If a pension plan delegates investment decision-making, this decision should estop it from proclaiming itself competent to make voting decisions over the same portfolio assets that it has delegated to professional management. At a minimum, the Department of Labor should require special justification of such a step, which suggests that the corporate sponsor is seeking to gain control of the plan's voting power.[313]

Indirectly, such an initiative might also create an increased market for the services of professional proxy advisers in order to justify the pension fund's ability to retain or reclaim voting discretion. Although corporate sponsors might desire to hire "tame" advisers whose advice would match their promanagement inclinations, one constraint could limit their ability to obtain cosmetic advice: Namely, professional advisers could be placed under a special obligation to report inconsistent advice given to different clients on the same issue. At least, this would

309. 29 U.S.C. § 1104(a)(1)(C) (1988).

310. Labor Department regulations under ERISA require a "screen or filter process" even in the case of an index fund to exclude companies that have suffered "significant, adverse financial developments." 44 Fed. Reg. 37,224 n.7, amending 29 C.F.R. § 2550,404a-1(b) (1990).

311. See Jeffrey N. Gordon, The Puzzling Persistence of the Constrained Prudent Man Rule, 62 N.Y.U. L. Rev. 52, 66–67 (1987); see also Black, supra note 12, at 553–54 for a similar conclusion.

312. See infra notes 336–347 and accompanying text.

313. Some evidence suggests that this practice is becoming more common and that its "conscious purpose is to ensure promanager votes." Black, supra note 12, at 598.

inhibit specially tailored advice for each client in keeping with its corporate sponsor's preexisting views.

3. *Deregulating the Proxy Adviser.* — The professional proxy adviser today operates in a legal limbo, because its activities are at the very edge of those permitted by law. Unlike earlier firms that played only a clearinghouse function, these new advisers expressly offer voting advice on proxy matters to their institutional clients. The best known of these new firms, Institutional Shareholder Services, Inc., not only gives voting advice, but is developing a database on outside directors and more technical issues, such as executive compensation.[314]

Potentially, these organizations could substantially reduce the collective action problem facing institutional investors. Both for financial and legal reasons, however, no institution will be eager to solicit proxies, particularly when it believes that other institutional investors are "free riding" on its efforts, and will benefit pro rata with it. As a result, collective action remains under-funded.[315] Yet, because the costs of their services are equitably prorated among all their institutional users, proxy advisers provide a means for taxing the institutional free rider and reducing the costs that an insurgent must bear to conduct an effective proxy solicitation. Equally important, because the proxy adviser plays a critical coordinating role, no institutional investor would have to bear the full political heat of publicly opposing management and coordinating shareholder resistance. Rather, each can remain seemingly passive, on the surface only paying an annual fee to its proxy adviser, but in reality subscribing to the costs of collective action.

At present, the problem with this simple scenario is that it may run afoul of the SEC's proxy rules. The legal issue is whether the provision of proxy advice amounts to a proxy "solicitation" under SEC Rule 14a-1.[316] Clearly, the definition of solicitation reaches this far, but an exemption can be justified on any of several rationales. First, there is an existing exemption for the "furnishing of proxy voting advice by any person (the 'advisor') to any other person with whom the advisor has a business relationship, if . . . the advisor renders financial advice in the

314. Founded in 1985 by Robert Monks, the former administrator of the Department of Labor's Pension and Welfare Benefits Administration, Institutional Shareholder Services was the first firm openly to offer voting advice to its clients on corporate governance matters. See Peter Riddell, A Crusader Takes on Corporate America, Fin. Times, June 6, 1990, at 7; see also Marcia Parker, New Tactics in Governance Wars, Pension & Investment Age, Nov. 12, 1990, at 1 (describing an affiliated company, Institutional Shareholder Partners, which seeks partners in the form of large individual corporate investors to engage in corporate governance activities).

315. For a discussion of collective action and "free-riding," see supra note 23 and accompanying text.

316. See 17 C.F.R. § 240.14a-1(l) (1991). This rule defines solicitation to include any "communication to security holders under circumstances reasonably calculated to result in the procurement, withholding, or revocation of a proxy." Id. at § 240.14a-1(l)(iii).

ordinary course of his business."[317] On its face, this exemption would seem to cover the new professional proxy advisor, except for the ambiguity in the requirement that the advisor render "financial advice in the ordinary course of his business." Unfortunately, the SEC has historically given a narrow interpretation to this exemption, and in 1988 it refused to grant a "no action" letter exemption to Institutional Shareholder Services, ruling that only an advisor who provides "separate and distinct" financial advice could utilize the exemption.[318] More recently however, the SEC has proposed an even broader exemption for proxy advice furnished by a "disinterested" person so long as the adviser does not seek to obtain a proxy.[319] This proposed exemption would expressly cover the new proxy advisory firms that have recently entered this field.[320] Either approach is adequate, but whether either will be actually adopted may test the validity of the overregulation thesis.

E. *Delegation to Professional Directors*

As earlier noted, direct monitoring of corporate managements by institutional investors quickly encounters a major logistical problem: Most institutional investors own too many stocks and have too small an in-house staff to be able to evaluate the quality or performance of the corporate managements in whose securities they have invested.[321] Delegating shareholder voting decisions to professional investment managers is a partial answer to this problem. Still, it is directors, not shareholders, who hold the real power in corporate governance. Here, the same overload problems re-appear, but they can potentially be solved by delegating the task of monitoring to outside directors. Yet, as most serious proponents of this approach acknowledge, there is considerable reason to doubt that, absent a crisis, outside directors today

317. 17 C.F.R. § 240.14a-2(b)(2) (1991).

318. See Institutional Shareholder Services, Inc., SEC No-Action Letter, 1991 SEC No-Act. LEXIS 17, (Jan. 2, 1991). In this no-action letter, the SEC staff advised Institutional Shareholder Services that: "Rule 14a(b)(2) seems to contemplate that the voting advisor will be rendering voting advice in the context of a relationship in which his role is primarily that of an advisor on financial matters separate and distinct from that of proxy voting." As a result, a bank trustee or a registered investment advisor can provide voting advice, but a specialized firm, such as Institutional Shareholder Services, Inc., apparently cannot.

319. See Release No. 29,315, supra note 290, at 28,990–92 (proposing Rule 14a-2(b)(1) to exempt proxy advice from a "disinterested" person).

320. Release No. 29,315 specifically refers to "organizations or associations comprised of securityholders or issuers that exchange information with members regarding such matters of common concern as proxy voting positions or views on corporate governance policy. Another category would be providers of shareholder advisory services, including organizations offering proxy voting information or recommendations . . . ." Id. at 28,991 (footnote omitted). The Release then names the principal existing proxy advisers and indicates that they would generally be covered by the proposed rule.

321. See supra notes 243–244 and accompanying text.

play an adequate monitoring role in the public corporation.[322] Critics point out that the vast majority of outside directors at Fortune 1000 firms are chief executives of other corporations,[323] who thus are subject to severe time constraints and other commitments. Such directors, they argue, may also share a group loyalty or "club ethos" that assumes that directors, like house guests, should not question or criticize the host.[324] Finally, outside directors are part time visitors to the corporation, who lack any permanent staff, depend on management for their factual information, and on average devote only fourteen days a year to each board on which they serve.[325]

Beyond these logistical, ideological, and social obstacles to effective monitoring, the greater problem again involves incentives. Even if the law could define independence in a meaningful way,[326] there is no assurance that an independent director would be an effective director. The outside director still has few incentives to challenge or criticize the incumbent management, particularly when the economic payoff from such conduct to the director will be minimal—and may get the director removed from office. Thus, for the outside director to be effective, incentives must be used to increase the director's willingness to monitor.

Recognizing the need for enhanced incentives to monitor, Professors Ronald Gilson and Reinier Kraakman have recently proposed a novel and provocative solution: Make the outside director economically dependent on the institutional investors that the director is expected to serve.[327] Under their proposal, institutional investors would identify a cadre of professional outside directors who would become specialists in monitoring. Each such director would serve on a full-time basis as the representative of institutional investors on the boards of a number of corporations in these institutions' portfolios. They suggest that a professional director could serve on, hypothetically, six boards and that, as a class, they would constitute a minority—probably a third—of the entire board. Through such multiple board memberships, the professional director could earn compensation equivalent to that of a partner in a law or an accounting firm, but, unlike most current

322. See Jay Lorsch, Pawns or Potentates: The Reality of American Corporate Boards (1989). Professor Jay Lorsch, a Harvard Business School professor, concluded that directors play an effective role in times of crisis, but seldom otherwise.

323. Lorsch finds 63% of outside directors at such firms to be other chief executives. Id. at 18.

324. Lorsch reports that many directors "still feel they are serving at the pleasure of the CEO-Chairman." Id. at 17. For the view that there is a "club ethos," see Elmer W. Johnson, An Insider's Call for Outside Directors, 68 Harv. Bus. Rev., Mar.–Apr. 1990, at 46, 47.

325. See Heidrick & Struggles, The Changing Board 9 (1987).

326. As Professor Brudney has noted, the law cannot assess the social and personal relationships that may exist between directors and those they are expected to monitor. See Victor Brudney, The Independent Director—Heavenly City of Potemkin Village, 95 Harv. L. Rev. 597, 613 (1982).

327. See Gilson & Kraakman, supra note 13, at 883–92.

outside directors, they would have no other major time commitments and would be dependent upon institutional investors for their continued service in that capacity. In effect, Professors Gilson and Kraakman discard the models of the outside director as an independent referee in favor of one under which the director becomes a full-time agent of an identifiable class of shareholders.[328]

In principle, such an idea could work because it solves the logistical and incentive problems that have long made monitoring by outside directors more an ideal than a reality. But the real problem is how to get there from here. From this Article's perspective, the Gilson and Kraakman proposal for institutional investors to elect a minority slate of professional directors is not feasible without (a) some deregulation and (b) enhanced incentives for institutional money managers to monitor. The problem is not with what Professors Gilson and Kraakman say, but with what they leave out. Their solution works to align the interests of principal and agent only at the directorial level, not at the institutional level. At the institutional level, there is considerable reason to believe that professional money managers would remain rationally apathetic about minority directors, because they would incur short-run costs to benefit free-riding shareholders but would not expect to share in the long-run benefits.[329]

This conclusion does not deny that a variety of legal obstacles should be reduced by the SEC through the deregulation of rules that curb the overreach of the proxy rules and reduce the prospect of section 16(b) and controlling person liability.[330] Still, even if these reforms were implemented, it remains doubtful that institutional investors would respond to the "voice" that the Gilson and Kraakman proposals would give them. The implicit premise to the Gilson and Kraakman proposals appears to be that if legal restrictions, particularly those on "exit," are eased, institutional investors will participate actively in corporate governance. Yet, from this Article's perspective, easy "exit" may mean diminished "voice"; and deregulation is not a cure for rational apathy.

To date, there is little evidence that institutional investors who rely on "exit" will participate in corporate governance, except on a short-term basis in connection with takeovers. Although sometimes institutional investors have successfully organized themselves to take collective action in favor of proposals that seek to unblock the market for corporate control, there are few instances in which they have success-

---

328. For precisely this reason the Gilson and Kraakman proposal presents the earlier noted legal issues surrounding deputization theory and controlling person liability in their least favorable light. See supra notes 253–262 and accompanying text.

329. See supra notes 194–198 and accompanying text. For a similar analysis, see Rock, supra note 9, at 474–75.

330. See supra notes 264–287 and accompanying text.

fully organized to pursue other goals.[331] Only in corporate control battles have the short-term gains to investors been sufficiently high—because success may be followed by a lucrative takeover bid—to outweigh the uncertain direct and indirect costs of opposing corporate management. Even in these cases, institutional activism has been on balance largely unsuccessful. In 1987–88, the Council of Institutional Investors organized a campaign to adopt shareholder proposals opposing the poison pill; thirty-two corporations were chosen as candidates for such proposals because they had particularly high levels of institutional ownership (averaging 56.6%).[332] Regardless, the average vote for the proposals was only 29.4%, implying that institutional investors only voted a little over half of their stock for the proposal.[333]

Holding aside the special case of public pension funds, a pessimistic evaluation thus seems necessary: The costs of opposing management are still perceived by many, perhaps most, institutional investors as too high. Many fear the unknown evil represented by insurgents more than they fear the known evil of incumbent management.[334] Still, over the next decade, pension funds will come to own approximately forty percent of the equity in American corporations.[335] The future of corporate governance will depend less on what the SEC does about the overreach of the securities laws and more on what the Department of Labor does about creating incentives through compensation systems, diversification restrictions, and the pricing of money management services to encourage long-term monitoring.

F. *The Case for Incentive Compensation*

The hardest problem has been saved for last. Repeatedly, this Article has suggested that even if institutional investors have a rational

331. According to the Investor Responsibility Research Center, there were twenty-six proxy contests for full or partial control of the board in 1989, of which only three were successful. As of mid-1990, there had been twenty actual or threatened proxy contests, of which only one had been successful. See Proxy Contests, supra note 234, at 1, 10. There has also recently been a decline in the number of proxy contests. See supra note 47.

332. See Gilson & Kraakman, supra note 13, at 868, 893 n.91.

333. Id. By 1988, this average increased to 39.5%. Id. Still, this data suggests that a substantial portion of institutional investors will not even support a provision that seeks to unblock the market for corporate control (in which they make very high short-term returns). Contests over directorial elections are even more controversial and offer no immediate returns.

334. See Proxy Contests, supra note 234, at 11 (institutional investors have "conservative" bias and tend to back only candidates they know). The Gilson and Kraakman proposals are intended to respond to this problem by seeking to elect only a minority of the board. Still, investors may fear that a divided board implies disharmony and conflict. This fear was always the justification offered by corporations for their opposition to cumulative voting, and the Gilson and Kraakman proposals may produce an equivalent end result.

335. See supra note 239 and accompanying text.

interest in corporate governance, their investment managers may not. Why? Both in the mutual fund and pension contexts, investment advisers tend to be compensated under mechanical formulas that pay them a small annual percentage of the assets under their control.[336] Clearly, such an unsophisticated flat formula does little to align incentives between the manager and the fund it serves, and incentive compensation based on capital appreciation would work far better.

Why isn't incentive compensation used? In the mutual fund context, the short answer is a legal one: The Investment Advisers Act of 1940[337] prohibits the use of any formula that "provides for compensation to the investment adviser on the basis of a share of capital gains upon or capital appreciation of the funds or any portion of the funds of the client."[338] Although this prohibition has been marginally relaxed in the case of an investment adviser to a mutual fund, index funds are, as a practical matter, unable to use the narrow authorization for incentive compensation.[339] Moreover, even if a broader exemption specifically tailored to the index fund could be adopted, a further problem still remains: Directors of mutual funds have little incentive to adopt

336. Usually, such formulas are a declining percentage of the assets under management in order to reflect economies of scale (for example, 1/2 of 1% of the first $500 million, 1/4 of 1% of the next $250 million, etc.). The actual formulas used appear in many of the well-known cases in this field. See cases cited supra note 197. For an overview of the factors considered in the fee formula determination, see Robert C. Pozen, Financial Institutions: Cases, Materials, and Problems on Investment Management 250–96 (1978).

337. 15 U.S.C. § 80b-1–80b-21.

338. Investment Advisers Act of 1940 § 205(a)(1) ("Investment advisory contracts"), 15 U.S.C. § 80b-5(a)(1) (1988). The policy problem underlying the statute is that incentive compensation can create an incentive for the fund manager to accept excessive risk. See 2 Tamar Frankel, The Regulation of Money Managers 285–300 (1978); Harvey E. Bines, The Law of Investment Management § 5.03[2] (1978). But see infra notes 346–347 and accompanying text (noting that pension fund managers would never take on excessive risk in any case).

339. Section 205(b)(2) of the Investment Advisers Act of 1940, 15 U.S.C. § 80b-5(b) (1988), relaxes the prohibition on incentive compensation with respect to a registered investment company if the contract "provides for compensation based on the asset value of the company or fund under management averaged over a specified period . . . in relation to the investment record of an appropriate index of securities prices or such other measure of investment performance as the Commission by Rule, regulation, or order may specify." The SEC has promulgated Rule 205-1 to define "investment performance." See 17 C.F.R. § 275.205-1 (1990). However, because index funds by definition do not exceed the performance of the market (or any other "appropriate index"), this Rule does not provide them with a relevant exemption. An expanded rule could seek to define the meaning of superior "investment performance" in the index fund context, but this is not an easy task. Finally, Rule 16a-1(a)(2)(ii)(C), 17 C.F.R. 240.16a-1(a)(2)(ii)(C) (1991), states that a performance-related fee received by any broker, investment adviser, or trustee gives such person an "indirect pecuniary interest" in the securities managed and thus triggers the application of § 16(b) of the Exchange Act, 15 U.S.C. § 78p(b) (1988). This rule, however, applies only when the securities of the issuer exceed 10% of the market value of the portfolio. See Rule 16a-1(a)(2)(ii)(C)(2).

novel or potentially excessive fee formulas, because, under the Investment Company Act of 1940, they are subject to private suit for permitting investment advisers to receive excessive or unreasonable compensation.[340] Derivative actions regularly raise such claims against mutual fund directors.[341]

In the case of pension plans, there is similar fiduciary liability for unreasonable compensation, whether the plan is subject to ERISA or not.[342] Moreover, incentive compensation contracts are strictly forbidden when the adviser is also a registered investment adviser under the Investment Advisers Act of 1940.[343] Possibly some means of circumventing these prohibitions can be devised, but pension and mutual fund trustees have little reason to take risks or to experiment. Rather, both are likely to follow the herd and avoid original but potentially litigable compensation arrangements.

How great an impact do these limitations on incentive compensation actually have? In the case of mutual funds, the answer is debatable, because superior performance by a fund manager will attract new money into the fund, thus increasing the adviser's compensation even though it is measured on the basis of a declining percentage of total assets. In short, the market may still work. In the case of a pension fund, however, the problem is more complicated. The corporate sponsor of a defined benefits plan, which includes most pension plans, does have an incentive to monitor its investment manager's performance, because the better the manager does, the less the sponsor has to contribute to the pension fund. Still, this incentive weakens to the extent that investment managers begin to become involved in proxy contests or show other indicia of shareholder activism. Here, all the evidence suggests that corporate managers resist such involvement and may

340. Section 36(b) of the Investment Company Act of 1940, 15 U.S.C. § 80a-35(b) (1988), creates fiduciary liability and gives a private cause of action to shareholders against both the fund's directors and the investment adviser for "breach of fiduciary duty in respect of . . . compensation or payments paid by such registered investment company . . . to such investment adviser."

341. See cases cited supra note 197. For a more recent case, see Kalish v. Franklin Advisers, Inc., 742 F. Supp. 1222 (S.D.N.Y. 1990).

342. Under § 1104(a)(1) of ERISA, a fiduciary "shall discharge his duties with respect to a plan *solely in the interests of the participants and beneficiaries* and . . . for the exclusive purpose of . . . defraying reasonable expenses of administering the plan." 29 U.S.C. § 1104(a)(1) (1988) (emphasis added). For a decision imposing civil liability, see Leigh v. Engle, 858 F.2d 361 (7th Cir. 1988). Criminal and civil penalties are also authorized for breach of this duty. Non-ERISA trustees are subject to virtually identical standards under the law of trusts. See Black, supra note 12, at 553–56.

343. Many pension advisers in fact are registered investment advisers. Where the investment adviser represents a pension fund, the exemption in § 205(b)(2) of the Investment Advisers Act of 1940 for an adviser to a mutual fund is made expressly inapplicable by § 205(b)(2)(B). 15 U.S.C. § 80b-5 (1988). Thus, incentive compensation seems to be strictly forbidden in this case.

withdraw voting discretion.[344] Put simply, corporate management's conflict of interest weakens its normal incentive to pressure its fund managers for performance in this area. Moreover, the investment manager may fear that aggressive monitoring will give it a reputation as an "activist" that will cost it additional pension fund accounts. In short, in the absence of incentive compensation that rewards it for successful monitoring, a pension fund investment manager probably has more reasons to avoid active monitoring than to engage in it.

So stated, the compensation problem seems to require regulatory intervention to encourage the use of incentive fee formulas that better align the investment manager's incentives with those of the fund. But here the real difficulty of the problem comes into view: In the case of the indexed fund manager, incentive compensation is difficult to devise because it is impossible to calculate how an index fund's performance exceeded that of the market when, by definition, it sought to match the market. In short, by choosing as its goal the matching of the market's performance, there is no yardstick for comparison or an obvious basis for measuring superior performance. Even if its monitoring improved the firms in its portfolio, a broadly diversified index fund will have thereby improved the entire market.

One answer to this "Catch-22" is possible and has already been discussed: Restricted diversification. A diversified portfolio of, say, 50 stocks can outperform a similar market index (i.e., the Standard & Poor 500)—largely to the extent that the firms in the smaller portfolio are better monitored. Indeed, the margin by which the smaller portfolio outperforms the larger, similarly selected portfolio is probably an approximate measure of the success, or failure, of monitoring. Ultimately, then, answers dovetail: a restricted diversification policy combined with incentive compensation to fund managers can raise the payoff from monitoring to both the institutional investor and its manager. Indeed, if prudent incentive compensation plans could be adopted, it might not be necessary to mandate restricted diversification, but only to relax the current rules that require a special level of diversification beyond that suggested by economic theory.[345] Money managers who saw an opportunity to profit would have a rational self-interest in assembling smaller portfolios based upon their perceptions of the potential for monitoring gains in these stocks. Finally, the traditional reason for avoiding incentive compensation—namely, that it will lead managers to accept excessive risk[346]—seems inapplicable here. ERISA's diversification requirements would continue to apply,[347] and the

344. See supra note 18 and accompanying text.

345. See supra notes 309–311 and accompanying text.

346. See supra note 338.

347. See 29 U.S.C. § 1104(a) (1988); supra notes 309–311 and accompanying text. While the phrasing of this standard should be revised, the continuation of a diversification rule for pension funds is a certainty.

pension fund's trustees would be under a duty to monitor the fund manager to ensure that it not accept excessive risk. Put simply, the pension investment manager's strategy under such a compensation formula should be to increase portfolio value through active monitoring; and nothing suggests that this requires it to accept additional portfolio risk.

G. *Summary*

Investors who rely on "exit" are likely to show little interest in "voice." As a result, actively trading institutional investors are apt to make poor corporate monitors. In contrast, indexed investors have largely abandoned "exit" and might therefore be induced to exercise "voice." For them, participation in corporate governance can be rational, because they are locked into the market. Yet, even if it is rational for the institutional investor to be interested in corporate governance, it need not be for its agent, the professional money manager. Here, deregulation will have little impact, and the critical steps are for the Labor Department and the SEC to increase the incentives to monitor, by restricting diversification and/or by authorizing incentive compensation formulas that better align the interests of external money managers with those of the institutions they serve.[348]

Restricting diversification under ERISA to the level at which the pension fund could show that it was still capable of monitoring its portfolio would be a sensible means to this end. However, mandating such a rule may be infeasible. Although it would impose little cost on most institutions (because efficient diversification is achievable with relatively few stocks, and market indexes can be constructed using only a fraction of the Standard & Poor's 500),[349] it does encroach on the sacred cow of the manager's investment discretion. Thus, if such a proposal is deemed politically infeasible, the second-best substitute would be to relax ERISA's diversification requirements to a level that is economically justifiable. Such a deregulatory step, if coupled with the authorization of incentive compensation, would give investment managers their own incentive to reduce their portfolio size so as to be able to outperform the market.

Still, if these steps were taken, how optimistic should we be that corporate governance would improve? It is difficult to make optimistic predictions, because adaptive responses by corporate managements are predictable. "Tame" proxy advisers would soon enter the market, and

348. As noted earlier, the Labor Department has begun to assert jurisdiction over pension voting decisions, but it has not gone much further than ruling that voting is mandatory. See supra notes 297–300 and accompanying text. The SEC has similar jurisdiction over mutual funds, but has taken no steps to date.

349. See supra notes 306–308 and accompanying text. Indeed, the net impact might be to reduce transaction and brokerage costs for institutions, as each would trade, monitor and focus on fewer stocks.

would characteristically counsel deference to the incumbent management. Assertive corporate managements can always find a variety of low-visibility means to induce their pension fund trustees to retain "safe" or "prudent" proxy advisers, if the law mandated their use. This does not mean that there would be no net gains because the foregoing proposals would likely activate public pension funds and indexed mutual funds. Still, the gains would be marginal. Only changes in the compensation formulas used for money managers promise significant short-term gains.

CONCLUSION

The trade-off between liquidity and control implies that overregulation is only one of the factors inhibiting institutional activism. More importantly, it also suggests that the reduction of agency costs cannot be the sole goal of corporate governance reform. Rather, monitors as well as managers can behave opportunistically. Indeed, the two can even collude to the disadvantage of minority shareholders (as may sometimes occur in the financial monitoring systems now in operation in Japan and Germany).

Once one recognizes the multilateral character of the relationships within the public corporation, the very concept of financial monitoring takes on a deeper ambiguity: (1) sometimes, the monitor may work on behalf of the minority shareholders to reduce agency costs (possibly in return for some benefit not made available on a pro-rata basis to all shareholders, such as above-market interest); (2) sometimes, the monitor may rebel against the tendency of minority shareholders to "free ride" on its efforts and instead align itself with management (again, possibly in return for some side payment); or (3) sometimes, the monitor may defect from one alliance to another and do so repeatedly. The result can be unstable and shifting coalitions.[350]

From this perspective, public policy should encourage some institutional investors more than others to assume a monitoring role. The profile of the optimal monitor seemingly includes the following elements: (1) an ability to hold large equity stakes; (2) an inclination to hold for the longer term over which improved monitoring can pay off; and (3) the absence of any substantial conflict of interest. On this basis, pension funds and closed-end mutual funds seem potentially superior to banks and other creditor-shareholders. Yet, what cannot be safely concluded is that monitoring will be adequately funded without the institutional investor occupying some other relationship to the corporation through which it can be compensated for the "excess" monitoring it provides the free-riding minority shareholders. Precisely this issue underlies, and confounds, any attempt to reach a bottom line evalua-

350. I have discussed this theme elsewhere. See John C. Coffee, Jr., Unstable Coalitions: Corporate Governance as a Multi-Player Game, 78 Geo. L.J. 1495 (1990).

tion of the efficiency of either the Japanese *keiretsu* or the German universal bank system of credit or/shareholder monitoring. The unwillingness of financial monitors to take and hold larger equity stakes that might justify greater expenditure on their part, even when legally permitted to do so, suggests that monitoring is costly and that these institutions do not consider themselves to have a major comparative advantage as equity investors.

The serious study of comparative corporate governance is still in its infancy. Yet, at least as a preliminary assessment, the liquidity/control trade-off seems readily discernible around the globe. Does this mean that it is unbridgeable? Not necessarily. This Article has focused on how to improve monitoring by those investors whose demand for liquidity is already limited. However, the longer term answer may lie in focusing on how public policy can reduce either the demand for liquidity or the demand for control. Much of the demand for liquidity may reflect managerial desires, rather than institutional needs.[351] Similarly, the demand for control may be moderated to the extent that close substitutes for control can be developed.[352]

Ultimately, monitoring is not neutral. Different monitors will behave differently in terms of their respective needs for liquidity, their time horizons, or their attitudes toward risk. Society either chooses the monitors it wants or accepts those that emerge by default. In this sense, the new political theory of the corporation is correct: Politics does and will continue to count.

351. The short-term trading of large portfolios, for example, produces brokerage commissions and justifies research fees, even though the large institutional investor may already be locked into the market and unable to outperform it.

352. This is essentially what the Gilson and Kraakman proposals would accomplish by allowing institutions to influence, but not directly control, corporate decision-making. See Gilson & Kraakman, supra note 13, at 883–905.

[17]

THE INSIGNIFICANCE OF PROXY ACCESS

Marcel Kahan and Edward Rock***

PROXY access is the right of shareholders to nominate directors and to have their nominees included in the company's proxy statement. Because proxy access is viewed as dramatically lowering the costs of an election contest, both proponents and opponents of proxy access predict that it will have a significant impact. Contrary to this conventional wisdom, we argue that proxy access will lead to few shareholder nominations, that most of these nominees will be defeated, and that the occasional nominee who may get elected will have little impact.

Based on past involvement in shareholder activism, we believe that neither mutual funds nor private pension funds would make significant use of proxy access. Certain large public pension funds have shown a modest interest in activism and may make some nominations. The entities with the greatest interests in activism—hedge funds and union-affiliated funds—would generally not satisfy the ownership and holding period requirements.

When compared to traditional proxy contests and to withhold campaigns, proxy access involves significant disadvantages while promising only modest advantages. The cost savings of proxy access compared to traditional contests are overstated because most proxy contest expenses are discretionary campaign expenses or relate to other expense items that are unaffected by the proxy access rule. By contrast, the limitations that come with proxy access are significant: the number of nominees a shareholder can propose is limited; the level of shareholder support required to gain a seat, as a practical matter, is increased; the company retains control over the design of

* George T. Lowy Professor of Law, New York University School of Law.
** Saul A. Fox Distinguished Professor of Business Law, University of Pennsylvania School of Law. We would like to thank Bill Allen, Jennifer Arlen, Marshall Babson, Michal Barzuza, Ryan Bubb, Emiliano Cattan, Jeff Gordon, Mike Levine, Mark Roe, and the participants at workshops at Columbia and NYU for helpful comments and Emily Schultz for her excellent research assistance. Marcel Kahan would like to thank the Milton and Miriam Handler Foundation for generous support. Edward Rock's research was supported by the University of Pennsylvania's Institute for Law and Economics and the Saul A. Fox Research Endowment.

the proxy cards; and the company retains exclusive access to preliminary voting information.

When compared to withhold-vote campaigns, proxy access has the advantage that, if it succeeds, it results in the election of a dissident director. But this benefit must be weighed against countervailing factors that reduce the likelihood of success: the higher level of shareholder support required for success, the greater challenge of positive versus negative campaigning, and the vulnerability of the dissident shareholders and their nominees to attacks by the company for lack of qualification or conflicts of interest. Such attacks will resonate especially for nominees by unions and public pension funds and may make it difficult to find qualified nominees.

Overall, we believe that proxy access would have some undesirable effects—it would result in some increase in company expenses and may, rarely, increase the leverage of shareholders whose interests conflict with those of shareholders at large—and some desirable effects—it may occasionally lead to the election of nominees to recalcitrant boards, where such nominees may have a modest impact on governance and a marginal impact on company value. None of these effects is likely to be very material, and the net effect is likely to be close to zero.

INTRODUCTION

Should shareholders in publicly traded corporations have the right to have their nominees to the corporate board included in the proxy statement and ballots mailed out by the company and at the company's expense? The highly controversial question has long been at the forefront of the corporate governance debate. The Securities and Exchange Commission ("SEC") first considered passing rules 60 years ago, and has since released several proposals.[1]

But although there is significant disagreement among observers over whether such "proxy access" is desirable, there appears to be a widespread expectation that proxy access would have major effects on corporate governance. Thus, John G. Finley, formerly a partner at Simpson Thatcher & Bartlett and now Senior Managing Director and Chief Legal Officer at Blackstone, remarked that proxy access is "the biggest change relating to corporate governance ever proposed by the SEC."[2] John Greenwald, in *Corporate Board Member* magazine, opined that "few things make boards more nervous" than proxy access.[3] The Chamber of Commerce viewed proxy access as "extremely significant" and having "enormous impacts"[4] and included killing it among its top 5 priorities.[5] David Katz and Laura McIntosh, two lawyers at Wachtell, Lipton, Rosen & Katz, see proxy access as having the "potential to wreak havoc with American business"[6] and an SEC adoption as "unwise and unnecessary."[7] Michael Garland of CtW Investment Group, a proxy advisory firm, called proxy access a "new and powerful tool."[8] *The Deal Magazine* notes that proxy access would make it "dramatically less expensive[] for shareholders to nominate direc-

[1] See Yin Wilczek, In Historic Rulemaking, SEC Allows Investors to Access Proxies to Nominate Directors, 42 Sec. Reg. & L. Rep. (BNA), 1617, 1621 (Aug. 30, 2010).

[2] John Greenwald, Hang On, 13 Corp. Bd. Member, First Quarter 2010, at 22, 24.

[3] Id.

[4] Sarah N. Lynch, Business Groups Gear Up To Fight SEC Proxy Access Proposal, Dow Jones Newswires, Aug. 18, 2009, available at Factiva, Doc. No. DJ00000020090818e58i000aq (quoting Tom Quaadman, Executive Director at the U.S. Chamber of Commerce).

[5] Kara Scannell, Proxy Plan Roils Talks on Finance Rules, Wall St. J., Mar. 17, 2010, at A2.

[6] David A. Katz & Laura A. McIntosh, Senate Bill Adversely Affects the Landscape, N.Y. L.J., May 27, 2010, at 5.

[7] David A. Katz & Laura A. McIntosh, Populists' Wish Lists Offer Legislative Parade of Horribles, N.Y. L.J., July 23, 2009, at 5; see also David A. Katz & Laura A. McIntosh, Proxy Access: Not Then, Not Now, N.Y. L.J., Sept. 28, 2006, at 5; David A. Katz & Laura A. McIntosh, SEC Revisits Shareholder Access to Director Nominations, N.Y. L.J., Aug. 30, 2007, at 5.

[8] Joann S. Lublin, New Rule on Proxies Puts Heat on Firms, Wall St. J., Aug. 23, 2010, at B1.

tors."[9] Brian Cartwright, the former general counsel of the SEC, regards proxy access as a "grand experiment in politicizing the leadership" of U.S. corporations.[10] *The Wall Street Journal* has called it a "high-stakes issue"[11] and headlined that proxy access would "put[] heat on firms."[12] Others call proxy access either "groundbreaking"[13] and "historic,"[14] or "fatally flawed"[15] and "a giant step backwards."[16] Some predict that proxy access would result in a "profound effect on the boardroom"[17] and help "restore shareholder confidence";[18] others predict that it would "handcuff boards,"[19] generate a "fair amount of litigation,"[20] and occupy the SEC for "years to come."[21]

On August 25, 2010, it looked like proxy access was about to become a reality. The Securities and Exchange Commission, over heavy opposition by corporations and after a close vote along partisan lines, finally adopted a rule granting shareholders proxy access.[22] But the Business Roundtable and the Chamber of Commerce promptly filed suit to enjoin and invalidate the rule.[23] On

---

[9] Steven Epstein & Matthew Soran, Uncle Sam: A Most Effective Shareholder Activist?, TheDeal.com (July 13, 2009, 2:24 PM), http://www.thedeal.com/newsweekly/community/uncle-sam-a-most-effective-shareholder-activist.php.

[10] Editorial, Alinsky Wins at the SEC, Wall St. J., Aug. 30, 2010, at A14.

[11] Scannell, supra note 5, at A2 (discussing Congressional response to the proxy access legislation).

[12] Lublin, supra note 8, at B1.

[13] Wilczek, supra note 1, at 1623.

[14] Id. at 1621.

[15] Id. at 1622 (quoting SEC Commissioner Kathleen Casey).

[16] Id. at 1623 (quoting U.S. Chamber of Commerce).

[17] David Calusdian, Proxy Access: Time to Get Ready for Profound Changes, The Podium (Nov. 18, 2009, 1:16 PM), http://blog.investorrelations.com/2009/11/18/proxy-access-time-to-get-ready-for-profound-changes.

[18] Walter Calls for Action on Proxy Access, Disclosure, Other Governance Topics, Corporate Law Daily (BNA) (Feb. 19. 2009), http://0-news.bna.com.pacman.law.du.edu/cldn/display/batch_print_display.adp?searchid=14113940 (attributing phrase to SEC Commissioner Elisse Walter).

[19] Wilczek, supra note 1, at 1623 (quoting Business Roundtable).

[20] Id. at 1622 (quoting John Olson, a partner at Gibson, Dunn & Crutcher LLP).

[21] Id. (quoting SEC Commissioner Kathleen Casey).

[22] See Wilczek, supra note 1, at 1621.

[23] Petition for Review at 2, Bus. Roundtable v. SEC, No. 10-1305 (D.C. Cir. Sept. 29, 2010). The SEC agreed to stay the effectiveness of the proxy access rules pending resolution of the lawsuit. See U.S. Chamber and Business Roundtable Commend SEC's Decision to Grant Stay on Proxy Access Rule, U.S. Chamber of Commerce

July 22, 2011, the U.S. Court of Appeals for the D.C. Circuit vacated the proxy access rule due to the SEC's failure to assess its economic effects adequately.[24] As of this writing, the SEC has yet to determine whether to appeal the court decision, revise or reissue the rule after performing the missing analysis, or drop its effort to grant proxy access.

In this Article, we will argue that, contrary to the views expressed by the commentators, proxy access would have little impact on corporate governance. Even if the SEC's rule is ultimately validated or a different rule is adopted, few shareholders would use proxy access to make nominations, very few of the nominees would succeed in getting elected to boards, and the rare nominee who does get elected would make little difference on the way companies are run and would have even less of an effect on company value. While the specifics of our analysis consider the rule adopted by the SEC in 2010, our general arguments apply to any revised rule that may be adopted by the SEC, which is likely to be narrower than the 2010 rule, as well as to the prior proposals, some of which were broader than the 2010 rule.

Rather, the whole concept of proxy access, in our view, is based on a fallacy: the erroneous belief that it is the costs associated with distributing a proxy statement that accounts for the failure of shareholders to wage more successful proxy contests. Accordingly, all the effort that shareholder activists have poured into proxy access, even if they ultimately succeed in getting a valid rule adopted, will be wasted.

In Part I of this Article, we discuss the history of the proxy access rule, describe the rule adopted by the SEC in greater detail, and place it in the context of some other recent developments related to the shareholder franchise. Part II analyzes the status quo of contested and uncontested shareholder votes and examines what type of shareholders are likely both to satisfy the qualifications for making proxy access nominations and to be interested in engaging in activism via proxy access. Parts III and IV assess the advantages and disadvantages of proxy access relative to, respectively, tradi-

(Oct. 4, 2010), http://www.uschamber.com/press/releases/2010/october/us-chamber-and-business-roundtable-commend-secs-decision-grant-stay-prox.

[24] Bus. Roundtable v. SEC, No. 10-1305, 2011 U.S. App. LEXIS 14988 (D.C. Cir. July 22, 2011).

tional proxy contests and withhold votes. In Part V, we discuss the marginal impact proxy access would have on corporate governance. We close with a brief conclusion.

I. THE HISTORY OF PROXY ACCESS

A. History

The recently enacted, and for the time being vacated, rules on proxy access are the product of a long and tortured history. In 1942,[25] and then again in 1977,[26] the SEC expressed some interest in giving shareholders the opportunity to use the company's proxy materials to solicit votes in director elections, but ended up taking no action. Things started heating up in 2003, when the SEC again issued a proposal on proxy access for comments. Under the 2003 proposal, shareholders would obtain proxy access for the two years following a triggering event—either a 35% or more "withhold" vote in a director election or a majority vote by shareholders electing to make the company subject to proxy access.[27] Under that proposal, shareholders who held at least 5% of the company's stock for a minimum of 2 years would have been able to make nominations for some of the board seats.[28]

From its beginning, the 2003 proposal was highly controversial. It was initially adopted by a vote of 3-2, with the Republican

[25] See Security and Exchange Commission Proxy Rules: Hearings on H.R. 1493, H.R. 1821, and H.R. 2019 Before the H. Comm. on Interstate and Foreign Commerce, 78th Cong. 17–19 (1943) (testimony of Chairman Ganson Purcell that the SEC solicited comments on staff proposal); Securities Act Release No. 2887, Exchange Act Release No. 3347, Holding Company Act Release No. 3988, Investment Company Act Release No. 417 (Dec. 18, 1942) (stating that "[a] number of the suggestions proposed by the staff were not adopted," including the suggestion related to shareholder access to the company's proxy material). No action was taken.

[26] Staff of U.S. Securities and Exchange Commission Rep.: Review of the Proxy Process Regarding the Nomination and Election of Directors 3 (July 15, 2003), available at http://www.sec.gov/news/studies/proxyreport.pdf.

[27] Security Holder Director Nominations, Exchange Act Release No. 48,626, Investment Company Act Release No. 26,206, 68 Fed. Reg. 60,790, 60,791 (Oct. 23, 2003), *reprinted in* [2003–2004 Transfer Binder] Fed. Sec. L. Rep. (CCH) ¶ 87,101, at 88,409, 88,410 (Oct. 14, 2003).

[28] Security Holder Director Nominations, Exchange Act Release No. 48,626, Investment Company Act Release No. 26,206, 68 Fed. Reg. 60,794 (Oct. 23, 2003), *reprinted in* [2003–2004 Transfer Binder] Fed. Sec. L. Rep. (CCH) ¶ 87,101, at 88,413–88,414 (Oct. 14, 2003).

Chairman Donaldson siding with the two Democratic commissioners.[29] The Business Roundtable (an association of CEOs of leading U.S. companies) and the Chamber of Commerce were strongly opposed.[30] Donaldson ended up not pushing for an adoption of the proxy rules and resigned in 2005.[31] His successor, Christopher Cox, was not regarded as a champion of proxy access, and proxy access was considered dead.

Dissatisfied champions of proxy access therefore decided to adopt an alternative strategy. In 2005, the American Federation of State, County and Municipal Employees (AFSCME) made a shareholder proposal under Rule 14a-8 to American International Group (AIG) seeking to implement a homemade proxy access regime through a bylaw amendment.[32] The SEC's Division of Corporate Finance took the position that AIG could omit this proposal under Rule 14a-8(i)(8).[33] AIG did, and AFSCME sued. In 2006, the U.S. Court of Appeals for the Second Circuit ruled that the proposal could not be excluded.[34] In its opinion, the court was highly critical of the SEC, berating it for changing its position on the meaning of its rules without either acknowledging so or explaining the reasons for it.[35] The Court of Appeals's ruling meant that the SEC had to act, both to clarify its rules and to remedy the shortcomings the court had noted.

And act it did—sort of. In July 2007, the SEC released for comment two alternative proposals. One resembled the 2003 proxy access proposal. The other would have provided a reasoned basis for the position that a shareholder proposal trying to implement proxy

[29] See Jonathan Peterson, SEC Offers Conflicting Shareholder Proposals, L.A. Times, July 26, 2007, at C3 (stating that Chairman Donaldson and the SEC's Democratic commissioners supported the SEC's 2003 proposal).

[30] See Bill Baue, Opening Up Pandora's Box: SEC Proxy Roundtable Questions Role of Non-Binding Resolutions, SocialFunds (May 15, 2007), http://www.socialfunds.com/news/article.cgi/2293.html ("The SEC allowed the rule it proposed in October 2003, allowing shareowners proxy access to nominate directors in certain circumstances, to die on the vine due to opposition by the Business Roundtable and the US Chamber of Commerce, which threatened a lawsuit.").

[31] Stephen Labaton, S.E.C.'s Chairman is Stepping Down from Split Panel, N.Y. Times, June 2, 2005, at A1.

[32] AFSCME v. AIG, Inc., 462 F.3d 121, 123–24 (2d Cir. 2006).

[33] Id. at 124.

[34] Id. at 129–30.

[35] Id. at 129.

access for a single company can be excluded under Rule 14a-8. Each proposal was supported by only 3 of the 5 commissioners—the first by the 2 Democratic commissioners and Chairman Cox, the second by Cox and the 2 other Republican commissioners.[36] In November 2007, the 3 Republican commissioners adopted the second proposal.[37]

A year later, Barack Obama was elected President. Cox resigned and was succeeded by Mary Schapiro.[38] With Cox having been replaced by an Obama nominee, the SEC, in June 2009, released another variant of a proposed proxy access rule—again in a 3-2 vote.[39] The 2009 proposal was broader than the 2003 proposal: it removed the requirement of a triggering event, it lowered the percentage ownership requirement for making a nomination to 1%–5%, depending on company size, and it shortened the required holding period to 1 year.[40] Predictably, reactions were mixed, with some groups strongly opposed and others strongly in favor. But even some of the market participants who favored proxy access in general suggested that the 2009 proposal be made more restrictive.[41] For example, in its comment letter to the SEC, Barclays Global Investors, a major institutional holder that manages $1.5 trillion in assets, favored both the reintroduction of the triggers in the 2003

[36] See Nicholas Rummell, SEC Splits Proxy Access Votes as Cox Says 'Yea' to Two Proposals, Fin. Wk. (July 25, 2007, 6:11 PM), http://www.financialweek.com/apps/pbcs.dll/article?AID=/20070725/REG/70725013/1036 (describing how the first proposal would allow shareholders to put forth proxy proposals calling for bylaw changes to allow shareholder-approved directors during corporate elections and how the second would restate the SEC's position prior to the Second Circuit's invalidation).

[37] L. Reed Walton, The SEC Denies Proxy Access, RiskMetrics Group Blog (Nov. 30, 2007, 10:33 AM), http://blog.riskmetrics.com/gov/2007/11/the-sec-denies-proxy-accesssubmitted-by-l-reed-walton-publications.html.

[38] See Randall Smith & Kara Scannell, Regulator Schapiro to Run SEC for Obama, Wall St. J., Dec. 18, 2008, at A1.

[39] Georgeson Inc. & Latham & Watkins LLP, Proxy Access Proposed Rules Published by SEC, Corp. Governance Comment. (June 15, 2009), http://www.georgeson.com/usa/download/corp_gov_commentary.html.

[40] Facilitating Shareholder Director Nominations, Securities Act Release No. 9046, Exchange Act Release No. 60,089, Investment Company Act Release No. 28,765, 74 Fed. Reg. 29,032, 29,037, 29,063 (June 18, 2009).

[41] See generally Corporate Law Daily (BNA) (Aug. 20. 2010), available at http://news.bna.com/cldn/CLDNWB/split_display.adp?fedfid=17646623&vname=ccdbulallissues&fn=17646623&jd=a0c4a1c0v3&split=0 (noting that institutional investors favor a 3% threshold).

proposal and an increase in the ownership threshold needed to make a nomination to 5%–15%, depending on the company's market capitalization.[42] T. Rowe Price Associates, a mutual fund complex with about $190 billion in assets, favored a 5% ownership threshold for all companies, noting that it owned more than 5% of the stock in more than 350 U.S. operating companies.[43] Moreover, managerial interests raised the argument that the proposed rule exceeded the SEC's rulemaking authority.[44]

To insulate any rule against such a legal attack, the SEC delayed action until Congress, as part of the financial reform bill, granted the disputed authority to the SEC.[45] President Obama signed the finance reform bill on July 21, 2010, and the SEC adopted the proxy access rule on August 25, 2010. Under the adopted rule, the ownership requirement was set at a uniform level of 3% for all companies.[46] Shareholders can pool their shares to form a group that satisfies the ownership threshold. If more than 10 other shareholders are solicited in the effort to form such a group, the soliciting shareholder must file a disclosure statement with the SEC. The 3% ownership requirement must be satisfied as of the date the nomination is made and for the preceding 3 years.[47] Since nominations must be made no later than 120 days before the anniversary of the company's mailing of the previous year's proxy statement,[48] and the nominating shareholders must intend to maintain their

---

[42] Annette L. Nazareth, SEC Urged to Defer Adopting Proxy Access Rules, Harv. L. Sch. F. on Corp. Governance and Fin. Reg. (Oct. 6, 2009, 9:01 AM), http://blogs.law.harvard.edu/corpgov/2009/10/06/sec-urged-to-defer-adopting-proxy-access-rules.

[43] Id.

[44] See Kevin Drawbaugh, US CEO Lobby Doubts SEC Authority on Proxy Access, Reuters, Jan. 16, 2004; Rachelle Younglai, SEC Aims for Proxy Access Rules in 2nd Quarter, Reuters, Apr. 27, 2010, available at http://www.reuters.com/article/idUSTRE63Q47T20100427.

[45] See Jeff Morgan, SEC Proxy Access Vote Delayed Until Early 2010, National Investor Relations Institute (Oct. 6, 2009), http://www.niri.org/Main-Menu-Category/advocate/Presidents-Note/SEC-Proxy-Access-Vote-Delayed-Until-Early-2010.aspx.

[46] 17 C.F.R. § 240.14a-11(b)(1) (2010). However, for very small issues (with a public float of less than $75 million), the effective date of the rule was delayed for 3 years. Facilitating Shareholder Director Nominations, Securities Act Release No. 9136, Exchange Act Release No. 62,764, Investment Company Act Release No. 29,384, 75 Fed. Reg. 56,668 (Sept. 16, 2010).

[47] 17 C.F.R. § 240.14a-11(b)(2) (2010).

[48] Id. § 240.14a-11(b)(10).

ownership until the date of the meeting,[49] the rule effectively imposes a 3-and-1/3-year holding period on nominating shareholders. As in the proposed rule, nominations may only be made for up to 25% of the board seats. No nominations may be made by a shareholder who seeks to change control of the company or to gain a number of seats in excess of the maximum permitted by the rule.[50] A nominee's candidacy may not violate the law or any stock exchange rules, the nominee must meet stock exchange rule independence criteria, and the nominating shareholder must file a new Schedule N containing certain disclosures.[51]

Promptly after the proxy access rule was adopted, the Business Roundtable and the Chamber of Commerce filed suit to enjoin and invalidate it.[52] On July 22, 2011, the Court of Appeals for the D.C. Circuit vacated the proxy access rule, holding that the rule was "arbitrary and capricious" due to the SEC's failure to assess its economic effects adequately.[53] As of this writing, the SEC has yet to determine whether to appeal the ruling, revise or reissue the rule after performing the missing analysis, or drop its effort to grant proxy access. But given the checkered history of proxy access, we would be surprised if the Court of Appeals opinion presented the last word in this long saga.

B. Other Developments

Between 2003, when the Donaldson commission released its proxy access proposal, and 2010, when the Schapiro commission adopted its variant of proxy access, several notable developments occurred. Shareholders realized the power they can wield by "just voting no." Many companies switched their election regime from

[49] Id. § 240.14a-11(b)(5).

[50] Id. § 240.14a-11(b)(6).

[51] Id. § 240.14a-11(b)(8)–(10). The requirements of Schedule N are further discussed at Table 4, infra.

[52] Petition for Review at 2, Bus. Roundtable v. SEC, No. 10-1305 (D.C. Cir. Sept. 29, 2010). The SEC has agreed to stay the effectiveness of the proxy access rules pending resolution of the lawsuit. See U.S. Chamber and Business Roundtable Commend SEC's Decision to Grant Stay on Proxy Access Rule, U.S. Chamber of Commerce (Oct. 4, 2010), http://www.uschamber.com/press/releases/2010/october/us-chamber-and-business-roundtable-commend-secs-decision-grant-stay-prox.

[53] Bus. Roundtable v. SEC, No. 10-1305, 2011 U.S. App. LEXIS 14988 (D.C. Cir. July 22, 2011).

plurality voting to some form of majority voting. Discretionary broker voting in director elections was eliminated. And finally, Delaware law was clarified to permit shareholders to adopt tailor-made, firm-specific proxy access rules. These developments have reduced—in our view, significantly—the impact, usefulness, and need for a federal rule on proxy access. In this Section, we describe these developments in greater detail.

In uncontested director elections—and the overwhelming majority of elections are uncontested—the only choice for shareholders who do not want to vote for a board nominee is to mark their proxy card (or voting instruction form) to withhold authority to vote for the director at issue. Shareholders have long had the ability to return a proxy card but withhold the vote for a director. Until recently, however, shareholders have taken little note of it.

The intellectual origin of shareholders withholding their votes lies in a 1990 presentation to large institutional investors by former SEC Commissioner, and then-professor at Stanford law, Joe Grundfest. Grundfest proposed that shareholders "just vote no" in director elections.[54] Though under the plurality voting system that prevailed at the time, withhold votes would have no legal effect no matter how many were cast,[55] he argued that the symbolic impact of withhold votes, especially when coupled with shareholder communications with management, could act as an annual referendum on managerial performance and "be a catalyst for improved oversight that would benefit all corporate constituencies, as well as the economy at large."[56] In particular, Grundfest expected that

> [a] successful "just vote no" campaign can induce internal reforms as a result of social pressures that lead board members to engage in more effective monitoring. Alternatively, a substantial "just vote no" turnout can increase the probability of a hostile proxy contest or tender offer that will be treated more kindly by

[54] Joseph A. Grundfest, Just Vote No: A Minimalist Strategy for Dealing with Barbarians Inside the Gates, 45 Stan. L. Rev. 857, 867 (1993).

[55] As discussed below, in an uncontested election under plurality voting, each nominee is elected as long as she receives a single affirmative vote. See infra text accompanying note 190.

[56] Grundfest, supra note 54, at 866.

the courts precisely because it follows a significant "just vote no" turnout.[57]

Although there was some early enthusiasm for the initiative,[58] it took a number of years before Grundfest's proposal caught on. The turning point probably was in the 2004 Disney board election,[59] when 45% of the shares were withheld from Disney CEO Michael Eisner.[60] This campaign was highly publicized for a variety of reasons: it involved a large entertainment company; it pitted Eisner against Roy Disney, the nephew of the legendary founder of the company; and Roy Disney spent more than $2 million in campaigning for shareholders to vote "no."[61] Even though Eisner received a majority of the votes cast, the board of Disney immediately stripped him of his position as chairman[62] and Eisner resigned as CEO the following year.[63] The Disney withhold campaign showed shareholders that, in the right circumstances, a high withhold vote is both achievable and effective in inducing governance changes.

In the wake of the rise of withhold campaigns, it also dawned on shareholders that there is something wrong with an election system in which a director can be elected even if a large majority of shareholders is opposed. As a result, shareholders began pushing for some form of majority voting. It seems that the arguments against plurality voting struck a chord. Within a short span, most large companies discarded the old plurality voting regime and adopted

[57] Id. at 927.

[58] Id. at 866–67 & n.33 (citing press reports commenting on the increased popularity of the initiative).

[59] See Andrew Countryman, Shareholders Renewing "Just Vote No" Campaigns, Chi. Trib., Feb. 11, 2005, § 3, at 4 (quoting Patrick McGurn, a corporate governance expert at Institutional Shareholders Service, as saying "[w]ithhold-vote campaigns came of age in 2004, and they emerged as the dominant tactic for shareholder activists . . . .").

[60] See Laura M. Holson & Geraldine Fabrikant, Disney Chief to Leave, Setting Off Race for Job, N.Y. Times, Sept. 11, 2004, at C3.

[61] See Matt Kelly, Proxy Access Update: A Review of Likelihood, Costs, Compliance Wk. (Oct. 12, 2004), http://www.complianceweek.com/article/1219/proxy-access-update-a-review-of-likelihood-costs.

[62] See Steven J. Spencer & Young J. Woo, Considerations for "Just Vote No" Campaigns, Activist Investment Developments, Schulte, Roth & Zabel, LLP 1 (Fall 2006), http://www.srz.com/files/News/5333c42b-1659-4caf-9540-c10b4a6a038c/Presentation/NewsAttachment/26d52d60-ac91-404e-8bbd-67bfae1332d0/filesfilesArticle%20-%20AI%20-%20fall06%20-%20Considerations.pdf.

[63] See Exit Eisner, L.A. Times, Sept. 30, 2005, at B10.

some form of majority voting. Thus, the percentage of S&P 500 companies with some form of majority voting increased from 16% in February 2006 and 66% in November 2007[64] to about 80% in 2010.[65] S&P 500 companies account for about 75% of the aggregate capitalization of the U.S. stock market.[66] Among smaller companies, majority voting so far remains much less prevalent: of 5930 companies outside the S&P 500 that are followed by RiskMetrics, only 17% had adopted some form of majority voting by 2009.[67] But still, it is clear that majority voting has been a big success, is already in effect for a majority of U.S. companies when weighted by capitalization, and is likely to be adopted by many more companies in future years.

A third change occurred with respect to the ability of brokers to vote shares held in their customers' brokerage accounts. Most individual shareholders in the U.S. hold their shares through brokers and are not the record holders of those shares.[68] When a company solicits proxies, it sends proxy materials to the brokers, which then forward them to their customers together with a form on which the customers can mark voting instructions.[69] If the customer does not return these instructions, and the issue is designated as "routine" by the NYSE, the broker can vote the uninstructed shares in its discretion—which usually means in accordance with management recommendations.[70]

---

[64] Claudia H. Allen, Study of Majority Voting in Director Elections, Neal, Gerber & Eisenberg, LLP i (Nov. 12, 2007), http://www.ngelaw.com/files/upload/majoritystudy 111207.pdf.

[65] See Press Release, California Public Employees' Retirement System, CalPERS 2010 Majority Vote Initiative Successful at Top Companies (Dec. 22, 2010), http://www.calpers.ca.gov/index.jsp?bc=/about/press/pr-archive/pr-2010/dec/2010-majority-vote.xml.

[66] See Data Series: SP500, S&P 500 Index, Federal Reserve Bank of St. Louis (Jul. 26, 2010, 10:01 AM), available at http://research.stlouisfed.org/fred2/series/SP500.

[67] See Lucian Bebchuk & Scott Hirst, Private Ordering and the Proxy Access Debate, 65 Bus. Law. 329, 343 (2010) (citing figures supplied to the authors by RiskMetrics).

[68] Marcel Kahan & Edward Rock, The Hanging Chads of Corporate Voting, 96 Geo. L.J. 1227, 1237 (2008) [hereinafter Kahan & Rock, Hanging Chads].

[69] Id. at 1243–48 (describing the process of how nominee shares are voted).

[70] Id. at 1250.

Until 2010, all uncontested director elections were treated as routine[71]—including the Disney board election in 2004 and subsequent elections in which active withhold campaigns were waged. As of January 1, 2010, the NYSE no longer treats *any* director election as routine.[72] As a result, when a shareholder does not return voting instructions to the broker, these shares are not voted in the election of directors.

Finally, while proxy access was waxing and waning at the SEC, Delaware law made clear that shareholders had broad powers to adopt bylaws governing proxy access. In 2008, the Delaware Supreme Court held in *CA, Inc. v. AFSCME Employees Pension Plan*[73] that provisions facilitating the nomination of director candidates by shareholders can be included in bylaws—which can be adopted by shareholders without board approval[74]—and need not be included in the certificate of incorporation (which can only be changed upon a board recommendation).[75] The following year, the Delaware legislature adopted a new Section 112 that explicitly allows corporations to adopt proxy access via bylaw.[76] Under that section, the bylaws may provide that individuals nominated by a stockholder will be included in the corporation's proxy solicitation materials and its form of proxy, subject to the procedures and con-

[71] NYSE Rule 451, 2 N.Y.S.E. Guide (CCH) ¶ 2451 (Dec. 2009); NYSE Rule 452, 2 N.Y.S.E. Guide (CCH) ¶ 2452 (Dec. 2009). Since NYSE exchange rules effectively govern all brokers, this rule applies to all publicly traded companies, regardless of where their stock is listed for trading.

[72] See Julie Connelly, What the Amended Rule 452 Means to You, Corp. Bd. Member, Third Quarter 2009, available at http://www.boardmember.com/MagazineArticle_Details.aspx?id=3880 (explaining the change in NYSE Rule 452 and ramifications for director elections).

[73] 953 A.2d 227, 237 (Del. 2008).

[74] Del. Code Ann. tit. 8, § 109(a) (Supp. 2010).

[75] See generally Marcel Kahan & Edward B. Rock, Corporate Constitutionalism: Antitakeover Charter Provisions as Precommitment, 152 U. Pa. L. Rev. 473, 495–96 (2003) (distinguishing between unilateral and bilateral governance changes).

[76] H.R. 19, 145th Gen. Assemb., Reg. Sess. (Del. 2009); see also Comment Letter from James L. Holzman, Chair, Council of the Corp. L. Section of the Del. Bar Ass'n, to Elizabeth M. Murphy, Secretary, Sec. & Exchange Commission 4 (July 24, 2009), available at http://www.sec.gov/comments/s7-10-09/s71009-65.pdf. For an analysis of the jurisdictional interaction between Delaware and the federal government regarding proxy access, see Mark J. Roe, The Corporate Shareholder's Vote and its Political Economy, in Delaware and in Washington (Paolo Baffi Centre Research Paper No. 2011-94, 2011), available at http://papers.ssrn.com/sol3/papers.cfm?abstract_id=1884110.

ditions provided in the bylaw. These conditions may include a minimum level or duration of ownership, submission of specified information, and limitations on parties seeking control. In principle, therefore, if a majority of shareholders of a company want proxy access, they have the power to adopt a proxy access bylaw, at least in most Delaware companies.[77] Unlike the SEC's proxy access rule, Section 112 embodies an "enabling" approach to corporate governance, as it permits each company to determine for itself whether to have proxy access, and if so, which shareholders should be eligible to make nominations, rather than imposing the same "one size fits all" approach on all companies.[78]

II. THE STATUS QUO: UNCONTESTED AND CONTESTED PROXY SOLICITATIONS

Before considering how proxy access may change the existing system, we need to describe briefly how the existing system works.

[77] Though Section 112 became effective in August 2009, we are not aware of any shareholder proposal during the 2010 proxy season that tried to use Section 112 to opt into a homemade proxy access rule. While this may indicate a lack of demand, it could also be due to the fact that shareholders' rights advocates were awaiting the likely adoption of the SEC proxy access rule. Moreover, without changes in federal law, a proxy access rule under Section 112 would have created some tensions with the antifraud provision in the proxy rules: to the extent that the company's proxy statement includes information provided by a nominating shareholder, and that information is materially false or misleading, the company would have violated Rule 14a-9. The new federal proxy access rule makes it a violation for a nominating shareholder to cause a company to include materially false or misleading information regarding a proxy access nomination under federal or state law, see 17 C.F.R. § 240.14a-9 (2010), and exculpates the company from any liability for false or misleading statements supplied by a nominating shareholder in Schedule 14N or otherwise, see 17 C.F.R. § 240.14a-11(f) (2010). It is not entirely clear whether this exculpation applies to information furnished under Section 112. However, prior to the adoption of the federal proxy access rule, the clear lack of any exculpation may have made a company wary of adopting proxy access under Section 112.

[78] The lack of any ability of companies to opt out of proxy access formed part of the basis for Commissioner Paredes's opposition to the SEC's approach. See, e.g., Troy A. Paredes, Comm'r, Securities and Exchange Comm'n, Speech at the 22nd Annual Tulane Corporate Law Institute (April 15, 2010) (transcript available at http://www.sec.gov/news/speech/2010/spch041510tap.htm).

A. Uncontested Solicitations

There are approximately 6000 firms listed on the NYSE, the AMEX, and the NASDAQ, including foreign issuers.[79] The Wilshire 5000 index, which now includes around 4000 companies,[80] endeavors to cover the entire U.S. equity market and includes every equity security with its primary market listing in the U.S. It drops issues which stop trading for 10 consecutive days (which then are typically listed, if at all, on the "Pink Sheets").[81] Most of these companies hold shareholder meetings once a year and solicit proxies for these meetings[82] under the federal proxy rules.[83]

All but a handful of these meetings are utterly routine. As one would predict, the solicitation of proxies for the uncontested an-

[79] NYSE: 2600 listed operating companies, including 450 from outside the U.S. See A Guide to the NYSE Marketplace, NYSE Group 3 (2006), available at http://www.nyse.com/pdfs/nyse_bluebook.pdf. AMEX: 539 listed companies, including closed-end funds and non-U.S. issuers. See NYSE and NYSE AMEX Equities Membership, NYSE Euronext, Inc., http://www.nyse.com/membership/equities/nyse (last visited Sept. 2, 2011). NASDAQ: 2852 listed companies as of December 31, 2009. See NASDAQ OMX Group, Inc., Annual Report (Form 10-K), at 2 (Feb. 18, 2010). Total: 6009 companies.

[80] Wilshire Fundamental Characteristics, Wilshire Indexes (April 29, 2011), http://web.wilshire.com/Indexes/Broad/Wilshire5000/Characteristics.html.

[81] See Description of Wilshire 5000 Total Market Index, Wilshire Indexes, http://web.wilshire.com/Indexes/Broad/Wilshire5000/ (last visited May 17, 2011). The "Pink Quotations" or "Pink Sheets"—an electronic quotation system that displays quotes for typically inactively traded over-the-counter securities—are so called because the quotes were originally published on pink colored paper by the National Quotation Bureau (NQB). They are currently published by NQB's successor, OTC Markets Group, Inc., which recently changed its name from Pink OTC Markets, Inc. See History of OTC Markets Group, OTC Markets, http://www.otcmarkets.com/about/otc-markets-history (last visited May 17, 2011).

[82] We have described this complex system previously. See Kahan & Rock, Hanging Chads, supra note 68 at 1233–47. It is also the subject of a recent SEC release. See Concept Release on the U.S. Proxy System, Exchange Act Release No. 62,495, Investment Advisers Act Release No. 3052, Investment Company Act Release No. 29,340, 75 Fed. Reg. 42,982, 42,984 (July 22, 2010).

[83] Other estimates indicate that there are somewhere around 13,000 shareholder meetings for public companies per year at which around 600 billion shares are voted. 2009 Proxy Season: Key Statistics & Performance Ratings, Broadridge Investor Communication Solutions 2 (2009), available at http://www.broadridge.com/investor-communications/us/2009ProxyStats.pdf. The difference between the 13,000 estimate of meetings and the 6000–7000 estimate of public companies is probably due to (1) the fact that companies sometimes hold more than one meeting per year, (2) the inclusion of companies that trade only on pink sheets, and (3) the inclusion of investment companies in the former figure.

nual meeting is likewise fairly routine. Counsel for the company must produce a proxy statement that complies with the requirements of Schedule 14A. That proxy statement along with a proxy card—or, in the case of indirect holding, a request for instructions (a VIF or "voting instruction form")—is then distributed to the shareholders, proxies and instructions are collected, votes are tabulated, and the results are reported.

Total costs of the annual proxy solicitation usually fall in the $10,000 to $100,000 range. For example, at Air Products & Chemicals (market capitalization $15.4 billion), the 2010 annual proxy solicitation cost around $80,000, of which $35,700 was paid to Broadridge[84] (covering the distribution to street holders, registered holders, and employee plan participants as well as hosting meeting materials on their website); $14,000 was paid to Morrow & Co. (for acting as proxy solicitor); and $30,000 was paid to RR Donnelley (for proxy printing and EDGAR preparation).[85] The proxy statement itself was produced in house.

B. Contested Solicitations

In contrast to the routine uncontested proxy solicitation for the annual meeting, a proxy contest for control, or even a "short slate" contest in which the dissidents seek to elect only a minority of directors, is much closer to a political campaign. It typically involves telephone solicitations, presentations to institutional investors, multiple mailings to shareholders, and sometimes newspaper advertisements and litigation.

Contested solicitations are relatively infrequent. According to data compiled by Georgeson, a proxy solicitation firm, the number of contested solicitations from 1981 to 2009 has ranged from a low of 3 (in 1993) to a high of 57 (in 2009), with a general trend upwards beginning in the mid 1990s. Since there are over 6,000 publicly traded companies, this means that over 99% of all votes are uncontested. In Table 1, we present data on the cost to dissidents

---

[84] Broadridge Financial Solutions, Inc. ("Broadridge"), formerly a unit of Automatic Data Processing, Inc. ("ADP"), is the market's leading provider of investor communications, including proxy mailing and vote processing services.

[85] Email from John Stanley, General Counsel, Air Products & Chemicals, Inc., to Marcel Kahan (July 30, 2010) (on file with the Virginia Law Review Association).

and companies of waging a contest in 2009.[86] Dissident costs varied widely, from a low of $30,000 to a high of $9 million for Ackman's (unsuccessful) contested solicitation at Target. Unsurprisingly, costs tended to be higher for larger companies (as measured by their market capitalization) than for smaller ones. For companies with a capitalization of less than $300 million, the average (median) costs amounted to $267,000 ($200,000); for companies with a capitalization between $300 million and $1 billion, the average (median) costs amounted to $643,000 ($275,000); and for companies with a capitalization of above $1 billion, the average (median) costs were $2.17 million ($1.15 million).

Table 1: 2009 Contested Solicitations (Source: Georgeson and Independent Research)

Company	Dissident	Market Cap $mil	Issue	Co. Costs $1000	Diss. Costs $1000	Diss. Stake	Outcome
Online Resources	Tennenbaum Cap Part	2	Directors	650	550	21.90%	Dissidents
Rancher Energy	Andrei Stytsenko	4	Directors	*	30	1.30%	Dissidents
Asure Software	Red Oak/ Pinnacle	9	Directors	*	100	10.30%	Dissidents
Wilshire Enterprises	Full Value Part.	9	Directors	150	30	18.60%	Settled
Advocat Inc.	Bristol Inv. Fund	15	Directors	175	150	7.40%	Mgmt
Whitney Inf. Network	Kingstown Part.	17	Directors	*	50	11.50%	Dissidents
Hooper Holmes, Inc.	R. V. Aprahamian	18	Directors	160	150	4.40%	Dissidents
VaxGen	VaxGen Full Value Comm.	23	Directors	*	*	*	Mgmt
Premier Exhibitions	Sellers Cap.	35	Consent to Elect Directors	350	500	16.30%	Dissidents
Fauquier Bankshares	D. M. Van Roijen	43	Directors	200	75–100	7.30%	Mgmt

(*continued overleaf*)

[86] We use the cost estimates provided by companies and challengers in their proxy statements, as required by Schedule 14A. 17 C.F.R. § 240.14a-101, Item 4 (2010).

(continued)

Company	Dissident	Market Cap $mil	Issue	Co. Costs $1000	Diss. Costs $1000	Diss. Stake	Outcome
Neuberger Berman Dividend Adv, Fd.	Western Investment	53	Directors; Opp. Mgmt Agr.	250	150	9.90%	Settled
ORBCOMM, Inc.	John C. Levinson	58	Directors	475	495	1.10%	Withdrawn
Trico Marine Services	Kistefos AS	59	Directors	1200	1700	21.00%	Mgmt
iPass Inc.	Foxhill Opp. Master Fd	62.5	Directors	750	300	7.00%	Settled
California Micro Devices	Dialectic Cap. Mgmt	64	Directors	350	375	8.80%	Dissidents
Penwest Pharmaceuticals	Tang Cap. Part.	64	Directors	875	450	21.10%	Dissidents
Tollgrade Comm.	Ramius LLC	67	Directors	400	200	15.50%	Dissidents
Mac-Gray Corp.	Fairview Cap. Inv.	71	Directors	250	350	6.30%	Split
Quigley Corp.	Ted Karkus	77	Directors	*	250	*	Dissidents
DWS RREEF Real Estate Fund	Susan L. Ciciora Trust	95	Vote Against Liquidation	330	55	16.50%	Dissidents/ Settled
Avigen Inc.	Biotechnology Value Fund	<100	Remove/ Replace Directors	*	150	30.00%	Mgmt
BellaVista Capital	MacKenzie Patterson Fuller	<100	Remove/ Replace Directors	79.5	20	12.40%	Mgmt
Cavalier Homes Inc	Cavalier Homes Comm. for Change	<100	Directors	*	225	9.60%	Settled
Charlotte Russe Holding	KarpReilly Cap. Partners	<100	Directors	*	295	8.90%	Withdrawn
CNS Response	Leonard J Brandt	<100	Remove/ Replace Directors	*	*	32.00%	Mgmt
Concord Milestone Plus	Everest Mgmt	<100	Remove Gen. Partner	*	10	11.30%	Dissidents

Company	Dissident	Market Cap $mil	Issue	Co. Costs $1000	Diss. Costs $1000	Diss. Stake	Outcome
Insured Municipal Income Fund	Bulldog Investors	<100	Directors/Inv. Policies	*	100	10.80%	Dissidents
IPC Holdings	Validus Holdings	<100	Opp. to Amalgamation	*	*	*	Dissidents
IPC Holdings	Validus Holdings	<100	Call Sp. Meeting	*	*	*	Dissidents
LCA Vision, Inc.	The LCA-Vision Full Value Comm.	<100	Remove/ Replace Directors	*	*	*	Withdrawn
Specialty Underwriters' Alliance	Hallmark Fin. Services	<100	Directors	275	250	9.90%	Split
Sun-Times Media Group	Davidson Kempner Cap. Mgmt	<100	Consent to Replace Directors	445	415	5.90%	Dissidents
TM Ent. and Media	Opportunity Part.	<100	Expand Bd; Directors	*	25	18.50%	Settled
Agilysys Inc.	Ramius LLC	100	Directors	*	250	12.50%	Settled
Tier Technologies	Discovery Equity Part.	119	Directors	*	162.5	9.90%	Dissidents
CPI Corp	Ramius LLC	122	Directors	*	200	23.00%	Mgmt
Providence Service Corp.	Prov Comm	128	Directors	445	250	17.90%	Mgmt
Tecumseh Products	Herrick Found.	171	Directors	*	700	15.20%	Dissidents
Consolidated-Tomoka Land Co.	Wintergreen Fund	204	Directors	*	100	25.90%	Split
Conseco	Otter Green Mgmt	233	Director	245	225	0.80%	Dissidents
Myers Industries	GAMCO Asset Mgmt	304	Directors	*	25	9.60%	Mgmt
Orthofix International	Ramius LLC	308	Directors	650	250	5.50%	Mgmt
Orthofix International	Ramius LLC	308	Consent to Call Meeting	*	*	5.50%	Dissidents
Adaptec, Inc.	Steel Part.	389	Remove/ Replace Directors	700	275	10.90%	Dissidents

(continued overleaf)

(*continued*)

Company	Dissident	Market Cap $mil	Issue	Co. Costs $1000	Diss. Costs $1000	Diss. Stake	Outcome
Federal Signal Corp.	W. B. Kanders	399	Directors	1800	750	2.60%	Withdrawn
Saks Inc.	P. Schoenfeld Asset Mgmt	781	W/hold on Directors/ Repeal Class Bd	*	575	1.50%	Mgmt/Dissident
Children's Place Retail Stores	E. Dabah & Comm.	908	Directors	1500	2350	21.80%	Settled
Emulex Corp.	Broadcom Corp.	922	Call Sp. Meeting	900	*	0.00%	Withdrawn
Chemed Corp.	MMI Investments	960	Directors	1500	275	3.60%	Mgmt
PHH Corp.	Pennant Cap. Mgmt	1000	Directors	325	600	9.90%	Dissidents
Texas Industries	Shamrock Activist Value Fund	1108	Directors	600	1000	10.20%	Dissidents
Amylin	Icahn	1619	Directors/ Reincorp	7000	650	9.20%	Split/Mgmt
Amylin	Eastbourne Cap.	1619	Directors	7000	2500	12.20%	Split
CF Industries Holdings	Agrium Inc.	4968	Withhold on Directors	250	1300	2.60%	Mgmt
NRG Energy	Exelon	6227	Dir.; Exp. Board	3000	1300	0.00%	Settled
Biogen Idec	Carl Icahn	14137	Directors	9200	1000	5.60%	Split
Target Corp.	Pershing Square	34909	Directors	11100	9000	7.80%	Mgmt

* Not disclosed.
Market capitalization "<100" is authors' estimate.

To examine contested solicitations more closely, we collected detailed information about all the contests waged between 2005 and 2009 as listed by Georgeson,[87] excluding contests that did not primarily involve the election of directors upon expiration of their terms, contests waged in connection with hostile takeover at-

[87] See Georgeson, 2009 Annual Corporate Governance Review (2009), available at www.georgeson.com/usa/download/acgr/acgr2009.pdf.

tempts, and contests involving closed-end mutual funds.[88] Our list consists of 129 contests. In about half of these contests (66), the dissidents obtained some board representation, either as a result of a ballot success or pursuant to a settlement.[89]

Our analysis shows that most of the target companies involved in these proxy contests are small. Only 8 companies (6%) had a market capitalization of more than $10 billion (a typical definition of large-cap), 9 had a capitalization of between $2 billion and $10 billion (mid-cap),[90] and another 40 had a capitalization of between $300 million and $2 billion, a standard range for small-cap companies.[91] About 60% of the companies (72) were micro-cap companies, with a capitalization of less than $300 million. The average and median capitalizations of these micro-caps were $93 and $66 million. Though micro-cap companies also constitute a large fraction of publicly traded companies, they account for less than 2.5% of the market capitalization of U.S. companies.[92]

That proxy contests are overwhelmingly a phenomenon of small and very small publicly-held firms is important, but rarely noted in the extensive literature on proxy contests. Corporate law scholars often seem to think of publicly held firms as a unitary phenomenon and focus mainly on the larger capitalization firms. But when a company falls below the $300 million market cap, it is extremely difficult to attract attention from analysts or investors.[93] These

[88] Contests about mergers, bylaw amendments, and director removal were excluded because proxy access would not be a vehicle through which such contests could be waged. Contests involving closed-end mutual funds were excluded because of the special nature of these contests, which usually relate to the opening or liquidation of a fund.

[89] In 3 contests, no election was held for reasons such as a lack of quorum or the acquisition of the company prior to the scheduled vote.

[90] Mid Cap, Investopedia, http://www.investopedia.com/terms/m/midcapstock.asp (last visited May 17, 2011).

[91] Small Cap, Investopedia, http://www.investopedia.com/terms/s/small-cap.asp (last visited May 17, 2011).

[92] See Russell 3000 Index, Russell Investments (Feb. 28, 2011), http://www.russell.com/indexes/data/fact_sheets/us/russell_3000_index.asp (stating that Russell 3000 companies account for 98% of the investible U.S. equities market).

[93] Justin Canivet, Small Cap Analyst Coverage: An "Under-the-Radar" Dilemma, Focus, Apr. 2009, at 4, available at www.world-exchanges.org/files/file/Focus%200409.pdf. As Demiroglu & Ryngaert describe,

> [i]n a press release dated July 7, 2005, Bob Greifeld, president and CEO of NASDAQ, noted that 35% of all publicly traded US firms had no analyst cov-

firms are lucky if a single analyst follows them.[94] With so little attention, the market for such companies' shares is far less informationally efficient than for mid-cap or large-cap companies.[95] Similarly, micro-cap companies present distinctive governance challenges. With most of the normal levers of accountability missing, many of them may be badly governed.

In terms of dissidents, of the 129 contests, 86 were waged by hedge funds; of the rest, most were waged by an individual or a group of individual investors. Mutual funds, public pension funds, and private pension funds did not wage *any* of these contests. Dissidents held on average 8.9% of the target company's outstanding shares. In 100 of the 129 contests, the dissidents held more than 5% of the shares of the respective target company. Only 13 dissidents held less than 1% of the shares. This group includes 9 dissidents that held stakes with a dollar value below $150,000, all of whom lost. We regard such low percentage and dollar value contests as nuisance contests. Outside of nuisance contests, there is no strong correlation between dissident stakes and success. Thus, in the 15 contests in which dissident stakes exceeded 15%, the dissidents won only 6 (40%), a success rate well below the sample average.

Segregating the sample into micro-cap and regular-sized (that is, non-micro-cap) companies yields some further insights. Among regular-sized companies, hedge funds constituted 82% of the dissi-

> erage. Additionally, he cited estimates by Reuters that from January 2002 to June 2005, 691 publicly traded US companies had lost all analysts' coverage. Almost all of these companies had market capitalizations under $1 billion. Greifeld also noted "a lack of research coverage impacts company valuation, liquidity, and ultimately the welfare and growth of public companies."

Cem Demiroglu & Michael Ryngaert, The First Analyst Coverage of Neglected Stocks, 39 Fin. Mgmt. 555, 555 (2010) (quoting Press Release, NASDAQ, NASDAQ and Reuters Launch New Venture to Help Companies Obtain Independent Analyst Coverage (June 7, 2005), available at http://www.nasdaq.com/newsroom/news/pr2005/ne_section05_056.stm).

[94] Indeed, one concern with the 2003 analyst settlement was that the new rules would mean that many of the smaller firms would go from one analyst to zero. See Susanne Craig, Firm to Research Stock "Orphans," Wall St. J., June 7, 2005, at C3 ("Reuters found that since 2002, 691 companies have lost analyst coverage altogether. The hardest hit sector: Almost 99% of the companies that have lost coverage are smaller companies with a stock market value of less than $1 billion.").

[95] See Demiroglu & Ryngaert, supra note 93, at 555, 567–69, 581 (documenting the price effects from the announcement of analyst coverage of a previously uncovered company).

dents, former insiders constituted 7%, and other dissidents constituted 11%. Among micro-caps, hedge funds accounted for only 54% of the dissidents, former insiders for 18%, and other dissidents for 28%.

Table 2: Proxy Contests 2005-2009*

	Contests	Hedge Funds	Former Insiders	Success Rate	Success Rate HF	Success Rate Insiders	Success Rate Others
All Companies	129	86	17	52%	60%	59%	21%
Microcaps (capitalization < $300m)	72	39	13	51%	63%	69%	28%
Regular (capitalization > $300m)	57	47	4	54%	56%	25%	0%

*Derived from Georgeson, Annual Corporate Governance Review, 2005 to 2009

As Table 2 shows, the overall success rate of the dissidents was similar in both groups. But this similarity masks important differences. Dissidents other than hedge funds had substantially higher success rates among micro-caps than among regular-sized companies, with former insiders doing better than other non-hedge fund dissidents. Hedge funds had high success rates in both groups, but accounted for a much larger fraction of the contests among regular-sized companies. Dissident stakes averaged 7.8% in regular and 9.7% in micro-cap companies. In both sets of companies, former insiders had the highest average stake (9.2% and 16.6%, respectively), followed by hedge funds (8.1% and 11%, respectively), and other dissidents (0.2% and 7.5%, respectively).

In sum, only two types of dissidents showed meaningful success in waging proxy contests: hedge funds and, for micro-cap companies, former insiders. Other investors—including institutional investors other than hedge funds and individual investors other than former insiders—either never tried or rarely succeeded.

C. Contested Lite: Shareholder Proposals

Under Rule 14a-8, any shareholder who holds a mere $2,000 worth of stock for one year can place a shareholder proposal in the company's proxy statement.[96] Rule 14a-8 proposals may relate to many important corporate governance matters, but they cannot be used as a vehicle to make a nomination for a directorship.[97] Given the trivial share ownership requirements and the short holding period, especially compared to the (adopted as well as proposed) thresholds for proxy access, a large number of shareholders are eligible to make Rule 14a-8 proposals. But most of them do not.

Georgeson publishes an annual list of all corporate governance-related proposals submitted at S&P 1500 companies. We examined the sponsors of the proposals for the five-year period 2005 to 2009 to determine what shareholder types make the most use of Rule 14a-8. In the 2005 to 2009 period, 1844 governance proposals were submitted. Of these, 47% were made by individual shareholders, 39% by labor-affiliated groups (unions, union funds, and employee organizations), and 5% by public pension funds.

Table 3: Governance Shareholder Proposal at S&P 1500*

Sponsor	2005	2006	2007	2008	2009	Combined
Total	375	384	375	339	371	1844
Individuals	158	180	177	163	181	859
Labor and Employee Groups	164	155	154	13	128	714
AFL-CIO	20	4	16	13	17	70
AFSCME	9	15	20	20	17	81
UBCJA	49	64	43	20	27	203
Public Pension Funds	15	19	19	19	25	97
CalPERS	3	2	5	6	5	21
NYC Pension Funds	0	9	10	10	11	40
Hedge Funds	3	7	0	3	2	15
Social Responsibility Funds	3	2	4	19	6	34
Charities and Religious Groups	24	16	15	9	13	77
Investment Managers	6	4	4	7	9	30
TIAA-CREF	0	0	0	2	4	6

*Derived from Georgeson, Annual Corporate Governance Review, 2005 to 2009

What is notable about this listing is, again, the absence of any private pension fund and the virtual absence (with the partial ex-

[96] 17 C.F.R. § 240.14a-8(b) (2010).
[97] Id. § 240.14a-8(i)(8).

ception of TIAA-CREF, which manages both retirement and mutual funds) of any mutual fund. Even public pension funds are underrepresented, and virtually all of the proposals in that category are sponsored by a handful of funds: New York City Pension Funds (40); CalPERS (21); Connecticut Retirement Plans (11); Massachusetts Laborers' Pension Fund (11); and New York State Retirement Fund (9).

By contrast, entities with economic or ideological interests that may deviate from maximization of company value—labor affiliated groups, religious and other charities, and social-responsibility oriented entities—are vastly overrepresented relative to their percentage shareholdings. As to the individual sponsors, a large percentage of proposals were made by a handful of individuals (such as John Chevedden, Gerald Armstrong, the Rossi family, and Evelyn Davis) with usually minimal ownership stakes.[98]

For most of these shareholder proposals, the proponent relies on the description of the proposal but engages in no outside campaigning. Institutional shareholders are familiar with most types of proposals and often have developed policies on how they vote on them. Indeed, the proposals that receive majority shareholder approval tend to fall into a narrow set, which includes recommendations to destagger the board, establish majority voting, or eliminate supermajority voting. Occasionally, shareholder sponsors may campaign through public speeches, press releases, and advertisements, which they can do without having to make any filings.[99] Very rarely, a sponsor also engages in a so-called exempt solicitation under Rule 14a-2(b), which permits a shareholder to mail materials to other shareholders without filing a proxy statement as long as that shareholder does not furnish a proxy form and does not seek to act as a proxy, but it requires the filing of the mailed materials if the sponsor holds more than $5 million in shares.[100]

[98] See, e.g., FedEx Corp., Definitive Proxy Statement (Form DEF 14A), at 85–87 (Aug. 16, 2010) (identifying shareholder John Chevedden as owner of 100 shares of FedEx stock); Bill Barrett Corp., Definitive Proxy Statement (Form DEF 14A), at 46–47 (Apr. 9, 2010) (identifying shareholder Gerald Armstrong as owner of 100 shares).

[99] 17 C.F.R. § 240.14a-1(l) (2010).

[100] Id. §§ 240.14a-2(b)(1), 240.14a-6(g). In 2009, 15 shareholders engaged in such campaigns in favor of shareholder proposals. Seven of these campaigns were led by CalPERS. Most consisted of a single short mailing to shareholders.

Under that rule, shareholders may also engage in oral solicitations of other shareholders. Since most oral solicitations require no filings with the SEC,[101] the exact number and scope of such solicitations are unclear. We doubt, however, that many proponents, with the possible exception of TIAA-CREF and public pension funds, engage in widespread oral solicitations.

D. Withhold Votes: Activism Without Activists

A final, more recent form of election "contests" relates to withhold votes in director elections. According to Georgeson's survey of S&P 1500 companies, there were 41 directors in 2010 who received a majority withhold vote and 317 directors who received a withhold vote in excess of 30% of the votes cast.[102] As described below,[103] many boards care about the percentage of withhold votes even if it does not affect the outcome of an election, and significant withhold votes often induce governance changes. Withhold votes thus represent an important form of shareholder activism.

Peculiarly, however, it is unclear who the activists behind withhold votes are. Most large withhold votes occur in companies in which no filings were made by backers of a withhold vote.[104] Thus, most large withhold votes are cast without any open campaigning. And, while it is true that most directors who receive large withhold votes received a withhold vote recommendation from ISS, the leading proxy advisor, it is equally true that most withhold recommendations by ISS do not result in large withhold votes.[105] Moreover, it is unclear whether an ISS withhold recommendation is the

[101] Moreover, under 17 C.F.R. § 240.14a-2(b), shareholders are exempt from the rules requiring filling, except as provided under § 240.14a-6(g):

> [N]o . . . submission need be made with respect to oral solicitations (other than with respect to scripts used in connection with such oral solicitations), speeches delivered in a public forum, press releases, published or broadcast opinions, statements, and advertisements appearing in a broadcast media, or a newspaper, magazine or other bona fide publication disseminated on a regular basis.

[102] Georgeson, 2010 Annual Corporate Governance Review 8 (2010), available at http://www.georgeson.com/usa/download/acgr/acgr2010.pdf.

[103] See infra Subsection IV.B.4.

[104] In 2009, only 5 proxy statements or notices of exempt solicitations were filed in relation to withhold votes. See Georgeson, 2009 Annual Corporate Governance Review 48–49 (2009), available at www.georgeson.com/usa/download/acgr/acgr2009.pdf.

[105] See Stephen Choi, Jill Fisch & Marcel Kahan, The Power of Proxy Advisors: Myth or Reality?, 59 Emory L.J. 869 (2010).

direct cause of withhold votes or whether an ISS withhold recommendation and withhold votes have the same underlying cause. A recent paper co-authored by one of us estimates that the ISS recommendation independently shifts only 6%–10% of the shareholder vote.[106] Large withhold votes may thus come about either spontaneously or from low-level coordination among institutional investors through oral communications and aided by recommendations by proxy advisors.

E. Who Will Use Proxy Access?

Predicting at this point what type of shareholders would use the proxy access rule to make nominations and how frequently they would do so is somewhat speculative. However, at least a good tentative sense of who would use proxy access can be obtained by looking at the activists who initiated full-fledged proxy contests and shareholder proposals under Rule 14a-8. Each of these types of activism bears some similarity to proxy access: full-fledged (or traditional) proxy contests share with proxy access the feature that they concern the election of directors; Rule 14a-8 proposals share with proxy access the feature that they entail low costs unless the proponent engages in outside campaigning.

Past participation in these forms of activism may be a predictor of future inclination to use proxy access for several reasons. First, proxy access may become a substitute for the other forms of activism: instead of, say, conducting a traditional proxy contest or making a shareholder proposal, a shareholder may make a nomination using proxy access. Second, participation in these other forms of activism indicates an interest in being and willingness to be an activist shareholder. Shareholders who, in the past, have remained passive when it came to voting are not likely to become active merely because—in addition to the existing avenues—a new way to become active presents itself. Relatedly, while proxy access represents a new, relatively cheap mode of activism, which may in principle be attractive to highly cost-conscious investors, making a Rule 14a-8 proposal is an equally cheap, and widely available,

---

[106] Id. at 906.

mode of activism.[107] Shareholders who have not made Rule 14a-8 proposals are thus unlikely to make proxy access nominations merely because it involves low expenses.

As discussed below,[108] the third type of activism, withhold votes, also resembles proxy access. However, since the activists behind large withhold votes, to the extent any exist, are unknown, and since any such activists seem to prefer to stay out of the limelight, we cannot and probably should not look at large withhold votes to predict who would use proxy access.

We start with proxy contests. As discussed, most (and most successful) proxy contests are initiated by hedge funds and former insiders. None were initiated by pension funds or mutual funds.[109] 85% of the dissidents in these proxy contests had a stake of more than 3% of the company when the contest commenced. However, under the rule adopted by the SEC, shareholders must also have held a 3% stake for the prior 3 years to qualify for proxy access.

A 3-year holding period is a particular problem for hedge funds, given their intense focus on internal rates of return. If a hedge fund buys a $100 million stake and, within 1 year, changes things enough to increase the share price by 20%, it has a gross annual return of 20%. If, to take advantage of the costs savings of proxy access, the hedge fund holds the position for 3 years, earns a "normal" return of 5% in the first 3 years and then gets the same outcome with a 20% return in the fourth, the gross annual return goes from 20% per year to 8.6% per year. The cost savings would have to be huge to justify the much longer holding period, far higher than is reasonable to expect. Indeed, a spot check of 12 hedge funds that initiated proxy contests, based on 13F and other filings, showed that only 1 fund satisfied the 3-year holding period. Former insiders, by contrast, were more likely to satisfy both the 3% threshold and the holding period.

Turning next to shareholders who submitted Rule 14a-8 proposals, the largest institutional investors, who are most likely to satisfy a 3% ownership threshold for proxy access, rarely made such submis-

---

[107] As discussed below, a dissident shareholder has to make extensive disclosures to become eligible for proxy access and satisfy high minimum holding period and ownership thresholds. See infra text accompanying notes 109–12 and 130–31.

[108] See infra Part IV.

[109] See supra Section II.B.

sions. Rather, most proposals were submitted by individual investors who hold trivial stakes in the respective companies.[110]

Labor-affiliated groups, which also frequently sponsor shareholder proposals, present a more mixed picture. Some labor groups that have been very active in submitting shareholder proposals have few investment assets. For example, the AFL-CIO sponsored 70 resolutions through its $28 million "Reserve Fund."[111] In comparison, a 3% stake in the median S&P 600 SmallCap company would have a value of about $18 million. These smaller funds will thus generally hold stakes far below the threshold for proxy access.[112]

The real union money is in joint union-employer pension funds subject to the Taft-Hartley Act (and thus known as "Taft-Hartley Plans" or "THPs"). THPs face two problems in utilizing proxy access: collective action and fiduciary duties.

There are approximately 1500 THPs[113] that collectively manage approximately $400 billion in assets,[114] of which approximately $100

[110] See supra note 98. Similarly, charities and social issue funds appear not to have assets that are likely to be significant enough to qualify them for proxy access. For example, the Unitarian Universalist Common Endowment Fund had an ending market value of $111.8 million as of June 30, 2010, and $21.8 million in domestic equity holdings. See Investment Performance Summary, Unitarian Universalist Common Endowment Fund (June 30, 2010), http://www.uua.org/documents/finance/uucef/100630_summary.pdf.

[111] See Georgeson, 2009 Annual Corporate Governance Review 15 (2009), available at www.georgeson.com/usa/download/acgr/acgr2009.pdf; see also AFL-CIO, AFL-CIO 2009 Financial Report (2009), available at http://www.aflcio.org/aboutus/thisistheaflcio/convention/2009/upload/ec_finreport.pdf (stating $28 million of investments by the Reserve Fund at 2008 year end).

[112] In addition, a few of the social responsibility-oriented funds have assets of above $1 billion. See Press Release, The Children's Investment Fund Foundation, The Children's Investment Fund Foundation Files Accounts for 2008/9 (May 28, 2010), available at http://www.ciff.org/assets/financial/CIFF_Financial_Statement_27_May_2010.pdf (stating 2009 year-end assets of £1,445 million, equivalent to over $2 billion).

[113] Private Pensions: Long-standing Challenges Remain for Multiemployer Pensions Plans, Testimony Before the S. Comm. on Health, Educ., Labor, and Pensions, 111th Cong. 1 (2010) (statement of Charles Jeszeck, Acting Director, Education, Workforce, and Income Security Issues, U.S. Gov't Accountability Office), available at http://www.gao.gov/new.items/d10708t.pdf (noting that there were approximately 1500 multiemployer plans in 2009); Pension Benefit Guar. Corp., 2010 PBGC Annual Report 2 (2010), available at http://www.pbgc.gov/Documents/2010_annual_report.pdf ("[The PBGC] multiemployer program protects about 10.4 million works and retirees in about 1,460 pension plans.").

[114] Pension Benefit Guar. Corp., Pension Insurance Data Book 2009, at 105 (2010), available at http://www.pbgc.gov/docs/2009databook.pdf (reporting total assets of $434.9 billion at the beginning of 2007).

billion is in common stock.[115] For comparison, TIAA-CREF alone controls approximately $420 billion. If all the assets of the activist $40 billion United Brotherhood of Carpenters and Joiners of America, which sponsored 203 Rule 14a-8 proposals, were spread proportionally over the S&P 1500 companies, the fund would only hold about 0.35% in each company. Accordingly, with the current, diversified asset allocation, THPs face a monstrous collective action problem in satisfying the proxy access thresholds.

Although, in principle, individual THPs or a small group could change their investment choices to build up stakes large enough to satisfy a 3 year/3% proxy access threshold, doing so would expose the plans and their fiduciaries to legal risk. THPs are subject to strict fiduciary standards under both the Taft-Hartley Act and ERISA, including ERISA § 404(a), which mandates that fiduciaries must discharge their duties "solely in the interest of the participants and beneficiaries and (A) for the exclusive purpose of: (i) providing benefits to participants and their beneficiaries; and (ii) defraying reasonable expenses of administering the plan."[116] In addition, fiduciaries must act "with the care, skill, prudence, and diligence under the circumstances then prevailing that a prudent man acting in a like capacity and familiar with such matters would use in the conduct of an enterprise of a like character and with like aims."[117]

In order to satisfy these mandates, many THPs hire outside money managers to manage their assets and delegate full authority to invest and vote. So long as this delegation is made prudently, THP trustees face minimal prospects of being sued.

But suppose that, to satisfy the eligibility requirement for proxy access, a large and active THP chose to override the investment discretion of its outside money managers and invested an outsized portion of its pension assets in a specific company for 3 years. In making the investment decision, the plan fiduciaries, and anyone else exercising discretion, would take on the fiduciary duties out-

[115] Emp. Benefits Sec. Admin., U.S. Dep't of Labor, Private Pension Plan Bulletin: Abstract of 2008 Form 5500 Annual Reports 27 (2010), available at http://www.dol.gov/ebsa/pdf/2008pensionplanbulletin.pdf (multiemployer pension plans with 100 or more participants had $107,637,000,000 in common stock in 2008).

[116] 29 U.S.C. § 1104(a)(1) (2006).

[117] Id. § 1104(a)(1)(B).

lined above,[118] and in doing so, would incur significant legal risk. Indeed, the resulting firm-specific investment risk is significant enough that it is considered highly unlikely that any THPs will change their investment policies in order to qualify for proxy access.[119] So long as the THPs remain widely diversified, the collective action problems are sufficiently severe that they are unlikely to qualify for proxy access under a 3% eligibility threshold.

By contrast, the few public funds that have sponsored more than a handful of shareholder proposals tend to be among the largest institutional investors. The New York City Pension Funds, CalPERS, and the New York State Retirement Fund—which, together, sponsored 70 proposals—have assets of $98 billion, $202 billion, and $134 billion, respectively.[120] Of course, only a portion of these assets are invested in U.S. equities, and, of those, some are managed by external managers. Thus, for example, CalPERS claims to have voting authority only for about $30 billion of equities that are publicly traded in the U.S.[121] TIAA-CREF has $415 billion in assets

[118] Id. § 1002(21)(A) ("[A] person is a fiduciary with respect to a plan to the extent (i) he exercises any discretionary authority or discretionary control respecting management of such plan or exercises any authority or control respecting management or disposition of its assets . . . .").

[119] Personal communication with Damon A. Silvers, Director of Policy and Special Counsel, AFL-CIO (Jan. 27, 2011).

[120] See CalPERS, 2010 Comprehensive Annual Financial Report 2 (2010) (valuing CalPERS at $201.6 billion as of June 30, 2010); Ciara Linnane, New York Comptroller Unveils Pension Fund Reform Plan, Reuters, Feb. 18, 2010, available at http://www.reuters.com/article/idUSTRE61H3SD20100218 (valuing New York City's pension fund at $98 billion); N.Y. State and Local Retirement System, 2010 Comprehensive Annual Financial Report 21 (2010) (valuing pension funds at $134.2 billion as of March 31, 2010).

[121] See CalPERS, Quarterly Report Filed by Institutional Managers (Form 13F-HR) (Jul. 22, 2010), http://www.sec.gov/Archives/edgar/data/919079/000114036110029935/form13fhr.txt. On its website, CalPERS claims to have $119 billion invested in global equities (which includes U.S. and international equities as well as alternative investments and hedge funds), and that 40% of its U.S. equities are managed externally. See Facts at a Glance: Investments, CalPERS, http://www.calpers.ca.gov/eip-docs/about/facts/investments.pdf (last visited May 18, 2011); U.S. Equities, CalPERS (Nov. 15, 2010), http://www.calpers.ca.gov/index.jsp?bc=/investments/assets/equities/usequities.xml. The discrepancy between these figures is likely due to the fact that outside money managers exercise voting authority over a portion of the CalPERS equity investments. The rule is not entirely clear as to whether shareholders like CalPERS can use all their shares in a company to meet the eligibility requirements even if some of these shares are managed by an outside money manager who has voting authority. The key is whether CalPERS has the "power" to vote the shares. If

under management[122] and voting authority for over $92 billion of equities that are publicly traded in the U.S.[123] Given their substantial asset size, the larger public pension funds and especially TIAA-CREF may well qualify for proxy access for several of their portfolio companies outright. As large institutional investors, these entities are also relatively well positioned to assemble a group of shareholders that so qualifies.

Of course, even these large institutional investors will not necessarily own the requisite shares in the specific company for which they would want to use proxy access. Thus, for example, CalPERS held between 0.4% and 1.3% of the shares in the 6 S&P 1500 companies to which it submitted a shareholder proposal in 2008.[124] In

CalPERS can at any time revoke the delegation of voting authority, one could argue that it either does have such authority already or that it could easily amend its contracts prospectively to give it the power, when it chooses, to vote shares held on its behalf by outside money managers. The practicability of such contracts may depend on the type of outside money manager that CalPERS employs. To the extent that equity is held via mutual funds or hedge funds, rather than in managed accounts, it may be difficult for CalPERS to obtain the requisite voting power.

[122] TIAA CREF, 2009 Annual Report 2 (2009), available at http://www.tiaa-cref.org/ucm/groups/content/@ap_ucm_p_tcp/documents/document/tiaa04018030.pdf.

[123] TIAA CREF Investment Management, LLC, Quarterly Report Filed By Institutional Managers (Form 13F-HR) (Aug. 10, 2010), available at http://www.sec.gov/Archives/edgar/data/887793/000088779310000005/r30-0630.txt.

[124] CalPERS owned 0.4% of Dollar Tree. See Dollar Tree, Definitive Additional Materials (Form DEFA 14A), at 2 (May 29, 2008), available at http://www.sec.gov/Archives/edgar/data/935703/000093570308000057/a.htm; California Public Employees Retirement System, Notice of Exempt Solicitation (Form PX 14A6G), at 1 (May 29, 2008), available at http://www.sec.gov/Archives/edgar/data/919079/000119380508001433/e603890_px14a6g-dollar.htm. CalPERS owned 1.3% of Tech Data Corporation. See CalPERS, Notice of Exempt Solicitation (Form PX14A6G), at 1 (May 15, 2008), available at http://www.sec.gov/Archives/edgar/data/790703/000118811208001684/t62731_px14a6g.htm. CalPERS owned 0.7% of Interpublic Group. See Interpublic Group, Definitive Proxy Statement (Form DEF 14A), at 2 (Apr. 18, 2008), available at http://www.sec.gov/Archives/edgar/data/51644/000104746908004848/a2184688zdef14a.htm; CalPERS, Notice of Exempt Solicitation (Form PX 14A6G), at 1 (Apr. 28, 2008), available at http://www.sec.gov/Archives/edgar/data/51644/000118811208001447/t62529_px14a6g.htm. CalPERS owned 0.4% of Hilb Rogal & Hobbs. See Hilb Rogal & Hobbs, Definitive Proxy Statement (Form DEF 14A), at 1 (Mar. 31, 2008), available at http://www.sec.gov/Archives/edgar/data/814898/000119312508070921/ddef14a.htm; CalPERS, Notice of Exempt Solicitation (Form PX 14A6G), at 1 (Apr. 23, 2008), available at http://www.sec.gov/Archives/edgar/data/814898/000091907908000007/hrh_filing.htm. CalPERS owned 0.5% of Standard Pacific. See Standard Pacific Corp., Definitive Proxy Statement (Form DEF 14A), at 1 (Apr. 2, 2008), available at http://www.sec.gov/Archives/edgar/data/878560/000119312508072676/ddef14a.htm; CalPERS, Notice of Exempt Solicitation (Form

the 3 companies for which CalPERS made an exempt solicitation in support of a shareholder proposal in 2010, it held, respectively, 0.2%, 0.4%, and 0.6% of the shares.[125] TIAA-CREF held slightly above 1% of the shares in the two companies in which it made proposals in 2008.[126] Presumably, the number of shares in these companies that has been held for the requisite 3-year period is even lower, perhaps substantially so. And the holdings of CalPERS are of a magnitude that suggests that even a group of several large public pension funds may not satisfy a 3% ownership threshold for a given company. Finally, both the large pension funds and, even more so, TIAA-CREF have been relatively restrained in offering shareholder resolutions under Rule 14a-8. In 2010, for example, TIAA-CREF did not make a single Rule14a-8 shareholder proposal in an S&P 1500 company, even though it would have been qualified to do so for most if not all of the companies in the index.

PX 14A6G), at 1 (Apr. 17, 2008), available at http://www.sec.gov/Archives/edgar/data/878560/000117152008000224/eps2936.htm. CalPERS owned 0.4% of Eli Lilly & Co. See Eli Lilly & Co, Definitive Proxy Statement (Form DEF 14A), at 3 (Mar. 10, 2008), available at http://www.sec.gov/Archives/edgar/data/59478/000095013708003475/c22930ddef14a.htm; CalPERS, Notice of Exempt Solicitation (Form PX 14A6G), at 1 (Mar. 28, 2008), available at http://www.sec.gov/Archives/edgar/data/59478/000119380508000951/e603562_pxa146g-calpers.htm.

[125] CalPERS owned 0.2% of Health Net. See Health Net, Definitive Proxy Statement (Form DEF 14A), at 5 (2010), available at http://www.sec.gov/Archives/edgar/data/916085/000119312510088007/ddef14a.htm; CalPERS, Notice of Exempt Solicitation (Form PX14A6G), at 1 (May 3, 2010), available at http://www.sec.gov/Archives/edgar/data/916085/000117152010000282/eps3791.htm. CalPERS owned 0.4% of Graco. See Graco, Inc., Definitive Proxy Statement (Form DEF 14A), at 6 (2010), available at http://www.sec.gov/Archives/edgar/data/42888/000095012310023365/c56457ddef14a.htm; CalPERS (Form PX14A6G), at 1 (Mar. 30, 2010), available at http://www.sec.gov/Archives/edgar/data/42888/000117152010000236/eps3761.htm. CalPERS owned 0.6% of Hospitality Properties Trust. See Hospitality Properties Trust, Definitive Proxy Statement (Form DEF 14A), at 5 (2010), available at http://www.sec.gov/Archives/edgar/data/945394/000104746910001257/a2196573zdef14a.htm; CalPERS, Notice of Exempt Solicitation (Form PX14A6G), at 1 (Mar. 25, 2010), available at http://www.sec.gov/Archives/edgar/data/919079/000117152010000222/eps3755.htm.

[126] See Johnson & Johnson, Definitive Proxy Statement (Form DEF 14A), at 2, 58 (Mar. 12, 2008), available at http://google.brand.edgar-online.com/DisplayFiling.aspx?TabIndex=2&FilingID=5794786&companyid=10313&ppu=%252fdefault.aspx%253fcompanyid%253d10313%2526amp%253bformtypeId%253d148 (Johnson & Johnson, 1%); PepsiCo, Definitive Proxy Statement (Form DEF 14A), at 1, 49 (Mar. 24, 2008), available at http://sec.edgar-online.com/pepsico-inc/def-14a-proxy-statement-definitive/2008/03/24/section2.aspx (PepsiCo, 1.4%).

This, of course, raises substantial doubt about their proclivity to make proxy access nominations. Still, on occasion, these investors may both have an interest in becoming active in a company and either meet the qualifications for proxy access for that company or be able to assemble a group of investors that does.

In sum, judging from their past actions, the set of shareholders that have shown both an interest in activism and have some potential to be eligible for proxy access is fairly limited. Select public pension funds and, to a lesser extent, TIAA-CREF, have shown a modest interest in activism and may qualify for proxy access for some of their portfolio companies. Labor affiliated groups have shown a more significant interest in activism, but would be less likely to qualify due to the percentage ownership requirement. Hedge funds have been active in full-fledged contests, but would usually not satisfy a 3-year holding period. Former insiders may satisfy both the ownership threshold and the holding period requirement for micro-cap companies (albeit generally not for larger companies).

Of course, if the SEC releases a revised rule on proxy access in an effort to cure the deficiencies noted in the Court of Appeals, it may adopt different eligibility thresholds. We would anticipate that such thresholds would make eligibility more restrictive than the 2010 rules. But even if the SEC decided to relax the eligibility standard and revert to the 1%/1-year standard applicable to larger accelerated filers under its 2009 proposal, the general thrust of our argument would remain: most large institutional investors have shown no interest in or inclination to types of activism similar to proxy access; and labor affiliated groups, which have shown themselves most interested in activism, would often fail to satisfy even a 1% threshold.

A remaining possibility is that some new player would emerge or an existing player would become a catalyst to organize the longer term shareholders such as mutual funds into a group large enough to meet the threshold for taking advantage of proxy access, similar to the way hedge funds have played a catalyst role in other areas of corporate governance and corporate control.[127] For reasons we discuss below,[128] we think this is unlikely.

Interest in activism and qualification for proxy access, of course, is just the beginning of the inquiry. The next steps are to determine whether it would make sense for these shareholders to pursue proxy access, as opposed to either a traditional proxy contest or a withhold campaign, and whether, if they were to pursue proxy access, they would have a significant chance of succeeding. These issues are taken up in the following Parts.

III. Proxy Access Versus Traditional Proxy Contests

In examining the impact of proxy access, one has to compare proxy access to the existing alternatives for shareholder activism to see what advantages it offers and what disadvantages it entails. The closest alternatives to proxy access are either the waging of a traditional proxy contest—in which a dissident submits its own proxy statement—or to withhold the vote for company nominees. In this Part, we will compare proxy access to a traditional proxy contest. In the next Part, we will compare it to withholding one's vote.

Before we commence our substantive discussion, we want to clarify the terminology we will be using. We will use the terms "dissident" and "dissident shareholder" to refer to the party who initiates (and pays for) a campaign and the terms "dissident nominee" and "company nominee" to refer to the persons running for seats on the board of directors nominated by the dissident or the board, respectively. We will use the terms "traditional proxy contest" and "proxy access contest" to distinguish between election contests in which the dissident, respectively, does not or does make use of proxy access. Finally, we will use the terms "withhold" or "just say no" campaign to refer to elections in which there is a large percentage of withhold votes, even if there is little or no observable campaigning.

[127] Marcel Kahan & Edward B. Rock, Hedge Funds in Corporate Governance and Corporate Control, 155 U. Pa. L. Rev. 1021, 1045 (2007).

[128] See infra Section IV.D.

A. Plusses of Proxy Access: Cost Savings

The principal direct effect of proxy access is to reduce the costs of conducting a contested election. This is achieved by forcing companies to include, under certain circumstances, shareholder nominees in the company's proxy statement. In this Section, we will discuss how significant these cost savings are. For purposes of this analysis, we will take as a starting point the costs of a traditional proxy contest and then analyze the extent to which these costs decline as a result of proxy access. As background, it is worth recalling the wide range of cost estimates for contested solicitations, from about $30,000 to approximately $9 million.[129]

1. Cost of Preparing a Proxy Statement That Complies with Schedule 14A

Proxy access obviously has the result of removing the requirement for a dissident to prepare her own proxy statement. Instead, however, under the rule adopted by the SEC, a dissident would have to prepare and submit to the company a newly established Schedule 14N.[130] But as we show, the net cost savings from having to prepare a Schedule 14N instead of a proxy statement are minimal.

The actual content of proxy statements can roughly be divided into 4 parts: required substantive information about the dissident and her nominees, certain technical information that identifies the issues and explains the basic ground rules, disclosures related to the company that duplicates the information provided by the company in its proxy statement, and additional information not required by the proxy rules.

Table 4 below contains our analysis of Schedule 14A, which governs the required contents of proxy statements. As to each item or sub-item, we categorized the information required as substantive, technical, or unnecessarily duplicative. Items that do not relate to the election of directors, or only to uncontested elections, or that generally require disclosure only by the company, are omitted.

[129] See supra Table 1.

[130] 17 C.F.R. § 240.14n-1 (2010). We believe that any revised rule would contain equivalent requirements. Otherwise, shareholders would have less information about dissidents and their nominees in proxy access contests than in regular contests.

Table 4: Schedule 14A Items

Item	Description	Category	14N
1a, b	Date, time, place of meeting; registrant's address; mailing date	Technical	
1c	Deadline for stockholder proposals for following year	Duplicative	
2	Proxy revocability	Technical	
4b	Solicitation methods, use of employees, contracts with other solicitation agents, total costs and costs to date, who pays/reimbursement, terms of any settlement	Substantive	Yes
5b	Interest and security holdings of any participant; name, address, convictions, share transactions in prior 2 years, source of funds, contracts re securities; ownership, related transactions, future employment or transactions by associates of participants	Substantive	Yes
6a–c	Share info: outstanding, votes, record date, cumulative voting	Technical	
6d	Ownership by management and 5% holders	Duplicative	
6e	Information regarding change of control	Duplicative	
7b	Only re nominees: bio, related transactions, 16(a)	Substantive	Yes
7c	Only re nominees: independence	Substantive	Yes
10–20	Other items	Duplicative	
21	Voting: required vote, abstentions and broker non-votes	Technical	
23	Documents where security holders share address	Technical	

Substantive information includes biographical information about the nominees, information about other "participants" (for example, the dissident entity) and their interest in the solicitation, and information about solicitation methods and expenses. Unlike technical and duplicative information, substantive information must be prepared from scratch by the dissident. Moreover, the information that must be disclosed, in particular with respect to items 5 and 7, can be extensive. The preparation of substantive information, therefore, entails the greatest regulatory compliance costs. The proxy access rule would do nothing to reduce these costs, however, since a dissident and her nominees must provide the same substantive information to the SEC and to the company on a newly created Schedule 14N.[131]

Technical information includes the name and address of the company, time and place of the annual meeting, information on how to vote, the record date, the effect of abstentions and broker no-votes, proxy revocability, the required vote, the number of shares outstanding, and some additional disclosure where one set of materials is sent to holders who share an address. Proxy access would save the costs associated with including this information in a proxy statement. But because technical information is of limited scope and basically copied from the company's proxy statement, these cost savings would be trivial.

Duplicative information includes information about shareholdings by 5% owners and by management, information about any issue for which the dissident does not engage in a counter-solicitation, as well as information as to whether a change of control has occurred and by what deadline shareholder proposals must be submitted for the annual meeting in the following year. Since all of this information is already included in the company's proxy statement, and as long as dissidents do not have private information indicating that the information provided by the company is incorrect, it is not clear why the SEC requires the disclosure of this duplicative information.[132] But since duplicative information can be

---

[131] Id. § 240.14n-101.

[132] As to agenda items other than the election of directors, as long as dissidents make no recommendation about how to vote or the same recommendation as the company, they also should be permitted to refer to the company's proxy statement for further information on these items. To be sure, this would mean that shareholders have to access the company's proxy statement to get such information. But the same is true whenever a company uses notice and access, where shareholders are given a voting form and told where they can get additional information on the item at issue. As to the other items, the SEC should not require their disclosure in dissident proxy state-

copied from the company's proxy statement, the regulatory compliance burden is minimal.

A significant portion of the proxy statement is taken up by information that is not required by SEC rules.[133] Such information is usually intended to influence shareholder votes. As such, it resembles other campaign expenses. Campaign information included in a proxy statement often consists of additional information about the dissident and her nominees,[134] the reasons for the solicitations,[135] and any business strategies that the dissident would want the company to explore;[136] the address of the proxy solicitor who can provide further information and assistance in voting;[137] and several boldfaced recommendations on how to vote.[138] Obviously, since these information items are provided voluntarily and serve a campaigning rather than a regulatory compliance function, proxy access does not result in any cost savings as to these items.

In sum then, the proxy access rule only reduces the costs associated with the preparation of a proxy statement that satisfies the regulatory requirements by eliminating the costs associated with the preparation of duplicative and technical information. As to substantive and campaign information, the dissident must either prepare a statement containing the same information even under proxy access or it does not have to provide the information to start with. The technical and duplicative information spans only a few pages and is copied from the company's proxy statement. The resulting cost savings will therefore be minimal.

ments (as it did, for example, for information in Item 8 of Regulation 14A) unless the dissident has access to information not available to the company which indicates that the information in the company's proxy statement is incorrect.

[133] See, e.g., Metropolitan Capital Advisors, Definitive Proxy Statement Filed by Non-Registrant (Form DEFN 14A), at 3–10 (Jan. 4, 2007) [hereinafter Metropolitan Proxy Statement], available at http://www.sec.gov/Archives/edgar/data/864683/000119312507001082/ddefn14a.htm.

[134] See id. at 10–11.

[135] See id. at 4–10.

[136] See Trian Fund Management, Definitive Additional Proxy Materials Filed by Non-Registrant (Form DFAN 14A) (May 23, 2006), available at http://www.sec.gov/Archives/edgar/data/46640/000095011706002372/ex1.htm (showing dissident Trian Group offering new business strategies for H.J. Heinz Company).

[137] See Metropolitan Proxy Statement, supra note 133, at 3.

[138] See id. at 3, 12.

2. Cost of Distributing the Proxy Statement to All Solicited Shareholders

Proxy access also eliminates the requirement for dissidents to distribute the proxy statement to all solicited shareholders. As a result, nominations under proxy access will save the costs of printing, mailing and distributing the proxy statement.

Printing and mailing expenses for a proxy statement depend on the length of the statement and the number of shareholders that are being solicited. A dissident proxy statement that contains only the required disclosures would typically be 10–15 pages long.

Printing and mailing expenses are further reduced in two ways. First, many shareholders do not receive printed proxy statements, either because they have signed up for internet delivery, because they participate in ProxyEdge (an electronic delivery system for institutional shareholders set up by Broadridge), or because a single statement is sent to a financial advisor for a managed account or to a household with multiple shareholders. In uncontested 2010 elections, these "suppressed" accounts total about 54% of all distributed proxy statements, and their percentage has been rising.[139] As to suppressed mailings, dissidents have no printing and mailing expenses, and instead just pay an incentive fee of 25 or 50 cents per account, depending on the size of the distribution.[140]

Second, the proxy rules do not require a dissident to provide a proxy statement to each shareholder. A dissident could, if it opted to do so, forego soliciting small shareholders and not send them a proxy statement either.[141] Data compiled by Broadridge suggest

[139] See Broadridge Financial Solutions, Inc., 2010 Proxy Season: Key Statistics & Performance Ratings 2 (2010) [hereinafter Key Statistics], available at http://www.broadridge.com/investor-communications/us/Broadridge_Proxy_Stats_2010.pdf (54.4% suppression in 2010); Compass Lexecon, An Analysis of Beneficial Proxy Delivery Services 14 (May 11, 2010) [hereinafter Beneficial Proxy Delivery Services], available at http://www.broadridgeinfo.com/ADPFiles/Compass%20Lexecon%20Report%20Final%2005-14-10.pdf (showing steadily increasing suppression percentages from 7.7% in 1998 to 53.2% in 2009).

[140] NYSE Rule 465, 2 N.Y.S.E. Guide (CCH) ¶ 2465 (June 2010).

[141] The recently enacted rules on internet availability of proxy materials offer dissidents another option. Under these rules, a dissident does not have to mail paper proxy statements to shareholders as long as they provide shareholders with a short (typically half-page) notice at least 10 days before a proxy form or other solicitation materials are sent to shareholders regarding the internet availability of the information, post the proxy statement on a website, and supply paper and email copies on re-

that accounts containing fewer than 1000 shares constitute about 90% of all accounts, but that the shares in these accounts constitute only 3.7% of the votes cast.[142] Moreover, over half of the shares voted that are held in such small accounts are voted through ProxyEdge, an electronic system established by Broadridge for institutional investors and investment advisors that permits the voting of shares held in different accounts on a consolidated basis.[143] ProxyEdge enables an investor or advisor to vote shares held in all accounts, whether or not the holder received a proxy statement for any particular account, at least as long as that holder also has shares in a different account for which it received a proxy statement. As a result, printing and mailing expenses can be dramatically reduced, with a minimal impact on the voting outcome, by not mailing proxy statements to holders of small accounts.

In addition to printing and mailing expenses, any person who distributes a proxy statement (or another mailing) to beneficial owners has to pay a unit fee to the securities intermediary through which the shares are held. In a contested election, this fee is $1 for the mailing of the proxy statement.[144] The unit fee is payable for accounts that receive hard copies of the proxy statement as well as for suppressed accounts, but is not payable for accounts that are excluded from a distribution (for example, because the number of shares held in the account is too small).

---

quest. 17 C.F.R. § 240.14a-16 (2010). Typically, less than 5% of the shareholders request paper copies. Personal communication with Charles V. Callan, Chief Regulatory Officer, Broadridge Financial Solutions, Inc. (Oct. 25, 2010). Thus, notice and access reduce the costs for printing and mailing the proxy statement. Notice and access, however, require the dissident to make one mailing (of the notice) without any campaign literature and impose a 10-day delay for the distribution of campaign materials. For that reason, most dissidents do not avail themselves of notice and access.

[142] See Key Statistics, supra note 139, at 3 (providing 3.7% of votes cast figure). That such small accounts constitute about 90% of all accounts is our estimate derived from the data on ballot share amounts and total shares processed in the Key Statistics and estimates of the total number of accounts derived from these statistics.

[143] Id.

[144] NYSE Rule 465, 2 N.Y.S.E. Guide (CCH) ¶ 2465 (June 2010). It is somewhat ironic that the largest expense component obviated by proxy access is a fee imposed by New York Stock Exchange Rules and sanctioned by the SEC. Much of the effect of proxy access thus could have been achieved by merely lowering this fee.

3. Costs of Collecting and Processing Votes

A third saving associated with proxy access relates to the costs of mailing separate proxy forms to shareholders and the costs of return postage and of processing the returned forms. In a traditional proxy contest, both the company and a dissident prepare their own proxy forms and forms of voting instructions. Proxy forms are sent to shareholders who are also listed as record holders in the company's register. These proxy forms are then typically returned to, respectively, the company's or the dissident's proxy solicitor. For shareholders who hold their shares through brokers and banks, Broadridge distributes voting instruction forms which are then returned to Broadridge, tabulated, and presented to the company's vote tabulator.[145] Under proxy access, however, there is only one form of proxy and one form of voting instructions that contains both the company's and the dissident's nominees. These forms are distributed to shareholders at the company's expense and, if mailed, returned at the company's expense. The dissident pays nothing.

In traditional proxy contests, the proxy statement and the voting forms are mailed out together. Compared to traditional contests, proxy access thus generates savings for the printing costs of voting forms and the costs associated with the return of the voting forms. In traditional contests, the latter costs obviously arise only (and the cost savings generated by proxy access thus extend only) with respect to the portion of the dissident's forms that are used to cast votes for the dissident.

4. Campaign Expenses, Including Associated Legal and Regulatory Expenses

Campaign expenses are, in most contests, by far the largest expense item. They include all campaign materials and information provided to shareholders that go beyond the required disclosures made in the proxy statement. While the proxy statement serves also as a regulatory compliance document with a lot of fine print, the other mailings to shareholders (so-called "fight letters") tend to be more catchy and reader friendly and to focus on the issues and

[145] Shareholders are also given the option to vote by phone or via the internet.

information likely to influence shareholders, rather than on disclosures required by the SEC.[146] In addition to drafting and sending fight letters, solicitors make personal phone calls to record holders, beneficial holders who have not objected to the disclosure of their names (so-called NOBOs), and other institutions who are known (as a result of their public filings or industry rumors) to hold shares in the company. For larger holders and proxy advisors, dissidents sometimes make detailed presentations of their future strategic plans for the company and the benefits they expect to reap. Other campaign expenses include the cost of strategic advice provided by proxy solicitors, the cost of legal advice related to campaign materials (for example, review of these materials for compliance with the anti-fraud rules), and litigation expenses concerning these materials. Proxy access has virtually no impact on these cost items and any associated legal and regulatory expenses. Even under proxy access, to the extent that a dissident engages in any such campaigning, all these expenses must still be borne by the dissident.

The only exception is that the dissident may include a supporting statement of up to 500 words in the company's proxy statement.[147] While the dissident bears the cost of preparing that statement, the costs of distributing it fall on the company. For a dissident who does not otherwise campaign, the supporting statement is the only campaign material that is provided to shareholders and the dissident is limited to the 500-word statement in explaining why shareholders should vote for the dissident nominee instead of a company nominee.

We doubt, however, that this supporting statement will be effective. First, a 500-word statement is very short to make both the negative case that the management nominees should not all be reelected and the affirmative case that the dissident nominee deserves election instead. While a 500-word statement in support of a shareholder proposal can be enough to identify a proposal as one of a standard type (for example, to declassify the board), director elections are a much more complex decision. Second, many share-

[146] See, e.g., The Committee for Concerned Cyberonics, Inc. Shareholders, Definitive Additional Proxy Materials Filed by Non-Registrant (Form DFAN 14A) (Jan. 12, 2007), available at http://www.sec.gov/Archives/edgar/data/864683/000119312507005900/ddfan14a.htm.

[147] 17 C.F.R. § 240.14a-11(c) (2010).

holders may never read the dissident's supporting statement. Company proxy statements are significantly longer than dissident proxy statements because of additional disclosure requirements imposed only on the company.[148] The company can thus easily bury the supporting statement somewhere in the long compliance document where it is unlikely to be noticed even by shareholders who receive a paper copy. Moreover, the company can use "notice and access" for distributing its proxy statement.[149] Under notice and access, the company mails a short notice to shareholders informing them how to receive a paper or electronic copy of the proxy statement.[150] Shareholders who do nothing thus never receive a copy of the proxy statement. But, while the proxy statement itself is mailed out only on request, the company can distribute its own fight letters, which will not contain the dissident's supporting statement, to all shareholders. For dissidents who do not otherwise campaign, this means that many shareholders will never read the supporting statement, though they may receive plenty of campaign materials from the company.

5. Assessment of Aggregate Cost Savings

Data on distribution size, total solicitation costs, and printing and postage expenses compiled by the former parent company of Broadridge for proxy contests from 2003 to 2005 enable us to evaluate the aggregate cost savings that would have been generated in these contests if the dissident had used proxy access.[151] We

[148] See, e.g., Id. § 240.14a-101, Items 8 and 9.

[149] Id. § 240.14a-16; Amendments to Rules Requiring Internet Availability of Proxy Materials, Securities Act Release No. 9108, Exchange Act Release No. 61,560, Investment Company Act Release No. 29,131, 75 Fed. Reg. 9073 (Feb. 26, 2010), *reprinted in* [2009-2010 Transfer Binder] Fed. Sec. L. Rep. (CCH) ¶ 88,866, at 84,708 (Feb. 22, 2010); Shareholder Choice Regarding Proxy Materials, Exchange Act Release No. 56,135, Investment Company Act Release No. 27,911, 72 Fed. Reg. 422,221 (Aug. 1, 2007).

[150] 17 C.F.R. § 240.14a-16 (2010); Shareholder Choice Regarding Proxy Materials, Exchange Act Release No. 56,135, Investment Company Act Release No. 27,911, 72 Fed. Reg. 422,221 (Aug. 1, 2007). In addition, the Commission has adopted the notice-and-access model that permits issuers to send shareholders a Notice of Internet Availability of Proxy Materials in lieu of the traditional paper packages.

[151] These data are contained in a letter from Richard J. Daly, Group Co-President, Automatic Data Processing, Inc., to Nancy M. Morris, Sec'y, U.S. Sec. & Exch.

used these data as input to a regression to estimate both the total solicitation expenses and the printing and postage expenses associated with the mailing of the proxy statement as a function of the size of the initial distribution and of any subsequent fight letters,[152] and calculated total cost savings as the sum of the saved printing and mailing costs, the $1 unit fee per account, and an additional estimate of $0.50 per account for the costs associated with the printing and collection of voting forms and other expenses. Reflecting the fact that many companies involved in proxy contests are small and that dissidents decide not to mail statements to shareholders who hold few shares, the 25th percentile, median, and 75th percentile of the actual distribution sizes were, respectively, about 1,600; 2,500; and 5,600. The largest distribution was made to 203,000 shareholders and the second largest to 32,000.

In dollar terms, the estimated cost savings for the 25th percentile, median, and 75th percentile distributions amounted to $7,000; $9,800; and $17,700, respectively.[153] Even for significantly larger distribution sizes of 20,000 and 50,000, the estimated cost savings are modest, $47,000 and $100,000, respectively. In percentage terms, the cost savings for the 25th percentile, median, and 75th percentile distributions account for 3.4%, 4.3%, and 5.8%, respectively, of solicitation expense estimates provided by dissidents in their proxy statements. For distributions above 10,000, percentage cost savings stabilize at around 6.6%.

Comm'n (Apr. 20, 2006), available at http://www.sec.gov/rules/proposed/s71005/ccallan1565.pdf.

[152] We removed one outlier in running this regression.

[153] These cost measures are not adjusted for inflation. Nevertheless, we believe that they reflect an overestimate of actual cost savings for several reasons. First, the percentage of suppressed accounts that do not receive hard copies of the proxy statement increased from 32.4% to 40.9% in the years 2003–2005 to 54.4% for 2010. See Key Statistics, supra note 139, at 1; Beneficial Proxy Delivery Services, supra note 139, at 14. Second, we believe that our allowance of $0.50 for the costs associated with voting is conservative, especially for larger contests and in light of the fact that only 82% of the shares are voted through ProxyEdge and 10% through the internet. See Key Statistics, supra note 139, at 3. Third, the Broadridge estimate concerned the cost of printing and mailing the actual proxy statements used by the dissident, rather than a minimal statement containing only the required disclosures and a 500-word supporting statement. Fourth, one large cost item, the unit fee payable to intermediaries, is based on 2010 cost levels. Note that the issuer's printing and mailing expenses are substantially higher since issuers often mail glossy (both expensive to print and to mail) annual reports to shareholders with their proxy statements.

B. Minuses of Proxy Access

1. Limitations on Nominees

In traditional contests, dissidents can make as many nominations as there are board seats up for election. For companies without a staggered board, this means that they can run nominees for the entire board and take over control in one proxy contest. In companies with staggered boards, this typically means that they can run nominees for the one-third of the board up for election each year.

Under proxy access, the number of nominees would be more confined. Only one shareholder dissident may use proxy access for any given election, and that shareholder may nominate directors for no more than 25% of the board seats.[154] Thus, for example, if the board has 7 members, the dissident may nominate one candidate; if the board has 12 members, the dissident may nominate up to 3 candidates. Any previously elected dissident candidates who remain on the board count towards that maximum.[155]

The limitations imposed by the proxy access rule would clearly be problematic for any dissident who, but for these limitations, would have wanted to nominate candidates for more than 25% of the board seats. Such a dissident may therefore prefer to run a traditional contest instead of a proxy access contest.

In our sample of contested elections, dissidents in 59% of the contests involving former insiders sought board control[156] and, in another 29% sought more than the 25% of the seats obtainable via proxy access. Particularly for former insiders, proxy access would probably not be a useful alternative to a full-fledged proxy contest.

But many dissidents run so-called "short slate" contests. In short slate contests, the dissident nominates fewer candidates than there are seats up for election and fills the remaining spots with company nominees. By definition, in short slate contests, a dissident does not nominate the maximum number of candidates possible. Short slate

[154] 17 C.F.R. § 240.14a-11(d) (2010).

[155] Id. § 240.14a-11(d)(2).

[156] We characterized dissidents as seeking board control if they contested more than a majority of the board seats. Hedge funds sought control in only 17% of the contests. For companies with staggered boards, even a dissident who contests all the board seats up for election will usually contest less than a majority of the seats. If such contests are redefined as control contests, the percentage of former insiders seeking control rises to 76%.

contests are often run by hedge funds that seek board representation but, intentionally, do not seek board control. Even though short slate contests sometimes involve more than 25% of the seats, the limitation on the number of candidates would seem to be less severe for short slate contests than for other contests.

However, even for short slate contests, and even for the subset of short slate contests involving no more than 25% of the seats, the limitation on nominees is significant. While a dissident in a short slate contest does not seek immediate control, the power of any elected dissident nominees depends on the *future* threat of a control contest. As discussed below,[157] minority representation on the board not coupled with such a threat may not amount to much. The minority can always be outvoted and even shut-out completely from the decision-making process by the delegation of decision-making power to board committees on which the minority is not represented. The power of a minority board member depends on her ability to persuade other directors and on the ability of the dissident to take over control if the majority is recalcitrant.

In a typical short slate contest in which dissident nominees are elected, the dissident has shown her ability to mount a successful contest and the shareholders have indicated that they want the dissident nominees' views to be taken into account. A majority that ignores the dissident acts at its peril.

In a proxy access contest, the situation is less stark. To be sure, the shareholders have shown support for the dissident. But the dissident cannot obtain board control via proxy access. The dissident may try to gain control through a traditional proxy contest in the year following the proxy access contest. But the threat of doing so would be undermined by the requirement in the proxy access rule that a dissident *not have the purpose* of changing control or gaining more board seats than the 25% threshold available via proxy access.[158] A dissident who, at the time of a proxy access nomination, claimed not to seek control and made nominations for less than 25% of the board and then, a year later, changed her tune arguing that her intentions had changed because the board majority ig-

[157] See infra Section IV.A.

[158] 17 C.F.R. § 240.14a-11(b)(6) (2010).

nored the dissident nominees' views would run significant litigation risk.

Even if this obstacle is overcome, the mere fact that a dissident used proxy access would make the threat of running a traditional proxy contest in the following year less credible. By using proxy access, a dissident signals that she is highly cost-conscious and willing, as we will show below,[159] to accept a significantly lower chance of winning in exchange for a small reduction in proxy contest expenditures. This is not a message of shock and awe and is much less likely than a successful short slate contest to induce cooperation by the majority.

2. Higher Voting Threshold

The practical effect of proxy access, and the way it is likely to be implemented, will raise the level of shareholder support that is required for dissident nominees to succeed. To see this effect, we have to delve deeper into the board election system and the design of voting forms. In contested board elections, the candidates with the most votes fill the available seats. Moreover, shareholders normally can vote for as many candidates as there are seats to be filled.[160]

In traditional contests, it generally takes the support of a majority of the shares that are voted to get a dissident nominee elected. In these contests, both sides—the company and the dissident—distribute separate voting forms listing the respective sides' nominees. In traditional short slate contests, the dissident completes the slate by listing specific company nominees in addition to the dissident nominees.[161] While a shareholder may decide not to vote for all of the dissident's or for all of the company's nominees listed on the respective form, it is very difficult for a shareholder to vote for some of the dissident's nominees and some of the company's nominees *not* listed on the dissident form.[162] Given this design of

[159] See infra Subsections III.B.2–6.

[160] We focus here on elections without cumulative voting. Cumulative voting is addressed infra Subsection III.B.5.

[161] See 17 C.F.R. § 240.14a-4(d)(4) (2010).

[162] To do that, the shareholder would have to show up in person at the meeting and, if the shareholder were not a record holder, would in addition have to get a proxy from the record holder before the meeting.

the voting forms, most shareholders vote either for all the company nominees or for all the dissident nominees (including, in a short slate contest, the company nominees listed on the dissident's proxy form). Some shareholders vote for a subset of the respective nominees. But, we believe, it is extremely rare for shareholders to split their votes. In this structure, if holders of a majority of voted shares—and occasionally even fewer—support a dissident nominee, the nominee will get elected.

By contrast, under proxy access, it may take substantially more votes to be elected. The reason is that both the dissident and the company nominees appear on a single ballot form. Consider a hypothetical election with 7 candidates for 5 seats to the board of a company with 1 million voting shares. The table below gives the votes received by each nominee. Even though Fred received the votes of holders of 69% of the voting shares, he is not elected.

Nominee	**Votes**
Alice	790,000
Bill	770,000
Claire	750,000
David	730,000
Emily	710,000
Fred	690,000
Gillian	560,000
Total	5,000,000

The difference in required votes between traditional contests and proxy access contests is due to the fact that, in traditional contests, shareholders cannot split their votes between dissident nominees and those company nominees that do not appear on the dissident ballot. In traditional short slate contests, the company nominee who is also named on the dissident ballot is virtually assured election. From the dissident's perspective, votes for this company nominee are harmless. The dissident only cares about the votes received by its nominees and by the company nominees who do *not* appear on the dissident's ballot, and the ballot design assures that supporters of the dissident do not vote for those nominees. In effect, the ballot design enables the dissident to coordinate the votes by its supporters and to assure that they do not cast any votes for the "wrong" company nominee. Under proxy access, a single voting form does not afford such coordination. Shareholders can vote for a dissident nominee and *any* company nominee and may not even know which company nominee the dissident is trying to defeat.[163] The likely result is that many shareholders who vote for dissident nominees will spread their remaining votes among *different* company nominees.

To see the effect of this feature of proxy access on the required vote, take the extreme case in which all shareholders vote for the maximum permissible number of nominees and in which shareholders who support the dissident vote for all dissident nominees and distribute their remaining votes evenly among the company nominees. Let S be the number of board seats up for election and V be the number of dissident nominees. To get elected, a dissident nominee must receive a fraction of votes $d > S/(S+V)$. The reason is that each company nominee will get the vote of the fraction $(1-d)$ of the shares that did not support the dissident, and, in addition, a fraction equal to $d*(S-V)/S$ from supporters of the dissident who distribute their remaining votes $(S-V)$ evenly among the S company nominees.

If a dissident makes nominations for all open seats (if $V=S$), it just takes the support of more than half of the voting shares to get the dissident nominees election. However, as the proxy access rule limits the number of nominees to 25% of the board, most proxy access contests would be for less than all of the open seats. If the whole board is up for election, V would be at most ($S/4$), and the support required to get elected would be 80% of the voting shares (or more if the number of open board seats is not divisible by 4). For companies with a staggered board and classes of equal size, V would be at most ($3S/4$), and the support required to get elected would be 57% (or more if the number of open board seats is not

[163] The 500-word limit on the supporting statement and the fact that it may not be read by all shareholders make it a rather ineffective vehicle for effecting such coordination. To be sure, to the extent that a dissident engages in additional campaigning, it can ask shareholders not to vote for specific (or any) company nominees. But the fact that such targeting is not automatically induced by the design of the voting forms is likely to make it much less effective.

divisible by 4). Most such staggered boards have 9 members, in which case the required support threshold would be 60%.

Admittedly, the assumptions we used to make these calculations represent an extreme case. Some dissident supporters may cast votes only in favor of the dissident nominees, even though they have additional votes they are permitted to cast. To the extent that dissident supporters also cast votes for board nominees, they may not do so evenly but rather based on factors such as the description of the board nominee in the proxy statement, the order in which the nominees are listed, or voting recommendations received by a proxy advisor. Thus, in reality, the effect of the ballot design under proxy access will be less strong than as presented in our calculations.

3. Design of the Proxy Card

Under proxy access, the single ballot forms sent to shareholders are prepared by the company. This, by itself, entails significant advantages for the company and disadvantages for the dissident. First, the adopting release for the proxy access rule makes clear that the company is permitted to note on these forms that it recommends that shareholders vote for its nominees and against the dissident's nominees.[164]

Second, if the proxy form is signed but no specific instructions are marked, the shares to which the proxy relates can be voted for the company's nominees.[165]

Third, when dissidents mail fight letters or other campaign materials to shareholders, they will not be able to include a ballot form with their materials. Inclusion of a proxy or voting instruction form would result in the dissident losing the exemption under Rule 14a-

[164] See Facilitating Shareholder Director Nominations, Securities Act Release No. 9136, Exchange Act Release No. 62,764, Investment Company Act Release No. 29,384, 75 Fed. Reg. 56,668, 56,723–24 (Sept. 16, 2010).

[165] See 17 C.F.R. § 240.14a-4(c) (2010); see also Facilitating Shareholder Director Nominations, Securities Act Release No. 9136, Exchange Act Release No. 62,764, Investment Company Act Release No. 29,384, 75 Fed. Reg. 56,668, 56,724 n.609 (Sept. 16, 2010) ("We anticipate that companies would continue to be able to solicit discretionary authority to vote a shareholder's shares for the company nominees . . . ."). Rule 14a-4(c) as amended prohibits proxy "slate voting" (on the grounds that it would unduly favor management) but anticipates the continuation of discretionary voting by management when authorized by shareholders. 17 C.F.R. § 240.14a-4(c) (2010).

2(b)(1) that would otherwise apply to the fight letters and would thus require the dissident to furnish its own proxy statement to all solicited holders.[166] Moreover, even if the SEC expands the exemption under Rule 14a-2(b)(1) to include solicitations where a dissident distributes only the *company's* proxy and voting instruction form, inclusion of such forms is not practical for beneficial holders. Voting instructions supplied to beneficial holders are not generic but carry unique, holder-specific control numbers.[167] The holder-specific numbers on the company's voting instruction form would ordinarily not be available to the dissident, and a shareholder who returns a form with the incorrect control number would not validly vote her shares.

Campaign materials not accompanied by a proxy or voting instruction form are less effective. Any shareholder who, after reading the materials, decides to vote for the dissident has to search for the ballot form sent to her by the company or, if that form has been lost or has already been mailed back, has to request a new form. If the shareholder neglects to do so, or changes her mind in the interim, the vote for the dissident is lost.

Finally, the design of the proxy card may result in a disproportionately large number of invalid votes from shareholders who support the dissident nominees. In a director election, the maximum number of votes is equal to the number of available board seats. As explained above, in a traditional proxy contest both the company's and the dissident's forms are designed to assure that shareholders do not overvote. In proxy access contests, however, a shareholder may mark "for" for more nominees than there are seats to fill. By definition, a shareholder who overvotes must have voted for at least some dissident nominees. Moreover, most of them presumably did so conscious of the fact that the company recommended a vote "against" all the dissident nominees. Dissidents will thus effectively lose the support from these shareholders.

---

[166] That rule exempts from the requirement to furnish a proxy statement certain solicitations where the person making the solicitation does not "seek . . . the power to act as proxy . . . and does not furnish . . . a form of revocation, abstention, consent or authorization." 17 C.F.R. § 240.14a-2(b)(1) (2010).

[167] Personal communication with Charles V. Callan, Chief Regulatory Officer, Broadridge Financial Solutions, Inc. (Oct. 25, 2010).

4. Fighting in the Dark

When shareholders submit their votes, they do not go into a black ballot box that is left unopened until the shareholder meeting, when the votes are counted and the winner is declared. Rather, information about who casts votes for whom becomes available throughout the duration of the contest.

In traditional contests, shareholders who hold their shares directly on the company's books ("registered holders") receive proxy forms directly from the company and from a dissident and return the proxy they execute to the company or the dissident, as the case may be. As to these proxies, each side will know who returned the proxy form to it and how they voted, but neither side will know—except by inference—who returned the proxy form to the other side and how they voted. That is, the company, for example, will see the proxies it receives, which will appoint some member of management as proxy and, for the most part, authorize that person to vote the shares as recommended by the company.[168] From the fact that certain proxies have not been returned, the company can deduce that these shares have either not been voted yet or that proxies were given to dissidents. Dissidents are in an analogous position.

Shareholders who hold shares through brokerage or bank accounts ("beneficial holders")—a category that includes holders of most of the outstanding shares—receive voting instruction forms mailed to them by Broadridge on behalf of the company and the dissident, with both sides using different forms, and return one of the forms to Broadridge. In traditional contests, Broadridge provides both sides with daily vote tallies and weekly reports showing, for each broker, how many shares have been voted and for whom they have voted.[169] We will refer to this information provided by Broadridge, together with the information obtained from directly returned proxies, as "preliminary voting information."

[168] In traditional contests, a shareholder may withhold authority to vote the shares in a certain way but cannot require the proxy to vote the shares for a director nominee not recommended by management.

[169] Personal communication with Charles V. Callan, Chief Regulatory Officer, Broadridge Financial Solutions, Inc. (Oct. 25, 2010).

Access to preliminary voting information is very important. Proxy solicitors and their clients use it for several purposes.[170] First, most generally, they use it to determine whether their overall strategy is successful. If the results are close, the client may decide to expend additional resources. If results indicate that the outcome is clear, management or dissidents may decide to settle or fold rather than spend more money on a hopeless campaign. Second, solicitors can use the information to figure out whether major institutional holders have voted their shares and how they voted. Even though these holders usually hold their shares through banks or brokerages and no direct information on their voting is provided, solicitors have some general ideas about how many shares an institution holds and which intermediary it uses. Thus, changes in the vote tallies provide a good indication of how certain institutions are voting. Solicitors can accordingly engage in more effective solicitations of these institutions. Third, solicitors can estimate how retail shareholders are voting and adjust their campaign message to this group of holders. Fourth, as to registered holders, solicitors can engage in targeted campaigns for holders who have not returned their proxy forms. Finally, proxy solicitors can police for mistakes. As we have discussed in an earlier article, the proxy voting system is prone to administrative and clerical errors that can easily—and, under applicable law, irreversibly—affect the ultimate outcome of close contests.[171] And, as discussed above,[172] mistakes involving overvoting may easily occur in proxy access contests.

In traditional contests, access to preliminary voting information is roughly symmetrical: Broadridge provides the same information to both sides, and, as to proxies directly returned by registered holders, each side sees the proxies it gets but not those the other

[170] Personal communication with Alan Miller, Co-chairman, Innisfree M&A, Inc. (June 4, 2010).

[171] See Kahan & Rock, Hanging Chads, supra note 68, at 1249–55, 1267–70. A recent, if extreme, example of such a mistake occurred in a proxy contest waged by Terra Industries on the board election for CF Industries Holdings. The night before the vote, a proxy solicitor noted that a vote by a large institutional holder who had indicated support for its client had not been tallied. After inquiries, the solicitor determined that RiskMetrics, who had been hired by the institutional holder to deal with the mechanics of voting, had mistakenly failed to vote the shares. RiskMetrics was alerted to the mistake and managed to cast the vote before the ballot closed.

[172] See supra Subsection III.B.3.

side gets. In proxy access contests, by contrast, information is likely to be completely one-sided. As to proxies sent directly to registered holders, shareholders can vote either for the company's or for the dissident's nominees, but either way these proxies are returned to, *and seen only by*, the company. The dissident sees nothing. As to beneficial holders, Broadridge generally provides preliminary voting information only to clients who mail out their own proxy forms. Dissidents who make no mailing to shareholders receive no information. Dissidents who mail fight letters and other campaign materials but who do not mail a separate proxy statement and voting form receive preliminary information on the aggregate votes cast with respect to the director or issue they target but no broker-specific voting information.[173] Unless Broadridge were to make significant changes in these policies, dissidents in proxy access would receive substantially less preliminary voting information than companies do or than dissidents would receive in traditional proxy contests.

That such disparate access to preliminary voting information is a material disadvantage is corroborated by Professor Yair Listokin's study of the voting outcome of management-sponsored proposals.[174] In these proposals, as under proxy access, shareholders can vote for or against the proposal on the company's proxy card, and shareholders can campaign without having to file a proxy statement.[175] As Listokin has shown, the voting outcome on these resolutions is highly skewed: management is overwhelmingly more likely to win votes by a small margin than to lose by a small margin. The most likely explanation is that management uses information about the votes cast prior to the close of balloting and, when it appears that the vote is close, makes enhanced efforts to obtain additional votes for its side. The data presented by Listokin suggest that these efforts are rather successful: of 68 "close" votes (with a final voting result of between 47% and 53% for the management proposal), management won 61 votes.[176] If one assumes that, with-

[173] Personal communication with Charles V. Callan, Chief Regulatory Officer, Broadridge Financial Solutions, Inc. (Oct. 25, 2010).

[174] Yair Listokin, Management Always Wins the Close Ones, 10 Am. L. & Econ. Rev. 159, 175–78 (2008).

[175] See 17 C.F.R. § 240.14a-2(b) (2010).

[176] See Listokin, supra note 174, at 179 tbl. 5.

out the strategic advantage conferred on management by unilateral access to preliminary voting results, management would have lost half (or 34) of the close votes, then the effect of the strategic advantage is that 27 of these 34 losses—or 79%—turned into management wins. Even this 79% estimate understates the significance of superior preliminary voting information since it assumes that there were no contests which were close but which ended up, due to enhanced efforts, not being close after all. Moreover, we believe that Listokin's study picks up mostly the effect of some last-minute use of preliminary voting information and thus understates the benefits of disparate access to such information.

5. Cumulative Voting

Proxy access involves a special disadvantage for the few companies that permit shareholders to use cumulative voting in the election of directors. In cumulative voting, a shareholder is given as many votes per share as there are board positions to be filled and is allowed to cast those votes for one nominee or to distribute them in any way among the nominees. Cumulative voting, if used strategically, permits a minority of shareholders to secure minority board representation by cumulating all their votes on a single nominee. Consider a company with 1 million shares and a 9-member, annually elected board. Under regular voting, each shareholder can cast 1 vote per share for up to 9 nominees. In such a system, a shareholder group that controls 500,001 of the shares can secure the election of all 9 nominees. Thus, even a group that controls 499,999 votes is not assured of getting even a single nominee elected. Under cumulative voting, a nominee who gets 900,001 votes is assured election.[177] Since any shareholder can cast all 9 of her votes for a single nominee, it takes only 100,001 shares—roughly 10%—to be assured of electing 1 nominee to the board.

To employ cumulative voting strategically, a dissident must ideally get proxies that give the dissident discretion to decide how to cast the votes after the dissident knows the approximate level of shareholder support for its nominees. In proxy contests in compa-

[177] There are a total of 9 million votes to be cast, and the nominees with the 9 highest vote levels are elected. If a nominee gets 900,001 votes, it is thus impossible that 9 other nominees each get more votes. Thus, that nominee is assured of being elected.

nies with cumulative voting, proxies and voting instructions are designed to provide such discretion. Under proxy access, this is unlikely to occur. The specific design of proxies and voting instructions for board elections involving cumulative voting is unclear. Most likely, however, the proxies and voting instructions would resemble those distributed in elections not involving cumulative voting, meaning that 1—and only 1—vote will be cast for each nominee marked on the ballot. After all, if votes are to be cumulated, then someone has to decide how to cumulate them, and there is no likely candidate for doing so in proxy access.[178] This means, in effect, that by using proxy access, a dissident would forego the significant advantage conferred by cumulative voting on dissidents seeking minority representation.

6. Adverse Signal

A final adverse effect of proxy access is that its use would convey a negative signal about the dissident. As discussed,[179] proxy access would generate modest cost savings but entail substantial strategic disadvantages. For larger holders, the only ones eligible to use proxy access under the SEC-adopted rule, these costs savings would represent a trivial percentage of the value of the their stakes. Take a typical midcap company, with a capitalization of about $5 billion. A 3% stake in that company would amount to $150 million. According to our estimates, the cost savings from proxy access would amount to 1 or 2 hundredths of 1% of that stake.

Now suppose that a dissident has a 3% stake, that the cost savings from proxy access are 0.03% of the dissident's stake, and that using proxy access would reduce the dissident's chances of winning by 10%. What would using proxy access signal about the dissident's view of the expected gains from winning a contest? If the dissident believed that winning the contest would increase the stock price by 0.3% or more, the dissident should forego proxy access and wage a traditional contest, because the benefits of using a traditional con-

[178] Normally the person who solicits the proxies or the appointed proxy decides how to cumulate the votes, but in proxy access this person has interests adverse to those of the dissident shareholder.

[179] See supra Section III.A; Subsections III.B.1–5.

test would outweigh the cost savings from proxy access. In such a case, a dissident's decision to opt *for* proxy access would convey a signal that the dissident does not believe that winning the contest would have a material effect on the stock price. Such a signal, of course, would be unlikely to attract votes.

C. Empirical Assessment

1. Number of Nominees

One important limitation of the proxy access rule is that a dissident may not nominate more than 25% of the board.[180] To assess the importance of that limitation, we examined the seats sought in traditional proxy contests. In our sample of 129 contests, the dissident sought a majority of the total seats in 23% of the contests and more than 25% of the seats in 91% of the contests. Hedge funds were less likely to seek control, or more than 25%, of the seats (13% and 88%, respectively), but dissidents other than hedge funds were substantially more likely to do so (44% and 95%, respectively). In sum, judging from traditional campaigns, the limitation on the numbers of seats sought is an important disadvantage, especially for dissidents other than hedge funds who often seek control.

2. Success Rates and Margins

As discussed, using proxy access rather than waging a traditional proxy contest entails several significant disadvantages that render it more difficult to gain the requisite shareholder support.[181] To estimate the size of these disadvantages and their impact on the outcome of proxy contests, we performed a number of calculations. First, for our sample of traditional proxy contests, we calculated the increase in the implicit vote threshold assuming (i) that the dissident nominates the maximum number of candidates permissible by the proxy access rule and (ii) that shareholders who support the dissident will cast their remaining votes for company nominees and spread these votes evenly among the nominees. Under these assumptions, the average level of support required to win increased

[180] See 17 C.F.R. § 240.14a-11(d) (2010).
[181] See supra Section III.B.

from a majority to 71% of the shares voted for a nominee. As discussed, the second of these assumptions is extreme.[182] More reasonably, the implicit vote threshold would rise by about half that amount to roughly 60% of the shares voted for a nominee. In addition, we estimate that not having one's own proxy card, having to fight in the dark, and sending an adverse signal, together would cost a dissident another 5% of the votes.

In our sample of proxy contests in which a vote was held, dissidents won outright in 35 contests, dissidents won some seats in 9 contests, and management won in 52 contests. In the 44 contests in which dissidents won some seats, 3 involved cumulative voting. In these contests, proxy access entails even more severe disadvantages. For the 41 other contests, we calculated the swing—that is, the percentage shift in votes from the dissident to the management nominees—necessary for a dissident nominee to lose.[183]

Table 5: Results of Proxy Contests

Swing Range	Number of Contests with Dissident Victories	Percentage of Total Dissident Victories—All Companies	Percentage of Total Dissident Victories—Capitalization > $500 million	Percentage of Total Dissident Victories—Capitalization < $500 million
< 1%	4	9.8	15.4	7.1
1% - 2%	4	9.8	23.1	3.6
2% - 5%	5	12.2	15.4	10.7
5% - 7.5%	5	12.2	7.7	14.3
7.5% - 10%	12	29.3	15.4	35.7
10% - 15%	3	7.3	7.7	7.1
15% - 20%	2	4.9	0	7.1
20% - 30%	5	12.2	15.4	10.7
30% - 35%	1	2.4	0	3.6

If our quantification of the disadvantages of proxy access is correct, these data indicate that dissidents would have lost 33 of the 41

[182] See supra Subsection III.B.2.

[183] The swing was calculated by taking half of the difference between the votes for the dissident nominee who got the lowest number of votes but still got elected (the marginal dissident winner) and the votes for the management nominee who received the highest number of votes but did not get elected (the marginal management loser) and then dividing the difference by the number of the outstanding votes.

contests that they won as a result of these disadvantages. Moreover, elections tend to be closer for regular-sized than for microcap companies.[184] For regular-sized companies, 50% of the dissidents who won would have lost had 5% of the votes swung the other way. And of the 4 contests in large companies (with a capitalization of more than $5 billion) in which dissidents gained board representation, 3 would have been lost had as little as 2% of the votes swung the other way. Thus, the disadvantages of proxy access are relatively more important for larger companies.

The data on success rates and margins also indicate the difficulty, if not futility, of winning a proxy access contest without actively campaigning. The level of campaigning varied greatly within the sample of traditional proxy contests, with some dissidents mailing several fight letters to all shareholders and making presentations to large holders and others relying mostly on the proxy statement. However, in each serious contest, the campaign material distributed went substantially beyond the 500-word supporting statement permitted by the proxy access rule. Judging by the results of traditional contests, and taking into account the other disadvantages of proxy access, the chances of victory for a dissident who uses proxy access and does not campaign would be remote.

3. Dissident Stakes and Savings

These limited costs savings resulting from proxy access have to be evaluated not only in relation to the effect on winning the contests but also in relation to the dollar value of the dissident stakes. As noted, these savings would normally amount to a few hundredths of 1% of the value of a 3% stake. Moreover, successful dissidents in traditional contests often seek and receive reimbursement of their costs for waging a proxy contest. As between, on the one hand, waging a traditional contest, expending some more resources, but having a material likelihood of succeeding and then possibly also getting the costs reimbursed; and, on the other hand,

[184] Just looking at the swing margins of prior contests probably understates the adverse impact of proxy access. In contests which dissidents won by a large margin, it is likely that management—looking at the preliminary voting results—realized that it had no chance to win and stopped campaigning. But if the dissidents in these contests had been burdened by the disadvantages of proxy access, the preliminary results would have been much closer, and management might well have campaigned harder.

waging a proxy access contest, expending fewer resources, and having a significantly reduced chance of succeeding and a correspondingly reduced chance of receiving reimbursement for any additional campaign expenditures,[185] the choice, we believe, would be an easy one.

D. Summary and Evaluation

Overall, for most dissidents, proxy access would not represent an attractive alternative. The reduced chances of winning associated with proxy access would generally outweigh the cost savings generated by it. For dissidents serious about winning, and who are considering significant outside campaigning (and spending the money on it), using proxy access makes little sense.

IV. Proxy Access Versus Withhold Votes

Proxy access may be attractive for dissidents who do not plan to engage in outside campaigning and who are not really serious about winning. For these types of dissidents, the major advantage of proxy access is not merely a cost reduction but the virtual absence of any expenses. This has two implications: first, because the costs of making a proxy access nomination are very low, it may make sense to make a nomination even if the chances of success are low. As a result, we would expect many of these nominations to be unsuccessful. Second, some nominations may be made by dissidents who are virtually certain that they will not win for reasons other than getting one's nominee elected. These reasons may include trying to propagate certain ideas through the supporting

[185] Dissidents in traditional contests state whether they will seek reimbursement in their proxy statement, the granting of which is within the discretion of the board. If dissidents obtain control, they have the power to award themselves the reimbursement. See Lucian Arye Bebchuk & Marcel Kahan, A Framework for Analyzing Legal Policy Towards Proxy Contests, 78 Calif. L. Rev. 1071, 1108–09 (1990). If they settle, the agreement sometimes provides for a reimbursement of expenses. If they obtain minority representation, they have at least an argument that shareholders wanted them to get reimbursed. Dissidents in proxy access contests can also seek reimbursement but, in our view, are less likely to obtain reimbursement since (i) they will never have board control, (ii) they will never have stated in the proxy statement that they will seek reimbursement, and (iii) the board may take the position that the company already subsidized the proxy contest by providing proxy access and that no further reimbursement is warranted.

statement and gaining publicity for the shareholder and/or the nominee.

But even for highly cost-conscious dissidents, another alternative presents itself. Instead of starting a proxy access contest, these dissidents could use another, equally low-cost strategy: withhold their votes from some of the company nominees and perhaps engage in low-cost efforts to induce other shareholders to withhold their votes.[186] In this Part, we examine this alternative. As we will show, even for highly cost-conscious dissidents, a withhold campaign will often be a better option than a proxy access contest.

A. Plusses of Proxy Access: Effect of Winning

A proxy access nomination entails one major plus over a withhold campaign: if the contest is successful, its effects are stronger, and more certain, than those of a withhold vote. The technical legal effect of a director receiving less than a majority of the votes cast in a withhold campaign depends on the voting rules in place at the corporation. Most companies subscribe to one of three different voting rules:[187] the old, unmodified plurality regime that remains the default rule in Delaware and most other states;[188] an official bylaw (or charter provision) that changes the default rule for uncontested elections to a majority standard; or a "policy" adopted by the corporation to require each nominee to submit an irrevocable offer to resign from the board should she receive less than the majority of the votes cast in an uncontested election.[189]

In companies with a plurality regime, in an uncontested election, a nominee who receives less than a majority of the votes is elected to the board just like a nominee who receives more than a major-

[186] Such low-cost efforts may take the form of a press release explaining why the dissident is withholding its votes, an amendment to the dissident's Schedule 13D or 13G making such points, or a letter to proxy advisors urging them to recommend a withhold vote. Most dissidents who qualify for proxy access would be subscribing to the services of proxy advisors and would have sufficient financial clout to have their press releases picked up by wire services.

[187] See, e.g., Marcel Kahan & Edward Rock, Embattled CEOs, 88 Tex. L. Rev. 987, 1010 n.152 (2010).

[188] Del. Code Ann. tit. 8, § 216(3) (Supp. 2010).

[189] See id. § 141(b).

ity.[190] In companies with a board policy, such a nominee is also elected, but the other board members have to decide whether to accept her resignation. Under a majority vote bylaw, the nominee who receives less than a majority is not elected. Nor, of course, is anyone else. But under Section 141(b) of the Delaware General Corporation Law, each director remains in office until her "successor is elected and qualified or until such director's earlier resignation or removal."[191] Thus, if the nominee who receives less than a majority is a member of the incumbent board,[192] she will remain in office until the vacancy created by her non-election is filled. Generally, the resulting vacancy can be filled by the board, and at least in theory nothing prevents the board from appointing that non-elected nominee to the vacancy created by her non-election.[193]

---

[190] In uncontested elections, the number of nominees is the same as the number of board seats to fill, so it technically takes just a single vote to get the requisite plurality.

[191] See Del. Code Ann. tit. 8, § 141(b).

[192] The nominee would not remain on the board as a holdover if she had not been an incumbent. Also, the statute is not clear as to who would remain as a holdover if two of the incumbent directors are not re-elected and a single vacancy is created. This can occur, for example, where one of the incumbents does not run for re-election and the other runs but fails to receive the requisite majority. Since directors run for the board as a whole, rather than for specific seats, there is no a priori way to distinguish between these two potential holdover directors. The latter hypothetical raises the issue of whether the statute ought to be applied at all to a situation where some nominees are elected and others are not. Though phrased in terms of an individual director ("[e]ach director shall hold office"), it may make more sense to view the provision as applying to the whole board; that is, a board remains in place until a successor board is elected. See id. An election where some, but not all, nominees fail to get a majority would then produce a vacancy without any holdover directors, which does not generate much of a problem. Moreover, such an interpretation would avoid several problematic scenarios, for example, one where several board members fail to get a majority, remain as holdover directors, and then appoint themselves to the vacancies over the objection of board members who were properly elected.

[193] For a recent Delaware opinion on majority vote bylaws, see *City of Westland Police & Fire Retirement System v. Axcelis Technologies., Inc.*, 1 A.3d 281 (Del. 2010). *Axcelis* involved a board-adopted bylaw that mandated that a director who did not receive a majority of the votes tender her resignation but which also gave the board discretion whether to accept the resignation. See id. at 283–84. In determining whether plaintiffs had established "proper purpose" to inspect books and records under Delaware General Corporation Law, tit. 8, § 220(b), the Delaware Supreme Court upheld the Chancery Court's finding that a board decision not to accept the resignation did not by itself establish a credible basis to infer wrongdoing. Id. at 291. In so holding, the Delaware Supreme Court held that such board decisions, without additional evidence showing an entrenchment motive, are to be analyzed under the business judgment rule and not the *Unocal* or *Blasius* tests, even if they take place

Moreover, independent of the technical effect, a nominee (and the company on the board of which he serves) who receives less than a majority without having an opponent, or even a substantial withhold percentage short of a majority, suffers substantial embarrassment. Shareholders are sending a message to such companies, and companies may respond to these messages regardless of the technical effect of the withhold vote. In addition, the threatened infliction of such embarrassment gives shareholders leverage.[194]

Compare these effects to the effect of a successful proxy access contest. Should the shareholder nominee receive more votes than one of the company nominees, the shareholder nominee would be elected and the company nominee who received fewest votes would not be elected.[195] How important this is in practice depends to a large degree on the level of recalcitrance of the board majority and on the person elected. Proxy access would not afford shareholders the opportunity to elect a majority of the board. By intention and design, shareholder nominees elected via proxy access would thus be a minority. Since board decisions are generally taken

during a battle for control. Id. at 288–91. The narrow ruling, however, may well not apply to shareholder-adopted majority voting bylaws or to better-crafted Section 220 requests that focus on investigating the suitability of directors whose resignations were rejected.

[194] It also deserves mention that, under the law of Delaware and some other states, shareholders can adopt a majority bylaw which could not then be amended by the board. See Del. Code Ann. tit. 8, § 216(b) (Supp. 2010) (codifying amendment adopted in 2006 to provide binding bylaws adopted by shareholders that prescribe vote requirements for director elections). Other states that have adopted legislation to enable shareholders to provide for forms of majority voting include California, Nevada, North Dakota, Ohio, Utah, Virginia, and Washington. See Claudia H. Allen, Majority Voting in Director Elections—An Activist Success Story, Neal, Gerber & Eisenberg LLP (Nov. 13 2007), http://www.ngelaw.com/news/pubs_detail.aspx?ID=777. Such a bylaw could be proposed via a binding shareholder resolution under Rule 14a-8. See Del. Code Ann. tit. 8, § 216 ("A bylaw amendment adopted by stockholders which specifies the votes that shall be necessary for the election of directors shall not be further amended or repealed by the board of directors."). Thus, to the extent that the plurality regime or a resignation policy is not sufficiently effective, in most companies shareholders can take action to adopt a more effective majority voting bylaw.

[195] In many instances, the board could place the non-elected company nominee on the board by expanding the board size and filling the resulting vacancy with the company nominee.

by majority vote,[196] the elected board nominees, if voting together, could always outvote the elected shareholder nominee.

Even having a seat at the table where decisions are made is, upon final analysis, contingent. The board could, at its first meeting, create a board committee—consisting of all board members except the shareholder nominee—and delegate to this committee most board powers, effectively shutting the shareholder nominee out of the discussion and information process.[197] While such an extreme measure may be unlikely, boards have significant discretion over what matters are primarily decided in committee and over who sits on which committee. Thus, through the proper work division and committee membership designation, the participation of the shareholder nominee in the discussion and information process could be reduced.[198]

B. Minuses of Proxy Access

While proxy access has an advantage over a withhold campaign, it also entails substantial disadvantages: the likelihood of winning a withhold vote is significantly higher than the likelihood of winning a proxy access contest, and a good showing short of victory in a withhold vote may have a greater effect than a close loss in a proxy access campaign.

---

[196] It is possible to change this by bylaw, but it would probably require an active solicitation.

[197] See Del. Code Ann. tit. 8, § 141(c)(2) (Supp. 2010) (permitting delegation of any power to such a committee other than the power to approve or recommend any action that requires shareholder approval and the power to amend bylaws).

[198] This could be done in a subtle and discreet manner so that the sidelining of the shareholder nominee would be less apparent. All of this, of course, presupposes that the shareholder nominee would differ significantly from the board nominees along dimensions other than the fact that she was selected by shareholders and that the other board members, for that reason, would want to sideline her. On this issue, as well, there are some doubts. Also note that directors have information rights under state law and thus cannot be shut out completely from the information process. Id. § 220(d). In public companies, however, the additional information that comes from these information rights, and the capacity to use it, are very limited.

1. Higher Voting Threshold

As explained in the preceding Part,[199] it takes more votes to succeed in the proxy access contest than in a traditional proxy contest. This is equally true when comparing a proxy access contest to a withhold vote. To generate a majority withhold vote that results in a nominee not being elected or triggers her resignation, shareholders must cast more "withhold" than "for" votes for a specific nominee, with abstentions and non-votes being ignored. As a result, it just takes a majority of the voting shares to generate a majority withhold vote. But, as discussed above, it will likely take a substantially greater fraction of the voting shares to get a nominee elected via proxy access.

2. Negative Versus Positive Campaigning

A further disadvantage of a proxy access campaign compared to a withhold vote is that it would be more difficult to get shareholder support for a proxy access campaign. First, and most fundamentally, it is easier to get other shareholders to agree to be against something than to be in favor of something. In a withhold campaign, other shareholders just have to agree to oppose a specific company nominee. By contrast, in a proxy access campaign, they are asked to put the dissident nominee on the board instead of a company nominee. Even if these other shareholders believe that the present board or a certain director has not done a good job and would thus want either to send a general message to the board to mend its ways or to remove a specific director, they may not necessarily agree that putting the dissident nominee on the board would lead to an improvement.

The purely negative structure of withhold votes also means that they involve little downside risk. So what if a qualified company nominee receives a majority withhold vote? Unless the nominee is the company's CEO, she can probably be replaced by another similarly qualified director. This may generate some work, but has no material impact on the company. Moreover, as explained below, a majority withhold vote may not result in the removal of the director from the board, but instead generate other sought-after

[199] See supra Subsection III.B.2.

changes.[200] In comparison, placing a dissident nominee who does not deserve election on the board is potentially more serious business. Put differently, the very advantage of a proxy access contest—that, if it succeeds, it is certain to replace a board member with a dissident nominee—may lead shareholders to be more guarded in voting for a dissident nominee than in withholding their vote from a company nominee.

It will be especially difficult to make the affirmative case for voting for the dissident nominee without significant campaigning. While dissidents would get to include a 500-word supporting statement in the company's proxy materials,[201] this is very limited space to make such an affirmative case. At the very minimum, we believe, the dissident would ordinarily have to supplement the supporting statement with low-level campaign efforts, such as press releases and letters soliciting the support from proxy advisors.[202] But even with such supplements, it will not be easy to explain convincingly to other shareholders why electing the dissident nominee would be in their interest.

Moreover, proxy access opens the door to more effective campaigning by the company. In withhold contests, the ability of the company to campaign is somewhat limited by the nature of the contest. The company nominee targeted for a withhold vote is running against no one. To campaign, the company has to argue, in effect, that the company nominee is doing a good enough job to deserve being elected. This positive campaigning can be difficult—usually nominees targeted for a withhold vote have been so targeted for a reason—and implicitly draws attention to the nominee's shortcomings. By contrast, in a proxy access campaign, the company could attack the dissident's nominees via negative campaigning. Even casual observation of political campaigns suggests that

[200] See infra Section IV.C.
[201] See supra text accompanying note 147.
[202] If the dissident goes much beyond such efforts and makes a mailing to shareholders, it will probably pay to wage a traditional contest rather than a proxy access contest.

this is much easier than positive campaigning.[203] In fact, in traditional proxy contests, such attacks are common.[204]

The company may not merely attack the dissident nominee. It may also attack the dissident shareholder who made the nomination. Such attacks are particularly likely to be credible and effective if the dissident shareholder has arguable conflicts of interest. Most evidently, allegations of conflicts can be made for dissident shareholders who are affiliated with labor and employee interests. Other shareholders, who are interested predominantly in maximizing the economic value of the stakes, may worry that a nominee put forth by such groups will push the company to pursue the labor interests at the expense of profit maximization or that lending support to such a candidate will provide leverage to labor groups to extract concessions in exchange for withdrawing the nomination. In addition, public pension funds and hedge funds are vulnerable to being attacked for alleged conflicts. The boards of trustees of public pension funds typically consist of political appointees, politicians serving *ex officio*, or beneficiary representatives.[205] Beneficiary representatives often have ties to organized labor.[206] Thus, public pension fund trustees, who have little personal financial stake in maximizing the returns of the funds, may plausibly pursue other interests. Politicians and political appointees may purse political

[203] See, e.g., Eric Ferkenhoff, Icahn Appears to Fall Short at Motorola, N.Y. Times, May 8, 2007, at C1 (detailing personal criticisms by Icahn of Motorola's board).

[204] See, e.g., The Committee for Concerned Cyberonics, Inc. Shareholders, Definitive Additional Proxy Materials Filed by Non-Registrant (Form DFAN 14A) (Jan. 18, 2007) [hereinafter The Committee for Concerned Cyberonics, Inc. Shareholders], available at http://www.sec.gov/Archives/edgar/data/864683/000119312507008489/ddfan14a.htm (containing a fight letter by dissidents citing to and refuting attacks by company).

[205] See, e.g., Board Members, CalPERS (Jan. 25, 2011), http://www.calpers.ca.gov/index.jsp?bc=/about/organization/board/members/home.xml; Structure and Responsibilities, CalPERS (Aug. 27, 2008), http://www.calpers.ca.gov/index.jsp?bc=/about/organization/board/structure-responsibilities.xml.

[206] See, e.g., Benn Steil, California's Sovereign Wealth Fund, Wall St. J., Mar. 7, 2008, at A14 ("Calpers is a political entity in every sense of the word. Its board is comprised of . . . six elected members—all six of whom have long ties to organized labor, including the board president . . . who is also executive vice president of the California Labor Federation. Calpers's investment policies are politically driven, often dictated by the legislature, and even involve foreign policy goals.").

goals such as increasing in-state investment,[207] getting favorable PR, or benefiting significant donors.[208] Beneficiary representatives may pursue labor goals.

These issues have particular salience for some of the most activist public pension funds. CalPERS, the New York State Retirement Fund, and the New York City Pension Funds have all been involved in "pay to play" scandals.[209] CalPERS has been criticized for the presence of union representatives on its board and the pro-union stance it has taken in various labor disputes.[210] The New York City Pension Funds, though making a fair number of governance proposals, make more than twice as many social and environmental proposals and tout the engagement of (former) Comptroller William Thompson—the *ex officio* chief investment advisor of the funds—on climate change.[211] Former New York State and

[207] See Roberta Romano, Public Pension Fund Activism in Corporate Governance Reconsidered, 93 Colum. L. Rev. 795, 796–98 (1993).

[208] See, e.g., Danny Hakim, Cuomo Issues 100 Subpoenas in Pension Fund Inquiry, N.Y. Times, May 2, 2009, at A17.

[209] See id. (discussing investigation by Attorney General Cuomo into pay to play in New York pension funds); Craig Karmin & Peter Lattman, Calpers Rocked By 'Pay to Play,' Wall St. J., Oct. 15, 2009, at A1 (discussing pay to play at CalPERS).

[210] See Calpers and Cronyism, Wall St. J., Oct. 18, 2004, at A18 (noting political and union ties of CalPERS board members and accusing board of basing investment decision on political goals of labor and the Democratic Party); Jim Carlton & Jonathan Weil, Ouster Isn't Expected to Alter Calpers Policy, Wall St. J., Dec. 2, 2004, at C3 (noting that CalPERS has been criticized for "meddling in political and labor-union issues with little connection to improving shareholder returns"); Jonathan Weil & Joann S. Lublin, Gadfly Activism at Calpers Leads to Possible Ouster of President, Wall St. J., Dec. 1, 2004, at A1 (noting controversial CalPERS actions in interceding on behalf of striking employees of a portfolio company).

[211] The New York City Pension Funds' 2006 Shareholder Proposals, The New York City Pension Funds 4–17 (2006), http://www.comptroller.nyc.gov/bureaus/bam/corp_gover_pdf/2006-shareholder-report.pdf; see also id. at 4 ("Comptroller Thompson has played a leading role in the efforts of the Investor Network on Climate Risk (INCR) . . . . INCR has taken steps to pressure Wall Street firms, securities regulators and companies to provide deeper analysis and disclosure on the business risks and opportunities of climate change. In June 2006, Comptroller Thompson joined with 27 members of INCR in a letter to SEC Chairman Cox expressing concern that climate change poses material risks to companies in which INCR members are invested . . . . On September 20, 2006, the New York City Comptroller's Office participated in a meeting between INCR members and SEC Commissioner Roel Campos in an effort to push the SEC towards the adoption of an SEC rule that would require companies to disclose climate change risks in their financial reports. Commissioner Campos expressed deep interest in the issue and offered his active participation in advancing the initiative."); Postseason Report 2007 Shareholder Proposal Programs & Other Share-

New York City Comptroller Alan Hevesi (and the head of the respective pension systems) pled guilty to charges of defrauding the government[212] and to more serious felony corruption charges for awarding pension investment business in exchange for gifts.[213] The current New York City Comptroller John Liu has been criticized for using a trip to Ireland to gain political, rather than investment, returns.[214]

3. Finding a Nominee

Given the possibility of highly one-sided campaigning and of getting attacked and not defended, one wonders who would agree to become a dissident nominee. The dissident would want to nominate a person with experience, a good track record, independence, and an unimpeachable character to minimize susceptibility to negative campaigning against the nominee or the dissident herself. Warren Buffet, to use an extreme example, may not have to worry much about negative ads and, even if nominated by a union pension fund, may receive a lot of shareholder support. The Warren Buffets of this world, of course, usually have better things to do than run as dissident nominees. Someone less famous and accomplished than Buffet may well have second thoughts about entering a campaign in which she can expect to be attacked and have her record presented in the least favorable light by a company with significant campaign funds, while the dissident who nominated her

ownership Initiatives of the New York City Pension Funds & Retirement Systems, The New York City Pension Funds & Retirement Systems 4 (2007), http://www.comptroller.nyc.gov/bureaus/bam/corp_gover_pdf/2007-Shareholder-report.pdf ("On March 19, 2007, Comptroller Thompson joined with Ceres, dozens of institutional investors, and a dozen leading U.S. companies and called on U.S. lawmakers to enact strong federal legislation to address global climate change . . . . The investors and companies emphasized their concerns that the uncertainty surrounding climate policy and the lack of federal regulations may be undermining the long-term competitiveness of companies by discouraging new investments in clean energy and energy-efficient technologies.").

[212] See Michael Cooper, Hevesi Pleads Guilty to a Felony and Resigns, N.Y. Times, Dec. 23, 2006, at B1.

[213] Danny Hakim & William K. Rashbaum, Hevesi Pleads Guilty in Pension Case, N.Y. Times, Oct. 7, 2010, at A19.

[214] See Michael Corkery & Michael Howard Saul, Comptroller's Ireland Trip Questioned, Wall St. J., Oct. 9, 2010, at A17.

will make little effort, and expend minimal funds, to defend her.[215] To be sure, for the right price, nominees can be found or the dissident can simply nominate one of its own officials. But this involves expense (if the dissident ends up paying the nominee), and, more importantly, it reduces the independence of the nominee from the dissident shareholder (if the nominee is paid or is an official with the dissident) and increases the credibility of accusations of conflict.

4. Effect of "Losing"

The final drawback of proxy access compared to a withhold campaign relates to the effect of losing. In a proxy access campaign, if the dissident nominees are not elected, the company can claim victory and vindication: shareholders have been offered a real choice between two live candidates and rejected the candidate nominated by the dissident.

In a withhold vote, by contrast, the company may be the de facto loser even if its candidate receives more "for" than "withhold" votes. Getting a substantial, but less than a majority, withhold vote is still an embarrassment and often induces board actions. Having, say, 40% of the shareholders withhold their vote from you in order to vote for no one is quite different from having an opponent in a contested election get 40% to your 60%. In the mother-of-all withhold campaigns—the 2004 campaign against Disney CEO Michael Eisner—Eisner received a majority "for" vote but was nevertheless ousted shortly thereafter.[216] This experience is not singular. For example, after some directors received a 25% withhold vote, International Paper decided to heed shareholder requests to dismantle its staggered board.[217] According to proxy solicitors, some companies regard withhold percentages of as low as 15-20% as problematic

[215] See The Committee for Concerned Cyberonics, Inc. Shareholders, supra note 204 (containing a dissident mailing defending the record of its nominees against attacks from company).

[216] See supra text accompanying notes 59–63.

[217] News Release, International Paper, International Paper Board of Directors Announces Annual Director Elections (Oct. 17, 2007), http://investor.internationalpaper.com/phoenix.zhtml?c=73062&p=irol-newsArticle_Print&ID=1064053&highlight=.

and will make additional solicitation efforts to increase the "for" votes.[218]

C. Empirical Assessment

Among Russell 3000 companies, 82 director nominees in 2009 and 31 directors nominees in 2008 received a majority withhold vote in uncontested elections.[219] Of these nominees, 7 were running for board seats at companies that had adopted a resignation policy, and one was running at a company that had implemented a majority standard for election to the board.

Of the 113 nominees with majority withholds, 4 (the director subject to a majority standard and 3 subject to a regular plurality standard) were not elected or resigned, and one director died within a year.[220] However, even for most of the other 108 directors, the majority withhold votes had a substantial impact that appears to have satisfied the concerns that triggered the withhold votes in the first instance.

To determine the basis for the withhold vote, we examined the voting recommendations by ISS, the most influential proxy advisor, which state the reason for any withhold recommendation.[221] These reasons fell into 6 categories: failure to attend at least 75% of the board meetings, membership on an excessive number of boards, lack of independence (often coupled with service on certain committees, adoption of a poison pill without shareholder approval, failure to implement shareholder proposal that received majority support, and compensation-related issues. This listing suggests that

[218] Personal communication with Alan Miller, Co-chairman, Innisfree M&A, Inc. (June 4, 2010).

[219] Gretchen Morgenson, Too Many 'No' Votes To Be Ignored, N.Y. Times, Sept. 20, 2009, at BU1. There were 84 directors in 2009 and 32 in 2008, but two of these directors (of Zapata Corp.) were not elected because different director candidates received a higher vote than they did, and for one further (of Alico), the company had agreed to support a different nominee in his stead. We thus disregarded these 3 directors.

[220] The respective companies with directors subject to a resignation policy did not accept any of the 7 resignations.

[221] See Choi, Fisch & Kahan, supra note 105, at 869, 871. We caution that the ISS rationale is not necessarily the only reason why directors receive withhold votes. In fact, many directors for whom ISS issues a withhold recommendation for the same reason, and sometimes at the same company and the same year as the nominees who received majority withholds, receive a majority "for" vote.

often the main aim of the withhold recommendation is to induce corporate changes, rather than to remove the director at issue from the board. The reaction of companies and shareholders we discuss below suggests that this is indeed the case.

For the nominees who did not leave the board within one year and whose companies were not acquired or about to be acquired by the next annual meeting (98 nominees), we considered whether they were re-nominated, whether the company had taken any steps to address the shareholder concern, and how the nominees at issue fared in the 2010 board elections. Specifically, for those nominees who were re-nominated, we judged whether the company had adequately addressed the issue by the percentage of withhold votes they received the following year. Generally, if the nominee received less than 10% withholds, we considered the company as having addressed the issue to the satisfaction of shareholders and if the nominee received more than 40% withholds, we considered the company as not having addressed the issue to the satisfaction of shareholders.[222] When the board was staggered and the nominee was not up for reelection the following year, or when the nominee received between 10% and 40% withholds, we considered several factors, including (i) our own evaluation of the company's response to the ISS basis for a withhold recommendation, (ii) the presence of a secondary reason that may have accounted for the majority withhold vote and whether the company addressed that reason, and (iii) the withhold percentage received by other board nominees. For nominees who received withhold votes in 2008, we further judged whether that reason was addressed in the second year following the withhold vote. Based on our evaluation, 67 of the 98 withhold votes resulted in a company response that was satisfactory (including 2 in which the nominee was not re-nominated and 7 relating to a 2008 withhold vote that were addressed in the second year following the vote);[223] 28 did not result in a satisfactory response (including 2 in which the nominee received another majority withhold vote in the following year); and in 3 instances, it was unclear whether the response was satisfactory or not.

---

[222] Note that for 2010 results, unlike for 2009 and 2008, shares voted by brokers without instructions from the beneficial owner are not included in the "for" vote count.

[223] 2 of these 7 directors received a second withhold vote in 2009.

Note that the cases in which the response was not satisfactory were concentrated among smaller companies. Of the 28 nominees in companies with unsatisfactory responses, none were directors at an S&P 500 large-cap company, 3 were directors at an S&P 400 mid-cap company, and 24 were directors at an S&P 600 small-cap company. By comparison, for the 10 nominees at S&P 500 companies, every company addressed the concerns that gave rise to the withhold vote. Another notable aspect of the data is the rarity of majority withhold votes at companies that had adopted a majority standard for the election of directors and, to a lesser extent, at companies with a resignation policy. This may be due to any of the following factors: companies with a majority standard for election or with resignation policies may be more successful in avoiding majority withhold votes because they campaign more heavily for "for" votes; shareholders at companies with a majority standard for election or with resignation policies may be more careful in voting "withhold" if this may result in a majority withhold vote since their real aim is to induce the company or the director to make changes, rather than remove the director from the board; companies with a majority standard for election or with resignation policies may address the shareholder concerns before they result in a majority withhold vote; or withhold campaigns may be used to pressure companies to adopt majority voting. To the extent that either of the first 2 reasons account for the scarcity of majority withhold votes, they would result, to an even greater extent, in a scarcity of successful proxy access contests.

When a withhold vote did occur, the margin tended to be narrow. The average (median) percentages of the shares voting withhold, relative to the shares voting either "for" or "withhold," were 56.25% (54.89%) in 2009 and were 55.11% (55.57%) in 2008. The withhold percentage exceeded 60% in only 24 votes and never exceeded 70%.[224]

[224] These figures, however, somewhat understate the degree of shareholder opposition. In 2008 and 2009, uninstructed shares held through brokers could still be voted for the company nominees. To estimate the degree to which such shares may have reduced the withhold vote margin, we considered whether another issue (such as a shareholder proposal) was on the ballot for which uninstructed shares could not be voted. This permitted us to estimate the number of uninstructed shares. We then assumed, conservatively, that all these shares had been voted for the board nominees. (During 2009, about one-half of uninstructed shares were voted, by each broker, in

The set of nominees who received majority withhold votes may represent a potentially fertile set of targets for proxy access. Obviously, these nominees already face substantial opposition from shareholders. Nevertheless, we do not believe that dissident nominees would have had an easy time prevailing against most of these nominees.

First, the principal reason for the withhold nominations may not be known by the time a dissident has to make a proxy access nomination. For example, the company discloses whether directors attended at least 75% of the meetings only when it files its proxy statement. At that point, however, it would be too late for a dissident to nominate someone else to defeat a director who had missed many meetings.

Second, as later developments indicate, many if not most of these withhold votes were aimed at achieving a corporate change other than the removal of the director at issue. Regardless of the reason for the ISS withhold recommendation, the nominees seem to be able to receive a large majority in the next board election as long as the company takes proper rectifying measures. Take, for example, Syniverse Holdings, where all 8 directors received majority withhold votes in 2009. The reason for the ISS withhold recommendation was that the company adopted a poison pill without shareholder approval. The company then promised that the pill would either be terminated or submitted to a shareholder vote in 2011, and the directors were reelected in 2010 with a 94% "for" vote margin.[225] Or take Sir Peter Bonfield, who attended fewer than 75% of the board meetings of Mentor Graphics and received a ma-

---

the same proportion as the actual instructions received by that broker. See Broadridge Financial Solutions, Inc., Broadridge Report on Rule 452: The Elimination of the Broker Vote for Director Elections—Analysis of the Impact During the First Proxy Season 25–31 (2010), available at www.broadridgeinfo.com/.%20.%20./MASTER%20Steering%20Comm%2010-19-10%20FINAL.pdf). We subtracted the respective number from the "for" votes received by the nominee and recalculated the withhold vote margin. Using this methodology for the 2009 withhold votes, the average and median withhold vote margins rose by about 6.5%.

Note, however, that once uninstructed broker shares may no longer be voted, the company may make enhanced efforts to induce holders to submit voting instructions. As a result, our methodology may result in an overestimate of the withhold vote margin.

[225] Syniverse Holdings, Inc., Current Report (Form 8-K) (May 6, 2010), available at http://www.sec.gov/Archives/edgar/data/1169264/000119312510112812/d8k.htm.

jority withhold vote in 2009. His attendance record improved in the following year and he was reelected in 2010 with 93% of the vote.[226] As a result, we do not believe that a majority withhold vote generally translates to majority support for a dissident nominee.

Third, even shareholders who would ideally like to oust a certain director from the board may not vote for a dissident nominee because they consider the dissident nominee to be even worse. This may be the case because the dissident nominee lacks the proper professional qualifications, because shareholders distrust the dissident shareholder who made the nomination, or because they believe that election of a dissident would reduce board effectiveness.

Fourth, as discussed, it is likely that a company would campaign more heavily—and more effectively—against a dissident nominee than it presently does when faced with a large withhold vote. At present, companies where nominees received a majority withhold vote engaged in little open campaigning.[227] A small minority of companies mailed an additional letter to shareholders explaining why they should vote for certain nominees, and a few more mailed reminders to shareholders to vote, but most engaged in no open campaigning at all. If faced with a dissident nominee, we believe that this would be likely to change.

In rare instances, however, a dissident nominee may succeed. Take Ralph Atkin, a director of Skywest who received a 63% withhold vote in 2009, presumably because of concerns about his independence. Apparently nothing was done, and in 2010 he received a 68% withhold vote.[228] Repeated ineffective withhold votes may eventually induce frustrated shareholders to support a dissident nominee. But then take Ralf Boer, a director of Plexus who received majority withhold votes in 2008 and 2009. Boer was a partner in a law firm that billed Plexus $500,000 in 2008, and, the following year, Plexus adopted a poison pill without shareholder

[226] Mentor Graphics Corp., Current Report (Form 8-K) (July 1, 2010), available at http://www.sec.gov/Archives/edgar/data/701811/000119312510153532/d8k.htm.

[227] By open campaigning, we mean campaigning that requires the company to make additional filings with the SEC.

[228] Skywest, Inc., Current Report (Form 8-K) (May 4, 2010), available at http://www.sec.gov/Archives/edgar/data/793733/000110465910027128/a10-6140_38k.htm. Though the withhold margin in 2010 appeared to have been higher, the withhold margin in 2009, when uninstructed broker votes are filtered out, as discussed supra note 222 and accompanying text, was 69%.

approval.[229] By the time of the 2010 annual meeting, Boer's law firm's billings had dropped to $5,000, and, although the poison pill appears to have remained in place, Boer was reelected in 2010 with 90% of the vote.[230] Even repeated majority withhold votes thus may generate no hard feelings if the company shapes up.

D. Summary and Evaluation

A proxy access nomination, without significant outside campaigning, may be a plausible alternative to a withhold campaign. In both cases, the costs are low, and success in a proxy access campaign assures a change in board composition. Moreover, the fact that a majority of shareholders sometimes withholds its votes without any open campaign shows that a proxy access nomination without campaigning is not necessarily doomed to fail.

Nevertheless, we believe that successful proxy access nominations will be extremely rare. It will be harder to obtain the requisite majority because proxy access involves an implicitly higher voting threshold. It will be harder to obtain shareholder support because of the affirmative nature of the support required and concern over the dissident's goals. It will be hard to find qualified nominees due to the lack of support they are receiving from the dissident. Finally, by the time proxy access nominations are due, it may not yet be clear which companies or company nominees would be most vulnerable to a proxy access campaign.

And even as to companies or nominees who are clearly vulnerable, there may not be a shareholder (or group of shareholders) who is both qualified to make a proxy access nomination and interested in doing so. As discussed, to be eligible to make a proxy access nomination, a shareholder (or a group of shareholders) must have a sizeable equity stake of 3% and must satisfy a lengthy holding period of 3 years. No such requirements apply to a shareholder who wants to withhold its votes or encourage others to do so. Moreover, most large institutional investors, who would most easily satisfy these requirements, have been reluctant to become openly active but are perfectly willing to withhold votes from com-

---

229 Other Plexus directors did not receive a majority withhold vote.

230 Plexus Corp., Current Report (Form 8-K) (Feb. 10, 2010), available at http://www.sec.gov/Archives/edgar/data/785786/000095012310012127/c56287e8vk.htm.

pany nominees. We thus predict that withhold votes will remain the preferred method for shareholders to signal dissatisfaction to the company.

V. MUCH ADO ABOUT LITTLE: THE MARGINAL IMPACT OF PROXY ACCESS

We would expect proxy access to result in few nominations. Of the nominations made, few would result in the election of dissident directors. And the dissident directors elected would have little impact on the companies. Thus, in our view, proxy access does not amount to much, and the statements made by the supporters and detractors of proxy access are greatly overblown.

This being said, proxy access would have some marginal consequences. In this Part, we discuss these effects: some positive, others negative. On the whole, the net effect of proxy access is likely to be close to zero and surely is not high enough to get very excited about.

A. Costs

Dissident nominations generate costs. Faced with the possibility that a dissident nominee will get elected to a board, the company may campaign against the nominee. In doing so, the company will, in effect, spend shareholders' money.

As we have argued before, we do not believe that proxy access would generate a slew of nominees. However, given the low costs of making a nomination and the possibility of goals other than getting the nominee elected, nominations might be made even if the chances of success are highly remote. In fact, as discussed, we would expect that more serious dissidents would opt for a withhold campaign or a traditional proxy contest rather than for proxy access and that proxy access would predominantly be used by dissidents with low chances of success.

On the other hand, the marginal cost to the company of including the nominee and the supporting statement in its material is trivial. For dissident nominees who stand virtually no chance of getting elected, the company would not need to expend material resources in assuring their defeat. As it is, companies already incur some—although, we believe, lower—expenses to generate a high percentage of "for" votes or to defeat shareholder proposals. This being said, any increase in campaign expenses generated by proxy access would be a downside that has to be weighed against any benefits produced by proxy access and companies, being risk averse, may end up spending a lot more than needed to defeat a marginal shareholder nominee.

B. Unholy Alliance

A second potential downside of proxy access relates to the possibility of dissident nominations by shareholder groups who pursue interests that diverge from the interests of shareholders as a whole. *The Wall Street Journal*, for example, editorialized that proxy access will empower unions to threaten to run opposition candidates to extract political concessions, such as support for health care reform.[231] Other groups, such as public pension funds, social-issue oriented funds, hedge funds, and former insiders, may have divergent interests and may be tempted to use proxy access to advance their personal agendas. This is the "proxy access" equivalent of greenmail—and leaves shareholders worse off.

While there is a possibility that proxy access may be abused by some shareholder groups, we do not think that any abuse would be likely to have a serious impact. First, any single union or union-affiliated fund would very rarely own the requisite amount of stock to make nominations, and hedge funds would rarely satisfy the 3-year holding period requirement. Thus, these shareholders would have to assemble groups of like-minded investors and even then would not easily be able to satisfy the thresholds. The same would be true, albeit to a lesser degree, for public pension funds.

If these shareholders succeed in forming a group that meets the proxy access threshold requirements, they will have difficulty succeeding in extracting political concessions. As we argued above, the presence of, or even the suspicion of, divergent interests by the dissident makes it unlikely that nominees will succeed. Efforts to extract political concessions, or otherwise pursue personal interests, would be unlikely to stay secret for long. First, the company asked to make concessions would have a strong interest in revealing any request in order to discredit the dissident group. Second, if

[231] See Editorial, Alinsky Wins at the SEC, Wall St. J., Aug. 30, 2010, at A14.

several shareholders must join the dissident group to satisfy the ownership threshold requirements, the likelihood of a leak from some member of the dissident group would increase. Third, the formation of a shareholder group would become public knowledge.[232] Once it becomes known that such a shareholder group was formed, that it threatened to make, but never did make, a proxy access nomination (or that it made one and withdrew it), and that around the same time the company changed its position on some matter of public policy or took some other action to benefit the special interests of these shareholders, then other market participants could deduce the link between these events. And once a shareholder has been publicly exposed, any future nominations by that shareholder would lack credibility.

Put differently, it is exactly because market participants would be attuned to the danger that some shareholders could abuse proxy access that it is unlikely that such abuse would result in more than sporadic harm.

C. Recalcitrant Companies

As we argued in Parts III and IV, we believe that withhold campaigns and traditional proxy contests are generally more effective ways for activists to achieve their goals than proxy access contests. Some companies, however, may lose a withhold campaign and still not mend their ways: the director at issue stays on the board and is re-nominated, and the board does not address the issue that prompted the high withhold vote or otherwise shape up. In these situations, the shareholders' only recourse will be to withhold their votes again or to start a traditional proxy contest. For these recalcitrant companies—which will overwhelmingly be micro-cap and small-cap companies—giving shareholders the additional option of proxy access may have some beneficial effects. Having snubbed shareholders once, the company stands an increased chance of losing in a proxy access contest. The case for the nominee is relatively simple and has some inherent appeal: the board ignored shareholder wishes expressed in a majority withhold vote and thus

[232] The knowledge will become public either because the attempt to form a group triggers filing requirements under Rules 14a-b(1) or (7) or because of the large number of persons who will become aware of the attempts to form a group.

stronger steps are needed. The threat of a specific board nominee generating such intense opposition from shareholders may induce the company to replace that nominee with a more acceptable candidate.

This being said, one should not overstate the resulting benefits of proxy access. First, the number of recalcitrant companies is small. For 2009, there were only 11 companies in the Russell 3000 in which one or more director received a majority withhold vote and the company failed to make a satisfactory response.

Second, for some recalcitrant companies, it may be difficult to satisfy the shareholder requirements for a proxy access nomination. The activist public pension funds and labor funds may not have sufficient shares, and mutual funds and other institutions may not be willing to make a nomination. Instead, it may be both easier and more promising to make a Rule 14a-8 proposal forcing these companies to adopt a majority standard for director election.

Third, it is not at all certain that recalcitrant companies would respond positively to the possible or actual election of a dissident director. Truly recalcitrant companies may just ignore the dissident director and push her to the sidelines by not putting her on any important board committee. Other companies may campaign heavily against the election of such a director.

Fourth, even if a minority of dissident directors were to be elected to the boards of some of these companies and succeeded in inducing some changes, it is unclear whether they will have major effects on company value. To be sure, such companies may make some actual or perceived improvements in their corporate governance such as destaggering the board, increasing the number of independent directors, or reducing excessive management compensation. But even to the extent that such changes are desirable, their effect on company value may be marginal.

As to changes that are likely to have a more significant impact on company value—such as agreeing to a hostile takeover offer, replacing management, substantially increasing payouts to shareholders, or making fundamental changes in operations or strategy—we doubt that a proxy access contest would be sufficient to induce them. Rather, for such changes, especially in recalcitrant companies, it takes a traditional proxy contest.

D. Emergence of New Activist

Another possibility is that proxy access would spur a new type of activism by a new type of activist. Maybe once proxy access is available, mutual funds and other large institutional holders who have credibility in the market place and are free of conflicts will finally use the power they have as large shareholders and come together to improve the way companies are run. Maybe proxy access would lead the Vanguards and Fidelities of the investment world to add respected and truly independent directors to the boards of their portfolio companies and to intervene quickly and aggressively when management fails. Maybe a group of professional independent directors would be assembled who are unaffiliated with dissident shareholders but have strong reputational reasons to act effectively as shareholder representatives and could easily be nominated by dissidents via proxy access. Maybe. But we think this is unlikely.

First, proxy access does not fundamentally change the corporate governance structure. Even without proxy access, mutual funds can sponsor shareholder resolutions, campaign for withhold votes, run an election contest, or ask a company and its nominating committee to place a certain person on the board. Many nominating committees will be perfectly happy to nominate a well-qualified and willing director candidate suggested by a Vanguard or Fidelity. Proxy access affords just one more option for activism. Though different from the existing options, we do not see why this option would induce activism by groups of shareholders who, in the past, have only become active in very limited circumstances where the activism had an immediate and material effect on the share price—such as pressuring boards not to block a hostile bid or to seek a higher price in a friendly merger.

Second, we do not think that most mutual funds are structured to become activists. Mutual funds largely compete on the basis of offering diversification, low expenses, and superior stock selection ability. They do not specialize in improving operations. Mutual funds like Third Avenue, which are more activist, behave like activist hedge funds: they identify companies with operational or strategic problems, take a significant equity stake, and then work to make improvements. But those mutual funds that specialize in activism will, just like hedge funds, prefer to pursue more expensive routes which offer higher chances of success.

Third, mutual funds have been, and will remain, reluctant to put their own portfolio managers or other employees on the board of portfolio companies. Having such directors would arguably give the fund access to non-public information, which would greatly impede its ability to trade in the company's stock. Mutual funds, of course, could nominate an unaffiliated outsider to the board. But even if a competent outsider could be found, it is unclear how much difference her presence on the board would make. If the presence of the dissident nominee makes little difference, why even bother nominating one?

Finally, the notion that mutual funds would commence waging successful proxy access contests requires significant leaps of faith. As discussed in Part II, mutual funds led not a single traditional contest between 2005 and 2009. Moreover, hedge funds and individuals who have started contests would have had a much lower success rate had they used proxy access rather than traditional contests. The notion that mutual funds will now wage successful contests via proxy access requires one to believe that (i) mutual funds would have been highly successful in the past had they waged traditional contests (and will thus remain reasonably successful even if they wage proxy access contests); (ii) funds nevertheless did not wage any traditional contests because the costs outweighed the benefits for every single fund and every single portfolio company; and (iii) the small reduction in costs generated by proxy access will change this calculus even though proxy access contests entail a lower likelihood of success. We are skeptical that anyone seriously holds these views.

In sum, we are highly doubtful that proxy access would be the start of a new dawn in mutual fund activism. If proxy access does anything, it would be an additional, but largely ineffective weapon in the toolbox of those investors who were already engaged in activism before the passage of proxy access.

Conclusion

There is something seductive about "ballot access" for shareholders. After all, as Chancellor Allen noted over 20 years ago, "[t]he shareholder franchise is the ideological underpinning upon which the legitimacy of directorial power rests."[233] Perhaps the ideological status of shareholder voting explains the vehemence of the battle over proxy access and has clouded the views of the partisans on both sides to the fact that proxy access would have minimal practical significance.

Any incremental reform to increase shareholder access to the corporate proxy must be evaluated against the backdrop of the existing structures and players in corporate governance. The impact of proxy access can only be understood in comparison to traditional proxy fights and other modes of shareholder involvement, including "just vote no" campaigns and shareholder proposals.

When one takes account of institutional detail, it becomes clear that, for multiple reasons, neither the proxy access rule adopted by the SEC nor any revised rule is likely to be important. Very few shareholders will qualify for proxy access. Of those who would qualify, the most important ones—mutual funds, private pension funds, and many public pension funds—have shown no taste for this type of activism. Even for those shareholders interested in activism, and even if shareholders not presently interested were to develop an interest, proxy access entails severe disadvantages. Thus, traditional proxy fights and other modes of shareholder involvement would often represent far better options for challenging incumbent management. Shareholders who *do* use proxy access would thus reveal themselves as busybodies, unserious about winning elections but all too happy to stir up publicity and controversy. What then, fellow shareholders may wonder, is their motivation? A union-affiliated fund may be seeking to advance labor interests. A social responsibility fund may be seeking publicity for its causes. Public pension funds may be pursuing political goals and publicity for board members who are elected officials or may be acting at the behest of union representatives on the fund's board. The inherent strategic disadvantages of proxy access, coupled with these concerns, mean that the few initiated contests would likely fail. As long as companies understand this, the threat of using proxy access would not be an effective tool to extract concessions.

But ultimately, the insignificance of proxy access turns on a more fundamental issue. According to urban legend, the famous

[233] Blasius Indus. v. Atlas Corp., 564 A.2d 651, 652, 659 (Del. Ch. 1988).

bank robber Willie Sutton, when asked why he was robbing banks, answered: "Because that's where the money is."[234] Willie Sutton has a lot to teach to proponents of proxy access. Even if all the other problems of proxy access could be magically overcome, it would still have a limited impact for one simple reason: *the cost savings targeted by proxy access are not where the money is.* Director election contests involve complex issues, much more than shareholder proposals and withhold campaigns. The cost savings entailed by proxy access involve such a small part of the expenses it takes to wage a serious contest, and such a small fraction of the stake of any dissident who would be taken seriously, that it is implausible that they would generate large effects.

Shareholder activists who support proxy access are barking up the wrong tree if they think that a proxy access rule is a useful way to energize board governance. At best, it is symbolic politics in a world in which there are already easier, cheaper, and more effective measures such as targeted "withhold vote" campaigns.

A more serious means to invigorate shareholder voting would provide a mechanism to reimburse successful dissidents—and perhaps even those who gain high levels, but less than a majority of, shareholder support—for all or part of their reasonable *campaign expenses*. That's where the money is. The recently enacted Section 113 of the Delaware General Corporate Law provides a roadmap for shareholders who want to adopt bylaws to provide for such reimbursement.[235] Rather than waste their time and energy on proxy access, shareholder activists could have developed model bylaw provisions and pushed boards to adopt them. The SEC, in turn, could have taken the much less controversial step of revising its rules to make sure that such bylaw amendments could be introduced as Rule 14a-8 shareholder proposals without violating the various procedural limitations (such as the 500-word limit of such proposals). Reimbursement that is contingent on success, but that covers a much greater share of expenses than those avoided by proxy access, would encourage those shareholders who have a real shot yet hold the publicity seekers at bay. Whether such a rule

[234] See generally, Willie Sutton, Wikipedia, http://en.wikipedia.org/wiki/Willie_Sutton (last visited Aug. 29, 2011).

[235] Del. Code Ann. tit. 8, § 113 (Supp. 2010).

would improve corporate governance or increase the value of firms is beyond the scope of this Article, but at least such a rule could make a real difference in getting shareholder nominees elected to corporate boards.

[18]

Empty Voting and Hidden (Morphable) Ownership: Taxonomy, Implications, and Reforms

*By Henry T. C. Hu and Bernard Black**

Most American publicly held corporations have a one-share, one-vote structure, in which voting power is proportional to economic ownership. This structure gives shareholders economic incentives to exercise their voting power well and helps to legitimate managers' exercise of authority over property the managers do not own. Berle-Means' "separation of ownership and control" suggests that shareholders face large collective action problems in overseeing managers. Even so, mechanisms rooted in the shareholder vote, including proxy fights and takeover bids, constrain managers from straying too far from the goal of shareholder wealth maximization.

In the past few years, the derivatives revolution, hedge fund growth, and other capital market developments have come to threaten this familiar pattern throughout the world. Both outside investors and corporate insiders can now readily decouple economic ownership of shares from voting rights to those shares. This decoupling—which we call "the new vote buying"—is often hidden from public view and is largely untouched by current law and regulation. Hedge funds, sophisticated and largely unfettered by legal rules or conflicts of interest, have been especially aggressive in decoupling. Sometimes they hold more votes than economic ownership, a pattern we call "empty voting." That is, they may have substantial voting power while having limited, zero, or even negative economic ownership. In the extreme situation of negative economic ownership, the empty voter has an incentive to vote in ways that reduce the company's share price. Sometimes hedge funds hold more economic ownership than votes, though often with "morphable" voting rights—the de facto ability to acquire the votes if needed. We call this "hidden (morphable) ownership" because under current disclosure rules, the economic ownership and (de facto) voting ownership are often not disclosed. Corporate insiders, too, can use new vote buying techniques.

---

* Professor Hu is Allan Shivers Chair in the Law of Banking and Finance, University of Texas Law School. Professor Black is Hayden W. Head Regents Chair for Faculty Excellence, University of Texas Law School, and Professor of Finance, University of Texas, McCombs School of Business. The authors thank workshop participants at the American Law and Economics Association annual meeting (May 2005), the Conference on Boundaries of SEC Regulation at the Financial Economics Institute of Claremont McKenna College (February 2006), the Weil, Gotshal & Manges Roundtable at Yale Law School (April 2006), the Corporate Law Roundtable at University of Pennsylvania Law School (April 2006), Iman Anabtawi, Richard Craswell, Jeffrey Gordon, Larry Harris, Linda Hayman, Gérard Hertig, Bruce Johnsen, Charles McCallum, Harold J. Mulherin, Jeff Netter, Ian Ramsay, Edward Rock, Roberta Romano, David Skeel, Janet Kiholm Smith, Leo Strine, and anonymous peer reviewers for comments and suggestions. We thank Catherine Bellah and Ryan McCormick for their research assistance.

This article analyzes the new vote buying and its corporate governance implications. We propose a taxonomy of the new vote buying that unpacks its functional elements. We discuss the implications of decoupling for control contests and other forms of shareholder oversight, and the circumstances in which decoupling could be beneficial or harmful to corporate governance. We also propose a near-term disclosure-based response and sketch longer-term regulatory possibilities. Our disclosure proposal would simplify and partially integrate five existing, inconsistent share-ownership disclosure regimes, and is worth considering independent of its value with respect to decoupling. In the longer term, other responses may be needed; we briefly discuss possible strategies focused on voting rights, voting architecture, and supply and demand forces in the markets on which the new vote buying relies.

CONTENTS

I. INTRODUCTION

The governance structure of the modern corporation emerged in a period characterized by two core concepts. One was the "separation of ownership and control," which has been central to thinking about corporate governance since the 1930s. In stylized form, as conceived by Adolph Berle and Gardiner Means,[1] and converted to modern language, the professional managers of public corporations hold few shares yet substantial control. Shareholder-owners face large collective action problems in overseeing managers. Constraining managerial autonomy and reducing the divergence between managerial and shareholder interests are key elements of an overall governance system.

The second core concept was that a "shareholder" has economic ownership coupled with voting power. For much of the period in which modern thinking about corporate governance developed, one-share, one-vote structures were nearly universal, enforced by New York Stock Exchange listing standards. Although dual-class structures became possible around 1990, they remain uncommon. Our views

1. ADOLPH BERLE & GARDINER MEANS, THE MODERN CORPORATION AND PRIVATE PROPERTY (1932).

of the ways in which institutional investor oversight and the market for corporate control can discipline management depend on the coupling of economic interest and voting power. Terminology reflects this coupling: we use a single term, "ownership," to refer to possession of both the economic return on shares and corresponding voting power. The deference that courts pay to shareholder votes is premised on the belief that shareholders have an economic interest in increasing share value and will vote to further that interest. Beyond the instrumental role of voting, Delaware courts treat the concept of shareholder-as-owner-and-voter as the core ideological basis for managerial exercise of authority over property the managers do not own.[2] Securities and Exchange Commission (SEC) "large shareholder" disclosure rules also largely assume the coupling of economic ownership and voting power.[3]

The assumption that votes are tightly linked to economic interest has become increasingly fragile over the past few years. The derivatives revolution in finance, especially the growth in equity swaps and other privately negotiated ("over the counter" or "OTC") equity derivatives, and related growth in the stock lending market, are making it ever easier and cheaper to decouple economic ownership from voting power.[4] Both company insiders and outside investors can take advantage of this opportunity. Hedge funds, the emblematic opportunistic investors, have been at the vanguard; the rapid growth of hedge fund assets has coincided with the increase in decoupling. Sometimes they hold more votes than shares—a pattern we call "empty voting" because the votes have been emptied of an accompanying economic interest. In an extreme case, an investor can vote despite having *negative* economic ownership, which gives the investor an incentive to vote in ways that *reduce* the company's share price.

Investors and insiders can also have economic ownership that exceeds their formal voting rights. This ownership is often "hidden" because current large shareholder disclosure rules often focus on voting power rather than economic interest. Thus, even significant economic ownership may not be known to the outside world. Often, this economic ownership is combined with *de facto* ability to acquire voting rights at any time. The informal, "morphable" nature of these voting rights lets investors plausibly deny the voting power that would trigger disclosure. We use the term "hidden ownership" to refer to undisclosed economic ownership and "hidden (morphable) ownership" to refer to undisclosed economic ownership plus probable informal voting power.

---

2. *See, e.g.*, Blasius Industries, Inc. v. Atlas Corp., 564 A.2d 651, 659 (Del. Ch. 1988); *cf.* MM Companies Inc. v. Liquid Audio, Inc., 813 A.2d 1118 (Del. 2003).

3. We provide citations to SEC rules and discuss these rules in Part III.

4. The complexities raised by the "new vote buying" are new examples of the challenges the derivatives revolution and modern financial innovation generally pose to corporate governance principles. For discussions of the overarching issue, see, e.g., Henry T. C. Hu, *New Financial Products, the Modern Process of Financial Innovation, and the Puzzle of Shareholder Welfare*, 69 TEX. L. REV. 1273 (1991) [hereinafter "Hu, *New Financial Products*"]; Henry T. C. Hu, *Behind the Corporate Hedge: Information and the Limits of "Shareholder Wealth Maximization,"* 9 J. APPLIED CORP. FIN. 39 (Fall 1996) [hereinafter "Hu, *Behind the Corporate Hedge*"].

We refer to empty voting and hidden (morphable) ownership together as "the new vote buying" or simply as "decoupling." In the past several years, this decoupling has affected takeover battles and control of public companies in (at least) Australia, Canada, Germany, Hong Kong, Italy, Japan, New Zealand, the U.K., and the U.S. How often decoupling has been used, and how often it has altered outcomes, is unknown. Policymakers abroad are beginning to confront the new vote buying, principally by requiring additional disclosure. Policymakers in the U.S. have barely begun to address it, but will soon need to.[5]

There are a number of ways to decouple votes from economic ownership. One common method relies on the stock lending market, which lets one investor "borrow" shares from another. Under standard lending arrangements, the stock borrower has voting rights but no economic ownership, while the stock lender has economic ownership without voting rights. A second approach relies in part on an equity swap, in which the person with the long equity side (the "equity leg") of the swap acquires economic ownership of shares, but no voting rights, while the short side (the "interest leg") often hedges its economic risk by holding shares, thus ending up with votes but no net economic ownership.[6] Finance-savvy readers will quickly see other possibilities, such as relying on put and call options or, where they exist, on single-stock futures.

Surprising results can flow from empty voting. A recent public U.S. instance illustrates the potential risks. Perry Corp., a hedge fund, owned seven million shares of King Pharmaceuticals.[7] Mylan Laboratories agreed in late 2004 to buy King in a stock-for-stock merger at a substantial premium. However, Mylan's shares dropped sharply when the deal was announced. To help Mylan obtain shareholder approval for the merger, Perry bought 9.9% of Mylan—becoming Mylan's largest shareholder—but fully hedged the market risk associated with its Mylan shares. Perry thus had **9.9%** *voting ownership* of Mylan but **zero** *economic ownership*. Including its position in King, Perry's overall economic interest in Mylan was **negative**. The more Mylan (over)paid for King, the more Perry stood to profit.

A second, potentially beneficial use of empty voting involves outside shareholders magnifying the voting power of an existing ownership position. Other things equal, this can reduce shareholder collective action problems. For example, a hedge fund can borrow shares just before the record date for a shareholder vote, then reverse the transaction afterwards. The first publicly reported instance of this "record date capture" strategy occurred in the U.K. in 2002.[8] Laxey Partners, a hedge fund, held about 1% of the shares of British Land, a major U.K. property

5. The only public sector recognition in the United States that we know of is a July 2005 speech by Vice Chancellor Leo Strine, where he stated that what we term "empty voting" and "related factors" are "making it difficult for corporate law makers to avoid a fundamental look" at corporate law. David Marcus, *Thinking Big Thoughts*, CORPORATE CONTROL ALERT, Aug.–Sept. 2005, at 6.

6. The U.K. instrument corresponding to the equity swap is known as a "contract for differences" or CFD. In this article, we use the term "equity swap" to refer to both instruments.

7. We provide citations and further details on this example in Part II.B.1, *infra*.

8. We provide citations on this example and further details in Part II.B.2, *infra*.

company. At the annual general meeting, Laxey emerged with voting power over 9% of British Land's shares, the better to support a proposal to dismember British Land. Just before the record date, Laxey had borrowed 42 million shares. Hedge funds may see record date capture as a tool for responding to incompetent or self-serving management. Company managers will have a different view.

Empty voting by institutions is a close cousin to hedging by managers and controlling shareholders who retain formal ownership of shares, while shedding some or most of their economic ownership.[9] In the U.S., these strategies have typically been driven by such insiders' desire to shed risk while deferring taxes, rather than by vote buying motives. But insiders can also use empty voting techniques to cement their control.

Conversely, investors can have greater economic ownership than voting rights—but with the *de facto* ability to acquire those rights quickly when they are needed. With these "morphable voting rights," the investor likely has full ownership has a practical matter. But under existing disclosure rules, the lack of formal voting rights may let the investor's position remain hidden. Perry's stake in a New Zealand company, Rubicon Ltd., which came to light in 2003, illustrates this.[10] Perry used equity swaps provided by derivatives dealers to hold an undisclosed 16% economic stake, despite New Zealand's large shareholder disclosure rules, which, like section 13(d) ("Section 13(d)") of the Securities Exchange Act of 1934 (the "Exchange Act"),[11] require disclosure by 5% shareholders. When an election came along, Perry went back to its derivatives dealers, unwound the swaps, acquired the "matched shares" held by the dealers to hedge the swaps, and thus obtained formal voting rights. Perry had morphed its *de facto* voting rights into *actual* voting rights. Its failure to disclose the swaps was held not to violate New Zealand law. Morphable voting rights can also be useful for reasons unrelated to disclosure; for example, to avoid "mandatory bid" rules requiring large shareholders to offer to buy all remaining shares.[12]

The new vote buying is largely unregulated and often unseen. Corporate case law relating to "classic" vote buying is generally unlikely to reach the new vote buying without major changes in doctrine.[13] In the leading Delaware case, *Schreiber v. Carney*, vote buying is defined as "a voting agreement supported by consideration personal to the [selling] stockholder, whereby the stockholder divorces

9. *See, e.g.*, Donoghue v. Centillium Communications Inc., No. 05 Civ. 4082 (WHP) 2006 U.S. Dist. LEXIS 13221 (S.D.N.Y. Mar. 28, 2006) (discussing variable prepaid forward contracts and how they are regulated under Section 16 of the Exchange Act); J. Carr Bettis, John M. Bizjak & Michael L. Lemmon, *Managerial Ownership, Incentive Contracting, and the Use of Zero-Cost Collars and Equity Swaps by Corporate Insiders*, 36 J. FIN. & QUANT. ANALYSIS 345 (2001) (discussing zero-cost collars and equity swaps).

10. We provide citations on this example and further details in Part II.C.1, *infra*.

11. Securities Exchange Act of 1934 (ch. 404, 48 Stat. 881) [hereinafter "Exchange Act"], § 13(d) (codified as amended at 15 U.S.C. § 78m(d) (2000 & Supp. III 2003)).

12. We discuss other uses of morphable voting rights in Part II.C, *infra*.

13. Vote buying by insiders can, however, sometimes be challenged under fiduciary duty rules. See *infra* Part V.B (discussing, for instance, *Hewlett v. Hewlett-Packard*).

his discretionary voting power and votes as directed."[14] The focus is on a *transfer of voting rights* to a vote buyer from a **vote seller**; the court then assesses the seller's motives. In contrast, the new vote buyer can often follow a two-step process, in which neither step involves a transfer of voting rights or a vote seller. *First*, the new vote buyer buys shares in the open market. *Second*, it offsets economic ownership of the shares through derivatives transactions. Thus, in the Perry-Mylan situation, Perry purchased Mylan shares, and then hedged its economic ownership through equity swaps. That is, with modern decoupling, the vote is often acquired not through the transfer to a vote buyer of *voting rights* **by a vote seller**; but through the transfer **by a vote buyer** of *economic ownership*. The vote buyer is left only with voting ownership. It has engaged in two ordinary market transactions—purchasing shares and using derivatives for hedging purposes—which are not individually suspect. A new vote buyer using record date capture rather than the foregoing two-step process is also generally not reached by existing case law.[15]

Federal disclosure rules scarcely touch the new vote buying either. Institutional investors must disclose their share positions in public companies on Form 13F,[16] but generally need not disclose transactions that offset the voting rights or economic interest conveyed by these positions. Nor must they disclose economic ownership acquired through equity swaps or other OTC derivatives. The Schedule 13D and Schedule 13G rules[17] governing disclosure by 5% shareholders are more extensive but with some attention to legal niceties, hidden (morphable) ownership and empty voting positions can often be structured in a way that arguably evades the 13D/13G disclosure requirements, and is commonly not disclosed. Even in Perry-Mylan, where Perry filed a Schedule 13D, it made only partial, rather opaque disclosure of its hedging agreements.[18] Disclosure by insiders and 10% shareholders under section 16 of the Exchange Act ("Section 16")[19] focuses on economic ownership and thus captures empty voting through hedging (since hedging affects economic ownership) but likely does not cover empty voting through stock borrowing (since economic ownership does not change).

Because the new vote buying is often not captured by disclosure rules, its scale is unknown. We did, however, find over twenty confirmed or publicly rumored examples, almost all of which have occurred since 2002. These are set out in Table 2. It is no accident that most of these examples are quite recent, nor that most

14. Schreiber v. Carney, 447 A.2d 17, 23 (Del. Ch. 1982). *See also* Robert Charles Clark, *Vote Buying and Corporate Law*, 29 CASE W. RES. L. REV. 776 (1979).

15. We discuss this in Part V.B, *infra*.

16. Form 13F, Information Required of Institutional Investment Managers Pursuant to Section 13(f) of the Securities Exchange Act of 1934 and Rules Thereunder, 17 C.F.R. § 249.325 (2005) [hereinafter "*Form 13F*"].

17. 17 C.F.R. §§ 240.13d-1–.13d-7 (2005); Schedule 13D, 17 C.F.R. § 240.13d-101 (2005); Schedule 13G, 17 C.F.R. § 240.13d-102 (2005).

18. News reports suggest that the SEC is considering an enforcement action against Perry, presumably under the 13D rules. *See, e.g.*, Ianthe Jeanne Dugan, *Hedge Funds Draw Scrutiny Over Merger Play*, WALL ST. J., Jan. 11, 2006, at C1.

19. Exchange Act § 16(b), 48 Stat. at 896 (codified as amended at 15 U.S.C. § 78p(b) (2000 & Supp. III 2003)).

involve hedge funds. The theoretical possibility of decoupling votes from economic ownership is not new.[20] What is new are investor ability to do so on a large scale, newer derivatives (such as equity swaps) which simplify decoupling, declining transaction costs, and a trillion dollar-plus pool of sophisticated, lightly regulated, hedge funds, largely free from the conflicts of interest and concerns with adverse publicity that may deter other institutional investors from using decoupling strategies.

The corporate governance challenges posed by new vote buying are clear, but the remedies are not. In the near term, we believe that enhanced disclosure (crafted with sensitivity to the costs of disclosure) is desirable, to let both regulators and market participants assess how much new vote buying occurs and how often it affects shareholder voting or transaction outcomes. If disclosures are made on a real-time basis (a step that goes somewhat beyond our proposal), they can also let the Delaware courts (the most likely venue) address voting rights on a case-by-case basis under general corporate law principles.

Four themes motivate our disclosure reform proposals. One is that disclosure rules should be internally consistent—they should treat substantively identical positions similarly, which current rules do not. In particular, given investors' ability to morph from economic-only to economic-plus-voting ownership, the rules must cover both economic and voting ownership. A second theme is to produce disclosure that is "good enough" to let regulators, companies, and investors assess how often vote buying occurs, without imposing large new costs on anyone. A third theme is to treat long and short positions symmetrically.

The fourth theme is simplification of the ownership disclosure rules. Currently, there are five distinct, idiosyncratic ownership disclosure regimes, applicable respectively to active 5% shareholders (Schedule 13D), passive 5% shareholders (Schedule 13G), institutional investors (Form 13F), insiders and 10% shareholders (Section 16), and mutual funds.[21] Our proposals would greatly simplify this complex scheme, and move toward an integrated system of share ownership disclosure, analogous to the current integrated disclosure regime for company disclosures. Moving toward integrated, consistent ownership disclosure could well be worthwhile independent of its role in addressing the new vote buying.

In proposing disclosure reforms, we take as given the rough economic and political logic behind the current rules. We do not revisit whether large shareholders or major institutions should disclose their share positions, nor the threshold levels for this disclosure. The optimality of these thresholds is contestable. We believe, however, that the thresholds are reasonable and that, whatever the thresholds are, the disclosure rules should be internally coherent, which at present they are not. Moreover, the political history of disclosure, in the U.S. and elsewhere, suggests that our political system will not tolerate hidden control of major companies, nor control contests waged behind closed doors. So disclosure there

20. For an example of how to hedge a share position with options, see, e.g., RICHARD A. BREALEY & STEWART C. MYERS, PRINCIPLES OF CORPORATE FINANCE 570–72 (7th ed. 2003).

21. *See infra* Part III.B.

will be. Our aim is to make that disclosure coherent, simple, and therefore relatively low-cost.

As a regulatory response to hidden (morphable) ownership, disclosure alone may suffice. For empty voting, other responses may also be needed. Still, we consider it premature to adopt proposals that go beyond disclosure at this point.

One reason is that empty voting can sometimes be beneficial and sometimes not, depending on the circumstances. On one hand, empty voting by insiders can increase entrenchment and undermine external oversight. Empty voting with negative economic interest is also troubling. On the other hand, hedge funds using empty voting can, under certain circumstances, strengthen shareholder oversight of company managers. Empty voting could let votes move from less to better informed hands and, thus, could enhance the effectiveness of shareholder oversight.[22] Of course, supporters of management discretion will have a different view. Martin Lipton, for instance, believes that hedge fund activism and "abusive" takeovers can cause managers to focus too much on short-term results.[23] Under this view, decoupling by outside investors would tend to exacerbate the problem. We do not address here the optimal level or type of shareholder oversight of managers; we merely note that many observers believe that more external oversight would be beneficial on balance.

Another problem with some regulatory responses stems from the multiple forms that new vote buying can take, and the need to understand these forms before regulating them. As yet, we know too little about the new vote buying to know what rules to write. Yet delegating rule-writing power to companies is problematic, because company managers may well write rules that block vote-buying forms used by outside investors, while allowing forms used by insiders. Moreover, some substantive responses may exceed the SEC's statutory authority.

Nonetheless, over a longer term, additional steps could prove useful in addressing empty voting. We discuss three families of possible strategies at the end of this article. One family focuses directly on voting rights. The key question is: under which circumstances should empty voters lose voting rights? A second family of strategies focuses on updating the mechanics of shareholder voting. A

22. *See* Susan E.K. Christoffersen, Christopher C. Geczy, David K. Musto & Adam V. Reed, Vote Trading and Information Aggregation (Jan. 20, 2005) (unpublished draft), *available at* http://ssrn.com/abstract=686026; Hu & Black, *New Vote Buying*, *infra* note 24, at 857 (our analysis of foregoing draft).

23. *See, e.g.*, Martin Lipton & Steven A Rosenblum, *A New System of Corporate Governance: The Quinquennial Election of Directors*, 58 U. CHI. L. REV. 187, 210 (1991); Martin Lipton, *Is This the End of Takeovers?*, WASH. POST, Nov. 6, 1988, at H2; Martin Lipton et al., Wachtell, Lipton, Rosen & Katz, *Be Prepared for Attacks by Hedge Funds* (Dec. 21, 2005) (on file with *The Business Lawyer*).

Concerns that hedge fund activism may lead to such corporate "short-termism" are closely related to issues like conflicts among "generations" of shareholders and differences between running a company to maximize shareholder wealth based on share trading prices (i.e., "actual shareholder wealth maximization") and running a company to maximize shareholder wealth based on share intrinsic values (i.e., "blissful shareholder wealth maximization"). *See e.g.*, Hu, *New Financial Products*, *supra* note 4, at 1278–87 & 1300–05 (discussion of such matters); Henry T. C. Hu, *Buffett, Corporate Objectives, and the Nature of Sheep*, 19 CARDOZO L. REV. 379, 392–95, & 397–407 (1997) [hereinafter "Hu, *Nature of Sheep*"] (discussion of such matters and in relation to how Warren Buffett and Charlie Munger run Berkshire Hathaway).

third family of strategies focuses on supply and demand forces relating to the new vote buying, such as rules that would encourage or require institutional investors to recall lent shares around voting record dates.

This article proceeds as follows. Part II proposes a taxonomy of the elements of empty voting and hidden (morphable) ownership, and provides details on the public examples we have been able to locate. Part III discusses the current ownership disclosure rules. Part IV presents our integrated ownership disclosure proposal. Part V offers a menu of possible additional longer-term responses. Part VI concludes.

This article is part of a broader research agenda relating to the new vote buying. In two companion articles, one directed at an academic legal audience and the second at a finance audience, we discuss the theoretical and empirical literature (principally in finance) that bears on the benefits and costs of decoupling, present more details on the known examples of new vote buying and on longer-term regulatory options, and provide fuller citations.[24] As far as we are aware, this article and its companions are the first attempt to systematically analyze the new vote buying and its corporate governance implications.[25]

II. The New Vote Buying: Taxonomy and Public Examples

A. Factors Underlying Decoupling and Decoupling's Functional Elements

In their classic 1983 article on voting in corporate law, Judge Frank Easterbrook and Professor Daniel Fischel stated that "[i]t is not possible to separate the voting right from the equity interest" and that "[s]omeone who wants to buy a vote must buy the stock too."[26] This was an oversimplification then, but only a bit. For the most part, voting rights were linked to shares.

With the new vote buying, in contrast, the economic return on shares can be easily decoupled from the related voting rights. Modern financial innovations,

24. *See* Henry T. C. Hu & Bernard S. Black, *The New Vote Buying: Empty Voting and Hidden (Morphable) Ownership*, 79 S. Cal. L. Rev. 811 (2006), *also available at* http://papers.ssrn.com/abstract=904004 [hereinafter "Hu & Black, *New Vote Buying*"]; Henry T. C. Hu & Bernard S. Black, *Hedge Funds, Insiders and Empty Voting: Decoupling of Economic and Voting Ownership in Public Companies* (working paper 2006), *available at* http://ssrn.com/abstract=874098 [hereinafter "Hu & Black, *Hedge Funds and Empty Voting*"].

An initial version of the research that led to this article and its companions was first presented publicly in May 2005, at the annual meeting of the American Law and Economics Association (held at New York University Law School). *See* Henry T. C. Hu & Bernard S. Black, *Empty Voting: Shareholder Voting Rights and Coupled Assets* (Feb. 2005). Subsequent versions were posted on SSRN, beginning on January 6, 2006.

25. *See, e.g.*, David Marcus, *Hedge fund voting: The devil we don't know*, Corporate Control Alert, Mar.–Apr. 2006, at 10. Other articles or working drafts in the legal literature that have either discussed or touched on the issue include Shaun P. Martin & Frank Partnoy, *Encumbered Shares*, 2005 U. Ill. L. Rev. 775; Marcel Kahan & Edward B. Rock, *Hedge Funds in Corporate Governance and Corporate Control* (preliminary draft, Apr. 9, 2006); David Skeel, *Behind the Hedge—In the Untamed World of Hedge Funds, Rigged Deals and Manipulated Markets Help the Wealthy Thrive While Ordinary Investors Wither*, Legal Affairs, Nov.–Dec. 2005, at 28.

26. Frank H. Easterbrook and Daniel R. Fischel, *Voting in Corporate Law*, 26 J. L. & Econ. 395, 410 (1983).

especially OTC derivatives, have played a central role in this decoupling.[27] OTC derivatives are customizable tools that can be engineered to facilitate decoupling. The rapid growth in share lending over the last decade pushes in the same direction.[28] Share lending underlies most current decoupling strategies, both directly (for record date capture and short selling) and indirectly, by helping derivatives dealers hedge their exposure on equity swaps. We can expect the "supply" of financial technology available for decoupling to continue to increase.

Demand factors have also been at work. Hedge funds have grown rapidly in the last decade and now have over $1 trillion in investor assets, compounded by many funds' use of leverage.[29] Hedge fund managers typically have wide leeway as to the strategies they can use; many are comfortable with equity derivatives and other sophisticated financial tools. Unlike mutual funds and pension funds, they also face few regulatory constraints. And, in the past year or two, some have adopted corporate governance activism as an investment strategy.[30] Hedge funds usually have fewer conflicts of interest than other institutional investors, and less concern with adverse publicity, so can be more aggressive in using decoupling strategies.

Understanding the new vote buying must begin with identifying its core functional elements. Throughout this article, we assume a simple context: a publicly held corporation with one class of equity (each share carrying one vote) and diversified shareholders with homogeneous preferences. We treat shareholder wealth maximization as a corporate goal and do not consider non-shareholder constituencies.[31] We sometimes refer to an outside investor who engages in new

27. For analysis of the modern process of financial innovation and the emergence of the OTC derivatives market in the 1980s, see, e.g., Henry T. C. Hu, *Misunderstood Derivatives: The Causes of Informational Failure and the Promise of Regulatory Incrementalism*, 102 YALE L. J. 1457 (1993) [hereinafter, "Hu, *Misunderstood Derivatives*"].

28. *See, e.g.*, Heather McKenzie, *Securities Lending Grows Up*, FIN. NEWS, Oct. 2, 2000; Gene Picone & Richard Warne, *Securities Lending—A Coming of Age*, PENSIONS MGMT., Sept. 1, 2003, *available at* http://www.pensions-management.co.uk/news/fullstory.php/aid/471/A_coming_of_age.html. For other sources on share lending, see *infra* note 130.

29. There is no reliable data on the number of hedge funds or their assets under management. *See* Securities and Exchange Commission, IMPLICATIONS OF THE GROWTH OF HEDGE FUNDS—STAFF REPORT TO THE UNITED STATES SECURITIES AND EXCHANGE COMMISSION 1 n.2 (Sept. 2003), *available at* http://www.sec.gov/news/studies/hedgefunds0903.pdf [hereinafter "SEC, HEDGE FUND REPORT"]. For the $1 trillion estimate in mid-2005, see *At Deadline*, PENSIONS & INVESTMENTS, Aug. 8, 2005, at 1 (reporting estimate by Tremont Capital).

30. *See, e.g.* Riva D. Atlas, *Some Funds Taking Role Far Beyond Just Investor*, N.Y. TIMES, Aug. 16, 2005, at C1; Lina Saigol, *Hedge Funds are Very Keen to Flex Their Secretive Shareholding Muscle*, FIN. TIMES, Aug. 9, 2005, at 19; Henny Sender, *Hedge Funds: The New Corporate Activists?*, WALL ST. J., May 13, 2005, at C1.

31. We also generally leave aside the distinctions between shareholder wealth maximization based on market prices and shareholder wealth maximization based on intrinsic share values, between the welfare of the corporation and the welfare of the shareholder, between shareholder welfare and shareholder wealth, and short-termism-related issues such as conflicts between short term and long term shareholders. *See, e.g.*, Henry T. C. Hu, *Hedging Expectations: "Derivative Reality" and the Law and Finance of the Corporate Objective*, 73 TEX. L. REV. 985 (1995); Hu, *New Financial Products*, *supra* note 4; Hu, *Nature of Sheep*, *supra* note 23, at 388–407; *supra* note 23 (on "short-termism" and related issues).

vote buying as a "hedge fund" and an officer, director or controlling shareholder who does so as an "insider."

To proceed further, it helps to define a set of terms. By **"formal voting rights,"** we mean the *legal* right to vote shares under company law (as supplemented by SEC and stock exchange rules governing voting of shares held in street name), including the legal power to instruct someone else how to vote. Thus, in the common situation where a broker holds shares in street name for a customer, the customer has formal voting rights because it has the right under stock exchange rules to instruct the broker how to vote the customer's shares. By **"voting rights"** or **"voting ownership"** of shares, we mean formal *or informal* rights to vote shares, including the de facto power to instruct someone else how to vote. In Perry-Rubicon, Perry had voting rights because it had the informal power to return to its derivatives dealers at any time, unwind its equity swaps, and obtain Rubicon shares from the dealers.[32] The company at which voting takes place is the **"host company."**

By **"economic ownership,"** we mean the economic returns associated with shares. This ownership can be achieved **directly** by holding shares, or **indirectly** by holding a **"coupled asset,"** which conveys returns that relate directly to the returns on the shares. Economic ownership can be either **positive**—the same direction as the return on shares—or **negative**—the opposite direction from the return on shares. Someone who owns voting shares has **"full ownership**," consisting of voting ownership plus direct economic ownership. Coupled assets include derivatives (such as options, futures, and equity swaps), contractual rights (such as rights under a stock loan agreement), and other financial products. A coupled asset can either increase or decrease economic ownership. Decoupling often involves owning both shares and a coupled asset.

By **"net economic ownership,"** we mean a person's combined economic ownership of host company shares and coupled assets. This net ownership can be positive, zero, or negative. We characterize as an **"empty voter"** a person whose voting rights substantially exceed his net economic ownership. Depending on the nature of the coupled assets, net economic ownership may depend on share price. Suppose, for example, that a company's shares trade at $50, and an executive enters into a zero-cost collar that caps the upside on the shares at $60 and limits the downside to $45. The executive will have higher net economic ownership for share prices within the $45–$60 range than outside this range.

An investor may also hold "**related non-host assets**"—assets, often securities of another company, whose value relate in some way to the value of the host company's shares. In Perry-Mylan, for example, Perry's shares in Mylan's target, King Pharmaceuticals, were a related non-host asset. The combined return on host shares, coupled assets, and related non-host assets produces what we call an **"overall economic interest"** in the host firm's shares. This overall economic interest can be positive, zero, or negative. In the Perry-Mylan example, Perry combined full ownership of the Mylan shares with coupled assets (equity swaps

32. We discuss the Perry-Rubicon example *supra* in Part I and *infra* in Part II.C.

and other hedges) that offset its economic ownership; this left it with **9.9%** *voting ownership* and **zero** *net economic ownership*:

[9.9% full ownership of shares] − [9.9% economic ownership (through coupled assets)]
= [9.9% voting + 9.9% economic ownership] − [9.9% economic ownership]
= [9.9% voting ownership]

But Perry also held a related non-host asset—shares of King Pharmaceuticals, which gave it a **negative** *overall economic interest*—it would profit if Mylan overpaid for King.

If a person has economic ownership that disclosure rules do not cover (or can reasonably be interpreted by the person as not covering), we call this **"hidden ownership."** If this hidden ownership is likely to include informal voting rights, we term this "**hidden (morphable) ownership.**" These "**morphable**" voting rights derive from market customs and the economic incentives of the pertinent participants; these rights will generally not be formally enforceable or verifiable by outsiders. Perry's hidden (morphable) ownership of Rubicon offers an example.

Notice that whatever form new vote buying transactions take, only the host company can alter the total level of voting rights or economic ownership. If one investor holds more voting rights than economic ownership, someone else must hold more economic ownership than voting rights.

Table 1 offers some illustrative examples of the forms that new vote buying can take.

Table 1. Some Forms of New Vote Buying

Examples of some of forms of new vote buying. These examples are illustrative only. The Perry-Mylan, Laxey-British Land, insider hedging, and Perry-Rubicon examples are discussed in the text above. The other examples are discussed below.

Example	Voting Ownership	Economic Ownership	Coupled Asset	Net Economic Ownership	Related Non-Host Asset	Overall Economic Interest
Empty Voting						
share ownership hedged with short equity swap (Perry-Mylan)	yes	direct	equity swaps, others	no	yes (target shares)	negative
share ownership hedged with options (Coles Myer proxy fight)	yes	direct	short call + long put	zero	no	zero
share ownership hedged with related non-host asset (MONY-AXA)	yes	direct	possible	not known	yes (acquirer bonds)	negative
record-date capture via stock borrowing (Laxey-British Land)	yes (high)	Direct (low)	share loan	yes (low)	no	low
record-date capture via stock borrowing in combination with short-sale (Henderson Investment)	yes	negative	share loan + short sale	negative	no	negative
insider hedging	yes	direct (lowered)	equity derivatives	positive (lowered)	no	positive (lowered)

(*continued overleaf*)

(continued)

Example	Voting Ownership	Economic Ownership	Coupled Asset	Net Economic Ownership	Related Non-Host Asset	Overall Economic Interest
Deutsche Boerse-London Stock Exchange (for hedge funds that were long acquirer shares and short target shares)	yes	direct	no	yes	yes (target shares)	positive or negative, depending on stake in target
Hidden (Morphable) Ownership						
voting rights exercised by acquiring shares (Perry-Rubicon)	informal right to acquire shares from derivatives dealers	indirect	equity swaps	yes	no	high
voting rights exercised by directing votes of others (Marks & Spencer)	informal right to direct voting by derivatives dealers' matched shares	indirect	equity swaps	yes	no	high

B. Empty Voting

We turn in this Section B to a closer examination of the mechanics of empty voting. Section C addresses hidden ownership. Section D addresses the extra complexities introduced by related non-host assets.

1. Empty Voting Through Equity Derivatives

a. Perry-Mylan and Similar Examples

The Perry-Mylan example, discussed briefly in the Introduction, offers a good case study of empty voting through the use of OTC equity derivatives. As of late 2004, Perry Corporation owned seven million shares of King Pharmaceuticals, a generic drug maker.[33] Mylan Labs, a rival, agreed to acquire King Pharmaceuticals in a stock-for-stock merger at a significant premium over King's trading price, and thus a large profit for Perry. However, Mylan's shares dropped sharply when the deal was announced, and Mylan needed shareholder approval for the merger. Perry therefore bought a 9.9% stake in Mylan, which it could vote in favor of the merger. At the same time, Perry hedged its economic exposure to Mylan by taking the short or "interest" leg of equity swaps with derivatives dealers and entering

33. Our descriptions in this article of new vote buying examples rely in some cases on news reports that refer to market rumors or other sources which may not be accurate. Our description of Perry-Mylan is based on Perry Corp., Schedule 13D as to Mylan Laboratories, Inc. (Nov. 29, 2004), *available at* http://www.sec.gov/Archives/edgar/data/69499/000116923204005932/d61489_sc13d.txt; Complaint, High River Limited Partnership v. Mylan Laboratories, Inc., No. 04-2677 (M.D. Pa. Dec. 10, 2004) [hereinafter "Icahn Complaint"]; Tara Croft, *Mylan: King Deal Doomed*, DAILY DEAL, Jan. 13, 2005; Christopher Faille, *Perry Plans to Sell Stake in Mylan*, HEDGE WORLD DAILY NEWS, Mar. 23, 2005; Jesse Eisinger, *Icahn Cries Foul at Perry's No-Risk Play in Takeover Fight*, WALL ST. J., Dec. 15, 2004, at C1; Andrew Ross Sorkin, *Icahn Accuses a Hedge Fund of Stock Manipulation*, N.Y. TIMES, Dec. 13, 2004, at C1; Andrew Ross Sorkin, *Nothing Ventured, Everything Gained*, N.Y. TIMES, Dec. 2, 2004, at C1.

into other unspecified transactions. The derivatives dealers who took the long or "equity" leg of the Mylan swaps likely hedged their Mylan exposure, perhaps by selling Mylan shares short. A second hedge fund, Citadel, acquired another 4.4% of Mylan's shares and was rumored to have followed a strategy similar to Perry's.

Carl Icahn, a major Mylan shareholder, opposed the acquisition. He sued Mylan and Perry under federal securities law, including Section 13(d). He claimed that Perry and other unnamed hedge funds following similar strategies held 19% of the Mylan votes, yet no economic interest. If so, Perry and kindred investors had a negative overall economic interest in Mylan. They would want Mylan to complete the deal even if Mylan's value were to suffer. Indeed, the more Mylan overpaid, the better. The lawsuit became moot when Mylan abandoned the acquisition because of accounting problems at King.

Several other anecdotes illustrate how hedged share purchases can be used to influence voting outcomes.

- In 2004, French insurer AXA entered into a merger agreement to acquire MONY. To finance the bid, AXA issued convertible bonds, which were convertible into AXA shares at a discount to AXA's price *only if* AXA acquired MONY. Holders of AXA bonds apparently acquired MONY shares to vote for the merger, while short sellers of the AXA bonds (including the Highfields Capital hedge fund) acquired MONY shares to oppose the merger, with neither group's vote turning on whether the merger was good for MONY. The AXA bondholders may have hedged some or all of their MONY positions.[34]
- During Hewlett Packard's 2002 acquisition of Compaq, some holders of Compaq shares were rumored to have engaged in empty voting of H-P shares to support the merger. The merger announcement led to a sharp drop in H-P's price and to a proxy contest by Walter Hewlett opposing the merger. Empty voting might have affected the outcome of this very close vote.[35]
- In a 2002 proxy contest at Australian firm Coles Myer, investor Solomon Lew held 3% of Coles Myer's shares. To support his proxy campaign, he acquired another 4% of Coles Myer's shares while hedging his economic ownership with (short call, long put) options positions.[36]

34. *See In re* The MONY Group, Inc., Shareholder Litigation, 852 A.2d 9 (Del. Ch. 2004) and 853 A.2d 661 (Del. Ch. 2004); Theo Francis, *AXA Launches Offensive to Woo MONY Holders*, WALL ST. J., Apr. 28, 2004, at C5.

35. *See* Icahn Complaint, *supra* note 33, at 4; Andrew Ross Sorkin, *Nothing Ventured, Everything Gained*, N.Y. TIMES, Dec. 2, 2004, at C1.

36. *See* Malcom Maiden, *Lew Confirms Hedging Coles Myer Shares*, ABIX—AUSTRALASIAN BUSINESS INTELLIGENCE—THE AGE, Oct. 24, 2002 (Lew confirmation that companies linked to him had hedged recent purchases); Mark Todd, *Lew Hedges Coles Gamble*, THE AGE, Oct. 10, 2002 (rumor that Lew had hedged recent share purchases); James McCullough, *The amazing war of Solomon Lew*, COURIER MAIL (Queensland, Australia), Nov. 9, 2002, at 77 (on Lew's 7% holding of Coles Myer).

These strategies are troubling. Many acquisitions turn out poorly for the acquirer.[37] The major U.S. stock exchanges require the acquirer's shareholders to approve a large stock-for-stock merger. Yet in practice, the acquirer's shareholders rarely vote down even apparently overpriced mergers. Empty voting on the acquirer's side by the target's shareholders, employed when the vote on a merger is likely to be close, could reduce the limited constraint the vote requirement now imposes on the acquiring firm's managers.

Moreover, these techniques can readily be extended to proxy fights for control. With control at stake, neither side can be counted on to play fair and simply solicit the votes of other shareholders. The temptation to buy votes quietly will be strong, especially if the other side may be doing so as well. Cleverness in vote buying—a characteristic not necessarily associated with either ability or incentive to run the company well—may become important for proxy fight success.

b. Insider Hedging and Entrenchment

Corporate executives are often ill-diversified. Both their human capital and much of their financial capital is tied up in the firm they manage. Controlling shareholders, often the founder's family, are similarly undiversified. These insiders often want to reduce their economic exposure to the firm's shares—hopefully without causing public concern that insiders are bailing out, triggering a tax bill, or, for controlling shareholders, giving up control. High levels of insider ownership are reasonably common. One survey of New York Stock Exchange-listed companies with 2001 revenues between $250 million and $1.5 billion found that more than one in ten had Chief Executive Officers who held more than 10 percent of the shares. About half of those companies had insiders who held more than 50 percent of the shares.[38] Lack of diversification will often cause insiders to be more averse to firm-specific risk than diversified outside shareholders.

Investment banks have developed strategies to accommodate the desire of insiders to hedge their economic exposure. Multiple techniques have emerged. One is a short equity swap position. Another, known as a zero-cost collar, involves buying a put option (to limit downside loss) and selling a call option (thus reducing potential gain).[39] Such a collar sharply reduces economic ownership but preserves voting rights. A 2001 study reports that senior executives in U.S. public companies, on average, use collars for 36% of their holdings and thereby reduced

37. *See, e.g.*, ROBERT BRUNER, DEALS FROM HELL: M & A LESSONS THAT RISE ABOVE THE ASHES (2005); Sara B. Moeller, Frederik B. Schlingemann & Rene Stulz, *Wealth Destruction on a Massive Scale? A Study of Acquiring Firm Returns in the Recent Merger Wave*, 60 J. FIN. 757 (2005).

38. Dennis Simon, *In splitting leadership, look at CEO ownership*, DIRECTORS & BOARDS, Jan. 1, 2004, at 24, 25.

39. If the put and call options have the same exercise price and expiration date, this transaction is a complete hedge, economically equivalent to selling shares. More commonly, the call option exercise price is somewhat above the put option exercise price, hence the term "collar." In a "zero-cost" collar, the proceeds from selling the call equal the cost of buying the put.

their economic ownership position by 25%.[40] In the past five years, the use of derivatives by executives appear to have increased dramatically.[41]

To be sure, there are other ways for insiders to retain control while shedding economic ownership, including dual-class common stock and pyramidal ownership structures.[42] There may be justifications for insiders to use dual-class stock to raise capital without relinquishing control. In particular, the buyers of low-vote shares know what they are getting, and will pay a market price. So too for buyers of shares in companies controlled through pyramids. The new vote buying, however, is more akin to the criticized and now-banned dual-class recapitalizations of the 1980s, in which insiders acquired control without paying a market price for doing so. In some respects, the new vote buying is worse than a dual-class recapitalization—the recapitalization was publicly known and required a shareholder vote, while new vote buying requires no vote and can sometimes be hidden.

2. Empty Voting Through Record Date Capture

Thus far, we have focused on empty voting strategies that involve holding shares and hedging one's economic ownership. A second strategy, known as *record date capture*, involves borrowing shares in the stock loan market. In a typical stock loan, the borrower obtains shares (and accompanying votes).[43] The borrower contracts with the stock lender to: (i) return the shares to the lender at any time at the election of either side; and (ii) pay to the lender the value of any dividends or other distributions on the shares during the borrowing period. The loan is secured with cash or Treasury securities. This borrowing contract (a coupled asset in our terminology) leaves the economic risk of the shares with the lender. The borrower holds votes but no economic ownership. The lender has economic ownership without votes.

A traditional use of stock borrowing is to facilitate short selling. The borrower sells the borrowed shares in the market,[44] ending up with no votes and negative net economic ownership. Later, the short-seller closes out the short position by

40. *See* Bettis, Biszak & Lemmon, *supra* note 9.

41. *See* Ronald Fink, *Overexposed*, CFO, Apr. 2006, at 85, *available at* http://www.cfo.com/printable/article.cfm/5674520?f = options.

42. *See, e.g.*, Heitor Almeida & Daniel Wolfenzon, *A Theory of Pyramidal Ownership and Family Business Groups* (working paper 2005), *available at* http://ssrn.com/abstract = 721801; Lucian Arye Bebchuk, Reinier Kraakman & George Triantis, *Stock Pyramids, Cross-Ownership, and Dual Class Equity: The Mechanisms and Agency Costs of Separating Control from Cash Flow Rights*, in CONCENTRATED CORPORATE OWNERSHIP 295–318 (Randall K. Morck ed., 2000).

43. For an overview of customary share lending practices, see, e.g., Bond Market Association, Master Securities Loan Agreement (2000) (under U.S. law); International Securities Lending Association, Global Master Securities Lending Agreement (2000) (under English law); Darrell Duffie, N. Garleanu & L. H. Pedersen, *Securities Lending, Shorting, and Pricing*, 66 J. FIN. ECON. 307 (2002).

44. By adopting Regulation SHO in 2004, the SEC sought to reduce the extent of "naked shorting," the practice of selling shares short without borrowing the necessary shares, thus creating the risk of failing to deliver shares to the buyer. Short Sales, SEC Rel. No. 34-50103 (July 28, 2004), 69 Fed. Reg. 48008 (Aug. 6, 2004); Aaron Lucchetti & Kara Scannell, *Despite SEC Rules, a Small Amount of Naked Shorting Appears to Persist*, WALL ST. J., Apr. 13, 2006, at C1.

buying shares in the market and delivering them back to the stock lender. But, omit the short sale, and stock borrowing becomes an easy route to empty voting.

Here is how the strategy works. Before a shareholder meeting, a company's board of directors establishes a voting record date.[45] Shareholders who hold shares on the record date have the right to vote at the meeting. The empty voter simply borrows shares before the record date, and returns them afterward. Efforts by pension funds and other stock lenders in the U.K. to respond to record date capture suggests that the practice is reasonably widespread in the U.K.[46] A recent working paper by Christoffersen, Geczy, Musto and Reed provides quantitative, albeit dated, evidence for the U.S. market. They report, based on stock loan data from a custodian bank in 1999 and a broker-dealer from 1996–2001, that stock loans spike on the record date, increasing on average from 0.21% to 0.26% of outstanding shares. The spike in borrowing is higher for firms that have had poorer financial performance, for meetings that result in a close vote, and for firms that experience higher support for shareholder proposals.[47]

The shares of most publicly traded stocks in the U.S. can be borrowed. A study by Gene D'Avolio of shares available from just one large financial institution found that the stocks that could not be borrowed accounted, in the aggregate, for less than 1% of market capitalization.[48] Borrowing shares is generally cheap: 91% of the stocks lent in this sample cost less than 1% per year to borrow. The number of borrowable shares is often large—during some recent corporate battles, up to 20% of a company's shares were held by borrowers.[49]

The Laxey Partners-British Land incident, discussed in the Introduction, offers an example of record date capture.[50] Laxey sought a breakup of British Land and opposed the reelection of British Land's chairman. British Land's chairman was a bit miffed at what he called Laxey's "rent-a-vote" strategy.[51] There was irony all around. British Land saw Laxey as abusing the corporate voting system, while Laxey perceived itself as calling weak management to account. Meanwhile, fund manager Hermes, one of the City's champions of good corporate governance, was (unknowingly) one of the stock lenders. Hermes did apologize.

45. *See, e.g.*, DEL. CODE ANN. tit. 8 § 213(a) (2001).

46. We discuss these efforts *infra* in Part V.D.3.

47. Christoffersen et al., *supra* note 22.

48. *See* Gene D'Avolio, *The Market for Borrowing Stock*, 66 J. FIN. ECON. 271 (2002).

49. *See* Kate Burgess & James Drummond, *Transparency finds a high-level champion*, FIN. TIMES, Apr. 22, 2005, at 1. Borrowing is cheap on average, but not for every company. In one recent case, Charter Communications took the unusual step of issuing 150 million shares in a public offering, supposedly to accommodate hedge funds frustrated by borrowing costs. *See* Peter Grant, *Charter's Unusual Issue May Have SEC Balking*, WALL ST. J., June 24, 2005, at C3; *Charter Share Issue Approved by the SEC*, WALL ST. J., July 19, 2005, at C3.

50. Our discussion of the Laxey-British Land encounter is based on Florian Gimbel, *The Big Picture: Uneasy Bedfellows with Money in Mind: Does Investing in Hedge Funds Compromise Pension Funds' Corporate Governance Activity?*, FIN. TIMES, Apr. 19, 2004; Jim Piccitto, *Laundering Money in the Free World*, GLOBAL INVESTOR, Dec. 1, 2004, at SS36; John Ritblat, Letter to the Editor, *British Land Buy-back Well Under Way*, FIN. TIMES, Jan. 13, 2003, at 18 (letter); Simon Targett, *Top Pension Funds Plan Securities Lending Code*, FIN. TIMES, June 14, 2004, at 1 (FT Report); John Waples, *Ritblat Hits at CSFB and Laxey for Vote 'Conspiracy,'* SUNDAY TIMES (LONDON), July 21, 2002, Bus. Sec., at 1.

51. Ritblat, *supra* note 50.

In early 2006, a far more questionable use of record date capture appears to have occurred in Hong Kong. Henderson Land wished to buy the 25% minority interest in Henderson Investment, a publicly held affiliate.[52] Henderson Investment's share price increased substantially, in anticipation that its shareholders would approve the buyout. Under Hong Kong law, however, the buyout could be blocked by a negative vote of 10% of the "free floating" shares—in this case about 2.5% of the outstanding shares. To everybody's surprise, 2.7% of the shares—75.5 million shares—were voted against the buyout. Henderson Investments shares fell 17% the day after the voting outcome was announced.

What happened? It appears that one or more hedge funds borrowed Henderson Investment shares before the record date, voted against the buyout, and then sold those shares short, thus profiting from its private knowledge that the buyout would be defeated. One hedge fund alone voted at least 72 million shares against the merger; that fund may have held enough shares by itself to defeat the buyout. Thus, a shareholder with negative economic ownership blocked a deal that would benefit other shareholders.

Consider next a variant on record date capture. An investor can buy shares just before the record date and sell them soon thereafter. The investor has economic exposure for a short period and can hedge some or all of this exposure through equity derivatives. The timing of the economic exposure further reduces any link between economic ownership and voting rights. The record date is well before the meeting date. There is no reason to expect company-specific news on the record date. By the meeting date, the investor will have sold his shares and will suffer no harm from voting in ways that reduce share price; indeed, as in Henderson Investments, the investor could even gain from doing so.[53]

C. Hidden (Morphable) Ownership

1. Morphing from De Facto to Formal Voting Rights

Equity derivatives can also be used to conceal ownership, against the background of disclosure rules that, as we discuss in Part IV, turn largely on voting rights rather than economic ownership. Perry has used equity derivatives for this purpose as well as for empty voting. In early 2001, Perry was a major holder of Rubicon Ltd., a New Zealand public company.[54] New Zealand has rules similar

52. This account draws on: *Asian hedge funds undermine lending*, Int'l Sec. Fin., Mar. 1, 2006, at 10(1); Patricia Cheng, *Hedge funds find loophole in H.K.*, Int'l Herald Trib., Feb. 16, 2006, at 18; Alex Frew McMillan, *Hong Kong studying voting issues on borrowed shares*, Infovest21 News, Jan. 25, 2006; Florian Gimbel & Francesco Guerrera, *Henderson stock lending fears*, Fin. Times (Asia Ed.), Feb. 15, 2006, at 15.

53. We thus disagree with Easterbrook and Fischel, who ignore the difference between the record date and the voting date. They claim that a person who buys shares "the day before the election, votes them, and sells the day after the election" will bear "the gains or losses attributable to the election." Easterbrook & Fischel, *supra* note 26, at 411 n.41. This is simply not so.

54. Our discussion of the facts is based on *Ithaca (Custodians) Ltd. v. Perry Corporation*, [2003] 2 N.Z.L.R. 216 (H.C.), *rev'd*, [2004] 1 N.Z.L.R. 731 (C.A.), *conditional leave to appeal refused*, [2004] 2 N.Z.L.R. 182 (C.A.).

to Section 13(d), which required disclosure of 5% ownership positions in public companies.[55] In June 2001, Perry gave notice that it had ceased to be a 5% holder. Then—to everyone's surprise—on July 11, 2002, Perry disclosed that it held 16% of Rubicon. It had bought 31 million shares from Deutsche Bank and UBS Warburg—just in time to vote at Rubicon's shareholder meeting.

What happened during the interim period? On May 31, 2001, Perry shed its voting rights but not its economic interest. It sold 31 million shares to Deutsche Bank and UBS Warburg and simultaneously took the long side of equity swaps covering these shares. Perry stopped reporting as a 5% owner because, it claimed, its equity swap position fell outside the New Zealand disclosure rules. When Perry needed voting rights, it terminated the swaps and bought the shares back from Deutsche Bank and UBS Warburg. Another major Rubicon shareholder challenged Perry's right to vote. Perry lost at trial but won on appeal.

How did Perry know that it had *de facto* ability to reacquire and vote Rubicon shares, when it chose to do so? The two banks needed to hedge their exposure on the swaps. Perry could expect them to do so by holding the shares they had bought from Perry. Another means of hedging was unlikely, given the thin market for Rubicon shares and the transaction costs to hedge in another way. Perry could also expect the banks to sell the shares back to Perry when Perry chose to unwind the equity swaps. Even the Court of Appeal, which ruled in Perry's favor, stated that:

> [I]t was almost certain that the shares would be sold to Perry Corporation upon the termination of the swaps if Perry Corporation wished to buy, provided the counterparties held the shares (. . . [which] was highly likely). We consider that this market reality would have been obvious to any reasonably informed market participant. Mr Rosen, head trader of Perry Corporation, said in evidence that he had always thought it likely that the shares would be held by the counterparties as a hedge. He also said that, if he wanted to terminate the swaps and purchase the shares, it would have been commercially sound for the . . . counterparties to sell him those shares.[56]

The Court of Appeal nonetheless concluded that disclosure was not required, partly because it believed disclosure would generally not be required in Australia, the United States, or the U.K.

Holding "matched shares" is a common way for a derivatives dealer to hedge the short side of an equity swap. Especially when the equity swap involves a large number of shares in a thinly traded company, alternative hedging strategies may be limited. When a dealer hedges through share ownership, a *de facto* practice is apparently emerging, at least in the U.K., in which the dealer, if asked, will either unwind the swap and sell the shares to its client (as in Perry-Rubicon) or vote the shares as its client wants (we cite some examples in Table 2). To refuse would risk the dealer's business relationship with its client, and perhaps its market reputation as a reliable counterparty. Indeed, dealers may hedge with matched shares precisely because doing so lets the swap dealer accommodate its client by un-

55. *See* New Zealand Securities Markets Act 1988, 1988 S.N.Z. Nos. 2, 5, 20–22.
56. *Ithaca (Custodians)*, [2004] 1 N.Z.L.R. 731, at ¶ 66.

winding the swap or voting the shares if needed. The Code Committee of the U.K.'s Panel on Takeovers and Mergers recently explained that it is "frequently the expectation" of a long equity swap holder that the derivatives dealer would "ensure" that the shares are available to be voted by its customer and/or sold to the customer on closing out the contract.[57] If the dealer hedged in another way, the holder would "normally expect" the dealer to acquire the necessary shares, even if this resulted in cost to the dealer.[58]

Market expectation that a dealer will unwind a swap, however, is not a guarantee. A 2006 buyout offer by Sears Holdings for the minority shares in its Sears Canada subsidiary, illustrates this.[59] A hedge fund acquired equity swaps in Sears Canada from Scotiabank. A unit of Scotiabank later became the dealer-manager for Sears Holdings' buyout offer. The offer required approval by a majority of the Sears Canada minority shareholders. The bid was opposed by Sears Canada's independent directors and by many Sears Canada shareholders. The hedge fund (presumably) thought it had morphable voting rights and asked Scotiabank to unwind the swap so it could vote against the offer. Scotiabank not only refused but committed to vote its Sears Canada shares *for* the offer. Scotiabank thus became an empty voter; perhaps with negative economic interest because of its relationships with Sears Holdings and Sears Canada. Another possible characterization is to see Sears Holdings as the empty voter, voting indirectly through its influence over Scotia Bank. The hedge fund complained about Scotiabank's failure to observe market conventions and said it was "looking forward to regulatory and legal scrutiny of this transaction."[60]

2. Other Uses of Hidden Ownership

An additional use of hidden ownership involves avoiding mandatory bid rules. In many countries, a shareholder who acquires more than a specified percentage of a company's shares must offer to buy all other shares at a formula price. Holding equity swaps instead of shares can let a shareholder avoid these rules.

In 2005, for example, the Agnelli family, which controlled Fiat, quietly entered into equity swaps for Fiat shares with Merrill Lynch.[61] The family wanted to retain

---

57. *See* Code Comm., Panel on Takeovers and Mergers, *Consultation Paper, Dealings in Derivatives and Options: Outline Proposals relating to Amendments Proposed to be Made to The Takeover Code and the SARS*, ¶ 3.3 (PCP 2005/1 Issued on Jan. 7, 2005), *available at* http://www.simmons-simmons.com/index.cfm?fuseaction = takeover.display&page = 1868.

58. *Id.* For a U.S. example where a customer was unhappy enough that Citibank had hedged equity swaps in a manner that the client had not expected to bring a suit, see Caiola v. Citibank, N.A., New York, 295 F.3d 312 (2d Cir. 2002).

59. *See* Jesse Eisinger, *In Canada, A Face-Off Over Sears*, WALL ST. J., Apr. 12, 2006, at C1.

60. *Id.*

61. On the Agnelli-Fiat transactions, see *IFIL-Exor Investigation Merrill Lynch Milan HQ Searched*, IL SOLE 24 ORE, Mar. 10, 2006 (IFIL is the Agnelli family vehicle that acquired the swaps); *IFIL Receives Consolb Equity Swap Report*, IL SOLE 24 ORE, Feb. 23, 2006; *Italian Stock Market Regulator Rules Against IFIL in Fiat Case*, WORLD MARKETS ANALYSIS, Feb. 23, 2006; *Italy's Consob Rules IFIL Not Obliged to Bid for Fiat, but Swap Deal Probed*, AFX INTERNATIONAL FOCUS, Feb. 8, 2006; *Still in the driving seat—Italian finance*, ECONOMIST, Oct. 15, 2005; *Three Investigated in IFIL-Exor Equity Swap Affair*, IL SOLE 24 ORE, Feb. 25, 2006.

control of Fiat after dilution of its stake through a forthcoming debt-for-equity swap, in which Fiat would issue shares to various banks. If the Agnelli family had bought shares directly, it would have crossed a 30% ownership threshold, thus triggering Italy's the mandatory bid rule. The Agnellis also would have had to disclose their purchases, which could have affected Fiat's share price. After Fiat completed its debt-equity swap, the Agnelli family unwound the swaps and obtained the "matched" Fiat shares. The Italian securities commission ruled that the Agnellis did not violate the mandatory bid rule; it is still investigating the propriety of nondisclosure.

Avoiding a mandatory bid rule also animated the earliest example of decoupling we are aware of. In 1997, Brierley Investments used equity swaps to increase its stake in John Fairfax Holdings from 19.98% to 25%.[62] If Brierley had acquired more than 20% of the shares, it would have had to offer to buy all of the Fairfax shares. Unlike the Agnellis, Brierley disclosed its swap position to market participants; it merely sought (successfully) to evade Australia's mandatory bid rule.

The Agnellis had a second goal—to acquire shares more cheaply, by evading large shareholder disclosure rules. This theme emerged as well in Australia, during the 2005 takeover bid by Centennial for Austral Coal.[63] Rival Glencore acquired a "blocking position" (sufficient to prevent Centennial from reaching 90% ownership and then squeezing out remaining shareholders), through a combination of shares and equity swaps (which the derivatives dealers hedged with matched shares). Glencore claimed that the equity swaps did not need to be disclosed under Australia's large shareholder disclosure rules (which are triggered by 5% share ownership), and disclosed its combined position only after crossing 10%. The Australian Takeovers Panel held that Glencore should have disclosed its combined position when its economic ownership crossed 5% and assessed damages based on Glencore's estimated savings from purchasing its full stake prior to disclosure. However, the Panel's decision was reversed on appeal by the Australian courts.

Hidden ownership may not always be undesirable from the standpoint of corporate governance. For instance, consider the possible use use of hidden ownership to obtain a "toehold" stake in a target company in advance of a takeover proposal. An unresolved puzzle in finance is why more takeover bidders do not acquire toeholds, since doing so would appear to be highly profitable.[64] The usual

62. *See* Louise McCoach, The Glencore Decision: A Case for Reform? (Nov. 2005) (unpublished manuscript, on file with authors); Louise McCoach, The Glencore Decision: A Case for Reform? An Update? (Feb. 2006) (unpublished manuscript, on file with authors).

63. Our discussion of Austral Coal is based on Nigel Morris, Dir., Takeovers Panel, Austral Coal Ltd. 02, Decision and Review Application (July 1, 2005), *available at* http://www.takeovers.gov.au/display.asp?ContentID=956 [hereinafter "*Austral Coal Takeovers Panel Decision*"]; Glencore International AG v. Takeovers Panel [2006] FCA 274 (Mar. 22, 2006) [hereinafter "*Austral Coal Federal Court of Australia Decision*"].

64. *See, e.g.*, Arturo Bris, *Toeholds, Takeover Premium, and the Probability of Being Acquired*, 8 J CORP. FIN. 227 (2002); Sandra Betton & B. Espen Eckbo, *Toeholds, Bid Jumps, and Expected Payoffs in Takeovers*, 13 REV. FIN. STUD. 841 (2000).

explanations are concern about prompting a price run-up, which could increase total acquisition cost, and concern that target knowledge of the toehold may make bidder resistance more likely. An equity swap offers a quiet toehold that need not be disclosed. Nondisclosure might reduce market impact cost, or simply avoid bidder resistance. In Australia, for example, BHP Billiton, before announcing a 2004 bid for WMC, acquired a 4.3% toehold through equity swaps.[65] BHP disclosed its toehold before crossing the 5% threshold at which a direct share position had to be disclosed. Its reasons for acquiring swaps rather than shares are not known. Perhaps it wanted to preserve the possibility of acquiring more than 5% before disclosing its position.

D. Related Non-Host Assets

We consider here some complexities that can arise when related non-host assets form part of a shareholder's overall economic interest.

1. Mergers

One recurring situation involving related non-host assets is a proposed merger. We have already seen several examples, including Perry-Mylan, AXA-MONY, and Hewlett Packard-Compaq, where the empty voter had a limited or negative overall economic interest in the acquirer. But economic ownership in both bidder and target can also increase a shareholder's economic interest, and thus reduce the collective action problems that often lead to shareholder passivity when an acquirer proposes an overpriced acquisition.

Actions by hedge funds to oppose Deutsche Boerse's proposed acquisition of the London Stock Exchange (LSE) illustrate. In December 2004, Deutsche Boerse proposed buying the LSE.[66] In January 2005, two hedge funds (Children's Investment Fund and Atticus Capital), together holding 8% of Deutsche Boerse's shares, publicly opposed the bid as against shareholder interests. (We cannot resist noting that the head of Children's Investment Fund is a Perry alumnus.[67]) The acquisition was eventually abandoned. What connects this story to vote buying is that certain hedge funds—perhaps including these two funds—shorted a significant number of LSE shares soon after the opposition was announced. Let us

65. Andrew Trounson, *BHP Bid for the Long Haul—Xstrata Outgunned in Showdown for WMC*, AUSTRALIAN, Mar. 9, 2005, at 35; Bryan Frith, *Cunning Predators Hide Behind Swaps*, AUSTRALIAN, Mar. 11, 2005, at 18.

66. Our discussion relies on Norma Cohen and Patrick Jenkins, *D Borse Acts to Heal TCI Rift*, FIN. TIMES, Apr. 21, 2005, at 25; *Winners and Losers: CEO Werner Seifert Sheds Some Light on the Reasons Why Deutsche Borse Decided to Drop its £1.3 Billion Bid for the London Stock Exchange*, GUARDIAN, Mar. 14, 2005, at 11; Norma Cohen, *Investors Warn D Borse Board*, FIN. TIMES, Feb. 22, 2005, at 21; William Hutchings, *Deutsche Boerse Affair Shows Way Ahead*, EFINANCIALNEWS.COM, Jan. 23, 2005; *Seifert's Second Proposal*, ECONOMIST, Dec. 18, 2004; Silvia Ascarelli, *A Market Marriage in Europe? Deutsche Boerse's Courtship of London Exchange May Elicit a Rival*, WALL ST. J., Dec. 14, 2004, at C18.

67. *See* Jason Singer, *Ivy Leave: Yale Parts Ways With Hedge Fund*, WALL ST. J., Mar. 29, 2006, at C1.

assume that some hedge funds went long Deutsche Boerse and short LSE, thus betting that the acquisition would fail—causing Deutsche Boerse shares to rise and LSE shares to fall. The LSE short positions would increase the hedge funds' net economic interest in the Deutsche Boerse vote, and might make it cost-justified for them to undertake a public campaign against the acquisition.

However, other combined Deutsche Boerse-LSE positions could have the opposite effect. For example, merger arbitrageurs who follow the "classic" strategy of betting on completion of a stock-for-stock merger by going long the target and short the acquirer (the opposite of the posited CIF and Atticus strategy) have an incentive to support a merger, even if it was bad for the acquirer or the combined firms. Thus, ownership of related non-host assets could, at the same time, empower CIF and Atticus to pressure Deutsche Boerse to make a "good" decision, and empower classic merger arbitrageurs to support deal completion regardless of the merits.

In a merger situation, it is not much of a stretch to imagine a subterranean battle for votes among investors with differing overall economic interests. In such a battle, the voting outcome might not reflect the acquisition's expected value to the acquirer, the target, or both companies together. The outcomes in Henderson Investments and Sears Canada were apparently altered by new vote buying; vote buying may also have been outcome-determinative in AXA-MONY and Hewlett Packard-Compaq, though no one knows for sure (at least not publicly).

2. Indirect Hedges

Other plausible related non-host assets can exist, in addition to positions in the other party to a takeover bid. The essential characteristic of a related asset is that its value relate in some way to the value of host shares. Thus, an executive at Ford who is concerned about the future of Ford and other American car companies, might buy put options on shares of General Motors or a Ford supplier, rather than put options on Ford (which would raise legal and perception issues).[68]

E. The Extent of New Vote Buying

Table 2 lists all publicly disclosed (or in some cases rumored) decoupling examples that we have been able to find, in rough reverse chronological order. The list suggests the potential scale of decoupling, while the dates suggest its recent advent. Other evidence, including data on executive hedging and record date capture, suggest that the new vote buying is reasonably common.[69]

68. On the related question of whether executives can use such substitutes without running afoul of insider trading laws, see Ian Ayres & Joseph Bankman, *Substitutes for Insider Trading*, 54 STAN. L. REV. 235 (2001).

69. *See* Hu & Black, *The New Vote Buying*, *supra* note 24, at 846–47.

Table 2. Decoupling Examples

This table lists, roughly in reverse chronological order, the known (or publicly rumored) instances of new vote buying we were able to collect. The list is surely partial: if readers know of instances not on this list, we would be grateful to learn of them.

Date	Host Company	Country	Vote Buyer	Empty Voting	Hidden (Morphable) Ownership	Coupled Asset or Related Non-Host Asset	Description	Source
2006	Sears Canada	Canada	hedge fund (Bill Ackman) and Scotiabank	X (by Scotiabank)	X (by Ackman's hedge fund: unsuccessful)	equity swap	See Part II.C	
2006	Henderson Investment	Hong Kong	hedge fund(s)	X	X (short position)	share borrowing + short sale	See Part II.B	
2005	Fiat	Italy	Agnelli family		X	equity swaps	See Part II.C	
2005	Austral Coal	Australia	Glencore		X	equity swaps	See Part IV.B	
2005	Fuji TV	Japan	Nippon Broadcasting		X	stock lending	Nippon lent its shares in Fuji TV to others as a defense to a takeover bid by Livedoor, producing a variant of hidden (morphable) ownership in which Nippon had economic ownership, but hoped to *deny* voting rights to Livedoor	70
2005	Deutsche Boerse	Germany	hedge funds	X		short sale of target shares	See Part II.D	
2005	Portman Mining	Australia	Seneca (hedge fund)		X	equity swaps	Seneca held 9% economic interest in Portman through equity swaps provided by CSFB.	71
2004–2005	WMC Resources	Australia	BHP Billiton		X	equity swaps	See Part II.C	

(*continued overleaf*)

70. *See, e.g.*, Kyodo News Service, *Japan: Investment Firm becomes Fuji TV's Largest Shareholder*, BBC Monitoring Media, Mar. 24, 2005; David Pilling, *White Knight New Villain of Fuji TV Saga*, Fin. Times, Mar. 28, 2005, at 1; Martin Foster, *Livedoor Suffers Blow in Bid*, Daily Deal, Mar. 25, 2005; *Softbank to Return Fuji Shares*, Daily Yomiuri (Tokyo), Apr. 23, 2005, at 8; Michiyo Nakamoto, *Historic Battle Establishes Combat Rules*, Fin. Times, June 27, 2005, at 5 (FT Report); Nippon Broadcasting, *Softbank Investment End Fuji TV Stock Loan Deal*, AFX–Asia, June 30, 2005. The defense was successful. Livedoor and Fuji TV agreed to a partnership, and Livedoor ended its effort to acquire Nippon. One borrower (Softbank) promptly returned the Fuji shares to Nippon; we have not found news reports discussing whether the other borrower (Daiwa Securities) also returned its borrowed shares.

71. *See* Bryan Frith, *Portman trading should be reviewed*, Australian, Mar. 4, 2005, at 22.

(continued)

Date	Host Company	Country	Vote Buyer	Empty Voting	Hidden (Morph-able) Ownership	Coupled Asset or Related Non-Host Asset	Description	Source
2004–2005	Mylan Laboratories	U.S.	Perry Corp. (hedge fund)	X		equity swaps	See Part II.B	
			Citadel (hedge fund) (possible)	X		unknown		
2004	DFS	U.K.	Polygon (hedge fund)		X	equity swaps	Polygon sought to influence DFS despite owning only one share of stock (it had 3% economic ownership through equity swaps).	72
2004	Alvis	U.K.	Hedge funds (helping BAe Systems to acquire Alvis)		X	equity swap	BAe Systems obtained commitments from hedge funds with equity swap positions in Alvis to either obtain shares or direct the voting of shares to support BAe's offer	73
2004	Marks & Spencer	U.K.	Hedge funds (helping Philip Green to acquire Marks & Spencer)		X	equity swap	Green announced support by 8.3% of target shares held by derivatives dealers as "matched shares" to support equity swaps	74
2004	Canary Wharf	U.K.	"Songbird" consortium (seeking to acquire Canary Wharf)		X	equity swaps	derivatives dealer UBS held 7.7% of Canary as matched shares to support equity swaps	75
2004	MONY Group	U.S.	holders and short sellers of AXA convertible bonds	X		convertible bonds of acquirer (AXA)	See Part II.D	

72. *See* Richard Fletcher, *US hedge fund builds up large stake in DFS*, SUNDAY TIMES (LONDON), Aug. 22, 2004.

73. *See* Panel on Takeovers and Mergers, *Consultation Paper Issued by the Code Committee of the Panel—Dealings in Derivatives and Options: Outline Proposals relating to Amendments Proposed to be Made to The Takeover Code and the SARS*, ¶ 3.3–3.4 (PCP 2005/1 Issued on Jan. 7, 2005), *available at* http://www.simmons-simmons.com/index.cfm?fuseaction = takeover.display&page = 1868.

74. *See* U.K. Takeover Panel, *January 2005 Proposal*, *supra* note 73, at § 3.4(b); Jeremy Warner, *Outlook: Uncharted Waters*, INDEPENDENT, July 14, 2004.

75. *See, e.g.*, Martin Dickson, *The secret City battle over Canary Wharf*, FIN. TIMES, Apr. 24, 2004; Linda Saigol, *UBS wins Takeover Panel appeal over Canary Vote*, FIN. TIMES, Apr. 24, 2004.

Date	Host Company	Country	Vote Buyer	Empty Voting	Hidden (Morph-able) Ownership	Coupled Asset or Related Non-Host Asset	Description	Source
2004	News Corp.	Australia & U.S.	Liberty Media	X	Hidden: yes Morphable: maybe	forward contract and equity swap	Liberty Media held voting and nonvoting News Corp. shares, also used derivatives to adjust its economic exposure	76
2002	P&O Princess	U.K.	Investors (favor Carnival bid for P&O Princess)	X	maybe	share borrowing	P&O shareholders who favored Carnival's bid reportedly borrowed shares in order to vote for acceptance	77
2002	Hewlett-Packard	U.S.	holders of Compaq shares (target of H-P merger bid)	X		target shares	See Part II.B	
2002	Coles Myer	Australia	Solomon Lew (proxy contestant)	X	no	options	See Part II.B	
2002	British Land	U.K.	Laxey Partners	X		share borrowing	See Part II.B	
2001	Rubicon	New Zealand	Perry Corp.		X	equity swaps	See Part II.C	
1997	John Fairfax Holdings	Australia	Brierley Investments			equity swaps	See Part II.C	

III. Current Ownership Disclosure Rules

A. General Considerations

We turn now to how current ownership disclosure rules treat the new vote buying. This Part III addresses the extent to which these rules require disclosure of empty voting or hidden ownership. Part IV presents our integrated disclosure reform proposal, which would require disclosure of both economic and voting

76. *See* Liberty Media Corporation, Schedule 13D as to The News Corporation Limited (Jan. 21, 2004), *available at* http://www.sec.gov/Archives/edgar/data/788509/000110465904001378/a04-1434_1sc13d.htm and (Amendment No. 1 to this Schedule (Nov. 12, 2004), *available at* http://www.sec.gov/Archives/edgar/data/788509/000104746904034156/a2146699zsc13da.htm; *Q3 2004 Liberty Media Group Earnings Conference Call—Final*, FD (Fair Disclosure) Business Wire, Nov. 9, 2004; US, *Liberty Media Corporation Announces Early Termination of Total Return Swap With Merrill Lynch,* PR Newswire (Dec. 20, 2004); Tim Burt, *Prince Pledges to Aid Murdoch*, Fin. Times, Nov. 18, 2004, at 32; Geraldine Fabrikant, *In Surprise, Liberty Media Fattens Stake in News Corp.*, N.Y. Times, Jan. 22, 2004, at C1; Geraldine Fabrikant, *Liberty Media Fuels Speculation By Adding to News Corp. Stake*, N.Y. Times, Jan. 23, 2004, at C3; Martin Peers, *News Corp.'s Net Increases by 27% on TV Strength—Liberty Media Gains Right to Boost Its Voting Stake in Murdoch-Led Concern*, Wall St. J., Nov. 4, 2004, at B3; Martin Peers, *News Corp. Offers About $5.7 Billion To Buy Rest of Fox*, Wall St. J., Jan. 11, 2005, at C4; *Why Liberty Halted Its 'Forward' Pass; Sale of 19 Million Shares Is Scrapped to Simply Structure, Show Faith in News*, Multichannel News, Sept. 26, 2005.

77. *See* Bank of England, Stock Lending and Repurchase Committee, Summary of Dec. 11, 2002 Meeting, *available at* http://www.bankofengland.co.uk/markets/gilts/slrcdec02.pdf.

ownership. Part V discusses additional possible steps for regulating empty voting. We are not yet ready to advocate taking any of these additional steps, but setting out a menu of regulatory choices may still prove helpful in the long run.

Currently there are five discrete ownership disclosure systems: for active 5% shareholders on Schedule 13D,[78] passive 5% shareholders on Schedule 13G,[79] institutional investors on Form 13F,[80] insiders and 10% shareholders under Section 16,[81] and mutual funds.[82] These systems, taken together, are bewilderingly complex. Different rules often apply in determining what triggers the disclosure requirements and what must be disclosed once the disclosure requirements have been triggered. Economically identical situations are often treated differently, depending on how an investor achieves a particular combination of voting and economic ownership. Positions involving OTC derivatives often escape disclosure, when an equivalent position involving exchange-traded derivatives would be disclosed. Ownership of call options sometimes requires disclosure, but (the nearly equivalent) sale of put options does not. And so on. A derivatives-savvy hedge fund can often avoid disclosure.

Table 3 summarizes the current ownership disclosure requirements. The complexity and illogic of the current rules is immediately apparent.

78. 17 C.F.R. § 240.13d-101 (2005).
79. 17 C.F.R. § 240.13d-102 (2005).
80. 17 C.F.R. §§ 240.13f-1, 249.325 (2005).
81. Exchange Act § 16 is codified as amended at 15 U.S.C. § 78p (2000 & Supp. III 2003).
82. *See infra* note 119.

Table 3. Current Ownership Disclosure Requirements Relating to New Vote Buying

This table summarizes how long positions in shares or equivalents, short positions in shares or equivalents, and stock lending and borrowing are treated under current U.S. ownership disclosure rules. The table addresses separately the use of long and short positions in shares and equivalents to *trigger* a reporting obligation, and the need to disclose these positions if a reporting obligation exists.

<table>
<tr><th></th><th></th><th colspan="4">Long Positions</th><th colspan="6">Short Positions</th><th colspan="2">Stock Lending and Borrowing</th></tr>
<tr><th></th><th></th><th colspan="2">As Trigger</th><th colspan="2">If Filing Required</th><th colspan="3">As Trigger</th><th colspan="3">If Filing Required</th><th colspan="2"></th></tr>
<tr><th>Reporting Scheme</th><th>Reporting Frequency</th><th>Equity Swaps; other OTC Derivatives</th><th>Shares and Exchange-traded Derivatives</th><th>Equity Swaps; other OTC Derivatives</th><th>Shares and Exchange-traded Derivatives</th><th>Equity Swaps; other OTC Derivatives</th><th>Exchange-traded Derivatives</th><th>Short Sales</th><th>Equity Swaps; other OTC Derivatives</th><th>Exchange-traded Derivatives</th><th>Short Sales</th><th>Lending</th><th>Borrowing</th></tr>
<tr><td>13D</td><td>current</td><td>generally no</td><td>yes</td><td>partial</td><td>yes</td><td>no</td><td>yes</td><td>no</td><td>partial</td><td>yes</td><td>partial</td><td>unclear</td><td>yes</td></tr>
<tr><td>13G</td><td>annual</td><td>generally no</td><td>yes (if held on reporting date)</td><td>no</td><td>yes</td><td>no</td><td>yes (if held on reporting date)</td><td>no</td><td>no</td><td>yes</td><td>no</td><td>no</td><td>yes (if held on reporting date</td></tr>
<tr><td>13F</td><td>quarterly</td><td colspan="2">status-based: $100M in 13F securities</td><td>no</td><td>partial</td><td colspan="3">status-based: $100M in 13F securities</td><td>no</td><td>partial</td><td>no</td><td colspan="2">no</td></tr>
<tr><td>Section 16 (director or officer)</td><td rowspan="2">current</td><td colspan="2">status-based</td><td colspan="2" rowspan="2">yes</td><td colspan="2">status-based</td><td rowspan="2">banned by Section 16(c)</td><td colspan="2" rowspan="2">yes</td><td rowspan="2">banned by Section 16(c)</td><td rowspan="2">probably no</td><td>probably no</td></tr>
<tr><td>Section 16 (10% holder)</td><td>generally no</td><td>yes</td><td colspan="2">no</td><td>yes (as trigger); probably no (in disclosure)</td></tr>
<tr><td>mutual funds</td><td>quarterly</td><td colspan="2">yes</td><td colspan="2">yes</td><td colspan="3">yes</td><td colspan="3">yes</td><td colspan="2">no (except by implication from disclosure of short sales)</td></tr>
</table>

B. Existing Disclosure Requirements

We review here the current disclosure requirements that affect the new vote buying. To avoid clutter that might obscure our main themes, we gloss over some complexities. Thus, our discussion should be understood as roughly but not wholly accurate. Outside investors, including hedge funds, are governed by large shareholder rules—any shareholder holding a 5% stake in a public company must make a Schedule 13D or 13G filing.[83] Institutional investors, including hedge funds, are also subject to status-based disclosure rules: an investment manager holding $100 million or more in U.S. equities must disclosure its holdings every quarter on Form 13F.[84] Corporate directors, officers, and 10% shareholders are also subject to separate disclosure of ownership on Forms 3, 4, or 5 under Section 16.[85] Finally, mutual funds must list all portfolio positions quarterly, and break down their holdings into various categories.[86]

1. Large Shareholder Disclosure (Schedules 13D and 13G)

a. Basic Requirements

Any person who "directly or indirectly" acquires "beneficial ownership" of more than 5% of a public company's shares is generally required to file Schedule 13D with the SEC within 10 days after crossing the 5% threshold.[87] Certain types of institutional investors who invest "passively" (in the ordinary course of business and without intent to influence control) and own between 5% and 20% of a company's shares can instead file a more abbreviated Schedule 13G (generally on February 15 of each year, reporting year-end positions with a 45-day lag).[88] Both Schedules are publicly available.

For both Schedules, disclosure is based on "beneficial ownership" of shares, as defined by Rule 13d-3. The focus is on sole or shared voting or investment power, which can be held "directly or indirectly, through any contract, arrangement, understanding, relationship, or otherwise." Beneficial ownership of shares includes "the right to acquire beneficial ownership . . . within sixty days, including . . . through the exercise of any option [or] warrant." The SEC seeks to discourage

83. *See* Exchange Act § 13(d), (g) (codified as amended at 15 U.S.C. §§ 78m(d), 78m(g) (2000 & Supp. III 2003)); SEC Rules 13d-1–13d-7, 17 C.F.R.§§ 240.13d-1–13d-7 (2005); SEC Schedules 13D, 13G, 17 C.F.R. §§ 240.13d-101–102 (2005).

84. *See* Exchange Act § 13(f) (codified as amended at 15 U.S.C. § 78m(f) (2000 & Supp. III 2003)); SEC Rule 13f-1, 17 C.F.R. § 240.13f-1 (2005); *Form 13F*, *supra* note 16.

85. *See* Exchange Act § 16 (codified as amended at 15 U.S.C. § 78p (2000); SEC Rules 16a-1–16e-1, 17 C.F.R. § 240.16a-1–16e-1 (2005); SEC Form 3: SEC Initial Statement of Beneficial Ownership of Securities, *available at* http://www.sec.gov/about/forms/form3.pdf [hereinafter "*SEC Form 3*"], Form 4: Statement of Changes in Beneficial Ownership, *available at* http://www.sec.gov/about/forms/form4.pdf [hereinafter "*SEC Form 4*"], and Form 5: Annual Statement of Changes in Beneficial Ownership of Securities, *available at* http://www.sec.gov/about/forms/form5.pdf [hereinafter "*SEC Form 5*"], OMB Nos. 3235-0104, 3235-0287, 3235-0362.

86. *See infra* Part III.B.4.

87. Rule 13d-1(a), 17 C.F.R. §§ 240.13d-1(a) (2005).

88. Rule 13d-1(b), 17 C.F.R. § 240.13d-1(b) (2005). When ownership first exceeds 10%, Schedule 13G must be filed by the 10th day of the next month.

gaming by providing that any person who uses any "contract, arrangement, or device" to evade the 13(d) reporting requirements is deemed to be a beneficial owner.[89]

Both Schedules require disclosure of the number and percentage of the shares beneficially owned, and any purchases or sales within the past 60 days.[90] Item 6 of Schedule 13D—which has no counterpart in Schedule 13G—also requires disclosure of "any contracts, arrangements, understandings or relationships (legal or otherwise)" relating to any securities of the issuer[91] as well as filing of certain related "written agreements" as exhibits. The scope of the exhibit requirement is not entirely clear. Short positions, whether in shares or derivatives, do not trigger disclosure. If disclosure is triggered by a large long position, some disclosure is required for partially offsetting short positions.

How Schedules 13D and 13G treat share lending and borrowing is unclear. Borrowing (which provides voting power) would likely both count toward triggering disclosure and be disclosable on both forms. However, as a practical matter, record date capture without a control intent is unlikely to be captured by Schedule 13G, because few record dates will fall around the year-end reporting date. Share lending might be disclosable on Item 6 of Schedule 13D, but is likely not disclosable on Schedule 13G.

b. Application to Hidden Ownership

Consider now whether the 13D and 13G rules would capture hidden (morphable) ownership. We will use Perry-Rubicon as an example. Perry held just under 5% of Rubicon's shares, plus equity swaps conveying an additional 11% economic ownership. Its equity swaps, by themselves, seem unlikely to trigger disclosure. They were cash-settled, and thus did not convey the right to acquire shares. Perry's equity swap position might be caught by the "arrangement, understanding, or relationship (legal or otherwise)" language in Rule 13d-3. This would depend on whether Perry had a sufficiently firm expectation that it could terminate the swaps and obtain shares from the derivatives dealers at any time. On this point, there is no clear guidance in SEC rules or no-action letters. Practitioners at law firms prominent in the OTC derivatives market have stated that in their view, disclosure of cash-settled equity swaps is normally not required. A partner at Allen & Overy, the primary outside law firm of the International Swaps and Derivatives Association (the main trade association for the OTC derivatives industry), has so stated.[92] Similarly, partners at Cleary Gottlieb have written that "a long position under an

89. Rule 13d-3, 17 C.F.R. § 240.13d-3 (2005).

90. Schedule 13D, Item 5, 17 C.F.R. § 240.13d-101 (2005); Schedule 13G, Item 4, 17 C.F.R. § 240.13d-102 (2005).

91. Schedule 13D, Item 6, 17 C.F.R. § 240.13d-101 (2005).

92. Chin-chong Liew, *Disclosure Requirements for Purely Cash-Settled Derivatives*, HONG KONG LAWYER, June 2000, *available at* http://www.hk-lawyer.com/2000-6/June00-59.htm.

equity swap would generally not be treated as beneficial ownership" under Rule 13d-3.[93]

The non-disclosure of cash-settled equity swaps can be questioned, if one looks beyond the swap itself to the economic dynamic surrounding it. The derivatives dealer that enters into the swap will almost surely want to hedge its exposure. A principal way to hedge is to hold matched shares. This was especially likely in Perry-Rubicon because Perry initiated the swap by selling Rubicon shares to Deutsche Bank and UBS Warburg. Thus, there was an excellent chance that Perry could return to its dealers, pretty much whenever it chose, and exchange its swap position for shares, even without a prior discussion with its dealers.[94] Is this a sufficient "arrangement, understanding, or relationship (legal or otherwise)," to trigger disclosure, especially in light of the extension of beneficial ownership to any person who uses any "arrangement, or device" to evade reporting?

Perry claimed not under New Zealand's rules, which are similar to U.S. rules. It lost at trial and won on appeal. Glencore similarly lost a similar argument before the Australian Takeover Panel in 2005 under Australia's similar ownership disclosure rules,[95] but the Panel's decision was reversed on appeal by the Federal Court of Australia.[96]

c. Application to Empty Voting

Consider next how Schedules 13D and 13G affect empty voting, using Perry-Mylan as an example. If Perry held less than 5% of Mylan, disclosure would not be triggered. Perry chose, however, to acquire 9.9% of Mylan's shares. Had Schedule 13G been available, no disclosure of the hedges would have been needed, and the Schedule 13G filing could be delayed until Feb. 15 of the next year. Perry initially took the position that Schedule 13G was available, and filed a Schedule 13D only after Icahn filed his own Schedule 13D, indicating an intent to acquire control of Mylan, a step that Perry opposed.[97] Perry's view that its own intent to support the merger did not involve a control intent might be debatable. But assume a Schedule 13D filing was required. What did Perry have to disclose about the hedges that offset its direct economic ownership?

Not much, or so Perry and its counsel decided. Item 6 of Schedule 13D requires disclosure of "any contracts, arrangements, understandings or relationships" re-

93. 2 Edward F. Greene, Edward J. Rosen, Leslie N. Silverman, Daniel A. Braverman & Sebastian R. Sperber, U.S. Regulation of the International Securities and Derivatives Markets § 13.02[2] n.25 (2004).

94. See the discussion of Perry-Rubicon in Part II.C *supra*. Access to the dealers' matched shares is not a certainty; the hedge fund in the Sears Canada situation, discussed in Part II.C *supra*, was surprised to find its dealer less accommodating than it had expected.

95. *See Austral Coal Takeovers Panel Decision*, *supra* note 63. The Takeovers Panel based this decision on the policy concerns underlying the large shareholder disclosure rules, rather than on the specific language of the statute.

96. *See Austral Coal Federal Court of Australia Decision*, *supra* note 63.

97. *See* Neil Whoriskey & Brandon W. Gardner, *Arbitrage in an M&A Context—Issues Raised by the* Mylan *Case*, M&A Report, Sept. 2005, at 15, *available at* http://www.cgsh.com/files/tbl_s47Details%5CFileUpload265%5C498%5CCGSH_MA_Newsletter_Sept2005.pdf.

lating to Mylan shares. Perry duly said that it had engaged in "security-based swap agreements" and other "hedging transactions" and that "to execute . . . certain hedging transactions," it had entered into stock loan transactions with Bear Stearns and Goldman, Sachs. But Perry disclosed neither the terms of the hedges nor the number of shares to which they pertained.

Consider finally the scenario in which an investor holds a stake in both acquirer and target, which affects its overall economic interest in the acquirer. Deutsche Boerse/LSE and HP-Compaq, discussed in Part II, provide examples. Assume that a hedge fund owns over 5% of a host company: must it disclose its position in the target's shares? Here the answer is clear—no disclosure is required by either Schedule 13D or 13G. For example, Item 6 of Schedule 13D requires disclosure of contracts or arrangements with respect to "any securities *of the issuer*" (emphasis added).

In sum, Schedules 13D and 13G provide only limited disclosure of the existence and nature of the new vote buying. One can quibble with level of detail that Perry provided, its initial decision that Schedule 13G was available, and its failure to attach the hedging agreements as exhibits to its 13D filing.[98] But from a policy perspective, picking at the language of disclosure rules that weren't written with empty voting in mind is beside the point. The real problem is that the 13D and 13G rules were written in the 1970s, when options markets were in their infancy and neither swaps nor other OTC derivatives existed.

2. Reporting by Institutional Money Managers (Form 13F)

The third ownership disclosure regime is under Section 13(f) of the Exchange Act ("Section 13(f)"). Institutional money managers must disclose their holdings at the end of each quarter by filing Form 13F with the SEC.[99] Form 13F, like Schedule 13G, is filed with a 45-day delay. For new vote buying, Form 13F offers little help. It requires disclosure of holdings of "section 13(f) securities" by every "institutional investment manager" who holds $100 million or more in these securities.[100] The term "institutional investment manager" is defined broadly to include (a) any person, other than a natural person, who invests in or buys or sells for its own account; and (b) any person, whether or not a natural person, who exercises investment discretion with respect to the account of any other person.[101] This captures hedge funds (whether located in the U.S. or offshore) but not Joe

98. Item 7 of Schedule 13D requires filing of "all written agreements, contracts, arrangements, understandings, plans or proposals relating to . . . (3) the transfer or voting of the securities, finder's fees, joint ventures, options, puts, calls, guarantees of loans, guarantees against loss or of profit, or the giving or withholding of any proxy as disclosed in Item 6." 17 C.F.R. § 240.13d-101 (2005). Perry's counsel presumably decided that its hedges were none of these.

99. The filings are publicly available. A manager may request confidential treatment, but only under narrow circumstances, and the SEC does not often grant such requests. *See Form 13F*, *supra* note 16, Instructions For Confidential Treatment Requests.

100. *See* Exchange Act §§ 13(f)(1), 13(f)(5)(A) (codified as amended at 15 U.S.C. §§ 78m(f)(1), (f)(5)(A) (2000 & Supp. III 2003)); Exchange Act Rule 13f-1, 17 C.F.R. § 240.13f-1 (2005).

101. *See* Exchange Act § 13(f)(5)(A) (codified as amended at 15 U.S.C. § 78m(f)(5)(A) (2000 & Supp. III 2003)).

Zillionaire, unless he exercises investment discretion over the accounts of others.[102] "Section 13(f) securities" are publicly traded U.S. equity securities included in the SEC's "Official List of Section 13(f) Securities." This list includes common shares and exchange-traded options.[103] Anything not on the list need not be disclosed. Form 13F is also quite narrow in what it calls for. The "Information Table" at its heart is simply a list of each security the managers owns, its CUSIP number (a standard means for identifying publicly traded securities), its type (for instance, shares, puts, or calls), and the number of securities held.[104]

Critically, Form 13F requires no disclosure for securities that are not publicly traded, even if they are economically equivalent to disclosable securities. For instance, holdings of exchange traded options are disclosable, but OTC option positions are not. Even for exchange-traded options, money managers need not report options they have *written* rather than *bought*. Long share positions are reported; short positions are not. Indeed, a manager who holds 1,000,000 shares and has separately sold 500,000 short will report owning 1,000,000 shares, and never mention the short position.[105] If shares have been lent, the loan is ignored. The lender reports owning the shares, while the borrower reports nothing.[106]

Form 13F requires reporting of voting power, and whether it is sole or shared. However, if a manager has voting authority over "routine" matters and no authority for "non-routine" matters, it reports as if it had no voting authority. Non-routine matters include a "contested election of directors, a merger or sale of all or substantially all assets, a charter amendment affecting shareholders' rights, and a change in fundamental investment policy" while routine matters "include" selection of an accountant, uncontested election of directors, and approval of an annual report.[107]

Consider now how 13F affects hidden (morphable) ownership positions. These positions commonly rely on OTC derivatives, which are not disclosed. Indeed, one reason why hedge funds hold equity swaps and other OTC derivatives rather than shares is to hide their ownership from public view.

Form 13F fares little better for empty voting. Empty voting through share borrowing will never be seen. If an investor holds shares directly, while hedging its economic ownership, the direct ownership will be reported, its empty character will not. Moreover, it is usually a simple matter to hide a voting stake altogether. All the investor need do is shed its direct holdings before quarter end. For example,

102. *See* Exchange Act § 13(f)(1) (codified as amended at 15 U.S.C. § 78m(f)(1) (2000 & Supp. III 2003)); Securities and Exchange Commission Division of Investment Management, Frequently Asked Questions About Form 13F (Question 4) (May 2005), *available at* http://www.sec.gov/divisions/investment/13ffaq.htm [hereinafter "*SEC 13F FAQ*"]. For an example of the use of Form 13F information to track hedge fund trading, see Markus K. Brunnermeier & Stefan Nagel, *Hedge Funds and the Technology Bubble* (working paper 2003), *available at* http://ssrn.com/abstract=423940.

103. See Exchange Act Rule 13f-1(c), 17 C.F.R. §240.13f-1; *SEC Form 13F FAQ*, *supra* note 102.

104. *See* Form 13F, *supra* note 16, Special Instructions 9–12.

105. *See, e.g.*, *SEC Form 13F FAQ*, *supra* note 102, Question 4 ("You should not report short positions on Form 13F. You also should not subtract your short position(s) in a security from your long position(s) in that same security; report only the long position.").

106. *SEC Form 13F FAQ*, *supra* note 102, Question 42.

107. Form 13F, *supra* note 16, Special Instruction 12(b)(viii).

a hedge fund could, in effect, exchange its shares for equivalent swaps before quarter end, and then unwind the swaps and require shares soon afterwards.

3. Insider and 10% Shareholder Disclosure (Section 16)

The fourth principal source of disclosure is Section 16, which covers officers, directors, and 10% shareholders of U.S. public companies.[108] Section 16 rarely covers outside shareholders, who avoid crossing the 10% threshold, partly because doing so triggers recapture of "short-swing profits" from buying and selling (or selling and buying) within a 6-month period. Avoiding coverage is straightforward. The 10% threshold is based on "beneficial ownership" in the 13D sense.[109] Thus, if a cash-settled equity swap lets a hedge fund avoid "beneficial ownership" for 13D purposes, this same swap should also let the hedge fund avoid Section 16 disclosure.

If disclosure is required, the positions to be disclosed are based on "beneficial ownership" in the Section 16 sense, and is reasonably extensive. The 13D definition of beneficial ownership focuses on voting power. In contrast, the Section 16 definition focuses on economic ownership.[110] The relevant forms (Forms 3, 4, and 5) require disclosure of most economic interests, regardless of their form. An initial filing must be made on Form 3 and changes reported on Form 4. Form 5 is an annual statement of changes. All Forms are publicly available. Form 3 must be filed with the SEC within 10 days after the event which triggers coverage.[111] Equity derivatives, whether exchange traded or OTC, must be disclosed. These include:

> any option, warrant, convertible security, stock appreciation right, or similar right with an exercise or conversion privilege at a price related to an equity security, or similar securities with a value derived from the value of an equity security.[112]

This definition is quite broad. The derivative's value need not precisely track share value; disclosure is required as long as the derivative's value is "derived from the value of an equity security." There is an exception for "broad-based" index options, futures, and market baskets of stocks.[113] By implication, derivatives whose value is based on a narrow index are covered. Thus, some related *non-host* assets are covered by Section 16—albeit with ambiguity about which ones. There is no disclosure of short sales of shares, but no need for any, because short sales

108. *See* Rules 16a-1(a); 16a-2, 17 C.F.R. §§ 240.16a-1(a), 16a-2 (2005).

109. Rule 16a-1(a), 17 C.F.R. § 240.16a-1(a) (2005). Registered broker-dealers, banks, and certain other persons are exempt so long as they hold shares without the purpose or effect of changing or influencing control of the issuer or entering into an arrangement that would violate the anti-gaming provisions of Rule 13d-3(b), 17 C.F.R. § 240.13d-3(b) (2005).

110. Rule 16a-(2), 17 C.F.R. § 240.16a-2 (2005). For non-experts in securities law, yes, the SEC has indeed defined the same term—beneficial ownership—in two different ways, once under Exchange Act § 13(d) (codified as amended at 15 U.S.C. § 78m(d) (2000 & Supp. III 2003)) and once under § 16(b) (codified as amended at 15 U.S.C. § 78p(b) (2000 & Supp. III 2003)).

111. Rule 16a-3, 17 C.F.R. § 240.16a-3 (2005); *SEC Form 3*, *supra* note 85, General Instruction 3.

112. Rule 16a-1(c), 17 C.F.R. § 240.16a-1(c) (2005).

113. Exchange Act Rule 16a-1(c)(4), 17 C.F.R. § 240.16a-1(c)(4) (2005).

are banned outright by Section 16(c). The information required for each derivative is also extensive, and includes the title, exercise or conversion price, date exercisable, expiration date, and the title and amount of securities underlying the derivative security.[114] Changes in ownership are reported on Form 4 using specific transaction codes. For instance, "S" indicates a sale, "C" indicates conversion, "O" indicates exercise of an out-of-the-money derivative, "X" indicates exercise of an in-the-money or at-the-money security, "K" indicates an equity swap or similar security.[115]

Because Section 16 disclosure focuses on economic ownership, it is much less developed for voting ownership without economic ownership. It seems likely that few Section 16 filers report share borrowing or lending.[116] The SEC does not directly require this, there is no relevant transaction code, and we have not found any SEC or practitioner guidance even discussing this question. Economic ownership, the focus of Section 16, is not significantly changed by lending or borrowing, and voting rights do not easily fall within the term "pecuniary interests" under Section 16. In the parallel situation of a voting trust which has voting power but no economic ownership, the trust does not report share ownership.[117]

For hidden (morphable) ownership, then, Section 16 disclosure does a good job. For empty voting, disclosure likely depends on how the empty voter acquires its votes. Shares hedged with derivatives would be disclosed; share borrowing likely would not be.

4. Mutual Fund Reporting

The final set of reporting rules applies to mutual funds, which report to the SEC quarterly on their portfolio holdings (the filing is public), and provide a summary list semiannually to investors.[118] Disclosure focuses on economic ownership and covers both long and short positions. For options, disclosure includes value, exercise price, and maturity date. There are no rules on what details to report for equity swaps and other OTC derivatives, but our spot check of several

114. *SEC Form 3*, *supra* note 85, General Instruction 5(c)(iii).

115. *SEC Form 4*, *supra* note 85, General Instructions 1(a), 4(a), 8.

116. Share borrowings would, however, clearly count toward triggering disclosure by 10% shareholders, which is governed by the separate Section 13(d) rules.

117. *See, e.g.*, 16 ARNOLD S. JACOBS, SECTION 16 OF THE SECURITIES EXCHANGE ACT § 7.31 (2005). The lender's tax position does change slightly, due to tax differences between dividends and payments by the borrower in lieu of dividends. *Cf. infra* note 171 (on another aspect of such tax differences). However, these seem too thin a reed on which to hang a disclosure obligation, especially since this difference has been significant only since the 2003 reduction in the tax rate on dividends.

118. The basic forms for mutual fund portfolio disclosure are Forms N-1A, N-CSR, and N-Q. *See* Shareholder Reports and Quarterly Portfolio Disclosure of Registered Management Investment Companies, SEC Rel. No. 33-8393 (Feb. 27, 2004), 69 Fed. Reg. 11244, 11254–57 (Mar. 9, 2004) [hereinafter "*SEC Mutual Fund Reports Adopting Release*"]; Form N-1A, Registration Statement Under the Securities Act of 1933, Items 22(b)-(c) (discussing annual and semiannual reports), *available at* http://www.sec.gov/about/forms/formn-1a.pdf; Form N-CSR, Certified Shareholder Report of Registered Management Investment Companies, Item 6 (Schedule of Investments), *available at* http://www.sec.gov/about/forms/formn-csr.pdf; Form N-Q, Quarterly Schedule of Portfolio Holdings of Registered Management Investment Company, *available at* http://www.sec.gov/about/forms/formn-q.pdf.

disclosure filings suggests that disclosure of counterparties and certain quantitative information such as notional amounts is common. There is no requirement to disclose share lending or non-short-sale-related borrowing.[119]

Thus, while the details are different, mutual fund reporting is similar to insider Section 16 reporting in: (i) its focus on economic ownership; (ii) its coverage of all forms of economic ownership, both long and short; and (iii) its failure to cover share lending and non-short-sale-related borrowing. Both systems thus cover hidden (morphable) ownership reasonably well, as well as some empty voting. However, mutual fund disclosure captures only quarter-end positions.

IV. A Proposal for Integrated Ownership Disclosure

A. General Considerations

As Part III has shown, the current ownership disclosure rules are highly complex, treat substantively identical positions inconsistently, both across and within disclosure regimes, and do not effectively address either empty voting or hidden (morphable) ownership. In big picture, current 13D and 13G disclosures turn largely on voting ownership while Section 16 and mutual fund disclosures focus on economic ownership. Form 13F disclosure covers only publicly-traded shares and long positions in exchange-traded derivatives. None of the disclosure regimes effectively addresses share borrowing and lending. Some of the differences between these sets of rules may have once made sense. Some omissions may once have been unimportant. But in a world of easy decoupling and massive OTC derivatives and share lending markets, these differences and omissions make sense no longer.

In this Part IV, we offer an "integrated ownership disclosure" reform proposal that would provide decent although still imperfect disclosure of both empty voting and hidden ownership, while greatly simplifying the current ownership disclosure rules. Our proposal builds on existing disclosure technology and requires only information readily accessible to investors. For the most part, we would simply extend existing disclosure requirements for insiders and mutual funds to a broader class of reporting persons. Thus, additional compliance costs should be limited, and will be offset for many reporting persons by adopting a single set of rules for what must be reported. We expect, but cannot prove, that overall reporting costs would decline.

We believe the new information will be useful to investors, as well as to corporations, judges, regulators, and legislators as they assess how else to respond to new vote buying. But even if our proposal had no other value, simpler disclo-

119. Mutual funds usually list the securities that they have lent in their schedule of investments with a footnote saying that "[a]ll or a portion of this security is on loan." Susan C. Peters, *Accounting Treatment of Loans of Securities*, in Securities Finance: Securities Lending and Repurchase Agreements 210 (Frank J. Fabozzi & Steven V. Mann eds., 2005). Mutual fund balance sheets disclose the total value of securities on loan. *Id.* Mutual funds must disclose any short positions; implicit in this disclosure is that the fund borrowed the shares that it then sold short.

sure—largely integrating what are now five discrete ownership disclosure systems—would likely be worthwhile.

Our proposal would: (i) move toward common standards for triggering disclosure and for disclosing positions once disclosure is triggered; (ii) provide a single set of rules for which positions to disclose and how to disclose them; (iii) require disclosure of both voting and economic ownership, however arising; and (iv) require symmetric disclosure of long and short economic ownership. We mostly leave for another day disclosure of related non-host assets. However, our proposals would often require disclosure of holdings in both acquirers and targets, which is one important instance of related non-host assets.

Our disclosure proposal should capture empty voting and hidden (morphable) ownership reasonably well for current Schedule 13D and Section 16 filers, who must report ownership and ownership changes promptly. Disclosure will be patchier for other filers due to the periodic nature of the reporting requirements, which let filers sell down their positions before the filing date. To capture significant empty voting by periodic filers, we would require disclosure of instances in which they voted when holding voting ownership that exceeded economic ownership by more than a threshold percentage (such as 0.5% or 1% of a company's shares). This will ensure that empty voting episodes such as Henderson Investments or Sears Canada are disclosed eventually.

In offering these proposals, we do not reassess here the current disclosure thresholds, disclosure frequencies, and delay periods, nor, to any significant extent, which investors must disclose their positions. Implicitly, then, we assume that there is rough economic or political logic supporting the current rules. We believe, however, that whatever the thresholds and delay periods may be, ownership disclosure rules should be internally coherent.

We recognize that ownership disclosure has both benefits and costs.[120] On the benefit side, share pricing is likely to be more efficient if investors know what major investors are doing and have advance notice of possible changes in control. Moreover, price-relevant information about securities often has greater private than social value. Requiring disclosure can reduce costly, often duplicative private search for it. On the cost side, private search for information can enhance share pricing efficiency, and the corporate control market is animated in part by private returns to search. Outside investors must receive some reward for searching for mispriced shares and mismanaged firms. Real-time disclosure would likely reduce the return to search. The current system, with near-real-time disclosure by insiders and large active shareholders (13D filers), but delayed disclosure by other shareholders, could well strike a decent balance among these competing concerns.

Beyond their potential economic logic, ownership disclosure rules reflect the intuition that investors want to know who a company's major shareholders are and whether those shareholders are buying or selling, and that company insiders should have an opportunity to respond to takeover attempts. Moreover, the his-

120. For more extended discussion of the benefits and costs of disclosure, see Hu & Black, *Hedge Funds and Empty Voting*, *supra* note 24, Part 4.3.

tory of ownership disclosure, in the U.S. and elsewhere, suggests that hidden control of major companies will not be politically acceptable for long, nor will secret contests for control. So disclosure of major positions there will be. Our aim is to make that disclosure coherent, simple, and therefore relatively low-cost.

Our proposed reforms build largely on the Section 16 rules. We would extend Section 16-type disclosure of economic ownership to institutions and other shareholders who now report on Form 13F and Schedules 13D and 13G. Short sales of shares would be disclosed in a manner similar to long positions, with a possible exception for "pure" short sales, discussed below. We would modestly expand the institutions who report on Schedule 13F by counting any economic ownership of equity securities or equity derivatives, long or short (on a gross basis) and exchange-traded or OTC, toward the 13D, 13F, and 13G triggering thresholds. For banks, broker-dealers and others who both hold proprietary positions and positions managed for clients, we would require separate reporting of each; subject perhaps to limited exceptions for short-term positions held in connection with market-making.

We would also require more complete disclosure of share lending, share borrowing, and voting ownership unaccompanied by economic ownership. Share lenders would report their loans; share borrowers would report borrowings and whether they retained the borrowed shares or sold them short. Money managers who have voting discretion for routine but not non-routine matters would so indicate.

We propose symmetric disclosure of positive and negative economic ownership. Whether a large "pure" short economic position, defined as negative economic ownership with no accompanying voting ownership, should require disclosure is, we believe, a very close question. Our proposal opts for simplicity and symmetry in providing that these short positions should be disclosed and count toward triggering a filing requirement.[121]

Regulators will need to develop guidelines for reporting derivative positions that are not addressed by the current Section 16 and mutual fund rules. As a lodestar principle, we believe that disclosure should allow a derivatives dealer, with access to market information on volatility and other pricing parameters, to estimate the derivative's value and its delta (how that value depends on share price). The reporting person need not provide the model it uses to value the derivative (that may be proprietary), only the raw material. For instance, for a typical OTC put option, disclosure would include the core contractual terms— the strike price, expiration date, and number of shares, the counterparty, and

121. The principal arguments for disclosure of pure short positions are the value of simplicity and symmetry, the practical difficulty in drafting an exception that is limited to a short position with no de facto voting rights, reduced gaming risk, and the value to investors of fuller knowledge of other investors' positions. The principal arguments against disclosure are that short selling is a valuable policing mechanism for share prices, our markets and regulatory systems already burden short sellers in various ways, and disclosure would add to these burdens. On how U.S. tax and regulatory rules raise the cost of short selling, see Michael R. Powers, David M. Schizer & Martin Shubik, *Market Bubbles and Wasteful Avoidance: Tax and Regulatory Constraints on Short Sales*, 57 TAX L. REV. 233 (2004).

whether the option was European style (exercisable only at expiration) or American style (exercisable at any time). This principles-based approach should be more robust to financial innovation than a traditional classification-based (i.e., "cubbyhole") approach such as that used in the 13F rules.[122]

These proposals would expand disclosure, but would also integrate and substantially simplify the current disclosure regime. Economically equivalent positions would be treated consistently. The distinction between positions that trigger disclosure and positions that must be reported once disclosure is triggered, would disappear.

Our proposals are consistent with recent regulatory changes made in the U.K. and Hong Kong in response to new vote buying. In November 2005, the U.K. began requiring large shareholder reporting by persons who have long economic ownership through derivative positions.[123] In 2003, Hong Kong similarly extended large shareholder disclosure to persons with both long and short equity derivatives positions.[124] The 2006 Henderson Investment incident, discussed in Part II.C, may prompt Hong Kong to take further action.[125] The most important difference between the U.K. and Hong Kong approaches is that Hong Kong does (as we do), while the U.K. does not, require disclosure of a *pure short* economic position.

Disclosure rules also need to be enforced. At present, there is some enforcement of Section 13(d) and Section 16 disclosure, but apparently minimal enforcement of Form 13F.[126]

Table 4 summarizes our integrated ownership disclosure proposal. Comparing Table 4 to Table 3 shows the significant simplification of the current rules.

---

122. For analyses of how financial innovation subverts traditional classification-based regulation, see Hu, *Misunderstood Derivatives*, *supra* note 27; Henry T. C. Hu, *Swaps, the Modern Process of Financial Innovation and the Vulnerability of a Regulatory Paradigm*, 138 U. PA. L. REV. 333 (1989) [hereinafter "Hu, *Regulatory Paradigm*"]; Edward D. Kleinbard, *Equity Derivative Products: Financial Innovation's Newest Challenge to the Tax System*, 69 TEX. L. REV. 1319 (1991) [hereinafter "Kleinbard, *Equity Derivatives*"].

123. Panel Executive (Panel on Takeovers and Mergers), *Summary of Changes to the Takeover Code* (Oct. 2005), *available at* http://www.thetakeoverpanel.org.uk/forms/summary%20of%207%2011%20 changes.pdf; Panel on Takeovers and Mergers, *Dealings in Derivatives and Options: Statement by the Code Committee of the Panel Following the External Consultation Processes on Disclosure Issues in PCP 2005/1 and PCP 2005/2* (Aug. 5, 2005), *available at* http://www.thetakeoverpanel.org.uk/new/statements/ DATA/2005/2005-34.pdf; Panel on Takeovers and Mergers, *Consultation Paper Issued by the Code Committeee of the Panel—Dealings in Derivatives and Options: Outline Proposals relating to Amendments Proposed to Be Made to The Takeover Code and the SARS* (PPCP 2005/1 Issued on Jan. 7, 2005), *available at* http://www.thetakeoverpanel.org.uk/new/consultation/DATA/PCP200501.pdf.

124. Hong Kong Securities and Futures Commission, *Consultation Paper on the Review of the Disclosure of Interests Regime under Part XV of the Securities and Futures Ordinance* (Jan. 2005), *available at* http://www.sfc.hk/sfc/notes/consult/EN/apps/som/direviewconsult.nsf/content/Download/1/$FILE/ Part%20XV%20Consultation%20Paper%20200105%20-%20English.pdf; Hong Kong Securities and Futures Commission, *Outline of Part XV of the Securities and Futures Ordinance (Cap. 571)—Disclosure of Interests* (Aug. 6, 2003), *available at* http://eapp01.sfc.hk/apps/cc/RegulatoryHandbook.nsf/lkup MainAllDoc/H339/$FILE/en_sfc_outline.pdf.

125. *See, e.g.*, Cheng, *supra* note 52.

126. On Form 13F enforcement, see James D. Cox & Randall S. Thomas, *Letting Billions Slip Through Your Fingers: Empirical Evidence and Legal Implications of the Failure of Financial Institutions to Participate in Securities Class Action Settlements*, 58 STAN. L. REV. 411, 445–48 (2005).

Table 4. Proposal for More Integrated Ownership Disclosure

This table summarizes the disclosure changes we propose, in a format similar to Table 3, which summarizes current ownership rules. The table addresses separately the use of long and short positions in shares and equivalents to trigger a reporting obligation, and the duty to disclose them once the reporting obligation has been triggered. For stock lending and borrowing, borrowing is relevant both for triggering disclosure (except for status-based filers) and for disclosure if a filing is required.

Proposed Disclosure Requirement	Reporting Frequency (Same as Current Law)	Long Positions (Shares, Equity Swaps, other OTC and Exchange-traded Derivatives)		Short Positions				Share Lending and Borrowing		Empty Voting (over Threshold Level, such as 0.5% of Company's shares)
		As trigger	If filing required	As trigger		If filing required				
				Equity Swaps, other OTC and Exchange-traded Derivatives	Short Sales	Equity Swaps, other OTC and Exchange-traded Derivatives	Short Sales	Lending	Borrowing	
13D	current	yes	yes	yes		yes		yes		yes
13G	annual	yes (if held on reporting date)	yes	yes (if held on reporting date)		yes		yes (if held on reporting date)		yes
13F	quarterly	status-based: $100M in economic ownership of equities and equity derivatives	yes	status-based: $100M in economic ownership of equities and equity derivatives		yes		yes		yes
Section 16 (director or officer)	current	status-based	yes	status-based	banned by Section 16(c)	yes	banned by Section 16(c)	yes		yes
Section 16 (10% holder)		yes		yes						
mutual Funds	quarterly	yes	yes	yes		yes		yes		yes

B. Large Shareholder Disclosure (Schedules 13D and 13G)

Currently, 13D and 13G disclosure focuses on voting ownership. Our proposed extension is simple: filers should report both voting and economic ownership and either form of ownership can trigger the reporting obligation. The Section 16 concept of economic ownership can be carried over to Schedules 13D and 13G. We would expand current Section 16 reporting to include stock borrowing and lending positions, since these positions affect voting ownership. Each position would be separately disclosed using transaction codes adapted from Section 16 reporting, including new codes for borrowing and lending. Schedule 13D filers would attach any contracts that convey or relate to their economic or voting ownership. We would also modestly move the line between 13D and 13G reporting, which currently turns on control intent, and require 13D reporting for positions held with a view to affecting a shareholder vote, even if the vote does not affect control.

To take Perry's position in Mylan as an example, Perry, once it passed 5% ownership of Mylan, would report on Schedule 13D because it sought to influence Mylan's vote on acquiring King. It would separately report each position conveying positive or negative economic or voting ownership, and attach related contracts as exhibits. Schedule 13G reporting would be similar to Schedule 13D reporting, but without exhibits. As at present, it would generally be due annually and include only year-end holdings. This will let some positions go unreported, but most institutional filers will have to report their positions quarterly on Schedule 13F.

In determining whether the 5% reporting threshold has been crossed, we would not allow netting of long and short positions. An example can show why. Assume that a hedge fund takes a 10% net short position and also enters into an equity swap conveying a 6% long position, so that its net short position is 4%. With netting, no filing would be required. But we would want the hedge fund to disclose its position. It would like to see the company's share price drop because its overall position is net short, and likely has de facto access to 6% voting rights if a shareholder vote arises.

For some derivative positions, questions will arise as to how to measure effective economic exposure. An equity swap conveying the economic return on 1,000,000 shares should count as economic ownership of 1,000,000 shares. That is simple enough. But how about a call option? The option holder's economic exposure depends on the share price. In derivatives terminology, δ (delta) is the change in option value for a small change in the price of the underlying asset.[127] If shares go up by $1, a call option with $\delta = 0.4$ will increase in value by $0.40. A call option's δ, however, changes as share price changes. How should this position be reported?

127. More technically, delta is the partial derivative of option price with respect to the price of the underlying asset. *See* E. Briys, M. Bellalh, H.M. Mai, F. De Varenne, Options, Futures, and Exotic Derivatives 124 (1998).

We believe that reporting the precise economic exposure for call options and other derivatives with deltas that vary with share price or other factors would add undue complexity and cost. We propose a cruder approach. Under current Rule 13d-3, option holders report the number of shares that would be acquired on exercise of the option, which is equivalent to assuming $\delta = 1$. We believe the number of "matched shares" for a derivative position should be computed in parallel fashion. Hong Kong uses a similar approach and its experience can be instructive.[128]

C. Institutional Money Managers and Mutual Funds

We propose that 13F disclosure should use the same format and contain the same information as revised Schedules 13D and 13G. The principal difference would be the trigger for reporting. We would change the threshold from $100 million in Section 13(f) securities to $100 million in economic ownership of U.S. equity securities (including equity derivatives). Otherwise, an institution could avoid disclosure by holding equity derivatives and keeping its direct equity holdings under $100 million.

Cost concerns are more important for Form 13F reports than for Schedules 13D and 13G because almost every institutional investment manager has to file Form 13F on a quarterly basis, as to all positions held. In contrast, Schedules 13D and 13G apply to a much smaller number of persons and positions. However, institutional money managers should have ready access to the basic information we propose to collect. Some hedge funds, for example currently provide quite detailed reports to investors.[129] Thus, there will be a one-time cost in revising internal reports to match the new reporting format, but ongoing filing cost should be similar to current cost, and similar to the costs that mutual funds now incur, without howls of outrage at compliance cost.

These changes to Form 13F would result in mutual fund advisory firms that manage a number of funds (such as Fidelity and Vanguard) providing greater information on the aggregate holdings of the funds they manage. Individual mutual funds would continue to provide fund-specific disclosures, much as they do currently. Both advisory firms and individual funds would be subject to the new empty voting disclosure rules we will address in Part IV.D.

The 13F and mutual fund disclosure is quarterly, and thus will not reach all instances of new vote buying. We also would not change the current reporting delays, in which 13F, 13G, and mutual fund reports are due some time after the end of the reporting period. The current reporting speeds and frequencies seem to us to offer an acceptable tradeoff between disclosure completeness and cost. The disclosures should offer an overall picture of the extent of new vote buying, even if they do not capture all instances.

128. *See* Hong Kong SFC, *Part XV Outline*, *supra* note 124, at 2.5 (section entitled "How many shares am I taken to be interested in if I hold equity derivatives?").

129. For a discussion of so-called "risk reporting" to hedge fund investors, see Leslie Rahl, Hedge Fund Transparency—Unraveling the Complex and Controversial Debate 65–81 (2003).

An important fringe benefit of our proposal is that Form 13F reporting covers a large fraction of the universe of stock lenders and borrowers. Currently, stock lending data is sparse. Even the aggregate size of the market can only be estimated.[130] The largest borrowers of stocks are prime brokerage firms; the largest lenders are major institutions. Beyond that, little is known, beyond individual anecdotes.[131] Simply aggregating 13F reports of lending and borrowing will provide valuable data, both in the aggregate and for particular firms.

The primary cost to investors will be indirect, from disclosing trading positions that are currently concealed. Yet, to some extent, we have already crossed the bridge. The intent of Form 13F was to require institutional money managers to disclose their equity holdings, with a delay to reduce the competitive impact of disclosure. Changes in the derivative markets have undermined the completeness of reporting but, as discussed earlier, we do not believe that the basic tradeoff between the value of disclosure to other investors and the value of competitive secrecy was seriously misdrawn.

D. Disclosure of Empty Voting

Our proposed stock lending and borrowing disclosure will provide a good aggregate picture of the stock lending market. But without more, periodic filers (i.e., mutual funds and those filing on Schedule 13G or Form 13F) could avoid disclosing most empty voting positions that are in place for a short period around that record date. For instance, consider an institution using record date capture; it could borrow up to 5% of a company's shares, vote them, reverse the borrowing before the quarter ends, and report nothing.

To address empty voting by periodic filers, we propose that these filers separately report any occasions where they cast votes which substantially exceed their economic ownership. To limit the reporting burden for filers who engage in ordinary hedging activities, we would require disclosure if a filer held voting ownership that exceeded economic ownership by at least 0.5% (or some other threshold amount) of the outstanding shares on a record date for a shareholder meeting. We would rely on the crude rules discussed above to measure economic ownership. Reporting would be on the usual forms, and thus would occur some time after the vote.

Consider the MONY-AXA merger as an example. Suppose that a hedge fund holds AXA convertible bonds, wants the merger to be completed, borrows 4% of MONY's shares shortly before the record date, votes for the merger, and reverses the borrowing soon afterwards. The hedge fund would report, in its next 13F

---

130. Thus, one recent estimate of the size of the U.S. institutional securities lending market drew on a combination of the firm's own internal client surveys and Federal Reserve statistics. *See* Phyllis Plitch, *Funds' Lending Sparks' 'Short' Debate*, WALL ST. J., May 25, 2005, at B2D; *cf.* Dan Barnes, *Learning the Cost of Stock Lending*, BANKER, May 2005, at 62 (the size of the global securities lending market is "fairly unclear").

131. *See* Jeffrey Cohen, David Haushalter & Adam V. Reed, *Mechanics of the Equity Lending Market*, in SHORT SELLING: STRATEGIES, RISKS, AND REWARDS 13–14 (Frank J. Fabozzi ed., 2004).

filing, that it had borrowed and voted the MONY shares, what issues it had voted on, how it had voted, and relevant dates (for borrowing, voting, and position reversal). It would also report its economic ownership at the time of MONY shares and any related non-host assets (in this case, the AXA bonds).

This empty voting disclosure will apply only to institutions that engage in large-scale vote capture. These are likely a small faction of the universe of 13G, 13F, and mutual fund filers. If vote capture is widespread, the filing burden will be higher, but so will be the need for the information.

E. Summary

As a response to hidden (morphable) ownership, the disclosure enhancements we propose above may well be sufficient. For empty voting, disclosure will be valuable, and may reduce the incidence of empty voting. Even hedge funds may be less likely to do publicly what they might do in the dark. Insiders might hesitate as well. Derivatives dealers could take "reputational risk" into account in deciding whether to facilitate a client's empty voting.

Disclosure should also provide the information base needed to assess the need for additional reforms to address empty voting. At the same time, much of the disclosure will be delayed, which limits its value for a contest at an individual company. It will often be possible to reconstruct instances in which vote buying may have affected voting outcomes, but usually too late to alter those outcomes. Delayed reporting is a tradeoff of disclosure cost against timeliness. If empty voting proves widespread, it could make sense to require periodic filers to provide "real-time" reports of significant empty voting positions.

The new information will also prove useful for efforts at international coordination, which is important for any regulatory response. The need for international coordination has been recognized in a current private effort to address new vote buying undertaken by the International Corporate Governance Network (ICGN), a group of major institutional investors from the U.S. (including CalPERS), U.K. (including Hermes), France (including Credit Agricole), and elsewhere.[132]

V. Toward Additional Responses to Empty Voting

A. General Considerations

We discuss in our companion works the theory and evidence bearing on the benefits and costs of linking shares to votes and on how a market for votes, decoupled from shares, might operate.[133] There are circumstances in which such

132. *See* International Corporate Governance Network—Securities Lending Committee, *ICGN Stock Lending Code of Best Practice* (2005) [hereinafter "ICGN, *Draft Stock Lending Code*"], *available at* http://www.icgn.org/organisation/documents/slc/code_final.pdf; Lintstock, *Share lending vis-à-vis voting—A report commissioned by the International Corporate Governance Network*, at 3 & 22 (May 28, 2004) [hereinafter "Lintstock, *Share Lending Survey*"], *available at* http://www.icgn.org/documents/share_lending_report_may2004.pdf.

133. *See* Hu & Black, *New Vote Buying*, *supra* note 24; Hu & Black, *Hedge Funds and Empty Voting*, *supra* note 24.

a market could be problematic, and circumstances in which it could enhance shareholder oversight of managers. For this and other reasons, including the difficulty in regulating an activity that can take many forms, about which little is yet known, we consider it premature to adopt additional rules to address empty voting.

Still, some simple examples can illustrate why it is likely that additional regulation will be needed. For takeover bids, an unregulated market for shares, coupled with votes, has well-known problems, driven by the high value of the marginal shares that just convey control, and the lower value of minority shares once control is assured. These problems have led to regulation of takeover bids, including a minimum offer period and a ban on two-tier offers. Similar problems would afflict a proxy fight waged by buying votes decoupled from shares. Thus, an unregulated market for votes seems unlikely to work well.

For record date capture, consider the Henderson Investments scenario. A hedge fund borrowed shares, voted them against an apparently beneficial transaction, and then sold them short, profiting while defeating an apparently beneficial transaction. Disclosure would not change the hedge fund's ability to profit at other shareholders' expense. Or consider Scotiabank's decision to vote the Sears Canada shares, held to support an equity swap, in favor of Sears Holdings' buyout offer.[134] It is arguable that, Scotiabank was an empty voter, akin to a nominal holder, while the hedge fund was the real economic owner. Perhaps the wrong party voted.

We therefore develop below a menu of regulatory options for addressing empty voting, and say a bit about their merits. There are three families of additional strategies. The most obvious strategies focus directly on voting rights (Section B). A second family focuses on improving an aging "voting architecture" (Section C). A third family involves regulatory interventions that affect supply and demand forces in the markets that support decoupling (Section D). We make no claim that particular rules we discuss are desirable, only that they are possible.

A further issue, which we do not detail here, is the locus of regulation. In particular, federal securities law focuses on disclosure. The SEC likely cannot, within its current statutory authority, directly regulate empty voting. Doing so would likely affect the "internal affairs" of corporations, traditionally governed by state law.[135] Moreover, especially in an area where the right response is uncertain, a federal response could lock in overregulation—as some scholars suggest may be the case with the Sarbanes-Oxley Act.[136] Thus, there could be reason to prefer responses that do not expand the SEC's regulatory reach.

---

134. Scotiabank apparently is claiming that the shares it pledged were not the "matched shares" supporting the swap. *See* Eisinger, *supra* note 59 (noting that shares are fungible).

135. *See* Business Roundtable v. SEC, 905 F.2d 406 (D.C. Cir. 1990) (invalidating SEC's effort to ban dual-class recapitalizations); Stephen M. Bainbridge, *The Short Life and Resurrection of SEC Rule 19c-4*, 69 WASH. U.L.Q. 565 (1991) (discussing said effort).

136. *See, e.g.*, Kate Litvak, *The Effect of the Sarbanes-Oxley Act on Non-US Companies Cross-Listed in the US* (working paper 2006), *available at* http://ssrn.com/abstract=876624; Roberta Romano, *The Sarbanes-Oxley Act and the Making of Quack Corporate Governance*, 114 YALE L.J. 1521 (2005).

B. Strategies Focused on Voting Rights

1. Direct Limits on Voting Rights

One way to address empty voting is to limit the voting rights of shareholders who hold greater voting than economic ownership. Thus, in a recent article, Professors Martin and Partnoy suggest that "shareholders with substantial short positions should not be entitled to vote" and that "corporations and their regulators should strongly consider taking away the votes of [shareholders who are also] options buyers and sellers."[137]

In the extreme case of negative economic ownership, this could be the right answer. But even here, the technology for enforcing such a rule is not obvious. To be effective, a rule must address the many ways to decouple votes from economic ownership. Martin and Partnoy address only short sales and option positions and do not offer guidelines for implementation. They do not discuss other decoupling techniques—including record date capture and hedging with equity swaps.[138] In addition, new strategies will no doubt emerge as financial innovation continues. The innovation process can easily undermine classification-based regulatory approaches such as theirs.

An additional problem with limiting voting rights is determining when a single "investor" holds equivalent economic and voting ownership. Say, for instance, that a fund management firm runs both a conventional, "long-only" mutual fund that holds General Motors shares, and a hedge fund, managed by a different portfolio manager, which is short General Motors. Should the conventional mutual fund lose its votes because of the hedge fund's short position? Should it matter whether the fund management firm centralizes its voting decisions, or delegates them to individual fund managers?

Bringing related non-host assets into a calculus of overall economic interests raises further complexities. Consider the AXA-MONY transaction, discussed in Part II.B. The problem was not that holders of AXA convertible bonds had greater voting than economic interest in MONY, but instead that they had an orthogonal interest in the AXA bonds, which was their primary concern.

Once one moves from a simple, rarely triggered on-off switch (Does an investor have negative economic ownership, or perhaps negative overall economic interest?) to a general rule that limits voting rights when votes would otherwise exceed economic ownership, the technical difficulties in measuring economic ownership become fearsome. One must grapple with complex derivative positions, in which economic exposure varies with share price. In developing the integrated disclosure proposal presented in Part IV, we initially attempted to invent a workable scheme for numerical disclosure of economic ownership for positions with deltas different than one. The effort became absurdly complex, and we gave it up as misguided. Substantive limits on voting rights when an investor holds related non-host assets would raise further complications.

137. Martin & Partnoy, *supra* note 25, at 794.

138. In effect, Martin and Partnoy deal with limited aspects of what we refer to as empty voting, and do not address hidden (morphable) ownership, the other half of the new vote buying.

Moreover, vote buying can sometimes move votes from passive or ignorant investors to investors who can cast informed votes. Insiders who hold partly hedged positions still have incentives to vote in ways that increase firm value. The proportions of "good" and "bad" empty voting are currently unknown.

In the end, a combination of factual uncertainty about when and how new vote buying occurs, how often it is beneficial or harmful, and concerns about how one might draft and enforce a rule that limits voting rights and thus requires measuring economic ownership with reasonable precision, persuade us to err on the side of caution. At this point, we are ready neither to recommend limiting voting rights when they would otherwise substantially exceed economic ownership, nor to argue that such a rule would be a serious error. Our disclosure proposal may provide the knowledge needed to draft a workable rule. It will also help courts assess whether to limit voting rights on a case-by-case basis.

2. Voting By Record Owners: Extension to Equity Swaps

Empty voting by shareholders with zero economic ownership deserves special attention, because it is common and, in part, already regulated. Our system of record ownership already decouples economic ownership from formal voting rights. The record owner is typically at least two persons removed from the economic owner of the shares.[139] Shares held in "street name" are generally held "of record" by Depository Trust Company or another securities depository, which holds the shares on behalf of another intermediary (such as a broker-dealer or bank), which holds the shares for economic owners. Our legal system has responded by partly recoupling voting and economic ownership. Depositories pass voting rights to their bank and broker clients, who must request voting instructions from economic owners. If the customer does not provide instructions, New York Stock Exchange (NYSE) Rule 452 allows a bank or broker to vote on routine matters, but not on a contested matter or on a merger or similar transaction which may substantially affect the value of the shares.[140]

These rules on when record owners can vote provide precedent for an effort to reconnect voting rights to economic ownership, when technology has severed them. Consider, for example, a derivatives dealer who holds shares to hedge a short equity swap position. As we discuss in Part II, the dealer will often either unwind the swap so that the holder of the long position can vote, or simply vote as the holder directs. This market convention reconnects voting and economic ownership in a manner similar to the rules governing record owners. In this situation, we should require disclosure of ownership that is currently hidden, but recognize that the market is generally placing voting rights where they ought to

139. On the current system and its origins, see, e.g., Issuer Restrictions or Prohibitions on Ownership by Securities Intermediaries, SEC Rel. No. 34-50758, 69 Fed. Reg. 70852, 70852 nn. 1–2, 70853 n. 21 (Dec. 7, 2004); MICHAEL T. REDDY, SECURITIES OPERATIONS—A GUIDE TO OPERATIONS AND INFORMATION SYSTEMS IN THE SECURITIES INDUSTRY 127–64 (2d ed. 1995).

140. NYSE RULE 452. *See generally* Task Force on Shareholder Proposals of the Committee on Federal Regulation of Securities, *Report on Proposed Changes in Proxy Rules and Regulations Regarding Procedures for the Election of Corporate Directors*, 59 BUS. LAW. 109 (2003).

be. One might also extend current rules governing record owners to dealers who hold matched shares to hedge short equity swap positions.

3. Corporation Opt-In

An obvious alternative to mandatory limits on voting rights would be to let corporations decide for themselves whether to require a link between economic and voting ownership.[141] Corporations could potentially do so through a board-adopted bylaw or a charter amendment.

Corporate opt-ins, such as only allowing shareholders with positive net economic ownership to vote or limiting votes to the amount of economic ownership, have the attractive feature of allowing corporations to experiment with different solutions. Still, they are subject to many of the measurement concerns we raised above. Opt-ins also raise additional concerns. A board-adopted bylaw can easily be structured to entrench insiders. It also is not clear whether board-adopted bylaws that restrict voting rights would be valid, given that corporate law currently grant voting rights to record owners, whether or not they are economic owners. Moreover, case law promises close scrutiny of unilateral board actions affecting shareholders.[142]

A charter amendment is more likely to be valid. Delaware section 212(a) states that "unless otherwise provided in the certificate of incorporation" and subject to certain record date limitations, "each stockholder shall be entitled to 1 vote for each share of capital stock."[143] The one share-one vote rule is merely a default rule and the corporation is not explicitly constrained in how it departs from this rule. Moreover, the most closely relevant case, *Williams v. Geier,* suggests that a charter amendment affecting voting rights will receive deferential business judgment review.[144] However, stock exchange rules that limit dual-class recapitalizations could block some charter amendments. Consider, for example, a time-phased voting plan, similar to the one approved in *Williams v. Geier*, which limits the voting rights of short-term shareholders. This would likely run afoul of NYSE rules, which state that voting rights cannot be "disparately reduced or restricted through any corporate action or issuance" and offers as examples "time phased voting plans" and "capped voting rights plans."[145]

Some vote-limiting strategies could also run afoul of the federal proxy rules. Consider, for example, a charter provision requiring a shareholder to attest that

141. We first raised the idea of an opt-in approach in the initial 2005 draft of this article. *See supra* note 24.

142. The Delaware Supreme Court has stated that Delaware courts "have remained assiduous in carefully reviewing any board actions designed to interfere with or impede the effective exercise of corporate democracy by shareholders, especially in an election of directors." MM Cos. v. Liquid Audio, Inc., 813 A.2d 1118, 1127 (Del. 2003).

143. DEL. CODE ANN. tit. 8, § 212(a) (2001 & Supp. 2004).

144. Williams v. Geier, 671 A.2d 1368 (Del. 1996). This case involved "time-phased" voting rights, in which shareholders who held shares for three years had 10 votes per share, while other shareholders had only one vote per share.

145. New York Stock Exchange, *Voting Rights*, LISTED COMPANY MANUAL, ¶ 313.00(A) (Oct. 10, 1998).

he has economic ownership "substantially equal" to the number of votes he proposes to cast. Given the SEC's broad power under Exchange Act section 14(a) to regulate the proxy process, such a provision would probably require SEC assent.[146]

Assuming that a charter amendment is permitted under current law, there remains the policy question: To what extent *should* companies be able to limit voting rights through charter amendments? The core problem is that for shareholders, voting rights are collectively valuable but individually worth little. Thus shareholders can sometimes be persuaded, as in the dual class recapitalizations of the 1980s, to part with these rights for little consideration.

There is usually a presumption that a charter provision adopted before a company goes public is probably not seriously inefficient, because if it is, the insiders should receive a lower price for their shares. This market price response presumably explains why most companies go public with a one share, one vote structure. Scholars debate, however, the extent to which IPO pricing is efficient for more subtle variations in shareholder rights.[147] Those doubts would likely include charter provisions that respond to empty voting. In addition, the usual arguments for the efficiency of corporate choice are weaker for midstream charter amendments, which can entrench management and can sometimes succeed despite reducing share value.[148] Companies might well opt for midstream amendments that allow vote buying techniques used by insiders while blocking techniques used by outsiders. Time-phased voting is a good example of a rule that limits vote buying but also entrenches insiders.

Thus, the "company choice" approach needs to be cabined. Yet it seems premature to assess how without knowing either the dimensions of empty voting or how companies might respond. Some possible charter amendments might be unobjectionable. Others might be acceptable at the IPO stage, but problematic midstream. The initial need is still for disclosure, to provide a base of knowledge against which potential charter amendments can be judged.

4. State Corporate Law

A separate question from whether companies can use charter amendments to limit vote buying by outside shareholders is whether corporate law limits vote buying by insiders. There are no direct legal constraints.[149] Insiders, however,

146. Exchange Act § 14(a) (codified as amended at 15 U.S.C. § 78n(a) (2000 & Supp. III 2003)).

147. *See, e.g.*, Robert Daines & Michael Klausner, *Do IPO Charters Maximize Firm Value? Antitakeover Protection in IPOs*, 17 J.L., ECON. & ORGANIZATION 83 (2001).

148. *See* Lucian Arye Bebchuk, *Limiting Contractual Freedom in Corporate Law: The Desirable Constraints on Charter Amendments*, 102 HARV. L. REV. 1820 (1989); Bernard S. Black, *Is Corporate Law Trivial?: A Political and Economic Analysis*, 84 NW. U.L. REV. 542 (1990).

149. In the Introduction, we sketched why traditional vote buying doctrine does not cover empty voting through the two-step process of purchasing shares and then hedging economic ownership. A new vote buyer using record date capture can generally also avoid being constrained by existing case law. The borrowed shares convey full economic and voting ownership. This is customarily coupled with the right of either the borrower or the lender to reverse the transaction on demand and, while the loan is outstanding, the borrower paying to the lender the cash return on the shares plus an agreed upon borrowing charge. No individual piece of this arrangement is seen as problematic under current doctrine.

might be constrained by fiduciary duty. At one extreme, given the rigor with which courts police shareholder elections, company officers or directors would likely breach their duty of loyalty if they used corporate funds or the promise of future business to procure votes. In the *Hewlett v. Hewlett-Packard* proxy fight case, for example, Walter Hewlett claimed that HP management had procured a favorable vote by Deutsche Bank through promises or threats related to future business dealings between the two companies. HP defended on the grounds that it had persuaded Deutsche Bank to support the merger on the merits, and effectively conceded that procuring votes through a promise or threat would be improper.[150] Suppose, instead, that HP management had engaged in new vote buying to swing the outcome. There would be no identifiable transfer of voting rights, and hence no classic vote buying, but the breach of fiduciary duty would be the same, and the courts would likely disallow the procured votes.

However, other efforts at new vote buying could be hard for courts to reach under current doctrine. Consider, for example, a company founder who hedges his economic ownership. Corporate law neither requires disclosure of the hedging nor questions the founder's exercise of voting rights. Disclosure comes from Section 16 rules. Managers could also acquire votes while hedging their economic interest, if they did so for the long term, rather than to influence a particular vote.

If empty voting is potentially outcome-determinative, judges will likely face pressure to update current vote-buying doctrine, which addresses only explicit transfers of voting rights by a vote seller. They may also have to examine a new vote buyer's transfer of economic ownership. They might well disallow voting by an empty voter such as Perry, or the hedge fund in Henderson Investments, with negative economic interest. This situation is analogous to voting by directors whose personal interests conflict with the corporation's interests.[151] In both situations, the usual presumption that the voter will seek to increase shareholder wealth is thrown into doubt. Zero or negative economic interest aside, it seems premature to speculate as to how courts should address empty voting, given the multiple factual contexts in which it can be used.

Another possible response is to reduce the importance accorded to shareholder votes as a guide to shareholder preferences. Ronald Gilson and Alan Schwartz have argued that elections are inferior to tendering decisions as a guide to shareholder preferences in a control battle.[152] The potential for empty voting strengthens their case. When some directors are conflicted, the Delaware courts channel decision-making to non-conflicted directors. Similarly, if some shareholders hold more votes than economic ownership, judges can give less deference to a voting

150. *See* Hewlett v. Hewlett-Packard Co., No. Civ. A. 19513-NC, 2002 WL 818091, at *9 (Del. Ch. Ap. 30, 2002) (finding that "no one from HP used any threats or inducements regarding future business relationships").

151. *See* Warner Fuller, *Restrictions Imposed by the Directorship Status on the Personal Business Activities of Directors*, 26 WASH. U.L.Q. 189 (1941); *cf.* Golden Rod Mining Co. v. Bukvich, 92 P. 2d 316 (Mont. 1939) (involving an outside director who was a competitor).

152. Ronald J. Gilson & Alan Schwartz, *Sales and Elections as Methods for Transferring Corporate Control*, 2 THEORETICAL INQUIRIES IN LAW 783 (2001).

outcome influenced by the votes of these shareholders. The degree of deference could change both for control contests and for shareholder proposals, for which an open question is how much attention a board should pay to a nonbinding shareholder proposal that receives majority shareholder support.[153]

C. Strategies Focused on Voting Architecture

The new vote buying has put stress on an aging "voting architecture," developed before the emergence of OTC equity derivatives and large-scale stock lending. One result is that even large institutional investors often misunderstand how share lending affects their voting rights. There are also mechanical problems; the simple act of properly counting votes would often fail if all shareholders entitled to vote did so.

Many institutional investors lend through agents and do not keep careful track of which shares have been lent.[154] For example, in 2004, the International Corporate Governance Network (ICGN) circulated among its members a questionnaire on their securities lending practices.[155] Of the 39 institutions which responded (including pension funds, mutual funds, banks, insurance companies, and other asset managers), 31 had lent shares. Most relied on agents and half reported that the agent could lend without the respondent's knowledge. A substantial majority (21 of 31) "[r]arely, only in special circumstances" recalled shares in order to vote them; moreover, attempts to recall shares for voting purposes sometimes failed.

Another recent analysis found similar results. In 2005, the Shareholder Voting Working Group—a financial industry group convened to improve the voting process in the United Kingdom—issued a report stating that some fund managers were not aware that their shares had been lent.[156] This was the case both for institutions that lent through agents and institutions that ran their own lending programs; because lending departments often do not report loans to portfolio managers. Some institutions were not even aware that lent shares cannot be voted. Working Group head Paul Myners stated that "[i]t is not well enough understood that the vote goes with the share."[157]

Fuller information may change lender behavior. CalPERS, a major lender which earns about $110 million a year from this activity, illustrates. Beginning in 2003,

153. *See, e.g.*, Andrew R. Brownstein & Igor Kirman, *Can a Board Say No When Shareholders Say Yes? Responding to Majority Vote Resolutions*, 60 Bus. Law. 23 (2004).

154. *See, e.g.*, Kit Bingham, *Myners rejects calls for curbs on stock lending*, eFinancialNews.com, Mar. 20, 2005 ("most portfolio managers are unaware that their shares have been lent"); Martin Dickson, *Myners' whiffometer*, Fin. Times, Mar. 15, 2005, at 22 ("some fund managers may not be aware that the shares have been lent, since the beneficial owners may contract directly with custodians to lend").

155. *See* Lintstock, *Share lending vis-à-vis voting—A report commissioned by the International Corporate Governance Network* (May 28, 2004), *available at* http://www.icgn.org/documents/share_lending_report_may2004.pdf.

156. Paul Myners, Review of the Impediments to Voting UK Shares 4–5, 11 (2005), *available at* http://www.investmentuk.org/press/2005/20050314-01.pdf.

157. Kit Bingham, *Concern Grows Over Borrowed Votes*, eFinancialNews.com, May 8, 2005.

CalPERS has sought to balance the income it receives from securities lending with its "shareholder responsibility" to vote shares. CalPERS currently will not lend shares of certain companies around voting record dates and claims that it will only lend shares to "those who have a legitimate right to the proxy as a benefit of true ownership."[158]

Institutional investors will vary in their interest in preserving voting rights. Any one investor can profit from lending, while its vote probably won't matter. Some institutional investors enter into "exclusives"—arrangements in which a lender makes some or all of its portfolio available to a particular borrower—usually with no exception for record dates and little consideration of the borrower's goals.[159] On the other hand, some institutional investors (such as Europe's largest pension fund) have decided to stop lending shares despite the impact on their returns.[160]

For annual meetings, a lender's effort to decide whether to hold shares and itself vote faces a technical problem. The record date will usually have passed before the company distributes its proxy statement. Hence, on the record date, investors may not know what is on the agenda (beyond the customary need to elect directors and approve the auditor). One could address this problem by requiring companies to disclose the expected voting agenda when they announce record dates. To be sure, however, this same information could encourage record date capture.

A further step for stock lenders, beyond knowing that they have lent shares and cannot vote, is knowing to whom they have lent. This too is not common. Lenders often lend through agents, or lend to broker-dealers who act on behalf of clients who are unknown to the lender. Efforts are currently under way to require U.S. banks or broker-dealers that arrange securities loans to advise the *borrower* of the *lender's* identity. The goal is to allow the borrower to assess the lender's credit risk, since the lender holds the borrower's collateral.[161] These efforts do not yet contemplate advising the lender of the borrower's identity.

Another concern is mechanical problems associated with voting.[162] Growth in short selling and stock lending are fostering an increasingly serious "over-voting"

---

158. *See* CalPERS, *Securities Lending as It Relates to Proxy Voting* (report prepared by CalPERS staff in response to May 16, 2005 Investment Committee meeting), *available at* http://www.calpers.ca.gov/eip-docs/about/board-cal-agenda/agendas/invest/200506/item08a-03.pdf. We confess to being unsure how CalPERS will decide which borrowers are legitimate and which are not.

159. *See* Gene Picone & Paul Wilson, *Lending Arrangements—Exclusive Risks, Exclusive Rewards*, Global Investor, Mar. 2005, at 1, 1–2.

160. See, e.g., *Super-hero or Super-villain? Is Securities Lending Unpatriotic and Detrimental to the Market, or Does It Improve Liquidity and Efficiency?*, Banker, Nov. 1, 2002.

161. *See DTC Begins Testing for Agency Lending Disclosure*, Business Wire, June 29, 2005; Shane Kite, *Deadline Looms for Securities Lenders-Two-year Agency Disclosure Initiative Still Trying to Fill Membership Gaps*, Sec. Industry News, Mar. 15, 2006; Department of the Treasury, Financial Crimes Enforcement Network, Frequently Asked Questions—Customer Identification Program Responsibilities Under the Agency Lending Disclosure Initiative (Apr. 25, 2006), *available at* http://www.fincen.gov/cip_faq.html.

162. For an introduction to over-voting issues, see Martin & Partnoy, *supra* note 25; Chris Kentouris, *Decisive Moment on Proxy Miscounts*, Sec. Industry News, Dec. 31, 2004; Robert C. Apfel, John E. Parsons, G. William Schwert, & Geoffrey S. Stewart, *Short Sales, Damages, and Class Certification in 10b-5 Actions*, Univ. of Rochester, Simon School of Business Administration, Bradley Policy Research

problem, which arises as follows. Currently, brokers who hold shares in street name must vote in accordance with their clients' instructions. Suppose that a broker holds 2 million shares in a pooled account on behalf of margin customers, lends 1 million shares, and receives voting instructions from holders of 1.5 million shares. There is no coherent way of ensuring that such a broker will cast only 1 million votes, nor for companies to decide what to do if a broker votes too many shares, nor for the broker to decide whose voting instructions count if it casts only 1 million votes. Instead, brokers and companies follow ad hoc procedures, with uncertain impact on proxy fights. The New York Stock Exchange issued a warning on over-voting in 2004.[163] Over-voting has been an issue in at least two lawsuits over the results of a proxy fight.[164] The Securities Transfer Association, a trade group for transfer agents, reviewed 341 shareholder votes in corporate contests in 2005—and found over-voting in all 341 cases.[165] One company specializing in the oversight of shareholder elections recently said that "[a] lot of the time we have no idea who's entitled to vote and who isn't" and called the situation an "abomination."[166]

The current formally correct response to overvoting is to limit the broker in our example to 1 million votes (presumably cast in proportion to the voting instructions the broker receives). But this would disenfranchise individual shareholders and *increase* the disparity between economic ownership and voting rights. What might contribute to a better solution would be a change in business practice in which economic owners could decide whether to allow their shares to be lent around record dates, or in which stock lenders could elect to retain voting rights. If some lenders retain voting rights, borrowers who need these voting rights would have to borrow from lenders who were willing to part with them, presumably at higher cost.

In sum, the current ways in which share lending affects voting need to be updated, both to ensure that those with voting rights can exercise them and to provide lenders and borrowers with the information they need to decide what to do with their voting rights.

D. Strategies Focused on Supply and Demand Forces in the Markets on Which the New Vote Buying Relies

A third family of regulatory interventions would focus on the supply and demand forces in the markets that support new vote buying, especially the share

Center Financial Research and Policy Working Paper No. FR 01-19 (July 2001), *available at* http://ssrn.com/abstract=285768.

163. *See* Kentouris, *supra* note 162.

164. *See* Seidman and Associates, L.L.C. v. G.A. Financial, Inc., 837 A.2d 21 (Del. Ch. 2003) (court upholds decision by election inspector to disallow all 232,000 votes cast by a broker dealer who had overvoted by less than 1,000 votes); Apfel et al., *supra* note 162 (discussing a proxy contest at Integrated Circuit Systems and associated voting actions taken by brokers).

165. Bob Drummond, *One Share, One Vote: Short Selling Short-circuits the System*, Int'l Herald Trib., Mar. 1, 2006, at 20.

166. *Id.* (quoting Thomas Montrone, CEO of Registrar & Transfer).

lending market. On the "supply" side, one could regulate share lenders, lending intermediaries, and derivatives dealers. On the "demand" side, one could regulate the purposes for which hedge funds and other investors could acquire voting rights decoupled from economic ownership. The primary actors here would be the SEC, the Federal Reserve Board, the U.S. Department of Labor, and other federal authorities.

1. Encouraging Institutional Shareholders to Vote on Important Matters

One approach would be to encourage institutional shareholders to vote on important matters. Voting could be made part of their obligation to their clients, perhaps with an exception for routine matters. Regulators have already gone part-way down this path for mutual funds and pension funds. An SEC guideline for mutual funds states that:

> We would not object if voting rights pass with the lending of securities. However, this does not relieve the directors of a fund of their fiduciary obligation to vote proxies. If the fund management has knowledge that a material event will occur affecting an investment on loan, the directors would be obligated to call such loan in time to vote the proxies.[167]

We are not aware, however, of SEC efforts to enforce this soft guidance. It has little bite for annual meetings, for the technical reason noted above—the record date has typically passed before the company distributes its proxy statement, thus informing shareholders about the voting agenda. Moreover, the SEC's controversial 2003 rules requiring mutual funds and investment advisers to disclose their voting practices are silent on stock lending. The adopting release states that mutual funds and investment advisers can choose not to vote if the costs of doing so outweigh the benefits, and offers examples involving voting of foreign shares.[168]

The Department of Labor (DoL), which regulates pension plans subject to ERISA (basically, company pension plans but not public sector pension plans), has adopted a similar approach. Interpretive Bulletin 94-2 encourages but does not require voting. For shares of foreign corporations, the Department interprets ERISA fiduciary duties:

> to require the responsible plan fiduciary to weigh the costs and benefits of voting on proxy proposals relating to foreign securities and make an informed decision with

167. *See, e.g.*, State Street Bank & Trust Company, SEC No-Action Letter, 1972 SEC No-Act. LEXIS 4607 (Sept. 29, 1972); *cf.* Susan C. Peters, *Accounting Treatment of Loans of Securities*, in SECURITIES FINANCE: SECURITIES LENDING AND REPURCHASE AGREEMENTS 209 (Frank J. Fabozzi & Steven M. Mann eds., 2005) (mutual funds "must have the ability to recall any security on loan to vote on a material event proxy").

168. *See* Disclosure of Proxy Voting Policies and Proxy Voting Records By Registered Investment Companies, SEC Rel. No. 33-8188 (Jan. 31, 2003); Proxy Voting by Investment Advisers, SEC Rel. No. IA-2106 (Jan. 31, 2003). On the circumstances when investment advisors need not vote, see Rel. No. IA-2106, *supra*, at § II(A)(2)(a) & n. 3.

> respect to whether voting a given proxy proposal is prudent and solely in the interest of the plan's participants and beneficiaries.[169]

A similar analysis presumably would apply to voting shares in U.S. companies.

At the same time, the DoL appears to expect that ERISA plan trustees will recall lent shares in order to cast important votes. In a 1979 advisory opinion on share lending, the Department stated:

> a breach of fiduciary responsibility . . . might result if the plan trustees do not terminate the loan in time to vote proxies in the event of an occurrence affecting the plan's interest in the security.[170]

It is not hard to imagine the SEC, the DoL, or other regulators strengthening this sort of informal guidance, and extending to other classes of institutional investors a requirement to recall lent shares in order to cast important votes. Regulators might also require institutions to disclose when they have lent shares rather than voting them. Some might find it embarrassing to have to disclose that they routinely lend shares around record dates.

2. Safe Harbor for Voting Instead of Lending Shares

A more modest step would address the dilemma faced by an institutional investor which must decide whether to lend or vote shares. Any one institution's vote is unlikely to affect the outcome, so lending will often be privately optimal. Yet collectively, institutional voting can benefit all shareholders. This externality will produce too much lending and too little voting. The SEC and DoL positions on share lending, discussed above, likely provide a quasi-safe harbor in terms of fiduciary challenges. If one's regulator is urging one to vote, it is hard for clients to object to a decision to do so. Still, there could be value in a safe harbor for all institutions which vote shares rather than lend them around a record date.

3. Reducing the Attractiveness of Lending Shares and Providing Equity Derivatives

There are also a variety of tax and regulatory changes that could be deployed to make share lending less attractive to lenders, or to make equity swaps less attractive to derivatives dealers. One set of changes could focus on the fact that if a mutual fund lends shares and receives a dividend-equivalent payment, the dividend would have qualified for a reduced 15% tax rate; but the substitute payment does not.[171] A similar tax issue arises for lending by broker-dealers. If a

169. *See* Department of Labor, Interpretive Bulletin 94-2 (July 29, 1994); *cf.* Clifford E. Kirsch, *Proxy Voting*, in MUTUAL FUND REGULATION § 11.4 (Clifford E. Kirsch ed., 2d ed. 2005) (describing DoL's approach to proxy voting).

170. Department of Labor—Pension & Welfare Benefit Programs, Opinion 79-11A, 1979 ERISA LEXIS 81 (Feb. 23, 1979).

171. For discussion of how these tax considerations may cause stock lending to flow from mutual funds to (tax-exempt) pension funds, see Phyllis Feinberg, *Reduced Supply: New Law to Slow Mutual Funds' Securities Lending: Pension Fund Programs Stand to Receive Benefits of Recently Passed Dividend Tax Cut*, PENSIONS & INVESTMENTS, Sept. 1, 2003, at 6.

broker lends customer shares and receives dividend-equivalent payments, the broker keeps the loan proceeds, while the customer receives "payments in lieu of dividends," which are taxed as ordinary income. These tax consequences should reduce the attractiveness of stock lending. For example, unless compensated for these tax consequences (which is not the current industry practice), investors could open cash accounts (from which shares cannot be lent) rather than margin accounts.

Many mutual fund investors and margin account holders are probably not aware of the tax consequences of share lending. Broker-dealers must disclose annually to their customers the portion of investment income that qualifies for the dividend tax rate, but not the reasons why. One can imagine better disclosure, for example, a statement that "we earned $X last year by lending shares from your account; this increased your ordinary income by an estimated $Y."

Other steps could affect the attractiveness of share lending and equity derivatives activities. Broker-dealers could be required periodically to obtain customer consent to lend shares held in margin accounts.[172] Pension funds and banks are already subject to constraints on their securities lending activities; these could be revisited.[173] Capital adequacy and general safety and soundness requirements applicable to commercial and investment banks provide additional regulatory levers. We make no claim that particular tax or regulatory tweaks are desirable, only that they are possible.

4. Imposing Responsibilities on Share Lenders and Derivatives Providers

Another possible approach would require share lenders and equity swap providers to know their clients, and how their clients will use the share borrowing or swap. In the Enron disaster, banks offered Enron a variety of financial products that helped Enron present a misleading financial picture to the public. One consequence has been multibillion dollar payments by major banks to settle class action lawsuits. Another is that regulators now expect financial institutions to do more to investigate their clients' use of financial products to game disclosure or tax rules.[174] The SEC, the Federal Reserve Board, and the Office of the Comptroller of the Currency have issued a joint statement warning financial institutions against creating complex financial products that let their customers artificially alter their

172. Rule 15c3-3(b)(3), 17 C.F.R. § 240.15c3-3(b)(3) (2005), specifies that the broker's borrowing of securities from its margin customer be pursuant to a written agreement that meets certain criteria; there is no requirement that the agreement be periodically renewed, or that the customer approve individual loans. *See* Michael P. Jamroz, *The Customer Protection Rule*, 57 Bus. Law. 1069 (2002).

173. For details on these constraints, see Hu & Black, *New Vote Buying*, *supra* note 24, at 903–04.

174. *See* In the Matter of Citigroup, Inc. SEC Rel. No. 34-48230, 2003 SEC LEXIS 1778 (July 28, 2003); In the Matter of J.P. Morgan Chase & Co., Lit. Rel. No. 18252 2003 SEC LEXIS 1775 (July 28, 2003).

public financial statements or evade taxes.[175] Regulators could take a similar interest in investment banks' creation of instruments designed to facilitate empty voting or evade ownership disclosure rules.

In one respect, current rules already limit the purposes for which shares may be lent. Under Federal Reserve Regulation T, broker-dealers who have material dealings with the general public are exempt from the usual margin rules that limit borrowing to acquire securities. Other broker-dealers enjoy a more limited "permitted purpose" exemption. They may "borrow or lend securities in case of short sales, failure to receive securities required to be delivered, or similar situations."[176] Under the "permitted purposes" exemption, broker-dealers are required to make a good faith effort to determine the borrower's purpose and cannot lend shares for voting purposes.[177] All the Federal Reserve need do to greatly limit record date capture is to either extend the permitted purpose approach to all broker-dealers or make share lending for vote capture purposes an illicit purpose for otherwise exempt broker-dealers. Such a ban on share lending to permit record date capture is already the informal norm in the U.K.[178]

A similar "know your customer's purpose" approach could affect the market for some other forms of vote buying. Suppose that a hedge fund comes to a derivatives dealer, seeking simultaneously to buy shares and hedge its economic exposure, ending up with pure votes. One could establish a presumption that the hedge fund's goal is empty voting, and bar dealers from entering into these swaps.

5. The Demand Side: Executive Hedging

The demand for vote buying and the products it depends on can be affected by techniques similar to some of those discussed above for the supply side. We offer here one example, involving executive hedging, which usually leaves executives with more voting power than economic interest. One could make this "lite voting" less attractive by increasing the tax consequences of hedging. By hedging, the executive has effectively sold a portion of his shares. Internal Revenue Code section 1259 taxes, as constructive sales, a limited set of hedges.[179] For example, an equity swap that offsets "substantially all" economic exposure would trigger taxation. Section 1259 is easy to avoid: standard zero-cost collars do not trigger

175. *See* Securities and Exchange Commission, Policy Statement: Interagency Statement on Sound Practices Concerning Complex Structured Finance Activities, SEC Rel. No. 34-49695, 2004 SEC LEXIS 1017 (May 13, 2004); Interagency Statement on Sound Practices Concerning Elevated Risk Complex Structured Finance Activities, 71 Fed. Reg. 28326 (May 16, 2006).

176. *See* Regulation T, 12 C.F.R. pt 220 (2006), especially 12 C.F.R. § 220.2 (2006) ("exempted borrower" exemption for major broker-dealers); 12 C.F.R. § 220.10(c) (2006) ("permitted purpose" exemption for other broker-dealers).

177. *See* Federal Reserve Board Rulings and Staff Opinions Interpreting Regulation T, 5-615.01, FRRS 5-615.01 (July 6, 1984) (regarding analogous situation of record date capture to let borrowers take advantage of company dividend reinvestment plans).

178. *See* Myners, *supra* note 156, at 13; Bank of England, Securities Borrowing and Lending Code of Guidance, at 17 (2004), *available at* http://www.bankofengland.co.uk/markets/gilts/stockborrowing.pdf (stating that there is "consensus in the market" that securities "should not be borrowed solely for the purposes of exercising the voting rights at [a shareholder meeting]").

179. 26 U.S.C.A. § 1259 (2002 & Supp. 2006).

it, nor would a swap that offset most, but not "substantially all" of an executive's economic exposure.[180] While it may be hard to develop an administrable rule that could not be easily gamed, one could try to move to a more easily triggered standard.

VI. Conclusion

The shareholder vote is a central means by which corporate governance systems constrain managers' discretion over other people's money. The vitality of that constraint, however, depends on a connection between votes and economic interest.

Financial innovation now allows large scale, low cost, often undisclosed decoupling of voting rights from economic ownership. This decoupling—the new vote buying—comes in two main forms, which we call empty voting (more votes than economic ownership) and hidden (morphable) ownership (undisclosed economic ownership accompanied by informal voting rights). The modern derivative, heretofore largely a risk management tool and an investment vehicle for investors and firms, can also affect voting outcomes. OTC derivatives, developed to trade risk, turn out to be well adapted for trading votes. A now-massive share lending market serves the needs of both short-sellers and empty voters.

Hedge funds have been among the pioneers in both forms of the new vote buying. Insiders have also used decoupling strategies to retain votes while shedding economic exposure. In the past several years, decoupling has played an increasing role in corporate governance worldwide. We have found more than twenty publicly known or rumored examples, almost all since 2002. Several involve empty voting by investors with negative economic interests, who would profit if the companies' share prices go down. Additional uses of decoupling have surely remained hidden.

Not all vote buying is bad. Some could move votes from less informed to better informed investors, and strengthen shareholder oversight. Still, unless there are ways to separate good vote buying from bad, and allow only the former, the new vote buying, as we call it, can potentially undermine the coupling between voting and ownership. Voting outcomes might be determined by hidden warfare among company insiders and major investors, each employing vote morphing and other financial innovations to swing a voting contest. Voting results are now increasingly close, a corollary to voting becoming an increasingly significant aspect of corporate governance. Winning a close vote could sometimes turn on cleverness in decoupling, rather than the merits of each side's position.

While the potential corporate governance threat posed by the new vote buying is serious, the extent and nature of the new vote buying is unknown. In addition, any regulatory response to decoupling must attend to potential effects on derivatives and short-selling. Derivatives serve good purposes, as well as ill. Short

180. *See, e.g.*, Alex Raskolnikov, *Contextual Analysis of Tax Ownership*, 85 B.U. L. Rev. 431 (2005); Deborah H. Schenk, *An Efficiency Approach to Reforming a Realization-Based Tax*, 57 Tax L. Rev. 503, 532–33 (2004) (noting that a "very limited number of taxpayers" pay tax under § 1259).

sellers play a valuable role in securities markets, and depend on the same share lending market that facilitates the new vote buying.

The first step is to better understand the new vote buying through enhanced disclosure. Empty voting and hidden (morphable) ownership should, we believe, be exposed to public view. This article's "integrated ownership disclosure" proposal would partially integrate and greatly simplify the five existing ownership disclosure regimes. The proposal is practical and indeed may reduce the direct costs of regulatory compliance. Indeed, we believe that our integrated ownership disclosure proposal is worth considering for its simplicity and internal consistency alone, even apart from its value in relation to new vote buying.

Disclosure may be a sufficient response to hidden (morphable) ownership. For empty voting, it will likely be only a first step, but a sufficient step to give regulators, judges, companies, and investors a good view of the nature and scale of this new activity. Eventually—perhaps soon—other responses to empty voting may be needed. One family of responses would involve focusing on voting rights themselves. Corporations can, for instance, amend their charters to condition voting rights of major shareholders on economic ownership. Other families of responses focus on voting mechanics and on the supply and demand forces in the OTC derivatives and share lending markets, on which the new vote buying relies.

Which additional reforms should be adopted, we cannot yet say. That will depend on information as yet unknown, which our disclosure rules are designed to collect. We do know that existing legal and economic theories of the public corporation depend on a link between voting rights and economic ownership that can no longer be relied on.

Part VI
Comparative Perspective

[19]

THE JOURNAL OF FINANCE • VOL. LXI, NO. 1 • FEBRUARY 2006

What Works in Securities Laws?

RAFAEL LA PORTA, FLORENCIO LOPEZ-DE-SILANES,
and ANDREI SHLEIFER*

ABSTRACT

We examine the effect of securities laws on stock market development in 49 countries. We find little evidence that public enforcement benefits stock markets, but strong evidence that laws mandating disclosure and facilitating private enforcement through liability rules benefit stock markets.

IN THIS PAPER, WE EXAMINE SECURITIES LAWS OF 49 COUNTRIES, focusing specifically on how these laws regulate the issuance of new equity to the public. Security issuance is subject to the well-known "promoter's problem" (Mahoney (1995))—the risk that corporate issuers sell bad securities to the public—and as such is covered in all securities laws.[1] We analyze the specific provisions in securities laws governing initial public offerings in each country, examine the relationship between these provisions and various measures of stock market development, and interpret the evidence in light of the available theories of securities laws.

For securities markets, alternative theories of optimal legal arrangements can be distilled down to three broad hypotheses. Under the null hypothesis, associated with Coase (1960) and Stigler (1964), the optimal government policy is to leave securities markets unregulated. Issuers of securities have an incentive to disclose all available information to obtain higher prices simply because failure to disclose would cause investors to assume the worst (Grossman (1981), Grossman and Hart (1980), Milgrom and Roberts (1986)). Investors can

* La Porta is at Tuck School of Business, Dartmouth College; Lopez-de-Silones is at the University of Amsterdam; and Shleifer is at Harvard University. We are grateful to the Inter-American Development Bank, the Gildor Foundation, the BSI Gamma Foundation, the NSF, the International Institute for Corporate Governance at Yale University, and the Doing Business project of the World Bank for financial support; to Alfredo Larrea-Falcony and Qian Sun for significant contributions to this work; to Constanza Blanco, John C. Coates IV, Luis Leyva Martinez, Carlos Orta Tejeda, Tuffic Miguel Ortega, Jorge Gabriel Taboada Hoyos, Annette L. Nazareth, and Robert Strahota for assistance in developing the questionnaire; to Douglas Baird, Jack Coffee, Frank Easterbrook, Richard Epstein, Merritt Fox, Edward Glaeser, Simon Johnson, Lawrence Katz, Paul Mahoney, Mark Ramseyer, Kevin Murphy, Eric Posner, Richard Posner, Roberta Romano, Luigi Spaventa, the editor, and two referees of this journal for helpful comments; and to Jeffrey Friedman, Mario Gamboa-Cavazos, Amy Levin, Anete Pajuste, and Vasudev Vadlamudi for excellent research assistance. The data used in this paper can be downloaded from http://post.economics.harvard.edu/faculty/shleifer/papers/securities_data.xls.

[1] Teoh, Welch, and Wong (1998) and Dechow, Sloan, and Sweeney (1996) present evidence consistent with the view that U.S. firms manipulate accounting figures to raise capital on favorable terms. Leuz, Nanda, and Wysocki (2003) show that earnings manipulation is more extensive in countries with weak investor protection.

rely on these disclosures when there are reputational, legal, and contractual penalties for misreporting, verification of accuracy is costless, or reporting accuracy is backed by warranties. When verification is costly, issuers of "good" securities can resort to additional mechanisms to signal their quality (Ross (1979)). For example, auditors and underwriters can credibly certify the quality of the securities being offered to safeguard their reputation and avoid liability under contract or tort law (Benston (1985), Chemmanur and Fulghieri (1994), De Long (1991)). Similarly, private stock exchanges can mandate optimal disclosure and monitor compliance by listed firms to facilitate trading (Benston (1973), Fischel and Grossman (1984), Miller (1991)). These market and general legal mechanisms suffice for securities markets to prosper. Securities law is either irrelevant (to the extent that it codifies existing market arrangements or can be contracted around), or damaging, in so far as it raises contracting costs and invites political interference in markets (Coase (1975), Macey (1994), Romano (2001)).

The two alternative hypotheses hold that securities laws "matter." Both reputations and contract and tort law are insufficient to keep promoters from cheating investors because the payoff from cheating is too high and because private tort and contract litigation is too expensive and unpredictable to serve as a deterrent. To reduce the enforcement costs and opportunistic behavior, the government can introduce a securities law that specifies the contracting framework.[2] The two alternative hypotheses differ in what kind of government intervention would be optimal within such a framework.

Under the first alternative, the government can standardize the private contracting framework to improve market discipline and private litigation. Without such standardization, litigation is governed by contract and tort law, with grave uncertainty about outcomes because such matters as intent and negligence need to be sorted out in court (Easterbrook and Fischel (1984)). We examine two aspects of standardization. First, the law can mandate the disclosure of particular information, such as profitability and ownership structure, in the prospectus. If followed, such mandates make it easier for investors to value companies and therefore more willing to invest. If violated, these mandates create a prima facie liability of issuers or intermediaries. Second, the law can specify the liability standards facing issuers and intermediaries when investors seek to recover damages from companies that follow affirmative disclosure rules but fail to reveal potentially material information. The law can thereby reduce the uncertainties and the costs of private litigation, in turn benefiting markets.[3]

Under the final hypothesis, even given a securities law that describes both the disclosure obligations of various parties and the liability standards, private enforcement incentives are often insufficient to elicit honesty from issuers. A public enforcer such as a Securities and Exchange Commission is needed to

[2] See Landis (1938), Friend and Herman (1964), Coffee (1984, 1989, 2002), Simon (1989), Mahoney (1995), Fox (1999), Stulz (1999), Black (2001), Beny (2002), and Reese and Weisbach (2002).

[3] This view is developed in Black and Kraakman (1996), Hay, Shleifer, and Vishny (1996), Hay and Shleifer (1998), Glaeser and Shleifer (2001, 2002), and Bergman and Nicolaievsky (2002).

support trade. Such an enforcer might be able to intervene ex ante, by clarifying legal obligations or ex post, by imposing its own penalties or bringing lawsuits. Public enforcement might work because the enforcer is *independent and focused* and thus can regulate markets free from political interference, because the enforcer can *introduce regulations of market participants,* because it can *secure information* from issuers and market participants—through subpoena, discovery, or other means—more effectively than private plaintiffs, or because it can *impose sanctions.*[4] Under this hypothesis, the strength of public enforcement introduced by securities laws is most beneficial for market development.

To distinguish these hypotheses, we cooperate with attorneys from 49 countries to assemble a database of rules and regulations governing security issuance. We use the data to produce quantitative measures of securities laws and regulations, with a focus on mandatory disclosure, liability standards, and public enforcement. Finally, we examine the relationship between our measures of securities laws and a number of indicators of stock market development. In the analysis below, we first motivate our data collection effort using an example of an actual dispute. We then present the data on securities laws around the world, and finally investigate whether and how these laws matter for stock market development.

I. A Motivating Example

We focus on the agency problem between prospective investors in an initial public offering and the "promoter" who offers shares for sale. In modern days, this promoter is usually the owner or founder of a private company acting in concert with his distributors (or underwriters) and accountants. But at least some of the law developed historically as a way to control share sales by specialized promoters, who bought companies and then sold their equity to the public (Mahoney (1995)). The promoter's problem is fraught with potential conflicts of interest. The promoter wants to sell the shares at the highest possible price while concealing bad information about the company and diverting its cash flows and assets to himself. Both the adverse selection and the moral hazard problems are severe, and if not addressed can undermine and possibly stop fund-raising in the stock market.

Grossman and Hart (1980) show, however, that with perfect law enforcement (i.e., automatic sanctions for not telling the truth), promoters have an incentive to reveal everything they know, at least in a particular model. The reason is that without such revelation, potential investors assume the absolute worst. To the extent that the circumstances of the company are better or the conflicts of interest less severe, promoters have every reason to disclose such information, and they cannot say anything more optimistic than the truth because of the automatic sanctions. Grossman and Hart also note that without perfect enforcement, these favorable results for the market solution do not hold.

[4] These themes are developed in Landis (1938), Becker (1968), Polinsky and Shavell (2000), Glaeser, Johnson, and Shleifer (2001), Glaeser and Shleifer (2003), and Pistor and Xu (2002).

Contrast this theoretical paradigm with an actual example of a securities issue from the Netherlands (Velthuyse and Schlingmann (1995)). In 1987–1988, the Dutch bank ABN Amro underwrote some bonds of Coopag Finance BV, a Dutch financial company wholly owned by Co-op AG, a diversified German firm. The bonds were guaranteed by Co-op AG. The prospectus was drafted in accordance with the requirements of the Amsterdam Stock Exchange and included audited annual accounts provided by the issuer to ABN Amro. In conformity with the law on annual accounts, the (consolidated) financial statements included in the prospectus omitted 214 affiliated companies of Co-op AG with debts of DM 1.5 billion. Shortly after the issue, Dutch newspapers published negative information about Co-op AG and the bond prices of Coopag Finance BV plummeted. The creditors of Coopag Finance sued the underwriter, ABN Amro, for losses due to its failure to disclose material information about the finances of Co-op AG. ABN Amro claimed in response that "the damages, if any, did not result from the alleged misleading nature of the prospectuses. . . . ," but rather from unfavorable events that took place after the offering. In addition, the distributor argued that "an investigation by ABN Amro, however extensive, could not have led to the discovery of deceit, because even the accountants appeared not to have discovered in time that something was wrong . . . " (Velthuyse and Schlingmann (1995), p. 233). The successive Dutch courts, however, ruled the distributor liable and recognized explicitly that the distributor's duty in presenting the prospectus to investors went beyond merely relying on the information provided by the issuer. Rather, to avoid liability, the Supreme Court ruled that a distributor must conduct an independent investigation of the issuer and prove that it cannot be blamed for the damages caused by the misleading prospectus.

As this example illustrates, a country as developed as the Netherlands, as recently as 15 years ago, did not have clearly defined responsibilities and automatic penalties for issuers and underwriters as required by Grossman and Hart (1980). Some of the differences between the example and their model are worth emphasizing. First, reputational concerns did not suffice to induce either the issuer to disclose the omitted information or the underwriter to carry out an independent investigation of the issuer's financial condition. Second, the problem for private enforcement was not that of inaccurate disclosure—in fact, the issuer complied with the affirmative disclosure requirements—but rather, the omission of material information from the prospectus. This omission did not cause investors to assume the worst; after all, they bought the bonds. Third, this omission raised the question for the court of whether the distributor or the issuer was liable, with the distributor rather than the bankrupt issuer having the assets to compensate investors. Fourth, and perhaps most importantly, the court had to resolve the crucial question of the standard of liability for the distributor, namely, what were its affirmative obligations to investors. The court did not presume, as in the model, that failure to disclose automatically caused liability. Resolving this issue required extensive and expensive litigation, leading to a particular standard of care. These differences between the case and the model suggest that in reality, enforcement of good conduct is costly, and hence we should not necessarily expect efficient outcomes from unregulated markets.

This enforcement-based reasoning forms the analytical foundation of the case for securities laws. Market mechanisms and litigation supporting private contracting may be too expensive. Since investors, on average, are not tricked, they pay lower prices for the equity when they are unprotected, and the amount of equity issued is lower (Shleifer and Wolfenzon (2002), La Porta et al. (2002b)). Securities laws, in so far as they reduce the costs of contracting and resolving disputes, can encourage equity financing of firms and stock market development. The Dutch example also suggests that solving the promoter's problem is important not only for equity markets but for debt markets as well.

II. The Variables

Our data on the regulation of the promoter's problem are based on answers to a questionnaire by attorneys in the sample of 49 countries with the largest stock market capitalization in 1993 (La Porta et al. (1998)). We invited one attorney from each country to answer the questionnaire describing the securities laws (including actual laws, statues, regulations, binding judicial precedents, and any other rule with force of law) applicable to an offering of shares listed in the country's largest stock exchange in December 2000.[5] All 49 authors returned answered questionnaires, and subsequently confirmed the validity of their answers as we recorded them. All the variables derived from the questionnaires and other sources are defined in Table I.

A. Disclosure and Liability Standards

As James Landis, the principal author of U.S. securities laws, recognized, making private recovery of investors' losses easy is essential to harness the incentives of market participants to enforce securities laws (Landis (1938), Seligman (1995)). Efficiency considerations suggest that the lowest cost provider of information about a security should collect and present this information, and be held accountable if he omits or misleads. In the Grossman and Hart model (1980), for example, the lowest cost providers are not the investors, but the issuers, distributors, and accountants.[6] An efficient system would provide these agents incentives to collect and present information to investors,

[5] We first approached authors who had published country reports on securities laws in publications such as *International Securities Regulation* and *International Securities Laws*. When countries were not covered in such publications or authors declined our invitation, we searched the *Martindale Law Directory* to identify leading law firms practicing in the area of securities laws and invited them to answer the questionnaire. The respondents received a questionnaire designed by the authors with the help of practicing lawyers in Argentina, Japan, and the United States.

[6] Two other features of initial public offerings make "buyer-beware" rules unattractive. First, the scope for fraud is very large. Second, the damages resulting from investing in reliance of a defective prospectus are much easier to calculate than those that result from, for example, the use of a defective appliance.

Table I

Description of the Variables

This table describes the variables in the paper. The *Supervisor* is the main government agency in charge of supervising stock exchanges. The *Issuer* is a domestic corporation that raises capital through an initial public offering of common shares. The newly issued shares will be listed on the country's largest stock exchange. The *Distributor* advises the *Issuer* on the preparation of the prospectus and assists in marketing the securities but does not authorize (or sign) the prospectus unless required by law. The *Accountant* audits the financial statements and documents that accompany the prospectus. Unless otherwise specified, the source for the variables is the questionnaire of law firms and the laws of each country. The edited answers to the questionnaire are posted at http://post.economics.harvard.edu/faculty/shleifer/papers/securities_documentation.pdf.

Variable	Description
	I. Disclosure requirements
Prospectus	Equals one if the law prohibits selling securities that are going to be listed on the largest stock exchange of the country without delivering a prospectus to potential investors; and equals zero otherwise.
Compensation	An index of prospectus disclosure requirements regarding the compensation of the *Issuer*'s directors and key officers. Equals one if the law or the listing rules require that the compensation of *each* director and key officer be reported in the prospectus of a newly listed firm; equals one half if only the *aggregate* compensation of directors and key officers must be reported in the prospectus of a newly listed firm; and equals zero when there is no requirement to disclose the compensation of directors and key officers in the prospectus for a newly listed firm.
Shareholders	An index of disclosure requirements regarding the *Issuer*'s equity ownership structure. Equals one if the law or the listing rules require disclosing the name and ownership stake of each shareholder who, directly or indirectly, controls 10% or more of the *Issuer*'s voting securities; equals one half if reporting requirements for the *Issuer*'s 10% shareholders do not include indirect ownership or if only their aggregate ownership needs to be disclosed; and equals zero when the law does not require disclosing the name and ownership stake of the *Issuer*'s 10% shareholders. We combine large shareholder reporting requirements imposed on firms with those imposed on large shareholders themselves.
Inside ownership	An index of prospectus disclosure requirements regarding the equity ownership of the *Issuer*'s shares by its directors and key officers. Equals one if the law or the listing rules require that the ownership of the *Issuer's* shares by *each* of its director and key officers be disclosed in the prospectus; equals one half if only the *aggregate* number of the *Issuer*'s shares owned by its directors and key officers must be disclosed in the prospectus; and equals zero when the ownership of the *Issuer*'s shares by its directors and key officers need not be disclosed in the prospectus.
Irregular contracts	An index of prospectus disclosure requirements regarding the *Issuer*'s contracts outside the ordinary course of business. Equals one if the law or the listing rules require that the terms of material contracts made by the *Issuer* outside the ordinary course of its business be disclosed in the prospectus; equals one half if the terms of only *some* material contracts made outside the ordinary course of business must be disclosed; and equals zero otherwise.
Transactions	An index of the prospectus disclosure requirements regarding transaction between the *Issuer* and its directors, officers, and/or large shareholders (i.e., "related parties"). Equals one if the law or the listing rules require that *all* transactions in which related parties have, or will have, an interest be disclosed in the prospectus; equals one half if *only some* transactions between the *Issuer* and related parties must be disclosed in the prospectus; and equals zero if transactions between the *Issuer* and related parties need not be disclosed in the prospectus.
Disclosure requirements index	The index of disclosure equals the arithmetic mean of (1) prospectus; (2) compensation; (3) shareholders; (4) inside ownership; (5) contracts irregular; and (6) transactions.

(*continued*)

Table I—*Continued*

Variable	Description
	II. Liability standard
Liability standard for the issuer and its directors	Index of the procedural difficulty in recovering losses from the *Issuer* and its directors in a civil liability case for losses due to misleading statements in the prospectus. We first code separately the liability standard applicable to the *Issuer* and its directors and then average the two of them. The liability standard applicable to the *Issuer's* directors equals one when investors are only required to prove that the prospectus contains a misleading statement. Equals two thirds when investors must also prove that they relied on the prospectus and/or that their loss was caused by the misleading statement. Equals one third when investors must also prove that the director acted with negligence. Equals zero if restitution from directors is either unavailable or the liability standard is intent or gross negligence. The liability standard applicable to the *Issuer* is coded analogously.
Liability standard for distributors	Index of the procedural difficulty in recovering losses from the *Distributor* in a civil liability case for losses due to misleading statements in the prospectus. Equals one when investors are only required to prove that the prospectus contains a misleading statement. Equals two thirds when investors must also prove that they relied on the prospectus and/or that their loss was caused by the misleading statement. Equals one third when investors must also prove that the *Distributor* acted with negligence. Equals zero if restitution from the *Distributor* is either unavailable or the liability standard is intent or gross negligence.
Liability standard for accountants	Index of the procedural difficulty in recovering losses from the *Accountant* in a civil liability case for losses due to misleading statements in the audited financial information accompanying the prospectus. Equals one when investors are only required to prove that the audited financial information accompanying the prospectus contains a misleading statement. Equals two thirds when investors must also prove that they relied on the prospectus and/or that their loss was caused by the misleading accounting information. Equals one third when investors must also prove that the *Accountant* acted with negligence. Equals zero if restitution from the *Accountant* is either unavailable or the liability standard is intent or gross negligence.
Liability standard index	The index of liability standards equals the arithmetic mean of (1) liability standard for the issuer and its directors; (2) liability standard for distributors; and (3) liability standard for accountants.
	III.1 Characteristics of the Supervisor of securities markets
Appointment	Equals one if a majority of the members of the *Supervisor* are not unilaterally appointed by the Executive branch of government; and equals zero otherwise.
Tenure	Equals one if members of the *Supervisor* cannot be dismissed at the will of the appointing authority; and equals zero otherwise.
Focus	Equals one if separate government agencies or official authorities are in charge of supervising commercial banks and stock exchanges; and equals zero otherwise.
Supervisor characteristics index	The index of characteristics of the *Supervisor* equals the arithmetic mean of (1) appointment; (2) tenure; and (3) focus.
	III.2 Power of the Supervisor to issue rules
Rule-making power index	An index of the power of the *Supervisor* to issue regulations regarding primary offerings and listing rules on stock exchanges. Equals one if the *Supervisor* can generally issue regulations regarding primary offerings and/or listing rules on stock exchanges without prior approval of other governmental authorities. Equals one half if the *Supervisor* can generally issue regulations regarding primary offerings and/or listing rules on stock exchanges only with the prior approval of other governmental authorities. Equals zero otherwise.

(*continued*)

Table I—*Continued*

Variable	Description
	III.3 Investigative powers of the Supervisor of securities markets
Document	An index of the power of the *Supervisor* to command documents when investigating a violation of securities laws. Equals one if the *Supervisor* can generally issue an administrative order commanding all persons to turn over documents; equals one half if the *Supervisor* can generally issue an administrative order commanding publicly traded corporations and/or their directors to turn over documents; and equals zero otherwise.
Witness	An index of the power of the *Supervisor* to subpoena the testimony of witnesses when investigating a violation of securities laws. Equals one if the *Supervisor* can generally subpoena all persons to give testimony; equals one half if the *Supervisor* can generally subpoena the directors of publicly traded corporations to give testimony; and equals zero otherwise.
Investigative powers index	The index of investigative powers equals the arithmetic mean of (1) document; and (2) witness.
	III.4 Sanctions
Orders issuer	An index aggregating stop and do orders that may be directed to the *Issuer* in case of a defective prospectus. The index is formed by averaging the subindexes of orders to stop and to do. The subindex of orders to stop equals one if the *Issuer* may be ordered to refrain from a broad range of actions; equals one half if the *Issuer* may only be ordered to desist from limited actions; and equals zero otherwise. The subindex of orders to do equals one if the *Issuer* may be ordered to perform a broad range of actions to rectify the violation; equals one half if the *Issuer* may only be ordered to perform limited actions; and equals zero otherwise. We disregard orders that may be issued by Courts at the request of a private party in a civil lawsuit.
Orders distributor	An index aggregating stop and do orders that may be directed to the *Distributor* in case of a defective prospectus. The index is formed by averaging the subindexes of orders to stop and to do. The subindex of orders to stop equals one if the *Distributor* may be ordered to refrain from a broad range of actions; equals one half if the *Distributor* may only be ordered to desist from limited actions; and equals zero otherwise. The subindex of orders to do equals one if the *Distributor* may be ordered to perform a broad range of actions to rectify the violation; equals one half if the *Distributor* may only be ordered to perform limited actions; and equals zero otherwise. We disregard orders that may be issued by Courts at the request of a private party in a civil lawsuit.
Orders accountant	An index aggregating stop and do orders that may be directed to the *Accountant* in case of a defective prospectus. The index is formed by averaging the subindexes of orders to stop and to do. The subindex of orders to stop equals one if the *Accountant* may be ordered to refrain from a broad range of actions; equals one half if the *Accountant* may only be ordered to desist from limited actions; and equals zero otherwise. The subindex of orders to do equals one if the *Accountant* may be ordered to perform a broad range of actions to rectify the violation; equals one half if the *Accountant* may only be ordered to perform limited actions; and equals zero otherwise. We disregard orders that may be issued by Courts at the request of a private party in a civil lawsuit.
Orders index	The index of orders equals the arithmetic mean of (1) orders issuer; (2) orders distributor; and (3) orders accountant.
Criminal director/officer	An index of criminal sanctions applicable to the *Issuer's* directors and key officers when the prospectus omits material information. We create separate subindexes for directors and key officers and average their scores. The subindex for directors equals zero when directors cannot be held criminally liable when the prospectus is misleading. Equals one half if directors can be held criminally liable when *aware* that the prospectus is misleading. Equals one if directors can *also* be held criminally liable when negligently *unaware* that the prospectus is misleading. The subindex for key officers is constructed analogously.

(continued)

Table I—*Continued*

Variable	Description
Criminal distributor	An index of criminal sanctions applicable to the *Distributor* (or its officers) when the prospectus omits material information. Equals zero if the *Distributor* cannot be held criminally liable when the prospectus is misleading. Equals one half if the *Distributor* can be held criminally liable when *aware* that the prospectus is misleading. Equals one if the *Distributor* can *also* be held criminally liable when *negligently* unaware that the prospectus is misleading.
Criminal accountant	An index of criminal sanctions applicable to the *Accountant* (or its officers) when the financial statements accompanying the prospectus omit material information. Equals zero if the *Accountant* cannot be held criminally liable when the financial statements accompanying the prospectus are misleading. Equals one half if the *Accountant* can be held criminally liable when *aware* that the financial statements accompanying the prospectus are misleading. Equals one if the *Accountant* can *also* be held criminally liable when *negligently* unaware that the financial statements accompanying the prospectus are misleading.
Criminal index	The index of criminal sanctions equals the arithmetic mean of (1) criminal director; (2) criminal distributor; and (3) criminal accountant.
	III.5 Summary index of public enforcement
Public enforcement index	The index of public enforcement equals the arithmetic mean of (1) supervisor characteristics index; (2) rule-making power index; (3) investigative powers index; (4) orders index; and (5) criminal index.
	IV. Outcome variables
External cap/GDP	The average ratio of stock market capitalization held by small shareholders to gross domestic product (GDP) for the period 1996 to 2000. The stock market capitalization held by small shareholders is computed as the product of the aggregate stock market capitalization and the average percentage of common shares not owned by the top three shareholders in the 10 largest nonfinancial, privately owned domestic firms in a given country. A firm is considered privately owned if the State is not a known shareholder in it. Source: La Porta et al. (1999b), Hartland-Peel (1996) for Kenya, *Bloomberg*, and various annual reports for Ecuador, Jordan, and Uruguay.
Domestic firms/pop	Logarithm of the average ratio of the number of domestic firms listed in a given country to its population (in millions) for the period 1996 to 2000. Source: International Finance Corporation (2001) and World Bank (2001).
IPOs	The average ratio of the equity issued by newly listed firms in a given country (in thousands) to its GDP (in millions) over the period 1996 to 2000. Source: *Securities Data Corporation,* World Bank (2001).
Block premia	"The block premia is computed taking the difference between the price per share paid for the control block and the exchange price 2 days after the announcement of the control transaction, dividing by the exchange price and multiplying by the ratio of the proportion of cash flow rights represented in the controlling block." We use the country's sample median. Source: Dyck and Zingales (2004, p. 547).
Access to equity	Index of the extent to which business executives in a country agree with the statement "Stock markets are open to new firms and medium-sized firms." Scale from 1 (strongly agree) though 7 (strongly disagree). Source: Schwab et al. (1999).
Ownership concentration	The average percentage of common shares owned by the top three shareholders in the 10 largest nonfinancial, privately owned domestic firms in a given country. A firm is considered privately owned if the State is not a known shareholder in it. Source: La Porta et al. (1998), Hartland-Peel (1996) for Kenya, *Bloomberg*, and various annual reports for Ecuador, Jordan, and Uruguay.
Liquidity	The average total value of stocks traded as a percentage of GDP for the period 1996 to 2000. Source: World Development Indicators at http://devdata.worldbank.org/dataonline/.

(*continued*)

Table I—*Continued*

Variable	Description
	V. Control variables and instruments
Anti-director rights	This index of anti-director rights is formed by adding one when: (1) the country allows shareholders to mail their proxy vote; (2) shareholders are not required to deposit their shares prior to the General Shareholders' Meeting; (3) cumulative voting or proportional representation of minorities on the board of directors is allowed; (4) an oppressed minorities mechanism is in place; (5) the minimum percentage of share capital that entitles a shareholder to call for an Extraordinary Shareholders' Meeting is less than or equal to 10% (the sample median); or (6) when shareholders have preemptive rights that can only be waived by a shareholders' meeting. The range for the index is from 0 to 5. Source: La Porta et al. (1998).
Efficiency of the judiciary	Assessment of the "efficiency and integrity of the legal environment as it affects business, particularly foreign firms" produced by the country risk rating agency International Country Risk (ICR). It may be "taken to represent investors' assessment of conditions in the country in question." Average between 1980 and 1983. Scale from 0 to 10, with lower scores representing lower efficiency levels. Source: *International Country Risk Guide* (Political Risk Services (1996)).
Log GDP per capita	Logarithmic of per capita GDP (in U.S. dollars) in 2000.
Legal origin	Identifies the legal origin of the company law or commercial code of each country. Source: La Porta et al. (1998).
Investor protection	Principal component of the indices of disclosure requirements, liability standards, and anti-director rights. Scale from 0 to 10.

and would hold them liable if they do not. In securities laws, this strategy generally takes the form of disclosure requirements and liability standards that make it cheaper for investors to recover damages when information is wrong or omitted—the two features we try to capture empirically.

We collect six proxies for the strength of specific disclosure requirements pertaining to the promoter's problem.[7] The first and most basic question is whether promoters can issue securities without delivering a prospectus describing the securities to potential investors in advance. Since every country requires a prospectus before securities are sold and listed, the operational word here is "delivering." In some countries, it is possible to sell securities after a prospectus is deposited at the company, or with the Supervisor, without delivering it to investors. Delivering a prospectus to potential investors is an affirmative step in making disclosures to them. In addition, we keep track of affirmative disclosure requirements in the following five areas: (1) insiders' compensation; (2) ownership by large shareholders; (3) inside ownership; (4) contracts outside

[7] A detailed study of the impact of substantive disclosure rules is beyond the scope of this paper. However, we examine the robustness of our findings to the inclusion of less selective measures of disclosure. Bushman, Piotroski, and Smith (2003) present data on firms' actual disclosures in the following four areas: (1) segments, R&D, capital expenditures, accounting policies, and subsidiaries; (2) major shareholders, management, board, director, and officer remuneration, and director and officer shareholding; (3) consolidation and discretionary reserves; and, (4) frequency of reporting, consolidation of interim reports, and number of disclosed items. None of these variables has additional explanatory power in our regressions.

the normal course of business; and (5) transactions with related parties. We calculate the index of "disclosure requirements" as the average of the preceding six proxies.

In addition to specific disclosure requirements, nearly every country has a residual disclosure requirement that the prospectus must include all material information necessary to assess the value of the securities being offered. When bad news hits after security issuance, the question becomes whether this information was known or knowable to the issuer, the distributor, and/or the accountant and omitted from the prospectus. As legal scholars including Black (2001) and Coffee (2002) emphasize, and as the Dutch example illustrates, the liability standard in the cases of such omission is central to private enforcement of securities laws.[8]

There are basically four liability standards. In the base case, the standard is the same as in torts, namely negligence: the plaintiff must show that the issuer, the distributor, or the accountant was negligent in omitting information from the prospectus. The tort standard also requires that investors prove that they relied on the prospectus to invest (reliance) or that their losses were caused by the misleading information in the prospectus (causality). Some countries rule out recovery in a prospectus liability case or make it harder than the tort standard by requiring the plaintiffs to show that the defendants either knew about the omission or acted with intent or gross negligence (e.g., while "drunk") in omitting the information from the prospectus. In contrast, the burden of proof is less demanding than tort in countries in which investors must prove reliance or causality or both, but not negligence. Finally, burden of proof is lowest where plaintiffs only need to show that the information in the prospectus was misleading (but not prove reliance or causality). The defendants are either strictly liable (i.e., they cannot avoid liability if the prospectus omitted information) or they must themselves show that they exercised due diligence in preparing the prospectus. This shift in the burden of proof from plaintiffs to defendants can, in principle, significantly reduce the cost to the former of establishing liability.

In our empirical analysis, we distinguish among these four liability standards in cases against issuers and directors, distributors, and accountants, and compute a "liability standard" index.

B. Public Enforcement

In the context of securities markets, a public enforcer can be a securities commission, a central bank, or some other supervisory body. For concreteness, we call the main government agency or official authority in charge of supervising

[8] We have been asked to examine whether the availability of class action suits and contingency fees is associated with the development of securities markets. A dummy equal to one if class actions are available in a prospectus liability case is an insignificant predictor of the development of securities markets. Similarly, a dummy equal to one if contingency fees are generally available is an insignificant predictor of the development of securities markets. Finally, the interaction of class actions and contingency fees is also insignificant.

securities markets the Supervisor. We focus on five broad aspects of public enforcement.

The first aspect covers the basic attributes of the Supervisor, which we capture with three variables. First, an effective Supervisor may need to be insulated from interference by the Executive, both to facilitate recruiting professional staff and to prevent political interference on behalf of influential issuers. To measure the Supervisor's independence, we keep track of whether its key members are appointed through a system of checks-and-balances or unilaterally by the Executive. Second, the independence of the Supervisor may be enhanced when its key members may be dismissed only after due process rather than at the will of the appointing authority. Third, an effective Supervisor may need to be focused on securities markets, rather than on both these markets and banking, so that his success is more closely tied to that of the securities market. Accordingly, we measure whether the Supervisor's mandate covers securities markets alone. We combine these three variables into a subindex of "Supervisor attributes."

The second issue is whether the power to regulate securities markets be delegated to the Supervisor, rather than remain with the legislature or the Ministry of Finance (Spiller and Ferejohn (1992)). We measure whether the Supervisor has the power to regulate primary offerings and/or listing rules on stock exchanges.

The third aspect covers the investigative powers of the Supervisor. Unless the issuer, the distributor, and the auditor are strictly liable for all false and misleading statements in the prospectus (which never happens), the question arises as to why the information revealed to investors was inaccurate. Did the issuer, distributor, or auditor have the information? If not, could they have had it? At what cost? Did the issuer hide the information from the distributor or the auditor? Answering these questions is costly, especially for private plaintiffs. A Supervisor can be empowered to command documents from issuers, distributors, or accountants, and to subpoena testimony of witnesses. Such powers can in principle enable the Supervisor to ascertain the reasons for inaccuracy which can then—as a public good—become the basis for sanctions, or for criminal or civil litigation. We summarize the powers of the Supervisor to subpoena documents and witnesses by forming a subindex of "Investigative powers."

The fourth aspect—perhaps most directly intended to substitute for the weakness of private enforcement—covers noncriminal sanctions for violations of securities laws. These sanctions may involve ordering the directors of a public firm to rectify noncompliance with disclosure requirements, to institute changes recommended by outside reviewers, and/or to compensate investors for their losses. Such sanctions could be imposed separately on issuers, distributors, and accountants, and we keep track of each category. We then average the scores for the sanctions against the various parties to create a subindex of "Orders."

Finally, the fifth aspect covers criminal sanctions for violations of securities laws. We keep track of whether criminal sanctions are applicable, to whom they apply, and what conduct invokes them. We average the scores for criminal sanctions against directors, distributors, and accountants to obtain a subindex of "criminal sanctions." These variables are of special interest since a popular sentiment sees criminal sanctions as essential to enforce good practices in security issuance. We average the preceding five subindexes to form the index of "Public enforcement."

C. Other Variables

We are interested in understanding the effects of the various provisions in securities laws on financial development. We use seven proxies for the development of securities markets in different countries. The first variable is the ratio of stock market capitalization to gross domestic product (GDP) scaled by the fraction of the stock market held by outside investors. (The results are qualitatively similar for the unadjusted ratio of market capitalization to GDP.) The second variable is the (logarithm of the) number of domestic publicly traded firms in each country relative to its population. The third variable is the value of initial public offerings in each country relative to its GDP. All three variables are 5-year averages of yearly data for the period 1996 to 2000. Theoretically, the first of these three measures is the most attractive, since in theory better investor protection is associated with both a higher number of listed firms and a higher valuation of capital (Shleifer and Wolfenzon (2002)). Except for some differences in scaling and timing, these three variables are used in La Porta et al. (1997) to study the consequences of investor protection through corporate law on stock market development.

The fourth variable is a qualitative assessment of the ability of new and medium-sized firms to raise equity in the stock market based on a survey of business executives by the *Global Competitiveness Report 1999* (Schwab et al. (1999)). The fifth variable is the (median) premium paid for control in corporate control transactions. In several theoretical models, this variable has been interpreted as a measure of the private benefits of control, which are higher in countries with weaker investor protection (Grossman and Hart (1988), Dyck and Zingales (2004), Nenova (2003)). The sixth variable is a proxy for ownership concentration among the largest firms in the country. Both theory (Shleifer and Wolfenzon (2002)) and prior empirical work (La Porta, Lopez-de-Silanes, and Shleifer (1999a)) suggest that ownership concentration is lower in countries with better investor protection. Finally, the seventh variable is a proxy for stock market liquidity, as measured by the ratio of traded volume to GDP. Levine and Zervos (1998) show that this variable predicts the growth in per capita income.

To isolate the effect of securities laws on financial markets, we control for several factors identified by previous research. The first of these is the level of economic development, which we measure as the (logarithm of) per capita GDP. Economic development is often associated with capital deepening. In addition, richer countries might have higher quality institutions in general, including better property rights and rule of law, which could be associated with better financial development regardless of the content of the laws (North (1981),

La Porta et al. (1999b)).[9] To further address this issue, we use the measure of the efficiency of the judiciary from the *International Country Risk Guide* (Political Risk Services (1996)) as an additional control.

La Porta et al. (1997, 1998) present evidence that measures of investor protection derived from corporate law are associated with stock market development. This evidence raises the question of which laws, if any, make a difference. Accordingly, in all our regressions, we include the anti-directors rights index of the protection afforded to shareholders through statutory corporate law as an additional control.

As in many other studies in this area, the causal effect of securities laws on financial development cannot be established with certainty. Following La Porta et al. (1997, 1998), we use the legal origin of commercial laws as an instrument. The commercial laws of most countries originate in one of four legal families: English (common) law, French civil law, German civil law, and Scandinavian law, which have spread throughout the world through conquest, colonization, and occasionally voluntary transplantation. England developed a common law tradition, characterized by independent judges and juries, relatively weaker reliance on statutes, and the preference for contracts and private litigation as a means of dealing with social harms. France, in contrast, developed a civil law tradition, characterized by state-employed judges, great reliance on legal and procedural codes, and a preference for state regulation over private litigation. This makes legal origin a suitable instrument for the stance of the law regarding alternative regulatory strategies.

Table II presents our data on securities laws. Countries are arranged by legal origin, and we report means by legal origin as well as tests of the differences in these means. There is large cross-country variation in our measures of securities laws. Common and civil law countries differ significantly in our measures of disclosure, liability standards, and public enforcement. Common law countries both have more extensive mandatory disclosure requirements, and make it easier for investors to recover damages. In the public enforcement area, these differences are smaller for Supervisor attributes and rule-making power, and greater for investigative powers, orders, and criminal sanctions. In the next section, we examine which aspects of the securities law, as well as corporate law, matter for financial development.

III. Securities Laws and Financial Development

Table III presents the results of regressions of our various measures of financial development on the anti-director rights index, efficiency of the judiciary, logarithm of GDP per capita, disclosure (Panel A), liability standards (Panel B),

[9] In practice, per capita GDP is very highly correlated with survey measures of the quality of institutions such as perceptions of property rights, rule of law, and the prevalence of corruption. In our sample, the pair-wise correlation of (log) per capita GDP with property rights, corruption, and rule of law is 0.754, 0.882, and 0.892, respectively. The results reported in the paper are robust to replacing log per capita GDP by any of these three measures.

Table II

Indices of Regulation of Securities Markets

This table classifies countries by legal origin and shows the securities law variables for each country covering the areas of (1) disclosure requirements; (2) liability standards; (3) supervisor characteristics; (4) rule-making power of the supervisor; (5) investigative powers of the supervisor; (6) orders to issuers, distributors, and accountants; (7) criminal sanctions applicable to directors, distributors, and accountants; and (8) public enforcement. All variables are described in Table I.

Country	Symbol	Disclosure Requirements	Liability Standard	Supervisor Characteristics	Rule-Making Power	Investigative Powers	Orders	Criminal Sanctions	Public Enforcement
English legal origin									
Australia	AUS	0.75	0.66	0.67	1.00	1.00	1.00	0.83	0.90
Canada	CAN	0.92	1.00	0.67	0.50	1.00	1.00	0.83	0.80
Hong Kong	HKG	0.92	0.66	0.33	1.00	1.00	1.00	1.00	0.87
India	IND	0.92	0.66	0.33	0.50	1.00	0.67	0.83	0.67
Ireland	IRL	0.67	0.44	0.00	1.00	0.00	0.00	0.83	0.37
Israel	ISR	0.67	0.66	0.67	0.00	1.00	1.00	0.50	0.63
Kenya	KEN	0.50	0.44	0.33	1.00	0.50	1.00	0.67	0.70
Malaysia	MYS	0.92	0.66	0.33	0.50	1.00	1.00	1.00	0.77
New Zealand	NZL	0.67	0.44	0.33	0.00	1.00	0.00	0.33	0.33
Nigeria	NGA	0.67	0.39	0.67	0.50	0.00	0.00	0.50	0.33
Pakistan	PAK	0.58	0.39	0.67	1.00	1.00	0.17	0.08	0.58
Singapore	SGP	1.00	0.66	0.33	1.00	1.00	1.00	1.00	0.87
South Africa	ZAF	0.83	0.66	0.33	0.00	0.50	0.00	0.42	0.25
Sri Lanka	LKA	0.75	0.39	0.33	1.00	0.50	0.00	0.33	0.43
Thailand	THA	0.92	0.22	0.67	1.00	1.00	0.33	0.58	0.72
USA	USA	1.00	1.00	1.00	1.00	1.00	1.00	0.50	0.90
United Kingdom	GBR	0.83	0.66	0.00	1.00	1.00	1.00	0.42	0.68
Zimbabwe	ZWE	0.50	0.44	1.00	0.00	0.00	0.08	1.00	0.42
Mean		**0.78**	**0.58**	**0.48**	**0.67**	**0.75**	**0.57**	**0.65**	**0.62**
French legal origin									
Argentina	ARG	0.50	0.22	0.67	1.00	1.00	0.08	0.17	0.58
Belgium	BEL	0.42	0.44	0.00	0.00	0.25	0.00	0.50	0.15
Brazil	BRA	0.25	0.33	0.33	1.00	0.50	0.75	0.33	0.58
Chile	CHL	0.58	0.33	0.33	1.00	0.75	0.42	0.50	0.60
Colombia	COL	0.42	0.11	0.33	1.00	0.75	0.33	0.50	0.58
Ecuador	ECU	0.00	0.11	1.00	1.00	0.25	0.08	0.42	0.55
Egypt	EGY	0.50	0.22	0.67	0.00	0.25	0.17	0.42	0.30
France	FRA	0.75	0.22	1.00	0.50	1.00	1.00	0.33	0.77
Greece	GRC	0.33	0.50	0.67	0.00	0.25	0.17	0.50	0.32
Indonesia	IDN	0.50	0.66	0.33	1.00	1.00	0.25	0.50	0.62

(*continued*)

Table II—*Continued*

Country	Symbol	Disclosure Requirements	Liability Standard	Supervisor Characteristics	Rule-Making Power	Investigative Powers	Orders	Criminal Sanctions	Public Enforcement
Italy	ITA	0.67	0.22	0.67	1.00	0.25	0.00	0.50	0.48
Jordan	JOR	0.67	0.22	0.33	1.00	1.00	0.67	0.00	0.60
Mexico	MEX	0.58	0.11	0.00	1.00	0.25	0.00	0.50	0.35
Netherlands	NLD	0.50	0.89	0.33	1.00	0.50	0.00	0.50	0.47
Peru	PER	0.33	0.66	0.67	1.00	0.75	1.00	0.50	0.78
Philippines	PHL	0.83	1.00	0.67	1.00	1.00	1.00	0.50	0.83
Portugal	PRT	0.42	0.66	0.67	1.00	1.00	0.25	0.00	0.58
Spain	ESP	0.50	0.66	0.67	0.00	0.50	0.00	0.50	0.33
Turkey	TUR	0.50	0.22	0.67	1.00	1.00	0.00	0.50	0.63
Uruguay	URY	0.00	0.11	0.67	1.00	0.25	0.50	0.42	0.57
Venezuela	VEN	0.17	0.22	0.33	1.00	1.00	0.08	0.33	0.55
Mean		**0.45**	**0.39**	**0.52**	**0.79**	**0.64**	**0.32**	**0.40**	**0.53**
German legal origin									
Austria	AUT	0.25	0.11	0.33	0.00	0.00	0.00	0.50	0.17
Germany	DEU	0.42	0.00	0.33	0.00	0.25	0.00	0.50	0.22
Japan	JPN	0.75	0.66	0.00	0.00	0.00	0.00	0.00	0.00
Korea	KOR	0.75	0.66	0.33	0.00	0.50	0.08	0.33	0.25
Switzerland	CHE	0.67	0.44	0.33	1.00	0.00	0.00	0.33	0.33
Taiwan	TWN	0.75	0.66	0.33	1.00	0.25	0.17	0.83	0.52
Mean		**0.60**	**0.42**	**0.28**	**0.33**	**0.17**	**0.04**	**0.42**	**0.25**
Scandinavian legal origin									
Denmark	DNK	0.58	0.55	0.00	1.00	0.50	0.33	0.00	0.37
Finland	FIN	0.50	0.66	0.67	0.00	0.25	0.17	0.50	0.32
Norway	NOR	0.58	0.39	0.00	0.00	0.25	0.33	1.00	0.32
Sweden	SWE	0.58	0.28	0.00	1.00	0.25	0.67	0.58	0.50
Mean		**0.56**	**0.47**	**0.17**	**0.50**	**0.31**	**0.38**	**0.52**	**0.38**
Mean of all countries		**0.60**	**0.47**	**0.45**	**0.66**	**0.60**	**0.38**	**0.50**	**0.52**
				Tests of means (t-stats)					
English vs. Civil Law		−5.01[a]	−2.45[b]	−0.60	−0.04	−2.23[b]	−2.60[a]	−3.18[a]	−2.72[a]
English vs. French		−5.31[a]	−2.48[b]	0.48	0.90	−0.92	−1.87[c]	−3.46[a]	−1.43
English vs. German		−2.19[b]	−1.44	−1.67	−1.59	−3.45[a]	−2.70[a]	−1.77[c]	−3.85[a]
English vs. Scandinavian		−2.60[b]	−0.99	−1.94[c]	−0.67	−2.17[b]	−0.80	−0.76	−2.22[b]
French vs. German		1.49	0.28	−2.13[b]	−2.27[b]	−3.32[a]	−1.87[c]	0.18	−3.66[a]
French vs. Scandinavian		1.03	0.58	−2.34[b]	−1.21	−1.94[c]	0.29	1.05	−1.82[c]
German vs. Scandinavian		−0.32	0.28	−0.75	0.48	1.26	3.70[a]	0.49	1.35

[a]significant at 1%; [b]significant at 5%; and [c]significant at 10%.

Table III

Securities Laws and the Development of Stock Markets

Ordinary least squares regressions of the cross-section of countries. The dependent variables are (1) external market capitalization; (2) log of domestic firms per capita; (3) value of the IPO-to-GDP ratio; (4) block premium; (5) access to equity; (6) ownership concentration; and (7) the stock-market-volume-to-GDP ratio. All regressions include anti-director rights, efficiency of the judiciary, and log of GDP per capita. In addition, regressions include disclosure requirements (Panel A); liability standards (Panel B); and public enforcement (Panel C). All variables are described in Table I. Robust standard errors are shown in parentheses.

Panel A: Disclosure Requirements

	Market Capitalization	Number of Firms	IPOs	Block Premia	Access to Equity	Ownership Concentration	Liquidity
Disclosure requirements	0.5813[a]	1.1103[b]	4.6983[a]	−0.2682[b]	1.8032[a]	−0.1930[b]	97.2050[a]
	(0.1377)	(0.4127)	(1.4395)	(0.1145)	(0.4834)	(0.0871)	(34.0413)
Anti-director rights	0.0420	0.1195	0.1371	−0.0180	−0.0715	−0.0209[c]	1.7897
	(0.0308)	(0.0946)	(0.2772)	(0.0204)	(0.0856)	(0.0123)	(5.5914)
Ln GDP per capita	0.0957[a]	0.2789[b]	1.1393[a]	−0.0028	0.1543[c]	−0.0285[b]	20.2746[a]
	(0.0229)	(0.1075)	(0.2439)	(0.0195)	(0.0903)	(0.0139)	(6.4414)
Efficiency of the judiciary	0.0386[c]	0.2302[a]	−0.0843	−0.0070	0.1824[a]	−0.0070	−4.0440
	(0.0204)	(0.0664)	(0.2106)	(0.0114)	(0.0649)	(0.0093)	(5.3761)
Constant	−1.2056[a]	−2.6758[a]	−9.5765[a]	0.4067[b]	1.4312[c]	0.9540[a]	−160.1500[a]
	(0.2037)	(0.6693)	(1.8551)	(0.1492)	(0.7266)	(0.1036)	(37.7904)
Observations	49	49	49	37	44	49	49
Adjusted R^2	54%	69%	38%	32%	52%	36%	27%

(continued)

Table III—*Continued*

	Market Capitalization	Number of Firms	IPOs	Block Premia	Access to Equity	Ownership Concentration	Trading
			Panel B: Liability Standards				
Liability standards	0.4481[a]	0.7522[c]	3.7150[a]	−0.1302[c]	1.4655[a]	−0.1104	90.3188[a]
	(0.1289)	(0.4245)	(1.3750)	(0.0673)	(0.4755)	(0.0699)	(31.4726)
Anti-director rights	0.0515	0.1474	0.2049	−0.0276[b]	−0.0545	−0.0277[b]	1.9140
	(0.0330)	(0.0883)	(0.3216)	(0.0133)	(0.0823)	(0.0125)	(5.3484)
Ln GDP per capita	0.0878[a]	0.2665[b]	1.0733[a]	−0.0121	0.1534	−0.0268[c]	18.5645[a]
	(0.0240)	(0.1089)	(0.2370)	(0.0219)	(0.1082)	(0.0150)	(6.0737)
Efficiency of the judiciary	0.0457[b]	0.2439[a]	−0.0275	−0.0040	0.1916[a]	−0.0095	−2.9061
	(0.0226)	(0.0768)	(0.2031)	(0.0126)	(0.0663)	(0.0106)	(5.0634)
Constant	−1.0818[a]	−2.4459[a]	−8.5704[a]	0.3950[b]	1.7065[b]	0.9152[a]	−138.5010[a]
	(0.2026)	(0.7360)	(1.7468)	(0.1647)	(0.8231)	(0.1000)	(35.2721)
Observations	49	49	49	37	44	49	49
Adjusted R^2	51%	67%	36%	22%	50%	31%	27%
			Panel C: Public Enforcement				
Public enforcement	0.3446[c]	0.6422	3.7220[b]	−0.0087	0.0069	0.0560	39.5648
	(0.1990)	(0.4813)	(1.5531)	(0.0651)	(0.5736)	(0.0940)	(30.0063)
Anti-director rights	0.0711[b]	0.1761[b]	0.3098	−0.0414[a]	0.0895	−0.0420[a]	7.8568
	(0.0347)	(0.0861)	(0.2434)	(0.0148)	(0.1056)	(0.0121)	(4.7260)
Ln GDP per capita	0.1041[a]	0.2949[a]	1.2210[a]	−0.0133	0.1835	−0.0289[c]	21.4326[a]
	(0.0218)	(0.1052)	(0.2687)	(0.0216)	(0.1222)	(0.0153)	(7.0790)
Efficiency of the judiciary	0.0518[b]	0.2551[a]	0.0355	−0.0041	0.1916[b]	−0.0090	−2.0959
	(0.0236)	(0.0750)	(0.2168)	(0.0120)	(0.0740)	(0.0112)	(5.4241)
Constant	−1.2999[a]	−2.8470[a]	−10.8554[a]	0.3898[b]	1.7103[c]	0.8912[a]	−165.9368[a]
	(0.2169)	(0.7578)	(2.0799)	(0.1791)	(0.9944)	(0.1173)	(40.4056)
Observations	49	49	49	37	44	49	49
Adjusted R^2	48%	66%	34%	15%	38%	29%	18%

[a]significant at 1%; [b]significant at 5%; and [c]significant at 10%.

and public enforcement (Panel C).[10] Both higher per capita GDP and efficiency of the judiciary tend to be associated with more developed stock markets, and these effects are quantitatively large. To interpret the results on Table III, note that when securities laws are excluded from the regression, stronger anti-director rights are associated with better stock market development for all dependent variables except the index of access to equity (results not reported). In contrast, anti-director rights are only significant in one of the regressions that controls for disclosure (ownership concentration) and two of the regressions that control for liability standards (ownership concentration and block premium). The results for anti-director rights are more consistent in the regressions that control for public enforcement. In those regressions, anti-director rights have predictive power for market capitalization, number of firms, block premium, and ownership concentration.

Perhaps most interestingly, both disclosure requirements and liability standards are positively correlated with larger stock markets. In Panel A, disclosure is associated with more developed stock markets for all seven dependent variables. The estimated coefficients predict that a two-standard deviation increase in disclosure (roughly the distance from the Netherlands to the United States) is associated with an increase of 0.27 in the external-market-to-GDP ratio, a 52% rise in listed firms per capita, a 2.22 increase in the IPO-to-GDP ratio, a 13 percentage point drop in the block premium, a 0.85 point improvement in the access-to-equity index, a 9 percentage point drop in ownership concentration, and a 45.9 point increase in the volume-to-GDP ratio.[11]

The results on liability standards are also consistently strong. The estimated coefficients predict that a two-standard deviation increase in this variable (roughly the distance from Denmark to the United States) is associated with an increase of 0.23 percentage points in the external-market-to-GDP ratio, a 28% rise in listed firms per capita, a 1.88 increase in the IPO-to-GDP ratio, a 6.6 percentage point drop in the block premium, a 0.75 point improvement in the access-to-equity index, a decrease of 6.6 percentage points in ownership concentration (but with a t-stat of only 1.58), and a 45.8 point increase in the volume-to-GDP ratio.

Figures 1 and 2 illustrate the impact on the external-market-capitalization-to-GDP ratio of disclosure and liability standards, respectively. In our sample, the external-market-capitalization-to-GDP ratio ranges from 0.002 in Uruguay

[10] We obtain similar results replacing each of our three indices of securities laws by the principal component of the variables included in the relevant index. The most important change is that the principal component of public enforcement only predicts IPOs.

[11] The effect of efficiency of the judiciary on financial markets is comparable to that of disclosure. The estimated coefficients predict that a two-standard deviation increase in the efficiency of the judiciary (roughly the distance from Korea or Mexico to the United States) is associated with an increase of 0.16 in the external-market-to-GDP ratio, a 94% rise in listed firms per capita, and a 0.75 point improvement in the access-to-equity index, a 12 percentage point drop in ownership concentration, and an 83 point increase in the volume-to-GDP ratio. The effect of efficiency of the judiciary on financial development is similar in the specifications that control for liability standards (Panel B) and public enforcement (Panel C).

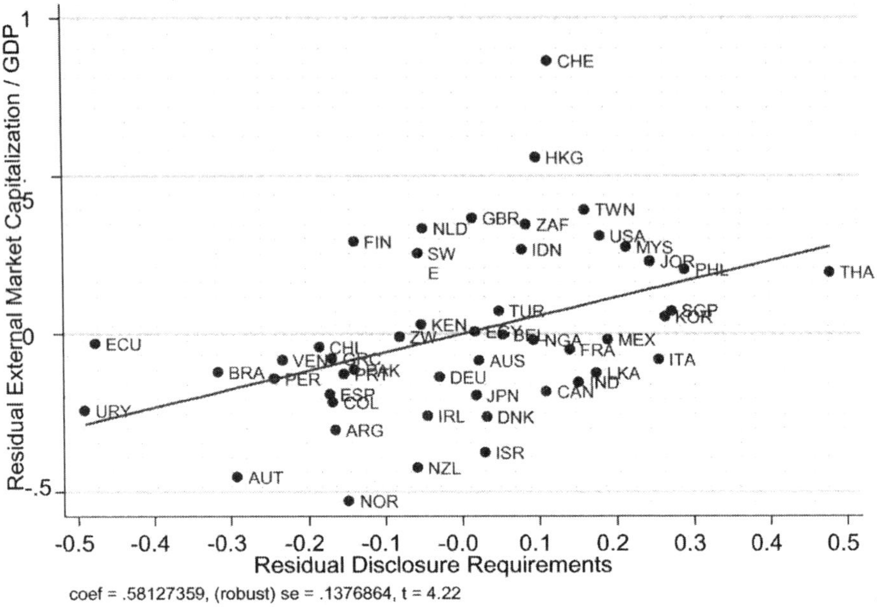

Figure 1. Partial regression plot of external-market-capitalization-to-GDP and disclosure requirements. The independent variables include anti-director rights, log of GDP per capita, and efficiency of the judiciary. Table II lists the country symbols.

to 1.44 in Switzerland. Thus, the roughly 0.25 point increase in the external-market-capitalization-to-GDP ratio associated with a two-standard deviation improvement in either disclosure or liability standards is economically large. Note also that the strength of disclosure and liability standards is not driven by outliers; we obtain qualitatively similar results using median regressions.

The results for public enforcement (Panel C) are less consistent. Public enforcement only matters for the external-market-capitalization-to-GDP ratio and IPOs, although it has a large economic effect on both variables (see Figure 3). A two-standard deviation increase in public enforcement (roughly, from the Netherlands to the United States) is associated with an increment of 0.15 points in the external-market-capitalization-to-GDP ratio and adds 1.6 firms in the IPO-to-GDP ratio. In contrast, anti-director rights, but not public enforcement, matter for the number of firms, block premium, and ownership concentration.

These results suggest a preliminary view of what works, and what does not, in securities laws. Public enforcement plays a modest role at best in the development of stock markets. In contrast, the development of stock markets is strongly associated with extensive disclosure requirements and a relatively low burden of proof on investors seeking to recover damages resulting from omissions of material information from the prospectus.

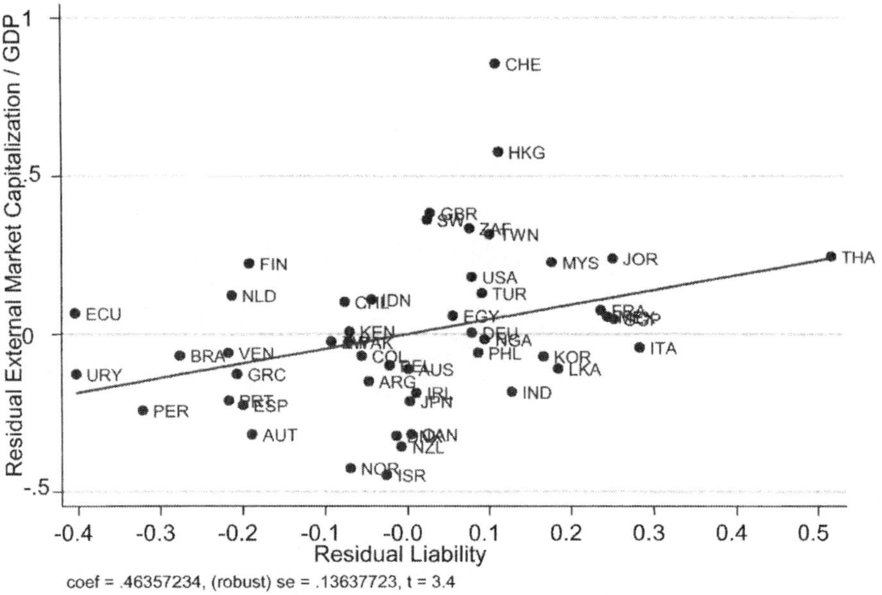

Figure 2. Partial regression plot of external-market-capitalization-to-GDP and liability standards. The independent variables include anti-director rights, log of GDP per capita, and efficiency of the judiciary. Table II lists the country symbols.

In the remainder of this section, we explore these preliminary findings from a range of perspectives. We first examine whether the weakness of public enforcement is due to our aggregation procedure. Table IV presents the results of regressing external market capitalization on the components of the public enforcement index. The power to make rules is the only element of public enforcement that is statistically significant. The results using other proxies for stock market development are similar (we do not report them to save space). First, neither the characteristics of the Supervisor (i.e., its independence and focus) nor its power to make rules matter for any of the other outcome variables. Second, the Supervisor's investigative power is only associated with more domestic firms. Third, the Supervisor's power to issue orders is only associated with more IPOs (and weakly—t-stat of 1.65—with more domestic firms). Fourth, criminal sanctions only matter for IPOs. Criminal deterrence may be ineffective because proving criminal intent of directors, distributors, or accountants in omitting information from the prospectus is difficult. In sum, no dimension of public enforcement consistently matters for the development of stock markets.

Table V presents the results of a horse race between disclosure requirements, liability rules, and public enforcement. Disclosure is significant in all regressions. In contrast, public enforcement is never significant. Liability standards

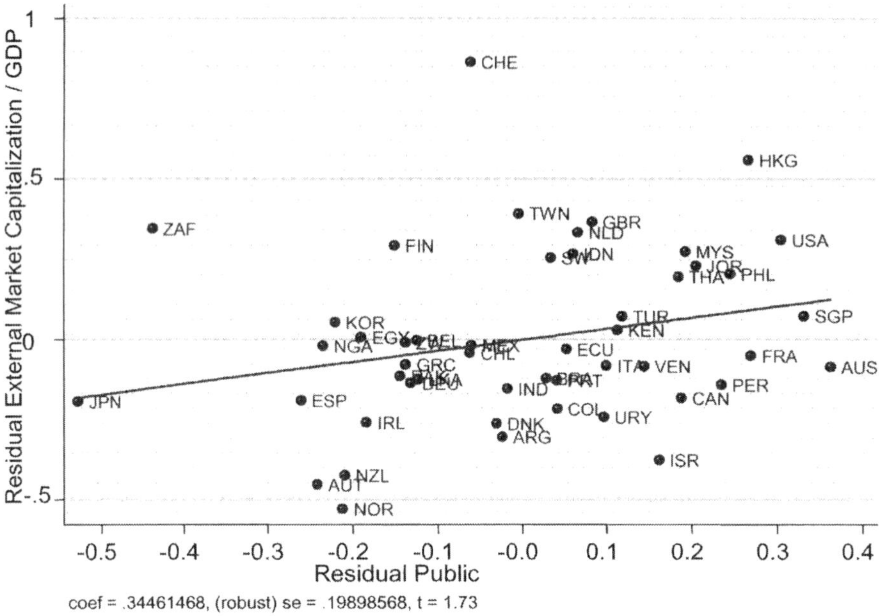

Figure 3. Partial regression plot of external-market-capitalization-to-GDP and public enforcement. The independent variables include anti-director rights, log of GDP per capita, and efficiency of the judiciary. Table II lists the country symbols.

are significant in the regressions for external capitalization, access to equity, and liquidity. However, multicollinearity between disclosure and liability standards may be of concern as the correlation between the two variables is 0.55 (the correlation between public enforcement and either disclosure or liability standards is only around 0.3). Finally, consistent with Table III, the anti-director rights index is never significant.

One of our key results is that disclosure and liability standards are stronger than the anti-director rights index. Why? One possibility is that we have found the "true" channel through which legal origin matters: it is correlated with the development of stock markets because it is a proxy for the effectiveness of private contracting as supported by securities laws. Note in this regard that legal origin typically loses its strong predictive power for the development of stock markets when we include anti-directors rights, disclosure, or liability standards in the regression. A second possibility is that investor protection through corporate law (which also works through private litigation) also matters, but we simply have cleaner measures of disclosure and liability standards. A third, more nuanced, possibility is that corporate and securities laws often rely on similar rules (e.g., regarding liability standards in civil cases), and it is the presence of these rules that is essential for the ability of private investors to seek remedy for expropriation by corporate insiders. For example, the U.S. system of mandatory disclosure evolved out of common law principles applicable

Table IV

External Market Capitalization and Public Enforcement

Ordinary least squares regressions of the cross-section of countries. The dependent variable is external market capitalization. We report five regressions successively controlling for the following securities laws variables: (1) supervisor attributes; (2) rule-making powers; (3) investigative powers; (4) orders; and (5) criminal sanctions. In addition to a securities laws variable, all regressions include anti-director rights, efficiency of the judiciary, and log of GDP per capita. Robust standard errors are shown in parentheses. All variables are described in Table I.

	Supervisor Characteristics	Rule-Making Powers	Investigative Powers	Orders	Criminal Sanctions
Securities regulation variable	−0.0111	0.1986[c]	0.1207	0.0525	0.1336
	(0.1312)	(0.1008)	(0.1112)	(0.1236)	(0.1643)
Anti-director rights	0.0944[a]	0.0889[a]	0.0803[b]	0.0878[a]	0.0877[a]
	(0.0325)	(0.0316)	(0.0312)	(0.0310)	(0.0303)
Efficiency of the judiciary	0.0465[c]	0.0590[b]	0.0412[c]	0.0496[c]	0.0430[c]
	(0.0247)	(0.0249)	(0.0243)	(0.0249)	(0.0252)
Ln GDP per capita	0.0990[a]	0.0992[a]	0.1041[a]	0.0987[a]	0.1018[a]
	(0.0245)	(0.0234)	(0.0219)	(0.0245)	(0.0265)
Constant	−1.1002[a]	−1.3177[a]	−1.1129[a]	−1.1377[a]	−1.1506[a]
	(0.2342)	(0.2350)	(0.2003)	(0.2021)	(0.2410)
Observations	49	49	49	49	49
Adjusted R^2	44%	50%	46%	45%	45%

[a]significant at 1%; [b]significant at 5%; and [c]significant at 10%.

to agents dealing adversely with their principals (Mahoney (1995)). In fact, the correlations of the anti-director index with disclosure requirements and liability standards are 0.52 and 0.50, respectively (see the Appendix). On this view as well, our results do not imply that corporate law is unimportant.

IV. Robustness

In this section, we address three issues of robustness using some additional data. First, is the weakness of our results on public enforcement due to inadequate measures of the Supervisor's strength? Second, what omitted variables may explain the strength of our results on disclosure and liability standards? Third, are securities laws endogenous?

Public enforcement may only be effective in countries with efficient government bureaucracies. To address this concern, we have rerun our regressions for the subsample of countries with per capita GDP above the median. We find that in these countries, public enforcement is correlated with more developed financial markets as proxied by the market-capitalization-to-GDP ratio, the number of listed firms, and the value of IPOs (and weakly—t-stat of 1.72—with stock market liquidity).[12] The effect of public enforcement in rich countries is

[12] Results are qualitatively similar if we break up the sample using survey measures of the quality of government (including either judicial efficiency or the Kaufmann, Kraay, and Mastruzzi (2003) proxy for bureaucratic quality). We also find that public enforcement is correlated with better access to equity markets in countries in which insider trading laws were enforced before 1995 (Bhattacharya and Daouk (2002)).

Table V

Disclosure, Liability Standards, and Public Enforcement

Ordinary least squares regressions of the cross-section of countries. The dependent variables are (1) external market capitalization; (2) log of domestic firms per capita; (3) value of the IPO-to-GDP ratio; (4) block premium; (5) access to equity; (6) ownership concentration; and (7) the stock-market-volume-to-GDP ratio. All regressions include disclosure requirements, liability standards, public enforcement, anti-director rights, efficiency of the judiciary, and log of GDP per capita. All variables are described in Table I. Robust standard errors are shown in parentheses.

	Market Capitalization	Number of Firms	IPOs	Block Premia	Access to Equity	Ownership Concentration	Liquidity
Disclosure requirements	0.4316[a]	0.8735[c]	3.2784[b]	−0.2667[b]	1.5815[a]	−0.1912[b]	68.5580[b]
	(0.1391)	(0.4919)	(1.6017)	(0.1296)	(0.4548)	(0.0887)	(30.0254)
Liability standards	0.2646[c]	0.3849	2.1213	−0.0790	1.1350[b]	−0.0656	64.9247[b]
	(0.1386)	(0.4961)	(1.6166)	(0.0713)	(0.4827)	(0.0647)	(30.4823)
Public enforcement	0.1900	0.3627	2.5228	0.0864	−0.7054	0.1130	9.9240
	(0.1812)	(0.4946)	(1.6761)	(0.0653)	(0.6908)	(0.0994)	(32.3549)
Anti-director rights	0.0176	0.0799	−0.1054	−0.0157	−0.1133	−0.0224	−2.4741
	(0.0333)	(0.0976)	(0.2861)	(0.0175)	(0.0847)	(0.0136)	(5.6187)
Ln GDP per capita	0.0925[a]	0.2757[b]	1.1296[a]	0.0025	0.1080	−0.0252[c]	18.9326[a]
	(0.0213)	(0.1071)	(0.2445)	(0.0205)	(0.0840)	(0.0132)	(5.9055)
Efficiency of the judiciary	0.0427[b]	0.2377[a]	−0.0341	−0.0070	0.1790[a]	−0.0053	−3.6729
	(0.0201)	(0.0684)	(0.2105)	(0.0114)	(0.0577)	(0.0099)	(5.3006)
Constant	−1.2694[a]	−2.8131[a]	−10.6035[a]	0.3437[b]	1.9522[a]	0.8872[a]	−156.8780[a]
	(0.2222)	(0.7724)	(2.2086)	(0.1611)	(0.6737)	(0.1219)	(39.7945)
Observations	49	49	49	37	44	49	49
Adjusted R^2	56%	68%	40%	31%	58%	37%	29%

[a]significant at 1%; [b]significant at 5%; and [c]significant at 10%.

narrowly confined to the rule-making power of the Supervisor. In contrast, public enforcement does not predict the development of securities markets in countries with below-median GDP per capita.

A related concern is that public enforcement may be ineffective if the Supervisor lacks adequate resources. To address this concern, we collect data on the number of employees that work for the Supervisor. We find that the (log of) the number of employees is insignificant in our regressions. To get at the interaction between public enforcement and the resources of the Supervisor, we break up the sample according to whether the number of employees working for the Supervisor is above or below the sample median and run separate regressions for both groups of countries. Public enforcement is statistically significant only for IPOs in countries with well-staffed regulators (and for domestic firms in countries with poorly staffed regulators). All the evidence suggests that relying on pubic enforcement is unlikely to be a useful strategy for jump-starting the development of securities markets in poor countries.

One set of omitted variable stories holds that investor protection picks up the effect of political ideology. Roe (2000) argues that the emphasis on investor protection for the development of financial markets is misplaced. In his view, social democracies have weak investor protection and arrest the development of financial markets. To examine this issue, we use the Botero et al. (2004) measure of political ideology as the fraction of years between 1928 and 1995 that the office of the chief executive is held by a member of a leftist party. This proxy for left power is uncorrelated with both disclosure and liability standards (correlations of −0.06 and −0.13, respectively). We find (results not reported) that the power of the left is associated with smaller external market capitalization when controlling for either disclosure or liability standards, and with a higher block premium when controlling for liability standards. However, including left power in the regressions does not diminish the strength of the results on either disclosure or liability standards.

It might also be argued that financial markets are small where the state is large. For example, few firms may be publicly traded in countries in which the state owns most of the capital. Omitted variable bias may account for the strength of our results if disclosure or liability standard is negatively correlated with the role of the state in the economy. To address this concern, we have included two measures of the role of the state in the economy in our regressions: (1) the fraction of the capital stock in the hands of state-owned companies from La Porta et al. (1999b); and (2) the fraction of the banking assets controlled by government-owned banks from La Porta et al. (2002a). Our results on securities laws remain qualitatively unchanged.

Another omitted variable story holds that countries with large capital markets may come to rely on disclosure and private litigation because their institutions are more democratically responsive to the interests of small investors. However, measures of democracy and political rights are uncorrelated with securities laws. Moreover, these measures are not significant predictors of financial development in our regressions. A related concern is that securities laws may proxy for social capital. The most commonly used measure of social

Table VI

Instrumental Variables Regressions

Panel A presents two-stage least squares regressions of the cross-section of countries. The dependent variables are (1) external market capitalization; (2) log of domestic firms per capita; (3) value of the IPO-to-GDP ratio; (4) block premia; (5) access to equity; (6) ownership concentration; and (7) the stock-market-volume-to-GDP ratio. Investor protection is the principal component of: (1) anti-director rights; (2) disclosure requirements; and (3) liability standards. In addition to investor protection, all regressions include efficiency of the judiciary and log of GDP per capita. Panel B presents results from the first-stage regression. The instrument is a dummy equal to one if the country's legal origin is common law. All variables are described in Table I. Robust standard errors are shown in parentheses.

	Market Capitalization	Number of Firms	IPOs	Block Premia	Access to Equity	Ownership Concentration	Liquidity
Panel A: Second Stage Regression Results							
Investor protection	0.5800[b]	2.0147[a]	6.3885[a]	−0.2118[b]	1.3533[b]	−0.1651[c]	55.9974
	(0.2615)	(0.6917)	(2.3353)	(0.0942)	(0.6068)	(0.0973)	(40.5738)
Efficiency of the judiciary	0.0443[b]	0.2137[a]	−0.1488	−0.0076	0.1638[b]	−0.0115	−2.6144
	(0.0211)	(0.0773)	(0.1961)	(0.0115)	(0.0704)	(0.0096)	(4.5972)
Ln GDP per capita	0.0908[a]	0.2741[b]	1.1539[a]	−0.0067	0.1762	−0.0253[c]	19.8192[a]
	(0.0209)	(0.1089)	(0.2468)	(0.0191)	(0.1049)	(0.0146)	(6.3732)
Constant	−1.0052[a]	−2.4332[a]	−8.9957[a]	0.3303[b]	1.6148[c]	0.8601[a]	−130.0414[a]
	(0.1855)	(0.7313)	(1.6992)	(0.1436)	(0.8141)	(0.0935)	(32.1144)
Observations	49	49	49	37	44	49	49
R^2	59%	71%	43%	36%	54%	39%	31%

Panel B: First Stage Regression Results for Investor Protection

English legal origin	0.3448[a]
	(0.0598)
Efficiency of the judiciary	−0.0064
	(0.0176)
Ln GDP per capita	0.0521[b]
	(0.0255)
Constant	−0.0644
	(0.1876)
Observations	49
R^2	0.45

[a]significant at 1%; [b]significant at 5%; and [c]significant at 10%.

capital—a survey measure of trust among strangers—is available for 27 of our countries and is always insignificant.[13]

Finally, it is possible that governments adopt better securities laws in countries with buoyant financial markets (Cheffins (2001, 2003), Coffee (2001)). This argument is undermined by the systematic differences in investor protection across legal origins. Reverse causality is also undermined by the fact that the dimensions of the law that are expensive to implement—for example, having an independent and focused regulator—do not seem to matter. On the contrary, what matters is legal rules that are cheap rather than expensive to introduce. A second reverse causality argument holds that regulators swarm toward large securities markets because there are bigger rents to secure from regulating them. This argument is also undermined by the fact that it is precisely the regulations that render the regulators unimportant, namely, those that facilitate private contracting and that have the tightest association with stock market development.

We can partially address endogeneity problems using instrumental variables. In practice, legal origin is the only suitable instrument, but we have several legal variables that influence stock market development. To get around this problem, we replace disclosure, liability standards, and anti-director rights with the principal component of these three variables, which we call investor protection. This principal component accounts for roughly 70% of the variation in disclosure, liability standards, and anti-director rights. Table VI presents the two-stage least squares results using common law as an instrument. Investor protection is statistically significant for all seven proxies of stock market development (Panel A). Moreover, legal origin is a strong predictor of investor protection (Panel B).[14] These results should partially mitigate endogeneity concerns.

V. Conclusion

In the introduction, we describe three hypotheses concerning the effect of securities laws on stock market development. Our findings provide clear evidence bearing on these hypotheses.

First, the answer to the question of whether securities laws matter is a definite yes. Financial markets do not prosper when left to market forces alone. Second, our findings suggest that securities laws matter because they facilitate private contracting rather than provide for public regulatory enforcement. Specifically, we find that several aspects of public enforcement, such as having

[13] We also use the percentage of the population that belongs to a protestant denomination as a proxy for trust (the correlation between the two variables is 0.762). In the specifications that include our three indices of securities laws, the percentage of the population that is protestant predicts more access to equity and a lower control premium but disclosure and liability standards retain their predictive power.

[14] The F-statistic for the exclusion of English legal origin from the first-stage regression is 33.3, suggesting that there is no problem of weak instruments (Staiger and Stock (1997)). The Hausman test rejects the unbiasedness of the OLS estimated coefficients in the regressions for domestic firms, IPOs, and trading.

an independent and/or focused regulator or criminal sanctions, do not matter, and others matter in only some regressions. In contrast, both extensive disclosure requirements and standards of liability facilitating investor recovery of losses are associated with larger stock markets. Our results on the benefits of disclosure support similar findings of Barth, Caprio, and Levine (2003), who find that their proxy for private monitoring is positively correlated with the size of the banking sector.

These results point to the importance of regulating the agency conflict between controlling shareholders and outside investors to further the development of capital markets. They also point to the need for legal reform to support financial development, and cast doubt on the sufficiency of purely private solutions in bridging the gap between countries with strong and weak investor protection. Finally, our findings further clarify why legal origin predicts stock market development. The results support the view that the benefit of common law in this area comes from its emphasis on market discipline and private litigation. The benefits of common law appear to lie in its emphasis on private contracting and standardized disclosure and in its reliance on private dispute resolution using market-friendly standards of liability.

Appendix
Table of Correlations

This appendix shows the correlations among the variables used in the paper. All variables are described in Table I.

	Disclosure requirements	Liability standards	Supervisor characteristics	Rule-making power	Orders	Investigative Power	Criminal sanctions	Public enforcement	Anti-Directors rights	Efficiency of the judiciary	Ln GDP per capita	UK Legal Origin	French Legal Origin	German Legal Origin	Scandinavian Legal Origin	Market capitalization	Domestic firms	IPOs	Block premia	Access to equity	Ownership concentration
Liability standards	0.5496[a]																				
Supervisor characteristics	−0.1099	0.0481																			
Rule-making power	0.0196	−0.0427	−0.0149																		
Orders	0.3847[a]	0.4082[b]	0.1399	0.2837[b]																	
Investigative power	0.3759[a]	0.3100[b]	0.2142	0.3465[b]	0.5750[a]																
Criminal sanctions	0.3121[b]	0.2184	−0.0053	−0.0778	0.3208[b]	−0.0292															
Public enforcement	0.3305[b]	0.3091[b]	0.3821[a]	0.6179[a]	0.8067[a]	0.7575[a]	0.3193[b]														
Anti-directors rights	0.5236[a]	0.4999[a]	0.0559	0.0177	0.4129[a]	0.3554[b]	0.2811[c]	0.3691[a]													
Efficiency of the judiciary	0.2542[c]	0.2241	−0.3128[b]	−0.2600[c]	0.2215	−0.1588	0.2038	−0.1130	0.2113												
Ln GDP per capita	0.1378	0.1805	−0.2821[b]	−0.1798	0.0263	−0.1263	0.0489	−0.1709	0.0349	0.6618[a]											
English Legal Origin	0.5902[a]	0.3369[b]	0.0878	0.0058	0.3548[b]	0.3091[b]	0.4212[a]	0.3687[a]	0.5890[a]	0.1826	−0.1967										
French Legal Origin	−0.5509[a]	−0.2830[b]	0.2297	0.2384[c]	−0.1322	0.1054	−0.3393[b]	0.0639	−0.4463[a]	−0.4742[a]	−0.1815	−0.6599[a]									
German Legal Origin	0.0005	−0.0687	−0.2267	−0.2771[c]	−0.3175[b]	−0.4259[a]	−0.1237	−0.4719[a]	−0.1925	0.1611	0.3078[b]	−0.2846[b]	−0.3235[b]								
Scandinavian Legal Origin	−0.0440	0.0006	−0.2983[b]	−0.1094	−0.0057	−0.2247	0.0198	−0.1996	0.0001	0.3428[b]	0.3059[b]	−0.2272	−0.2582[c]	−0.1114							
Market capitalization	0.5412[a]	0.5046[a]	−0.1773	0.0885	0.3030[b]	0.0691	0.2447[c]	0.1869	0.3909[a]	0.5771[a]	0.5646[a]	0.2041	−0.4058[a]	0.1828	0.1552						
Domestic firms	0.4596[a]	0.4152[a]	−0.1876	−0.2464[c]	0.3378[b]	0.1476	0.2209	0.0805	0.3598[b]	0.7454[a]	0.6760[a]	0.2681[c]	−0.4770[a]	0.1084	0.2602[c]	0.6315[a]					
IPOs	0.4372[a]	0.4241[a]	−0.1209	0.0637	0.2813[c]	0.0037	0.4162[a]	0.2021	0.2459[c]	0.3960[a]	0.5426[a]	0.1795	−0.3407[b]	0.2181	0.0387	0.7144[a]	0.5664[a]				
Block premia	−0.5845[a]	−0.4523[a]	−0.1100	0.1326	−0.1658	−0.1439	−0.2334	−0.1309	−0.4662[a]	−0.3103[c]	−0.2586	−0.3209[c]	0.3936[b]	0.0592	−0.2258	−0.5334[a]	−0.5058[a]	−0.4641[a]			
Access to equity	0.5173[a]	0.4802[a]	−0.1462	−0.2757[c]	0.2103	−0.0425	0.1891	−0.0443	0.2659[c]	0.6234[a]	0.5498[a]	0.3401[b]	−0.5624[a]	0.1121	0.2892[c]	0.6727[a]	0.6985[a]	0.5139[a]	−0.5942[a]		
Ownership concentration	−0.5005[a]	−0.4159[a]	0.1634	0.0535	−0.1080	−0.0335	−0.0147	0.0093	−0.4024[a]	−0.4301[a]	−0.4243[a]	−0.1572	0.5163[a]	−0.3526[b]	−0.2343	−0.5623[a]	−0.4267[a]	−0.4743[a]	0.4993[a]	−0.5390[a]	
Liquidity	0.4154[a]	0.4404[a]	−0.0647	0.0968	0.1028	−0.0287	0.2766[c]	0.1187	0.2165	0.2829[b]	0.4390[a]	0.0269	−0.3233[b]	0.4180[a]	0.0365	0.7571[a]	0.4329[a]	0.6967[a]	−0.3944[b]	0.4736[a]	−0.5297[a]

[a]significant at 1%; [b]significant at 5%; and [c]significant at 10%.

REFERENCES

Barth, James, Gerard Caprio, and Ross Levine, 2003, Bank supervision and regulation: What works best? *Journal of Financial Intermediation* 13, 205–248.

Becker, Gary, 1968, Crime and punishment: An economic approach, *Journal of Political Economy* 76, 169–217.

Benston, George, 1973, Required disclosure and the stock market: An evaluation of the Securities Market Act of 1934, *American Economic Review* 63, 132–155.

Benston, George, 1985, The market for public accounting services: Demand, supply and regulation, *Journal of Accounting and Public Policy* 4, 33–79.

Beny, Laura, 2002, A comparative empirical investigation of agency and market theories of insider trading, Harvard University mimeo.

Bergman, Nittai, and Daniel Nicolaievsky, 2002, Investor protection and the Coasian view, Harvard University mimeo.

Bhattacharya, Utpal, and Hazem Daouk, 2002, The world price of insider trading, *Journal of Finance* 57, 75–108.

Black, Bernard, 2001, The legal and institutional preconditions for strong securities markets, *UCLA Law Review* 48, 781–858.

Black, Bernard, and Reinier Kraakman, 1996, A self-enforcing model of corporate law, *Harvard Law Review* 109, 1911–1981.

Botero, Juan, Simeon Djankov, Rafael La Porta, Florencio Lopez-de-Silanes, and Andrei Shleifer, 2004, The regulation of labor, *Quarterly Journal of Economics* 119, 1339–1382.

Bushman, Robert, Joseph Piotroski, and Abbie Smith, 2003, What determines corporate transparency? *Journal of Accounting Research* 42, 207–252.

Cheffins, Brian R., 2001, Law, economics and the UK's system of corporate governance: Lessons from history, *Journal of Corporate Law Studies* 1, 71–89.

Cheffins, Brian R., 2003, Law as bedrock: The foundations of an economy dominated by widely held public companies, *Oxford Journal of Legal Studies* 23, 1–23.

Chemmanur, Thomas, and Paolo Fulghieri, 1994, Investment bank reputation, information production, and financial intermediation, *Journal of Finance* 49, 57–79.

Coase, Ronald, 1960, The problem of social cost, *Journal of Law and Economics* 3, 1–44.

Coase, Ronald, 1975, Economists and public policy, in J. F. Weston, ed.: *Large Corporations in a Changing Society* (New York University Press, New York).

Coffee, John, 1984, Market failure and the economic case for a mandatory disclosure system, *Virginia Law Review* 70, 717–753.

Coffee, John, 1989, The mandatory/enabling balance in corporate law: An essay on the judicial role, *Columbia Law Review* 89, 1618–1691.

Coffee, John, 2001, The rise of dispersed ownership: The roles of law and the state in the separation of ownership control, *Yale Law Review* 111, 1–82.

Coffee, John, 2002, Understanding Enron: It's about the gatekeepers, stupid, *Business Lawyer* 57, 1403–1420.

Dechow, Patricia, Richard Sloan, and Amy Sweeney, 1996, Causes and consequences of earnings manipulations: An analysis of firms subject to enforcement actions by the SEC, *Contemporary Accounting Research* 13, 1–36.

De Long, Bradford, 1991, Did J.P. Morgan's men add value? An economist's perspective on financial capitalism, in Peter Temin, ed.: *Inside the Business Enterprise: Historical Perspectives on the Use of Information* (University of Chicago Press, Chicago, IL).

Dyck, Alexander, and Luigi Zingales, 2004, Private benefits of control: An international comparison, *Journal of Finance* 59, 537–600.

Easterbrook, Frank, and Daniel Fischel, 1984, Mandatory disclosure and the protection of investors, *Virginia Law Review* 70, 669–715.

Fischel, Daniel, and Sanford Grossman, 1984, Customer protection in futures and securities markets, *Journal of Futures Markets* 4, 273–295.

Fox, Merritt, 1999, Retaining mandatory disclosure: Why issuer choice is not investor empowerment, *Virginia Law Review* 85, 1335–1419.

Friend, Irwin, and Edward Herman, 1964, The S.E.C. through a glass darkly, *Journal of Business* 37, 382–405.

Glaeser, Edward, Simon Johnson, and Andrei Shleifer, 2001, Coase versus the Coasians, *Quarterly Journal of Economics* 116, 853–899.

Glaeser, Edward, and Andrei Shleifer, 2001, A reason for quantity regulation, *American Economic Review Papers and Proceedings* 91, 431–435.

Glaeser, Edward, and Andrei Shleifer, 2002, Legal origins, *Quarterly Journal of Economics* 117, 1193–1230.

Glaeser, Edward, and Andrei Shleifer, 2003, The rise of the regulatory state, *Journal of Economic Literature* 41, 401–425.

Grossman, Sanford, 1981, The informational role of warranties and private disclosure about product quality, *Journal of Law and Economics* 24, 461–483.

Grossman, Sanford, and Oliver Hart, 1980, Disclosure laws and takeover bids, *Journal of Finance* 35, 323–334.

Grossman, Sanford, and Oliver Hart, 1988, One share-one vote and the market for corporate control, *Journal of Financial Economics* 20, 175–202.

Hartland-Peel, Christopher, 1996, *African Equities: A Guide to Markets and Companies* (Euromoney Publications, London, U.K.).

Hay, Jonathan, and Andrei Shleifer, 1998, Private enforcement of public laws: A theory of legal reform, *American Economic Review Papers and Proceedings* 88, 398–403.

Hay, Jonathan, Andrei Shleifer, and Robert Vishny, 1996, Toward a theory of legal reform, *European Economic Review* 40, 559–567.

International Finance Corporation, 2001, Emerging Markets Database, located online at: http://www.ifc.org/EMDB/EMDBHOME.HTM.

Kaufmann, Daniel, Aart Kraay, and Massimo Mastruzzi, 2003, Governance matters III: Updated governance indicators for 1996–02, Working paper draft for comments, Washington, D.C.: World Bank.

Landis, James, 1938, *The Administrative Process* (Yale University Press, New Haven, CT).

La Porta, Rafael, Florencio Lopez-de-Silanes, and Andrei Shleifer, 1999a, Corporate ownership around the world, *Journal of Finance* 54, 471–517.

La Porta, Rafael, Florencio Lopez-de-Silanes, and Andrei Shleifer, 2002a, Government ownership of banks, *Journal of Finance* 57, 265–301.

La Porta, Rafael, Florencio Lopez-de-Silanes, Andrei Shleifer, and Robert Vishny, 1997, Legal determinants of external finance, *Journal of Finance* 52, 1131–1150.

La Porta, Rafael, Florencio Lopez-de-Silanes, Andrei Shleifer, and Robert Vishny, 1998, Law and finance, *Journal of Political Economy* 106, 1113–1155.

La Porta, Rafael, Florencio Lopez-de-Silanes, Andrei Shleifer, and Robert Vishny, 1999b, The quality of government, *Journal of Law, Economics, and Organization* 15, 222–279.

La Porta, Rafael, Florencio Lopez-de-Silanes, Andrei Shleifer, and Robert Vishny, 2002b, Investor protection and corporate valuation, *Journal of Finance* 57, 1147–1170.

Leuz, Christian, Dhananjay Nanda, and Peter Wysocki, 2003, Earnings management and investor protection: An international comparison, *Journal of Financial Economics* 69, 505–528.

Levine, Ross, and Sara Zervos, 1998, Stock markets, banks, and economic growth, *American Economic Review* 88, 537–558.

Macey, Jonathan, 1994, Administrative agency obsolescence and interest group formation: A case study of the SEC at sixty, *Cardozo Law Review* 15, 909–949.

Mahoney, Paul, 1995, Mandatory disclosure as a solution to agency problems, *University of Chicago Law Review* 62, 1047–1112.

Milgrom, Paul, and John Roberts, 1986, Relying on the information of interested parties, *Rand Journal of Economics* 17, 18–32.

Miller, Merton, 1991, *Financial Innovations and Market Volatility* (Blackwell, Cambridge, MA).

Nenova, Tatiana, 2003, The value of corporate voting rights and control: A cross-country analysis, *Journal of Financial Economics* 68, 325–351.

North, Douglass, 1981, *Structure and change in Economic History* (Norton, New York).

Pistor, Katharina, and Chenggang Xu, 2002, Law enforcement under incomplete law: Theory and evidence from financial market regulation, Columbia Law School, mimeo.

Polinsky, Mitchell, and Steven Shavell, 2000, The economic theory of public enforcement of law, *Journal of Economic Literature* 38, 45–76.

Political Risk Services, 1996, *International Country Risk Guide* (Political Risk Services, East Syracuse, NY).

Reese, William, and Michael Weisbach, 2002, Protection of minority shareholder interests, cross-listings in the United States, and subsequent equity offerings, *Journal of Financial Economics* 66, 65–104.

Roe, Mark, 2000, Political preconditions to separating ownership from corporate control, *Stanford Law Review* 53, 539–606.

Romano, Roberta, 2001, The need for competition in international securities regulation, *Theoretical Inquiries in Law* 2, 1–179.

Ross, Stephen, 1979, Disclosure regulation in financial markets: Implication of modern finance theory and signaling theory, in Franklin Edwards, ed.: *Issues in Financial Regulation* (McGraw-Hill, New York).

Schwab, Klaus, Michael Porter, Jeffrey Sachs, Andrew Warner, Macha Levinson, The World Economics Forun of Geneva, and The Harvard University Center for International Development, eds., 1999, *The Global Competitiveness Report 1999* (Oxford University Press, New York).

Seligman, Joel, 1995, *The Transformation of Wall Street: A History of the Securities and Exchange Commission and Modern Corporate Finance* (Northeastern University Press, Boston, MA).

Shleifer, Andrei, and Daniel Wolfenzon, 2002, Investor protection and equity markets, *Journal of Financial Economics* 66, 3–27.

Simon, Carol, 1989, The effect of the 1933 Securities Act on investor information and the performance of new issues, *American Economic Review* 79, 295–318.

Spiller, Pablo, and John Ferejohn, 1992, The economics and politics of administrative law and procedures: An introduction, *Journal of Law, Economics and Organization* 8, 1–7.

Staiger, Douglas, and James Stock, 1997, Instrumental variables regression with weak instruments, *Econometrica* 65, 557–586.

Stigler, George, 1964, Public regulation of the securities market, *Journal of Business* 37, 117–142.

Stulz, René, 1999, Globalization of equity markets and the cost of capital, *Journal of Applied Corporate Finance* 12, 8–25.

Teoh, Siew Hong, Ivo Welch, and T. J. Wong, 1998, Earnings management and the long-run market performance of initial public offerings, *The Journal of Finance* 53, 1935–1974.

Velthuyse, Heleen, and Francine Schlingmann, 1995, Prospectus liability in The Netherlands, *Journal of International Banking Law*, 229–236.

World Bank, 2001, *World Development Indicators 2001*, [CD-ROM] (World Bank, Washington, D.C.).